the sexual experience

To Our Families

the sexual experience

EDITED BY

Benjamin J. Sadock, M.D.

Professor of Psychiatry, Director, Division of Group Process,
and Director, Continuing Education in Psychiatry,
New York Medical College;
Attending Psychiatrist, Flower and Fifth Avenue Hospitals;
Visiting Psychiatrist, Metropolitan Hospital;
New York, New York

Harold I. Kaplan, M.D.

Professor of Psychiatry and Director of Psychiatric
Education and Training, New York Medical College;
Attending Psychiatrist, Flower and Fifth Avenue Hospitals;
Visiting Psychiatrist, Metropolitan Hospital, and Bird S. Coler
Memorial Hospital and Home, New York, New York

Alfred M. Freedman, M.D.

Professor of Psychiatry and Chairman of the
Department of Psychiatry, New York Medical College;
Director of Psychiatric Services,
Metropolitan Hospital and Flower and Fifth Avenue Hospitals,
Chairman, Department of Psychiatry,
Grasslands Hospital, Valhalla, New York

THE WILLIAMS & WILKINS COMPANY
Baltimore

Copyright ©, 1976
THE WILLIAMS & WILKINS COMPANY
428 E. Preston Street
Baltimore, Md. 21202, U.S.A.

Made in the United States of America

Library of Congress Cataloging in Publication Data
Main entry under title:

The Sexual experience.

    1. Sex—Addresses, essays, lectures. 2. Sexual disorders—Addresses, essays, lectures. 3. Sexual deviation—Addresses, essays, lectures. 4. Sex (Psychology)—Addresses, essays, lectures. I. Sadock, Benjamin J., 1933–   II. Kaplan, Harold I.
III. Freedman, Alfred M. [DNLM: 1. Sex behavior. 2. Sex disorders. HQ21 S5155]
HQ21.S4736   612.6   75-41350
ISBN 0-683-03374-3

Preface

Sexuality is one of the most intriguing subjects in the area of human behavior and has been so since antiquity. As this book attests—for one thing, by virtue of its size—the serious body of knowledge about human sexuality is considerable. As editors, we have attempted to bring together in one book a survey of the entire field.

This book is intended for a variety of readers—from the professional who requires a comprehensive, in-depth survey of the field to the educated general reader who recognizes the importance of sex and sexual knowledge in his or her life. Accordingly, all the facts relating to normal and abnormal sexuality are presented, as well as an overview of various hypotheses and speculations relevant to the goal of sexual enrichment. By so doing, we hope to make the reader aware of and more sensitive to what others do, have done, or want to do in the sexual sphere. The professional and nonprofessional alike are too often unschooled in the varieties of sexual experience, so we have gathered a wide range of information to fill what gaps and blind spots exist. Knowledge gained from this text can be of inestimable value not only in the management of sex-related problems but also in the prevention of the distress that originates in the sexual sphere.

Many of the chapters of this book are derived from *Comprehensive Textbook of Psychiatry-II*, the major psychiatric text in use throughout the world. That two-volume textbook was edited by the editors of *The Sexual Experience*. For this volume, we have selected material from *Compre-*

hensive Textbook of Psychiatry-II that is relevant to the field of sexual behavior. In addition, we have added new chapters, especially written for this book by various experts. We wish to acknowledge our debt to the contributors whose work we have used. At the same time, *The Sexual Experience* presents a new and modified integration of their work, and for these changes we must accept the responsibility.

This book is organized into sections that cover sex and sexual behavior from historical, developmental, biological, functional, and social points of view. However, in the chapter on sex through the ages, more than history is presented. It is, indeed, a testimonial to sex as a central issue in life throughout all human history. And in the section on sexual research, some of the investigators who pioneered the scientific study of sex are described and their major contributions discussed. The reader will also find a complete discussion of the anatomy and physiology of sex; ignorance in this area is widespread, and without such knowledge a satisfactory understanding of sexuality is impossible. An overview of sexual development from infancy through old age is presented, as well as surveys of the various schools of psychology as they relate to each phase of sexual development and stage of life. The reader will find suggestions on how to respond to questions that may arise in regard to childhood sexuality, masturbation, sex in adolescence and young adulthood, the menopause, and the male climacteric.

Unique to a book of this type is a detailed description of the techniques of intercourse and the art of love. Often, it is necessary to teach what is erroneously thought to come naturally. We have also included a large section on abnormal sexual behavioral—real or imagined—and another section on the recent advances in the treatment of sexual disorders, describing both individual and group therapeutic approaches, including a detailed description of the technique developed by Masters and Johnson. Also included are sections on marital therapies, treatment techniques designed to alleviate the problems of the nuclear family in today's complex society. The varieties of marriage, from the traditional to the open marriage model, are described, and sex before, during, and after marriage is also discussed. Sex and its relation to pregnancy, abortion, contraception, sterilization, and physical and mental illness are covered in depth, as are the effects of various drugs on sex and sexual performance.

The influence of sexual factors on all aspects of the society has been immense. Sex affects all social institutions—education, religion, the arts. All are discussed thoroughly in a variety of chapters, each of which deals with the effect of sexuality on a particular cultural issue. In addition, the more circumscribed areas of pornography and prostitution are examined. The two areas are not unrelated; the word "pornography" stems from the Greek word meaning "writing of prostitutes," and the reader may find that they still share common ground. Finally, we have included an extensive survey of the women's movement, which has produced sexual, psychological, economic, political, and social changes in American life. Only now are the profound effects of the women's movement on society being realized as man's view of woman and woman's view of herself undergo constant change and re-evaluation.

In addition to expressing our thanks to the contributors, all of whom are outstanding workers in their respective fields, we wish to thank Virginia A. Sadock, M.D., whose work in sex therapy and in the training of sex therapists helped provide the organizational structure for this book. As director of one of the country's largest graduate training programs in human sexuality at New York Medical College, she made us keenly aware of the need for a book of this type, one that would provide a thorough overview of the field and one that sex trainees from various walks of life—medicine, clergy, nursing, social work, and psychology, among others—would find useful. The clarity of the writing in the book makes it equally useful for the college or medical student attending a course on sexuality.

In addition, we want to thank our close friend Joan Welsh, who has done outstanding editorial work in this volume, as she has done in the past in other books. Lois Baken headed our secretarial staff with her usual and most appreciated dedication and skill. We thank her and Eva Washington for their help. Batya Bauman directed the proofreading staff, to whom we also extend our appreciation. Finally, we wish to thank our publishers, Williams & Wilkins—especially Charles Reville, the President, and James Gallagher, the editor-in-chief—for their unwavering support in all our mutual endeavors.

New York   B.J.S.
                                              H.I.K.
                                              A.M.F.

Contributors

Theus N. Armistead, M.D.
Superintendent, East Louisiana State Hospital, Jackson, Louisiana

Hrair M. Babikian, M.D.
Clinical Associate Professor of Psychiatry, New York Medical College; Chief, Division of Psychosomatic Medicine and Liaison, Flower and Fifth Avenue Hospitals and Metropolitan Hospital Center; Associate Professor of Psychiatry, New York School of Psychiatry, New York, New York

Barbara E. Bess, M.D.
Assistant Professor of Psychiatry, New York Medical College; Assistant Attending Metropolitan Hospital; Staff Attending, Gracie Square Hospital; Associate Director, Residency Training Psychiatry, New York Medical College, New York, New York

Paul Bohannan, D.Phil. (Oxon)
Professor of Anthropology, Northwestern University, Evanston, Illinois

John Paul Brady, M.D.
Professor and Chairman, Department of Psychiatry, University of Pennsylvania School of Medicine; Medical Research Scientist, Eastern Pennsylvania Psychiatric Institute, Philadelphia, Pennsylvania

Edward M. Brecher, M.A.
Author, *The New Sex Researchers;* Coauthor, *An Analysis of Human Sexual Response;* Fellow, Society for the Scientific Study of Sex, West Cornwall, Connecticut

Mary S. Calderone, M.D.
Executive Director, SIECUS (Sex Information and Education Council of the U.S.), New York, New York

Michael Joe Daly, M.D.
Professor and Chairman, Department of Obstetrics and Gynecology, Temple University Health Sciences Center, Philadelphia, Pennsylvania

Stephen Fleck, M.D.
Professor of Psychiatry and Public Health; Psychiatrist-in-Chief, Yale Psychiatric Institute, Yale University School of Medicine, New Haven, Connecticut

Abraham N. Franzblau, M.D., Ph.D., L.H.D.
Professor of Pastoral Psychiatry (Emeritus) and Dean (Emeritus), Hebrew Union College-Jewish Institute of Religion; Preceptor in Psychiatry, Mount Sinai Hospital; Lecturer in Psychiatry, Mount Sinai School of Medicine, City University of New York, New York, New York

Alfred M. Freedman, M.D.
Professor of Psychiatry and Chairman, Department of Psychiatry, New York Medical College; Director, Psychiatric Services, Flower and Fifth Avenue Hospitals; Chairman, Department of Psychiatry, Metropolitan Hospital and Bird S. Coler Memorial Hospital and Home, New York, New York; Chairman, Department of Psychiatry, Grasslands Hospital, Valhalla, New York

Robert E. Gould, M.D.
Professor of Clinical Psychiatry, New York Medical College; Director and Visiting

Psychiatrist Out-Patient Department, Metropolitan Hospital, New York, New York

Richard Green, M.D.
Professor of Psychiatry and Behavioral Sciences; Coordinator, Projects in Human Sexuality, Health Sciences Center School of Medicine, State University of New York at Stony Brook, Stony Brook, New York

Robert B. Greenblatt, M.D.
Professor of Endocrinology (Emeritus), Medical College of Georgia, Augusta, Georgia

Jay Haley, M.A.
Director, Family Therapy Research, Philadelphia Child Guidance Clinic, Philadelphia, Pennsylvania

D. James Henderson, M.D.
Honorary Lecturer, Department of Psychiatry, University of Toronto, and Active Medical Staff, Sunnybrook Hospital, Toronto, Canada; Active Medical Staff, Mental Health Care Center, Penetanguishene, Ontario, Canada; Private Practice, Barrie, Ontario, Canada

Elizabeth Janeway, B.A.
Author and Social Historian, *Man's World, Women's Place, A Study in Social Mythology; Between Myth and Morning: Women Awakening;* New York, New York

Samuel S. Janus, Ph.D.
Clinical Assistant Professor, Department of Psychiatry, New York Medical College; Codirector of Group Psychotherapy, Continuing Education Program, New York Medical College, New York, New York

Gordon D. Jensen, M.D.
Professor of Psychiatry in Pediatrics and Head, Section of Child Psychiatry, University of California Davis School of Medicine, Davis, California

Harold I. Kaplan, M.D.
Professor of Psychiatry and Director, Psychiatric Education and Training, New York Medical College; Attending Psychiatrist, Flower and Fifth Avenue Hospitals; Visiting Psychiatrist, Metropolitan Hospital and Bird S. Coler Memorial Hospital and Home, New York, New York

Simon M. Koenig, LL.B.
Faculty, Post Graduate Instruction, New York Medical College, New York, New York; Member American Bar Association and American Academy of Matrimonial Lawyers

Klaus Laemmel, M.D.
Assistant Clinical Professor of Psychiatry, New York Medical College; Assistant Attending Psychiatrist, Flower and Fifth Avenue Hospitals, Metropolitan Hospital, St. Vincent's Hospital, New York, New York, and Westchester County Medical Center (Grasslands Hospital), Valhalla, New York

Harold I. Lief, M.D.
Professor of Psychiatry; Director, Division of Family Study; Director, Marriage Council of Philadelphia; Director, Center for the Study of Sex Education in Medicine, University of Pennsylvania School of Medicine, Philadelphia, Pennsylvania

Morris A. Lipton, M.D., Ph.D.
Sarah Graham Kenan Professor of Psychiatry and Director, Biological Sciences Research Center, Child Development Institute, University of North Carolina, Chapel Hill, North Carolina

Paul D. MacLean, M.D.
Chief, Laboratory of Brain Evolution and Behavior, National Institute of Mental Health, Bethesda, Maryland

Virginia P. McNamara, M.D.
Assistant Professor of Obstetrics and Gynecology, Associate Director, Outpatient Clinic, Department of Obstetrics-Gynecology, Medical College of Georgia, Augusta, Georgia

Edward C. Mann, M.D.
Chief, Department of Obstetrics and Gynecology, Earl K. Long Memorial Hospital, Baton Rouge, Louisiana; Psychiatrist, East Louisiana State Hospital, Jackson, Louisiana; Associate Clinical Professor of Psychiatry, Louisiana State University School of Medicine, New Orleans, Louisiana

Judd Marmor, M.D.
Franz Alexander Professor of Psychiatry, University of Southern California School of Medicine; Senior Attending Psychiatrist, Los Angeles County-University of Southern California Medical Center, Los Angeles, California

Jon K. Meyer, M.D.
Assistant Professor of Psychiatry and Assistant Professor of Surgery (Psychiatric), Johns Hopkins University School of Medicine; Director, Sexual Behaviors Consultation Unit and Gener Identity Clinic, Johns Hopkins Medical Institutions, Baltimore, Maryland

Daniel Offer, M.D.
Associate Director, Institute for Psychosomatic and Psychiatric Research and Training, Michael Reese Hospital; Professor of Psychiatry, University of Chicago Pritzker School of Medicine, Chicago, Illinois

George O'Neill, Ph.D.
Associate Professor of Anthropology, City College of New York; Co-author, *Open Marriage*; New York, New York

Nena O'Neill, B.A.
Lecturer, Division of Continuing Education in Psychiatry, New York Medical College; Co-author, *Open Marriage*; New York, New York

Ira B. Pauly, M.D.
Professor of Psychiatry, University of Oregon Medical School, Portland, Oregon; Visiting Lecturer, Department of Psychiatry, University of Melbourne Medical School, Melbourne, Victoria, Australia

David M. Reed, Ph.D.
Associate Professor of Family Study, Department of Psychiatry, Assistant Director, Marriage Council of Philadelphia and Center for Study of Sex Education in Medicine, University of Pennsylvania School of Medicine, Philadelphia, Pennsylvania

Benjamin J. Sadock, M.D.
Professor of Psychiatry; Director, Division of Group Process; Director, Continuing Education in Psychiatry; New York Medical College; Attending Psychiatrist, Flower and Fifth Avenue Hospitals; Visiting Psychiatrist, Metropolitan Hospital, New York, New York

Virginia A. Sadock, M.D.
Assistant Professor of Psychiatry and Director, Human Sexuality Program, New York Medical College; Assistant Attending Psychiatrist, Flower and Fifth Avenue

Hospitals; Assistant Visiting Psychiatrist, Metropolitan Hospital, New York, New York

Robert L. Sadoff, M.D.
Associate Clinical Professor of Psychiatry, University of Pennsylvania School of Medicine; Director, Center for Studies in Social-Legal Psychiatry, University of Pennsylvania, Lecturer in Law, Villanova University School of Law, Villanova, Pennsylvania

Eugene C. Sandberg, M.D.
Associate Professor of Gynecology and Obstetrics, Stanford University School of Medicine, Stanford, California

William Simon, Ph.D.
Director, Social Science Division, Institute for Juvenile Research, Chicago, Illinois

Iver F. Small, M.D.
Professor of Psychiatry, Indiana University School of Medicine; Assistant Medical Director, Larue D. Carter Memorial Hospital, Indianapolis, Indiana

Joyce G. Small, M.D.
Professor of Psychiatry, Indiana University School of Medicine; Director of Research, Larue D. Carter Memorial Hospital, Indianapolis, Indiana

Henry Ian Spitz, M.D.
Assistant Clinical Professor of Psychiatry, New York Medical College; Assistant Attending Psychiatrist, Flower and Fifth Avenue Hospitals; Assistant Visiting Psychiatrist, Metropolitan Hospital, New York, New York

Robert J. Stoller, M.D.
Professor of Psychiatry, University of California (Los Angeles) School of Medicine, Los Angeles, California

Norman Sussman, M.D.
Lecturer, Division of Continuing Education in Psychiatry, New York Medical College, New York, New York

Walter Taub, M.D.
Clinical Associate, Department of Medicine, Mount Sinai School of Medicine of the City of New York; Assistant Professor of Medicine, New York Medical College, New York, New York

Joseph D. Teicher, M.D.
Professor of Psychiatry, University of Southern California School of Medicine; Director, Children's and Adolescents' Psychiatric Services, Los Angeles County, University of Southern California Medical Center; Director, Los Angeles Child Guidance Clinic, Los Angeles, California

Edward A. Tyler, M.D.
Associate Dean and Professor of Psychiatry, Northwestern University Medical School, Chicago, Illinois

Hans H. Zinsser, M.D. (deceased)
Associate Professor of Clinical Urology, Columbia University College of Physicians and Surgeons, New York, New York

Contents

chapter 1 Introduction to Sexuality

HAROLD I. LIEF, M.D.

Introduction

Although psychiatrists have always had a great concern with sexuality—"sexuality" covers far more territory than does "sex," which properly denotes physical sexuality or aspects of the sex act—interest in the subject has had an exponential increase in the last decade. Why? The factors contributing to the upsurge of attention in this area of human behavior may be summarized as follows:

1. Professional interest parallels the remarkable societal changes in the openness and candor with which sex is discussed and displayed in the communications, artistic, and entertainment sectors of society.

2. Quasirevolutionary movements such as women's lib and gay lib have challenged old, strongly held beliefs, values, and stereotypes. Traditional male and female roles and concepts of homosexuality as a disease (recall that in the first edition of *Comprehensive Textbook of Psychiatry,* homosexuality was part of a section on sexual deviations) are under strong attack. Professionals are forced to rethink traditional notions.

3. A striking increase in sex research has taken place in the last 10 years. Most notable has been the research in therapy by Masters and Johnson, following up their ground-breaking physiological research of the early 1960's. Also of signal importance have been the studies of· gender development by Money and Ehrhardt and by Stoller and Green and their associates. This work has implications for the theory of sexual development and disorder and is probably opening new areas of additional investigation. Biological research, notably the effect of fetal androgens on organizing the brain for later sexual behavior, has been expanding at a significant rate. Sociological studies have added greatly to the understanding of changing cultural and social values, attitudes, and behavior. Clinical researchers have tended to concentrate on the problem of the causes of homosexuality and transsexualism, but their clinical studies have created intense interest and controversy.

4. The therapeutic methods of Masters and Johnson, with the possibility of more effective sex therapy than ever before, have excited professionals and have made many people, including psychiatrists, decide to specialize in sex therapy. It is estimated that there are more than 2,000 sex therapists in the United States, but many of them are unqualified, and some are outright quacks. The issues of adequate training for sex therapy and of quality control are of increasing concern. A consortium of medical schools in the eastern part of the country, organized in part by the Center for the Study of Sex Education in Medicine of the University of Pennsylvania, is moving toward establishing standards for sex therapy, as is the American Association of Sex Educators and Counselors (AASEC).

5. National professional organizations have aided in the dissemination of information to professionals. The Center for the Study of Sex Education in Medicine has contributed primarily to medical school teachers and students; AASEC has helped with other professions. The pioneering organization in the sexual health field and one most well known is the Sex Information and Education Council of the United States (SIECUS). Its publications, notably its study guides, have been a great help to workers in the field. Recently, meetings of the American Psychiatric Association and the American Orthopsychiatric Association have devoted more and more time to aspects of human sexuality. The National Sex Forum has helped educational developments by its creation of films dealing with explicit erotic material. The American Association of Marriage

and Family Counselors has helped by its integration of marital, family, and sex therapy, augmented by similar activities of the National Council on Family Relations.

6. The medical profession has accepted human sexuality as a legitimate area for investigation and therapy. In 1960 only 3 medical schools had formal programs for the teaching of human sexuality. In 1968, when the Center for the Study of Sex Education in Medicine was formed, about 30 schools had started programs. Now it is a rare school that has no teaching program in the field of sexuality. The American Medical Association's Committee on Human Sexuality has published a volume, *Human Sexuality (1972)*, a handbook for students and practitioners. The speciality organizations, expecially the American College of Obstetrics and Gynecology, have devoted much needed time to the subject of sex counseling. For the first time, the thirteenth edition of the *Cecil-Loeb Textbook of Medicine* includes a section on sexuality in medicial practice.

Normal and Abnormal Sexuality

A decade ago psychiatrists were more certain than they are today about what constitutes healthy sexuality, for it was this perspective of normality, rather than the statistical one, that dominated psychiatric thought. At that time, the majority of psychiatrists seemingly believed, for example, that homosexuality is an illness. Currently, there is a sharp debate between 2 polarized groups—one still claiming that homosexuality is a disease, the other claiming that it should not even be regarded as a deviation, since that word implies psychopathology, but simply as a sexual variation that should be removed from the official American Psychiatric Association's nomenclature of psychiatric disorders.

Gadpaille (1972) states the illness viewpoint succinctly:

Preferential homosexuality is clearly the result of some disorder in the normally programmed sequence of psychosexual differentiation and development, however early or subtle the interference may be.

Gadpaille labels homosexuality "an abiological maladaptation." Arguing for this point of view are Bieber et al. (1962), Hatterer (1970), and Socarides (1970), with each

of them stressing a somewhat different aspect of family interaction as a pathological factor in faulty psychosexual development.

Arguing that homosexuality should not be considered a mental illness or disorder is, among others, Green (1972), who—reviewing the biological, psychological, and sociological considerations—finds no clear-cut evidence of superiority of the heterosexual and says that the essential issue is whether the "given state or attribute . . . homosexuality—is, *in itself,* an illness, not whether all the other systems are in order." Green cites the famous 1935 passage of Freud, in which he wrote

Homosexuality is assuredly no advantage, but is nothing to be ashamed of, no vice, no degradation; it cannot be classified as an illness: we consider it to be a variation of the sexual functions produced by a certain arrest of sexual development.

Marmor (1965) stated the position without any equivocation:

Homosexual behavior and heterosexual behavior are merely different areas on a broad spectrum of human sexual behavior . . . and neither can be assumed to be intrinsically more or less "natural" than the other.

Theoretical considerations affect one's concept of normality. In the 1960's, the physiological research of Masters and Johnson (1966) and the theoretical review by Sherfey (1966) made the issue of the vaginal versus the clitoral orgasm a debating point for dozens of workers in the field.

Until then, except for a few debunkers, the vaginal transfer theory of Freud had led therapists to the mistaken notion that the woman who fails to transfer the seat of excitability from the clitoris to the vagina is immature. Here Freud's famous dictum, "Anatomy is destiny," must be re-examined. What if his anatomical ideas were erroneous, as a consequence of which it has been the destiny of many women to be iatrogenically damaged by the followers of this theory? To be sure, the inability to have a coital orgasm clearly does signify an inhibition, but the clitoral-labial mechanism has to work as a unit to produce orgasm, and the therapist needs to recognize the central importance of the clitoris in the orgastic process, realizing the error of Freud's 1905 statement that the vaginal "anesthesia may become permanent if the clitoric zone refuses to give up its excitability." In what now appears to be a moralizing statement, Freud attributed clitoral responsivity in the adult to "profuse sexual activities in infantile life."

Time passes, and the issues change somewhat, but it is curious how controversy can always find an anchoring point in Freud's writings, in a position to be strongly endorsed or challenged.

The last few years have created the "primacy of the orgasm," where more and better orgasms have been sought by patients and therapists (for their patients, if not for themselves). Now the entire process of sexual excitement and pleasure is being emphasized, not only the end result. What did Freud say about this?

The fore-pleasure is thus the same as that which can already be furnished by the infantile sexual instinct, albeit on a reduced scale, while the end-pleasure is new and is probably associated with conditions which first appear at puberty.

Freud argues that forepleasure or foreplay is infantile and only the end pleasure (orgasm) is mature. Actually, orgasm, although without ejaculation, occurs in early infancy. Freyhan (1973) points out that in Freud's view the mechanisms through which forepleasure is attained are an obstacle to the mature achievement of the sexual aim. Most sexologists now take the opposite view.

The entire process of sexual relatedness, touching and being touched (the haptic sense), looking, smelling, listening, rubbing, caressing, and kissing all parts of the body that are pleasing to self and partner are as important as the orgasm. Current professionals are not nearly as worried about fixation points and compulsions as was Freud and the generation of psychoanalysts after him, provided the sexual activity is pleasurable and noninjurious to both partners. Hence, the range of normal sexual behavior has broadened enormously from the rather restricted one of Freud's time and place. Although psychiatrists must always retain a concern for compulsive, stereotyped sexual

behavior that limits the freedom and flexibility of the patient, yesterday's perversion, as far as society is concerned, is today's deviation and tomorrow's variation.

What is true of sexual relations seems to be equally true of sexual relationships. As Comfort (1972) puts it:

Contraception has, for the first time, wholly separated the three human uses of sex—sex as parenthood, sex as total intimacy between two people ("relational" sex), and sex as physical play ("recreational" sex).

Normal functioning, that is, what society judges to be normal, has shifted from reproductive sex to relational sex and is now moving toward the sanctioning of recreational sex (physical pleasure accompanied by no more than affection). Men have always enjoyed all three levels; now women are discovering that they also have the capacity to enjoy sex at all three levels, including the initiation of recreational sex.

The concept of complete one-to-one sufficiency is shifting, changing the nature of family relationships, increasing the variety of possible patterns—some old, some new—from total involvement with one person to central but not exclusive involvement and to recreational sex as a source of bonding between friends. The rigid patterns of all-or-none involvement and the institutionalization of adultery or middle-class, middle-age swinging may be or are being replaced by new patterns. Although intimacy today is very difficult for many people to attain, will it become more or less difficult to achieve if society reduces the unrealistic expectation of complete involvement and one-to-one sufficiency? If these new patterns develop among ever-broadening sectors of the population and people truly become nonpossessive, what will happen to sexual jealousy? Will the extreme reaction of adolescents in their first love relationship in which complete possession is desired, an emotion that still persists into adult life for most, still be normal in the 21st century, or, as Comfort puts it, will our grandchildren be completely bewildered by 19th century opera because it is emotionally unintelligible?

Today's concepts of normality are affected by new discoveries and new facts, new technological inventions and improvements, and shifting social patterns, belief systems, and attitudes—all of which affect people's thinking and feeling. Normality is a process, a dynamic, shifting, changing interplay among discovery, invention, dissemination of information, and behavioral and attitudinal changes.

Sexual System

Sexuality may be described in terms of a system analogous to the circulatory or respiratory system (Lief, 1971). The components of the sexual system are set forth in Table I.

BIOLOGICAL SEX

The basic characteristics of the organism are the result of the interaction between the environment and the genetic code transmitted by the parents. The fetal environment may itself be highly significant in shaping sexual development and differentiation. A deficiency or excess of maternal hormones, viral infections, trauma, toxicity, nutritional deficiency, or maternal stress may affect the fetus adversely even before the environment at and after birth becomes effective. Ordinarily, the XX or XY chromosomal combination programs the undifferentiated gonad to become ovaries or testes. If testes, the gonad secretes androgen, which programs the fetus to become a male. Money and Ehrhardt (1972) write:

In the total absence of fetal gonadal hormones, the fetus always continues to differentiate the reproductive anatomy of a female.

TABLE I
Sexual System (Sexuality)

Biological sex—chromosomes, hormones, primary and secondary sex characterists.
Sexual identity (sometimes called core gender identity)—sense of maleness and femaleness.
Gender identity—sense of masculinity and femininity.
Sexual role behavior: sex behavior—behavior motivated by desire for sexual pleasure, ultimately orgasm (physical sex); gender behavior—behavior with masculine and feminine connotations.

The primordial fetus is, then, female. If one wishes to be mythically symbolic, one might say that Eve preceded Adam and that the biblical story is a reflection of ancient male chauvinism. Testicular secretions (or their absence) program the brain into patterns of organization, subsuming later sexual behavior.

Abnormalities in biological sex may be minor or major. Major anatomical or physiological—that is, androgen insensitivity—abnormalities create problems of intersexuality that may, if not corrected early in life, lead to conflicts in sexual or gender identity.

SEXUAL IDENTITY

At times, sexual identity has been referred to as core gender identity. Sexual identity may be defined as the person's inner feeling of maleness or femaleness continued over time. The sense of one's maleness or femaleness is more or less reinforced by the ways in which people, notably parents, react. Blue or pink is one of the earliest manifestations of such a response.

Of equal importance to the role of fetal androgens in organizing the brain for later masculine behavior (if androgen is present in sufficient amounts) or for female behavior (if androgen is insufficient) is the assignment of sex to the infant. Even in the presence of ambiguous biological characteristics, unambiguous sex rearing usually leads to a firm sexual and gender identity. A change in sex assignment is generally unwise after the child is older than 18 months. As Money and Ehrhardt (1972) point out:

by the age of 3 to 4 years, it is typically as difficult for an hermaphroditic child as it would be for an ordinary child, or an adult for that matter, to negotiate an imposed change of sex.

Almost everyone goes through sexual development differentiation without serious defects in sexual identity. The exceptions are some children with ambiguous sexual morphology who have ambiguous sex rearing and transsexuals who have the conviction that they belong to the opposite sex and reject their own body appearance and social status.

GENDER IDENTITY

With the relatively rare exceptions noted above, the development of sexuality leads to a secure sense of maleness or femaleness, which is generally complete by the age of three years. However, in American culture, doubts and conflicts about masculinity and femininity are ubiquitous. Serious disturbances lead to sex deviations, such as transvestitism, fetishism, voyeurism, and exhibitionism. Homosexuality is a special case of disturbance of gender identity; homosexuals do not have doubts about their maleness or femaleness (sexual identity).

The variations in behavior created by doubts and conflicts about one's femininity or masculinity are many. The reparative efforts at reassurance cover a wide spectrum, from compulsive promiscuity in both sexes to nonsexual competitiveness, as in sports or in dress and appearance. Inhibitory or avoidance responses are equally common. Attitudes and behavior toward the other sex are strongly influenced by the sense of security or insecurity about one's gender identity. Most problems in marriage, played out in the battle of the sexes, have their roots in gender insecurity.

SEXUAL ROLE BEHAVIOR

Sexual role behavior is divided into sex behavior and gender behavior. Sex behavior is based on a desire for sexual pleasure, ultimately for orgasm (physical sex); gender behavior is behavior with masculine and feminine connotations. The sexual response cycle and dysfunctions in performance come under the first category; sexual relatedness or relationships come under the second category. Gender role behavior was once handed down or assigned by tradition; today, roles are negotiable, and problems may become serious if negotiation is impossible to attain because of faulty communication (communication often breaks down because of disturbed perception or the fear of compromise) or conflicts over rights and privileges.

One may separate sexual behavior and gender behavior for the purposes of analysis and study, but, in actual functioning, sex and sexuality are intimately connected. With rare exceptions, sexual relations and relationships are different facets of a mosaic, with complex patternings and interfaces.

REFERENCES

American Medical Association Committee on Human Sexuality. *Human Sexuality.* American Medical Association, Chicago, 1972.

Bernard, J. *The Future of Marriage.* World, New York, 1972.

Bieber, I., Dain, H. J., Dince, P. R., Drellick, M. G., Grand, H. G., Gundlach, R. W., Kremer, M. W., Rifkin, A. H., Wilbur, C. B., and Bieber, T. B. *Homosexuality: A Psychoanalytic Study.* Basic Books, New York, 1962.

Broderick, C. B., and Bernard, J., editors. *The Individual, Sex, and Society: A SIECUS Handbook for Teachers and Counselors.* Johns Hopkins University Press, Baltimore, 1969.

Calderone, M. S., editor. *Manual of Family Planning and Contraceptive Practice,* ed. 2. Williams & Wilkins, Baltimore, 1970.

Christensen, H. T., and Gregg, C. F. Changing sex norms in America and Scandinavia. J. Marriage Fam., *32:* 616, 1970.

Comfort, A. Sexuality in a zero-growth society. Center for the Study of Democratic Institutions, *5:* 12, Dec. 1972.

Diamond, M., editor. *Perspectives in Reproduction and Sexual Behavior.* Indiana University Press, Bloomington, 1968.

Freud, S. Letter to an American mother. Am. J. Psychiatry, *107:* 786, 1951.

Freud, S. Three essays on the theory of sexuality. In *Standard Edition of the Complete Psychological Works of Sigmund Freud,* vol. 7, p. 221. Hogarth Press, London, 1953.

Freyhan, F. A. Scientific models for sexual behavior from the clinician's point of view. In *Contemporary Sexual Behavior: Critical Issues in the 1970's,* J. Zubin and J. Money, editors, p. 259. Johns Hopkins University Press, Baltimore, 1973.

*Gadpaille, W. J. Research into the physiology of maleness and femaleness. Arch. Gen. Psychiatry, *26:* 193, 1972.

Gagnon, J. H. Sexuality and sexual learning in the child. Psychiatry, *28:* 212, 1965.

Green, R. Homosexuality as a mental illness. Int. J. Psychiatry, *10:* 94, 1972.

Green, R., and Money, J., editors. *Transsexualism and Sex Reassignment.* Johns Hopkins University Press, Baltimore, 1969.

Harlow, H. The heterosexual affectional system in monkeys. Am. Psychol., *17:* 1, 1962.

Harris, G. W. Sex hormones, brain development, and brain function. Endocrinology, *75:* 627, 1964.

Hatterer, L. *Changing Homosexuality in the Male.* McGraw-Hill, New York, 1970.

Kagan, J. Acquisition and significance of sex typing and sex role identity. In *Review of Child Development Research,* M. L. Hoffman and L. W. Hoffman, editors, vol. 1, p. 137. Russell Sage Foundation, New York, 1964.

Kinsey, A. C., Pomeroy, W. B., and Martin, C. E. *Sexual Behavior in the Human Male.* W. B. Saunders, Philadelphia, 1948.

Kinsey, A. C., Pomeroy, W. B., Martin, C. E., and Gebhard, P. H. *Sexual Behavior in the Human Female.* W. B. Saunders, Philadelphia, 1953.

Lief, H. I. New developments in the sex education of the physician. J. A. M. A., *212:* 1864, 1970.

Lief, H. I. Medical aspects of sexuality. In *Cecil-Loeb Textbook of Medicine,* P. Beeson and W. McDermott, editors, ed. 13. p. 129. W. B. Saunders, Philadelphia, 1971.

Lief, H. I. Obstacles to the ideal and complete sex education of the medical student and physician. In *Contemporary Sexual Behavior: Critical Issues in the 1970's.* J. Zubin and J. Money, editors, p. 441. Johns Hopkins University Press, Baltimore, 1973.

MacLean, P. D. New findings on brain function and sociosexual behavior. In *Contemporary Sexual Behavior: Critical Issues in the 1970's.* J. Zubin and J. Money, editors, p. 53. Johns Hopkins University Press, Baltimore, 1973.

Marmor, J., editor. *Sexual Inversion.* Basic Books, New York, 1965.

*Masters, W. H., and Johnson, V. E. *Human Sexual Response.* Little, Brown, Boston, 1966.

*Masters, W. H., and Johnson, V. E. *Human Sexual Inadequacy.* Little, Brown, Boston, 1970.

*Money, J., and Ehrhardt, A. A. *Man and Woman, Boy and Girl.* Johns Hopkins University Press, Baltimore, 1972.

Rainwater, L. Some aspects of lower-class sexual behavior. J. Soc. Issues, *22:* 96, 1966.

Reiss, L. *The Social Context of Premarital Sexual Permissiveness.* Holt, Rinehart & Winston, New York, 1967.

Sherfey, M. J. The evolution and nature of female sexuality in relation to psychoanalytic theory. J. Am. Psychoanal. Assoc., *14:* 28, 1966.

Socarides, C. N. Homosexuality and medicine. *J. A. M. A., 212:* 1199, 1970.

Sorensen, R. C. *Adolescent Sexuality in Contemporary America.* World, New York, 1973.

Stoller, R. J. *Sex and Gender.* Random House, New York, 1968.

*Stoller, R. J. Overview: The impact of new advances in sex research on psychoanalytic theory. Am. J. Psychiatry, *130:* 241, 1973.

Vincent, C. E., editor. *Human Sexuality in Medical Education and Practice.* Charles C Thomas, Springfield, Ill., 1968.

Young, W. C., Goy, R. W., and Phoenix, C. H. Hormones and sexual behavior. Science, *143:* 212, 1964.

*Zubin, J., and Money, J., editors. *Contemporary Sexual Behavior: Critical Issues in the 1970's.* Johns Hopkins University Press, Baltimore, 1973.

chapter 2

History of Sexuality

2.1 Sex and Sexuality in History

NORMAN SUSSMAN, M.D.

Introduction

Patterns of sexual behavior have varied widely throughout the course of history. Activities accepted as normal and openly engaged in during one era have been severely condemned and considered too abnormal to be tolerated during another. In some cultures, certain forms of behavior achieved such widespread popularity or deviated so drastically from the commonly accepted sexual customs that they, in fact, characterized the sexuality and reflected the character of a time and place.

Prehistoric Europe

An awareness of, concern with, and, some suggest, preoccupation with sex can be traced back to prehistoric times. Analyses of surviving European cave paintings, combined with studies of today's primitive cultures in other parts of the world, indicate that by the early Stone Age, some 30,000 years ago, sex had already become something more complex than a compulsive, uninhibited activity motivated by pleasure and little else. Evidence suggests that patterns of sexual thought and behavior foreshadowing modern sexual practices and beliefs were being formed in these early social units.

CAVE PAINTINGS

Some of the oldest material evidence related to human sexuality is found in the Stone Age cave paintings of France and northern Italy. One painting from an epoch ending some 15,000 years ago at the Trois Freres cave in Ariege, France, has been interpreted as showing a human male figure with an accentuated erect phallus protruding beneath the flowing tail of an unidentifiable animal. Engravings dated at roughly 8,000 B.C. and found in several caves are suggestive of human copulation. Many prehistoric works show women with large breasts, prominent hips, protruding buttocks, and exaggerated vulvae. Such figures are often found in association with renderings of horses and other animals. A relief of three female figures at the Roc aux Sorciers in Vienne, France, for example, clearly shows the pubic triangles on each of the women, with a rendering of bisons situated next to one of the women.

Various explanations have been offered as to the meaning of these works, and interest has focused on what they reveal about actual sexual practices. The frequent portrayal of women in a forward bending position, for example, has given rise to speculation that this was a customary position in offering oneself to a man. Similarly, art showing human beings next to or in juxtaposition with animals has been said to be evidence of bestiality. These theories, however, are considered highly speculative. The most plausible interpretation is that cave art was not intended to, did not, and does not accurately reflect the prevalence and popularity of specific sexual practices. What it does show, most scholars agree, is that sex had already been endowed with magical qualities in the minds of humans and that these pictures, constituting sympathetic magic or fertility tokens, were symbolic of that fact.

ANIMISM AND SYMPATHETIC MAGIC

The emergence of sex as a social activity with both emotional and instinctual significance was the result of an early human exercise in the powers of reason and intellect and the development of two related concepts: animism and sympathetic magic. Animism was a system of thought in which nature and all objects, animate and inanimate, were conceived of as having spirits and conscious lives of their own. It represented an attempt to explain the causes of natural events. Natural phenomena were seen in terms of human experience, and human experience was seen in terms of cosmic events. The two were inseparable; nature and humans did not stand in opposition to one another. The destiny of the world and its creatures was ascribed to personified forces of nature, to beings with impulses, motives, and patterns of behavior similar to those of humans.

Consonant with animistic thought was the belief in sympathetic magic. Since providence was seen as incorporated in anthropomorphic beings, it, like humans, was open to persuasion. Specific thoughts, verbalizations, associations, gestures, postures, or visual representations might in some manner lead to the fulfillment of certain wishes or to the warding off of certain evils. The cave paintings may have been an attempt to express desires in visual form; perhaps they were appeals for such things as a successful hunt, a plentiful harvest, and the ability of women to bear children. According to magical thinking, death can be warded off by bartering the life of a human being or an animal in the form of a sacrifice. Done at a circumscribed time, in a specific place, and in a particular fashion, sex served as a way to placate and communicate with the forces of nature and to imitate nature. The spirits, too, were thought to copulate. In this fashion, sex attained a ritual character, in addition to its natural, impulsive expression. Sex came to serve the social unit as well as the individual. And there was a subordination of the instinctive drives of the individual to the larger concerns of the group. A sexual act committed against the accepted customs of the group was thought to offend the supernatural and in this way caused famine, sterility, and disease. Sex became subject to inhibitions and prohibitions; it became a sacred act with cosmic overtones.

Ancient Near East

In contrast to the speculative nature of theories concerning prehistoric man, concrete evidence of the connection in the human mind between sex, fertility, and belief in the supernatural appears in the religions of the ancient Near East. As documented by the written words of the cultures in Egypt and Sumer some 6,000 years ago, sympathetic magic had evolved into fertility cults.

FERTILITY CULTS

In Egypt, for example, a multitude of deities existed within the context of an institutionalized system of attitudes, beliefs, practices, and worship. The god Osiris was one important personification of the divine providence that permeated the world and gave it life and increase. The rhythm of nature was seen as a consequence of the periodic withdrawal or absence of this divine providence. Religious rites were designed to secure divine blessings. In all of these activities sexual symbolism played an important role. Phallic statues were a part of festivals. When depicted taking an oath,

Osiris is shown clutching his penis, by this gesture making his word more sacred. This custom was widespread throughout the ancient Near East. When Osiris was being revived from the dead, as portrayed in the *Book of the Dead,* the goddess Isis is shown kneeling before him, her mouth around his sacred phallus. Other gods and goddesses appear as representations of human forms, endowed with sexual attributes.

The goddess of the sky, Nut, is described in an Egyptian coffin painting at the Rijks-Museum in Leiden, Holland, as follows: "Her mouth is the western horizon, her vulva the eastern horizon." Papyrus drawings and coffin paintings explicitly show her arched above the erect phallus of the earth god, Geb (see Figure 1), a representation so common that some scholars have concluded that the Egyptians greatly favored the female superior position during sexual intercourse. But such speculations are highly questionable. The fact is that in Egypt, in Sumer, and in numerous other societies creation was imagined, by analogy with human conditions, as a process of copulation and birth, with a supernatural primeval couple as the parents of all that exists. It is, therefore, best to think of these renderings as evidence that sex was considered something sacred, rather than to take them as representations of sexual intercourse between ordinary men and women. Their significance was essentially symbolic.

The sacred nature of sexual intercourse was most evident in the fact that copulation itself

FIGURE 1. The sky (Nut) shown above the earth (Geb). Geb impregnates Nut with the stars. This drawing is based on the Papyrus of Tameniu (21st dynasty) at the British Museum. (Courtesy of Carol Simon)

was, at times, regarded as an act of worship. This view was the rationale for the customs of ritual intercourse and sacred prostitution, both of which were major features of the fertility cults.

Special importance was attached to the initial intercourse of a virgin, whose hymen, the guardian at the gateway of generation, represented a sacrifice dear to the deities. At some point in her life—at birth, at puberty, or before marriage—a female was expected to be ritually deflowered. Most often, this deflowering took place in a temple and was done by an artificial phallus, a priest, or a stranger. These practices were almost universal in the ancient Near East.

The prevalence of such defloration customs in various societies has prompted speculation as to the underlying psychological meaning inherent in the practice. It has, for example, been ascribed to fear and superstition surrounding contact with hymenal blood. Certain scholars, of whom Freud is one, speculate that, by having the bride deflowered by some man other than her spouse, the husband is relieved of any associations with the trauma of the first sexual act. Freud maintained that, since the first intercourse is more likely to bring disillusion than satisfaction, such customs prevent feelings of alienation by transferring the bride's hostility to some other man.

Sacred or temple prostitution was one form of ritual intercourse. Male and female prostitutes, serving temporarily or permanently and performing heterosexual, homosexual, oral-genital, bestial, and other forms of sexual activities, dispensed their favors in behalf of a temple. The prostitute and the client acted as surrogates for the deities, representing, in the words of Rawson (1973),

both fertility and sexuality in an erotic sense, the two being interdependent and mutually enhancing.

Eventually, secular forms of prostitution arose, but the generally high status of prostitutes throughout antiquity may be due to the sacred origin of the practice.

Despite uninhibited references to sex and the widespread acceptance of prostitution, extramarital coitus was not totally free of restrictions. The *Book of the Dead,* the code of Hammurabi, various Assyrian laws, and the Hittite code—all penalized coitus outside of marriage. Middle Assyrian laws, for instance, stated that, if a man kissed the wife of another,

they shall draw his lower lip along the edge of the blade of an ax and cut it off.

Prohibition against adultery represents one of the oldest known moral dictates.

Modesty also appears to have been an early element in relations between the sexes. Paintings from the Egyptian pyramids show that female servants working for men were fully clothed but that female servants working for women went about in the nude.

Most societies, however, were relatively free of prohibitions in the exercise of sexual functions. Only among the ancient Jews did calls for sexual restraint overshadow the ideals of sexual permissiveness.

ANCIENT JEWS

In its early history the Jewish religion exhibited many of the same interests and practices evident in neighboring Near Eastern cults. Only gradually did ascetic tendencies develop, reaching their full expression around the 7th century B.C. The Jews ultimately rejected temple prostitution and the excessive sexuality of fertility religions. Their god, Yahweh, had no sexual attributes and was not expected to participate in sexual rites, even symbolically.

The dominating factor that shaped the Judaic sexual outlook was a strong belief that procreation was the primary reason to exercise the sexual function. The essence of this morality is expressed in the following passage from the Talmud, a codification of Judaic laws:

Our Creator and Maker ordered us to be fruitful and multiply, and whoever does not engage in reproducing the race is likened unto one who is shedding blood, thus diminishing the essence of the deity, and he is the cause that the holy spirit shall depart from Israel; his sin is great indeed.

Masturbation, considered a form of contraception, was contrary to the ideal of procreation. Celibacy was sinful. Marriage was encouraged during the childbearing years; therefore, prepubescent girls did not marry. Sterility and failure to marry were stigmas worthy of exclusion from the religious and social community. Nonprocreative activities, such as homosexuality and bestiality, were forbidden. In Leviticus 18:22–23, the Bible tells men:

You shall not be with a male as with a woman; it is an abomination. And you shall not be with any beast and defile yourself with it.

Women are warned not to give themselves to a beast, since "it is a perversion."

Despite these restrictions, sex was not meant to be a joyless act. Pleasure was merely subordinate to reproductive functions. Sex could, however, coexist with passion. The tractate Niddah of the Talmud tacitly approves of pleasure during sex, stating that, if a woman takes part in copulation more passionately than the man, a son will be born, but, if the man takes part more passionately than the woman, a daughter will be conceived.

Passion could also coexist with affection. One of the most romantic works of antiquity, the *Song of Solomon,* comes from the Judaic culture.

Behold, you are beautiful, my love,
Behold, you are beautiful! . . .
Your lips are like a scarlet thread,
And your mouth is lovely . . . .
You have ravished my heart, my sister, my bride.
You have ravished my heart with a glance of your
    eyes,
With one jewel of your necklace,
How sweet is your love, my sister, my bride!

Women were, nevertheless, held to be inferior to men. A woman who bore a son needed 33 days to purify herself, but after the birth of a daughter, the woman needed 55 days before she could again engage in sexual intercourse.

As a rule, sexual relations between unmarried persons was condemned. When such activity was uncovered, it was viewed as both a religious and a secular transgression, since all women were treated as possessions, and a daughter belonged to her father. If she was used sexually, the responsible man had to compensate the father monetarily or take the daughter in marriage.

One custom that underscored the importance placed on the preservation of property and the continuation of the family line was the practice called levirate marriage. According to this custom, if a Jewish husband died without heirs, his closest male relative was compelled to take the widow as a bride and provide her with children.

Levirate marriage is mentioned in the book of Genesis (38: 7-10) in the narrative of Onan, son of Judah. The father tells Onan to go to his slain brother's wife

and perform the duty of the husband's brother unto her, and raise up seed to thy brother.

But Onan, knowing that the seed would not be his, spilled the seed on the ground when he went to his brother's wife, "lest he should give seed to his brother." This act was offensive to the Lord, and Onan paid for his sin with his life. Not only had he refused to adhere to the custom of levirate, but he had practiced coitus interruptus, a form of contraception through the centuries. Onanism has thus come to be used as a term for coitus interruptus, although it is sometimes used in reference to another nonprocreative act, masturbation.

The Jews were unique among the peoples of the ancient Near East in their rigid sexual outlook. They stood in contrast to the prevalent belief that sex was embued with sacred meaning and to cultures whose institutions facilitated the exercise of sexual functions and enhanced sexual enjoyment.

Ancient Greece

With the civilization of ancient Greece, a clear picture of the common patterns of sexual behavior and morality in a Western society emerges for the first time. From the 8th century B.C., when Homer produced the *Iliad* and the *Odyssey,* down through the cultural outburst of classical Athens in the 5th century B.C., references to sex in literature and visual art are extensive and straightforward.

SECULARIZATION OF SEX

At the height of Athenian civilization, sensuality and a relative lack of sexual in-

hibition were characteristic of Greek life. Athenians looked at sex and beauty as values. More than any previous society, the Greeks gave increased emphasis to everything human, including sex, changing a fearful world into a world full of beauty and without fearful powers to be propitiated in fearful ways (Hamilton, 1958). The Greeks desacralized society, taking the domain of the intellect away from the priests, and, by taking the domain of sex away from the gods, they desacralized sex as well.

No feature of Greek society more vividly reflects the joyous quality of sexual life and the general disinterest of the gods in human sexual morality than the attitudes and the activities ascribed to the gods themselves. Very human divine creatures were portrayed as seductive, wanton, flirtatious, and philandering. The gods enjoyed themselves. Zeus, the most powerful god in the pantheon, engaged in numerous sexual escapades. He married at least seven times and had innumerable affairs with mortal and immortal women and men. When companionship was lacking, he masturbated. When infatuated with the beauty of a young male, as in the case of the beautiful Ganymede, he pursued him with a fervor equal to that shown in the pursuit of women.

The goddess Hera, wife of Zeus, also practiced seduction, but her efforts, in keeping with the then-prevailing double standard, were directed toward her husband. As described by Homer in the *Iliad,* when Hera decided to intervene in behalf of the Achaean Greeks in their war with Troy, she chose sex as her weapon. In a highly sensuous passage Homer related Hera's efforts to distract Zeus from the battles below by means of seduction. As Zeus succumbed, Homer wrote,

the gracious earth sent up fresh grass beneath them, dewy lotus and crocuses, and a soft crowded bed of hyacinths to lift them off the ground. In this they lay, covered by a beautiful golden cloud from which a rain of glistening dew drops fell.

The Greeks used an ancient idea—that the gods' intercourse brought fertility—to emphasize beauty and pleasure.

Apart from such portrayals of overt sexual activity, mythological themes described many of the unconscious fears and drives associated with sexual behavior. One example, the Oedipus myth, a tale of parricide and incest in which Oedipus unwittingly slays his father and marries his mother, has repeatedly drawn the interest of writers, philosophers, and artists. Freud, who interpreted the story as a revelation of the universal unconscious urge of a young male to take the place of his father and possess his mother, wrote that, if psychoanalysis

> could boast of no other achievement than the discovery of the repressed Oedipus complex, that alone would give it a claim to be counted among the precious new acquisitions of mankind.

But Sophocles, in his *Oedipus Tyrannus,* indicated that an awareness of this psychological phenomenon already existed among the ancients. He wrote:

> Many a man in his dreams has seen himself in his mother's arms.

Sophocles also revealed, through metaphor, another element of the Oedipus complex, the fear of castration by the father. Sophocles ascribed sterility of men, women, cattle, and land to the consequences of Oedipus' act. The deed of Oedipus offended the gods, he wrote, leading them to physically prevent all things and people under his domain from reproducing.

Other insights into human sexual psychology were contained in the tale of Electra, who displayed the tendency of a daughter to be attached to her father and hostile to her mother (the Electra complex); in the story of Narcissus, who loved himself so much he could love no other (narcissism); and in the story of Cronus, who severed his father's genitalia with a flint sickle (fear of castration). Cronus, as Chronos or Father Time, still wields his relentless sickle.

In classical Athens, there was a growing tendency, at least among intellectuals, to view mythological stories and characters as symbols or conventions. The Greeks, more than any earlier civilization, were able to separate the symbolic from the real and the sacred from the secular. This ability is seen in the lapse of sacred prostitution. In classical Athens prostitution was a purely secular activity. This thinking is also reflected in the Greek language. The phallus, for example, had a symbolic importance, as in many earlier societies. But the Greeks could and did make distinctions between the artificial phallus and the anatomical organ. The term "phallus" was used only in the religious context; such words as peos, meaning tail, were used to describe human genitalia.

Artificial phalluses were, nevertheless, very much a part of the Greek landscape. Hermas, four-sided columns with the head of Hermes at the top and a protruding phallus in the middle (see Figure 2), stood in large numbers before Athenian homes, shops, and shrines and at all crossroads. Originally, the hermas were used as fertility symbols and to ward off evil spirits. The mutilation of virtually all of the Athenian hermas during a single night in 415 B.C. was a major episode in Athenian political and social history. The city was outraged at this act. Athenians saw it as a manifestation of the irreverence for sacred things, a consequence of the moral decay

FIGURE 2. Greek vase showing a bird perched on the phallus of a herma. (Bettmann Archive)

during the classical enlightenment. Viewed by many as a sacrilege and an offense to the divinities, the breaking of the phalluses was, nevertheless, recognized as a social transgression more than a religious transgression. The episode was, in fact, used as an opportunity to exile Alcibiades, a controversial general and politician who was held responsible for the mutilations.

The movement away from absolute acceptance of mythology as reality is reflected in the transformation of roles and ideas concerning Dionysus, the god of wine and fertility. When the worship of Dionysus first came to Greece, probably from Thrace, it was an excessive type of worship, characterized by sexual license and abandon, that contrasted markedly with daily sexual behavior and the worship of other gods. Dionysia, the festivals to honor Dionysus, consisted of drunkenness, nudity, wild dances, music, and orgies. The mystic doctrines and extravagant rites of the Dionysian cults had a tremendous appeal but were essentially foreign to the Greeks. The Greek emphasis on moderation in sexual activity eventually altered the character of the god and his worship. The orgiastic Dionysia continued to be held, but they were overshadowed by the emphasis placed on the role of Dionysus as the patron of choral song and drama. To the Athenians, at least the educated ones, he came to represent the inspiring force behind writing and acting. The annual Dionysia became cultural events, for which great plays like those of Euripides, Aeschylus, and Sophocles were written and performed. This change in the priorities assigned to Dionysus, as surely as any feature of Greek life, symbolized the secular tendencies of Greek society.

SEXUAL PRACTICES

The Greeks were totally free to show in their art and describe in their writings every form of sexual activity. And they did. Moreover, in classical Athens both art and literature were virtually devoid of symbolism. On this basis, several scholars have attempted to reconstruct the spirit and nature of common sexual practices.

Licht, for example, in *Sexual Life in Ancient Greece,* created a composite descrip-

tion of what typical love play may have been like. He concluded that a tender embrace, a kiss, and a caress were initial activities in a sexual encounter. Kissing between lovers was done with open mouths, tongues intermingled. One particular type of kiss, called the handle kiss, consisted of the man's pulling a woman's mouth toward his own by pulling on her ears.

Throughout ancient Greece, there was a cult of the bosom, and it was considered highly sensual for a man to clasp the breast of the woman and wantonly touch her "plump apples." Nonnus (Licht) described a male lover's pressing the "heaving globe of the plump breast" and a male god's accidentally touching the prominent roundness of the dress of a woman standing before him, feeling the heaving breasts, and having his hands start to quiver.

A man was expected to disrobe his partner. In general, this act was a simple matter, since a woman wore only a single garment. A bride, however, also wore an ornamental girdle, representing her virginity, that the groom loosened and removed. Kisses and tender bites on the shoulders and breasts usually accompanied the act of disrobing. On the wedding night, the love play took place somewhere other than the bed, which was adorned with flowers for the occasion. When the time for the completion of the act of love was at hand, the husband carried his bride to the bed.

Particular significance has been attached to the kiss for the purpose of expressing affection or sexual emotion. The kiss for this purpose is not found in all cultures. As Havelock Ellis noted, it is a comparatively new discovery in Europe, rarely being mentioned by Homer and other early Greek poets. In Celtic language, there was no word for kiss, and in some societies, according to Ellis, it is

regarded as a serious matter and very sparingly used, being by law only permitted on special occasions.

In the ancient Near East the kiss was largely monopolized for sacred uses. Among the early Egyptians, it had an all but sacramental significance. Thus, the kiss used in an erotic context is a significant aspect of Greek sexual expression and is certainly in harmony with the sensual climate of the Greek sexual outlook.

Acts of fellatio, which commonly appear on figure cups and vases, were, according, to Melville, a preliminary to full intercourse, not an alternative. Commenting on a scene from a cup at the Louvre, he writes:

It seems unlikely that the man whose penis is being sucked by the woman kneeling on a table will forgo the pleasure she is affording to a man at the other end and will expect to change places with him in due course.

This conclusion is reinforced, according to Melville, by another illustration on the same figure cup.

If one can assess the situation by the way in which the man is grasping his penis, it would appear that he intends only its head to enter the woman's mouth, and it provides another reason for supposing that, if ejaculation occurs, it will be considered preliminary to a further ejaculation in the vagina. Fellatio would not be an entirely satisfactory substitute for ordinary sexual intercourse unless the entire length of the penis passed between the woman's lips and its head pressed against the back of her throat.

Copulation was portrayed in an infinite variety of positions. The most frequently represented position of sexual intercourse shows a man taking a woman from behind. But it is difficult to know whether this position was simply a useful convention for showing the penis entering a woman or a generally accepted sexual custom. It is, moreover, a highly ambiguous position because it is impossible to tell whether the penis is entering the vagina or the anus.

Another common motif in Greek art is seen on a red figure jug attributed to the Shuralov painter. As shown in Figure 3, an attractive young couple are shown naked and about to make love. The man sits on a low chair, and the woman faces him, her arms around his neck, preparatory to sitting down on his erect penis. The sensual and emotional qualities present in this work mirror these qualities as they were present in Greek society. As Athenian society progressed, art became less stylized, contained more themes of feminine

FIGURE 3. Sensuality and frank eroticism were features of Greek life and Greek art, as reflected in the scene on this ancient Greek vase. (Bettmann Archive)

inspiration, and generally showed sexual activity as a joyful or tender event.

The Body

Nudity was commonplace at many public occasions, and the naked body was a favorite subject of Greek artists. Sculptors and painters studied human anatomy and, as part of their art, developed an image of ideal beauty that persists to the present day. In addition to a well proportioned muscular body, the Greeks concerned themselves with the matter of body hair. In the literature it is clear that body hair was considered unattractive. Various writers of the time describe the "troublesome" body hairs, and Clearchus recounted how in one town it was common practice to remove every hair from the body and go about in transparent purple-bordered garments. Among young men, hairiness of the legs was the most disliked, but facial hairs, especially those of puberty, were viewed as sensual, since they marked a youth's coming of age. On women, pubic hair and hair on the breasts were considered ugly. Visitors to brothels could watch dancing girls described as "naked and clean-plucked" (Licht). This attitude toward women was not, however, universal. On Greek statues, female pubic hair is depicted, if only rarely; on vase paintings, female pubic hair is commonly displayed. Depilation was accomplished by the plucking or singeing of hairs.

Before sexual intercourse, it was customary to make the body supple with olive oil. It is not clear whether this oiling was done for hygienic reasons or to heighten enjoyment of the sexual act or both. One of Solon's laws, forbidding slaves from rubbing freeborn boys with oil after exercises in the palaestra, and several other sources indicate that rubbing with oil often preceded a pederastic relationship.

There was concern with bodily odors. Numerous accounts in Greek literature describe the bath and the lavish use of perfumes by men and women. In the view of Plautus, an ancient Greek writer,

a woman only smells as she should when she does not smell at all. For those vamped up, toothless old women who besmear themselves with ointments and hide their bodily defects with dye, when once perspiration has united with the cosmetics, such a smell arises from the hags as when a cook mixes together a number of soups.

One courtesan had the nickname Hys, meaning swine, possibly to describe her lack of cleanliness.

Homosexuality

Sexual intimacy between men was widespread throughout ancient Greek civilization. Although not considered perverse or shameful, homosexual behavior as a substitute for or to the exclusion of heterosexual relationships was considered abnormal. On this point one must differentiate between the overt behavior and the preferred arousal pattern. It was accepted that one could be strongly aroused by a member of one's own sex, but the Greek man whose erotic impulses were directed only toward other men was universally scorned. What was accepted and practiced among the leading citizens was bisexuality; a man was expected to sire a large number of offspring and to head a family while engaging a male lover.

The male homosexual act usually involved anal intercourse with a boy. In reality, the boy was a young man, since puberty, marked by the first growth of facial hairs, represented the legally and socially acceptable developmental stage at which the male could become the object of sexual advances. Sexual intercourse with underage youths was a punishable offense.

Pederasty was closely linked to an idealized concept of the man as the focus of intellectual and physical activities. The relationship was a major element in the upbringing of boys and was used to impart to the youth the desirable qualities of his lover. The semen served as the carrier of these qualities. It was considered a reflection of some weakness of character if a boy or man was unable to enter into a satisfactory relationship. Pairs of lovers were held to have another quality of importance to the state: They made good soldiers. As expressed in numerous tales, most notably the account of the Theban band, lovers fighting side by side made formidable warriors.

Physical intimacy between women—termed tribadism by the Greeks, after the word trib, meaning to rub—occupied a position of little importance in the accounts of Greek sexual life. In contrast to male homosexuality, female homosexual relationships seemed to have no high ethical purpose to justify them as being beneficial for either the individual or the state. The woman was seen as serving but two roles. As a wife, she bore children and ran the home. As a courtesan, she satisfied male sexual desires. The spiritual qualities of the male homosexual relationship did not extend to such practices among women. Women are regarded and treated as inferior to men, and this misogynistic attitude colored the view of female homosexuality.

Nevertheless, some of the most famous accounts of the intensely emotional qualities of love between women come from the remaining works of the Greek female poet Sappho, who lived with a group of women on the island of Lesbos during the 6th century B.C. It is because of the association between Lesbos, Sappho, and female homosexuality that the terms "lesbianism" and "sapphism" came to be used for this sexual preference.

Many bowls and vases portray female homosexual activity and the use of artificial penises. These are shown being held in the hand or attached to the thigh with a leather strap. They were also used for the purpose of masturbation.

Prohibitions

Although sexually permissive by modern standards, Greek society was subject to moral pressures that served to limit violent or excessive acts. From the time of Homeric Greece through the period of classical Athens, written laws and public opinion curbed rape, sexual assault, adultery, exhibitionism, and sexual abuse of young children. In the first written Athenian code of law, promulgated by Draco in 621 B.C., rape and seduction were crimes punishable by death. These oppressive laws, said to have been written in blood instead of ink, were later modified or replaced by other legislation governing sexual conduct. For a time, a rapist was forced to marry the person he ravished in order to escape more severe punishment.

The most comprehensive laws governing sexual matters were passed by Solon between 600 B.C. and 500 B.C. They created state brothels called dicteria that were run and taxed by the government, made fornication by freeborn women a serious offense, forbade sexual intercourse between slaves and freeborn boys, deprived those who encouraged male prostitution of their civil rights, and punished by death those who sold a freeborn girl into a brothel. No Athenian laws made incest a punishable offense, but a union between sister and brother or parent and child was viewed as a sexual transgression. As expressed by Plato, such incestuous activity violated an unwritten law and was a cause of anguish to the gods.

Perhaps the most idealistic moral code or prohibition applied to physicians. The Hippocratic oath—believed to reflect the ethical principles of Pythagoras, a 6th century philosopher—provided a standard of sexual behavior for youths entering their apprenticeship to a physician. In the performance of his duties, the physician vowed to remain free of all intentional injustice, of all mischief,

> and, in particular, of sexual relations with both female and male persons, be they free or slaves.

Normally, slaves, an important feature of affluent households, were expected to engage in sexual relations with their masters or with those to whom the masters abrogated their privileges. Privileges accorded to free men and women included the right to exploit slaves, physically or sexually. The values contained in the Hippocratic oath thus stand apart from the usual standard of morality.

SPARTA

Athens is frequently compared with Sparta, another of the many city-states in the Greek-speaking world. Sexual life in Sparta differed from that of Athens in many respects. The military nature of the Spartan state, always preoccupied with preparation for war or engaged in some combat, meant that women assumed great responsibilities and freedom. They were seen more in public, in contrast with the Athenian women, who lived in virtual seclusion. Female homosexual activity was more visible, if not more widespread, than in Athens. Girls and young women were able to exercise in the nude, together with males.

Male homosexuality was idealized and practiced as a matter of course. Lycurgus, who, according to legend, was the promulgator of Spartan laws, encouraged pederasty as an important element of a boy's upbringing. This practice was especially common in the state military schools between the young soldiers and their officers. Lycurgus is also said to have advocated another Spartan custom, the temporary transfer of conjugal rights. To insure the superiority of Spartan children, a husband loaned his wife to a more vigorous man. Prostitution never flourished in Sparta, probably because partners were readily available and sexual life was relatively promiscuous.

Ancient Rome

The sexual attitudes and practices of ancient Rome contrasted markedly with those of Greece. In their daily lives, the Romans were far more coarse than the Greeks and were generally less concerned with abstract thought and esthetic ideals. Accordingly, sex was viewed in more physical terms.

FARMER-SOLDIER ORIGINS

From the time of Rome's founding in the 8th century B.C. until the last emperor was deposed in the 5th century A.D., the Roman sexual outlook was shaped by the temperament and character of the earliest Romans, a tribe of farmers turned soldiers who had a simple but persistent and profound belief in divine powers.

To the early Roman, the life of the fields was his life, and he saw himself as subordinate to the personified forces of nature that governed his harvest and later his fortunes in war. To assure a plentiful harvest, the Roman farmer went out to the fields at the beginning of the planting season and ritually copulated with his wife. When, in the course of events, the farmer became a soldier, the god of the fields, Mars, underwent a similar transformation, changing into the god of war. Against this background, there evolved crude patterns of sexual behavior, simple in character and sometimes cruel in practice.

VIRGINITY

Until late in the history of Rome and even then to a lesser extent, magical qualities were attached to female virginity. Virgins were carried across fields to sanctify the earth. As in other cultures, a virgin bride was more valued than a bride already deflowered, although virginity was not universally expected by men. Roman religious belief offered the worshiper little in the way of spiritual concepts or codes of sexual morality, but it glorified the virtues of virginity. The cult of Vesta and the vestal virgins who served Vesta are examples of the extraordinary powers that virgins were thought to possess in dealing with the gods. The vestal virgins were responsible for guarding the sacred objects and sacred fire in the round temple of Vesta, on whom the safety of Rome depended. If the sacred fire went out, the responsible virgin was suspected of unchasteness.

According to Roman law, no virgin—be she citizen, slave, pagan, or Christian—could be executed. It was thus necessary to rape a virgin before the sentence of death could be carried out. In another ingenious circumvention of the law, virgins were entombed alive with enough food to survive just a few days. Their deaths could then be attributed to starvation, instead of human conspiracy.

In some marriages, reportedly in the upper classes, brides were still ritually deflowered, sacrificing their hymen and thus their virginity to the god of fertility. This ritual involved a marble representation of the god Mutinus Tinitus or Priapus; it was placed in the bridal chamber or was contained within a sacred chamber of a temple. St. Augustine, describing these statues and the ritual, wrote of their immense and unsightly members, on which the bride was commanded to sit

according to the most honorable and most religious custom of nations.

In the most ancient times, the first sexual intercourse took place in the presence of witnesses or with the husband's friends' having intercourse with the bride first. A cloth stained with hymenal blood was displayed as proof of bridal virginity.

SADISM

The sadistic tendencies of the ancient Romans became most visible during the late empire in the form of spectacular combats and circus games. Commonly cited as examples of sexual sadism, these events were highly attended, and they represented a major source of amusement, even being called the national sport of Rome. But it was a sport in which thousands of human beings lost their lives. In Latin the word "arena" means sand, a material that was used because it easily absorbs blood.

The origins of these games can be found in the Etruscan funeral games and similar practices in other parts of the ancient world. The glorification and institutionalization of cruelty as a source of pleasure has been variously attributed to several causes. One is the basic violent and inhumane outlook of a warrior society, with its strong physical appetites. It has also been attributed to the influence of the emperors, who were often known for their infliction of physical and psychological pain on others in both official and private affairs. Another factor was the frustration of the lower classes, whose feelings of social impotence and joyless existence made the games a form of sexual excitement and release.

Many of the events themselves involved sexual activity. Couples were forced to perform sexual acts before the spectators. Women were raped by any one of a variety of animals as they were tied spread-eagled on a bed. At the conclusion of these displays, wild beasts were turned loose. During the reign of Augustus, casting prisoners to wild beasts was a statutory form of execution.

The intermingling of sex and sadism was seen in the stands surrounding the arena floor. The circuses were places to meet. Ovid, for example, advises young men to sit beside women in order to take advantage of them as they became engrossed in the bloody spectacle below.

Outside the stadium, other expressions of this sadism were seen. Crowds leaving the savage events made excellent patrons of prostitutes. The area around the Circus Maximus, one of the earliest arenas, housed a dense prostitute population, a phenomenon directly related to the high state of sexual arousal that the events caused in the spectators.

Sadism was also present on the Roman theatrical stages. Plays portraying adultery and incest carried out in fact what was to be done in pretense. And a character called on to die in the play would, indeed, die on the stage—by crucification, by being eaten by wild beasts, or by being burned alive. Tales of mythology were sometimes acted out with a bull, horse, or other animal playing the part of Zeus or another god in the seduction of a young woman.

IDEALS OF BEAUTY

The Romans appreciated the beauty of a well proportioned body. Unlike the Greeks, they made no effort to separate this appreciation from sexual thoughts. The body was primarily an instrument of sex. It is, therefore, logical that the constant depreciation of nakedness found in Roman literature is based on the view that nakedness is synonymous with indecency and impropriety. Only with the later popularity of the public baths did nudity become more accepted.

Ideals of male and female beauty differed.

A woman was favored if her skin was soft, smooth, and unmarred by blemishes. Her body was slender, with firm, plump thighs. She dyed her hair, usually to a red or yellow. Her skin was softened by olive oil, and the use of makeup was essential. Cosmetics were applied to the body, as well as to the face. The Romans, like the Greeks before them, were lavish in their use of perfumes, and, as Ellis has commented, they disliked personal odors. A personal odor was almost always an unpleasant odor, and Ovid wrote,

it is scarcely necessary to remind a lady that she must not keep a goat in her armpits.

The ideal man was muscular and, in contrast with the women, deeply bronzed by the sun. The appearance of his muscles and tan was enhanced by the application of olive oil to make the skin shine.

SITES OF SEXUAL ACTIVITY

Potential sites for sexual union were ubiquitous. Wherever people could meet was apparently an acceptable place to satisfy erotic desires.

Arches beneath aqueducts, houses, temples, circuses, and arenas were particularly favored as locations for rendezvous. So commonly did prostitutes solicit and entertain their customers beneath the arches that eventually the arches, termed "fornices" in Latin, became synonymous with the word for brothel and gave rise to the verb "to fornicate," a word that still retains a crude connotation with respect to sexual intercourse.

Within the home, sexual encounters generally took place in the bedroom, but they were not restricted to the sleeping areas. The Roman custom of dining on a couch in a reclining position, with men and women sharing one couch, encouraged and resulted in intimate activities. Affluent citizens had rooms reserved specifically for sex. For example, Messalina, wife of the emperor Claudius, had a room in the imperial palace where she forced ladies of the nobility to engage in intercourse with men of her choosing, sometimes while the woman's husband watched. Rooms intended for sexual activity often had obscene paintings and statues. The emperor Tiberius and the poet

Horace were two notables who decorated rooms in their homes with erotic frescoes.

In later Rome, the public baths became a site identified with sex. The opportunities for erotic practices were fully explored, with men and women bathing together and prostitutes of both sexes working as attendants in the baths.

HOMOSEXUALITY

In contrast to the self-conscious and elaborate efforts of the Greeks to glorify and idealize homosexuality, the Romans simply accepted it as a matter of fact and as an inevitable part of human sexual life. Pederasty was just another sexual activity.

Many of the most prominent men in Roman society were bisexual if not homosexual. Julius Caesar was called by his contemporaries every woman's man and every man's woman. Other emperors of questionable sexual perference were Nero, Augustus, Tiberius, Hadrian, Domitian, and Trajan. So prevalent was the practice of anal intercourse, primarily between men, that one Roman writer cited this activity as the major cause of hemorrhoids.

Transvestism seems to have been more common in Rome than in Greece. Cross-dressing was known in other ancient societies, mainly as part of wedding rituals, but in Rome the practice was more overtly secular and removed from ritual. One head of state, Elagabalus, who was, according to Ellis,

the most homosexual of all the company; a true invert of the feminine type,

is reported to have dressed as a woman, to have bathed with the women in the baths, to have depilated his body and facial hair, and to have been devoted to the men he loved.

GALEN AND SORANUS

Galen (ca. 130 to ca. 200 A.D.), a Roman physician of Greek parentage, influenced the practice of medicine through his many treatises and extensive teaching and was an undisputed authority until the 16th century. He had a great curiosity in and addressed himself to many of the problems surrounding generation and sexual activity.

In *De Sanitate Tuenda,* his discourse on hygiene, he discussed the ways a person can avoid the fatigue and exhaustion that may follow sexual activity. Before intercourse, exercise and the taking of only moderate quantities of food are advised. Galen also advocated the taking of baths after intercourse. Two chapters of his treatise *On the Preservation of Health* are devoted to techniques of anointing the body with oil before copulation. Galen sometimes used dummies as part of his lectures to apprentice physicians to demonstrate the roles of men and women in sexual activity (see Figure 4).

His most striking observations with respect to sexual functions involve the physiological and psychological aspects of sex. Galen coined the term "gonorrhea," translated as flow of seed. He pointed out that male retention of sperm and female delay of uterine discharges contributed to psychic imbalance and to the manifestations of anxiety. He detected a correlation between hysterical symptoms and the absence of sexual relations and noted the curative effect of sexual relations and the release of tension provided by masturbation. These observations, according to Mora, are but some of the clinical descriptions given by Galen of the interaction between psychic components and somatic illness.

Galen also directed his attention to the subject of birth control, suggesting among other practices violent postcoital movements to prevent conception. But Galen was surpassed in his expertise on birth control by another Roman physician, Soranus of Ephesus (98–138), whose *Gynaecology* has been described by Himes as

the most brilliant and original account of contraceptive technique written prior to the nineteenth century.

Among the methods Soranus suggested were the use of occlusive pessaries, vaginal plugs, astringent solutions to contract the cervical os and thus make impregnation less likely, gumlike or oily substances to occlude the os and reduce sperm motility, and strong acid or alkaline douches to create an unfavorable environment for sperm. His observations on abortions included the view that the

FIGURE 4. Shown within the illuminated initial of the Dresden Galen manuscript is a scene of the Roman physician Galen lecturing his students on the physiology of sex. (Fourteenth century. Preserved in the former Royal Library of Dresden.) (Bettmann Archive)

need for repeated abortions is a primary indication for future contraceptive efforts. The potential of a dangerous birth was the single most important indication for abortion. Abortions were not to be done, according to Soranus, simply to prevent the birth of unwanted children or to maintain a chaste figure.

The extensive use of contraceptives and abortives has been cited as a factor leading to the fall of Rome. This theory is but one of countless assertions that sexual degeneracy and a decline in the popularity of marriage undermined the empire and led to its collapse. It is not a view supported by the weight of historical evidence.

OVERVIEW OF ROMAN SEXUALITY

On balance, the Romans were matter-of-fact in their approach to sex. They had few pretensions about sexual activity being anything more than a physical activity. It could be sacred but not spiritual in the sense or to the degree evident in Greek homosexuality. Also in contrast with the Greeks, the Romans who wrote of and pictured sexual themes were less serious about the subject, satire and cynicism being the prevalent genres in presenting erotic subjects.

The ancient Romans traditionally resisted attempts to regulate sexual conduct. When, in 186 B.C., the Senate forbade the Bacchanalia, the Roman version of the Dionysian orgies, enforcement of the decree proved to be impossible. A later effort to govern morality, the Julian laws, passed by Augustus between 18 B.C. and 9 B.C., met a similar fate.

This importance accorded to sex as a physical and often impersonal activity did not prevent the Romans from appreciating the sensual, tender, and intimate nature of love play and coitus. This fact is evident in the works of Ovid, Horace, Martial, Lucius Apuleius, Petronius, and other writers.

Ovid, to cite but one example, in his manual of seduction and adultery, *The Art of Love,* repeatedly described lovers' kisses with tongues intermingled or with the tongue of one partner thrust within the mouth of the other. These kisses he distinguished from those a "sister gives her sober-minded brother."

The Romans, noted Ellis, had words for at least three kinds of kiss: the *osculum,* for friendship, given on the face; the *basium,* for affection, given on the lips; and the *suavium,* given between the lips, reserved for lovers.

Ovid and others mentioned the use of the thigh, pressed against a lover's genitalia, as an early act of sexual stimulation. Caressing and handling of the whole body, the pressure of female breasts, and the fondling of private parts apparently stimulated Ovid and his contemporaries, just as they have stimulated men of other generations.

On the basis of graphic and literary evidence, three coital positions appear to have been favored: the male superior position, the female superior position, and the taking of the woman from behind. Particular significance has been attached to the female dominant position, since it is said to reflect the enhanced status of women in Roman society. Indeed, women were not expected to be passive participants in sexual activities. Numerous writers depict women who initiate encounters and are aggressive in the sex act. In performing fellatio, women are shown as violent and devouring, acting out a visible inner desire to perform the act for personal satisfaction. The male partner is often portrayed as being "pumped dry" (Legman). Recognition and acceptance of female passion is found in numerous Roman works but is best expressed in Lucretius' *On the Nature of the Universe.* He wrote:

> Do not imagine that a woman is always sighing with feigned love when she clings to a man in a close embrace, body to body, and prolongs his kisses by the tension of moist lips. Often she is acting from the heart and in longing, for a shared delight tempts him to run love's race to the end.

Interest has also focused on the taking of the woman from behind. This position is by far the one most frequently shown in visual renderings (see Figure 5). A possible explanation for this fact, and it holds for Greece as well, is found in Book IV of Lucretius' treaties. According to Lucretius, it was

FIGURE 5. Fragment of a late Roman relief, showing a man taking a woman from behind, a common portrayal in ancient art. (Bettmann Archive)

thought that women conceived more readily when they used the *more ferarum,* the way that four-footed animals copulate,

in a prone posture with loins uplifted so as to give access to the seed.

Possibly, then, it was customary to use this position when procreation was an objective. Or perhaps it had a symbolic significance as an act of favor to the fertility gods.

Rare insight into sexuality in Roman civilization during the period of the Empire is provided by the city of Pompeii, a settlement to the south of Rome on the Italian peninsula that was buried in a volcanic eruption of Mount Vesuvius in 79 A.D. Protected by hardened lava and ashes, evidence of daily life and sexual attitudes—evidence in the form of frescoes, statues, and graffiti—has been preserved almost perfectly intact. Grant analyzes the nature and meaning of sex in Pompeii based on these remaining bits of evidence, writing:

The feelings of the average Pompeian were a kind of easy-going Epicurianism . . . the general Pompeian belief could be summed up by the doctrine of having a good time while you can.

Since life was generally shorter for most people than it is today, there was, Grant notes, a feeling that life should be enjoyed before it is too late. He adds:

It is in order to ensure enjoyment of the fleeting hour that the graffiti of Pompeii revert continually to the words for luck and happiness—*felicitas* and *felix.* And since sex ranked as an unsurpassed way of enjoying oneself, that is one of the main explanations of the powerful atmosphere of sexuality that is detectable in the city.

This positive attitude toward sex and the frank and uninhibited nature of its discussion and practice characterized not only Pompeii and Rome but most of the ancient world.

The Middle Ages

The period of European history from the fall of the western part of the Roman empire in 476 A.D. until the beginning of the Renaissance, some 1,000 years later, is by convention called the Middle Ages.

Throughout this period, the Roman Catholic Church, having stepped into the void of the destroyed Roman civilization, endeavored to create a new society guided by such Christian principles as virtue, compassion, charity, and love. Also included among Christian ideals were asceticism and chastity—ideals that not only devalued sex but separated sex from other spiritual and social values.

Church morals were formulated largely from the writings of the early Church fathers. St. Jerome wrote:

A wise man ought to love his wife with judgment, not passion. He who too ardently loves his wife is an adulterer.

St. Augustine struggled to separate affection from sexual passion, and several chapters in *The City of God* attempt to solve this problem and to answer the question of how children might have been purely propagated, had Adam and Eve remained free of original sin. And St. Paul argued:

It is good for a man not to touch a woman.

Eventually, these theological writings were transformed into doctrine. Celibacy came to be viewed as a chief virtue of the Christian faith, and only procreation could justify physical relations. Two major objectives of Church morality emerged: to create a population of celibate clerics and to restrict all sexual activity to those joined in holy wedlock and, even then, to make it as joyless and perfunctory as possible.

CELIBACY

It has been estimated that one person in 12 during the 13th century was in the service of the Church. Efforts to impose ascetic and celibate life-styles on so large a group represented a constant source of difficulty for the Church.

Chastity was not always a requisite for entry into the service of God. In the early years of Christianity, celibacy was considered ideal, but clerics were able to take wives. Some customs were devised that permitted cohabitation between priests and women but without conjugal relations. One such attempt was inspired and called by the Greek concept of spiritual love, agape. According to this practice, also known as synesaktism, a priest entered into a spiritual marriage with a virgin, who became his spiritual bride, or agapeta. The couple could live together and even share the same bed, but, in theory, the relationship remained chaste. Tertullian, for one, advocated this arrangement for those men, lay and clergy, who wished to be celibate but were unable to live without women. For himself, Tertullian chose traditional marriage. It is difficult to say how successful the agapetae (spiritual lovers) were in adhering to their lofty ideal. Some irregularities were publicized by advocates of absolute asceticism. But even the thought of a man and woman living together was offensive to some of the early Church fathers. Cyprian (Taylor), for example, asked:

Shall Christ be composed, seeing the virgin that was dedicated to him sleeping with another, and not become wrathful? And not threaten with the severest punishments for such unclean relationships?

St. John Chrysostom wrote a polemic, *Against Those Who Keep Virgins in Their Houses,* in which he described a perverse form of pleasure in the chaste marriage, a pleasure "more ardent than conjugal union." St. Jerome, on the other hand, was skeptical about the custom. How, he asked, could one help but draw certain conclusions. By the 7th century several Church councils had declared the practice of agape a heresy, and it gradually declined as a formal custom among clerics.

But the problem of achieving a celibate clergy did not end. St. Benedict of Aniene, a 9th century reformer, described numerous cases of ecclesiastical transgressions. Marriage among the lower clergy was still prevalent during this period, as it was in 1215, when the Fourth Lateran Council met and vigorously denounced, among other things, clandestine marriage, immorality, and drunkenness among clerics. The council also attempted to resolve a major theological issue that had been used by opponents of the rule of clerical celibacy, namely, that no scriptural authority for this requirement existed. The council proclaimed that celibacy was henceforth an absolute duty for the priesthood.

Nevertheless, many clerics continued to marry and fornicate, a situation that was not due solely to irrepressible libidinal drives or disregard for Christian precepts. It was encouraged by tacit acceptance of breaks with vows of celibacy. Despite repeated, unequivocal official statements that rules of sexual continence be observed, a review of court records of the medieval period indicates that these efforts were spasmodic, that enforcement was rare, and that penalties upon conviction were invariably light. If the issue was pressed, public penance or forced seclusion was considered an appropriate punishment. No one wanted scandal, and only the most scandalous episodes, involving rape and other excesses, resulted in harsh sentences.

Reacting to this state of affairs, the presiding archbishop at the Council of Ravenna in 1261 rose before the attending prelates and announced his revulsion at the fact that women were being led behind the altar under the pretense of confession and there being dealt with as the "sons of Eli dealt at the door of the tabernacle." The confessional box had not yet been introduced; its use was suggested by the Council of Valencia in 1565 partially for the purpose of preventing physical access to women during confession. The archbishop also spoke out against those priests at the council who had houses full of sons and daughters. In Germany at the time this situation was so common that the word *pfaffenkinder*—parson's children—became a synonym for bastard. He could have added that many Church councils, themselves convened to deal with the problem of sexual incontinence, regularly attracted prostitutes. About 700 courtesans came to Constance for a meeting held between 1414 and 1418. The papacy itself set a bad example. Many popes only grudgingly accepted celibacy for themselves. Others made no secret of their affairs.

What was true of the men was also true of the residents of the convents. In the satirical style of Ovid, whose *Art of Loving* was a popular feature in many monastic libraries, Andreas Capellanus, a 12th century chaplain to the king of France, alluded to this fact. He warned against

> seeking lonely places with nuns or looking for opportunities to talk with them, for if one of them should think that the place was suitable for wanton dalliance, she would have no hesitation in granting you what you desire and preparing for your burning solaces, and you could hardly escape that worst of crimes, engaging in the work of Venus.

Brothel keepers and whores frequently complained that the keen competition of the convents was ruining their business. As de Riencourt notes:

> Those were the days when nun and whore were almost synonymous expressions.

Convents were frequently described by writers of the period as brothels. For example, Nicolas Clemangis (Christian, 1959), a physician at the Sorbonne in Paris, made the following observation:

> I am prevented by modesty from making too detailed accusations; but in all truth can our monasteries, which I cannot call sanctuaries of God, at present be called anything but the mere abodes of Venus? And nowadays is it not recognized that, if a girl takes the veil, she is going to perdition?

Further evidence of persistent ecclesiastical interest in sex was also revealed in the sculptures, furniture carvings, and missals of various medieval churches. Often visible to the clergy but not to the worshipers, these works of art portrayed riotous monks, with monastic robes bulging over erect penises, and nuns carnally entertaining the devil. A sculpture of the elect and the damned at the Cathedral of Amiens showed in such great detail the specific sexual vices committed by those going to hell and so shocked the clerics of the 18th century that they had many portions of the panel chiseled out.

There were many reports of homosexuality in monasteries and convents. As with heterosexual excursions into eros, the extent of sexual release between ecclesiastical members of the same sex cannot be conclusively documented. But this sort of lapse in celibacy might be expected among persons deprived of normal outlets. In any event, it is known that members of many orders were preoccupied with homosexuality. This aspect of medieval male celibate psychology was revealed in the charges that monks frequently brought against accused heretics. One notable example of this obsession is found in the accusations made against the Templars, a wealthy and powerful fellowship of knights. When arrested in 1307, the members of the knightly order were confronted with an indictment, prepared by Dominican and Franciscan monks, that described Templar initiation rites in which neophytes were stripped naked and obliged to kiss the presiding officer, who was also said to be naked, on the mouth, navel, and anus. The candidate, according to the charges, was then forced to submit to anal intercourse. No respectable scholar has ever been able to provide evidence that corroborates this account, a fact that leads to the general conclusion that these charges, although possibly based on rumors, had no basis in fact.

When discovered, homosexuality rarely provoked severe penalties. Conviction on charges of sodomy usually resulted in demotion or the prevention of future advancement within the ecclesiastical hierarchy. Reports of lesbianism among nuns caused at least two Church councils, one in Paris in 1212 and another at Rouen in 1214, to forbid residents of convents from sharing the same bed.

In summary, the gulf between official Church theory and the actual practice of individual ecclesiastics was, in the words of Huxley (1952), "enormous, unbridged, and seemingly unbridgeable." Abuses among the lower clergy were not checked from above, since the highest prelates, like the humblest friars, could in many instances hardly offer themselves as exemplifications of sexual virtue. It was this open and cynical license among clerics that prompted the laity to say, "I'd rather be a priest than do such a thing" (Christian).

Such accounts of ecclesiastical conduct should be kept in perspective. Those who chose to ignore or were unable to abide by their pledges of sexual continence were not, as the writings of moralists often suggest, any more lecherous or dissolute than their secular contemporaries. Moreover, conclusions as to the extent of clerical sexual activity cannot be offered with accuracy. All that can be said is that it was common and that its pervasiveness varied from country to country. For many persons, vows of celibacy represented a formality, a required statement for admission to Holy Orders. The laity seemed to understand, since the departures from sexual abstinence were considered ordinary and were almost taken for granted. A frequent humorous theme of the period involved the father who offered a traveling priest lodgings for the night but made sure to keep an eye on his daughter or wife. Violations of celibacy rarely caused scandal. In the eyes of ardent supporters of Church doctrine, these lapses were sins. To everyone else, they were hypocrisy.

SECULAR BEHAVIOR

As a rule, people in the general population were not torn away from their instinctual drives or their classical and barbaric inheritance of sexual freedom. Like officers of the Church, they mouthed adherence to the concept of sexual restraint but continued to lead sexual lives not markedly different from their pagan ancestors. Rape did not disappear. People kissed, caressed, and copulated. The nobility exchanged concubines, youths mischievously fornicated in churches, students kept mistresses during their stay at the universities, and prostitution flourished.

Church teachers, most historians agree, had little impact on the prevalence or frequency of marital and extramarital intercourse. They may, however, have modified some attitudes toward coital technique, largely through the use of guilt and fear.

It was during the Middle Ages that the Church began to advocate the man-above-and-woman-below position as the only proper copulatory position for those joined in holy wedlock. Approaching the woman from behind, even for the purpose of vaginal insertion, was especially discouraged. This technique was most frequently attributed to demons by accused victims of demonic advances and by their clerical inquisitors. Medieval physicians, mirroring current social values, also described *coitus a posteriori* as the demon's method and reported an associa-

tion between taking the woman from behind and abortion. At one time, 40 days' penance was prescribed for such practices in England.

So strongly did the Church advocate the missionary position—as it later came to be known, after the missionaries who urged converts to adopt this technique—that some theologians suggested that God prohibited demons from using it. All other techniques, they said, were those of the devil, and the lower the demon, the more perverse his postures in coitus. The lowest type of demon engaged in oral or anal intercourse. A common feature on some chastity belts, brought to Europe by returning Crusaders, was a shield for the anus as well as the vagina. This attempt to insure inviolable fidelity revealed an awareness or, at least, a concern by the absent husband that sodomy was practiced by mortals or demons.

Ecclesiastical opposition to erotic pleasure, the underlying motive behind Church advocacy of one coital position, resulted in the development of the *chemise cagoule,* a thick nightshirt that had a single, suitably placed hole through which it was possible to impregnate one's wife with the minimum possible contact and pleasure.

Absolute condemnation of contraception and abortion—physicians were told,

Do not allow women to persuade you to give abortives, and do not be a party to any such plan

—did not stop the use of various techniques to prevent childbirth. Coitus interruptus, a measure that the Crusaders encountered in Islam, was an important contraceptive technique. Drugs to increase sexual ardor were marketed in all countries throughout Europe, as were drugs to cure impotence. By these indexes alone, sexual intercourse was as commonly engaged in during the Middle Ages as it had been during other eras and with many of the same attendant practical concerns.

Canon law considered homosexuality an abomination and called for punishment by death. Homosexuality was, nevertheless, as widespread during the Middle Ages as it was during preceding and subsequent periods in European history. There is some evidence that the Church had partial success in its attack on sodomy during the early Middle Ages, at least as far as its public practice was concerned. But homosexual promiscuity reappeared during the Crusades—in part, the result of exposure to Oriental tolerance of such practices and the camaraderie of the fashionable young warriors. Anal intercourse between men was not necessarily taken as a sign of effeminacy. Among the Crusader kings, Richard III and Edward II of England and Philip IV of France made no secret of their practices. Anal intercourse was so widespread among the Crusaders that burning as a punishment for it was legislated at a council held in Nablus in 1120 under Baldwin II of Jerusalem. One 12th century abbot complained that anal intercourse had become so common that ancient Sodom was rising from her ashes in Europe. A 13th century Frenchman, Jacques de Vitry, observed that sodomy so filled the city of Paris

that it was held a sign of honor if a man kept one or more concubines.

The Crusaders can be credited with having reintroduced the bath to Europe. The Church regarded the body as shameful, a view that expressed itself in manifold ways over the years. In art, nudity was discouraged. During the early Middle Ages, pictures of genitalia—with penises, testicles, and prominent pubic hair—had been evident. But by the 11th century the pubis in both men and women was nearly always covered or effaced. When nudes did appear, they were stiff, stylized, and sexless. The Church also discouraged baring of the body, even in private. Clerical associations of sex with the great baths of Rome had caused bathing to become identified with lustful thoughts and deeds. Cleanliness and godliness were not yet neighbors. Purity of the body and its garments sometimes meant impurity of the soul. Some pilgrims did not wash their faces after the time of their baptism, so as not to remove the holy chrism. So, in some instances, dirtiness was a sign of holiness (Green).

Ecclesiastical fears were justified with respect to public bathing. The Moslem-style steam baths, brought to Europe by the Crusaders, became, in many instances, sources of sexual temptation and encounters

comparable to the great baths of Rome but on a smaller scale. In several cities and towns, men, women, boys, girls, monks, and nuns bathed together quite naked. Charges of shameless abuse of the baths in England resulted in the mandatory use of drawers or smocks by patrons at some establishments. A 15th century Florentine visitor to Aargau wrote that baths were common to both sexes. Ploss and Bartels note that the wooden partitions between male and female sections

had so many openings that people on both sides could see and even, as happened frequently, could touch each other.

Many bath houses, in fact, became disguised brothels, containing tubs large enough for two people but small enough to insure intimate enjoyment.

Medieval sexuality can thus be viewed in terms of Church failure to achieve universal acceptance of its officially restrictive regulations of moral behavior. It was a futile and sometimes half-hearted battle to impose the ideal of sexual restraint on the population of Europe. But a large group within society did take the concepts of chastity and asceticism quite seriously. They lived in a world of fear, and the very thought of sex put terror into their hearts. Their lives were devoted to worship, and they had no room for the sensual joys that the flesh could provide. It was among these people that the untoward manifestations of prolonged sexual abstinence appeared. Not permitted to function openly and naturally and forced underground, sex, as Brill put it,

behaved like an outcast, plying his trade secretly and sneakily, often causing confusion by popping up where and when least expected.

FLAGELLANT SECTS

Denied outward expression, sexuality may turn inward. In both a literal and a symbolic Christian revolt against the body and its sensual potential, some persons, like St. Fidelis, wore uncomfortable shirts made of hair and burdened themselves with heavy iron girdles. Others slept on hard wooden boards or, like St. Francis, made sure they never completely satisfied their hunger and thirst.

Such harsh physical austerity was masochism in its most benign form. In its most malignant form, masochism appeared among the faithful ascetics who wore painful belts of nails and the nuns who proved their contempt for the sensual interests of young women by scarring their faces and cutting off their hair and, sometimes, their breasts (Cleugh, 1955).

The exemplification of such self-inflicted castigation of the flesh was found among the flagellant sects that swept over Europe during the 13th century. Most of these sects were headed by monks, who, as described by Goldberg,

claimed to have received letters from heaven, demanding that people punish themselves for the wickedness in the world by striking their bodies with thongs.

These letters were said to threaten terrible punishments on the whole earth if the commands were not filled. It was both a curative and a prophylactic masochism. Many sect leaders set themselves up as examples. St. Dominic, for example, immortalized himself by inflicting 300,000 strokes on himself in 6 days. The flagellants marched from town to town, using heavy leather scourges on themselves until blood streamed from their open wounds.

Flagellantism assumed the proportions of a mania. According to one estimate, there were 800,000 flagellants in 14th century France alone. Even if exaggerated, this figure underlines the magnitude of the practice. Eventually, even the Church became alarmed. In 1349 Pope Clement VI issued a bull that declared the practice of self-torture a heresy, and several flagellant leaders were burned at the stake. Although diminished somewhat, the mania continued into the 15th century.

WITCHCRAFT

The disguised or sublimated eroticism that was manifested in flagellantism appeared in another medieval phenomenon—the great fear of witchcraft that appeared early in the 14th century. In itself, the belief in the reality of evil nonhuman and semihuman spirits was neither new nor unique to the Middle Ages. Such beliefs had their origins in prehistoric times. They formed the basis of the old fertility cults. The concept of malevolent supernatural agents is, in fact, no more than a variation of the magical thinking found in all religions and mythologies throughout the world. Christianity itself was based on the belief that a benevolent God can perform supernatural acts, and the belief in the devil was simply the converse of this view. References to Satan and the devil are present in both the Old Testament and the New Testament, and all the trappings and rituals of witchcraft, as described by Apuleius in *The Golden Ass* during the 2nd century, were already present in the Roman empire. These beliefs were merely adopted, altered, and given a new life during a period of tremendous social and psychological stress—the 14th century, a time when Europe began to emerge from the Middle Ages.

In the summer of 1348 the bubonic plague, the Black Death, killed between one-third and one-half of the population of the continent. Two subsequent epidemics struck with less violence in 1362 and 1374. A series of defaulted loans had, by 1350, caused most of the great banking houses of Florence and Siena to fall. Controversy over the papacy had continually undermined church power. The result was the Great Schism, during which two lines of popes, one at Avignon and another at Rome, ruled a divided Christendom from 1378 to 1409. In 1409 a third pope was added, and not until 1417 was the Church reunified under a single pope in Rome. Throughout this period numerous dissenting heretical sects challenged the validity of ecclesiastical structure and practice. If one takes into consideration the opinion, expressed by Mora and commonly held by other scholars, that witchcraft and belief in occult and supernatural powers tend to prevail in times of social stress and the decline of traditional institutions, as the 14th century was, a partial understanding of the rise of witchcraft fears can be obtained.

Still another aspect of medieval life had a direct bearing on witchcraft. Anything mysterious or seemingly unexplainable could be and was attributed to magic or the supernatural. Intense emotional feelings, like lust and passion, were said to result from evil spirits. Mental illness was felt to be supernatural, and the sick were accordingly called "fiend sick" or were said to be suffering from "devil sickness" and "witch disease." Mental disease was not recognized as such. It was a time of psychological ignorance and unsophistication about human behavior. Society was thus susceptible to those who played on popular passions, credulity, subconscious urges, and fears. As revealed in medieval witchcraft, many of these fears and passions dealt with sex.

The most convincing proof of the intimate connection between witchcraft and sexuality is the *Malleus Maleficarum* (Witches' Hammer), the textbook of the Inquisition. Written between 1484 and 1486 by two Dominican priests, Jacob Sprenger and Heinrich Kramer, at the request of Pope Innocent VIII, this disputation attempted to rationalize, legalize, and make uniform the theories and practices of the witch trials. Evident within its text is an anxiety about sexual function (specifically impotence, failure to conceive, and abortion), an unconscious fear of women, and deep-seated and apparently prevalent sexual frustrations.

The papal bull giving Sprenger and Kramer their authority to produce the *Malleus Maleficarum* made reference to the supernatural cause of impotence. In *Summis desiderantes affectibus,* issued in 1484, Innocent VIII declared that incubi (male demons) and succubi (female demons)

hinder men from performing the sexual act and women from conceiving, whence husbands cannot know their wives nor wives receive their husbands.

Elaborating on this ascription of impotence and infertility to demonic spells, the authors of *Malleus Maleficarum* distinguished between natural and supernatural varieties of impotence. Natural impotence was the inability to have sexual relations with any member of the opposite sex. Supernatural impotence was the inability to have sexual relations with only one person while able to perform normally with other persons of the opposite sex.

Lust itself was said to be evident of bewitchment. And, since women inspire lust, women were seen as natural agents of the devil. The seductive qualities of women,

which were said to injure humanity through the induction of "evil love in man," were thus literally perceived as being, in their supernatural sense, charming, bewitching, and enchanting. This bewitchment was said to explain the intense, mysterious, and overwhelming emotional effect that women have on men, sometimes driving them into irrational acts.

The witch trials themselves have been described as outlets for impulses that were otherwise socially and morally unacceptable. A physical test of witchcraft was intended to find the devil's mark, visible evidence of a compact or transaction with the devil, or to discover hidden amulets. According to *Malleus Maleficarum:*

The hair should be shaved from every part of the body. The reason for this is the same as that for stripping her of her clothes—they are in the habit of hiding some superstitious object in their clothes or in their hair or on the most secret part of their bodies which must not be named.

As instructed by *Malleus Maleficarum* and under the guise of religious purpose, countless women were stripped, shaved, and subjected to vaginal and rectal searches by their inquisitors. As for the devil's mark itself—which could be any birthmark, mole, or supernumerary nipple—it was said to be anesthetic, and long pins were stuck into these areas. Countless victims were subjected to this degrading and painful treatment (see Figure 6).

Tortures used to extract confessions were unbelievably cruel. Legs were mangled by a viselike Spanish boot. The eye gouge and thumb screw were common. Flagellation and squassation were mild tortures compared with these and other methods.

Thinly disguised misogyny was given justification by theology. This misogyny could explain why witches were invariably believed to be women and why those actually accused of transactions with the devil were almost always women. *Malleus Maleficarum* contains endless quotations from the Church fathers and other authorities on this point, such as these:

Now the wickedness of women is spoken of in *Ecclesiasticus XXV:* All wickedness is but little to the wickedness of a woman . . . . What else is a

FIGURE 6. An accused witch about to be tortured. (Bettmann Archive)

woman but a foe to friendship, an unescapable punishment, a necessary evil, a natural temptation, a desirable calamity, a domestic danger, a delectable detriment, an evil of nature, painted with fair colors!

Terrence says: Women are intellectually like children . . . the natural reason is that she is more carnal than a man, as is clear from her many carnal abominations. And it should be noted that there was a defect in the information of the first woman, since she was formed from a bent rib, that is, rib of the breast, which is bent as it were in a contrary direction to a man. And since through this defect she is an imperfect animal, she always deceives.

Justly we may say with Cato of Utica: If the world could be rid of women, we should not be without God in our intercourse. For truly, without the wickedness of women, to say nothing of witchcraft, the world would still remain proof against innumerable dangers . . . a woman is beautiful to look upon, contaminating to the touch and deadly to keep.

The point is clear, and the logic is simple: Carnal lust is the source of all witchcraft; lust

is in women insatiable . . . the mouth of the womb never being satisfied;

more women than men are witches.

Tying in the underlying social and psychological elements of the witchcraft mania with its sexual aspects, psychologists have constructed several hypotheses. One is that the fantasies of the accused persons— which were, almost without exception, about sexual activity—were the manifestation of guilt-ridden consciences or the projections of wishful thinking related to lives of sexual frustration. Another is that the attitudes and the activities of the inquisitors were, as noted by Mora,

dominated by an unconscious fear of women and lustful gratification of their repressed sexual desire.

There is a general consensus that these factors played an important part in shaping the concepts and practices of the witch trials.

STATUS OF WOMEN

The obviously misogynistic attitudes revealed in the witchcraft mania were also apparent in other medieval customs and practices. Women were generally held in low esteem. A wife existed to bear sons, a mistress to satisfy lust, but women had little value otherwise and were of no interest to men.

The nobility generally had total freedom to use women of the lower classes for sexual purposes. There was no need to justify these acts, and, moreover, there was no recourse in feudal law for victims of sexual assault. This attitude toward women has been described by Bullough and Bullough as resulting in the treatment of many women as slaves, who could be violated with impunity.

The more powerful often slept with the less powerful without paying much attention to the legal niceties. It was an honor to be a king's mistress or a king's whore, and while the honor was somewhat less for being a mistress to lesser nobility, there was still prestige attached to the position . . . . A lascivious lord, or even a lascivious abbot, and there were a few of these, quite clearly could have the pick of a whole flock of possible companions.

Women, not protected by law or moral opinion, could be freely brutalized and even killed. In this respect, the witch trials did not depart radically from prevailing custom. This fact is illustrated in the story of John Arundel, an English military officer, who, according to Cleugh, carried off some 60 women and girls from a convent to serve as field whores during a campaign in France.

Raping started immediately aboard the ships. But a storm sprang up in the channel. In order to lighten his dangerously overloaded and tossing vessels, Arundel had all his wretched captives thrown into the sea, where no one dreamed of trying to rescue them.

There are no records that Arundel or any of his troops were ever punished for this massacre of their countrywomen.

Apart from their procreative potential, women were valued as either sources of sexual gratification or, like slaves, pieces of property. This view was evident in the *jus primae noctis*, the right of a lord to sleep with every maiden under his jurisdiction on the first night of her marriage. The right of the first night—also known as *culagium, gam-*

bada, jambage, and *droit du seigneur*—was based on the idea that every woman belonged to the master of the estate before her marriage. In order to wed, a woman was obliged to appear before the lord and obtain his consent. If permission was granted, she was required to offer, in return, her one-time conjugal privileges. The lord could relinquish his rights for a fee, or he could insist on exercising his right.

There has been a scholarly debate over the years as to the origins of the *jus primae noctis*. At one extreme are those, like Goldberg, who see it as a vestige of the pre-Christian defloration rites, with the feudal lord performing intercourse by proxy. In the middle of this debate are those who see it as a purely Christian phenomenon. Westermarck, for instance, relates its development to the ecclesiastical advocacy in some parts of Europe of 3 nights of chastity after the wedding day. Permission to engage in conjugal activity within 3 days could be obtained through the payment of a fine to the Church. At the other extreme are those who see the practice as a rationalization for the use of these women as bedmates. In any event, the *jus primae noctis* was further evidence of the degrading treatment accorded the majority of medieval womanhood.

A contradiction, at least superficially, to the misogynistic spirit of the times appeared in the form of courtly love, *l'amour courtois,* a term coined by Gaston Paris in the 19th century to describe a new ideal, philosophy, or set of sentiments about the male-female relationship that appeared in France during the 11th and 12th centuries. In contrast to generally held views of the time, this ideal placed the beloved (woman) in a position superior to that of her aspiring lover (man). It put the woman on a pedestal.

The exact origins of *l'amour courtois* or, as it is also known, *cortezia, courtesie,* and *Frauendienst* are vague and much disputed. It may have started as a game or a literary movement, but—popularized by the lyrical poems of the troubadours, immortalized in the romances of the chivalric epics, and finally codified by Andreas Capellanus (Andrew the Chaplain)—it became both custom and law among the middle and upper classes of Europe until the 16th century.

The apparent contradictions of courtly love and the prevalent societal attitudes are seen in *Love and Its Cure,* the most authoritative treatise on the subject to come out of the period. Written by Capellanus between 1184 and 1186, this book sets forth the principles of courtly love in 31 rules for lovers. These laws of love advocate fidelity ("A true lover does not desire to embrace in love anyone except his beloved"), difficulty in the attainment of love ("The easy attainment of love makes it of little value"), good character ("Good character alone makes any man worthy of love"), and the impermanence of love ("A new love puts to flight an old one"). The last

point reveals perhaps the most intriguing aspect of courtly love: It applied only to the unmarried. Love between husband and wife was held to be impossible, simply because its legal permanence was incompatible with passion. Several courts of love, using these rules as their guide, were established in various parts of Europe to enforce the chivalric codes of conduct (see Figure 7).

Lovers were bound by a formal and complex system of courtship. These protocols had the effect of dragging out the period of courtship and in this way, at least theoretically, were intended to discourage anyone whose only motivation was sex. A

FIGURE 7. An ivory carving on a mirror back titled, "Siege of the Castle of Love." The scene is an allegory of the rules of courtly love. In the style of the Ile-de-France, Paris, ca. 1320–1350. (Seattle Art Museum)

man was expected to pass through four stages—*fegnedor* (aspirant), *precador* (supplicant), *entendedor* (recognized suitor), and *drut* (accepted lover)—before being privileged with intimacy. The process could be long, since a woman could love only one man at a time.

Another feature of courtly love was based on the ideal of *amor purus,* pure love. Put simply, *amor purus* scorned the completed sex act. The highest form of love was seen to exist only when the temptations of the flesh were resisted. Abstinence in the face of temptation was regarded as the greatest virtue. Unrestrained passion was incompatible with *amor purus,* and copulation represented false love. Sometimes the concept of pure love took the form of a test, which, like the protocols of courtship, tested the motivation and powers of denial. Lovers stripped naked and spent extended periods of time together in bed, free to engage in any form of sex play but obliged to refrain from actual intercourse. Although this custom seems improbable, a substantial body of historical literature testifies to its existence. Taylor and Denomy present evidence that in many instances restraint was, indeed, exercised.

But courtly love was not as contradictory as it appeared to be. It was full of internal contradictions, exalting at one and the same time adultery and chastity, suffering and delight. Yet with respect to medieval morality it was more a microcosm than an inconsistency. Despite its exaltation of spiritual, as opposed to lustful, relationships, chivalric thinking was permeated with sexuality. Themes of medieval romance and balladry were preoccupied with sex. Surviving verses of the troubadours often verge on the obscene. Similarly, the exaltation of the woman is deceptive. It has frequently been observed that putting women in a place of veneration and respect was a measure of the rise in status of women in the Middle Ages. Indeed, it was a better state of affairs than had existed before the advent of courtly love. If nothing else, it nurtured such refinements in male manners as courtesy and gentleness. But the chivalric woman—perfect, pure, and almost unattainable—was unreal, and, like the protocols of love themselves, she was artificial. She never displayed passion, an emotion reserved for men. Men, as Firestone notes, were encouraged to view women as objects "whose resistance to entrance must be overcome." Rather than elevating women, the mock workship, typified by courtly love, served through false flattery, she observes,

> to keep women from an awareness of their lower-class condition.

Courtly love—like asceticism and, indeed, like Christian sexual morality—was an ideal more than a reality. None of these ideals became universally adopted patterns of behavior, but they were not without their effects. In the words of Nietzsche,

> Christianity gave Eros poison to drink; he did not die of it but degenerated into a vice.

What had been an activity with sacred associations became the cause of many a troubled conscience, a source of anxiety and guilt.

The Renaissance

In the early 15th century, at first in Florence and later in other parts of Italy and Europe, the nature of human existence took on a new meaning. People began to think of themselves as individuals and to accept as natural their perceptions, desires, and impulses. This period, the Renaissance or rebirth, was characterized by a conscious movement away from medieval ideals of devoutness, faith, and concern with the future and by a movement toward ideals of secularism, skepticism, materialism, and individualism. Paralleling these changes was a relaxation of constraints on sexual expression in art, literature, and everyday life. There was a new social reality: Sex could be overtly pursued, idealized, and enjoyed.

DECLINE OF FAITH AND RISE OF HUMANISM

The Renaissance was sparked by a group of Florentine scholars calling themselves *umanisti,* the humanists, who looked back to ancient Greece and Rome as a source of inspiration for contemporary society. Two events were instrumental in triggering this renewed interest in classical culture. The first event, the Council of Florence, begun in 1439, brought together representatives of the Greek Orthodox and Roman Catholic churches to discuss doctrinal differences. It exposed the Florentines to learned scholars from Constantinople and created a new awareness of the classical roots of Italian society. The second event, the fall of Constantinople in 1453, brought an influx of scholars from the collapsed Byzantine empire, many of whom took positions as lecturers in Florence and further generated interest in and knowledge of antiquity. Eventually, a new philosophy that embodied classical ideals and values developed. Known as neoplatonism, it formed the intellectual fabric of the Renaissance.

During the Middle Ages, the Church had denounced any such glorification of pagan culture. As guardian of the faith, dominating intellectual force, chief patron of the arts, and master of all learning centers, the Church had been able to impose its restrictions.

But in Florence a new class had arisen. Families like the Strozzi and the Medici, who had grown wealthy through trade and industry, became sponsors of the arts, letters, and learning. There was a reversal of the relative importance of religious and secular forces in society. A new civilization, more secular in its orientation, came to act as a major political and social power. It supported the work of intellectuals with humanist values. Thus, one of the Medici commissioned the painter Botticelli to create one of the first important Renaissance works to use a theme from classical mythology. This painting, the Birth of Venus, was not only an artistic landmark but a milestone of the Renaissance spirit. It was as if, by accepting classical values in art, the Renaissance was also accepting the more permissive sexual values of antiquity.

But the Renaissance was not an abrupt and absolute break with the social matrix and sexuality of the medieval period. Florence, on the eve of the great cultural outburst that marked the 15th century, was a city where most people had resolved in their minds the basic conflicts between sexual reality and the Christian ideal. They had decided, in the words of Eimerl, "to keep their own moral counsel." The humanists merely provided an attractive and legitimate philosophy that could be invoked as an intellectual justification for existing conduct.

This pragmatic approach to personal needs was evident as early as 1364, when the importation of slaves was made legal. Enormous mortality rates in the plagues had caused a shortage of domestic servants, prompting Florentines to venture to the slave markets of Venice and Genoa. Slaves could be easily and inexpensively obtained. Most of the slaves were teenage girls from Russia, Turkey, and Greece. Brucker quotes a letter, dated February 13, 1392, and addressed to Piero Davanzanti in Venice, that reminds him of a request for two slave girls:

> You can transport them from Venice and send them to me . . . . These slave girls should be between twelve and fifteen years old, and if there aren't any available at that age, but a little older or younger, don't neglect to send them.

The writer of this letter was not concerned "if they are pretty or ugly," but other slave-owners displayed interest in physical appearance. The owner of a young female slave had the right, by law, to "enjoy" her, and, as noted by Hibbert:

> Many of them became pregnant by their masters; the correspondence of the time is full of disputes arising from such inconvenience; and the foundling hospitals were continually being presented with little bundles of swarthy or Slavic-looking babies.

The use of slaves as concubines did not provoke official censure. Neither did other practices that could be considered unchristian. Such vices as homosexuality, for example, were seen as nuisances in need of regulation but not elimination. In reviewing official records from the latter part of the 14th century, Brucker concluded that, as a rule, efforts to control public mores were more closely tied to social consideration than to the doctrines of the Church. There was, then, an abandonment of the faith even before neoplatonism made its appearance. "They thought," one Florentine of the period wrote, "that God's hand was unstrung."

In a marked change from the medieval mentality, more than practice, it became socially and psychologically acceptable to think of sex in positive terms, not as an activity that inevitably led men and women into perdition. The cosmic fear that had haunted medieval persons was dispelled, thus enabling people of the Renaissance, as noted by de Riencourt

> to focus without restraint on the plastic beauty of the human body, searching now for the *superhuman* rather than the supernatural; sexual life began to pattern itself on a revived paganism without much restraint from religion. In the process, the church became more catholic but far less Christian: the classical Greco-Roman almost eliminated the Jewish biblical one.

The decline of spirituality that characterized the 14th, 15th, and 16th centuries was intimately tied to the low spiritual reputation of the Church. This reputation reached its nadir during the pontificates of Alexander VI (1492–1503) and his successor, Julius II (1503–1513).

At the time of his election as Alexander VI, Rodrigo Borgia was 61 years old, the father of at least seven illegitimate children, one of the richest and most flamboyant cardinals in Italy, and outspoken in his opinion that clerical celibacy was a mistake. Rome, as described in a letter written by Lorenzo de' Medici in 1492, the year of Alexander's election, was the "sink of iniquity." Out of a population of less than 90,000 people, 7,000 were estimated to have been prostitutes, many working in Church-licensed brothels. Cellini called syphilis a "kind of illness very common among priests," and many priests who might in preceding years have denounced sexuality as the "act of Venus" spoke, instead, of the "glories of Venus." Soon to be painted on the walls of Cardinal Bibiena's bathroom were pagan scenes of Venus and her triumphs, portrayed in the most visually explicit terms by Raphael.

Still, the cardinals who assembled in Rome to select one of their number as the head of Christendom were less interested in the moral temper of a potential leader than in his strength as a secular leader. After the disarray of the Church in the years of the Great Schism and the loss of papal authority and prestige to the king of France, the deliberating College of Cardinals looked for someone who could consolidate Church power and increase Church authority. They chose a determined and energetic Rodrigo Borgia.

As Alexander VI, he succeeded in achieving almost all the secular objectives the Church had hoped for. The authority of the papacy over affairs of state was stronger at the end of his reign than it had been before his pontificate. Yet it is not for his political successes that Alexander is best remembered. He has become known to posterity as the most notorious of the scandalous popes, the Renaissance counterpart of the sacrilegious Alcibiades.

How justified is this reputation? Alexander VI's failure to observe celibacy—even as Pope, he fathered two illegitimate children, one in 1498 and another in 1503—his publicized liaisons with a series of mistresses, his associations with prostitutes, his encouragement of his daughter Lucrezia to use sex as a means of winning support for papal policies, and his tolerance of sexual looseness by those in his court have been well documented. However, the most sensational and most frequently cited examples of his practices are based on a single source, the diary of the papal master of ceremonies, Burckhard of Strasbourg. According to Burckhard, Alexander VI regularly had sexual intercourse with Lucrezia and was in the habit of inviting prostitutes to his private chambers (one evening in 1501, Burckhard noted in his diary, 50 women were ordered) and there encouraged lewd displays between male and female guests. There are no corroborating accounts of the extremes described by Burckhard, and most serious scholars question the reliability of Burckhard's reports and his possible motivations.

Many persons in the papal court both feared and resented Alexander VI. The most influential Roman families—like the Orsinis and Colonnas—were aware of the Pope's plans to turn the pontificate into a hereditary monarchy, with his ambitious son Cesare Borgia (whom Machiavelli, in *The Prince*, especially praised for being deceitful and unscrupulous) intended as the first to inherit the throne (see Figure 8). It was, thus, in the interest of many to play up Alexander VI's notoriety as a moral anarchist.

Whatever the degree and extent of Alexander VI's actual transgressions of Church doctrine, his lack of concern about public opinion and popular gossip in itself represented an abdication of papal moral and spiritual leadership. The result was a lowering of respect for the highest office in Christendom.

Alexander VI's successor, Julius II (see Figure 9), did little to salvage the spiritual reputation of the papacy, even though his private life caused little scandal. To have three illegitimate children, as Julius II did, was unexceptional for the time. Few people were aware, moreover, of the reason behind his abandonment of a traditional act of homage to the popes—the kissing of the papal foot by worshipers. Julius II's toes were reportedly so deformed by syphilis that this custom could not be continued.

Julius II was an egotist. Not only was he

FIGURE 9. Pope Julius II.

ambitious for the Roman Catholic Church, but, as Clark has observed, he was ambitious for Julius II. He was obsessed with the idea of tearing down the old St. Peter's and replacing it with a new and magnificent basilica, the one that stands in Rome today. His motive was, more than anything else, to create a temple that would house his tomb, which, says Clark, was to be

the greatest tomb of any ruler since the time of Hadrian.

He commissioned Michelangelo to design a structure three stories high, with more than 40 figures at least life size. Although the monumental scale of the new seat of Christendom served to restore, if only symbolically, the grandeur and power of the papacy, the decision to build a new St. Peter's committed the Church to a prohibitively expensive undertaking and had far-reaching consequences.

MANNERS AND MORALS IN ITALY

Egotism, extravagance, sensuality, and individualism, qualities evident in the per-

FIGURE 8. Cesare Borgia, second son of Pope Alexander VI. He was the model for Machiavelli's *Prince*.

sonalities of Alexander VI and Julius II, were found in persons at every level of society. These characteristics typified the men and women of the Renaissance, distinguished them from people of the medieval period, and to a great extent made the ambitious artistic achievements of the Renaissance possible.

Indeed, the artists, both in their art and in their character, revealed much about the manners and morals of the 15th and 16th centuries in Italy. The artist was the great hero of the Renaissance. He gave visual expression to the ideals and spirit of his age. His achievements remained as the most conspicuous evidence of the change that was taking place in attitudes toward life and toward sex. In their personal lives, as in their art, artists enjoyed tremendous freedom to indulge their own passions, physical and esthetic.

Benvenuto Cellini (1500–1571), an admired goldsmith and sculptor, wrote an autobiography of his amorous and artistic adventures in Renaissance Europe. Boastful and egotistical, Cellini described a society where adultery and intercourse were almost synonymous and nearly universal. About his relations with the wife of an acquaintance, Cellini wrote:

I used to send for her to make use of her as my model. Every day I gave her thirty soldi; and I made her pose in the nude. First, she wanted to be paid in advance, and then she wanted to make a good meal, and then I had my revenge by having intercourse with her, mocking at her and her husband for the various horns I was giving him.

According to Cellini, he made it a point, whenever possible, to make love with his models between poses.

Cellini declared that artists were above the law, a view that was no doubt inspired by the Renaissance idea of the artist as a genius, a concept borrowed from Platonic theory. One testimonial to this prestige of the artist was the tremendous popular appeal of Giorgio Vasari's *Lives of the Painters*. Published in 1550, this series of biographies of the most important Renaissance artists became an immediate bestseller. It has remained an important historical source of information on the men who created the paintings and sculp-

tures of the Renaissance, but it has also served as a source of insight into the raw sexuality of the times and the tolerance of sexuality at the highest levels of society.

As recounted by Vasari, for example, Raphael (1483–1520), a "moral god," was a very amorous man with a great fondness for women, whom he was always anxious to serve. He constantly indulged his sexual appetites and pursued his pleasures, with no sense of moderation. He reportedly became so obsessed with sex at times that he was unable to concentrate on his painting. On one occasion, his mistress had to be brought to the house where he was at work so that he could complete the task he had started. Raphael was also in the habit of using his current mistress or a prostitute as the model for some of the approximately 50 Madonnas he painted. This fact did not diminish the popularity of the works. Neither did his conduct diminish his reputation as a good Christian. At the time of his death, he had been promised a cardinal's red hat by Pope Leo X. As Vasari commented, several men less deserving than Raphael had already been so honored.

Vasari's narratives on the lives of other artists could also be used to demonstrate the general disregard for ideals of restraint in sexual matters. Fra Filippo Lippi (1406–1469), one of the first great Renaissance painters, appears to have shared Raphael's temperament. It is said that Fra Filippo was so lustful that he would give anything to enjoy a woman he wanted if he thought he could have it his way; and if he couldn't buy what he wanted, he would cool his passion by painting her portrait and reasoning with himself. His lust was so violent that, when it took hold of him, he could never concentrate on his work. At one time, when he was doing something for Cosimo de' Medici in Cosimo's house, Cosimo had him locked in so that he wouldn't wander away and waste time. After he had been confined for a few days, Fra Filippo's amorous desires drive him to seize a pair of scissors, make a rope of his bedsheets, and escape through a window one night to pursue his pleasures for days on end.

While using a young convent novice,

Lucrezia Buti, as the model for a painting of the Madonna, Fra Filippo seduced her, carried her off, and got her pregnant. Through the intervention of his patron Cosimo de' Medici, Fra Filippo received permission from the Pope to marry Lucrezia.

A question that arises, in dealing with Renaissance art, is whether the works, which were clearly sensual in style and subject, were actually erotic or even pornographic. If pornography is defined as the explicit depiction of sexual organs and sexual acts in a manner designed to elicit a strong erotic response in the viewer, most Renaissance art represented what has been called "erotic realism" (Kronhausen and Kronhausen). In their classic studies of sexual behavior, Kinsey and his co-workers explored the erotic elements of nudes painted by Raphael and other artists. Many of these artists, they said, portrayed the human form in a fashion that indicated an erotic interest in that form. They concluded:

Even though there may be no portrayal of genitalia and no suggestion of sexual action, the nude body itself may be drawn or painted in a fashion which is erotic to the artist and to most males, who subsequently observe the drawing or painting.

Raphael's favorite pupil and assistant, Giulio Romano, took the freedom of expression and sensuality of Renaissance art beyond previously accepted limitations. He set about to depict in drawing every sexual practice that the period would tolerate. Romano's work qualifies as hard-core pornography. The 20 drawings he made of various sexual activities were taken to Marcantonio Raimondi, who engraved them. The poet Pietro Aretino then added erotic sonnets, *Sonetti Lussuriosi,* to the engravings. When these works were published in 1524 as the *Sedici Modi,* they represented the first mass-produced commercial pornography. Commented Vasari, in reference to their lewdness:

I cannot say which is worse, the drawings or the words.

The drawings were, indeed, explicit, showing some dozen variations of coital tech-

nique. Widely circulated among the upper classes, the works even came to the attention of Pope Clement VII. This attention caused Aretino, not universally admired to start with, some difficulties, and he voluntarily left Rome for a period. Nevertheless, the Pope eventually made Aretino a Knight of Rhodes and gave him a comfortable pension. Giulio Romano also continued to enjoy freedom and popular demand.

Moral outlook was also reflected in dress. Extroversion of intellect was mirrored in the extroverted body and the decline of modesty in dress.

The codpiece, a flap or bag that concealed an opening in the front of a man's breeches, became a popular feature of clothing, especially during the 15th and 16th centuries. It was certainly functional and convenient, but it also served to accentuate the natural bulge of the male genitalia. Sometimes men gave further emphasis to their anatomical endowments by padding or stuffing the codpiece. And it could greatly simplify the act of coitus, since only the codpiece needed to be removed. A character described by the monk Francois Rabelais declared:

I am in a rage after lust, and after a wife, and vehemently hot upon untying the codpiece point.

Modesty and decency in female dress also declined. Bosoms became more visible. In portraits and in formal dress, uncovered breasts became major adornments.

It was hardly a shame to be illegitimate. A large segment of the population, from all social and economic classes, were bastards. Moreover, these children were generally treated and given recognition by their parents and the state as equals to those born of marriage. Leonardo was the illegitimate son of Piero da Vinci and a peasant girl known as Caterina. This climate of tolerance toward birth out of wedlock was seen in a Florentine tax register, which in an entry dated 1457 matter of factly mentions a 5-year-old *figlio di Piero illegittimo,* an illegitimate son of Piero.

A passage in the autobiography of Cellini also shows that birth out of wedlock carried little stigma. In a casual manner Cellini tells of a beautiful 15-year-old model who especially stimulated his desires. He boasted:

This young girl was untouched, and a virgin, and I got her pregnant.

Evidence that illegitimacy was no great civic stain is reflected in the fact that the daughter born of this union was baptized and at the baptism was held by the royal physician, her godfather. All it took in many instances to become legitimate was the payment of an ecclesiastical fee in return for dispensation. Cellini fathered at least eight children, legitimate and illegitimate.

Like its classical predecessors, Renaissance society in Italy witnessed the open practice of male homosexuality. Venice seems to have been notorious in this respect. One 16th century Frenchman, Henriques (1963) notes, made the following observations:

however easy may be the commerce with women and however beautiful they may be, would you believe it but the Venetians mistrust them, and attach themselves rather to a boy, even if he be as ugly as a monkey, rather than to the most pleasant girl . . . there are even those who go to the infamous excess of paying porters and gondoliers to bestialize themselves.

Numerous Venetian laws intended to suppress sodomy reflect the prevalence of and concern with this practice. Such efforts were not helped by Pope Sixtus IV, who reportedly granted the family of a Venetian cardinal permission to engage in anal intercourse.

Members of Florentine society even began to think of their city as excessively corrupted by sodomy. Municipal records of judicial convictions and penalties during the Renaissance relate some examples of homosexual activities. One Jacopo di Cristofrano called to a boy who was standing next to his house. The records state:

He coaxed the boy into his house and then fed him a meal. Afterwards he committed the unnatural act of sodomy on the table where they had previously eaten.

Piero de Jacopo, a Bolognese coppersmith, was reported to have similarly invited a 10-year-old boy into his house, then threw him

on the bed and placed a gag in his mouth . . . then with force and violence he committed the act of sodomy with him.

As these accounts indicate, laws against homosexuality were applied primarily to those cases involving the seduction of a youth. Unless an episode provoked outrage or produced public scandal, prosecutions were almost always limited to lesser members of the community.

Leonardo was accused but not convicted of homosexual activities with a boy. There is dispute as to whether Leonardo was homosexual or asexual. In either case, he took a dim view of physical intimacy, as expressed in the following statement:

The act of procreation and the members employed therein are so repulsive that if it were not for the beauty of the faces and the adornments of the actors and pent-up impulses, nature would lose the human species.

Freud, in his psychobiography of Leonardo, subtitled *A Study in Psychosexuality,* wrote that Leonardo channeled his sexual drives into intellectual pursuits. Freud maintained that Leonardo's genius

resulted from his particular tendency to repress his impulses [and from] his extraordinary tendency to sublimate primitive impulses.

Leonardo's art does reveal an avoidance of the erotic. His only known drawing of human intercourse was done in the dehumanized and technical style of the anatomist—as a sagittal section—and is totally asexual (see Figure 10).

The Renaissance social atmosphere provided an opportunity for persons to chart their own course. For some, that course led to prostitution.

During the Renaissance and for the first time since ancient Rome, prostitutes could live and work in their own houses. They openly entertained the famous and influential and were admired for their intelligence, charm, education, and manner. In Rome and Venice, especially, there was a rebirth of the *cortigiana onesta,* genteel courtesan, as a respectable member of society.

A famous Roman courtesan of the period,

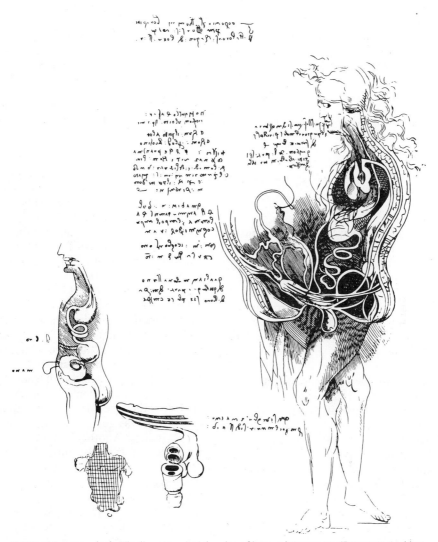

FIGURE 10. Leonardo da Vinci's anatomical drawing of human intercourse. (Bettmann Archive)

Catherine of San Celso—popularly known by the classical name Imperia, in keeping with the neoplatonic spirit—welcomed many men of stature. When she died at age 26 in 1511, Imperia was mourned by many (some say half the male population of Rome) and, as a sign of the esteem in which she was held, was buried in the Chapel of San Gregorio.

Another courtesan, Veronica Franco of Venice, was a friend and lover of the artist Tintoretto. Henry III of France knew her pleasures during a visit to Venice and sent a portrait of himself as a sign of his affection. She was in many ways the female counterpart of the Renaissance man; she spoke several languages and was highly cultivated. Despite her marriage to a physician, she openly practiced her trade, even writing a book of verses in honor of one lover, the Duke of Mantua.

Although the Renaissance was an age of renewed status and enhanced prestige for prostitutes, it was also a time when the attitude toward the oldest profession took a distinctly negative turn. The precipitating factor in this change of view was the appearance of a new disease that played havoc with 16th century European society—syphilis. Only with this development, Benjamin and Masters remark, did "an authentic antipathy toward prostitution" become widespread and find itself able to gain influence. As a way to prevent the spread of the ailment, they note,

> stringent measures were taken to supress prostitution, and brothels were closed down, and individual harlots pursued and penalized in large numbers. It was upon the fear of venereal infection in Italy and elsewhere, and not upon morality, that the modern censorious approach to prostitution was based, later overlaid with moralistic and pietistic rationalizations.

Syphilis, most evidence suggests, was a consequence of the New World explorations. It is widely but not universally held that sailors on the West Indian voyages of Columbus contracted syphilis and, on their return home, spread the infection to European prostitutes. The absence of its mention in earlier literature, coupled with its sudden appearance, serves as the basis for the conclusion that syphilis was a new disease in Europe.

A disorder with the signs and symptoms of syphilis first appeared in epidemic proportions during the seige of Naples in 1494. Particularly hard-striken were the soldiers of the French army. By 1500 the pathogenic agent, *Treponema pallidum,* appears to have spread throughout western Europe. Reports of the disease appeared in every nation.

As with any new disease, there was a problem of nomenclature. At first it was customary to call the malady after the name of a neighboring state. To the French it was the Italian or Neapolitan disease; to the Italians it was the French or Spanish disease; to the Russians it was the Polish disease. This confusion was largely resolved by the publication in 1530 of *Syphilus sive Morbus Gallicus,* a poem by Girolamo Fracastoro (1478–1553). Fracastoro, an Italian, used as the main character in this work, a shepherd named Syphilus, who contracted the French disease. From Syphilus, the malady received its name. Despite the popularity of the poem, it was overshadowed by a later work by Fracastoro, *De Contagione et Contagiosis Morbis,* thought to be the greatest single study of infectious disease in the 16th century. Referring to the disorder by the name syphilis, Fracastoro discussed its symptoms and its contagion. He accurately stated:

> It was contracted by contagion; but not from every kind of contact, nor readily, but only when two bodies in close contact with one another became extremely heated. Now this happened in sexual intercourse especially, and it was by this means that the great majority of persons were infected.

The toll of human suffering caused by syphilis in later centuries was already evident during the Renaissance. Hospitals were opened solely to treat victims of the disease. One institution in Venice, its name reflecting the inefficacy of available therapies, was called the Incurabili. Brothels, viewed as the major site of infection, were closed in many parts of Europe. All skin lesions became a source of anxiety. Cellini, despite assurances by doctors that he did not have a syphilitic infection, wrote that he, indeed, "had got the sickness." Blisters "the size of sixpences and rose-colored," Cellini reported, covered his flesh. Others, too, spoke of the horrible pox.

By far, the most popular remedy of the period and the one that Cellini reported had cured him, was guaiacum, imported from the West Indies. Another countermeasure was developed by the anatomist Fallopius. He is credited with devising the first condom, a linen sheath to be worn under the prepuce. Although others may have improvised similar methods for the purpose of contraception, Fallopius' description of the linen sheath in *De Morbo Gallico* (see Figure 11) popularized the use of the condom.

Reformation and Counterreformation

As syphilis became an unwanted fact of life, some Europeans, like John Calvin, suggested that the malady was ordained by God to punish the promiscuous. One thing was certain: This visible evidence of sexual encounter focused attention on another fact of life—European sexual mores and behavior were virtually unbridled. Ecclesiastical concern with sins of the flesh had receded into the background, although there had been no official change in Christian dogma. Papal Rome, moreover, resisted reform from within. Girolamo Savonarola, a monk who

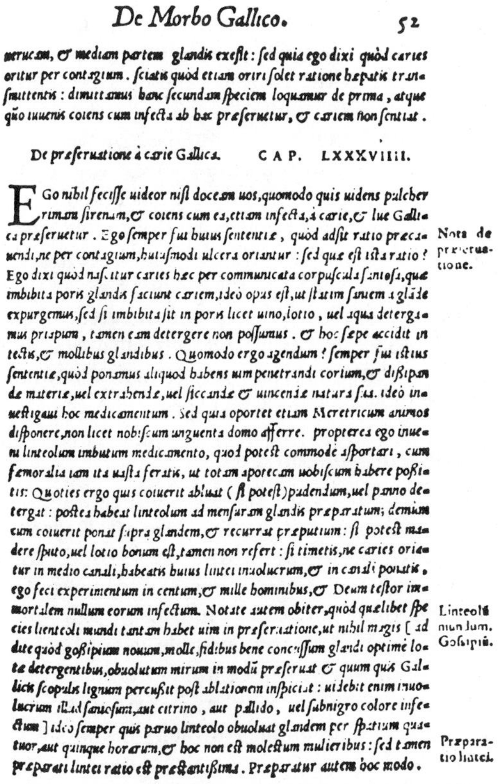

De Morbo Gallico.   52

uerrucam, & mediam partem glandis exeſit: ſed quia ego dixi quòd caries oritur per contagium. ſciatis quòd etiam oriri ſolet ratione hepatis tranſmittentis: dimittamus hanc ſecundam ſpeciem loquamur de prima, atque quo iuuenis coiens cum infecta ab hac præſeruetur, & cariem non ſentiat.

De præſeruatione à carie Gallica.   CAP. LXXXVIIII.

EGo nihil feciſſe uideor niſi doceam uos, quomodo quis uidens pulcher rimam ſirenam, & coiens cum ea, etiam infecta, à carie, & lue Galli ca præſeruetur. Ego ſemper ſui huius ſententiæ, quòd adſit ratio præca uendi, ne per contagium, huiuſmodi ulcera oriantur: ſed quæ eſt iſta ratio? Ego dixi quòd naſcitur caries hæc per communicata corpuſcula ſanioſa, quæ imbibita poris glandis faciunt cariem, ideo opus eſt, ut ſtatim ſaniem à glāde expurgemus, ſed ſi imbibita ſit in poris licet uino, lotio, uel aqua deterga mus priſpiam, tamen eam detergere non poſſumus. & hoc ſæpe accidit in tectis, & mollibus glandibus. Quomodo ergo agendum? ſemper ſui iſtius ſententiæ, quòd poſſimus aliquod habens uim penetrandi corium, & diſſipan de materie, uel extrahende, uel ſiccande & uincende naturæ ſuæ. ideo in ueſtigaui hoc medicamentum. ſed quia oportet etiam Meretricum animos diſponere, non licet nobiſcum unguenta domo afferre. propterea ego inue ni linteolum imbutum medicamento, quod poteſt commode aſportari, cum femoralia tam ita uſta feratis, ut totam aporecam nobiſcum habere poſſi tis: Quoties ergo quis coiuerit abluat (ſi poteſt) pudendum, uel panno de tergat: poſtea habeat linteolum ad menſuram glandis præparatum; demùm cum coiuerit ponat ſupra glandem, & recurrat præputium: ſi poteſt man dere ſputo, uel lotio bonum eſt, tamen non refert: ſi timetis, ne caries oria tur in medio canali, habeatis huius lintei inuolucrum, & in canali ponatis, ego feci experimentum in centum, & mille hominibus, & Deum teſtor im mortalem nullum eorum infectum. Notate autem obiter, quòd quælibet ſpe cies lintei coli mundi tantam habet uim in præſeruatione, ut nihil magis [ad dite quòd goſſipium nouum, molle, fidibus bene conciſſam glandi optime lo ta detergentibus, obuolutum mirum in modū præſeruat & quum quis Gal licki ſcopulis lignum percuſſit poſt ablationem inſpiciat: ut debit enim inuo lucrum illud ſanieſuat, aut citrino, aut pallido, uel ſubnigro colore infe ctum] ideo ſemper quis paruo linteolo obuoluat glandem per ſpatium qua tuor, aut quinque horarum, & hoc non eſt moleſtum mulieribus: ſed tamen præparati lintei ratio eſt præſtantiſſima. Præparatur autem hoc modo.

[margin notes: Nota de præſerua-tione. — Linteoli mundum. Goſſipiū. — Præpara-tio lintei.]

FIGURE 11. Fallopius' description of his linen sheath to prevent infection with syphilis. (From N. E. Himes, *Medical History of Contraception,* Williams & Wilkins, Baltimore, 1936.)

had denounced the moral laxity of the Church and established a puritanical regime in Florence, was excommunicated and burned.

Indicative of the Church interest in temporal matters, almost to the exclusion of the spiritual, was the construction of the new St. Peter's. Its cost necessitated the indiscriminate and self-serving sale of indulgences, remissions of punishment for sins. The appearance of a Dominican preacher in Wittenberg, Saxony, to raise funds for St. Peter's by selling indulgences provoked a German priest, Martin Luther, to express his resentment and thus helped speed the Reformation—a revolt that split Christendom into Catholic and Protestant churches, each with disparate views of sex and sexuality.

Luther posted his 95 theses on the doors of All Saints church in Wittenberg in 1517.

Among the many differences he had with the doctrines of papal Rome were ones that involved celibacy, virginity, and marriage. On the basis of the scriptures and in light of Christian experience, Luther argued, official doctrine was both theologically invalid and practically unrealistic.

Basic to Luther's attitude was his belief that faith alone, to the exclusion of good works, can bring salvation. Good works in themselves, he said, could not earn salvation. Since chastity and celibacy were Church-imposed good works, there was no legitimate reason for these practices, and, Luther maintained, they were no indication of virtue.

Hardly an advocate of sexual promiscuity—his writings reveal a suspicious, prudish, and somewhat shameful view of sex—Luther did think that sex was not inherently sinful. He recognized the existence of sexual drives and saw intercourse as a necessary part of marriage. Priests, monks, and nuns who could not live in chastity, Luther wrote, should marry and relieve themselves of any burden of guilt. Sex and marriage, both created by God, were good and, moreover, a natural state of affairs. Whoever do not marry when they so desire, he declared, must misconduct themselves. Luther thus agreed with St. Paul, who declared:

It is better to marry than to be consumed with passion.

Vows of celibacy, Luther held, only aggravate the tendency to be evil. He wrote:

It is impossible to be alive and to have flesh and blood without sinful inclination.

A second major figure of the Reformation, John Calvin, agreed with Luther on the issues of marriage, virginity, and chastity. But Calvin, unlike Luther, maintained that people should work to overcome their inherent weaknesses and sinful impulses. This view gave Calvin's ideal of Christianity a much more austere coloring, especially with respect to sex, than did Luther's concepts.

Calvin shared Luther's distaste for the tacit Catholic acceptance of sexual looseness. Calvin declared:

It is scarcely possible to find one convent in ten that is not rather a brothel than a sanctuary of chastity.

Calvin saw the task of Christianity as lying in its ability to eliminate sin, and he developed a rigid code of Christian life to foster this ideal. In *Institutes of the Christian Religion* Calvin laid the groundwork for the theocracy he established in Geneva, his native city. Although Calvin opposed abstinence, he opposed promiscuity as well. Singing, dancing, cursing, gluttony, the wearing of ostentatious clothing, and other pleasurable activities were cause for a fine or imprisonment. Adultery was punishable by death.

Calvin was convinced that the entire community had a common responsibility for sin, just as all members shared in the gifts God had given them. In contrast to sin, hard work was seen as a sacrament, and a vocation was seen as a divine blessing.

Outward evidence of adultery, profane dress and speech, intoxication, gambling, and other transgressions were difficult to find in Calvin's Geneva. But there were, in official records, accounts of numerous illegitimate births. Calvin's stepdaughter and son-in-law were among those condemned for adultery.

Ironically, Calvinism had its most spectacular success in England, a nation that broke away from the Church of Rome because of papal adherence to Catholic divorce laws. Henry VIII, the English monarch, wanted his marriage to be declared invalid by the Church so that he might remarry and sire a male heir to the throne. Largely for political reasons, the Pope refused, and the Reformation in England became a fact.

The Catholic Church, in response to the Reformation's growing success, held a council to deal with the issues raised by men like Luther and Calvin. The problems of sex and marriage were major issues.

Meeting at Trent and Bolzano intermittently between 1536 and 1563, the council ultimately reaffirmed existing Catholic ideals. It declared marriage a sacrament that was indissoluble, called for absolute adherence to rules of celibacy, and denounced expressions of overt sexuality among the general population. As if to symbolize this turn of events,

Pope Paul IV, whose reign began in 1555, ordered Michelangelo's Last Judgment taken off the wall of the Sistine Chapel. Dissuaded from this act by numerous protests, he hired one of Michelangelo's pupils, Daniele da Volterra, to paint clothing over the nude figures, a commission that earned Volterra immortality and ridicule as Il Brachettone, the breeches maker. In 1566, Pope Pius V, acting in the spirit of the Council of Trent, called for the abolition of prostitutes in all papal states but was forced to relent when the extent of the opposition to this action among Roman men was made clear.

The Age of Reason

The 17th and 18th centuries are commonly considered together as the Age of Reason. The 18th century alone is called the Enlightenment. Both terms are used to describe the changes in European thinking that grew out of the remarkable scientific discoveries in the 17th century by men like Descartes, Galileo, Kepler, Newton, Boyle, and Hooke. The impact of their findings was seen in the redefinition of many existing ideals of human affairs, including sexuality.

Throughout the Renaissance and Reformation the supreme arbiter of all questions—moral, religious, and physical—had remained the Scriptures. The Bible provided explanations for events that could not otherwise be explained. The scientific discoveries, however, provided answers to many of nature's mysteries, and, accordingly, European intellectuals turned away from dependence on the Scriptures. Faith in reason, belief in absolute truth, and the concept of natural laws marked all aspects of later 17th and 18th century life. With the mystery of sex diminished and the fear of supernatural retribution for sexual transgressions all but eliminated, the Age of Reason became, as well, the age of license. *Laissez-faire, laissez-passer,* live and let pass, an attitude toward economic matters, became applicable to sexual behavior and mores.

SEVENTEENTH CENTURY ENGLAND

Seventeenth century England was a land of revolution, both politically and sexually, before it became a nation of reason. In the political domain it underwent transformations from a stable divine-right monarchy to a theocratic republic to a monarchy that ruled at the pleasure of the people. In sexual matters the changes were equally dramatic. From a society with a loose but unremarkable pattern of sexual morality, it went to an era when the word puritanism was popularized and then to a period when unrestrained licentiousness prevailed.

Elizabethan era

In the year 1600, Elizabeth I, daughter of Henry VIII, had been on the English throne for 42 years. The Virgin Queen, as she was called, once told Parliament that her most ardent desire was to have a marble stone

> declare that a Queen, having reigned such a time, lived and died a virgin.

Although the monarch tried to perpetuate her reputation as a virgin, a reputation that has never been conclusively disproved or confirmed, she did not encourage or expect those in her court to emulate her conjugal status. As a nation, England was, by most measures, a place where sex, with the exception of homosexuality, was uninhibited and seen as an enjoyable part of life.

Elizabethan England was also the age of Shakespeare, whose works reflect the moral climate and sexual outlook of the late 16th and early 17th centuries. Although prostitution was outlawed by Henry VIII, prostitutes continued to be standard features of English cities. Rowse remarked:

> Shakespeare's plays are sufficient evidence of that, with the brothel scene in *Pericles*, the realistic happenings at the Boar's Head in East Cheap, the characters of Mistress Quickly—with the suggestiveness of the name—Doll Tearsheet, Mistress Overdone, poor Kate Keepdown, Pandarus, and the goings-on in *Troilus and Cressida*.

A commentary on the prevailing mores was the great frankness that was not merely tolerated but expected by Elizabethan audiences. Thus, Shakespeare's plays make direct references to cuckoldry, cuckold-makers, dildos, fornication, upraised cocks and their flashing fire, pistol-proof women

(immune to impregnation), virgins pure, men given to fornication, copulation, whores, whoremasters, whoremongers, and other sexual matters. The English could laugh at sex, and it appears that there was no generalized anxiety associated with its practice.

Another current of sexuality during the reign of Elizabeth I ran in a direction quite opposite that of Shakespeare's admirers. Almost coinciding with Elizabeth's rise to the throne, a group of religious reformers appeared. Their primary objective was to purify the Church of England of all remaining Catholic influence and ceremony. These Puritans, as they were called, were for the most part close to the Calvinistic view of life, and they spoke out not only against ecclesiastical affairs but against the profanity of the theater, the immoral conduct in the royal court, and the debased lives of the upper classes. Elizabeth opposed and resisted the Puritans but did not persecute them. Throughout her reign they grew increasingly vocal and gained popular support.

James I and Charles I

With the death of Elizabeth I in 1603, the Tudor dynasty ended, and King James VI of Scotland was proclaimed King James I of England. Most distasteful to the new monarch was his rigid Calvinistic upbringing. He had a cordial dislike for the Calvinists and made it clear that these dissenters were not welcome in England unless they conformed. To emphasize his feelings, he began a program of harassment. Some Puritans took flight. Among these was a group who went to Leyden, Holland, and then in 1620 to America. Thus James I, who profoundly influenced literary English by commissioning the version of the Bible that still bears his name, profoundly affected the sexuality of a future nation.

James I was succeeded in 1625 by his son, Charles I. His policies led to a civil war between the Cavaliers (those loyal to the king) and the Roundheads (those loyal to Parliament). In 1649, after a civil war of 7 years, Charles I was executed, and the Puritans, led by Oliver Cromwell, established the Commonwealth of England. Loose manners and morals gave way to the strictly regulated life-style of Calvinism.

Puritanism

The reign of Cromwell was marked by repeated attempts to impose the austere values of Calvinism on the entire English populace through inhibitory social legislation. Sex in itself was not the major target of Puritan efforts to alter social habits. Pleasure in any form was seen as diminishing one's ability to serve the glory of the Lord. As a foremost source of enjoyment, sexual expression was limited. In this respect, the Puritan view of sex differed from asceticism, a distinction that Passmore described this way:

> Asceticism attempts to withdraw from the world as a whole; Puritanism condemns the world only insofar as it is sinful, not, for example, commerce, or political service, or marriage, but characteristically, the theatre, the consumption of alcohol, any form of sensual delight.

Starting in 1650, legislation was adopted that forbade such profane amusements and works of the devil as dancing, singing, and the theater. Fornication became punishable by imprisonment, and adultery could lead, on conviction, to death. Long hair and makeup on women, not to mention naked breasts, were described as the badge of a harlot. Fast days, which to the Puritans meant total abstinence from food, replaced traditional religious and secular holidays. Celebrations involving that remnant of phallic worship, the maypole, were banned. Measures were taken against swearing, displays of affection between men and women, drinking, and gambling. All activities on Sundays not related to worship were banned. Even in marriage, sex was supposed to be for procreation, not for pleasure. Clothing and hairstyles were to be plain.

However, the sentiments of most Englishmen were against the harsh regulations enacted by the Calvinists. Records of the period indicate that juries were reluctant to convict on charges of adultery. Only three instances are known in which conviction was followed by infliction of the death sentence. Despite adequate evidence, juries regularly

returned verdicts of not guilty. The extreme penalty worked to the opposite of its intended effect: It was so severe that punishment was avoided altogether.

Most people found the laws and ordinances and their enforcement obnoxious or repulsive. On fast days, for instance, soldiers were instructed to enter homes without warrants to determine whether abstinence was being observed. In assessing the outcome of the Puritan attempt to legislate moral standards, Davies wrote:

> The general effect of the repressive measures of the puritans, their inhibitions and prohibitions, was exactly what would be expected—that they imposed a yoke heavier than most Englishmen would bear . . . . It had been possible to overthrow institutions but not fundamentally to change habits. The attempts to interfere with daily social customs met with little success and irritated men beyond endurance. The consequence was that the puritans, in their endeavors to compel men to be good (as they understood goodness), defeated their own ends.

This fact became abundantly clear when, just 2 years after the death of Cromwell, Parliament recalled the exiled son of Charles I. An English fleet set out for the continent to fetch Charles II.

The Restoration

After 11 years of Calvinistic austerity and repression, the English populace eagerly received Charles II and his entourage. The returned king and the aristocrats around him, given a mandate for license, made certain that hedonism replaced Puritanism. Released from moral tyranny, many persons, from the throne to the slums of London, indulged in lustful sensuality, sexual chaos, and promiscuity of a degree almost unequaled in history. The maypoles used in many of the Restoration celebrations were, significantly, of an unprecedented height.

Adultery, previously held to be an affront to God and an offense in the law, became an important index of loyalty to the monarch. Success and social prestige were enhanced, rather than destroyed, by scandal. It was, as Macauley noted, evidence that unbridled debauchery was the natural consequence of unnatural severity.

The king and his court set the permissive tone for the rest of society. Married to a barren queen, Charles II had no legitimate children, but he kept a series of mistresses, including the immensely popular Nell Gwyn, and had 14 children with these various royal bedmates.

Nell Gwyn—raised in a brothel and herself a prostitute, barmaid, and sometime actress—had become by age 19 the favorite of Charles II. She made no secret of being the royal whore, as she called herself on numerous occasions, but was proud of her position, and countless stories have come down through the years that attest to her pride in this respect. They also attest to the nature of the times. One episode in particular reveals the moral temper of the Restoration period. It was said that, while riding through London one afternoon in 1675, Nell's carriage, a gift from Charles, was mistaken for the carriage of Louise de Keroualle, a Frenchwoman sent by Louis XIV to service Charles II. An angry crowd gathered around the coach, incensed that a Catholic should venture not only into England but into the king's bed. After much shouting, cursing, and jostling, Nell could no longer bear the insults. She ordered the coach to stop. Putting her head out the window, she called for the crowd to be civil and let her pass. "I am the Prostestant whore!" she yelled. Delighted, the crowd wished her well and let the carriage continue on its outing. Noting the significance of this anecdote, Wallace emphasized that

among the hundreds watching, not one thought it improper that the king's mistress had so plainly and openly announced her station.

The most outstanding men of the Restoration were often the most notorious rakes, defined as dissolute and perverse persons. John Wilmot, Second Earl of Rochester, was perhaps the foremost debauchee of his time. An accomplished writer and scholar—he earned a master's degree from Oxford at age 14—he was lecherous, drunken, and known for his coarse humor. He opted for the licentious life. One of Rochester's poems, "Maim'd Debauchee," has been described by Greene as a possible self-portrait:

I rise at eleven, I dine about two,
I get drunk before seven, and the
    next thing I do,
I send for my whore, when for
    fear of a clap,
I dally about her, and spew
    in her lap.

One of Rochester's plays, *Sodomy*, exemplified Restoration taste and commented on the openly tolerated practice of homosexuality, a practice that was particularly widespread in the army. Said to have been performed at the royal court, the title page of the script, dated 1665, read:

Sodom or the Quintessence of Debauchery
by E. of R.
Written for the Royal Company of Whoremasters

The play dealt with the consequences of a proclamation issued by the King of Sodom to his Buggermaster General that in the future buggery should be the order of the day. Important characters included Queen Cuntigratia, Prince Pricket, Pimps of Honor, and a Merkin and Dildoe Maker to the Royal Family.

Rochester's *Sodomy* was not a departure from existing standards of theatrical taste. To the Puritan, the theater was a waste of time and an escape from the duties of life. To the society of Charles II, the theater accordingly became the delight of London, permeated with sex at every level. On stage, backstage, and in the audience, immorality was evident and glorified.

Themes in the plays expressed prevailing moral attitudes. William Congreve's *Love for Love* advocated calculated seduction and emotional callousness. George Farquhar's *The Inconstant, or the Way to Win Him* dealt with the joys of adultery. William Wycherley's *The Country Wife* depicted the adulterer as hero. John Dryden's *Mock Astrologer* stressed the necessity of sufficient wenching, a view also presented in Congreve's *The Way of the World* and Farquhar's *The Beaux' Stratagem*.

Acting was a disreputable occupation, and most leading ladies played two roles each evening—one on stage and one as courtesans. Prostitutes solicited members of the audience during performances. Hoping to end such practices, Queen Anne, who came to the throne in 1702, decreed that members of the audience could not go backstage or onstage before or during a play and that women could not, as had been the custom, wear masks to the theater. The masks were used by prostitutes to disguise their identities.

The Restoration was notable in English history for the absence of prosecutions for homosexuality. A number of private clubs for homosexuals flourished. The Mollies Club was among the first to open, and it appears to have catered to transvestites or, at least, highly effeminate men.

However, Puritanism and sobriety did not disappear altogether. While Charles II and his court ran the sexual riot of London, the lower classes and those in the countryside continued to live by many Calvinistic ideals. The Puritan ethic had become deeply rooted. Many people considered two major disasters in 1665 and 1666—the plague and the great fire of London—to be expressions of the Lord's displeasure at the wickedness rampant in the city.

More important than any sexual morality implanted by the Puritans or destroyed by the rakes was the outlook the Puritans fostered toward work. The Puritan ethic was a work ethic that many scholars feel made possible the eventual economic dominance of England.

As noted by Smith, the reaction of the Restoration period was, in fact, largely superficial, and the licentiousness, although highly visible, did not reflect the real character of the period. Smith wrote:

On deeper view it is a long pause, to allow the settlement and digestion, to allow a general infiltration of great movements . . . . The energy evoked by the great events of that earlier time and by the searching controversies which laid bare the very foundations of politics and religion now passed off into scientific enquiry, into industrial commercial and agricultural enterprise, into economic and financial speculation . . . . Even the bitter anti-Puritanism of the first years of the reign [of Charles II] dies out into mere cynicism and disgust as it realises that worse even than a rule of saints can be a fatal brand and signature of nothing else but the impure.

Overshadowed by social developments was the great movement that took place in the realm of science. The Royal Society of London, the first major organization dedicated to the advancement of science, was founded during the reign of Charles II and was the object of his interest. It was the age and the society in which Isaac Newton and Robert Boyle made their great discoveries. The habeas corpus act was also passed during the Restoration.

These advances made themselves felt in attitudes toward sexuality as they became incorporated into the social consciousness of an age they helped make possible, the Age of Reason.

RATIONAL SEXUALITY

The Royal Society of London was, without question, the foremost institution devoted to science in 17th century Europe. Virtually every new discovery or theory was routinely sent to London for recognition and criticism. Thus, when Leeuwenhoek discovered spermatozoa under his microscope in 1677, it was to the Royal Society of London that he sent a manuscript on his finding, and it was this society that authenticated his work. England was then the center of Enlightenment science. But France, and the court of Louis XIV, was the focus of European morals and manners. And France, the home of Descartes, witnessed the first deliberate application of the rational approaches used in science, mathematics, and geometry to social, moral, philosophical, and sexual issues.

Reason, as extended to physical and emotional relations between the sexes, resulted in what might be termed rational sexuality. It came to mean the control of the heart by the head and the rule of passion by the will. There was a definite effort not to be carried away by emotions and to keep feelings under control. Among the upper classes this rationality became not only an ideal but a way of conducting daily activities.

It is hard to say which more profoundly influenced the manners and morals of France, the intellectual arguments of the Enlightenment philosophers or the clearly defined tastes of Louis XIV. The two held views that were mutually enhancing. And both were willingly followed, first by the closely knit group of aristocrats in the court at Versailles and in Paris and eventually by all Europe.

Voltaire called the late 17th and the 18th centuries the Age of Louis XIV to emphasize how completely the Sun King, *le Roi Soleil,* dominated his time. Others have called the period the great age of the mistress, and here again the stamp of Louis XIV was evident. Less than a year had passed since his marriage to Marie Thérèse, daughter of the Spanish king, when Louis replaced her as his companion in public ceremonies and in his bed chamber with the first of several mistresses he was to keep. Durant and Durant (1963) wrote:

The morals of the court were decorous adultery, all carried on a rhythm of external refinement, elegant manners, and compulsory gaiety.

Men of the Age of Reason, according to Hunt, wanted a new kind of woman, one

who combined sex and intellect [and] who could be detached and perfectly cool about love.

Important to Louis XIV "was the avoidance of all true feeling," and the etiquette at his court was intended to suppress all evidence of emotion. Those who could abide by these rules were most favorably received; those who could not were viewed with disfavor. Eventually, Hunt continues,

upper-class men and women of the late seventeenth and eighteenth centuries concealed their feelings by the aid of cold reason and carefully rehearsed manners; after a while they almost forgot they had any feelings.

By these values, Ninon de Lenclos exemplified the ideal woman in the age of Louis XIV, and, indeed, she was one of the most admired women in France, a favorite of the king and of the aristocracy.

Ninon de Lenclos operated a school of gallantry at her home, where, in addition to entertaining the most powerful figures in French society, she taught young aristocrats the art of lovemaking and the conduct of sexual relationships. As described by Wallace, her instruction included

the care and handling of a mistress or wife, the psychology of women, the correct approach to courting and seduction, the acceptable ways of ending an affair, and the physiology of artful sex

. . . . When words would not do and more earthy instruction was required, Ninon took her young men to bed to demonstrate the techniques of foreplay and sexual intercourse.

On occasion, Ninon also offered advice to young girls whose mothers sought her guidance.

Above all else, Ninon instructed her students and expected of her lovers to suppress any expressions of passion and to maintain refined manners. Every act, every gesture, every display of emotion was to be carefully and reasonably measured.

By her popularity, Ninon de Lenclos testified to the emergence of a new kind of woman, a development that in itself was a major event of the period. Women became involved in the culture of a Western society to a degree previously unknown. Through salons, like those of Ninon, they controlled French social life.

The salons flourished during the reign of Louis XIV but grew even more numerous and influential after his death and the subsequent decline of Versailles as a social focus. Louis XIV has been credited with the rise of the salon system of the 18th century by bringing men and women together in a social setting and investing women with the responsibilities of teaching men refined manners.

Summarizing the dispassionate nature of rational sexuality during the Age of Reason, de Riencourt notes that this outlook was based on the absence of any felt need to interfere with private morals,

so long as they conformed to the well-established patterns of traditional *amorality* and in no way threatened the social organism.

Each person could, it was held, formulate his own moral code. Thus, de Riencourt concludes:

The French saw in sexual activity a tool of the intellect that it was imperative to keep at all times under rational control; hence it was more a matter of self-regulation than of repression. Sexual passion, regulated by the intellect, could always be proclaimed openly because it was *sous contrôle* of the rational faculty.

In the human search for perfection, passion was seen as a destructive force, a force that stood in opposition to reason and logic.

NATURAL SEXUALITY

A previously lacking warmth was injected into the Enlightenment sexuality in 1750 by Jean Jacques Rousseau. Cold and rational ideals were infused with a somewhat more emotional, romantic, and even sentimental spirit. Rousseau declared:

Man is good; only our institutions have made him bad.

This view formed the basis of his back-to-nature philosophy, a view that was promptly extended to sexual behavior.

In *Emile* (1762) Rousseau maintained that every person

brings with him at birth a distinctive temperament, which determines his spirit and his character. There is no question of changing or putting a restraint upon this temperament, only of training it and bringing it to perfection.

Not long after Rousseau's ideas had become known, European sailors discovered the islands of the South Pacific, finding what many people considered to be nature in its most pure and perfect form.

Captain James Cook, who reached Tahiti in 1769, discovered and later reported examples of sexual promiscuity and female beauty that intellectuals seized to support their back-to-nature views. Much publicized was the reception accorded the European sailors; white skin was considered highly attractive by the Tahitians, and the welcome was, therefore, particularly enthusiastic. Attention was also focused on the rites of Venus, a custom in which young men and girls copulated publicly so that more experienced members of the community, usually women, could offer their advice and directions. Girls as young as 11 years received their sex education in this way. Similar coming-of-age rites were found elsewhere in Polynesia. A Frenchman, Louis Antoine de Bougainville, also sailed to the South Seas and reported similar examples of sexual morality.

Denis Diderot—editor of the *Encyclopédie,* chronicler of his age, spokesman of the Enlightenment, and friend of Rousseau—seized on the accounts cf Tahitian practices to support his attacks on conventional Christian morality. He cited the primitive society of Tahiti as an example of natural goodness and sexuality, unhampered by ideas of chastity or the restraints of marriage. In *Supplément au voyage de Bougainville* and other works, Diderot enviously discussed the innocent and uninhibited sexuality of Polynesia. In one of his major works, *La Religieuse,* Diderot similarly attacked traditional sexual standards and practices, specifically the continued Catholic practice of clerical celibacy. In this novel about the love of a mother superior for a young novice, Diderot made the point, as noted by Wilson,

that celibacy is unnatural and that the cloistered life is socially wasteful, that the warping of personality in the convent is inescapable.

Both Diderot and a fellow Frenchman, Choderlos de Laclos, were part of another development of the late 18th century, the emergence of modern psychology and psychiatry. Their works on sexual themes coincided, in terms of insight, with the pioneering efforts of such men as Tuke, Pinel, and Chiarugi, whose views changed attitudes toward the nature and treatment of mental illness. Freed from moral prejudice by the nihilistic intellectual climate of the Enlightenment and able to present sexuality as part of the common and natural human condition, Diderot and Laclos described human sexual drives with remarkable acuity. Their works, in a sense, anticipated the clinical studies into human sexuality.

In *La Religieuse,* for example, Diderot provided a realistic, detailed, and clinical study of homosexual behavior. In *Les Liaisons Dangereuses* Laclos described the sexual impulses of women, descriptions that, says Lewinsohn, are noteworthy for their subtlety of psychological analysis.

During the late 18th century, an era when sexual excess and even violence were accepted features of society, one man, the Marquis de Sade (1740–1814), through his personal exploits and published works, was able to earn immortality and provoke public outrage as a sexual deviant.

Several major scandals brought de Sade to public attention. One, called the Arcueil scandal, occurred in 1768 and involved an unemployed seamstress, Rose Keller, who was flogged and otherwise assaulted by de Sade. Another, known as the scandal of the young girls, was an outgrowth of de Sade's procurement and use of teenage girls, mostly 15-year-olds, for orgies at his chateau during the winter of 1773. These were not isolated undertakings. When not in prison for his activities, de Sade regularly whipped prostitutes, organized orgies, and experimented with aphrodisiacs.

Had de Sade not been gifted as a writer and intellect, he might have been remembered merely as an eccentric or psychopath. But he presented his views in such works as *Justine, Histoire de Juliette,* and *The 120 Days of Sodom.* Moreover, prevailing Enlightenment philosophy provided de Sade with a convenient rationalization for his impulses and activities. He attempted to justify his views by surrounding them with the terms and concepts of natural law and presenting them as part of the back-to-nature ideal. He stated that traditional morality was antinatural, that man's natural desires were evil, and that natural man existed, as Rousseau said, but that man was inherently cruel, as mother nature was cruel. De Sade exalted sex, stating that

there is nothing greater or more beautiful than sex, and no salvation without it.

But the most natural and intense form of sexual activity, especially for women, he concluded, was pain. By its very existence in nature, de Sade maintained, sexual deviation was natural. Just as Rousseau became identified with the back-to-nature ideal, de Sade, as the inspiration of the word "sadism," has come to be identified with the attainment of sexual excitation from the suffering of others.

EIGHTEENTH CENTURY ENGLAND

The 17th century had been an age of revolution in England; the 18th century was a period of transformation. Without violent social or moral upheavals, public attitudes toward sexuality changed so profoundly that standards of behavior evident at the end of the 18th century were almost nonexistent at the beginning of the century. Limits of tolerance narrowed, spontaneity gave way to inhibition,

and, in general, sexuality became subdued. Few measures indicate any changes in actual practices, but the alteration of mores was tremendous.

Early in the Georgian era, English sexuality was reminiscent of the immediate post-Restoration years. Brothels that had sprung up in London's Covent Garden were notorious throughout Europe. These bawdy houses, said to have employed some 50,000 prostitutes, often attempted to fashion themselves along the lines of the salons in Paris but were generally unsuccessful. The closest thing to the salons were the bluestocking clubs of London. Other clubs, which catered to sexual activity, were so numerous that the early 18th century has been characterized as the age of English clubs. The names of such fashionable whores as Anna Bellamy, Fanny Murray, Lucy Cooper, Harriet Errington, and Kitty Fisher were as well known to London society and as acceptable in high social circles as officials of state and members of royalty. John Fielding, one of London's most eminent magistrates and the half-brother of the author Henry Fielding, lived next door to the Covent Garden brothel run by Mother Cocksedge. Little or no effort was made by justices of the peace to interfere with prostitutes.

Marriage was a frivolous undertaking for many persons, as evident in the so-called Fleet marriages. Named after London's Fleet prison, in whose shadows disreputable ministers conducted clandestine marriage ceremonies, they were without church sanction and often impulsive, lasting only long enough for the bride and groom to become sober. As one woman (Jarrett) complained,

drunken swearing parsons with their myrmidons that wear black coats and pretend to be clerks and registers to the Fleet [ply about] pulling and forcing some people to some peddling Alehouse or Brandyshop to be married.

According to Bloch:

From October 1704 to February 1705, 2,954 weddings were performed; often twenty or thirty couples were mated in a single day . . . . The Governor of the prison and the Registrar got handsome incomes from these weddings.

Starting in 1738, John Wesley preached the gospel of his Methodist movement. His sermons and those of his fellow preachers had great appeal. They denounced the convivial excesses of society, the empty rationalism of the Church of England, and the lack of religious feeling among the populace. By 1840, the Methodists were having a perceptible impact on public opinion.

That England was receptive to the puritanical preachings of an evangelical movement can be surmised from the art and literature of the period, particularly the graphic work of William Hogarth and the novels of Daniel Defoe, Samuel Richardson, Henry Fielding, and John Cleland. The series of etchings by Hogarth, "The Rake's Progress" and "The Harlot's Progress," Defoe's *Moll Flanders* and *Roxana,* Richardson's *Pamela,* Fielding's *Tom Jones* and *Joseph Andrews,* and Cleland's *Fanny Hill* were, at one and the same time, erotic and moralistic.

Morality and sexual restraint were not seen as being synonymous. It was not outrageous that the main character of *Fanny Hill,* a girl with a totally guiltless and uninhibited preoccupation with sex, reached respectability in the end. Any criticism directed to Cleland was equaled by criticism of Richardson's *Pamela,* in which the heroine defends her virtue by preserving her virginity. It has long been held by scholars of English literature that *Fanny Hill* was written as a response to *Pamela* and that Fielding's *Joseph Andrews* was a similarly motivated parody of Richardson's novel. To a great extent, Cleland and Richardson defined morality as truth, lack of self-deception, and the absence of hypocrisy. Female chastity was not considered a major index of moral virtue. Meanness and cruelty were viewed as greater sins.

After 1750, in part because of the success of the Methodists, a moralistic cast of mind was increasingly evident. In terms of sex, men and women began to conduct their affairs more privately and discreetly. Value was placed on moral virtue and the avoidance of an expanding number of activities, including fornication, that came to be considered vices. The fear of scandal became very real.

Respectability began to hinge on subdued sexuality.

Among the official efforts to restrain English morals—efforts that in themselves reflect the new outlook—was the Marriage Bill of 1753. All future marriages—except those among the royal family, Jews, and dissenters—were held to be invalid unless solemnized by an Anglican clergyman. Moreover, the banns had to be cried for three successive Sundays in the parish church before the ceremony could be performed. In this fashion, the Fleet marriages were put to an end and the status of matrimony enhanced.

Other developments indicative of the concern for morals were the creation of the Society for the Reformation of Manners in 1757, the proclamation against vice issued by George III, and the Proclamation Society, founded in 1789 to support its goals.

Popular attitudes about homosexuality further illustrate the movement away from Restoration values. The permissive attitude toward homosexuality all but disappeared. The publication of *Fanny Hill* in 1749, in the words of Plumb,

did not unduly disturb the tough-minded public of eighteenth century London.

But, he adds, when

a disreputable publisher . . . wrote into it a long, explicitly homosexual scene in 1757,

the authorities began to take notice of and to object to the book. By 1780 homosexuals are reported to have been put to death by angry crowds. Attempted homosexuality was punishable by the pillory and several years in jail, and the act itself could be punished on the gallows.

These harsh measures caused the politician Edmund Burke to protest in Parliament. Burke brought before Parliament the story of a coachman named Read and a plasterer named Smith, who in 1780 were sentenced to the pillory after being convicted on charges of sodomy. While in the pillory, they were both stoned to death. For his efforts to prevent such abuses, Burke was accused of having some personal interest in these matters and, in fact, had to bring a libel action to clear his name. So strong had the prejudice against homosexuality once again become that even the upper classes made sure to conceal their sodomitical practices, although the penalties for them inevitably fell short of prison or death.

Lesbianism, according to Tomalin, was considered

a dirty little vice of servant girls, boarding schools, and actresses,

a view continually presented in publications aimed at women. To the refined sensibilities of the period, it was almost inconceivable that sophisticated women would engage in such an activity.

In England, as in France, etiquette and restraint were major concerns in relationships between the sexes. Among those to record this fact about midcentury society was Giovanni Giacomo Casanova, the Italian whose name has since become a synonym for great lover. The tale of the Lady of Ranelagh, a passage in Casanova's memoirs, relates an episode in London during 1763.

Ranelagh was one of London's pleasure gardens, elaborate halls where the upper classes dined, danced, and otherwise socialized. One midnight, after an evening at Ranelagh, Casanova emerged to find that his hired carriage had left without him. A woman, seeing Casanova's plight, offered to take him home in her private coach. Once in the cab, Casanova and his benefactor had sexual intercourse. But, when asked her name, the woman would not give it. Some time later, Casanova saw the woman again at a gathering. Approaching her and getting no sign of recognition, Casanova inquired as to whether she had forgotten him. She replied,

I remember you perfectly, but a piece of folly is not the same as an introduction.

In 1789, the English concern for Christian morals was reinforced. Always looking to France as a source of social fashion, the English had, throughout the 18th century, modeled their own institutions and practices on those in France. But 1789 witnessed the start of the French Revolution, and many people in Britain wondered whether the same fate awaited their nation. Describing the mood in the last decade of the century and the interrelationship of the events across the channel with sexuality in England, Jarrett wrote that the English saw themselves as inhabiting a

green and pleasant land [that] was a reservoir of virtue which was in danger of being poisoned by the foul effluents from the Frenchified high society of London . . . . The natural functions of the human body no longer seemed a fit subject for humor. The same applied to its natural pleasures. In Hogarth's world fornication had been accepted as something which went on all the time and which was generally fairly amusing in a squalid kind of way . . . . By the 1790s it seemed that fornication, perhaps even sexual pleasure itself, was something which was always to be deplored and never to be made fun of.

By 1800, most persons were conforming with this new sexual morality, at least as far as their public behavior was concerned. That English morals and manners should rise so dramatically in the 18th century, when the Puritans had been unsuccessful in achieving this objective during the previous century, can be ascribed to the fact that 18th century morals were not imposed. They evolved in a society that was in sympathy with ideas of restraint.

Romantic and Victorian Eras

During the first half of the 19th century, reason (the Enlightenment) and revolution (French, industrial, scientific) sparked reaction. Protest movements agitated for such radical ideals as socialism, free love, eugenics, birth control, equal rights for women, and marital reform. By midcentury the negative analogue of the reformist causes appeared in the form of a puritanical and rigid code of behavior known as Victorianism. Toward the end of the century, another reversal took place as men like Havelock Ellis and Sigmund Freud initiated a revolution of human sexuality by introducing a clinical approach to the study and analysis of sexual behavior.

ROMANTICS AND REFORMERS

Romantics, predominantly literary and artistic people, and a cluster of social reformist groups were in the forefront of efforts to change the conventional climate of sexual opinion and mores. While espousing different causes, many groups had shared and overlapping ideals.

Romanticism

Romanticism represented the great intellectual revolt of the early 19th century. Above all, it was a reaction against the Enlightenment. The omnipotence of reason was replaced by an emphasis on emotion and instinct. It was, in this sense, a rebellion of the heart against the mind. Individual desires and passions were accepted as driving forces in human behavior, personal feelings and thoughts were emphasized, and artificiality in relations between the sexes was rejected.

The modern notion of marriage as the natural outcome of an intense love relationship was born of the romantic rebellion. Marriage was seen as a union between equals based on reciprocal love. The view of marriage as a total relationship, providing both emotional and sexual needs, was another outgrowth of the romantic ideal. Psychological and physical elements were seen to be of equal importance. Shelley, for example, wrote that all sympathies should be "harmoniously blended," with sexual intercourse requiring "the entire consent of all the conscious portions" of both partners.

Romanticism ended the fragmentation of female roles. A woman was no longer seen as either a mother and wife or a mistress or whore. Indeed, traditional distinctions between men and women in terms of sexual traits and characteristics were de-emphasized. The image of delicate and dreamy men, free and daring women emerged.

The emphasis on both emotional and physical compatibility was, in part, the cause and the consequence of another ideal of the early 19th century—namely, that only lovers who were emotionally, intellectually, and sexually attracted to one another had legitimate relationships. Any protocols or moral restraints that delayed gratification were considered artificial. Passions led to coitus. Impulses were to be followed, and expressions of desire could be immediate. The conventional value of premarital chastity was rejected.

Emotion was idealized as an end in itself. This primacy of feeling in romantic sensibilities is reflected in Goethe's *The Sorrows of Young Werther*. The loss of Werther's one true love—the idea of one love was an important romantic concept—evoked anguish and loss of value and meaning and ultimately led to his suicide. A passage in Werther's diary proclaimed:

Oh this fearful void which I feel here in my breast! I often think to myself—if you could press her just once to this heart, just once, then this entire void would be filled.

Another entry declared:

I have so much, and my feeling for her engulfs it all; I have so much, and without her I find everything turned into nothing.

Napoleon said that he had read *Werther* seven times, weeping whenever he read of the hero's suicide. This fact underscores an important aspect of the romantic movement. It was a movement of a few, a small group of artists and writers. But these few were among the most eminent figures in the arts, including such writers as Byron, Wordsworth, Coleridge, Keats, and Shelley. The pathos, suffering, and unhappiness that the romantics associated with love apparently appealed to the sense of alienation that people experienced in the early 19th century. And it inspired many radical thinkers to seek changes in society to improve the nature of human existence. Many of these efforts were directed toward sex and the relationship between man and woman.

Reformers

Various social reformers echoed romantic sentiments and ideals. A foremost advocate of marital reform, free love, the redefinition of male-female relationships, and equal rights for women was Mary Wollstonecraft. Her major work, *Vindication of the Rights of Women*, was published in 1792 and provided for many 19th century marriage reformers and women's rights protagonists what Ditzion called "a source of exciting and convincing quotations."

Equality for women was a major concern

of Wollstonecraft. About male chauvinism, she wrote:

> I scarcely am able to govern my muscles when I see a man start with eager and serious solicitude to lift a handkerchief or shut a door when the lady could have done it herself had she only moved a pace or two. I do earnestly wish to see the distinction of sex confounded in society, unless where love animates behaviour.

Wollstonecraft also espoused free love, contending that partners should be able to satisfy one another sexually and that premarital and extramarital sexual activity was not inherently sinful. Others expressed similar views. The Saint-Simonians, a Utopian socialist movement founded by Henri, Comte de Saint-Simon, considered sexual relations outside of marriage as natural. Friedrich Schlelermacher, a German writer who was widely read in England, declared that a suitable partner could be found only through sexual experimentation before marriage. Shelley, in his poem *Queen Mab* (1813), discussed his ideas on free love. He wrote:

> Love withers under constraint, its very essense is liberty; it is compatible neither with obedience, jealousy, nor fear . . . . Love is free: to promise forever to love the same woman is not less absurd than to promise to believe the same creed.

William Godwin was among the most outspoken of Englishmen on the contemporary ills of the marital institution. Godwin considered monogamous marriage an odious monopoly. Couples should not be bound for a lifetime to feelings and attitudes experienced for a few moments, he wrote.

Other reformers mixed theory with practice. Robert Owen, a British businessman, developed a model for a utopian community, the Agricultural and Manufacturing Village of Unity and Mutual Co-operation. Influenced by both Shelley and Godwin, he shared many of their views on free love and marriage. Charles Fourier, a Frenchman, developed a theory of utopian socialism that included a system of license to serve human passions and desires. Owen and Fourier profoundly affected American utopians.

Many of the ideas advanced by European reformers found an ideal testing ground in the United States. Although America retained its basic puritan outlook on sexuality through the 19th century, the period after the War of 1812 saw some loosening of official moral restraints. As noted by Carman et al., in the years between 1820 and 1860, many 18th century institutions were dismantled. Conflicts arose in the minds of Americans between what the nation had been and what it might become. Many persons joined reform movements that hoped to set the country right, and by 1840 few phases of American life had not been held up to some ideal standard by the nation's reformers. This particularly held true for sex life.

The elaborate socialist plans of Charles Fourier generated considerable interest in America, largely through Albert Brisbane's newspaper column in *The New York Tribune.* Horace Greeley, publisher of the *Tribune,* was himself a strong supporter of Fourierism.

According to Fourier, the ills of society resulted from its failure to harness human passions for productive purposes. People will not work and be happy, he contended, so long as their satisfaction is thwarted. He devised a scheme for a new form of society that would permit full realization of human potential by providing a pleasurable existence.

Central to Fourier's utopia was the idea of transforming labor into pleasure. The transformation of social institutions called for by Fourier—including the

> distribution of the social product according to need, assignment of functions according to individual faculties and inclinations, constant mutations of functions, and short work periods

—the creation, in brief, of attractive labor *(travail attrayant),* was, according to Marcuse, derived "above all, from the release of libidinal forces." Marcuse explains:

> Fourier assumes the existence of an *attraction industrielle* which makes for pleasurable co-operation. It is based on the *attraction passionnée* in the nature of man, which persists despite the opposition of reason, duty, prejudice. This *attraction passionnée* tends toward three principal objectives: the creation of "luxury, or the pleasure of the five

senses"; the formation of libidinal groups (of friendship and love); and the establishment of a harmonious order organizing these groups for work in accordance with the development of the individual "passions" (internal and external "play" of faculties).

To accomplish his ideal of strength through joy, Fourier intended to create working communities based on the phalanx, a unit of 1,620 persons. People would live in communal buildings designed to maximize opportunities for various forms of socialization, including sex. Indulgence of sexual desires and easy access to partners was encouraged. A system of license, Fourier maintained, served human passions and desires far better than did the system of traditional matrimony.

Called Associationists in the United States, the Fourierists established about 40 *phalanstères* by 1843, the peak year of their movement. None of the communities did well.

Best known of all 19th century American communes was the Oneida Community. Founded and run by John Humphrey Noyes, (see Figure 12), at Oneida, New York, the community had objectives found in many other social experiments of the time: improvement of the quality of sexual and social relations between men and women, control of the birth rate, and improved quality of offspring. Noyes called his philosophy perfectionism, and his followers were known as perfectionists (see Figure 13).

Oneida had a system of complex marriage, in which any male or female member could, with the consent of a central committee, live as man and wife. Relationships could be readily dissolved, previous commitments and attachments being of no concern. In effect, all community members were potential conjugal partners. Complex marriage included stirpiculture, an exercise in controlled eugenics. This practice—based on Noyes' philosophy that excessive, random, involuntary procreation was less desirable than intelligent, well ordered procreation—called for Oneida residents to participate in arranged matings. Offspring from these scientific combinations, it was hoped, would be biologically superior to the offspring of nonscientific propagation. Also a part of Noyes' teaching was the use of coitus reservatus as a contraceptive method. This form of self-control was taught to the teenage males in the community by experienced, older women. Oneida also had a system of ascending fellowship, which gave the men of the central committee first choice in selecting female partners.

Among the other noteworthy examples of 19th century sexual ventures were George Rapp's Harmony in Indiana, where his Rappites practiced celibate marriage; Robert Owen's New Harmony, on the site purchased from the Rappites, where intercourse was seen as an important aspect of male-female relations; Fruitlands and Hopedale in Massachusetts, where nudism and sexual equality were major concerns; and Josiah Warren's Modern Times, in New York, which experimented with free love. Two religious groups, the Shakers and the Mormons, stood at opposite extremes on the matter of sex. The Shakers, who had about 6,000 members during the 1840's, insisted on celibacy, which made it necessary for them to recruit new members constantly. The Mormons, on the other hand, permitted polygamy.

FIGURE 12. John Humphrey Noyes, founder of the Oneida Community. (Oneida Ltd. Silversmiths)

FIGURE 13. Members of the Oneida Community around 1860. John Humphrey Noyes stands in the *right foreground* with his hands crossed. (Oneida Ltd. Silversmiths)

Such deviations from prevailing patterns of matrimony and sexuality were quite limited, even in America. In all, about 200 utopian communities were established. These efforts were highly publicized and in some instances, as in the case of the Mormons, persecuted. Most utopian sexual ventures were an indication of the social pluralism in England and America in the first half of the 19th century and not an indication that the societies were abandoning their sexual mores.

Birth control

Thomas Robert Malthus (1766–1834), an English clergyman, presented a theory that considerably alarmed people and motivated them to act on the issue of birth control. In *An Essay on the Principle of Population*, published anonymously in 1798, Malthus contended that population was growing in a geometric progression, while sources of subsistence were growing in an arithmetic progression. Eventually, he argued, the world would be unable to feed itself. Concern about the real and imagined ailments of industrialized society was immediately exacerbated. Malthus' ideas were put to propagandistic use by numerous groups interested in limiting population. The problem they confronted was stated by Malthus in one of his postulates:

that the passion between the sexes is necessary, and will remain nearly in its present state.

This fact, he wrote, appears to be a fixed law of human nature. A solution proposed by Malthus was for people to spend their youth—which meant into their thirties—in total sexual abstinence. By marrying late, they would have fewer children. In brief, his prescription was moral restraint.

Sexual abstinence was not encouraged by most activists concerned with the limitation of population. Francis Place (1771–1854), considered the founder of the birth control movement, separated the sexual instinct from the reproductive instinct and gave contraception a body of social theory. His view, as outlined in *Illustrations and Proofs of the Principle of Population* (1822), was that contraceptive measures, instead of moral restraint, should be used. Place distributed a series of handbills that educated the masses about such specific birth control techniques as coitus interruptus, the sponge, and the tampon—but not the condom. Contraception eventually became popularized as Malthusianism, neo-Malthusianism, and other organized movements dealt with the issue of population control.

The appearance of Charles Darwin's *Origin of Species* in 1859 further fixed attention on the quality of human existence. Darwin's theory of evolution—with its references to the struggle for existence and the survival of the fittest, along with discussions of natural selection and artificial selection—provoked interest in eugenics.

Apart from its religious and physiological aspects, contraception was of paramount psychological and social significance. Natural sexuality—as espoused by Wollstonecraft, Godwin, and others—was largely impossible for most women. The lack of effective birth control techniques made naturalness and promiscuity tremendously risky. As pointed out by Tomalin, "the idea that one false step was irretrievable," leading to the unwanted birth of a child, was in itself a strong inhibiting factor.

Material dealing with contraception provoked strong public reactions, in contrast to other causes, which produced only ridicule. This fact was borne out by the events surrounding Charles Knowlton, an American physician, and the publication of his works in both England and America. Knowlton had a distinctly modern view of sexual behavior, a view that was unacceptable to official society in his time. In the *Fruits of Philosophy*, which first appeared in 1832, Knowlton expressed the idea that sexual desire was a normal body appetite whose reasonable indulgence was both satisfying and healthy. He was opposed to celibacy, calling it unwholesome, and he was against sexual denial, considering it harmful. What most disturbed people, though, was Knowlton's detailed descriptions

and advocacy of contraceptive practices, including the use of the diaphragm, then called a vaginal tent, and the postcoital douche. Describing the general attitude toward the *Fruits of Philosophy,* Ditzion has written:

With knowledge of contraception in the hands of all, female virtue was on the way out.

This fear motivated the city of Cambridge, Massachusetts to imprison Knowlton for 3 months of hard labor. It led some years later to the conviction of Henry Cook, a bookseller in Bristol, England, on the charge of disseminating obscene literature. Freethought advocates Charles Bradlaugh and Annie Besant, who challenged the government by reprinting the *Fruits of Philosophy,* were likewise convicted and sentenced in England, but their conviction was later reversed by the courts.

VICTORIANISM

By 1840 the spirit of romanticism and reform was overshadowed by Victorianism, a moral ethic that had as its central ideal the denial or repression of sexual drives. It was an ethic of purity that, in the words of May, "sought to have love without falling into sex." Accepted by a large and influential segment of English society, this moral code characterized the public life-style of the nation in the latter half of the 19th century.

Origins

Actually, the term "Victorianism" is misleading. Although named after the reigning monarch of the time, Queen Victoria, the ethic was not the product of the throne. The roots of the Victorian outlook can be traced back to the moralist trend begun nearly 100 years before, when, obscured by the publicity and controversy of the radical thinkers, the evangelical movements, like the Wesleyans, had initiated a resurrection of the Puritan inheritance. The major factors involved in the development of Victorianism relate to the consequences of industrialization. The need for labor, male and female, enabled women to earn independent incomes, freed them from the home and the need to use prostitution as a source of income, and gave women a new economic power. The double standard of sexuality became all but obsolete, and the gender confusion evident in romanticism was compounded. It is often suggested that the new complex society threatened to break down the traditional family structure. A newly formed middle class was sensitive to this possibility. Many saw within the grasp of their hands a life of pleasure and comfort denied to earlier generations of workers. Stability became a primary desire. Thus, a combination of sexual license, advocated by the romantics and the social radicals, and the economic liberation of women may have prompted the Victorian sexual ethic and its attempt to repress sexuality completely.

Victorian ethic

A review of Victorian literature and private correspondence reveals the nature of the Victorian ethic. There was, foremost, a constant stress on the sanctity of the home. A wife's first duty was to serve her husband. Sermons described world-weary men who needed wives who would make a home something like a bright, serene, restful, joyful nook of heaven in an unheavenly earth.

This increased emphasis on the importance of the home and the institution of matrimony (see Figure 14) was coupled with a renewed stress on economic and social factors as considerations in marriage. Love took second place as society became highly conscious of class distinctions.

Men were encouraged to delay marriage until they had achieved success and had acquired money. This meant marrying late, all the while suppressing their passions. It was perversely maintained that true virility was evidenced by the ability to delay sexual gratification beyond the age of 30.

The ideal Victorian woman was like the title of a poem by Coventry Patmore, *The Angel in the House.* She was literally perceived as an angel—delicate, totally pure, and exalted to the point of adoration. Nice women, like those one married or like one's sister, were incapable of sexual feeling, and any suggestions to the contrary were considered vile aspersions. Only wicked and depraved women had erotic drives.

Men differed from women, it was held, in that at puberty, the male manifested inherent and spontaneous sexual desires. The woman, by contrast, had dormant or nonexistent sexual drives that did not arise spontaneously but needed excitation by "undue familiarities." Women could pass through life without being cognizant of the promptings of the senses—if, of course, they were protected from exciting causes.

Children, like women, were thought to be virtuous by nature and devoid of innate sexual feelings. Only through bad associations and habits was virtue lost. A foremost 19th century authority on sex, William Acton, a physician, saw youth as a virgin page in most healthy and well-brought-up children. He wrote:

No sensual idea or feeling has been entered into their heads, even in the way of speculation.

Youthful curiousity, Acton maintained, was

the result of suggestion by persons older than themselves.

Prudery

To keep the virtue of women and children from being endangered, all possible avenues of temptation needed to be policed. Efforts to suppress sexual references in books, conversation, and the general environment were carried to extremes, leading to what has been called the great age of the stork.

In some Victorian homes, piano legs were draped with crinolines or pantalets, so as not to evoke thoughts of their human counterparts. In much of the literature, Victorian women had no legs—they had limbs—and these were covered by layers of petticoats. Women also lacked breasts—they had bosoms, instead. Up until the 1860's halters were used to remove any outward evidence of the breast. At the dinner table, one spoke of a chicken's neck, instead of its breast. Some persons even suggested that works by authors of the two sexes should not be kept side by side on the bookshelf, unless the authors happened to be married. A physician who asked to see a female patient's "belly" was chastised for using this dreadful word and was asked to use the word "stomach" in the future.

Protection of the moral welfare of the reading public was felt to necessitate rigid

FIGURE 14. A wedding in Victorian England. This painting by William Powell Firth, done in 1881 and titled, "For Better, For Worse," epitomizes the 19th century concern with the sanctity of marriage and proper decorum. (The Forbes Magazine Collection, New York)

literary censorship. Thomas Bowdler was so notorious and ambitious in his attempts to eliminate sex from literature that his name became synonymous with expurgation. Among his many achievements was *The* *Family Shakespeare,* a version of Shakespeare's works fit for the young and female. Today the term "bowdlerize" has a distinctly offensive connotation. But to the Victorians this sort of work carried the blessings of society. One 18-year-old woman entered in her diary the following reference to a book by George Eliot:

> Granny began yesterday to spout to us the new novel about which the world raves, *Adam Bede*, to be duly bowdlerized for our young minds.

It is worth noting that *Adam Bede*, like the novels of Thomas Hardy and other popular 19th century fiction writers, was not laden with eroticism. Without resorting to bowdlerization or other forms of censorship, the Victorian atmosphere constrained the freedom of novelists in their portrayal of sexuality.

Scientific and medical journals that were considered obscene or likely to corrupt the morals of Her Majesty's subjects were often seized and kept from circulation. It was on these grounds that the second volume of Havelock Ellis's *Studies in the Psychology of Sex* was confiscated by English police in 1899. By maintaining prudent standards, the Victorians attempted to ignore sex as an aspect of reality.

The secret sin and spermatorrhea

Victorians displayed a near obsession with the practice of masturbation. Using various euphemisms—like the secret sin, self-pollution, self-abuse, and the solitary vice—they denounced what was sincerely believed to be a highly pernicious activity.

Before the 18th century, masturbation was held to be morally wrong, the sin of Onan. Then, around 1700, a number of theologians and medical quacks began to describe various untoward emotional and physical consequences of masturbation and nocturnal emissions. As early as 1708, Hermann Boerhaave, a Dutch physician, wrote that

> the rash expenditure of semen brings on a lassitude, a feebleness, a weakening of motion, fits, wasting, dryness, fevers, aching of the cerebral membranes, obscuring of the sense and above all the eyes, a decay of the spinal chord, a fatuity and other like evils.

By the early 19th century, Claude Francois l'Allemand, a French physician, had coined the term "spermatorrhea" to describe wet dreams. In several books published between 1836 and 1842, he equated nocturnal emissions with gonorrhea, saying that the same pathological outcome results from the two disorders. The work of l'Allemand influenced the English medical establishment, and one physician, Charles Drysdale, wrote a treatise on these involuntary seminal discharges. He observed that spermatorrhea was a progressive disorder that assumed a horrible character in its terminal stages. After years of suffering, the patient, he said, sinks into the lowest stages of mental and physical deterioration, finally dying of

> a kind of apoplexy . . . induced by the exhausted state of the brain.

Most influential and authoritative of all Victorian physicians was the urologist William Acton. More than any other person in the 19th century, Acton legitimized morally colored medical misconceptions about sexual activity and thus caused a tremendous amount of needless anxiety. Acton was greatly impressed by the work of Samuel Auguste Andre David Tissot (1728–1797), a Swiss physician who claimed that blindness, impotence, insanity, and acne were but some of the consequences of masturbation. This doctrine was echoed by Acton in his textbook, *Functions and Disorders of the Reproductive Organs in Childhood, Youth, Adult Age, and Advanced Life Considered in their Physiological, Social, and Moral Relations* (see Figure 15). Of masturbation, he wrote:

> I cannot speak of the many wrecks of high intellectual attainments, and of the foul blot which has been made.

In his text Acton also maintained that sexual intercourse during pregnancy produced depravity, epilepsy, and sexual precocity in the child. Any prolonged or intense activity by any part of the mother's body, be it her brain or her vagina, he wrote, would result in a disproportionate growth of that area in the developing fetus.

With such severe consequences believed to result from the loss of semen, it was inevitable that drastic treatment methods arose. By 1900 physicians were advocating castration of sexually active children, clitoroidectomy,

FUNCTIONS AND DISORDERS

OF THE

REPRODUCTIVE ORGANS

IN

Childhood, Youth, Adult Age, and Advanced Life

CONSIDERED IN THEIR PHYSIOLOGICAL, SOCIAL, AND
MORAL RELATIONS.

BY WILLIAM ACTON, M.R.C.S.,

LATE SURGEON TO THE ISLINGTON DISPENSARY, AND FORMERLY EXTERNE TO THE VENERAL HOSPITALS,
PARIS, FELLOW OF THE ROYAL MED. AND CHIR. SOCIETY, ETC., ETC.

FOURTH AMERICAN

FROM THE LAST LONDON EDITION.

PHILADELPHIA:
LINDSAY & BLAKISTON.
1875.

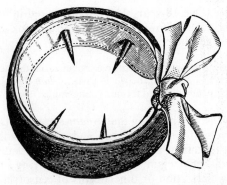

FIGURE 16. A four-pointed urethral ring, which was used to treat spermatorrhea during the 19th century. This engraving shows how the ring was tied to the penis.

FIGURE 15. The title page of an American edition of William Acton's highly influential textbook, which was first published in 1857.

cauterization of the genitals and prostate, the severing of nerves leading to the penis, and the use of various mechanical devices to obstruct access to the genitalia or to make sexual arousal extremely painful. These sexual restraints consisted of bandages (onanism bandages), belts, corsets, and spermatorrhea rings—instruments similar to chasity belts but for men. Spermatorrhea rings consisted of spikes that made contact with the penis only when it was erect, causing considerable discomfort during involuntary arousal (see Figures 16 and 17). One English surgeon, J. L. Milton, described the various available therapies in his book *On Spermatorrhea.* One especially ingenious ring caused a bell to ring when an erection broke an electrical circuit (see Figure 18). Between 1881 and 1887 Milton's book ran through 12 editions.

Popular medical opinion thus reflected and reinforced misconceptions based on prevailing Victorian morality. Since, by the 19th century, medicine had become a more scientific, less quack-infested profession, these views by physicians considerably influenced societal beliefs. Fear of masturbation and nocturnal emissions became almost universal, and, in a sense, the scientific establishment helped to institutionalize a high pitch of sexual anxiety by wrongly ascribing mental anguish and disease to activities that, it would one day be recognized, are natural and often necessary forms of sexual release.

Masturbation and spontaneous emission were unquestioned as the leading causes of impotence. This belief is seen in the attention given to neurasthenia, a disorder that concerned physicians in England, France, and

FIGURE 17. A toothed urethral ring, which was used during the 19th century to treat spermatorrhea.

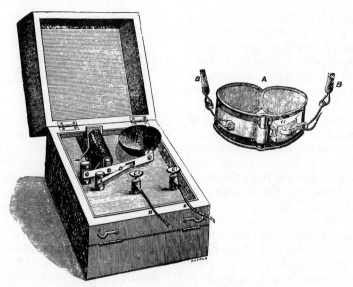

FIGURE 18. A device that was marketed to prevent spermatorrhea. When there was a nocturnal erection, a bell would ring, awakening the sleeper or his parents.

America in the late century. First described by George Miller Beard in 1869 as an epidemic of nervous exhaustion among middle-class persons in urbanized, industrial areas, neurasthenia was viewed as both a major cause and a manifestation of sexual dysfunction. This thesis was contained in Beard's *Sexual Neurasthenia: Its Hygiene, Causes, Symptoms, and Treatment with a Chapter on Diet for the Nervous* (1884).

Central to the imagined physiological and psychological derangements of neurasthenia and to their treatment was the theory of nervous energy. According to Beard, the body contains a finite amount of potential energy, which can be depleted as a consequence of excessive expenditures of nervous force. Overstrain of a particular nerve cell, organ, or organ system can impair functions in other portions of the body by draining them of their energy.

To Beard and other physicians, the sex organs were often the site of energy depletion. A variety of therapeutic techniques were developed to restore the body's vital force. In keeping with the concept of stored energy and the loss of natural charge as a precipitating factor in neurasthenia, physicians used the application of electrical shock as a standard treatment method (see Figure 19). Electrodes

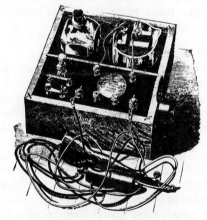

ONE OF THE FORMS OF APPARATUS FOR FARADIZATION.

Small size, for family use.   Large size, for professional use.
ELECTRO-MAGNETIC MACHINES.

FIGURE 19. Some of the electrical devices used to treat neurasthenia.

were inserted into the rectum and urethra and on the scrotum, penis, inner thigh, and spine.

It was generally held that neurasthenics, particularly women, were incapable of having normal sex lives. Neurasthenia was thought to deprive women of their sexual instincts and their ability to bear children. The female nervous system was thought to be inferior to that of the male and was, therefore, less able to withstand the expanded and more demanding duties of industrialized and emancipated life. Departure from the traditional sex role, it was maintained, led to the deterioration of sexual function. S. Weir Mitchell's rest-cure treatment for neurotic women was an outgrowth of these concepts.

Freud was in agreement with Beard about many features of neurasthenia, including the view that neurasthenia is a disturbance in sexual functioning. It results, said Freud, from the inadequate discharge of sexual energy, which occurs whenever less-than-adequate relief, like masturbation or nocturnal emission, takes place instead of adequate relief—normal intercourse.

Sexual subculture

Behind the prudence and modesty was another side of English society—the extensive sexual underworld, the so-called sexual subculture. As measured by the high numbers of illegitimate births, the prevalence of prostitution, the volume of pornography, and the periodic scandals that shocked 19th century England, a substantial portion of society lived a sexual life far different from the facade presented to others and, often, to themselves.

The anonymous sexual memoirs of a Victorian gentleman, *My Secret Life,* described this other side of 19th century sexual behavior. It portrays a man who is able to engage in an endless variety of sexual experiences in the very society that presented itself as relatively free of such vice. Opportunities, like the experiences, appeared to be infinite. According to Marcus, *My Secret Life* is more than merely an erotic work. It shows us, Marcus wrote:

that amid and underneath the world of Victorian England as we know it—and as it tended to represent itself to itself—a real, secret social life was being conducted, the secret life of sexuality. Every day, everywhere, people were meeting, en-

countering one another, coming together, and moving on. And although it is true that the Victorians could not help but know of this, almost no one was reporting on it; the social history of their own sexual experiences was not part of the Victorians' official consciousness of themselves or of their society.

Over the years, as new evidence has surfaced, it has become clear that many Victorians, of high and low station, led secret lives. William Gladstone (1809-1898), four times prime minister of Great Britain and a pillar of Victorian society, patronized the brothels and regularly flagellated himself. None of this was known in his lifetime, and only the publication in 1975 of his diaries, covering 29,915 days between 1840 and 1854, made these facts public. This revelation has been of special interest because Gladstone devoted himself to doing rescue work for prostitutes, an activity that earned him recognition as a philanthropist. It also raised a number of eyebrows and caused consternation among his associates. The following passage by Henriques, written before Gladstone's diaries came to light, illustrates the puzzlement caused by the statesman's behavior, behavior that is now better understood:

Gladstone throughout most of his life had concerned himself with the reclamation of prostitutes. At times this exposed him to serious risks of blackmail and public scandal. His advisers and friends remonstrated with him again and again that he should give up his dangerous hobby. His practice was to take walks late at night in the West End and accost any likely looking female, and ask her to accompany him home to meet his wife, and thus start the process of reform. Clearly this was behaviour which could be misinterpreted. What is interesting is that he kept up this practice when it could have accomplished his political ruin . . . . It remains curious that his monumental respectability allowed him to consort with the most famous kept women of his day.

Writing how he read pornography, a craving that revulsed him but that he could not resist, and visited prostitutes to indulge in "strange and humbling acts," Gladstone also made reference to his masochism. One entry rhetorically asked:

Has it been sufficiently considered how far pain may become a ground of enjoyment? How far satisfaction and even an action delighting in pain may be a true experimental phenomenon of the human mind?

Various places in his diaries contain a small sketch of a whip, instead of a direct reference to flagellation. The English vice, as flagellation was called on the continent, was a favorite theme of a large body of pornographic literature and art, was evident in the use of the rod to discipline school children, and appears to have been very common in 19th century England. Gladstone was not unique in his passion. Flagellation was far from uncommon in the sexually repressed Victorian society. A number of high-class brothels catered to those with a taste for whipping as a sexual stimulant.

Discretion was a key word in Victorian society. Actions contrary to the official public image were not tolerated. The Cleveland Street case, a scandal involving a homosexual brothel at the end of the 19th century, illustrates this fact, as does the fact that sexual misconduct, by Victorian standards, reached into Buckingham Palace itself.

There had been rumors in the mid 1880's about a homosexual brothel on Cleveland Street in the West End on London. The two men who ran it and staffed it with post office messenger boys were tried and jailed. Rumors circulated that some people in the highest ranks of Victorian society had patronized the establishment, but no member of the aristocracy was taken to court. Not until 1975, when the British government made available official papers from the years 1882 to 1889, did the reason for both the rumors and the lack of aristocratic prosecutions become known. The official documents reveal that the high Victorian establishment closed ranks and exerted all conceivable pressures to protect its own, particularly Prince Albert Victor, a son of the Prince of Wales and the queen's grandson. Also involved were Lord Arthur Somerset, the personal aide to the Prince of Wales (the future King Edward VII), and several other members of the nobility. Records show that the Prince of Wales, the prime minister (the Marquess of Salisbury), and two of his ministers fought with the police and the attorney general to keep aristocratic offenders out of the court. Their chief motive appears to have been to

keep information about Prince Albert Victor's homosexual activity from coming out at a trial. One newspaper editor, whose paper reported court testimony by one boy that the Earl of Euston frequented the brothel, was promptly arrested and jailed 1 year for libel. Some messenger boys were bribed to go abroad and thus avoid testifying.

Hypocrisy and promiscuity were not limited to the upper classes. According to official statistics, about 42,000 illegitimate children were born in England and Wales during 1851. If correct, this figure means that more than 8 per cent of all women beyond puberty had given birth out of wedlock, a figure that does not account for unreported births and abortions. There was an almost unquenchable appetite for prostitution and pornography. Brothels flourished, and expensive limited editions of erotic works were much in demand. As in the case of illegitimacy, figures suggesting the extent of these elements in society are astonishing. There were estimated to have been 5,000 procurers in London in 1850 and some 400,000 people directly or indirectly connected with prostitution. In 1857 police records suggest that there were nearly 25,000 prostitutes in London, and the number of prostitutes prosecuted for criminal offenses in England and Wales at about the same time totaled just under 31,000.

By its very existence, Victorian pornography also contrasted markedly with the views of official society. The character of the pornography, moreover, stood in complete opposition to the moral tone of the period. A novel like *The Romance of the Lust,* published during the 1870's, for example, excluded all human considerations from its descriptions of sexual activity, just as society erased sexuality from other human concerns. Marcus used the example of Victorian pornography as a source of insight into the real mentality of the late 19th century and into the reasons why Victorianism broke down from within. Noting that the view of human sexuality held by the official culture and the subculture of pornography were reversals of one another, Marcus wrote:

For every warning against masturbation issued by the official voice of culture, another work of pornography was published; for every cautionary statement against the harmful effects of sexual excess uttered by medical men, pornography represented copulation in excelsis, endless orgies, infinite daisy chains of inexhaustibility; for every assertion about the delicacy and frigidity of respectable women made by the official culture, pornography represented legions of maenads, universes of palpitating females; for every effort made by the official culture to minimize the importance of sexuality, pornography cried out—or whispered—that it was the only thing in the world of any importance at all. It is essential for us to notice the similarities even more than the differences between these two groups of attitudes or cultures. In both the same set of anxieties are at work; in both the same obsessive ideas can be made out; and in both sexuality is conceived of at precisely the same degree of consciousness. It was a situation of unbearable contradiction. And it was at this point that the breaking through began.

Twentieth Century

Schopenhauer wrote:

The relation of the sexes is really the invisible point of all action and conduct, and peeps out everywhere in spite of all veils thrown over it.

This was one lesson drawn from Victorianism. With the nominal end of the Victorian era on the death of the queen in 1901, sex began to emerge from the domain of secrecy. From the start, the 20th century was characterized by people and events that served to make sex and sexuality increasingly visible as part of the common human experience. From 1900 to the present day, the veil of ignorance, reticence, guilt, and misconception has gradually been drawn back.

1900 TO 1954

Escape from the confines of Victorian sexuality was given tremendous impetus during the first part of the 20th century by four developments: psychoanalytic theory, World War I, the increased social and economic freedom of women, and the tremendous growth of mass communications and means of rapid transportation. The tradition of prudery lingered, but these factors loosened Western attitudes toward sex.

At the turn of the century, Sigmund Freud had already published several works that would form the foundation of the psychoanalytic movement, and he was in the

process of formulating his theories of human sexuality. In *Three Essays on the Theory of Sexuality* (1905) Freud introduced the libido theory. Not only did Freud reject the Victorian notion that children are little innocents devoid of innate sexual impulses, but he went further, stating that sex is a major factor in human development from the time of infancy onward. In a sense Freud discovered the sexual life of the child by pointing to the presence of sexuality where it had not previously been seen.

The repercussions of Freud's writings transcended the circle of physicians and patients directly involved with psychoanalysis. His theories caused, to say the least, considerable animosity. Yet even so, it drew attention to sex. Freud brought sex into the arena of intellectual debate. Another consequence, as noted by Zilboorg, was that Freud's observations on sexuality were

mistaken for an assertion and proselytic attitude with regard to sexual behavior.

During the 1920's in America, the gospel of Freud was interpreted in a way that lent support to the spirit of sexual rebellion that followed World War I. According to Allen's *Only Yesterday,* an account of the 1920's by one who lived through the era:

A fertile ground was ready for the seeds of Freudianism . . . . One began to hear even from the lips of flappers that "science taught" new and disturbing things about sex. Sex, it appeared, was the central and pervasive force which moved mankind. Almost every human motive was attributable to it: if you were patriotic or you liked the violin, you were in the grip of sex—in a sublimated form. The first requirement of mental health was to have an uninhibited sex life. If you would be well and happy, you must obey your libido.

Freud, of course, was anything but an advocate of sexual anarchy. That society chose to interpret his theories of sexuality as threats to conventional morality or as excuses for amorality were indications of the extremes that existed.

A relaxed and rebellious atmosphere was evident in sexual matters in the aftermath of World War I. Berlin, Munich, and Paris were meccas of sexual tolerance. It was in America, however, that the most striking changes were occurring. A daring few captured the imagination of the world with their rejection of the puritanical tradition that had dominated American sex life since the nation's founding. They were the Jazz Age youth—the flappers, the red-hot babies, the flaming youth. Movies gave further impetus to this development with the introduction of sex queens like Clara Bow, the It girl. No longer were women the sheltered ladies of the Victorian era, and chaperons—an almost constant feature during meetings between single people from respectable homes—almost disappeared.

People of the roaring twenties felt that much of what they perceived to be the new promiscuity was related to the automobile. The number of registered cars increased from 2.5 million in 1915 to 9 million in 1920. By 1930 their number was more than 26.5 million. Describing contemporary thinking on the consequences of the motor car, Allen wrote:

The automobile offered an almost universally available means of escaping temporarily from the supervision of parents and chaperons, or from the influence of neighborhood opinion. Boys and girls now thought nothing of jumping into a car and driving off to a dance in another town twenty miles away, where they were strangers and enjoyed a freedom impossible among their neighbors.

Other forces that contributed to the more permissive atmosphere of the 1920's, particularly with respect to the accepted conduct of women, included the ratification of the 19th amendment to the Constitution in 1920, giving women the right to vote, and prohibition, which fostered a mood of defiance. To many people, the rising hemlines, as evident in flapper dresses, were evidence of a decline in morals.

A major publication dealing with sex and sexuality, *Ideal Marriage,* was published in 1926. Written by Theodor Van de Velde, a Dutch gynecologist, the book gained immense popularity and interest because of its straightforward and un-Victorian discussion of sexual techniques. Alternatives to the missionary position, the pleasures of cunnilingus and fellatio, and other previously taboo subjects were explored. Variations of coital postures and oral-genital sex were presented

as healthy and normal. Van de Velde also stressed the mutuality of the sex act, citing it as an important form of communication between two persons.

1945 TO THE PRESENT

Soon after the end of World War II a report on investigations into human sexual behavior by Alfred Charles Kinsey (see Figure 20) and his colleagues was published. *Sexual Behavior in the Human Male* appeared in 1948, and its companion volume, *Sexual Behavior in the Human Female,* was published 5 years later. Together, they represented the most extensive, methodical, and objective study of sexuality ever undertaken. In all, the sexual case histories of 5,300 males and 5,940 females were used in preparing the final report.

Before Kinsey's survey, investigations of human sexual behavior were, according to Brecher,

characterized by certain uneasiness, even prissiness, in approaching sexual material. Rarely

FIGURE 20. Alfred Kinsey. (Institute for Sex Research, Bloomington, Indiana)

would questions deal with fellatio or cunnilingus, as was the case in the Kinsey study.

Moreover, Brecher adds:

Questions were often worded so discreetly that respondents might miss their meaning—or might perceive and give the "proper" answer expected by the interviewers. A study of 1,029 North Carolina males aged fifteen to twenty, published in 1926 by a state health officer, included such questions as this one, which can surely be labeled as "loaded":
"Has anyone ever tried to give you the mistaken idea that sex intercourse is necessary for the health of the young man?"

Kinsey undertook his research in response to a need—the need for accurate information on human sexual functions and patterns of sexual behavior. As noted by one of his associates, Wardell B. Pomeroy, Kinsey went to the library to learn about human sexual behavior in order to answer many questions posed by his students that dealt with sex. He felt ill-prepared to provide answers, but

he soon discovered that no one else knew very much either.

Even the well known work of Ellis and Freud was limited to their focus on persons with sexual problems and by their lack of scientific and statistical methods. Thus, Kinsey and his co-workers wrote in 1953, their research was prompted by the fact

that the scientific understanding of human sexual behavior was more poorly established than the understanding of almost any other function of the human body.

Describing the inadequate nature of sexual knowledge and some of the problems confronting researchers, they added:

There seemed to be no sufficient studies of the basic anatomy or the physiology of sexual response and of orgasm. Both the biologists and the philosophers had confused reproductive function with sexual behavior, and had taken it for granted that the reproductive organs, and particularly the external reproductive organs (the genitalia), were the only part of the anatomy that were involved with either of these functions. Heretofore, in attempting to interpret sexual behavior, we have been as handicapped as one might be if he attempted to understand the processes of digestion

before he knew anything of the anatomy of the digestive organs, or attempted to understand respiratory functions without realizing that the lungs and the circulatory system were involved.

In the course of their routine history-taking, interviewers for the Kinsey investigation found several people who expressed an intense desire to actually be members of the opposite sex. In the early 1950's the physical change of sex from male to female became a possibility as surgeons developed sex-conversion operations. While remaining genotypically male and lacking female reproductive organs, the feminized transsexuals had female external genitalia. Through the use of estrogens, plastic surgery, and depilation, other female characteristics were induced. One of the more notable persons to undergo sex reassignment during the 1950's was Christine Jorgensen. Various terms came to be applied to the underlying psychological condition that prompted persons to undergo sex-change operations. Gender identity disturbance, gender role disorientation, and cross-gender identity are among the terms that were and still are most commonly used.

Was there any significant relationship between societal forces and the desire to have a sex reassignment? Probably not. Green showed that this tendency has existed in some people throughout history. During the 1950's, however, the surgical techniques were perfected. A 1972 *New York Times* survey on surgical sex change indicated

that such operations have been successful in achieving their goals—relative contentment and peace of mind for persons whose lives before surgery were marked by depression, isolation, despair and often attempted suicide.

The advent of sex-conversion operations underscored the role of science and technology during the 20th century in potentiating pleasure among those with diverse sexual preferences and dysfunctions.

In 1953 Hugh Hefner published the first issue of *Playboy,* a magazine whose success has been phenomenal the world over. *Playboy* made sex and nude photographs respectable material to sell on newsstands next to copies of *Time* and *Newsweek.* Hefner linked sex with upward mobility. Put differently, hedonism and sensuality were among the rewards of success and could in themselves be viewed as measures of economic and social achievement. In this respect, the magazine reflected and further encouraged a tendency to view sex in positive terms. As presented in the words and pictures of *Playboy,* sex was wholesome. Although the concept of sex as depicted in *Playboy* was unrealistic—airbrushes were used to obliterate pubic hair and blemishes, genitalia were never shown, men and women never appeared together in the nude, and the models were perfect to the point of being unrealistic—that concept was in harmony with the prevailing atmosphere of toleration in the 1950's. Hard-core pornography was still cause for prosecution and had to be sold under the table.

In 1956 the first reports of successful ovulatory inhibition by orally administered norethynodrel were published. Within a decade more than 7 million women were taking oral contraceptives. The birth control pill represented the most effective method of fertility control, short of castration, yet devised. However, its introduction had an impact that transcended purely reproductive considerations. The pill made possible the complete separation of human reproductive functions from sexual activity motivated by social and libidinal factors. In essence, it emancipated people from the fear of conception and from the anxiety that surrounded sexual encounters. For many women, the risk of unwanted pregnancy had been sufficient reason to abstain from coitus or had served to diminish their enjoyment of the sex act because of their anxiety about its consequences. But the pill largely removed this aspect of concern.

One resulting change in male-female relationships, as noted by Montagu, involved the traditional female resistance to male sexual advances. This resistance, he observed, had forced men to adopt a predatory exploitative attitude toward women. The pill, however, provided the possibility of engaging in sex for purely enjoyable purposes and thus altered this traditional view of the put-on woman. It challenged the sexual double standard and shifted much of the responsibility for preventing conception to the woman. Many clinicians have observed that the availability

of simple and effective birth control measures—which include, in addition to the pill, the intrauterine device (IUD) and male vasectomy—has been partially responsible for increased premarital coitus.

Coincidental with their emancipation from the fear of unwanted impregnation, women have experienced a greater freedom in all sectors of business and social activity. Women have demanded equality and greater responsibilities and have, since 1960, obtained many of these objectives. Sexual manifestations of the new liberated women have included the appearance of magazines that are the female counterpart of *Playboy.* These magazines have included *Viva, Playgirl,* and *Foxylady.* Other evidence of the altered outlook toward male and female sexual roles has appeared in the quality and spirit of sexual activity.

A number of psychiatrists have cited a relationship between changes in social attitudes toward premarital sexual activity, especially among women, and changes in patterns of sexual dysfunction, particularly male impotence. William Masters and Virginia Johnson offered hope to those who suffer from impotence and a number of other sexual complaints through their research into the physiology of the human sexual response and their development of successful treatment methods for sexual problems that had been refractory to traditional medical psychological therapies. Work done at the Reproductive Biology Research Foundation in St. Louis, Missouri, has served as the prototype for sex therapy programs throughout the country. Sexual counseling has become an effective and acceptable method for dealing with most forms of sexual inadequacy. Masters and Johnson have reported a success rate of more than 80 per cent with their techniques.

A basic concept in the Masters and Johnson approach is that of the couple as a unit. The interrelationship of sex and sexual problems with the over-all communications and feelings between the involved persons is stressed in their therapy. In any form of sexual inadequacy, they note, there is no such entity as an uninvolved partner. In itself, this view is an exemplification of the sexual mores in the late 1960's and early 1970's.

By the late 1960's and early 1970's there

was considerable evidence of a new, uninhibited sexual spirit. This spirit was striking not so much because of its rebellious or revolutionary nature but because of its seemingly experimenting character. Rudi Gernreich, for example, introduced his topless bathing suit in the mid 1960's. Some daring swimmers challenged local ordinances against indecency. Most women took their cue from this development, and by the mid 1970's topless bathing, although not prevalent, was not unusual.

Experiments in living that were reminiscent of those in the 19th century also appeared. Communes developed, most notably in the Haight-Ashbury district of San Francisco during the summer of 1967. In 1972 more than 1,000 communes had been set up in the United States. On a smaller scale were countless groupings and extended families. Serial marriage, multiple love relationships, and coupling—premarital trials in living together—also increased. Terms such as "swingers," couples who exchange sexual partners and engage in generally promiscuous sex, and "groupies," adolescent girls and boys who offer their sexual services to touring rock-and-roll musicians, became part of the American vocabulary.

Everything You Always Wanted to Know About Sex but Were Afraid to Ask and *The Joy of Sex* became two of the most successful books of the early 1970's, an indication of the public's desire to learn more about sex. Devices that enhanced sexual pleasure gained increased acceptance. Flavored and scented vaginal douches were advertised and marketed. Feminine deodorant sprays appeared. Vibrators, used for masturbatory reasons or to supplement sexual relations, were on sale by 1975 on the counters of most drug stores and were offered in the Sears Roebuck catalogue. The waterbed, commercials that rely on sexual suggestions to sell goods or services that have nothing to do with sex, pornographic films in neighborhood movie houses, and sexually explicit publications like *Screw* on local newsstands are but a few measures of the more liberal sexual attitude of the 1970's.

Conclusion

Patterns of human sexual behavior have remained remarkably constant through the course of Western history. Although the spirit of sexuality has differed from period to period and there have been variations in what is or is not officially sanctioned, at no point, it would appear, has any sexual activity ceased to be performed. Depending on whether it is considered sacred or sacrilegious, a sexual act can be performed on the altar of a temple with the blessings of society or in the privacy of a locked room so that society does not learn what is being done. To the average normal person throughout history, as Malinowski commented,

attraction by the other sex and the passionate and sentimental episodes which follow are the most significant events in his [or her] existence, those most deeply associated with . . . intimate happiness and with the zest and meaning of life.

Regardless of public values, private impulses overrule prohibitions.

A total reevaluation and redefinition of sex and sexuality is currently in progress. Over the years, sex has lost most of its cosmic, supernatural, sacred, and mystical associations. It has recently lost much of its identity as a sacrilegious activity. A major trend in the sexual morality of the 1970's has been the decline in reliance on sexual conduct as an index of virtue or character. The range of acceptable sexual experience and expression is expanding. Whether there will be a reversion to the more inhibited and self-conscious standards that have characterized Western society throughout most of its history cannot be determined. The dialectical process has surely been evident in the history of sexuality, and history itself suggests that periods of moral looseness eventually give way to times of restriction.

Never before, however, have science and psychology so dominated culture as they do today. Never before has the understanding of sex and sexuality been as sophisticated as it is today. Although it is an overstatement to call this age an era of sexual revolution, it is an age of sexual enlightenment. If newly gained insights into human sexual behavior serve no other function, they may serve as insurance against the use of misconception, superstition, and ignorance to deny that sexual pleasure is a normal part of human existence, a part that is important to all people and their development.

REFERENCES

Allen, F. L. *Only Yesterday.* Harper & Brothers, New York, 1931.

Anonymous. *My Secret Life.* Grove Press, New York, 1966.

Apuleius, L. *The Golden Ass.* Collier, New York, 1962.

Augustine, St. *Confessions.* Penguin Books, Baltimore, 1961.

Barrow, R. H. *The Romans.* Pelican Books, London, 1949.

Benjamin, H., and Masters, R. E. L. *Prostitution and Morality.* Julian Press, New York, 1964.

Bloch, I. *Sexual Life in England Past and Present.* Arco, London, 1958.

Brasch, R. *How Did Sex Begin?* Signet, New York, 1973.

Brecher, E. *The Sex Researchers.* Andre Deutsch, London, 1970.

Brinton, C., Christopher, J. B., and Wolff, R. L. *Civilization in the West.* Prentice-Hall, Englewood Cliffs, N. J., 1964.

Brucker, G. *The Society of Renaissance Florence.* Harper & Row, New York, 1971.

Bullough, V. L., and Bullough, B. *The Subordinate Sex.* Penguin Books, Baltimore, 1974.

Capellanus, A. *The Art of Courtly Love.* Columbia University Press, New York, 1941.

Carman, H., Syrett, H., and Wishy, B. *A History of the American People,* vol. 1. Alfred A. Knopf, New York, 1961.

Cellini, B. *Autobiography.* Penguin Books, Baltimore, 1956.

Chesser, E. *Strange Loves.* William Morrow, New York, 1971.

Christian, P. *Magic.* Citadel Press, New York, 1969.

Churchill, W. S. *The New World.* Dodd, Mead, New York, 1956.

Clark, K. *A Guide to Civilization.* Time-Life, New York, 1970.

Cleugh, J. *The Marquis and the Chevalier.* Little, Brown, Boston, 1952.

Cleugh, J. *Love Locked Out.* Crown, New York, 1955.

Davies, G. The early Stuarts, 1603–1660. In *The Oxford History of England,* G. N. Clark, editor, vol. 9, p. 452. Clarendon Press, Oxford, 1959.

Denomy, A. J. *The Heresy of Courtly Love.* Declan X. Macmillan, New York, 1947.

*de Riencourt, A. *Sex and Power in History.* David McKay, New York, 1974.

Ditzion, S. *Marriage, Morals, and Sex in America.* Bookman Associates, New York, 1953.

Durant, W. *The Story of Civilization.* Simon & Schuster, New York, 1935.

Durant, W. *The Life of Greece.* Simon & Schuster, New York, 1939.

Durant, W. *Caesar and Christ.* Simon & Schuster, New York, 1944.

Durant, W. *The Renaissance.* Simon & Schuster, New York, 1953.

Durant, W. *The Reformation.* Simon & Schuster, New York, 1957.

Durant, W., and Durant, A. *The Age of Reason Begins.* Simon & Schuster, New York, 1961.

Durant, W., and Durant, A. *The Age of Louis XIV.* Simon & Schuster, New York, 1963.

Durant, W., and Durant, A. *The Age of Voltaire.* Simon & Schuster, New York, 1965.

Eimerl, S., and the editors of Time-Life Books. *The World of Giotto.* Time, New York, 1967.

Ellis, A., and Abarbanel, A., editors. *The Encyclopedia of Sexual Behavior.* Jason Aronson, New York, 1973.

Ellis, H. *Studies in the Psychology of Sex: Sexual Selection in Man.* F. A. Davis, Philadelphia, 1905.

Ellis, H. *Studies in the Psychology of Sex: Erotic Symbolism.* F. A. Davis, Philadelphia, 1906.

Ewart, A. *The Great Lovers.* Hart Publishing, New York, 1968.

Ferm, D. W. *Responsible Sexuality Now.* Seabury Press, New York, 1971.

Firestone, S. *The Dialectic of Sex.* Bantam Books, New York, 1970.

Frankfort, H., Frankfort, H. A., Wilson, J., and Jackson, T. *Before Philosophy.* Penguin Books, Baltimore, 1946.

Frazer, J. *The New Golden Bough.* New American Library, New York, 1964.

Freud, S. *Totem and Taboo.* Vintage Books, New York, 1946.

Freud, S. *Leonardo da Vinci: A Study in Psychosexuality.* Random House, New York, 1947.

Freud, S. *The Future of an Illusion.* Doubleday, New York, 1961.

Goldberg, B. Z. *The Sacred Fire.* Citadel Press, Secaucus, N. J., 1958.

Grant, M. *Eros in Pompeii.* William Morrow, New York, 1975.

Green, V. H. H. *Medieval Civilization in Western Europe.* St. Martin's Press, New York, 1971.

Greene, G. *Lord Rochester's Monkey.* Viking Press, New York, 1974.

Hale, W. H. *Ancient Greece.* American Heritage Press, New York, 1970.

*Haller, J. S., and Robin, M. *The Physician and Sexuality in Victorian America.* University of Illinois Press, Chicago, 1974.

Hamilton, E. *The Greek Way.* Discus Books, New York, 1958.

Hamilton, E. *Mythology.* Mentor Books, New York, 1969.

Hays, H. R. *The Dangerous Sex.* Pocket Books, New York, 1964.

Heer, F. *The Medieval World.* Mentor Books, New York, 1961.

Henriques, F. *Prostitution and Society,* vol. 1: *Primitive, Classical, and Oriental.* MacGibbon & Kee, London, 1962.

Henriques, F. *Prostitution and Society,* vol. 2: *Prostitution in Europe and the New World.* MacGibbon & Kee, London, 1963.

Henriques, F. *Prostitution and Society,* vol. 3: *Modern Sexuality.* MacGibbon & Kee, London, 1968.

Hibbert, C. *The House of Medici: Its Rise and Fall.* William Morrow, New York, 1975.

Himes, N. E. *Medical History of Contraception.* Williams & Wilkins, Baltimore, 1936.

Homer. *The Iliad.* Penguin Books, London, 1950.

*Hunt, M. *The Natural History of Love.* Minerva Press, New York, 1959.

Huxley, A. *The Devils of Loudon.* Harper & Row, New York, 1952.

Hyde, H. M. *The Love That Dared Not Speak Its Name.* Little, Brown, Boston, 1970.

Jarrett, D. *England in the Age of Hogarth.* Viking Press, New York, 1974.

Kiefer, O. *Sexual Life in Ancient Rome.* Abbey Library, London, 1934.

Kinsey, A., Pomeroy, W., and Martin, C. *Sexual Behavior in the Human Male.* Saunders, Philadelphia, 1948.

Kinsey, A., Pomeroy, W., Martin, C., and Gebhard, P. *Sexual Behavior in the Human Female.* Saunders, Philadelphia, 1953.

Kronhausen, E., and Kronhausen, P. *Pornography and the Law.* Ballantine Books, New York, 1969.

Legman, G. *Ora-Genitalism.* Causeway Books, New York, 1969.

Lennig, W. *Portrait of DeSade.* Herder & Herder, New York, 1965.

*Lewinsohn, R. *A History of Sexual Customs.* Green & Co., London, 1958.

Licht, H. *Sexual Life in Ancient Greece.* Abbey Library, London, 1932.

Lucretius. *On the Nature of the Universe.* Penguin Books, Baltimore, 1951.

Macauley, T. B. *History of England from the Accession of James II.* AMS Press, New York, 1915.

Maisch, H. *Incest.* Stein & Day, New York, 1972.

Malinowski, B. *Sex and Repression in Savage Society.* Harcourt, Brace, New York, 1927.

Marcus, S. *The Other Victorians.* Basic Books, New York, 1966.

Marcuse, H. *Eros and Civilization.* Beacon Press, Boston, 1966.

Masters, R. E. L. *Eros and Evil.* Penguin Books, Baltimore, 1962.

May, R. *Love and Will.* Dell, New York, 1969.

Melville, R. *Erotic Art of the West.* Weidenfeld & Nicolson, London, 1973.

Montagu, A. *Sex, Man, and Society.* G. P. Putnam, New York, 1969.

Mora, G. Historical and theoretical trends in psychiatry. In *Comprehensive Textbook of Psychiatry,* ed. 2, A. M. Freedman, H. I. Kaplan, and B. J. Sadock, editors, p. 1 Williams & Wilkins, Baltimore, 1975.

Morison, S. E. *The Oxford History of the American People.* Oxford University Press, New York, 1965.

*Murstein, B. I. *Love, Sex, and Marriage Through the Ages.* Springer, New York, 1974.

Nietzsche, F. *Beyond Good and Evil.* Vintage Books, New York, 1966.

Ovid. *The Art of Love.* Grosset & Dunlap, New York, 1959.

Paine, L. *Sex in Witchcraft.* Taplinger, New York, 1972.

Passmore, J. *The Perfectability of Man.* Scribner's, New York, 1970.

Peckham, M., editor. *Romanticism: The Culture of the Nineteenth Century.* Braziller, New York, 1965.

Ploss, H., and Bartels, M. *Woman.* W. Heinemann, London, 1935.

Plumb, J. H. Introduction. In *Memoirs of Fanny Hill,* J. Cleland, p. vii. New American Library, New York, 1965.

Rawson, P. *Primitive Erotic Art.* Weidenfeld & Nicolson, London, 1973.

Rowse, A. L. *The Elizabethan Renaissance.* Macmillan, London, 1972.

Schopenhauer, A. *World as Will and Representation.* Dover, New York, 1966.

Simons, G. L. *Sex and Superstition.* Abelard-Schuman, London, 1973.

Smith, A. L. English political philosophy in the seventeenth and eighteenth centuries. In *The Cambridge Modern History,* A. W. Ward, G. W. Prothro, and S. Leathes, editors, vol. p. 785. Cambridge University Press, Cambridge, 1909.

*Taylor, G. *Sex in History.* Thames & Hudson, London, 1953.

Todd, J. M. *Reformation.* Doubleday, New York, 1971.

Tomalin, C. *The Life and Death of Mary Wollstonecraft.* Harcourt Brace Jovanovich, New York, 1974.

Vanggaard, T. *Phallos: a Symbol and Its History in the Male World.* International Universities Press, New York, 1972.

Vasari, G. *Lives of the Painters.* Penguin Books, Baltimore, 1965.

Wallace, I. *The Nympho and Other Maniacs.* Simon & Schuster, New York, 1971.

Weinstein, L., editor. *The Age of Reason.* Braziller, New York, 1965.

Westermarck, E. *The History of Human Marriage.* Allerton, New York, 1922.

Wilson, A. M. *Diderot.* Oxford University Press, New York, 1972.

Zilboorg, G. *A History of Medical Psychology.* W. W. Norton, New York, 1941.

2.2 History of Human Sexual Research and Study

EDWARD M. BRECHER, M.A.

Krafft-Ebing

Richard von Krafft-Ebing (1840-1902) was a scion of the minor German nobility who became professor of psychiatry in the German University of Strassburg at the age of 29. Under the influence of an uncle, a renowned Heidelberg lawyer, Krafft-Ebing specialized in forensic psychiatry and was soon recognized as an authoritative witness on sex crimes by criminal courts throughout Europe. Krafft-Ebing's powerful and terrifying masterpiece, *Psychopathia Sexualis,* was first published in 1886; revised editions and translations poured from the presses of many countries, including the United States, throughout his lifetime and continued to appear as recently as the 1960's.

Krafft-Ebing viewed human sexual behavior as a collection of loathsome diseases. For more than three quarters of a century, his *Psychopathia Sexualis* was the chief vehicle for transmitting that doctrine from country to country and from generation to generation. It probably did more to elicit a disgust with sex than any other single volume.

In Krafft-Ebing's Germany, as in Victorian England, most people had a clear view of what constituted healthy or normal sexuality. A young man is attracted to a young woman. They marry and live happily ever after. From time to time during the early years of the marriage, the husband inserts his penis into his wife's vagina for the purpose of procreation; he experiences orgasm, but she does not. Deviations from this "normal" pattern Krafft-Ebing viewed as perversions, diseases to which he and others applied such names as sadism, masochism, zoophilia, urolagnia, fetishism, nymphomania, saty-riasis, homosexuality, voyeurism, and exhibitionism.

To make sure that readers would start off with a proper attitude toward these matters—that is, with Krafft-Ebing's attitude—*Psychopathia Sexualis,* in an early chapter, presents the most lurid case histories of the particular form of deviation most likely to arouse horror and disgust: stories of lust-crazed rapist-torture-murderers whose chosen victims are innocent children. Here are some examples:

Case 15. A four-year-old girl was missing from her parents' home, 15 April, 1880. On April 16th, Menesclou, one of the occupants of the house was arrested. The forearm of the child was found in his pocket, and the head and entrails, in a half-charred condition, were taken from the stove. Other parts of the body were found in the water-closet. The genitals could not be found . . . . The circumstances, as well as an obscene poem found on his person, left no doubt that he had violated the child and then murdered her. M. expressed no remorse, asserting that his deed was an unhappy accident.

. . . Convulsions at the age of nine months. Later he suffered from disturbed sleep; was nervous and developed tardily and imperfectly. With puberty he became irritable, showed evil inclinations, was lazy, intractable, and in all trades proved to be of no use. He grew no better even in the House of Correction. He was made a Marine, but there, too, he proved useless. When he returned home, he stole from his parents, and spent his time in bad company. He did not run after women, but gave himself up passionately to masturbation, and occasionally indulged in sodomy with dogs. His mother suffered from *mania menstrualis periodica.* An uncle was insane, and another a drunkard. The examination of M.'s brain [after his execution] showed morbid changes of the frontal lobes, of the first and second temporal convolutions, and of a part of the occipital convolutions.

Case 16. Alton, a clerk in England, went for a

walk out of town. He lured a child into a thicket. Afterward at his office he made this entry in his notebook: "Killed today a young girl; it was fine and hot." The child was missed, searched for, and found cut into pieces. Many parts, and among them the genitals, could not be found. A. did not show the slightest trace of emotion, and gave no explanation of the motive or circumstances of his horrible deed. He was a psychopathic individual, and occasionally subject to fits of depression with *taedium vitae*. A near relative suffered from mania with homicidal impulses. A. was executed.

Case 22. A certain Gruyo, aged forty-one, with a blameless past life, having been three times married, strangled six women in the course of ten years. They were almost all public prostitutes and quite old. After the strangling he tore out the intestines and kidneys *per vaginam*. Some of his victims he violated before killing; others, on account of the occurrence of impotence, he did not. He set about his horrible deeds with such care that he remained undetected for ten years.

Of these many lust murders, Krafft-Ebing himself described as "the most horrible" the case of Andreas Bichel, who violated little girls, killed them, and butchered them.

With reference to one of his victims, on his examination he expressed himself as follows: "I opened her breast and with a knife cut through the fleshy parts of the body. Then I arranged the body as a butcher does beef, and hacked it with an axe into pieces of a size to fit the hole which I had dug up in the mountain for burying it. I may say that while opening the body I was so greedy that I trembled, and could have cut out a piece and eaten it."

Having thus ensured in his opening chapters that his readers will react with nausea to the loathsome diseases called perversions, Krafft-Ebing then proceeds to review similarly many other forms of deviation. Thus, fetishists, voyeurs, and homosexuals become tainted with the same stench of disgust aroused by the rapist-tor-turer-murderers. Krafft-Ebing considered homosexuals, for example, as victims of an "antipathic sexual instinct"; here are two case histories:

Case 156. S.J., age thirty-eight, governess. Came to me for medical advice on account of nervous trouble . . . . From the earliest youth she was subject to sexual excitement and spontaneously practiced masturbation. At the age of

fourteen she began to menstruate . . . . With the age of eighteen she gave up masturbation successfully.

The patient never experienced an inclination towards a person of the opposite sex. Marriage to her only meant to find a home. But she was mightily drawn to girls. At first she considered this affection merely friendship, but she soon recognized from the intensity of her love for girl friends and her deep longings for their constant society that it meant more than mere friendship.

To her it is inconceivable that a girl could love a man, although she can comprehend the feeling of man toward woman. She always took the deepest interest in pretty girls and ladies, the sight of whom caused her intense excitement. Her desire was ever to embrace and kiss these dear creatures. She never dreamed of men, always of girls only. To revel in looking at them was the acme of pleasure. Whenever she lost a "girl friend" she felt in despair.

Patient claimed that she never felt in a defined role, even in her dreams towards her girl friends. In appearance she was thoroughly feminine and modest. Feminine pelvis, large mammae, no indication of beard.

Case 135. V., age twenty-nine, official; father hyponchrondiac, mother neuropathic, four other children normal; one sister homosexual.

V. was very talented, learned easily and had a most excellent religious education. Very nervous and emotional. At the age of nine he began to masturbate of his own accord. When fourteen he recognized the danger of this practice and fought with some success against it; but began to rave about male statuary, also about young men. When puberty set in, he took slight interest in women. At twenty, first coitus . . . but though potent, he derived no satisfaction from it. Afterward only *faute de mieux* (about six times) heterosexual intercourse.

He admitted to have had very frequently intercourse with men . . . . He took either the active or passive role.

At the consultation he was in despair and wept bitterly. He abhorred his sexual anomaly, and said that he had desperately battled against it, but without success. In women he found only moderate animal satisfaction, psychical gratification being totally absent. Yet he craved for the happiness of family life.

Excepting an abnormally broad pelvis (100 cm.) there was nothing in his character or personal appearance that lacked the qualities of the masculine type.

Along with such homosexual cases, Krafft-Ebing presented histories of transvestites and transsexuals; he mistakenly concluded that they are all successive stages in one progressive disease.

The pattern of *Psychopathia Sexualis* thus becomes clear. Having first aroused horror by detailed accounts of lust murders, Krafft-Ebing seeks to lead his readers step by step to a similar feeling of horror toward all sexual variations and then toward almost all manifestations of sexuality. He rightly points out, for example, that even the simplest and most harmless acts of sexual love are related to aberrations. He notes that it is not uncommon for husband and wife during sexual foreplay or intercourse to "strike, bite, or pinch each other." He notes that kissing sometimes

degenerates into biting. Lovers and young married couples are fond of teasing each other; they wrestle together "just for fun," and indulge in all sorts of horseplay.

Havelock Ellis, in his treatment of precisely this subject, used such examples to help his readers understand from their own experience the more extreme pathological forms that these impulses sometime take in others. Krafft-Ebing, in contrast, uses these commonplace examples to arouse forebodings of the most terrible kind. The simple tussling and the gentle love bite, he warns, may be a prelude to lust murder.

The transition from these atavistic manifestations to the most monstrous acts . . . can be readily traced.

But it was in his insistence on masturbation as a factor in the development of all sexual deviations from fetishism and homosexuality to lust murder that Krafft-Ebing accomplished the most harm. Indeed, for Krafft-Ebing, masturbation is the soil out of which all the sexual variations seem to grow. Against the background of the lust murders, for example, he tells the story of

a girl eight years old, who was devoid of all childlike and moral feelings, and who had masturbated from her fourth year; at the same time she consorted with boys of ten or twelve. She had thought of killing her parents, that she might become her own mistress and give herself up to pleasure with men.

In such cases, Krafft-Ebing generalizes,

the children begin early to masturbate; and since they are greatly disposed constitutionally, they often sink into dementia, or become subjects of severe degenerative neuroses or psychoses.

Such evils, moreover, may be visited upon subsequent generations as well. Thus, one young girl who began to masturbate at 8

continued to practice masturbation when married, and even during pregnancy. She was pregnant twelve times. Five of the children died early, four were hydrocephalic, and two boys began to masturbate—one at the age of seven, the other at the age of four.

The outcome of the twelfth pregnancy he did not record.

Even heroic measures, Krafft-Ebing stressed, could not deter these tainted children from their obstinately degenerate behavior. Thus he tells what he calls "the disgusting story" of a girl who began to masturbate at 7, taught her sister to masturbate also, and "at the age of ten was given up to the most revolting vices. Even a white-hot iron applied to the clitoris had no effect in overcoming the practice.

Sexual manifestations in old age, like sexual manifestations in children, Krafft-Ebing viewed with dire suspicion. His message may be simply paraphrased: Beware of sexuality in your parents as well as in your children and your neighbors. Even though an old man may appear honorable and rational in all other respects, the appearance of sexual desire should warn you against him, for sexual desire "may be the precursor of senile dementia, and may make its appearance long before there are any other manifestations of intellectual weakness." The aftermath can prove disastrous.

A lustful old man killed his daughter out of jealousy and took delight in the dying girl's wounded breast.

Psychiatry has come a long way since Krafft-Ebing. Indeed, psychiatrists today might dismiss Krafft-Ebing altogether as merely an aberration in the history of their speciality were it not for a most unfortunate phenomenon: Krafft-Ebing's writings and views still remain amazingly popular. Newspaper accounts of sexual offenses continue to cast a Krafft-Ebing-like aura around sexual deviation, and *Psychopathia Sexualis* itself continues in demand at bookstores. Here are 2 recent advertisements:

Krafft-Ebing's *Psychopathia Sexualis.* 624 pages. Startling case histories of unnatural sex practices, weird auto-erotic methods, sex—lust—torture—much, much more! Many of the hundreds of sex case histories are from secret files and hushed-up court proceedings. Monstrous strange, almost unbelievable sex acts! For mature adults only! $1.

Psychopathis Sexualis [by] Richard von Krafft-Ebing. Nearly every book ever written about abnormal sex has used this book as a reference. It is presented here, for the first time, in its complete unexpurgated and authoritative translation into English. Previous editions had important phrases and paragraphs in Latin or French, but this classic edition is now entirely in modern English. Orig. published at $10.00. Hardbound collectors edition—Over 400 pages. $5.49.

Some physicians still keep a copy of Krafft-Ebing on their shelves and refer to it on occasion. Two new editions were published in the United States in 1965. Both carried introductions by reputable psychiatrists, introductions that casually conceded that perhaps Krafft-Ebing was a little out of date but that failed to alert readers sufficiently to the deeply damaging nonsense—such as the alleged relation between childhood masturbation, lust murder, and homosexuality—with which his pages are filled. The cauterization of a little girl's clitoris with a white-hot iron has gone out of style, but the ideas that provoked such savagery still circulate widely.

Freud

Sigmund Freud (1856-1939) was educated in the shadow of Krafft-Ebing's doctrines, and, at the age of 40 he earned a personal rebuke from that eminent professor. Krafft-Ebing chaired the meeting in Vienna at which Freud first presented his theory that, in every case, hysteria in an adult patient results from a seduction or sexual assault at an early age. These hysteriogenic assaults, Freud reported, were often homosexual, often occurred during

a child's second or third year, and were often perpetrated by a parent. Krafft-Ebing's rebuke was not gentle: "It sounds like a fairy tale." Four months later, Freud retracted his theory. Krafft-Ebing, he conceded, had been right; those infantile seductions and assaults had been reported by patients but had not, in fact, occurred.

Like Krafft-Ebing, Freud throughout his life saw sexual deviations as diseases or as symptoms of disease. Unlike Krafft-Ebing, he neither saw nor portrayed them as *loathsome* diseases. This was a major step forward in the history of psychiatry.

Like Krafft-Ebing, Freud, through most of his life, saw masturbation as pathological. He did not, however, link masturbation to sexual deviations; instead, he viewed it as a cause of neurasthenia. In this view, he followed in the tradition of the eminent Swiss authority, Samuel Auguste André David Tissot (1728-1797), who had announced, a century earlier, that the loss of 1 ounce of semen through masturbation was as debilitating as the loss of 40 ounces of blood. This loss Freud accepted as the cause of neurasthenic weakness, and he sought to persuade his neurasthenic patients to stop masturbating. He reported some successes. When persuasion failed, he did not hesitate to resort to stronger measures. One adolescent girl, on Freud's prescription, was placed under prolonged round-the-clock surveillance so that she would have no privacy for masturbation. This represented a significant step forward from clitoral cauterization as a treatment for masturbation.

Not all cases of neurasthenia, Freud concluded, could be explained or cured in this way. Some male neurasthenics insisted, despite Freud's initial skepticism, that involuntary nocturnal emissions of semen (wet dreams) were their only sexual outlet. This information led Freud to the same conclusion announced in France a generation earlier by Claude Francois l'Allemand (1790-1853): Involuntary nocturnal emissions must be as damaging as masturbation and must lead to the same debilitating neurasthenia. Thus, Freud's early patients were caught, like countless other males in the 18th and 19th centuries and like some today, between the Scylla of masturbation of the Charybdis of involuntary nocturnal emissions. Freud continued to hold this dismal view until 1925, when he was 69. He changed his mind the next year.

In one respect, Freud went well beyond Krafft-Ebing. In addition to teaching that sexual deviations are in fact diseases, he taught that such sexual practices as masturbation, coitus interruptus, and the use of birth control devices are the causes of diseases that, at first blush, do not appear sexual at all, diseases that he called "the actual neuroses."

If Freud had stopped there, he might, like Krafft-Ebing, be dismissed without further consideration. But Freud then went on to study the psychoneuroses, the broad collection of conditions that are today subsumed under the heading neurosis. He sought the causes of neuroses in the childhood of his patients and in their initial family constellations. This is the primary meaning of the Freudian tradition today.

Freud was among the first physicians in history who *listened* to patients. (Havelock Ellis was another.) Freud also sometimes *talked* with patients, and, in the process, he demonstrated the therapeutic effectiveness of psychotherapy. He discovered and made known the overwhelming significance of unconscious forces in daily lives, in decisions, and in emotional conflicts. He called attention to the critical importance of the child's first few years and of his relations with his parents during those years. Children in many countries are brought up a bit differently, even by parents who have never heard Freud's name, because Freud's central views have seeped so convincingly through the culture.

Freud's doctrines have also been a factor in the somewhat less vengeful attitudes common today toward those who deviate moderately from Victorian standards of sexual normality, especially toward homosexuals. Freud taught that many perversions are signs of immaturity—failures to repress on schedule those polymorphously perverse responses common to all young children. Being stigmatized as immature is hardly a welcome characterization, but, for homosexuals and many others, it marked a long step forward from being denounced as sinners, punished as criminals, and feared as the carriers of loathsome psychosexual diseases.

The Freudian tradition has through the years been purified of much dross. Few Freudians, for example, now warn against masturbation or nocturnal emissions. There are signs, moreover, that another Freudian bastion may be crumbling. Today, homosexuality is no longer considered an illness per se by the American Psychiatric Association. This and other signs of change suggest that—at least with respect to some of the perversions—American psychiatry is slowly and painfully shifting from the tradition of Krafft-Ebing and the tradition of Sigmund Freud to the tradition of Havelock Ellis.

Havelock Ellis

Henry Havelock Ellis (1859-1939) has, through the generations, been somewhat less influential than either Krafft-Ebing or Freud. Yet his day may soon be dawning. Most of the recent changes both in psychiatric thinking and in popular thinking about human sexuality are changes in the direction of the Havelock Ellis tradition.

Everyone brings to the considerations of human sexuality his personal sexual attitudes, experiences, and responses. He also brings his notions of the sexual behavior of his friends and neighbors—who, he assumes, must resemble him quite closely. Out of this he shapes a central institution of what is sexually normal—usual, reasonable, and acceptable. What he thereafter reads, or hears about the sexual behavior of Hottentots, hippies, homosexuals, and orgy participants he arranges around the periphery at a greater or lesser distance from the norm, much as the sun, moon, stars, and planets were deployed around the earth in Ptolemy's geocentric astronomy. Havelock Ellis was one of the first and one of the most forthright challengers of this egocentric perspective. In place of the Ptolemaic model, he presented concepts of individual and cultural relativism that are currently beginning to come into their own.

Ellis illustrated his views with voluminous data, but his central theses were simple in the extreme:

With respect to human sexuality, everyone is not like you, your loved ones, and your friends and neighbors.

Even your loved ones, friends, and neighbors, moreover are probably not as much like you as you suppose.

The almost limitless diversity of human sexuality that Ellis unearthed was recorded in splendidly flowing prose in a monumental series of volumes, *Studies in the Psychology of Sex,* which he published and periodically revised between 1896 and 1928. Many of Ellis's insights, like many of Freud's, came from his personal experiences and recollections.

Born to a mother with a narrowly pietistic Victorian outlook, young Havelock and his four sisters were brought up in the strictest asexual tradition. None of his sisters ever married, and Havelock himself remained a virgin until his marriage at 32. With a few exceptions that he frankly set forth in his autobiography, *My Life* (1939), he said: "I cannot recall that I heard or saw anything that would have shocked an ordinarily modest [Victorian] schoolgirl" until his sixteenth year.

Yet these were years of sexual stress. He never masturbated, but his involuntary nocturnal emissions filled him with the terror ordinarily associated in those times with masturbation. In adolescence, he read a book by Charles Drysdale that warned that, as a result of involuntary emissions, "the organs lose their natural powers . . . . the semen becomes thinner and deteriorated in quality," (1854). There follows

a feeling of weakness on rising in the morning . . . a sort of mistiness or haze in the thoughts, and dimness in the sight, while the eye loses its luster.

This disease, spermatorrhea, Drysdale wrote,

has in many cases progressed to insanity, and idiocy. [It often terminates in death] by a kind of apoplexy, characteristic of this disease, and induced by the exhausted state of the brain.

One common treatment of spermatorrhea in those days was

the armed bougie . . . through which a stilet is passed, containing at its end the caustic nitrate of

silver, with which [the physician] slightly touches the tender part of the urethra.

This remedy, however, Drysdale warned, should in no case be applied more than twice since it might produce stricture of the urethra, "a disease often more difficult to cure than spermatorrhea itself."

Living under the daily threat of spermatorrhea, young Havelock reported that

all the obscure mysteries of sex stirred dimly and massively within me; I felt myself groping helplessly among the difficulties of life.

He contemplated the possibility of suicide or of becoming a monk. Instead, he resolved to devote his life to the study of human sexuality—to "penetrate those mysteries and enlighten those difficulties, so that to those who came after me they might be easier than they had been for me."

As his first project in sex research, Ellis kept for many years a daily record of his own involuntary nocturnal emissions, a record that refuted the allegations of l'Allemand and Drysdale that spermatorrhea is a progressive disease, characterized by a steadily increasng frequency of involuntary emissions.

Unlike either Krafft-Ebing or Freud, Ellis's primary interest was in normal human sexuality. In this, he was a pioneer, pointing the way for Kinsey and for the laboratory studies of Masters and Johnson. As he himself explained in his *Studies in the Psychology of Sex:*

It is a very remarkable fact that, although for many years past serious attempts have been made to elucidate the psychology of human perversions, little or no endeavor has been made to study the development of the normal sexual emotions. Nearly every writer seems either to take for granted that he and his reader are so familiar with the facts of normal sex psychology that any detailed statement is altoghether uncalled for, or else he is content to write a few fragmentary remarks . . . . Yet it is unreasonable to take normal phenomena for granted here as in any other region of science.

Ellis's definition of "normal," moreover, was very broad. He included under that rubric many phenomena that his predecessors saw as perversions, and he pointed out the ways in which they can serve to enrich rather than impoverish sexual experience. In this, too, he was a pioneer.

Many of Ellis's findings have a startlingly contemporary flavor. Here are a few examples:

Sexual activities and responses set in long before puberty in both girls and boys.

Masturbation is a common phenomenon at all ages in both sexes.

Homosexuality and heterosexuality are not opposites, like up and down; they are present or absent in varying degrees.

The absence of sexual desire among women in a Victorian myth. Indeed, some women are more highly sexed than most men and take the active role in initiating sexual relations.

A well-known physician in Chicago informs me that, on making inquiry of twenty-five married men in succession, he found that sixteen had first been seduced by a woman.

The orgasm is remarkably similar in women and in men.

Multiple orgasm is a common phenomenon among women.

. . . A woman who experiences the sexual act several times in succession often experiences more intense orgasm and pleasure with each repetition.

Male impotence and female frigidity are of psychological rather than physiological cause in the vast majority of cases.

But it was in his treatment of the *perversions* that Ellis's doctrines flowered.

So far from the facts of normal sex development, sex emotions, and sex needs being uniform and constant . . . the range of variation within fairly normal limits is immense, and it is impossible to meet with two individuals whose records are nearly identical.

Ellis's own record contained numerous examples of sexual variation. As a boy of 12, walking by the side of his mother at the zoo, he noted that his mother dropped behind

and soon I heard a very audible stream falling to the ground. When she moved on I instinctively looked back at the pool on the path, and my mother . . . remarked shyly: "I did not mean you to see that."

The experience was repeated a little later; this time his mother confided in him beforehand. Havelock "spontaneously played a protective role and watched to see that no one was approaching." Throughout his life thereafter, Ellis reported, he enjoyed "a slight strain of what I may call urolagnia"—sexual arousal at the fantasy or sight of a woman urinating, preferably in a standing position. But his urolagnia, he added, "never developed into a real perversion nor ever became a dominant interest, and formed no distinguishable part of the chief love interests of my life." Nevertheless

my vision of this function became in some degree attached to my feeling of tenderness toward women—I was surprised how often women responded to it tenderly.

The other common deviation he treated with as much sensitivity and acceptance as his own urolagnia was homosexuality.

His understanding of homosexuality was enriched by 2 minor homosexual incidents—both involving sex-play—in his childhood and by his insight into his wife's homosexual experiences. Edith Lees Ellis, during her marriage to Havelock, engaged in a series of homosexual relationships and encounters. One of them was a passionately emotional attachment rivaling Edith's attachment to Havelock. Ellis took both her casual lesbian encounters and her enduring lesbian relationships in his stride. After Edith's death, he wrote:

I never begrudged the devotion, though it was sometimes great, which she expended on them, for I knew that it satisfied a deep and ineradicable need in her nature.

To a far greater extent then either Krafft-Ebing or Freud, Ellis captured in his writings the poignancy of sexual experience. He described the tragic wastes resulting from sexual ignorance and sexual repression—the bachelors and spinsters, the blighted love affairs and unfulfilled marriages. He described the sufferings of the damned imposed by a callous and ignorant society on masturbators, adulterers, homosexuals, devotees of flagellation, and many more. His studies also persuaded him that these wastes and these tragedies are avoidable. He threw himself wholeheartedly into movements for sexual reform and for sexual freedom.

He urged, for example, that sexual manifestations during infancy and childhood be accepted casually, as a routine matter of course. He argued for the frank sexual education of both sexes. He favored greater freedom of sexual experimentation during adolescence and trial marriage as a prelude to actual marriage. He demanded equal rights—including equal sexual rights—for women, greater ease of divorce, and a repeal of the laws against contraception. And he stated with clarity the legal principle governing "consenting adults in private" that is only today beginning to reach the statute books:

If two persons of either or both sexes, having reached years of discretion, privately consent to practice some perverted mode of sexual relationship, the law cannot be called upon to interfere. It should be the function of the law in this matter to prevent violence, to protect the young, and to preserve public order and decency.

The Three Traditions Today

The extent to which these three major sexual traditions, these three stances toward human sexuality, continue to infuse psychiatrist-patient relationships can hardly be overestimated.

In the course of taking a history or during subsequent therapy, psychiatrists daily come face-to-face with the countless sexual variations that Krafft-Ebing excoriated, Freud sought to cure, and Havelock Ellis calmly accepted as a part of the texture of life. The outcome of therapy necessarily turns in considerable part on the tradition to which the therapist adheres.

The Freudian tradition has, through the decades, stood therapists in good stead. In recent years, however, changes have been occurring in patients themselves and in the culture from which they are drawn. An increasing proportion of patients under the age of 30 are coming in for therapy with essentially Ellis's views of human sexuality. They themselves do not see sexual variations as a collection of loathsome diseases. Indeed, they do not recognize variation as pathology. They may never have heard of Ellis, but they stand firmly in the Ellisian tradition.

Can the Freudian tradition provide effective therapy for this new generation of patients? Only time will tell. At the very least, however, psychiatrists must understand Ellis's tradition and his stance toward sexual variation if they are to understand their young patients.

REFERENCES

l'Allemand, C. *Des Pertes Seminales Involuntaires.* 3 vols. Becher-Jeune, Paris, 1936-1842.

*Brecher, E. *The Sex Researchers.* Little, Brown, Boston, 1969.

Drysdale, C. *Elements of Social Science.* E. Pruelove, London, 1854.

*Ellis, H. *Studies in the Psychology of Sex,* 2 vols. Random House, New York, 1936.

*Ellis, H. *My Life.* Houghton Mifflin, Boston, 1939.

Freud, S. *An Autobiographic Study.* W. W. Norton, New York, 1935.

Freud, S. *An Outline of Psychoanalysis.* W. W. Norton, New York, 1949.

Freud, S. *Standard Edition of the Complete Psychological Works of Sigmund Freud.* 23 vols. Hogarth Press, London, 1953-1966.

Freud, S. *Collected Papers (1893-1938),* 5 vols. Basic Books, New York 1959.

*Jones, E. *The Life and Work of Sigmund Freud,* 3 vols. Basic Books, New York, 1953-1957.

*Krafft-Ebing, R. *Psychopathia Sexualis,* ed. 12. 1906.

Tissot, S. *Onanism.* M. Chapvis, Lausanne, 1760.

Tissot, S. *Advice to the People in General with Regard to Their Health.* T. Becket and P. A. Dehondt, Lausanne. 1765.

chapter 3 Anatomy and Physiology of Sexuality

3.1 Sexual Anatomy and Physiology

VIRGINIA A. SADOCK, M.D.

Introduction

The sex of a human being is determined at the time of fertilization. Within the broad limits defined by normal variation, individual heredity, and environmental influence, the physiology, anatomy, and physical development of a person are, therefore, forecast at conception. To the extent that society dictates social and cultural roles according to sex, psychological development is also affected. Sexual physiology goes beyond reproduction, and hormonal changes affect libido, physical well-being, and behavior. These physical facts are also important contributions to the psychological development of a person.

Embryology

Gonadal structures are recognizable in the embryo by the fourth week of development. However, these structures do not assume male or female morphological characteristics until the seventh week of development. They begin as genital ridges, 5 mm. in length, and lie on either side of the embryonic midline.

Around the sixth week, primordial germ cells migrate from the wall of the primitive gut to this gonadal area. The germ cells that migrate to the area seem to have an inductive effect that influences the differentiation of the gonad into a male or a female gland (see Figure 1). The sex glands are attached by cords to the surface epithelium, and male and female differences are still not apparent.

In addition to indifferent gonads, male and female fetuses have identical genital tubes. The development of the testes causes the female tubes, the Müllerian duct, to shrink away in the male fetus, and development of the ovary causes the disappearance of the male tubes, the Wolffian duct, in the female fetus. In the male, the Wolffian duct, arising from the primitive kidney, eventually forms the ductus deferens, seminal vesicles, and epididymis. In the female, the Müllerian duct arises as an epithelial invagination on the urogenital ridge and eventually forms the oviducts and the uterus. The vagina is currently believed to be formed from evaginations of the urogenital sinus that join the fused Müllerian ducts (see Figure 2).

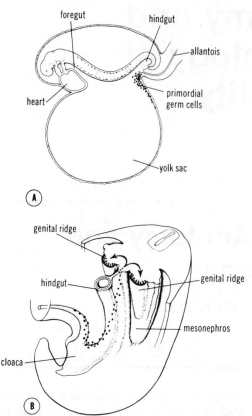

FIGURE 1. *A*. Schematic drawing of a 3-week-old embryo, showing the primordial germ cells in the wall of the yolk sac, close to the attachment of the allantois (after Witchi). *B*. Drawing to show the migration path of the primordial germ cells along the wall of the hindgut and the dorsal mesentery into the genital ridge. Note the position of the genital ridge and mesonephros. (Reproduced from Langman, J. *Medical Embryology*, ed. 2. Williams & Wilkins, Baltimore, 1972, by permission.)

DEVELOPMENT OF THE TESTES

Between the sixth and eighth weeks of development, the primitive sex cords in the male embryo proliferate and anastomose with one another in the medulla of the sex gland forming the testis cords. These become the seminiferous tubules of the adult. The cords remain solid until puberty, at which time they canalize. While the testis cords are proliferating in the medulla of the sex gland, the cortex degenerates. The germ cells disappear from the cortex, and a dense layer of fibrous connective tissue, the tunica albuginea, separates the testis cords from the surface

epithelium. This surface epithelium then disappears, leaving the tunica albuginea as the capsule of the testes. During the fourth to eighth months of development, the interstitial cells of Leydig are formed from the mesenchyme between seminiferous tubules. The tubules themselves have formed from primitive germ cells and epithelial cells from the surface of the gland. The epithelial cells eventually develop into the sustentacular cells of Sertoli (see Figure 3).

At this time the testes' initial attachment to the primitive kidney is reduced to a mesentery-like attachment called the gubernaculum testis, which extends from the caudal pole of the testes to the genital swelling of the fetus. In the second month of life, the fetus grows rapidly. The gubernaculum testis does not grow correspondingly, with the end result that the testes seem to descend. By the end of the third month, they lie near the inguinal region. At this time the prostate glands and scrotal sac form. The final descent through the inguinal ring into the scrotal sac form. The final descent through the inguinal ring into the scrotal swelling occurs in the seventh month of development. Hypotheses as to the final cause of this descent include shortening of the gubernaculum testis and hormonal influence (see Figure 4).

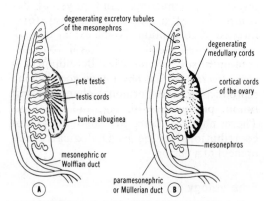

FIGURE 2. Diagram of the genital ducts in the sixth week of development in the male *(A)* and in the female *(B)*. The Wolffian and Müllerian ducts are present in both the male and the female. Note the excretory tubules of the mesonephros and their relationship to the developing gonad. (Reproduced from Langman, J. *Medical Embryology*, ed. 2. Williams & Wilkins, Baltimore, 1972, by permission.)

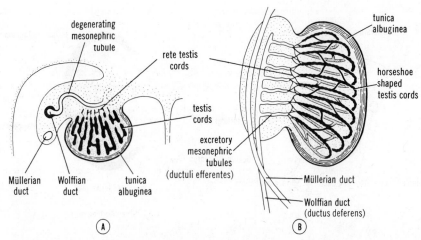

FIGURE 3. *A.* Transverse section through the testis in the eighth week of development. Note the tunica albuginea, the testis cords, and the rete testis. The glomerulus and Bowman's capsule of the mesonephric excretory tubule are in regression. *B.* Schematic representation of the testis and the genital ducts in the fourth month of development. The horseshoe-shaped testis cords are continuous with the rete testis cords. Note the ductuli efferentes (excretory mesonephric tubules), which enter the Wolffian duct (modified after Giroud). (Reproduced from Langman, J. *Medical Embryology,* ed. 2. Williams & Wilkins, Baltimore, 1972, by permission.)

DEVELOPMENT OF THE OVARIES

The development of the ovaries, in contrast to the testes, involves primarily the development of the cortex of the gland. The sex cords of the medulla eventually disappear and are replaced by vascular stromata, which form the ovarian medulla. The surface epithelium of the gland thickens and proliferates, giving rise to cords that push into the gonad. These cords then split into clusters of cells that surround the primitive germ cells. The cord cells eventually develop into follicular cells; the germ cells develop into oogonia and then oocytes. At birth the follicles are very similar to the young follicles in the adult ovary (see Figure 5 and 6). Only at puberty, however, do the primordial follicles develop into mature Graafian follicles and do the primary oocytes continue maturation to become mature oocytes (see Figure 7).

DEVELOPMENT OF THE EXTERNAL GENITALIA

Until the seventh week, the external development of the genitalia appears the same in the male and female fetuses. In the presence of androgens, male development occurs; in the absence of androgens, female development occurs. These changes can occur under the influence of fetal testosterone or of exogenously administered androgens. Table

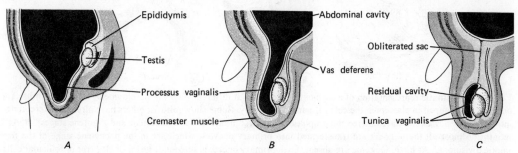

FIGURE 4. *A.* Descent of the human testis and its subsequent relations, shown in diagrammatic hemisections. (Reproduced from Arcy. *Developmental Anatomy,* ed. 7, p. 333. W. B. Saunders, Philadelphia, 1965, by permission.)

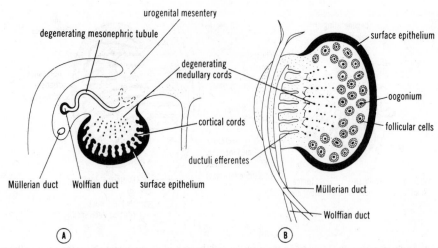

FIGURE 5. *A*. Transverse section through the ovary at the seventh week of development, showing the degeneration of the primitive (medullary) sex cords and the formation of the cortical cords. *B*. Schematic drawing of the ovary and genital ducts in the fifth month of development. Note the degeneration of the medullary cords. The excretory mesonephric tubules (ductuli efferentes) do not communicate with the rete. The cortical zone of the ovary contains groups of oogonia surrounded by follicular cells. (Reproduced from Langman, J. *Medical Embryology,* ed. 2. Williams & Wilkins, Baltimore, 1972, by permission.)

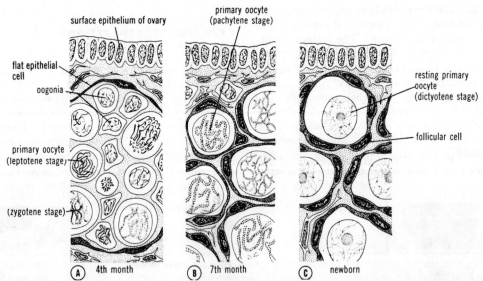

FIGURE 6. Schematic representation of a segment of the ovary at different stages of development. *A*. At 4 months. The oogonia are grouped in clusters in the cortical part of the ovary. Some show mitosis; others have already differentiated into primary oocytes and have entered the prophase of the first miotic division (leptotene and zygotene stages). *B*. At 7 months. Almost all the oogonia are transformed into primary oocytes, which are in the pachytene stage of the first miotic division. *C*. At birth. Oogonia are absent. Each primary oocyte is surrounded by a single layer of follicular cells, thus forming the primordial follicle. The oocytes have entered the dictyotene stages, in which they remain until just before ovulation. Only then do they enter the metaphase of the first miotic division (modified after Ohno et al.). (Reproduced from Langman, J. *Medical Embryology,* ed. 2. Williams & Wilkins, Baltimore, 1972, by permission.)

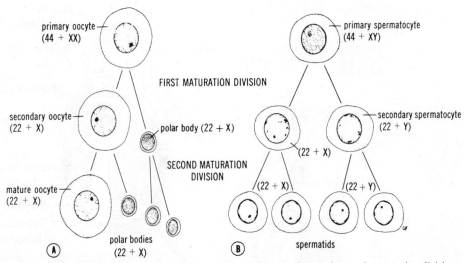

FIGURE 7. Schematic drawing showing the events occurring during the first and second maturation divisions. *A*. The primitive female germ cell (primary oocyte) produces only one mature cell, the mature oocyte. *B*. The primitive male germ cell (primary spermatocyte) produces four spermatids, all of which develop into spermatozoa. (Reproduced from Langman, J. *Medical Embryology,* ed. 2. Williams & Wilkins, Baltimore, 1972, by permission.)

I and Figure 8 summarize the changes that occur.

Anatomy
MALE

The external genitalia of the normal, adult male include the penis, scrotum, testes, epididymis, and parts of the vas deferens. The internal parts of the genital system include the vas deferens, seminal vesicles, ejaculatory ducts, and prostate.

The testis or male gonad is an oval gland measuring approximately 1½ inches by 1 inch by ¾ inch. There are two testes, each with an epididymis attached to its upper pole and posterior border. Each testis is surrounded by two coats—the tunica vaginalis and the tough, outer tunica albuginea—and is enclosed in the scrotal sac (see Figures 9 and 10).

The scrotum, the bag of skin and tissue in which the testes lie, hangs between the thighs. Externally, it is a single pouch. Internally, it is divided by subcutaneous tissue into right and left compartments, each containing a testis and epididymis. The left testis usually hangs lower than the right. The scrotal sac is responsive to temperature changes and responds with elevation to sexual stimulation. In cases of undescended to ectopic testes, the scrotal sac may be empty.

Within the testes are the seminiferous tubules that produce the sperm cells. Between these tubules lie the cells of Leydig, which are involved in the production of testosterone. Testosterone is the male hormone responsible for development of masculine secondary sex characteristics. Recent studies have shown an inverse correlation between stress and the testosterone blood levels in adult males. The

TABLE I
Differentiation of the External Genitalia from Indifferent Primordia

Primordial Structure	Structures that Develop with Androgen Exposure	Structures that Develop without Androgen Exposure
Genital tubercle	Penis	Clitoris
Urethral folds	Corpus spongiosum (penile urethra)	Labia minora
Labioscrotal swellings	Scrotum	Labia majora
Urogenital sinus	Prostatic utricle	Lower two thirds of vagina
	Bulbourethral glands	Skene's glands
		Bartholin's glands

Sexual Differentiation

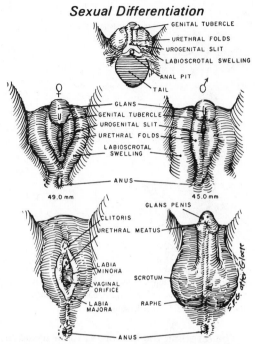

FIGURE 8. Differentiation of male and female external genitalia from indifferent primordia. Male differentiation occurs only in the presence of androgenic stimulation during the first 12 weeks of fetal life. (Redrawn from Van Wyk and Grumbach, 1968. Reproduced from Brobeck, J. R. (editor). *Best & Taylor's Physiological Basis of Medical Practice,* ed. 9. Williams & Wilkins, Baltimore, 1973, by permission.)

seminiferous tubules join to form the straight tubules and then the rete testis at the apex of the gland. These, in turn, give rise to efferent ductules, which coil to form the head of the epididymis. They then empty into the duct of

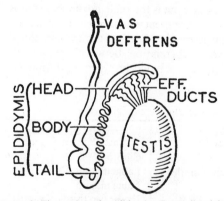

FIGURE 9. The testis and epididymis. (Reproduced from Dickinson, R. L. *Atlas of Human Sex Anatomy,* ed. 2. Williams & Wilkins, Baltimore, 1949, by permission.)

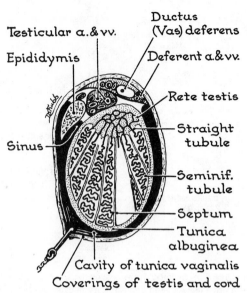

FIGURE 10. Right testis in transverse section. (Reproduced from Dickinson, R. L. *Atlas of Human Sex Anatomy,* ed. 2. Williams & Wilkins, Baltimore, 1949, by permission.)

the epididymis (the head and tail). The tail of the organ continues as the vas deferens. It is through this network that the spermatozoa must travel.

The vas deferens passes over the pelvis into the lower abdomen and is here connected to the seminal vesicle. This vesicle secretes a substance believed to add motility to the sperm. The vas deferens, now called the ejaculatory duct, continues from its connection with the seminal vesicle into the prostate. Within the prostate the ejaculatory duct enters into the urethra. The duct is usually closed, opening to allow the passage of semen into the urethra under strong sexual stimulation (see Figure 11).

This passage of fluid into the urethra—sperm from the testicles and epididymis, fluid from the seminal vesicles, and fluid released by contraction of the prostate itself—provides the man with a sensation of impending climax. Indeed, once there is contraction of the prostate, ejaculation is inevitable. The ejaculate is propelled through the penis by urethral contractions. The ejaculate consists of about one teaspoon of fluid (2.5 cc.) and contains about 120 million sperm cells.

The urethra, through which the ejaculate travels, is 8 to 9 inches long, originating in the

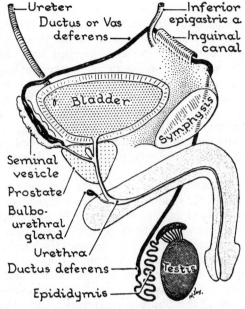

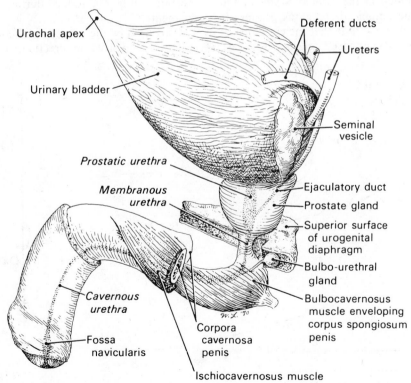

FIGURE 11. Diagram of the ductus (vas) deferens. (Reproduced from Dickinson, R. L. *Atlas of Human Sex Anatomy,* ed. 2. Williams & Wilkins, Baltimore, 1949, by permission.)

bladder and passing through the prostate (prostatic urethra), and following the ventral surface of the penis to the glans (penile urethra) (see Figure 12).

The prostate is a gland weighing about 20 gm.; it surrounds the urethra and shares the bladder bed near the neck of the bladder. It can be palpitated rectally. The gland is composed partially of smooth muscle cells and elastic tissue fibers. During sexual excitation this smooth muscle contracts, and prostatic secretions are emptied from the gland's ductules into the urethra.

Cowper's glands, two pea-size structures located behind the membranous urethra, may provide a small amount of additional lubrication during sexual excitation.

The penis has been referred to by Freud as the executive organ of sexuality. The word "penis" has been traced from the Latin as meaning variously "tail" or "to hang," referring to the pendant position of the organ in its resting or flaccid state. Its size varies within a range that is fairly constant, although various

FIGURE 12. The male urethra and its relation to the urogenital organs. (Courtesy of R. F. Becker, Ph.D., Michigan State University.)

sex researchers over the years have diverged in their findings. All agree, however, that concern over the size of the penis is practically universal among men. The most recent data, those of Masters and Johnson, indicate a range of 7 to 11 cm. in the flaccid state and 14 to 18 cm. in the erect state. Of interest was their further observation that the flaccid dimension bears little relation to the erect dimension; the smaller penis erects to a proportionally greater size than does the larger penis (see Figure 13).

The penis consists of the glans, shaft, and root and is composed primarily of erectile tissue. It comprises three parallel tubes: two corpora cavernosa, which lie side by side, and beneath them the single corpus spongiosum, which is traversed by the urethra. The anterior end of the corpus spongiosum fits over the corpora cavernosa and is called the glans. The foreskin covering the glans is known as the prepuce (see Figure 14).

The rite of circumcision, in which the prepuce is surgically removed, has been practiced as a religious rite by Jews and Moslems and is common in the United States at the present time among all religious groups. It was believed at one time that the circumcised penis, with its exposed glans, was less

sensitive as a result of cornification of the epithelium. In studies by Masters and Johnson, no difference in tactile threshold was found between the circumcised penis and the uncircumcised penis. A further finding was that, intravaginally, the prepuce of the uncircumcised penis remains retracted behind the glans during penile thrusting, dispelling the myth that premature ejaculation may be more common in uncircumcised men because of increased stimulation as a result of preputial movements.

All three fibrous tubes of the penis have innumerable spaces that can become engorged with blood, causing the penis to become erect (see Figure 15). The three tubes extend backward, each corpus cavernosum attaching to an arm of the pubis and the corpus spongiosum extending into the urethral bulb. The muscles covering these backward extensions (the bulbocavernosus and the ischiocavernosus) by their contractions, respectively, propel ejaculate through the urethra at the point of sexual climax and prevent blood from leaving the penis, so that erection can be maintained during sexual excitement.

Activation by the parasympathetic nervous system is involved in erection. The pelvic

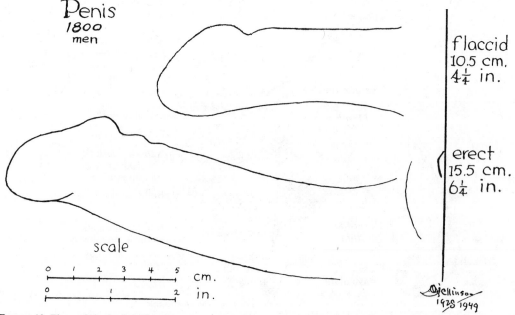

FIGURE 13. The penis in the flaccid and erect state with average size as surveyed and drawn by Dickinson. (Reproduced from Dickinson, R. L. *Atlas of Human Sex Anatomy,* ed. 2. Williams & Wilkins, Baltimore, 1949, by permission.)

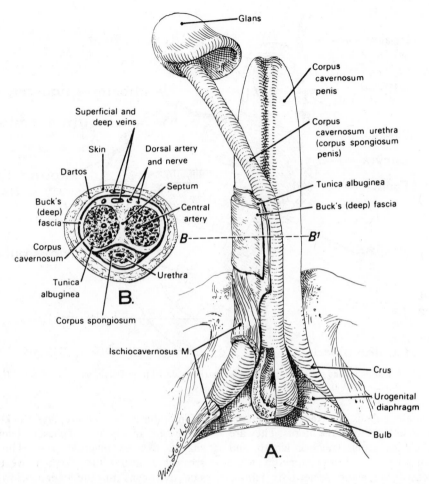

FIGURE 14. *A*. Crural relationships and tunics of the penis. *B*. Cross-section taken through *A* at *B-B*¹. (Courtesy of R. F. Becker, Ph.D., Michigan State University.)

splanchnic nerves (S2, 3, and 4) stimulate the blood vessels of the area to dilate, causing the penis to become erect. The sympathetic nervous system is involved in ejaculation. Through its hypogastric plexus, the sympathetic nervous system innervates the urethral crest and the muscles of the epididymis, vas deferens, seminal vesicles, and prostate. Stimulation of this plexus causes ejaculation of seminal fluid from these glands and ducts into the urethra.

FEMALE

The internal female genital system comprises the ovaries, fallopian tubes, uterus, and vagina. The external genitalia or vulva includes the mons pubis, major and minor lips. clitoris, glans, vestibule of the vagina, and vaginal orifice (see Figure 16).

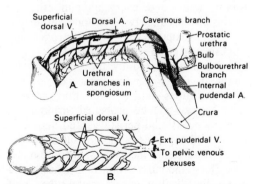

FIGURE 15. Blood supply of penis. *A*. Arterial. *B*. Venous. (Courtesy of R. F. Becker, Ph.D., Michigan State University.)

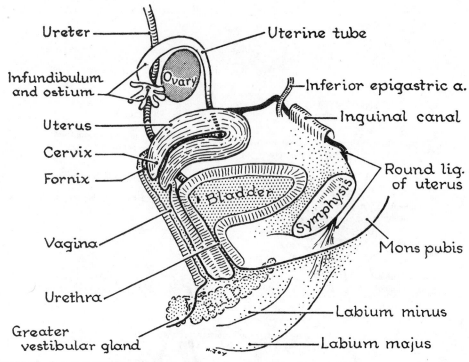

FIGURE 16. The female pelvis and perineum, median section. (Reproduced from Dickinson, R. L. *Atlas of Human Sex Anatomy*, ed. 2. Williams & Wilkins, Baltimore, 1949, by permission.)

The female gonads are the two ovaries, which lie on either side of the uterus. They are spherical glands, about 1 inch in length, and are supported by a fold of peritoneum called the suspensory ligament. A newborn female has about 200,000 immature ova in each ovary. These ova decrease in number with age and disappear after menopause. Throughout her reproductive life, from puberty to menopause, a woman usually releases a total of 400 ova into the peritoneal cavity. Release of ova usually occurs once every lunar month. The ovaries also produce two hormones important to female sexual development, estrogen and progesterone (see Figures 17 and 18).

The ovum released by the ovary can be caught in the finger-like processes of the fallopian tubes—either tube may service either ovary—and be propelled through the tubes by occasional peristalsis and action of the hair like processes in the tubes to the uterus. The tubes themselves are about 4½ inches long and curve from the ovaries to the uterus. Fertilization occurs in the tubes, and tubal secretion may be nourishing to the released ovum (see Figure 19).

The uterus is a muscular, thick-walled, hollow organ about 3 inches in length and shaped like an inverted pear. The uterus receives a uterine tube from above on each side and opens into the vagina below. When not harboring a fetus, the uterine cavity remains collapsed. It is held in place by two broad ligaments and two round ligaments. The endometrium, the internal mucous surface of the uterus, is composed of glands and stromata and goes through stages each month: (1) postmenstrual, (2) proliferative or nonsecretory, (3) secretory or progestational shedding of the upper two thirds of the endometrium. It regenerates from the remaining basales, composed of stromata and stumps of glands (see Figure 20).

The word "vagina" is derived from the Latin word meaning sheath. It is usually in a collapsed state, a potential rather than an actual space. It is about 3 inches long and extends from the cervix of the uterus above (see Figure 21) to the vestibule of the vagina or the vaginal opening below. In most virgins a membranous fold, the hymen, separates the vestibule and opening from the rest of the

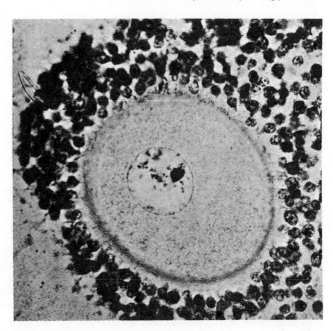

FIGURE 17. Human oocyte from a large graafian follicle (x 480). (Reproduced from Eastman and Hellman. *Williams Obstetrics,* ed. 13, p. 60. Appleton-Century-Crofts, New York, 1966, by permission.)

vaginal canal. The mucous membrane lining the vaginal walls rests in numerous transverse folds. This lining can stretch during the birth process. To accommodate the penis during sexual intercourse, the vagina expands in both length and width. In addition to its other functions, the vagina offers a passage for the release of menstrual fluid from the uterus. After menopause, the vagina loses much of its elasticity.

Figure 22 shows the blood supply to the internal genitalia. The ovarian artery derives from the aorta, and the vaginal and uterine arteries arise from the internal iliac. Congestion of small vessels surrounding the vagina results in a transudate that lubricates the vaginal walls during sexual excitement.

The hypogastric plexus of the sympathetic nervous system supplies the uterus, tubes, and part of the vagina. The lower part of the vagina is supplied by the pudendal nerve. During sexual climax these nerves stimulate the genitalia to contract rapidly.

The most superficial aspect of the female external genitalia is the mons pubis (see Figure 23), a mound directly in front of the pubic bone. Hair growth occurs here at puberty. The pattern of hair growth in the mature woman varies but follows roughly the shape of an inverted triangle.

The major lips are two broad cutaneous ridges that meet in the midline of the body and cover most of the other external genitals. They extend backward to the perineum.

Inside the major lips lie the minor lips, thinner folds devoid of fat, that lie alongside the vaginal orifice and form the angle limiting the vestibule. Opening into the vestibule are the urethra, vagina, paraurethral glands, and

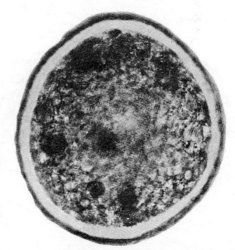

FIGURE 18. A fresh ovum washed from the tube; the protoplasm is enclosed by semitransparent zona pellucida and consists largely of lipoid masses (x 405). (Reproduced from Eastman and Hellman. *Williams Obstetrics,* ed. 13, p. 60. Appleton-Century-Crofts, New York, 1966, by permission.)

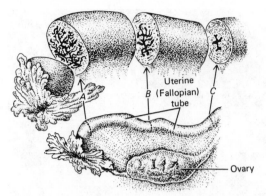

FIGURE 19. Uterine tube. *A.* Infundibular. *B.* Ampullar. *C.* Isthmic. (Reproduced from Eastman and Hellman. *Williams Obstetrics,* ed. 3, p. 31. Appleton-Century-Crofts, New York, 1966, by permission.)

vestibular gland. The minor lips are free posteriorly but join anteriorly to form the prepuce and frenulum of the clitoris.

The clitoris was first described in the medical literature by Hippocrates, who referred to it as the site of sexual excitation. Masters and Johnson have described the clitoris as the primary female sexual organ in that orgasm is dependent, physiologically, on adequate clitoral stimulation. Clitoris is

derived from a Greek word meaning "closure" or "to hide" and anatomically it has a nerve net that is three times as large as that of the penis in proportion to its size. Sherfey cites recent embryological evidence that indicates that the mammalian embryo is female during its early development; the differentiation of the male from the female results from the action of fetal androgen at about the sixth week and is completed by the third month of embryonic life. On the basis of this evidence and the similarity in certain anatomical structures—both the clitoris and the penis have corpora cavernosa, an anatomical shaft, and a glans, and both are erectile—she states that, whereas the clitoris has been considered a rudimentary penis, there is evidence to suggest that the penis may more accurately be considered an enlarged clitoris.

Kinsey found that in masturbatory techniques most women prefer stimulation of the clitoris above all other sites. This finding was refined further by Masters and Johnson, who reported that the shaft of the clitoris is preferred to the glans, which is subject to a particular type of hypersensitivity if stimulated excessively. An important anatomical finding is that the clitoral prepuce is

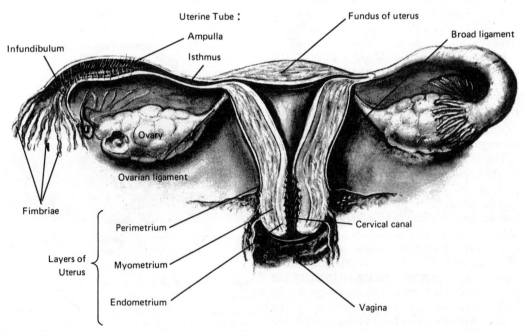

FIGURE 20. Internal female reproductive organs. (Reproduced from Dienhart. *Basic Human Anatomy and Physiology,* p. 215. W. B. Saunders, Philadelphia, 1967, by permission.)

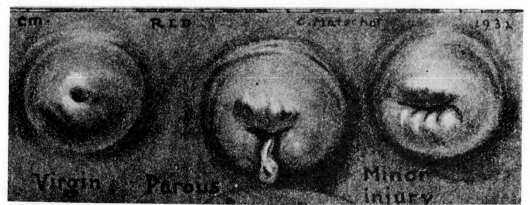

FIGURE 21. The cervix in the nulliparous and multiparous female. (Reproduced from Dickinson, R. L. *Atlas of Human Sex Anatomy*, ed. 2. Williams & Wilkins, Baltimore, 1949, by permission.)

contiguous with the labia minora and that during coitus there is no direct stimulation of the clitoris by the penis. Rather, traction exerted on the minor lips as a result of penile thrusting accounts for stimulation of the clitoris necessary for orgasm to occur. They also noted the retraction of the clitoris under the clitoral hood during the plateau phase as a result of the contraction of the ischiocavernosi muscles. Retraction of this type moves the clitoris away from the vaginal barrel, thus making clitoral-penile contact impossible.

The size of the clitoris varies considerably (see Figure 24) and is unrelated to the degree of sexual responsiveness of a particular woman. A controversial medical procedure advocated by some workers at the present time for the treatment of frigidity or dyspareunia is the clearance of peputial adhesions to the clitoris, as illustrated in Figure 25.

Breasts are not specifically sexual organs but are mentioned in this discussion because of their importance in sexual play and as erogenous areas. Breasts are much more fully developed in the human female than in the male (see Figure 26). They function as suckling organs but respond in a definitive physiological pattern during intercourse as well. There is a wide variation in size, shape, and sensitivity of breasts in women. The breasts are attached to the chest muscles and are composed of glandular, fibrous, and fatty tissue. The nipple and surrounding areola possess a darker pigmentation than the rest of

the breast. This pigmentation increases with pregnancy and childbirth.

Physiology

Neurological and hormonal factors are enmeshed in the development of human sexuality. Gonadal sex is chromosomally determined at the time of fertilization, and chromatic bodies (or lack of them) appear as indications of genetic sex in nonsexual body cells as well. These chromatin bodies are present only in the female (see Figure 27).

Unlike the gonads, which are under chromosomal influence, the fetal external genitalia are very susceptible to hormones, and exogenous hormonal administration could cause external genital development in-

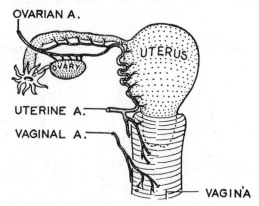

FIGURE 22. The uterine vessels. (Reproduced from Dickinson, R. L. *Atlas of Human Sex Anatomy*, ed. 2. Williams & Wilkins, Baltimore, 1949, by permission.)

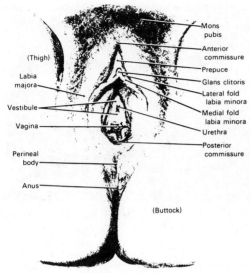

FIGURE 23. Female external genitalia. (Courtesy of R. F. Becker, Ph.D., Michigan State University.)

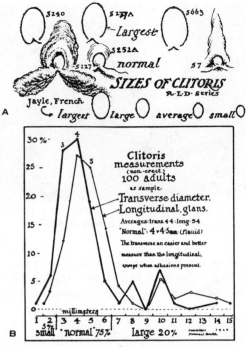

FIGURE 24. Size of clitoris. *A.* Anatomical drawings showing location and dimensions of clitoris (life size). *B.* Range of clitoral measurements in nonerect state. (Reproduced from Dickinson, R. L. *Atlas of Human Sex Anatomy,* ed. 2. Williams & Wilkins, Baltimore, 1949, by permission.)

consistent with the fetal sex gland development. A female fetus, possessing an ovary, could develop external genitalia resembling that of a male if the pregnant mother received sufficient exogenous androgen.

In normal development, spermatogenesis and oogenesis begin embryonically and are continued and completed when the male and female reach puberty (see Figures 28 and 29).

Figure 30 summarizes the normal hormonal effect at the time of puberty. Deprived of male and female gonads and the respective hormones, testosterone and estrogen, the human adult does not develop normal secondary sexual characteristics, is incapable of reproduction, and, in the case of the female, does not develop a normal menstrual cycle.

The onset of menstruation during puberty marks the expulsion of the unfertilized egg from the ovary and the uterine bleeding that

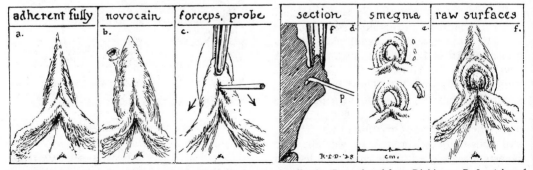

FIGURE 25. Procedure for clearance of preputial adhesions to the clitoris. (Reproduced from Dickinson, R. L. *Atlas of Human Sex Anatomy,* ed. 2. Williams & Wilkins, Baltimore, 1949, by permission.)

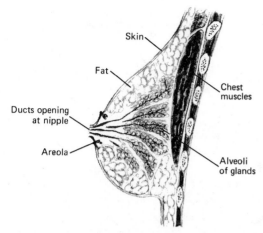

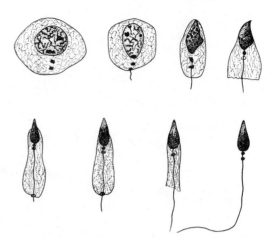

FIGURE 26. Vertical section of the breast. (Reproduced from Dienhart. *Basic Human Anatomy and Physiology*, p. 217. W. B. Saunders, Philadelphia, 1967, by permission.)

FIGURE 28. Eight successive stages in the transformation of a spermatid cell into a mature sperm. (After Stieve, *Habch. d. Mikroskop. Anat. d. Menschen*, 7, 1930. Reproduced from Stern. *Principles of Human Genetics*, ed. 2, p. 11. W. H. Freeman, San Francisco, 1960. Copyright of W. H. Freeman and Company and reprinted by permission.)

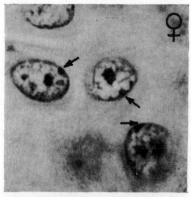

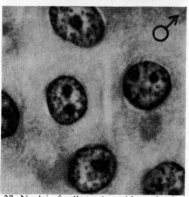

FIGURE 27. Nuclei of cells in the epidermal spinus layer of a genetic female *(left)* and a genetic male *(right)*. The sex chromatin bodies are indicated by *arrows* in the female. (Redrawn from Grumbach and Barr, 1958. Reproduced from Brobeck, J. R. (editor). *Best & Taylor's Physiological Basis of Medical Practice*, ed. 9. Williams & Wilkins, Baltimore, 1973, by permission.)

follows. At menarche, however, the female does not always release an egg and may not, at first, be fertile. The process of menstruation, involving ovulation and uterine changes, is intricately involved with hormonal changes (see Figures 31 to 34). According to Masters and Johnson, many women are particularly sexually responsive just prior to menstruation due to the pelvic congestion which occurs at that time.

The hypothalamic-testicular interaction resulting in the release of sperm is also intimately connected with hormonal regulation and is graphically demonstrated in Figure 35.

FERTILIZATION

For fertilization, the mature ovum and sperm must meet in the fallopian tube. The sperm is viable for about 36 hours and may be present in the tube before the egg arrives. Conception must occur within 48 hours of ovulation. Many sperm may enter the fallopian tubes, but only one can penetrate the capsule of the egg. Once this penetration has occurred, the egg becomes impenetrable to other sperm. The final maturation of the egg occurs after it has been fertilized. The egg divides and continues to divide into greater numbers of cells. The sperm determines the

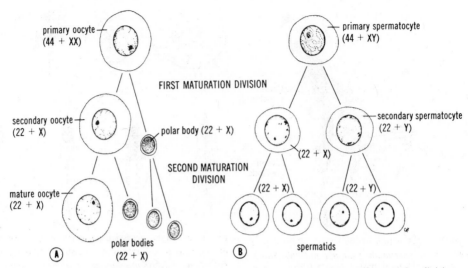

FIGURE 29. Schematic drawing showing the events occurring during the first and second maturation divisions. *A*. The primitive female germ cell (primary oocyte) produces only one mature cell, the mature oocyte. *B*. The primitive male germ cell (primary spermatocyte) produces four spermatids, all of which develop into spermatozoa. (Reproduced from Langman, J. *Medical Embryology*, ed. 2. Williams & Wilkins, Baltimore, 1972, by permission.)

sex of the child. The egg always contains an X or female chromosome. If the sperm adds a male or Y chromosome, the embryo is a male. If the sperm adds another X chromosome, the embryo is a female. After about 3 days of division of the fertilized egg, at the 16-cell stage, the fertilized egg enters the uterine cavity.

PHYSIOLOGICAL RESPONSES

In the normal man or woman, a sequence of physiological sexual responses exists that has been described by Masters and Johnson. These levels of sexual arousal consist of four discrete phases, each accompanied by unique physiological changes (see Tables II and III). These phases can be understood physiologically as increasing levels of vasocongestion and myotonia (tumescence) and the subsequent rapid release of this vascular activity and muscle tone as a result of orgasm (detumescence).

Stage I: excitement. This phase is brought on by psychological stimulation—fantasy, the presence of a love object—or physiological stimulation—stroking, kissing—or by a combination of both. It is characterized by erection in the man and vaginal lubrication in the woman, both occurring within 10 seconds

of effective stimulation. The nipples of both sexes become erect, although this erection is more common in the woman (see Figure 36). The clitoris becomes hard and turgid, and the labia majora and minora become thicker as a result of venous engorgement (see Figure 37). The excitement phase may last several minutes to several hours.

Stage II: plateau. As stimulation continues, the testes increase in size 50 per cent and elevate. The vaginal barrel shows a characteristic constriction along the outer third, known as the orgasmic platform. The clitoris elevates and retracts behind the symphysis pubis and, as a result, is not easily accessible. Breast size in the woman increases 25 per cent. Continued engorgement of the penis and vagina produces specific color changes, most marked in the labia minora, which spread and become a deep purple red color (see Figure 38). Voluntary contractions of large muscle groups occur. The plateau phase last 30 seconds to several minutes.

Stage III: orgasm. In the man, orgasm is triggered by a subjective sense of ejaculatory inevitability, followed by the forceful emission of semen. In the woman, orgasm is characterized by 3 to 12 involuntary contractions of the vaginal orgasmic platform. Te-

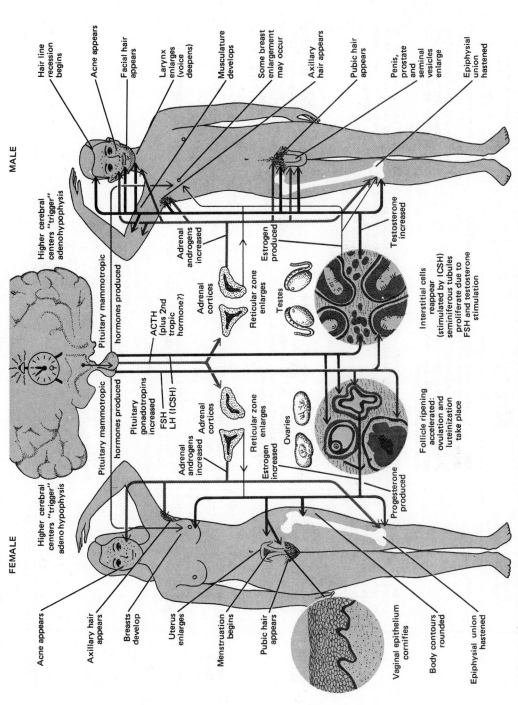

FIGURE 30. Effects of sex hormones on development of puberty. (Copyright 1965 by CIBA Pharmaceutical Company, Division of CIBA-GEIGY Corporation. Reproduced with permission from the Ciba Collections of Medical Illustrations, by Frank Netter, M.D. All rights reserved.)

TABLE II
*The Male Sexual Response Cycle**

	I. Excitement Phase (several minutes to hours)	II. Plateau Phase (30 sec. to 3 min.)	III. Orgasmic Phase (3–15 sec.)	IV. Resolution Phase (10–15 min.; if no orgasm, ½–1 day)
Skin	No change	Sexual flush: inconsistently appears; maculopapular rash originates on abdomen and spreads to anterior chest wall, face, and neck and can include shoulders and forearms	Well developed flush	Flush disappears in reverse order of appearance; inconsistently appearing film of perspiration on soles of feet and palms of hands
Penis	Erection within 10–30 sec. caused by vasocongestion of erectile bodies of corpus cavernosa of shaft. Loss of erection may occur with introduction of asexual stimulus, loud noise	Increase in size of glans and diameter of penile shaft; inconsistent deepening of coronal and glans coloration	Ejaculation: marked to 3 to 4 contractions at 0.8 sec. of vas, seminal vesicles, prostate, and urethra; followed by minor contractions with increasing intervals.	Erection: partial involution in 5–10 sec. with variable refractory period; full detumescence in 5–30 min.
Scrotum and testes	Tightening and lifting of scrotal sac and partial elevation of testes toward perineum	50 per cent increase in size of testes over unstimulated state due to vasocongestion and flattening of testes against perineum signaling impending ejaculation	No change	Decrease to base line size due to loss of vasocongestion. Testicular and scrotal descent within 5–30 min. after orgasm. Involution may take several hours if there is no orgasmic release
Cowper's glands	No change	2–3 drops of mucoid fluid that contain viable sperm	No change	No change
Other	Breasts: inconsistent nipple erection	Myotonia: semispastic contractions of facial, abdominal, and intercostal muscles. Tachycardia: up to 175 per min. Blood pressure: rise in systolic 20–80 mm.; in diastolic 10–40 mm. Respiration: increased	Loss of voluntary muscular control. Rectum: rhythmical contractions of sphincter Up to 180 beats per min. 40–100 systolic; 20–50 diastolic Up to 40 respirations per min. Ejaculatory spurt: 12–20 inches at age 18 decreasing with age to seepage at 70	Return to base line state in 5–10 min.

*Table prepared by Virginia A. Sadock, M.D., after Masters and Johnson data.

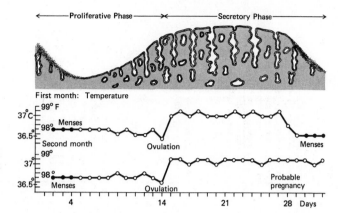

FIGURE 31. The phases of the menstrual cycle. (Reproduced from Benson. *Handbook of Obstetrics and Gynecology,* ed. 3, p. 26, Lange Medical Publications, Los Altos, Calif., 1968, by permission.)

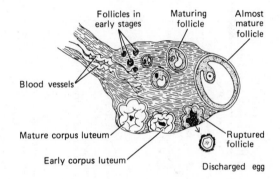

FIGURE 32. Composite view of ovum. (Reproduced from Crawley, Malfetti, Stewart, and Vas Dias. *Reproduction, Sex, and Preparation for Marriage,* p. 16. Prentice-Hall, Englewood Cliffs, N.J., 1964, by permission.)

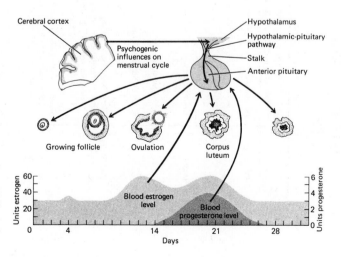

FIGURE 33. Ovulation during the menstrual cycle. (Reproduced from Benson. *Handbook of Obstetrics and Gynecology,* ed. 3, p. 26. Lange Medical Publications, Los Altos, Calif., 1968, by permission.)

TABLE III
*The Female Sexual Response Cycle**

	I. Excitement Phase (several minutes to hours)	II. Plateau Phase (30 sec. to 3 min.)	III. Orgasmic Phase (3-15 sec.)	IV. Resolution Phase (10-15 min.; if no orgasm, ½-1 day
Skin	No change	Sexual flush inconstant except in fair-skinned; pink mottling on abdomen, spreads to breasts, neck, face, often to arms, thighs, and buttocks—Looks like measles rash	No change (flush at its peak)	Fine perspiration, mostly on flush areas; flush disappears in reverse order
Breasts	1. Nipple erection in two thirds of subjects 2. Venous congestion 3. Areolar enlargement	Flush: mottling coalesces to form a red papillary rash Size: increase one fourth over normal, especially in breasts that have not been nursed Areolae: enlarge; impinge on nipples so they seem to disappear	No change (venous tree pattern stands out sharply; breasts may become tremulous)	Return to normal in reverse order of appearance in ½ hr. or more.
Clitoris	Glans: half of subjects, no change visible, but with colposcope, enlargement always observed; half of subjects, glans diameter always increased 2-fold or more. Shaft: variable increase in diameter; elongation occurs in only 10 per cent of subjects	Retraction: shaft withdraws deep into swollen prepuce; just before orgasm, it is difficult to visualize; may relax and retract several times if phase II is unduly prolonged Intrapreputial movement with thrusting: movements synchronized with thrusting; due to traction on labia minora and prepuce	No change (Shaft movements continue throughout if thrusting maintained)	Shaft returns to normal position in 5-10 sec.; full detumescence in 5-30 min. (if no orgasm, clitoris remains engorged for several hours)
Labia Majora	Nullipara: thin down; elevated; flatten against perineum Multipara: rapid congestion and edema; increases to 2-3 times normal size	Nullipara: totally disappear (may res- well if phase II unduly prolonged.) Multipara: become so enlarged and edematous, they "hang like folds of a heavy curtain"	No change	Nullipara: *increase* to normal size in 1-2 min. or less Multipara: *decrease* to normal size to 10-15 min.
Labia Minora	Color change: to bright pink in nullipara and red in multipara Size: increase 2-3 times over normal; prepuce often much more; proximal portion firms, adding up to ¾ inch to functional vaginal sidewalls	Color change: suddenly turn bright red in nullipara, burgundy red in multipara. Signifies onset of phase II. Orgasm will then always follow within 3 min. if stimulation is continued Size: enlarged labia gap widely to form a vestibular funnel into vaginal orifice	Firm proximal areas contract with contractions of lower third	Returns to pink blotchy color in 2 min. or less; total resolution of color and size in 5 min. (decoloration, clitoral return, and detumescence of lower third all occur as rapidly as loss of the erection in men)

98

Bartholin's Glands	No change	A few drops of mucoid secretion form; aid in lubricating vestibule (insufficient to lubricate vagina)	No change	No change
Vagina	Vaginal transudate: appears 10-30 sec. after onset of arousal; drops of clear fluid coalesce to form a well lubricated vaginal barrel. (aids in buffering acidity of vagina to neutral pH required by sperm)	Copious transudate continues to form; quantity of transudate generally increased only by prolonging preorgasm stimulation (increased flow occurs during premenstrual period)	No change (transudate provides maximum degree of lubrication)	Some transudate collects on floor of the upper two thirds formed by its posterior wall (in supine position); ejaculate deposited in this area forming seminal pool
Upper two-thirds	Color change: mucosa turns patchy purple	Color change: uniform dark purple mucosa Further ballooning creates diameter of 2½-3 inches; then wall relaxes in a slow tensionless manner	No change; fully ballooned out and motionless	Cervical descent: descends to seminal pool in 3-4 min.
Lower third	Dilation of vaginal lumen to 1-1¼ inches occurs; congestion of walls proceeds gradually, increasing in rate as phase II approaches	Maximum distension reached rapidly; contracts lumen of lower third and upper labia to ½ or more its diameter in phase I; contraction around penis allows thrusting traction on clitoral shaft via labia and prepuce.	3-15 contractions of lower third and proximal labia minora at ¾-sec. intervals	Congestion disappears in seconds, (if no orgasm, congestion persists for 20-30 min.)
Uterus	Ascent: moves into false pelvis late in phase I Cervix: passively elevated with uterus (no evidence of any cervical secretions during entire cycle)	Contractions: strong sustained contractions begin late in phase II; have same rhythm as contractions late in labor, lasting 2 + min. Cervix: slight swelling; patchy purple (inconstant; related to chronic cervicitis)	Contractions throughout orgasm; strongest with pregnancy and masturbation	Descent: slowly returns to normal Cervix: color and size return to normal in 4 min; patulous for 10 min.
Others	Fourchette: color changes throughout cycle as in labia minora	Perineal body: spasmodic tightening with involuntary elevation of perineum Hyperventilation and carpopedal spasms: both are usually present, the latter less frequently and only in female-supine position	Irregular spasms continue Rectum: rhythmical contractions inconstant; more apt to occur with masturbation than coitus External urethral sphincter; occasional contraction, no urine loss	All reactions cease abruptly or within a few seconds

*From *The Nature and Evolution of Female Sexuality*, by Mary Jane Sherfey. Copyright 1966, 1972 by Mary Jane Sherfey. Reprinted by permission of Random House, Inc.

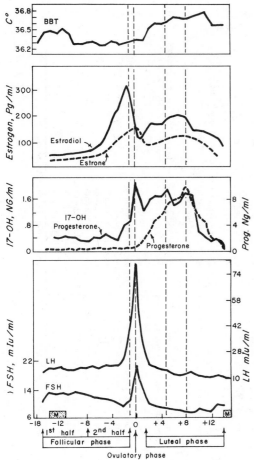

FIGURE 34. The hormonal events of the reproductive cycle are centered on the midcycle LH peak (day 0). Basal body temperatures *(BBT)* are shown on the *top line.* Plasma levels of luteinizing hormone *(LH)* and follicle-stimulating hormone *(FSH)* are shown on the *bottom two lines.* Gonadal steroid levels (estradiol, estrone, 17-hydroxyprogesterone, and progesterone) are shown in the *center.* Days of menstrual bleeding are indicated by *M.* (Redrawn from Ross et al. 1970, and Koreman et al., 1970. Reproduced from Brobeck, J. R. (editor). *Best & Taylor's Physiological Basis of Medical Practice,* ed. 9. Williams & Wilkins, Baltimore, 1973, by permission.)

tanic contractions of the uterus, flowing from the fundus downward to the cervix, also occur. Both sexes show involuntary contractions of the internal and external anal sphincter. The male orgasm is associated with four to five rhythmic spasms of the prostate, seminal vesicles, vas, and urethra. In both sexes the contractions of the various organs occur at in-

tervals of 0.8 second. Other changes consist of further voluntary and involuntary movements of the large muscle groups, including facial grimacing and carpopedal spasm. Blood pressure rises 20 to 40 mm. (systolic and diastolic), and the heart rate rises to 120 to 160 beats a minute. Orgasm lasts 3 to 15 seconds and is associated with a slight clouding of consciousness.

The orgasmic potential in men is highest at about age 18 and in women at about age 35. The 18-year-old man may achieve as many as eight orgasms in a 24-hour period. In the man over 30, one orgasm in a 24-hour period is more common. The increased orgasmic potential in the woman of 35 has been explained on the basis of less psychological inhibition.

Orgasm is a true psychophysiological experience in that there is a subjective per-

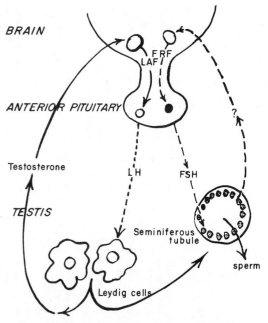

FIGURE 35. Testicular function in man. The hypothalamo-pituitary-Leydig cell axis is shown on the *left* with pituitary luteinizing hormone stimulating testosterone secretion. The hypothalamo-pituitary tubular axis is shown on the *right* with follicle-stimulating hormone and testosterone stimulating spermatogenesis. A factor from the seminiferous tubules (?) is believed to regulate follicle-stimulating hormone secretion. (Reproduced from Brobeck, J. R. (editor). *Best & Taylor's Physiologic Basis of Medical Practice,* ed. 9. Williams & Wilkins, Baltimore, 1973, by permission.)

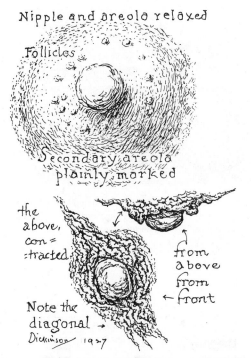

FIGURE 36. As sexual excitement increases, nipple erection and impingement of the areolar on the nipple is a finding in two thirds of women, as illustrated. (Reproduced from Dickinson, R. L. *Atlas of Human Sex Anatomy,* ed. 2. Williams & Wilkins, Baltimore, 1949, by permission.)

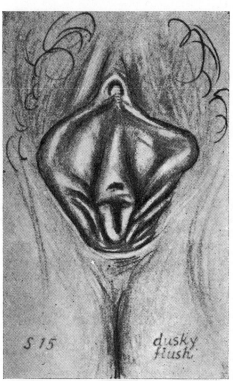

FIGURE 38. In the plateau phase of sexual responsivity, the labia minora elongate, spread, and thin out; the clitoris enlarges and elevates. (Reproduced from Dickinson, R. L. *Atlas of Human Sex Anatomy,* ed. 2. Williams & Wilkins, Baltimore, 1949, by permission.)

FIGURE 37. In the excitement phase of sexual responsivity, the labia majora and labia minora become thickened as a result of vasocongestion, as illustrated. (Reproduced from Dickinson, R. L. *Atlas of Human Sex Anatomy,* ed. 2. Williams & Wilkins, Baltimore, 1949, by permission.)

ception of a peak of physical reaction to sexual stimuli and a brief episode of physical release from vasocongestion and myotonia built up during the excitement and plateau phases.

Stage IV: resolution. Resolution consists of the disgorgement of blood from the genitalia (detumescence), which brings the body back to its resting state. If orgasm occurs, resolution is rapid; if it does not occur, resolution may take 2 to 6 hours and be associated with irritability and pain in the genitalia (see Figure 39). Successful resolution in both sexes is characterized by a subjective sense of well-being and a specific perspiratory reaction—a generalized excretion of sweat over the entire body including the palms and soles.

Refractory period. After orgasm, men have a refractory period that may last from several minutes to many hours; in this period they cannot be stimulated to further orgasm. The

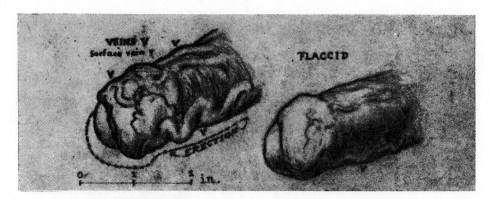

FIGURE 39. Venous engorgement without orgasm produces partial involution of the penis with associated pain *(left).* Complete involution occurs after orgasm, and the penis returns to its flaccid state *(right).* (Reproduced from Dickinson, R. L. *Atlas of Human Sex Anatomy,* ed. 2. Williams & Wilkins, Baltimore, 1949, by permission.)

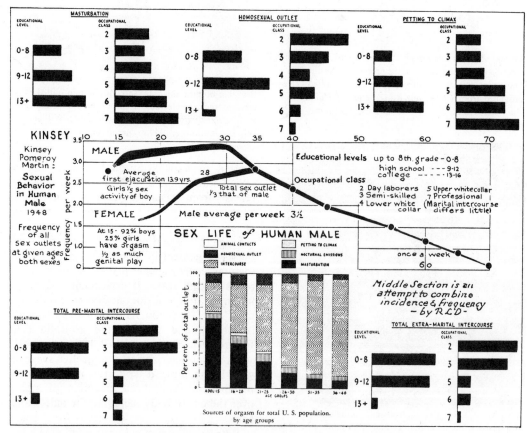

FIGURE 40. Sex life of human male. (Reproduced from Dickinson, R. L. *Atlas of Human Sex Anatomy,* ed. 2, Williams & Wilkins, Baltimore, 1949. Adapted by permission, from Kinsey, Pomeroy, and Martin, *Sexual Behavior in the Human Male.* Courtesy of W. B. Saunders, Philadelphia.)

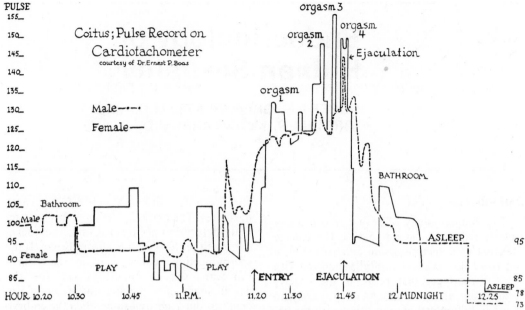

FIGURE 41. Coitus was performed with both partners monitored for pulse rate. Note the increased rate in both the man and the woman, the length of foreplay, the multiple orgasmic return of the woman, and the orgasm and resolution to the resting state with sleep. (Reproduced from Dickinson, R. L. *Atlas of Human Sex Anatomy,* ed. 2. Williams & Wilkins, Baltimore, 1949, by permission.)

refractory period does not exist in women, who are capable of multiple and successive orgasms. Some women are capable of experiencing 20 to 30 orgasms by continued penile or manual stimulation, barring exhaustion. Psychosexual development and psychological development and psychological attitude toward sexuality are directly involved with and affect the physiology of human sexual response (see Figures 40 and 41).

REFERENCES

*American Medical Association. *Human Sexuality.* American Medical Association, Chicago, 1972.

*Basmajian, J. V. *Grant's Method of Anatomy,* ed. 8. Williams & Wilkins, Baltimore, 1971.

Becker, R. F., Gehweiler, J. A., and Wilson, J. W. *The Anatomical Basis of Medical Practice.* Williams & Wilkins, Baltimore, 1971.

Brobeck, J. R. (editor). *Best & Taylor's Physiological Basis of Medical Practice,* ed. 9. Williams & Wilkins, Baltimore, 1973.

*Dickinson, R. L. *Atlas of Human Sex Anatomy,* ed. 2. Williams & Wilkins, Baltimore, 1949.

Ellis and Arbanel, *The Encyclopedia of Sexual Behavior.* Jason Aronson, New York, 1973.

Langman, J. *Medical Embryology,* ed. 2. Williams & Wilkins, Baltimore, 1972.

*Masters, W. H., and Johnson, V. E. *Human Sexual Response.* Little, Brown, Boston, 1966.

*Masters, W. H., and Johnson, V. E. *Human Sexual Inadequacy.* Little, Brown, Boston, 1970.

Novak, E. R., Jones, G. S., and Jones, H. W. *Novak's Textbook of Gynecology,* ed. 7. Williams & Wilkins, Baltimore, 1965.

*Sherfey, M. J. *The Nature and Evolution of Female Sexuality.* Random House, New York, 1972.

3.2

Endocrinology of Human Sexuality

ROBERT B. GREENBLATT, M.D., and
VIRGINIA P. McNAMARA, M.D.

Introduction

The endocrinology of sexuality is a many splendored saga, beginning with the chance meeting of a spermatozoon and an ovum, a microscopic merger of two cells endowed with genetic messages that result in the orderly progression and development of two cells into a many billion-cell human being with the capacity of repeating this continuing miracle. With the event of birth, the first question asked is, "Is it a boy?" or "Is it a girl?" Usually, the answer is arrived at by a quick glance at the external genitalia. But in this day of intense interest and preoccupation with the subject of sex, even the most unsophisticated physician realizes that at birth maleness or femaleness involves not only the morphology of the external genitalia but also that of the gonads and the internal genitalia.

Ultimate gender identity and behavior emerges from a combination of physical and psychosocial factors. The sum total of the individual makeup depends on many facets, including chromosomal endowment, gonadal adequacy, childhood rearing, environmental influences, hormonal factors, degree of maturation of the external genitalia, and possible hypothalamic sensitization. The harmonious interplay of these many properties results in a normal man or woman; lack of uniformity of one or several of these factors can create sexual dysfunction.

Chromosomal Sex

In the normal progression of events, the sex of a person is determined at the moment of the union of the sperm and egg cells. In each human cell, there are 22 pairs of autosomal chromosomes and one pair of sex chromosomes. The ovum contributes the X or female-determining chromosome; the sperm carries either an X or a Y chromosome. If the sperm meeting the ovum contains the X chromosome, the blueprint is set for the development of a female, but if the sperm contains the Y chromosome, then the embryo is destined to become a male.

According to Jost, maleness is imposed on a basically female fetus. The embryonal gonadal structures begin developing as ovaries, and the growth of the male gonad transpires consequent to the intrusion of the Y chromosome. This concept contradicts the traditional theory, which holds that the developing sex organs of a fetus are orginally made up of male and female components. Early in fetal development, the struggle for supremacy takes place, and one component suppresses the other, allowing the organs of one sex to begin development. When dominance fails, then both components persist in the same gonad resulting in ovo-testis (see Figure 1), or an ovary and a testis develop independently (see Figure 2), resulting in true hermaphroditism (see Figure 3). Here is seen the result of faulty chromosomal endowment—that is, both XX and XY sex chromosomal lines—gondal inadequacy, ambiguous external genitalia, and confused gender identification. The inherent difficulties in childhood rearing and environmental influences leave an indelible mark on future sexual comportment.

In an orderly progression of events, birth takes place some 270 days after conception, and the infant is phenotypic for its genetic sex with gonads and internal and external

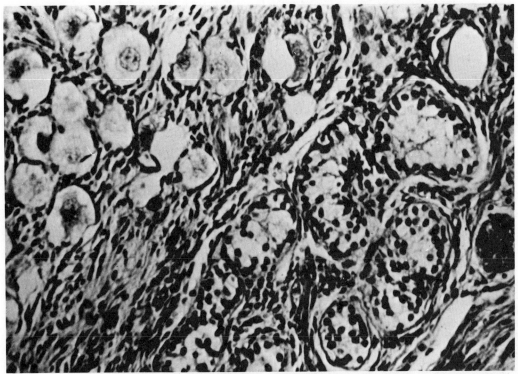

FIGURE 1. Photomicrograph of a histological section of an abdominal ovotestis removal from a phenotypic female, 5 years of age, with normal vaginal canal and enlarged clitoris. Note the cortical primordial follicles containing oocytes and the medullary portion composed of testicular tubules.

genitalia. In a list of sex determinants, the definition of human sexuality must be a complex of many interrelated and interdependent factors. That the first determinant is listed as chromosomal is valid. The gonad then programs the path of growth and development of internal and external genitalia.

The male gonad is believed to produce an organizing or inductor substance sometimes referred to as a fetal androgen, different from testosterone, that induces regression of the Mullerian structures and permits the full development of the Wolffian duct system. In the absence of this inductor substance, the basic femininity of the fetus persists, and a person resembling more or less completely a phenotypic female results. Thus, one endowed with an XY chromosomal pattern but lacking the organizer emerges as a phenotypic female. An excellent example is the phenotypic female, seen in Figure 4, with rudimentary gonadal streaks (gonadal dysgenesis),

negative Barr bodies, and an XY chromosomal pattern. This particular person is feminine in her attitudes and aptitudes. She experiences menses at monthly intervals on sequential estrogen and progestogen medication.

Some writers list chromosomal or genetic sex as diagnostic of sexuality when a person's several sexual characteristics are not consonant. Barr described, within the cells of a buccal smear of the normal female, a deeply staining chromatin conglomerate located immediately beneath the nuclear membrane (see Figure 5). In a normal male or XY person, these chromatin masses are absent; however, in males with Klinefelter's syndrome (gynecomastia and testicular dysgenesis), an extra X is found; as a result, such a person possesses an XXY chromosomal pattern. Some of these males may appear normal; others may be eunuchoid; all are infertile (see Figure 6). Incidentally, every female Olympic

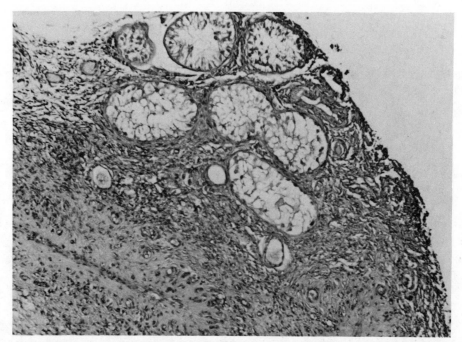

FIGURE 2. Photomicrograph of a histological section of a scrotal ovo-testis obtained by biopsy from a phenotypic male, 21 years of age, with ambiguous external genitalia and gynecomastia. Karyotype of the blood was XX, but a gonadal tissue culture revealed two cell lines—XX and XY. Note that the cortical zone contains testicular tubules; primordial follicles are seen immediately below the tubules.

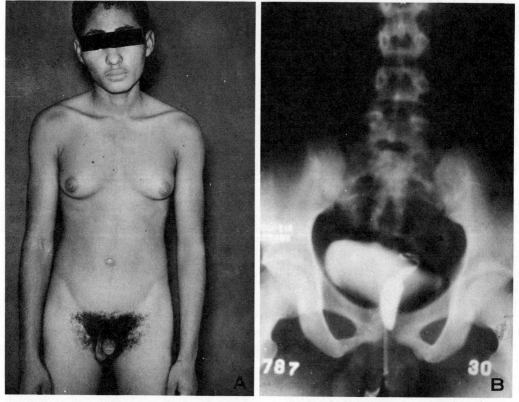

FIGURE 3. A true hermaphrodite. An abdominal ovary and a scrotal testis were found on biopsy of gonadal structures. Menses occurred each month from the urogenital sinus. *A*. Note gynecomastia. *B*. A cystogram and vaginal-uterosalpingogram revealed separate openings for the urethra and vaginal tract. The unicollis uterus and the Fallopian tube are outlined.

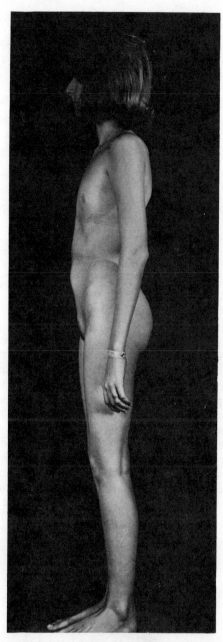

FIGURE 4. A phenotypic female with XY karyotype. The vaginal canal was normal without clitoral enlargement. At laparotomy, dysgenetic gonads and a uterus with Fallopian tubes were present. On cylic estrogen-progestogen therapy, menses were induced at regular intervals, and good breast development resulted.

athlete is routinely examined for the presence of Barr bodies in a buccal smear.

It appears, then, that chromosomes and fetal androgen or inductor substance are of much significance in the early weeks of fetal life; however, in this strange story, time enters the picture. Fetal hormones, maternal hormones, or exogenous hormones administered to pregnant women may alter the external genital development, depending on the time in fetal development during which these hormonal influences come to bear. In congenital adrenal hyperplasia, the excessive androgens produced by the fetal adrenal may prevent the formation of a complete vagina, resulting in a urogenital sinus and an enlarged clitoris at birth; if the hormonal influence was mild or later in its appearance, then a normal vagina is formed, and only the clitoral enlargement is indicative of unnatural fetal hormonal influences (see Figure 7). So too, a woman harboring an arrhenoblastoma or a virilizing tumor of the adrenal or receiving large doses of testosterone or androgenic progestational substances (norethindrone, ethisterone) during pregnancy may give birth to an infant with anomalous external genitalia (see Figure 8).

The picture of human sexuality as revealed to the clinician and the layman is a complex tapestry with interweaving and meshing of many discrete threads, the origin of which may arise from the moment of conception or at any point in the life span of the person. Today's clinician, to understand such complexity, needs much and varied knowledge, including a few facts concerning the structural formula of the male and female sex hormones.

All steroid hormones have a four-carbon ring skeleton known as cyclopentenophenanthrene derivatives (see Figure 9a). The basic structural formula for natural estrogen contains 18 carbon atoms (see Figure 9b). Estradiol is the primary estrogen, with estrone and estriol representing other metabolically active estrogens. Androgens are 19-carbon steroids with a hydroxyl or oxygen at position three and 17 and a double-bond at position four (see Figure 9c). When oxygen is found at position 17, the androgens are called 17-ketosteroids. Androsterone was the first 17-

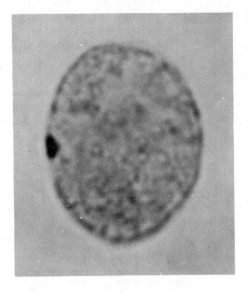

FIGURE 5. Barr body. A deeply staining chromatin mass just below the cellular membrane of the nucleus is found in more than 30 per cent of somatic cells in the normal female.

ketosteroid with androgenic properties to be isolated from human urine. In the male, urinary 17-ketosteroids are the metabolites of adrenal and testicular steroid secretion; in the female, they are of adrenal and ovarian origin. It should be emphasized that 17-ketosteroids are not a measurement of testosterone, the true masculinizing hormone. It appears very likely that the effect of testosterone on the target tissue is mediated by its reduction to dihydrotestosterone. Plasma testosterone levels in young men vary from 5

to 8 mg. per ml.; in elderly men, the range is from 3 to 5 mg. per ml. The hirsute female, with a few exceptions, has higher plasma levels than the normal female and may experience, as a result, greatly increased libido. Progesterone (see Figure 10) is the ubiquitous hormone in the synthesis of all gonadal and adrenal steroids; it is produced in large quantities by the corpus luteum and placenta. It is a 21-carbon compound, measured in the urine as pregnanediol. Synthetic C-18 and C-19 compounds used as

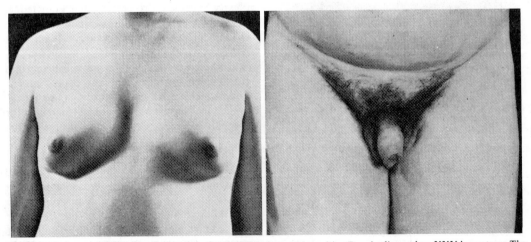

FIGURE 6. Gynecomastia in a male with Klinefelter's syndrome, with positive Barr bodies and an XXY karyotype. The testes are very small and show typical seminiferous tubule sclerosis.

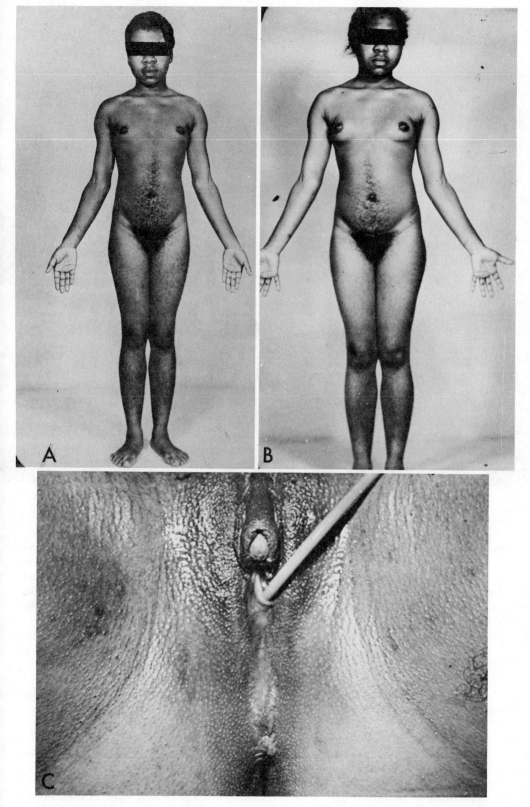

FIGURE 7. *A*. Female pseudohermaphroditism due to congenital adrenal hyperplasia. *B*. Note the breast development after 6 months of cortisone therapy; normal cyclic menses began within a few months. *C*. Note the enlarged clitoris and urogenital sinus.

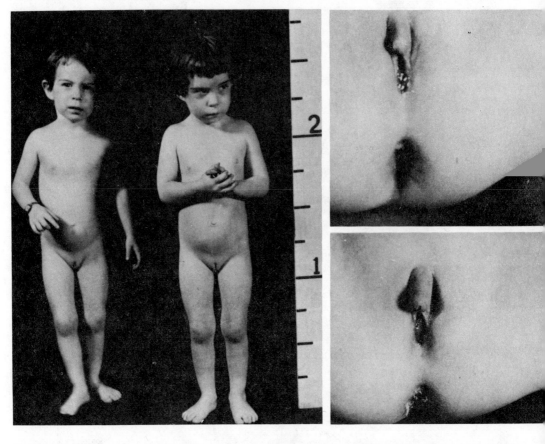

FIGURE 8. Twins born to a mother who received ethisterone during pregnancy. Not the enlarged clitoris in each child.

progestational agents bear a resemblance to testosterone in their chemical conformation. This relationship explains why certain progestational agents may have some androgenic properties and masculinize a female fetus when administered to the mother early in pregnancy (see Figure 11).

Maleness and Femaleness

"Male and female created He them." These biblical words represent an over-simplification of human engineering; the discussion here emphasizes the endocrinal aspects of masculinity and femininity in the presence of normal, overabundance of, or absence of sex steroids. Other factors also play a part in the human being's sex interest. In childhood, gonadal hormones are barely measurable, yet eroticism displays itself quite early in life. Little boys have erections; little

girls frequently show sexual awareness—rhythmic rubbing of thighs or sometimes inserting small objects into the vagina. Is such behavior hormonal? Most likely, it is instinctive, exploratory, and pleasurable. And what about the young boy who is innocently drawn to female dress and playing with dolls? Could this early manifestation of things to come bespeak some kind of specific hypothalamic conditioning? Such trends cannot be wholly explained on the basis of child rearing or environmental influences. Many a transvestite, sexual apostate (those with a compulsive desire for sex reassignment), or homosexual may have had such simple but harmless beginnings. Hormones in themselves have little to do with such conditioning, since hormonal levels in these people are, as a rule, within normal limits. On the other hand, hypogonadal males and hya

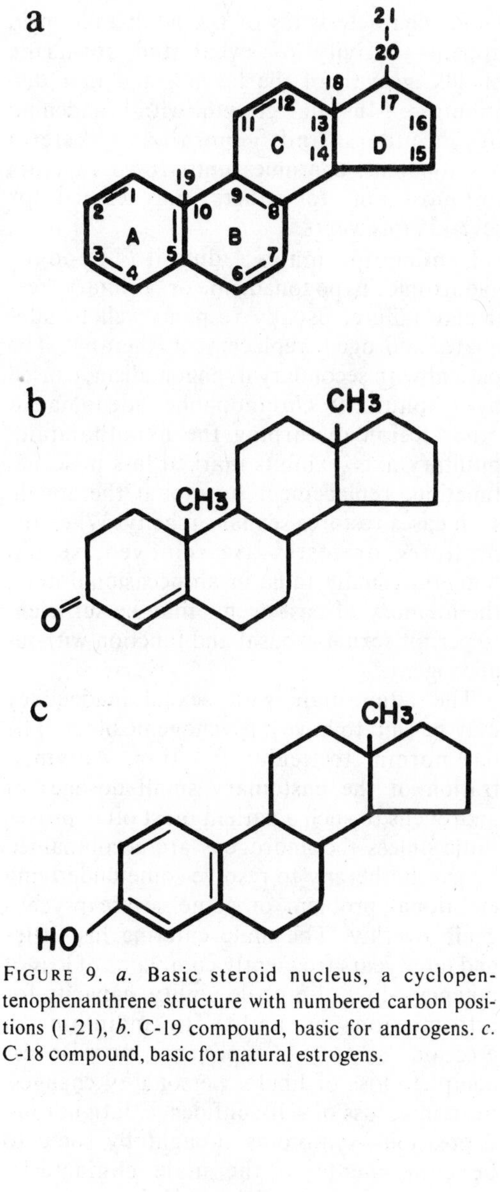

b

c

FIGURE 9. *a.* Basic steroid nucleus, a cyclopen-tenophenanthrene structure with numbered carbon positions (1-21), *b.* C-19 compound, basic for androgens. *c.* C-18 compound, basic for natural estrogens.

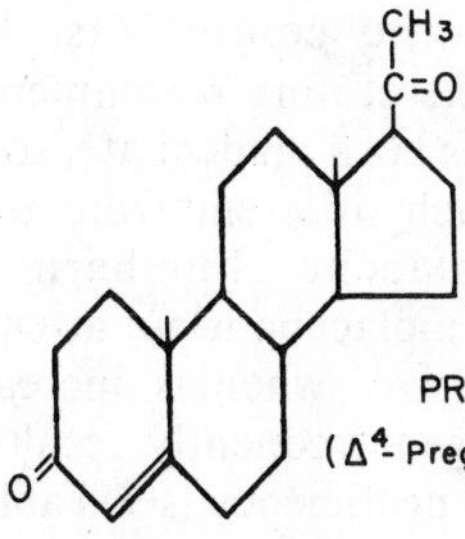

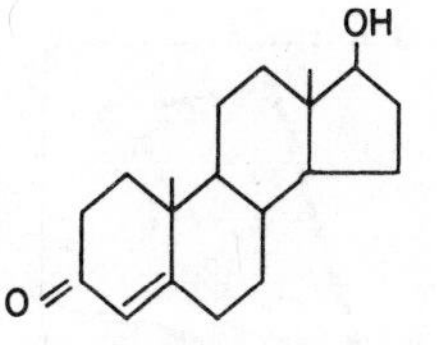

Testosterone

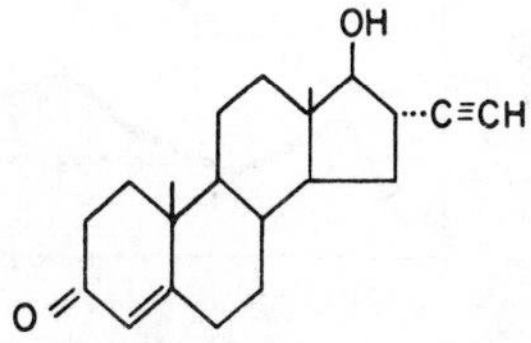

17alpha-ethynyl-testosterone
(Ethisterone)

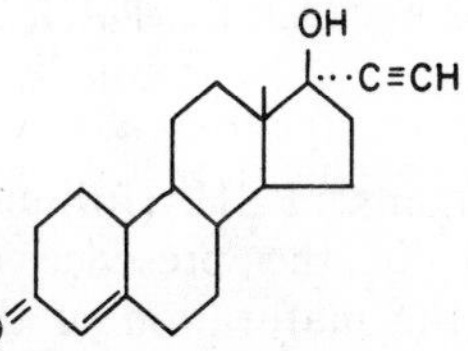

19 nor–17 alpha ethynyl –
testosterone
Norethindrone

FIGURE 11. Note the similarity to testosterone of C-19 compound, ethisterone, and C-18 compound, norethindrone (norethisterone). Both C-18 compound and C-19 compound are progestogens with slightly androgenic properties.

perandrogenized females are easily led into homosexual alliances, so that, in a small proportion of such persons, it may be said that hormonal levels are of significance.

MALE ENDOCRINOLOGY

After the male gonad develops as the result of chormosomal endowment and fetal androgen, the testicular androgens permit the maturation of the external genitalia and masculine bodily habitus. Urinary 17-ketosteroid levels remain low in the male infant until the prepubertal age, at which time there are increments, reaching a peak at 18 to 20 years (see Figure 12), then tapering off to a fairly constant level. After the age of 50, plasma testosterone levels begin slowly to decline.

Pituitary interstitial cell-stimulating hormone stimulates the testes to produce

PROGESTERONE
(Δ⁴ Pregnene - 3, 20 - Dione)

FIGURE 10. Progesterone, a C-12 compound.

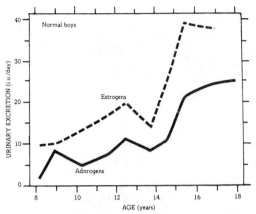

FIGURE 12. The excretion of sex hormones in boys (i.u., international units), (Data are from Greulich, W. W. et al. Somatic and endocrine studies of puperal and adolescent boys. Mongr. Soc. Res. Child Develop., *7:* 26-27, 1942.)

androgens and estrogens. FSH (follicle-stimulating hormone), in the presence of testosterone, permits the maturation of the germ cells lying in between the sustentacular cells of the tubule to mature into spermatogonia. The Sertoli or sustentacular cells are thought by some to be capable of producing estrogen. Others postulate a specific kind of inhibitory property as a system for the control of hormonal secretion. Androgens affect other than sexual activities: nitrogen retention, skeletal growth, increase in muscle mass and somatic organ size (kidney, liver, spleen), salt and water retention, and fat metabolism. The Leydig cells of the testis release androgens during the first 6 months after birth and then become active again around the tenth to the thirteenth years of age with early manifestations of pubescence. At puberty, when the body is suffused with androgens in increasing amounts, sex drive and libido develop as a part of the total picture. Extensive changes take place in the nervous system; in addition, there is growth of the secondary sex characteristics and maturation of the organs of reproduction.

The age of puberty varies widely within the normal range and may be conditioned by genetic background and by nutritional and environmental factors. Boys reach puberty (defined as the ability to ejaculate and produce spermatozoa) in the age bracket from 9 to 17 years, 15 being the average age.

Other characteristics of the adult male also appear—activity of sweat and aprocrine glands, growth of the larynx, and hair distribution. Muscular growth, with broadening of shoulders and generalized skeletal development, continues until 16 to 18 years for most but, for others, may extend for several more years.

Eunuchoid males, due to hypogonadotropic hypogonadism or primary testicular failure, usually respond well to adequate androgen replacement therapy. The patient with secondary hypogonadism, caused by a pituitary chromophobe adenoma or other lesion disturbing the hypothalamic-pituitary axis, exhibits marked loss in sexual function; replacement hormonal therapy in such cases restores sexual capacity. When the pituitary or testes are removed, sexual potentia usually fails; in an occasional man, the memory of past events may be sufficient to permit sexual arousal and function without androgens.

The adult male with sexual inadequacy may be said to have a psychogenic block if he has normal testicular function. Administration of the customary small dosages of androgens to such a patient most often proves futile unless the androgens are accompanied by psychotherapy to resolve some underlying emotional problem or some severe psychogenic overlay. The male entering his fifties and later years frequently complains of loss of potency—loss of erectile ability, capacity for intromission, or ability to maintain an erection. Some men experience more or less complete loss of libido, personality changes, insomnia, loss of self-confidence, fatigue, and depression—symptoms thought by some to be components of the male climacteric. Testosterone, in sufficiently large amounts, may satisfactorily, although not completely, alleviate many of the complaints. Unfortunately, dosage heretofore recommended for this syndrome has been inadequate, so the results were not much different from those obtained with a placebo. Furthermore, increasing dosage of a placebo is not attended by increasing sex drive, whereas increased dosage of an androgen frequently results in restoration of sexual proficiency (see Tables I and II).

Men with uncontrollable sexual appetites

TABLE I

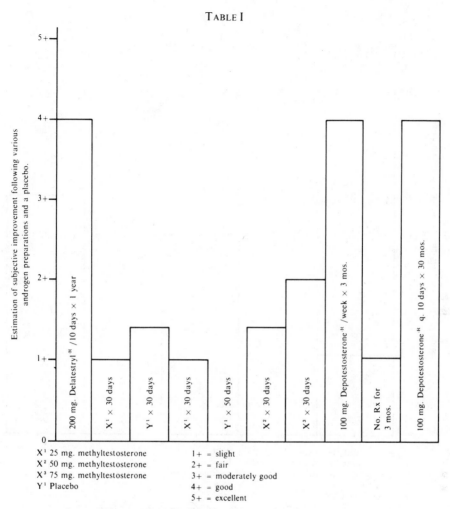

X¹ 25 mg. methyltestosterone   1+ = slight
X² 50 mg. methyltestosterone   2+ = fair
X³ 75 mg. methyltestosterone   3+ = moderately good
Y¹ Placebo   4+ = good
                                    5+ = excellent

Loss of Potentia and Personality Changes in a 50-Year-Old Man

(satyriasis) may be suffering from a compulsive neurosis. Excessive coitus in itself does not constitute satyriasis; the drive for sexual gratification must be so overpowering that it becomes the one dominant thought and purpose of the person's life, not unlike the animal in rutting season. The afflicted person seeks and demands gratification of his unbridled passion in a promiscuous, impulsive, and insatiable succession of sexual indulgences. The object of his attentions may be man, woman, child, or beast.

Some believe that satyriasis is symptomatic of a grave psychosis; others believe that it is a pathological condition of sexual hyperesthesia. Huhner (1942) considers satyriasis a clinical entity resulting from local, cerebral, or psychic causes. Genetic factors may be implicated. The recent finding of an XYY chromosomal pattern in markedly aggressive males with tendencies to commit sex crimes and murders adds another dimension to the problem. Therapy in the form of estrogens has been tried, but estrogens also stimulate nipple and breast development. However, ¼ to ½ tablet of an estrogen-progestogen contraceptive pill administered daily or every other day is effective in reducing the uncontrollable sex drive without too much breast stimulation. In Europe, cyproterone acetate, an antiandrogen, is being employed for this purpose, with promising results.

TABLE II

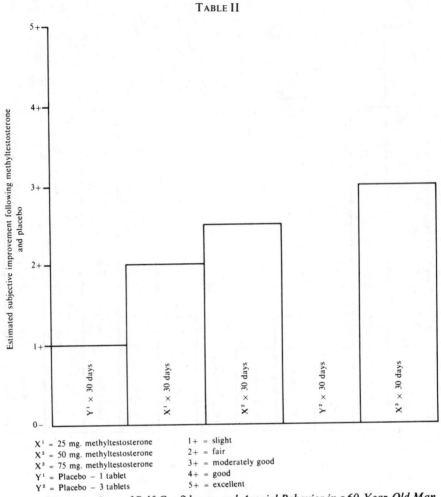

X¹ = 25 mg. methyltestosterone   1+ = slight
X² = 50 mg. methyltestosterone   2+ = fair
X³ = 75 mg. methyltestosterone   3+ = moderately good
Y¹ = Placebo − 1 tablet   4+ = good
Y² = Placebo − 3 tablets   5+ = excellent

Loss of Potentia, Loss of Self-Confidence, and Asocial Behavior in a 60-Year-Old Man

The inherent variables in response to suppressive hormonal therapy in males, particularly sex criminals, provide an insight into the manner in which motivation or resentment may modify effectiveness. For instance, if castration is performed by administration of female sex hormones or by orchidectomy, results will differ, depending on whether it was done to relieve the man of a tormenting urge or it was forced on him as a punishment for his crime. In the former case, there may be a rapid and welcome release from the uncontrollable drive; in the latter, there may be little abatement, and the obsession for sexual assault may even increase.

FEMALE ENDOCRINOLOGY

The girl-woman story is not too dissimilar from that of the boy-man epic except that the time clock initiates feminine body growth, development, and maturation of the organs of reproduction 1½ years earlier than in males, or at about 13½ years of age. A second variation occurs in the woman's fifth decade, when sex hormone production in the woman, in contrast to the man, comes to a virtual halt.

In the female, pubescence begins with the budding of the breasts, the appearance of sexual hair, and growth of the internal and external genitalia. As with males, great variation in age of onset of puberty exists, varying from 9 to 17 years of age. The most dramatic case of very early onset of menstruation (precocious puberty) thus far recorded is that of Lina Medina of Peru, who began menstruating at age 3, became pregnant at 4 years 10 months of age, and was delivered by cesarean section at 5 years 7 months. Menarche in the young girl frequently occurs without the release of an ovum during the early phase of this maturing process. Usually, several months to years elapse before optimal reproductive efficiency (monthly ovulation) is established.

Ovulatory menstruation. The estrogens produced by maturing follicles stimulate the proliferation of the endometrium. This proliferation is made possible by the FSH and luteinizing hormone released from the pituitary. The Graafian follicle chosen for ovulation releases an ovum as a result of a marked surge of luteinizing hormone and a minor surge in FSH secretion. The ruptured follicle is rapidly converted into a corpus luteum, and now the estrogen and progesterone produced by it arrest further proliferation and induce secretory changes of the endometrium, preparing it for nidation of the ovum. If fertilization does not take place, the corpus luteum regresses; the ovarian hormonal levels drop as a signal to the pituitary to begin a new cycle. When fertilization does occur, minute amounts of chorionic gonadotropin keep the corpus luteum viable to secrete the hormones requisite for maintenance and nutriment of the developing embryo while minimizing uterine contractions. The corpus luteum continues to function for about 3 months; thereafter, the placenta assumes hormonal responsibility for gestation. At a point in time not precisely established, the fetal endocrinological system begins to function as dictated by fetal chromosomal inheritance.

The human engineering is exquisitely timed and ordered. Within the miracle of the beginning of life, errors can and do happen. The wonder is not that some occur but that, from such a complex system, so many persons develop normally and gain entrance to this world, sound of cerebral and physical endowment, with capability for insuring the infinite continuation of human sexual func-

tioning and the perpetuation of the human race. Ovulation, menstruation, pregnancy, parturition, lactation, and the constantly changing physiological faces of Eve keep the endocrinological system of woman in a constantly changing state.

Disorders due to inborn error in the enzymes needed for hormonal synthesis and utilization by the fetus may result in many endocrinopathies, such as congenital adrenal hyperplasia, resulting in pseudohermaphroditism in the female and macrogenitosomia precox in the male. How this hormonal disorder affects the sexual behavior of the adult female is strikingly illustrated in Table III, which summarizes the hormonal, physical, and behavioral responses in three sisters suffering from this disorder. Today, early treatment with glucocorticoids from childhood onward prevents the virilization of the afflicted person by dampening excess androgen and pregnanetriol production by the adrenals. All the untoward effects of excess androgens can be thwarted or avoided, and normal feminine development, menstruation, and even conception may be expected.

Another example of an inborn enzymatic error interfering with proper progression of maleness is the insensitive androgen syndrome or the syndrome of feminizing testes. The estrogens but not the testosterone produced by the testes are effective in stimulating target tissues. The insensitivity to endogenous or even exogenous testosterone results from failure of the receptor sites to utilize this hormone. Such persons appear as well-breasted females, without pubic or axillary hair, acne or oily skin, and with a normal but blind vaginal canal (see Figure 13). The absence of a uterus and fallopian tubes indicates that the Y chromosome and the fetal androgens effectively caused regression of the Mullerian duct structures. Such persons are feminine in outlook, sexual behavior, and response, despite the absence of menstruation and the presence of testes.

Sex interest of the woman. Women frequently have heightened sex interest at the time of ovulation; others have heightened sex interest during the week prior to menstruation. However, many women find sexual relations during the latter part of the luteal phase

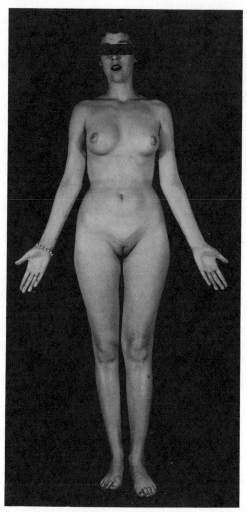

FIGURE 13. A phenotypic female with abdominal testes and an XY chromosomal karyotype. Note the excellent breast development and the absence of pubic hair. A normal blind vagina was present without clitoral enlargement.

less than appealing. Experiments indicate that the baboon behaves in a similar manner. The female baboon's sex skin is red during the peak of the follicular phase, a visual signal of sexual preparedness. The sex skin blanches during the luteal phase, and the female baboon fights off male advances. But the adult woman is not a baboon; she may have normal sex drives or suffer from frigidity or an overabundance of urges for sexual gratification—all independent of the phases of the menstrual cycle.

For many women, interest in sex wanes at the time of the menopause and thereafter. With the marked estrogen deficiency of the postmenopausal period, the vaginal mucosa thins and atrophies, and intercourse is frequently attended by dyspareunia. On the other hand, many women, freed from the fear of pregnancy, enjoy flight of fancy and fantasy; sex drive may increase—in some, to nymphomaniacal proportions.

Endocrine treatment of the menopausal woman. The everchanging activity of the ovarian hormones of the woman finally comes to a halt in the fifth or sixth decade; sometimes the activity ceases abruptly with cessation of menses and sometimes with much troublesome menstrual irregularity, emotional changes, and depressive reactions that veer from slight to intense. Just how many of the personality changes are due to psychogenic reasons, inability to conceive, and fear of expendability to the family is not a subject of concurrence among physicians. Nevertheless, most endocrinologists agree that estrogen depletion is attended by not only severe vasomotor disturbances and psychosexual upheaval but also a raft of metabolic changes. It is now considered good medical practice to correct the hormonal deficiency with estrogen replacement therapy. Many clinicians add a small amount of androgen to this regimen because it adds to well-being and rekindles waning sex drive. The menopausal woman often yearns for a last chance at sexual fulfillment. Adequate hormonal replacement therapy facilitates the attainment of her hopes.

Sexual inadequacy and sexual gluttony. Frigidity may be primary or secondary. Primary frigidity is regarded as psychogenic in origin and frequently necessitates the efforts of the endocrinologists, the psychiatrist, and a competent team of sex counsellors. Secondary frigidity usually results from manifold causes and is far easier to manage. After a woman has had several pregnancies, she may become sexually inadequate. Fatigued and bored by household chores, the glow of the sexual encounter fades. Her sexual response may be revived readily in most instances. Certainly, correction of environmental problems is of utmost importance, but, despite these untoward influences, testosterone administration restores the capacity for sexual gratifi-

TABLE III

Personality Disorder	Age (yrs)	Ur. Excretion (mg/24 hrs)		Response to Cortisone	Age at:			
		17-Keto steriods	Pregnanetriol		Menarche	Cessation of menses	Appearance of pubic hair	Onset of virilization
#1 Nymphomania with homosexual tendencies*	34	35.9 18.6	24.5	Good	10	18	4	18
#2 Religious fanatic	44	75.2	—	Good	11	15	?	15
#3 Alcoholic†	51	43.0	23.5	Refused Rx	0	—	9	?

*During cortisone therapy, libido returned to normal and homosexual tendencies disappeared.

†Surgery (abdominal) was performed at age 17. She had not menstruated before operation and did not menstruate afterward. (Possibly the operation was a panhysterectomy).

Reproduced from Greenblatt, R. B., and Leng, J.-J. Factors influencing sexual behavior. J. Am. Geriatrics, 20: 49, 1972, with permission of the authors.

Personality Changes and Biochemical Data—Three Sisters with Congenital Adrenal Hyperplasia.

TABLE IV

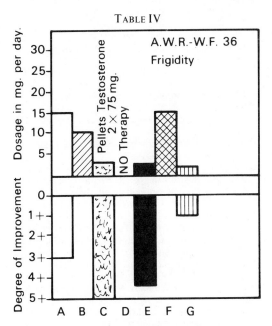

Comparative Effects of Various Hormones on Libido in a 36-Year-Old Woman Who Complained of Frigidity.

The responses (ranging from 1+ to 5+) are shown in the lower part of the graph. The sequence of hormone dosages is shown in the upper part of the graph. From left to right, *(A)* methyltestosterone, *(B)* placebo, *(C)* testosterone by implantation, *(D)* no therapy, *(E)* testosterone propionate subcutaneously, *(F)* progestogens, and *(G)* estrogens.

cation in almost all women who have once known libido. Estrogens alone are less effective but occasionally do as well as testosterone (see Table IV).

A third type of frigidity, amenable to gynecological therapy, is occasionally seen. This type of frigidity may be a defensive mechanism because of dyspareunia due to endometriosis; bacterial, protozoal, or fungal vaginitis; atrophic (senile) vaginitis; or scarring of the introitus. Correction of these conditions frequently overcomes the problem. Antibiotic and fungicidal agents cure the usual vaginal infections; the use of estrogens locally, orally, or parenterally restores the mucosa to a healthy state in women with senile vaginitis. Kraurosis vulvae, a moderately rare but advanced form of senile vaginitis, is complicated by atrophy of the perigenital skin, narrowing of the vaginal introitus, and unrelenting pruritus. The local use of ointments of hydrocortisone or its analogues and of estrogens, orally or parenterally, ameliorates the discomfort, assuages the pruritus, and tends to overcome the defensive frigidity. Women suffering from endometriosis frequently experience dyspareunia and avoid sexual relations. The use of progestational agents or testosterone may bring temporary relief.

Nymphomania may be regarded as a form of sexual gluttony. Some women cannot be sexually satisfied and continually search for sexual gratification. Some are unable to reach an orgasm, and they keep seeking yet another mate, believing that relief or the golden goal is just around the corner, but somehow the perfect mate is rarely found. Other women have multiple orgasms, but satiety escapes them, and they are in constant pursuit of more of the same. Progestational agents and tranquilizers, such as reserpine, may be employed over a prolonged period of time to dampen their sexual ardor and to provide them with an opportunity to readjust to their new and decreased needs for sexual activity. Nymphomania, encountered at any time from adulthood to late in the menopausal years, is rarely the result of excess hormones; in most, the condition is of psychogenic origin, although women who harbor a virilizing tumor of the adrenal or ovaries may have excessive sexual drives.

Conclusions

Human endocrinopathies have aided the endocrinologist to delineate the role of the gonads, chromosomal endowment, socio-environmental factors, and exogenous and endogenous hormones not only in sexual development but also in human sexuality. Human behavior involves all sorts of mental processes not subject to experimental control. Libido and sexual gratification may depend mostly on the proper amatory prelude or on the proper mechanics of coitus.

In human beings, the urge for sexual gratification may be sublimated and modified by learning, experience, and culture. The intrusion of so-called psychic factors merely modifies sexual arousal and responsiveness. Androgens appear to increase the responsiveness of certain central nervous system mechanisms to peripheral excitation; progestogens seem to diminish that response. In adults with established patterns of sexual behavior, androgens do not alter the form of the motor acts involved in courtship and mating; androgens merely increase susceptibility to sexual excitement. However, to judge from animal and nature's human experiments, excess androgens, particularly during the fetal life of the female, may alter sexual direction of libidinous drive later on in life.

Discussion in this section of the endocrinal

aspect of human sexuality represents one, though admittedly a very important one, of the many components that make up masculinity and femininity. Embryology, anatomy, physiology, and socio-cultural and psychogenic elements of manhood and womanhood are also involved. The clinician, confronting a patient with problems in sexual function and adequacy, would be like the Man of La Mancha, jousting with windmills, were he to attempt amelioration of the dysfunctional or diseased state without a careful search and intensive investigation not only into the endocrinal but also into the many facets of human sexuality as well.

REFERENCES

Brogger, A., and Aagenaes, O. The human Y chromosome and the etiology of true hermaphroditism. Hereditas, *53:* 231, 1965.

*Dmowski, W. P., and Greenblatt, R. B. Abnormal sexual differentiation. Am. Fam. Physician, *3:* 72, 1971.

Ferguson-Smith, M. A. X-Y chromosomal interchange in the aetiology of true hermaphroditism and of XX Klinefelter's syndrome. Lancet, *2:* 475, 1966.

*Greenblatt, R. B. Clinical aspects of sexual abnormalities in man. Recent Prog. Horm. Res., *14:* 335, 1958.

Greenblatt, R. B. Endocrinology of sexual behavior. Cincinnati J. Med., *40:* 49, 1959.

Greenblatt, R. B., editor. The ovary as a source of androgens in hirsutism. In *The Hirsute Female,* p. 179. Charles C Thomas, Springfield, Ill., 1963.

Greenblatt, R. B. In *Ovulation.* J. B. Lippincott, Philadelphia, 1966.

*Greenblatt, R. B., Mortara, F. Torpin, R. Sexual libido in the female. Am. J. Obstet. Gynecol., *44:* 658, 1942.

Greulich, W. W. Somatic and endocrine studies of puperal and adolescent boys. Monogr. Soc. Res. Child Dev., *7:* 26, 1942.

Huhner, M. *Sexual Disorders.* F. A. Davis, Philadelphia, 1942.

*Jost, A. Problems of fetal endocrinology: The gonadal and hypophyseal hormones. Rec. Progr. Hormone Res., *13:* 379, 1953.

Jost, A. "Maleness" is imposed upon a basically female fetus. Science Digest, *73:* 4, 1973.

*Masters, W. H., and Johnson, V. *Human Sexual Response.* Little, Brown, Boston, 1966.

Money, J. Problems in Sexual Development: Endocrinologic and Psychologic Aspects. N. Y. State J. Med., *63:* 2348, 1936.

*Shepard, R. S. *Human Physiology.* J. B. Lippincott, Philadelphia, 1971.

Wilkins, L. Masculinization of female fetus due to use of orally given progestins. J. A. M. A., *172:* 1028, 1960.

3.3

Brain Mechanisms of Elemental Sexual Functions

PAUL D. MacLEAN, M.D.

As opposed to neuroendocrinological aspects of sexual behavior, almost nothing was known until recent years about specific brain structures involved in such elemental sexual functions as penile erection and seminal discharge. Although the brain had been extensively explored by electrical stimulation, there was hardly a reference to the present topic. In his classical treatise of 1909 von Bechterew referred to a finding by Pussep that electrical stimulation of the anterior thalamus in dogs resulted in penile erection.

The present author undertook work on this problem in connection with experiments suggested by his elaboration on the Papez theory of brain mechanisms of emotion (Papez, 1937; MacLean, 1949). Because of the highly organized forms of behavior required for the preservation and procreation of the species, it seemed probable that systematic exploration of the forebrain by electrical stimulation might reveal structures involved in elemental, and perhaps more complex, forms of sexual behavior.

Relevance of Animal Experimentation

Since animal experimentation provides us our only systematic knowledge of brain functions, we must consider the justification of the use of such material for drawing inferences about the workings of the human brain. In this section, for example, we not only deal with the question of the cerebral representation of elemental sexual functions, but also suggest the relevance of the findings to oral-genital relationships in feeding, aggressive, and other behavior of animals and man. At the molecular or cellular levels, discoveries in animals are readily acknowledged as applicable to human biology. In the field of psychiatry, neurochemical and neuropharmacological discoveries in animals have radically changed the treatment of certain neuropsychiatric disorders. But somewhat ironically, many people refuse to admit that behavioral and neurological observations on animals have human relevance. This attitude is perhaps engendered by a failure to realize that in its evolution the human brain expands in hierarchic fashion along the lines of three basic patterns, which in Figure 1 are labeled reptilian, paleomammalian, and neomammalian. Markedly different in chemistry and structure, and in an evolutionary sense countless generations apart, the three cerebrotypes constitute, so to speak, three brains in one, a *triune* brain (MacLean, 1970, 1973c). Because of the respective similarities in chemistry and anatomical organization of the three basic evolutionary formations, the comparative experimental approach can give important leads in regard to primal neural functions of the human brain.

The following review starts with the findings on penile erection, presenting them with respect to each of the 3 main evolutionary formations. Then the results are given pertaining to somatosensory aspects of genital function and seminal discharge. Implications of the work in regard to oral-genital behavior are discussed. Finally, in describing ablation experiments on the mammalian counterpart of the reptilian brain, it is pointed out that in social communication genital manifestations have other than purely sexual significance.

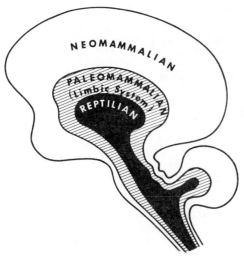

FIGURE 1. Diagram of the hierarchy of the three basic cerebrotypes that provide the anatomical and chemical "blueprints" for the evolution and growth of the human brain. (From MacLean, P. D. The brain in relation to empathy and medical education. J. Nerv. Ment. Dis., *144:* 374, 1967.)

METHODS

Since the direct evidence of cerebral representation of sexual functions is largely based on experiments on squirrel monkeys, a brief description is given of the methods. In order to avoid the depressant effects of anesthesia, animals were prepared for chronic experimentation under waking conditions. A stereotaxic platform with electrode guides was chronically fixed above the scalp on four screws cemented in the skull (Mac-Lean, 1957). This device avoided open surgery at the time of an experiment and provided a closed system for millimeter by millimeter exploration of the brain with stimulating and recording electrodes while the monkey sat in a special chair. During an experiment animals were given their favorite forms of nourishment and at the end of each session were returned to their home cages. For the reasons explained in the original papers, stimulation was performed with a wide range of stimulus parameters. The magnitude of genital tumescence was graded on a scale of ± to 5+. A positive response was characterized as one that could be obtained repeatedly at a regular latency. When stimulation elicited seminal discharge, the presence of spermatazoa was confirmed by microscopic examination. Animals were sacrificed after exploring 8 to 10 tracks during a period of about 2 months. The location of all points of stimulation

was confirmed by histological examination of the brain.

Neocortex and Related Structures

In all mammalian forms, the neomammalian formation consists of the most highly evolved form of cortex called neocortex and structures of the brain stem with which it is primarily connected. In operations for treatment of epileptic disorders, Penfield stimulated the greater part of the human neocortex, as well as limbic cortex of the insulotemporal region, but never elicited signs or symptoms of a sexual nature (Penfield and Jasper, 1954). Woolsey et al. (1942) showed in the macaque that tactile stimulation evoked potentials in the parietal cortex on the medial wall of the hemisphere. In the squirrel monkey, MacLean and co-workers (MacLean and Ploog, 1962; Dua and MacLean, 1964) explored all of the medial frontal and parietal neocortex. As illustrated in Figure 2,

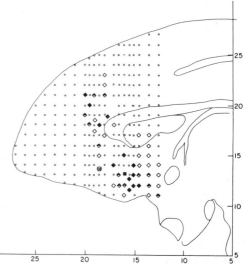

FIGURE 2. Diagram of medial frontal lobe of squirrel monkey with *diamond* and *square* symbols indicating loci at which electrical stimulation resulted in penile erection. *Squares* give added information that stimulation was followed by hippocampal afterdischarges. *White, half black,* and *solid black* symbols refer, respectively, to gradations of erection of 1+, 2 to 3+, and 4 to 5+. Rows of *small circles* overlie regions explored and found negative. Marginal scales in millimeters give distances forward and above zero axis of stereotaxic atlas. (From Dua, S., and MacLean, P. D. Localization for penile erection in medial frontal lobe. Am J. Physiol., *207:* 1425, 1964.)

stimulation of the transitional region between medial frontal cortex and limbic cortex of the anterior cingulate gyrus evoked full erection (Dua and MacLean, 1964). In this respect it is significant that stimulation within the medial part of the cerebral peduncles also elicited erection (see below). The somatomotor areas of the lateral convexity were not explored, but stimulation of the middle segment of the cerebral peduncle which contains efferent fibers from that region failed to induce erection.

Limbic System

In all existing mammals, most of the phylogenetically old cortex is contained in a large convolution which Broca (1878) called the great limbic lobe because it surrounds the brain stem. In 1952, the term "limbic system" (MacLean, 1952) was suggested as a designation for the limbic cortex and structures of the brain with which it has primary connections. This anatomically and functionally integrated system represents an inheritance from paleomammalian forms. In the last 30 years, evidence has accumulated that the limbic system derives information in terms of emotional feelings that guide behavior required for self-preservation and the preservation of the species (MacLean, 1962, 1973c).

In the discussion it helps to visualize oral-genital relationships if the functions of the limbic system are described with respect to the three main subdivisions of the limbic system shown in Figure 3. The figure illustrates that the limbic lobe has the shape of a ring and that the medial forebrain bundle is a major line of communicaton between the limbic cortex and structures of the brain stem. In contrast to the neocortex, the limbic cortex has numerous connections with the hypothalamus which plays a major role in integrating the performance of brain mechanisms involved in self-preservation and the preservation of the species. It can be noted that the two upper branches of the medial forebrain meet with descending fibers from the olfactory bulb and feed into the lower and upper halves of the ring through (1) the amygdala and (2) the septum. In contrast, the third large pathway branches lower down

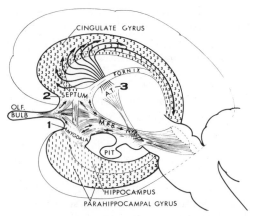

FIGURE 3. Diagram of three main corticosubcortical subdivisions of the limbic system discussed with respect to genital and oral functions. *HYP*, hypothalamus; *M.F.B.*, medial forebrain bundle; *OLF.*, olfactory; *PIT*, pituitary. (Based on MacLean, P. D. Contrasting functions of limbic and neocortical systems of the brain and their relevance to psychophysiological aspects of medicine. Am. J. Med., *25:* 611, 1958.)

from the hypothalamus and bypasses the olfactory apparatus.

Clinical and experimental findings have indicated that the lower part of the ring (including parts of the frontal, insular, temporal, and hippocampal cortex) is concerned with feelings and behavior that ensure self-preservation. Neural excitation in this circuit results in responses related to feeding, fighting, and self-protection.

In 1939, Klüver and Bucy reported that following temporal lobe excisions including this part of the brain, wild monkeys seemed to become tame and engaged in bizarre sexual behavior. The latter finding suggested the release of other parts of the brain involved in sexual functions. Such an assumption is supported by findings on the two other main limbic subdivisions. In preliminary experiments it was found that chemical or electrical stimulation of parts of the septal division in male cats resulted in behavior suggestive of feline courtship, and, in some instances, penile erection (MacLean, 1957). Since then the author and co-workers have stimulated virtually all of the limbic system of squirrel monkeys except the cortex in the orbitoinsular region.

The structures and pathways of the limbic

system involved in penile erection are schematically shown in Figure 4. Stimulation of the lower part of the septum and the contiguous medial preoptic area elicited full erection (MacLean and Ploog, 1962). In a number of instances, stimulation within the dorsal psalterium or fimbria of the hippocampus resulted in recruitment of hippocampal potentials and penile erection (MacLean et al., 1961). Additional evidence of the role of the hippocampus in sexual functions is described below.

In the third subdivision of the limbic system positive loci for erection were found in the mammillary bodies, along the course of the mammillothalamic tract, in the anterior thalamus, and in the pregenual cingulate and subcallosal cortex which are known to receive projections from the anterior thalamic nuclei (see Figure 2). The third subdivision articulates with the part of the medial dorsal nucleus that projects to the posterior part of the gyrus rectus. Stimulation at loci in either of these structures was highly effective in eliciting penile erection.

As diagrammed in Figure 4, the results of stimulation indicated that the main effector pathway from the medial septopreoptic

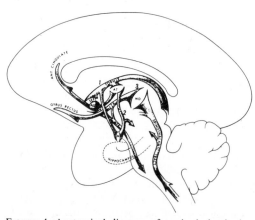

FIGURE 4. Anatomical diagram of cerebral circuits involved in elemental sexual functions. *AC,* anterior commissure; *AT,* anterior thalamic nuclei; *ITP,* inferior thalamic peduncle; *M,* mammillary bodies; *MD,* medial dorsal nucleus; *MFB,* medial forebrain bundle; *MT,* mammillothalamic tract; *SEPT,* septum. (From MacLean, P. D. New findings relevant to the evolution of psychosexual functions of the brain. J. Nerv. Ment. Dis., *135:* 289, 1962.)

region follows the medial forebrain bundle, while that from the midline thalamus runs in the inferior thalamic peduncle before joining the medial forebrain bundle. In the macaque, Showers (1959) found evidence of cingulate projections passing through the medial part of the cerebral peduncle and distributing to the ventral tegmental area and medial part of the substantia nigra. Since penile erection was elicited by stimulation of these same structures, the effector fibers from the pregenual cingulate and medial frontal cortex may be located in the medial part of the internal capsule and cerebral peduncle.

Traced along the medial forebrain bundle to the ventral tegmental area, the main effector pathway turns abruptly toward the lateral part of the substantia nigra, then descends through the ventrolateral part of the pons, and enters the medulla near the exit of the sixth nerve and lateral to the pyramids.

Hippocampal Influences

The hippocampus contains the so-called archicortex of the limbic lobe. Stimulation at positive points in the pregenual cingulate cortex and subcallosal region resulted in a build-up of high voltage potentials in the hippocampus that coincided with the appearance of penile erection (Dua and MacLean, 1964). Stimulation at positive sites in the septum and anterior thalamus commonly led to the development of self-sustained hippocampal afterdischarges associated with throbbing of the penis and an increase in size of the erection (MacLean and Ploog, 1962). Afterward spiking activity might appear in the hippocampus and persist for periods up to 10 minutes, during which time there would be waxing and waning of penile erection. In view of the known hippocampal projections to the septum and anterior thalamus, these findings suggested that the hippocampus exerts a modulatory influence on genital tumescence. Recently, it was shown in the squirrel monkey that hippocampal volleys elicit discharges of single units in the septum and the contiguous parts of the medial preoptic area (Poletti et al., 1973). It was also shown anatomically for the first time in a primate that the fornix projects to the medial preoptic region. As mentioned above, stimulation in the medial preoptic region elicits full erection. In recent years, it has been found that the medial septo-preoptic region plays an important role in sexual differentiation of some rodents and that it exerts a regulatory influence on the tonic and cyclic secretion of gonadotropin, respectively, in the male and female (see Gorski (1971), for review). Therefore, it seems likely that, in addition to its influence on genital function, the hippocampus may also affect the regulation of the release of gonadotropin. In view of limbic system involvement in emotional behavior, these findings suggest neural mechanisms by which either the agreeable or disagreeable aspects of affective experience could influence genital and gonadal function.

The Striatal Complex

The major counterpart of the reptilian forebrain in mammals is represented by the corpus striatum (caudate and putamen) and globus pallidus. The corpus striatum projects to the pallidum, as well as to the substantia nigra, which in turn projects back to the striatum by a recently discovered dopaminergic system. The medial segment of the globus pallidus projects principally to the ventral anterior, lateral ventral, and centromedian nuclei of the thalamus and to the peduncolopontine nucleus of the midbrain (Nauta and Mehler, 1966). The lateral segment projects to the subthalamic nucleus which projects back to the medial segment. There continues to be uncertainty about pallidal connections with the hypothalamus.

The author has not systematically explored the striatal complex, but stimulation at many points within the caudate, putamen, and globus pallidus elicited no genital responses. A paper by Robinson and Mishkin (1968) shows a few loci in the putamen of the macaque at which stimulation elicited partial erection. MacLean and Ploog (1962) found strongly positive loci within parts of the substantia nigra; the location of the electrodes was such that the current could have spread to excite the descending effector pathway described above.

Robinson and Mishkin (1968) have confirmed in the macaque most of the localizations for penile erection that have been described in the squirrel monkey. Ploog and co-workers (Maurus et al., 1965) have reported that the representation for clitoral tumescence in the upper brain stem of the female squirrel monkey is similar to that for penile erection in the male. The original papers must be consulted for other manifestations such as vocalization, urination, cardiac changes, and so forth, that may at times be elicited in conjunction with penile erection.

Genital Sensation and Seminal Discharge

As already noted, stimulation at some sites resulted in throbbing penile erection that persisted for many seconds after the termination of the stimulus. Despite the orgastic appearance, ejaculation was never observed under these conditions. Seminal discharge, sometimes preceding erection, was elicited only in those cases in which the electrodes proved upon reconstruction to lie along the course of the spinothalamic pathway (Figure 4) and its ancient medial ramifications into the caudal intralaminar region of the thalamus (MacLean et al., 1963). Characteristically, as the electrode approached one of these points, the monkey would begin to scratch in the region of the chest or abdomen and then, with the electrode at the critical locus, scratch the genitalia. It was shown, however, that emission containing motile sperm could occur independently of scratching. The thalamic structures involved in these manifestations lie in close relationship to the part of the midline thalamus involved in penile erection. These experiments provide a first inkling of pathways and brain structures involved in sensorimotor aspects of elemental sexual functions.

Robinson and Mishkin (1966) reported a single case of a macaque that ejaculated following self-stimulation through an electrode in the medial preoptic area. According to Herberg (1963), stimulation in the posterior hypothalamus of rats may induce ejaculation.

Oral-Genital Relationship in Feeding

In regard to oral-genital relationships, it is significant that slow frequency stimulation of the amygdala may elicit first either facial or alimentary responses such as biting, chewing, and salivation followed 30 or more seconds later by penile erection (MacLean, 1962). Such a behavioral sequence may be owing to recruitment of neural activity in the septum, mediodorsal nucleus, and hypothalamus with which the amygdala is reciprocally connected. These observations give insight into mechanisms underlying erection seen in human infants and animals during feeding or attempts to feed.

In the neocortex, the representation of the head and tail are at opposite poles, whereas in the limbic lobe structures involved in oral and genital function are in close proximity and intimately connected. The close relationship between oral and genital functions seems attributable to the olfactory sense, which dating far back in evolution is involved in both feeding and mating.

Orosexual Factors in Aggression

The above findings are also relevant to orosexual factors in aggressive and combative behavior. In Figure 5 the shield and sword of Mars are used to indicate, respectively, the pathways from the amygdala and septum that are involved in oral and genital functions.

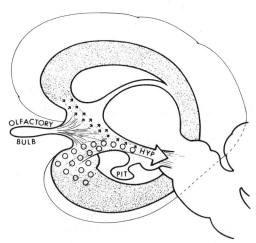

FIGURE 5. Diagram of medial view of squirrel monkey's brain illustrating convergence in hypothalamus of amygdala and septal pathways involved in oral (O) and genital (7374) functions. *PIT,* pituitary; *HYP,* hypothalamus. Adapted from MacLean, P. D. Mao and his animal brains. Mod. Med., *32:* 95, 1964.)

Traced caudally, the symbols show a reconstitution of the warrior Mars in a region which Hess and Brügger (1943) proved to be involved in the expression of angry and defensive behavior. In the squirrel monkey, stimulation within a narrow compass of this region elicits penile erection, angry behavior, biting, and chewing (MacLean and Ploog, 1962; MacLean et al., 1963). Since fighting is a preliminary to both feeding and mating, the same mechanisms for combat appear to be involved in each situation. Elsewhere the author has discussed these findings with respect to Freud's "Three Contributions to the Theory of Sex," in which he comments on the relationship between sexual and agonistic behavior (MacLean, 1962).

Penile Erection in Aggressive and Other Behavior

During the bucking and locking of horns while defending its territory, called a lek, the Uganda kob often develops penile erection (Buechner et al., 1966). The same autonomic manifestation may be seen in the chimpanzee during its raucous display (J. Van Lawick-Goodall, personal communication). The squirrel monkey, which the present author has extensively studied, provides an excellent example of multiple ways in which the genital organ may be used in social communication. This species variously uses a genital display in a show of aggression, courtship, and greeting. After a description of the display, a brief summary is given of ablation experiments showing that the striatal complex plays a basic role in its performance. These results are of great interest because experimentation over a period of 150 years has failed to reveal the functions of the corpus striatum and globus pallidus. The traditional view that these structures have a purely motor function is out of harmony with the finding that large bilateral lesions (provided there is no injury of the internal capsule) may result in no apparent motor deficit.

In the communal situation, the displaying monkey vocalizes, spreads one thigh, and directs the fully erect penis toward the head or chest of the other animal (MacLean, 1962; Ploog and MacLean, 1963). It is of comparative interest that the display may involve grinding of the teeth, recalling that bruxism and penile erection have been observed in man during rapid eye movement sleep correlated with dreaming (Fisher et al., 1965). If a new male is introduced into an established colony of squirrel monkeys, all the male monkeys approach it and display, and if the stranger does not remain quiet with its head bowed, it will be viciously attacked. Showing a remarkable parallel to reptiles and some lower forms, the male squirrel monkey displays to a female during courtship in the same manner as in an aggressive encounter with other males.

A variation of the display is also used as a form of greeting, and the author has described one variety of squirrel monkey that will display to its reflection in a mirror (MacLean, 1964). The mirror display is so predictable that it has been formalized as a test in an investigation attempting to identify structures involved in genetically constituted, species-typical behavior. Other manifestations recorded in the display test are urination, vocalization, "thigh spread," and scratching.

In observations on more than 90 animals, it has been found that large bilateral lesions in many structures (including neocortical and limbic structures and the superior colliculus) may have only a transient or no effect on the display. It was shown, however, in a study of 14 subjects that following large bilateral lesions of the globus pallidus monkeys no longer were inclined to display (MacLean, 1972, 1973a, 1973b). Yet these animals were capable of defending themselves, and even overpowering the dominant animal, when introduced into an established colony of squirrel monkeys. It has since been found that small bilateral lesions of pallidal projections in the ansa lenticularis may interfere with the somatic components of the display whereas small lesions of the medial forebrain bundle affect the genital response.

The foregoing findings support the hypothesis that the striatal complex provides a neural repository for species-typical forms of behavior (MacLean, 1972, 1973a, 1973b).

Although squirrel monkeys in the wild are not territorial in the strict sense, they will, as mentioned above, defend their enclosure against the intrusion of strange animals. Wickler has described "sentinel" monkeys in troops of baboons and green monkeys that sit at lookout sites with their thighs spread and a display of partial erection while the troop feeds or naps (1966). He regard this display as an optical marker of boundaries, warning other animals not to intrude. In mythology the phallus of such gods as Pan, Priapus, Amon, and Min is symbolic both in regard to fertility and territorial protection. Phallic representations, for example, used to be placed at various vantage places as a protection against robbers. The god Pan (to whom we owe the word panic) found amusement in terrifying "travelers" (i.e., strangers, intruders). In primitive cultures in different parts of the world the territorial aggressive implications of penile display are illustrated by house guards—stone monuments showing an erect phallus—used to mark territorial boundaries. It would seem "as though a visual, urogenital symbol is used as a substitute for olfactory, urinary, territorial markings of animals" that possess an acute olfactory sense (MacLean, 1973a).

Gajdusek (1970) has described a genital display in New Guinea tribes suggestive of the display in squirrel monkeys, while I. Eibl-Eibesfeldt (1971) has presented cinemographic documentation of adolescent children in a primitive tribe elsewhere who display in a self-assertive manner while everting one thigh. These recent observations raise again the following question: It is possible that primitive man may have learned that by covering himself he reduced the unpleasant social tensions arising from the archaic impulse to display and that this, rather than modesty, has led to the civilizing influence of clothing (MacLean, 1962).

Possible Altruistic Implications

In the evolution of primates, the septum of the second limbic subdivision illustrated in Figure 3 shows relatively little change compared with the thalamic structures connected with the third division that undergo progressive development and reach their greatest size in man. The lemur, which represents a primitive primate with a well developed septum, has a greeting display in which the male and female mutually lick the anogenital region (Andrew, 1964). This behavior recalls what was said earlier about the close functional relationship of the olfactory apparatus with the amygdala and septum. In contrast, the display of the squirrel monkey, which occupies an intermediate position on the phylogenetic scale of primates, involves primarily visual communication. It has been suggested that the great development of the third subdivision of the limbic system in higher primates and man may reflect a shifting in emphasis from olfactory to visual factors in socio-sexual behavior (MacLean, 1962). This subdivision articulates with the medial dorsal nucleus, the phylogenetically old and new parts of which project to the orbitofrontal cortex. The representation of genital function in these neural circuits has already been described above. It is of further significance in regard to socio-sexual behavior that after large lesions of the medial dorsal nucleus the squirrel monkey no longer shows an inclination to display (MacLean, 1973c). There is some experimental evidence that the cingulate gyrus is involved in maternal behavior (Stamm, 1955; Slotnick, 1967).

On the basis of clinical evidence, it is believed that the functions of the prefrontal neocortex include the capacity for both foresight and insight involved in planning for the welfare and preservation of the species. It is said that some individuals are vaguely aware of tingling or partial tumescence in the genital region when experiencing altruistic feelings or engaging in an altruistic activity. In the hierarchical organization of the phylogenetically old and new structures under consideration, there would appear to be a neural substrate for creating a span between a most elemental sexual feeling and the highest level of altruistic sentiments.

REFERENCES

Andrew, R. J. The displays of the primates. In *Evolutionar and Genetic Biology of Primates*, J. Buettner-Janusch, editor, vol. 2. Academic Press, New York, 1964.

Broca, P. Anatomie comparée des circonvolutions cérébrales. Le grand lobe limbique et la scissure limbique dans la série des mammiferes. Rev. Anthropol., *1:* 385, 1873.

Buechner, H. K., Morrison, J. A., and Leuthold, W. Reproduction in Uganda kob with special reference to behavior. In *Comparative Biology of Reproduction in Mammals,* J. W. Rowlands, editor. Academic Press, New York, 1966.

Dua, S., and MacLean, P. D. Localization for penile erection in medial frontal lobe. Am. J. Physiol., *207:* 1425, 1964.

Fisher, C., Gross, J., and Zuch, J. Cycle of penile erection synchronous with dreaming (REM) sleep. Arch. Gen. Psychiatry, *12:* 29, 1965.

Gajdusek, D. C. Physiological and psychological characteristics of Stone Age man. Symposium on biological bases of human behavior, California Institute of Technology, Pasadena, March, 1970. Eng. Sci., *33:* 26, 1970.

Gorski, R. A. Sexual differentiation of the hypothalamus. In *The Neuroendocrinology of Human Reproduction,* H. C. Mack, editor. Charles C Thomas, Springfield, Ill., 1971.

Herberg, L. J. Seminal ejaculation following positively reinforcing electrical stimulation of the rat hypothalamus. J. Comp. Physiol. Psychol., *56:* 679, 1963.

Hess, W. R., and Brügger, M. Das subkortikale Zentrum der affektiven Abwehrreaktion. Helv. Physiol. Pharmacol. Acta, *1:* 33, 1943.

Klüver, H., and Bucy, P. C. Preliminary analysis of functions of the temporal lobes in monkeys. Arch. Neurol. Psychiatry, *42:* 979, 1939.

MacLean, P. D. Psychosomatic disease and the "visceral brain": Recent developments bearing on the Papez theory of emotion. Psychosom. Med., *11:* 338, 1949.

MacLean, P. D. Some psychiatric implications of physiological studies on frontotemporal portion of limbic system (visceral brain). Electroencephalogr. Clin. Neurophysiol., *4:* 407, 1952.

MacLean, P. D. Chemical and electrical stimulation of hippocampus in unrestrained animals. II. Behavioral findings. Am. Med. Assoc. Arch. Neurol. Psychiatry, *78:* 128, 1957.

MacLean, P. D. New findings relevant to the evolution of psychosexual functions of the brain. J. Nerv. Ment. Dis., *135:* 289, 1962.

MacLean, P. D. Mirror display in the squirrel monkey, Saimiri sciureus. Science, *146:* 950, 1964.

*MacLean, P. D. A chronically fixed stereotaxic device for intercerebral exploration with macro and micro electrodes. Electroencepalogr. Clin. Neurophysiol. *22:* 180, 1967.

MacLean, P. D. The triune brain, emotion and scientific bias. In *The Neurosciences Second Study Program,* F. O. Schmitt, editor. Rockefeller University Press, New York, 1970.

MacLean, P. D. Cerebral evolution and emotional processes: New findings on the striatal complex. Ann. N.Y. Acad. Sci., *193:* 137, 1972.

MacLean, P. D. Effects of pallidal lesions on species-typical display behavior of squirrel monkey. Fed. Proc., *32:* 384, 1973a.

MacLean, P. D. New findings on brain function and sociosexual behavior. In *Contemporary Sexual Behavior: Critical Issues in the 1970's,* J. Zubin and J.

Money, editors. The Johns Hopkins University Press, Baltimore, 1973b.

MacLean, P. D. A triune concept of the brain and behavior. Lecture I: Man's reptilian and limbic inheritance. Lecture II: Man's limbic brain and the psychoses. Lecture III: New trends in man's evolution. In *The Hincks Memorial Lectures,* T. Boag and D. Campbell, editors. University of Toronto Press, Toronto, 1973c.

MacLean, P. D., Denniston, R. H., and Dua, S. Further studies on cerebral representation of penile erection: Caudal thalamus, midbrain, and pons. J. Neurophysiol., *26:* 273, 1963.

MacLean, P. D., Denniston, R. H., Dua, S., and Ploog, D. W. Hippocampal changes with brain stimulation eliciting penile erection. In *Physiologie de l'hippocampe.* Colloq. Int. Cent. Natl. Rech. Sci., *107:* 491, 1962.

MacLean, P. D., Dua, S., and Denniston, R. H. Cerebral localization for scratching and seminal discharge. Arch. Neurol., *9:* 485, 1963.

MacLean, P. D., and Ploog, D. W. Cerebral representation of penile erection. J. Neurophysiol., *25:* 29, 1962.

Maurus, M., Mitra, J., and Ploog, D. Cerebral representation of the clitoris in ovariectomized squirrel monkeys. Exp. Neurology, *13:* 283, 1965.

Nauta, W. J. H., and Mehler, W. R. Projections of the lentiform nucleus in the monkey. Brain Res., *1:* 3, 1966.

Papez, J. W. A proposed mechanism of emotion. Arch. Neurol. Psychiatry, *38:* 725, 1937.

Penfield, W., and Jasper, H. *Epilepsy and the Functional Anatomy of the Human Brain.* Little, Brown, Boston, 1954.

Ploog, D., Hopf, S., and Winter, P. Ontogenese des Verhaltens von Totenkopf-Affen (Saimiri sciureus). Psychol. Forsch., *31:* 1, 1967.

Ploog, D. W., and MacLean, P. D. Display of penile erection in squirrel monkey (Saimiri sciureus). Anim. Behav., *11:* 32, 1963.

Poletti, C. E., Kinnard, M. A., and MacLean, P. D. Hippocampal influence on unit activity of hypothalamus, preoptic region, and basal forebrain in awake, sitting squirrel monkeys. J. Neurophysiol., *36:* 308, 1973.

Robinson, B. W., and Mishkin, M. Ejaculation evoked by stimulation of the preoptic area in monkey. Physiol. Behav., *1:* 269, 1966.

Robinson, B. W., and Mishkin, M. Penile erection evoked from forebrain structures in *Macaca mulatta.* Arch. Neurol., *19:* 184, 1968.

Showers, M. J. C. The cingulate gyrus: Additional motor area and cortical autonomic regulator. J. Comp. Neurol., *112:* 231, 1959.

*Slotnick, B. M. Disturbance of maternal behavior in the cat following lesions of the cingulate cortex. Behavior, *24:* 204, 1967.

*Stamm, J. S. The function of the median cerebral cortex in maternal behavior of rats. J. Comp. Physiol. Psychol., *48:* 347, 1955.

von Bechterew, W. *Die Funktionen der Nervencentra,* vols. 1, 2, and 3. Gustav Fischer, Jena, 1909-1911.

Wickler, W. von. Ursprung und biologische Deutung des Genitalpräsentierens männlicher Primaten. Z. Tierpsychol., *23:* 422, 1966.

Woolsey, C. N., Marshall, W. H., and Bard, P. Representation of cutaneous tactile sensibility in the cerebral cortex of the monkey as indicated by evoked potentials. Bull. Hopkins Hosp., *70:* 399, 1942.

chapter 4 Sexual Development

4.1 Stages of Sexual Development

**DANIEL OFFER, M.D., and
WILLIAM SIMON, Ph.D.**

Introduction

Sexual behavior and sexual development are varied and multifaceted topics. Behavior is the end product of interacting systems that change over time. The interacting systems are biopsychosocial. Development depends on constitutional factors, environmental influences, and the accidental, including the traumatic. As researchers have been able to study human sexuality directly, they have been able to better understand its place within the context of general personality functioning and development.

Freud

No discussion of the stages of sexual development in men and women can be undertaken without reviewing Freud's momentous contribution to the understanding of human sexuality. Freud was basically a clinician who built his theory on the patients he treated. Beginning his work in the intellectual context of Victorian Europe, he discovered that unconscious forces were operating in his patients. Many of these patients were suffering from conflicts rooted

in sexual development. When these conflicts could be understood and brought to the awareness of the patient, the conflicts could be dealt with, and the patient was helped, if not cured. Although Freud's initial writings concerning the role of sexuality in human life were ignored or ridiculed, he was able to document his clinical work. Freud's intellectual honesty, his courage, and the strength of his clear and convincing writing slowly began influencing the scientific community. His theories could no longer be ignored, and they ushered in a new era in the understanding of human sexual behavior.

Libido was defined by Freud in 1905 (1953) as a quantitative force that measures the intensity of the sexual drives. This instinct represents the psychic counterpart of the biological (hormonal) sources and originates from within the person. It can, of course, be stimulated by outside forces. Adults have, in general, had no problems in analyzing and measuring the sexual pressures intricately interwoven with the psychological and social aspects of living. In "Three Essays on the Theory of Sexuality," Freud was able to argue persuasively that the libido theory is just as applicable to children. They derive protoerotic pleasure in specific ways from given experiences or conditions. Freud called this "infantile sexuality." It is qualitatively different from adult sexuality. The similarity is in the fact that the source of pain and pleasure, as well as the response to stimuli, gives rise to a specific set of responses. Freud did not say that the kind of feelings associated with sexuality in the child are fully analogous to the adult's sexual feelings and impulses. He did want to stress, however, that sexual feelings do exist in the child; although they may have a different meaning for the child, they are intricately related to sexual matters. Freud stressed the necessity of studying and understanding the manifestation of sexuality throughout the life cycle—from the inception of life through the final years.

The three essential characteristics of infantile sexuality are these: (1) At its origin, it attaches itself to one of the vital somatic functions. (2) It has as yet no sexual object; therefore it is autoerotic. (3) The sexual aim is dominated sequentially by erotogenic zones. Because of these characteristics, a child goes through different stages in his psychosexual development—oral phase, anal phase, phallic phase, and genital phase.

During the genital stage of development, the Oedipus complex is initially resolved. With the passing of the Oedipus complex, the child has developed an independent, internalized superego. He or she now has a relatively well functioning ego that is able to keep the id drives in check. The child can go to school and learn, study, and play. The important defense of sublimation is beginning to develop. As the child goes through latency, sexual feelings, according to Freud, are held to a minimum. With the onset of puberty, the sexual drives re-emerge with considerable strength, threatening the relatively weak ego. The Oedipus complex re-emerges for the second and final time; the adolescent forever relinquishes the sexual attachment to the parent of the opposite sex and finds his sexual partner among peers, outside the home environment.

These stages can be observed by studying children. Freud and other psychoanalysts have attempted to correlate adult psychopathology to an unsuccessful resolution of one or more of these phases. Not much solid information has been accumulated to support this point of view. The meaning of those stages to adult feelings and behavior remains, at best, unclear.

Freud stressed, in addition, that the bedrock of bisexuality is the biological substrate to which all later psychosexual and sociosexual developments are related. His theory does, therefore, leave much room for environmental influences on the development of the sexual potential in men and women. The development of neurotic conflicts results, to a large extent, from the libido's inability to obtain satisfaction along normal developmental lines. Freud strongly believed that sexual deviancy originates from a combination of three factors: (1) constitutional-biological, (2) accidental-environmental, and (3) internal-unconscious. In other words, sexual conflicts and neurotic conflicts are, at least in part, propelled by psychological mechanisms within the person himself.

A summary of Freud's sexual theory would be incomplete without at least a passing reference to the concepts of penis envy and castration anxiety. Few psychoanalytic theories have raised such a furor as these concepts. Briefly stated, Freud's basic assumption was that the male sex was the superior and more intelligent and creative one. Hence, he believed that little girls feel that they are injured because they lack a penis. Similarly, little boys get intense castration anxiety when they observe that they have something that little girls do not possess. Much libido is cathected by children onto this early factual observation, leading, according to Freud, to many subsequent psychological developments in males and females. Much ink has been spilled over the past few years of this subject.

The question remains: How and to what extent does it affect the sexual development of boys and girls? It is the authors' opinion that the extent of its psychological impact on children depends, to a large degree, on the cultural values of the family and the society into which the child is born. Freud, no doubt, was reflecting the Victorian point of view. How important is the discovery of the difference in the anatomy of genitals in himself or herself and the other sex? Is the concept of penis envy meaningless? Is sexuality viewed today differently from the way it was viewed 70 years ago?

Closely tied to the concept of penis envy is Freud's statement concerning the different kinds of orgasm. It was Freud's opinion that as long as the girl or woman retains her wish for a penis, she focuses on her clitoris, the "damaged penis." Hence, clitoral orgasm in the woman is not as healthy or as developmentally mature as vaginal orgasm. It is only when the woman has given up her wish for a penis and settled for her feminine role function—to bear children—that a significant psychic shift can take place. The shift is from cathecting or fixating onto the clitoris to cathecting the reproductive female organs, namely the vagina and the womb. As this shift takes place, the woman has accepted her sexual role identity and can enjoy the highest level of sexual fulfillment, namely vaginal orgasm.

Kinsey

The major influence on thinking about human sexuality after Freud was clearly the work of Alfred Kinsey and his associates. A comparison, however, between these two major figures is a difficult matter. Kinsey's work, in comparison with that of Freud, is less an intellectual event than a socio-historical event. Freud was self-consciously concerned with the development of a general theory of character development and functioning, within which the sexual was merely one dimension—albeit one of considerable significance. Kinsey was more narrowly concerned with the sexual, with only a minimal number of nonsexual, contextual concerns. This isolated view of the sexual may have been necessary to bring sex research out of the clinical setting and into the larger society. Kinsey's work appears as essentially descriptive empiricism, with only minimal concerns for theory.

The major contribution of Kinsey, beyond that of opening the way for nonclinical research, remains the broad imagery of sexual behavior within contemporary society, against which given theories can be examined.

As is true for many pioneering ventures, this initial research was flawed by a number of methodological shortcomings (Cochran et al., 1953; Hyman and Sheatsly, 1954).

A number of methodological criticisms have been raised from psychiatric and psychoanalytic perspectives. Among these is the question of the reliability of conscious recall in the sexual or any other complex and historically derived aspect of human behavior. Recall is particularly suspect in the areas of childhood and adolescent sexuality, where repression has often occurred—coloring, if not changing, the response of the person being interviewed. Additionally, the unconscious fantasies regarding sexuality are difficult, if not impossible, to obtain in a single interview. However, Kinsey's gross, approximate view of sexual behavior in American society appears to have held up (Ehrmann, 1959; Reiss, 1967; Christianson, 1966; Simon et al., 1972a). When differences emerge, they are, with few exceptions, more suggestive of incremental or evolutionary changes than of radical and disconfirming differences.

Of the four works completed by the Institute for Sex Research, founded by A. C. Kinsey, the first two, *Sexual Behavior in the Human Male* (1948) and *Sexual Behavior in the Human Female* (1953), had the greatest impact on the scientific and lay communities. Yet even these represented such a massive accumulation of information that they were only partially assimilated into a tradition of continuing research or development. The second two works—*Pregnancy, Birth, and Abortion* (Gebhard et al., 1958) and *Sex Offenders* (Gebhard et al., 1965), possibly owing to their narrower focus, had far less impact than did the initial volumes.

Kinsey's view of childhood experience, like Freud's view, pointed to the possibilities of infant and childhood sexuality. Kinsey's data suggested the occurrence of prepubertal orgasm in a small number of girls and a smaller number of boys. A substantial proportion of people reported prepubertal sex play, making it something of a conventional aspect of development, but far fewer who reported sex play reported erotic arousal. This finding suggests that a considerable part of childhood sex play may more nearly reflect conventions of childhood play rather than early direct sexual interest. For both genders, this play occurred in homosexual contexts only slightly less often than in heterosexual contexts, but this finding may have to be read as situational and not characterological. For young girls, this early sexual experimentation is markedly different from that exhibited by young boys. For most girls, the experiences were confined to very brief periods in their childhoods, usually within a single year or less. Additionally, there is a dramatic decrease as adolescence is approached. For boys, on the other hand, the sexual experiments are more continuous, and they increase with proximity to adolescence.

For less than 10 per cent, preadolescent experience includes some sexual contact with adults. For most, this contact represented an isolated experience. Even when the child reacted negatively, the reaction was, for most, rather mild. In Kinsey's (1953) words:

In most instances the reported fright was nearer the level that children will show when they see insects, spiders, or other objects against which they have been adversely conditioned.

Past puberty, masturbation becomes a critical part of the experience of males and something dramatically less than that for females. Ultimately, almost all males masturbated to orgasm (92 per cent), but only 58 per cent of females reported masturbation to orgasm. More significant is the phasing of this component in the sexual development between the two genders. For males, the experience peaks during adolescence; by age 12, masturbation to orgasm has been experienced by about one-fifth of all boys; by age 15, the proportion is over four-fifths. After adolescence, it declines in significance for men, although it remains a minor source of sexual outlet for a large number of men during the rest of the life cycle. Female patterns are much different, particularly with reference to the age of first experiences. By age 12, only 12 per cent reported masturbating to orgasm; at age 15, this percentage rises to 20 per cent; and at age 20, it includes one-third of all females. Moreover, for those who are active, rates of activity are substantially lower for females than for males

during adolescence. About one-half of all females who do masturbate to orgasm do so after having experienced orgasm in some form of sociosexual activity; this is unlike the male experience; for boys, masturbation is almost universally the introduction to orgasm. Frequencies of the activity among women tend to increase to middle age. Fantasy is more common among males than among females, but among those females who both masturbate and use fantasy, the context of fantasy tends to be more realistic than that among males. Females who engage in early masturbatory activity also tend to be generally more sexually active and report a higher rate of orgasm in subsequent marital intercourse.

In American society, as well as in much of the Western world, what has been called petting behavior—essentially the same behavior that is subsequently labeled foreplay—is most typically the mode of entry into sociosexual activity, but boys are more likely to engage in this behavior than are girls during midadolescence; at age 15, it is reported by 39 per cent of girls and 57 per cent of boys. By age 18, four-fifths of both males and females have engaged in the behavior. However, at 15, the activity culminates in orgasm for about one-fifth of the boys (18 per cent) but for very few girls (3 per cent). By the early twenties the percentages even out, and orgasms occur for about 30 per cent of both genders.

Coital activity becomes the most significant potential determinant of sexual status on the levels of both self-conception and social standing. The question of premarital coital patterns probably received most of the attention that followed the publication of the first two volumes and has remained a major focus of attention in much of the research and discussion that followed. Kinsey established the normative nature of premarital activity for both genders. About one-half of all women reported premarital intercourse, with little difference across varied social levels. For men, it was an even more common event, with more marked social level differences. When educational backgrounds were considered, premarital coitus was reported by 98 per cent of the men with educational attainment of eighth grade or less, by 85 per cent of those with 9 to 12 years of school, and by 68 per cent of those with 13 years or more. During the ages 16 to 20, social level differences for both genders were observed, with premarital coital activity reported by 38 per cent of the women with grade school backgrounds, 32 per cent of those who had gone to high school, and 17 per cent of those who had gone to college. Comparable figures for men were 85 per cent, 76 per cent, and 42 per cent. These differences, particularly for women, reflect differences in terms of age of marriage rather than differences in moral standards. Indeed, about one-half of the women who reported engaging in premarital coital activity had only one partner; in 43 per cent of the cases, it occurred only with the fiance. More recent research (Simon et al., 1972a) has suggested rather consistently a moderate increase in premarital intercourse rates for women, but the activity is still disproportionately confined to relationships marked by strong emotional involvement.

More striking than the effect of social background, as measured by educational attainment, was the effect of religiosity. Rates of premarital intercourse for the devout of both genders were about one-half those of the less devout. And, consistent with what was observed with reference to masturbation and petting, orgasm almost always accompanied premarital intercourse for men, but only two-thirds of the women reporting premarital intercourse reported ever reaching orgasm. The difference, however, is not substantially different from a similar difference observable in reports of early marital coitus.

Most adults in American society spend most of their adult years within one or more marital relationships, and it is in marriage that sexual intercourse becomes a regularized part of life. Frequencies of coital activity in marriage range from about 2.5 times a week for those couples in their twenties to 1.5 times a week for those in their forties to 0.5 times a week for those in their sixties. This decline tends to coincide with declining male interest in marital coitus, but it does not coincide with female interest, which increases, in an association with greater orgasmic capacity. In the context of marital intercourse, multiple orgasm becomes a measurable factor, occur-

ring among about 14 per cent of the women Kinsey studied. It was also reported as a male experience, predominantly during younger years, declining significantly with age.

Stages of Sexual Development

This discussion does not consider the various social, cultural, and ethnic differences in sexual development; rather, it concentrates on those factors believed crucial and probably shared by the majority of people. Nor does it discuss alternative sexual routes, previously called deviant sexual development; rather, it discusses normal sexual development, normal behavior being described in terms of averages—what is most typical for the majority of the group at a certain point in time.

INFANCY (BIRTH TO 18 MONTHS)

It is extremely difficult to discuss the nature of sexuality in infants and children, whose sexual apparatus has not yet developed biologically. The years leading to puberty, nonetheless, are crucial if the person is to develop a normal sexual response to a person of the opposite sex. The foundations for all future behavior, sexual behavior included, are decided, to a large extent, in childhood. Freud used the term "infantile sexuality" to stress the fact that children do have sexual-like feelings and curiosities.

In the first year of life, the major channel for libidinal satisfaction is through the mouth. Hence, Freud called this the oral stage, stressing the importance of oral gratifications for the infant. The erotic attachments and pleasures achieved from self-stimulation and relationships with important others are forerunners of future development. If the normal curiosity of the young child is thwarted and his relationship with the other persons is fragile, anxiety and uncertainty will develop in the child.

Psychiatrists know least about the intricate factors that are important for the normal psychological development of infants. Since the infant cannot tell anyone his feelings, adults must make many deductions based on their own feelings and observations. For example, it has been noted that, even in the first few weeks of life, parents treat boys and girls differently. Fathers play roughly with their sons and gently with their daughters. Mothers seem to be warmer and more affectionate with their daughters (Kagen, 1964). It appears that this treatment is a covert, possibly unconscious, form of imprinting. It is hard to imagine that this behavior, which is repeated hundreds of times during the first 18 months, does not communicate itself to the young child. Many other social customs help form the core gender identity in the infant, things such as the color of the room, clothes of the infant, and stress on cleanliness (Stoller, 1968; Money and Ehrhardt, 1972).

The autoerotic experiences of pleasure from touch and oral exploration are probably similar in both boys and girls. Also, the internalized world of object representations develops along similar lines. Separation anxiety, primitive affects of satiation, and rage are not different. Since the verbal mode of communication is nonexistent, it is difficult for the adult to be more specific in his understanding of the infant.

EARLY CHILDHOOD (18 MONTHS TO 5 YEARS)

With the development of language and motor autonomy, the child can be understood better and begins the long road of learning to decode the adult world. An important part of becoming a member of the adult world is to learn to control one's bladder and bowels. During the toilet-training period, the child first learns to associate the genitalia with privacy and cleanliness or dirt. Freud called this period the anal period, to stress the libidinal concentration of the child on the anal area. The act of releasing the contents of the bowel and the bladder is a source of enjoyment for the child. He learns that he has control of these functions. The parent interferes with the sense of pleasure the child receives from the acts of evacuation by teaching him that his productions are not beautiful and worthwhile but dirty and in need of control. Much of the fantasy life of the child at this stage is attached to his production. Nonsensitive child rearing can traumatize the child and give rise to future conflicts, which, on the emotional level, are tied to acts of giving and receiving.

Together with the developing sense of privacy, children experience a phallic exhibitionistic period. The pride in one's genitals and the wish to share this feeling with others is stressed. Sexually, the child discovers his genitalia and finds that they can bring him pleasure. This discovery is probably the beginning of the lifelong association between sexual feelings and the genitals. The communication between the parents and the child concerning this exploratory sexual behavior is another milestone in the sexual development of the child. If parents are too strict and shame the child for his behavior or if they are too encouraging—by giggling when he does explore or, in extreme cases, by demonstrating to him how they engage in sexual behavior—the child associates negative feelings, such as guilt and shame, with something that gives him pleasure and is associated with the genitals. The fantasy life of the child is vivid and, although different in character and content from the adult, may give rise to unwarranted conclusions by the child. For example, if a boy enjoys fondling his genitalia yet feels that he should not enjoy it, he may develop undue anxiety associated with his natural fears of losing something he cherishes (castration anxiety). If the parents verbalize threats in this area—"We'll cut off your hand if you don't stop playing with yourself"—major neurotic problems concerning sexuality may develop in the child in later life.

For the girl, who does not develop as intense a castration anxiety as the boy, there does not seem to be as great a psychological need to give up the sought for object, the parent of the opposite sex. Hence, her sexual development is not tied as intrinsically to castration anxiety as is the boy's. Her wish for a penis is modified, and she learns to want a child to compensate for what she perceives as a loss of a penis. It is unclear whether cultural factors can sway the psychological developments of the two sexes. Only future research will lead to better understanding of the relationship between social factors on the one hand and biopsychological factors on the other hand.

During the last 2 years of this stage, the child works through the beginning relationships with the parent of the opposite sex. In this relationship, the child lays the foundation for future healthy relationships with people of the opposite sex. The Oedipus complex, as Freud called it, vividly illustrates the drama that is often enacted in the triangular relationship. The child has to realize that he cannot possess, emotionally or sexually, the parent of the opposite sex. This first love relationship has to be given up in favor of possible future gratifications. Only by giving up the struggle within the familial environment can the child proceed to develop healthy relationships beyond the family confines.

The social, familial, environmental, and cultural settings continue to stress the differences between the role models for boys and girls. In many instances, the growing child continuously observes, in his own parents, different role models that later take on sexual connotations.

Much of the warmth that the child experiences from the close relationship with his parents is later transferred to his relationship with persons of the opposite sex. The child needs the physical closeness and feelings of security to feel positively about his own body. The child's relationship to the world outside his family is limited to occasional playing with friends and watching the immensely complex adult world as seen on the TV screen. If he goes to nursery school, his emotional investments, in general, are not there. Only when the child enters officially into school at age 5 does the experience with peers become crucial for his normal development.

LATE CHILDHOOD (5 TO 11 YEARS)

With the passing of the Oedipus complex, the period of latency is ushered in. Sex play, usually quite harmless, begins between boys and girls. The boys continue to be curious about sex; among girls, the curiosity is merely episodic. As the children grow older, parental concern regarding sexual matters increases. In particular, girls must sometimes get the feeling that they walk around with "a time bomb between their legs" (Gagnon and Simon, 1970), so great is the parental concern communicated explicitly to them. Besides the explicitly sexual, crucial psychological developmental issues are closely tied to the sexual.

The psychological task of the child and, in turn, the parental figure is to allow for a smooth transition from the home environment to the school. The child has by now internalized the parental image enough that he can tolerate the short separation from the care-giving figure. The child also slowly develops meaningful relationships with peers of the same sex with whom he or she shares interest, hobbies, activities, and, later on, fantasies relating to sexuality. These homosocial friendships solidify the sexual identity of the child. Of course, children are strongly influenced by the social and cultural expectations of the environment in which they grow up. So far, the women's liberation movement has made no significant inroads into the cultural mode from which roles develop. If there are to be major changes in the role models available to both sexes, the basic changes will eventually have to come in child-rearing practices.

In addition, the child between 5 and 11 years is ushered into the adult sexual world by means of fiction, movies, television, and general day-to-day observations. Latent erotic inquiry is developed. Moral categories are learned. All the above information is absorbed by the child. However, the cognitive and affective meanings of the words and symbols are not understood and are possibly distorted by the child. Thus, "fucking" is a bad word, used to degrade another child. It is a cause for a fight. But the sexual referent of the word either escapes the child or follows vaguely the nonsexual cluster of associations. Sexual information is not available and is mixed with personal nuances and fantasies. Much learning has to take place later in life to straighten out the false information obtained by the child.

EARLY ADOLESCENCE (12 TO 15 YEARS)

The beginning of adolescence has both a socio-cultural and a biological referent, both characterized by a profound lack of specificity. The biological referent, puberty, develops slowly and, in its major aspects, can occur between 11 and 15 and still fall within the normal range, although earlier or later development need not imply pathology (Tanner, 1971). The socio-cultural referent represents a new set of age-graded expectations; the application of these new expectations is generally applied with relatively greater uniformity, but there is still substantial variation within and between social class groups in terms of the content of these new expectations and the age at which they are applied.

Essential to these new role expectations are a granting of greater autonomy and a lessening of direct adult supervision (the enlargement of the testing of superego formation as the primary source of behavior control); greater involvement in and importance of peer groups, predicted largely on same-sex (homosocial) membership; and the social recognition of sexual interest and capacities, even if premature in terms of biological development.

Puberty, beyond the outward manifestations of secondary sex characteristics, has a direct impact on what may be termed the intrinsically sexual, although this differs dramatically for the two genders. For males, the major development, the capacity to ejaculate, is directly linked to the experiencing of sexual pleasure. Indeed, all but a few males experience orgasm within 2 years of puberty (Kinsey, 1948), and this experience initiates a pattern of masturbation that occurs at fairly high levels of frequency during early, middle, and late adolescence. This pattern is particularly characteristic of middle-class males, who generally engage in limited direct sociosexual activity during this period. The essentially privatized nature of masturbation leads to an independent commitment to sexuality—that is, the capacity to engage in sexual activity without social or emotional attachments—to the elaboration of sexual scenarios of varied and highly elaborative content (frequently expressive of dominance needs and aggressiveness and involving behavior that most never perform except vicariously—and to reinforced commitments to genitality and heterosexual behavior. Lower-class and working-class males are substantially more likely to engage in heterosexual activity, including coital activity. However, this activity, occurring during a period of maximum homosocial peer involvement, does little to allow heterosexual

commitments to reinforce heterosocial competence; the heterosexual behavior involved remains referential to one's male peers and not necessarily to one's female partner. This pattern of combined heterosexuality and homosociality continues to characterize patterns of sexual behavior during the rest of adolescence and much of adulthood. It is reinforced by and continues to reinforce the sexually segregated character of lower-class and working-class social life on many levels besides the sexual.

For females, on the other hand, the most direct expression of puberty, menses, is predominantly negative. Periodic flows heighten already existing ambivalences about their genitalia, and serve as direct reminders of the potential reproductive consequences of coital activity. The most general pattern is to avoid genital involvement or exploration. Masturbation to orgasm is exceedingly rare during this period; when it occurs, it does not appear to have the committing powers the equivalent behavior has among males, as marked by infrequent repetitions of the behavior. In terms of overt social behavior, the females resemble males in the basically homosocial nature of peer involvement, but the content of this homosocial interaction heavily reflects a commitment to anticipated heterosocial roles as girlfriends, wives, and mothers.

Much of the sexual behavior of adolescents—masturbation, necking, petting, and, especially, heterosexual intercourse—is performed with intense feelings of anxiety and guilt on the part of the adolescent. Optimally, adolescence brings with it the resolution of unconscious incestuous attachments to one's own parents. The shift from pregenital zones to genital-sexual pleasure is on the road to being attained. However, one often sees regression to earlier stages of development because of a variety of unresolved unconscious conflicts. Guilt, shame, or anxiety is partly the reason that it takes an adolescent many years to work his way through the maze of fantasy and reality and eventually achieve his own resolution.

LATER ADOLESCENCE (16 TO 18 YEARS)

Later adolescence begins a point of still further autonomy and detachment from adult supervision—for example, the right to hold a driver's license, to leave school, and, in many jurisdictions, to consent to coitus. It is also a time, for both genders, when heterosociality becomes fairly normative in terms of both adult and youth culture expectations; it is a time when the rating-and-dating system becomes an important—if not the central—aspect of adolescent society.

For males, particularly in the middle class, a commitment to masturbation persists—for the middle class, it remains the major source of sexual outlet as it will well into youth or young adulthood—with an increasing commitment to sociosexual activity. Borowitz (1973) has theorized that, from a psychoanalytic point of view, the capacity to masturbate alone during adolescence is a developmental achievement. It is, he says,

an important way station in the transition from infantile sexuality to adult genitality and from narcissism to object relatedness.

On all class levels, this sociosexual activity is colored by homosocial attachments, with much of the activity being referential to the judgment of male peers; much of this sexual activity is organized around the language of "getting points" or "scoring," reflecting attempts at masculinity confirmation and, as such, possibly serving ego more than libido (Simon et al., 1972b). The effects of this homosocial component are more temporary for middle-class adolescents, where the general norms of social life are more heavily heterosocial, than among lower strata, where such behavior is more consistent with such general norms.

Most males, by this time, have engaged in heavy petting—genital involvement without coitus. A majority or near majority of lower-class and working-class males have experienced coitus, as have something less than that of middle-class males. For the most part, early entry into coital behavior is associated with density of involvement within peer social life—general popularity, frequency of dating, number of partners dated. Initial coital acts tend to occur in relatively nonserious relationships that do not generate numerous repetitions, one to three times being the mode for numbers of times males had coitus with their initial partners. Pre-

viously, this casual introduction to coital behavior reflected both a prevalent double standard and what was called the good girl-bad girl syndrome, where initial contact was either with prostitutes or with local girls who had bad reputations. However, both of these categories appear to have significantly declined for recent and current cohorts. The relatively short duration of the relationship within which coitus occurs during this stage may increasingly reflect an inability to manage the emotional requirements of partners who are social and near-age peers. The most recent data suggest that, although there has been a moderate increase of the proportion of females at this stage who are no longer virgins, there has been a measurable increase in the proportion of males who are still virgins (P. Y. Miller, W. Simon, and C. B. Cottrell, unpublished data).

For both males and females during later adolescence, the negotiation of this increased sexuality is rendered difficult by the conflicting pressures of parental attachment and peer attachment. This conflict remains somewhat simpler for the male than for the female. Not only is the male adolescent given more freedom by parents, but he also finds within the family new opportunities for confirmation of his increased sexual experiences or claims for masculinity. The female has more restrictions placed on her by parents, but she is able to rehearse and get confirmation for her more adult-like femininity through quasiseductive interaction with her father or other near-father figures. However, she receives what are, at best, ambivalent responses from her parents or peers, who are rejecting if she is either too little or too boldly sexual (Rheingold, 1964). The older male adolescent in some sense gets almost too much peer support for his sexual commitments, frequently feeling pressured into escalating his movement through the several sexual thresholds; his female counterpart has to navigate a far more confused route, where her sexual attractiveness is valued, except in rare circumstances, but not her activity—either internally or externally.

YOUTH (18 TO 23 YEARS)

The proximity of marriage, which, on all social class levels, is the end of this period—

except perhaps at the upper middle-class level and higher, where youthful marriage partners may still retain a protected and dependent status—makes this a period of maximum interpersonal and intrapsychic sexual self-consciousness. It is also the period when one's sexual status is a matter of public concern or when one's sexual status is part of one's public status. The establishment of capacities for intimacy is facilitated by the legitimacy of romantic commitments on the part of men as well as women. At the same time, this shared rhetoric of romantic love and near-adult status effectively neutralizes conventional moral constraints, giving sociosexual activity a more explicitly genital or coital emphasis. Premarital intercourse becomes virtually normative during this period, occurring for most men and a majority of women—the women extending greater degrees of physical intimacy in return for greater emotional commitment by the men (Simon et al., 1972a).

The increased potential for regularized but not fully conventionalized sexual access tends to create a number of problems for men. Superficial problems of sexual competence—secondary impotence, premature ejaculation, and anxieties about penis size—commonly appear in otherwise normal men. Moreover, unresolved problems of relating the erotic to the sentimental, possibly reflecting residual forms of the good girl-bad girl syndrome, and the prior training through masturbation add additional difficulties. As female partners become more emotionally secure in the relationships, their interest in and capacity to enjoy sexual activity increase, but the very same emotional commitment creates an uncertain complexity of motivation for many men. Not only is it apparently easier to add an erotic component to more diffuse emotional attachments than it is to do the reverse, but the lesser commitment of women to orgasm, either as a pleasure in its own right or as testimony to one's gender competence, gives fewer direct anxieties. A woman's anxieties focus on unintended pregnancy and concerns for the effect on her reputation if the relationship does not culminate in marriage.

EARLY ADULTHOOD (23 TO 30 YEARS)

With formal engagement and marriage, sexual access is fully legitimated and regu-

larized. For both sexes, sexual attractiveness and acceptance of the sexual facilitate an elaboration of sexual techniques, although this elaboration varies greatly across social class lines. As sexual access ceases to be problematic, more attention is focused on the activity itself.

The appearance of problems of sexual adequacy or anxieties about adequacy on the part of the man now becomes more meaningfully symptomatic. However, it is not unusual for many women to fail to be consistently orgasmic, although existing gaps between rates of activity and rates of orgasm should narrow during these early years of marriage. The recent emphasis on female orgasm may pose it as a simultaneous problem of gender competence for both partners.

The very regularization of sexual access—with the addition of the sheer density of interaction and, in many cases, the pressures of early pregnancy and child rearing—frequently creates a problem of declining eroticism for many men. For middle-class men, the complicated and lush eroticism cultivated by long periods of masturbation typically leads to a sense of erotic deprivation. For many such men, masturbation persists as a source of sexual outlet, allowing them to more fully tap their otherwise unexpressed and unconventional erotic imagery. Moreover, their training in and commitment to heterosociality and their commitments to careers prevent, except in rare circumstances, the exploration of extramarital activity during these early years. However, working-class and lower-class men, although they are less trained in erotic imagery by earlier abandonment of masturbation for sociosexual activity, living in a less heterosocially oriented social world and being less committed to occupational success, experience a loss of homosocial masculinity confirmation by an abandonment of public sexual activity. For these men, both the pressures and the practice of extramarital sex appear fairly early in the marriage.

MIDDLE ADULTHOOD (31 TO 46 YEARS)

Surrounding the sexual at any point in the life cycle are the other activities and attachments that shape the relative significance of the sexual. This period, particularly for middle-class people, is a point of maximum involvement in careers, family, child rearing, and the social life of the surrounding community. During this period, rates of marital intercourse decline, reflecting a decline of interest on the part of husbands; decline or change in the organism plays only a secondary role. Much of the decline in marital intercourse has to do with a de-erotization of the wife-mother role and with the husband's alternative attachments. In recent years, especially after the publication of the initial work of Masters and Johnson (1966), sexual activity as an essential aspect of a complete marriage has been stressed. There is little systematic evidence as yet to indicate any resultant shift in patterns of sexual behavior.

On a more intrinsically sexual level, this declining rate of male interest in marital coitus frequently reflects an inability to connect marital sexual activity with (in the case of higher social strata) the elaborate sense of the erotic developed during adolescence or with (in the case of the lower strata) homosocial validation. For women, however, on all but the lowest social level, interest in marital competence increases. Typically, not having had a long period of privatized elaboration of the erotic, the woman's commitments to the sexual derive heavily from the sensual and from continuing confirmation of an emotional attachment. This partial reversal of gender-linked interest in coital activity is generally resolved in terms of the greater power of the husband—in general social terms and in the assumption that the sexual is more important to him.

Marital intercourse rates during this period remain higher among higher social class groups. This reflects several elements: the greater sharing of power and communication in higher social class groups, a greater concern for maintaining sexual attractiveness and resources with which to express the concern, and men who are trained to be more responsive to external erotic stimuli. There are possibly fewer unconscious conflicts regarding sexuality that originate in childhood. For persons whose sexual identity is well established, these years do not give rise to new sexual conflicts. Problems in other areas, such as work and home life, do not weaken the sexual life of the person. They basically make very little difference.

For both genders, this is the period of rising extramarital activity, with well over one-half of all men and about one-fourth of all women reporting at least one instance. The frequencies of such occurrences remain fairly low; for very few can it be said to serve fully as a replacement for declining marital rates. For both sexes, the patterning of extramarital sexual activity continues to be expressive of earlier patterns of psychosexual development. For men, it predominantly has the capacity for detachment that in adolescence was directly related to the pursuit of sexual fantasies and the homosocial validation of masculinity. For women, on the other hand, it resembles a quest for circumstances that justify and confirm a romantic self-image, rather than a quest for lost orgasms. In very few marriages do extramarital activity and declining rates of interest in marital intercourse become the direct basis for a marital crisis. Still less frequently do they become the basis for divorce, although they may well play a critical role in the explanation of divorce.

LATE ADULTHOOD (46 TO 60 YEARS)

As the biological drives decrease in intensity, there is less need for the same level of sexual activity that the person engaged in previously. It takes the man longer to reach orgasm, and the pleasure associated with orgasm is no longer as powerful an event for him. In the woman, the decline in coital activity is not as marked; rather, she stabilizes at about the same level she was at previously. For both sexes, though, it is imperative to continue in sexual activity. Long sexual abstinence makes it harder for either sex to continue to function, even on a reduced level (Masters and Johnson, 1966). The initial crisis of aging, in this youth-oriented society, makes it doubly difficult for the older adult to adjust his sexual feelings and impulses to what is considered normal by his culture. If he or she has sexual feelings that do not find an easy outlet because of the early death of the spouse, guilt is often associated with these feelings. In addition, anxiety concerning adequate performance complicates the possibility for an easy solution for many older adults.

Menopause occurs sometime during this stage. According to Kinsey (1953), the average age of menopause is 50. There is no evidence to suggest that it has changed in the past 20 years. The biological changes may result in normal psychological problems for women, particularly those in the middle class. The fact that pregnancy can no longer occur often increases the woman's interest in sex, just at the time when the man's interest is often on the decline. The woman can no longer transfer her conflicts, feelings, and gratifications onto her children, since they have left the home (empty-nest phenomena). Thus, husband and wife are compelled to resolve their problems directly.

OLD AGE (60 YEARS AND OVER)

The arc of life turns back and descends on the older persons. Just as children were in the past not supposed to have feelings that adults often associate with sex, so the older generation, those over 60, are denied the possibilities of expressing their sexual feelings and impulses in a socially accepted way.

Grown children often react with horror or humor when Grandaddy, 82 years old, begins to date a 60-year-old woman. The guilt feelings in the elderly concerning sexuality, according to Weinberg (personal communication), are phenomenal. Although the desire and the ability have realistically decreased, the sexual feelings are very much with them. As Masters and Johnson (1966) have pointed out, married couples in their seventies can have an active sexual life and enjoy it. Those who had sexual difficulties earlier—say, in their teens—often experience a re-emergence of the negative old feelings and problems.

But it is not only the society. The older person, who feels that he is at the end of the road, often believes that he does not deserve to have a continuous, happy sexual life. The older person rarely believes that he or she can be or deserves to be looked at as a sexual object. Even when masturbation occurs, it is with guilt and shame. The fact that for each 100 men over 65 there are 138 women further complicates the picture.

Better sexual education for the young and their children is often advocated. The authors believe that an even more important area is the sexual re-education of citizens over 60. It is particularly important to stress that the older generation of today is much healthier physically and younger in spirit than a comparable group two or three generations ago. The older people are often financially independent, and their self-esteem is high, which makes it all the more important that they be treated with new understanding and compassion.

Conclusion

Freud and Kinsey remain the figures that dominate the intellectual landscape of sex research and theory development, but other strains have emerged that continue to command serious attention. One such strain runs from the relatively early psychoanalytic revisionists, from Wilhelm Reich to Herbert Marcuse. Sharing with Freud and Kinsey a sense of the powerful and primitive nature of the sex drive, they saw the repression or sublimation of the sexual as a major source of pathology, both individual and collective. At the other extreme, there was the tendency, best typified by Erik Erikson, that, responding to the growing tradition of child development research, conceptualized psychosexual development in less dramatic terms, in terms more immediately responsive to changing role expectations that mark movement through childhood and adolescence.

The legitimacy accorded scientific concepts of sexual matters that followed Freud and Kinsey prompted a moderate increase in research by anthropologists and sociologists. Anthropology, with a major tradition of research in the area of culture and personality, found Freud playing the role of critical pivot for a series of studies and disputes. Two emergent themes accounted for much of this research: first, a preoccupation with the question of the universality of the role of the sexual in personal and social life; second, playing off the tradition of cultural relativism, which provided a broadened tapestry of ways of organizing and defining the sexual (Ford and Beach, 1951; Marshall and Suggs, 1971). Sociologists, on the other hand, found Kinsey's commitment to quantification and his implicit relativism the basis for a narrow but continuing tradition of research focusing on the impact of social location (particularly as influenced by social class), attitudes and values, and changing patterns of social relationships (Ehrmann, 1959; Reiss, 1967).

In the last decade, there developed two additional lines of research rich with implications for theories of psychosexual development and, in both instances, implications for clinical practice. The first, centering on the work of Masters and Johnson, resembled Kinsey in the questioned scope of generalization, the massiveness of the societal response, and the attendant debate on methodology. However controversial these findings may be, the research did make significant contributions on several levels. From the vantage point of history, it represented a dramatic crossing of what previously appeared to be an impenetrable barrier for sex research: the consideration of the physical activity associated with the sexual in the most direct ways; from an almost exclusive preoccupation with the "being" of sex, the field enlarged to include a concern with the "doing" of sex. Sex as a physical act need no longer be shrouded in an exchange of verbal tokens. Moreover, the research of Masters and Johnson (1966) was a major, although not exclusive, occasion for a radical reassessment of the nature of female sexuality, which was previously largely encapsulated in conceptual language organized by descriptions of the male experience and which had long been a source of uneasiness for theoreticians. Masters and Johnson demonstrated that the link between physiology and behavior is neither direct nor well understood. This ground-breaking function also extended to focusing attention on the question of sexual feelings and behavior on the part of the aged, who had previously been sheltered from the sexual in ways only shared by young children. And the research led to a vastly widened concern for the treatment of sexual dysfunction on the clinical level, giving rise to a growing number of competing approaches to therapy.

The second line of research, beginning with a concern for sexual anomalies and centering most commonly on what has been called

"transsexualism," posed the general question of the effects of gender role learning as the larger framework within which more specifically sexual commitments evolve. For some researchers working in this tradition, particularly Stoller (1968, 1973), there was a continuing commitment to psychoanalytic conceptions, as core gender identity was seen as something shaped in crude but powerful outlines during the early months of life, shaped in psychologically complex relations to parents and parent-like figures. At the same time, much of the research pointed to the greater determination of postnatal experience and learning over genetic factors. Unfortunately, little research has focused as intensively on seemingly normal people. What research is available tends to point in the direction of a relationship between gender role learning and subsequent patterns of sexual development (Kagen and Moss, 1962).

Following this line of research and reflecting still further the traditional sociological concerns for social learning within the context of social relationships, others (Simon and Gagnon, 1969; Gagnon and Simon, 1973) have moved toward what has been called an appetitional theory of sexual behavior (Beach, 1956; Hardy, 1964). This view tends to view the sexual as being not a terribly urgent, biologically rooted drive but a diffuse and unfocused biological potential that can be organized—amplified or diminished—in terms of available social definitions of the sexual. The capacity to be sexual is then seen as being organized by available scripts that describe self, others, and given contexts as erotic or sexual. These sexual scripts, in turn, are organized by still more persuasive elements of the social scripts that make up conceptions of self. Among these are the definitions of gender role identity, incorporating both societal and subcultural elements, specific life cycle stage expectations, normative definitions of the sexual, and the state of development of relevant institutions, such as the family. From this perspective, sexual learning is seen as a continuous process that extends virtually over the entire range of the life cycle; early infant and childhood experiences are influential in shaping potentials and do not form a basic outline of capacities and needs for which later sexual activity becomes either a direct or an indirect expression.

Just as medical scientists and social scientists have begun to study domains in human sexuality, psychologists and psychiatrists have concentrated on the unconscious as a motivating force in sexual behavior in normal people. Clinicians have developed their theories based, to a great extent, on studies of patients. Recently, clinicians have begun extensive studies of sexual behavior and development in nonpatient populations (Offer, 1973). This approach, together with sociological studies of sexual behavior among large, nonpatient populations, may bring about a greater understanding of the complexities and vicissitudes of sexual behavior throughout the life cycle in the normal man and woman.

REFERENCES

Beach, F. Characteristics of masculine sex drive. In *Nebraska Symposium on Motivation,* vol. 4, M. R. Jones, editor, pp. 1-32. University of Nebraska Press, Lincoln, 1956.

Borowitz, G. H. The capacity to masturbate alone in adolescence. In *Annals of Adolescent Psychiatry.* S. C. Feinstein and P. Giovacchi, editors. Basic Books, New York, 1973.

Christianson, H. T. Scandinavian and American sex norms: Some comparisons with sociological implications. Soc. Issues, *22:* 60, 1966.

Cochran, W. G., Mosteller, F., and Tukey, J. W. Statistical problems of the Kinsey report. J. Am. Statistical Assoc. *48:* 673, 1953

Ehrmann, W. *Premarital Dating Behavior.* Holt, Rinehart and Winston, New York, 1959.

Ford, C. F., and Beach, F. A. *Patterns of Sexual Behavior.* Harper & Row, New York, 1951.

*Freud, S. Three essays on the theory of sexuality. In *The Standard Edition of the Complete Psychological Works of Sigmund Freud,* vol. 7, p. 135. Hogarth Press, London, 1953.

Freud, S. Analysis terminable and interminable. In *The Standard Edition of the Complete Psychological Works of Sigmund Freud,* vol. 23, p. 230. Hogarth Press, London, 1964.

Gagnon, J. H., and Simon, W. *Sexual Encounters Between Adults and Children. Sex Information and Education Council of the United States, New York, 1970.*

*Gagnon, J. H. and Simon, W. *Sexual Conduct: The Social Sources of Human Sexuality.* Aldine-Atherton, Chicago, 1973.

Gebhard, P. H., Gagon, J. H., Pomeroy, W. B. and Christenson, C. V. *Pregnancy, Birth, and Abortion.* Harper & Row, New York, 1958.

Gebhard, P. H., Gagnon, G. H., Pomeroy, W. B. and Christenson, C. V. *Sex Offenders.* Harper & Row, New York, 1965.

Hardy, K. R. An appetitional theory of sexual motivation. Psychol. Rev., *71:* 1, 1964.

Hyman, H., and Sheatsly, P. B. *An Analysis of the Kinsey Reports on Sexual Behavior in the Human Male and Female.* New American Library, New York, 1954.

Kagen, J. Acquisition and significance of sex typing and sex role identity, in *Review of Child Development Research,* vol. 1, M. L. Hoffman and L. W. Hoffman, editors, pp. 137-167, Russell Sage Foundation, New York, 1964.

*Kinsey, A. C., Pomeroy, W. B., and Martin, C. E. *Sexual Behavior in the Human Male,* W. B. Saunders, Philadelphia, 1948.

*Kinsey, A. C., Pomeroy, W. B., Martin, C. E., and Gebhard, P. H. *Sexual Behavior in the Human Female,* W. B. Saunders, Philadelphia, 1953.

Marshall, D. S., and Suggs, R. C., editors. *Human Sexual Behavior: Variations Across the Ethnographic Spectrum.* Basic Books, New York, 1971.

*Masters, W. H., and Johnson, V. E. *Human Sexual Response.* Little, Brown, Boston, 1966.

Money, J., and Ehrhardt, A. A. *Man and Woman, Boy and Girl: Differentiation and Dimorphism of Gender Identity.* Johns Hopkins Press, Baltimore, 1972.

Offer, D. *Psychological World of the Teen-ager: A Study of Normal Adolescent Boys.* Harper & Row, New York, 1973.

Reiss, I. L. *The Social Context of Sexual Permissiveness.* Holt, Rinehart, & Winston, New York, 1967.

Rheingold, J. C. *The Fear of Being a Woman: A Theory of Maternal Destructiveness.* Grune & Stratton, New York, 1964.

Simon, W., Berger, A. S., and Gagnon, J. H. Beyond anxiety and fantasy: The coital experiences of college youth. J. Youth Adolescence, *1:* 203, 1972a.

Simon, W., and Gagnon, J. H. Psychosexual development. In *Handbook of Socialization Theory and Research,* D. A. Goslin, editor, p. 733. Rand McNally, Chicago, 1969.

Simon, W., Gagnon, J. H., and Buff, S. A. Son of Joe: continuity and change among white working class adolescents. J. Youth Adolescence, *1:* 13, 1972b.

*Stoller, R. J. *Sex and Gender: On the Development of Masculinity and Femininity.* Science House, New York, 1968.

*Stoller, R. J. Overview: the impact of new advances in sex research on psychoanalytic theory. Am. J. Psychiatry, *130:* 241, 1973.

*Tanner, J. M. Sequence, tempo, and individual variation in the growth and development of boys and girls aged twelve to sixteen. Daedalus, *100:* 907, 1971.

4.2   Adolescent Sexuality

GORDON D. JENSEN, M.D.

Introduction

Puberty, the dramatic body and psychological changes brought on by the surge of sex hormones, comes upon the children of this society at a younger age every year. Today it is not at all unusual for girls under 10 years of age to begin breast development. Adolescence is becoming less and less synonymous with the teen years. The changes of puberty bring on adolescence—a psychological, social, and maturational process that presents the child with new tasks to master and presents his parents with new crises to weather. Among the adolescent's most challenging tasks is to learn to live with himself or herself as a highly sexual person. Sex urges come upon them like a 10-ton truck. The urges are inescapable; something must be done with them.

For the adolescent, sexual adjustment inevitably presents worries and stresses if not problems. It almost always produces a lot of pleasure as well. In this society repression and negative attitudes toward sex fuel some of the worries and problems. Inadequate knowledge about the bodily changes—such as breast enlargement, menstruation, and nocturnal emissions—generally creates worries. Taboos about masturbation cause guilt. Prevailing cultural attitudes that sex is dirty produce anxiety and detract from the pleasure of sex. Societal mores against premarital intercourse produce conflict. Difficulties in obtaining contraceptives present teen-agers with frustration, decrease their use, and contribute to unwanted and unwed pregnancy, which leads to more problems.

An adolescent, sexually active or not, presents anxieties for the parents either about too little sexuality or too much. Parents feel that their own moral code is the one their adolescent should follow, and this code definitely does not include premarital intercourse, especially for girls. Parents are angered when their adolescents ignore their moral code or rebel against it. At the same time, they ignore their own tarnished adolescence. Their own sexual transgressions as adults make it harder to deal with their sexually maturing adolescents. Parents are anxious about losing control over their children just at the time when they feel it is needed most.

Sexual development of adolescents is heavily influenced by forces in the adolescent himself, his family, his subculture, and his peers. The basic factors are behavior, knowledge, and attitudes. Intertwined with sexual behavior is the whole matter of morality. Making adolescent sexual development a little more complex are developmental stages of early, middle, and late adolescence—the last stage often termed youth. Together, they cover an age span beginning as early as 10 years of age and sometimes extending to age 30, although most adolescents begin young adulthood in their twenties.

Sex education and counseling involve many people in the community, including parents, teachers, ministers, agencies such as Planned Parenthood, general physicians, pediatricians, obstetricians, and psychiatrists. Each has a role to play. Although many cop out or are unprepared or unskilled, the psychiatrist has no excuse. He becomes involved in sex education at schools, counseling parents and adolescents, and helping medical colleagues deal better with cases presenting sexual problems.

Early Adolescence

BODILY CHANGES OF PUBERTY

Puberty comes on with a series of bodily changes that take several years. The major changes and the nature of the process are covered to some degree in good sex education courses in elementary school. This information needs to be presented by the time children have reached the fifth grade. Because of better education and greater freedom to discuss sexuality, adolescent girls are much less likely to be totally surprised by their first menstruation than were the women of previous generations. Even today, however, girls and boys are frequently puzzled and worried about the events of puberty. Girls who begin puberty before their peers do may be embarrassed or feel self-conscious. Those older girls and boys who, unlike their peers, are not yet in puberty often have a harder time feeling adequate. Girls may worry desperately about such things as acne, the size of their breasts (either too small or too large), and height, especially when they are tall. Unfortunately, they do not feel comfortable in sharing their worries with anyone or in asking for reassurance. Boys may also worry desperately about acne and height, especially when they are short. In addition, they are concerned about spontaneous erections and nocturnal emissions. Very few parents, doctors, or schools provide the opportunity for reassuring discussions about these matters. Pubertal adolescents carry around a load of worries about little things that they feel are wrong or unacceptable about their anatomy and physiological functioning. Often, not until adulthood are such such dissatisfactions and concerns overcome.

Once the adolescent is through puberty, he must come to grips with the image of his body as it has finally turned out. Most growth is complete by 2 years after the onset of menses in the girl and when the voice has finally changed in the boy. The adolescent then begins to realize what he or she will be like forever: short or tall, stocky or slender. Girls may be self-conscious about tallness; a boy may be disappointed or feel inadequate about his lack of height. Because of this society's stereotypes, a tall girl has a harder time feeling feminine and desirable, and a short boy has a harder time feeling masculine. It takes years to fully accept one's own body image and some people never do.

MASTURBATION

In early adolescence the spontaneous erections in boys seem puzzling, sometimes a bit embarrassing or even frightening. Boys find it hard to be cavalier about an erection in class, for example. The penis of the young adolescent is likely to erect at chance stimulation, such as rubbing past a chair. There are generally pleasurable feelings with erections also. Boys and girls may experience sexual arousal and even orgasm from nonsexual activities, such as riding bicycles, riding horses, and climbing trees. These genital sensations often invite further self-stimulation or masturbation.

Between 80 and 90 per cent of men have masturbated to orgasm by the time they have completed adolescence. This makes it normal behavior, and yet society at large still considers it unacceptable. All modern books clearly state that masturbation is not wrong and that it is normal, but they often put in a statement cautioning against too much, which opens the door for guilt. Because of the deep-seated taboos about masturbation, most males and females feel some guilt. However, this guilt does not generally create psychopathology. Neurosis or psychosis with a preoccupation about masturbation or overwhelming guilt is not caused by masturbation. Rather, it is only one of the symptoms of the illness, which has other causes. Yet the myth persists.

Masturbation is far less common in females than in males. About one adolescent girl in three has masturbated to orgasm. For reasons not entirely clear, females have the sexual equipment and probably the responsiveness, but, in contrast to males they do not use it. Possibly this is because females in this society are not encouraged or expected to be sexual. Unlike the penis, the clitoris is not as subject to chance stimulation. A popular recent book, *The Sensuous Woman,* recommends masturbation for women and describes in detail how to do it. Kinsey found that girls who had masturbated to orgasm were more likely to enjoy intercourse when they reached sexual maturity. Sexual therapists recommend and sometimes teach masturbation to women with sexual dysfunction such as anorgasmia. Masturbation is helpful both for women who have difficulty in allowing themselves to respond to sexual stimulation with arousal and for women who become highly aroused but do not climax. Masturbation may relieve the symptoms of premenstrual tension and dysmenorrhea. It seems likely that the incidence of women who masturbate will increase during the years of the current sexual revolution.

With masturbatory experiences, many adolescents come into their first acknowledged conflict over morals. Subsequently, many other sexual behaviors present moral dilemmas. Adults can help young adolescents develop their own set of moral values, but few do. At most, adults tell adolescents what they regard as acceptable, and unacceptable. This is of some help, except that the adolescent has to adjust to the fact that he or she is thinking about and probably engaging in some activities that his parents and other adults disapprove of. Adolescents can benefit by being told what society thinks about masturbation and by being given the known facts, such as commonness, harmlessness, acceptability, pleasure, and advantages. Psychiatrists regard masturbation as normal for adolescent development and even necessary for the control and integration of sexual urges and for mastery of one's sexual capacities.

IMPULSES WITHOUT OVERT SEXUAL BEHAVIOR

Most young adolescents are not yet dating or interacting heterosexually, although they are experiencing strong erotic impulses. Boys may notice their sister's underpants and may peek at them while they are dressing or try to touch their bodies. They struggle to control these impulses and feel guilty about them. Boys, particularly, seek out pictures of nude women from magazines and pornographic literature. When a group of boys are together, they may brag about masturbation and discuss embellished sexual experiences.

The heterosexual peer group is ideal for trying out ways to get along and communicate with the other sex. Young adolescents do not want to be pushed into situations where they are alone or where sex is expected. They need time to be together and just talk in order to develop the skills of interpersonal relations.

Fantasies become an important part of sexual development at adolescence, and they play a significant role in sexual arousal throughout the rest of the life-span into old age. Males differ from females in the nature of their fantasies, and this difference relates to a difference in their sexual attitudes.

There is little data on adolescent sexual fantasies because research in this area is difficult. As with all sexual research on adolescents, there is the necessity of explicit informed consent by parents; in addition, adolescents find it hard to remember and difficult to relate their sexual fantasies.

Sexual arousal of adolescents generally occurs when they are alone. Masturbation, particularly for boys, leads to a state of arousal generally accompanied by fantasies. These fantasies are predominantly erotic; they include scenes of naked women, particularly their breasts and genitalia, and involve looking, kissing, and petting. Males are oriented toward discovery and exploration. Their fantasies are derived from pictures and from seeing live nude women and couples engaging in sex. Fantasized erotic objects are often amalgamated with images of beautiful and sexy girls they know, with movie actresses or teachers. Fantasies may evoke an erection, may commence after an erection has begun, or may accompany masturbation. Here is an adolescent boy's description of one of his favorite fantasies:

We would be riding in the back seat of the car, and I would reach over and fondle her breasts. She would reach into my pants and begin to caress my penis and finally suck me off.

Female fantasies emphasize romance and love, rather than or in addition to erotic elements. They think, for example, about a boy being interested in them, falling in love, and proceeding to hold and touch them. For example:

Our eyes met across the room. He came over and asked me to go to the beach with him. We went walking along the beach, held hands, and he kissed me under the starry sky.

Contrary to popular belief, girls are also aroused by pictures of nude men and women, but it is not known to what extent such pictures are a part of their sexual fantasies. Like boys, they fantasy touching, kissing, necking, and petting. Here are some examples:

I read the book *Candy* and envisioned myself in her place, making it with the gardener, her uncle, and so on.

I once had a crush on a high school teacher, who I dreamed of loving and kissing in deep passion.

The character of fantasies changes as the adolescent grows and gains more sexual experience and, particularly, after the adolescent becomes sexually active with intercourse. Additional experience is woven into sexual fantasies. For example, males commonly fantasize having sex with more than one woman at once or engaging in an orgy. Females, after intercourse experience, tend to include more explicit aspects of lovemaking in their fantasies.

The different characters of the fantasies of males and females are consistent with a characteristic difference in orientation to the other sex. Males are eager to become physically involved for the purpose of having sex; they wanted to experiment and explore. Girls, in contrast, are more interested in having a boyfriend and in falling in love. They look forward to this and less toward sexual involvement.

Those girls who gain sexual experience and find it exciting begin to seek it, as do boys, but the girls still desire a committed relationship. It is frequently not until late adolescence that males combine a love relationship with the person with whom they are sexually active. In fact, male adolescents, particularly of the lower class, are inclined to view female sexual partners as bad girls and nonsexually active ones as good girls. Boys precede girls in their sexual activity by about 2 years but are later to integrate love and sex.

RUSHING OVERT SEXUAL BEHAVIOR

Although it is common in this society for adults to try to retard any adolescent expression of sexuality, some parents and the mass media in general tend to encourage it. Parents may convey their encouragement to a very young teen-age daughter in terms of concern about getting dates. They may encourage the use of cosmetics, pantyhose, and a bra. The girl may respond by dating before she feels ready and may get involved sexually before she wants to, even though she does not enjoy it. Anxieties borrowed from parents and stemming from such situations often carry over to later sexual function.

SEXUALLY ACTIVE YOUNG ADOLESCENTS

Some adolescents begin dating and become sexually active early, as young as 12 or 13 years of age. Because girls have a full 2-year advance on puberty over boys, they are likely to date boys a few years older than themselves. Sexual activity with intercourse as young as 12 years of age is often a symptom of maladjustment, particularly in the parent-child relationship, and unwanted pregnancy compounds the problems. However, contrary to popular belief, sexual behavior that includes intercourse can be adaptive, rather than pathological or pathogenic, provided the young adolescent girl accepts her sexuality and acts responsibly. It is possible for some to enjoy sexual intercourse at this age and to avoid getting into trouble, physically and psychologically. In accordance with the double standard of society, adults show little concern about the psychologically harmful effects of sexual intercourse on young adolescent boys.

The peer group is very powerful in adolescence. If the group norm is sexual activity, a girl or boy may be urged into it. This is often the case with juvenile delinquent adolescent girls of any age, who as a whole are sexually active. Some young adolescent girls who are engaging in intercourse to gain acceptance from their peers do not enjoy sex. It takes considerable ego strength for the young person to behave counter to the expectations of the peer group. It is surprising that more sexually active 12- and 13-year-olds do not get pregnant. A partial explanation is the 6-month to 1-year period of infertility that normally follows menarche.

At this age the predominant pattern of peer

and parent pressure is not to become sexually involved to the extent of intercourse. This peer support is most helpful in controlling natural sexual urges.

Although professional help seldom reaches promiscuous girls, they can be helped enormously by psychotherapy (Meeks, 1971) or group therapy (Jensen, 1973).

SEXUALLY UNINTERESTED YOUNG ADOLESCENTS

Some adolescents threatened by sexual urges can only handle them by continuing to act like sexually disinterested preadolescent children. Others keep sexual urges under control by avoiding any contacts with the opposite sex. They become sexless and lose themselves to excess in a variety of nonsexual activities in order to avoid peers, except on a superficial level; they sublimate their sexual urges by becoming totally involved in hobbies or time-consuming sports, music, and arts. These activities are important for normal development as long as they are not carried to the point of excluding good interpersonal relationships. This kind of adjustment can become a pattern for years to come, or it may just function in the service of a temporary adjustment, followed by sexual maturity in late adolescence or in the twenties. For example, a girl who had lived and breathed swimming all summer and skied for the ski patrol in winter in order to avoid heterosexual involvement came to the point at 22 years of age of accepting dates and being interested in men. This pattern is one variation of sexual development.

SEX EDUCATION

Young adolescence is a ripe age for schools to offer relevant education about sex because parents lack information or are uncomfortable in conveying it and because social institutions, including churches, are reluctant to deal with the nitty gritty. Adolescents get the majority of their sex education from each other, an education highly distorted and fraught with misinformation. Adolescents are not very interested in reproduction or the body changes of puberty because they have heard quite a bit about these things in their prepubertal years. However, they still harbor a surprising amount of misinformation, and they do not know how anatomical and physiological events relate to sex. For example, few know the time in the menstrual cycle in which a woman is most fertile. They are interested in talking about the following: (1) Moral issues. Is sexual behavior of any kind, including petting and intercourse, all right or not? (2) Homosexuality. How does a person know if he is one? Why do people get that way? Is it acceptable or not? (3) Contraceptives. (4) Sexual variations like voyeurism. There is less interest and perhaps less willingness to talk about masturbation.

Sexuality is only one part of personality, but it is a significant part as the young search for identity. It is most helpful if sex educators give the young a chance to discuss their views of themselves and their feelings in relation to the opposite sex and the same sex. In addition to facts, they want to understand and develop their own values regarding sexuality. They are very responsive to communication with nonmoralizing sympathetic adults who understand their attitudes, behavior, and needs.

Mid-adolescence

Experimentation with heterosexuality is characteristic of the 15- to 18-year olds. Males are still primarily interested in sex without love. Love and intimacy for both sexes comes later, during the stage of late adolescence or youth. Heterosexual crushes—one-sided infatuations, often with an unattainable person of the same age or older, such as a teacher or movie star—are common but usually transient.

SEXUAL BEHAVIOR

There is controversy over the degree to which patterns of sexual behavior have changed in recent years. Most authors believe there has been a relatively small increase in sexual activity. Several recent surveys contrast with data obtained more than 25 years ago by Kinsey.

Sorenson's report, based on a nationwide sample (although small and perhaps not fully representative) of adolescents aged 13 to 19, showed that 52 per cent had had sexual intercourse (59 per cent of the boys and 45 per cent of the girls). In the 13 to 15 age group, 37 per cent had had intercourse, and in the 16 to 19 age group, the proportion was 64 per cent. Among those who had experienced intercourse, the age of first coitus was as follows: 13 per cent (17 per cent of the boys and 7 per cent of the girls) were 12 years of age or under; 71 per cent of the boys and 56 per cent of the girls had had first coitus by age 15; only 5 per cent of the boys and 17 per cent of the girls waited until age 19 for their first experience.

A study for the President's Commission on Population Growth and the American Future found that, by 19 years of age, 46 per cent of the girls had had intercourse. The age of greatest increase for first sexual experience for girls was 16.

Compared with data of 25 years ago (Kinsey, 1948, 1953), these figures of the prevalence of premarital intercourse are about 20 per cent higher for females and 10 per cent higher for males. This finding has led to the general consensus that the sexual revolution of the present era is manifested by a change in attitudes, particularly a willingness of adolescents to talk about sex, rather than by a marked change in sexual behavior of any kind.

Use of contraceptives

The pill is generally credited with the increased incidence of sexual activity among teen-agers. It may possibly account for an increase in frequency of intercourse by those who are sexually active, but the fact that most sexually active adolescents do not regularly use any kind of contraception suggests that the pill has not been a major factor in promoting sexual activity at a younger age. Several surveys have reported that about 70 per cent of sexually active teen-agers have used contraceptives at one time or another, but regular use is much less common. Only 20 per cent of unmarried sexually active female teen-agers used any kind of contraceptive regularly (Kantner and Zelnik, 1972). Lack of information and nonuse of contraceptives are apparently no deterrent to sexual activity. Teen-agers rely on many of the following ineffective means of contraception: Coke douches, laxatives, avoidance of orgasm, withdrawal, standing up, and prayer.

In recent years Americans have increasingly favored dissemination of birth control information for teen-agers. In 1972 between 70 and 80 per cent of adults approved of such information being given in public high schools, and there was little difference between Catholics and non-Catholics. The majority of adults also approved of free contraceptive services to teen-agers, in spite of the commonly held belief that the pill encourages sexual activity or promotes promiscuity (Blake, 1973). Most people are pragmatic and regard contraception as a major preventive of unwed pregnancy. Still, some adults have taken a moralistic stance and disapprove of contraceptives for unmarried adolescents.

Counselors need to know why adolescents are not using contraceptives as much as they should: (1) The adolescents do not believe they will become pregnant if intercourse is infrequent. (2) They do not believe they can get pregnant easily—that is, they doubt their fecundity. (3) They think they are having intercourse in the safe period. (4) Some contraceptives are difficult to get; the pill and the intrauterine device require a doctor's prescription and, legally, a parent's permission. Most teen-agers are afraid to face their parents with the fact that they are sexually active, knowing that their parents disapprove of premarital sex. Few teen-agers feel comfortable talking with their parents about any aspect of sex. (5) Because of the general disapproval of premarital sex, and because it is often against the law, teen-agers do not want to admit to their parents or themselves that they are sexually active. Unmarried teen-age girls deny the realization of past, present, or future sexual activity. "Nice girls don't plan ahead," is a common belief, and taking the pill would be an admission of intent. "It won't happen to me" is the typical attitude toward the possibility of pregnancy from unprotected intercourse. (6) Contraceptives are considered by many to be unnatural. About 25 per cent of teen-age girls regard the pill as potentially harmful. Boys, particularly, believe that a condom decreases the pleasure of intercourse. (7) Some adolescents hope to get pregnant, although this wish is usually unconscious. (8) Adolescents are afraid that clinics and physicians will not be confidential and will tell their parents.

Parents often resist their adolescent's request for contraceptives or information about contraception, equating it with sexual promiscuity. They refuse to allow their adolescent to obtain the pill, naively believing that their adolescent daughter will not be sexually active if she is not taking it.

Minors may obtain contraceptives without parental permission (1) if they are emancipated minors, which means living away from home and primarily self-supporting; (2) at most Planned Parenthood clinics; (3) by asking the right physician; many M.D.'s prescribe the pill without a parent's permission and maintain confidentiality.

Although the pill is the most popular contraceptive, it is not necessarily the best choice. For adolescents who have infrequent intercourse, a combination of the condom and foam, also nearly 100 per cent effective and highly efficient, may be better. The condom is inexpensive, obviates exposure to the undesirable side-effects of the pill, and is the only contraceptive that prevents the spread of venereal disease.

Pregnancy

Unwed pregnancy is one complication of sex. It is often only one symptom of an emotional disturbance, but in and of itself it creates severe emotional distress. Every adolescent with an unwanted pregnancy should have the benefit of counseling. She and her family need help to weather the stress of pregnancy—including a decision about abortion, adoption, or parenthood—help to prevent a subsequent unwanted pregnancy, and help in returning to school, free of emotional and educational handicaps.

One in every 10 babies born in the United States is illegitimate. The frequency of unwed pregnancy in the United States is increasing every year. At present, there are about 400,000 unwed pregnancies each year, and more than half of these are in teen-agers. There is a rising use of abortion to terminate these pregnancies; a diminishing percentage are carried to term to be placed in adoption.

For the purposes of counseling, it is useful to know the causes of unwed pregnancy. Whereas it may appear at first glance that most adolescent pregnancies are the result of accidents of contraception or misinformation, repeated studies have shown that the great majority of teen-age girls get pregnant because they want to. Most knew about contraceptives but did not use them. Generally, the motivation for the pregnancy is unconscious, although some girls readily admit that they wanted to become pregnant. The most common reasons are: (1) to prove that she is a woman and that her body works the way it should; (2) to have someone, the baby, to love; (3) to please a man who wanted to impregnate her; (4) to get back at her parents for hassling her about her sexual behavior; (5) to get away from her rejecting home environment, her boring school, and the "awful town" she lives in; (6) to satisfy her parents' covert wish for her to get pregnant and have the baby; (7) to get a man to marry her; and (8) to relieve loneliness and depression. Usually, pregnancy accomplishes few of these aims, and none turn out to the adolescent's advantage. She often can be helped to see this in early stages of pregnancy. Many of these women select abortion and a few, adoption. However, for those unmarried mothers who give birth, a majority choose to keep their baby and raise it as a single parent. A marriage entered into because of an unwed, unwanted pregnancy has a high probability (over 50 per cent) of ending in divorce within 1 year.

Studies of unwed teen-age boys have shown clearly that they, too, desire to create the pregnancy. Indications are that many deliberately select the girl they wish to impregnate. The majority of these boys disapprove of abortion for "their child." Whereas many of these boys drop the girl after she becomes pregnant, at least as many act responsibly. Although they do not generally desire to get married, some want to assist their girl friends through the stressful period of pregnancy or abortion and even help pay the expenses. Boys, too, need counseling assistance at this time and should be considered in the over-all program of services for the girl and her family (Robbins, 1975).

After pregnancy begins, many of these

adolescents discover that this is not the answer to their problems and that it just complicates their lives and their relationships. Many adolescent girls choose abortion now that it is legal and readily available.

Counseling and sometimes psychotherapy is needed to help the girl resolve her anguish and relieve the guilt she inevitably feels—guilt about the trouble she has created for her parents and, at the same time, resentment of her parents because of their lack of understanding, their punishment of her, and their uncooperativeness. These young women need support to cope with disappointment when their pregnancy fantasies are not fulfilled. Many need to work through the grief over the loss of their babies by abortion or adoption. Some need support and guidance in order to keep up with their school work, so that they will be successful in re-entering school and will be able to recover important peer relationships. It is essential that they be given help to avoid a repeat unwed pregnancy; without counseling, they are likely to continue using ineffective contraception. When teen-agers are asked how they will avoid another pregnancy, they say, "I won't do it again [have intercourse]," but this is an example of denial. Both the girl and her parents—and the boyfriend, if possible—have to be helped to realize that they will have intercourse again and that they will have to learn to accept and use contraceptives.

Without adequate counseling help from community agencies and physicians, unwed teen-age girls who carry their pregnancies to term are high risks for dropping out of school, being forced into a welfare life-style, physically abusing (battering) their children, entering unsatisfactory marriages, getting divorced, and repeating unwed or unwanted pregnancies. Comprehensive programs for unwed pregnant girls have demonstrated that all the undesirable consequences can be prevented (Osofsky, 1968).

Homosexuality

Homosexual experiences are common in adolescent boys but less common in girls. In this discussion, homosexuality refers to sexual behavior rather than a deep emotional attachment, which is also common in adolescence and is sometimes called a homosexual crush. This crush is mostly a friendly alliance or an intense nonsexual companionship, primarily for the satisfaction of dependency needs. The homosexual crush or homosexual experiences in adolescence rarely presage the kind of behavior patterns and psychological relationships seen in homosexuals. In other words, it is common for persons who eventually establish a clear heterosexual identity to have had at least one homosexual experience in adolescence.

In boys the experience is usually between peers and generally involves genital manipulation or masturbation. Fellatio may occasionally occur. Homosexual experiences are more likely to occur when youth of the same sex congregate, such as on boy scout outings, and in sexually segregated institutions, such as boarding schools. In girls the homosexual experience is also generally between peers and is usually limited to touching, caressing, or kissing. Although such experiences are generally erotic, heterosexually oriented adolescents do not persistantly seek them out. Persons who repeatedly and eagerly seek out homosexual experiences are more likely to establish a homosexual identity later in life. The majority of homosexuals establish their homosexual identity between the ages of 15 and 25 years. The gay subculture refers to this as "coming out" (Dank, 1973).

In adolescence, particularly late adolescence, some youth develop profound guilt feelings about homosexual experiences and occasionally an acute anxiety reaction, referred to as "homosexual panic." A case in point is a young male missionary whose religion regarded the expression of homosexuality as highly sinful. He traveled and lived together with a male peer for an extended period and had no heterosexual outlet. After being involved in a single act of homosexual behavior with his friend, he became extremely conscience-stricken and later deeply depressed. Many adolescents need reassurance about the normality of a homosexual experience and need to learn that it does not necessarily mean one is a homosexual. Those who harbor a neurotic guilt benefit from counseling or psychiatric therapy.

IDENTITY

The adolescent's critical task is to obtain an awareness of himself as a person independent from his parents and to arrive at a sense of ego identity (Erikson, 1968). He is in the process of sorting out what he stands for morally—what he values, cares about, and dislikes—and is attempting to attain an unconfused image of himself as a sexual being. In this process he balances the pros and cons derived from attitudes held by parents, adults who are role models, and peers. He struggles with the heavy load of expectations held by his parents. Some degree of rebellion against parents is essential in order to identify with peers, and this process is central to the development of identity. Peers, more than parents, play the primary role in helping an adolescent resolve his identity crisis. One manifestation of this primacy: The peer group or gang is typical of this age. This natural proclivity for group relationships is one reason why group therapy (Berkowitz, 1972) is especially effective with adolescents.

The young person who forms no peer relationships through which he can integrate his past and present identifications or whose parents have imbued him with a basic anxiety about such relationships is likely to have a prolonged identity conflict, often manifested by low self-esteem and periodic depression.

The adolescent who recognizes his sexuality and accepts his sexual behavior, rather than denying it, and who is aware of its consequences, regardless of the extent of it, has made a major step in the attainment of identity.

It is not until late adolescence, usually after 18 years of age, when identity is reasonably well achieved, that they are ready to pursue an intimate relationship with another person.

SEXUAL PROBLEMS

In spite of the fact that youths and their parents commonly have concerns about sexuality, few bring them to the attention of the medical profession. Rarely does a mother request that her daughter be told about menstruation. Some parents appear with their adolescent to obtain contraceptive advice or a prescription to take the pill. Parents are more often worried about the sexual activity of their daughters than they are about their sons, and they may seek advice regarding their daughters. An occasional mother expresses concern about her son's masturbation. The problems associated with unwed pregnancy are generally brought to the physician or psychiatrist. Promiscuity, prostitution, homosexuality, and other sexual variations are present in adolescents, but they seldom come to medical professionals as presenting concerns. Rather, they generally come to light in the process of legal, medical, or psychological involvement for other reasons. For example, promiscuity is common among delinquent girls, but it is rare for physicians or psychiatrists to be involved in treatment. Cases of rape and child molestation are also generally processed by the juvenile justice system, and few adolescents receive more than a psychological evaluation. This is unfortunate because, for the majority of these adolescents, mental health treatment is indicated and could be highly therapeutic and preventive if instituted.

Most of the sexual variations and/or deviations seen in adults have their onset in the teen years or before. These include transvestism, exhibitionism, prostitution, and child-molesting. However, relatively few persons with these variations come for therapy during this period of their lives.

Late Adolescence

Most of the information researchers have gathered about sex in this age period stems from studies of college youth, and, although they account for about 50 per cent of the population in this age group, they doubtlessly differ to some extent from their noncollege age-mates. In addition to displaying patterns general to the largest portions of the population, special subgroups have their own variations. For example, a large motorcycling group in the West engage in sadomasochistic gang-bang sex encounters with female members of their gang. By most standards this behavior would be considered deviant, but it is an accepted ritual by this group.

SEXUAL BEHAVIOR AND ATTITUDES

Christensen (1971) studied students at a Midwest university in 1958 and again in 1968.

Over that decade there was little change in the percentage of men who experienced premarital intercourse—50 per cent. However, the percentage of unmarried women experiencing intercourse had risen from 21 per cent in 1958 to 34 per cent in 1968.

A study of unmarried students at a U. S. college in the Southwest (Eastman, 1972) showed a slightly higher prevalence of sexual activity than at the above midwest university: 55 per cent of the men and 49 per cent of the women had had sexual intercourse. These figures are still somewhat lower than Sorenson's data on younger adolescents. It should also be noted that sexual permissiveness differs by geography, with the West and East coasts being more permissive than the Midwest and central U.S.

College men are more likely to have had their first intercourse experience with someone with whom they are not emotionally involved. In contrast, most women (about 80 per cent) have their first intercourse within a love relationship. The overwhelming majority of both men and women desire a close relationship and in fact may prefer it but men are willing to have sex without affection. Women are less willing; they are desirous of sex in the context of a committed relationship, often in line with the goal of marriage.

There is, however, a trend toward a reduction in the differences between male and female sexual behavior and attitudes. Among youth today, the double standard is less evident, and a sharp rise in sexual experience among women is expected in this era. Women are becoming increasingly willing to have sex for its own intrinsic value. As one 19-year-old high school graduate put it:

A woman can score just as many times as a man if she wants to. I've gone to bed with ten in the past few years. It's a natural nice thing, and a great high. It sure does clear up the blues.

Compared with their fathers and grandfathers, young men today are less likely to visit prostitutes and are aware of the possibilities of sex with affection. Virginity is less prized among men and women; young men are more accepting of a nonvirgin marital partner, and women are more accepting of themselves as nonvirgin brides.

Peer pressure plays a considerable role in shaping sexual behavior. Among some peer groups, virginity is deplored, and this attitude can place unfortunate and even harmful pressure on youth. As a young woman from an Eastern college related:

I found my virginity to be so burdensome that I just decided to get rid of it. So when I was in Italy I looked for any old Italian and just screwed with him. Now, thank heavens, it's not an issue any more.

A prevailing attitude that favors sexual intercourse for youth makes it difficult for virgins to be comfortable about their own sexuality. Virgin men may feel that their masculinity is threatened, and virgin women may feel apologetic about themselves or somehow less than adequate. These youths need sources of support for themselves and for their beliefs that sexual intimacy should be reserved for marriage. Belonging to a peer group, often a church group, whose members hold similar values is the most effective source of support.

Kinsey's data showed significant differences between the lower and middle classes in patterns of sexual behavior, the lower class having had sexual experience earlier and being more liberal about premarital intercourse. In the past decade this has changed; the middle classes are now just as liberal as the lower classes about accepting premarital intercourse. However, for the middle class, affection with sex, especially for women, is a key value. Race and some religious affiliations do make for differences in the proportion of women who have had intercourse at any age.

INTIMACY

Erikson's theory of psychosocial development emphasizes the achievement of intimacy as the crucial developmental challenge of youth. Those who do not attain it in this stage of development are destined to live out the rest of their lives in relative isolation. This concept is amply verified when one looks at the consuming thoughts of youth. In addition, many youths are still struggling with leftover needs in establishing their identity, the task of the preceding phase.

Youth describe intimacy with a variety of terms; the most frequently used words are "trusting" and "caring." In addition, they describe it in terms of mutual sharing, honesty, communicating, being open, taking risks of exposing your own frailties, taking chances, really liking a person, physical attraction, giving of yourself, being happy with making your partner happy, really getting to know the other person and yourself, being comfortable with the other person, fulfilling the needs of the other person, and love.

Once two people are attracted to each other, it takes several months or even a year or more to become intimate. There is no such thing as instant intimacy. Some married persons do not become intimate for several years after their marriage, and other marriages fail for lack of intimacy. Some relationships last only months, but others may last for years, even though the couple rarely see each other. Most intimate relationships do not eventuate in marriage, nor are they necessarily entered into with a goal of marriage in mind.

The rewards of intimacy are clearly very great and are described in such terms as feeling good, fantastic, mellow, warm, happy, and a satisfying feeling but one that is hard to come by. The breaking up of an intimate relationship often produces hurt, but the intimacy is usually considered worth the hurt. Some fear a repetition of hurt feelings, but most say they are willing to take a chance. It appears that most people who are sexually intimate find it very difficult to tolerate their partner's being involved in another intimate relationship.

Youth may date and be involved with many persons without becoming intimate with any of them. People who have never been intimate often express a longing for it, and some feel that they are depressed because it is absent.

Sex is generally a part of the relationship, and probably for most it is essential. However, some have intimate relationships without sex; others mutually agree to omit sex from their relationship, even though they are sexually attracted to each other. Sex occasionally destroys an intimate relationship when the sex is not mutually desired or truly shared. People in this society often have difficulty in distinguishing an intimate nonsexual relationship from a relationship that involves sex. Many people erroneously assume that sex is involved if two people are close and are seeing each other.

In order to obtain intimacy, youths advise, do the following:

Let things happen as they may, and don't try to stop them. Somehow a bad relationship dies anyway, so why not enjoy it until it does?

Let yourself get to that scary point where, when in doubt, give to the other person.

Don't give up your values, but give love, even if there is danger of your being hurt.

It's worth being hurt to really share and care for someone else.

First you need to develop a basic feeling of trust in people.

You also need to work at a relationship so that you don't let walls be built up between you.

Perhaps the best thing that one in a position of counseling can do is to help youths realize that they first need to accept themselves without a facade. At this point they will communicate more effectively and have the potential to develop meaningful interpersonal relationships.

CO-ED DORMS AND LIVING TOGETHER

There is a trend toward co-ed dorms on college campuses and toward unmarried men and women living together off campus in couples or groups.

Sexual behavior is apparently little changed by co-ed dorm living. There is no evidence that students living in such residences engage in more overt sexual behavior than do those students living in the usual segregated residence halls. There is an intensification of socialization, but they commonly use the term "brother-sister relationship." There may, in fact, be less overt sexual behavior in the co-ed dormitories, compared with the segregated residence hall. And there is probably less homosexual behavior also. There is, however, a change in the location of the sexual behavior, with more of the co-ed residents using the residence hall facilities.

Co-ed residence halls do promote an increased opportunity for relationships with the opposite sex. There is more expression of feelings and opinions as they engage in long talks with groups of men and women and visit more in each other's rooms. In those co-ed dorms where both sexes share the same bathroom, there is no evidence of irresponsible sexual behavior. It is rare for men and women to shower together. The most uncomfortable aspect of co-ed bathrooms is changing for a shower in full view of the opposite sex. Women encounter less adverse reaction by the men in the bathroom on the co-ed floor that originally had been a male bathroom before being converted, than do men on the co-ed floor where the bathroom was originally for women. Reservations are based on a feeling of encroaching on the other sex's territory. It appears that both sexes are seeking to get used to the idea of co-ed bathrooms, and few suggest ways of changing those arrangements that make them uncomfortable. As one said:

I think it would be beneficial, hearing your friend pee or shower. It's really down to earth, and brings you closer.

Most men and all women living in the co-ed dorms express satisfaction with co-ed bathrooms. One male co-ed dorm resident said:

If the females feel that there is no need for modesty with the males in the co-ed dorm, then we have attained a remarkable goal of unity, but I don't think the females feel confident of us now. I like the idea of co-ed showers and bathrooms only as long as it is natural and relaxed. To put up a hip front to solve all the problems is completely artificial and just won't work.

In contrast to the co-ed dorms, it appears that college youth who choose to live together off campus are likely to be involved in a sexual relationship with their living partner. These liaisons generally do not have negative effects on academic, social, or personal adjustment. In fact, they can be positive and supportive. One danger is becoming too close or dependent on the other person and spending virtually all free time with that person, thereby cutting off the opportunity to develop a range of satisfying and growth-promoting relationships.

SEXUAL PROBLEMS

Most adolescents and youth do not seek professional help for their sexual problems because they do not feel they can afford it and because they fear the labels of psychiatry. Furthermore, they do not feel comfortable in this kind of formal relationship. They do, however, seek help from community agencies like Planned Parenthood, church groups, telephone sex counseling services, and college peer counseling services. There is currently a trend toward nonprofessional college youth counseling their peers. Some college campuses have many peer counselors who are part of established groups recognized by the students as sources of help with all sorts of personal problems, including sexual concerns. Peer counselors generally refer severely disturbed persons to professional services.

Under such readily available and accepting circumstances, college students bring up the following concerns:

Many simply want to talk about sex to a listening, understanding person. Some women want to admit that they are sexually active, and they do not yet feel comfortable talking with a roommate or friend about their intimate sexual concerns. It comes as a relief to know that they are not the only ones of their age who engage in intercourse or masturbation. Others feel scared or guilty about intercourse. Some express a fear of becoming involved in sex at all. Although some women talk about masturbation rather freely and accept it, they are often not yet ready to do it themselves. Commonly, women want to talk about orgasm. They ask, "What is it?" They are concerned that they are not experiencing it, and they want to know how to become orgasmic. Education about sexuality is most reassuring and helpful with all these concerns.

Women ask, "Should I have sex?" Regarding virginity, they ask, "Is it valuable or not?" They want to learn what the standards of their peer group are and to formulate their own moral values. A woman peer counselor is more suitable than a man to help a woman talk and develop her own answers.

A common question is, "How can I have sex?" These young people want to become sexually active but feel unable or inadequate. Many of them need help in developing basic interpersonal skills. Group activities facilitate learning to relate to the opposite sex. These activities may be through craft workshops, personal exploration groups led by peer counselors, and other structured community or campus social activities.

There are many requests for birth control information. College health services are beginning to provide contraception services. Planned Parenthood clinics in many large cities throughout the U.S. are highly effective in fulfilling the contraceptive needs of adolescents. The trend is for county health agencies to provide these services to adolescents of all ages.

There are increasing requests for abortion and venereal disease information. Again, many college campuses and communities have well known volunteer-run groups or hotlines which answer questions, give information, and offer referral sources.

Concerns about impotence generally turn out to be situational. Examples are being at a friend's house and fearful of interruption or discovery at any moment, being drunk, being under the influence of drugs, or being anxious about pregnancy or venereal disease. Education and reassurance are usually sufficient.

Occasionally, women complain about the absence of sexual desire after an abortion. These women benefit by talking over the conflicts about the abortion and the relationship with their boyfriends and families. They respond to reassurance that their sexual interest will return in time.

"I don't like sex anymore" is a complaint that may signal multiple emotional problems or depression. Peer counselors generally refer these persons for professional help.

Homosexual expression and life-style are a concern for many. Both men and women who desire to relate in a friendly and even affectionate way with a person of the same sex have anxieties and puzzlements about the normality of their feelings and behavior and about their general acceptance.

Women want to talk about how they relate to men. They are struggling with new lifestyles, especially those ideas brought out by the feminist movement, such as not being dependent and not letting others make their decisions for them. All-female groups are popular vehicles for exploring ideas.

COMMUNICATING WITH AND HELPING ADOLESCENTS

Talking with young people about sex requires distinct skills. Adolescents will talk with persons who have certain qualities:

Trust is of prime importance. Sex is a subject about which the young people fear being betrayed—having their parents told. For an adolescent, being frank about sex with an adult or authority figure is comparable to going to the police to discuss your problems with thievery. Sometimes it takes many visits for an adolescent to develop trust.

Patience to listen and be comfortable and not shocked by whatever the adolescent has to say. This takes considerable time, and general physicians are usually not prepared to give it.

Adults who do not moralize. If there's one thing adolescents particularly dislike, it's having someone else's morals laid on them. They do not mind hearing—they even like to hear—what adults' own morals and values are, but they do not accept moralizing.

Adults who reassure and give factual information about sexual topics, where to go and what to do for help—for example, how to get a pregnancy test.

Those who give support and accept the adolescent as is and are careful not to place heavy expectations on him. Adolescents are already burdened by expectations of parents and society, and they feel frustrated in their inability to meet these expectations.

A peer is in some ways a more acceptable counselor to adolescents than is a physician. Peers can share feelings and empathize in ways not possible for professionals. The simple sharing of feelings is highly therapeutic to adolescents; they are reassured to know that others like themselves have similar feelings and needs. Adolescents have a powerful need to grow through communication, which is primarily an exchanging of meaningful thoughts and feelings.

Professionals who can talk with youth are sought out by them and are fully capable of playing the roles of educator, advisor, counselor, and therapist.

REFERENCES

Ald, R. *Sex Off Campus.* Grosset & Dunlap, New York, 1970.
Berkowitz, I. H. *Adolescents Grow in Groups.* Brunner-Mazel, New York, 1972.
Blake, J. The teenage birth control dilemma and public opinion. Science, *180:* 708, 1973.
Boston Women's Health Book Collective. *Our Bodies, Ourselves.* Simon and Schuster, New York, 1971.
Christensen, H. T. Scandinavian versus American sex patterns. Sex. Behav., 4, 1971.
Corbett, J., and Summer, S. Anatomy of a coed residence hall. J. Coll. Stud. Personnel, 215, 1972.
Dank, B. M. Coming out in the gay world. In *Human Sexuality: Contemporary Perspectives,* E. C. Morrison and V. Borosage, editors, p. 222. National Press Books, Palo Alto, Calif., 1973.
Eastman, W. F. First intercourse. Sex. Behav., 22, 1972.
Erikson, E. H. *Identity: Youth and Crisis.* Norton, New York, 1968.
Group for the Advancement of Psychiatry. *Sex and the College Student.* Group for the Advancement of Psychiatry, New York, 1965.
*Group for the Advancement of Psychiatry. *Normal Adolescence.* Scribner, New York, 1968.

Halleck, S. L. Sex and mental health on the campus. J. A. M. A., *200:* 684, 1967.
Jensen, G. D. *Youth and Sex: Pleasure and Responsibility.* Nelson-Hall, Chicago, 1973.
Jensen, G. D., and Robbins, M. B. How sex talks with adolescents go wrong. Med. Aspects Hum. Sex., July, 1975.
*Kantner, J. F., and Zelnik, M. Sexual experience of young unmarried women in the United States. Fam. Plann. Perspect. *4:* 4, 1972.
Kantner, J. F., and Zelnik, M. Contraception and pregnancy: experience of young unmarried women in the United States. Fam. Plann. Perspect. *5:* 1, 1973.
Kinsey, A. C., Pomeroy, W. B., and Martin, C. E. *Sexual Behavior in the Human Male.* Saunders, Philadelphia, 1948.
Kinsey, A. C., Pomeroy, W. B., Martin, C. E., and Gebhard, P. H. *Sexual Behavior in the Human Female.* Saunders, Philadelphia, 1953.
*Meeks, J. E. *The Fragile Alliance,* Williams & Wilkins, Baltimore, 1971.
Osofsky, H. J. *The Pregnant Teenager.* Charles C Thomas, Springfield, Ill., 1968.
*Reiss, I. L. Premarital sex codes: the old and the new. In *Sexuality: A Search for Perspective,* D. L. Grummon, and A. M. Barclay, editors, p. 190, National Press Books, Palo Alto, Calif., 1973.
Robbins, M. B. Dynamics of Unwed Fatherhood, Ph.D. Dissertation, U. of Cal., Davis, 1975.
Sorenson, R. C. *Adolescent Sexuality in Contemporary America.* World, New York, 1973.

4.3

The Family

STEPHEN FLECK, M.D.

Introduction

The family is the universal primary social unit and, therefore, must occupy a central position in any consideration of social psychiatry. As current psychiatry and medicine encompass the study and understanding of the cell and its elements, of cellular organization and integration into organs and organ systems, and of their orchestration into a biopsychological whole that is the organism, so is that organism's behavior in and interaction with its environment important for the understanding of health and disease. Knowledge of the social elements and parameters of this environment is as essential to diagnosis and treatment as is reliance on laboratory data on body chemistry and the nature of food, water, and air supply.

The first social environment for every human being is his biological family, or its substitute. If the latter, ideally it will be adoptive parents who take over at the earliest possible time after birth. Usually, however, one family provides offspring with biological and cultural heritages.

The family is, therefore, an important socio-cultural institution—the keystone of society—and every human group has devised traditional prescriptions and proscriptions to ensure that the family fulfills its biological and enculturating tasks. In this way, the family is both a link between generations that ensures the stability of the culture and also a crucial element in culture change. The biological functions of the family are usually, but not always, left to the nuclear family, and especially to the mother; the enculturating functions may be assigned to members of the extended family or even to nonrelated persons in the community. In Western society, both of these tasks have rested with the primary family, although not always with the primary nuclear family, as is most usual today.

Socio-cultural Perspectives

Scientific study and knowledge of the family have a rather recent history, especially in the context of psychiatry, but preoccupation with the family as a socio-cultural institution is as ancient as human history. Three of the 10 Commandments specifically concern family relations, and every religious doctrine contains many specific rules and taboos about family structure and family duties. Equally ancient are concerns about family dysfunctions. Athenians deplored the alleged decline of family tradition and cohesion as endangering the state and society; the decline of the Roman Empire has been attributed to, among other causes, the family's failure to inculcate the earlier moral standards and discipline. Throughout history major social upheavals have been examined in the light of changes in family life. Today this age-old thesis finds expression in more scientific endeavors, such as the current interest in cross-cultural comparisons, which seek precise correlation between national characteristics and family practices, and in the studies of socio-economic class variables and familial role structure and behavior.

The causal relationships between family characteristics and social change or human history are circular and complex rather than unidirectional. Because of the family's central importance in human development, not only historians and social anthropologists but also legal scholars, economists, philosophers, and sociologists have studies and written about the family. However, some of our most perspicacious insights derive from literature, for instance, *Oedipus Rex, Hamlet,* Strindberg's *The Father,* and O'Neill's *Long Day's Journey into Night.*

Psychiatric Studies

Although the medical profession has prided itself on its family physician, now elevated to the status of specialty, this designation is based on his identical role with all members of the family and not until recently on any formal knowledge of group dynamics and their institutional characteristics. Historically, such endeavors in Western medicine can be measured in decades. Freud, although aware that his discoveries pertained primarily to family processes, chose to study and treat family pathology only in individuals. He concentrated on the investigation and conceptualization of his patients' psychic apparatus isolated from its usual environment in the stark setting of the analyst's office. He thereby limited the social parameters to the analyst-patient dyad, a situation in which a person can relive family experiences through the phenomenon of transference.

Not until 25 years after Freud's first accounts of family-related unconscious processes—such as his reinterpretations of Oedipus and Electra—of the family romance and incest, did the first psychoanalytical effort to conceptualize family processes appear in print (Flugel, 1921). At about the same time, investigation and clinical consideration of individual family members began in the American child guidance clinics. But, in clinical medicine and psychiatry, family histories have continued to focus mostly on familiar incidence of disease and on hereditary patterns, not on family dynamics. In psychiatry some investigation of socio-cultural constellations in families of patients according to diagnosis began in the 1930's (Middlefort, 1957), but systematic clinical study and research of the family as a group did not begin until the 1940's. Despite the existence of an extensive sociological literature on family life, despite scholarly studies of family law, and despite anthropologists' preoccupations with non-Western family systems during this century, medicine and psychiatry continued to focus on the individual patient and the doctor-patient relationship.

Only in the last 25 years has there been rapidly increasing clinical scientific interest in and appreciation of the family as the most significant social force in human development, specifically in personality development, and hence as a potent agent in personality disorders. The family, therefore, is not only the keystone of society, but also a key to understanding the humanness of the human being, including his failures as a human, whether labeled psychopathology, social deviance, or alienation. In line with scientific developments in other specialties, the study of the abnormal, that is, disturbed, families, forced consideration and study of the normal. The Lidzes' (1949) discovery of the frequency of abnormal family backgrounds of schizophrenic patients, Ackerman's findings that the families of disturbed children needed study and treatment as a group, Hilde Bruch's observations of the mother's role in the obesity of children and the related unusual family frame, and other clinical data could not be ordered without some concept of normal, or culture-typical family life. In the meantime, sociologists like Parsons, Merton, and Rainwater had elucidated some of the institutional characteristics of the family as well as the different paradigms of family behavior according to socio-economic class, whereas anthropologists contributed information about family structure in very different cultures.

A General Systems Viewpoint

In terms of general systems theory, the family constitutes an open system with many subsystems; among them are the marriage as such, the marriage as parental coalition, the triads of parents and each child, sibling coalitions, and possibly subsystems involving grandparents or other significant relatives or friends. Within the boundaries that differentiate the family system from its environment, each family must effect its structure and organization appropriate to the family mission and to boundary control and management. The boundary enables each family to become a distinct unit, sharing affection and tending to the nurturance, rearing education, and enculturation of the children. Private and shared rituals serve to connect the family with the larger cultures as well as to related lineal and collateral families. Such interactions require boundary management and regulation in addition to governing internal familial subsystem relationships.

Originally the family was the primary unit for subsistence, and all family functions subserved the goal of survival. In industrial societies, the family's economic role has become less critical, and the issues of the interpersonal and subsystem relationships, together with the everyday familiar tasks of nurturance and education, work, and recreation, constitute the main mission of each family.

Unlike other systems or groups, family goals and tasks are predetermined largely by the culture and society in which the family exists. Although these family goals cannot be as clearly or simply defined as was possible when subsistence constituted the overriding task, the less tangible tasks of guiding the younger generation into adulthood remain as vital as ever. Moreover, in modern developed societies, the younger generation must not only be educated far beyond earlier levels in order to participate in societal processes, but must also enter into a much more rapidly changing adult world and, therefore, cannot be guided into rigidly charted adult roles and functions. These system goals now change within the time span of a generation as, for instance, role paradigms in the current realignment of gender relationships in Western countries. Already in this century the family as an institution has had to undergo a radical transformation by abrogating the major system paradigm of its own survival and continuance, at least as a tangible group. The nuclear family in industrialized nations usually begins as an isolated dyad in terms of living space, economics, and kinship supports, and after fulfilling its mission of guiding the younger generation into similarly isolated adult roles, again becomes a dyad.

These evolutionary changes also demand

different boundary management by the family. The boundary must not only be expansible and contractible without undue trauma to the members, but also more permeable. For instance, if women are to maintain extrafamilial roles and functions throughout most of their married state, small children also must experience and master extrafamilial life in day care centers or nurseries. In intangible spheres there must be a parallel readiness and capacity for family members to separate and reunite. Until quite recently in the United States only the breadwinner crossed the family boundary daily in this fashion, so that there was more opportunity for preschool children to establish relatively firm ego boundaries before negotiating the family boundary regularly with school entry. Interpersonal and intergroup boundary dynamics are a key element in social organization, of which the family is the basic unit. Investigation and elucidation of boundary functions and control, therefore, should lead to fruitful insights into intra- and interpersonal functioning and malfunctioning, and concomitantly to therapeutic and preventive applications.

From all these sources have emerged concepts of structural and functional essentials that, despite varying socio-cultural factors, must be fulfilled to accomplish the family's institutional mission. These family tasks include the nurturance of the young, their enculturation into family life and the larger society, that teaching of the cultural tools of survival and communication, and preparing the young in general to assume adult gender-appropriate membership in their community.

For purposes of clarity of discussion, family structure and functions are considered separately, but it must be kept in mind that such a separation is as artificial in understanding an institution as it would be to treat cellular competence as if structure and function were not interdependent. As noted, effecting certain structural paradigms are basic parental and familial tasks. Because marriage is usually basic to family formation (whether legally sanctioned or not), and because marital functions are also to some extent independent of family issues, obviously so while there are no progeny, marriage is discussed

first and is followed by presentations of family structure, dynamics, and functions.

Marriage

Marriage is, of course, an integral part of and constitutes the basis for the family in most societies. But it also needs to be considered somewhat apart from the family, and it must be evaluated in each instance along a range of socio-cultural and idiosyncratic contingencies.

PURPOSES OF MARRIAGE

A universal biopsychosocial need for completion and fulfillment of oneself through the intimate life with another exists among humans and some other species, and two people may undertake marriage solely for their mutual satisfaction, without intent or capacity to establish a family. In Western society today this definition of mutual satisfaction could be exclusively that of the two partners, although their definitions would necessarily reflect the cultural and psychological norms or deficiencies they have absorbed into their personalities during their respective developments. Western society would not actively interfere with a decision or plan not to produce offspring, the needs or demands of spouses' parents or collateral relatives to the contrary notwithstanding. Other cultures may dictate in these matters. In extended family systems, parents may achieve neither full independence in these respects nor full authority over their own offspring, and failure to produce offspring can lead to dissolution of the marriage by either partner or by outsiders. On the other hand, marriage may also be undertaken solely for the purpose of procreation, and in some religions it is indeed so prescribed, even if not always practiced.

From the clinical vantage point, most marriages fall somewhere between these extremes of intent and purpose, one "nonfamilial" and the other 100 per cent family-oriented. It is most important for the clinician to appreciate that the spouses' respective explicit intents and beliefs may be at variance with the implicit or subconscious intents and wishes that lead them to marriage. For instance, one spouse may agree to marriage determined not to have children, and the other spouse may accede to this conditon, quite prepared not to honor the agreement after marriage or vice versa. Such behavior need not be a conscious or designed betrayal; both spouses may intend to honor their agreements but later find that they cannot resist their own subconscious opposite desires, needs, or fears. For example, Catholics may have increasing guilt feelings over birth control, or one or more parents who aspire to the status of grandparents may exert pressure on the couple. In the United States, in particular, subtle pressures operate to establish a family; childless couples are often pitied.

Depending on the partners' culture, they unite in marriage because they want to, or because it has been arranged for them by their parental families, usually for economic reasons, or because of a combination of these prescriptions. In the West, partners choose each other by and large on the basis of their feelings and hopes, be they realistic or not. Among the less conscious motivations and unrealistic factors that lead to marriage are many neurotic tendencies or needs. Most common among these is probably the use of marriage to achieve independence from the family or procreation which the young person cannot accomplish as an individual. This brings to the marriage dependency needs that are likely to result in expecting parental care from the spouse. Another factor is social pressure, especially on girls, from families or peers that marriage at a certain age is an essential earmark of success.

Not all unconscious or external determinants need be unsound; the choice of a marital partner is a complex process, and a certain intuitive sense of personality fit between two people seems to operate effectively at times, even if neither spouse can account for it explicitly. There are many paths to marriage, sound and unsound foundations for family life, but spouses can build sound relationships even if they have united for ill-considered reasons, or if the marriage was arranged for them. One of the chief criteria for a successful marriage is that it furthers individual growth and growth as a unit, especially as a parental team (see Figure 1).

MARRIAGE IN INDUSTRIALIZED SOCIETIES

The personalities and the socio-cultural values that two individuals bring to marriage determine the nature of their relationship more than do their hopes, dreams, and inten-

FIGURE 1. A beginning.

tions during courtship. This is particularly so now in industrialized societies where marriage has shifted during this century from being an economic advantage and even a necessity (including having offspring) to being an economic liability. The basis for marriage and for marital continuity has changed from tangible issues to the intangible necessities and requisites of companionship, encompassing physical, intellectual, affectional, and social facets. Conventions and traditions no longer serve these societies as behavioral and relational guideposts as they did, for instance, in Victorian times. Although the partners can share the economic burdens, they rarely can do so side by side as they would have in working on complementary tasks on the farm. Maintaining a house and household can be reduced to a minimum of labors, leaving as the major shared goal family life itself, together with the care of the offspring. Work roles for women are important therefore, especially if the family is to remain small in size.

Sharing family responsibilities, however, has been made more difficult by the absence of the husband during working hours, and if he is ambitious, working hours may approach the entire waking hours of the family on many days. Hence, when there is concern in present-day America about the husband's declining role in the family, these socio-cultural givens of an industrial society are probably more responsible and pertinent than speculative cliches about the decline of masculinity or the ascendancy of masculine strivings on the part of women. It must be appreciated that, in our age, after a school day with women teachers, a boy does not return to a home where a father works. Such a youngster may hardly ever see his father at work, the nature of which may be very difficult for a young child to comprehend. The burden of making an absentee husband a live and appropriate image for children often falls on the wife and depends, therefore, on the spouses' views of each other.

The recent upsurge in communes may, in part, represent an interest in re-establishing synthetically an extended family system. It provides for wider familial task-sharing, and also for adult models in the family besides the child's parents. So far it is not a widespread phenomenon. Although some regard it as evidence of the demise of the family, communes are yet another form of family constellation, neither new nor unknown in other parts of the world, for example, Israel.

MARITAL COALITION

This may be defined as those interactional patterns that the spouses evolve to provide at first for their mutual satisfaction. Later, in the structure and dynamics of the family, this coalition must serve the age-appropriate needs of the children and still maintain an area of exclusive relationship and mutuality between the parents. One of these parental sectors is sexual activity, interdicted to children in our society. Mutuality denotes the spouses' interactive patterns on implicit and explicit levels, the sharing of feelings, and the conveying of respect and appreciation of the spouses to each other as well as to others.

Marital roles. An important function of this coalition in family life is the mutual reinforcement of the spouses' complementary sex-linked roles. As parents they represent, respectively, culture-determined masculinity and femininity not only as individuals but through the other spouse's support and approval. Another facet of the coalition is the conjugal role divisions and reciprocities the spouses establish for themselves. These role allocations and the decision-making methods vary with each socio-economic class. According to Bott (1957) and Rainwater (1965), upper-class spouses believe that their role divisions are equal and complementary, but that husbands make more decisions. Lower-class spouses, except for the lowest group, also state that their role allocations are joint and complementary, but that wives make more decisions than husbands.

However, currently sex-linked roles and role paradigms are changing very rapidly in response to two significant socio-dynamic forces. One is the women's liberation movement, and the other, not related, is the tendency toward small families. These reinforce each other, because familial tasks tend to be shared more equitably, freeing women with few children for extrafamilial work and professional pursuits. Moreover, small families will eventuate as a prototype only if women have such opportunities for work and careers other than being housewives and mothers.

Effects of isolation. Industrialization and social and geographic mobility have isolated the nuclear family, adding to the critical importance of the marital coalition in the life of the family. Newlyweds may well seek isolation initially, but in the process of adjusting to married life, friends and relatives can be useful. Nowadays, marriage is often followed by a move to new surroundings, strange for both partners. Whereas living apart from one's family of origin is considered desirable, letters are not the ideal forum in which one inquires about a recipe for tonight's supper, or in which one reports and gains perspective about the first marital altercation. These items may seem trivial, but professional experience with marital problems indicates otherwise; minor problems and disharmonies can accumulate and fester. Physicians can help as marriage counselors, but young people have few occasions to seek out health resources until pregnancy occurs. Prenatal care, therefore, offers an important opportunity for remedial marital counseling and for the prevention of future marital and family disorders.

Because the marital partners usually become the sole or at least the major sources of identification for their young, the spouses' personalities and the marital coalition are much more critical today for the personality development of the children than in the past. In extended family systems a child has many adults of his or her sex to use for identification, and this is still true to some extent in subcultures where grandparents and the parents' collaterals live nearby, albeit in separate households. Living isolated from close relatives deprives the spouses of the advantage of sharing parental functions with an extended family group and leaves each child with little alternative but to view his parents and their relationship as exemplary. Spouses must depend on each other in crises without ready availability of a relative to assume the tangible household or income-producing duties of a disabled partner. In this sense, the demand for individual adjustment and

maturity and for effective role complementarity is more stringent than in earlier times. Moreover, most offspring will have no other adults as models in a continuing way at home to compensate for model deficits in one or the other parent. Problems in the isolated nuclear family, therefore, tend to become circular; marital difficulties affect children adversely and a difficult or ill child strains the marital coalition.

In a free society, spouses depend still more critically on their inner resources because, compared with other cultures, there are relatively few social rules or rituals concerning marriage. In the West, society and religion concern themselves primarily with the beginning of marriage and with death and divorce. Aside from registration of the newborn, society intervenes with a family only if gross undercare or mistreatment of the young is made evident. Otherwise marital partners are on their own to mesh their personalities into the kind of bond and coalition they desire and are capable of, but their capabilities may fall short of their desires. If this happens, they may seek help through counseling, which is available only to a very limited extent, they may live in conflict and disharmony, or they may seek divorce.

Marital Problems and Counseling

Marriage in the United States now depends primarily on the personalities the spouses bring to it. Their personalities are shaped largely by their parents and by the marital modes to which they have been exposed, modes that often do not serve or suit a younger generation of newlyweds. From these circumstances, plus the greatly prolonged duration of the average marriage, derive some specific burdens of marriage in current industrial societies.

Whether the prevalence of marital maladjustment is absolutely greater or only proportionally so compared with other periods is uncertain. Because the marriage now depends so greatly on the partners' personalities, the high prevalence of individual emotional maladjustment must be taken into account. If every tenth person spends some time in a mental hospital, and if the prevalence of symptomatic personal maladjustment is still higher, marital adjustment, which depends so largely on personality factors, obviously carries a commensurate incidence of instability. Of course, marriage can also lend support and stability to an unstable partner, but the doubling of the marriage life-span also requires that the marital relationship be adaptable to more stages and meet the challenge of longer lives.

Because marital and familial maladjustment tends to be so encapsulated, the parents in need of help must seek it actively outside the family. In extended family systems remedial influences might have arisen spontaneously from within the group through the efforts or the mere presence of one or more of the other adults. In this way the marital problem as such might have been contained and never have become quasi-public and statistical.

From the clinical standpoint, a marriage should be evaluated as a singular undertaking of two people. It should be examined in the contexts of their respective personalities and the motivations for marriage and family, and of the family they have already created. Their socio-cultural milieu must be taken into account, and their coalition evaluated according to the class-specific modes of marital interaction.

Although a marriage between two disturbed partners can be satisfactory to them, this does not ensure a good prognosis for a healthy family. Furthermore, a marital coalition adequate for the nurturance of a few children may deteriorate if the family enlarges every year. Family planning through contraceptive control, to avoid offspring, to plan and space them, or to limit family size, is, therefore, an essential element of marital counseling and health care and of preventive psychiatry.

PREMARITAL SEXUAL ACTIVITY

Two topics relevant to marital problems deserve further discussion: sexual patterns within and without marriage, and divorce. Premarital and extramarital sexual intercourse is difficult to assess statistically and cannot be discussed meaningfully as a single phenomenon. In particular, these practices must not be confused with normality or morality, as societies that permit complete freedom of sexual activity after puberty are no less stable or less successful than we are in living up to their cultural norms and preserving their continuity. The same is true of societies that condone extramarital sexual activity implicitly or explicitly.

The changes in premarital sexual activities in our society may be less marked in practice than are the attitudes toward such practice. Young people have gained freedom in recent decades to know and talk about sexual matters; they also expect tolerance with regard to their activities. This has led to the present-day demand of adolescents for their elders to take an open and nondefensive stand about rules and guidelines for sexual behavior outside marriage. There are serious advocates of complete license in this respect and there are equally serious advocates of Victorian rules of behavior and thought.

The physician, however, should not take positions of generalities. When called on to advise or educate on matters of sex and marriage, he should inform about sexual matters and reproductive control, but it is also incumbent upon him to consider to whom he is talking and why. The patient's health needs, his or her life situation, and the capacity of the individual or couple for mature relationships, be the goal marriage or not, should concern the physician who must be especially aware in this part of his work that the patient is apt to attribute to him a parental role. He must use such "transference" elements for the welfare of his patients in these emotionally charged instances just as skillfully as in any other facet of doctor-patient interactions.

Clinically, there is no evidence that premarital sexual relationships either promote or detract from successful marital adjustment. However, one reason for early marriage seems to be the desire for legitimate sexual union, even though emotional and socio-economic independence may not have been achieved by the couple. This can create special problems if they become parents while still dependent on others; also they may not be as mature and certain in their identities as they might be a few years later, when they might seek different partners. In general, the younger marital partners are at the start, the less good is the prognosis for marital success and stability.

Sexual adjustment in marriage is a favorite topic for amateur psychologists. Like other aspects of marriage it is not static or a single given or symptom but varies with the evolution of a marriage. In particular, the physician should know that sexual competence is not automatic and that two partners have to find their way. One of the important elements in satisfactory sexual relationships is that partners must learn how to communicate with each other about their sexual experiences, which is also an important preparation for the sex education of children. When sexual dissatisfaction becomes a complaint, it is rarely an isolated problem in the marriage and, if so, readily remediable by appropriate discussion with both spouses and even by specific instruction (Masters and Johnson, 1966).

Divorce

Divorce is popularly considered as a kind of barometer of familial and societal stability, but divorce too must be understood in appropriate context. Marriages are dissolved; families persist. Divorce as a social phenomenon is susceptible to customs, to legalistic vogues and changes in the law, and to religious codes. It is fashionable to point out that the divorce rate in this country has risen 5-fold in this century from 0.7 to 3.7 per 1,000 population and that the number of divorces has risen more than 7 times. But these figures must be considered in the light of the changed basis for marriage, the modern risks to marital stability, and the freer attitudes toward the dissolution of marriages so beset by problems and suffering that present-day counseling or therapeutic agencies find them beyond salvage.

In particular, the marriage counselor must examine critically a common rationalization designed to avoid divorce for the sake of the children. Children's needs and how they are served by a particular marital pair must be carefully assessed without assuming a priori that two parents under the same roof are better than one, although neither divorce nor its causes are of any benefit to children. In the past a very disturbed marriage might have been continued because there was no real avenue open or even known to the partners on how to dissolve it (except through desertion),

and economics often dictated its continuance. Even today, severe economic liabilities are usually imposed on the divorcing parties by circumstances or by the court or both.

The peak divorce rate in the United States of 4.5 per 1,000 (population) occurred in 1945, when many hastily undertaken war marriages were dissolved, often by spouses whose life together could be counted in days or months. But, from the over-all statistical standpoint, the divorce-risk time has doubled, because with an increased life expectancy in this century from 47 to 70 years, the duration of marriages (over 90 per cent of which take place before the age of 30) has more than doubled. The real divorce rate for the population may have at most doubled if the rate is corrected for risk, which has doubled in terms of duration, and also because the proportion of the population ever married has increased 20 per cent. The lowering of the average marriage age requires a further correction, so that the corrected rate increase may be only ⅓ of the gross 5-fold rate increment. Considering again that 10 per cent of the population will require temporary psychiatric hospital care and that most but not all divorces involve one or two emotionally unstable partners, the present divorce rate is not even commensurate with the estimated prevalence of emotionally disturbed individuals.

Family Structure and Dynamics

In this and the following sections, the term "family" refers to the Western nuclear family, the "isolated" family of industrial society, unless otherwise specified.

From the socio-dynamic standpoint, the family is a small group to which most small group dynamics apply, but it is also a very special group. The special group features pertain to the family's biosocial evolution in a particular culture and to its axial divisions into two generations and two sexes. These axes are important psychological and behavorial boundaries. The parents form the generation that leads and are implicitly obligated to relate sexually to each other. Sexual relations, however, are interdicted to all other members by the archetype of all taboos, the taboo against incest. The generation of offspring follows and learns from the parents as gender-typical models.

As a group the family moves from the parental dyad to a triad and larger group, and later contracts again. Because the family is divided into two generations, each child's relationship to the parents is, to some degree, exclusive and unique and can be represented by an inverted triangle. The family consists of a series of overlapping triangles, each child forming a unique subsystem with the parents, and these triangular relationships are not identical. It cannot be overemphasized that no child lives in the same family in a dynamic sense, sometimes tangibly so because of changing family fortunes. Even identical twins are ascribed different roles and characteristics by parents, by siblings, and eventually by themselves, so that each has different relationships with parents and with the parental unit (see Figure 2).

The family as a whole also constitutes a structural and functional unit, and one important task of the marital coalition consists in mastering the family's evolutionary transitions or crises. Besides the arrival of children, such critical phases include each child's oedipal phase, school beginnings, puberty, adolescence, and eventual emancipation as he leaves his family of origin physically and emotionally. Adversities such as illnesses or economic or political misfortunes may produce other crises and even temporary or permanent separations.

These evolutionary crises can also be viewed as a succession of separations that all family members must learn to master. These separations can be tangible or intangible; that is, they may be on only an emotional plane, as when a child in early adolescence withdraws from closeness to parents. The evolutionary expansion of the family also involves issues of emotional separation and lessened dependency gratifications for the older members of the family. Family life, therefore, requires the capacity to forego individual gratifications for the sake of the group, whose cohesion depends on the example being set by the parents' foregoing some degree of their individuality and certain gratifications for the benefit of the marital coalition and of the family. Each evolutionary step or crisis results in a new equilibrium and realignment of the family's emotional forces, and sometimes this leads to role changes and different task distribution.

ROLE DIVISIONS

Compared to the Victorian prototype of the autocratic patriarch, the role of the father in present-day America has weakened, but more in appearance than in substance. Typically the father's role is still that of the leader; his activities, his productivity, and his education usually determine the position of the family in the community and larger society, and these same factors also correlate with the character of the marital coalition. He provides the instrumental model of how things are done in society in matters of acquisition and survival. It is true that he can be pushed by his spouse's ambitions or even be overshadowed by her accomplishments in all these respects, but such a family may pay a

FIGURE 2. Becoming a triad.

price in suffering, disturbance, and pathology. The fact that the father's activities today occur mostly away from home, unshared and unobserved by the family, is a disadvantage.

The mother's primary role concerns the affective life of the family, and she also tends to its biological needs in health and sickness. Her role is expressive in that she not only tends to affective needs, but identifies them and helps the children to learn about and understand feelings and, therefore, is more responsible for their self-expressive communication. She also guides the child toward self-awareness. This is distinct from instrumental communication—"how to get things done," which is more the father's domain. Although such role differences are becoming more blurred, the basic biologically engendered infant-mother symbiosis persists.

Otherwise, role divisions are not absolute; they only indicate a dominant role for each parent. However, it must be appreciated that the mother's ability to help a child gain self-awareness and body consciousness and to perceive and establish boundaries between himself and the world outside him is more crucial than the father's ability to do this, whereas the father's role as a leader and activator in matters of communal relationships is more important to the family than the mother's social competence and instrumental skills outside the home.

These role divisions are not only important for reasons of example, but also essential in the children's acquisition of communicative skills. For instance, a father working away from home cannot be relied upon to teach about intimate feelings in a detailed way, but he can bring to this and other family tasks a perspective that a mother, harassed by the demands of young children throughout the day, may not maintain for seven days a week.

Parental role divisions should be flexible and complementary rather than fixed, because in crises role complementarity may be essential, and even temporary role reversal may be necessary. Permanent role reversal of the spouses occurs also. It may be mutually satisfactory to the parents, but it provides offspring with unsuitable models for their future life in society, unless society does indeed move toward psychosocial gender equality to the greatest possible extent. Parental role reversals are particularly disadvantageous to the child if the reversal is covert, although desired by both parents. Parents must provide gender-typical role models that are in some harmony with the larger society in which they live. Otherwise, a child may fail to acquire and incorporate role attributes and expectations of himself that have utility when he moves into the community, even as the new generation may alter role stereotypes.

FAMILY STRUCTURE AND PERSONALITY DEVELOPMENT

Dynamically, the triangular structure of the family is epitomized by the oedipal phase of each child. Its adequate and appropriate resolution, which determines important salients of the child's psychic structure, depends more on the family structure and behavior than on biological determinants as postulated by Freud. This appears to be true of all phases of psychosocial development, although parental attitudes and behavior are both reactive and interactive with the child, so that a child's equipment at birth, his temperament, and the parents' capacity to cope with infantile needs all coincide to establish the family's interactional patterns. From these patterns derive much of what the child sees and observes in terms of what kind of people his parents are, indeed, how they are human. Personality development proceeding through identifications and limitations depends as much on the parents' individual characteristics as on their correlated marital and familial interactive behavior. The child observes and absorbs the defensive modes of those around him and in this way evolves his secondary processes from familial examples and interaction modes.

After a child has learned body awareness and body management, including the correlated communicative facility, his relational learning begins. The task for the family is to help each child establish his place in the family and to make him feel sufficiently secure in it so that he can begin to move beyond the family circle without undue anxiety. To attain this place of nearly equal emotional distance from both parents, he must not only master body competence and competence in feeding, clothing, and toileting himself, but he also must master the oedipal issues of having desexualized his close primary object relations to his parents. Only then can he turn to his peers as an increasingly important source of relationships. This step, in one sense the internalization of the incest taboo, the family must accomplish with him. The family accomplishes much of this not only nonverbally, but almost unconsciously. The personalities, especially the degree of security in sexual identity which the parents bring to their union, and their coalition are more crucial to this task than in any other phase of family life, most of which can be more explicit and verbally directed.

Further personality development of the child will be less directly dependent on family structure and dynamics. But in subtle and not so subtle ways, the oedipal issues are relived in adolescence in terms of dependence-independence issues. These problems begin with the internal imbalances of puberty and continue into the prolonged path toward heterosexual competence and personal identity. The parental models play a role during this phase, often as an antipodal fulcrum for the offspring. To achieve a workable ego integration and identity, the offspring must be able to overcome his negativistic stances, which serve the separation from his elders but do not serve in themselves the reintegration of an independent and inner-directed personality. If the antipodal position is very ambivalent and remains emotionally charged, it may become fixed. The child then remains partially identified with a parent whom he also rejects, a shaky foundation for ego integration and ego ideal.

Family Functions

As stated before, it is artificial to separate structure, relationships, and functions and, indeed, the formation of a family structure is one of its inherent functions for its own sake. It is also an implicit charge from the larger community. Society expects the family to prepare children for their lives as adults in the wider community, enabling them in turn to procreate and form their own families. Procreation is essential to the survival of any

species, but the human species must also teach its heritage and thus ensure its continuity and future development. The family as the basic socio-cultural unit is the embryo of social organization, and the parents are the socio-cultural gametes.

The biological heritage demands a set of vital family tasks to be performed for the infant, such as feeding, sanitation, teaching him body management, and the utilization of survival tools. All this, many animals do for their young, and social organization is also a characteristic way of life of some species. For the human race another dimension is added through the development of the culture-typical symbols and their utility, not only in the survival tasks, but in planning for the future through an understanding of one's individual past and the group's collective past. Moreover, the symbolic communication among humans does not require physical proximity of the communicators in time or space, a prerequisite to communication among animals.

For the purpose of discussion, family functions are separated as follows: (1) marital; (2) nurturant; (3) relational; (4) communicative; (5) emancipational; and (6) recuperative—keeping in mind that in vivo they all overlap and to some extent are continuous. Only the predominance of one function against another may be discernible in actual life at a particular time. Also, all except the marital interaction itself involve educational tasks, even though formal education is assigned to extrafamilial institutions in many societies.

MARITAL FUNCTIONS

Marriage must serve the respective needs and satisfactions of the spouses and enable them to effect an appropriate family constellation in order to fulfill their tasks. Beyond the familial obligations, the marital partners must jointly prepare to renounce their close ties to their children when they are ready to emancipate themselves physically and emotionally from the family. The "family" ultimately becomes a dyad again and must turn its concerns from productive engagement in the community to issues of retirement and the concomitant aging processes.

NURTURANT FUNCTIONS

The nurturant functions of the family encompass more than nursing and food supply, although these are basic at first. Beyond nursing, there are the other forms of physical care that the helpless infant needs. Their performance requires the mother's motivation as well as some degree of security on her part in performing these tasks. This security derives from her quasi-instinctual propensity for mothering coupled with the almost symbiotic union with the newborn, such as the mutual and simultaneous relief of the baby's hunger and the mother's breast turgor, and from the support of her spouse and other family members if any. The less specific nurturant activities of the mother continue throughout the life of the family. Eating together as a family at least once a day is not only a caloric ritual but a significant landmark in family life for communication, learning, interacting as a group, and relaxing together (see Figure 3).

The psychological and symbiotic aspects and overtones of nursing and feeding grow from, and with, the earliest mother-infant interaction. Here the infant acquires his initial trust in his human environment, and therefore nurturance is also the beginning of enculturation. Because the entire family is involved, their interaction with the mother-infant unit determines much of the nursing atmosphere. The broader nurturant tasks concern almost every aspect of the young child's development as he acquires body awareness and learns body management, sphincter competence, and self-care with regard to feeding and clothing. All these myriad activities, feeding with its symbiotic and symbolic implications, caring for the baby, helping the child to walk and talk, getting things that he cannot reach, supplying him with appropriate visual, auditory, and kinesthetic experiences, can be at times carried out by any family member or by other substitutes.

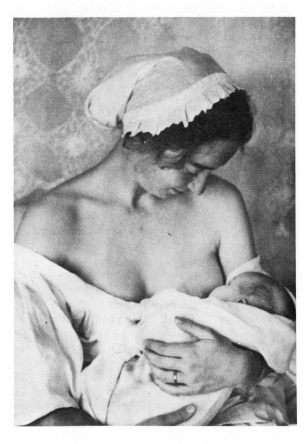

FIGURE 3. Biosocial nurturance.

RELATIONAL FUNCTIONS

Weaning. This is part of nurturing but implies more than withdrawing bottle or breast. The intimate physical closeness with the mother must be weaned and an increasingly nonphysical intimacy established with all family members. Weaning involves still more, in that both the process of weaning and its accomplishment are foundation stones in the acquisition of ego boundaries. In reverse a mother may fail to wean a baby adequately and at the appropriate age, because her ego boundaries are blurred and because she overidentifies with the infant. She then also violates the generation boundary. In all these functions the mother plays the dominant role, but the entire family atmosphere and interaction are also crucial. For instance, parents already locked in an energy-consuming struggle with each other or with one child will necessarily neglect another child proportionally. It should be noted in passing that in terms of ultimate mental health, the underattended child may fare better than the overinvolved one.

Weaning, the cessation of sucking in the narrow sense, also has important relational implications as the prototype of a succession of separation crises that characterize personal development and family life evolution. Nurturant competence on the part of the parents implies not only providing for needs and their satisfaction, but also the capacity to frustrate and deny the child without provoking undue feelings of rejection and without undermining his natural propensity to grow and master problems, often painful problems. When frustrated or punished, the child may find his anger and hostility quite overwhelming and lose faith in a parent temporarily. Nurturant and weaning competence in the family teaches the child that his temper tantrum does not overwhelm others in the family and that he is separate but not alone. In reverse, a parent's anger and frustration with a child teach him the limits of his provocative power and are another essential lesson in grasping limits between himself and others and in establishing his own ego boundaries. Here the parental coalition counts. Ideally the uninvolved and nonangry spouse would support both the upset parent and the child.

Mastery of separation can be defined as the child's experiencing the pain of acute loss of good feeling toward, or dissatisfaction with, another significant person, the parent, without losing faith and trust in the continuity of the relationship and the ultimate restoration of good feeling. Through these experiences he also learns and grows, becoming more able to avoid the same impasse and less vulnerable to and threatened by subsequent separations or emotional distance. This mastery must be facilitated by the opportunity to observe, imitate, and eventually internalize how other family members cope with frustration and this kind of separation anxiety.

The relational issues involved in the feeding and weaning experiences culminate in each child's oedipal phase. Its successful passage includes the central issue of effecting the incest taboo as a rather unconsciously directed inhibitory force within the child and within the family. Conscious incestuous preoccupations beyond the oedipal phase interfere with subsequent successful personality integration and growth, especially in adolescence. The child's omnipotent sense of exclusive relationship with the mother must be curbed and frustrated, enabling the child to wish to grow up like the same-sex parent and to relate to both parents as individuals and as a unit.

Peer group relationships. After the child has been helped to find his place in the family, permitting him to feel comfortable and safe in intrafamilial relationships, his relational learning turns to peer groups. Here the familial guidance becomes more distant and indirect, but familial facilitation and support of peer relationships are as essential as restraint against undue familial intrusion into peer activities. After six or seven, the child's relational learning depends increasingly on extrafamilial examples and on the family's social activities with relatives and friends.

Not only are the culture-typical distance and closeness to various people in differing situations learned that way, but extrafamilial persons are important as alternate figures for imitation and identification. Such experiences complement the parents' unique examples as members of their gender and their society and provide alternate and corrective models for parental shortcomings as people. Even if such shortcomings are not severe, teen-agers often find their friends' parents or other adults superior and preferable as examples to follow in the service of emotional separation from the family.

Parents and the family as a whole must be able to tolerate such disloyalties lest the emancipating adolescent bear an undue degree of guilt, burdening him with intense conflict between his needs and society's (that is, his peer group's) expectations that he be an individual like them on the one hand, and parental demands to conform to their standards on the other. Such an impasse may occur because of his inner unresolved dependency-independency conflicts or because of parental resistance to his independence, or both. The parents' respective values and expectations for their offspring must be in sufficient harmony so that the child can integrate parental objectives and standards, and parents and children must reconcile these values and goals with the realities both of the child's capabilities and of the community in which they live or wish to live.

COMMUNICATIVE FUNCTIONS

The central element in the family's educative mission concerns communicative competence. This includes nonverbal and verbal interchange, and there must be culture-typical congruence between the two. Otherwise messages are inconsistent and contradictory. Talking with the child about his earliest internal and external experiences is essential to his beginning to talk and to communicate meaningfully. What he says and what is said to him must be meaningful to him and to others, so that through such validation he comes to rely on the utility and consistency of language to express himself and to impress others. Only through language and the symbols basic to it does body awareness become body knowledge, and only through language can the basic trust of the mother-infant relationship be reinforced and broadened to include other family members and people outside. Without language (or equivalent symbols), prediction and a grasp of the future are almost impossible; for

instance, only by very rigid timing could a child feel assured that he will be fed when hungry. Language allows for flexibility, such as, "supper will be late," or "after your bath tonight instead of before."

Familial communication must, of course, be related to the communication styles and symbol usages of the family's community. Language plays a role in personality and concept formation beyond its communicative utility. Language reflects the culture's conceptual heritage and determines thought and concept organization across the generations, that is, the cultural system of logic and institutionalized beliefs.

The jargon on any younger generation combines elements of both the emancipative striving for separateness and of evolutionary changes in language and culture. In some immigrant families special problems arise because school-age children often surpass their parents in vocabulary and linguistic mastery, depriving both generations of certain communicative dimensions.

EMANCIPATIVE FUNCTIONS

The ultimate goal for each child is to grow up and take his place as a full-fledged member in the society into which his family has placed him. In Western industrialized society this usually means that the offspring must attain physical, emotional, and economic independence from his family, being motivated and able to originate his own family.

In other societies emancipational tasks may not be as stringent and extensive, but the family still serves to guide the child toward the position society expects him to occupy as an adult. The process of emancipation of each child demands a compensatory re-equilibration of the family after each departure until the spouses return to a dyadic existence, free to enjoy parental prerogatives as grandparents without the continuing responsibilities of a nuclear family. Obviously each step toward emancipation poses the recurrent issue of separation, until it is final and definitive, ideally without rupture of emotional ties (see Figure 4).

The degree of mastery of the earlier and more limited separations, beginning with

FIGURE 4. Separate, but not alone.

weaning and later the beginning of school, separate vacations, and possible hospitalizations of members, indicates and to some extent determines the ease or difficulty experienced by the family when a child leaves for college, to get married, and for military service. But geographic separation is only a part of the issues to be mastered; more important are the emotional components, the sense of loss experienced by all involved and the inner capacity of each member, and the capacity of the family as a group, to do the work of mourning appropriately without becoming pathologically depressed. The departing member must accomplish this alone or with his spouse; the remaining family group can work it out together, the parents demonstrating appropriate mourning, faith in everybody's ability to master separation, faith in the continuity of life, and altered yet rewarding relationships.

The modern family is handicapped with regard to total separation experiences, as the death of a parent or child within the life-span of the nuclear family is now rare, whereas it was rather usual only 50 years ago. Often now the four grandparents are still living at the time when a young adult emancipates himself from his family. And grandparents often live at a distance, so that the impact of their deaths on the nuclear family does not carry the immediacy and intensity of the permanent loss of a regular participant in family life. The time when the first child leaves may be the first occasion for all family members to mourn together, in contrast to the experience of a youngster of earlier generations who usually would have shared mourning with his family incident to the death of a close relative, often a sibling.

Family bonds continue, of course, beyond the emancipation of the young. Rejoining one's family temporarily is a mutually enjoyable and relaxing experience, provided the family has done its tasks well. Opportunities for mutual support are also likely to arise after parents have become grandparents (see Figure 5).

RECUPERATIVE FUNCTIONS

The family must provide for the relaxation of its members, relaxation of manners and behavior and even of defenses essential to interaction in the community. Most mothers are familiar with the need of an elementary school child for strenuous physical activity, even for a fight, on his return from school, and the home must serve as a controlling environment for such socially nonadaptive, possibly regressive, relaxation of behaviorial standards.

In the family circle, parents shed formal attire, actually and symbolically. If a man's house is his castle, his family is the one group in which he can be king or at least president, but in which he can also exhibit dependency needs. The same is true for the wife, especially if she works outside the home. For such mundane reasons alone the family might have to be invented if it did not exist, as no other living arrangements could provide for so many individuals these opportunities to forego formal behavior and recover energy for the work in the community that requires more formal and defensive interpersonal demeanor.

To some degree the family also permits its members to engage in creative or other activities that afford relief by contrast from the monotony of many jobs. By setting limits on relaxing activities, the family as a group also demands and teaches impulse control, in games for instance, and all members may have to defer individual hobbies to family group activities at times. Children experience discipline in this way, as with other frustrat-

FIGURE 5. Grandparents.

ing experiences, first as outer control and eventually as inner restraint.

Effects of Impoverishment on Family Functions

If the family is so burdened by its own tasks that relaxation and enjoyment as a group become jeopardized, because of emotional conflicts or ill health or because the size of the family overtaxes its emotional, nurturant, educational, or tangible resources and reserves, indications for family limitation through birth control and for outside assistance with family tasks are at hand.

Besides exhaustion of family resources because of family size, any disproportion between essential resources and the magnitude of family tasks must lead to family dysfunction and distorted or inadequate task performance. If familial resources are limited in this way, primarily through external social and economic circumstances, such families should be considered impoverished as opposed to pathological, which is related primarily to deviant parental personalities or coalition, or other intrafamilial distortions in relationships and interaction without undue exterior stresses or disadvantages. This somewhat arbitrary distinction between deviant family design and interaction modes, which are more or less externally engendered and often characteristic of a class or minority group and structural and functional deviances arising primarily from within the family, has clinical value and leads to very different therapeutic measures. While both types of families may benefit from family group treatment, the impoverished family needs many communal supportive and remedial measures, and treatment for tissue abnormalities and defects may be as urgently needed as restoration of family function competence.

ONE-PARENT FAMILIES

Impoverishment in the form of one-parent families is of three origins, each leading to different problems. Widowed parents must cope with the loss of spouses, not only within themselves but also with the children's grief and sorrow. If not adequately resolved the ensuing depression, whether masked or overt,

may become pathological for that family member and a pathological focus for the family as a whole. Obviously the problem varies depending on the age of the children, the nature of the death, and other factors such as support resources from outside the family, including possible remarriage. The crucial issue, however, is the surviving parent's mode of dealing with the loss and mourning and his or her representation of the deceased parent to the children.

Divorce or desertion presents a different problem although the sense of loss may be equally intense. However, the feeling of abandonment may be quite realistic and the likelihood for resentment is great. The remaining spouse may have great difficulty in representing the absent parent realistically, and opportunities abound for the children to be confused about what each parent is really like. The acme of such conflicts and confusion is custody fights between divorcing or divorced parents, often compounded by the introduction of stepparents.

Parenthood outside marriage is an increasing occurrence and is class-related in that its prevalence is higher in the lowest socio-economic class, although its incidence is increasing only in the middle and higher classes. The impoverishment, therefore, is often not only that of single parenthood but is compounded by the characteristics of family life in the poverty sector of the population.

POVERTY

Economically and educationally underendowed parents obviously are handicapped in their enculturating missions, and because certain patterns are characteristically common in such families the term "poverty culture" has been coined. This seems incorrect and misleading because the transmission of life on the welfare rolls is not the cross-generational passing on of a set of beliefs and values that have served well or are believed to have served preceding generations well. On the contrary, it is the transmission, if any, of deficiencies such as undereducation for success in an industrial society combined with pessimism about and resentment toward an environment that is, or is perceived as, hostile and repressive.

Nurturance in such families is often distorted by a literalness, in that all discomfort in infants is sought to be alleviated by feeding. This practice often is continued beyond infancy, and instead of a child's complaints or discomfort being explored, he is offered food or, if old enough, sent to the candy store or scolded. Thus, relational issues are met tangibly and often orally, or by verbal or physical punishments. Neither type of interaction invites need-consideration or thought development, thus interfering with emotional growth, communicative development, and the capacity to postpone need-satisfaction, so basic to the attainment of long range goals, especially along educational lines.

CULTURAL DEPRIVATIONS

Further enculturing deficiencies in poor families are the lack of toys and of play space and the common disinterest or inability of adults to interact meaningfully with children beyond infancy. In a one-parent family, that parent often is working and the child is then left to the care of a grandmother or aunt or older sibling, none of whom is as motivated to stimulate and interact with the child as a mother could be if supported by a spouse who shares parental tasks. This set of familial deficiencies in enculturation leads to a circular handicap when formal education begins, and it has been demonstrated now that even the Head Start program could not compensate for the earliest deprivations and under-stimulation of an impoverished family environment. Racial or other group discrimination may further impair the slim opportunities for developing self-esteem and hope for mastery over one's fate.

A second deficiency cycle then develops with formal education. Children ill-prepared to begin school are not only hampered or discouraged by their own backwardness but are likely to be stamped as poor students from the beginning, which leads to educational neglect in many school systems. The feedback from school to family then further depreciates an already underendowed family, enhancing their pessimism and likely apathy toward education and social betterment.

Such a family is likely to be beset by many problems, economic ones, conflicts with authority, as well as health problems. It can be seen that these deficiencies, although largely externally engendered and reinforced, become internalized, especially as seen by mental health professionals, in the form of defective communication about inner experience and as so-called lack of motivation for treatment. The salient family dynamics are those of predominantly reactive interaction and defective development of thought and language, because of disbelief and even mistrust in the utility of abstract and symbolic mentation and communication. Moreover, there is impaired capacity for pleasures that are not immediate; generally such family members know and exploit how to make one another feel bad, but not how to make each other feel good, except by granting immediate satisfaction regardless of long-range consequences. Emancipation in a sense occurs early in such families because older children are usually left to be with their peers in school and out, or are called upon to tend younger siblings or other small children in the neighborhood. However, such early "emancipation" occurs at the expense of further education and emotional and relational development, and hence bodes ill for more mature family formation and parenthood when sexual activity begins, usually at an early age.

Impoverished families—and that is all families whose tangible and emotional resources fall short of adequate family task performance—must be supported by the community through many agencies, among them day care centers for children, special school programs, and social and welfare services for the family as a unit. Health Services must include birth control and abortion counseling (see Figure 6).

Relevance of the Family to Clinical Psychiatry

The family physician is generally not an expert in family dynamics and functioning, although the establishment of a specialty in family practice can fulfill its promise only if physicians of the future become family experts in this sense. The same holds for psychiatrists, who furthermore must become

FIGURE 6. A family beyond its resources.

proficient in family treatment. Psychiatric illness does not occur in a vacuum, and whether or not the social environment of which a patient's family is the most crucial sector engenders psychiatric disturbance, the psychiatric patient always interacts with significant others who interact with him more or less helpfully or pathogenically. Almost always these significant others are the family, whether that of origin or progeny. Spouses are, of course, the most significantly involved persons, but it must be kept in mind that any significant relationship carries subterranean and prototypical elements of familial relationships.

Another important aspect is the family's reaction to a member's serious illness of any type. If it is a psychiatric condition, and especially if it requires institutionalization, the family deserves therapeutic attention for three general reasons. First, they may be involved in the genesis of the illness and this must be understood by clinicians who want to help the patient and his family. Second, if this is so, the patient should not return to his family unless they are helped to change or unless it is ascertained that the family is supportive and helpful without major pathogenic in-

fluences. Third, the moment of hospitalization of a family member is a crisis that affects all members and that demands therapeutic consideration.

The psychiatrist must balance the advantages of returning the patient promptly to the community against the possible pathogenic effects of his return upon him or his family. Moreover, a family may be sufficiently relieved by the removal of a sick member that they eagerly establish a new equilibrium that may interfere with the patient's discharge from the hospital. The problem arises particularly often with disturbed elderly patients.

Family pathology will be considered in two sections: first, familial problems related to or associated with specific clinical entities and, second, an outline of family function deficiencies that is a more general but also a more promising approach to the clinical study of families.

FAMILY PATHOLOGY IN CERTAIN PSYCHIATRIC ENTITIES

Precise correlations between family pathology and psychiatric syndromes must comprise all the many levels of personal and social integration, and the conceptualization of these processes ranging from genetic coding to group dynamics is difficult and complex. The exception is psychiatric entities with a familial incidence based on chromosomal and inborn defects, whether hereditary or not, which will not be considered here in detail. However, familial malfunctioning can ensue from severe guilt and other unrealistic reactions to the birth of a defective child. Because there is need for further clinical investigation and standardization of diagnostic terminology and classification, and for correlations among family disorders, psychopathology and psychiatric syndromes are, therefore, outlined only briefly.

Mental subnormality. This tends to run in families apart from genetic factors. Below certain intelligence levels, parental functioning, especially the communicative performance, does not suffice to accomplish the enculturation of offspring. Educational inadequacies and inferior social position in a given subculture can also result in ineffectual family structure and dynamics, especially if the family belongs to a group against which the surrounding community discriminates actively.

Depression and manic-depressive illness. Parental overinvestment in the achievement of children, especially parents' social prestige aspirations, are commonly found in the backgrounds of these patients. Such parental attitudes are introjected and they predispose the child to intense ambivalence and a sense of being loved and worthy only on the basis of superior performance and achievement. Resentment and punitive attitudes toward the self supervene when failure in terms of internalized overstringent expectations occur. Often a parent is deceased at the time of the overt illness and early loss of one parent occurs in 10 per cent of psychotically depressed patients. This is only a fragmental sketch of the genesis of depression and the detailed biological and intrapsychic phenomena, and their familial and possible genetic transmission cannot be considered here.

Psychopathy. Asocial behavior is often associated with family pathology where children have been found to carry out covert or overt needs or wishes of parents. The young sociopath's behavior may express directly such propensities of a parent in exaggerated form; in other instances the child behaves like a sociopathic parental collateral, whom one parent secretly—or not so secretly—admires. Emphasis on proper appearance and denial of any problem in the face of evident malfeasance by a family member is often encountered in the families of psychopaths.

Addictive behavior, especially alcoholism, also is related to certain family problems. In general, parental examples of unrestrained indulgence in smoking or drinking or drug intake to alleviate habitually acute or chronic discomfort and stress are likely to be followed by offspring, although not necessarily in the identical form of overindulgence. Such habits may form a source of family conflict, but equally often are employed to bypass it instead of resolving family stress. The same is true of the current epidemic of drug abuse among the young; in general it serves to avoid growth pains and emancipation anxieties instead of mastering them.

Schizophrenia. This psychosis has been investigated most intensively with regard to family pathology, and according to Alanen (1958), Lidz et al. (1965), and Singer and Wynne (1963) the outstanding findings are that families with schizophrenic offspring evidence faulty structure and functioning in almost every parameter of essential family tasks. These include frequent and severe parental personality disorders resulting especially in gender model deficiency, deficient parental coalition, violation of generational and sexual boundaries, paralogical or dissimulating communication modes, interference with a child's development of ego boundaries and with his maturing. In some cases the parental model paradigms are so irreconcilable that the offspring must fail in integrating an identity.

DEFECTS IN ORGANIZATION AND DYNAMICS

A more meaningful approach to family pathology than the specificity search, that is, correlating phenomenological entities with a particular family constellation or dysfunction, is the study and discernment of how a family succeeds or fails in accomplishing the essential family tasks and how it operates as a system (Fleck, 1972). Yet as iterated above, family structure and functions or dysfunctions cannot be separated operationally as clearly as they can for the sake of clear discussion. For instance, a disturbed or immature parent may or may not satisfy the spouse but is apt to blur the generation boundaries, besides being a poor model for the same-sexed child. Parental communication inadequacies will likely pervade the family and handicap children, if not encourage them to continue a life in fantasy uncorrected by reality presentation from the older generation, without unduly handicapping the latter.

Marital and parental dysfunction. Intrapersonal parental inadequacies cover a wide range of difficulties. For instance, severe immaturity may lead one spouse to seek a dependent position in the family akin to that of an offspring. Such a spouse expects parental care from the partner or even from a child. Almost any form of neurosis or psychosis in one parent is apt to produce defective parental coalitions, which in turn will handicap the nurturant and enculturating tasks on which the children depend.

Model deficit. Inability or failure of a parent to serve adequately as a gender model appropriate to the larger society leads to increased developmental vicissitudes for a child of the same sex, and more so if, as is often the case, the posture of such a parent is further weakened and undermined by the mate's critical and contemptuous attitudes. The insecure gender identity of a parent predisposes the same-sex child to gender uncertainty and confusion and to social ineptness, important elements in the development of perversions and schizophrenia.

Parents with severe hysterical or obsessional or other neurotic characteristics are apt to produce offspring with like defensive structures if not symptoms.

Nuclearity failure. Another form of family pathology peculiar to the nuclear family and due to parental problems can be viewed as the surreptitious need for an extended family system. This occurs overtly or covertly when one parent or both remain primarily attached to and dependent on their parents or a parental substitute, and the center of gravity for authority, decision-making, and emotional investment rests outside the nuclear family group. This distorts family structure and functions, especially if both parents feel primarily beholden to their respective families of origin and no workable coalition for the younger family becomes established. An extended family system is quite workable with differential role assignments across three generations, but it is damaging to a nuclear family that intends or aspires to such designation, a family that lives geographically but not dynamically as a nuclear family.

Incompetent boundaries. Family boundaries can be impaired in the form of undue rigidity or excessive porosity or undue elasticity. The last, originally described by Wynne and colleagues in families of schizophrenic patients as a "rubber fence," allows no real negotiation of the family boundary into the community. A departing member is somehow engulfed by an extension of the family, which allows no one to leave or emancipate from it. For instance, a father shadowing a daughter on her dates like a detective or a mother who accompanies a child on his or her honeymoon are pathological examples of this.

Overly rigid boundaries are established by some pathological families, leading to isolation from and fear of the larger community. This may occur in the form of physical and geographical isolation, or through shared paranoidal suspiciousness of extra familial humanity, or both. Obviously such a family is over isolated, deprived of friends and of other communal participation.

Porous and inadequate boundaries are found in ghetto and broken families. Often such defective external boundaries coincide with or reflect chaotic internal organizations of the family with faulty subsystem organization, for instance, violations of the generation boundary.

Older siblings may be expected to function as parent figures for younger ones, and there may be age overlap between uncles or aunts and nephews or nieces in three-generation households.

Family boundaries may be blurred because kitchens and bathrooms have to be shared, and there may be neither a pattern nor opportunity for family gatherings. Children of school age may often be left to their own devices if parents are working during the day, which undercuts a clear sense of moving from the organized setting of the school, to another supportive system, that is, a family home and atmosphere.

Parental break. Broken families are the grossest but not necessarily the psychiatrically most devastating form of family pathology. Broken families are disproportionally frequent in the backgrounds of sociopaths, unmarried mothers, and schizophrenics, regardless of whether the fracture is through death, desertion, or divorce.

Schism. Probably more pathogenic than actual parental separation is family schism. Here, the family is divided overtly or covertly into warring camps, usually because of chronic conflict and strife between the parents. The children are forced to take sides to the detriment of their personality development and integration. This type of family pathology is found in the background of schizophrenic patients.

Skews. In a skewed marital relationship one spouse expects the other to be a parent to him or her, or one disturbed parent dominates the other and family life absolutely and rigidly. Such a marital coalition often preempts parental functions and emotional resources, and the children's affective and psychological needs are neglected. However, a family may be skewed when a dyad other than the parental one dominates the group emotionally and often tangibly. Most often this is a symbiotic mother-child relationship.

In both schismatic and skewed families violations of the generation boundary abound, and in both, the intense relationship between one parent and one child may have seductive and incestuous components, an additional violation of sex role requisites, if not of the incest taboo.

Incest. Overt incest is evidence of gross parental psychopathology and of defective family structure. Father-daughter incest is commonest, but both parents are psychologically involved since incest often bespeaks a tenuous equilibrium in a family that seeks to avoid overt disintegration. The involved daughter has assumed many parental functions, while the parents maintain a facade of role competence. The family often breaks up after incest is brought out into the open, usually by the involved child.

Family Task Deficits
NURTURANT DEFICIENCY

In its grossest form, this occurs because of parental neglect and disinterest, and infant victims of malnutrition are known to pediatricians in large municipal hospitals. The worst manifestation is the battered child syndrome, although such victims are not necessarily malnourished. More discrete nurturant disturbances occur because of maternal illness or anxiety and empathy failure in that a mother fails to distinguish between an infant's hunger-borne crying and other bodily needs, discomforts, or pain. Such mothers may also tend to overfeed the baby or try to do so, thus coupling pain and discomfort with oral input. Such problems may have occurred in the backgrounds of psychosomatic patients including obese ones. It is likely that the marital coalition is also deficient in such families.

ENCULTURATION DEFICITS

Failure in separation mastery. This may begin with a mother's inability to wean a child effectively, due to the mother's symbiotic propensities or, more generally, the parents' incapacity to effect inhibitions and adequate frustration tolerance in the offspring. This becomes crucial in the failure to help a child through his oedipal conflicts, a basic family task in effecting the incest taboo. This does not mean that overt incest behavior will ensue, but rather that the offspring is prone to develop one of the more classical neuroses. If coupled with other family function deficits the defective separation competence may be important in the development of schizophrenia and will be a handicap at all stages of personality development.

Aberrant communication. This is a common finding in families with psychiatric problems. Although usually secondary to parental psychopathology, notably thought disorders, faulty communication also builds up a pathogenic autonomy of its own. Young children learn the defective communication modes, which distort their linguistic development, perception, and concept formation. If communication is confusing within the family and ineffectual as expressive or instrumental tools, children are deprived of a critical socializing instrument outside the family. They may never gain basic faith in and reliance on the utility of communication. The seeds of autism may be sown in this way.

Severely amorphous or fragmented modes of communicating have been found in families of schizophrenic patients and may be pathognomonic for schizophrenia (Wynne and Singer, 1963). Parental examples of paralogical thinking and of fear and mistrust of their social environment affect offspring by creating confusion and anxiety, and children may internalize the faulty ideation, the mistrust of the world, and externalize their problems by habitual projection. This is the familial counterpart of Cameron's pseudocommunity; paranoidal suspiciousness can be "learned" in this way, or it can also be viewed as the transmission of irrationality (Lidz et al., 1965).

Scapegoating. A special clinical problem in some families is the scapegoat phenomenon. This pathological family constellation is discernible only if the family as a unit is considered and studied, because the pathological character of the scapegoat's behavior and personality is usually blatant, and his diagnosis in traditional terms is easy, although it is not identical from case to case. The scapegoat, regardless of whether he is schizophrenic, psychopathic, an underachiever, or shows neurotic trait disturbances, serves to bind family anxiety and to mask family deficiencies. "If it were not for him," so the family saga goes, "this would be a happy family." However, it can often be demonstrated, for instance by the scapegoat's institutionalization if this is required, that the family is not only unhappy, but more overtly disturbed without the presence of the scapegoat, unless another family member can be scapegoated soon. The scapegoat serves to divert parents from their own conflicts or provides an alibi for deficient parenting of all offspring in terms of warmth and nurturant

care. The scapegoated child suffers more because his needs are neglected and he is made to feel that it is all his fault and his siblings may believe this too. They in turn suffer not only insufficient care and attention, but they also either learn a distorted view of the scapegoat or must covertly oppose the parents' view, leading to conflict and a sense of guilt. In addition, the family as a whole does not escape unscathed, because the scapegoat may indeed cause the family tangible harm and suffering.

Clinical Evaluation

Besides the history of psychiatric disorders in the family, clinical assessment concerns family functions, but function and structure cannot be separated as neatly by the clinician as by the textbook writer. Observations about functioning and coping force inferences about structure and vice versa. Just as the clinician can draw inferences about lung structure or pathology from breathing patterns, so also can he infer on a statistical basis that chronic sociopathic behavior in an offspring, for instance, is likely related to certain structural and functional family defects.

Symptoms aside, the clinician seeks information about the basic elements of family structure, notably the maintenance of the generation boundary and the gender-linked role divisions and complementarities, and about the manner in which the family copes with its major tasks and functions. He pays special attention to their communication modes.

Diagnostic investigation and therapeutic influences overlap in the establishment of family diagnosis, as they do in psychiatry generally. Only the referential framework for evaluation through family history and direct observation is outlined here.

INFORMATION SOURCES

Ideally the individual histories and statements of all family members are combined and examined for confluent and contradictory data, and these individual records are complemented by participant observation of the family as a group. There are many methods available for this, ranging from open-ended family interviews to more structured formats, including the possibility of having the family do specific tasks or tests together while being observed, and preferably videotaped.

SPOUSES

The referential framework begins with an examination of the marital relationships, the pertinent data concerning the spouses' respective backgrounds, their personal developments, educational levels, socio-economic class positions, and the cultural and ideological value patterns of their respective families of origin. Significant discrepancies in these parameters should alert the examiner to potential conflict areas, and he should investigate the resolution of such discrepancies. For instance, he should explore differences with regard to religion, social class ambitions, desired family size, and rearing methods of and goals for the children.

FAMILY ORGANIZATION

Data about family structure can be obtained through inquiries about living and sleeping arrangements, activities of the family as a group and as part-groups, role divisions incident to various family tasks and crises, and about the decision-making processes. As far as possible, these items should also be examined directly through group observations, as should the possible existence and nature of dominant dyads other than that of the parents. In observing the family as a group, the diagnostician gains impressions about the extent and methods of parental leadership, and whether it is united or not, that is, data about the effectiveness of the parental coalition and the integrity of generational division. Gender appropriateness in manners and conversational content can be established impressionistically in family interviews, or inappropriate seductiveness can be documented, for example.

FAMILY COPING

This can be assessed by learning about crisis behavior. The normal crises of family evolution are important sources of understanding the family's coping patterns, coping reserves, and coping deficiencies. Among such crises are possible resistance or reservations of the spouses' families to the marriage and how this was resolved; the first pregnancy; the original triad formation; subsequent pregnancies and births; evolutionary separations such as the first day of school or nursery; economic misfortunes or deaths of relatives or friends. In psychiatric practice, the examination often takes place in a crisis situation, such as that incident to the hospitalization of a family member as a mental patient.

SOCIAL NETWORK AND BOUNDARY COMPETENCE

The nature of the family's social network should be examined to establish social isolation or the nature of family relatedness within the community. The network must fit to some degree the class position and the patterns of the community and subculture of which the family is a part. The involvement with the spouses' families of origin and collaterals also must fit to some degree their cultural pattern, or conflict should be presumed and the resolution of it examined. A parent's intense attachment to either family of origin should alert the examiner to the possibility that a truly nuclear family has not been established.

Related to the issue of the family's social interactions is the issue of how family boundaries are managed. Properly permeable boundaries permit age-appropriate exit from and entry into the family circle without undue conflict. For instance, how do children and parents behave when the examiner wants to see the parents without the children or wants to interview a child by himself? Kindergarten and school entries are items related to boundary adequacy or difficulties, as are, of course, emancipation events. Crisis coping also indicates boundary difficulties, if a family cannot tolerate the introduction of a helper or if a potentially manageable problem quickly spills into the larger community, such as a parental quarrel always ending with a neighbor's involvement.

CHILDREN'S DEVELOPMENTS

Evaluation of the children depends on their respective ages. Is their behavior age-appropriate? Are their educational achievements and social participations within the range of community expectations for them? Pediatric histories, including well child care data, may be the only source of information available from outside the family. For older children, kindergarten and school adjustments, records from recreational agencies, and, when indicated, information from neighbors and friends as to the socialization of a child can be utilized. School phobias are a classic manifestation of deficient separation mastery in the family, and school failures are a problem to families and may bespeak family problems.

In families with older children, attention must be paid to their emancipating efforts and the parents' reactions to these. Adolescence, notoriously a stage of uneasy family truce in many respects, should be just that, a family dissolution process, at least on an emotional plane. Adolescents must experiment with greater independence and each step carries a potential for disagreement and conflict for all concerned. Also, the adolescent's dissatisfaction with and opposition to parental standards are an intermittently necessary stance for him in his strivings for emotional distance and independence. Examining and evaluating the family with adolescent offspring are, therefore, especially difficult because of this evolutionary state of imbalance.

INTRAFAMILIAL COMMUNICATION

Here recordings or films are essential for detailed analysis. But grossly or impressionistically, the clarity of communication or lack of it can also be seen and heard. Contradictory statements in the same verbal passage or discrepancies between verbal content and nonverbal communication may confuse rather than convey meaning or may have a double bind effect. Scapegoating of a member becomes readily apparent, as do ambivalences, such as the more or less covert condoning of a member's behavior that also constitutes the family's complaint. Careful analysis of verbal passages or special tests given singly or to the group will disclose thought disorders and ideational defects.

TOOLS

Questionnaires and schedules of family process items are available or can be com-

posed for specific assessment modes, but in general they are ancillary diagnostic tools. They are most useful for the examiner who wants to standardize examinations, for data retrieving purposes, for research, or for didactic purposes. Their major value, therefore, rests with the organization of data and not with the information-gathering segment for clinical evaluation, which depends primarily on the clinician's skill and art and his ability to order the data within conceptual frameworks such as outlined here.

REFERENCES

*Ackerman, N. W. *The Psychodynamics of Family Life.* Basic Books, New York, 1958.

Ackerman, N. W. Family diagnosis and therapy. In *Current Psychiatric Therapies,* J. Masserman, editor, vol. 3. Grune & Stratton, New York, 1963.

Alanen, Y. O. The family in the pathogenesis of schizophrenia and neurotic disorders. Acta Psychiatr. Neurol. Scand. (Suppl. 189) *24:* 75, 1966.

Anokhin, P. K. Functional system as unit of organism integrative activity. In *Systems Theory and Biology,* M. D. Mesarovic, editor. Springer-Verlag, New York, 1968.

*Anthony, E. O., and Benedek, T., editors. *Parenthood. Its Psychology and Psychopathology.* Little, Brown, Boston, 1970.

Bell, N. W. Extended family relations of disturbed and well families. Fam. Process, *1:* 175, 1962.

Bell, N. W., and Vogel, E. Toward a framework for functional analysis of family behavior. In *A Modern Introduction to the Family,* N. W. Bell and E. Vogel, editors. The Free Press (Macmillan), New York, 1960.

Benedek, T. Parenthood as a developmental phase. J. Am. Psychoanal. Assoc., *7:* 389, 1959.

Bertalanffy, L. von, *Organismic Psychology and Systems Theory.* Clark University Press, Worcester, Mass., 1968.

Bibring, G. L., Dwyer, T. F., Huntington, D. S., and Valenstein, A. F. A study of the psychological processes of pregnancy and of the earliest mother-child relationship. Psychoanal. Study of Child, *16:* 9, 1961.

Bott, E. *Family and Social Network.* Tavistock Publications, London, 1957.

Bowlby, J. *Maternal Care and Mental Health.* World Health Organization, Geneva, 1952.

Bowlby, J. *Child Care and the Growth of Love.* Penquin Books, Baltimore, 1965.

Cameron, N. *Personality Development and Psychopathology: A Dynamic Approach.* Houghton Mifflin, Boston, 1963.

Christensen, H. T., editor. *Handbook of Marriage and the Family.* Rand McNally, Chicago, 1964.

Erikson, E. *Childhood and Society.* W. W. Norton, New York, 1950.

Erikson, E. *Insight and Responsibility.* W. W. Norton, New York, 1964.

Fishbein, M., and Burgess, E. W., editors. *Successful Marriage.* Doubleday, New York, 1948.

Fleck, S. Family welfare, mental health and birth control. J. Fam. Law, *3:* 241, 1964.

Fleck, S. Some basic aspects of family pathology. In *The Manual on Child Psychopathology,* B. Wolman, editor. McGraw-Hill, New York, 1972.

Fleck, S., Lidz, T., Cornelison, A., Schafer, S., and Terry, D. The intrafamilial environment of the schizophrenic patient: Incestuous and homosexual problems. In *Individual and Familial Dynamics.* J. Masserman, editor. Grune & Stratton, New York, 1959.

Flugel, J. *The Psychoanalytic Study of the Family.* Hogarth Press, London, 1921.

Frenkel-Brunswik, E. Differential patterns of social outlook and personality in family and children. In *Childhood and Contemporary Culture,* M. Mead and M. Wolfenstein, editors. University of Chicago Press, Chicago, 1955.

Freud, S. Der Familieuroman der Neurotiker, Gesellschaff Weker VII. Imago Publishing Co., London, 1941.

Group for the Advancement of Psychiatry. *Human Reproduction.* GAP Report No. 86. (New York: Group for the Advancement of Psychiatry 1973.) pp. 383.

*Howells, J. G. *Theory and Practice of Family Psychiatry.* Brunner-Mazel, New York, 1971.

Johnson, A. M. Sanction for superego lacunae of adolescents. In *Searchlights on Delinquency,* K. Eissler, editor. International Universities Press, New York, 1949.

Keniston, K. *The Uncommitted.* Harcourt, Brace and World, New York, 1965.

Kluckhohn, F. *Variants in Value Orientations.* Row, Peterson, Evanston, Ill., 1957.

Leighton, A. H. *My Name Is Legion.* Basic Books, New York, 1959.

Lidz, R. and Lidz, T. The family environment of schizophrenic patients. Am. J. Psychiatr., *106:* 332, 1949.

Lidz, T. *The Family and Human Adaptation.* International Universities Press. New York, 1963.

*Lidz, T. *The Person.* Basic Books, New York, 1968.

Lidz, T., Fleck, S., and Cornelison, A. *Schizophrenia and the Family.* International Universities Press. New York, 1965.

Masters, W. H., and Johnson, V. E. *Human Sexual Response.* Little, Brown, Boston, 1966.

Merton, R. K. *Social Theory and Social Structure.* The Free Press (Macmillan), New York, 1949.

Middlefort, C. F. *The Family in Psychotherapy.* Blakiston, New York, 1957.

Minuchin, S., Montalvo, B., Guerney, Jr., B. Rosman, B., and Schumer, F. *Families of the Slums.* Basic Books, New York, 1967.

Morris, G., and Wynne, L. Schizophrenic offspring and parental styles of communication. Psychiatry, *28:* 19, 1965.

Parsons, T. The incest taboo in relation to social structure and the socialization of the child. Br. J. Sociol, *5:* 101, 1954.

*Parsons, T. *Social Structure and Personality.* The Free Press (Macmillan), New York, 1964.

Parsons, T., and Bales, R. F. *Family, Socialization and Interaction Process.* The Free Press (Macmillan), New York, 1955.

*Rainwater, L. *Family Design.* Aldine Publishing Company, Chicago, 1965.

Richardson, H. B. *Patients Have Families.* Commonwealth Fund, New York, 1948.

Riesman, D. *The Lonely Crowd.* Yale University Press, New Haven, 1950.

Rossi, A. S. Transition to parenthood. J. Marr. Fam. Living, *30:* 26, 1968.

Rossi, A. S. Family development in a changing world. Am. J. Psychiatr., *128:* 47, 1972.

Singer, M. T. and Wynne, L. C. Differentiating characteristics of parents of childhood schizophrenics, childhood neurotics, and young adult schizophrenics. Am. J. Psychiatr., *120:* 234, 1963.

Strodtbeck, F. L. The family as a three-person group. Am. Sociol. Rev., *19:* 23, 1954.

Vogel, E. F., and Bell, N. W. The emotionally disturbed child as the family scapegoat. In *A Modern Introduction to the Family,* N. W. Bell and E. F. Vogel, editors, The Free Press (Macmillan), New York, 1960.

Vygotsky, L. S. *Thought and Language.* Wiley and M.I.T. Press, New York, 1962.

Weinberg, S. K. *Incest Behavior.* Citadel Press, New York, 1955.

Whorf, B. L. *Language, Thought, and Reality: Selected Writings of Benjamin Lee Whorf.* Wiley and M.I.T. Press, New York, 1956.

Winnicott, D. W. *The Family and Individual Development.* Tavistock Publications, London, 1965.

Wynne, L. C., and Singer, M. T. Thought disorder and family relations of schizophrenics. II. A classification of forms of thinking. Arch. Gen. Psychiatr., *9:* 199, 1963.

Zimmerman, C. *Family and Civilization.* Harper & Row, New York, 1947.

Zimmerman, C., and Cervantes, L. *Successful American Families.* Pageant Press, New York, 1960.

chapter 5 Sexual Identity

5.1 Gender Identity

ROBERT J. STOLLER, M.D.

Development

INTRODUCTION

Gender identity is a term used for one's sense of masculinity and femininity; it was introduced to contrast with the term "sex," which summarizes the biological attributes adding up to male or female (Stoller, 1964; 1968). Gender identity is the product of three kinds of forces: biological, biopsychic, and intrapsychic responses to the environment, especially the effects due to parents and to societal attitudes.

ORIGINS

Biological. For mammals, the resting state of tissue is female, and male organs are produced only if an androgen pulse is added (Jost, 1958; 1972). Likewise, androgens at the critical period specific for each species are needed for the brain to be organized to maleness (Money and Ehrhardt, 1972). Such organization then produces a reaction in lower animals typical of the males of that species, that is, masculine behavior. Natural experiments in human beings confirm the general rule that maleness and masculinity

depend on fetal and paranatal androgens (Money and Ehrhardt, 1972). As one observes animals in an ascending evolutionary scale, however, the general rule of behavior is that the organism is granted greater flexibility of response to a larger spread of environmental stimuli. This is also true for gender behavior—masculinity and femininity as contrasted with maleness and femaleness. No species more than man so often breaches the rule that maleness and masculine behavior or femaleness and feminine behavior go together (Money et al., 1957; Stoller, 1968).

To account for this last observation and to assist in the understanding of the development of gender identity, one must turn to the environmental forces to determine their contribution to the development of masculinity and femininity.

Biopsychic. By this term is meant the result of those forces originating in the environment and exerting their influence throughout life outside awareness, conscious or unconscious; they are nonmental (nonpsychic). Environment here means not just stimuli coming from outside the organism but also those to which it responds that come from within and that set up changes in the nervous system, more or less permanently instigating behavior. These processes are so far poorly understood in human beings; clear evidence for their action—or even evidence that they exist—is still to be found, and it is not known to what extent they contribute to habitual adult behavior (identity). Those processes described so far are imprinting, classical conditioning, and visceral conditioning.

Environmental-intrapsychic. The third category of forces contributing to the development of gender identity is made up of two parts. The first is the effects of shaping—reward and punishment that do not leave deposits of intrapsychic conflict. The second, familiar largely because of Freud's work, is made up of the effects of trauma, frustration, conflict (at first with objects in the outside world and then with one part of oneself attempting to control another), and the efforts the person makes to resolve these conflicts in order to ensure gratification and tranquility. This prolonged childhood development, eventually leading to masculinity and femininity, is known in psychoanalytic circles as the oedipal conflict and its resolution.

The most notable description of the development of gender identity is Freud's. In brief, he believed that maleness and masculinity were the primary and more natural states and that both males and females considered femaleness and femininity to be less valuable (Freud, 1964). Both maleness and femaleness, however, are invaded by attributes of the other sex, and this innate bisexuality has its consequences for both normal and abnormal development (Freud, 1953).

According to Freud, masculinity develops in males as follows. From the start, the biologically normal infant boy is attached literally and figuratively to his mother, a person of the opposite sex. As his awareness of himself and the outside world grows, what at first was attachment in the life-preservative sense becomes libidinized—that is, affection and erotic desire are focused exclusively on his mother. One zone followed by another becomes a source of his libidinal needs, giving rise to stages—oral, anal and urethral, phallic, and, finally, in the fortunate few, according to Freud, mature genitality. The last

stage is defined by a full capacity for orgasmic and loving satisfaction with a person of the opposite sex.

This unfolding of erotic life cannot proceed quite without hazard, however, because the boy's primary love object, his mother, is already committed to his father or other father figures. The boy simply cannot compete on an equal basis. In the typical situation, Freud says, a father serves as a too powerful rival whose threats, open or implied, are seen by the boy as directed at his maleness. For phylogenetic and ontogenetic reasons, that maleness is invested in his genitals; and so, castration anxiety—its source being especially his father, who blocks the boy's access to his mother—forces the boy to detour in his search for an ideal sex object. If the threats are not too great, the boy in time surmounts the danger and, in deferring his hopes, eventually finds other women as gratifying substitutes for his mother. In this process, his father not only serves to threaten but, when himself wholesomely masculine, serves as a model for the boy.

That castration is not just an idle word, Freud says, the boy learns as he becomes aware of the anatomical distinctions between the sexes; when he observes females—his mother, his sisters, or neighborhood girls—he learns first hand of penisless creatures and then has confirmed for him his belief that castration is a reality in the world (Freud, 1955).

The little girl, on the other hand, has a more devious and uncertain gender development, Freud believed. First, her original love object is a person of the same sex, so that, beyond the innate bisexuality already present, she also has from the start another obstacle to surmount, the homosexuality of her first love. Then, too, she is supposed to possess an organ inferior for erotic pleasure. Smaller in size, the clitoris does not serve adequately for dependable erotic pleasure; even worse, in time the girl must shift her genital erotic experiences to the vagina, at first an almost unknown organ, inept for pleasure. And her genitals do not visibly support a sense of pride and power. For these reasons, especially after she has seen one, she wants a penis and fantasies having one, since it is needed for loving mother. Yet, to fulfill biological destiny, she must give up her wish for a penis and her primary love for her mother, renunciations made difficult by the intense experience of the mother-infant relationship. This great permutation requires efforts so monumental that few women, according to Freud, can succeed. In the attempt, the girl has to learn masochism and passivity, these psychological states augmenting already present biological tendencies. The rare and fortunate girl who accomplishes this task loosens the desire for her mother and, on renouncing it and her wish for a penis, turns to her father for comparable, although attenuated, erotic and loving gratifications (Freud, 1964).

To attain proper gender identity, the boy achieves masculinity, said Freud, on resolving the oedipal conflict: the desire for his mother versus the threat of castration from his father. The girl, on the other hand, finds her femininity by entering into the oedipal conflict—that is, by turning to her father and risking her mother's wrath.

The dangers in this development make a bisexual solution possible. Not only is the potential there innately, but, for each sex, sufficient frustration or danger may force the child to give up the desire for the parent of the opposite sex. If the boy is too threatened, he may put on the disguise of femininity; in developing too great an attachment for his father, he may identify with his mother and offer himself, as if a female, to his father. If the little girl, on the other hand, cannot renounce desire for a penis and for her mother, she is also forced to a bisexual solution.

There are data and concepts, however, that reorder Freud's theories. Perhaps crucial is the fact that, for both male and female infants, the first months of life are spent in a state of symbiosis in which the child has not yet separated out himself or herself from the dimensions of the mother's body or psyche. This state of merging, long known to analysts, suggests that the earliest stages of infancy are not experienced as a loving object relationship with mother but rather as if one were part of her. To be part of her is to partake of her being a mother, which is femaleness and femininity. It may be, therefore, that a sort of protofemininity is the first stage in the development of both boys and girls (Stoller, 1973).

Is there evidence of such a stage of protofemininity? If so, one should find forms of behavior recognized as feminine in both male and female infants. However, no behavior clearly recognizable as masculine or feminine is consistently found in infants of either sex before a year or so of age, by which time the process of separation is already underway (Mahler, 1968). One cannot look to females for evidence of this alleged early femininity, for there is no shift from another gender state that could mark the onset of femininity. But if one studies males, one can perhaps find clues.

There are three classes. The first is the most extreme form of femininity found in males, transsexualism. In this rare condition, an excessively close, blissful symbiosis between the mother and her infant son is established from birth on and maintained for years, until modulated by the boy's moving from his mother's embrace in order to start school. When the mother-infant son symbiosis is not relaxed, as it is in the boys who become masculine, no masculinity develops; rather, from the time one can first measure any sort of gender behavior, the boy is feminine.

The second clue is found in the ubiquitous fear in men of being unmanly. In this fear, the castration anxiety of psychoanalysis, and in the transformations of this fear that make up the perversions in men, one finds that—once a male has developed a sense of masculinity, achieved in part in the struggle to separate from the symbiosis with his mother and to create for himself a distinct identity (individuation)—an inner vigilance must be established in the boy. Only this vigilance keeps him from the temptation to regress to that Garden of Eden—the blissful, frustrationless, traumaless experiences in the symbiosis with mother. Thus, the boy (and man) is more or less at risk (depending on how well his parents helped him handle the process of separation and individuation) of having the achievement of masculinity weakened or wiped out. This risk may help account for the facts that the variety and number of perversions are much greater in men than in women and that men are more belligerent in protecting their masculinity than are women in protecting their femininity. It may even help explain the odd finding that accusations of homosexuality in paranoid psychoses are almost universal in males, although, in females, the accusations far more frequently concern heterosexual misdemeanors.

The third clue for the hypothesis of protofemininity comes from a rare group, female transsexuals. If the rule is that femininity is the first stage in the development of gender identity for both males and females and if the achievement of masculinity requires an additional effort on the part of males—breaking from the symbiosis and from the mother's femaleness and femininity—it should also be true that females whose symbiotic relationship with the mother is ruptured are in danger of masculinity. That seems to be the case in female transsexualism. It has been found in such girls that their mothers were unable to establish a true symbiotic relationship, due to severe depression or other pathology that removed these mothers from the mothering care of these infant daughters. In addition, these little girls are encouraged by their fathers to be independent, tough, aggressive, and forceful—that is, to be what the father thinks is masculine. And, as this hypothesis predicts, these little girls become the most masculine of females.

A concept—core gender identity—may help organize the data. Core gender identity is the sense of maleness or the sense of femaleness (Stoller, 1968). It is the conviction, established in the first 2 or 3 years of life, that one belongs to the male or to the female sex. A psychological state, a part of identity, it is not synonymous with belonging to one's sex but, rather, with the conviction that one does so belong. These are not just pedantic minutiae; in the rare case of assignment to the wrong sex, core gender identity almost always follows that assignment rather than the biological state.

Core gender identity is created by the following forces: biological factors (embryological and central nervous system centers); genital anatomy (a signal to parents that they have a boy or a girl and a source of sensation, confirming at all moments the existence, dimensions, and functions of the genitals); sex assignment and rearing (parents' personalities and attitudes—conscious, preconscious, unconscious—about *this* son's or daughter's maleness and masculinity or fe-

maleness and femininity and other people's (society's) attitudes about maleness and masculinity or femaleness and femininity); and "imprinting" (so far, imprinting, to the extent that it is known in some birds and mammals, has not been shown in man, but something like it may play a part in creating core gender identity) and classical, visceral, and operant conditioning (the effect of being raised from birth by a female, the mother).

In the genetically and constitutionally normal female, the brain is not androgenized *in utero* nor are the internal and external sexual organs. As a result, on the basis of the appearance of the external genitals, the mother is informed by unquestioned authority, the person delivering the infant, that the baby is a female. From then on, the reaction of the parents and the manner in which they respond to the infant's sex is that she is a female. Regardless of the variability of attitudes that mothers and fathers must have about a new daughter, one attitude is fixed: "This is a female, our daughter."

The case is not quite as simple for the boy. Although, in the usual case, he, too, brings his normal male biology to his birth and, on the basis of his external genitals, is unequivocally assigned to the male sex, he has an effect playing on him from birth on that has potential consequences different from the girl's. Both sexes are in an intimate relationship with the mother; although this relationship can augment the girl's femininity, it threatens the boy with femininity. So his core gender identity may be a little less absolute; from the start he may not be as unequivocally fixed in his conviction of belonging to his anatomical sex.

These, then, are the circumstances that usually hold; however, there are conditions in which core gender identity formation is invaded from the start with elements of belief that one is not just a member of the male or the female sex. In some intersexed people—those with hermaphroditic external genitals—the assignment of sex by the authorities may be equivocal from the start; the physician delivering the infant may tell the parents that their child is neither a male nor a female or that their child has elements of both. If the parents continue to believe this dictum about their child, the child develops a hermaphroditic identity, in which is permanently laid down a sense that one belongs to neither the male nor the female sex, as do others, but that one is, in his sex, a freak, a hermaphrodite. Another example of a bisexual core gender identity is the transsexual, who, although clearly assigned to the proper anatomical sex, develops a belief that he or she is a member of the opposite sex, regardless of the information given by sex assignment, appearance and sensations of one's genitals, one's name, and one's parents' recognition of one's sex.

The two main factors in creating gender identity—whether it is the gender congruent with anatomy and with what one's culture defines as the proper behavior for one's sex or a distorted gender identity —are the silent effects of learning and the more sharply experienced modifications resulting from frustration, trauma, conflict, and the attempts to resolve conflicts. Thus, parents, siblings, and in time others outside the family may shape masculine and feminine behavior in boys and girls by complicated systems of reward and punishment, subtle and gross. Additionally, prohibitions, threats, and complicated and mixed communications that combine both reward and punishment are taken up by the developing child and, with different stages of maturity and experience, are interpreted to have different meanings. The oedipal conflict and its resolutions are filled with such development.

Disorders

The gender disorders can be divided into two groups, deviations (variants) and perversions (sexual neuroses). The first group is made up of those aberrations of masculinity and femininity that are not the result of intrapsychic conflict; the latter disorders are the result of intrapsychic conflict. For instance, an aberration due to an unusual core gender identity development is a variant, for it is not the result of intrapsychic conflict, avoidance of trauma, or unconscious (repressed) awareness that one has compromised and erected personality attributes to disguise one's true self. An unexpectedly powerful force—biological or early postnatal—that shifts the balance in core gender identity development can produce a variant, such as a transsexual male, who

chooses an object of the same sex but of opposite gender identity. So, too, may sexual styles that change with cultures and eras produce a variant; for example, women's ankles had great fetishistic power 70 years ago in Western society but have none now. Deprivation may also produce a variant, such as the use of animals *faute de mieux* in an adolescent.

Although most modern sex research seems aimed at showing that sex aberrations are merely variants (with the additional benefit that the term "perversion," with its pejorative connotations, could be gotten rid of), the evidence from these researches in this regard is weak (Stoller, 1972). Yet it is almost universally argued these days that the perversions are not created by man's personality but by forces outside his psyche. The argument takes several forms.

The perversions and the marked disorders of gender identity, it is argued, are the result of genetic or constitutional factors or both. Because, in the laboratory, manipulation of the function of animal brains causes reversal of gender behavior, it is argued that the same reversal occurs silently and out of the reach of the researcher's observation in producing gender disorders in man. Ignored is the fact that gender reversal and sexually aberrant behavior for genital gratification are almost unknown in free-ranging lower animals, except when the paranatal hormonal disorder is so great that it produces gross anatomical changes as well. In addition, in most of those natural experiments in man in which prenatal sex hormones cause gender behavior changes—for example, females with hyperadrenalism (Money, 1969), some cases of Klinefelter's syndrome (Money and Pollitt, 1964; Baker and Stoller, 1968), and sons of certain diabetic mothers (Yalom et al., 1973)—the hormonal central nervous system defect produces no perversion and only mild gender change, certainly not gender reversal, except in the androgen insensitivity syndrome and perhaps in rare cases of hypogonadism in males.

The argument that aberrant sexual behavior in man is simply an extension of the same tendencies found throughout the animal kingdom is based on false report. Although lower animals perform bits and pieces of sexual behavior considered aberrant in man, such as members of the same sex mounting each other, there are almost no reports of sexual excitement accompanying this ubiquitous behavior, much less of sexual intercourse leading to ejaculation. The behavior is almost never motivated, as in man, by sexual excitement.

Then there are those who believe that nonconflictual, learning factors are responsible for the development of masculinity and femininity and of gender disorders, not just in core gender identity but throughout life. They explain this normal and aberrant development as the result of conditioning, especially shaping by reward and punishment applied by parents and, especially, by society. They do not find that, for instance, conflict over one's hostile feelings toward desired objects also determines lifelong sexual behavioral patterns.

One might consider almost all the perversions as gender disorders, for, except for the sexual orientation disturbances, most of the perversions are either rare or unknown in women. Whether perversion is sex-linked (biologically determined) or gender-linked (associated with nonbiological forces that influence the development of masculinity and femininity) has not been demonstrated. There are, however, suggestions that the findings may be gender-linked; as yet, the laboratories have produced no evidence for sex linkage.

A clue may be found, as noted above, in the added work required of males, as compared with females, in creating a clear-cut core gender identity. Little boys must successfully separate from their mothers' bodies and personalities. As a result, boys and men are more sensitive than girls and women are to real or imagined threats to their gender identity. It may not be coincidence that manifest or latent hatred of women is found in many of the perversions, with the act of the perversion styled for revenge. This dynamic of hostility is present in the perversions suffered and enjoyed almost exclusively by men—for instance, rape; necrophilia; coprolalia, in which one becomes excited by speaking what one feels is filthy, insulting language to women; exhibitionism, in which one exhibits his penis only to women who are expected to be shocked by it, never to those who would

welcome the view and encourage intercourse; voyeurism, in which one imagines he is peeping at a woman who does not know and would not approve of her being so viewed; excretory perversions, in which one becomes excited by defecating or urinating on one's object. In perversions such as these, sadism is overt. But even in that disguise of sadism known as masochism, hostility and triumph (revenge), this time buried out of sight but still influencing behavior, play their part. In such a situation, the memory of having been the victim of sadism (the power of women to inflict punishment on the boy) is scattered throughout the perverse practice, in which one comes to believe (keeps proving in the perverse act) that he was not, in fact, demolished by the woman but has survived and triumphed; the mark of the triumph is his presumed masculinity, especially his capacity for erection and orgasm, bent but not destroyed the women's power. These mechanisms are planted in the depictions of pornography, which provides a constant source of perverse fantasies tailored to any taste (Stoller, 1970a).

TRANSSEXUALISM

The most extreme form of gender reversal is transsexualism, the belief by an anatomically normal person that he or she is a member of the opposite sex. The gender reversal in both sexes is present as soon as any behavior that can be called masculinity or femininity begins, even as early as 1 year of age. As gender identity develops, there are no episodes of behavior appropriate to one's sex; rather, the person continues unchanged from the femininity present since earliest childhood. Because of the ever sensed incongruity between one's sex and one's gender identity, in time, even as early as adolescence, the transsexual seeks "sex change" procedures, surgical and hormonal techniques aimed at making the body appear and function like that of the opposite sex.

In the literature, the term "transsexual" is usually used simply to indicate anyone who wishes a sex reassignment. But that usage covers different personality types and has no defining quality in regard to a clinical syndrome, cause, indicated treatment, and prognosis. In the following descriptions, transsexual means only someone who has extreme reversal of gender identity; transsexuals make up a much smaller group than all those people who at one time or another may wish to have a sex transformation. The incidence of transsexualism is unknown. If the persons called transsexuals are selected only by the above criterion of being the most feminine of males and the most masculine of females, then a rather clear-cut clinical syndrome (more so in males than in females), with distinguishing dynamics and causes, is found in each sex.

Male transsexualism

Clinical features. At his birth, the male transsexual is clearly recognized as a male, and his mother is overjoyed to have given birth to this son. She gives him a masculine name. Sex assignment is clear-cut. Thrilled to have this infant, she establishes an extremely close and loving symbiosis with him, trying to allow no circumstances or people to interfere. By the time he is a year or two of age, the first intimations of femininity appear; they please his mother, who, however, defines them to herself not as feminine but only as graceful, lovely, appealing, gentle; by rewarding the behavior, she permits it to flower, and it does.

As soon as the child can manage, he spontaneously begins putting on girls' clothes (it is not first done by his mother) and, in all his play, takes girls' parts. He has no interest in masculine activities and, in his choice of stories read to him or of television programs, shows that his fascination is with females. When old enough to play with other children, he joins girls in girls' games. The girls diagnose his femininity accurately; a masculine boy would be excluded from games played only by girls, but the feminine boy insinuates himself effortlessly into their group, and the girls sense that he is one of them. By 3, 4, or 5 years of age, he has given himself a girl's name and is talking of becoming both a girl (an identity and a role) and a female (a biological state) when he grows up. He may even announce that he wishes his penis to be removed.

School becomes increasingly painful, since his femininity marks him for teasing by the other boys but, interestingly, not often by girls. Sooner or later, under the pressure of

his peers, teachers, or neighbors—but not his parents—he may try to hide his femininity, but he does not succeed, and so he finds himself almost friendless. The ensuing state of sadness and loneliness leads to poor school performance, further isolation from other people, and a picture of a generalized neurosis. This, however, is only an appearance, for the "neurosis" is not generated from inner conflict but is, rather, a collection of symptoms, the result of a painful external reality. The proof is that, as soon as the transsexual is given permission by some authority in society, such as a physician, to embark on the task of passing into membership in the female sex, the anxiety, depression, and withdrawn behavior disappear. But lasting relationships with others seem beyond the transsexual's grasp.

Perhaps the commonest diagnosis given the transsexuals, after sexual orientation disturbance, is schizophrenia, a label attached to them by diagnosticians who feel that such a gross turning from one's anatomical reality must be evidence of a delusional system. There is, however, none of the signs and symptoms typical of schizophrenia in these transsexuals, nor would one expect schizophrenia to be cured if one granted the delusional person the reality that his delusion demands. Yet that is what occurs with transsexuals; they need only be told that they will be allowed to pass, and the neurotic symptoms disappear.

Feeling as if he were a girl, although not denying the anatomical maleness, the transsexual single mindedly seeks out "sex change" procedures and, with this desire overriding all other wishes of existence, in time manages to arrange for the following: estrogens to create breasts and otherwise feminize his body contours, electrolysis to remove the male hair distribution, and surgery to create female-appearing genitals by means of castration of the testes, amputation of the penis, and creation of an artificial vagina. Now, "she" can fully pass in society as a female; in fact, "she" has done so for months or years before these procedures. With no rehearsal, often in their teens, transsexuals are able to go into the world and be accepted by society at large unsuspectingly as a female (Benjamin, 1966; Stoller, 1968; Green and Money, 1969).

Causes. What factors cause male transsexualism? There is no point in discussing causes if, in searching for them, one studies several different conditions. This discussion, therefore, is restricted to the most feminine of males, those who have been so since any gender behavior appeared and who have never had a period of masculinity, such as heterosexual liaisons, marriage, employment in masculine professions, military service, fetishism, or other evidence of valuing one's penis. With that restriction, one now has to consider only a small but homogeneous group of persons, all with a similar clinical picture, underlying psychodynamics, and etiological complex.

The boy's mother is a woman with a strong bisexual component in her personality. In childhood, her femininity was flawed because her mother felt no regard for this girl's femaleness and femininity. The mother—a cold, distant, harsh woman—was unable to give the girl a sense of worth, and so the child, although knowing that she was a girl, had the conviction that being a girl was of no value and far inferior to being a boy. Her father and she, on the other hand, started with a good relationship, and so she was able to feel loved by one parent. Unfortunately, in their close relationship, he encouraged her to share in his interests. Since these interests were masculine, the feeling she acquired from her mother that boys were better than girls was augmented by her father's encouraging her in athletics and boys' hobbies, and by dressing in a boyish manner. Then, usually sometime before puberty, her father abandoned her, by separation or divorce, by his dying, or by his turning to one of her younger siblings. When that happened, the girl's masculinity broke out. She decided that she would grow up to be both a male and a man, wear only males' clothes, play only with boys in boys' sports in which she excels in equal competition with them. She even hoped and expected someday to have a penis. In other words, for several years, she looked as if she would be a female transsexual.

Then, however, with the feminizing changes of puberty, her hopes were wrecked, and so she put on a feminine façade. In time—without heterosexual impulse, love, or romance—she married.

She chose a man, the transsexual-to-be's father, who was distant and passive; only occasionally do these men have an effeminate tinge. He would not, therefore, inflict on her the masculinity or maleness for which she has such great envy. Instead, he offered himself up to her as an object for her scorn. His function was to provide the family with a never ending example of male ineptitude; he was to work and support his family, but his presence was to be evidenced only in her outspokenly disparaging attitude, not by his being physically present. And so, when this son was an infant, his father was not there. The man left home in the morning for work before the boy had awakened and came home after his son was asleep; on the weekends, he was willingly absent from his son's presence by being occupied in his hobbies, solitary television watching, or other forms of removal.

These, then, are the parents who produce the transsexual. Yet, almost invariably, only one son in the family is the transsexual (Stoller and Baker, 1973). Why is that? What precipitates the femininity only at this time in the family? This boy is chosen because his mother finds him beautiful. All the mothers report that in infancy these sons appear physically lovely and cuddly, with a graceful quality their mothers adore.

Contrary to what one might predict, these mothers, despite their envy of maleness, are thrilled when they give birth to this son. They do not wish a daughter and, in fact, give this boy a markedly masculine, heroic, warrior, or king-like name; there is no intimation of a wish for a girl, as may be seen in a softer or bisexual name. Now begins the process out of which develops the boy's femininity. Having in her arms, possessing, having brought forth from her own body this beautiful male child—this phallus—the mother finally has a cure for her lifelong sense of worthlessness. Her desire for loving completeness with this son is profound; in her joy at holding in her arms a cure for her sadness, she finds herself unable to let go. And so, usually skin-to-skin, in the most loving embrace, she keeps her infant against her body and psyche for months and then for years. An excessively close, blissful symbiosis develops. Although within this embrace she allows the boy to develop in an otherwise unremarkable manner—he learns to walk, talk, and relate to others and even becomes artistically creative—the two are all too close in the sharing of mother's femaleness. This is not heterosexual; rather, it is an endless continuation of the merging of their two bodies from earliest infancy.

The child's femininity begins to appear as soon as any gender behavior is manifested; when it does so, the second part of the process of its creation is underway: the positive reinforcement of all behavior that the mother finds graceful, lovely, clean, tender—that is, what she would define as not masculine. To allow her son masculinity would arouse in her the envy that would ruin their love.

The feminizing process is uninterrupted; she has ensured that in her choice of husband. He is not there to disturb the obviously intense symbiosis or to serve as a model for his son's masculinity, as other fathers do. And so the process goes on until the boy goes to school. By then, without treatment, it is too late. As committed to his gender identity as are nontranssexual children of 5 or 6, he does not give it up because people tell him to; instead, he tries to cope with their taunting. But, his femininity fixed, he is not about to change, and so, as the years pass, he can only wish to find a way that will allow him to be a girl. He does find that way because now there are techniques for making his body appear female.

Although experts speculate that transsexualism must be the result of genetic, hormonal, or central nervous system factors, or a combination of these factors, no evidence has been found in human beings. In fact, no complete gender reversal is found in anatomically intact animals, except in the laboratory. The only biological contribution to etiology known at present is the boys' beauty and grace, and very few beautiful boys become transsexuals.

Treatment. Although few cases have been reported, one can be cautiously optimistic that treating the very feminine boy may stop the progress of his developing femininity (Greenson, 1966; Stoller, 1970b; Green et al., 1972). In essence, the treatment is behavior modification, although the guidelines are drawn from a more dynamic approach—an understanding of the interplay of forces in the family. In addition to treating the boy, encouraging the pleasures of masculinity and discouraging femininity, the mother must

also be treated. The minimal hope in her treatment is that the inevitable depression ensuing as such a mother gives up her beautiful, feminized phallus can be made bearable and that she, in her pain, will not sabotage the boy's treatment and draw him back to her. Attempts to involve the fathers in treatment have so far failed, which is not surprising, since these men habitually remove themselves from their families. There is no report of an adolescent being treated by behavior modification alone and then developing masculinity and heterosexuality (Barlow et al., 1973); further work is necessary to corroborate this.

So far, no treatment has been reported that will make the adult transsexual masculine; with adult transsexuals, one can either do nothing or comply with the patient's wish for a "sex change." Some have felt that doing the latter is the same as treating delusions by giving a patient what he delusionally demands, but their suggestion that the patient be treated by psychotherapy or psychoanalysis has yet to meet with success (at least none has been reported). On the other hand, when sex change procedures are used on these most feminine males (although by no means is this true for all patients receiving such treatment), the results seem uniformly successful; the patients are more content, become employable, and establish sturdier relationships with others.

Female transsexualism

Clinical features. Female transsexuals are the most masculine of females. These anatomically normal females have been masculine since early childhood and have not had episodes in their lives when they expressed femininity. Like the males, they are exclusively homosexual if measured by the anatomy of their sex objects but heterosexual if measured by identity. They, like the males, do not deny their anatomical sex but are, nonetheless, unendingly preoccupied with the sense of really being men and with the desire to have their bodies changed to male. Although males can surgically receive a genital that can function in a female manner—even including, at times, capacity for orgasm—it is not yet possible to give to a female functioning testes or a penis. However, with testosterone, mastectomy, and panhyste-rectomy, the patient can pass as a man.

When a child, this girl refuses to be a girl. She gives herself a boy's name, dresses completely in boys' clothes, and is interested in and skillful in the same activities as are boys. For instance, in sports, she is one of the best athletes, fully competitive with the most skillful boys. As soon as she can, often in adolescence, she passes as a young man. As with the male transsexuals, she successfully appears as a male, without rehearsal and the first time out in public, no one suspecting the true sex. Even before a sex change, the patient has found a partner with whom she lives for a long time, perhaps permanently. This partner is not an overt homosexual but is usually a woman who has not had homosexual relations, who has been married and had children, and who responds to the patient as if she were a man without a penis, not as if she were a homosexual.

Causes. Although the evidence is fragmentary, the following may account for female transsexualism (Stoller, 1972). At the time this infant is born—an infant seen by her parents as not pretty or cuddly but as strong and vigorous—or in the early months of life, her mother is unavailable for mothering. This is usually because the mother is clinically depressed, although in some cases the mother has been absent from her mothering (but not physically absent) because of a severe physical illness or other invaliding psychological illness. That she is physically but not psychologically present sets up a poignant situation, more intense than if mother were completely gone and replaced by an adequate substitute. At this time in the relationship between her parents, the infant's father is either unwilling or unable to move in and by himself carry the burden of his wife's problem. The little girl is used for that; she is to be a comfort and a cure that the father will not provide. Her task, she comes to sense, is to restore her mother. In doing this, she is supported by her father, with whom she has a close and happy relationship, but, in order to do so, she becomes her father's substitute. He encourages her in behavior he considers masculine, and so she spends much time with him successfully learning to be like his little boy. His joy when she is physically adept and

then athletically skilled and his pleasure in having her accompany him when he works around the house or at his hobbies, when he hunts or fishes, augments the encouragement to be masculine she already senses in having been chosen as father's substitute in her mother's suffering.

This process is furthered from the start by the girl's unlovely appearance. Had she been considered feminine, she would not have served as well for molding into masculinity.

As with male transsexualism, there is no reported evidence of biological factors in the etiology other than the appearance just noted.

Treatment. There are no cases reported in the literature of child, adolescent, or adult female transsexuals being successfully treated by any method that would make them feminine. As with the males, they establish a clear-cut core gender identity, and it is difficult later in life to instill attributes of an opposite gender identity. Whether behavioristic techniques in the future will succeed in doing this or not is still unknown.

FETISHISTIC CROSS-DRESSING (TRANSVESTISM)

Clinical features. Sexual excitement produced by garments of the opposite sex is found exclusively in males; only one exception appears in the whole literature in English (Gutheil, 1964). Although this deviation starts most often in adolescence, it has been seen in prepubertal boys and may even first manifest itself in adult men in their thirties or forties. There are two groups, those men who prefer a single type of garment, such as shoes, throughout their lives and those who, starting with a single garment, eventually prefer to dress completely as women and who, in addition to the penile gratification, also have the nonerotic pleasure of feeling themselves temporarily to be women with penises.

The terms "transvestism" and "transvestitism" have been used in the literature to cover any sort of cross-dressing. In the *Diagnostic and Statistical Manual of Mental Disorders* (DSM-II), transvestitism is neither defined nor discussed, only listed. This lack of definition obviously leads to confusion if one is searching for causes or choosing treatments. Cross-dressing is an outstanding feature of all gender disorders, but the rest of the clinical features, dynamics, and causative factors can so differ that no useful purpose is served by giving them all the same label (Stoller, 1971a). It is suggested herein that the term "transvestism" be used only for fetishistic cross-dressing.

By whatever chance circumstances the boy or man himself spontaneously first puts on women's clothes, he is astonished to find himself intensely excited sexually. From that experience on, he recognizes this to be his greatest and sometimes only mode of sexual gratification. Because of the risks involved of being found in women's clothes, the activity is usually secretive. In time, however, the man may find other men who share his interest or, if married, may be able to enlist his wife in the activity.

Most transvestites are overtly heterosexual and marry (Prince and Bentler, 1972). They work in professions requiring masculine interests and behavior; they dress, except when cross-dressed, in masculine clothes; and they have masculine interests and hobbies and engage in masculine sports. They do not wish to be females, except for a few whose fetishistic desires are weaker than most and whose wish to be feminine is stronger, and even these come to this wish hesitatingly, after many years, with many rehearsals; then, if not quickly granted a "sex change," they usually back away, satisfied to be women with penises. By far the greatest number cross-dress only intermittently, spending most of their time willingly as masculine-enough men. Perhaps, however, if society gets more lenient, we shall learn that the natural history for these transvestites is to end up, in their later years, living fully as women with penises. When doing so, however, they do not feel themselves to be females. Quite the opposite. Nothing could emphasize their maleness more than their intense, gratifying erection when dressed in women's clothes (Stoller, 1971b).

Causes. Although the causative factors are less clear in transvestism than in transsexualism, many transvestites or their families or both report that the first episode of cross-dressing occurred when a female dressed the boy in girls' clothes in childhood, at which time he was not sexually excited. The cross-dressing was done to humiliate

him; that is, it was done by a female attacking an essential of the boy's identity, his masculinity. Years later, however, the fetishism—erotic cross-dressing—surfaced. In all cases of transvestism, as differentiated from transsexualism, there is a history of some masculine development and present-day masculinity (Stoller, 1968; Stoller, 1970). One could not humiliate a transsexual at any age by putting him into girls' clothes.

If this history is part of the cause of transvestism, it accounts for the finding that these men are otherwise masculine, enjoy their penises, and do not usually request a sex change. The pornography of transvestites gives further evidence that this thesis may be correct. Therein is found a recapitulation of the life history; in many of these illustrated stories, a masculine young man is forced by women into their clothes in humiliating circumstances. Later, the hero finds this cross-dressing enjoyable; encouraged by the women, who are now his friends as he becomes cooperative, he establishes a happy pattern whereby he can continue this behavior when he wishes and with their joyful cooperation (Stoller, 1970b).

Evidence of a biological cause has not surfaced. The suggestion that an abnormal electroencephalogram exists in some transvestites (Walinder, 1967) has not been corroborated.

Treatment. There are no reports of the treatment of a series of fetishistic cross-dressers who lost the perversion after psychotherapy or psychoanalysis. However, recent reports show that behavior modification techniques can be successful (Marks and Gelder, 1967). Although the follow-up time in these reports is too short for a final decision about efficaciousness, the aberrant sexual behavior can be removed in some of those who choose to have it removed. The more purely fetishistic the patient is, the better is the prognosis with this treatment. The more his condition consists also of desires to pass in public as a woman, the poorer the results (Gelder and Marks, 1969).

CROSS-GENDER HOMOSEXUALITY

Many male and female homosexuals (no reports tell how many) have cross-gender qualities. One sees a continuum among homosexuals of each sex, the males ranging from having no effeminate qualities to having a marked and persistent effeminacy, the females from being nonmasculine to being in states approaching female transsexualism. The prime feature stressed herein for distinguishing these people from others with gender disorders is that those considered here are overt homosexuals, acknowledging, at least to themselves, that this is the case and clearly preferring people of the same sex. That last qualification can be underlined by stating that the homosexual feels that he prefers a person of the same sex; the transsexual, in contrast, feels himself heterosexual.

Homosexuals like their own genitals and feel that these organs are appropriate. Sexually, they prefer people with the same genitals. Homosexuals are, in the vast majority, uninterested in sex change. Fetishistic excitement from clothes of the opposite sex is rare in homosexual males and unknown in transsexuals. Cross-dressing in homosexuals is not for the purpose of passing as a member of the opposite sex. In males, it derives from identification with women and hostility toward them; the undercurrent of mimicry reveals the disturbance in identifying with women that helps save the male homosexual from being transsexual. In butch female homosexuals, cross-dressing is used to increase the sense of masculinity, but it is not carried to such an extent that one would think the person is a male. The male homosexual, like the transvestite and unlike the transsexual, has developed a degree of masculinity that is threatened in childhood by either or both parents, who make a sustained development of comfortable masculinity impossible.

PSYCHOSES AND BORDERLINE STATES

Although flagrant cross-gender behavior is not typical of psychoses and borderline states, it is occasionally seen. The gender disorder is sometimes only a minor element in the patient's style of behavior and at other times dominates it, creating a bizarre picture indeed. The gender disorder may be found with or without homosexuality and with or without fetishism; the main features, as in any psychosis, are the signs and symptoms of psychosis that always define the state. That criterion distinguishes this present category from transsexualism, in which the signs and symptoms commonly accepted as those of

psychosis are very rare and the femininity is natural and easy, rather than the psychotic's bizarre appearance when cross-dressed.

A mild form of gender disorder typically found in paranoid males, psychotic or borderline, are accusations of homosexuality; on closer examination, these accusations are seen to be threats of transsexual disintegration; the hallucinations or delusions threaten the patient with losing attributes of the sex or gender he prizes. This finding is uncommon, however, in women; for them, the paranoid content is usually of heterosexual jeopardy and accusations.

INTERSEXUALITY

Today, the term "intersexuality" is used in discussing those with gross anatomical or physiological aspects of the opposite sex. These aspects may be found in the chromosomes (such as XXY and XO), external genitals (such as pseudohermaphroditism), internal sexual apparatuses (such as absent uterus and proximal vagina with concomitant masculinized external genitals in a female), gonads (such as ovotestes), and hormonal state and resultant secondary sex characteristics (such as androgen insensitivity syndrome). The discussion here need only be concerned with those intersexualities in which there are concomitants in gender identity. These patients serve as natural experiments who test rules related to the influence of biological forces on gender identity development.

Two distinct factors contribute to the development of gender identity in intersexed patients. The first is that sex assignment and parental influences during rearing account for the core gender identity in most patients, given an uneventful fetal hormonal-central nervous system development (Money et al., 1957; Stoller, 1968). The second factor is that, when abnormal fetal hormonal-central nervous system development occurs, gender identity is bent in the direction predictable from animal studies—androgenization of the brain turns the child toward masculinity, and absence of androgenization tends the child toward femininity (Money and Ehrhardt, 1972). One can see these rules at work in the following syndromes, which are the major intersexualities in which gender identity can be an issue.

Turner's syndrome. In this condition, one

sex chromosome is missing (XO), and so only a female chromosome is present to influence sex development. The result is an absence (agenesis) or minimal development (dysgenesis) of the gonads; no significant sex hormone, male or female, is produced in fetal life or postnatally. The sexual tissues thus retain a female resting state. Since the second X chromosome, which seems to be responsible for full femaleness, is missing, these girls are incomplete in their sexual anatomy and, lacking adequate estrogens, develop no secondary sex characteristics without treatment. They often suffer other stigmata, such as web neck. The infant is born with normal appearing female external genitals and so is unequivocally assigned to the female sex and thus reared. All these children develop as unremarkably feminine, heterosexually oriented girls, although later medical management is necessary to assist them with their infertility and absence of secondary sex characteristics (Money and Ehrhardt, 1972).

Klinefelter's syndrome. This person (usually XXY) has a male habitus, under the influence of the Y chromosome, but this effect is weakened by the presence of the second X chromosome. Although he is born with a penis and testes, the testes are small and infertile, and the penis may also be small. In adolescence, some of these patients develop gynecomastia and other feminine appearing contours. Sexual desire is usually weak. Sex assignment and rearing should lead to a clear sense of maleness, but these patients often have gender disturbances, ranging from a complete reversal, as in transsexualism, to homosexuality or an intermittent desire to put on women's clothes (Money and Pollitt, 1964; Baker and Stoller, 1968). It seems that, as a result of lessened androgen production, the fetal hypogonadal state in some patients has failed to produce fully the central nervous system organization that should underlie masculine behavior. In fact, there is a wide spread of psychopathology in many of these patients, well beyond that of gender (Money and Pollitt, 1964).

Adrenogenital syndrome. When this condition occurs in females, excessive adrenal fetal androgens cause masculinization of the external genitals, ranging from mild clitoral enlargement to external genitals that look like a normal scrotal sac, testes, and a penis; hidden behind these external genitals are a vagina and a uterus. These patients are otherwise normally female. At birth, if the genitals look male, the child is assigned to the male sex and is so reared; the result is a clear sense of maleness and unremarkable masculinity; but if the child is diagnosed as a female and so reared, a sense of femaleness and femininity results (Money, 1955). If the parents are uncertain as to which sex their child belongs, a hermaphroditic identity results. Although these patients show the power of rearing, the resultant gender identity seems to be also the effect of fetal androgens, organizing the fetal brain in a masculine direction, for what results in those children raised unequivocally as girls is a tomboy quality more intense than found in a control series but with the girls nonetheless having a heterosexual orientation (Ehrhardt et al., 1968).

Male pseudohermaphroditism. Different conditions can lead to hermaphroditic external genitals in otherwise normal males. The genitals' appearance at birth, not the true biological maleness, determines the sex assignment, and the core gender identity is male, female, or hermaphroditic, depending on the family's conviction as to the child's sex (Money et al., 1955).

Androgen insensitivity syndrome. This congenital (probably genetic but not chromosomal) disorder results from an inability to target tissues to respond to androgens. Unable to respond, the fetal tissues remain in their female resting state, and the brain is not organized to masculinity. The infant at birth appears an unremarkable female, although she will later be found to have cryptorchid testes, which produce the testosterone to which the tissues do not respond, and minimal or absent internal sexual organs. Secondary sex characteristics at puberty are female because of the small but sufficient amounts of estrogens typically produced by the testes. These patients invariably sense themselves as females and are feminine (Money, 1969).

Temporal lobe abnormality. There are a handful of cases of gender disorders, all in males, associated with temporal lobe dysfunction and remitted when the brain disorder is treated—for example, impulsive cross-dressing (Blumer, 1969). Perhaps related are reports stating that electroencephalograms show dysrhythmias in transsexuals and transvestites more frequently than in control groups. These reports need corroboration before one speculates on the role of the temporal lobes in gender behavior.

Treatment. Obviously, these different disorders require different medical and psychiatric management. The first rule, however, is that attempts to change gender orientation should be based on careful investigation of the patient's present gender identity. The somatic state should not cause one to inflict arbitrarily on the patient an attempt at creating a new personality; judgments about somatic state must be made on the basis of identity.

There are two truths in dealing with such patients. The first is biological and is the scientist's concern. The second is psychological and is of crucial concern to the patient. When the two truths lead to incompatibility, such as that the chromosomes are male but the identity is fixed in femininity with a sense of femaleness, then the identity truth should prevail.

Decisions about sex reassignment must be based on the patient's sense of self. When the physician has made this decision, then the decisions about surgery and hormones—about the ultimate anatomical appearance of the body—fall into place. In the newborn, however, where no gender identity has yet formed, one can take comfort in the finding that gender identity, except in the rare cases noted above, is the result of sex assignment and rearing. In practice, this means that, since it is easier to create a female than a male body because a functioning penis cannot yet be contrived, the easier decision in the newborn, hormonally and surgically, is to attempt reconstruction that results in female morphology.

If a hermaphroditic core gender identity has formed, decisions to reassign sex are usually easy enough. Since, with this identity, the patient is not firmly fixed with either a sense of maleness or a sense of femaleness, it is generally possible to suggest that the patient change sex in either direction if such a change is indicated for somatic reasons.

REFERENCES

American Psychiatric Association. *Diagnostic and Statistical Manual of Mental Disorders* (DSM-II), ed. 3. American Psychiatric Association, Washington, 1968.

Baker, H. J., and Stoller, R. J. Can a biological force contribute to gender identity? Am. J. Psychiatry, *124:* 1653, 1968.

Barlow, D. H., Reynolds, E. J., and Agras, S. Gender identity change in a transsexual. Arch. Gen. Psychiatry, *28:* 569, 1973.

Benjamin, H. *The Transsexual Phenomenon.* Julian Press, New York, 1966.

Blumer, D. Transsexualism, sexual dysfunction, and temporal lobe disorder. In *Transsexualism and Sex Reassignment,* R. Green and J. Money, editors, p. 213. Johns Hopkins Press, Baltimore, 1969.

Ehrhardt, A. A., Epstein, R., and Money, J. Fetal androgens and female gender identity in the early-treated adrenogenital syndrome. Johns Hopkins Med. J., *122:* 160, 1968.

*Freud, S. Three essays on the theory of sexuality. In *Standard Edition of the Complete Psychological Works of Sigmund Freud,* vol. 7, p. 135. Hogarth Press, London, 1953.

Freud, S. Analysis of a phobia in a five-year-old boy. In *Standard Edition of the Complete Psychological Works of Sigmund Freud,* vol. 10, p. 5. Hogarth Press, London, 1955.

Freud, S. Psycho-analytic notes on an autobiographical account of a case of paranoia (dementia paranoides). In *Standard Edition of the Complete Psychological Works of Sigmund Freud,* vol. 12, p. 9. Hogarth Press, London, 1958.

Freud, S. Femininity. In *Standard Edition of the Complete Psychological Works of Sigmund Freud,* vol. 22, p. 112. Hogarth Press, London, 1964.

Gelder, M. G., and Marks, I. M. Aversion treatment in transvestism and transsexualism. In *Transsexualism and Sex Reassignment,* R. Green and J. Money, editors, p. 383. Johns Hopkins Press, Baltimore, 1969.

*Green, R., and Money, J., editors. *Transsexualism and Sex Reassignment.* Johns Hopkins Press, Baltimore, 1969.

Green, R., Newman, L. E., and Stoller, R. J. Treatment of boyhood "transsexualism." Arch. Gen. Psychiatry, *26:* 213, 1972.

Greenson, R. R. A transvestite boy and a hypothesis. Int. J. Psychoanal., *47:* 396, 1966.

Gutheil, E. Case report. In *Sexual Aberrations,* W. Stekel, vol. 1, p. 281. Grove Press, New York, 1964.

Jost, A. Embryonic sexual differentiation. In *Hermaphroditism, Genital Anomalies, and Related Endocrine Disorders,* H. W. Jones and W. W. Scott, editors, p. 15. Williams & Wilkins, Baltimore, 1958.

*Jost, A. A new look at the mechanisms controlling sex differentiation in mammals. Johns Hopkins Med. J., *130:* 38, 1972.

Mahler, M. *On Human Symbiosis and the Vicissitudes of Individuation.* International Universities Press, New York, 1968.

Money, J. Hermaphroditism, gender and precocity in hyperadrenocorticism: psychologic findings. Bull. Johns Hopkins Hosp., *96:* 253, 1955.

Money, J. Sex reassignment as related to hermaphroditism and transsexualism. In *Transsexualism and Sex Reassignment,* R. Green and J. Money, editors, p. 91. Johns Hopkins Press, Baltimore, 1969.

*Money, J., and Erhardt, A. A. *Man and Woman/Boy and Girl.* Johns Hopkins Press, Baltimore, 1972.

*Money, J., Hampson, J. G., and Hampson, J. L. An examination of some basic sexual concepts: The evidence of human hermaphroditism. Bull. Johns Hopkins Hosp., *97:* 301, 1955.

Money, J., Hampson, J. G., and Hampson, J. L. Imprinting and the establishment of gender role. Arch. Neurol. Psychiatry, *77:* 333, 1957.

Money, J., and Pollitt, E. Cytogenetic and psychosexual ambiguity: Klinefelter's syndrome and transvestism compared. Arch. Gen. Psychiatry, *11:* 589, 1964.

Prince, V., and Bentler, P. M. Survey of 504 cases of transvestism. Psychol. Rep., *31:* 903, 1972.

Stoller, R. J. A contribution to the study of gender identity. Int. J. Psychoanal., *45:* 220, 1964.

*Stoller, R. J. *Sex and Gender.* Science House, New York, 1968.

Stoller, R. J. Pornography and perversion. Arch. Gen. Psychiatry, *22:* 490, 1970a.

Stoller, R. J. Psychotherapy of extremely feminine boys. Int. J. Psychiatry, *9:* 278, 1970b.

Stoller, R. J. The term "transvestism." Arch. Gen. Psychiatry, *24:* 230, 1971a.

Stoller, R. J. Transsexualism and transvestism. Psychiatr. Ann., *1:* 61, 1971b.

Stoller, R. J. Etiological factors in female transsexualism: A first approximation. Arch. Sex. Behav., *2:* 47, 1972.

Stoller, R. J. The impact of new advances in sex research on psychoanalytic theory. Am. J. Psychiatry, *130:* 241, 1973.

Stoller, R. J., and Baker, H. J. Two male transsexuals in one family. Arch. Sex. Behav., *2:* 323, 1973.

Walinder, J. *Transsexualism.* Akademiförlaget, Göteborg, 1967.

Yalom, I. D., Green, R., and Fisk, N. Prenatal exposure to female hormones. Arch. Gen. Psychiatry, *28:* 554, 1973.

5.2   Atypical Sex Role Behavior During Childhood

RICHARD GREEN, M.D.

Introduction

Cross-dressing by children, accompanied by other cross-gender behavior, has existed in many cultures. In recent Western society there has been considerable augmentation of interest in such behavior, with the publicity given to adults who undergo surgical sex change (Green and Money, 1969). These adults typically recall that their cross-gender behavior began during childhood. The fact that harbingers of adult atypical sex role behavior may be identifiable during childhood has provoked an interest in atypical children. Thus, developmental studies have been initiated to better understand the causes of atypical adult behavior and also to interdict such an outcome.

Cross-cultural Aspects

A subgroup of boys and girls in many societies has adopted the dress and activities more typical of other-sexed children. This behavior is typically reported to begin early in life and to remain an enduring personality feature. Cultures other than our own have generally accommodated such behavior, at times affording these children priority status.

Among the Cocopa Indians of North America, males called "e L ha" were reported to show feminine character from babyhood. As children, they were described as talking like girls, seeking the company of girls, and doing things in women's style. Girls known as "warhemeh" played only with boys, made bows and arrows, had their noses pierced, and later fought in battles (Gifford, 1933). The Yuma Indians recognized young boys who would later be "transformed into women." "Berdache," a nonpejorative term, was applied to those males who behaved like women (Bulliet, 1928). Devereux (1937) described Mohave Indian boys who were destined to become shamans, (priest-doctors who used magic.) They would pull back their penis between their legs and then display themselves to women, saying, 'I, too, am a woman; I am just like you are!' " These boys refused to play with boys' toys or wear boys' clothes. Similarly, there were girls who rejected dolls, copied boys' behavior, and refused to wear skirts.

In Madagascar, among the Sakalavas, boys who were noted to be delicate and girlish in appearance were raised as girls. And, on the Aleutians, very handsome young boys would also be brought up as girls, with their beards being plucked at puberty. They would later be married to wealthy men (Westermarck, 1917).

Of especial interest in these accounts is the early onset of a lifelong cross-gender identity.

Causes

Various theories exist as to the development of atypical gender role behavior. A clinical research project conducted by the author is assessing 50 families with preadolescent boys who prefer the dress, activities, toys, and companionship of girls. These boys and their families are being compared with control families with boys showing typical gender role behavior. Some early life experiences of the feminine boys include:

1. Parental encouragement or unconcern for feminine behavior in the boy during his first years.

2. Lack of psychological separation of the boy from his mother, resulting from factors that include excessive holding of a cuddly baby.

3. Maternal overprotection of the young boy, with marked inhibition of rough-and-tumble play and male peer group interaction.

4. Lack of availability of male playmates during the earliest years of socialization, coupled with the accessibility of female companions.

5. Absence of an older male to serve as an identity model during the boy's first years.

6. Gross rejection of the young boy by his father.

7. Unusual physical beauty in the boy, which influences adults to treat him as though he were a girl.

The above factors have been extensively detailed by Green (1973), with considerable clinical documentation. What appears to be necessary for the development of a strong feminine identity is that during the first 2 to 4 years of life, while the boy shows culturally feminine behavior, the parents consider the behavior to be cute or a normal passing phase. The parents make no attempt to discourage it.

The foregoing early life experiences of boys who develop feminine identities should not be construed as meaning the child's behavior is a derivative purely of these experiences and contains no contribution from innate or constitutional factors. Children are not all the same at birth. They differ with respect to temperamental features, such as neonatal cuddliness and activity levels and early childhood activity and aggressivity levels. Mothers of feminine boys typically describe those sons as having been the cuddliest of their children. The boys tend to avoid rough-and-tumble play, complaining: "Boys play too rough." They seek the companionship and activities of girls and women.

Although the bases of such innate differences are not fully known, there is a body of data pointing to a neuroendocrine contribution. Preadolescent girls exposed to large amounts of androgenic hormones before birth are unusually rough-and-tumble and culturally unfeminine (Ehrhardt et al., 1968; Ehrhardt, 1973). These are girls with the adrenogenital syndrome, with its excessive production of adrenal androgenic steroids, or girls whose mothers received an androgenic synthetic progesterone during pregnancy. Conversely, the author, with Yalom and Fisk, has studied two populations of boys, aged 6 and 16, whose mothers received large doses of estrogens and a lesser amount of progesterone during pregnancy. The results must be interpreted with caution, because of the inability to control for all variables in the contrast (no hormone) populations, but those boys exposed to female hormones *in utero* were found to be less athletic, less assertive, and less aggressive (Yalom et al., 1973).

Postnatal experiences that influence gender identity must not be obscured by neuroendocrine data. Anatomically intersexed children typically develop an identity consistent with their sex of assignment, even when that assignment contradicts such anatomical criteria for sex as chromosomal configuration and internal reproductive structures (Money et al., 1955 and 1957; Stoller, 1968). A classic example is that of two chromosomally female patients with the adrenogenital syndrome, both born with ambiguous external genitalia, with one being assigned male at birth and one being assigned female. Each developed a gender identity consistent with the assigned sex (Money and Ehrhardt, 1973). Additionally, the author, in collaboration with Stoller, has reported two sets of monozygotic twins discordant for gender identity. One is a set of 8-year-old anatomically normal boys, one of whom wants to be a girl. The other is a set of 24-year-old anatomically normal females, one of whom wants to be a man. In both sets of twins, it was possible to identify differential early life socialization experiences that could explain their divergence in psychosexual development (Green and Stoller, 1971).

Cross-gender Behavior
BOYS

Many preschool boys occasionally put on girls' or women's dress-up clothes during nursery school play or in make-believe games at home. Similarly, they may from time to time role play as women, usually as mother or teacher. They may also occasionally play with dolls. Typically, such play becomes increasingly rare with the start of grade school. However, a small group of anatomically normal boys show, from the first years of life, an enduring, overriding interest in the clothes, activities, and toys of girls; they role play almost exclusively as females, strongly prefer girls as playmates, and overtly state their wish to be girls.

As stated, the onset of this strong cross-gender role orientation is early. In about two-thirds of the feminine boys, the enduring interest in cross-dressing commenced by the fourth birthday. The remainder began before 6. The extent to which these boys wish to cross-dress is evidenced by the ingenuity with which they improvise feminine attire. When denied access to genuine women's articles—such as high heeled shoes, dresses, and wigs—they create them from available materials.

Large towels become long dresses, small towels become long hair, T shirts become dresses, building blocks convert slippers into high heeled shoes, and felt-tipped marking pens are pressed into service to simulate cosmetics.

Peer group preference is atypical. These boys avoid male agemates, asserting, "Boys play too rough." Role playing reveals their basic identity. When they play house, they do not play the father but insist on being the mother, in spite of their having girls as playmates. Should little girl playmate insist on being the mother, the boy compromises; he role plays as the teacher or a little girl. The television characters imitated are usually female; they are Batwoman, not Batman.

Toy preference is atypical, Barbie doll being the favorite. Should the parents gradually attempt to reorient their son's play by providing Ken dolls (Barbie's male counterpart), the boys continue to insist on Barbie, costuming and recostuming her by the hour. Figure drawings also give a clue to the boys' basic identity. When pictures are drawn, they are replete with females; males are rarely, if ever, included. Feminine fashions are also of considerable interest. The boys are exquisitely sensitive to their mothers' clothes, helping them select new ones at the store and advising them on what to wear at home. In a very direct manner, many ask their mothers why they cannot be girls, with some asserting that they are girls while cross-dressed.

Teasing by male agemates is considerable. The presence of feminine gestures, coupled with a strong preference for girl playmates and an aversion to rough-and-tumble play, results in these boys being labeled sissies.

Parents of the feminine boys typically see their sons' behavior, at least during its initial years, as a normal passing phase. Some consider it cute and show it off to relatives and friends, posing and photographing their children in dresses and wigs and laughing at them in a supportive way. During these years no effort is made to interdict the atypical behavior. Only when the child enters grade school and his behavior comes to the attention of others, children who tease him and teachers who express concern to the parents, may parental attitudes change. Fathers more than mothers continue to deny the potentially enduring nature of their sons' behavior, asserting, "He'll outgrow it." As pressure on the boy and his parents mounts in consequence of the family's interface with the larger community, professional consultation may be sought, usually at about age 7 or 8.

A 7-year-old boy was brought for evaluation by his parents because he wanted to wear high heeled shoes and women's clothes and stated that he wished he were a girl.

The mother was 32 years old. She had been moderately tomboyish as a girl, enjoying participation in rough-and-tumble play and sports, but she also enjoyed cooking and reading. Her relationship with both parents had been rather distant, and she was happy to leave home in her late teens and marry. The father was 34 years old and had had a moderate interest in sports as a child but participated less than most boys his age. He recalled a close relationship with his mother and a somewhat distant one with his father. He had no recollection of ever having worn girls' clothes as a child and stated that he had never participated in any male-male sexual contact after the onset of his teens.

The marital relationship was described as irregular, with the couple having considered divorce on a few occasions. The wife asserted that her husband took too little interest in the family and that most decision making was left to her. The husband asserted that his work took up most of his energy.

The couple had an older boy and a younger daughter. Before the birth of this child, the father had wanted a boy, the mother a girl.

The mother described her son as an infant this way: "He was pretty. You know, you don't associate pretty with a boy, but he was a pretty baby. He had really big eyes and long lashes. He loved to be held."

She then recalled the onset of the boy's atypical behavior: "At about 18 months, he began wearing high heeled shoes. I thought it was funny. I didn't think much of it. Then at 2, 2½, he liked to put things on his head, dish towels, anything that looked like long hair."

When asked about the current frequency of his wearing high heeled shoes, the mother replied, "Every day, if you let him." Regarding his make-believe games, she noted: "He has a towel on his head, and he's Batgirl, not Batman, or he's the Flying Nun or Cinderella. He loves the Wizard of Oz, and he's always Dorothy." Other concerns centered about his drawings: "Always girls, only girls. He says, 'I don't know how to draw a boy. I can't do it.'" His toy preference had also begun to worry her: "Just Barbie. He's got a Ken doll, but he doesn't play with it."

The father described his son as having no interest in rough-and-tumble play or sports, in contrast to the older brother. The mother added: "He says that boys play too rough. And he has also said he wished he were a girl. He's told me that."

The boy's atypical behavior had been in evidence for several years. The mother described why she sought professional consultation: "I got tired of people always saying something about it. Also, he's getting laughed at by the other kids, especially the boys." The father was less concerned: "I still think he'll outgrow it. I think she's making more out of it than necessary."

GIRLS

Many preadolescent girls show varying degrees of culturally masculine behavior. However, cross-gender behavior in girls has not been well studied. Tomboyishness is much more common than is its counterpart of feminine behavior in young boys. To a considerably greater degree, parental statements that "she'll outgrow it" are valid predictions. Additionally, this sexist pediatric age group affords a higher priority to boys. To be a tomboy is upwardly mobile, whereas to be a sissy is downwardly mobile, resulting in ostracism. Thus, mothers of tomboys do not usually seek professional consultation.

Some preadolescent tomboys do not outgrow their masculine orientation. How can one discriminate this subgroup from the larger population of masculine behaving young girls whose teen-age behavior will be feminine? To date there is insufficient clinical experience in this regard. A few preadolescent girls who insist on wearing boys' clothes, refuse to play with girls, insist on sports and trucks and guns, and say that they want to be boys have been evaluated. They appear to have a stronger degree of masculine identity than do most tomboys, and their behavior begins to approximate that retrospectively described by adolescent and adult women who request a sex change. However, this research is in a preliminary stage.

An 8-year-old girl was brought by her parents because she insisted on wearing boys' clothes, would not participate in girls' activities, and had a secret girl friend.

The mother was 30 years old and, as a child, had enjoyed doll play and helping her mother about the house. She had been emotionally closer to her mother and had not known her father after age 8.

The girl's father was also 30 years old and through adolescence had been moderately athletic and rough-and-tumble. He had been emotionally close to both parents. The marriage was described as presently comfortable but previously strained, due to a serious medical illness of the wife and her separation from the family. There were no other children.

The mother described her daughter as an infant in this way: "She was an active baby. She was never cuddly, always squirmish." The father added: "She would push you away."

The onset of atypical behavior was then recalled by the mother: "When she started school, she refused to wear dresses. She would spend all her time playing baseball with the boys. Before that, she had never liked to play with dolls."

Regarding current behavior, the father added: "She insists she will grow up to become a boy." Fantasy games were described by the mother: "When she watches 'The Brady Bunch,' she's always the middle boy. When she plays house, she's the father."

The parents' initial attitude toward their daughter's behavior was summarized by the father: "I always played active games with her. We enjoyed it. I think I encouraged her into rough-and-tumble play." The mother added: "She took to it. We thought she would outgrow it."

The parents then acknowledged the reasons for their seeking professional consultation: "She has one close girl friend. We know that she lies to us that she doesn't sneak off to see her. We're worried about later homosexuality."

Course and Prognosis

BOYS

Five previously feminine preadolescent boys have been followed into young adulthood by the author in collaboration with Money. Four of the boys appear to be primarily or exclusively homosexual, and the fifth is bisexual. A sixth feminine boy initially seen at the onset of puberty was reinterviewed during his later teens. At that time he requested sex change surgery. Another study has also re-evaluated six men during late adolescence and early adulthood in they had previously been seen for boyhood femininity. Three were homosexual and one was possibly transsexual (Zuger, 1966). A third project assessed 16 men who had been feminine as young boys. Three were transsexual, one was transvestic, two were homosexual, and 10 were heterosexual (Lebovitz, 1972).

Thus, boys who show a considerable degree of cross-gender behavior appear to have a greater than average probability of later manifesting one of three patterns of atypical sexuality—homosexuality, transvestism, and transsexualism.

What effects does treatment have on these boys? The answer is uncertain. The boys in the Green and Money pilot study were not systematically treated; rather, the parents were advised to no longer encourage feminine behavior where this had been the case, and the boys were confronted with the irreversibility of being born male. The extent and type of treatment intervention in the other two studies are unclear from the published reports.

GIRLS

As noted, most tomboys become feminine during adolescence. Their social milieu may afford advantages for boyish behavior during preadolescence, but with puberty the social system changes. Then, advantages accrue from being feminine. However, a few tomboys remain masculine. How can one identify those who will? The critical variable may be differentiating two components of gender or sexual identity—a basic identity of being male or female and a preference for masculine or feminine gender role behavior. Most tomboys know they are female and do not wish to be male, but they perceive their current social system as providing more rewards for boyish behavior. Once the social system begins to provide them with greater rewards for feminine behavior, such as courtship by males, their role behavior changes. However, those masculine behaving young girls whose basic identity is male do not respond to the change in social rewards occurring during the teens and remain masculine.

Psychological Testing.

Both traditional and innovative psychological testing have been used with boys manifesting cross-gender behavior. The traditional tests include the It Scale for Children (Brown, 1956) and the Draw a Person Test (Machover, 1949). Innovative procedures have included the Family Doll Preference Test, the Parent and Activity Preference Test, and a playroom observation period. In these procedures, boys described as showing cross-gender behavior have been compared with typical boys and typical girls.

The It Scale presents a child with a gender-neutral stick figure drawn on a card. The figure is presumed to serve as a projection of the child. "It" then selects choices from a series of cards that depict culturally feminine or masculine toys, household articles, and activities, as well as male or female playmates and ultimately a masculine or feminine representation of "It."

In the Draw a Person Test the child draws a person and then designates whether the figure is male or female. The Family Doll Preference procedure presents the child with a set of realistic dolls representing a grandmother, a grandfather, a mother, a father, a young boy, a young girl, and an infant. The child is then instructed to make up a story using these dolls and to hold the appropriate doll while that person is involved in the story. The time each doll is held during a 10-minute period is recorded. The Parent and Activity Preference probedure presents the child with a series of two-card picture sets that constitute the first two pictures in a three-card sequence. One picture depicts a man engaged in an activity and the other depicts a woman engaged in an activity. The activity may be gender-typical (such as a woman sewing), gender-atypical (such as a woman repairing a car), or gender-neutral (such as a woman or a man reading). The child then selects the third card from two options. One depicts a child of the same sex as the subject having joined the man; the other depicts the child having joined the woman. In the playroom observation period the child is permitted access to a variety of culturally masculine and feminine toys. The time spent with each toy is recorded through a one-way observation mirror.

Boys described by their parents as behaviorally feminine score differently from typical boys their age and similarly to same aged girls. On the It Scale, they select culturally feminine toys and activities and girl playmates. Their score is within the range for girls as reported by the test's developer and is significantly different from boys described as masculine. When asked to draw a person, boys described as feminine are more likely to draw a female, whereas masculine boys more often draw a male (Green et al., 1972). Normative data demonstrate that children of this age typically draw their own sex first, the sex of the first drawn person presumably being a reflection of the drawer's identity. When constructing a story using dolls representing family members, boys described as feminine employ the female family members more than male figures, as do girls. Feminine boys (and girls) also use the infant doll significantly more than do masculine boys (Green and Fuller, 1973). When completing a picture sequence depicting a child of their sex having joined a man or woman engaged in a masculine or feminine activity, boys described as feminine more often select the woman and feminine activities; so do girls (Green, 1973). When given free access to a variety of toys, boys described as feminine choose culturally feminine toys (typically a Barbie doll), whereas typical boys more often select culturally masculine toys (typically a truck). Girls select similarly to feminine boys (Green, 1973).

The results of psychological procedures reveal the degree of similarity between the feminine boys and same aged typical girls and the distinctness of these feminine boys from typical boys. These atypical boys do not emerge as a third sex but, rather, are socializing in a manner similar to most girls. The tests support the impression that these boys have an identity that is feminine and an activity preference that is feminine, and they prefer to associate with women and their roles.

Psychological testing of very masculine girls is in a preliminary stage. Currently, the results indicate that the girls typically draw a male first on the Draw a Person Test and score in the masculine range on the It Scale.

Treatment

Decisions regarding intervention into the behavior of children with extremely atypical gender role behavior engage both research and ethical considerations. At the outset it should be stressed that true nonintervention is impossible once a referral has been made and an evaluation conducted. By the very nature of these procedures, a change has occurred in the child's life. Typically, the parents have been ignoring or reacting neutrally to the atypical behavior. With the interface of the child and his peer group and the negative attitude of adults outside the family, the parents become concerned and begin to respond differently. The professional evaluation focuses on the child's gender role behavior, and thus a new message is transmitted by the parents and the evaluating facility. An alteration has been effected in the milieu in which the atypical behavior occurs.

Research questions arise as to the potential results of this nonspecific treatment intervention and other more systematic efforts at modifying behavior.

As noted earlier, adult male-to-female transsexuals report feminine behavior since childhood. Almost none of those seen by the author was treated prior to adolescence, and few were evaluated. These absences may have reflected parental unconcern for the behavior or reassurance by a family physician that the behavior was of no enduring consequence. Untreated, the boys evolved into transsexuals. Adult transsexualism can be considered a logical extension of early femininity. A second outcome possibility is homosexuality. The adult transsexual is homosexual by strict anatomical definition, at least prior to surgery, but he considers sexual attraction to persons of the same genetic sex as heterosexual. Additionally, about two-thirds of male homosexuals in one series reported some degree of feminine behavior during boyhood (Bieber, 1962). A third outcome possibility is transvestism. About one-half of a sample of adult transvestites report having initiated their cross-dressing prior to puberty (Prince and Bentler, 1972). Thus, some developmental overlap exists between the phenomena of transsexualism, homosexuality, and transvestism.

The relationship between early gender role behavior and later genital sexuality is not well understood. Gender or sexual identity may be defined as encompassing three fundamental components: (1) basic morphological sexual identity—whether a person's self-concept is male or female; (2) gender role behavior—whether the person is culturally masculine or feminine; and (3) genital orientation—whether the person prefers male or female sexual partners. Since, on a statistical basis,

more females than males are sexually attracted to males, boys with at least one component of cross-gender identity (feminine role behavior) might be expected to have a higher probability of also manifesting another component (male partner preference).

This is not to say that all feminine boys mature into homosexuals or that all masculine boys become heterosexual. Rather, some boys have a higher than average probability of later showing some type of atypical adult sexuality. The relationship also suggests a strategy for understanding the early developmental routes to several varieties of adult behavior.

Ethical considerations exist with respect to attempting to modify the very feminine boys' behavior. The parents request help with their child. They are concerned about his poor relationship with other boys and his being teased and bullied. The boy is unhappy. He may despair because he wants to be a girl, or he may be unhappy because other children tease him. Parents have not only immediate but also long range concerns. They may ask what the adult outcome of their son's behavior will be without treatment. To this, the therapist can give only approximate answers. He can say that the most extremely feminine of men (transsexuals) report having been feminine as boys and that some homosexuals also report behaving in a related way when they were children. The therapist can also say that he does not know the percentage of children like their son who, without intervention, will mature into heterosexual men. He must also say that the long term effects of treatment are not yet known.

If these children are pretranssexual, pretransvestic, or prehomosexual, what is the therapist's responsibility to them? In this society, there are distinct advantages in being satisfied with one's anatomical sex (nontranssexual), in not feeling compelled to wear clothes of the other sex (nontransvestic), and in being sexually attracted to persons of the other sex (nonhomosexual).

The transsexual experiences years of profound distress as he or she grapples with an identity in conflict with anatomy and with the social expectations deriving from that anatomy. If he or she is successful in finding physicians who will administer contrasexed hormones and perform genital reconstructive surgery, that person can never be fully of the sex aspired to, can never ignore the awareness of being anatomically incomplete, and can never escape the scars of the past. The transvestite may experience hardship if his wife and children object to his cross-dressing, and, if his behavior becomes public knowledge, he risks job loss and legal consequences. The homosexual continues to be socially stigmatized and experiences job discrimination and legal harassment. The homophile movement has made progress in challenging discriminatory employment and police procedures, and some new religious groups endorse the homosexual's behavior, but stigmatization continues. If extrapolation from other societal biases, such as religious and racial prejudice, is valid, it will take more than legal reform and public educational efforts to afford the homosexual equal status in Western society.

Although the clinician may privately feel that the important variable in an adult's sexuality is the emotional feeling for others and not the genital configuration of the partner or that a person should be able to dress any way he or she prefers or live in a sex role opposite to that expected from anatomy, his civil libertarian ethic confronts reality when talking with the atypical child. Even if one discounts the adult consequences of a persistent cross-gender identity, the child's immediate situation needs to be considered. He is already being teased and ostracized. Much is read and said about the blurring of sex roles and the unisexed or unigendered ethic of child rearing, but, by and large, this blurring of sex roles has so far had little effect on the pediatric population being seen. The feminine boy of today is experiencing the same social hardship that the atypical boy of a generation ago experienced. The changing culture is not modifying quickly enough for these boys. What then is the therapist's responsibility toward these families? How can he be of assistance to them?

For the boy who wants to be a girl and magically believes this to be possible, the therapist can help him see the unrealistic nature of that wish and can help him to be happier as a boy. For the boy whose behavior is so atypical as to be causing him social distress, the therapist can help him integrate more comfortably into his peer group. For parents who are concerned about their child's behavior and its possible consequence, the therapist can investigate whether they are in part responsible for promoting the behavior and can help them encourage alternate behaviors.

Toward these ends therapists have primarily attempted two types of intervention: (1) a one-to-one play relationship with the boy and counseling of his parents, either singly or conjointly, and (2) group meetings with several atypical boys and separate group meetings with their parents.

Over the years the author and his associates have evolved certain basic principles in their approach to these children (Green et al., 1972). First, they have used male therapists. The therapist serves as a role model for the boy. Frequently, there has been an absence of such a model in the boy's life, as a result of paternal abandonment or rejection. Second, they have attempted to reduce the social distress of the boy by alerting him, if he is not already aware, to the causes of his being teased. If his gestures are feminine, these are spotlighted. He may be unaware of the physical behavior that labels him a sissy. If he asserts that "boys play too rough" and, therefore, has gravitated toward girl playmates, the therapist helps him find boys and activities within his range of comfort and competence. Male friends, also not rough-and-tumble, with whom he will enjoy playing are recruited from his school and neighborhood. Board games and handicrafts are encouraged as a replacement for hours with the Barbie doll, an activity that results in stigmatization.

With the parents, it may be evident that they have encouraged the boy's atypical behavior. An attempt is made to sensitize them to their role. Some parents may be inhibiting their son's male peer group integration. Others may look on his strong preference for girl playmates as a sign of his later being a ladies' man. They do not see his peer group preference as a reflection of a basic sexual identity and ignore the fact that the typical boy prefers boy playmates.

Considerable alienation may exist between the feminine boy and his father. The father may see his son's behavior as a personal rejection and evidence of his own failure. He may defensively withdraw from father-son interaction. If there is another boy in the family who enjoys the father's activities, he may become the favored son. The father may defensively dismiss the boy's behavior as something he will outgrow and be reluctant to participate in the clinical program. To such fathers, the therapist attempts to point out the special need for their boys to have a sharing relationship with a man and his key position. The therapist attempts to engage the two in mutually enjoyable activities. No effort is made to make the boys into star athletes or to thrust them with zealous fathers into exceptionally competitive activities, such as Little League baseball. These activities may be so far beyond the boy's competence that they cause him to retreat even more from male group interaction. By contrast, the Indian Guides, a YMCA program, is preferable. This is a group father-son experience that stresses such outdoor activities as camping and cooking and such indoor activities as handicrafts (Green, 1973).

One-to-one contact permits tailoring to individual family needs, but group patient experience has also demonstrated some advantages, other than the economy of time. For the boys, the group is their initial social experience with other boys that has not been grossly threatening. Whereas prior experiences have been with rough-and-tumble boys with whom they do not keep pace, this group is comfortable. As they become increasingly close to the adult male therapist, they begin to imitate his behavior and respond positively to his suggestions for group interaction. Consequently, they develop a facility for more effective male peer group integration. The boys also become critical of others in the group who display grossly feminine behavior (identifying with the aggressor) and thus promote behavioral change in each other.

For the parents, the group is their initial opportunity to share common concerns and experiences. The parents have usually viewed the boy's atypical behavior positively. When mothers have been reinforcing a son's femininity, it may be easier for them to see such behavior in another group member.

Thus, projection helps the group become more sensitive to parental reactions that are causing difficulty for the children. The age scatter of the boys is also of value. A mother of a 9-year-old boy who ignored her son's feminine behavior at 5 may be able to point out to a mother of a 5-year-old a strategy previously ineffective in her own family.

For the fathers, the group offers considerable needed support. These fathers usually feel they are being held responsible for their son's femininity by not being available enough for father-son interaction. They feel they now have to perform as superfathers. The awareness that they are not alone is reassuring. The positive report by a father of his initially reluctant engagement in a father-son function such as Indian Guides, surprisingly found to be enjoyable, may help spur on other group members (Green and Fuller, 1973).

Treatment of masculine girls has not been systematically undertaken. In a pilot program, a feminine female therapist, herself engaged in an occupation more typically associated with men (combined M.D.-Ph.D. program), has served as a role model. Because of the imprecision with which the diagnosis of an enduring masculine identity in a preadolescent girl can be currently made, no assessments can yet bear any validity.

What will be the effects of treatment? These procedures are directed at teaching the boy social skills that will result in less stigmatization, permitting him to engage in more typically boyish activities and promoting more comfort in being anatomically male. The boys enter treatment as a consequence of their feminine identity and behavior; they do not enter because they are homosexually oriented. The intervention of the therapist is not directed specifically at genital sexual orientation. To the degree to which gender role behavior and genital sexuality are related, the therapists are also intervening with respect to genital sexuality. On the other hand, their intervention may do little to affect genital sexuality. If such is the case, early intervention, if effective in modifying feminine behavior, may preclude a transsexual outcome but not affect a later homosexual orientation. Thus, only one component of gender or sexual identity may be modified in the previously feminine 7-year-old boy who now appears to be a typical 9-year-old. However, there may well be an interrelation between the degree to which one behaves in a masculine way during late childhood and early adolescence, one's social experiences during these years, and one's later genital sexuality.

The feminine teen-age boy may experience greater difficulty in establishing heterosexual dating relationships than does the masculine teen-ager, and he may be more attractive as a romantic and sexual partner for homosexually oriented males. The image one has of oneself is, in part, a product of patterns of social feedback, and comfort in sexual relationships is, in part, a product of early successes and failures. Thus, the effect of more effective male peer group integration during late childhood and early adolescence may diminish the possibility of an exclusively homosexual orientation and permit bisexuality or heterosexuality. By instituting treatment during boyhood, the therapist hopes to make the child happier during childhood and permit him a wider range of social and sexual options during adulthood.

REFERENCES

Bieber, I. *Homosexuality.* Basic Books, New York, 1962.

Brown, D. G. Sex role preference in young children. Psychol. Monogr., *70:* 000, 1956.

Bulliet, C. *Venus Castina: Famous Female Impersonators Celestial and Human.* Covici, Friede, New York, 1928.

Devereux, G. Institutionalized homosexuality of the Mohave Indians. Hum. Biol., *9:* 508, 1937.

Ehrhardt, A. A. Maternalism in fetal hormonal and related syndromes. In *Contemporary Sexual Behavior,* J. Zubin and J. Money, editors, p. 99. Johns Hopkins Press, Baltimore, 1973.

Ehrhardt, A. A., Epstein, R., and Money, J. Fetal androgens and female gender identity in the early-treated adrenogenital syndrome. Johns Hopkins Med. J., *122:* 160, 1968.

Gifford, E. The Cocopa. In *University of California Publication in American Archaeology and Ethnology,* vol. 31, 1933.

*Green, R. *Sexual Identity Conflict in Children and Adults.* Basic Books, New York, 1974.

Green, R., and Fuller, M. Family doll play and female identity in preadolescent males. Am. J. Orthopsychiatry, *43:* 123, 1973.

Green, R., and Fuller, M. Group therapy with feminine boys and their families. Int. J. Group Psychother., *23:* 54, 1973.

Green, R., Fuller, M., and Rutley, B. It-scale for children and draw-a-person test: 30 feminine vs. 25 masculine boys. J. Pers. Assess., *36:* 349, 1972.

*Green, R., and Money, J. *Transsexualism and Sex Reassignment.* Johns Hopkins Press, Baltimore, 1969.

*Green, R., Newman, L., and Stoller, R. Treatment of boyhood transsexualism: An interim report of four years experience. Arch. Gen. Psychiatry, *26:* 213, 1972.

Green, R., and Stoller, R. Two pairs of monozygotic (identical) twins discordant for gender identity. Arch. Sex. Behav., *1:* 321, 1971.

Lebovitz, P. Feminine behavior in boys: Aspects of its outcome. Am. J. Psychiatry, *128:* 1283, 1972.

Machover, K. *Personality Projection in the Drawing of the Human Figure.* Charles C Thomas, Springfield, Ill., 1949.

*Money, J., Hampson, J. G., and Hampson, J. L. An examination of some basic sexual concepts: The evidence of human hermaphroditism. Bull. Johns Hopkins Hosp., *97:* 301, 1955.

Money, J., Hampson, J. G., and Hampson, J. L. Imprinting and the establishment of gender role. Arch. Gen. Psychiatry, *77:* 333, 1957.

Prince, V., and Bentler, P. M. Survey of 504 cases of transvestism. Psychol. Rep., *31:* 903, 1972.

*Stoller, R. J. *Sex and Gender: On the Development of Masculinity and Femininity.* Science House, New York, 1968.

Westermarck, E. *The Origin and Development of the Moral Ideas.* Macmillan, London, 1917.

Yalom, I., Green, R., and Fisk, N. Prenatal exposure to female hormones: Effect on psychosexual development in boys. Arch. Gen. Psychiatry, *28:* 554, 1973.

Zuger, B. Effeminate behavior in boys present from early childhood. J. Pediatr., *69:* 1098, 1966.

chapter 6 Techniques of Coitus

BENJAMIN J. SADOCK, M.D.,
and VIRGINIA A. SADOCK, M.D.

Introduction

Sir James Paget, who is best known for the disease that bears his name, was a crusader for sexual education. In the 19th century he stated:

Ignorance about sexual affairs seems to be a notable characteristic of the more civilized part of the human race. Among ourselves, it is certain that the method of copulating needs to be taught, and that they to whom it is not taught remain quite ignorant about it.

It is for this reason, among others, that an explicit and descriptive manual on the elementary facts of the varieties of sexual activity is included here. The art of love depends not only on the quality of the emotional union between the two people involved but also on the knowledge the two persons have of sexual techniques and of their own and each other's anatomy and biology. That this knowledge is now deficient in our society and greatly sought after is best illustrated by the recent growth of centers around the country that offer such information in the course of sexual counseling and therapy. Societies considered primitive by us along a variety of parameters are not primitive in the sexual sphere. Certain tribes in central Africa, for example, teach girls the different positions for sexual intercourse as part of their puberty rites. And various age-old love manuals, such as the *Kama Sutra* and the *Perfumed Garden,* are still avidly read, for they contain much information that is both accurate and pertinent.

Coital Positions

The 100-odd positions of sexual intercourse eagerly imagined and frequently attempted condense rapidly into a handful of basic positions with minor but almost unlimited variations. The basic positions are often divided in a number of ways: face-to-face positions as opposed to front-to-back positions, man-on-top as opposed to woman-on-top, penis-vagina positions as opposed to manual and oral-genital positions, lying down as opposed to sitting or standing, and so forth.

The custom shared by most experienced men and women is that of moving freely from position to position, beginning with a kind word or a knowing look, kissing, and fondling. They move to increased desire by touching the partner's erogenous zones until momentum for orgasm is produced and one or more orgasms on the part of one or both of the partners occur. At the final point, each partner is spent and contented in a quiet communion with the other. This procedure can involve starting to touch in one position, inducing an orally stimulated orgasm in another position, inserting the penis into the vagina in a third position, and reaching an orgasm in a fourth. It is difficult to describe positions in other than a static form, but it is important to remember while reading the following descriptions that each position may be thought of as fitting into a flow of movements.

Accordingly, the traditional breakdown of before, during, and after can be forgotten. Before, after all, can extend back to one's childhood, when sexual behavior was being patterned after parental attitudes and behaviors. Before, at any rate, surely begins with the emotional tone existing between the man and the woman at the time the sexual coming together is activated.

Coming together is close to the Latin meaning of the word coitus (*coire,* derived from the combination of *co,* together, and *ire,* to go). Coitus is generally taken to mean a coming together of male and female sexual organs, of penis and vagina. "Having sex," "making love," and similar terms bring to virtually everybody's mind the image of penis in vagina. This is both natural and cultural. It is only through penis in vagina that reproduction occurs, and the whole evolutionary history of life has produced in us a drive to do whatever we can and to move our bodies however we may to bring about reproduction—therefore, the great urge. The steps to reproduction give us great pleasure, but the great pleasures of sexual intercourse need not result in reproduction; in our time of overpopulation, it is even wiser that they do not. But from this typical and cultural bias comes the sense that penis in vagina is more sexual than oral-genital contact, for instance. In the course of this section, however, the authors use an informal definition that what produces orgasm between male and female is coital. This definition has the fallacy of putting too much emphasis on orgasm, but, just as there is no beginning to sexual acts, there is also no limit to what can be considered sexual. The carefully worded valentine may produce a profoundly sexual response. All such points of communication cannot possibly be discussed here, but they should be kept in mind as a large part of the sexual aura in which every man and woman lives. Genital communion is a part of sexual communion, which, in turn, is a part of human communion.

GENITAL-GENITAL POSITIONS

Describing first those penis-vagina positions that, without contraception, would normally and with varying degrees of probability lead to conception, one comes to the first division, that of positions where the man and the woman can see each other's faces, as op-

posed to the front-to-back or rear-entry positions, where the pair cannot see each other's faces. In 1906 Havelock Ellis made the point that the primary and essential characteristic of the specifically human method of coitus is the fact that it takes place face to face. The rear-entry or flight-and-pursuit position reminds human beings of animals in copulation. When persons think to vary their sexual techniques, they may, as Van de Velde points out, turn to the rear-entry position, thinking it is a spontaneous, uncivilized, natural way of human copulation.

Face-to-face positions. For centuries, the Western world's *idée fixe* on intercourse began and ended with a single face-to-face position, that of the man on top. Its appeal in less reproduction-oriented societies has, no doubt, been relatively lower, but the man on top position has a certain universality for all male and female pairs because it can be easily modified in tone, is highly stimulating to the man and only slightly less so to the woman, and suggests the psychological situation of the man as initiating and controlling sexual intercourse, a psychological statement that reflects the estimation of Western civilization's only recently changing sense of how it ought to be.

Man-on-top position. This position is the most common. The woman lies on her back with her legs parted and knees slightly bent; the man lies between her legs but supports his weight on his elbows and knees. The erect phallus can make an easy entry into the vagina either on its own accord or with the guidance of his or her hand (see Figure 1). With insertion completed, the man then thrusts the penis in and out—sometimes vigorously, sometimes with more subtle movements. This is done without actually removing the penis from the vagina, although, when lubrication and combined movements are good, actual exit and re-entry may take place. Such thrusting is highly stimulating to the penis, and the man may find himself approaching ejaculation quickly. The woman moves her pelvis away from and toward the erect penis as it moves away from and toward her. Or she may move in more of a horizontal manner, a supine version of the bump and grind, which charts something of a sideways

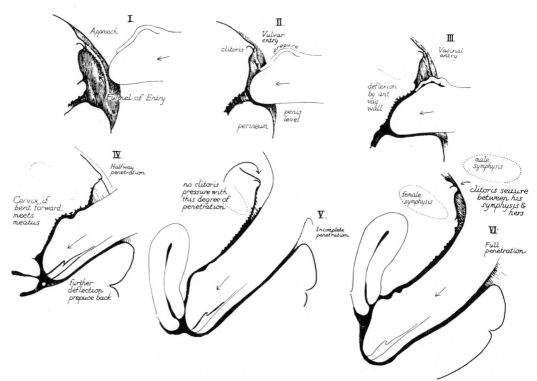

FIGURE 1. In this series of illustrations, the stage of entry *(I)* and stages of penetration *(II to V)* are depicted in the man-on-top position. At full penetration *(VI)* the clitoris is stimulated by male-female symphysis pressure rather than by the penis itself. (From Dickinson, R. L., *Atlas of Human Anatomy,* Williams & Wilkins, Baltimore, 1949.)

figure-eight on the surface beneath her. She may contract and relax the vagina and, indeed, contract the general body musculature.

This position provides an easy opportunity for men and women to kiss each other's mouths, faces, and shoulders, and the man may fondle, kiss, or suck at the woman's breasts. The woman has her hands free and may reach the testicles of the man to enclose them or hold the base of the penis. Or she may prefer to caress the more reachable face, torso, and hair of her partner. This position may be tiring for the man, and for this reason the pair may choose to move into other positions or to delay male orgasm; some couples tend to finish up in this position rather than to begin with it. If the man does ejaculate and lose his erection, the woman can close her thighs and extend her legs while the man moves his legs to the outside of her. With the flaccid penis held tightly between her thighs, the woman finds increased contact with her vulva from the penis and may reach orgasm; sometimes the pressure of her thighs causes a re-erection of the penis (see Figure 2).

The man-on-top position—the "missionary position," as it has been called—is more difficult when the man is fat or the woman pregnant, when the man has an incomplete erection or the woman has lost the elasticity of the vaginal barrel, which may happen as a result of multiple childbirth. In the case of this last condition, the woman may lie on her back and bend her knees to bring them toward her shoulders, or she may raise her legs and wrap them around the shoulders of the man. These positions place the vagina in a more vertical position. A pillow placed under the buttocks of the woman further raises the vulva. The man, who remains on hands and knees, inserts his erect penis in a horizontal plane; the entry of the penis into the vagina thus provides increased friction. The man supports himself on legs, arms, and hands and may then thrust while the woman, because of

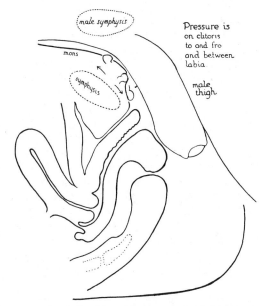

FIGURE 2. The flaccid penis is in contact with the vulva in this illustration. Note the excursion of the clitoris in the vertical plane which is produced by pelvic thrusting and which may lead to female orgasm. (From Dickinson, R. L., *Atlas of Human Anatomy,* Williams & Wilkins, Baltimore, 1949.)

her flexed position, remains relatively immobile. Although there is no direct contact of the clitoris by the penis, there is pressure upon it from traction of the minor lips of the vagina. If the woman entwines her legs around the man's back rather than his shoulders or if she keeps them bent and to the sides of her partner, she is better able to move her pelvis (see Figure 3).

Woman-on-top position. The fall of Rome, so ardently discussed by educated people over the years, has been attributed to 100 causes, including that of the favored Roman position of intercourse with the woman on top or astride the man. On top can perhaps best be taken to mean free to move and thus freer to set the pace and determine the action of intercourse. For years it was said that the man-on-top position was more natural because the psychological orientation of society was that the man should be in control. With recent sexual flexibility, however, increasing numbers of couples make their choice of sexual position or positions depending on how they feel at the moment. If the man feels active

and ready while the woman feels more passive, the man-on-top position is a natural one. But if the man is tired or anxious or somewhat indifferent and the woman feels ready and active, the woman-on-top position is the obvious choice. Or they may start in one position and then change to the other. The woman-on-top position is used at one time or another by about 45 per cent of couples.

The erect penis may be inserted from the male-dominant position and then the woman-dominant position rolled into; or the man may lie on his back with legs straight or slightly bent, and the woman may kneel with her legs on either side of man and with his or her hand guiding the penis. She may then lower herself onto the erect penis until it is contained within her vagina. This procedure is used in the dual-sex treatment of impotence or frigidity. After entry or containment, the woman may slowly, so as not to bend the erect penis, stretch her legs out between those of the man and support her weight on elbows or hands in a position exactly the reverse of the man-on-top position (see Figure 4). Or the

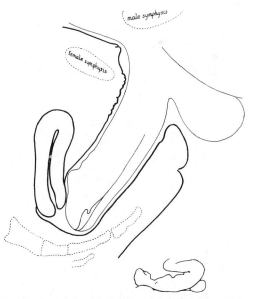

FIGURE 3. Coitus with the hips elevated and the thighs against the abdomen limit the pelvic movements of the woman while providing maximum movement of the man. (From Dickinson, R. L., *Atlas of Human Anatomy,* Williams & Wilkins, Baltimore, 1949.)

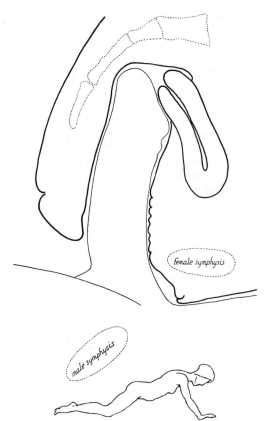

FIGURE 4. In this position, the woman lying above can regulate the rate and depth of penile penetration. Maximum clitoral stimulation is provided in the woman-on-top position. (From Dickinson, R. L., *Atlas of Human Anatomy*, Williams & Wilkins, Baltimore, 1949.)

woman can place more of her weight on him, or she can sit on her knees and the man's pubic area. She can even turn completely around, so that she is no longer facing the man. The man may remain supine or raise himself onto elbows or hands or raise his knees to support the woman if she leans back. The woman then begins to pace the movement of the pair. Although there is a chance of too-deep penetration, the woman is aware of this and can easily control it. She may move up and down, causing the vagina to almost exclude the penis, or she can move sideways. She can move her hips in a circular or figure-eight motion. When she leans forward to press her vulva against the man's pelvic area, she increases her clitoral

stimulation and also slows the movement of the penis. Virtually any movements made in this position provide stimulation for both the woman and the man. If the man is nearing orgasm, the woman may want to raise her hips to support her weight on her knees while she allows the man to set his own pace (see Figure 5).

The woman-on-top position probably provides the greatest degree of stimulation for a woman and, if done with skill and good vaginal control, is highly enjoyable for the man. The man has his hands free to caress the woman's breasts, clitoris, buttocks, and face, and there is also an opportunity for kissing. He is less pinned down by her weight than she would be by his, and, depending on her position, he is free to move and thrust from below.

At times, the woman-on-top position is prescribed by a physician.

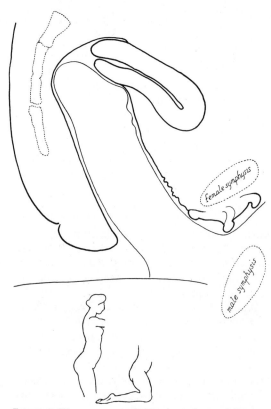

FIGURE 5. Woman on top, sitting across the man's knees as illustrated. (From Dickinson, R. L., *Atlas of Human Anatomy*, Williams & Wilkins, Baltimore, 1949.)

A 38-year-old man reported that he would lose consciousness for a few seconds during coitus. This loss of consciousness was unrelated to orgasm, a history confirmed by his wife. Two years earlier, he had an aortic valve prosthesis inserted; this prosthesis was able to function and maintain cerebral blood flow only if his pulse rate remained below 160 per minute. Coitus in the man-superior position and with vigorous large-muscle movements by the man pushed his pulse rate above this level, thus compromising the prosthetic device and producing cerebral hypoxia. In the woman-superior position, the husband was discouraged from active pelvic thrusting, his pulse rate remained under 160, and the distressing symptoms disappeared.

Another variation is recommended by Masters and Johnson. The woman lies at a 30-degree angle across the man and with one of her legs between his. In this position he is free to thrust, and she is free to thrust and to make pelvic movements.

Side-by-side positions. Genital intercourse tends to be leisurely in the side-by-side positions; penetration is relatively shallow, and movement is somewhat inhibited. The man and the woman can position themselves in a number of ways, with effort sometimes being needed to relieve weight pressure on the thigh—his or hers—that is bearing the other's weight. If the woman lies half on her side and half on her back with one leg extended, the man may rest both thighs on top of her bottom leg and she may raise her upper leg to encircle his top thigh; from this position, the penis can be inserted. If the weight of the man's thighs becomes too great on the woman's bottom thigh, they can trade positions. Pillows can help in all these variations. With his thigh between hers, the man can press against the clitoris. When a couple works out a comfortable version of the side-by-side position, they often find it restful, good for fatigue or pregnancy, and pleasant just for prolonging sexual activity. If the man finds it hard to enter a woman in this position, entry can be made in another position first and then a side-back position rolled into. A side-by-side position is used by about 30 per cent of couples as an occasional variant.

Sitting and standing positions. These positions have been used by 10 per cent of couples. Sitting positions provide very close body contact and moderate movement potential. The man may sit on a chair or on the edge of the bed, with the woman sitting suspended on his thighs. She can lower herself onto his erect penis, or containment can be achieved after she is sitting with her thighs across his. The man keeps his knees apart; movements of his knees further open the woman's thighs. He should insert the erect penis with a downward pressure. The man takes hold of the woman's hips and thighs and presses them toward him. The man also moves his pelvis forward and upward, pressing the penis more deeply up and down. The woman can encircle the man's back or lock her feet behind the chair to provide more penetration. She can lean back while he pulls her pelvis toward him.

Variations include that of the woman lying on her back on the bed while the man squats between her thighs, inserts his penis, and combines the pulling and pushing of the woman's hips with pelvic thrusts on his own. Or the man lies on his back with his legs apart, and the woman squats between his thighs, contains the penis, and moves her pelvis in a circle. Or she sits on the edge of the bed, spreads her thighs, and leans back while the man stands, bends, or kneels by the side of the bed and makes entry.

Another variation is the standing position. The woman can raise one leg onto the man's shoulder; or he can pick her up onto his erect penis, and she can wrap her legs around his waist and her arms around his neck while he is holding her by the buttocks.

Rear-entry positions. Genital intercourse may be achieved with the penis entering the vagina from the rear in any of the basic positions (see Figure 6). If the woman lies on her stomach, raises her pelvic area, and arches her back, the man may kneel astride her thighs and insert the erect penis through her thighs; if she kneels so that her head and breasts are touching the bed and her pelvic area raised higher than in the lying position, he may kneel behind her. If she lies on her side on the bed in a curved position, he may curve his body around hers and enter between the thighs; in the side-by-side position there is increased chance of the penis slipping out of the vagina; this can be countered if the woman presses her thighs together. The man

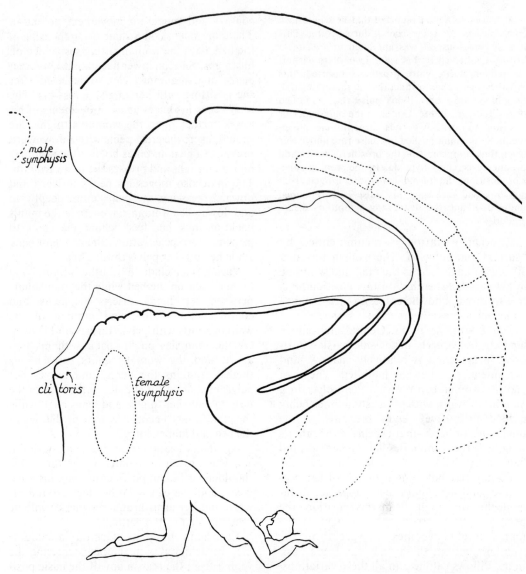

FIGURE 6. Rear-entry position with the woman in knee-chest position. The penis makes entry in a horizontal plane. Indirect clitoral stimulation results from traction on the minor lips with penile thrusting. Direct stimulation results from the testicles pressing against the clitoris. (From Dickinson, R. L., *Atlas of Human Anatomy*, Williams & Wilkins, Baltimore, 1949.)

may sit on a chair or the edge of the bed, and the woman may stand astride his thighs and lower herself onto his erect penis but with her back to him; she spreads her thighs wide when sitting astride him and leans forward, and he leans slightly backward. Or, while standing on the floor, the woman bends over, placing her hands on a low chair, and the man stands behind her. Rear entry can also be accom-

plished with the man lying on his back and the woman kneeling astride him but facing his feet.

If both partners are not slim, there will be difficulties with rear-entry positions. In the kneeling position a small amount of air may enter the vagina and expand its walls, reducing friction and sometimes producing a surprising noise when it later rushes out.

In rear-entry positions the man's hands are free to fondle the woman's body. He can easily reach her breasts and clitoris in these positions. Or the woman may stimulate her own clitoris or reach behind, either around her thighs or between them, and stroke the man's testicles. Rear-entry positions provide psychological and physical stimulation that is different from the stimulation provided in face-to-face encounters.

GENITAL-ORAL POSITIONS

Cunnilingus. Literally translated, cunnilingus means: "He who licks the vulva" (*cunnus* is Latin for vulva, and *lingere* means to lick). The man generally begins by kissing and fondling the inner thighs or the mons veneris, then kissing on the outside of the vaginal lips, arriving at the point where he puts his tongue inside the minor vaginal lips and moves it in various ways. He may begin by locating the clitoris and moving the tongue from side to side across it, slowly at first, then moving at a more rapid speed. He may move his tongue upwards from the entrance of the vagina to the clitoris and then across the clitoris. He may explore the clitoral shaft. The mouth as a whole is used as well as the tongue. Often the vaginal lips are taken inside the mouth and sucked, or the clitoris itself may be sucked. The man may then stiffen and harden his tongue and insert it into the vaginal opening itself in imitation of the penis, or he may use the same licking motions at the opening of the vagina. The insertion of one or two fingers into the vagina while he is licking or sucking the clitoris produces high stimulation for the woman.

When to do what depends on the woman, since what feels good to a woman in cunnilingus changes very rapidly. What is highly satisfying one minute can be painful the next, what is too fast at the beginning may be too slow toward climax, and what is satisfactory one night may be unsatisfactory a week later. Verbal and nonverbal communication must be relied on for satisfaction. Cunnilingus is particularly suited for producing multiple orgasms.

A specific technique of cunnilingus may be hazardous to the woman. Cases of fatal air embolism caused by mouth inflation of the vagina during pregnancy have been reported. In this technique the man covers the introitus with his mouth and forcefully expels his breath so that the vagina fills with air. For some women, such distention is highly pleasurable. Where death has occurred, autopsy revealed air in the uterine veins, trauma to the placenta, and evidence of gas embolism. The frequency of this technique is unknown; but, in view of the hazard involved, it should be used with caution and certainly not during pregnancy.

Fellatio. Fellatio stems from the Latin word *fellare,* meaning to suck. The word has been used to refer to the sucking of the infant at the woman's breast as well as to the woman's sucking the man's penis. This oral-genital activity has many variations. The woman kneels at the side of the man, who lies on his back, or she kneels between his legs and, perhaps after a short manual caressing, licks the glans of the penis, the shaft of the penis itself, and sometimes the testicles, gently taking them partly into her mouth. If the penis is not erect or fully erect, strong sucking combined with a gentle pulling by hand helps produce a full erection. She may then move her mouth, being careful that the penis is not scratched by her teeth, down to the base of the penis or partway down. She may move gently at first and then more rapidly. Or she may change from the in-and-out motion that imitates the thrusting of the penis in the vagina and move her tongue in a circular fashion around the top of the penis or flick her tongue horizontally across the corona. She may move from penis to testicles from time to time, taking them or portions of them into her mouth, or she may combine movements.

To bring a man to orgasm through fellatio, the woman then proceeds to encourage a deeper penetration of the penis into her mouth and returns to the familiar in-and-out motion. She may keep her hand loosely encircling the base of the penis and move the penis up and down rhythmically in a motion involving hand and mouth, the hand acting in a sort of milking fashion as it tightens around the penis. Thrusts deepen, bringing the penis well back into the mouth, approaching and coming into contact with the throat itself.

Here women may experience a gag reflex and may confuse hesitancy about receiving the imminent ejaculation in the mouth with the gagging reflex that is being physically rather than psychologically produced. To counteract the gag reflex, the woman can concentrate on relaxing her throat muscles while keeping the front part of her mouth firm enough to provide stimulation to the man. The ejaculated semen gives a sensation of warmth in the woman's mouth; the semen has little taste at first, but later tastes salty. Some women choose not to swallow the semen; others swallow it with pleasure.

A combined fellatio-cunnilingus results when the man and woman lie side by side or one above the other so that the mouth of one is opposite the genitals of the other. This position is known as *soixante-neuf* (69) and allows both persons to be active at the same time.

HAND-GENITAL POSITIONS

Hand-genital positions in which one person stimulates the genitalia of the other with his or her hand is the most common type of sexual activity between two people. It may be referred to by the term mutual masturbation, and it should be differentiated from self-stimulation, in which the person achieves sexual excitement alone.

It is perhaps simpler to describe how both the man and the woman masturbate than it is to describe hand-genital stimulation of one sex by the other. Coupled with this is the fact that, if the man can be taught to stimulate the woman in the same manner that she has been used to doing it to herself, both are assured of a satisfactory and gratifying experience. Similarly, the woman can be instructed to masturbate the man, using the same technique with which he has become familiar as a result of self-stimulation. For one to educate the other, there must be not only open and honest communication between the two but also, and perhaps even more important, a history of effective masturbation. It has been said that 99 per cent of young men and women masturbate occasionally, and the hundredth conceals the truth. But Kinsey found that by age 25, only 50 per cent of all women have masturbated, as compared to 95 per cent of all men. Kinsey's figures are now

20 years old, and it can be assumed that this discrepancy is no longer as great, although no reliable figures are available.

Female masturbatory techniques. The clitoris is the masturbatory site most preferred by women, and orgasm depends on adequate clitoral stimulation. Masters and Johnson reported that stimulation of the shaft of the clitoris is preferred to stimulation of the glans, which is subject to a particular type of hypersensitivity if stimulated excessively. This finding is especially important for the man to be aware of because undue concentration on direct clitorial stimulation may produce irritation, pain, and impatience. Masters and Johnson also reported that right-handed women usually prefer the right side of the clitorial shaft, and left-handed women the left side.

Since the clitoris is contiguous anatomically with the minor lips, any type of stimulation that applies direct or indirect traction to the inner lips is sexually exciting. Accordingly, a woman may masturbate by tugging or pulling on one or both minor lips, rubbing or squeezing the thighs together, massaging the mons veneris, or inserting one or more fingers into the vagina with an ensuing thrusting or circular motion. A combination of these methods may be used sequentially or simultaneously. Sexual feelings may be heightened further during masturbation by voluntary contraction of the anal sphincter, insertion of a finger into the rectum, or breast massage. A few women are able to achieve orgasm by fantasy alone (2 per cent) or by breast massage alone (11 per cent).

In general, once a woman finds a satisfactory technique, she uses it repeatedly, but a variety of techniques may be used by the same woman on different occasions. Women are capable of continuous masturbatory or hand-genital stimulation, so one orgasm can run into the next, and 25 to 100 orgasms in an hour have been reported.

Male masturbatory techniques. The man's organ of masturbation is the penis, but the sites of stimulation are less varied than in the woman. For example, the act comparable to pulling at the labia to achieve orgasm is pulling at the skin of the scrotal sac. But the latter action, although it may enhance sexual pleasure in some men, does not, in and of it-self, produce orgasm. Men masturbate by stroking the shaft and glans of the penis. The rate of stroking of the shaft may vary considerably from very slow to very rapid up-and-down movements. The stroking may oc-cur from the base to the tip, or the man may prefer to concentrate his movements at a particular area along the way. Some men especially prefer stroking the corona of the glans, which is the most sensitive area of the organ. The man may make a tube of his hand to encircle the penis or make a ring with finger and thumb. At the beginning of masturbation, quick movements are often considered more desirable, but they quickly become more vigorous and are applied with a varying degree of pressure. Many women tend to masturbate a man too gently. Increased sexual stimulation may be achieved by a variety of techniques, such as inserting a finger into the rectum and massaging the anus, scrotum, testicles, and whole body. Many men masturbate with one hand (some-times with both), but others prefer to thrust or rub the penis against an object, such as a pillow, and do not touch the penis with their hands at all.

Only a small percentage of men continue stroking the penis during ejaculation and or-gasm. Rather, at the time of ejaculation the man applies a continuous constrictive grip on the shaft of the penis with his hand. In-variably, there is an exquisite type of hypersensitivity of the glans and coronal ridge after orgasm that causes the man to withdraw the penis away from any source of stimulation. This refractory period varies with age, and in young men it may be nonexistent. Successive orgasms without loss of erection are most uncommon in men. Usually a refractory period of 15 to 20 minutes ensues, after which the man be re-stimulated to erection and orgasm. In general, after the age of 30 one orgasm in a 12-hour period represents the usual male physiological demand.

PENIS-ANUS POSITION

The man or the woman may wish to insert a finger into the anus of the partner at various stages of sexual contact, with insertion aided by a lubricant. It may be done before or at the moment of orgasm with an in-and-out movement. Fingers that have been so inserted must not come in contact with the vagina, since vaginitis can result. The tongue can also be used to stimulate the anus as a variant of sexual activity (anilingus).

Anal intercourse may be opted for during an extremely heavy menstrual flow or simply out of a will by both to explore and to be ex-plored for variety or to provide more stimulation than that afforded by an overly slack vagina. The woman may lie down with a pillow under her hips, or she may kneel on el-bows and knees, and the man may spread her buttocks and moisten the anal area with his tongue or a lubricant and place a lubricant on his penis. After such preparation, he gently inserts the well lubricated penis into the lubri-cated anus and begins controlled thrusts. If the woman can relax, there is no pain. Manual manipulation of the clitoris by the man or by the woman generally produces or-gasm in the woman being anally penetrated.

Conclusion

No single coital position or sex act means the same thing for all people or even for the couple involved at all times. To attempt to infer psychological states from such positions is, more than likely, unproductive. That a person may be anxious about a specific act is certain; although there is much to be learned in the analysis of that anxiety, the avoidance of an activity is not, in and of itself, pathological. Conversely, for some couples a particular coital style may be preferred and used extensively to the partial or complete ex-clusion of others. The most important considerations are that the flow of sexual activity be mutually acceptable and the ability to speak openly with one another about thoughts and feelings be unimpaired (see Figure 7).

REFERENCES

American Medical Association. *Human Sexuality.* American Medical Association, Chicago, 1972.
Comfort, A. *The Joy of Sex.* Crown, New York, 1972.
Ellis, H. *Studies in the Psychology of Sex.* Random House, New York, 1936.
Katchadourian, H. A., and Lunde, D. T. *Fundamentals*

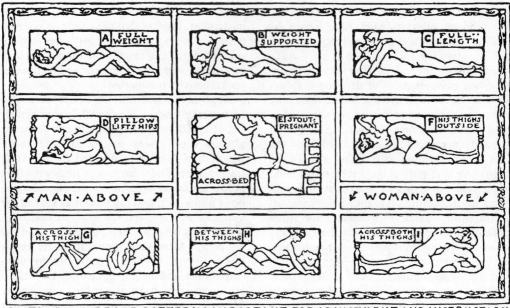

FIGURE 7. Positions of coitus. (From Dickinson, R. L., *Atlas of Human Anatomy,* Williams & Wilkins, Baltimore, 1949.)

of Human Sexuality. Holt, Rinehart, & Winston, New York, 1972.

Masters, W. H., and Johnson, V. E. *Human Sexual Response.* Little, Brown, Boston, 1966.

Masters, W. H., and Johnson, V. E. *Human Sexual Inadequacy.* Little, Brown, Boston, 1970.

Van de Velde, T. *Ideal Marriage: Its Physiology and Technique.* Random House, New York, 1930.

chapter 7 Marriage

7.1 Traditional Marriage

DAVID M. REED, Ph.D.

Introduction

Marriage has been described as a state that those on the outside are trying to enter and those on the inside are trying to leave. It has always created considerable ambivalence in the minds of people, both attracting and repelling those who take part in it. It has also been an integral part of society as an utilitarian component that has contributed immeasurably to group survival. Thus, it has been one of the great preoccupations of people, not only for the time it fills in the life cycle but for the implications it has for the happiness of the individual person and the success of his culture. In the past it has been extolled or derided by theologians and philosophers, and it has been scrutinized by all students of human beings.

All have agreed that the human being is usually a marrying animal. Whether marriage is traced to innate dependency needs or conditioned responses to psychosocial demands, people tend to seek out a mate and procreate. In so doing, they undertake one of the most complex of all experiences. On the one side are the intricate features of the per-

sonality of the husband, with the variables of his past history and future anticipations. On the other side are the same complexities of the wife, and for each there are the physiological components that direct how their psychological patterns respond. And there is the marriage institution itself, which is a product of the beliefs of both partners and of the society within which they live. The marriage lives as an entity between the two spouses, presenting its own series of complex demands and combinations of role behavior, which vary according to their places in the power structure and to the challenges of the life cycle. Therefore, it is remarkable not that so many marriages end in divorce but that so many last as long as they do.

It is now generally agreed that general practitioners need to understand the components of marital behavior in order to diagnose psychosomatic distress. People with problems related to sexual or marital life turn to their local clergymen first and to their family physicians second, typically developing masked symptoms or responding to interpersonal crises that are consistently rooted in an unhappy home life. Physicians have no choice but to recognize the highlights of marital behavior within the traditions of society in order to diagnose ailments if not to manage them by counseling or education (Vincent, 1968).

To describe the traditional marriage is as dangerous as describing the traditional American woman. It all depends on one's experience and one's point of view. There are some cautions to be observed. For example, most of the data pertaining to marriage and this society are taken from middle-class Americans who are psychologically minded, well educated, and motivated to reply to the questions of researchers. The body of information that supports most inferences about marital behavior is derived from comparatively few research studies. And there is even less information concerning marital behavior outside the middle class. Nevertheless, because of the immense hunger in society for answers to the problems of marital life, experts in the field have been tempted to give simple answers to complex questions, purporting that one way or another is the road to conjugal happiness. Furthermore, when the topic of sexuality arises, there is an emotional overlay that further distorts the opinions of the experts and the questioners. In the end, rhetoric often outweighs reason by a large margin.

The fact is that no one in the field of marriage and family counseling can say for sure what it is that makes a marriage work, except for the willingness of the participants and a smattering of good luck. Some like to say that love conquers all. Others reply that love is blind. Still others say that to marry for money is more sensible than to marry for love, since one's affectionate needs change over time. And with the modern emphasis on self-satisfaction and the realizing of one's potential, to stay married merely for utilitarian reasons—for the sake of avoiding divorce or for the sake of the children—is scorned as counter to the new American ideals.

The role of science is not to articulate ideals but to outline reality. There are no definitive roadmaps to marital happiness or success. Studies of sex and marriage manuals from 1830 to the present indicate that impressions of marital happiness and techniques

for more effective coping always tend to reflect currently popular sexual attitudes (Gordon, 1971). The student of marriage needs to recall that the data on which he relies are quite limited and the inferences to which he is exposed are often extensive. He should know that marriage has three interrelated components: sociological patterns within which marriage occurs, psychological patterns that each spouse brings to the relationship, and adaptational factors that shape marital behavior over the life cycle.

Sociological Factors

Anthropologists disagree as to when marriage began. They do agree, however, that the first reason for its existence has been the survival of society. Societies tend to be only as strong as the marriages they perpetuate because the marriage institution makes a number of crucial contributions.

First, marriage provides a clear definition of sexual domain. Husband and wife are able to identify each other as sexual partners and are able to establish their family. Historians agree that indiscriminate sexual activity leads to social chaos. Without the guidelines and demands of marriage, society would not be able to establish the rituals by which the group can organize, interpret the world, and survive. Freud indirectly pointed out the universal importance of marriage in his study of the incest taboo. He noted that this taboo was the reaction to a universal instinct for incestuous behavior, which he inferred to be at the root of neurosis. Whether or not one adheres to this psychoanalytic theory, the adaptational value of marriage as a discriminator of sexual choice is incontrovertible (Udry, 1971).

Second, marriage has contributed to society the roots of its economic system through the distribution of property. By defining the rights of spouses and offspring and by outlining the distribution of wealth, marriage forced societies to deal with complex economic structures, enabling groups to grow, subdivide, and create economies that contribute to survival.

Third, marriage has been of value in combining the responsibility of sexual relations with that of reproduction and socialization. Spouses are typically expected to become parents. As parents, they are expected to transmit to their offspring the values of their culture. Children are expected to learn from their forebearers the way of life to which their society subscribes, thus ensuring the survival of the group. Furthermore, since most marriages continue after the children leave the home, the institution provides a framework for socialization in the aging years, dealing with existential anxieties concerning helplessness and the inevitability of death. This factor relates closely to the fourth contribution of marriage to society, religion.

Most cultures have attached some religious significance to the marriage ceremony. This significance is rooted in the mystical view of sexuality and procreation. It also relates to the existential problems of the passage of time, the search for individual meaning and happiness, and the ultimate experience of death. Religious symbols are projections of the psychosocial needs of individual persons and groups, and they reinforce the clarity of group expectations and the techniques of individual adjustment (Kardiner, 1945). The adaptive value of the institution of marriage thus deals with both the needs of the group to survive and the needs of the individual to adapt.

FORMS OF MARRIAGE

History has indicated that changes have occurred in traditional marriage. But the extent to which actual changes have occurred has not been made clear in studies. Because Americans are in a society that advocates change as a source of improvement, sometimes to the point of worshiping change for its own sake, they are told by the public press that everything is different. It is commonly predicted that the marriage and family of the future will be vastly different from what is seen today. But there is little information to support this kind of contention, certainly none drawn from a representative sample (Libby and Whitehurst, 1973).

Sociologists see two forms of marriage in the Western world. On the one side is the traditional marriage, which is measured by the criterion of stability. Success is the survival of the marriage without divorce. On the other side is the companionship marriage, which is measured by the quality of the

spouses' personal happiness. It is comparatively easy to make a statistical measurement of divorce rates but nearly impossible to evaluate individual happiness. Therefore, the data on which opinions about marital behavior are based are difficult to validate.

Today the companionship marriage is heavily favored. Western people are accustomed to marrying for love, but this emphasis on romance is comparatively new. It was not until about two centuries ago that Western men and women married for the sake of love. Previously, they carried on a love affair with someone outside the marriage and chose a spouse according to the traditional contract, which assured the maintenance of class lines and the extension of the kinship system. The great majority of societies relied on the planned marriage, wherein the young did not run their own courtship system but had to respond to the blessings of the elders in the choice of a mate. When in the past two centuries a series of social revolutions began to blur class lines, the upper classes began to advocate marriage for the sake of romantic love. The lower classes followed suit. But no nation has followed it as fervently as the United States. Americans are known as the people who marry for love. Linton, the well known anthropologist, made an ironic comment about this several years ago (Udry, 1971):

All society has recognized that there are occasional violent emotional attachments between persons of opposite sex, but our present American culture is practically the only one which has attempted to capitalize these and make them the basis for marriage. Most groups regard them as unfortunate and point out the victims as horrible examples. Their rarity in most societies suggests that they are psychological abnormalities.

It seems to most observers that Americans seek companionship marriages more than traditional ones and place a higher value on love and happiness than on family stability. The American courtship system is a consistent series of pressures, whereby the young gradually escalate from casual dating to intense committed relationships, which finally evolve into the marriage vow itself (Broderick, 1969). All this is done under the rubric of romantic love, which is constantly espoused in television soap operas, movies, myths, romantic novels, and modern music. In many middle-class families, the parents are made helpless by the romantic involvements of their children, under the social standard that love is the reason for wedlock. By the same token, the problems of love outside of marriage become intensely difficult when a spouse falls in love with another and then must deal with the incredibly complex series of decisions as to how to manage the marriage, what to do with the children, what to tell the spouse and family, whether or not one is infatuated or really in love. And a considerable amount of energy is expended by the young on the always unclear questions of whether one is falling in love or out of love, is undergoing the real thing or is simply in love with love.

Such is the advocacy of companionship marriage today that it seems to be a minority opinion to try to maintain a marriage for the sake of the children. And few choose to stay together because there is no place else to go, their financial and emotional investment in the family estate is too extensive to give up, or they simply prefer the known to the unknown (O'Neill and O'Neill, 1973).

Actually, the data are not at all clear on any of these points. Do Americans marry for love, or is it that they need to say that they do? Studies indicate that it is impossible to predict who will marry whom in this society except for two factors. The first factor is geographic locale, and the second is the unconscious pattern of mate selection. Americans tend to marry those from their childhood neighborhoods and to stay within their own social class. They go through a series of dating experiences that constantly add to the pressure to get married. They finally make the decision to marry not so much on the basis of a decision that they are now in love but rather because everyone thinks that it is about time. The decision to marry is far more a response to group pressure and unresolved emotional needs than a response to the delights of love itself (Ryder et al., 1972). The familiar saying that a man tends to marry his mother and that a woman tends to marry her father has some merit; it relates to unconscious factors in mate selection. Such are the complexities of personalities that it is im-

possible to leave the unconscious behind when going through the crucial decision-making process as to whether or not to wed (Ottenheimer, 1971).

Most Americans marry in their mid-twenties, although a considerable portion are still working through adolescent turmoil problems. The decision to marry often comes as a result of an effort to resolve fears of living alone, unresolved rebellion against the family, identity crises left over from teen-age years, or an unwanted pregnancy. (One of every six brides going down the aisle in America is pregnant). In addition, the pressures to marry put on by friends and family attack the young person when he or she is unusually vulnerable. The question of whether or not Americans actually do marry for love or simply describe it that way is, thus, a complex one that cannot be simply answered.

The entry into marriage is a transitional experience in which both parties agree that to get married now is the thing to do. Pressure is put on those who become emotionally attached to get married once they have entered their twenties. As Ryder et al. (1972) point out, once a person has been perceived by his peers and family members as having met the right one, the pressure begins. In a series of soft sells, parties or meetings are arranged so that the lovers are subtly but consistently pushed toward marriage. Although entry into traditional marriage in this society is publicly proclaimed as done for the sake of love, it actually occurs as a result of a series of experiences that are far more complex. Americans seem to have a participant-run courtship system, but it is a moot question whether or not the participants do run the system. Thus, the view of observers that Americans marry for love deserves to be questioned. The covert pressure to marry may be perceived as leading to an arranged marriage as much as the traditional planned weddings do in other cultures. A further aspect of the conforming nature of entry into marriage is seen in the fact that the children of conventional family-oriented surroundings grow up to build traditional marriages. They thus repeat history. Many spouses admit that they marry for utilitarian reasons—everyone else was doing it—but love was more an ideal or a purely sexual expression than a relationship reality (Cuber and Harroff, 1966).

SEXUAL RENAISSANCE

Traditional marriage must respond to historical changes more than it has in the past. Specifically, there is an awakening in society today concerning sexuality. This awakening to sexuality as a component in one's life-style, particularly with reference to the modification of old attitudes, has been termed a sexual renaissance by Reiss and others (Broderick, 1969). Interlocking factors form the backdrop on which the drama of traditional marriage is acted out today.

Observers consistently conclude that American sexual mores are different now from what they were before World War I. The Kinsey studies indicated that there was far more sexual activity before and outside of marriage than had hitherto been believed. Americans have always advocated premarital chastity for women and exclusive monogamy. Kinsey found that 65 per cent of the men and 50 per cent of the women he studied had intercourse before marriage. He concluded that the incidence of female virginity was lower than had been supposed. The majority of premarital sexual intercourse took place with those who intended to get married. Other studies replicated this impression.

Two points of view have emerged. On the one side, some say that people are moving toward an ethic of "permissiveness with affection," to use Reiss's (1967) term. He believes that the future will show a decrease of female chastity and increased sanction for sex outside of marriage. Some have concluded that the ideal of virginity is now disappearing from the American scene. But statistics do not support this contention. Instead, the context within which sex before marriage occurs remains that of commitment toward marriage. The pressures toward affection do not mean purely recreational sex; instead, they imply that the participants should be thinking about the marital commitment itself (Gagnon and Simon, 1970).

Although some predict that the sexual renaissance will take people consistently toward a more liberal society and a Scandinavian ethic, which tolerates sex before marriage and outside of it, others predict that, as has often happened in the past, this liberal generation of attitudes will be followed by a conservative one. This point of view is supported by a more conservative interpretation of the data than is typically brought to the light of day in the popular press. This view holds that the studies quoted regarding liberality and sex are derived from middle-class and upper-middle-class college-educated respondents, who are themselves the offspring of liberal citizens of the 1920's era. They are not randomly selected, representative, or in the majority.

Sexuality in this society, it is argued, always occurs within the context of traditional marriage. Thus, premarital sex is valued in reference to the marital role. Pressures among the young to undertake sex tend to occur within the context of who will marry whom. By the same token, extramarital sex is regarded and valued according to its effect on the marriage itself. The sexual value system still adheres to the traditional model of chastity and exclusive monogamy.

It is also argued that these typical middle-class conservative standards of sexual restraint are expanding and not decreasing in scope as a perceived standard for socially acceptable behavior. A large body of citizens in the lower socio-economic classes is striving to enter the middle class. They can do this by absorbing the conservative values of the middle class as a part of their social aspirations. Mothers in lower-class families who aspire to middle-class standards teach their daughters female sex roles and conservative sexual ethics by adhering strictly to traditional middle-class sexual standards regarding chastity and fidelity (Kagan, 1964). Thus, the restlessness in society concerning sexual attitudes and behavior, although it is extensive, is not one that totally covers the social landscape. Large plateaus of conservative behavior thrust up above the flood and remain unchanged by its ebb and flow.

Regardless of how one interprets statistics or what conclusion one derives as to the future of marriage and the family, certain factors must be absorbed by those actors in the traditional marriage as they play their parts. Each of these singly and in sum contribute to the sexual renaissance.

First, there is a general blurring of family

traditions in most American homes today. Children often do not know what it is their family tradition seeks to uphold. Parents in a permissive atmosphere neglect to rear their young with a clear articulation of their own value systems. Consequently, particularly among teen-agers, the right to individual decision making without regard for past models of behavior is consistently acted on, often to the detriment of the young. In particular, the young are not well prepared for marriage. The only education given them is through the peer standards of romantic love, which is heavily laced with sex appeal. Nothing is taught them concerning responsibilities in role relations between husbands and wives. They grow up in what Bronfenbrenner (1969) calls the "split level family," which is only peer oriented. The adults spend time with the adults, and the young spend time with the young. There is little crossing of age lines and little viewing of extended family traditions in the kinship system. As a result, those who enter into marriage are not effectively modeled by those who have already been in it.

The only corrective to those families with unclear traditions are those who openly advocate the traditional marital relationship and espouse stability as a basic value for personal and social success. Families in which there is a high degree of permissiveness or a tendency toward distancing between the generations do not have the ability to correct ignorance based on misinformation, lack of information, and myths.

The second factor that must be understood in this sex-conscious society is the increase in expectations placed on the marital dyad. This increase is a result of the nuclear family; the average American home contains parents and their own offspring at a distance from grandparents and other kin. At least 20 per cent of the American population move every 2 years, and the extended family of the past tends to be less prevalent today. These nuclear families include a significant number of spouses who feel trapped because their responsibility in the family is to satisfy so many emotional needs that they are unable to succeed. In the extended family it was possible for a child to gain emotional support from a parent surrogate, such as a grandfather, when conflict with his own parent had become unavoidable.

An additional source of pressure on the American marriage relates to the emphasis on companionship and its success. The current value system that advocates marriage for the sake of personal happiness, as opposed to family stability, is appealing, but it is, at the same time, an emotional threat. Whether or not one lives in a nuclear family today, one must respond to this cultural drumbeat that advocates marching to a tune of self-fulfillment, love, openness, and affection, nearly to the exclusion of everything else. Like most ideals, it presents a crisis when overinterpreted. And there is a real question as to whether or not the average American really responds to the love and affection ideal or simply pretends to do so.

The third factor that must be absorbed in this sexually awakening world is the incredible emphasis on performance. In place of the Protestant ethic, which advocates commercial success and material reward as justification for long hours of industry, there is now a sex ethic. Couples consistently report to physicians and marriage counselors with a variety of sexual dysfunctions based on pressures to perform (Masters and Johnson, 1970). This performance code attached to sexual behavior has produced a plethora of guilt over men unable to bring their women to orgasm or fearful of losing their potency due to age or anxious lest their genitalia be of insufficient size. It has produced an equal amount of anxiety among women as to their own sexual satisfaction and orgasmic potential, as well as debates over whether or not their orgasms are clitoral or vaginal and over what a woman should do with a sexual appetite if it is greater than that of a man. This increasing emphasis on sexual performance and potency has created an artificial guideline by which many people strive to measure not only their sexual competency but their personal worth. And as the pressure is applied to sex, so it occurs in marriage. It may be that marital happiness is now being defined as sexual compatibility with the availability of birth control information and devices, comparative freedom from venereal disease, and general acceptance of sexuality as an ordinary component of living. This development has led to a new dimension in the traditional battle of the sexes, the fourth factor in the sexual renaissance.

It is in the area of role relations that traditional marriage has been most affected by changing sexual attitudes. There has been a marked change over the past three generations concerning perceptions of role behavior and the norms of performance ascribed either to men or to women. In the past, sexual roles were more ascribed than achieved.

A man had roles ascribed to him by virtue of his sex, age, position in the family, and place in the social power structure. Thus, when married, he became husband, lover, father, and master of the home. He fulfilled what has been defined as the instrumental role. It was his task to perform, to make decisions, to undertake a career by which the security of the family was measured. In the past, this emphasis on the instrumental male role produced a male-dominated society. With it came the double standard, derived from centuries of practice. In essence, the double standard stated that a man was allowed to have sexual adventures outside of marriage, but a woman was not allowed to have them. Sex was seen as something a man does to a woman. It was his responsibility to be the effective lover, to undertake the right sort of foreplay, and to allow the woman to respond sufficiently to please both of them. He, in effect, often regarded her orgasm, if there was one, as the result of his work.

The ascribed role of the woman has always been an expressive one in the traditional relationship. She was expected to nurture the young, give affection and support to her husband, and maintain the home in response to the needs of those around her. She was to combine the responsibilities of wife, lover, mother, and homemaker in order to satisfy the emotional needs of those depending on her. Because the man was the dominant social figure and had the instrumental responsibilities, she could accept the double standard and, in fact, appreciate it. For the man to have sex outside of marriage was seen by her as his prerogative, due to the fickleness of his sexual appetite, the easy accessibility of his sexual drive, and the presumed sexual skill he could bring into their own relationship.

The women's liberation movement has been a profound challenge to this model. Women have challenged the right of the man to the double standard and have pointed out that emphasis on the woman's keeping a passive and nurturing role in the home was not only debasing to her pride as a social person but debilitating to her integrity psychologically (Boston Women's Health Book Collective, 1971). Male chauvinism has been attacked not only as social tyranny but as emotional disaster. The demand has been that roles no longer be ascribed by virtue of sex but be achieved by virtue of ability. Within the American home, therefore, responsibilities are much more negotiable than has ever been the case in the past. This has been a highly significant source of change and has placed a primacy on the ability of spouses to communicate, compromise, and change. It has also produced considerable role conflict, not only between husband and wife as to who should do what but within persons as they appraise their own social behavior.

Here again, one must discriminate between what is advocated and what is done, what is preached and what is practiced. A great many people advocate the negotiation of roles and increased equality between the sexes, but an equal or greater number are satisfied with the differences between the two sexes. There are exaggerations on both sides, ranging from the old male dominance of the past, in which no questions are asked by the passive wife, to a constant exchange of new marriage contracts with multiple division of labor and a variety of incentive systems for total equality between the spouses. Between these two extremes are a number of traditional Americans who will always conform to the way things were done by their parents.

UTILITARIAN MARRIAGE

The most common conclusion by sociologists in the field is that the American marriage, with its traditions, is essentially a utilitarian arrangement. People get married because it is the thing to do at a particular time in life, and no one wants to be left out. They recall moments of love, but they share far more years of relatively calm coexistence. They stay together not because there is a great deal of romance or sexual excitement but because there is too much emotional and financial investment in the family to risk change. They are somewhat devitalized and more than a little bored. Although they may not make do just for the sake of the children, they do stay together essentially because it is both practical and, occasionally, deeply satisfying. But there are few illusions (Cuber and Harroff, 1966).

The same utilitarian approach may apply to individual role relations. It is likely that most spouses in the American marriage decide who does what based on the convenience of the moment, not by deep soul searching as to the psychological ramifications of a particular act. Most women spend 85 cents of the dollar because most expenses circle around the home. Most wives define the friendship circle of the family because they live in the neighborhood at hand most of the time. Most men dedicate their energies to work because it is important to succeed. They leave the responsibilities of childrearing and nurturing to their wives not only because the women may be better suited but because the men have less time and energy. Most wives end up taking care of the children and the home. Most husbands end up going out to work and bringing in the money. Decisions about the future of the family are usually acted on at the moment, with or without extensive negotiation, depending on the personal habits of the persons involved. In later years, after the children have gone, the dependency needs of childhood are resurrected. When aging and ill health and death approach, those in the traditional marriage lean on each other simply because they face a human need. There is no indication that the future will ever be much different. The perceptions of society may vary with time in the same sense that language alters as new insights are developed and old ones, seemingly discarded, are actually reshaped. But this variation may not be the same as an actual change in performance.

It is in the sphere of role behavior that the sociological factors behind marriage overlap into the psychological factors.

Psychological Factors

If traditional marriage satisfied only the needs of society, it probably would not survive. There are also areas in which it contributes to individual happiness, although without the emphasis on companionship at all costs that is popularized today.

ROLE RELATIONS

The psychology of this form of marital relation is primarily seen in role relations. Roles are beliefs that have two effects. First, they affect the perceptions of the person toward himself and others; second, they touch on performances that are believed by the group to represent marital responsibility.

Role perceptions are at the root of communication in marital relations. These perceptions filter the messages between spouses. For example, a woman may infer one thing when a single man says, "I love you." But, when her husband says the same thing, she may react quite differently because she sees three overlapping components: herself, her spouse, and the marriage itself. The perceptions one has of any of these components markedly affect communication and related behavior. Thus, most communication problems treated in marital therapy are rooted in perceptual distortions. Vincent (1968) summarizes the overlap of these perceptual problems, as shown in Figure 1.

The self's view of the self (S-S) is the way by which one likes to think one lives. For example, a husband sees himself as a problem drinker. He sees his wife as a nag (S-O). He thinks she sees him as a frustrated sex maniac (S-O-S). On the other side, a woman sees herself as depressed and afraid of being left alone (S-S). She sees her husband as a washed up alcoholic (S-O). And she thinks he sees her as a castrating woman who never trusted anybody (S-O-S). Both are partially right; there is hostility. But both are either projecting or second guessing. Constant petty fights, withdrawal into hurt feelings, and a viscious cycle of retaliation ensue because of this communications error.

The additional factor not shown is the model of the marriage itself, to which each spouse attaches a belief system. The husband

Husband	Wife
S—S	S—S
S—O	S—O
S—O—S	S—O—S

FIGURE 1. Perceptions of one's self (S-S), of the other spouse (S-O), and of how one thinks the spouse sees one (S-O-S).

believes that all wives are like that, since his mother was; that marriage is not what he expected it to be; or that all husbands have a right to a binge sometimes. The wife may believe that history is repeating itself, and it tends to in marriage; that she has failed as a wife, who should be able to keep her husband happy; or that no wife should have to take this much abuse. What each believes is a product of his own past and of his own level of aspiration. How each handles these beliefs is a product of his own personality. At all events, when there is role conflict in the traditional marriage, a large segment of the evaluation of one's role comes from socially defined codes regarding the normally accepted standards of one's social class. Perceptions between traditional spouses rely heavily on role performance criteria.

In a traditional marriage, role performance is the primary quality to which its participants respond. There are two general categories: the instrumental and the expressive. The husband is expected to perform the instrumental role—to achieve, work, perform in his career, and bring in prestige and success for his family. By the standards of the present society, this instrumental performance is a crucial aspect in the stability of the American marriage. Americans adhere to the Protestant ethic and do not tolerate male failure in the marketplace. Families are judged—and they judge themselves—by how well the husband is educated, how much he earns, and how much social power he wields. On the opposite side, the social standard for the traditional wife is in the demands of the expressive role. She is to nurture and feed, to feel more than to do. Her performance is closely attached to how her offspring grow—for example, "lack of it reflects on your mother." The performances of both husband and wife are critical to mutual esteem and cooperation within the marriage. Today, most of these roles are negotiated. But all judgment still returns to the perception of performance. What one does and what one says one does are never ending challenges.

The marriage relation is operated rather like a three-dimensional chess game in which a series of perceptions is constantly exchanged. The complexity extends even beyond the three levels and soon becomes a mutual guessing game. One of the most typical coping patterns in role conflict is second guessing, assuming that one knows how one is perceived in one's role, without taking the risk of actually finding out. Marriage problems typically arise when a spouse acts on a second guessing basis, assuming that he knows what his spouse is really thinking or really believes and then going ahead to perform a role based on that perception. In turn, the observed spouse reacts to inferential behavior and may covertly agree to respond as though this inference were, indeed, the way things are perceived. Typically, a passive spouse pretends to agree with an over domineering partner in order to avoid a fight. The game concept develops, and time goes by, allowing each player in the game to pretend that everything is all right while one secretly feels oppressed and unloved and the other is secretly disdainful of his easy victory. The result is a loss of intimacy and an ever expanding vicious cycle of emotionally distressing compensatory responses. This game was pointed out in Berne's (1964) best seller, *Games People Play*.

In studies of role perceptions as contributing to marital happiness in the traditional relation, an interesting double standard comes to the surface. It appears to be important to marital satisfaction that the wife accurately perceive her husband but not important in itself that the husband understand his wife (Stuckert, 1963). This same pattern carries over to role performance. Traditional marriages typically place a great deal of emphasis on the success of the husband in terms of satisfaction with the marriage. The husband, since he is maintaining an instrumental and task-oriented role, is expected to demonstrate high occupational status, income, and educational level as indicators of success and stability. According to these criteria, nonwhites who are not able to keep up with these standards have different and essentially less happy marriages. Data indicate that, in deference to the pressure placed on the husband to perform in the traditional relation wives tend to conform more to husband's expectations than husbands do to wives (Hurvitz, 1960). Repeated studies indicate that the most important source of marital satisfaction for the wife tends to be the husband's prestige. The higher the status, the greater the wife's satisfaction. Thus, it can be seen that traditional marriage is a direct descendent of the Protestant ethic, around which most of the incentive system in today's capitalistic society exists. It is also found that the double standard in favor of the man remains an important factor by common consent.

EMOTIONAL ADJUSTMENT

An important psychological feature is whether or not the sociological pattern within which a marriage stands does satisfy the emotional needs of its participants. Thus, it is important to review exactly what aspects of emotional adjustment can be derived from the rather rigid role relation in the traditional marriage.

Most studies concur that happiness in a marriage implies happiness in the general relationship. However, those who report very happy marriages tend to dwell on their relationship in surveys, and those who are unhappy tend to indicate external sources of stress. None of this research includes objective observation of actual behavior. In relations in which need satisfaction is measured, researchers are inconclusive as to how emotional adjustment is achieved. It has become popular to advocate communication and verbal confrontation as important ingredients in emotional adjustment in marriage. Advocates of this view proselytize that openness, more talking, increased sensitivity to feelings, personalizing of language symbols, and keeping the communication channels open all contribute to happiness. Some studies agree with this view (Navran, 1967). However, other studies report that communication can disturb a relationship, particularly when there is an emphasis on verbal overkill. Complete openness can be destructive. There may be a secret intolerance of weakness or an inability to perceive accurately the emotional strength of one's spouse. In such a relationship the verbally active partner becomes the better fighter who always wins. Thus, conflict is never well handled, and fights become a chronic source of despair. The need for more effective coping with the art of fighting has been articulated by Bach and Wyden (1969).

In marriage counseling, couples commonly complain that they are unable to communicate. But it is often found that marriages are troubled not by a lack of communication but by a misuse of it. Spouses who suffer from poor emotional adjustment suffer not because they are receiving no communication but because the message they are getting is not the one they can handle, and the message that they send is not the one that gets received. Moreover, there is usually a profound difference in conflicted relationships between the verbal and the nonverbal. Data consistently indicate that the bulk of messages and stimuli exchanged between human beings is more behavioral and nonverbal than word oriented. The modern vogue in favor of the open exchange of emotions as the hallmark of intimacy is like any form of self-help: For some it works, and for others it fails. Most spouses find that actual behavior is a far better substitute than verbal communication. Problems arise when a spouse says one thing and does another. The key to adaptive communication in marriage is its selective quality (Udry, 1971).

Psychological need satisfaction and social stability and adjustment may not have a direct positive correlation. As Cuber and Harroff (1966) indicated in their study of upper-middle-class couples who had been married at least 10 years and who had never considered divorce or separation, stability is not necessarily satisfying. As they wrote:

A "stable" married pair may on the one hand be deeply fulfilled people, living vibrantly, or at the other extreme, entrapped, embittered, resentful people, living lives of duplicity in an atmosphere of hatred and despair.

However, it is likely that there is a general correlation between happiness and stability. It is likely that in most relationships some form of success precedes general emotional fulfillment. By and large, this means that the husband needs to succeed in his role performance before there is an overwhelming concern with companionship. This is particularly true in disadvantaged families in which survival is an issue of far greater importance than pleasure. Moreover, satisfaction should not be confused with bliss, for satisfaction may include overt hostility more than peaceful companionship (Jackson and Lederer, 1968).

A psychoanalytically oriented view of emotional adjustment in marriage is described by Lidz (1968). He states that marital success is a combination of stability (the satisfaction of role perception and performance) and emotional adjustment (self-realization). Marriage demands a reorganization of the personalities of both partners. Each spouse's ego must expand pertaining to his view of himself, his partner, and the marriage relationship itself. Moreover, one's spouse should become one's alter ego when there is optimum mutuality of need satisfaction. He notes that a prototype for an effective husband-wife relation is the mutuality of the mother and the child.

Lidz also notes that each spouse needs to have some change at the superego level in order to cope with the id of his spouse, an apparent reference to the modification of a value system that tolerates the basic emotional demands of a partner without necessarily giving in to them. The impulses that are most crucial for recognition in a relationship involve assertion and self-preservation. And both need to respect ego defenses. Lidz notes that there is often a transference of parental traits to one's spouse and that this psychological factor is an important ingredient in dealing with the dependency needs and the learning of social roles. He also indicates that within the marriage there is a normal exchange of parental roles between spouses whenever a life cycle crisis places one or the other in an overdependent state. Finally, marriage involves a fusion of the original families of both spouses, a factor that brings role relations back into play.

Such a perspective of the complexities of the marital relationship by psychiatrically trained observers raises the question as to whether or not there is a deeper psychological rationale for the role relationship of the traditional marriage. Is there psychological justification for the double standard of the traditional marriage? Are there innate trends in men to be instrumental in life tasks and interpersonal relationships? Are there similar deep needs in women to nurture?

The first adaptive value of the separation between male and female roles in the traditional marriage concerns the process of reinforcement. This reinforcement is applied essentially to sexual identity. In the traditional home the husband is expected to be the dominant partner in regard to assertive behavior, decision making, and role modeling for the young the characteristics that define masculine behavior. Essentially, he is the model of appropriate aggression applied to decision making in the home and to competing in his work or career. Assertion is a crucial psychological strength that allows for individual survival and the maintenance of a person's inner satisfactions in a competitive world. Assertion can also become destructive aggression or, when turned in on the self, the source of depression. Psychometric data compiled by Fisher (1973) show that men tend to demonstrate a need for mastery, are strongly achievement oriented, and are likely to be aggressive under changing conditions. Studies into body image fantasy patterns and relative behavior support the contention that men are likely to be aggressive. In particular, the man tends to see his body image as a state of extended motion that brings a feeling of vulnerability in the environment. To ward off this state of vulnerability, the man acts assertively, emphasizing achievement and mastery as a compensatory response. These data have obvious sexual connotations. One may infer that the man's self-perception is not only a product of psychosocial conditioning but also an innate response to his physiology, insofar as his sexual build is extended and vulnerable when responsive to an arousing situation.

In contrast, the responses of women to psychological testing show an orientation far more toward feelings and the sensitivity of people than toward the mastery of tasks. The woman relies primarily on the experience of interdependency and tends to avoid aggressive behavior that might reveal sexual interest (Fisher, 1973). Furthermore, the female body image is not phallic but, rather, is turned in on itself and is reluctant to be moved. Sexual fantasies among women show a difference between those who are orgasmic and those who are not. The orgasmic woman tends to have fantasies that are turned in on herself and centripetal in motion, with a heavy emphasis on the affective or aesthetic in color, sound, and imagery. There is a sense of letting go from the outside world and responding only to one's inner needs. By contrast, the nonorgasmic woman tends to reveal a fantasy pattern that is always punctuated by real-life concerns, centrifugal in motion, and likely to imply that the male partner with whom she is making love is emotionally unpredictable or undependable. She is unable to let go of herself in the deepest sense, and a short circuiting of her physiological sexual arousal by her psychological inhibitions occurs. These data imply that the traditional role of the woman as nurturing and comparatively passive, following an expressive mode, and responding to the needs and perceptions of the husband has either permeated the female psyche to an extensive degree from centuries of psychosocial conditioning or was there in the first place, and societies have only responded to this natural role. There are no such indications of psychological limits from psychosocial conditioning placed on the man. His fantasies are unpredictable and usually irrelevant to the outcome of his sexual physiological response.

The role relationships of the traditional marriage provide useful reinforcement for deep psychological needs. This information is useful in discriminating between the sociopolitical arguments alive in today's society regarding equality of the sexes. There is often a great deal of confusion between the rights of the sexes and their innate needs. If the traditional mode has validity, it may be that it responds to a basic drive for mastery to compensate for extended vulnerability in the man. It also reinforces his most adaptive sexual response. And, since the traditional marriage provides a rather protected position for the woman, she is then free to nurture, gain dependency satisfaction, and feel free enough with her unpredictable man to enhance need satisfaction for both of them.

Adaptational Factors

The final evaluation of traditional marriage refers to responses in the dyadic relation to life cycle crises. Since the measurement of satisfaction tends to be stability, what tends to hold the traditional American marriage together? The answer includes the value system within which the spouses live, the degree of inner need satisfaction, and the available alternatives for change.

VALUE SYSTEM

Value systems have already been described as sociological variables. From the adaptational point of view, the importance of a value system is that it presents distinctions between right and wrong and offers the means for cooperation. As Rieff (1966) puts it:

Culture is another name for a design of motives directing the self outward, toward those communal purposes in which alone the self can be realized and satisfied.

In adapting to life cycle crisis, the traditional spouse must typically respond to a level of aspiration for his own behavior. It is this standard by which he judges himself to be a success or a failure and by which he is judged in the eyes of others. Although numerous studies purport to describe the values of typical Americans, none of them are conclusive or representative. Americans value their marriages on the basis of the family tradition they inherit and choose to represent, their place in the social power structure, and their religious behavior.

The most common reason given for the loss of a stable marriage is the lack of companionship. The second most common reason is sexual difficulty, usually infidelity. The third most common reason is money. Most spouses stay in a marriage as long as there is a modicum of companionship. This is not the same as romantic love or sexual success. It is, instead, a generalized belief that home should be a resting place from the workaday world, not an idyllic castle across whose moat no troubles ever come.

A second value in American culture refers to the maintenance of the family as long as the children need parental guidance. This idea of staying together for the sake of the children is related both to feelings of responsibility toward child rearing, which is highly prized in this society, and to financial obligations. Even though couples may feel that their relationship has become increasingly devitalized and boring, they tend to put off divorce until the husband is in his early forties. About 20 per cent of American divorces occur at that time, when the children are usually well into their teen-age years and are able to demonstrate emotional self-sufficiency. And by that time the divorcing partners may have collected enough financial security to start a new life successfully.

The value system of companionship is closely allied to inner need satisfaction. However, spouses—especially wives—tend to love those who succeed in work more readily than those who are career failures. Part of the marital mythology is that spouses typically decide whether to marry for love or for money. With the habitual American emphasis on material success, it is realistic to infer that far more people marry and stay together for money than ever acknowledge this motivation as fact. The great majority of marriages occur within similar social class lines or the choosing partner seeks to climb to a higher level. Only a small minority of lovers ever choose to decrease their social status by marriage.

INNER NEED SATISFACTION

Inner need satisfactions can be broken down into three aspects with related adaptational values: intimacy, dependency, and dominance. The intimate needs of partners need to be satisfied—needs regarding sex, love, affection, emotional support, and constant reinforcement of their identity. Intimacy is the product of sexuality and assertiveness. The adaptive challenge of marriage is to gain enough love to be satisfied, yet not so much that one is smothered; enough to like what one has, yet enough to give much away. This last factor allows for a reciprocal response between lovers as well as between parents and children.

Satisfaction of dependency needs involves breaking away from past parent-ideals and accurately perceiving one's partner as an equal, not as an authority or a subordinate. One of the most common areas of role conflict in the dependency sphere is in the tendency of couples to relate on a parent-child level rather than on an adult-adult level. Both spouses tend to play games to avoid confrontation with other aspects of their personality. As argued before, this is not always inappropriate.

Dominance refers essentially to role differentiation and decision making. It also includes a tolerance of weakness and the capacity for effective conflict resolution. It is here that role relationships are constantly negotiated in the modern marriage. The traditional marriage does not abrogate the need for husband and wife to negotiate as to dominance and decision making. It infers, however, that final responsibility tends to end with the husband and that the ideal of equality in decision making and responsibility is more an ideal than a reality. When this approach is taken in too rigid and domineering a fashion, compensatory behavior develops in both the husband and the wife—for example, the man becomes too aggressive and tyrannical, and the woman becomes too passive and depressed. The most adaptive response is an exchange of roles over time, when this exchange is realistically possible.

ALTERNATIVES FOR CHANGE

The availability of alternatives indicates that the husband or the wife may dissolve the relationship if he or she finds someone else. Because there are more women than men in the population and because men die at an earlier age than do women, the options for alternative partners are typically available far more to husbands than to wives. This discrepancy places an existential dilemma on the woman, since she must deal with a life of anticipated loneliness, individual decision making, and single parent functioning. In the middle years of marriage, the woman usually has two decades of life ahead of her. Her husband, in his midforties, who has just left her is able to enter the marriage marketplace and select a younger woman from the ranks in order to start a new family. When there are no other partners available, couples maintain the stability of the marriage to all outward appearances.

The availability of alternatives also includes the ever present problem of money. Many lower-class and lower-middle-class marriages cannot break up simply because the couples' financial futures would be destroyed if they did break up. Much of the advocacy of easy divorce and quick termination of a marriage if one is dissatisfied comes from upper-middle-class persons with the financial means to make their wishes become reality.

LIFE CYCLE CRISES

Life cycle crises to which traditional marriage responds in this culture can be labeled by common sayings:

"And so they married and lived happily ever after." This familiar last line to the average fairy tale indicates the emphasis in this society on marriage as the termination of romantic love and implies the high expectations placed on marriage for personal happiness and social success. Courtship behavior needs to be evaluated on the basis of what young adults expect when they marry.

"The honeymoon is over." Shortly after the wedding, the romance tends to change when role responsibilities are encountered. The special sexual liasion that was approved for the couple now encounters daily difficulties and preoccupation with other demands, including child rearing in the early years of the marriage. Many wives become wrapped up in their children and respond to their place in the family, thus slowly but surely turning away from their husbands. Husbands become preoccupied with their work and turn away from their wives.

"He looks just like you." The arrival of the first child is as significant as the departure of the last. The first child changes a dyad into a triangle and can seriously disrupt emotional need satisfaction.

"Keeping up with the Joneses." Husbands are expected in their instrumental role to bring in money and demonstrate upward mobility. The fear of failure is excessively high in this society and permeates every home. The marriage is challenged to devise a value system concerning the definition of success and to evolve financial abilities for the survival not only of the family but of the offspring.

"The nest is empty." When the children leave home, couples who have been preoccupied with careers and child rearing are now thrust on each other and need to devise ways of coping with the remaining years. Statistically, most of the married years are lived after the children have departed, although many couples ignore this fact (Duvall, 1971). Communication problems and perceptual distortions that have been hidden now tend to come into the light of day. Conflicts arise as they wonder whether or not they are still able to find the companionship in the marriage that they thought they once had.

"You're not getting any younger." The experience of aging is a profound one in this youth-oriented culture. A constant source of challenge in the middle years is the fear of loss of a partner to a younger and more attractive person. This fear begins to affect the sexual responsivity of both partners. Men feel that age will wither and women are concerned that the approach of menopause will reduce their sexual potential. This fear can affect the capacity for intimacy. General health problems also become a difficulty. In addition, there is an existential experience; the death of one of the spouses' own parents forces them to reconsider their value system and to raise the perennial question, "Is it all worth it after all?"

Conclusion

All in all, marriage is the most complex of human relationships. Having begun with the comparatively simple experience of falling in love, the couple takes on role responsibilities and adds the challenges of procreation and the transmission of values from their own generation to the next. The tradition of sex-differentiated role behavior, fidelity, and commitment to family ties has many adaptive assets beyond companionship.

REFERENCES

Bach, G. R., and Wyden, P. *The Intimate Enemy.* William Morrow, New York, 1969.

Berne, E. *Games People Play.* Grove Press, New York, 1964.

Boston Women's Health Book Collective. *Our Bodies, Our Selves: A Book by and for Women.* Simon & Schuster, New York, 1971.

*Broderick, C. B., editor. *The Individual, Sex, and Society.* Johns Hopkins University Press, Baltimore, 1969.

*Bronfenbrenner, U. The split level American family. In *Perspectives in Marriage and the Family,* J. R. Eshleman, editor, p. 521; Allyn & Bacon, Boston, 1969.

*Cuber, J. F., and Harroff, P. B. *Sex and the Significant American.* Appleton-Century, New York, 1966.

*Fisher, S. *The Female Orgasm.* Basic Books, New York, 1973.

Gagnon, J. H., and Simon, W. Prospects for change in American sexual patterns. Med. Aspects Human Sexuality, *4:* 100, 1970.

Gordon, M. Sex manuals: Past and present. Med. Aspects Human Sexuality, *5:* 21, 1971.

Hurvitz, N. The marital roles inventory and the measurement of marital adjustment. J. Clin. Psychol., *16:* 377, 1960.

Jackson, D. D., and Lederer, W. J. *The Mirages of Marriage.* W. W. Norton, New York, 1968.

Kagan, J. Acquisition and significance of sex typing and sex role identity. Rev. Child Dev. Res., M. L. Hoffman and L. W. Hoffman, editors, p. 137. Russell Sage Foundation, New York, 1964.

Kardiner, A. *Psychological Frontiers of Society.* Columbia University Press, New York, 1945.

Libby, R. W., and Whitehurst, R. N., editors. *Renovating Marriage: Toward New Sexual Life Styles.* Consensus Publishers, San Ramon, Calif., 1973.

Masters, W., and Johnson, V. *Human Sexual Inadequacy.* Little, Brown, Boston, 1970.

O'Neill, N., and O'Neill, G. *Open Marriage.* J. B. Lippincott, Philadelphia, 1973.

Ottenheimer, L. Unconscious factors in choice of a mate. Med. Aspects Human Sexuality, *5:* 130, 1971.

Ryder, R. G., Kafka, J. S., and Olson, D. H. Separating

and joining influences in courtship and early marriage. Med. Aspects Human Sexuality, 6: 13, 1972.

Stuckert, R. P., Role perception and marital satisfaction: a configurational approach. Marriage Family Living, 25: 415, 1963.

Udry, R. J. *The Social Context of Marriage.* J. B. Lippincott, Philadelphia, 1971.

Vincent, C. E., editor. *Human Sexuality in Medical Education and Practice.* Charles C Thomas, Springfield, Ill., 1968.

7.2 Marriage: A Contemporary Model

NENA O'NEILL and GEORGE O'NEILL, Ph.D.

Introduction

In the wake of major technological and social changes in contemporary society, numerous alternative experimental styles of marriage and relationships have emerged (Neubeck, 1969; Otto, 1970; Sussman, 1972). These experimentations vary from those involving more than two persons in the basic pattern—which include group marriage, communal life styles, and polygamous patterns (often triadic and more often polygynous than polyandrous)—to innovations and changes in the traditional pattern of monogamous marriage. These modifications, deletions, and additions to standard behavior and expectations for those legally married include such various patterns as separate domiciles, dual career couples, consensual extramarital sex in various contexts, and reversal of traditional role patterns—that is, the woman provides and the man keeps house. With frequent divorce and remarriage, serial or progressive monogamy has become common. In addition, there is a tremendous increase in nonmarriage arrangements, in which couples live together without being legally married. Some of these couples make long term commitments and have children, others use this arrangement as a trial or learning period for subsequent marriage, and still others remain together for short periods, with no intention to marry.

The proliferation of these alternative patterns and the motives that have impelled more and more men and women to seek new innovations are, perhaps, indicative of a need for revision in the marriage format. Enormous alterations in society have resulted in behavioral changes in marriage, yet the ideals, themes, and beliefs—the "shoulds" and "should nots" of behavior—concerning marriage have not changed. This cultural lag is customary in times of rapid social flux and movement.

One can catalogue all the sociological and technological forces that contribute to these changes in marriage, but an understanding of these forces offers little to the person in the way of ameliorating the problems he faces when he comes to grips on a personal basis with the fact that the old mores and established patterns of institutions have not changed, although his needs and the external socio-cultural conditions affecting his behavior have changed (Crosby, 1973; Slater, 1970). For many, this discrepancy creates confusion, an inability to deal with resultant problems, and a pervasive dissatisfaction with marriage and the self. It was to this problem that the authors directed their research, which has resulted in a new model for contemporary marriage.

Action Model

This new model, embodying the concept of open marriage (O'Neill and O'Neill, 1972a), is primarily based on the expression of a desire for change and the perceived routes for change drawn from interviews conducted with more than 400 respondents and from observations of actual changes already taking place in many relationships. The research the authors conducted was used to create a model for change, which has involved stepping beyond the role of an objective researcher reporting the data and findings, and into what has been termed action anthropology (Peattie, 1970; Piddington, 1970). This means delineating a model for change that places the problem areas in their present and past cultural context and presents various available options for change in marital behavior and attitudes.

An attempt has been made to present the traditional marital configuration in its societal setting and to delineate the cultural imperatives and values implicit in these imperatives for examination by those involved in marriage relationships. The first purpose was to make it possible for marriage partners to become aware of the idealized precepts of the institution of marriage and the forces influencing their attitudes toward and their behavior in marriage. Without an awareness of the present conditions, they cannot perceive the pathways to change. Some couples choose to remain within the traditional marriage, where the perimeters and dimensions are defined for them by the norms. But for those who feel a need for change, awareness and insight are necessary first steps to determining or discovering what pathways are available. The second objective was to outline those options for change in marital interaction that the authors had found in their research.

The Problem

During the course of the authors' research (O'Neill and O'Neill, 1972b), it became apparent that the central problem in contemporary marriage is relationship. With the breakdown of many external supports for traditional marriage, the pressures on the interpersonal husband-and-wife relationship are intensified. There is an increasing need for that relationship to provide more fulfillment and benefits on both a personal and an interpersonal level. Problems in marriage are

manifested by the inability of the majority of persons to find in the marital relationship both intimacy and opportunity for developing their personal potential.

It was found that marital partners and those contemplating marriage expressed a need for intimacy and growth in a relationship in which they could actualize their individual potential without destroying the relationship. Most people did not have the skills in relating and in communication that would facilitate growth in a noncritical atmosphere. The typical dyadic marital role relationships had already been precut for them, locking them into a negative, involuted feedback system. The most important impediments to growth were the unrealistic expectations and myths stemming from the traditional marriage format.

Closed Marriage Model

Many of the expectations for the traditional marriage format limit the development of individual potential and are out of step with changes in a contemporary society that have inevitably altered needs, flexibility, and perspectives on human equality. The rigidities of a patriarchal and monolithic style of marriage—based on an agrarian past, with husband and wife roles solidified into stratified positions—do not readily permit growth or change. Many factors in the contemporary world—including a longer life span, more education, greater mobility, rapid communication, and technological innovations—have changed the position of women and have created new needs for greater parity in marriage and in man-woman relationships. These factors have also created a need for a marriage format that can incorporate change.

To understand the difficulties that people may have in effecting change in marriage, one must understand some of the underlying themes in the traditional marriage format, which the authors have termed "closed marriage." The closed marriage model incorporates themes, ideals, and patterns resulting from the fusion of several traditions in the past—among them romantic love, a puritan ethic, and a patriarchal and authoritarian family structure. A profile of closed marriage follows.

Exclusivity and possession are the

hallmarks of closed marriage. The marital partners are possessive romantic lovers, and they belong to each other. Therefore, they have the right to make demands and to secure obligations from each other. Since they own each other, they can control each other. There is a rigid role dichotomy for husband and wife, reinforced by the cultural beliefs about masculinity and femininity. He is the breadwinner; she is the housewife. She runs the vacuum cleaner; he runs the lawnmower. She takes care of the children and does the dishes; he balances the checkbook and takes care of the car. He has the opinions; she keeps quiet. He is aggressive; she is passive. She is a full time mother; he is a part time father. There is an unequal status attached to these roles, best symbolized by the words of the traditional wedding ceremony: "I now pronounce you man and wife." Equal status might better be measured by the words, "husband and wife."

Some of the expectations, ideals, and misbeliefs associated with closed marriage are: Marriage offers the partners security, comfort, and happiness—and it will last forever. The partners will always appear as a couple; they must share the same friends, spend all their time together, and enjoy the same things. Each will have the constant consideration, undivided attention, and admiration of the other. Neither will change except gradually through the maturity of age. They will never be lonely again, and neither will ever be attracted to another person of the opposite sex. Fidelity is the proof of their love for each other. Sex will improve with time or by learning the right techniques, and good sex will solve all their problems in marriage. Jealousy means that they really care, and sacrifice is the true measure of love. They will adjust to each other gradually, without conflict or arguments. Neither is a complete person without becoming a parent. The ultimate proof of their love will be having a child. And last, but most important, each will be able to fulfill all of the other's needs.

The nature of these expectations leads to a concern in closed marriage with conformity to externals, fulfilling the expectations and living up to the prescribed roles. The common result is that the self becomes subsidiary to the role assumed in marriage. The rigidity of the roles may mean that motherhood deprives the wife of a personal career in the outside world, and work or a career for the husband deprives him of a larger role in parenthood. Structured roles lead to the process of bargaining over the exchange of rights and privileges and a feeling of constant compromise. Husband and wife are supposed to have a joint identity in marriage; they are enjoined to "become as one." This spiritual ideal is then transformed into concrete behavioral reality with the contemporary mystique of togetherness and the couple-front. Being constantly together within the marriage and maintaining a couple-front outside the marriage deprives them of their individual identities as persons, eliminates any personal privacy or time to be alone, and limits their contexts for growth. Time off for anything besides their mutual interests or concerns is interpreted as personal rejection. If infidelity (either sexual or psychological) occurs, then they either live with it in what Cuber and Harroff (1965) have described as conflict-habituated, passive-congenial, or devitalized relationships, or they divorce. Since there is no expectation or acceptance of new modes of behavior or provision for change—either in the individual marriage partner or in the larger world around them—the partners feel trapped. The themes, expectations, and restrictive clauses effectively lock the partners into a closed system that resists change and sets up a static framework that encourages frustration, hostility, boredom, and monotony. The entire framework actually works against the development of individual potential and a mutually fulfilling relationship of commitment.

Open Marriage Model

The concept of open marriage offers a model for a marital relationship that is flexible enough to not only permit but encourage growth for both partners. It is directed to the persons on whom the marital relationship depends—the husband and the wife. Inherent in this model is the authors' belief that people can and ought to be the focus for change (O'Neill and O'Neill, 1973). Also inherent in the way the authors have presented open marriage is their belief that, in a complex and bureaucratic society, the best human service system may well be the individual's own.

Open marriage is presented as a model with a two-fold purpose: to provide insights concerning the past patterns of traditional marriage, which, as a closed system model, presents few options for choice or change; and to provide guidelines, based on an open systems model, for developing an intimate marital relationship that can provide for change and growth for both partners.

Open marriage is defined as a relationship in which the partners are committed to their own and to each other's growth. It is an honest and open relationship of intimacy and self-disclosure, based on the equal freedom and identity of both partners. Supportive caring and increasing security in individual identities make possible the sharing of self-growth with a meaningful other who encourages and anticipates his own and his mate's growth. It is a relationship that is flexible enough to allow for change and that is constantly being renegotiated in the light of changing needs and consensus in decision making, in acceptance and encouragement of individual growth, and in openness to new possibilities for growth. Important guidelines for achieving this relationship are "living for now" and realistic expectations, privacy, role flexibility, open and honest communication, open companionship, equality, identity, and trust.

Compared to the themes and expectations described for closed marriage, the following expectations are seen as realistic for open marriage. The partners will share most things but not everything; each partner will change, sometimes through conflict as well as through gradual evolvement; each will accept responsibility for himself and grant it to his mate; neither partner can be expected to fulfill all the needs of the other or do for the other what he or she should be doing for himself or herself; each partner will have different needs, capacities, and potentials; the mutual goal is the relationship, not the status of marriage or material goals; should they choose to have children, they will undertake the role of parenthood willingly and with the understanding that this role is the greatest responsibility in life; liking and loving will grow out of the mutual respect they have for each other.

A comparison by Sargent (personal communication, 1972) between the two models of open and closed marriage can be seen in Table I.

Open marriage stresses a process in which dynamic interaction takes place between husband and wife and in which expectations frequently change. As an open systems model, open marriage, through positive feedback, provides for change and growth; closed marriage does not. Since these are models, they do not reflect the nuances or complexities of individual variation. Both are ideal models and stress an extreme contrast, like black and white. In reality, most marriages probably lie somewhere in the gray area midway between the extremes.

The first step in developing an open marriage relationship is for the partners to reassess the marriage relationship they are in or anticipate, in order to re-evaluate expectations for themselves and for their partner. Each person's needs and capabilities should be taken into consideration. Partners should be able to rewrite their contract—by "contract" is meant a verbal agreement about certain behaviors, division of tasks, and so on, not necessarily a written contract—according to their own particular situation, background, and needs, rather than accepting without question the predetermined role behavior outlined for them in closed marriage. They should be able to modify this agreement when conditions bring about a change in either their internal or their external environment, should they so desire or find it possible to do so. The flexible quality of the marital couple's working agreement is the essence of open marriage.

Even this initial step may be difficult to take, since couples are not educated for marriage or the requisites of a good human rela-

TABLE I
Comparison of Closed Marriage and Open Marriage

Closed Marriage	Open Marriage
Contracts set by tradition	Contracts developed by and for the person involved
Role-to-role relating	Person-to-person relating
Fighting over issues	Fighting for mutual growth
Compromise (sacrifice)	Synergy (union of differences)
Security based on rules	Security based on trust

tionship, nor are they generally aware of the psychological and myriad other commitments that the typical closed marriage contract implies. Awareness of these commitments and expectations and a realignment more in accord with a realistic appraisal of their capabilities are fundamental to instituting change.

The following 8 guidelines are designed to help give an understanding of the elements in interpersonal relationships that allow for change, for increasing responsibility for the self and for others, and for increasing intimacy in the relationship (see Figure 1).

1. "Living for now" involves relating to the present, rather than in terms of the past or in terms of future goals that are frequently materialistic and concrete rather than emotional and intellectual in nature.

2. The granting of time off or privacy can be used for examination of self and for psychic regeneration.

3. A way out of the typical husband-wife role bind involves working toward a greater role flexibility by exchanging roles and role-associated tasks on either a temporary or a part time basis and using role reversal as a device for greater understanding of the self and of the position of the other partner.

4. Open and honest communication is perhaps the most important element in an open relationship. The lack of communication skills creates a formidable barrier between husband and wife. These skills are essential in sustaining a vital relationship, promoting understanding, and increasing knowledge of self. Becoming sensitive to nonverbal communication, understanding the timing and context of verbal messages, and being able to distinguish such elements as sensing, feeling, interpretation, intention and expression in communication (Miller, Nunnally, and Wackman, 1972) can help partners to develop the true dialogue and self-disclosure necessary to intimacy.

5. Open companionship involves relating to others, including the opposite sex, outside the primary unit of husband and wife as an auxiliary avenue for growth.

6. Equality involves relating to the mate as a peer in terms of ways to achieve stature rather than in terms of the status attached to traditional husband and wife roles. Decisions are made by consensus, rather than bargaining on a 50-50 basis.

7. Identity involves the development of the individual partner through interaction with the mate and others, through actualizing his own potentials, and through building toward autonomy and personal responsibility.

8. Trust, growing through the use of these other guidelines and based on mutuality and caring, creates a climate for growth. Liking and respect for each other's integrity grow through the exercise of these guidelines.

Love, sex, and fidelity play extremely important parts in any marriage relationship, but they are not guidelines in the open marriage model. Many of the problems in closed marriage stem from the inordinate emphasis placed on the part that love, sex, and fidelity play in a marriage. The elements for a relationship of caring, respect, responsibility, and growth described in these guidelines form the basis on which love, sex, and fidelity achieve their meaning, not vice versa. Love grows out of one's own fulfillment, and the ability to

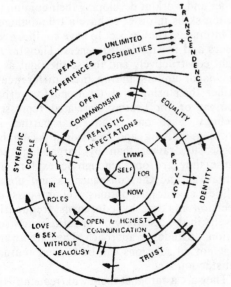

FIGURE 1. The open marriage.

give and to care equally for each other's well-being and growth; fulfilling sex is an affirmation of this love. Since the externally imposed sexual exclusivity of closed marriage may not fit into the framework of a relationship of equality, honesty, freedom and mutual responsibility, voluntary sexual exclusivity and nonexclusivity are options in the open marriage model.

The system of guidelines for open marriage can be seen as an expanding spiral of evolving steps in complexity and depth in the marital relationship (see Figure 1). The model begins with the self and the premise that internal communication is necessary to attain disclosure of inner feelings to one's self and, subsequently, disclosure to one's mate. Once open and honest communication is established with the mate, including feedback and disclosure from both, the partners' relationship can evolve through the guidelines, with multilevel feedback reinforcing each phase. The system operates through the principle of synergy, a concept drawn from medicine and chemistry, first used by Benedict (Maslow and Honigmann, 1970) in cultural contexts and later by Maslow (1964, 1965, 1968) in interpersonal contexts. In open marriage, the concept of synergic build-up is defined as a mutually augmenting growth system. Synergy means that two partners in marriage can accomplish more personal and interpersonal growth together than they could separately—without the loss of their individual identities. Synergic build-up defines the positive augmenting feedback that can enhance mutual growth and dynamism in the man-woman relationship.

Since only a limited few may be able to use all these guidelines in their totality or simultaneously, the open marriage model can best be considered a resource mosaic from which couples can draw according to their needs and their readiness for change in any one area. The following profile of open marriage is offered for comparison with the profile of closed marriage.

Couples in an open marriage enjoy each other as companions and intimate lovers. They share their joint and separate interests, discoveries, problems, and pleasures, learning from each other through an exchange of opinions, insights, and curiosity. Each is in-volved and busy in a career, work, or some activity (hobby, interest, or a cause) that requires a personal commitment. They respect each other's need for privacy and have the capacity to be alone, either together or in a separate place, without feeling rejected. They may even take a day off alone or take separate vacations. They do not feel a compulsion to go everywhere as a couple or to have only mutual friends. They can have friendships and work relationships with members of their own and the opposite sex without their being a threat to the partner.

They relate to each other as persons in terms of equal stature rather than unequal status. They may reverse roles and exchange household tasks; their roles will be according to their capacities or changing conditions rather than according to a preset role dichotomy. They may share parenthood more closely and even completely reverse the traditional roles of husband-provider and wife-housekeeper. They may choose not to have children. If they do choose to have children, these children become an integral part of their life, with a consideration for the consequent responsibility and time involved. They consider their children's needs, interests, and involvements as important as their own, judging carefully how both are commensurate with the child's development and age, yet they do not form a child-centric family.

They have developed a sensitivity to each other and work at developing their communication skills in order to have a true dialogue of intimacy. They expect to have conflict over issues and inevitable differences. They try to fight constructively and to use the fight as a means of understanding their differences, rather than using it as an arena for verbal combat or for venting unrelated repressed feelings. Each one is an equal partner in problem solving and decision making by consensus, rather than by bargaining. Because they are open enough to explore alternatives and the consequences and possibilities of various options, the process of decision making by consensus frequently results in the discovery of an entirely new solution, attitude, or approach. They are aware that not all solutions will be to their mutual satisfaction.

They are aware that there will frequently be

pain and uncertainty in mutual growth and self-development, but this pain and uncertainty will be more than compensated for by the rewards. They help each other and are supportive when their individual dependencies and insecurities are greatest, but they try to avoid acting as crutches for each other. They have knit together their commitment with intimacy, liking, and a continuity of shared experiences. With true caring for each other, they have developed a supportive and abiding love that is based on respect for their mutual integrity and an authentic concern for the other equal to concern for self.

Implications of the Model

Open marriage is a flexible model that offers insights and guidelines for developing more intimate and vital marital relationships. An open relationship in marriage, as in any interpersonal matrix, involves becoming a more open person. Since the open minded person (Rokeach, 1960) is one who can perceive options and alternatives and make decisions about the paths to change, efforts to help the marital partners in perception and skills should increase their ability to deal with emerging problems in marriage. However, it will not be easy for most couples. Emotional maturity and the development of responsibility and confident identity cannot emerge overnight. But clinging to the old format or merely exploring experimental structural forms without attention to the interpersonal factors only increases the number of problems in marriage and decreases the benefits to be gained from it. Open marriage is not a solution or panacea for marital problems; but, by using the open marriage model, the couple may at least substitute problems that promote growth and learning for problems that currently lead only to an impasse.

It is in the arena of interpersonal relations that marriage and the family will have to find new meaning and gain greater strength, no matter what the configuration of the marriage format may be. Children cannot be taught the value of supportive love and caring, responsibility, and problem-solving and decision-making skills unless the parents have first developed these qualities in their own relationship. The inadequacy of organized institutions to instill these values and skills is only too apparent. Therefore, intimate, long term relationships, such as those of marriage and the family, must provide them. To do this, they must be more rewarding and fulfilling for their members, and there must be feedback and caring for each other's welfare. By making marriage more open and by encouraging personal responsibility, self-growth, and bonding through a synergic relationship, marital couples may find more fulfillment and challenge in marriage.

REFERENCES

*Crosby, J. F. *Illusion and Disillusion: The Self in Love and Marriage*. Wadsworth, Belmont, Calif., 1973.

Cuber, J. F., and Harroff, P. B. *The Significant Americans*. Appleton-Century-Crofts, New York, 1965.

Maslow, A. H. Synergy in the society and in the individual. J. Individ. Psychol., *20:* 153, 1964.

Maslow, A. H. *Eupsychian Management*. Richard D. Irwin, Homewood, Ill., 1965.

Maslow, A. H. Human potentialities and the healthy society. In Human Potentialities. H. A. Otto, editor, p. 64. Warren H. Green, St. Louis, 1968.

Maslow, A. H., and Honigmann, J. J. Synergy: Some notes of Ruth Benedict. Am. Anthropol., *72:* 320, 1970.

*Miller, S., Nunnally, E. W., and Wackman, D. B. *The Minnesota Couples Communication Program Couples Handbook*. The Minnesota Couples Communication Program, Minneapolis, 1972.

Neubeck, G., editor. *Extra-marital Relations*. Prentice-Hall, Englewood Cliffs. N.J., 1969.

*O'Neill, N. and O'Neill, G. *Open Marriage: A New Life Style for Couples*. M. Evans, New York, 1972a.

*O'Neill, N., and O'Neill, G. Open marriage: a synergic model. Fam. Coordinator, *21:* 403, 1972b.

O'Neill, N., and O'Neill, G. Open marriage: implications for human service systems. Family Coordinator, *22:* 1973.

*Otto, H. A., editor. *The Family in Search of a Future*. Appleton-Century-Crofts, New York, 1970.

Peattie, L. R. The failure of the means-end scheme in anthropology. In *Applied Anthropology*, J. A. Clifton, editor, p. 121. Houghton Mifflin, Boston, 1970.

*Piddington, R. Action anthropology. In *Applied Anthropology*. J. A. Clifton, editor, page 127. Houghton Mifflin, Boston, 1970.

Rokeach, M. *The Open and Closed Mind*. Basic Books, New York, 1960.

Slater, P. *The Pursuit of Loneliness*. Beacon Press, Boston, 1970.

Sussman, M. B., editor. *Non-traditional Family Forms in the 1970's*. National Council on Family Relations, Minneapolis, 1972.

chapter 8 Pregnancy and Sexual Behavior

EDWARD C. MANN, M. D.,
and THEUS N. ARMISTEAD, M.D.

General Considerations

Many factors influence human sexuality synchronously and asynchronously, but pregnancy—whether in fact, in retrospect, or in prospect—may modify human sexuality in largely unpredictable ways, be these affiliative or disaffiliative.

As a physical condition and at a purely biological level, the pregnant state confers on the pre-existing self of the woman new biogenetic ferment. Estrogen and progesterone are produced in markedly increased quantities; at least 2 protein hormones are produced by the placenta (chorionic gonadotropin and chorionic somatomammotropin); and, among many other changes, there are increases in estrogen-binding and androgen-binding globulins, alterations in the renin-angiotensin system and in carbohydrate metabolism, increased insulinase and aldosterone production, and inhibition of certain pituitary functions. Along with these internal changes are the more obvious external changes in mammary and abdominal contour that progressively increase with advancing pregnancy (see Figure 1). Unbalancing, both literally and figuratively, as these changes are, they, from the standpoint of feminine sexuality, are usually compensatorily contained within the homeostatic bounds of nongravid parameters.

This is not to say that the pregnant state is, sexually speaking, unencumbered, for frequently it is (see Figure 2). In the first trimester, pregnancy is almost always accompanied by some degree of gastric distress, if not by nausea and vomiting. In some women,

the usually mild and fleeting bouts of nausea of early pregnancy are severe and continuous, rendering sex as well as food unappetizing. The ordinarily self-limiting nature of this probably hormonal phenomenon and its well known prevalence attenuate its disruptive impact on the sexual desires of the husband and—except in extreme instances, which are usually characterized by an overlay of psychic determinants—pose no prolonged threat to bed or board.

Another aspect of pregnancy that borders on feminine mystique but that, in the experience of the authors, may interfere with marital sexuality is the so-called introversion of pregnancy. This entity, although elusive and gossamer in quality, tends to be retrospectively minimized by the wife but defensively perceived by the husband. In essence, it consists of self-absorbing, in-and-out preoccupations that approximate fantasies but that, in the main, are without substantive content. These self-distant lapses are readily confused in the mind of the husband with some vague kind of communicative alienation, which he equates with loss of his wife's desire to sustain her intimacy with him both conversationally and sexually. Curiously enough, the wife is, for the most part, unaware of her causative role in this couple-at-odds syndrome, which is frequently amenable to a council with the husband, where patience is advised.

Proceeding apace with psychoendocrine effects are the volumetric effects of later pregnancy. The progression of "with child" to "heavy with child" is attended by physical changes that, in many instances, constitute

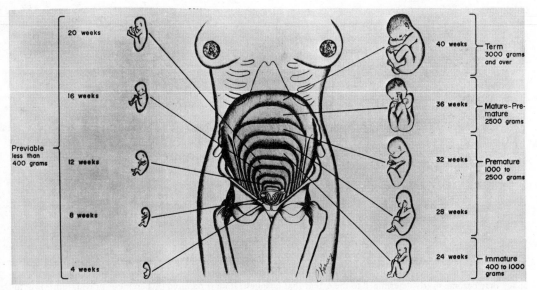

FIGURE 1. Uterofetal relationships as they develop during pregnancy. There is, in the world literature, only one recorded instance of a conceptus weighing less than one pound 397 gm. that survived. In most premature and intensive care nurseries, the chance for survival of a fetus weighing even 800 gm. is minimal. In consequence, the statistical tendency is to categorize the conceptus by weight. Thus, a fetus weighing 400 gm. (about 20 weeks gestational age) is, on the experiential basis of almost certain previability, termed an abortus. A fetus weighing, at birth, between 400 and 1,000 gm., again on the basis of improbable viability, is still termed an abortus by some institutions and, primarily by those institutions that have had statistical occasion to contend with an "abortus" who lived, immatures. With each 100-gm. increment of weight, beginning at about 1,000 gm., there is a progressively better chance for survival; therefore, prematures are usually defined as those infants weighing between 1,000 and 2,500 gm. Although an infant weighing more than 2,500 gm. is not statistically classified as premature, a 36-week-old fetus has less of a chance for survival than does the 3,000 gm. fetus close to term. Postmaturity is generally defined as a fetus born 2 weeks or more beyond the expected date of confinement. Since pregnancy at term is calculated as being 40 weeks from the last menstrual period and since the exact time of fertilization varies, the incidence of "post-maturity" is high when based on menstrual history alone. The truly postmature baby typically has long nails, scanty lanugo hair, more scalp hair, and increased alertness.

sexual impediments. The sheer abdominal bulk and height of the uterus and its contents near term often engender postural restlessness in futile search of comfort, along with exertional respiratory distress. Coupled together, these 2 physical factors may form a distracting presence that places sexuality beyond enjoyable reach.

Before leaving the subject of sexual offsets more or less indigenous to normal pregnancy, one should mention other clinical encounters connected with the pregnant state that have retained or gained currency and that, in different ways and at different physical and psychobiological levels, affect sexuality. The following illustrations have been encountered on the obstetrical service of Earl K. Long Memorial Hospital since its opening in 1968 and are included here because they generically

exemplify the varied kinds of pregnancy related and sex-related problems that are largely unheralded but that confront and often tax the managerial resources of the involved clinician.

INTRAUTERINE FETAL DEATH

Retention of the products of conception after loss of fetal life may occur at any time in pregnancy. In the absence of expulsive uterine activity, the patient, if in the early months of pregnancy, is ordinarily without subjective awareness of the fetal demise and usually learns of it as a result of pelvic examinations that reveal an absence of uterine growth and, frequently, a hardening of the normally soft cervix. The diagnosis is, at the outset, difficult to confirm, and the tendency is for the doctor to equivocate before announcing his doubts or

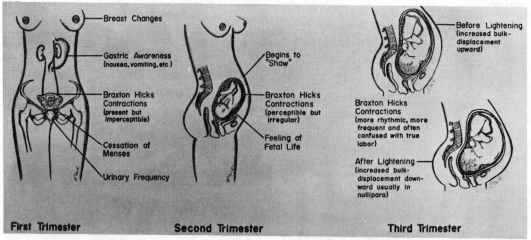

FIGURE 2. The symptoms most common to each trimester of pregnancy. The hormonally determined symptoms of pregnancy are often placed in the secondary service of emotional determinants. Thus, the nausea and vomiting of early pregnancy may become overly determined to the extent that hospitalization is required (hyperemesis gravidarum). Braxton Hicks contractions are apparently physiological and occur throughout most of pregnancy. Usually imperceptible in early pregnancy and painless in midpregnancy, these contractions, although expulsively ineffective, are frequently and at times exasperatingly confused with true labor during the last weeks of pregnancy. Lightening occurs during the last weeks of pregnancy and is due to downward descent and accommodation of the fetal head into the pelvic inlet. Upward displacement of the diaphragm by the encroaching uterus is correspondingly reduced, resulting in greater ease of respiration. With this downward displacement of the abdominal bulk, symptoms become targeted to the pelvic girdle, the lumbosacral area, and the lower extremities. Lightening is more obvious in first pregnancies and may not occur in multiparas until the onset of labor.

pronouncing final judgment. Later in pregnancy, after the uterus becomes abdominal and fetal movements and heart tones are discernible, the diagnosis is more easily made by both patient and doctor. Even here, however, despite recent diagnostic advances, the medical tendency is to withhold confirmation of the patient's fears until the diagnosis is no longer in doubt and then, in view of problems relating to induction, to wait for the spontaneous onset of labor, which usually occurs within a month.

The resultant periods of equivocal and watchful waiting are difficult and trying for the patient and her husband. Along with the feelings of loss is the frequently encountered conviction on the part of the wife that she must rid herself of this dead thing inside her and the companionate belief, on her part and on the part of the husband, that sexual relations under such circumstances are not only undesirable but insupportable to the point of ghoulishness.

POSTORGASMIC CONTRACTIONS AND PREMATURE LABOR

In some patients, particularly during the last trimester of pregnancy, orgasmic sexual activity may be followed by uterine contractions of a painfully prolonged order. Although the authors have seen premature labor occur in the conjunctive wake of such contractions and, in one compelling instance, on a basis that was operative in recurrent pregnancies, it has been seen infrequently and has been viewed in an idiosyncratic light. Others, however, who have recently studied the phenomena more searchingly, are convinced that postorgasmic contractions are a relatively frequent cause of premature labor or membrane rupture in the last trimester of pregnancy.

What role the prostaglandins may play in term and premature labor remains a continuing object of rewarding inquiry. The prostaglandins, first described and much too parochially named in the 1930's, are now known to be ubiquitous and to include a family of 20-C hydroxy-fatty acids that apparently have basic biological functions. With respect only to pregnancy, it is known that some of these compounds are present in male ejaculate, that some have been successfully used to induce expulsive uterine contractions in all 3 trimesters of pregnancy, that some have been found to be present in amniotic fluid and in maternal circulation during spontaneous labor, and that their effectiveness increases with advancing pregnancy.

Ignorance as to the genesis of premature labor is abysmal; the over-all incidence of premature labor has remained virtually static over the years, and the traditional way of seeing in this uncertain etiological area may prove to be a way of not seeing. The psychiatrist, from his intimate point of discursive vantage in his frequently continuing relationships with patients who become or are pregnant, could help illuminate this darkened area by noting and reporting any temporal relationships between orgasmic intercourse and premature labor.

PTYALISM

This very distressing condition, typified by round-the-clock salivation, is, in its severe form, disabling from almost every social aspect. Unlike the nausea of early pregnancy, it may persist until delivery. Handkerchiefs or their paper equivalents are constantly in evidence during the days, and at night the unabated drooling of the patient may literally soak her pillow. The copious secretion of saliva—some of which, particularly during sleep, is partially swallowed and regurgitated—frequently leads to nausea and vomiting. Sexual malaise is a frequent concomitant on the part of the wife and, for the admixed reasons of empathy and esthetics, on the part of the husband.

Although it is an unusual complication, this syndrome has in the past been intransigent to a variety of therapeutic regimens, such as starch restriction, atropine, and phenothiazine. Recently, however, one of the authors used doxepin (Sinequan) on a patient who had been semi-invalided by ptyalism throughout four previous pregnancies and who was similarly incapacitated in the early course of her fifth pregnancy. The results were dramatic and sustained. Since this initial success, two other ptyalism patients have been encountered, both of whom have responded in equally dramatic fashion. The authors have also used doxepin frequently in depression associated with pregnancy (100 to 200 mg. per day) and, with close follow-up, have not to date seen any adverse fetomaternal effects.

SYMPHYSIAL SEPARATION

Relaxation of the supporting ligaments of the bony pelvis normally occurs preparatory to labor and in apparent response to the hormone relaxin. This relaxation is most frequently subclinical and, when clinical, predominantly sacroiliac, but occasionally it is targeted to the connective elements that bind and immobilize the symphysis pubis. When this occurs in exaggerated form, the patient experiences severe pain on pelvic motion, which renders movement, locomotor or sexual, extremely uncomfortable. A tightly supportive hip binder provides some palliative relief, but such patients almost always sexually bench themselves for the duration of pregnancy, in the almost certain knowledge that their pelvic disabilities will disappear after delivery (see Figure 3).

PHEOCHROMOCYTOMA

This adrenal tumor, when coexisting with pregnancy, can be deadly. It is frequently confused with toxemia, in which event, death, as a result of hypertensive crisis, may result. Since the extreme hypertension associated with this tumor is paroxysmal and is usually detected at the time of crisis, anxiety, particularly of a recurrently severe nature, is a leading and all too frequently overlooked symptom.

One such patient was highly instructive in this regard; primarily as a result of her disclosure of alarming levels of anxiety, the diagnosis of pheochromocytoma was made and, 2 months before delivery, was surgically treated. Since surgical removal of the tumor more than 2 years ago, this patient has remained well and free of pathological anxiety.

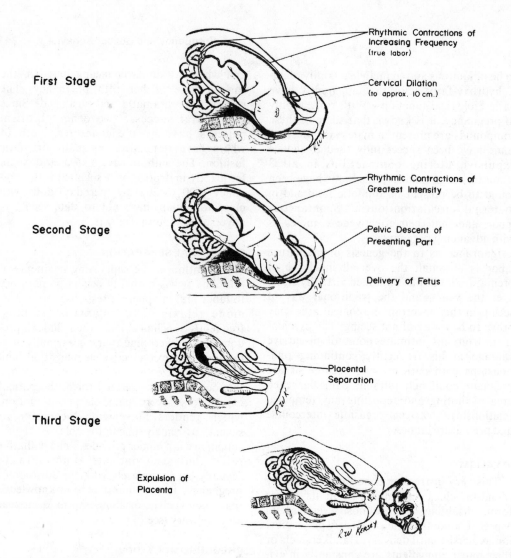

First Stage

Rhythmic Contractions of Increasing Frequency (true labor)

Cervical Dilation (to approx. 10 cm.)

Second Stage

Rhythmic Contractions of Greatest Intensity

Pelvic Descent of Presenting Part

Delivery of Fetus

Placental Separation

Third Stage

Expulsion of Placenta

FIGURE 3. Stages of labor. Prodromal events: Usually, and fairly consistently, labor is preceded by loss of a blood-tinged mucous "plug" from within the endocervix. This loss occurs in precursive relation to "silent" cervical effacement and cervical dilatation. The loss of this cervical barrier to ascending infection usually presages the imminence of labor and is referred to as a "bloody show." Occasionally, the first stage is preceded by premature rupture of the membrane as well. First stage: The first stage of labor is signaled by uterine contractions of a progressively more frequent and regular order. Unlike false labor, true labor is characterized by contractions that are productive of increasing cervical effacement and dilatation. Initially of short duration and occurring as much as 20 minutes apart, the intervals between contractions steadily decrease until they recur every 3 to 5 minutes. Complete cervical dilatation (10 cm.) marks the end of the first stage of labor. The length of the first stage of labor is highly variable, depending primarily on the progression and quality of labor. It is longer with primiparas than with multiparas, usually by some 4 to 5 hours. The usual primipara can ordinarily count on her first stage of labor lasting 12 to 14 hours. Second stage: This stage is defined as that portion of labor transpiring between complete cervical dilatation and the birth of the baby. Typically, the contractions during the second stage are of greatest frequency, intensity, and duration. The contractions occur every 2 to 3 minutes and last about 1 minute. During this stage, the patient, with the descent of the presenting part through the completely dilated cervix and into the birth canal, begins using her abdominal muscles to bear down during each contraction. Her efforts are, in time, followed by crowning (appearance of the widest diameter of the presenting part through the vulvar ring) and by delivery. Some 95 per cent of vaginal deliveries are vertex, with only 3 to 4 per cent being breech and less than 1 per cent being of the more unusual variety, such as face presentation. The second stage of labor is longer for primiparas than for multiparas. On the average, it entails a matter of an hour for primiparas; for multiparas, it may entail only a matter of minutes, usually not more than 30. Third stage: This terminal stage of labor begins immediately after delivery of the infant and ends with delivery of the placenta. It is generally of short duration, lasting less than 10 minutes.

Of interest relating to the present discussion was the relationship between her anxiety and sexual relations. Indeed, sexual intercourse was the only predictable situation that the patient associated with a paroxysmal bout of anxiety. The anxiety did not manifest itself until the immediate postcoital period, when she became subject to palpitations, tremulousness, panicky feelings, and severe headache. The association was so indelible that she came to regard sex in an almost phobic light and governed her sexual fears accordingly, through sexual avoidance.

Since apprehension is a prominent feature in pheochromocytoma, it is a symptom that should be thoroughly explored with pregnant hypertensives. The determination of urinary vanillylmandelic acid levels is a diagnostic must; this readily available test, although not entirely specific for increased circulating catecholamines, remains the first step in diagnosis. Urine analyses specific for epinephrine and norepinephrine (conjugated glucoronide or sulfate forms or metanephrine and normetanephrine) are more exact but may be influenced by exogenous compounds. Other corroborating procedures include suprarenal radiography, blood sugar levels, and provocative (histamine) and blocking (phentolamine) tests. Caution in the use of provocative and blocking tests must be exercised, inasmuch as extreme and possibly lethal swings in blood pressure may occur.

BLEEDING AND SEXUAL PROSCRIPTION

Bleeding may occur at any point in pregnancy, but it is most apt to occur in the first and third trimesters. Since bleeding early in pregnancy is frequently, but by no means invariably, followed by spontaneous abortion, precautionary interdiction of sexual relations on a temporary basis is usually recommended by the attending physician.

Bleeding in late pregnancy, because of its hemorrhagic potential—for example, placenta previa and abruption of the placenta—usually requires at least an evaluatory period of hospitalization as well as sexual proscription.

Proximate Considerations

More proximately connected with pregnancy are related considerations that frequently affect human sexuality in both the woman and the man. The infertile couple, for example, may separately or collectively react to childlessness in highly individualized ways.

The man, for example, in the course of a protracted medical work-up designed to overcome sterility, may dutifully conform to the masturbatory claims made upon him for repeated sperm analyses, to scheduled sex, and to posthaste delivery of his wife to the doctor for postcoital cervical examination; and yet he may inwardly rebel at the medicated tenor of this prescriptive style of sexual life by becoming subject to premature ejaculation or to impotence or by seeking more spontaneous sexual pastures. The wife, on the other hand, may, in consequence of the unflagging currency of her motivation, become so ritualistically involved in becoming pregnant that she becomes decreasingly concerned with wifely domesticity and increasingly preoccupied with fecundity. In the self-absorbing process, her capacity for erotic temperature is superseded by the temperature chart.

The variations on and extensions of this theme are legion. Occasionally, wives are pawns in the barren marriage contest that originates in heir-minded in-laws.

One patient, after repeated visits to the infertility clinic, finally and tearfully admitted that she had come to the clinic only at the behest of her overpowering mother-in-law and that, throughout the period of her work-up, she had surreptitiously, out of fear of pregnancy, been using a contraceptive.

Another patient, whose husband was azoospermic, decided, with the concurrence of her husband, on artificial insemination. The donor, a resident physician, whose routine was to obtain a fresh ejaculate in the office of the gynecologist doing the insemination, was observed by the patient on several occasions after leaving the rest room and delivering his specimen to the nurse. The patient, putting two and two together, inquired as to the name of the resident, and an unsuspecting receptionist naïvely obliged her with the requested information. After pregnancy and delivery, the patient, who theretofore had been a faithful wife, began—in the manner of an adopted child who, on learning the identity of her natural mother, seeks to meet her—telephoning the donor-resident and importuning him for a meeting. He consistently refused, only then to be openly propositioned. No meeting ever took place, but the telephone calls continued on an intermittent and in a progressively more brazen manner until the donor, after completing his residency, left the geographic area.

This "reverse english" type of response is encountered in other conceptional contexts. Habitual aborters, for instance, as a result of frustration and despair attending a succession of spontaneous abortions, frequently eventually blame their husbands for their reproductive disabilities and, in projection, translate, "What am I doing wrong with his seed?" to "What is wrong with his seed?" Armed with such transposed logic, they take the easy step to a self-curative extramarital pregnancy, which is almost always foredoomed to another abortive failure.

On the other side of the proximate coin are those women who, on the basis of what they consider to be hyperfertility, attested by a rapid succession of successful pregnancies, undergo tubal sterilization. Many of these women, particularly among the educationally and financially deprived, come to regard sexuality as the instrumentality that keeps them "knocked up and barefooted." The sexual act becomes invested with more anticipatory dread than participatory pleasure. After tubal ligation, and usually only after months of cautious appraisal, they frequently begin to experience their role as a sexual partner in a markedly enhanced way.

One such patient, in mock sincerity, recently complained of having, some months after tubal ligation, become regularly subject to hot flashes. On questioning, she made it clear that she was referring to the change of life occasioned by increased sexual responsiveness and not to premature menopause.

Enhanced sexuality of this order is, of course, not a ruling sequel to sterilization. Many notice no change in their sexual responsiveness, and some, particularly if sterilization was predicated on a medical complication aggravated by pregnancy, feel somehow deprived and complain of decreased libido.

Contingent Considerations

Sexuality, as it is affected by pregnancy, is related to a community of variables. The personalities of the wife and the husband, their desire for the pregnancy, financial circumstances, family size, material and nonmaterial aspirations, and unforeseen situations may separately or severally impose on pregnancy sexually cordant or discordant patterns. Of essence, particularly in this age of contraceptive options, is desirability. When the pregnancy is mutually desired and there are no medical complications, sexuality is usually unaffected. Without desirability, in the minds of either or both of the partners, there frequently appears an element of recriminatory disaffection that, to some degree, is carried over into sexuality. The couple with marginal financial resources and with the education of their other children foremost in mind, when confronted with an unplanned pregnancy, tend to blame themselves less than they blame each other. The immediate emotional tension of unacceptance, short of an induced abortion, is ordinarily followed by forced, grudging, and resigned acceptance. During the period of resolving accommodation to the reproductive fait accompli and before figurative restitution of in-bed-we-cry from unreconciled complaint to a more conciliatory plaint, there is often a disruption of the normally affiliative sexual relationship. The disruptiveness may take the form of pouting or punitive abstention. Or the husband may contentiously desensualize sex by dispensing with his usual amenities and foreplay. The wife may respond in kind by adopting a "try-me" rather than a "fly-me" demeanor and, as it were, be peeling an orange or eating an apple while they sexually go it alone together.

Just as sexual behavior may be adversely influenced by counterparental factors surrounding pregnancy, it may also be altered in converse fashion. Perhaps the most frequently encountered instance is that of the wife whose feminine security hinges on a bride-like figure or facsimile thereof. Despite her desire for and satisfaction with pregnancy, with the growth of her pregnancy, she becomes increasingly concerned over her disfigurement and, in compensatory consequence, more needful of husbandly reassurance, particularly sexual reassurance. Some such patients place the emotional lability of pregnancy, such as tearfulness at the slightest provocation, in the dominating service of their increasing sexual sensitivity and more or less extract sexual overtures from the husband; others, at subtle levels of awareness, regale the husband with an unaccustomed kind of sexual come-on that uniquely engages his arousal potential and that, in the absence of a motivated need specific to pregnancy, may be curiously inconspicuous in the nonpregnant state.

Pregnancy is ideally regarded as the leading method by which woman and man fulfill their unmet need for creative self-realization, but it is all too often, on a rationalized basis, overidealized as a vehicular device for meeting outsized or aberrant emotional needs. The lonely and dejected wife who feels that her unfaithful husband can be erotically recaptured and the gulf between her and her progressively more independent teenage children can be bridged by a familial event that in the past was always blessed usually compounds her difficulties when she perceives and attempts to resolve her problems in this way.

At other emotional levels, the woman may, more subliminally, become caught up in a variety of need-related conceptional webs.

The patient, 18 years old and unmarried, was first seen in the prenatal clinic after she had missed her second period. She was extremely anxious and related her anxious plight not so much to pregnancy as to the events that culminated in conception. These events included many sexual exposures, for most of which she was partially amnestic, as a result of almost daily and excessive drug usage ("acid, pot, speed, and God knows what else").

Her rumored sexual misbehavior and her recent shoplifting and forgery of checks had totally alienated her from her parents, particularly her father. Because of her increasing anxiety and her lack of financial and supportive resources, she was advised to enter East Louisiana State Hospital for care. After voluntary commitment, the history that follows was elicited.

The patient as a child was headstrong and fractious in minor matters, but she was without major behavioral problems. After puberty, she dated infrequently and was somewhat tomboyish. When she was in her early teens, her peer-aged sister was found to have a malignancy, and this fact was kept from both the patient and the afflicted sister by the parents. The mother and, more notably, the father, believing the sister's condition to be terminal, began showering her with solicitude and with gifts. Theretofore, the sisters had been treated impartially, and the patient reacted to this increasingly close relationship by becoming openly hostile toward her sister and by becoming rebellious around the house. After the death of her sister, more than a year later, the patient became increasingly estranged from her parents. She began keeping late hours, bar hopping, and taking up with a variety of men. Her sexual drive became overriding, and, as she turned to drugs, she became quite promiscuous. Significantly, and not necessarily related to her drug taking, she could achieve profound orgasm simply by being embraced or by being nongenitally touched.

After her admission to the state hospital and despite the earliness of her pregnancy, she wore maternity clothes, and in the recreation hall she was conspicuously unflirtatious in her demeanor with the male patients. Instead, she adopted a nonsexual buddy role with the men and women alike.

Although she approached reconciliation with her parents matter of factly, on the basis of financial need, and equivocally talked of either keeping her unborn child or placing him through an agency, she evidenced a strong and nonmaterial need to effect peace with her parents, particularly her mother. To this end, she circuitously importuned the therapist and social worker to intercede in her behalf to contact her mother regarding clothes and money for cigarettes and candy. As the mother began arriving with the requested items, the visits became longer, more cordial, and more transactional. When the mother brought up the possibility of her and her husband adopting the baby, the patient, for the first time, showed signs of unprecedented satisfaction, however disguised. She became more outgoing and entertainingly mischievous with other patients. She was allowed weekend passes with her parents, and these weekends went well until, during one pass and against a parental admonition to the contrary, she telephoned the boy by whom she had become pregnant but whom she did not want to marry, along with other drug-scene consorts. After her return to the hospital, the parents voiced second thoughts about adopting the baby. The patient became incensed and signed herself out of the hospital. Within a few days, she was arrested for passing forged checks and was jailed. Because of her pregnancy and through the intercession of the hospital social service workers, she was returned to the hospital, where, after some rather stormy sessions between the patient and her mother, agreement was again reached for her parents to adopt the child. Thereafter, the patient did well until just prior to delivery, when she developed cervical lymphadenopathy, the symptom that had led to the diagnosis of lymphoma in her sister. A diagnostic lymphadenectomy revealed chronic inflammation, with no other definitive findings.

After delivery and the adoption of her child by her parents, the patient, after a short period of living with them, left home and moved in with friends. When last heard from, some 5 months after delivery, she was running a low grade fever and was recurrently subject to cervical lymphadenopathy, for which she was going to seek private medical care.

The preceding case history illustrates several points worthy of comment. Perhaps the most revealing constructs relate to the pregnancy-by-proxy theme and to the matched motivational waxing and waning of sexual drive in the prepregnant and pregnant periods. In the afterlight, it seems that the child was a gift to replace a dead sibling for reasons of self-accusatory blame and self-effacing expiation. Of added interest is the symbolism attaching to the shoplifting and forgery. It could be formulated that the shoplifting symbolically related to admitted guilt on the part of the patient (the sister, prior to her death, received gifts that the patient enviously perceived to be stolen) and that the forgeries symbolically related to deceptive misrepresentation, on the part of the parents, in not informing the patient of the dying plight of her sister.

That expiative, propagative, and sexual determinants become inter-related and clinically manifest is amply documented in many instances of habitual abortion. In a combined psychiatric-obstetric study of more than 500 women, each of whom had experienced at least 3 successive spontaneous abortions, it was found that about one third had undergone a criminal abortion prior to marriage. When this historical finding began to emerge early in the investigation, it was impossible to state, with any degree of certitude, whether it was or was not of contributory significance in habitual abortion or, if contributory, whether the relatedness derived from anatomical (sphincteric) or psychological trauma. The investigators were unable to demonstrate, by way of hysterographic and intrauterine balloon studies, the presence of sphincteric or, for that matter, any discernible abortigenic pathology in the vast majority of this subgroup. It soon became apparent that unresolved guilt complexes associated with the criminal abortion represented a continuing unconscious conflict that, in somatic

translation and after marriage, culminated in recurrently expiative spontaneous abortions. Of corroborating significance in this regard was the frequently compelling psychodynamic meaningfulness of the temporal coincidences connected with the spontaneous abortions. One patient, for example, recurrently aborted on Mother's Day, and another repeatedly aborted on the anniversary date of the criminal abortion. Despite such imposing evidential patterns, most of these patients initially resisted insightful acceptance of any possible relatedness between the criminal abortion and their more current abortive difficulties. Some, however, before entering into the study, had considered the guilty connection. One of the anniversary aborters, after spontaneously aborting on the anniversary date of her criminal abortion on two successive occasions, became convinced of a causation other than coincidental. She attempted to forestall fate by becoming pregnant 9 months prior to the anniversary date, which, through the contrived correlation of the anniversary date with her expected date of confinement, would, magically, turn unexpectant to expectant motherhood. When this calendar-inspired pregnancy ended in an early spontaneous abortion, she, despairing of a self-cure, entered into the study. After months of preconceptional psychotherapy, she entered into another pregnancy and, like most of the other habitual aborters in the study, successfully completed the pregnancy.

This group of patients is not representative of women who seek and obtain induced abortions. Rather, they, more than most somatic compliers, were in difficult emotional straits of unusually high specificity at the time of the premarital pregnancy. The most striking historical feature common to their preabortive backgrounds was the seductive and game-like quality of the relationships between the patients and their fathers. The seductive interest was usually veiled until the patient entered into puberty, when it became operative at the level of sexual suspicion and punitive distrust. By way of paternal "sinnuendo," the patient was given to understand that she was a sexual temptress whose imminent loss of virtue bore constant watching. Placed by her father under a voyeuristic type of heterosexual surveillance of a cat-and-mouse kind, the patient—after such reinforcing affronts as keeping menstrual calendars for her sexually accusatory father or, on returning from a date, enduring grueling replays as to who did what to whom—began to act the role that her father, on projection, had defined for her. Her cued sexual role was experienced as coming from within herself and, after the "doing" of pregnancy, had to be self-punitively undone.

Puerperal Considerations

The terminative climax of pregnancy, with the living birth of a healthy infant, ideally marks, in the mind of the family unit, both a festive end and an auspicious beginning. Under these circumstances the climactic features, personified in the new addition to the family, clearly outweigh the anticlimactic features. The joys connected with the stimulating advances being made by the newly emerging personality and the pride of reproductive claimship and kinship are unifying ingredients that serve to reduce, in a kind of rose-colored retrospect, the travail and tensions that may have occurred during pregnancy. The wife becomes oblivious to cutting or recriminatory remarks leveled at her husband, say at the ligatory accessibility of his vas deferens, or by him at her during some period of objective or subjective incapacitation during pregnancy. The husband, in turn, is usually able to look back on the disconcerting aspects of pregnancy in an increasingly nonpersonal and good-humored way. Taken together, these ameliorative tendencies are reaffirmative, particularly in the sexual area.

Although these reaffirmative tendencies are usually dominant and they ultimately prevail, they are frequently delayed by unaffirmative feelings experienced by the wife after her delivery. In minor form, the postpartal blues usually become manifest early in the postpartal period, perhaps in initial response to hormone withdrawal, and take the anticlimactic form of unredeemed let-down. Although usually of a self-limiting nature, these unaccountable feelings of dejection may translate into more self-accountable feelings of doubt and worth. Depression at this discomfiting but nonprogressing level and in this postpartal context is not usually brought to the attention of the doctor. Instead, the wife toughs it out and only later, after it has been overcome, brings it to his attention. In the interim, however, there is an accompanying sexual detachment.

Much more infrequently, depressive reactions of a less concealable type develop. Along with the classic depressive hallmarks, including loss of libido, more contextual symptomatic features appear that typically interrelate maternal shortcomings with the newborn child. Phobic fears of hurting or dropping the baby while caring for it are almost invariable concerns and may be superseded by ruminative thoughts of willfully acting out such fears or by hallucinatory voices urging the mother in this direction. Functional psychoses of virtually every variety consonant with reproductive age may coexist with or follow pregnancy.

Conclusion

In the usual course of events, sexual behavior is only marginally affected by pregnancy. But its psychoendocrine effects, volumetric claims, and puerperal aftereffects exert, to some extent, a moderating influence on sexual activity.

In the unusual course of events, physical, hormonal, emotional, psychosocial, or situational determinants may more disruptively modify sexual behavior to the extreme extent of elective or medical proscription.

REFERENCES

*Asch, S. Mental and emotional problems. In *Medical, Surgical, and Gynecologic Complications of Pregnancy*, J. Robinsky and A. Guttmacher, editors, p. 461. Williams & Wilkins, Baltimore, 1965.

Flynn, V. T. Coitus and premature labor. Med. J. Aust., *1:* 1350, 1971.

*Goodlin, R. C., Keller, D. W., and Raffin, M. Orgasm during late pregnancy: Possible deleterious effects. Obstet. Gynecol., *38:* 916, 1971.

Greenson, R. R. On sexual apathy in the male. Calif. Med., *108:* 275, 1968.

Heitman, M. A psychoanalytic view of pregnancy. In *Medical, Surgical, and Gynecologic Complications of Pregnancy*, J. Robinsky and A. Guttmacher, editors, p. 473. Williams & Wilkins, Baltimore, 1965.

*Heitman, M. Pregnancy interwoven with people and problems. Med. Insight, *2:* 16, 1970.

Horton, E. *Prostaglandins.* Springer-Verlag, New York, 1972.

Kistner, R. *Gynecology Principles and Practice.* Year Book Publishers, Chicago, 1971.

Liswood, R. Variety, the spice of marital sex. Med. Aspects Human Sexuality, *3:* 105, 1969.

Mann, E., and Cunningham, G. Coital cautions in pregnancy. Med. Aspects Human Sexuality, *6:* 14, 1972.

Masters, W. H., and Johnson, V. E. Ten sex myths exploded. Playboy, *17:* 124, 1970.

*Meares, R., Grimwade, J., Brickley, M., and Wood, C. Pregnancy and neuroticism, Med. J. Aust., *1:* 517, 1972.

Rainwater, L. *And the Poor Get Children.* Quadrangle Books, Chicago, 1960.

*Sawin, C. *The Hormones: Endocrine Physiology.* Little, Brown, Boston, 1969.

*Shader, R., and DiMascio, A. *Psychotropic Drug Side-Effects.* Williams & Wilkins, Baltimore, 1970.

Von Euler, U. S. Uber die spezifische blutdrucksenkende substanz des mens chlichen prosta und samenblasensekretes. Klin. Wochenschr. *14:* 1182, 1935.

chapter 9 Sexual Behavior in the Separated, Divorced, and Widowed

DAVID M. REED, Ph.D., M.P.H.

Introduction

Much attention has been paid to patterns of sexual behavior before and during marriage, but relatively little data exist pertaining to the postmarital state. This is ironic, since a large proportion of our population is involved. Nearly one-half of the people married today will go through a separation or divorce. Virtually all will be widowed. Yet few normative data exist concerning sexual patterns among this group. Discussions of the psychology of postmarital behavior refer only to situational depressive reactions, with little or no attention paid to sexual adjustment itself. To evaluate the subject comprehensively, one must approach it from sociological, physiological, and psychological perspectives.

Sociological Factors

Statistics pertaining to the dissolution of marriage have been used by some observers to support the pessimistic conclusions that the institution of marriage has been critically wounded and that the family of the future will be increasingly disorganized. It can be indicated, for example, that divorce increased 13 times faster than the population did over the past 100 years; it can be added that the cumulative figures will show close to 10 million divorces in the decade between 1970 and 1980. There are flaws in this reasoning, however. It can also be shown that American divorce rates look high because America has recently emerged from a period of very low divorce incidence. The peak of divorce activity was 1946, a product of hasty wartime marriages; since 1950 the rate has remained stable but above the pre-World War II level. Moreover, the data were obscured by remarriage trends and increased longevity. Although divorces have increased in number, they have done so at a rate slower than the rate at which the average life expectancy has lengthened. When the rates are examined differentially, it appears that marital and family stability is not declining at a precipitous pace (O'Neill, 1967). Currently, about 50 per cent of all marriages are dissolved, but this rate includes second and third marriages. Only 25 per cent of first marriages end in divorce, desertion, or annulment, with the remainder finally being dissolved by the death of one spouse (Udry, 1971).

The ambience within which separation and divorce occur today is increasingly permissive. This fact may mean that persons recovering from this experience are able to effect a sexual adjustment with less social anxiety. Where laws and attitudes about divorce are very restrictive, only upper-class, well-to-do persons are able to afford a divorce. Where the laws concerning divorce are liberal, the rates are highest among the less privileged (Goode, 1963). In American society today, with increasingly liberal divorce laws, low income is more characteristic of divorcing couples than is low education.

Statistics on postmarital sexual behavior show that the dissolution experience appears to affect women more than men. Data from Kinsey indicate that the separated or divorced man is likely to carry on with the same frequency and type of sexual activity, and he reports the same level of orgastic satisfaction as occurred before his marriage. Nothing is noted concerning loss of a spouse by death (Kinsey, 1953).

Postmarital sexual behavior among women shows, in Gebhard's study of 632 white women, that the majority of women whose marriages have ended continue to have intercourse. These women, whether divorcees or widows, most commonly begin their postmarital coitus within 1 year after the end of the marriage. Usually, divorcees are more sexually active than widows. This difference can be attributed to age, response to trauma, previous sexual habits, and religious differences. Anywhere from 33 to 51 per cent more divorcees have sexual intercourse than do widows of the same age. Roughly two-thirds to three-quarters of the divorced have intercourse, in contrast to one-third to one-half of the widows. Interestingly enough, there is some statistical support for the stereotypes of the gay divorcee and the merry widow. The incidence of sexual activity after termination of the marriage shows an early drop after the event, followed by a higher incidence when the trauma has worn off. The rate of sexual activity—80 per cent being heterosexual coitus—tends to be higher than the rate before marriage. This increase is traceable to stronger motivations to remarry and to the general reduction of sexual inhibitions that occur in most women in their early thirties. Once a woman begins postmarital coitus, she is extremely likely to have it with more than one man. The percentage of women who have multiple partners is likely to be 12 per cent among the divorced and nearly 16 per cent among the widowed. These data, however, are limited, referring to women younger than age 45; separate consideration must be given to widows and widowers in the older age brackets (Gebhard, 1971).

Remarriage is a common form of sexual adjustment after divorce or widowhood. Divorced persons are more likely to remarry within a given period than are single or widowed persons of the same age. Of those who remarry from divorce two-thirds are women, and three-quarters are men. The motive for remarriage may be a desire for sexual companionship, the effort to overcome loneliness, or a desire to find a home for the children, but there are no statistics to differentiate among these motives. Those who do remarry tend to rate their second liaison as better than the first (Udry, 1971).

Widowhood obviously occurs because of the death of the spouse. Because of the differences in longevity between the sexes, there is a preponderance of widows in the aged population. Options for adjustment vary between men and women. Widowers have a greater opportunity, because of traditional male freedom and mobility in society, to effect sexual contact with a variety of women. They are also able to carry on with their habitual patterns of masturbation, sexual fantasy, or homosexuality. Because there are more widows than widowers available, widowers are, in effect, in a buyer's market. However, widowers are also more likely to be cut loose from their previous family. Studies of family kinship systems indicate that there is less tolerance for maintaining an elderly man in the home than for keeping a grandmother within the family residence. This may be one reason for the higher rate of remarriage among men than among women. Not only do the men have a better chance of finding a mate, but they have been cut loose from their previous family ties and are expected to re-establish their own liaisons (Troll, 1971).

The elderly widow has an option for both remarriage, which may deal with her sexual adjustment, and turning to other kin within her particular family, which enables her to effect an emotional adjustment. Women tend to define family social patterns and, with their mothers or mothers-in-law in the home, can exchange a reciprocal relationship relating to social interaction and child rearing. Because men work away from the home and generally rely on their wives' friends as sources of social exchange, this option is less available to them as widowed parents.

Statistics concerning widowhood include the following age and sex differences. Half the women between 70 and 75 are widows, but it is not until 15 years later in life that one half of the men are widowers. Between 60 and 64 more than one quarter of women are widows and only 6 per cent of the men. When a women loses her husband, she loses a love object and her social identity, derived from her husband's occupation. When a man loses his wife, he not only loses a love object but also suffers a marked change in his social interaction system. The loneliness during the first year or so after the death of a spouse is severe, and the death rate during this time tends to increase. There is also an apparent increase in suicidal gestures. During this time, sexual adjustments may move in any direction, based on the personal makeup of the widowed person and the opportunities that exist in his or her place in the social power structure (Troll, 1971).

In recent years, there has been increased tolerance for public sexual affection among the aged. Widows and widowers are now living together without marriage, presumably because of financial considerations. It is not clear that social approval has a direct effect on personal emotional adjustment or sexual behavior, but social pressures undoubtedly play a reinforcing role.

Physiological Factors

Sexual behavior is inevitably monitored by physiological capabilities. In dealing with postmarital sexual behavior, one is dealing with the effect of age on the sexual response and, in turn, with the problem of general health. Aging affects the man's sexual capability more than the woman's. The average marriage begins at age 25 for the man and at 23 for the woman—slightly past the peak of sexual interest for the husband and approaching the peak of sexual interest for the wife. When the couple reach their thirties, the man senses a reduction in his sexual interest and urgency. He may be satisfied with fewer orgasms, one or two coital contacts a week are satisfactory, and there is less preoccupation with sexual fantasies in the absence of a sexually stimulating situation. A man can physically attain an erection quickly; the refractory period, however now begins to lengthen—up to ½ hour by the late thirties. By contrast, women phasing through the twenties into the thirties are likely to be increasing their sexual responsivity (Kinsey, 1953).

Orgasmic response in women may be speeded up and more consistent in the mid-thirties than it was in the twenties. There are no clear explanations for this change. It may relate to the increased feeling of security for the woman or to the feeling of confidence in her motherhood, since most births are completed by this time, or to a general lowering of inhibition due to consistent contact with her husband and other men. Physically, there is a capability for early vaginal lubrication as a corollary to the male erection. And in the mid-thirties there is a higher frequency of multiple orgasms reported. When marriage ends in this decade, the woman is likely to be sexually active and considered to be sexually attractive within the cultural market-place for sexual partners. Those accustomed to a high rate of sexual satisfaction are likely to continue. Those with a pattern involving extramarital partners are likely to seek more than one partner after the end of the marriage. More women than men are likely to have multiple partners.

The rate of coital orgasm among formerly married women appears to be higher than among wives of the same age. Widows and divorcees who have postmarital coitus are generally orgastic more often than they were while they were married. Among the divorced, this fact is likely to be explained by feelings of relief in emerging from a painful relationship, since it has been shown that unhappy marriages include lower orgasm rate for wives. Among the widowed, this increase in orgasm may refer to a general reduction of inhibitions over time or to the same sense of release experienced by the divorcee, since so many marriages seem to be based on utilitarian motives and to suffer from a lack of happiness as time goes by (Gebhard, 1971).

By their forties, men continue to attach less importance to the orgasm itself and seem to prefer more general sexual or sensual experience. The two physical indices that are most sensitive to aging in men are frequency of orgasm and length of the refractory period. In a man of 50, there is a decline to two orgasms a week, with a refractory period that commonly lasts from 8 to 24 hours. This slowdown contributes to a diminished sexual drive in the older years. There is also some decline of erotic response to sexual stimulation, with a tendency to be more absorbed in work than in sex.

Women in their forties, approaching the

menopausal years, may lose responsiveness, in that there is less preoccupation with sex. However, there is still the capability for responding to sexual situations. The decrease of sexual appetite in the forties is greater for men than for women, but a crucial intervening variable is the nature of the sexual relationship itself.

In the decades of the fifties and sixties, men continue to function at a lower level of sexual interest, and there is a statistical increase in general health problems, such as difficulties with prostate glands. A common response to a surgical or health trauma is loss of sexual function. However, the crucial factor is the nature of the relationship with the sexual partner. Among women in the fifties and sixties, there is some chemical change that involves a slowing down of vaginal lubrication and less vigorous contractions of the pelvic platform during orgasm. Erotic sensations are reported to be less intense. However, elderly women remain capable of multiple orgasms, in contrast to men, who are likely to report an increase in impotence. It appears that the man, more than the woman, is a prisoner of chemistry. But the woman is vulnerable to psychosocial conditioning factors.

Psychological Factors

Sexual behavior over the life cycle may return to a median rate of activity and particularly favored style, but it is necessary to allow for the effect of the marital dissolution crisis itself. In separation, divorce, and widowhood, the obvious effect is that of a grief reaction and related depression. Where there is loss of a love object and a high degree of ambivalence, there may be a prolonged depressive response, with related loss of function. Where ambivalence is at a tolerable level and conflicting feelings allow one to complete his grief work in a reasonable length of time, return to the previously stable level of function is likely to occur. This is true in sex as well as in other areas of activity. Studies of family crisis show that the process of crisis evolution has 4 steps: the crisis event, disorganization, recovery, and reorganization (Eshleman, 1971). The pattern of adjustment varies among individual persons and according to the particular crisis.

SEPARATION CRISIS

Most marriages in which a separation occurs go through a precritical phase that may be termed "emotional separation." During this time the husband and the wife tend to lose contact with each other. The husband who wishes to leave is suddenly busier than ever and both physically and emotionally hard to reach. The wife who is uncomfortable withdraws into overconcern with the children or other situations that preoccupy her. The communications pattern is typified by avoidance and withdrawal. Hidden resentments mount, and hostilities create episodic explosions. At the time of physical separation, the experience of alienation is common. However, the anxiety that also comes into play involves an existential conflict as to whether or not one really wishes to live what may be the rest of one's life alone. Months of agonizing reappraisal can pass before the unhappy spouse makes the final move. He or she may be inhibited by financial realities or by emotional insecurities. During this time the sexual pattern can become unpredictable. The emotionally separated husband can commit adultery and use it to upset his wife and drive her further away, perhaps even to provoke a divorce. He may commit adultery for revenge at her not loving him enough, or, as a sociopath, he may try to cause a divorce, which, if he initiated it, would be excessively expensive. Other couples refuse to let their interpersonal antagonism affect the sexual relationship. In fact, this antagonism seems to add a new flavor to their sex life, and previously anorgasmic women become exciting bedmates.

After separation, periods of remorse or attempts at reconciliation may result in occasional intercourse between husband and wife. The incidence of pregnancies among recently divorced women is an important indication of this form of reparative behavior (Vincent, 1968).

However, in the typical relationship there is a general withdrawal from sexual responsivity as well as from other patterns of intimacy. At this time the hidden wounds in the marriage are becoming exposed, and previously sup-pressed hostilities are being brought into the open. The average wife tends to have a lowered sexual response and is unable to be orgastic in coitus. Masters and Johnson have indicated that one of the keynotes of sexual dysfunction is psychological withdrawal. During the emotional separation crisis, this sexual dysfunction is likely to be intensified. On the part of the husband, this dysfunction often results in secondary impotence. The bulk of impotence problems among men tends to be in the marital relationship (Pearlman, 1972).

DIVORCE CRISIS

Divorce after separation tends to be a climax to preceding anxieties. Alienation is increased by the dissolution of the family and by arguments over responsibilities. An un-fortunate catalyst to antagonism is the de-mand by law that those seeking a divorce function as adversaries within the court. Blame must be placed, and charges that one partner is right and one partner is wrong must be verified. This is typically a very destructive time for both parties (Rheinstein, 1972). The period of time needed to adjust to the divorce in practical matters, such as the woman's run-ning the home alone or the husband's es-tablishing a new locale, can take as long as 1½ years. The sexual response is unpredictable and depends on personal attitudes, the role of the divorce in one's life, and social options. Some spouses abandon sex for several months; others become promiscuous; still others cohabit with each other even while their case is in court.

Those outside the marriage counseling field often do not appreciate the intensity of the di-vorce struggle. Ordinary men and women who would never come to a psychiatrist for help can demonstrate a great virtuosity in sadistic behavior in the way they are able to manipulate their spouses and families when it comes to deciding who gets what, how one governs the children or whether one's reputation within the family is sullied.

All these emotional responses may have no relevance to the legal definition of the divorce cause. Adultery is often engineered in those states—now a minority—where it is the only

grounds for divorce. Courts are willing to go along with the new conception of mental cruelty in marriage and are, therefore, easily convinced. It is probably the most convenient cover-up for incompatibility, now acceptable in a few states (Bohannan, 1971).

WIDOWHOOD CRISIS

Loss of a spouse by death invariably produces conflicting emotions. These emo-tions affect the sexual response and behavior pattern. In general, the response to death creates a more definitive and prolonged grief reaction than does the experience of divorce, which may be heavily laced with hostility. In-sofar as widowhood occurs in an aged popu-lation, the nature of the anxiety involved is existential. The death of one's spouse tends to produce anxiety about one's own death. Questions about the meaning of life, the challenge of change, and the significance of passing time create a level of anxiety that has been well described by existential thinkers. Such observers as Sartre speak only of the quality of the sex act and tend to place it in an atmosphere of alienation, wherein sexual contact represents an effort to find oneself through another. Among the aged popu-lation, where widowhood is common, the at-tempt at recovery from alienation or existential despair through sexual activity seems doomed to failure. This failure is derived essentially from the view that, among the aged, sex is more a matter of memory than of ability. As de Beauvoir comments:

> The old person often desires to desire because he retains his longing for experiences that can never be replaced and because he is still attached to the erotic world he built up in his youth or maturity— desire will enable him to renew its fading colors. And again it is by means of desire that he will have an awareness of his own integrity. We wish for eternal youth, and this youth implies the survival of the libido.

The sexual adjustment here is, as elsewhere, liable to evolve in any direction, based on attitudes, appetites, and opportu-nities. For some, sex is an escape; for others, it is a rescue; for still others, it is an ir-relevance.

CRISIS CHARACTERISTICS

The termination of a marriage and the entrance into postmarital sexual behavior involve recovery from a psychological crisis, regardless of whether it is separation or divorce or loss through death. A crisis is a stressful situation that is perceived by the person as a threat to the self. It may derive from an external source, such as the spouse who suddenly threatens divorce or is killed in a traffic accident. It may come from an internal source, where hostility replaces love or exploitative demands countermand a past history of affection. When the crisis achieves significant proportions, the person is likely to go through a series of perceptual distortions. He cannot perceive clearly what is happening to him or what is likely to happen next. The disequilibrium into which he is thrown affects his coping mechanisms. The crisis becomes a combination of what actually is occurring and how the person responds to it (Rado, 1969). The most typical clinical response to crisis is depression; most studies indicate that with depression comes a lowering of the libido or a loss of sexual interest.

The sequence through which a person goes and his response to the crisis are roughly as follows. First, there is a rise in tension because of a pervasive feeling of helplessness. Then there is cognitive confusion, in which the person cannot clearly evaluate reality. This phase is followed by difficulty in formulating possibilities for problem solving. In extreme cases this phase results in perceptual confusion, in which one loses track of time and space. Feelings of anxiety, somatic symptoms, or use of denial or repression may occur. The key point here is the cognitive confusion of dissonance, to use Festinger's phrase, wherein there is a loss of reality testing (Festinger, 1957). The person is unable to understand either why the event has come about or what the event is going to do to him. Of the two concerns, loss of the ability to predict seems to be the crucial factor. During this time, reparative behavior patterns may develop, and these new patterns may include sexual responses.

Put most simply, a crisis tends to bring out the best in some people and the worst in others. This response defines the motivational state within which the person functions. From this state, sexual adjustment may derive. The clinician needs to infer whether or not a patient is depressed and to what extent. Then he needs to deal with the predictive anxiety factor, based on what it is the patient fears will happen to him next. It is within these two swings of the emotional pendulum that sexual acting out in its most destructive form or with the least control of impulses is likely to occur. It is impossible to predict sexual behavior according to the patient's psychological profile or the nature of the personal crisis because it is impossible to pinpoint individual motivations or to evaluate what kind of strength a person may generate in response to a crisis. Many sexual acts have nonsexual reasons.

Sexual behavior among the separated and divorced, although it emerges as statistically similar to preceding levels of adjustment and satisfaction, may have remarkable differences regarding the motivational state. If the separation and divorce is viewed as an extreme threat to oneself and if one feels that he or she has been abandoned and must, therefore, deal with great amounts of hostility, feelings of rejection, and impotent rage, one may latch onto any relationship as a source of rescue. It is typical for women subconsciously to blame themselves for the failure of their marriages, particularly if they have been convinced to do so for years by their husbands. As a result, many divorcees undertake sexual escapades to prove their sexual attractiveness to men and to convince themselves that, if they were this attractive, the failure of the marriage could not be their fault. They must also put up a front for their friends and acquaintances, who constantly wonder whether or not the divorced women are going to remarry. It becomes difficult to have a casual relationship with a man, since the ambience of the situation constantly implies that one or the other is likely to be recommitted to a marital situation. This makes it difficult to develop a relaxed relationship that offers maximal opportunity for personal growth and enrichment. Among women who have emerged from a relationship in which they instigated the divorce, their sexual liaisons may demonstrate a mood of triumph and a search for pleasure never attained with their inadequate former spouses.

The divorced man can go through as intense a grief response as the divorced woman, although social stereotypes do not lend themselves to this picture. Men have been known to retreat from social interaction for a year or so, leading virtually monastic existences while trying to put their lives back in order after a divorce. During this time their sexual pattern becomes virtually solitary, with a general emphasis on masturbation or nocturnal fantasies. The stereotype that the husband, now free, can hop into every available bed is inaccurate, and is usually propagated by the anxious wife who is left at home handling the kids, convinced that her former spouse has the better of the deal. Although it is true statistically that the man is more mobile and can make contact with a greater variety of women in a shorter period of time, many men in this critical phase develop drinking problems, become depressed, lower their work efficiency, or otherwise demonstrate psychological traumatic responses. In metropolitan areas, women who are divorced often have a particular difficulty in establishing a relationship with an unmarried man. Since the logistics of the situation typically call for the man to remove himself from the home and establish a new residence, the woman is left with her old circle of friends. This means that her male companionship is often derived from spouses of former friends within her social class. Therefore, she presents a threat to her peers who remain married. She often becomes the fifth wheel in social situations, and humor abounds that depicts the gay divorcee as someone likely to steal the local husbands. Often, the divorced woman has a clandestine affair with a married man who cannot dissolve his current marriage because of religious, financial, or emotional obligations. Many observers feel that an important reason behind this type of postmarital behavior is the fact that the average American marriage is emotionally empty and thus vulnerable to other options for romantic interest.

REFERENCES

*American Medical Association. *Human Sexuality.* American Medical Association, Chicago, 1972.

*Bohannan, P. *Divorce and After.* Doubleday, New York, 1971.

de Beauvoir, S. *The Coming of Age.* Putnam, New York, 1972.

Festinger, L. *A Theory of Cognitive Dissonance.* Harper & Row, New York, 1957.

Gebhard, P. H. Postmarital coitus among widows and divorcees. In *Divorce and After,* P. Bohannan, editor, p. 89. Doubleday, New York, 1971.

Goode, W. J. *World Revolution and Family Patterns.* Free Press of Glencoe (Macmillan), New York, 1963.

Kinsey, A. C., Pomeroy, W. B., and Martin, E. C. *Sexual Behavior in the Human Male.* Saunders, Philadelphia, 1948.

Kinsey, A. C., Pomeroy, W. B., Martin, C. E., and Gebhard, P. H. *Sexual Behavior in the Human Female.* Saunders, Philadelphia, 1953.

O'Neill, W. L. *Divorce in the Progressive Era.* Yale University Press, New Haven, 1967.

*Pearlman, C. K. Frequency of intercourse in males at different ages. Med. Aspects Hum. Sex., *6*:92, 1972.

*Rado, S. *Adaptational Psychodynamics: Motivation and Control.* Science House, New York, 1969.

Rheinstein, M. *Marriage Stability, Divorce, and the Law.* University of Chicago Press, Chicago, 1972.

Rosenstock, F., and Kutner, B. Alienation and family crisis. In *Perspectives in Marriage and the Family,* J. R. Eshelman, editor, p. 644. Allyn & Bacon, Boston, 1969.

Troll, L. E. The family of later life: A decade review. In *A Decade of Family Research and Action,* C. B. Broderick, editor, p. 187, 1971.

*Udry, J. R. *The Social Context of Marriage,* ed. 2. Lippincott, Philadelphia, 1971.

*Vincent, C. E. *Human Sexuality in Medical Education and Practice.* Charles C Thomas, Springfield, Ill., 1968.

chapter 10 Premarital and Extramarital Intercourse

IRA B. PAULY, M.D.

Premarital Intercourse

The term "premarital intercourse" covers a vast area that is extremely heterogeneous. The clinical implications of this behavior are quite different if one is talking about premarital intercourse by a 13-year-old girl or a 40-year-old bachelor. The problems often associated with the sexual behavior of the very young are not usually problems with the sexual activity itself—problems such as primary impotence and lack of orgasm—but problems with the consequences of this behavior, such as venereal disease, pregnancy, abortion, and peer or societal reactions. This discussion focuses primarily on premarital intercourse by late adolescent and young adult middleclass men and women.

From as early as 1915, Exner reported on studies of premarital intercourse by college-level men. Subsequently, other pioneer studies were reported in the literature (Davis, 1929; Hamilton, 1929; Bromley and Britten, 1938; Terman, 1938; and Landis et al., 1940). These early efforts culminated in the monumental work of Kinsey and his collaborators (1948, 1953). These early data are now several decades old, and their relevance to the present and future are somewhat questionable. However, they do give some impression of the pervasiveness of this form of sexual activity.

The incidence of premarital intercourse reported retrospectively by married men is reported to be from as low as 54 per cent (Hamilton, 1929) to as high as 98 per cent for men who never went beyond grade school

(Kinsey et al., 1948). For married women, the incidence varies from as low as 35 per cent (Hamilton, 1929) to as high as 50 per cent (Kinsey et al., 1953). Subsequent data indicate that college-level men and women are engaging in premarital sex more frequently than before (Ehrmann, 1961).

A recent survey sponsored by the Playboy Foundation has documented the impressions of many that premarital sexual activity of all kinds has significantly increased since Kinsey's study (Hunt, 1973). This increase is particularly true among the very young, that is, for those under the age of 25 years. In this category, 95 per cent of the married men and 81 per cent of the married women had had intercourse before marriage. Most of this increase has occurred within the last 15 years, and "in five to ten years, premarital coitus will be all but universal among the young" (Hunt, 1973). Associated with this increase in premarital coitus is an increase in petting, oral-genital sex, the duration of both foreplay and intercourse itself, the frequency with which intercourse takes place, and the frequency with which orgasm is achieved in the premarital situation.

Remarkable as these figures are, they by no means imply a total break with the cultural values of the past. Today's unmarried young, by and large, are not indiscriminate, they do not practice kinky sex and while they want sex to be physically intense, they also want it to be emotionally meaningful . . . . There is undoubtedly more casual coitus among single people today than a generation ago, but most of it seems to occur among those who are 25 and older (Hunt, 1973).

It is difficult to be certain whether this increased incidence is real or the result of a more open climate, in which respondents more readily reveal their sexual activity without guilt or shame. There is reason to believe that this increase in premarital sexual behavior may be partially attributable to the availability of contraceptive measures and to the more ready access to abortion. However, the magnitude of the increase does not appear to be such that one could properly say that there is a sexual revolution or a new era of sexual freedom and permissiveness.

Ellis (1973) predicts that, within the next 25 years,

from 80 to 90 per cent of those who legally wed will have enjoyed each other (not to mention other partners!) before marrying.

It is one thing to give figures that describe the extent of premarital relations and to realize their pervasiveness; it is another thing to question the motivation of those engaging in this behavior or to discuss the social-psychological environment in which this behavior takes place. Kirkendall (1961) underscores the importance of understanding the interpersonal relationship of those engaging in premarital intercourse, and he points out some differences between sexual intercourse with a casual partner and premarital sex with a partner who shares a considerable emotional attachment. Reiss (1967) and others have discussed the social context in which this behavior takes place. Ellis (1973) makes it clear that he feels this increase in premarital sexual behavior is good from the emotional or psychological point of view. He describes some 10 distinct advantages, from simple release of sexual tension to providing the necessary training to choose a suitable marital partner and to enjoy better sex-love relations with this partner.

The moralist may hope that the sexual act has some significance in terms of the intensity and meaning of the total relationship between the partners. But one holds a rather naive view of the current sexual scene if one does not accept the fact that motivations are varied and mixed and that, for some, premarital sexual relations—or marital intercourse, for

that matter—may mean little more than a release from sexual tension. From the viewpoint of a physician seeing a young woman for a premarital examination, it is reasonable for him to assume that she has already engaged in sexual intercourse and to explore whatever questions or problems she may have about this activity.

PHYSICIANS' ATTITUDES

One survey has attempted to ascertain physicians' attitudes and practices regarding a number of sexual issues (Pauly, 1972). Of particular significance are physicians' attitudes toward premarital intercourse. Physicians were asked to complete the following statement: "I believe that premarital intercourse by males (and females) is acceptable . . . ," with possible responses being "always," "often," "sometimes," "seldom," or "never" (Pauly and Goldstein, 1971). The responses of 937 physicians are summarized in Figure 1.

Individually, most physicians do not hold a decided double standard with reference to their attitudes toward premarital intercourse for men and women. Roughly one-third of the physicians feel that premarital intercourse is acceptable for men ("always" or "often"), another third fall into the neutral "sometimes" category, and the remaining third hold that such behavior is unacceptable ("seldom" or "never" acceptable). For women, the same

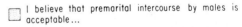
I believe that premarital intercourse by males is acceptable...

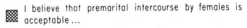
I believe that premarital intercourse by females is acceptable...

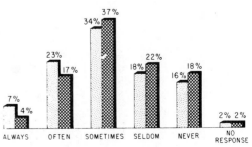

FIGURE 1. Physicians' attitudes toward the double sexual standard.

group of physicians feel that premarital intercourse is somewhat less acceptable.

When one looks at these same data from the viewpoint of the physician's specialty, one sees some striking and statistically significant differences between psychiatrists and the other specialists. This information is summarized in Figure 2 for men and in Figure 3 for women. The responses of specialists regarding premarital intercourse by women (see Figure 3) indicate a significant difference between the permissive attitude of psychiatrists and the negative attitudes of all other physicians.

A similar permissive or accepting attitude by psychiatrists, in contrast to other physicians, is seen with reference to other forms of sexual behavior. For example, psychiatrists show greater acceptance of oral-genital contact between married partners, greater acceptance of masturbation by the husband when the wife is unavailable, and more comfortable feelings in treating homosexuals (Pauly, 1972).

Among younger physicians, there has been a decline and fall of a double sexual standard and a more accepting attitude toward premarital intercourse. Recent graduates profess a better understanding of normal sexual behavior than do their predecessors, yet they are more likely to question their competence in treating sexual problems of a psychogenic nature. In addition, younger doctors feel

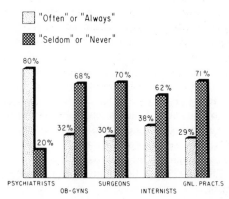

FIGURE 3. Specialists' attitudes toward premarital intercourse by women.

more comfortable in treating male homosexuals, more often feel that time spent in the discussion of sexual problems is warranted, and more frequently obtain a sexual history from their patients (Pauly and Goldstein, 1970 a, b, c, and d).

CLINICAL IMPLICATIONS

Since premarital intercourse occurs with a high frequency, the question now arises as to how often problems related to this sexual behavior are brought to the physician's attention. One study indicates that about 1 in every 10 persons who consult a physician has a significant sexual problem (Pauly and Goldstein, 1970c). Burnap and Golden (1967) have shown that problems related to premarital and extramarital intercourse rank ninth on a list of some 20 sexual problems for which patients seek medical advice or treatment. Although less frequent than problems related to lack of orgasm, dyspareunia, or impotence, concern about premarital intercourse is brought to the physician's attention more frequently than are problems with premature ejaculation, homosexuality, and other sexual variations and sexual problems related to disease or surgery.

But how does the physician respond to such requests for help with sexual problems generally? Until the last decade or so, the physician has had little or no training in human sexuality (Pauly and Goldstein,

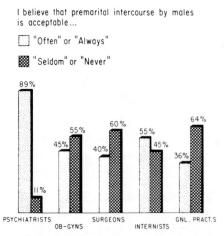

FIGURE 2. Specialists' attitudes toward premarital intercourse by men.

1970a). Thus, he has fallen back on whatever personal experience with these problems he may have had. This unfortunate situation places the physician in the untenable position of being vulnerable to his own bias and personal attitudes about such sexual behaviors as premarital intercourse. It has been shown that the physician's personal comfort in discussing sexual matters is a very critical factor, affecting how frequently he obtains a sexual history, how often he identifies significant sexual problems in his patients, whether he feels time spent in the discussion of sex is warranted, and how competent he feels he is to treat sexual problems. Patients with sexual problems become very aware of their physician's attitude when they see him for such common problems as venereal disease, contraceptive counseling, and therapeutic abortion, as well as problems directly related to sexual functioning. The physician's response is quite varied and improves with the trial-and-error learning he acquires as a clinician in practice. However, at the present time, only one-third of physicians feel they are more than adequate to treat their patients' sexual problems, another one-third consider themselves less than adequate, and the remaining third respond in the neutral, just adequate category (Pauly and Goldstein, 1970a).

There is reason to feel optimistic about the future. Lief has pioneered the effort in this country to improve and expand sex education for physicians in both medical school and postgraduate training programs. As a result of his effort and others, most medical schools in the United States now have at least some courses in human sexuality in their core curriculum. Not only is certain necessary content taught, from sexual anatomy and physiology to marital and premarital counseling, but students are exposed to various media in which overt sexual behavior is depicted in visual form. These desensitization procedures and the students' opportunity to discuss their personal reactions to this material provide a forum in which attitudes can be examined, compared with attitudes of peers, and modified if they are potentially antitherapeutic. This breakthrough in medical education was largely facilitated by Masters

and Johnson and other sex researchers, who have provided sex educators with the basic data they required in order to teach this topic.

Future physicians will no longer reject a role as sexual counselors (Pauly, 1972). Armed with knowledge that something positive can be accomplished, the physician need not feel that he has to refer all patients with sexual problems to the specialist. He will have found out that a number of sexual problems are quite easily resolved with specific information and education. He will become more of a sex educator than he has been in the past and even something of a sexual counselor. Every time he performs a pelvic examination, he has an opportunity to educate his female patient about her sexual and reproductive anatomy.

The physician has an opportunity to practice preventive medicine when he performs a premarital examination. Trainer (1973) and others have written about the use of this routine examination as an ideal opportunity for learning for both partners, rather than as a simple ritual to uncover venereal disease. At least one state, California, requires premarital counseling for minors. It is well known that adolescent marriages are fraught with problems and result in a very high incidence of divorce. The problems go beyond the fact that many of these marriages are precipitated by premarital pregnancies, most of which are unwanted. Some physicians have experimented with the use of premarital counseling for engaged couples in a group setting (Glendening and Wilson, 1972). The chances are better than 50 per cent that the couple about to marry has already engaged in premarital intercourse. It would be most unusual if certain sexual problems or simple ignorance did not still exist at the time of the marriage. An ounce of prevention at this point is certainly worth a pound of cure later, by which time the sexual problems may well result in an irreversible rift that ends in divorce. The physician can have an extremely important role as a sex educator for young couples because of his access to couples who requested a premarital examination. In the past, this opportunity has been missed because the physician has not been prepared for this role and has felt uncomfortable in this function (Pauly, 1972). Recent improvements in sex education and training for medical students cause one to feel optimistic about the future.

The previous discussion of the permissive attitudes of psychiatrists toward such sexual behaviors as premarital intercourse indicate that the psychiatrist is in a unique position to deal with premarital problems by virtue of his training and the personality characteristics that determined his choice of specialty. Patients are often referred to those psychiatrists who choose to function as sexual counselors. This is not to imply that other nonpsychiatric physicians or nonmedically trained people are not qualified to function in this capacity. The important variables are interest, a positive and therapeutic personal attitude, and adequate training and preparation for this role, rather than one's specialty or the possession of a particular degree. On the other hand, the need for such professional help and the paucity of trained personnel to provide such services have created a demand that has been met by many who are not qualified or adequately prepared to offer such counseling.

Certain common sexual problems arise during this early, premarital period of human interaction. In today's society there is considerable peer pressure to perform sexually. Young people are reluctant to admit that they are virgins, rather than, as in the past, seeing virginity as an asset or virtue. Under this kind of social pressure and in a spirit of high adventure and great expectation, disappointment is almost universal (Gagnon and Simon, 1973). The earth does not shake, and the experience is not as fantastic as may have been anticipated from peer recountings of their great sexual initiations. The award-winning movie "The Last Picture Show" was superb in its portrayal of the all too common initial failure at premarital intercourse. Only 4 of 10 young men and 2 of 10 young women find the first sexual experience "very" pleasurable (Hunt, 1973). The frequency of impotence during the young man's first attempt at sexual intercourse is unknown, but in the author's opinion this phenomenon is very common. Unfortunately, this initial failure often begins a vicious cycle,

in which each subsequent sexual opportunity is anticipated with increasing tension and fear of repeated failure. The situation is compounded by tremendous embarrassment, a tendency to avoid the same partner again, a need to hide the problem, and an unwillingness to communicate with anyone about this problem for fear of further humiliation.

This performance anxiety often leads to what Masters and Johnson (1970) have labeled "primary impotence." If the problem does not finally correct itself through trial-and-error learning, some of these young men seek medical consultation, often thinking their impotence has a physical basis. The vast majority of these young men are experiencing simple performance anxiety and can be helped quite simply and quickly. Reassurance is given by telling the young man that such initial failure is very common and that the problem is often compounded and prolonged by fear of repeated failures. If the young man is encouraged to stop hiding the problem, to begin accepting it for what it is, and not to generalize this failure to mean that he is totally inadequate as a man, he usually responds in short order.

It is very important for the young man and his partner to come to understand that sexual intercourse per se, that is, the penis inside the vagina, has been tremendously overemphasized as the only legitimate form of sexual expression. All other sexual behaviors have been denigrated to the level of "foreplay" or "warm-up" activities, which are justified only as precursors to the "real thing." This attitudinal relic from Victorian times, when the only acceptable motivation for sex was procreation, is obviously inappropriate in our contraceptive era. Nonetheless, this procreative motivation or justification for sexual intercourse is still prevalent and places undue pressure on the young man to perform with his penis. As this motivation shifts from one which emphasizes procreation to one concerned with the giving and receiving of pleasure and with communicating one's affection, couples will be freer to engage in a variety of sexual behaviors without hang-ups or guilt. In particular, the young man can learn to experience satisfaction as a competent sexual partner without relying entirely on his ability to get and maintain an erection. Often, this knowledge is enough to diminish his performance anxiety so that he is able to relax and thus achieve an erection. This attitudinal change can be positively reinforced by indicating to the young man that Masters and Johnson (1966) have found that intercourse itself is not as physically stimulating as other forms of more direct sexual contact.

Sometimes, however, these young men have other problems of a more long standing nature. Thus, the young man with low self-esteem is more uncertain and tense when approaching his first sexual adventure. Add to this the unfortunate set of circumstances that often surrounds the initial sexual encounter, such as being in the back seat of a parked car or in the parents' living room, and one has a situation in which the chances for success are very slim indeed. In any event, counseling may need to deal with the issue of the underlying inadequate personality, and for these young men the therapy is more prolonged— several weeks or a few months. The author feels strongly that one should not assume that all such initial sexual failures represent symptoms of early neurotic disturbances that are treatable only by long term psychoanalysis. The almost universal nature of this problem and the situational factors that surround this phenomenon belie the psychoanalytic interpretation often made in such cases.

If the young man is fortunate enough to achieve an erection, he may have some difficulty in sustaining it very long on his initial and early attempts at sexual intercourse. Premature ejaculation during premarital intercourse is very common among young men and is a source of some embarrassment for those sensitive enough to be concerned about their partner's satisfaction. There has been some speculation that premature ejaculation results from the enhanced stimulation brought on by the transition from masturbation to the more exciting involvement with a partner. Others propose that premature ejaculation is simply another manifestation of anxiety or tension. Whatever the cause, a fairly simple training procedure is highly successful in alleviating the condition. The method was originally described by Semans

(1956) and then modified by Masters and Johnson (1970); it is called the squeeze technique. An excellent movie and instructional manual of this procedure is available and is very useful in therapy (Vandervoort and McIlvenna, 1972a). Although it was designed for use by both partners together, very often a young man has no steady partner with whom it is feasible to use this method. Therefore, the squeeze technique can be used during masturbation, in the manner originally described by Semans. The previously mentioned de-emphasis on sexual intercourse is often helpful in reducing anxiety related to premature ejaculation.

For young women, the lack of sexual response in the form of orgasm is common during the initial and early experiences with premarital or marital intercourse. Perhaps her disappointment is even greater as a result of the romantic expectations she may have. Her ability to respond is largely related to the extent to which her sexual response system has been previously activated through self-stimulation or masturbation and to the extent to which she feels safe in the relationship. Masters and Johnson (1966) have shown that a woman's subsequent sexual adjustment and rate of orgasm is related to her having engaged in masturbation premaritally. Not only does this fact place a positive value on masturbation, a far cry from previous myths of masturbatory insanity and other adverse consequences of masturbation, but it has resulted in the therapeutic uses of masturbation in the treatment of orgasmic dysfunction (LoPiccolo and Lobitz, 1972). Even with the advent of the women's liberation movement, in the premarital situation it is the man who is usually the initiator of sexual contact. The pressure for sexual performance is felt more acutely by him. But this does not minimize the woman's concern about her own performance or her disappointment if she does not respond with orgasm.

For the young woman, as well as the young man, there are available highly effective behavioral methods for treating this primary lack of orgasm. The initial steps include a simple getting in touch with her genital anatomy and localizing the sensitive area in and around the clitoris. There is available a very useful pamphlet for illustrating various masturbatory techniques (Vandervoort and McIlvenna, 1972b). Then the woman is asked to proceed in a step-wise fashion, with the increasing use of fantasy formation, as well as a concentration on the physical technique of stimulating the clitoris. Through the use of fantasy, the woman can bridge the gap between a solitary self-stimulating experience to a live encounter with her partner (Brady, 1966). In most cases, women who have never been able to achieve orgasm can reach such a climax within a short period of time. The use of a vibrator is suggested when the previous steps have not been successful (LoPiccolo and Lobitz, 1972). An important point to make clear to the woman being treated by such a method is that the ultimate goal of this treatment is to set into motion her sexual response system, so that she can then transfer what she has learned about herself to her partner, present or future. It is important to realize that many people have significant reservations about masturbation, and it makes little sense to suggest such a method, no matter how potentially successful, if one's patient is not ready or able to accept it. Ironically enough, a woman who has never been able to reach an orgasm, one experiencing primary orgasmic dysfunction, has a better prognosis than does a woman who has or does achieve orgasm under one set of circumstances (i.e., through masturbation or with a previous partner) but not with her present partner. In this latter instance, a different set of emotional factors pertain, and treatment may be more complicated and prolonged.

She is likely to be more concerned about certain consequences of premarital intercourse, especially pregnancy. The mere fact of being on the pill does not completely eradicate the fear of an unwanted pregnancy, and the awareness of this disastrous possibility may be enough to prevent the relaxation necessary to enjoy the premarital experience, let alone reach a climax. Often the young woman is in the dilemma of refusing intercourse and running the risk of being dropped. Or she may give in to her own desires and those of her partner and fear that her reputation will be ruined. If she is not using some birth control method, she is taking considerable risk, which is difficult or impossible to ignore sufficiently to enjoy the sexual activity to any great extent.

Much of the statistical increase in premarital intercourse is accounted for by young women who have intercourse with their intended husbands. The *Playboy* survey indicates that 54 per cent of those married women born from 1948 to 1955 had premarital intercourse only with their fiance, and this is compared with Kinsey's figure of 40 per cent for those married women born before 1900 (Hunt, 1973). Because these couples have a commitment to one another and are engaging in a trial marriage or living together, they may well seek premarital counseling conjointly. Chances for a successful outcome are greatly enhanced if both partners are willing to assume some responsibility for the problems. The combination of premature ejaculation and primary lack of orgasm is the most common premarital sexual problem or marital problem that a couple present. This dual approach—in which the focus is on the couple, rather than on "the one at fault"—can be used by either a man-woman cotherapy team or by a single therapist of either sex. The therapist has the greatest success, using whatever technique, if he or she accepts these problems as situationally determined, very common, and more the result of anxiety, ignorance, inexperience, or faulty learning than as symptoms of deep seated, long standing neuroses or personality disorders for which only intensive, prolonged therapy is indicated.

Sexual problems that occur premaritally can often continue into marriage and become chronic and difficult to treat at a later time. Or a couple may have a relatively good sexual relationship premaritally, at a time when the relationship is new and exciting and before the other problems of marriage and children add their heavy burden of responsibility. Each set of circumstances requires a somewhat different approach, which may focus initially on the relationship and subsequently on the sexual interaction or vice versa.

Extramarital Intercourse

Like premarital intercourse, the term "extramarital intercourse" is very broad and requires specification if any generalizations are to be made. Cuber and Harroff (1965) attempt to provide this specification by discriminating between at least three types of relationships in which adultery take place.

In American culture, extramarital intercourse is a common theme, and yet research into this phenomenon is very recent. Almost no hard data existed on this subject before Kinsey's study in 1948. His reported figures of accumulative incidence (by age 40 years) of 26 per cent for women and 50 per cent for men shocked middle-class America. He went on to explain that this was probably a minimal figure and that "the actuality may lie 10 to 20 per cent above the figures now given." Beyond these global rates is the progressive increase in the accumulative incidence of extramarital intercourse for women by age 25, from 4 per cent for those women born before 1900 to 8 per cent for those born from 1900 to 1909, to 10 per cent (1910 to 1919) to 12 per cent (1920 to 1929). Extramarital intercourse among women under 25 is up to 24 per cent in the recent *Playboy* survey, and appears to be approaching the under-25 male infidelity rate of 32 per cent (Hunt, 1973). These figures of accumulative incidence by age 25 rise even more by age 40—to 22 per cent for those women born before 1900, compared with 30 per cent for those born after 1900 (Kinsey et al., 1953). The recent survey by *Playboy* indicates that the figure for accumulative incidence of extramarital coitus for men is 41 per cent, as compared with 18 per cent for married women (Hunt, 1974). The survey goes on to say that,

. . . contrary to popular belief, sexual liberation has had little impact on traditional attitudes toward or adherence to the ideal of marital fidelity. In Kinsey's time, married people had only two alternatives to life-long sexual exclusivity: divorce and secret extramarital relations. Since then, we find, sexual liberation has made the divorced far freer in postmarital sexual behavior, but it has had little effect on secret extramarital sex. As for the new alternatives about which there is so much talk—open marriage, mate swapping, group sex, group marriage, etc.—the data suggest that they are mostly just talk.

Other studies indicate different rates of extramarital involvement among middle-class couples (Cuber and Harroff, 1965; Neubeck and Schletzer, 1969; Whitehurst, 1969; Johnson, 1970). Ellis (1973) predicts that this behavior will increase even more in the next 25 years and says it will be much more accepted by the mates of the extramarital adventurers, as well as by people in general."

But it is one thing to state figures and another to understand motivations and the variety of socio-cultural circumstances in which this behavior takes place. It is often assumed that extramarital affairs are the result of impulsive acting out of neurotic conflicts or occur in sick marriages. Some recent data indicate that extramarital involvement is not necessarily related to the marital adjustment or happiness of the couple but, rather, to perceived opportunity and other factors and that this behavior is often agreed to in advance and amazingly well tolerated by the spouse (Neubeck and Schletzer, 1962, 1969; Cuber and Harroff, 1965; Whitehurst, 1969; Ellis, 1969; Cuber, 1969; Johnson, 1970; Bartell, 1971; Olson, 1972; O'Neill and O'Neill, 1972).

The rising divorce rate, having reached the 25 per cent mark, calls into question the viability of the institution of marriage. Yet the popularity of marriage continues, and in 1970, for the third consecutive year, there were more than 2 million marriages (Olson, 1972). Quantity is one thing; quality is another. Alternative and innovative marriage styles have evolved, in which extramarital involvements are expected and agreed to in advance. (Olson, 1972; O'Neill and O'Neill, 1972). As Ramey (1972) points out,

Free love, dyadic marriage with or without nonconsensual adultery, swinging, open marriage, intimate friendship, evolutionary communes, and group marriage are points on a continuum of increasing complexity in interrelationship.

Perhaps the most widely discussed style is the open marriage (O'Neill and O'Neill, 1972). Ellis (1973) has called this "civilized adultery" and defines it as follows:

a couple agreeing before or after legally mating, that the husband and wife probably will engage in extramarital affairs with the full consent of the other and, with relatively little insane jealousy, will back up this agreement.

Although this concept of open marriage is still quite new and those who agree to such a marital arrangement in theory or practice are relatively few, some predict that open marriage will increase and become relatively common. Many if not most of those married at this time have not freed themselves of the anxiety and guilt that have always surrounded adultery or infidelity. Even for those couples who have achieved the enviably mature position of being free of these traditional moral hang-ups regarding extramarital intercourse, the possibility that a frequent and long standing extramarital sexual involvement will develop into a serious relationship that may compete with the marital relationship is real and threatening.

PHYSICIANS' ATTITUDES

The study by Pauly and Goldstein (1971) included one statement regarding extramarital intercourse. In response to the statement, "I believe that extramarital intercourse by the husband during periods of unavailability of the wife is acceptable sexual behavior . . . ," the possible responses were "always," "often," "sometimes," "seldom," or "never." The surveyed physicians' responses are summarized in Figure 4. Most physicians consider this behavior to be seldom (35 per cent) or never (39 per cent) acceptable.

Unlike the situation regarding premarital intercourse, there is no significant difference

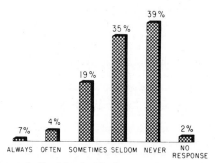

FIGURE 4. Physicians' attitudes toward extramarital intercourse by men.

between psychiatrists and other specialists with reference to their attitudes regarding the acceptability of extramarital intercourse. Nor is there any significant difference among physicians with reference to age. There was a positive correlation between physicians' convictions that their religious beliefs strongly affect their medical treatment of patients with sexual problems and the attitude that extramarital intercourse is unacceptable. Psychiatrists claim they are less affected by their religious beliefs in dealing with patients with sexual problems than are other specialists (Pauly and Goldstein, 1971).

CLINICAL IMPLICATIONS

One may well ask what is the clinical significance of these attitudes by doctors, especially when they are consulted by a patient experiencing a problem related to extramarital intercourse. It is hoped that most physicians discriminate between their own value or belief systems and what may be best for another person. Under circumstances of minimal exposure to the wide range of attitudes toward various sexual behaviors that most physicians currently in practice had during their training, it appears that people with sexual problems are at some risk of running into a doctor whose attitude causes him to be more judgmental and punitive than therapeutic.

It is difficult to be certain whether marital discord is the result of significant sexual problems or whether the disturbed marital relationship leads to secondary sexual problems. Masters and Johnson (1970) estimate that one in two marriages is complicated by serious sexual problems. Many may assume that the risk of extramarital involvement is greatest when dissatisfaction in the primary sexual relationship is greatest. Apparently, this holds true more for the husband than for the wife (Johnson, 1970). A substantial proportion of those engaging in extramarital relations are neither dissatisfied with their marriage or sick in any emotional or psychiatric sense. Some who are dissatisfied may choose to deal with their unhappiness through fantasy involvement, rather than real involvement, depending on their superego (Neubeck and Schletzer, 1969). Others may get involved physically but not engage in intercourse. Kinsey et al. (1953) reported that 16 per cent of their sample engaged in various forms of noncoital petting.

Whether he likes it or not, the physician is seen as an appropriate marital and sexual counselor, and many patients seek him out at times of marital crisis (Pauly, 1972). There is no question that the discovery of an extramarital affair is a serious crisis in some marriages today. Such an episode is not an infrequent precipitating event for a person or couple who seek psychotherapy. On the other hand, some reported results of adulterous activities call into question the almost universal assumptions about the deleterious effects of extramarital involvement (Cuber, 1969).

No single therapeutic tactic pertains to every such clinical situation. In some instances, the uninvolved partner is confused and uncertain about what he or she wants to do with his marriage. Often there is so much hostility that a conjoint approach is not feasible. In other cases, the spouse who has been involved is confused and troubled, being uncertain whether he wants a divorce or whether he should give up his outside relationship. Even if one prefers an approach that focuses on the couple, rather than a single partner, it is well to be flexible enough to allow for either or both partners to come in individually, should they wish to do so. Frequently, such a request for an individual appointment is for the purpose of disclosing an extramarital affair. The therapist should be very cautious in recommending that the patient inform his partner about this affair. Such a recommendation can have disastrous consequences, even if it is suggested with honorable intentions.

The author cannot refrain from making the analogy between an extramarital affair and the psychotherapeutic situation in which a spouse is in intensive and long term therapy with an opposite-sexed therapist. Often the partner in therapy develops an intensity of feeling and a level of communication that is envied by even the most secure spouse. One wonders whether most therapists are aware of the tremendous strain that prolonged individual therapy puts on the untreated spouse

and, thus, on the marriage itself. Add to this the high risk of a difficult transference situation in such an unhappy spouse, and the result is an "extramarital affair" of great intensity in fantasy if not in physical reality. Those who practice such therapy defend this state of affairs by stating that the resolution of this transference relationship is a constructive and even necessary pàrt of therapy. An important advantage of the conjoint approach is the fact that such a doctor-patient relationship is usually avoided. In addition, there seems to be an advantage in seeing first hand how these partners interact and communicate with each other.

In various psychopathological states, extramarital involvements occur with some frequency. The excess use of alcohol comes first to mind, a situation in which an underlying desire and a temporary loss of control result in a sexual relationship. Often, however, the decision to engage in such an affair precedes the use of alcohol, which is used as an excuse or rationalization. This situation is to be distinguished from that of the chronic alcoholic, in which the sexual acting out may be a significant feature of the alcoholism. The social environment in which he or she often drinks is conducive to this involvement with partners who are also looking for companionship of a social or sexual nature.

Depression is another emotional state in which sexual involvement may occur with greater frequency than would otherwise occur for that same person. If the depression is profound, there may be too much withdrawal and retardation to pursue actively an extramarital relationship. But short of such an extreme depression, there may be a reaching out for a new and hopefully exciting partner as a means of escape from the quicksand of depression. Related here are the common suspicions and jealousy, which can be prominent features of serious depressive reactions in both male and female patients, and such reports of infidelity by the spouse can be very convincing. Often a joint session with the spouse helps to clarify the situation.

Less frequently, one encounters sexually inappropriate behavior as a result of psychotic decompensation. Acute manic episodes or schizophrenic reactions may result in a breakdown of judgment or control, which results in sexual acting out in a person who would not otherwise engage in such behavior. On a more chronic basis, one sees lonely and inadequate schizoid persons whose only capacity to interact socially centers around their physical or sexual attractiveness.

But it should not be assumed that extramarital intercourse is necessarily the result of emotional disturbance. It happens all too frequently to assume that extramarital involvement is always to be understood in psychopathological terms. Perhaps the problem is better explained by the fact that many partners initially have some unrealistic notions of marriage (Lederer and Jackson, 1968). There is considerable question as to whether one man or one woman can satisfy all the intellectual and emotional needs of his partner and, therefore, whether they were ever meant to be exclusively monogamous or to mate for life with one partner. The current American marital scene and the evolution of variant marital styles challenge this notion.

As the transition from traditional marriage or closed marriage, as the O'Neills refer to it, to alternatives continues, couples may come to accept extramarital involvement to an even greater extent than is already evident. The popularity of the best-selling book *Open Marriage* is obvious, and this concept has caused many couples to question their marital agreements (O'Neill and O'Neill, 1972). An important dimension of this concept is open communication, in which partners make an agreement in advance that they are both free to pursue outside social or sexual relations. As long as both partners are playing the game by the same ground rules, theoretically there will be fewer casualties.

Until now most marriage partners have been exposed to traditional rules, and they find it more difficult than Ellis acknowledges to live with the new guidelines. Some spouses have been unable to cope with their original contract, in which they agreed to permit or engage in outside sexual involvement but subsequently became emotionally disturbed. The author has seen some situations result in the husband's impotence or the wife's lack of sexual responsiveness when the spouse becomes involved. One can certainly postulate

that this inability to live by the open contract is the result of immaturity or other personality inadequacies. It is the author's opinion, however, that such human frailty, under whatever psychiatric label it may be disguised, is so common that many if not most couples struggling with this transitional marital concept find the open contract more palatable in theory than in practice. In any event, it is an issue with which psychiatrists should be prepared to cope.

REFERENCES

Bartell, G. D. *Group Sex.* Wyden, New York, 1971.

Brady, J. P. Brevital-relaxation treatment of frigidity. Behav. Res. Ther., *4:* 71, 1966.

Bromley, D. D., and Britten, F. H. *Youth and Sex.* Harper & Brothers, New York, 1938.

Burnap, D. W., and Golden, J. S. Sexual problems in medical practice. J. Med. Educ., *42:* 673, 1967.

Cuber, J. F. Adultery: Reality versus stereotype. In *Extramarital Relations,* G. Neubeck, editor, p. 190. Prentice-Hall, Englewood Cliffs, N. J., 1969.

Cuber, J. F., and Harroff, P. B. *The Significant Americans: A Study of Sexual Behavior among the Affluent.* Appleton-Century-Crofts, New York, 1965.

Davis, K. B. *Factors in the Sex Life of Twenty-two Hundred Women.* Harpers & Brothers, New York, 1929.

*Ehrmann, W. W. Premarital sexual intercourse. In *The Encyclopedia of Sexual Behavior,* A. Ellis and A. Abarbanel, editors, vol. 2, p. 860. Hawthorn Books, New York, 1961.

Ellis, A. Healthy and disturbed reasons for having extramarital relations. In *Extramarital Relations,* G. Neubeck, editor, p. 153. Prentice-Hall, Englewood Cliffs, N. J., 1969.

Ellis, A. Sexual mores a quarter of a century from now. Psychiatr. Opinion, *10:* 17, 1973.

Exner, M. J. *Problems and Principles of Sex Education. A Study of 948 College Men.* Association Press, New York, 1915.

Gagnon, J., and Simon, W. *Sexual Conduct: Human Sources of Sexuality.* Aldine Atherton, Chicago, 1973.

Glendening, S. E., and Wilson, A. J. Experiments in group premarital counseling. Social Casework, *53:* 551, 1972.

Hamilton, G. V. *A Research in Marriage.* Boni, New York, 1929.

*Hunt, M. Sexual behavior in the 1970's. Playboy, *20:* 85, 1973.

*Hunt, M. Sexual behavior in the 1970's. Playboy, *21:* 60, 1974.

Johnson, R. E. Some correlates of extramarital coitus. J. Marriage Family, *32:* 449, 1970.

Kim, Y. H. The Kinsey findings. In *Extramarital Relations,* G. Neubeck, editor, p. 65. Prentice-Hall, Englewood Cliffs, N. J., 1969.

Kinsey, A. C., Pomeroy, W. B., and Martin, C. E. *Sexual Behavior in the Human Male.* W. B. Saunders, Philadelphia, 1948.

Kinsey, A. C., Pomeroy, W. B., Martin, C. E., and Gebhard, P. H. *Sexual Behavior in the Human Female.* W. B. Saunders, Philadelphia, 1953.

Kirkendall, L. A. *Premarital Intercourse and Interpersonal Relationships.* Julian, New York, 1961.

Landis, C., et al. *Sex in Development.* Paul B. Hoeber, New York, 1940.

Lederer, W. J., and Jackson, D. D. *The Mirages of Marriage.* W. W. Norton, New York, 1968.

LoPiccolo, J., and Lobitz, C. The role of masturbation in the treatment of orgasmic dysfunction. Arch. Sex. Behav., *2:* 163, 1972.

Masters, W. H., and Johnson, V. E. *Human Sexual Response.* Little, Brown, Boston, 1966.

Masters, W. H., and Johnson, V. E. *Human Sexual Inadequacy.* Little, Brown, Boston, 1970.

*Neubeck, G., editor. *Extramarital Relations.* Prentice-Hall, Englewood Cliffs, N. J., 1969.

Neubeck, G., and Schletzer, V. M. A study of extramarital relationships. J. Marriage Family, *24:* 279, 1962.

Neubeck, G., and Schletzer, V. M. A study of extramarital relationships. In *Extramarital Relations,* G. Neubeck, editor, p. 146. Prentice-Hall, Englewood Cliffs, N. J., 1969.

Olson, D. H. Marriage of the future: Revolutionary or evolutionary change? Fam. Coord., *21:* 383, 1972.

O'Neill, N., and O'Neill, G. *Open Marriage: A New Life Style for Couples.* Evans, New York, 1972.

O'Neill, N., and O'Neill, G. Open marriage: A synergic model. Fam. Coord., *21:* 403, 1972.

*Pauly, I. B. Influence of training and attitudes on sexual counseling in medical practice. Med. Aspects Hum. Sexual., *6:* 84 (March), 1972.

Pauly, I. B., and Goldstein, S. G. Physicians' perceptions of their education in human sexuality. J. Med. Educ., *45:* 745, 1970a.

Pauly, I. B., and Goldstein, S. G. Physicians' ability to treat sexual problems. Med. Aspects Hum. Sexual., *4:* 24 (Oct.), 1970b.

Pauly, I. B., and Goldstein, S. G. Prevalence of significant sexual problems in medical practice. Med. Aspects Hum. Sexual. *4:* 98 (Nov.), 1970c.

Pauly, I. B., and Goldstein, S. G. Physicians' attitudes in treating male homosexuals. Med. Aspects Hum. Sexual., *4:* 26 (Dec.), 1970d.

*Pauly, I. B., and Goldstein, S. G. Physicians' attitudes toward premarital and extramarital intercourse. Med. Aspects Hum. Sexual., *5:* 32 (Jan.), 1971.

Playboy Panel. New sexual life styles. Playboy, *20:* 73, 1973.

Ramey, J. W. Emerging patterns of innovative behavior in marriage. Fam. Coord. *21:* 435, 1972.

Reiss, I. L. *The Social Context of Premarital Sexual Permissiveness.* Holt, Rinehart & Winston, New York, 1967.

Semans, J. H. Premature ejaculation: A new approach. South. Med. J., *49:* 353, 1956.

Terman, L. M. *Psychological Factors in Marital Happiness.* McGraw-Hill, New York, 1938.

Trainer, J. B. The physician as a marriage counselor. Fam. Coord., *22:* 73, 1973.

Vandervoort, H. E., and McIlvenna, T. *You Can Last Longer.* Multi Media Resource Center, San Francisco, 1972a.

Vandervoort, H. E., and McIlvenna, T. *Masturbation Techniques for Women.* (Multi Media Resource Center, San Francisco, 1972b.

Whitehurst, R. N. *Extramarital sex: Alienation or extension of normal behavior. In Extramarital Relations,* G. Neubeck, editor, p. 129. Prentice-Hall, Englewood Cliffs, N. J., 1969.

chapter 11 Divorce

PAUL BOHANNAN, D.Phil. (Oxon)

Natural History of a Marriage

Most people who get involved in divorce are primarily concerned with what they are getting out of, not what they are getting into. Comparatively few seek help to deal with postdecree problems, although that may come later. Rather they seek help because they messed up in what they think ought to be a sacred institution. At whatever point they seek help, all these people are participating in a stage of the natural history of a marriage.

The natural history of a marriage has five major steps or conditions that can be diagrammed (Figure 1). Each of these steps or conditions can be broken down into many substeps.

All marriages begin after an initiatory procedure of courtship or some other means of matchmaking. Almost everywhere, the change is marked by a specific event—a ceremony or a celebration. All marriages end, either in a death or a divorce—again, an event. Between beginning and end, each marriage must go through a series of stages if it is to be satisfactory to the partners or socially recognizable as complete—so must a divorce.

The natural history of a marriage can, then, be seen as three processes and two events. The events—the wedding and the decree—are of less interest than the processes. What is important is what happens before the wedding, between the wedding and the decree, and after the decree. That is—courtship, marriage, and divorce.

The Divorce Case History

Three processes must be observed in taking a history from a person who is being or has been divorced. (1) Take a genealogy—overtly and in writing. Discover the age and attitudes of the subject at the time of other divorces in the family. (2) Plot the course of the marriage. (3) Take a psychiatric case history.

THE COURSE OF THE MARRIAGE

It is possible to lay out the course of a marriage on a piece of graph paper, allowing one section for every 3 months of the duration of the marriage (see Figure 2). On the top horizontal line, one can project the medical history of the husband, on the next line that of the wife. In the same way, one projects the job history of the husband and the wife, and their residential history—the number of times they have changed houses or communities. One must then plot the birth date and figure back to the conception date of all the children of both parties, whether of this marriage or earlier ones. A medical history of all the children may lead to some interesting discoveries. So may the medical histories of the spouses' parents. One has only to make a small x at the time point of any major illness or change in health, any promotions or major job changes, or major moves from one community to another.

The investigator presently sees that the x's on the chart are not random. Of the author's samples of marriages that ended in divorce (n = about 200), in none were the x's scattered at random on the page.

The major crises. Each x stands for a crisis. Each crisis obviously demands libidinal realignment, some alteration in object relationships, and a changed view of the self. But when the x's stack up, the petty crises are

FIGURE 1. Natural history of a marriage.

compounded into a major crisis. Even if the people involved could handle each petty crisis, the overload factor might mean that the major crisis is overwhelming.

In a healthy and viable marriage, the major crisis is just as important as it is in a marriage that ends in divorce. However, there is 1 important difference. When the people involved get through the major crisis—that is, make satisfactory resolutions of all the petty crises—they look back on the major crisis as a time of challenge and growth. They may see it as something "we won through." Although these kinds of data are not yet available from intact marriages to document this point, one can expect it to be true.

The marriage partners, who do not win through, however—who do not satisfactorily (in the definition of the spouses themselves) resolve the major crisis—are in double jeopardy. They may repair the surface but not the foundation of the relationship. The mar-

riage can continue, but the relationship has a hole in it. There are places in the totality of the relationship that must now be avoided. The spouses must step carefully around the trap.

Regression. With less security and with less trust, the couple proceed with their lives together—then the next major crisis occurs. In the new situation, there is likely to be a regression to the unsatisfactorily resolved elements of the first major crisis. The unresolved difficulties from the first are added to the second, making it that much more difficult.

Probably when one spouse regresses in such a situation, both do so. Obviously, these regressions do not stop at the first major crisis of the marriage; both spouses are likely to regress even farther to the difficulties of their lives before marriage. Earlier marriages of the spouses may add to the difficulties; unresolved difficulties in the marriages of their respective parents may become relevant.

Thus, the marriage is in jeopardy not only with the present situation and with the earlier crisis but with the early experiences and crises of both parties. In order to understand how

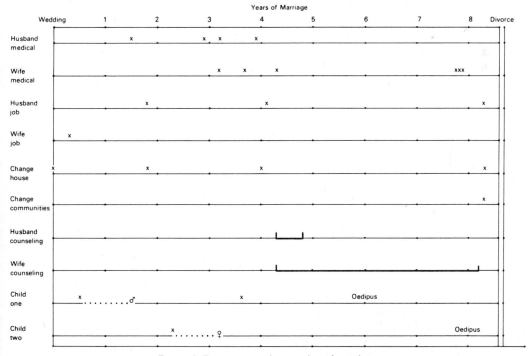

FIGURE 2. Event sequence in a terminated marriage.

two people act in marriage, one must know their personal histories, the history of their own marriages, and their version of the history of the parents' marriages. A marriage in a state of crisis has not only its own difficulties to bear, it has problems of the past to deal with as well.

Figure 2 shows the crisis points in the marriage of Kenneth and Alice. Theirs is a highly instructive case because there are three major crises, each made more serious by the fact that earlier crises were not adequately resolved.

Kenneth was 27 when he and Alice were married. When he was 40 and his divorce decree was almost 4 years old, he said that it had been her idea to get married, but, at 27, he had felt that he was ready to get married, and so he might as well. He had a Master's degree in business administration and a good job. She was 2 years younger; she had a Master's degree in psychology and a good job.

At the time of the wedding, Alice left her apartment and moved into his. It was 12 miles from her job, so she soon found another job closer to "home." The new job bored her. She was restive, and, less than a year later got pregnant.

As Kenneth put it, "Early troubles and struggles getting started and building up—furniture and all the things you need—we got through all that all right. Money was short, but we didn't have any trouble about it. Things were pretty good."

Within 3 or 4 months of the birth of their oldest child, Kenneth decided to go to graduate school to get a Ph.D. He felt that it would be worth more to him than the effort it would cost him. He was in graduate school for 2 years. Alice did not go back to work. She stayed home with the baby, being— he said—bored and resentful. A second child was born—she had become pregnant again within weeks of his entering graduate school. His words are vivid in their flatness: "I think that during this 2-year period our marriage ended. I supported the family while doing graduate work. At the end of the 2 years, I was on the edge of a nervous breakdown. She was, too. She attempted suicide. She had even *me* seeing psychiatrists! We just fell apart. And then things went from bad to worse. Whatever belief she had in me just disappeared. And what belief I had in her also disappeared. That was it."

The 2 years of graduate school did not produce the desired Ph.D., but "only another M.A." He was "out of school," he was 31 years old, he had 2 children—and he needed a job. Kenneth's failure to earn his Ph.D. undoubtedly shook his faith in himself. When he talked about their "losing their belief" in each other, he was certainly projecting the shattering of his self-image.

However, these were tough and intelligent people. Both proved, in the long run, to be very able. He got a good job in an eastern city. They moved and pulled themselves together with the aid of therapists. He saw a psychiatrist once a week for about 8 months; she spent over 3 years with a social worker whom Kenneth called "her marriage counselor." Even after the 3 years, she did not break off her dependency on her counselor; she continued to see him irregularly until they left the community.

As Kenneth reported it, her general efficiency and good humor went completely to pieces. And instead of trying to help her do her job, he simply took over all the tasks she did not or could not complete. In his version, at least, he did much of the cooking and all of the marketing, taking the children with him because she was either too sick or too crazy to keep them. He overlooked the fact that the children were with her when he was at work during the week; he seemed not to see the contradiction between her actions on weekdays and Saturdays.

The marriage continued for almost 5 years after Kenneth took the new job. A third child was born, but there seems to have been no development or maturation in the marriage. The "maturation" was a false one based on Alice's relationship with her therapist. Whatever was involved in that relationship, Kenneth saw it as a dyad "against" himself. "They talked about psychology and he gave her all these high flown ideas" was his envoi as he recounted it. The triad was not completed by the children, but by the therapist.

Another important fact came out in a different context. In response to a question about how much he had seen of his parents and siblings since his divorce, he said that he did not like his parents. They were, he said, immature and difficult to get along with and he saw as little of them as possible. During the period that Kenneth was seeing a therapist, his oldest child, a son, was about 3 years old. His wife stayed on with her marriage counselor. Probably the child was a threat, making Kenneth into a "parent." (The children remained shadowy characters—he said he might remarry but would not marry a woman with children, adding that he loved his own because they were his, but he did not like children.) From his point of view, there seemed to be a triad made up of himself, his wife, and her "marriage counselor." The children were incidental.

Then Kenneth was transferred to the midwest. They bought a "large house in a good neighborhood"—he had, by now, a good income. (Quite a lot of divorcees seem to have bought new houses or made substantial improvements just before the divorce occurred.) Kenneth had to take a trip east, back to company headquarters, 2 months later.

The night before he left, they had a ritual bout of sexual intercourse—he said that they both knew it would be the last. Yet, a few sentences later, he claimed to be amazed when he returned to find himself locked out of the house, a restraining order against his entering tacked on the door, and his wife and children gone.

The divorce was bitter; it went on for almost a year.

Kenneth went through what he himself called a "long period of postmarital satyriasis." He claimed in different contexts that it was disgusting and that it was delightful. Alice went back to graduate school and got a Ph.D. in psychology.

This marriage illustrates several important points: role reversal, ineptitude in drawing boundaries, general lack of autonomy on the part of both spouses, fear of aggression within the marriage, the third adult who replaced the child as the third element of a triad, oedipal implication, and, most important, the fact that the petty crises piled up into major crises.

Before the Wedding: Courtship

To understand the response to a major crisis, we must know something about the psychic development of the spouses before the wedding and something about the development of each in the course of the marriage.

Deutsch (1944) has shown magnificently and, at least for the generations of her patients, definitively that when girls begin to break away from their dependency relationships with their mothers and the rest of their families, they turn to other girls. During prepuberty, a girl is likely to form a close friendship with one other girl her own age; the two share secrets and ultimately give each other strength to continue breaking the bonds of dependency. Although these friendships sometimes mature (and occasionally continue without maturation as a sign of atrophy of development in both women), usually they are outgrown as the girls reach puberty and each becomes interested in boys.

During early adolescence comes a longer or shorter phase of romantic dreaming, in which the girl learns to depend even further on herself and to give up, even further, her dependency on her mother. Deutsch has documented the way in which such girls often turn against their mothers for short periods, only to turn hurriedly back to them if they become afraid in their developing relationships with boys.

Only after boy-girl relationships have been developed to the point that self-confidence can be said to have been achieved do we stop talking about boys and girls and begin talking about men and women—and the phase of courtship and "marriage" that follows such maturation. Many of today's teen-age marriages are made during this early adolescent developmental phase of experimentation between girls and boys—a situation that can be disastrous.

The developmental phases of boys are a little less obvious—mainly because, although they form same-sex friendships, these friendships are seldom as intense and seldom as exclusive. Boys are somewhat more inclined to form groups (perhaps even gangs) during this period, although they do have favorite friends. Girls form groups, too, obviously, but they tend to be smaller and to be better described as cliques.

Boys have to experiment with forming social relationships with girls, and they too are likely to take these experimental relationships as "the real thing"; if there is a push from home as well as this attraction, they may marry. And—it cannot be said too often—the situation may be disastrous. Today, with the marriage age being lowered, young people sometimes marry as a road to adult status. That is, they use marriage as some tribal societies use an initiation ceremony. The result does not work either as an initiation or as a marriage.

BEFORE COURTSHIP

There are, thus, three stages before one is ready for serious courtship. When the capacity for mature love is achieved, courtship can proceed. It may begin a psychic process that Benedek (1959) calls an exchange of ego ideals. This—if it happens—is a genuine test of one's sexual identification. If a person looks back to his own early years, he realizes that he had to make peace, about the end of the first year of his life, with being the sex he is. Then, during the oedipal crisis, it is necessary to become comfortable not merely with being the sex one is; one has to become comfortable with *not* being the sex that one is not. Not only is one content to be male or female, one must now also be content not to be the other. Most people, not quite all, manage the first part of this sexual identity. They do not object to being the sex they are. Many, however, cannot manage the second stage of sexual identification with equal security.

In the process of learning not to mind not being the sex that one is not, one has to put out of mind not only certain biological incapacities, but,—much more important, one must give up the social jobs that are assigned to the other sex. Freud discovered this under the idea of penis envy; others have extended it to womb envy and other such concepts. A male has to get used to the fact that in the ordinary division of social labor, he will never get to be a protected and efficient housekeeper or a loving mother; a female has to get used to the fact that she must give up certain roles in the external world if she is to take on those that traditional society assigns her. These assignments are cultural and hence subject to change. Sex role distinctions beyond those of reproduction are present wherever there is culture, and it seems likely that they will remain, even as specific distinctions change or disappear. Today, the division of social roles is changing; to try to say anything more specific would be foolhardy. But the cultural choice is nevertheless clear—one must either accept the assignments or else alter one's life by working to change them.

In the process, then, of growing up and getting one's sexual identity, one represses inclinations to do the tasks assigned to the other sex. Then, years later, when a person meets someone of the other sex who seems to have the capacity to do these things in a way that is harmonious with the way he would have done them himself (without the accident of being the sex he is), those qualities can be loved in objects rather than in the self.

It is this stage of falling in love that Benedek refers to as an exchange of ego ideals. She points out that the greatest enemy of such an exchange is imperfect repression. If, however, one has found a spouse in whom one can love in well tested reality those attributes that one would have carried in one's self were one of the other sex, then a major foundation of the love relationship has been laid.

The enemy of this particular exchange is what is usually called romantic love. Romantic love, as both Benedek (1959, 1970)

FIGURE 3. Preparation for marriage. Note that the right-hand box indicates capacity for mature love (that is, hooking the sexual drive to the emotion of love).

and de Rougemont (1956) have insisted, is not a love that is tested against reality; there is no reality testing in romantic love. Such people do not see what is there but, rather, what must be there in order for them to love at all. Many divorced people are confused on this very point. They do not see the reality of the spouse. Therefore, when the spouse begins to act "outside the script," such a person is likely to see this as perversity on the part of the spouse, not as a real personality attribute of the spouse.

THE MECHANICS OF FALLING IN LOVE

As people fall in love, in their journey toward the exchange of ego ideals, each one reveals a little of himself. If what is revealed is approved by the other, the rewards are tremendous. Then, when the other reveals something, one approves if one possibly can. In what may sometimes seem a positive ecstasy of revelation, the falling in love proceeds. Obviously, however, such revelation cannot go on indefinitely. The boundary must be drawn between self and object. Some aspects of the self cannot be joined with object under any conditions and other aspects cannot be so joined without a severe sense of loss. It is certainly true that many people in love affairs and marriage expose so little of themselves that they cannot achieve identification; it is also true, at least among the divorced population, that some expose so much of themselves, refusing to draw boundaries between self and spouse, that they end up feeling exploited and worthless.

The boundary drawing most often does not occur until after the wedding. The exchange of ego ideals is never complete. If there is a wedding, the process may well continue.

Before the Divorce: Marriage

In the prototype natural history of a marriage, a wedding takes place when the exchange of ego ideals is successful. Whether or not the relationship has included sex before the wedding seems to make little difference, at least to divorced people.

IDENTIFICATIONS

The next stage in the processes of marital love is, according to Benedek, identification with the spouse. After one has maintained a marriage for some time, one begins to realize that one is judged not merely by one's self, but by one's spouse.

There are two dangers at this point. (1) The person may feel that his spouse is so revealing of himself that he is unable to maintain the relationship—that is, the need he has for a kind of feedback from the world comes to include the spouse as part of himself. All of those things he does not like about himself are pushed off on the spouse. He thinks the spouse reveals a great deal more about him than is in fact the case to the casual or even the trained observer. (2) No boundaries are drawn between the two spouses. That is, one tries to manipulate the spouse in the same way one manipulates his foot or his arm. This is not an object relationship any longer. This means that communication falls to pieces and, ultimately, the first time a boundary is drawn may be the last.

Toby was a good-looking woman of 33 who described herself as a "two-time loser." She had played the same drama twice. Her first husband was a small businessman. She began to help him in the business; it became apparent that she was efficient and a good salesperson. She pushed him systematically into a position of inadequacy in his own business, which has been successful even before she began and became more so. He took to other women. She did not tell him she objected; she did not make demands. She claimed that she knew him well enough to be sure that if she had said anything he would have become angry and left. "I didn't want to ruin my marriage." When his behavior finally got too insulting, she got angry and left—her first boundary was the last.

Her second husband was a tax accountant. She moved into his office to help with the typing. Before long, he stayed in the back office, while she dealt with the public, which she did well. He began drinking and swearing at her. Again, she drew no boundaries about what she would and would not put up with. As she said, she made no "demands." Again, when he got no signals from her, his behavior became more and more preposterous until

she left him—again without warning and without any possibility of reconciliation.

Toby had one son from each marriage; she had decided that she did not want to marry again and was establishing her own business.

If, however, the identification is of a sort that the spouses can both say, "How glorious it is that the world knows what a good person I am because I can attract and keep such a wonderful person for a spouse," the identification gives good feedback, and has nothing to do with boundary drawing between self and other.

Benedek further points out that when a child is born, both parents identify with the child. Thereupon, unconsciously if not consciously, each spouse becomes identified with his own parent of the opposite sex. One finds in old-fashioned families that the spouses even address each other not by spouse terms but by their children's parental terms. This means, of course, that the relationship with the spouse is likely to be muddied by the unresolved problems in the relationship with the parent of opposite sex.

Further, identification of the spouse with the parent of opposite sex underscores the identification of self with the parent of same sex.

Marilyn had problems of identification with her own mother. Her mother was, in her view, a loud, vulgar alcoholic who hated men, although she had married four of them. The mother's first marriage occurred at the age of almost 30. When Marilyn was 16, she decided that the reason her mother had so much trouble in marriage was that she was too old when she married. So Marilyn married at 17. She confused her mother's being aggressive with her own drawing any boundaries. "Looking back now," she said, "I think he [the first husband] was emotionally unstable and was looking for someone to be the strong member of the marriage—make the decisions for him and make him succeed. Also, somebody to play the mother role. But, you see, I didn't want to be the strong member of the marriage—to make decisions and push him to success. My mother was aggressive and domineering, and I have leaned over backwards all my life not to be that way." She divorced him when he demanded children to avoid the draft. She was single for 5 years, then married a man with whom she had had a stormy affair. Only later did she find out that he made his money illegally—she had not even known his occupation before marriage. When the police began to watch the house, she left. He was later arrested.

Marilyn went into once-a-week psychotherapy for almost 3 years. She broke it off, thinking it successful, to marry her third husband. He was 39 and had never been married. He, too, was looking for someone to be strong. After a few months, she realized she had made the same mistake again; she left him and went into psychoanalysis. At the time of the interview, she claimed that the analysis was successfully terminated. She said she had no inclination to marry again—but that didn't mean that she had given up men.

DYADIC AUTONOMY

When the exchange of ego ideals is successful and all the identifications have been negotiated, it is a pretty good sign that the couple have come to a state that can be called dyadic autonomy. In order for a human being—or any other animal—to carry out some of his inherent behavior, he needs conspecifics. In dyadic autonomy, two people have selected each other in order to enhance best the behavioral and emotional capacities of each. Dyadic autonomy is what sees a couple through the "empty nest" syndrome and into the mutual dependablenesses of old age.

"Causes" of Divorce

What has been said so far surely provides conclusive evidence that the search for "causes" of divorce is simplistic. One often hears it said—sometimes even by people who spend much of their professional lives counseling divorcees—that sex and money are the causes of more divorces than anything else. Although differences over money matters and differences in sexual proclivities and capacities may sometimes lead to imperfect exchange of ego ideals, poor identification of the spouses, and even a disastrous identification of the spouse with the opposite-sex parent, sex and money are not so much the main causes of divorce as they are the recognized arenas of combat in our culture. The causes are much more subtle. They have to do with the psychic maturity of the spouses and those aspects of the relationship—after all, marriage is a very complex form of pair-bonding—that they can or cannot perform adequately with one another.

The Decree

Different societies disengage people from the institution of marriage by different cultural means. A few, (like ourselves), do it legally, some do it economically, some do it ritually—there is a Muslim ceremony of divorce and a Jewish ceremony of divorce, although in the Western world Jews seldom use it. There are also some societies that do divorce by contract. The societies of the Western world, however, have overwhelmingly legalized the matter of divorce—although this began only in the 17th century. Divorce has become a matter of the law and lawyers, handled by the judicial institutions of the society.

At least six separations take place at the time of the divorce. (A fuller discussion will found in Bohannan, 1970.)

PSYCHIC DIVORCE

This involves the renunciation of the object and the accompanying mourning. It often occurs, in at least one of the spouses, before any other aspect of the divorce.

LEGAL DIVORCE

This is fairly simple. Only one thing can be done by a legal divorce that cannot be done better by other legal means—make the partners remarriageable. (This is not true, obviously, in societies that practice plural marriages.) All the rest of the separations have been culturally associated with the legal problem because they are handled by the legal institutions.

Until the middle 1960's, the legal divorce in all American states and most, but not quite all, European countries was a judicial matter based on the adversary process. One partner had to be the injured party, the other the guilty party. Grounds had to be determined. At least nine tenths of divorces in all jurisdictions used the least incriminating grounds available—mental cruelty, incompatibility, and the like. In the 1960's, the "irretrievable breakdown of the marriage" became the basis for "dissolution of the marriage," first in California, later in other states. Some states have inserted "irretrievable breakdown" as one of the grounds (a logical contradiction and surely a temporary stage). Emphasis is shifting from guilt and punishment to the viability of the relationship itself.

ECONOMIC DIVORCE

In the Western world, the married couple is an economic unit—indeed, a property-owning unit. Even in those states that do not have community property laws, the couple is the legal owner of more or less property. At the time of divorce, the property that had belonged to a unit comparable to a "corporation aggregate" must be divided into two lots of property, each belonging to a "corporation sole." This is almost never easy. There is almost never enough to go around, no matter how much or how little there may be. Having more property never hurt anything in a divorce suit—but it probably never solved anything, either.

Obviously, certain cathexes toward things are disrupted at the time of divorce. That means that the psychic realignment of energies and forces has to be made to encompass the new situation; and it may have to be done without the possessions around one that have in the past been a part of one's self-image.

COMMUNITY DIVORCE

At the time of marriage, a couple enters into a new community. Some individual relatives and friends are likely to overlap from the old communities. But many new friends are added, besides new sets of in-laws. At that time, the change of community is experienced as growth, as emergence into a new and satisfactory status.

At divorce, part of the marital community must be given up, and still another new community must be acquired. At that time, it may be hard to regard the change of community as a process of growth. Indeed, although in many divorces it is, it may not be a process of growth.

Many divorced people regret that divorcing the spouse involves "divorce" from their ex-spouses' relatives: "Your in-laws become your out-laws," in the words of 1 informant. If there are children, many divorced people keep in touch with those they now call "the children's relatives." Some women say that they miss a good and friendly mother-in-law; some men miss the atmosphere that

absorption into the ex-wife's extended family had given them.

In the community divorce, one is thrust back on techniques of making friends and getting rid of nonfriends that one may not have used for a long time. The result is that many divorcees may be lonely or badgered or both.

CO-PARENTAL DIVORCE

"Co-parental" refers to separation of a parent from the child's other parent ("parental" implies the separation of children from parents). Being a single parent is very different from being a married parent. It is often more difficult, no matter how inadequate the other parent may have been. The difficulty does not arise merely because one is not morally supported as a parent. It is an alteration in the division of actual parenting.

All noncustodial parents must eventually realize a number of things about their situation. First, and psychically most important, they must realize that they no longer have any say in what the co-parent does to and with the children. The only exception arises if, in the eyes of the court, the actions of the co-parent are not in the best interests of the child, as legally determined. A man who is a noncustodial parent cannot say what his ex-wife will or will not do about training the children, disciplining them, giving them allowances, or anything of the sort, as long as the court does not have any complaint against the way the job is done. In the same way, the custodial parent has no control over what the children do with the noncustodial parent during vacations or visitation—unless it can be proved to the satisfaction of the court that the noncustodial parent is corrupting the child or is exposing the child to influences that are not in the best interests of the child.

Thus, the parents are no longer in collusion about child rearing. They may not even be in agreement—indeed, in a few cases, it may even have such differences that triggered the divorce action in the first place. Such a situation may be, for some people, the most difficult of all the divorces. They experience the ex-spouse not merely as turning against the self, but as turning against their personal definition of the best interests of the child. When the child is becoming something other than what the divorced parent thinks he or she should become, it becomes quite easy to blame it on the co-parent—no matter what the efficient cause of the change. Much bitterness between ex-spouses arises from differences in views about child rearing. It is also an area into which defensive projections can readily be made.

SEPARATION FROM DEPENDENCY

The last of the separations is the separation from a dependency that has allowed one not to be autonomous. The overwhelming number of divorces seem to occur between people who have not achieved a state of autonomy. It is quite true, of course, that some divorces occur because one or both members have become autonomous and recognize the inadequacy of the marriage. Some occur because one spouse is fed up with the dependence of the other. But in many, both are dependent.

This particular aspect of separation may not be easy to achieve. Indeed, the marriage originally may have been made in order to avoid becoming autonomous. Some people who remarry immediately seem never to achieve the autonomy that is necessary to run a good marriage. One informant asked the author, "You didn't think I'd jump without a parachute, did you?" A large but unknowable proportion of second marriages do not work out precisely because autonomy has not been achieved before the first marriage, during it, after it, or during the second.

In summary, at the time of a decree, there are likely to be two people who are angry because in the psychic divorce they have been rejected, in the economic divorce they have been cheated, and in the legal divorce they have been misrepresented. They may be bitter in the co-parental divorce, lonely in the community divorce, and afraid in the divorce from dependency.

When the institutionalization of the decree of divorce is legalized as it is in our society, and when in the laws of most states (all of them until a few years ago) it is necessary to assume that one party is guilty and the other innocent and the flaws in the relationship translated into faults of the partners so that the adversary process can proceed, it is no wonder that getting a divorce decree may be one of the most unpleasant experiences of a person's life.

The Divorce

Now that they have it, what do they have? It is not merely that divorced people are out of something (which they are); they are also into something. And many divorcees do not know what it is that they are getting into.

Divorce is an institution just as much as marriage is. However, it is not nearly as neat or efficient an institution. The institution of divorce may be less intense if there are no dependent children, but the ex-spouse can never become the nonspouse. It was Joe DiMaggio who made the funeral arrangements for Marilyn Monroe; divorced men often go back to perform household tasks for their ex-wives, particularly if those tasks concern the well-being of children or grandchildren.

The problems that face divorcees are obviously very real.

MONEY

American society is in a state of change in regard to the financial responsibility of the ex-spouses and co-parents. Ideas of child support are changing daily; ideas about alimony have changed vastly in the last 30 years. In a society in which the single-family household is the norm and in which the division of responsibility says that men support their children, the solutions seemed fairly clear. In a society in which men and women assume more or less equal responsibility, the solutions are not at all clear.

There is seldom enough money, and it is the focus of many disputes between ex-spouses. The ex-spouse relationship is likely to become a debtor-creditor relationship, with no real sanctions but the court. Part of the problem is lack of clear institutions.

THE HOUSEHOLD

American economy is set up so that services for either single people or marital households are available. However, there seems to be no way in our present economy for a single-parent household to be made adequate. This fact leads people into a constant struggle to discover new forms of household, with enough members to do all the jobs that have to be done.

Sometimes a woman moves back in with her parents. Her mother, the child's grandmother, takes care of her child while she works. Getting through the autonomy phase of separation is not easy in such a situation and, in some cases, may not be achievable at all. Two women, both with children, may try to create a pseudofamily life-style. Households in which an uncle and niece or other kinsmen have done the same thing can be found. All of these households leave something to be desired; many contain serious psychic traps that may be sources of distress to everybody in them.

The most controversial solution is the day care center. It remains to be seen whether day nurseries in America will be psychologically healthful places for young children. If we look at the day nurseries in Sweden or Israel, it is obvious that the job can be done. Whether it can be done in a society like the United States, with its high mobility of people—including children, social workers, teachers, nurses, and lunchroom attendants—is still an unanswered question.

Parenting. Probably the most discussed and most worried-about aspect of the institution of divorce is parenting. After the remarriage of the spouses, the problem may become even more acute.

In the monogamous family, there is a possibility of eight types of relationships (husband-wife, father-son, father-daughter, mother-son, mother-daughter, brother-brother, sister-sister, brother-sister). Some may, of course, not be present; all except the husband-wife relationship may be duplicated.

After divorce, if both spouses remarry people with children and if both have more children, there are 22 possible types of relationships. The situation is, in short, extremely complicated. Parents get involved with stepparents. Stepsiblings, half-siblings, and children who are not kinsmen at all (and hence are not protected by either incest taboos or laws) may be living in the same household. In 1962, it was computed by actuaries that one American child in nine has a stepparent. Certainly, the stepparent-stepchild relationship is not unusual. Culturally, however, it is not well delineated. Most of the etiquette books suggest that attempts be made to treat them all equally. Seldom is such advice workable.

The problem of stepparents is extremely complex and has been only minimally examined in the literature, although a full scale study is under way as this is written (Western Behavioral Sciences Institute).

SEX

Many divorced people—more men than women—move into a new sexual life that may be better by any criteria than the one they had in marriage. Material on this aspect is hard to come by, but many divorcees claim it to be the case. Gebhard (1970) has shown that a greater proportion of sexual acts by divorced women lead to orgasm than for the same women during their marriages, as, indeed, is also the case among widows.

If sex was a factor in the disruption of the marriage, it may well remain a problem after divorce. If sex is closely associated with marriage in the moral or religious convictions of the divorcee, then sex may be a difficult moral problem after divorce. Some women and a few men have little sexual activity after divorce. Some of them state that they are glad this is so—that they are free of sexual demands. Others say that partners are scarce or nonexistent; many blame it on their age or their appearance. The cause usually lies deeper.

Some men of 30 cannot find women, some men of the same age say that they have never had it so good, and some men of the same age say it is disgusting the way women throw themselves at a man. The range in women was as great.

COMMUNITY

Many divorcees remain lonely. Some join organizations, of which the best known are Parents Without Partners, United States Divorce Reform, Inc., A.D.A.M., and Divorcees Anonymous. Some few even become what can be called professional divorcees—people who devote their entire social and sexual lives to helping the newly divorced adjust to the status. Many of these people do admirable jobs of helping; a few may be parasites. One woman, a social worker of about 50, devoted all her evenings and weekends to discussion groups made up of the newly divorced; a handsome divorced man of about 35 belonged to several such organizations, found attractive women in the early stages of the divorce process, had affairs with them, and instructed them in how to be divorcees—he seems to have given as much as he got.

Some people, including some divorcees, think that only unsuccessful divorcees join organizations. The attitude among members runs all the way from the dependent people who are one of the staple character types in the organizations, to the young divorced woman who is a legend, if not a myth, in many chapters of Parents Without Partners; she came to a coffee and conversation hour and left in no more than an hour stating, "I came here to scout a good lay; obviously I am wasting my time."

Children of Divorce

Children of divorce must learn some things that other children simply pick up in the processes of living—what Gregory Bateson (1942) has called "deutero-learning." Freud himself said that he had great difficulty remembering what he had learned and almost as much difficulty forgetting what he had experienced.

AMBIVALENCE

A good informant in these matters was a woman psychoanalyst who had been divorced; her parents were divorced and both were psychoanalysts; both sets of her grandparents were divorced, but they were too early to have been psychoanalysts. She reported that there are two primary things that children of divorce have difficulty in learning which they might have experienced or deutero-learned quite readily in an intact household. One of these is ambivalence. Ambivalence in a divorce situation is difficult because the child can say that one parent is right and the other is wrong—that one caused the trouble and the other did not. If the child is living with both, the vacuity of a division of fault usually becomes immediately apparent. The other point is that children who grow up in a single-parent household do so in an atmosphere that this psychoanalyst called "dessicated." She went on to say that there is an undertone of sexuality in a well run household based on a good marriage, and that this undertone is completely lacking and cannot be supplied in a single-parent household. All other aspects of marriage, she claimed, can be taught to children in single-

parent households so that they grow up without any serious disadvantage. This requires, of course, a parent who has successfully finished the separations and is dealing with present reality as reality. It also requires a culturally recognized need and an adequate mode for providing the information and training to the children of one-parent households.

Teen-age Marriage and Divorce

The rate of divorce for teen-age marriages is higher than that for any other age group. One important reason is that some young people marry as a device for declaring themselves adult; they see the wedding as an initiation ceremony rather than as a marriage ceremony. The result, obviously, is that when they proceed into marriage, none of the psychic experiences—exchanging ego ideals, identifications that lead to a successful bonding—can develop.

Does Divorce Run in Families?

Divorce does indeed run in families, although quantitative information on this matter is lacking; it would be quite easy to get thorough genealogical studies but this has not actually been done. There seem to be two patterns. In one, the child has vicariously experienced the divorce of his parents and realizes that divorce does not bring the end of the world. Such a child is apparently somewhat more ready to solve his own marital difficulties by divorce than in other ways—he is not afraid of divorce. The other pattern is, of course, that the children of people who do not deal with the various separations and with the reality of the institution of divorce may not have the patterns or the emotional equipment to deal with those problems themselves—that is, their parents' difficulties are added to their own at the time of major crises in their own marriages.

What is true, however, is that some people get more than their share of divorces. If one marriage in four, one in three, or one in two (depending on what figure one uses to compute the rate) ends in divorce, that certainly does not mean that one person in every three or four who marries will get divorced. Every divorce lawyer has regular clients. There are no data available on which recidivism rates for divorce can be computed. We only know that they are high, and that, like the divorce rate itself, recidivism rates vary inversely with socio-economic status and education.

Remarriage

Since 1960, the annual number of remarriages has risen by 40 per cent, whereas the number of all marriages has risen by about 33 per cent. In the same period, the annual number of divorces has risen by 80 per cent (Glick and Norton, unpublished data, 1972). With more divorces, one can expect more remarriages. About one fifth of the remarriages also end in divorce (Glick and Norton, 1972).

Conclusion

In order to deal with the psychology of divorcees, it is necessary to know something about the sociology and the cultural context of divorce. Each case is, of course, psychologically unique. But divorce is not an entity, even in the sense that schizophrenia may be. It may not even be a symptom. Divorced people have failed at one of our favorite institutions—but they are also people who would not settle for less than they thought they deserved.

REFERENCES

Bateson, G. Social planning and the concept of deutero-learning. In *Science, Philosophy and Religion, Second Symposium.* Harper & Row, New York, 1942. Reprinted in Bateson, G. *Steps to an Ecology of Mind.* Ballantine Books, New York, 1970.

Benedek, T. The emotional structure of the family. In *The Family: Its Function and Destiny,* rev. ed., R. N. Anshen, editor, Harper & Row, New York, 1959.

*Benedek, T. The psychobiologic approach to parenthood. In *Parenthood: Its Psychology and Psychopathology,* E. J. Anthony and T. Benedek, editors. Little, Brown, Boston, 1970.

Bernard, J. *Remarriage.* Dryden Press, New York, 1956.

*Bernard, J. *The Future of Marriage.* World Publishing Co., New York, 1972.

*Bohannan, P., editor. *Divorce and After.* Doubleday, New York, 1970.

de Rougemont, D. *Love in the Western World,* 1956.

Deutsch, H. *The Psychology of Women: A Psychoanalytic Interpretation.* Grune & Stratton, New York, 1944.

*Egleson, J., and Egleson, J. F. *Parents Without Partners.* E. P. Dutton, New York, 1961.

*Gebhard, P. Postmarital coitus among widows and divorcees. In *Divorce and After,* P. Bohannan, editor. Doubleday, New York, 1970.

Nader, L. and Maretzki, T. W. *Anthropology and Mental Health.* In press.

*Steinzor, B. *When Parents Divorce.* Pantheon Books, New York, 1969.

Western Behavioral Sciences Institute. *The Stepfather: A Neglected Person in Mental Health Research.* In press.

chapter 12

Society and Sexuality

12.1 Socio-cultural Roles of Male and Female

ROBERT E. GOULD, M.D.

Freudian Theory

Modern concepts of normal psychosocial roles for men and women derive mainly from Freud's theories of the Oedipus complex and the castration complex. Throughout Freud's writings on sexuality and its psychic and social derivatives, from 1898 to 1939, he elaborated on the Oedipus and castration phases, clearly delineating his view of male and female patterns of behavior.

According to Freud, the difference in anatomy between the sexes provides both the foundation and the rationale for sexual role development. ("Anatomy is destiny.") For both the boy and the girl, the mother is the first love object. The little boy desires his mother sexually and would like to have his father out of the way. When the boy becomes aware that he has a penis and that a girl lacks one, he assumes that she has lost it for doing something wrong, most probably in the sexual area. He worries that his father may do the same to him, should he learn of the boy's wishes for his mother. To overcome his castration anxiety, the little boy learns to identify with his father and give up his mother, with the idea that in the future he will find a woman like his mother. This is a successful resolution of the oedipal conflict, and it heralds the beginning of superego development (conscience, feelings of guilt, and ability to determine right from wrong).

The little girl also starts life with the mother as her first love object. When the girl discovers that she has no penis and the boy does, she, too, believes that she has lost something and envies the boy for having it. She resents her mother, whom she holds responsible for bringing her into the world less complete than the boy. She loosens her ties to her mother and turns for a love object toward the father, whose penis she covets. Later, realizing that she cannot have her father's penis, she substitutes a desire to have a baby from him, which would be the equivalent of a penis. When that wish is frustrated, she decides to marry a man as the next best thing she can do in striving to possess the male organ.

The little girl proceeds from a castration phase to an oedipal phase, the reverse of the sequence of events for the boy. Since she is not actually threatened with castration, believing that it has already happened to her, she gives up the oedipal phase less completely and less urgently than the boy does. This incomplete resolution hampers the development of the superego, which is based on the resolution of the oedipal conflict. Thus, in Freud's view the superego remains weaker in the girl than in the boy.

According to Freud, the girl can never develop into a whole person because she has no penis. The best resolution of the situation she can manage is to overcome her envy of the penis by renouncing her competitiveness with the boy, since she cannot hope to beat or even equal him, and to develop her feminine nature. This means having babies (still regarded as a penis substitute), taking care of home and hearth, and developing her nurturing qualities. If this process is successful, the girl gives up an early interest in her clitoris, which Freud regards as a stunted penis and a homologue of the penis. The mature woman shifts her focus of erotic interest and pleasure to the vagina, which represents the truly feminine organ—a hole, round and receiving.

Virtually all the personality traits typically seen in men and women are explained by Freud on the basis of these theories. Freud postulated that man is the aggressor and all active traits are rightfully male, whereas all passive traits are female. The masculine nature was defined as objective, analytical, tough minded, intellectual, rational, aggressive, independent, active, and confident. The feminine nature was thought to embody opposing traits, such as subjectivity, emotionality, irrationality, illogical thinking, empathy, sensitivity, intuition, receptivity, passivity, and dependency.

In seeing man as mover, creator, and innovator, Freud actually felt that civilization is the business of men and that maintaining the home and nurturing the family (support functions) is woman's place. In a 1937 philosophical treatise, "Civilization and Its Discontents," he concluded that men are responsible for the survival of the race because only man can give up or sublimate instinctual needs for the benefits of civilization. Woman, because of her poorly developed superego, has "less sense of justice; her judgment is influenced by feelings of affection or hostility . . . ." Women are by nature less sincere, less moral, and less motivated by conscience than are men.

In the sexual area, Freud felt that the inhibitions of sexuality (shame, disgust, pity) take place in girls earlier than in boys and meet with less resistance; the tendency to sexual repression seems, in general, to be greater in girls, and this tendency contributes to the female preference for the passive role in sex.

Further sample thoughts of the different psychosexual social roles played by men and women as elaborated by Freud follow:

Women, since they have to move their erotogenic zone from the clitoris (representing "childish masculinity") to the vagina, are more prone to neurosis, especially hysteria, than are men, who have not had to change their primary erotogenic zone, the penis.

Woman suffers an original narcissism due to her "wound"—the lack of a penis—and so is unable to develop a true object choice with its accompanying overvaluation. In "On Narcissism," Freud wrote: "Women, especially if they grow up with good looks, develop a certain self-contentment which compensates them for the social restrictions that are imposed upon them in their choice of object. Strictly speaking, it is only themselves that such women love with an intensity comparable to that of man's love for them."

Woman's need lies in the direction of being loved (passive) rather than in loving (active). Freud further postulated that this "feminine" and "passive" state of a woman is the basis of her appeal to men; the man is attracted to the woman with "inaccessible narcissism and self-contentment." Freud compared this appeal of woman with "the charm of a child." Throughout his writings, Freud mentioned several times that traits of women resemble those of children.

Woman's innate passivity, combined with her mode of sexual expression, manifests itself in a tendency toward masochism, whereas man's fusion of aggressiveness and his sexual drive leads to sadism.

Freud's contention is that the presence of the penis in the boy makes him feel superior to the girl, who, noting her own lack of this impressive organ, feels inferior to the boy. The subsequent development of character and personality resulting from the oedipal and castration stages confirms the superiority of man to woman, since most of the traits defined as male are more valued in society than are those categorized as female.

Freud made it clear in one of his last statements ("Analysis Terminable and Interminable") that woman must come to accept her secondary status and compensate for her lack of a penis by having a baby and a husband; but something is always lacking. Man has to overcome his castration fear, which can reflect itself in passive traits; but, if successful, man emerges as a complete human being; the woman can never achieve this.

Following Freud's lead, male and female analysts of the classical tradition reaffirmed his delineation of normal male and female roles. Bettelheim (unpublished data, 1965) states that women want first to be "womanly companions of men and to be mothers, then engineers and scientists." Erikson (1964) felt that there is a biological, psychological, and ethical commitment to take care of human infancy: "Women are destined to bear children." Deutsch (1944) pointed out that

woman's intellectuality is, to a large extent, paid for by the loss of valuable feminine qualities: it feeds on the sap of the affective life and results in impoverishment of this life either as a whole or in specific emotional qualities . . . for intuition is God's gift to the feminine woman; everything relating to exploration and cognition, all the forms and kinds of human cultural aspiration that require a strictly objective approach, are with few exceptions the domain of the masculine intellect, of man's spiritual power, against which woman can rarely compete.

Freud observed keenly the differences in role function of men and women in the Western world from Victorian times through 1939. There was little argument with these observations. What became an issue was his theoretical framework, which suggested that these functions are based on biology and anatomy and are, therefore, inevitable and universal. Various groups—including, neo-Freudian psychoanalysts, social anthropologists, sociologists, sex researchers, and, most recently, militant feminists—have postulated that the traits Freud and his followers delineated as inherently masculine and feminine are actually induced by cultural attitudes of the society, rather than by any biological givens.

Interpersonal or Cultural View

Among the first psychoanalysts who challenged Freud's theories were Clara Thompson and Karen Horney. Thompson (1943) stressed that it is not the penis itself that women envy but, rather, the dominant position that the man holds in society. This privileged position of superiority is merely symbolized by the possession of a penis. Thompson also maintained that Freud, despite his extraordinary perceptiveness, was still a product of his culture and, as such, readily subscribed to the theory of male superiority. She pointed out that Freud was compromised in his understanding of the experiences and feelings of women. Indeed, Freud himself on many occasions admitted his lack of understanding of women. Jones's

biography of Freud (1955) quotes him as saying to Marie Bonaparte:

The great question that has never been answered and which I have not yet been able to answer, despite my 30 years of research into the feminine soul, is, "What does a woman want?"

Horney (1926) challenged Freud as having imposed a male orientation and bias in offering the theory that little girls believe themselves castrated and invariably envy boys their penises. Although she allows that a girl's lack of a penis may activate a boy's latent anxiety about his own organ, she claims it does not necessarily follow that the girl feels more insecure for not having a penis.

When Freud discussed masochism as a part of female sexuality, he used evidence from the fantasies of passive male homosexuals, and this material is not necessarily equatable with the female sexual experience. From clinical experience, this writer finds no relationship between a healthy woman's sexual life and that of a passive male personality.

Of the anthropologists, Margaret Mead has been one of the most persuasive in challenging the notions of what is naturally male and female. She readily admits, as do virtually all the so-called culturalists, that there certainly are biological differences between men and women, since there is an indisputable difference in organs, functions, and hormones, but she believes these differences may not be relevant in determining sex-linked traits. Mead pointed out in *Sex and Temperament* (1935) that the characteristics of three tribes she studied did not conform to the commonly held notions of masculine and feminine.

Among the Arapesh, men were trained to be cooperative, responsive to the needs and demands of others, and unaggressive. Sex was not felt as a driving force by either men or women. This contrasted sharply with the Mundugumor tribe, in which both men and women developed aggressive, ruthless, and highly sexed personalities. There were virtually no maternal feelings in Mundugumor men or women, whereas such feelings were commonly seen among both men and women of the Arapesh tribe. Mead pointed out not only that traits traditionally regarded as feminine are commonly seen in both male and female members in one tribe and that these same traits are absent from both men and women of a second tribe but that in a third tribe, the Tchambuli, there was a reversal of the position of dominance in the sexes.

One can deduce from this study that the contrasting cultural conditions are responsible for various traits that are thought to be sex-linked. Mead concluded that, whatever instincts human beings have toward certain behavior patterns, they seem minute compared to the tremendous influence of culture.

It appears from Mead's work that the malleability of human nature for men and women is so great and cultural forces so insistent and pervasive that the influence of instincts or biological factors in producing traits that are considered masculine or feminine is apparently quite small. The delineation of the different traits among neighboring tribes was quite clear-cut because, with less variety and complexity of stimuli, the personality traits of the individual members were more uniform.

Sex Research

Sex researchers have contributed new knowledge on the characteristics of male and female sexuality. The biologist Kinsey and his associates made the first wide scale study of sexual behavior in men (1948) and women (1953), and their findings challenged and revised many generally accepted theories about human sexuality. Among Kinsey's many findings was the fact that women enjoy sex more than had been generally thought. He also found that men reach their physical peak for sexual performance at about age 18 and slowly decline after that. Women's peak for sexual responsiveness occurs later but lasts much longer, with virtually no decline in powers.

Whereas Kinsey's studies were based mainly on extensive interviews, although he also had information based on observed data, Masters and Johnson (1966), who observed sexual behavior directly, added another important body of findings. They demonstrated, through laboratory work, the nature of female orgasm and found that orgasm derived from clitoral stimulation and orgasm after vaginal stimulation are physiologically indistinguishable.

In another study of female sexuality, "The Nature and Evolution of Female Sexuality" (1966), Sherfey pointed out that there is an unseen clitoral system under the visible glans and shaft, which together make this organ as large and impressive as the penis, both in size and, more importantly, in sexual responsiveness to stimulation. Sherfey also rejected Freud's theory of clitoral (immature) versus vaginal (mature) orgasm.

These studies indicate that the cause of woman's sexual problems lies neither in the difficulty of shifting her erotic center from the clitoris to the vagina nor in the liability of possessing a clitoris that is an inadequate penis. The notion of woman's sexual inferiority is, according to these theories, simply another manifestation of a general inferiority imposed on her by society.

Both Masters and Johnson and Sherfey have expanded on Kinsey's conclusion that women enjoy sex more than has been generally supposed. They point out, in fact, that women are multiorgasmic and that their potential for sexual fulfillment exceeds that of men. Women are capable of experiencing a series of orgasms of great intensity in a short period of time. Furthermore, they are capable of more frequent orgastic activity than are men, sustaining this capacity far later in life.

The implication is quite clear that, if woman's sexuality were not inhibited or dampened by external pressures or influences, it is highly unlikely that one man could satisfy her completely. This concept of woman's sexual capacity and needs surpassing that of the man's is the reverse of what had been generally thought to be the norm.

Changing Socio-cultural Roles

The fact that socio-cultural roles of men and women are changing is reflected in varying ways, including the obvious and dramatic recent trend toward unisex. This term is popularly used by the mass media to mean that outward differences between the sexes seem to be diminishing in many areas, most notably in styles of dress and personal appearance. This blurring of the external traditional distinctions seems to symbolize the blurring of other lines as well, characteristics that clearly separated male from female in the past.

"Unisex" is actually a misnomer for this trend. The dictionary defines the term "unisexual" as (1) of or pertaining to one sex only and (2) having only male or female organs in one person. "Androgyny" would more accurately convey the intended meaning; an androgynous person is one who possesses characteristics of both sexes, being in nature both male and female. The implication of androgyny is that human traits are not rigidly assigned to either the man or the woman but that, to be truly human, a person of either sex must have the qualities traditionally thought of and described as masculine and feminine.

In the last few years men have been dressing with more care and color and variety, and women, especially those active in the liberation movement, have tended to downplay frivolous and unnecessary adornments. It is becoming more common to see men wearing their hair longer; adopting adornments, such as bracelets, rings, and necklaces; form-fitting clothes; higher heels; and, in short, moving in the direction of what had been traditionally considered female attire.

The writer believes that these dramatic changes in style are deeply reflective of dynamic changes occurring in men and women relating to their socio-cultural roles. Historically, women's position in society could be deduced from a study of their clothes and appearance. Elaborate dress and adornment emphasized their objectness; they were to be admired for their decorative value. The consciousness of their dress, with its ever-changing styles, extolled trivia and emphasized woman's role as consumer. Women were enslaved by a system that maintained them essentially as playthings. High heeled shoes, dresses that inhibited movement, and the binding of feet in China all hampered woman's mobility, emphasized her helplessness, and further restricted her ability to function in society. When not overdressed (bustles, corsets, hoop skirts), women have often been underdressed (bikinis, see-through dresses, hot pants). Either way, fashion emphasized woman's role as sex objects.

Lacking an intrinsic sense of worth as a result of the influence of a sexist society, women acquired a sense of identity based primarily on how they appeared in public and, particularly, how they looked to men. Often the amount of time and concern spent on outer trappings such as dress and hair style reflects the level of insecurity in the woman (or man).

Women's recent shift from dresses to pants and to simpler functional clothes, such as jerseys and jeans, emphasizes their emergence as active, free persons rather than as ornamental and helpless objects. Many women are allowing more hair to appear under their arms and on their legs and some natural odors to emanate from their bodies. The hairless, odorless woman was reduced in her individuality and humanness and adultness—"smooth and clean; complexion like a baby's."

Meanwhile, the man, whose dress has been traditionally bland, conservative, and conformist (with certain exceptions, such as blacks and homosexuals, where other dynamics are operating), is also being liberated from the stereotyped roles imposed on him by the culture. It was not previously considered manly for men to show much concern over their looks; and so, many men have been inhibited from expressing their aesthetic natures in this manner. That men can take readily to all the personal grooming aids (deodorants, hair driers, jewelry) once thought to be particularly female underscores how great a part culture played in determining these attitudes initially.

Women's Liberation Movement

The women's liberation movement has exerted a profound influence on the changing perception of sex roles in society. Although the movement embraces many groups with diverse aims, the central thrust is to gain equality for women in all areas of living. The movement's leaders maintain that it is not more natural for women than for men to perform household chores and child care. They further maintain that women should be given equal career opportunities, that professions in which women have been traditionally excluded should change this policy, and that women should be permitted to enter any field and advance to leadership and power positions.

Many of the new militant feminists have made the movement a central part of their lives, thus creating for themselves an immediate new socio-cultural role of crusader. Important movement writers have exhorted women and men to challenge the sexual traditions and to effect radical changes. Among the most influential books in the burgeoning field of women's studies, offering both new insights into women's historical role and new models for changing it, are the works of de Beauvoir (*The Second Sex,* 1952), Friedan (*The Feminine Mystique,* 1963), Millett (*Sexual Politics,* 1970), and Greer (*The Female Eunuch,* 1971).

Early Training

Rearing children is training by indoctrination of cultural values through parental expectation, approval, encouragement, and the opposites of these sanctions. This training begins as early as the birth of the baby and often even before birth, in the choice of different color schemes in nursery and clothing for boys and girls. For this reason, even studies of infants to determine whether there are sex-linked biological differences are already contaminated. From the moment of birth, the handling, physical and verbal, is different for boys and girls. When a newborn baby boy yells or kicks or is loud and vigorous, he is "all boy," and the behavior is approved and encouraged. "Boys don't cry" or "girls don't play rough" and similar expressions inhibit emotional reactions and certain expressions of feelings even before the boy or girl can understand the words. Attitudes and feelings, however, are effectively communicated through nonverbal means.

Although very young boys and girls are treated differently in countless ways, it is surprising that even so perceptive a feminist as Germaine Greer, as well as Freud, minimized the importance of cultural influences in the first years of life.

Parents and relatives indoctrinate the child according to stereotyped notions of what boys and girls do simply because they are one sex or the other, and toys, books, games, television, and movies all reinforce the stereotypes. Boys are expected to be active; to show leadership, strength, bravery; and to go into so-called male professions (doctor, policeman, pilot); girls are encouraged to be docile, passive, dependent, and helpless and to go into so-called female professions (nurse, secretary, stewardess).

Not unexpectedly, the few studies on sex differences in newborns as reported by Korner (1973) do not show clear-cut biological differences. The constant reinforcement of what the culture considers appropriate behavior makes studies even on babies a few months old difficult to evaluate unless the findings of differences are more persuasive than they appear to be in the meager literature on the subject.

The continuous training that encourages girls to behave one way and boys another and, more significantly, the superior status conferred on the boy makes it difficult for boys and girls to relate as friends and equals. They grow up together physically, but they grow apart socially and psychologically. During adolescence, the onset of sexual drives only aggravates the situation. Boys, behaving in accord with cultural values, continue to treat girls as inferior beings, regarding them primarily as sex objects.

Girls are taught to inhibit their sexual feelings, to play the feminine role, which includes using guile and wile, to win the boy. There is little in this exchange that enhances the self-esteem of anyone involved. Love feelings that the boy experiences at this stage are primarily feelings of lust, without much regard for the needs and wishes of the girl, except as her satisfaction may help him get what he wants. The girl, for her part, is so involved with playing a part which can only be demeaning to her that the transaction between her and the boy is not designed for a shared social or sexual experience between two equal human beings. It is rare, indeed, for a boy and a girl to develop the kind of closeness and shared intimacy with each other that they often do with peers of the same sex.

Although, in Western society, love is extolled as the sine qua non for marriage, this love is often largely a romantic feeling that seldom lasts if it is not part of a larger concept of love. Love is difficult to define, and there are many kinds of love. Sullivan (1953) offered a definition stipulating that love exists only if each of the persons involved cares as much for the other's satisfaction and security as for his or her own. This state is not likely to occur, given the early and ongoing training and experiences of boys and girls in this culture. The problem is that loving another person as much as one loves oneself requires a mutual respect and liking on which the more intimate and emotional component of love can be built.

The author feels that true, mature love can only exist between two people who regard each other as equals. The very nature of the development of the socio-cultural roles of men and women precludes two people from reaching that state. What one sees in many marriages is the endless search by both partners for intellectual and recreational stimulation, often among same-sex peers. Men have their work, their night out for bowling or poker, and their weekend golf games or fishing trips. Women are relegated to taking care of traditional family chores, to telephone gossip, and to shopping trips with women friends. If a woman has a career or any other interests outside the home, it often must take second place to her wifely role, but the man usually has the option of living more fully outside the home, as well as taking advantage of all the satisfactions that home and family afford. The problem is not merely that work and responsibilities are not divided equally but that there is little reason, given childhood experiences and cultural values, for a man and a woman ever to regard each other as friends or equals.

To the extent that a woman must hide or repress her ambitions, intelligence, and sexual needs and interests and must playact to fulfill the feminine role and thus appeal to the man, she is compromised in the realization of her human potential. Women can react in many ways to this situation, depending on many particular factors. Boredom, drinking or any drug dependency, resentment, hostility, and surreptitious sexual affairs are among the countless ways women may express dissatisfaction with the marital state and with themselves.

Men, too, are compromised by the socio-cultural bind they are in. It is more difficult to appreciate their distress, since they have the dominant role in society, but their role is as rigidly defined and stereotyped as the woman's. So long as men must also play roles that do not necessarily reflect their essential individual selves, they are not realizing their full humanity either.

Many marriages, of course, do seem to work. The socio-cultural roles that men and women adopt are such that marital partners may achieve a neurotic fit. There are sadomasochistic pairings and power-dependency, father-daughter, and mother-son couples, where the needs of the two people dovetail. If one asks whether this is not a satisfactory state, the answer would be a qualified "yes," in that it does maintain the relationship. But the price paid lies in the fact that such a marriage permits neither person to grow and change. If such a potentially positive change occurs, it throws the neurotic unit out of balance, and neither person can remain satisfied or able to satisfy the other.

Current Trends

Evidence gathered from the diverse fields of comparative anthropology, sociology, history, sex research, and clinical observance of changing socio-cultural roles indicates that the distinctive traits of men and women observed by Freud were probably culturally determined, rather than biologically sex-linked, as he suggested. Comparative studies of men and women at different periods in history and others conducted during the same period but in different cultures support the thesis that there are no patterns of behavior peculiar to one sex which cannot also be observed in the opposite sex. These role reversals, furthermore, are based not on disturbances of development but on differing cultural patterns of training.

In the Victorian era, women often fainted when overcome by shame, embarrassment, grief—almost any unpleasant emotion. This behavior was considered a normal, feminine response and was culturally acceptable. Freud, seeing so much hysteria in women, concluded that this was a more natural condition for women than for men. But in Western society today one sees relatively little hysteria in women. Obsessiveness has become the more prevailing neurosis for both women and men. One does not see women fainting these days. Yet, in the Arab countries—where men are free to express emotion openly, as a result of more permissive cultural standards—there was a wave of hysterical crying in the streets when President Nasser died. Men showing physical expressions of friendship, such as kissing and embracing, are a common phenomenon in other countries, yet only women display affection in this manner in the United States.

Similarly, traditions vary in the area of work assigned to one or the other sex. More and more it appears that there is really no form of labor that is either masculine or feminine by its essential nature.

In this culture, women generally do the cooking and kitchen chores in the house. Yet chefs in leading restaurants are men, and even the lower paid jobs of kitchen cleaning and serving are held by men, usually of minority groups.

Men can handle a needle deftly in surgery and in tailor shops, but needlework is considered woman's domain in the home. Men are thought to be naturally clumsy at darning socks or sewing buttons. The essential difference is really not any intrinsic quality that makes the task male or female but, rather, whether it is a paying job, what the prestige value is, and tradition.

Under special circumstances these male-female barriers break down quickly. In World War II, when women were urgently needed in factories, Rosie the Riveter was welcomed; when the war was over and there was competition for the job, the differentiation between man's work and woman's work came back into style.

But under the impetus of the women's movement, which is spreading to other countries, the stereotypes are now breaking down rather dramatically. In New York, women have become state troopers, subway transit patrolwomen, and policewomen on the beat. A commercial airline has hired its first woman pilot. Almost daily a new barrier is broken in sports, politics, government, business, and work in general.

Marriage and family, the bedrock of the cultural system, appear to be, in their present form, irreconcilable with female equality. It is the writer's opinion that this problem is at the root of much that troubles marriages and families.

The failure of so-called normal marriage as a satisfying way of life has been highlighted recently by the women's liberation movement and its vast literature, expressing dissatisfaction with woman's role in society today. The divorce rate has been climbing steadily (between one fourth and one third of all marriages end in divorce), and among those marriages that do remain intact, many do so because of inertia, religious strictures, or neurotic fears or bindings. These intact unions are, in fact, often quite unhappy, and many young people who have grown up in such homes are choosing not to marry but to search instead for new alternatives to traditional family life, as in the communal living experiments.

The women's movement has spawned a number of women's groups whose members meet and undergo a process of consciousness raising, which a psychiatrist might consider a form of self-therapy. In these groups, women attempt to bring into awareness the traumas, humiliations, and oppression they have suffered as women; their feelings of helplessness and rage; and their developing insights into the destructive pattern of rigid sex role training.

From studies of individuals and consciousness-raising groups, the author feels that such vigorous efforts on the part of women are necessary if women are to achieve lasting changes within themselves and society—the institutions and men who, for the most part, set policy and run these institutions and who must ultimately relate to the changing role of women.

Some changes in socio-cultural roles are already occurring and with unsettling reactions. Not all women and, certainly, not many men are as yet actively seeking a profound revision of the man-woman relationship, although many members of both sexes have been affected more than they realize. The innate human tendency to resist change, a trait traditionally seen as a defense in the therapeutic endeavors of psychiatrists, is an unavoidable problem.

Many women are not prepared for different and more responsible social roles, and some men are, predictably, threatened by the idea of women acquiring more power and independence. There is also a marked cultural lag in conservative institutions, such as marriage and the law. As in psychotherapy, when a lifelong defense becomes threatened, there may be a period of transition, in which the patient often feels more anxious and upset than before he or she undertook therapy.

Some psychiatrists, such as Odenwald in his book *The Disappearing Sexes* (1965), feel that, without clear-cut sexual distinctions between men and women, the heterosexual ties will be weakened and, as a result of confusion over sexual identity, there will be a rise in homosexuality. The writer, taking a different view, considers the drive toward androgyny as essentially a healthy phenomenon and multidetermined, differing somewhat for each person. What may be lost in the fit of two opposite types of the traditional masculine man and feminine woman will be more than compensated for by the close rapport that can be achieved only by breaking down the enforced barriers of estrangement that culture has erected.

The author postulates that, even as women's socio-cultural role changes and expands in society—so that she achieves more independence, responsibility, and, indeed, maturity—man's role is not diminished but is, in fact, also expanded. Released from the rigid constraints of stereotypical masculine behavior, man becomes freer to express himself more fully. Should he have passive, intuitive, soft, gentle areas in his personality, he need no longer suppress them as weak or unmanly. Instead, these characteristics will be acceptable both to himself and to women, who will be free to express the active, assertive, and dominating aspects of their natures. The point is that if men and women relate more directly and honestly to each other, free of stereotyped roles that diminish their humanity there will be a gain in the richness and potential vitality in both sexual and social relationships.

Implications for the Psychiatrist

It seems extremely important to the writer that psychiatrists use the findings of sex researchers, anthropologists, and others when these data affect current psychiatric theories of personality development and types. Psychiatry has tended to resist change, as does any established institution. The newer understandings of what would be humanly normal rather than culturally normal should be incorporated in the theory and practice of psychiatry.

For example, the evidence that women physiologically are more capable of living an active sexual life in middle and old age than are men may cause one to wonder, in the interests of producing a more satisfying

marital relationship, if the long standing tradition and cultural acceptance of the husband's being older than the wife ought not to be reversed.

It is the writer's feeling that too few psychiatrists, male or female, have realized the extent to which women's mental health has been compromised by the socio-cultural role society has imposed on them, a role that psychiatry has reinforced. By the same token, psychiatry, in accepting man's aggressive role as natural, has failed to understand fully the damage done by exaggerated cultural emphasis on male dominance and power postures. Man's human potential has also been crippled by these assumptions of sex-linked behavior patterns.

Psychiatrists ought to question whether the cultural values are healthy as human values; they also ought to look at the institutions that shape people's lives.

Marriage, as an example, has institutionalized and thereby made rigid the roles that men and women are expected to play. As these roles change, responding to the human needs of individual persons, the expectations and rules of marriage must also change if marriage is to be relevant and congruent with those needs.

What the writer is suggesting is that psychiatry must recognize the fact that institutions need changing as much as people do. Two persons with intrapsychic problems may make a bad marriage, but it is also possible that two reasonably healthy people may suffer in a conventional marriage which may inhibit the growth of the partners or otherwise interfere with healthy self-expression.

REFERENCES

de Beauvoir, S. *The Second Sex.* Knopf, New York, 1952.

Deutsch, H. *The Psychology of Women,* 2 vols. Grune & Stratton, New York, 1944.

Erikson, E. Inner and outer space: reflections on womanhood. Daedalus, *93:* 582, 1964.

*Freud, S. Three essays on the theory of sexuality. In *Standard Edition of the Complete Psychological Works of Sigmund Freud,* vol. 7, p. 219. Hogarth Press, London, 1953.

Freud, S. The claims of psycho-analysis to scientific interest. In *Standard Edition of the Complete Psychological Works of Sigmund Freud,* vol. 13, p. 182. Hogarth Press, London, 1955.

Freud S. On narcissism. In *Standard Edition of the Com-*

plete Psychological Works of Sigmund Freud, vol. 14, p. 88. Hogarth Press, London, 1957.

Freud, S. Some psychical consequences of the anatomical distinction between the sexes. In *Standard Edition of the Complete Psychological Works of Sigmund Freud,* vol. 19, p. 256. Hogarth Press, London, 1961.

Freud, S. Civilization and its discontents. In *Standard Edition of the Complete Psychological Works of Sigmund Freud,* vol. 21, p. 103. Hogarth Press, London, 1961.

Freud, S. Female sexuality. In *Standard Edition of the Complete Psychological Works of Sigmund Freud,* vol. 21, p. 231. Hogarth Press, London, 1961.

Freud, S. The sexual life of human beings. In *Standard Edition of the Complete Psychological Works of Sigmund Freud,* vol. 16, p. 318. Hogarth Press, London, 1963.

Freud, S. An outline of psychoanalysis. In *Standard Edition of the Complete Psychological Works of Sigmund Freud,* vol. 23, p. 155, 193, 250. Hogarth Press, London, 1964.

Freud, S. Analysis terminable and interminable. In *Standard Edition of the Complete Psychological Works of Sigmund Freud,* vol. 23, p. 250. Hogarth Press, London, 1964.

Friedan, B. *The Feminine Mystique.* Norton, New York, 1963.

Greer, G. *The Female Eunuch.* McGraw-Hill, New York, 1971.

Horney, K. Flight from womanhood. Int. J. Psychoanal., *7:* 324, 1926.

Jones, E. *The Life and Work of Sigmund Freud.* Basic Books, New York, 1955.

*Kinsey, A. C., Pomeroy, W. B., and Martin, C. E. *Sexual Behavior in the Human Male.* Saunders, Philadelphia, 1948.

Kinsey, A. C., Pomeroy, W. B., Martin, C. E., and Gebhard, P. H. *Sexual Behavior in the Human Female.* Saunders, Philadelphia, 1953.

Korner, A. Sex differences in newborns with special reference to differences in the organization of oral behavior. J. Child Psychol. Psychistr., *14:* 19, 1973.

*Masters, W. H., and Johnson, V. E. *Human Sexual Response.* Little, Brown, Boston, 1966.

*Mead, M. *Sex and Temperament.* New American Library, New York, 1935.

Millett, K. *Sexual Politics.* Doubleday, New York, 1970.

Odenwald, R. P. *The Disappearing Sexes.* Random House, New York, 1965.

*Sherfey, M. J. *The Nature and Evolution of Female Sexuality.* Random House, New York, 1966.

Sullivan, H. S. *The Interpersonal Theory of Psychiatry.* Norton, New York, 1953.

*Thompson, C. Penis envy in women. Psychiatry, *6:* 123, 1943.

12.2

Cross-Cultural Studies and Animal Studies of Sex

GORDON D. JENSEN, M.D.

Introduction: Other Cultures and Other Species

For most people, sex is a highly personal and even a highly secret matter. Human beings behave as sexual people and few know much about how they got the way they are and why they behave as they do. Many therapists assume that their patterns of sexual behavior and their code of morals are the right ones. This egocentricity and ethnocentricity stands in the way of becoming a good therapist for patients with sexual problems, not to mention slowing down one's own sexual growth and limiting sexual satisfactions.

A broader perspective can be helpful in getting beyond the limitations imposed by one's own personal set on sexual behavior. This section deals with 2 perspectives: other cultures and other species.

There is a lot more to sex than instinct or biological urges. A great deal is primarily learned and culturally transmitted from generation to generation. For example, the most intelligent of the nonhuman primates, the chimpanzee, has one position of intercourse, whereas the human animal with all his intelligence and ingenuity has managed to figure out hundreds (some say over 2,000) of different positions. The favorite ones or sometimes the "proper" ones are a matter of what a person has learned as a participant in his own culture.

But there is also much more to sex than cultural factors. There are the biological or animal aspects, which many people know nothing about, or would like to forget because our particular culture degrades "raw" animal-like sex. For example, the thrusting with intercourse and the orgasm with its automatic convulsive movements are genetically programmed into our physical apparatus. Sexual arousal, for that matter, is an automatic physiological reaction, to some extent not under conscious control; a man cannot usually call forth an erection by thinking about it or wishing it. Rather, whether or not an erection occurs depends on a complexity of feelings, sensations, and psychological stimuli. The incest taboo, a cultural universal, may be in part a heritage passed on through evolution from our primate ancestors. Chimpanzees and monkeys have an incest "taboo," particularly between mothers and sons. In naturally living rhesus monkey groups and chimpanzees, no mother has ever been observed to mate with her sons. If a biological factor does exist, it is still recognized that there is a large learned component of the incest taboo.

It is common to emphasize cultural and learned determinants of sex to the exclusion of the genetic and evolutionarily acquired determinants. However, a combination and synthesis of these provides the most complete understanding.

Anthropology and Sexuality

MORALITY: WHAT IS RIGHT AND WRONG

America is not a single culture; as a nation, it is multiethnic. Generalizations usually refer to the broad middle class of puritan heritage and Protestant ethic. Americans have a curious and atypical moral code about sexual intercourse that profoundly affects the sexuality of its people. In a survey of 250 cultures scattered throughout the world, Murdock (1960) found that the United States is one of three that has the following broad prohibition on sexual intercourse: Sexual intercourse is approved of only in the context of marriage. This blanket prohibition on sexual intercourse outside of marriage is a very unusual restriction of sexual expression. For most people in the world, sex is tied up with many other aspects of living besides marriage, including kinship, special holidays, ceremonies, social status, and reproduction. Since we sanction sexual intercourse only within the narrow bounds of the marriage bed, it is not hard to understand why, in our society, sex in general takes on an air of wrongness or badness.

In contrast to our condemnation of intercourse outside of marriage, we are one of the most permissive in marital sex relations. For example, some societies restrict intercourse of the spouse of a deceased wife or husband and of relatives of the deceased, of a person who is ill, and, in a few cases, relatives of the ill person. We also impose no restriction on intercourse in connection with ceremonies, feasts, and hunting and farming activities as is the custom in many preliterate societies.

What is right or wrong and normal or abnormal in sexual behavior depends on the customs of the country one lives in. Studies of different cultures throughout the world show that there are a lot of ways of loving, that is, courting and copulating. Although it may appear that societies select their patterns of behavior arbitrarily, in fact the patterns develop in connection with the network of customs, traditions, ideas, and beliefs about many aspects of living in the society. Each society develops its own code of morals and each society regards behavior other than that prescribed by this code as unacceptable or deviant. Some societies have a long list of such behaviors and some have a short list. These include such activities as close dancing, certain positions of intercourse, and homosexuality. The deviant behaviors serve to regulate sex in the culture just as the rules of normal behavior are part of the system for regulating sex.

REGULATING SEX

Societies have a problem achieving the proper balance in regulating sex. In the United States, inhibitions and regulations are imposed so that sexual relations will not disrupt the nuclear family structure and so that they will not lead to illegitimate pregnancy or to too much venereal disease.

Moreover, our work-oriented society disapproves of anything suggesting hedonism, and particularly sex, to the point that people might be so satisfied with life that they would not be motivated to work hard. Rather than believing that sexuality invigorates, we have a general notion that sex drains strength and therefore one should not engage in too much of it or at certain times. For example, it is a custom that athletes should not engage in sex before their matches.

A society must not repress and frustrate basic sexual instincts. This has happened to some Irish subcultures and the consequences have been virtually to eliminate sexual satisfaction for most of the population. In Inis Beag, a small island community off the coast of Ireland, late marriage and celibacy are common. At marriage, the average age for men is 36 and for women 25; 29 per cent of eligible men and women are single. All behaviors suggestive of sex, such as dancing and nudity, are highly restricted. Intercourse is perfunctory and female orgasm unknown. In contrast, in a society highly permissive of sexuality such as the Mangaia in the Polynesian islands of the South Pacific 100 per cent of the females achieve orgasm.

SEXUAL RULES FOR WOMEN

In most cultures, rules about sex are especially evident for females. The double standard is pancultural. Females' interest in sex and their participation in sexual behavior is closely regulated by what is culturally appropriate. There are more restrictions on the female sex than the male. For example, there is a common taboo of intercourse during menstruation, lactation, and pregnancy—a prohibition that represents a great deal of a woman's lifetime. However, there are no biological reasons that a woman cannot have intercourse during these times. She is perfectly capable of having orgasm during any of these periods and there is little or no scientific evidence that intercourse at these times is in any way harmful. In some cultures, males are also prohibited from having intercourse at certain times such as before or after hunting, before going to war, or before or after harvesting crops. However, in most monogomous cultures, males are allowed more leniency for extramarital affairs, and may even be allowed to have concubines. In the United States, the feminist movement is expressing considerable resentment over the greater amount of sexual restriction for females. The general tendency seen in all cultures for greater control of female sexual behavior may be but 1 expression of male control of the power in societies.

SEXUAL RULES FOR CHILDREN

Our society is generally horrified at many kinds of sexual behavior that are accepted as perfectly normal in other cultures. For example, American parents are usually very upset when they discover that their children engage in sex play. This is in spite of what Freud taught about infantile sexuality and the fact that child sex play is common enough statistically to be considered normative. It should be reassuring to look at sexual behavior in African and Oceanian cultures, where children are allowed a great deal of sexual freedom. In many of these cultures, children of any age up to puberty are allowed to show open curiosity and imitation of mature sexual behavior. They explore each other's body freely and they imitate sexual intercourse that they have observed adults performing. Children of 4 to 10 years of age actually have intercourse. There is little reason to doubt this, because males of any age are capable of having erections. In cultures where overt childhood sexuality is practiced and accepted, there are apparently no detrimental long term consequences. However, these societies are also permissive about adolescent sexual behavior. It is possible that suppression of infantile and childhood sexuality, as presently practiced in our society, can be harmful for eventual sexual adjustment. As Erikson has pointed out, it is during childhood that permanent personality traits of shame, doubt, and guilt are most easily imposed.

RULES ABOUT HOMOSEXUALITY

In the United States, homosexuality is high on the list of morally wrong behaviors. Many forces, including activist groups, are trying hard to change this. These advocates of sexual freedom would like to convince their society that homosexuality is normal behavior. However, morals are deeply rooted and slow to change. In the United States, the taboos against homosexuality are so great that the behavior is shrouded in discomfort and even fear. Homosexual panic in young men is an example of extreme anxiety. A perspective from other cultures can lead to a calmer view. Certainly the psychiatrist who treats homosexual patients needs to be objective and personally comfortable about homosexuality.

Homosexuality is not universal. In 28 of 76 societies reviewed by Ford and Beach (1951), homosexual activities by adults were either rare, absent, or secret. Although many of these societies have customs or laws that maintain social pressure against homosexuality, this does not always account for its absence. For example, in the Siriono in Bolivia and the Mangaia in the South Seas, two societies in which there is maximal sexual permissiveness from our point of view and minimal social pressure against homosexuality, little or no homosexuality exists.

In 49 of the 76 societies reviewed (68 per cent), homosexuality was accepted to some extent for certain members of the society. In these societies, the homosexual person is generally given a clearly special role. In societies where male homosexual behavior is accepted, as for example in the Siwans of Africa and some of the Australian Aborigine groups, it is generally only one part of sexuality practiced by persons who are predominately heterosexual.

The *berdache* of the Plains Indians and the *bate* of the Crow Indians are examples of the special roles of which homosexuality is one part. These males dress in women's clothes and play the role of a woman. In the Siberian Chukchee, a homosexual man puts on women's clothing and takes the role of a shaman who has high status and supernatural power in a community. In some cases, this person is bisexual.

If the advocates of new sexual freedom are asking that exclusive homosexuality be accepted as entirely normal behavior by people who have usual roles, they are asking for something rather special, even unique. No society exists in which exclusive homosexuals are accepted without being given special roles clearly differentiated from those of heterosexuals; and, even then, the homosexuality aspect of the role is derided.

In all societies, female homosexuality is more accepted than male homosexuality. This suggests the operation of biological factors and inborn differences between the sexes. Possibly, affection and sexual behavior are more closely linked in females than they are in males and, therefore, it is more acceptable for females to participate in homosexual behavior.

In all societies, homosexuality is apparently more common in adolescents than in adults and is more common in males than it is in females. These facts also suggest biological determinants.

SEXUAL DIVERSITY

The same behavior does not mean the same thing in all cultures. For example, in East Africa, a young adult male couple can be seen strolling down the street holding hands. It appears affectionate and is entirely friendly behavior; it has no sexual connotation. However, if two males were seen walking down the street holding hands together in a Western country they would immediately be considered homosexual. A more subtle example is the case of the young Scandinavian woman. In common, ordinary, social interchange her manner of frankness, friendliness, and openness in communication, together with the cultural stereotype of sexual freedom in Scandinavia, lead Americans to believe that she is sexually interested or even promiscuous. Even in our own country, the same behavior has different meanings depending on the subculture group. For example, among some ethnic groups, a kiss and an embrace are common and are simply a friendly greeting, whereas among others these behaviors are reserved as part of sexual behavior. Among youths today, a warm embrace generally means friendliness, but very few adults feel comfortable engaging in this behavior because for them this kind of hugging has sexual connotations.

Sexual variations. In the United States, sexual behaviors that have been called deviations or perversions are being looked upon more liberally and less moralistically, and the word "variations" is increasingly being applied to such behavior patterns as homosexuality, pederasty, pedophilia, voyeurism, exhibitionism, bestiality, transvestism, and fetishism.

Only a few non-Western societies have been studied extensively in regard to social behavior. There is more knowledge about the United States than any other culture. Therefore, it is difficult to make cross-cultural comparisons about the sexual variations. In those preliterate cultures where sexual behavior has been carefully studied, such as the Trobriand Islanders, sexual variations are either rare or unknown. When present, they are treated with contemptuous amusement. Trobrianders ridicule persons who engage in sexual variations and make them the subjects of invective and comic anecdotes. Presumably, these attitudes are intended to reduce the frequency of sexual variations.

Sexual inadequacy or sexual dysfunction. In preliterate cultures, the incidence of sexual dysfunctions such as impotence, premature ejaculation, and nonorgasmic females is probably very low. At least, very few of these dysfunctions, so well known in Western culture, are mentioned in anthropologists' studies. One exception is the Mangaian society, where impotence is recognized as a "disease" and is said to be common. In this society, as in the United States, sexual intercourse is highly performance oriented, which could have etiological significance.

The relative infrequency of sexual dysfunction in other cultures is surprising in view of the fact that it is so prevalent in the United States. Masters and Johnson (1970) estimate that 50 per cent of American marriages are sexually dysfunctional or imminently so. Perhaps anthropologists have not looked at sexuality in terms of the many kinds of sexual inadequacies, or possibly what we consider an inadequacy may not be important to people of other cultures. For example, on the Irish island of Inis Beag, all women are nonorgasmic but, perhaps because they do not know about orgasm, they do not consider it a problem. If, however, sexual dysfunction is indeed rare in preliterate societies, we might look for the role of culture and our attitudes in producing the sexual dysfunctions so troublesome in our society.

Gender role. Most cultures have clear expectations of what males and females should do. Expectations begin at birth and continue through the years of primary and secondary education. An analysis of the readers currently used in the United States elementary schools shows a striking bias in terms of what little boys can do and are competent at in contrast to little girls. The stories portray boys as independent and capable in contrast to girls who stay at home with mother and need help, even to roller skate. Most of our adult roles for males and females are narrowly defined. For example, in the United States, males traditionally do not expect to clean house, wash dishes, and take care of the children. However, access to occupations by both sexes is beginning to be liberalized with the passage of the Civil Rights Act in 1964.

It has recently been established that males can be airline stewards and can compete with female airline stewardesses, and more females feel it is possible to enter the professions of medicine. Our society still has no acceptable roles for the transvestite, the homosexual, or even the feminine male, with the exception of some of the art and dance professions.

Some societies that define gender role very narrowly have built-in, specific, identified roles for males who do not or cannot fit into the expected role. The Plains Indians offered several options for males who did not want to join the ranks of the adult males, those who were total warriors oriented toward killing other men, collecting scalps, and capturing women and horses. LaBarre (1971) describes the Plains Indian's alternative:

At puberty, he set out on a long vision-quest, to fast and pray for four days and nights, so that (he hoped) he would obtain "medicine power": a kind of packaged virility that would help him carry out his various male roles. If he was lucky he actually got this package, i.e., his "medicine bundle" of supernatural magical malehood. Perhaps he would find a feather or a strange-looking stone or bone, or a weasel would run by and he would shoot it for his medicine-bundle container. The Blackfoot actually had so many medicine bundles that they constituted the major wealth that was traded back and forth in the tribe for other commodities. There was a variation to this pattern: Some men got medicine power, not to kill, but to cure. These individuals became "medicine men," or shamans, and they could do everything from curing wounds, discovering the persons causing disease, and sucking out disease-producing objects to seeing the enemy impossibly far off in space or distant in future time, supernaturally protecting the war party, and controlling the weather. There were only two kinds of male gender-role in the Plains: warrior and medicine-man.

In actual fact, there was still a third kind of male, the "not-man," or *berdache.* Lewis and Clark and other early explorers and scouts gave us many accounts of the *berdache* in the tribes they encountered. Many thought that they were "hermaphrodites" or at least sexually perverse, when as a matter of fact they were not necessarily either. The *berdache,* or not-man, was first and foremost only a social transvestite. That is, he wore women's clothes and performed women's roles. His "not-man" status of not being either a warrior or a medicine-man was announced simply by his wearing women's clothes. Like everyone else, he knew perfectly well the male gender-role, but he had a stubborn preference for his own gender-orientation. Psychologically, it is fairly easy to explain the *berdache* to a generation that can imagine other things a male might do besides (a) going off to be killed in Vietnam and (b) collecting a lot of green paper.

Traits that we usually think of as masculine and feminine are characteristic behaviors matching the culturally defined roles of the sexes. There is no doubt that most masculine and feminine behaviors are learned; there are numerous examples of this in various cultures. However, the most striking demonstration occurs when a person is assigned an incorrect gender identity at birth and is raised contrary to his genetic and anatomical sex. Gender identity becomes so well fixed early in life that by 2 or 3 years of age it is nearly impossible or unsatisfactory to change gender identity even when the sexual assignment was incorrect.

Diversity of sexual behavior. Although there are many commonalities across cultures in courtship rituals and the physical aspects of sexual behavior, societies tend to develop customs that limit certain expressions of sexuality and permit others only under certain circumstances. For example, some societies discourage or prohibit intercourse during menstruation, lactation, and pregnancy. This has been true to some extent in our own society, although such restrictions are gradually being eased. In some preliterate societies, anal intercourse (sodomy) is a part of the initiation rituals of adolescent males.

Positions of intercourse have been controlled to some extent by custom. It is hard to believe that 100 years ago in the United States intercourse with the male on top was considered just about the only correct position. It is called the missionary position because, supposedly, American missionaries in the South Sea Islands were shocked at seeing the natives perform intercourse sitting up or in other unfamiliar positions and told them that the proper position was the man on top. In this country, various intercourse positions are beginning to be accepted as entirely proper, even though there are still laws against them. For example, at present, the rear entry position ("dog position") is considered entirely normal.

Handling and mouthing of the partner's genitals, the most widespread type of precopulatory behavior, is acceptable in most cultures. However, not so many years ago, oral sexuality was considered abnormal in the United States and even today laws against it remain in effect in nearly every state. However, in spite of this, oral sex is now considered a normal part of lovemaking. Americans are approaching the point of view that anything in sex is normal and acceptable if it is done by mutual consenting people. However, myths, beliefs, and customs take a long time to change and it is not surprising that some people in today's society feel painfully guilty about oral sex.

Our culture tends to consider males the initiators of sexual activity, but this is not always the case, even in our culture, nor is it true in all cultures. For example, Trobriand Island women may go on ceremonial escapades into another village seeking out males. They also may form into groups for making orgastic assaults on men. Malinowski (1929) described it:

If they perceive a stranger, a man from any village but their own, passing within sight, they have the customary right to attack him, a right which by all accounts they exercise with zeal and energy.

The man is the fair game of the women for all that sexual violence, obscene cruelty, filthy pollution, and rough handling can do to him. Thus first they pull off and tear up his pubic leaf, the protection of his modesty and, to a native, the symbol of his manly dignity. Then, by masturbatory practices and exhibitionism, they try to produce an erection in their victim and, when their manoeuvres have brought about the desired result, one of them squats over him and inserts his penis into her vagina. After the first ejaculation he may be treated in the same manner by another woman. Worse things are to follow. Some of the women will defecate and micturate all over his body, paying special attention to his face, which they pollute as thoroughly as they can. "A man will vomit, and vomit, and vomit," said a sympathetic informant. Sometimes these furies rub their genitals against his nose and mouth, and use his fingers and toes, in fact, any projecting part of his body, for lascivious purposes. The natives from the north are very much amused by this custom, which they despise or affect to despise. They love to enter into details, and to demonstrate by convincing mimicry. Local informants from the south confirmed this account in all essentials. They were by no means ashamed of their custom, regarding it rather as a sign of the general virility of the district, and passing on any possible opprobrium to the stranger-victims.

Trends in morality. In every culture, reproduction has been highly valued and for obvious survival reasons. The reproductive drive, has no doubt been passed on to man in the course of evolution from lower animals. In the past few years, we have witnessed the first challenge in history to this time-honored cultural universal. Many young people have decided not to have children or are at least questioning what was once standard practice. At no time in our history has reproduction been so little valued. Many youths take the prospect of world catastrophic overpopulation seriously. A change away from valuing reproduction should have major consequences for our views of sexuality. One possibility is a shifting of greater value onto sexual behavior per se for pleasure rather than for reproduction.

Premarital intercourse is accepted in a majority of societies (70 per cent of 250 reviewed by Murdock, 1960). In those societies where it is not accepted, the main reason has been concern about pregnancy out of wedlock. In the past decade, new contraceptives have removed this concern for many people. Today, more youths in America are having premarital intercourse than was true a decade ago. In the past decade in Denmark, premarital intercourse has risen to an incidence

of about 9 per cent and it might be expected to approach this level in America. Sexual freedom in the United States is increasing, and there will be increasing permissiveness regarding premarital intercourse. This does not mean more promiscuity. As Reiss (1971) has shown, the trend of youth is toward "permissiveness with affection." It is also likely to become permissiveness with contraception.

Animal Studies and Human Sexuality

Much of human social and sexual behavior is the product of the slow process of evolution. Man shares some patterns of behavior with all mammals, the most striking of which is nursing of young. However, one can find parallels in human sexual behavior as well. When human behavior is viewed in the perspective of evolution, one can better understand how man came to be the way he is today.

A CONCEPT FROM ETHOLOGY: SEXUAL RELEASERS

The male stickleback fish is sexually attracted by the red color on the belly of the female. He will direct his copulatory behavior toward any spot that resembles this, even if it is an artificial one painted on a rock or a ball. The red color releases his sexual response. Sexual releasers also operate in primates. For example, baboon and chimpanzee females show a prominant swelling of their genital region during estrus, the sexually receptive period of their cycle. The swollen genitals, their light pink color and the odor eminating from the vagina are all powerful sexual attractants to the male. (It is not certain whether males have physical releasers that attract females, but they have courtship behaviors that attract.)

The human female also has clearly visible physical characteristics that act like sexual releasers. These include the breasts, red lips, the hips, and perfume or sometimes natural body odors that have the same effect. Although the breasts are not covered in all societies, they generally always have erotic qualities. However, this may be suppressed by cultural taboos. In all but a few societies, the vulva is covered. This is true even in societies where the males are entirely naked. This sug-

FIGURE 1. A male baboon (right) sits near the sex swelling of his estrous female with whom he is in consort relationship (at the Gombe Stream National Park, photo by J. R. Morris).

gests that the vulva also has powerful sexual releasing qualities. Certain female behaviors or postures are also sexual releasers. One example is the legs spread apart. Most cultures require that females keep their legs together and not expose their genitals except under the most restricted circumstances. In almost all mammals, exposure of the genitals by a receptive female is an invitation for sex.

EFFECTS OF CROWDED LIVING CONDITIONS ON MICE

Calhoun (1973) has shown the detrimental effects of crowding and overpopulation on sexual behavior and survival of mice. When the population rose to the point that no space for new groups was left, young mice tried to join existing groups. The defending male of a group rejected many of these newcomers and,

in the process, wore himself out from the added stress. When he stopped defending the territory, the adult females took over. They became abnormally aggressive in order to exclude mice attempting to join their group in their space. This aggressiveness generalized to their own young. They killed some young, raised some normally, and attacked and rejected others. When these mice grew up, their behavior was grossly abnormal. They did not develop affective bonds, there was a fragmentation and loss of behavior patterns, and some appeared to be autistic-like, passive, and withdrawn. They did not show courting behaviors, did not mate, and therefore did not conceive and produce young. After a few months, the entire colony became extinct. There does not appear to be a human parallel to this experiment but, conceivably, elements of this process will be seen in man under conditions of comparable runaway population growth leading to severe overcrowding.

FAMILY PATTERNS OF SEXUALITY

Of all the species of nonhuman primates, the chimpanzee most closely resembles man and genetically is his closest primate relative. It is for this reason that studies of chimpanzee behavior are particularly relevant for understanding human behavior. Although man is not an ape, both share common ancestors; thus, human sexual behavior is basically determined by some of the same processes that govern such behavior in the primates living today. There are some major differences between sexuality of man and nonhuman primates, one of the most striking of which is the continual receptivity of human females, not found in any other primate. However, such differences do not negate the value of the similarities in pointing up possible evolutionarily acquired characteristics in man.

In her observations of the wild chimpanzees, van Lawick-Goodall (1971) mentioned the great differences in the way that two adolescent females acted when they first became fully sexually mature and were approached by males. One, Fefe, became very sexually active as soon as she completed puberty; she copulated eagerly with all interested males. Another, Pooch, was initially very frightened by the males' aggressive sexual approaches. These differences may be related to certain characteristics of their mothers. Fefe's mother, Flo, was one of the highest ranking females in the dominance hierarchy and, although she was physically very ugly, she was one of the most sexually desirable and sought-after females in the chimpanzee community. Pooch's mother was

FIGURE 2. Typical position of baboons copulating; the male mounted on the female (photo by J. R. Morris).

FIGURE 3. A typical interaction between a consort pair. The female baboon presents her genitals to the male who grooms her (photo by J. R. Morris).

not known and probably died when Pooch was about 6 years old. Possibly Flo's high rank, self-confidence, and sexual desirability were acquired by her daughter. It has been observed in monkey societies that offspring tend to assume the rank of their mothers. These data are insufficient to generalize, and more observations of situations like this will be necessary before it can be definitely established that daughters acquire sexual behavior characteristics from their mothers. If so, they are no doubt acquired through learning. Human mothers may transmit sexual patterns to their daughters.

PRECOCIOUSNESS OF SEXUAL BEHAVIOR

There appears to be a striking precociousness of sexual behavior in primates. Puberty in chimpanzees occurs at about 8 to 10 years of age, but by one year of age the male chimpanzee has acquired nearly his full repertoire of sexual and copulatory behaviors and is seen practicing them on females of all ages. In the United States, many people are surprised by the sexual curiosity and imitative sexual behaviors of preschool children, and parents and other authorities punish this behavior, encourage its repression, and induce guilt over it. It is not at all far-fetched to regard such experiences as a source of lifelong guilt, sexual inhibition, and a decrease of any kind of sensuousness in regard to sexual expression.

OLFACTION IN PRECOITAL BEHAVIOR

Male monkeys and apes often sniff the female genitals prior to copulation. They may also insert a finger into the vulva or vagina and smell it. Experimental studies have shown that the odors emitted from the vulva are very powerful sexual excitants to the male. If the active chemical, which is a fatty acid, is painted on the genitalia of a female monkey who is not in the sexually receptive period of her cycle (estrus), the male is attracted to copulate as if the female were in full estrus. Many human males find cunnilingus highly sexually arousing. It is thus not surprising that the odor and possibly the taste of the vulva operate on the human male in much the same way that they do in the primates and by a similar chemical-neural mechanism.

INHIBITION OF SEXUAL BEHAVIOR

The sexual behavior of male monkeys has been found to be inhibited when they are confronted with a higher ranking male alongside the female they desire. The same male alone with a receptive female would copulate freely, but he is totally inhibited when a high ranking male is introduced. There may be a parallel in instances of human sexual inadequacy, particularly in the case of impotence. This could arise because the human being has a unique ability to fantasize and fantasies can contribute sexually inhibitory affects such as anxiety and fear. A fantasy involving a more dominant person of either sex could have an inhibiting effect comparable to that which the monkey experiences in the actual presence of a higher ranking animal. Fantasies may be a major cause of sexual inhibition through their triggering of fears of inadequacy, which Masters and Johnson (1970) have identified as the greatest deterrent to effective sexual functioning.

PROMISCUITY

Promiscuity is a normal pattern for female primates. Van Lawick-Goodall (1968) has observed a female chimpanzee copulate a dozen times with a dozen different males in the same number of minutes. On the other hand, chimpanzees and other monkeys may be selective of mates and are often very private in their consort and copulatory behavior. A chimpanzee couple may disappear for a week or longer during the female's period of sexual receptivity. In man, the consort pattern has been extended by marriage customs. Other cultural traditions discourage any remaining evolutionarily acquired inclinations to promiscuity. However, without marriage exerting a controlling force, it is expected that a human female will engage in sex with several male partners, a behavior that some would label promiscuous.

SECRECY

A consorting pair of chimpanzees is entirely secretive in their sexual behavior. Monkeys and baboons in consort relationships are less secretive, but the social organization of these species demands that all members of the troop always stay within close visual range of each other. Although secrecy during copulation is already developed, to some extent, in the nonhuman primate, it is most highly developed in man and it is virtually a cultural universal. Possibly the reason for this is that human beings are exceptionally sensitive to extraneous stimuli when they engage in sexual behavior. The male can lose his erection when disturbed by a

FIGURE 4. A common courtship gesture of the male chimpanzee; arm extended tugging at a branch; knees apart; erect penis fully visible; posture and gaze directed at the receptive female in foreground. The female generally responds by approaching and sexually presenting to the male (at the Gombe Stream National Park, photo by M. J. A. Simpson).

FIGURE 5. A male chimpanzee touches and inspects the genitalia of a female (photo by Gombe Stream Research Center).

door slam or lights being turned on. Perhaps the main function of seclusion is to reduce distracting stimuli, and cultural taboos serve to reinforce seclusion behavior.

EFFECTS OF EARLY EXPERIENCE

Many primate studies point to the first year of life as crucial for the sex differentiation. Harlow and Harlow (1967) have shown dramatically how infant monkeys raised in isolation for the first 6 months of life develop severely disturbed emotional behaviors and are totally inadequate sexually when they grow up. Rehabilitation of these animals, severely damaged by social isolation in the first half year of life, has been partially successful through the use of younger infant monkeys. Simply allowing the deprived infant monkey to be in the same cage with the younger "therapist" monkey for 1 hour per day facilitates the development of normal play and social behavior and diminishes the frequency of autistic and withdrawn behavior. The crucial factor in the rehabilitation is an infant who has a less complex repertoire of behavior that is less threatening than an agemate. This principle may have important implications for therapy of human childhood behavior disorders.

GENDER ROLE DIFFERENTIATION

This takes place prenatally as well as postnatally. Parallel studies in the monkey and the human being demonstrate the prenatal effects of hormones. Goy (1970) injected pregnant mother monkeys with high doses of androgen and produced female infants who were physically pseudohermaphroditic. Behaviorally, they showed a number of male behavior traits such as rough-and-

FIGURE 6. Picture taken immediately after Figure 5. The male smells the finger he has used for inspection of the genitalia (photo by Gombe Stream Research Center).

FIGURE 7. The typical position of chimpanzees copulating. The female (crouching) emits a unique vocalization heard only with copulation as she shows a grinning face (photo by Gombe Stream Research Center).

tumble play. Ehrhardt (1973) studied human females who had been exposed to excessive amounts of androgen in utero because their mothers had been administered hormones to prevent miscarriage. These female children developed significantly greater amounts of masculine play and masculine interests compared to normal control subjects. They also showed slightly higher I.Q.s than the control subjects.

A REPRODUCTIVE SEASON

Most nonhuman primates have a sexual season or mating season, which means that most births also occur seasonally. The determining factors are not known, but the weather is probably most important. Man has an apparent continual sexuality throughout all seasons. In spite of this, it has been recently found that human beings show a slight but significant tendency toward seasonality of birth. The yearly variation in peak of birth throughout the world suggests that the tendency toward human seasonality is determined by meteorological factors. That is, the two hemispheres of the earth have opposite seasons and have corresponding opposite peaks of birth.

SEXUAL VARIATIONS

Although homosexual behavior has been seen in primates living in captivity, it is virtually absent in naturally living primates. Mounting behavior is frequent among monkeys and apes of the same sex, but this is not necessarily a sexual behavior. Mounting can be a greeting, a dominance display, or it can be a part of copulatory behavior. However, the complete repertoire of copulatory behavior including anal intromission has never been observed in naturally living primates.

EXHIBITIONISM

A certain amount of exhibitionism is normal, and most of it is satisfied in socially acceptable ways. Females dress in ways to expose sexually stimulating amounts of legs, breasts, and so on. Males wear pants fitted so that their genital and body shapes can be seen. However, few people have the impulse to expose their naked genitals to total strangers as do exhibitionists. The exhibitionist gets sexual stimulation and gratification from exposing himself or herself, and the observers often do, too. Male exhibitionists describe an inexplicable urge to display their penis. In addition to producing sexual excitement, it gives them a feeling of power of sexually influencing the observers.

One primate species, the squirrel monkey, has a clear pattern of penile display that is a part of male-male dominance behavior. The chimpanzee uses penile display sexually. In one courtship gesture, he displays a swaggering upright gait with an erect penis as he approaches a receptive female. He may also sit with legs spread apart displaying his erect penis to a receptive female who then will approach him for copulation. In nonsexual situations he may also have a clearly visible erection. For example, at the feeding area he arrives with his hair erect, a confident gait, and an erection, bright pink and up to 6 inches long. The erection lasts anywhere from 10 seconds to 20 minutes. The feeding situation is one in which dominance and confidence occurs. It is not known what effects the erect penis has aside from the other dominance display behaviors on his chimpanzee observers, but possibly it enhances the overall effect.

The human male exhibitionist uses his display to shock and excite his female observer. It gives him a feeling of power. Yet, unlike the monkey or ape, he does not use it in the context of pursuing his sexual approach to intercourse. Rather, the act of exhibitionism is used for sexual release. In this respect, there is no counterpart of the behavior in a nonhuman primate.

THE ROLE OF DOMINANCE IN PRIMATE SEXUALITY

In baboon troops, the young adults and adolescents must wait until the full adult males have had their choice of sexually receptive females. More dominant males may displace subordinate ones from their consort relationship with a female in estrus. When a group of chimpanzees copulate with an estrus female, there is a suggestion that the higher ranking males precede the lower ranking males. In man, status is the equivalent of animal dominance. In human societies, status also plays a role in males' accessibility to desirable females. In those societies where there are exceptions to the incest taboo, it has been by the persons of the highest status, namely, nobility or ruling class. This includes the Inca royal family and the old Hawaiian aristocracy in which there was preference for marriage between brother and sister.

REFERENCES

Calhoun, J. B. Death squared: The explosive growth and demise of a mice population. Proc. R. Soc. Med. *6:* 80, 1973.

Ehrhardt, A. A. Maternalism in fetal hormonal and related syndromes. In *Contemporary Sexual Behavior:* J. Zubin and J. Money, editors. Johns Hopkins Press, Baltimore, 1973.

*Ford, C. C., and Beach, F. A. *Patterns of Sexual Behavior.* Ace Books, New York, 1951.

Goy, R. W. Experimental control of psychosexuality. Philos. Trans. R. Soc. Lond. Biol. Sci., *259:* 149, 1970.

Harlow, H., and Harlow M. The young monkeys. In *Readings in Developmental Psychology Today.* CRM Books, Del Mar, Calif. 1967.

Jensen, G. D. Primate sexual behavior: Its relevance to human sexual behavior. Med. Asp. Hum. Sex., *6:* 112, 1972.

*Jensen, G. D. Human sexual behavior in primate perspective. In *Contemporary Sexual Behavior: Critical Issues in the 1970's,* J. Zubin and J. Money, editors. Johns Hopkins Press, Baltimore, 1973.

Karlin, A. *Sexuality and Homosexuality.* W. W. Norton, New York, 1971.

LaBarre, W. Anthropological perspectives on sexuality. In *Sexuality: A Search for Perspective,* D. L. Grummon and A. M. Barclay, editors, p. 38. Van Nostrand Reinhold, New York, 1971.

Lieberman, B. *Human Sexual Behavior: A Book of Readings,* pp. 289-357. John Wiley, New York, 1971.

*Malinowski, B. *The Sexual Life of Savages.* Harcourt, Brace and World, New York, 1929.

*Marshall, D. S., and Suggs, R. C., editors. *Human Sexual Behavior.* Prentice-Hall, Englewood Cliffs, N. J. 1971.

Masters, W. H., and Johnson, V. E. *Human Sexual Inadequacy.* Little, Brown, Boston, 1970.

Mead, M. *Male and Female.* Dell Publishing Co., New York, 1949.

*Murdock, G. P. *Social Structure,* p. 260. Macmillan, New York, 1960.

Reiss, I. L. Premarital sex codes: The old and the new. In *Sexuality: A Search for Perspective,* D. L. Grummon and A. M. Barclay, editors. Van Nostrand Reinhold, New York, 1971.

Van Lawick-Goodall, J. *The Behavior of Free-living Chimpanzees in the Gombe Stream Reserve.* Anim. Behav. Monog., vol. 1 (part 3), 1968.

Van Lawick-Goodall, J. *In the Shadow of Man,* p. 180. Houghton Mifflin, Boston, 1971.

*Wickler, W. Socio-sexual signals and their introspecific imitation among primates. In *Primate Ethology,* D. Morris, editor, p. 89. Doubleday, New York, 1969.

13.1 ## Sex and Surgical Procedures in the Male

HANS H. ZINSSER, M.D.

Introduction

Surgical procedures threaten potency, fertility, and excretory control. Many of the procedures are urological, but the general surgeon as well as the urologist may stray into areas that impair one or more of these functions.

Each operative procedure may have unusual medical and surgical complications, depending on route and type of operation, which may vastly affect the self-image of the patient and the reflected image imposed by the environment on the patient. An example is the sudden loss of dignity and social sanction caused by fecal or urinary incontinence in the elderly. Similar sanctions within some ethnic groups are imposed on the infertile couple, whatever the cause of the infertility. One husband with excellent sexual function and high sperm levels was given a rough time on the job because his wife was a habitual aborter. This hazing led to considerable loss of confidence in the husband, who required steady reassurance. His self-confidence was finally restored and the nagging was stopped by his wife's first full term pregnancy.

The framework of such interactions is complex even when no surgery is involved, but when a conscious decision by the patient and often his spouse or close relatives is involved, doubts, guilt, recrimination, and even hate appear.

The surgeon, as a key figure in bringing on the loss of function, has to weigh benefits and possible losses, but he usually accepts more readily than the patient the dysfunctions involved. The surgeon usually does not knowingly or willingly jeopardize potency, fertility, or excretory control except to save the patient's life. Occasionally, he may hesitate to explain to the patient the life-threatening nature of the disease, and this silence leaves the patient with a mutilation difficult for him to accept. When such losses occur as unusual or unexpected accidents in the course of usually benign procedures, malpractice suits are common, and the depth of resentment against the surgeon by the patients is amplified by the legal profession.

Sterilization
CASTRATION

This operation, carrying with it the certainty of loss of fertility. can have profound depressing effects on a man of any age. Before puberty, the lack of testicular androgen can lead to exaggerated long-bone growth, eunuchoid facies, and small genitalia, in themselves sources of anxiety. Androgen replacement judiciously administered brings about salutary secondary sexual characteristics and allows normal potency.

After puberty, castration does not reverse male characteristics, and such eunuchs are usually potent, since adrenal androgen output is adequate. With the implantation of testicular protheses, a sexual partner may be led to believe that the patient is intact. The man after 60 usually accepts infertility cheerfully—but not impotence.

The diseases requiring castration as therapy are malignancies that are fanned in the fire of testicular androgen, just as is potency. Even medical castration by the administration of estrogen carries the consequences of surgical castration.

Castration can be carried out by ligation of the vas and cord structures and amputation below. More desirably, the surgeon can explain to the patient that he is going to remove only the hormone-producing portion and remove the testicular pulp intracapsulary, leaving the tunica, epididymis, and vas intact in the scrotum as a prosthesis. The patient is left with what on casual examination appears to be moderately atrophic testes.

The castrated man is likely to be severely depressed immediately after the operation. How big a contribution to this depression comes from the knowledge that serious disease is involved, how much from the loss of fertility, how much from the foreknowledge of impotence, and how much from acute male hormone withdrawal are matters difficult to quantitate.

A contrasting situation produced by excessive androgen or gonadotrophin administration resulting in sterility (the male pill) is accompanied by increased sexual desire, entirely satisfactory intercourse, and much patient satisfaction. At the termination of such therapy, vasomotor episodes, mental depression, and feelings of muscular weakness and temporary loss of potency occur almost uniformly, in a close approximation of female menopausal symptoms. All these symptoms disappear in about 2 months as normal testicular function returns. Patients with initially low sperm counts take longer to return to the pretreatment level of fertility. Occasionally, a rebound to higher sperm counts can occur.

VASECTOMY

With increasing social pressure to limit family size, adverse publicity given the pill, and the acknowledged failure rates of the intrauterine device, diaphragm, and foams, male sterilization by means of vasectomy is becoming more popular (see Figure 1). The acceptance by the men undergoing the operation is greater than the social acceptance of the patient by the society as a whole. Similar couples have a much higher regard for the man who insists that his wife use a contraceptive than for one who meekly undergoes vasectomy (Rodgers et al., 1965, 1967).

Because of the poor prognosis for reversibility (25 per cent), an in-depth interview with both partners is essential before any major step is taken.

There is abundant evidence that patients who already have difficulties with sexual function before vasectomy are likely (5 per cent) to have increasing difficulties postoperatively. A smaller number have alleviation of sexual dysfunction when that dysfunction was in any part due to fear of impregnation.

To avoid pregnancies after a vasectomy, the man must have adequate follow-up with at least 2 entirely sperm-free semen specimens on record. Histological proof of vasectomy by submission of the excised tissue gives patients and the physician greater reassurance about the success of the procedure.

Spontaneous reanastomosis is extremely rare but has been reported, and this possibility should be communicated to the patient. The psychological effect of knowing that the male childbearing years are ended can lead to depression akin to the familiar situation in menopausal women.

Disorders of Ejaculation

RETROGRADE EJACULATION

Many operative procedures lead to retrograde ejaculation, procedures such as prosta-

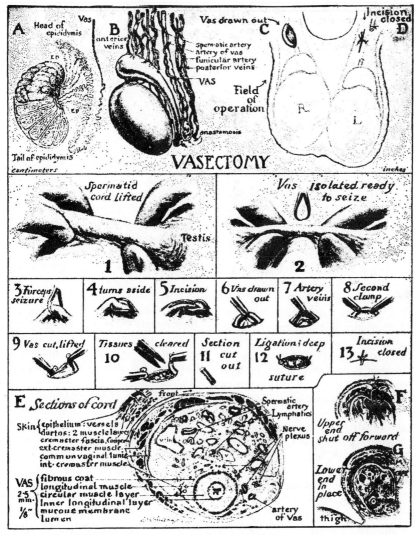

FIGURE 1. The increase in the number of vasectomies performed is related to the ease of the procedure, which can be done in the physician's office under local anesthesia in about 30 minutes to 1 hour. The technique and anatomy of vasectomy are illustrated. (From Dickinson, R. L. *Atlas of Human Sex Anatomy*, ed. 2. Williams & Wilkins, Baltimore, 1949.)

tectomy by either the suprapubic, retropubic, or transurethral route. Extensive dissections at the posterior bladder wall can lead to retrograde ejaculation or even absent ejaculation. The man with retrograde ejaculation complains of losing the urethral phase of orgasm but is usually reconciled to the idea of the infertility accompanying this condition by the life-threatening nature of the initial pathology, be it prostatic or testicular.

Dibenzyline phenoxybenzamine can also produce this condition (Phoenix, 1973).

ABSENT EJACULATION

In the course of aneurysm repair, back fusion, or sympathectomy for hypertension, the fourth lumbar sympathetic ganglion may be damaged, resulting in ejaculatory impotence. The condition arises unexpectedly in the postoperative period. The impact on the patient is violent and intractable. The bitterness and vengefulness of these patients toward their surgeons is only matched by that of women suffering from vesicovaginal fistula. The lesion, as far as is known, is irreversible and leads to long standing frustration and depression.

Disorders of Potency Secondary to Surgical Procedures

In cases of impotence of whatever cause, the honest assurance by the physician that he can truly help everyone can often be the turning point in the management of a recalcitrant man who feels he has been ruined by his surgeon.

Perineal prostatectomy or radical prostatectomy by any route carries a high incidence of impotence and, in some unfortunate cases, loss of urinary control because of damage to the perineal nerves and their branches. These complications are not well accepted by patients and reinforce the impression that they are falling into senescent decline. Depression is profound, and patients strive desperately for any procedure holding out any hope for repair.

The perineal plication operation originally invented for Diamond Jim Brady carries a good chance of restoring potency for impotence of neural or vascular origin. Although less satisfactory for incontinence, it is the therapy of first recourse. Implantation of a silicone splint in the penis or fitting the patient with an external dildo (some are even equipped with vibrators) is to be preferred only for very poor-risk patients.

Frank discussion of the risks of the operation rarely makes acceptance of abrupt impotence any more likely. The loss of the penis as an offensive weapon is difficult for many men—who view it as such— to accept.

Loss of the uterine cervix was once thought to interfere with the capacity for orgasm in hysterectomized women (Munnell, 1947). Although we know now that this is not the case, the destruction of the perineal nerves in poorly planned clitoral recessions certainly does result in loss of sensitivity and a frustrating situation in women whose original adrenogenital syndrome already posed a threat to their developing womanhood. With painstaking understanding in these women, alternate trigger areas for sexual stimulation can usually be found.

For carcinoma of the penis or urethra, amputation of the penis and dissection of associated nodes is usually the treatment of choice. The procedures are not well accepted by most men, and a marked change in attitude after the operation is the rule. Most men who have lost their penises involuntarily are anxious, for even after extensive and often unsatisfactory reconstructive plastic surgery they are acutely ashamed of their altered genital profile.

The loss of social face and masculinity in war-induced amputations ("Vietcong circumcision") has been a powerful propaganda weapon. The incidence of suicide in this group of victims has been high.

Quite the reverse is true when amputation has been at the patient's own hands. Usually, complete self-immolation with amputation of penis and scrotum is performed, often with surprisingly little blood loss. The underlying guilt is relieved by the amputation, and the patient feels enobled and inspired by his change. An analogy can be made to the changes in John Jay Chapman, who burned his right hand after accidentally killing a close friend (Goldfield and Glick, 1973).

The response to penile inversion (the Christine Jorgenson operation) in true transsexuals is extremely gratifying. They have battled with physicians, psychiatrists, surgeons, and peers for the right to assume what they are convinced is their true mission in life, to be women. Their breasts have been built up by estrogen and silicone, their androgen output dropped by orchiectomy, and, after vaginal construction, they put up with temporary and long term discomfort willingly. These patients have, in almost all cases, had a trial of conventional homosexual life and found sodomy to be unrewarding, unesthetic, and demeaning. Many of them have earned the price of the operation by putting on the public as topless go-go dancers.

After a lifetime of living without a penis, owing to an overzealous circumcision, a patient presented himself to a urologist after a transurethral resection had severed his external sphincter. He had a weeping excoriated scrotum with a normally placed urethral stump at the top of the scrotum. The urologist's primary purpose was to produce a penile conduit that would serve as a basis for a clamp to make the patient continent. After the second operation—which had an excellent cosmetic result, although the penis was functionally inadequate—the patient developed extreme modesty about his newfound apparatus. His wife, virginal to this time, developed extreme anxiety, lest this penis become potent and she be subjected to sexual contact. The patient's severe cardiac status made this possibility highly unlikely, and she was reassured. Without a silicone implant, potency in reconstructed penises is, at present, impossible.

With an attack of priapism, which is usually due to underlying hematological disease (sicklemia is the most common), the untreated patient is left with a fibrotic, painful, and distorted penis. The most effective early treatment involves end-to-side shunt of the saphenous vein to the evacuated corpora cavernosa. This procedure results in impotence unless pressure is applied to the shunt. Some positions in intercourse apply such pressure, and manual pressure can be used to restore erection in all positions.

Ostomies

The attitude of patients to the permanent placement of an abdominal stoma is universally one of horror. The assault on human dignity and body image is severe. The loss of a breast can be overcome, since the erogenous component of nipple stimulation is a minor one. But the attachment of a collecting device, however artfully disguised under clothing, leaves no retreat in the bedchamber.

COLOSTOMY

The usual placement of the stoma in the left upper quadrant, the potential with constipating diets, and the option of daily irrigation to yield a dry colostomy make adjustment to this procedure the best of any stoma operations. The colostomy is, however, usually performed for serious conditions of the rectum; if the rectum has been resected by the combined abdominoperineal approach, damage to the perineal nerves and the perivesical plexus is common, and disorders of potency in the man and of orgasm in both sexes occur.

ILEOSTOMY

Whether used as a urinary conduit or to bypass the colon, the ileum functions as a continuously draining stoma that needs a continual collecting device. By presenting a continuously wet surface, the stoma makes normal sexual contact messy. The victims of these stomas are a remarkably well adjusted group and are much reinforced by a self-help association that reviews and invents stratagems to deal with their new life pattern. One route of adjustment is to give the stoma a personality, often a nickname, and speak of the ileostomy fondly, almost as of a wayward child who must be catered to and humored. On the other hand, the continuous care that this type of stoma demands changes many of these patients into emotional cripples, demanding and, in many instances, unable to give any real measure of love. A new ileostomy reservoir which can be drained by catheter every 8 hours with subsequent improvement in social acceptance has been developed by Nils Krock.

Renal Transplant

The association of peripheral neuritis with uremia, even with dialysis therapy, may underlie the loss of potency that accompanies severe renal disease. This loss of potency may trigger the loss of libido that persists even after successful renal transplant (Levy, 1973). The adjustment of women is vastly better than that of men, but some loss of sexual response is apparent.

REFERENCES

Goldfield, M. D., and Glick, I. D. Self-mutilation of the genitalia. Med. Asp. Hum. Sex., 7: 219, 1973.
Krock, N. Ileostomy catheter, Med. World News, 15: 38, 1974.
*Levy, N. B. For dialysis patients, sex, too, is a washout. Med. World News, 14: 15, 1973.
*Munnell, E. Total hysterectomy. Am. J. Ob. & Gynecol., 54: 31, 1947.
*Phoenix, C. H. Sexual behavior in Rhesus monkeys after vasectomy. Science, 179: 493, 1973.
*Rodgers, D. A., Ziegler, F. J., Altrocchi, J., and Levy, N. A longitudinal study of the psycho-social effects of vasectomy. J. Marriage Fam., 27: 59, 1965.
*Rodgers, D. A., Ziegler, F. J., and Levy, N. Prevailing cultural attitudes about vasectomy: A possible explanation of postoperative psychological response. Psychosom. Med., 29: 367, 1967.

13.2   Psychological Impact of Surgical Procedures on Women

MICHAEL JOE DALY, M.D.

Introduction

Few things are more emotionally stimulating to women than sexuality and conception. Both of these potentials can be affected by surgery on the reproductive tract of women. This effect may be real or fantasied. Both men and women develop anxieties related to their reproductive organs, although the literature has emphasized castration anxieties in men much more than anxieties in women. In addition, women's reproductive organs are internal, so that inspection is not as possible as it is in men. This anatomical fact is one of the reasons why women fantasize more about their reproductive organs and why they have more mistaken notions concerning their potentiality and lack of potentiality. All these fantasies can stimulate emotional responses at the time of any surgery performed on women's genital organs. These emotional stimuli can result in the production of anxiety or guilt or can leave women with feelings of inadequacy, mutilation, and depression. With these attitudinal changes, the behavioral patterns of women after surgery on their reproductive tracts can be markedly changed.

Castrating and Sterilizing Operative Procedures

In this general category one may include tubal ligation, cauterization by laparoscopy, bilateral oophorectomy, and hysterectomy—all of which bring about some emotional responses in the women on whom these operative procedures are carried out.

STERILIZATION

Sterilization of a woman may produce either positive or negative emotional responses. In a study performed at Johns Hopkins University on a large group of women undergoing sterilization with follow-up, it was found that women who requested sterilization had few negative emotional sequelae, such as depression, anxiety, and the development of psychosis. Women for whom sterilization was recommended by physicians for such disorders as rheumatic heart disease and renal disease frequently responded with anxiety, guilt, depression, or psychosis. Some of these depressions were potentially suicidal. Similar experiences have been reported in many areas of the world, and the degree of the negative responses seems to depend on the cultural attitude concerning reproduction.

As the world becomes more cognizant of the fact that birth rates and the world population must be controlled, cultural attitudes concerning reproduction and the women's role have begun to change, and more options are available. In the past there was a need to imprint on women the importance of reproduction, so that the human race could not only exist but multiply. With changing attitudes and the movement of women into multiple roles, fewer negative responses are being noted in tubal sterilizations.

In those women who have strong cultural ties to the past and to religious beliefs, occasional severe depression and the development of anxiety and guilt are noted. Most depressed patients seem to have a combination of anger and guilt, and the anger is turned inward on themselves through the force of their guilt. In the case of sterilization, the anger stems from the surgeon's interference with their ability to reproduce and the guilt from the fact that the physician may have been trying to improve their health.

Preoperative recognition of this type of patient may be helpful in preventing the sequelae. In addition, women develop concerns about aging changes in their body because of a lack of hormonal stimulation.

BILATERAL OOPHORECTOMY

When a bilateral oophorectomy is performed, additional fantasies may result in abnormal responses, such as feelings of loss of femininity and loss of libido, depending on how the individual woman feels about the loss of her potential as a reproductive human being. Many women still feel that their sexuality is located in their ovaries, despite improved educational programs about female reproduction.

In addition, after having a bilateral oophorectomy, a woman may develop concerns about aging changes in her body because of a lack of hormone stimulation. There is some reality to this concern; however, substitutional estrogen may, for the most part, prevent these changes, and a woman who has had a bilateral oophorectomy should be made aware of this potential. One of the interesting facts about changing body responses is the increasing length of function of the ovaries. The natural menopause or cessation of menstruation is occurring well up into the fifties, as compared with the forties at the turn of the century. This fact has led to the notion that women are younger longer. This can also be true of the oophorectomized woman who is placed on estrogen.

HYSTERECTOMY

In recent years hysterectomies have been increasingly performed for elective reasons, in addition to the classic reasons, such as the presence of benign and malignant tumors. Side effects, psychological as well as physical, have become an increasingly pertinent issue. A psychological relation between the uterus and the emotional responses of women goes back to the ancient Greeks, from whom the word "hysteria" was adopted (*hystera* means womb in Greek).

Freud regarded the uterus as a significant symbol of femininity, and he reported on studies of women institutionalized for severe emotional illnesses, pointing out that a large number of them had previously undergone hysterectomies. Drellich and Bieber, in an extensive study, developed the following conclusions: Disease and surgery of the female genital organs are sometimes viewed as punishment for guilt-laden activities involving these organs; chiefly but not exclusively, sexual activities were identified by the women as the culprit. Recently, some obstetricians and gynecologists have developed the position that the uterus has but one function—reproduction. After the last planned pregnancy, the uterus becomes a useless, bleeding, and potentially cancerous organ and, therefore, should be removed.

Somewhere between these two extremes may lie the answer concerning emotional sequelae after a hysterectomy. The response to the operation depends on the emotional maturity of the woman involved, on her cultural attitudes about the importance of reproduction relative to her own concept of being a woman, and on the preparation for this operative procedure that her physicians gave her. Especially pertinent is the approach to her fantasy concerning this organ and what the removal of the organ means to her. Those gynecologists and surgeons who pay little heed to emotions and feelings report few emotional sequelae; but those physicians who provide more comprehensive care for their patients not only identify emotional sequelae that may be dealt with but may also use preventive means to prevent such sequelae.

In an attempt to compare the emotional sequelae to hysterectomy with the emotional reactions to other operations, researchers have studied more than 1,600 patients who had their uteruses removed and 1,100 women who had their gallbladders removed. No significant differences were found in the number of patients who were subsequently admitted to mental hospitals. It was found, however, that the hysterectomized woman markedly differed from the cholecystectomized women in several ways; the hysterectomized women were three times as likely to be single, and 21 per cent of them had recorded family histories of mental illness, as compared with none in the gallbladder group.

In a similar comparison of the two operative procedures, it was found that women who underwent hysterectomies had a much higher incidence of postoperative agitated depression, although the depression was sometimes mild. A similar study by Montague Baker of the same operative comparison used psychiatric referrals and hospitalizations as the point of the study and found that 7 per cent of 729 women who had undergone hysterectomies had been given psychiatric referrals a mean period of 4½ years after this operation. This percentage was 2½ times as high as the percentage of psychiatric referrals given the gallbladder group and 3 times as high as the incidence of psychiatric referrals in the general population. The individual characteristics of the women were of importance. It was noted that the incidence of psychiatric referrals after a hysterectomy was twice as high among patients without significant pelvic pathology as among those with significant pelvic pathology. This point becomes a crucial issue, since many uteruses have been removed as a solution to problems of pelvic pain without defined pathology, rather than looking at the emotional conflicts of the particular patient. When real pathological changes occur in the uterus and the patient is properly prepared, the surgeon can anticipate much less difficulty in the postoperative period, both immediate and extended.

Further studies suggest that women who have had difficulty in forming a meaningful relationship in marriage and those with previous psychiatric histories are at greater risk than those women who do not fall into this category. Nulliparous hysterectomized married women show no greater risk of emotional sequelae than do those who have had children.

Husbands of women who have undergone hysterectomies also show emotional difficulties. In a study at Temple University Medical Center, it was found that 18 per cent of the black men studied, became impotent with a woman who had had her uterus removed, although they could function well sexually with women who had not had hysterectomies. This pattern may well change when reproduction, both for men and for women, is not as important as it has been in the past to prove one's manhood or womanhood. In another study, husbands of women who received psychiatric referrals after a hysterectomy showed disturbed behavior; about 20 per cent of these

changes in behavior included impotence, suicide, irritability, promiscuity, and tormenting the wife with being only half a woman. In a psychosocial study carried out at Harvard by Doris Menzer, 26 patients were studied preoperatively and postoperatively in depth. The majority of women studied fell into a moderate reaction group. Behavior in the recovery room, Menzer felt, was a prognostic yardstick of later adjustment. Those who had the worst reaction later on were extremely restless at this time—having irregular breathing, sobbing, screaming, whining, and showing greater immobility, even to the point of not being able to open their eyes. The poorest reaction of all involved women whose lives were built exclusively on their reproductive function and their motherhood.

The goal of zero population growth and the active women's liberation movement will decrease the imprintings of the importance of reproduction in the years to come. Women who require hysterectomies will probably suffer fewer emotional sequelae. In addition, with better evaluation of the women, fewer hysterectomies will be performed and fewer symptoms produced by emotional conflicts, so that, it is hoped, emotional sequelae to this operative procedure will be brought to a minimum.

Harold Schulman has pointed out the many medical reasons for not doing routine hysterectomies as a form of sterilization. And the author does not think that statistical evidence supports the concept that the uterus needs to be removed to prevent malignant disease. In addition, effective and less traumatic—both physically and emotionally—methods of contraception may be provided.

The type of person who was apt to seek a hysterectomy in the past has been studied by Ralph Patterson in an extensive computer survey of 1,071 women. These women represented the total female population at Columbia Psychiatric Institute and Hospital over a 5-year period. Patterson found that social class, as measured by education, is significantly related to hysterectomy. In all age levels under age 54, the hysterectomized patient had spent less time in school than had those who did not have their uteruses removed.

In making a decision to perform a hysterectomy, the physician needs to evaluate the total patient and needs to give the patient an opportunity to express her fantasies, anxieties, and other emotional responses preoperatively. The physician should take care to correct any abnormal ideas if they exist. In addition, a hysterectomy should not be performed as a routine method of sterilization and should not be performed on women as an answer to symptoms related to emotional conflicts. The hysterectomy procedure should be limited to those women who have organic disease of the uterus and related structures.

Vaginal Procedures

DILATATION AND CURETTAGE

Dilatation and curettage is the most common operative procedure performed on the pelvic organs of women. There is a great degree of disparity between the fantasies that women have concerning this operative procedure and the reality of the operation. Frequently, this operation is performed on women who have been infertile, with pregnancy occurring after the diagnostic procedure. One of the explanations for this occurrence is that the operative procedure solves the guilt over sexuality and pregnancy in these women. For other women this operation may represent a sadistic assault on their genitalia and internal organs. The most usual conception that women have concerning this operative procedure is a positive emotional response; they feel that the operation either cleanses their reproductive organs or accomplishes a manipulation to improve the function of these organs. The other significant emotional response to this operation is one of anger, which results from disappointment when the operative procedure does not cure their symptoms, as in a woman with menometrorrhagia. It is, therefore, important for the physician to differentiate between the woman's fantasy and the reality of what the operative procedure will accomplish.

ABORTION

In women who have spontaneous abortions in the first trimester, a dilatation and evacuation is frequently carried out after the spontaneous abortion. For these women the procedure may represent a cleansing type of operative procedure, relieving their guilt related to the negative feelings they may have had concerning their pregnancy. In women who have had abortions performed in the first trimester by suction curettage, few emotional sequelae are noted if they are fairly well adjusted emotionally. However, women who do not have good emotional adjustment before the suction curettage may develop depression related to the guilt and anger they feel about the termination of the pregnancy. Women in whom abortion is brought about by saline instillation show a somewhat greater degree of depression because they frequently feel fetal movement before the termination of the pregnancy. This reaction is especially true in women who look on reproduction as a central part of femininity; feeling life within their bodies may generate guilt when the pregnancy is ended. However, even in this group of women, marked emotional depression is not a frequent occurrence.

VAGINAL PLASTIC PROCEDURES

Anterior and posterior colpoperineorrhaphy is a frequent operative procedure on women in the middle years, and the procedure is usually followed by a positive emotional response. However, some of these women become depressed because the expectations of their fantasies, such as the expectation that this operative procedure will enhance their sexuality, are not met.

COLPOCLEISIS

A colpocleisis is frequently performed in older women who have a large cystocele, rectocele, or uterine prolapse. Frequently because the effect of the operation is not properly explained to the patient—the physician may not be cognizant of the fact that older women still enjoy intercourse—this operative procedure results in a great deal of anger, feelings of inadequacy, and disappointment in women who wish to continue their sexual life. When physicians become cognizant of the fact that sexuality is desired throughout the life-span of most men and women, this operative procedure will be used less frequently. When it is used, the patient must be properly evaluated and prepared for the closing off of her vagina.

CREATING AN ARTIFICIAL VAGINA

Many a woman who is born without a vagina or with just a pouch may have an artificial vagina developed for her. If properly performed, the procedure has a great deal of success. Again, the expectations of the patient must be well discussed, and she must be cooperative during the postoperative period for the artificial vagina to become a useful structure. When the operation is unsuccessful, the failure is usually caused by the patient's emotional reactions of fear and anxiety. If the fear and anxiety can be overcome, so that the woman with the artificial vagina uses it with determination, the results may be excellent.

Obstetrical Operations

The episiotomy is frequently performed in this country for three basic reasons: to shorten the second stage of labor; to prevent tearing of the endopelvic fascia, thus preventing the development of a cystourethrocele or a rectocele; and to relieve compression of the baby's head. This concept has been challenged because of results in Europe, where episiotomies are not routinely used. There, women are delivered by midwives, and these countries have not reported a higher incidence of pelvic relaxation or abnormal development of the newborns. Many women feel that episiotomies are assaults on their bodies. Certainly, an episiotomy increases a woman's discomfort during the postpartum period, and the benefits of this procedure are not immediately obvious to many of these women. Some, therefore, respond with anger.

Women also have reactions to the use of forceps. Sometimes a woman fantasizes that these instruments are destructive to her and to her baby, and on occasion she feels that the necessity for forceps represents a failure on her part as a woman. These feelings and attitudes can result in depression during the postpartum period. Again, proper evaluation and communication with the patient can prevent many of these emotional responses.

A cesarean section can be associated with old fantasies related to the umbilicus. Some little children fantasize that birth occurs through the umbilicus; later, this fantasy becomes unconscious. A cesarean section can restimulate these early concepts, resulting in the production of anxiety and thereby further complicating the postpartum period. In addition, women on whom cesarean sections are performed may feel threatened by the fact that they could not have their babies normally.

Radical Pelvic Operations

Radical pelvic surgery is frequently performed when cancer of the pelvis is present. These operative procedures are some of the most destructive performed on human beings. Pelvic exenteration leaves the woman with a colostomy and an artificial urinary bladder, so that she has to wear a collection system for both bladder and bowel excreta. If these operations are performed on women who do not fully understand the postoperative effects, severe depression may occur. When women who require pelvic exenteration must choose between life and death and they choose life, some of the radical distortion may be more acceptable. Some women who have had colostomies and no longer have their vaginas have found other sexual outlets. But in the majority of women who have had radical pelvic exenterations and even in some women who have had less radical operative procedures, a significant degree of depression results. However, well motivated women are able to continue leading useful lives after this type of surgery.

Conclusion

Operations on the reproductive organs of women are associated with emotional sequelae. Women's fantasies concerning operative procedures on their reproductive organs are enhanced because of the fact that these organs are internal and cannot easily be inspected. Many of the emotional responses to these operative procedures may be prevented if the physician identifies the fantasies and expectations that women have about the operations and brings these fantasies into line with reality. Depression, anxiety, and guilt should also be recognized and dealt with during the immediate postoperative period.

Operative procedures performed on women's pelvic organs should be done for organic disease only. The incidence of postoperative depression and the need for psychiatric treatment in women who have had hysterectomies will probably decrease as options other than motherhood become more available to women. Proper preoperative evaluation for any pelvic surgery should be comprehensive, dealing with fantasies and expectations, so that the resulting emotional response will be positive. In this way the postoperative recovery of women will be enhanced.

REFERENCES

*Deutsch, H. *Psychology of Women,* vol. I. Grune & Stratton, New York, 1900.

*Freud, S. *The Basic Writings of Sigmund Freud,* p. 907. Modern Library, New York, 1938.

*Kistner, R. W. *Gynecology: Principles and Presentations.* ed. 2. Year Book Medical Publishers, Chicago, 1900.

*Osofsky, H., and Osofsky, J. *The Abortion Experience.* Harper & Row, New York, 1973.

*Richards, D. H. *Depressive Illness after Hysterectomy.* Physicians International Press, 1973.

13.3   Sex and Medical Illness

EDWARD A. TYLER, M.D.

Introduction

There is an increasingly widespread recognition that a reciprocal relationship probably exists between most medical illnesses and patients' sexual behaviors, attitudes, and expectations. The current medical literature suggests that the physician should accept the responsibility for anticipating potential sexual problems, preventing problems from developing, offering early treatment for problems that surface, and seeking consultation for his patients' more severe and long lasting sex problems. The initial responsibility definitely rests with the physician who diagnoses and treats the primary medical illness when the sexual behavior problem could be related to or precipitated by the medical illness or a surgical procedure. A sexual incapacity therapist may be indicated later as a consultant or referral source. Although there is an abundance of literature advising, speculating, and philosophizing on the relationship between medical illness and sexual performance, there is, as yet, a paucity of hard data based on carefully designed research to validate these assumptions.

Classification

A simple classification to conceptualize the kinds of sexual problems that present to a physician can be useful. Theoretically, any classification should consider a transient-permanent or a reversible-irreversible dichotomy. In real life, however, almost all sexual behavior changes are transient, reversible, or adaptable. Patients with spinal cord injuries, the best source of reported data, have been found to make ingenious, spontaneous adaptations to compensate for their irreversible neurological lesions. Likewise, health care professionals familiar with nursing home patients have observed the adaptive capabilities of the senile and invalid when the expression of sexual behavior is not suppressed by the professional staff. A concept of permanent or irreversible sexual incapacity seems an appropriate description only of those patients whose total interest, energy, and attention have become occupied with their painful, debilitating terminal illnesses. On the other hand, many apparently permanent sexual behavior incapacities do go untreated, but they are not irreversible or nonadaptable. These neglected problems result from patients' ignorance, naivete, guilt, and embarrassment and from professionals' embarrassment, naivete, and lack of training. When the therapist is capable of accepting the wide variety of sexual behaviors that can meet the patient's expectations, most sexual behavior problems must be considered transient. If the permanency of sexual behavior problems associated with terminal illness is excluded, then all other sexual problems related to medical illness can be classified usefully into four general groups: disinterest or lack of desire for sexual activity; physical incapacity or discomfort with sexual performance; fear of causing, precipitating, or aggravating a physical illness by sexual behavior; and use of medical illness as an excuse to avoid feared or undesired sexual experience.

DISINTEREST

Transient disinterest or lack of desire for sexual activity occurs in most persons whenever they become sufficiently preoccupied with the symptoms of their primary medical illnesses. This occurs in acute infectious diseases, acute trauma, acute asthma, other acute allergies, brittle diabetes, migraine, anemia, thrombophlebitis, herpes, acute myocardial infarction, drug or alcohol intoxication, endocrine disorders, and severe nutritional disorders. The presenting symptoms are typically those of the primary medical illness, and the altered sexual behavior is a secondary complaint, if the patient notices it at all. If there is a complaint, it most commonly comes from the patient's sexual partner. Therapy is typically directed toward the primary illness, and the sexual problem disappears or lessens as the primary

medical illness improves. When the sexual symptoms continue after the primary medical illness is relieved, the patient must be classified in another way and managed accordingly.

PHYSICAL INCAPACITY

Physical incapacity, pain, and distortion of body image should be further classified into two sub groups of sexual behavior problems. They are the problems related to the acute symptoms of the primary medical illness and the crippling sequelae.

Acute symptoms. Acute trauma to bones, muscle, skin, or internal organs frequently makes the patient's familiar sexual behaviors uncomfortable or embarrassing. A leg bone fracture in a plaster cast, a painful-on-motion low back muscle strain, arthritis, neuralgia, a groin bruise or strain, a widespread weeping contact dermatitis, severe acne, an acute sunburn, acute vaginitis, urethritis, cystitis, a Bartholin cyst, endometriosis, a tumor mass in the uterus or intestinal tract, late pregnancy, marked obesity, a post coital hemorrhoidal prolapse, a hydrocele, a hernia, varicosities of the legs, a breast abscess—all are examples of medical illnesses likely to interfere with the performance of a patient's customary and familiar patterns of sexual behavior. When the duration of the medical illness is expected to be brief, treatment consists of reassurance and appropriate therapy for the primary medical illness. When the duration is predicted to be longer but the prognosis is for eventual total recovery, additional understanding and reassurance are indicated. The patient frequently needs the physician's permission to experiment with new or modified patterns of sexual behavior. The physician can initiate this experimentation by low key education about how similar sexual problems have been solved by other patients. However, unless the physician communicates to the patient the feeling that a discussion of sexual behavior problems is welcome, the patient is frequently too embarrassed to mention the fact that sexual problems exist. If the physician is reluctant, uncertain, or "too busy," the patient is unlikely to introduce the topic a second time. When the problem is handled early by the physician responsible for the medical illness, these patients should not need a referral to a sex therapist. All physicians managing primary medical illnesses should prepare themselves to prevent or treat the common transient sexual problems that occur in the kinds of medical illnesses they usually manage.

Crippling sequelae. Other medical illnesses produce crippling and incapacitating sequelae that interfere with the patient's familiar and normal or "proper" sexual behaviors. The primary illness and its sequelae may be permanent and irreversible, but the sexual problems are usually transient or subject to acceptable adaptations if the physician is interested in the rehabilitation of the patient's sexual activities as well as in the rest of his medical illness sequelae. Work in rehabilitating paraplegics and quadraplegics has revealed the marked ability of human beings to adapt their behavior to fit anatomical limitations imposed by their physical incapacities. Sexual behavior has not been an exception for these patients. The drive for sexual gratification led to spontaneous experimentation by patients long before most physicians found this area an acceptable and worthy therapeutic task. Now some rehabilitation specialists enlist the assistance of former patients who have solved their own sexual problems. They serve as therapeutic assistants through reassuring rap sessions, frank open permissive discussions, and films of their own paraplegic sexual behaviors to educate new patients presenting these kinds of sexual problems. Most paraplegic and quadraplegic patients are sexually adapted to an able bodied partner. There is no evidence to show that marriages between paraplegics or quadraplegics and able bodied spouses are less stable or less sexually gratifying than other American marriages.

The progressive crippling of arthritis, emphysema, diabetes, cardiovascular disease, menopausal vaginal mucosal changes, Peyronie's disease, Klinefelter's syndrome, hydrocele, and many neuromuscular illnesses results in painful or awkward sexual behavior problems. The unsightly scarring of severe burns, chronic skin lesions, mastectomy, amputations, and colostomy openings, and the congenital, genetic, or endocrine disorders, such as gynecomastia, infantile genitalia, hermaphrodism, and chronic foul-looking or foul-smelling vaginal and pelvic infections all cause body image changes that make the patient ashamed of being touched or seen. In this group of sexual behavior problems, therapy is directed at rehabilitation from the primary incapacitating illness, permission to experiment sexually, and education about the adaptive solutions used by other patients with comparable problems.

FEAR

Fear that any sexual behavior may cause, precipitate, or aggravate a new or existing physical illness is common in patients recovering from life-threatening illnesses, like myocardial infarction or cerebral vascular accident. The fear may last long after recovery and convalescence from the primary illness, unless the managing physician inquires about any changes in the patient's sexual attitude, desire, or performance. The complaint may be expressed first by the patient's partner, rather than by the patient. The sexual partner may believe that requesting or demanding sex is likely to lead to homicide, and the patient may silently fear that allowing himself to become sexually aroused is risking suicide. One or both of the partners may become tense, guilty, and irritable and may seek permanent separation. The able bodied spouse may seek extramarital sexual gratification. Whether this gratification is sought secretly or openly, guilt, resentment, hostility, and self-esteem problems complicate the sexual performance problems. Conscientious but extremely conservative medical management unwittingly aggravates the fear. Statements like, "Your heart's okay now, but take it easy," are bewildering to the patient. Moralistic relatives and friends may even see the original primary medical illness as punishment for sexual and other pleasurable indulgences. This unintentional conspiracy of silence blocks exploration of the sexual problems being experienced. Therefore, at a very early stage of convalescence, the physician managing the medical illness is obligated to explore what help the patient and the partner need in re-establishing the premorbid patterns of sexual behavior. When this invitation is not offered and the problem becomes chronic, more specific psychiatric or sex therapy is likely to be needed. Unfortunately, many physicians, including psychiatrists, are not comfortable enough to inquire at the early stage, when preventive reassurance and patient education are likely to be sufficient. The attitude of assuming that no problem exists if the patient does not initiate questions is not the model used for discovering other complications of medical illnesses and is equally inappropriate for sexual complications.

Similar problems develop around less life-threatening medical conditions that are commonly associated with morality in this society. These problems occur most often in patients who believe that human sexual behavior should be primarily or exclusively a procreational activity, not a recreational activity. Overly cautious physicians reinforce this view with their admonitions about giving up all sexual activity during the last several weeks of pregnancy and for several weeks postpartum. The fear of injuring the fetus or of causing a life-threatening postpartum infection must be answered with 1970, not 1870, medical sophistication.

When the medical problem has been abortion or a venereal disease, the punishment-guilt-abstention feelings frequently rob the patient of sexual gratification, precipitate performance difficulties, or even bring about total cessation of all sexual behavior. Such a problem carried silently for months or years rarely disappears simply as a result of a legitimizing marriage ceremony or belated simple reassurance. The physician managing medical problems commonly associated with moralistic attitudes is obligated to consider and explore the potential problems at the time he is initially consulted for management of the patient's medical illness. At this early period, preventive reassurance and education can inexpensively influence the long term outcome. Later, time consuming and expensive psychotherapy or sex therapy will become necessary. Unfortunately, many patients who have suffered sexual problems for a long time have lost any belief that their incapacity is treatable. They suffer silently and not longer complain or seek help.

EXCUSE

It should be mentioned that human beings with latent or overt problems about expressing sexual behaviors and feelings may welcome their physical illnesses as acceptable shields and justifications against having to perform sexually. However, physical illnesses or their sequelae can rarely be blamed for permanent sexual abstinence, as evidenced by patients with severe irreversible physical incapacities who do adapt to new overt expressions of sexual behavior.

The patient's awareness of this relationship varies from total unconsciousness to total awareness. In either case, the patient is prone to resist public recognition of the fact that his medical illness is self-serving to a primary sexual problem and that the first step in the improvement of either is separation of the two health problems. Until the public recognition occurs, the physician managing the medical illness finds himself in a trap. His patient does not follow the prescribed treatment plan, subjectively reports incapacities that do not correspond with the physician's objective observations and findings, plays one physician against another, enlists the unsophisticated sympathy of friends and family, and continues to suffer. The physician's elaborating or repeating his examination beyond his reasonable medical judgment does not help and frequently compounds the problem by strengthening the patient's belief that serious medical problems justify the sexual behavior limitations. The physician's scolding, moralizing, tricking, or dismissing the patient is rarely helpful to the patient, even though it may relieve the physician.

Management

The management of the patient with a physical medical illness plus a sexual hang-up problem is always difficult, and sudden miraculous cures rarely occur, even in the hands of the most skillful and experienced therapist. An essential first step is that the physician privately recognize and publically state that he sincerely knows the patient hurts and would like to be helped. He must be willing to protect the patient from the immediate demands of the sexual partner when the patient publicly separates the medical illness and the sexual behavior problems. If the physician's competence is limited to the management of the medical illness, he must refer the patient for treatment of the sexual problem and maintain a cooperative liaison with the sex therapist. He must also be prepared for remissions of both the medical illness and the sexual behavior problems and remissions in the patient's recognition that medical illness is not causing the sexual incapacity. The physician with patience, humanistic concern for his patients, and a tolerance of sexual variation in others will be most successful in the management of this last group of complicated problems.

Conclusion

Medical illness and sexual behavior are commonly interrelated. When the patient experiences the changes in his sexual behavior as a problem, he needs a forum and a sophisticated, willing, listening ear from the physician managing his medical illness. Early management by prevention through reassurance, education, and permission to experiment is frequently successful. When the sexual behavior problem has been allowed to become chronic, time-consuming sex therapy or psychotherapy are frequently necessary. When a latent sexual problem becomes manifest during medical illnesses, the physician managing the medical illness must recognize the relationship of the two problems and refer those he does not feel competent to treat.

REFERENCES

Belt, B. G. Some organic causes of impotence. Med. Asp. Hum. Sex., *7:* 152, 1973.

Bennett, R. G. Gonorrheal proctitis. Med. Asp. Hum. Sex., *7:* 188, 1973.

*Birnbaum, M. D., and Eskin, B. A. Psychosexual aspects of endocrine disorders. Med. Asp. Hum. Sex., *7:* 134, 1973.

Blumer, D., and Walker, A. E. Sexual behavior in temporal lobe epilepsy. Arch. Neurol., *16:* 37, 1967.

Comarr, A. E. Sex among patients with spinal cord and/or cauda equina injuries. Med. Asp. Hum. Sex., *7:* 222, 1973.

Currey, H. L. F. Osteoarthrosis of the hip joint and sex activity. Ann. Rheum. Dis., *29:* 488, 1970.

Cushman, P. Jr., Sexual behavior in heroin addiction and methadone maintenance. N. Y. State J. Med., *72:* 1261, 1972.

Dlin, B., and Perlman, A. Sex after ileostomy or colostomy. Med. Asp. Hum. Sex., *6:* 32, 1972.

*Dwyer, J. T. Psychosexual aspects of weight control and dieting behaviors in adolescents. Med. Asp. Hum. Sex., *7:* 82, 1973.

Ellenberger, M. Impotence in diabetes: The neurological factor. Ann. Intern. Med., *75:* 2, 1971.

Finkle, A. L. Diagnosis of sexual problems in urology. In *Advances in Diagnostic Urology,* J. J. Kaufman, editor. Little, Brown, Boston, 1964.

Greenblatt, R. B., and Perez-Ballester, B. Gynecomastia. Med. Asp. Hum. Sex., *3:* 52, 1969.

Grimes, J. H. Hematospermia. Med. Asp. Hum. Sex., *4:* 115, 1970.

*Hastings, D. W. *Impotence and Frigidity.* Little, Brown, Boston, 1963.

Hellerstein, H. K., and Friedman, E. H. Sexual activity and the post coronary patient. Scand. J. Rehabil. Med., *2:* 109, 1970; and Arch. Intern. Med., *125:* 987, 1970.

Hollender, M. A. Hysterectomy and feelings of feminity. Med. Asp. Hum. Sex., *3:* 6, 1969.

Huffman, J. W. The effect of gynecological surgery on sex relations. Am. J. Obstet. Gynecol., *59:* 915, 1970.

Jackson, R. W. Sexual rehabilitation after cord injury. Paraplegia, *10:* 50, 1972.

Jochheim, K. A. A study of sexual function in 56 male patients with complete irreversible lesions of the spinal cord and cauda equina. Paraplegia, *8:* 166, 1971.

Kalliomaki, J. L., Markkamen, T. K., and Mustonen, V. A. Sexual behavior after cerebral vascular accident. Fertil. Steril., *12:* 156, 1961.

Kass, I., Updegraff, K., and Muffy, R. D. Sex in chronic obstructive pulmonary disease. Med. Asp. Hum. Sex., *6:* 33, 1972.

Kerr, C. H. Obstetrical trauma and subsequent sex relations. Med. Asp. Hum. Sex., *4:* 90, 1970.

Kolodny, R. Sexual dysfunction in diabetic females. *Diabetes, 20:* 557, 1971.

Levenson, R. M. A summary of a symposium on counseling the cardiac on work and sex. The Ohio State Med. J., *66:* 1003, 1970.

Levine, J. The sexual adjustment of alcoholics. Q. J. Stud. Alcohol, *16:* 675, 1955.

Linton, E. B. Honeymoon cystitis. Med. Asp. Hum. Sex., *5:* 110, 1971.

Loewe, S., and Puttuck, S. L. Anti-ejaculatory effect of sympatholytic, gangliolytic, and spasmoltyic drugs. J. Pharmacol. Exp. Ther., *107:* 379, 1953.

Mann, E., and Cunningham, G. Coital cautions in pregnancy. Med. Asp. Hum. Sex., *6:* 14, 1972.

Marbach, A. H. Sexual problems and gynecologic illness. Med. Asp. Hum. Sex., *4:* 48, 1970.

May, A. G., DeWeese, J.A., and Rob, C. G. Changes in sexual function in men following operation on abdominal aorta. Surgery, *65:* 41, 1969.

McDonald, D. Peyronie's disease. Med. Asp. Hum. Sex., *6:* 65, 1972.

Money, J. Phantom orgasm in paraplegics. Med. Asp. Hum. Sex., *6:* 90, 1972.

Oaks, W. W., and Moyer, J. H. Sex and hypertension. Med. Asp. Hum. Sex., *6:* 128, 1972.

Parades, A. Marital sexual factors in alcoholism. Med. Asp. Hum. Sex. *7:* 98, 1973.

Pinderhughes, C. A., Grace, E. B., and Reyna, L. J. Psychiatric disorders and sexual functioning. Am. J. Psychiatry, *130:* 1276, 1972.

Rubin, D. Sex in patients with neck, back, and radicular pain syndromes. Med. Asp. Hum. Sex., *6:* 14, 1972.

Sadoughi, W., Leshner, M., and Fine, H. L. Sexual adjustment in a chronically ill and physically disabled population: A pilot study. Arch. Phys. Med. Rehabil., *52:* 311, 1971.

Scheffling, K., Wilschumeit, H. Disorders of sexual function in male diabetics. *Diabetes, 12:* 519, 1963.

Shader, R. Sexual dysfunction associated with thioridiazine hydrocholoride. J. A. M. A., *188:* 1007, 1964.

Singh, J. Sex life and psychiatric problems after myocardial infarction. J. Assoc. Physicians India, *18:* 503, 1970.

Sohval, A. R. Klinefelter's syndrome. Med. Asp. Hum. Sex., *3:* 69, 1969.

Steele, R., Lees, R. E., Kraus, A. S., and Rao, C. Sexual factors in the epidemiology of cancer of the prostate. J. Chronic Dis., *24:* 29, 1971.

Tuttle, W. B., Cook, W. L. and Fitch, E. Sexual behavior in post-myocardial infarction patients. Am. J. Cardiol., *13:* 140, 1964.

Wershub, L. P. *Sexual Impotence in the Male.* Charles C. Thomas, Springfield, Ill., 1959.

Wigfield, A. S. Attitudes to venereal disease in a permissive society. Br. Med. J., *4:* 342, 1971.

13.4 Sex and Infection: Venereal Diseases

WALTER TAUB, M.D.

Introduction

The venereal diseases are worldwide in distribution and a difficult problem for the medical profession. Despite the advent of antibiotics, major epidemics continue to occur.

The major venereal diseases are syphilis, gonorrhea, chancroid, granuloma inguinale, lymphogranuloma venereum, and herpesvirus 2. In addition, hepatitis A and B are gaining recognition as likely venereally transmitted diseases.

Traditionally, the venereal diseases have been approached as though sexual intercourse were the exclusive mode of transmission. This idea is no longer tenable. Sexual behavior encompasses all the possible mucocutaneous appositions and, therefore, includes oral-oral, oral-genital, oral-anal, genital-genital, genital-anal, oral-cutaneous, and genital-cutaneous. These variations must be appreciated and understood to allow for a better understanding of how these diseases are transmitted.

Syphilis

Syphilis is a chronic systemic disease caused by the organism *Treponema pallidum.* There are four phases—primary, secondary, latent, and tertiary. After infection there is an incubation period, averaging 3 weeks, followed by a primary phase, consisting of a chancre associated with regional lymphadenopathy. This phase is followed by a secondary phase, marked by bacteremia and characterized by mucocutaneous manifestations. Thereafter, a latent period of subclinical infection may persist. This phase is divided into two stages—early latent and late latent. The early latent stage is arbitrarily dated up to 4 years from the presumed onset of infection. During this stage, organisms may re-enter the blood from subclinical sites and re-emerge as secondary syphilis—that is as mucocutaneous lesions. After 4 years, unless there is spontaneous or therapeutic cure, the disease may enter a late latent stage and remain asymptomatic. Eventually, the final or tertiary phase may become manifest as neurosyphilis or cardiovascular syphilis.

CAUSE, HISTORY, AND EPIDEMIOLOGY

The causative agent is *Treponema pallidum,* a thin spiral organism that is 6 to 14 spirals in length. It was discovered by Schaudinn and Hoffman in 1905.

The first recorded pandemic occurred at the end of the 15th century and spread over Asia and Europe. Historians attribute the pandemic to the return of Columbus and his men from the New World in 1493 or to the invasion of Italy by France in 1494.

Mercury was the first method of treatment. Salvarsan, an arsenical, was introduced in 1910 by Ehrlich and became the mainstay of treatment until 1943, when penicillin came into use. To this day, penicillin is the treatment drug of choice. There has been no convincing evidence that resistance of the spirochete to penicillin has ever been encountered although treatment failures have occurred.

The annual incidence of syphilis in the United States has been recorded since 1941. Reportable cases reached a count of 6,000 in 1957. In 1972 the reportable cases approached 100,000, including 24,000 primary and secondary cases. Since only about 15 per cent of all syphilis cases are actually reported, it is extremely difficult to estimate the syphilitic population.

Liberalized sexual views and a failure to recognize early syphilis undoubtedly account for the marked increase in syphilis cases in recent years. In addition, the pill, the diaphragm, and the intrauterine device have brought about the almost total discontinuance of the condom, which provided protection against venereal disease, as well as against pregnancy. Traditionally, the most effective health measures have been related to tracing the contacts of reported cases. This method obviously has serious defects. Therefore, all persons seen in hospital, clinic, and college and university health centers should have a routine serological test for syphilis.

It appears that only one of every two persons exposed to syphilis contracts it. Reportable syphilis is 20 times more frequent in blacks than in whites. This difference partly reflects the reporting trend—indigent blacks go to clinics, where reporting occurs, and not to private doctors' offices, where it often doesn't.

NATURAL COURSE OF UNTREATED SYPHILIS

The course of untreated syphilis was studied retrospectively in 2,000 patients with primary and secondary syphilis in the Oslo study (1891 to 1951). A prospective study of 431 black men with seropositive latent syphilis was started in 1932 and terminated in 1972. The latter study, known as the Tuskegee study, stirred considerable controversy because the researchers continued to observe these patients, rather than offer them penicillin, after this antibiotic had been shown to be effective in practically all stages of the disease. The proponents of the study stressed that they did not discourage their patients from seeking other medical attention, which many of them did. However, the researchers' rigid adherence to the original format of the study drew widespread criticism and resulted in the discontinuance of the study.

Within a few hours after contact, the organism can be found within the blood stream. Thus, blood from an incubating patient is infectious. The incubation period lasts from 10 to 90 days but averages 3 weeks. The primary lesion appears at the inoculation site and persists for 2 to 6 weeks, healing spontaneously. The lesion starts as a single painless papule, which rapidly ulcerates. The regional lymph nodes are involved and are firm, nonsuppurative, and painless. The chancre is usually located on the external genitalia, but it may be located wherever contact has occurred—mouth, breast, perineum, rectum.

The secondary stage usually includes symmetrical mucocutaneous lesions and nontender generalized lymphadenopathy. The skin rash consists of maculopapular nonpruritic lesions spread bilaterally on the trunk and proximal extremities. In moist areas, condylomata latum appear. Split papules and mucous patches are seen in the mouth. Patchy alopecia may be present.

Latent syphilis implies the finding of a positive serological test for syphilis, the absence of clinical disease, and a past history of infection. Early latent syphilis comprises the first 4 years after the onset of the infection. Late latent syphilis includes any period thereafter and may continue as long as the patient remains untreated. This stage is associated with partial immunity and a noninfectious state. Although this stage may intermittently be associated with spirochetemia, the lesions of secondary syphilis are not present and hence the transmission of disease is unlikely. However, it is not impossible for infection to occur in circumstances of rectal intercourse, when there may be erosion of the penile skin and rectal mucosa, with intermingling of blood. The appearance of immunity is an accommodation between host and organism. But, although this stage is an immune one that prevents reinfection, the lesions already present can progress.

Possibly 30 to 40 per cent of all untreated late syphilis cases go on to spontaneous cure. These people have no evidence of disease, are no longer seropositive, and are, therefore, not immune. This condition renders them susceptible to reinfection. Those latent cases who remain seropositive can be presumed to have

gummatous disease. The gummas are solitary lesions that range from microscopic size to several centimeters in diameter. Histologically, they consist of nonspecific granulomatous inflammations with secondary necrosis surrounded by mononuclear, epithelioid, and fibroblastic cells, occasional giant cells, and perivasculitis. *T. pallidum* can rarely be demonstrated in these lesions which are thought to represent sites of cellular hypersensitivity to relatively few Treponemes. The enhanced activity of the gummatous deposits may be related to periodic seeding of these areas with Treponemes.

Late syphilis is divided into symptomatic and asymptomatic neurosyphilis. In asymptomatic neurosyphilis, cerebrospinal fluid abnormalities are present, but there is no clinical disease; 20 per cent of these patients go on to symptomatic neurosyphilis in the next 10 years. This percentage rises with time.

Symptomatic neurosyphilis, which is 2 to 3 times more frequent in whites than in blacks and is twice as common in men as in women, includes meningovascular and parenchymal syphilis. Meningovascular syphilis is associated with inflammation of the pia and arachnoid. Parenchymal syphilis includes general paresis and tabes dorsalis. General paresis occurs 20 to 25 years after the initial infection and is associated with widespread parenchymal changes. Tabes dorsalis presents symptoms and signs of demyelinization of the posterior column, dorsal roots, and dorsal root ganglia. It develops 25 to 30 years after the onset of infection. Cardiovascular syphilis is another form of parenchymal syphilis. It occurs where the large blood vessels are supplied by vasa vasorum, as is the case in the aortic arch, resulting in aortitis, aortic regurgitation, saccular aneurysm, or coronary ostial stenosis. These complications do not occur after congenital syphilis or syphilis acquired before the age of 14. The onset of cardiovascular syphilis occurs 10 to 40 years after the infection and is more common in black men than in white men. The incidence is 10 per cent of all untreated cases. In the Tuskegee study 50 per cent of the black men in the untreated latent group had evidence of aortitis at autopsy, although many of them died of unrelated disorders.

CONGENITAL SYPHILIS

Congenital syphilis occurs after the fourth month of gestation, when immunological competence is developed in the fetus, suggesting an immune basis for the pathogenesis, rather than a direct effect of *T. pallidum*. The manifestations of early congenital syphilis occur within the first 2 years of life and consists of a rash, which can take any form from minute petechiae to bullous lesions, hepatosplenomegaly, hemolytic anemia, jaundice, and osteochondritis of the long bones. Thrombocytopenia and leukocytosis are common. Pathological findings include interstitial and perivascular inflammation, followed by variable fibroblastic activity involving whatever organ is affected.

Late congenital syphilis is defined as disease that remains untreated after the patient is 2 years of age. About 60 per cent of these cases remain latent and, therefore, unrecognized. In the symptomatic cases, the most common manifestations are interstitial keratitis, Hutchinson teeth, and, rarely, saber shins, eighth-nerve deafness, juvenile paresis, and tabes dorsalis.

LABORATORY DIAGNOSIS

Dark-field examination of suspected lesions and serological tests for syphilis constitute the diagnostic tests for syphilis. Dark-field examination of active lesions offers the most definitive means of diagnosis. The serological tests for syphilis are of two types—reaginic and antibody-specific. The Venereal Disease Research Laboratory test (VDRL) and the Wassermann test measure reaginic antibodies—immune γ-globulin (IgG) and immune γ-macroglobulin (IgM), immunoglobulins directed against a lipoidal antigen that results from *T. pallidum* interaction with host tissues. The reaginic tests are nonspecific, and it is estimated that 20 to 40 per cent of these tests are false positive. In the event of a positive reaginic test finding, a more specific antitreponemal antibody test must be used. Three of these

tests are important: The fluorescent treponemal antibody-absorption test (FTA-ABS) uses fluorescein-labeled antigammaglobulin as a marker to detect patient anti-Treponema antibody (γ-globulin) complexed with added *T. pallidum*. The treponemal immobilization test (TPI) is less frequently used. It demonstrates the immobilization of *T. pallidum* by the addition of patient serum and complement; the serum contains presumed Treponema antibody. The *Treponema pallidum* hemagglutination antibody test is not widely used in this country.

False positive test findings of syphilis with reaginic antibodies occur in cases of atypical pneumonia, malaria, autoimmune and granulomatous disease, aging, and narcotic addiction. Except in rare instances, the FTA-ABS test confirms the presence of syphilis; it is rarely positive in systemic lupus erythematosus. IgM FTA-ABS tests must be done in newborns if their mothers have syphilis. The presence of IgM is proof of intrauterine infection, since maternal IgM is large and cannot pass the placental barrier; IgM can only be made in the fetus. Standard (IgG) FTA-ABS tests would likely be positive because of passive transfer of maternal antibodies of IgG size. These antibodies would most likely be present in a mother with a recent infection albeit adequately treated.

TREATMENT

Benzathine penicillin G, given intramuscularly, is recommended for the treatment of syphilis. A total dose of 2.4 million units is given for early or early latent disease; 6 million to 9 million units of benzathine penicillin G are required for late latent or tertiary syphilis; and 50,000 units per kg. of benzathine penicillin G are given for congenital syphilis. Aqueous penicillin or procaine penicillin G may be substituted for benzathine penicillin in doses of 6 million units for early or early latent syphilis over a 10-day period and 9 million units in 15 days for late latent or late syphilis. For congenital infection, a total dose of 100,000 units per kg. is given over a 10-day period. Patients who are allergic to penicillin may be given tetracycline or erythromycin in a total dose of 30 to 40 gm. over a 10-day period. Late infection may require several treatment periods.

After the successful treatment of seropositive primary or secondary syphilis, the VDRL (reaginic) titer should progressively decline, becoming negative after 3 to 12 months in 75 per cent of all primary cases and in 40 per cent of secondary cases. After 2 years, nearly all primary cases have converted to seronegativity; 25 per cent of all secondary cases and a higher percentage of all latent cases maintain a persistent but low-titer VDRL. If the titer does not reach or maintain a fixed low in 2 years, retreatment is indicated. In addition, it is necessary to do a spinal tap to rule out asymptomatic neurosyphilis.

Treatment of all stages of syphilis is always indicated. Even long-standing cerebral disease may benefit from treatment, although tabes dorsalis and optic atrophy are known to be especially resistant to treatment. Generally, the longer the duration of the disease, the harder it is to eradicate. There is no vaccine currently available against syphilis.

Gonorrhea

Gonorrhea is an infection of the columnar and transitional epithelium that is caused by the organism *Neisseria gonorrhoeae*. It is almost always transmitted sexually. Common sites of infection are the endocervix, urethra, anal canal, pharynx, and conjunctivae. Local spread causes salpingitis, tubo-ovarian abscess, endometritis, and peritonitis in women. Men may develop periurethral abscess and epididymitis. Hematogenous spread may result in dermatitis, arthritis, myocarditis, endocarditis, pericarditis, and meningitis.

EPIDEMIOLOGY

Gonorrhea is the most common venereal disease; 2.5 million cases were reported in 1972, which means that 10 to 15 million cases are occurring yearly. The incidence has risen markedly in recent years, which is a direct reflection of three major changes in sexual behavior discussed earlier—the use of modern contraceptives, the discontinuance of use of the condom, and the relaxation in sexual mores.

Teen-agers account for 25 per cent of all cases of gonorrhea, and 90 per cent of cases occur in those under 35 years of age. This latter figure may be a reflection of mucosal aging, especially in women. Thus the declining incidence with age is not necessarily because of decreasing sexual involvement but is more likely due to an unfavorable environment for the growth of the organism. Gonorrhea, therefore, is rarely seen postmenopausally, and at that time it occurs as a vaginitis rather than a cervicitis.

Men are susceptible to gonorrheal disease at any age. Indeed, recent studies have shown that the organism may remain in their prostatic secretions without symptoms, rendering them important sources of infection. In one study, the examination of prostatic secretions of asymptomatic men exposed to known gonorrhea cases revealed the incidence of the carrier state to be 40 per cent. Women are often sources of asymptomatic infection. Organisms obtained from cervical swabs can be cultured or viewed directly under the microscope. The incidence of transmission of the disease is reported to be from 5 to 30 per cent from *known* sources.

GONORRHEA IN MEN

The usual incubation period is 2 to 7 days. In symptomatic patients, this period is followed by a purulent urethritis. In the preantibiotic era, this symptom lasted for about 8 weeks. Thereafter, 10 to 15 per cent of men would go on to get unilateral epididymitis. Urethral stricture was often a later sequela. Homosexual men are prone to develop anal and pharyngeal tonsillar infections. Heterosexual men and women may develop pharyngeal lesions through fellatio and cunnilingual acts.

GONORRHEA IN WOMEN

The major symptoms include dysuria and vaginal discharges. Asymptomatic carriers are common, and their numbers range from

15 to 50 per cent in various surveys. Symptoms may disappear spontaneously or after curative and subcurative treatment. The major complication in cases of female gonorrhea is acute salpingitis, which represents a spread from the endocervix and which occurs in 10 to 15 per cent of all untreated cases. Acute infection of the Bartholin glands results in a unilateral swelling of one side of the vulva. This condition should not be confused with a chronic Bartholin cyst. Acute inflammation of Skene's ducts may result in dysuria and, occasionally, acute urinary retention—a symptom that is rare in women; when it occurs it should suggest acute gonorrhea. Anal and pharyngeal infection is not uncommon. Anal infection tends to be chronic and may result in a carrier or symptomatic state, unless treated. Systemic infection may arise from both anal and pharyngeal sites. Gonorrhea in children can occur during childbirth. Areas of infection include the conjunctivae, pharynx, respiratory tract, and anal canal. Before puberty, gonorrhea occurs as a vulvovaginitis.

Systemic gonorrhea is often manifested by fever, polyarthralgias, and centrally necrotic pustular skin lesions. The arthritis accounts for 50 per cent of all infectious arthritides and is usually manifested as a tenosynovitis of the wrist and fingers or knee and ankle pain and swellings. Endocarditis is the most dangerous manifestation of disseminated disease, although it has become a rarity in the antibiotic era.

DIAGNOSIS

The demonstration of the organism is through direct Gram stain methods or through culture techniques, which are by far the more reliable. *N. gonorrhoeae* is notable for its absence on direct staining. This remains the most expedient technique *only when it is positive.*

TREATMENT

Penicillin remains the drug of choice, although drug-resistant strains of the organism are an increasing problem. More resistant forms have developed in the Far East, and

servicemen returning from Vietnam have been a source of these resistant infections. For uncomplicated gonorrhea, 4.8 million units of procaine penicillin G, given intramuscularly, are required. Variations of penicillin therapy have resulted in penicillin or ampicillin being combined with probenecid to maintain higher and longer blood levels of antibiotics. Spectinomycin (Trobicin) is specific for gonorrhea, although it is apparently ineffective for pharyngeal lesions. Treatment of disseminated disease should be in the hospital, where 6 million to 10 million daily units of penicillin G should be given intravenously over a 14-day period.

PREVENTION AND CONTROL

There appears to be no immunity after infection, and, indeed, certain patients fall into predictable patterns of reinfection. Recurrence applies to those who, after treatment, relapse with disease without contact. This recurrence likely has to do with dormant organisms and an apparently cured or subclinical state. Prophylactic penicillin is useful in preventing acquisition of the disease if the drug is taken shortly before or after infectious contacts; 500 mg. of potassium penicillin V, taken orally, is effective. Penicillin G should not be given orally because it is unstable in the presence of gastric secretions. Attempts to evolve a gonococcal vaccine are in the formative stages. Newborns are routinely given silver nitrate drops in the conjunctivae to treat gonorrhea contracted in the birth canal.

Chancroid

Chancroid is an acute infection transmitted sexually by the organism *Haemophilus ducreyi*. It is characterized by painful genital ulcers, associated frequently with suppurative inguinal adenopathy.

CAUSE

The causitive organism is a Gram-negative rod that can be cultured from enlarged inguinal lymph nodes called bubos. Under the microscope, the rods are seen to be arranged in chains. Insignificant spirochetes grow synergistically and are often confused with *T. pallidum*.

CLINICAL MANIFESTATIONS

Three to 5 days after infection is contracted, a small papule appears, usually on the preputial orifice or on the internal surface of the prepuce in men and on the labia and fourchette in women. The papule develops into an ulcer in 2 to 3 days and results in an acute inflammatory lymphadenitis in most instances. Untreated cases result in matted lymph nodes called bubos, which often go on to rupture.

INCIDENCE

The true incidence of chancroid is unknown, since reporting tends to be unreliable. In the armed forces, chancroid occurs as frequently as syphilis. Troops stationed in Vietnam had a high frequency of chancroid.

DIAGNOSIS

Chancroid must be differentiated from herpesvirus 2, syphilis, and lymphogranuloma venereum. There is no fever in chancroid, although tender lymphadenopathy is common in both herpesvirus and chancroid. Syphilis produces nontender lymphadenopathy. Ultimately, the diagnosis depends on isolation of the organism *H. ducreyi* from an infected node or demonstration on Gram stain.

TREATMENT

Sulfonamides and tetracycline remain the drugs of choice, Sulfadiazine or sulfasoxazole is given in doses of 4 gm. per day for 10 to 14 days. Tetracycline, 1 to 2 gm. per day, may be tried in sulfonamide-resistant cases.

Granuloma Inguinale

Granuloma inguinale is a chronic and progressive ulcerative disease involving the skin and lymphatics of the genital or perianal regions. It is often sexually transmitted and is associated with the presence in affected tissues of an intracellular microorganism known as the Donovan body.

CAUSE

Granuloma inguinale was described by McLeod in India in 1882, and Donovan described the intracellular bodies in 1905. Bacteria known as *Calymmatobacterium granulomatis* have been recovered from lesions, and they resemble Donovan bodies. It is not yet certain whether these are the responsible agents, although this is a strong possibility.

EPIDEMIOLOGY

Granuloma inguinale is endemic in the tropics. The disease is unusual in the United States. Only 103 cases were reported in the United States in 1971. It is uncommon in Caucasians and seems to affect mostly black male homosexuals. There appears to be a high incidence of anorectal involvement.

CLINICAL MANIFESTATIONS

The incubation period appears to range from 1 to 12 weeks. The disease begins as a papule, which ulcerates and evolves as an elevated zone of friable granulation tissue. It spreads by continuity or by autoinoculation of approximated skin surfaces. Secondary infection produces a painful and often foul-smelling exudative lesion. In men the lesions are located on the glans, prepuce, or shaft of the penis, or in the perineal region. The labia are most often affected in women. Intradermal and subcutaneous swelling produces pseudobubos, which are often mistaken for carcinomas. Dissemination may occur after many years of chronic infection and may involve the bones and joints. Fatalities have occurred.

DIAGNOSIS

As stated, granuloma inguinale is often mistaken for carcinoma. A punch biopsy must be obtained from the periphery of the lesion. The deep portion of the biopsy is removed, squeezed between two slides, air-dried, and stained with Wright-Giemsa stain.

Donovan bodies are seen as coccobacilli, which are present within cystic spaces in the cytoplasm of large mononuclear cells. A large mononuclear cell whose cysts contain Donovan bodies is pathognomonic of the disease.

TREATMENT

Tetracycline is given in a dose of 2 gm. daily and is continued until healing occurs. As an alternative, 1 gm. of streptomycin may be given intramuscularly every 12 hours for 10 to 15 days.

Lymphogranuloma Venereum

Lymphogranuloma venereum is a systemic infection caused by sexually transmitted bacteria. It is characterized by the presence of a small genital ulcer, followed by suppuration of the regional lymph nodes. There is usually a mild systemic reaction, although a severe reaction may occur. After a latent period of years, complications such a genital elephantiasis or rectal stricture may occur.

CAUSE

Although previously classified as a virus of the psittacosis-lymphogranuloma group, the agent is now thought to be a small bacterium, since it divides by binary fission and possesses both RNA and DNA. The bacterium belongs to the group known as Chlamydia.

EPIDEMIOLOGY

The southwestern U.S. remains an endemic source, although the disease is worldwide, especially in developing countries. Women and homosexual men tend to be carriers in whom infection may reside on a subclinical basis.

CLINICAL MANIFESTATIONS

The incubation period is 3 days to 4 weeks, after which a small painless ulcer appears at the site of the inoculation, on the penis, vagina, or rectum. Oral lesions have not been reported. These initial manifestations may go unnoticed. Healing usually occurs within a few days. In 2 to 6 weeks painful inguinal lymphadenopathy begins and progresses to contiguous unilateral or bilateral matted masses above and below the inguinal ligament. Within days, these areas may suppurate with the formation of multiple draining sinuses. It is at this time that systemic reactions occur, such as fever, malaise, myalgias, and arthralgias. On rare occasions, meningitis and pericarditis may occur. The organism Chlamydia may be cultured from the cerebrospinal fluid, bubo, or, rarely, blood. Complications include perirectal abscess, fistula-in-ano, and rectovesical, rectovaginal, and ischiorectal fistulae. A rare late complication is genital elephantiasis, which is an induration or edema of the penis or vulva caused by chronic lymphatic obstruction.

Lymphogranuloma venereum must be differentiated from chancroid and other conditions producing inguinal lymphadenopathy, such as syphilis, pyogenic infection, and neoplasm. Finding the organism by culture is the surest means of diagnosis. The lymphogranuloma venereum complement fixation test is positive in 85 to 90 per cent of all cases of lymphogranuloma venereum, although it is also positive in other Chlamydia infections, such as trachoma. The traditional Frei skin test is positive only 34 to 70 per cent of the time.

TREATMENT

Tetracycline, 2 gm. per day orally for 1 to 2 weeks, is used. Prolonged treatment may be necessary with proctitis. Sulfasoxazole or sulfadiazine is effective at a dosage of 4 gm. per day for 2 weeks.

Herpesvirus 2

DEFINITION, PATHOLOGY, AND EPIDEMIOLOGY

In 1960 a new wave of research began in the area of viral research and venereal disease. Since then, two naturally occurring variants of herpesvirus (HSV)—1 and 2— each with different biological and epidemiological characteristics, have been firmly established. HSV 1 was found to be primarily involved in nongenital sites and is responsible for a variety of oral and eye lesions. Herpesvirus 2 is a venereal disease transmitted presumably by the genital to genital route. The virus particle consists of DNA, protein, lipid, and carbohydrate.

During primary infections, fever, malaise, and adenopathy may be seen, and viremia may follow. In men, tiny vesicles may appear on the glans or shaft of the penis. These vesicles are associated with a burning, urgency, frequency, and watery discharge. In women, tiny vesicles appear on the labia minora and inner surfaces of the labia majora and cervix. These vesicles ulcerate and form coalescent gray-white lesions.

Recurrent attacks are associated with neurological pain. Vesicles may be seen at this time on the penis, vulva, thigh, or buttocks. If the cervix or the vulva is infected at the time of delivery, neonatal viremia may occur. The outcome is usually fatal because of extensive internal fetal disease. The virus may be recovered from the vesicles. Typical cytological changes of infection may be recognized on a Papanicolaou preparation.

Herpes progenitalis is now considered to be an extremely common form of venereal disease in women. It may actually exceed gonorrhea in frequency. Certainly, this is the case in private gynecological practice and may well be taking place in the clinic as these lesions are being sought and identified as the cause of nongonorrheal and nonleutic infection. In men, this vesiculoulcerative disease is seen almost as commonly as syphilis.

The average incubation period is 2 to 6 days for a primary infection. These lesions last from 3 to 6 weeks, causing considerable pain and disability. Recurrent disease lasts 7 to 19 days and may be aroused by reinfection, but this is by no means certain, as other factors—such as emotions, heat, hormones, and immunity—appear to be playing a role. There is considerable evidence that herpesvirus persists in noninfectious forms at the site of recurrence. Persistence in lymphocytes has been noted. The virus has been noted to remain in nerve cells, which accounts for the neurological pain of recurrence. The nerve cells may also serve as a common pathway for the various factors that participate in the reactivation of the disease.

TREATMENT

The most effective treatment to date is photodynamic inactivation of the lesions. Proflavine solution or ether is used to soak the lesions after the vesicles have been ruptured. The virus absorbs the solution and, on exposure to white fluorescent light, appears to inactivate the virus. This technique has value in that it may shorten the illness and possibly reduce the incidence of recurrence. Proflavine usage is now in question since its alteration of DNA may be carcinogenic.

Another method being used to prevent recurrence is repetitive smallpox or BCG (Bacillus Calmette-Guérin) inoculations. The inoculations apparently arouse the immune system with some specificity against herpesvirus. Idoxuridine may be topically applied and has been used intravenously in the viremic fetus.

A vaccine has been used in Europe but has not been tried in the United States. Of increasing importance to oncologists is the circumstantial evidence linking cervical cancer with HSV 2. Whether or not these viruses are carcinogenic remains to be determined.

Venereally Transmitted Hepatitis A and B

Hepatitis B, formerly called serum hepatitis, has been found in a large proportion of patients in whom no history of parenteral transmission can be obtained. This occurrence was initially noted in a number of patients institutionalized with Down's syndrome. Recently, good evidence has implicated hepatitis B as often being venereally transmitted. Hepatitis B antigen and antibody have been found in high frequency in sexual partners of hepatitis patients. It is assumed that hepatitis A, formerly called infectious hepatitis, is transmitted similarly. No measurable antigens or antibodies yet identify this virus. There appears to be an increased incidence of the disease among male homosexuals. Little hepatitis has been reported among lesbians—excluding bisexuals—and the incidence here seems to be less than in heterosexuals. Perhaps this difference is due to the technique of transfer—vaginal or rectal intercourse introducing infected semen on mucous membrane made permeable by the friction of coitus—but this speculation awaits further proof.

Psychological Effects of Venereal Disease

Few studies have been made of the reaction of the patient infected with venereal disease. However, Farnsworth, in a study of sexual morality on the campus, notes:

because cure of venereal disease is no longer the agonizing process it was when the only treatments were of long duration and uncertain value, most young people feel that the chance of contracting a venereal disease is no deterrent to intercourse and that, even if they do contract one, it can be cured quickly and with little trouble.

Some clinical investigators have reported marked anxiety about venereal disease in many patients, and others have described a phobia in some about becoming infected by such a disease. However, there seems to be minimal published material on this subject.

REFERENCES

Abrams, A. J. Lymphogranuloma venereum. J. A. M. A., *205:* 199, 1968.
*Blankenship, R. M., Holmes, R. K., and Sanford, J. P. Treatment of disseminated gonococcal infection. N. Engl. J. Med., *290:* 267, 1974.
*Clark, E. G., and Daubolt, N. The Oslo study of the natural course of untreated syphilis. Med. Clin. North Am., *48:* 613, 1964.

Davis, C. M. Granuloma inguinale: clinical, histological and ultrastructural study. J. A. M. A., *211:* 632, 1970.
Farnsworth, D. L. Sexual morality and the dilemma of the colleges. Int. Psychiatry Clin., *7:* 133, 1970.
Fulford, K. W. M., Dane, D. S., Catterall, R. D., Woof, R., and Denning, J. V. Australian antigen and antibody among patients attending a clinic for sexually transmitted disease. Lancet, *1:* 1470, 1973.
Hansfield, H. H., Lipman, T. O., Harnisch, J., Tronca, E., and Holmes, K. K. Asymptomatic gonorrhea in men: diagnosis, natural course, and prevalence, N. Engl. J. Med., *290:* 117, 1974.
Hersh, T., Melnick, J. L., Goyal, R. K., and Hollinger, F. B. Nonparenteral transmission of Australia Antigen associated hepatitis. N. Engl. J. Med., *285:* 1363, 1971.
Heyman, A. The clinical and laboratory differentiation between chancroid and lymphogranuloma venereum. Am. J. Syph., *30:* 279, 1946.
Holmes, K. K. Lymphogranuloma venereum. In *Principles of Internal Medicine,* T. R. Harrison, editor, ed. 7, pp. 982-985. McGraw-Hill, New York, 1974.
Holmes, K. K. Syphilis. In *Principles of Internal Medicine,* T. R. Harrison, editor, ed. 7, pp. 877-885. McGraw-Hill, New York, 1974.
Holmes, K. K., Counts, G. W., and Beaty, H. N. Disseminated gonococcal infection. Ann. Intern. Med., *74:* 979, 1971.
*Kampmeier, R. H. Editorial: Tuskegee study of untreated syphilis. South. Med. J., *65:* 1247, 1972.
Kerber, R. E., Rowe, C. E., and Gilbert, K. R. Treatment of chancroid: a comparison of tetracycline and sulfisoxazol. Arch. Dermatol., *100:* 604, 1961.
*Nahmias, A. I., and Roizman, B. Infection with herpes simplex virus 1 and 2. N. Engl. J. Med., *289:* 667, 719, 781, 1973.
*Rockwell, D. H., Yobs, A. R., and Moore, M. B. Tuskegee study of untreated syphilis. 30th year of observation. Arch. Intern. Med., *114:* 792, 1964.
Schroeter, A. L., and Pazin, G. J. Gonorrhea, Ann. Intern. Med., *72:* 553, 1970.
Sherlock, S., and Heathcote, J. Spread of acute type B hepatitis in London. Lancet, *1:* 1468, 1973.
Sparling, P. F. Diagnosis and treatment of syphilis, N. Engl. J. Med., *284:* 642, 1971.
*Sutnick, A. L., London, T. J., Gerstley, B. J., Cronlund, M. M., and Blomberg, B. S. Anicteric hepatitis associated with Australian antigen. J. A. M. A., *205:* 670, 1968.
Weisner, P. J., Tronca, E., Bonin, P., Pederson, A. H. B., and Holmes, K. K. Clinical spectrum of pharyngeal gonococcal infection. N. Engl. J. Med., *288:* 181, 1973.

13.5

Drugs and Sexual Behavior

ALFRED M. FREEDMAN, M.D.

Introduction

In all cultures and times, people have used chemical agents to relieve tension, to lessen anxiety, to increase self-awareness, and to heighten sensation. For thousands of years, alcohol, peyote, opium, and similar substances have been used to alter human consciousness and distort the sense of reality. One of the most elusive goals of those who seek drugs to alter their state of mind is the chemical that enhances sexual activity or increases one's ability to perform sexually. At one time or another, almost every well known drug—everything from the harsh irritant Spanish fly to the ubiquitous marijuana—has been thought to be endowed with aphrodisiac powers. Alcohol, despite its depressant qualities, is clearly associated with sexual activity, although its values probably lies most in its social lubricant qualities.

A complex assortment of social and cultural factors influence sexual behavior. Most drugs vary in their effects from person to person; a great deal depends on a person's expectations and on the current mythology surrounding a particular drug. Some people look for ways to relieve sexual tension; others are constantly looking for a magical potion that will yield fantastic sexual gratification. Needs, desires, expectations, and knowledge—all interact with the specific effect of a particular drug.

There are few reliable scientific studies of the relation of most drugs in use today to sexual performance and desire. A fact that does emerge from psychopharmacological research is that the variety of drug responses in a population may be largely the result of the situation in which the drug is used. Some persons given a sedative but told that it is a stimulant do, in fact, react as if they had actually taken a pep pill (Uhlenhuth, 1966). Similar behavior has been demonstrated with placebos. Paradoxically, some people find their sexual drive and activity increased by such depressant drugs as barbiturates. Others are completely inhibited by barbiturates. Lysergic acid diethylamide (LSD) impairs the sexual performance of some people; others have found it to be the wonder drug that finally brings full potency after years of humiliating failure. This effect may be the result of some of the mystique that surrounds the taking of drugs. A person who has been told that LSD will cure his impotence is likely to respond differently from someone with contrary expectations. The musician or artist who takes LSD or marijuana expects to improve his creativity and usually feels that his performance has been enhanced, even in the face of contrary objective evidence. In the same way, a person who wants or needs to improve his sexual competence may describe his sexual experience under drugs as "the greatest," an evaluation very difficult to verify objectively.

One young man claimed that when he crushed a vial of amyl nitrate just before having an orgasm his experience was extraordinary, better than his experiences with any other drugs. However, when he was closely questioned, it became clear that he was so preoccupied with crushing the capsule at the right moment and sniffing the vapor, thereby altering his mental state, that he was scarcely aware of what really happened.

Diversity of Sexual Effects

Some drugs have a powerful effect on sexual functioning. Sufficient doses of heroin, for example, nearly always depress desire and ability to perform (Isbell, 1965). However, with most drugs, there is no clear relation between drug ingestion and sexual behavior.

The following cases illustrate the diversity of sexual effects reported by a number of young drug users. These cases have been chosen because they emphasize sexual activity. However, more typically, drug use is associated with lack of interest in sex and a total concentration on the drug scene—obtaining and administering the drug. Male-female relations are often exploitative, with the woman caring for the drug-addicted and dependent man.

Carlos is 24 years old and came to this country from Puerto Rico when he was 3. When Carlos was 10, his father was hospitalized as a paranoid schizophrenic, and his mother, who was devoted and attentive, could not manage to keep the family together.

Although he was popular with his male schoolmates, Carlos was extremely shy with girls. His friends urged him to try marijuana when he was 14, and he found that he was much more comfortable around girls while under the influence of marijuana. At 15, he dropped out of school and again found himself anxious around girls. Encouraged by friends to try skin-popping heroin, he found that it relieved his anxiety more effectively than marijuana did. He was able to approach girls, dance with them, and, for the first time, engage successfully in sexual intercourse. Gradually, he became a mainline heroin user, which led to delayed ejaculation and, eventually, to indifference and impotence.

While addicted to heroin, Carlos married a woman who tried to get him to give up the habit but was willing to tolerate his impotence. When he abstained from drugs, he was able to perform sexually, but he was once again impotent when he went back to drugs.

Rose, the only child of a successful suburban businessman, moved to Greenwich Village after graduating from high school. She drifted from job to job and halfheartedly pursued an artistic career. Her parents supported her but were displeased with her behavior.

When she was 19, Rose began trying amphetamines and barbiturates. She also drank liquor and occasionally tried LSD, marijuana, and heroin. She had her first sexual relations at 18 and reported no significant change in her sexual behavior as a result of taking drugs. Barbiturates made her less interested in sex, and amphetamines, alcohol, and marijuana made her more interested in it, but none made any real change in her feelings or her performance. Only twice did she engage in sexual relations that she claimed would not have occurred without drugs.

George, 19 years old and the son of divorced parents, is a college student who has been addicted to heroin for 1½ years. He has also tried a great variety of other drugs, including barbiturates, amphetamines, marijuana, LSD, mescaline, psilocybin, cocaine, phenothiazines, meprobamate, and chlordiazepoxide (Librium). He does not drink alcohol.

George feels that drugs have allowed him to achieve sexual satisfaction. He claims that he has orgasms when he takes heroin, whereas he was unable to have an orgasm before taking the drug. Hashish, cocaine, and marijuana also increase his sexual drive. Amphetamines and LSD decrease it.

It is clear from these cases that a person's current psychological status and his total personality makeup must be considered in evaluating the effects of drugs on his sexual behavior. Thus, Carlos found that heroin initially facilitated his relations with women but ultimately destroyed his sexual abilities. George, on the other hand, found heroin to be an aphrodisiac. And Rose seemed to note little change in her sex life as a result of taking drugs.

Patterns of Drug Use

Today's young drug user—and the addict population gets younger every year—has a great variety of drugs at his disposal (Freedman and Brotman, 1969). The mind-altering or psychoactive drugs include alcohol, caffeine, and nicotine—which at least 38 per cent of the adult population use in the form of cigarettes—as well as amphetamines, barbiturates, narcotics, tranquilizers, marijuana, LSD (and associated drugs like psilocybin, mescaline, and dimethyltryptamine) and synthetics (2, 5-dimethoxy-4-methylamphetamine and MDA). Although statistics in this area are usually unreliable, it is estimated that there are between 5 and 7 million alcoholics in this country; that more than 10 million people commonly use sedatives, stimulants, and tranquilizers; that there are several hundred thousand people suffering from barbiturate or amphetamine abuse. At least 20 million people have tried marijuana.

Despite harsher laws, the trend seems to be clearly toward more use of mind-altering drugs, the use of more kinds of drugs in more combinations, and the widening of the drug-using population to include people from all socio-economic classes. The publicity associated with drug use surrounds it with a lurid sensationalism that is associated in the minds of many people, particularly the young and impressionable, with sexual freedom and exotic pleasures. These magical expectations are rarely fulfilled.

Sexual Effects of Various Drugs

ALCOHOL

Although many people do not consider alcohol a drug in the sense that such dangerous substances as amphetamines and heroin are drugs, it is, nonetheless, an addicting and potentially dangerous drug. The National Commission on Marijuana and Drug Abuse (1973) points out that it is the most important drug of abuse in the United States today. Many persons who consider themselves to be social drinkers consume a quantity of alcohol sufficient to have depressive effects, particularly on sexual activity. Impotence in middle-aged men is often the result of excessive alcohol intake. In addition to the physiological effect, alcohol may contribute to an inhibition of sex on an interpersonal basis. One partner may be so repelled by the other's alcoholic behavior that he or she avoids sex.

Although it is well known that alcohol impairs sexual performance, it may foster the initiation of sexual activity, heterosexual or homosexual, by removing inhibitions and social restraints. Alcohol can lead to promiscuity in some cases and the cycle continues with the promiscuous person often turning to alcohol to relieve his anxiety and guilt feelings.

The relation of alcohol, as well as many of the other drugs being discussed, to sexual performance has never been better described than by Shakespeare in *Macbeth*:

Macduff: What three things does drink especially provoke?

Porter: Marry, sir, nose painting, sleep, and urine. Lechery, sir, it provokes and unprovokes; it provokes the desire, but it takes away the performance.

MARIJUANA

The sexual effects of marijuana are related to dosage and to expectations. There is no clear indication that it is an aphrodisiac; there is some evidence that it can contribute to impotence. It must be remembered that marijuana is commonly smoked in a social context in which the conspiratorial atmosphere itself heightens perception, reduces sexual inhibition, and helps to enhance sexual experience. Changes in sexual behavior are often the result of the letting go of controls and inhibitions, so that, in fact or fancy, desired states can be achieved.

There is a learning factor involved in marijuana use. Users unaccustomed to smoking it report milder effects than do habitual users. Halikas et al. (1971), in a study of 100 regular users, state that 33 per cent reported that they usually performed better sexually; 46 per cent said that they occasionally experienced better sexual performance. Some users report that, while high on marijuana, they feel a sense of time distortion accompanied by prolonged orgasm.

There is no evidence to indicate that marijuana contributes significantly to sexual promiscuity or immorality.

LSD AND RELATED DRUGS

In its heyday in the mid-1960's, LSD was firmly linked with sexual experience, being credited with everything from producing multiple intense orgasms in previously nonorgasmic people to curing homosexuality. At the least, it was said to expand consciousness so that the user experienced the true nature of love.

The sexual promise of LSD and similar psychedelic substances, splashed enticingly across major magazines and newspapers, undoubtedly motivated many people to try it. But, as with marijuana, there is no pharmacological evidence that LSD is sexually stimulating in and of itself. In this sexually preoccupied society, such drugs may increase or decrease sexual functioning, depending on individual expectations and conscious and unconscious forces.

In discussing a hallucinogenic drug called sixty-eight, Raymond Naft (1967), the public health coordinator for Cape May County, New Jersey, commented:

> In many cases, with this drug, as with LSD and others, the increased sexual drives are in the user's mind. One man we heard of who claimed phenomenal sexual powers while under the influence of drugs was observed during his entire trip crouched in a corner.

Timothy Leary (1966), the high priest of the LSD cult, claimed that LSD was definitely the most powerful aphrodisiac known to man. Although he does not attribute the drug's remarkable powers to exclusively physiological or psychological factors, he does say that it can help the person with serious problems as well as those suffering from sexual inhibition. Despite his unbridled enthusiasm for the sexually enhancing qualities of LSD, Leary admits that social and sexual responses vary from person to person.

> One man may take LSD and leave his wife and family and go off to be alone on the banks of the Ganges. Another may take LSD and go back to his wife.

Ungerleider and Fisher (1966), commenting on the LSD scene in Los Angeles, described community dances at which the drug seemed to replace personal contact and to substitute for the drives of sex and aggression.

> We watched seven or eight sailors dancing with one girl. There was little male-female awareness or physical contact. Each was in his fantasy world.

The authors suggest that LSD helps to solve the problems of the adolescents who are struggling with feelings of aggression and sexuality, along with their need to establish an identity. LSD can seem to be a magic solution to such problems. Thus, they are able to achieve a ready-made identity with fellow users. The introspection they experience helps to deny the feelings of both aggression and sexuality.

AMPHETAMINES

Amphetamines have inconsistent but dose-related effects. Sexual behavior may be bizarre, and violent sexual abuses have been reported. In stimulating the central nervous system, amphetamines reduce fatigue and increase alertness and mental clarity. Amphetamines such as methamphetamine are extremely dangerous, and, although they produce a sense of thrill and excitement, there is no evidence that the sexual drive or sexual performance is enhanced.

High doses of some amphetamines can alter sensation. In one case, a dose of 40 mg. of dextroamphetamine was claimed to have enabled a frigid woman to achieve orgasm. A high dose, say 1 gm. given intravenously in 24 hours, commonly leads to a lack of interest in sex. In men, there are usually two stages: (1) an ability to maintain an erection for a long time without ejaculation and (2) a gradual loss of ability to achieve an erection.

HEROIN

Confusion of sexual identity and of identity in general is one of the social and individual factors associated with the heroin addict (Mathis, 1970). Among imprisoned heroin addicts, the usual sexual talk one is accustomed to finding in cohesive groups of young men is replaced by a solitary interest in heroin. Observers have found that heroin addicts show less interest in sex than do others their own age; imprisoned addicts even have fewer homosexual experiences than one would expect.

The typical addict, unable to deal with the conflicts and anxieties of normal life and of interpersonal relations, finds in heroin the ideal tranquilizer. Alcohol, on the other hand, removes inhibitions and allows sexual acting out. In its very early use, heroin may act similarly if skin-popped or sniffed. However, once addiction is well established, heroin removes the desire and thus the anxieties associated with desire. The marijuana user and the LSD user seek to heighten their feelings; the heroin addict wants to reduce sensory stimulation as much as possible. Sexual feelings may be absent, but sexual activity is often very much a part of an addict's daily life. Many female addicts must resort to prostitution to support their habits, and many male addicts act as pimps or homosexual prostitutes out of economic necessity.

Some observers have speculated that the addict's life-style imitates the rhythms of female sexual excitement and gratification—the procuring of the drug, the injecting of it *into* the body, and the peak of excitement, followed by the postorgasmic stage of relaxation. These observers further suggest that the male addict has a confused sexual identity, possibly as a result of an early disturbance in the mother-child relation. The addicts' report that they can function sexually while on a mild high—but only if their partner initiates the sexual activity—is cited as evidence to support this view.

Amenorrhea, infertility, and lowered libido have been associated with heroin addiction and are believed to be a direct result of the physical action of the drug (Isbell, 1965). It is possible that the sexual impairment resulting from heroin use is partly a psychological disturbance associated with the sedative and euphoric effects of the drug itself.

Cushman (1972) notes that the "inhibitory effects of heroin use in sexuality are usually rapidly reversible." In a study of four groups—control subjects, active heroin addicts, abstinent former addicts, and former addicts in a methadone program—Cushman notes that, after enforced withdrawal, all groups reported normal sexuality, as measured by libido, potency, and ejaculation time. All groups reported normal sexual experience before addiction; the abstinent group reported a return to normal after withdrawal, and the methadone-maintained group reported improved or normal performance and desire.

CYCLAZOCINE

Cyclazocine is an opiate antagonist used in the treatment of heroin addiction. A sufficient amount of cyclazocine blocks the action of opiates, and an opiate addict, if given the antagonist, has withdrawal symptoms. The purpose of administering cyclazocine is to extinguish the need for drugs in addicts who have been withdrawn from opiates (Freedman, 1966; Freedman et al., 1967).

Male addicts receiving cyclazocine during the initial phase, while the drug level is being built up, report markedly increased sexual interest and drive, more frequent erections, particularly on awakening, and the first wet dreams in years.

Although one cannot conclude that cyclazocine is an aphrodisiac, this intensified sex drive has been noted consistently and at relatively low dosages. However, the effect may be due to a release phenomenon. Opiate addicts have reduced sex drives and slight heroin effects for a considerable period of time after complete withdrawal of the drug. The cyclazocine may quickly neutralize these effects and thus free the sex drive.

METHAQUALONE

Methaqualone was introduced in 1965 under the trade name Quaalude as a nonbarbiturate, nonaddicting sedative-hypnotic. Unfortunately, in spite of claims, it has turned out to be addicting, capable of producing varying degrees of toxicity and an abstinence syndrome. In short, it manifests all the hazards of abuse and addiction of the short acting barbiturates (Inaba et al., 1973).

What was different about methaqualone was the glamorous reputation it achieved in the 1970's as the love drug, the Dr. Jekyll and Mr. Hyde drug, the heroin for lovers. Methaqualone swept the West and rapidly became the hottest drug on the streets, bigger than marijuana (Inaba et al., 1973). Methaqualone achieved widespread use because it was at first freely available; other companies manufactured it under such trade names as Sopor, Parest, and Optimil. More recently, its sale has been sharply restricted as a class II drug.

Methaqualone was widely reputed to be a powerful aphrodisiac, particularly by so-called street pharmacologists and drug experts.

Like the depressants previously described, including alcohol in small doses, methaqualone may reduce inhibitions and thus facilitate the initiation of sexual activity. However, with larger doses and continued use, anaphrodisiac effects are reported. Difficulty in obtaining an erection and maintaining it and inhibition of ejaculation are described by men on significant doses of methaqualone. Women describe various depressions of sexual drive and difficulties in achieving orgasm.

Thus, methaqualone—known on the street as sopes, ludes, and sopars—rapidly went through the cycle of fame as the greatest aphrodisiac of all time to its recognition as just another dangerous, addicting, short acting sedative-hypnotic.

PSYCHOTROPIC DRUGS

Antipsychotic drugs

Phenothiazines. Phenothiazines, such as chlorpromazine (Thorazine) and trifluperazine (Stelazine), may produce impotence as a result of their atropine-like effects. Thioridazine (Mellaril) causes dry ejaculation, in which erection and orgasm occur but no ejaculatory spurt. In some cases the ejaculate is inspissated, and in other cases retrograde ejaculation may occur.

Butyrophenones. The major drug in this group is haloperidol (Haldol), which acts similarly to the phenothiazines in producing occasional episodes of impotence. In addition, libido may be decreased. A particular side effect—catalepsy, in which loss of muscle tone occurs with strong emotional states—may affect coitus adversely.

Antianxiety agents. No specific side effects relate to the genitalia with these classes of drugs, which include chlordiazepoxide (Librium) and diazepam (Valium). Sexual functioning may improve as the anxiety, which may inhibit sexual expression, is reduced.

Antidepressants. The two major groups of antidepressants, tricyclics and monoamine oxidase inhibitors, both have atropine-like side effects and may produce potency problems. In general, however, sexual performance improves as the depression lifts.

MISCELLANEOUS SUBSTANCES

Cocaine. In small doses, cocaine produces an intense euphoria that may enhance libido and increase erection time but only for a short period. With chronic use, however, restlessness, tremors, and a toxic psychosis occur. Tolerance, habituation, and a continued need for the drug eventually produce a complete loss of sexual interest.

Cantharides. Derived from the Spanish fly (*Cantharis vesicatoria*), these drugs have an intensely irritant action on mucous membranes. They may be absorbed from the skin or from the gastrointestinal tract when taken orally. Cantharides produce bladder irritation, urinary frequency, and possible priapism. Large amounts of the drug are poisonous and cause vomiting, abdominal pain, renal damage, shock, and death.

Yohimbine. Because of its parasympathetic effect of increased vasodilation, this drug was believed to help induce erection. It is still to be found in a variety of proprietary nostrums, but no evidence of effectiveness has been demonstrated.

Amyl nitrate. A strong peripheral vasodilator used in the treatment of angina pectoris, amyl nitrate causes massive peripheral vasodilation and, when inhaled or "popped" at the moment of orgasm, is reported to enhance orgastic pleasure. This effect may be related to an altered state of consciousness.

Camphor. Camphor is a mild respiratory and circulatory stimulant, as well as a local rubefacient when rubbed on the skin. Accordingly, attempts have been made, without success, to find aphrodisiac effects.

Levodopa. L-Dopa is an agent used for the relief of Parkinson's disease. In rare instances, increased libido has been observed in persons receiving the drug. The mechanism of action is unclear and may be the result of the enhanced sense of well-being as the patient's tremor, dysphagia, and depression abate.

Pheromones. Pheromones are chemical substances produced by a member of a species that stimulates a response, usually sexual, in another of the same species. First found in the inframammalian world, these chemicals may play a role in human sexuality. Substances from the glands of various animals—musk oil, civet oil, ambergris—form the chemical base of many of the perfumes made throughout the world. The human animal may produce similar substances that account for mutual attraction; but human pheromones have yet to be demonstrated.

Ideological Factors in Drug Use

Man has searched since antiquity for substances that enhance sexual response. But, as noted above, no true or effective aphrodisiac exists. Indeed, in his search, man often found substances that were eventually abused because of effects that, although pleasurable, had little or nothing to do with sexual response.

With the increase in drug use and with more and more social problems being connected to the issue of drug abuse, many experts have speculated on the causes of the problem. The middle-aged may be motivated by a need to rejuvenate themselves, to impress one another with their sexual prowess, but this is presumably not a motive for the younger drug users, who clearly make up the majority of the drug population. Some observers think that drug abuse is related to the fact that this is a drug culture, that young people are taught at an early age to take medicine for all kinds of disorders, major and minor, physiological and psychological—a fact well illustrated by the average, middle-class, bathroom medicine cabinet. Most experts agree that drug abuse may be caused by such factors as social deprivation, peer pressure, alienation, and rebellion. And they agree that the typical drug user has problems of socialization and little tolerance for frustration and is extremely immature sexually.

In attempting to chance sexuality the person resorting to drugs will seek any kind of alteration; it doesn't matter if one takes ups or downs as long as sensation is altered. The barbiturate user extols the virtues of the drowsy high, and the speed freak raves about the amphetamine high. All that matters is one's subjective state, and all behavior, including sexual behavior, is encompassed in this belief.

REFERENCES

*Cushman, P. Sexual behavior in heroin addiction and methadone maintenance. N.Y. State J. Med., *27:* 1961, 1972.

*Freedman, A. M. Drug addiction: An eclectric view. J. A. M. A., *197:* 878, 1966.

Freedman, A. M., and Brotman, R. E. Multiple drug use among teenagers: Plans for action research. In *Drugs and Youth,* J. R. Wittenborn, editor, p. 340. Charles C Thomas, Springfield, Ill., 1969.

Freedman, A. M., Fink, M., Sharoof, R., and Zaks, A. Cyclazocine and methadone in narcotic addiction. J. A. M. A., *202:* 191, 1967.

*Halikas, J. A., Goodwin, P. H., and Guze, S. B. Marijuana effects: A survey of regular users. J. A. M. A., *217:* 692, 1971.

Inaba, D. S., Gay, G. R., Newmeyer, S. A., and Whitehead, C. Methaqualone abuse. J. A. M. A., *224:* 1505, 1973.

Isbell, H. Prospectus in research on opiate addiction. In *Narcotics,* D. M. Wilner and G. G. Kassebaum, editors. McGraw-Hill, New York, 1965.

Leary, T. Interview. Playboy, p. 100, Sept. 1966.

*Mathis, J. L. Sexual aspects of heroin addiction. Med. Asp. Hum. Sex., *4:* 98, 1970.

Matza, D. *Delinquency and Drift.* John Wiley, New York, 1964.

Naft, R. Quoted in New York Times, p. 27, Aug. 12, 1967.

National Commission on Marijuana and Drug Abuse. *Drug Use in America: Problem in perspective.* United States Government Printing Office, Washington, 1973.

*Uhlenhuth, E. H., Rickels, K., and Fisher, S. Doctor's verbal attitude and clinic setting in the symptomatic response to pharmacotherapy. Psychopharmacologia, *9:* 392, 1966.

*Ungerleider, J. T., and Fisher, D. D. LSD: Research and joy ride. Nation, May 16, 1966.

13.6   Psychological Aspects of Contraception

EUGENE C. SANDBERG, M.D.

Introduction

Contraception is the prevention of fecundation or fertilization of the ovum. It is ubiquitously available, in one form or another, to all who choose to use it.

Contraceptive Methods

Obviously, both celibacy and sterilization prevent the meeting of sperm and egg and are technically contraceptive. In general, they do not have the popularity of the other methods (see Table I), although sterilization of either partner is becoming more popular in those situations in which permanent contraception is desired.

Although celibacy is rejected by most people, temporary or intermittent celibacy in the form of timed abstinence (the rhythm method) is used by a huge number of couples. Since normally only one egg is released a month and this egg has a life-span of only 12 to 24 hours, avoidance of intravaginal ejaculation during that time should theoretically and regularly prevent conception. But difficulties in predicting the time of ovulation, uncertainties in ascertaining the duration of survival of previously introduced spermatozoa, and inconsistencies in the resolve to abstain are all sufficiently great to render the method notoriously unreliable.

The prevention of intravaginal insemination by withdrawal of the penis from the vagina before ejaculation is another contraceptive method that theoretically should have nearly absolute efficiency. For many couples it is a highly successful and totally acceptable method. But an uncommon alertness and a constancy of motivation are absolutely essential. In addition, the degree of emotional and physical control required of both partners by this method is not a universal attribute. Nor is the willingness to accept full sexual gratification by this coital technique universally acceptable.

The chemical methods of contraception include various spermicidal and sperm-immobilizing materials. These are constituted in the form of jellies, creams, foams, and suppositories and are inserted into the vagina precoitally or before ejaculation. They are rarely allergenic or harmful, but for some people they increase the degree of coital lubrication to an objectionable level. Theoretically, their uncertain dispersal about and out of the vagina with coition renders them less than absolutely efficient. They do have a respectable order of effectiveness, but they must be used correctly and with consistency. Of this group, the foams are the most efficient and are seemingly the least objectionable from the point of view of excess lubrication.

Obstructions to the flow of semen into the woman and to the upward motility of spermatozoa within the woman are also used to prevent the meeting of sperm and egg. The condom or penis-covering sheath (see Figure 1A) effectively and demonstratively prevents the intravaginal deposition of semen. It is simple to understand and use, rarely breaks, and is quite economical. For some, its use is erotic. For others, however, it is disruptive and interferes with pleasure. As with all other coitally connected methods, it must be used for every intravaginal ejaculation. It has widespread availability, but its commercial purchase in most areas still requires a potentially embarrassing request at the

TABLE I

Features of Current Methods of Contraception

Type	Method of Action	Effectiveness*	Advantages	Disadvantages	Potential Complications
Rhythm	Timed abstinence	Low	No cost Always available No professional help required	Imposed coital timing (lack of spontaneity)	Essentially none
Withdrawal	Prevention of insemination	Low (but theoretically high)	No cost Always available No professional help required	Regular coital use required Requires considerable attention and control	Essentially none
Intravaginal foams, creams, jellies, and suppositories	Spermicidal	Low	Inexpensive Generally available No professional help required	Regular coital use required Possible messiness Possible interference with enjoyment	Essentially none
Condom	Sperm barrier	Medium	Inexpensive Generally available No professional help required Decreased acquisition of coitally transmitted diseases	Regular coital use required Possible interference with enjoyment	Essentially none
Diaphragm	Sperm barrier (plus spermicidal with jelly)	Medium	Inexpensive	Regular coital use required Possible interference with enjoyment Requires professional fitting Not anatomically adaptable to everyone	Essentially none
Intrauterine device (IUD)	Unknown (possibly prevents zygote implantation)	Medium	Inexpensive Only single decision required Not coitally connected	Possible increase in bleeding and cramping. Requires professional insertion	Uterine perforation, pelvic infection, spontaneous expulsion
Oral (hormonal)	Prevention of ovulation (possible interference with sperm mobility)	High	Inexpensive Potential absolute efficiency Not coitally connected	Possible side effects Daily ingestion Requires professional visit (Rx)	Thromboembolism, neuro-ocular disturbances, hypertension

*Effectiveness is rated roughly as follows: low: more than 20 pregnancies per 100 woman-years of use; medium: 1 to 20 pregnancies per 100 woman-years of use; high: less than 1 pregnancy per 100 woman-years of use.

counter, and this factor modifies not only its absolute availability but also its frequency of use.

The intravaginal diaphragm (see Figure 1B) is the method most commonly used by women to prevent the upward progress of spermatozoa after the intravaginal deposition of semen. Historically, a large number of other items have been used, and anything that temporarily occludes the upper vagina and prevents direct contact of the ejaculate with the cervix will have some degree of efficiency. The diaphragm is quite effective, especially when it is used with a spermicidal jelly or cream. It is a relatively economical purchase and is simple to use once the woman is fully instructed and practiced. Its use does, however, require a degree of intellect, an initial and possibly an intermittent fitting for appropriate size, and steadfast diligence in insertion for every ejaculatory encounter.

The method requiring the least diligence and having exceptional advantages from this point of view is the intrauterine device (IUD). Once it is correctly inserted by a physician or other skilled person, it may remain in place indefinitely, maintaining its effectiveness throughout. Absolutely no tending is required. The devices are manufactured in numerous forms and are most commonly composed of highly flexible, preformed plastic. They have considerable, although not absolute, efficiency and probably prevent pregnancy by interfering with zygote implantation. At least, the incidence of tubal pregnancy in wearers of the IUD is essentially identical to that noted in the general population. This fact implies that ovulation and

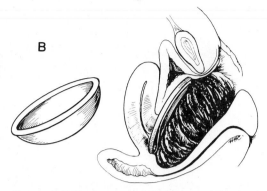

FIGURE 1. *B.* The intravaginal diaphragm and its correct position as viewed during coition.

sperm migration are not impeded, nor is sperm vitality apparently modified in the presence of IUDs. Each type of intrauterine device has its own rate of spontaneous expulsion, pregnancy failure, pelvic infection, uterine perforation, and requested removal because of excessive or abnormal uterine bleeding. For the models pictured in Figure 1C, these rates are all so low that the devices are universally applicable. They are most comfortably inserted during menstruation and should never be inserted in the presence of a pelvic infection or before sounding the uterus. Nulligravidity is not a contraindication.

Only celibacy, uterine or gonadal excision, and the dual oral contraceptive pill have absolute contraceptive efficiency. The combination and dosage of estrogen plus progestin present in dual oral contraceptive tablets consistently prevents ovulation when the tablets are taken daily for 3 of every 4 weeks. Neither 21 days of progestin alone (the minipill) nor 16 days of estrogen followed by 5 days of estrogen plus progestin (sequential oral contraceptives) have the absolute reliability of the dual contraceptive pill. A list of the oral contraceptives available in the United States and their hormonal contents is presented in Table II. A great host of side effects has been ascribed to the use of these medications; all these side effects are essentially minor, with the exception of thromboembolism, neuro-ocular disturbances, and protracted anovulation. Although the causative role of oral contracep-

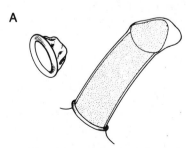

A

FIGURE 1. Pictorial representation of certain contraceptive modalities. *A.* The condom before and after being unrolled onto the erect penis.

C

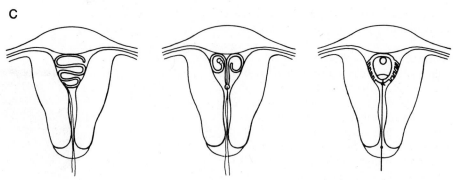

FIGURE 1. *C.* Examples of intrauterine devices in situ; from *left* to *right:* the Lippes loop, the double coil, and the Dalkon shield.

TABLE II
Oral Contraceptive Agents Currently Available in The U.S.A.

Trade Name (Pharmaceutical Company)	Estrogen	Progestin
	Dual or Combined Oral Contraceptives	
Norinyl 1 + 50 (Syntex)	Mestranol 0.05 mg.	Norethindrome 1.0 mg.
Norinyl 1 + 80 (Syntex)	Mestranol 0.08 mg.	Norethindrone 1.0 mg.
Norinyl-2 (Syntex).................	Mestranol 0.1 mg.	Norethindrone 2.0 mg.
Ortho-Novum 1/50 (Ortho)	Mestranol 0.05 mg.	Norethindrone 1.0 mg.
Ortho-Novum 1/80 (Ortho)	Mestranol 0.08 mg.	Norethindrone 1.0 mg.
Ortho-Novum-2 (Ortho)	Mestranol 0.1 mg.	Norethindrone 2.0 mg.
Ortho-Novum-10 (Ortho)	Mestranol 0.06 mg.	Norethindrone 10.0 mg.
Enovid-E (Searle)	Mestranol 0.1 mg.	Norethynodreal 2.5 mg.
Enovid-5 (Searle)	Mestranol 0.075 mg.	Norethynodrel 5.0 mg.
Ovulen (Searle)	Mestranol 0.1 mg.	Ethynodiol diacetate 1.0 mg.
Demulen (Searle)	Ethinyl estradiol 0.05 mg.	Ethynodiol diacetate 1.0 mg.
Ovral (Wyeth)	Ethinyl estradiol 0.05 mg.	Norgestrel 0.5 mg.
Norlestrin-1 mg. (Parke-Davis)	Ethinyl estradiol 0.05 mg.	Northindrone acetate 1.0 mg.
Norlestrin-2.5 mg. (Parke-Davis)......	Ethinyl estradiol 0.05 mg.	Northindrone acetate 2.5 mg.
Loestrin 1/20 (Parke-Davis).........	Ethinyl estradiol 0.02 mg.	Northindrone acetate 1.0 mg.
	Sequential Oral Contraceptives	
Norquen (Syntex)	Mestranol 0.08 mg.	Norethindrone 2.0 mg.
Ortho-Novum SQ (Ortho)	Mestranol 0.08 mg.	Norethindrone 2.0 mg.
Oracon (Mead Johnson)	Ethinyl estradiol 0.1 mg.	Dimethisterone 25 mg.
	Minipill (Pure Progestin) Oral Contracptives	
Nor-Q-D (Syntex)		Norethindrone 0.35 mg.
Micronor (Ortho)		Norethindrone 0.35 mg.
Ovrette (Wyeth)...................		Norethindrone 0.35 mg.

tives has not been firmly established in these circumstances, the Food and Drug Administration has recommended that the pill not be given to women who have a history of thrombophlebitis or embolic phenomena, impaired liver function, breast cancer, estrogen-dependent tumors, or undiagnosed genital bleeding. The Food and Drug Administration has also recommended discontinuation of oral contraceptives in the event of migraine headaches, hypertension, modification of vision, or development of ocular abnormalities. The incidence of severe complications or death associated with oral contraceptive ingestion is about one fifth to one tenth that associated with pregnancy.

With the exception of the intrauterine device, each of the methods requires sustained motivation and has a higher innate or theoretical effectiveness than is demonstrated in actual usage. Error and inconsistency in use are far more commonly the cause of contraceptive failure than is failure of the method itself. Studies of contraceptive efficiency are constantly marred by this uncontrolled and uncontrollable aspect—human behavior. Contraceptive availability and proclaimed motivation do not foreordain consistent and effective contraceptive use.

Contraceptive Use

In considering the psychology of contraception, one should consider the impact of religious teaching on its use and its lack of use. Many religious groups have historically opposed pregnancy prevention on practical as well as ideological grounds. As world communications increase, however, and as more and more global concern develops in regard to the dangers of overpopulation, contraceptive use is becoming increasingly acceptable as a matter of religious dogma and as a matter of individual belief, regardless of stated faith. Such changes do not occur instantaneously, however, and many persons caught in the process of change suffer varying degrees of guilt. This guilt emanates primarily from conflict between the deeprooted, childhood-imbued religious restrictions against contraception (often reinforced by orthodox elders) and the person's own modern, in-tellectualized belief in the inappropriateness of those restrictions. This guilt is magnified when both partners are subject to such conflicts but to different extents and degrees.

Persons who are efficient and effective users of contraceptives have been characterized as mature, independent, self-reliant, secure, ambitious, decisive, and intelligent. They have a good self-image, assume responsibility with ease and confidence, carry accepted tasks through to completion, control their impulsiveness, and have the capacity to tolerate frustration. They establish and appreciate long range goals and have a capacity to establish good communication and usually good sexual adjustments with their partners. Success in life, in business, and in marriage correlates well with success in contraceptive usage.

Such a generalization, although possibly acceptable as an introduction to the subject of contraceptive psychology, is much too broad, superficial, and intuitively understood to be of much interest or use. A more specific and exceptionally intriguing approach, at least to the personality of the female contraceptive user, has been described in the March 1973 edition of *Ms.* magazine by Aline House. Assuming that personality dictates choice of contraceptive method, she has attempted to characterize the female personality that chooses and presumably effectively uses each of the currently available contraceptive methods.

The user of the rhythm method is characterized as somewhat rigid regarding her religious and social attitudes. She frequently feels "overworked, unappreciated, and lonely." She suffers from low self-esteem, a "paralysis of will," and a "pervasive sense of guilt." Bad luck is considered to be deserved. She sees men as exploitative and unloving and, fearing rejection, is herself "ungiving and unyielding." Sex is a duty. Sexual drive is low, and body image is negative. She denies her sexual instincts and denies her partner's as well. The rhythm method allows her freedom frequently to escape intercourse and simultaneously to punish her partner for arousing her sexual feelings. Because of its precarious inefficiency, the rhythm method "suits her fatalism" and her desire for martyrdom.

The user of the withdrawal method is characterized as having an excessive faith in luck, a denying attitude regarding fertility, and feelings of guilt if she is contraceptively prepared for coitus. She feels a "doomed dependence" on men. Although she has low self-esteem, she is obsessive about her beauty, believing that only beauty can attract. She resents men and considers them to be "unreliable, perfidious, and unfaithful," but, being dependent on them and feeling dependent on sex appeal to attract them, she is caught in conflict. She must inspire sexual activity that she does not want. Compelled to indulge, she can still mentally and emotionally reject sex and the male as well. Withdrawal deprives each partner of pleasure, but, inasmuch as pleasure and orgasm are not her goals, the method is punitively directed. Furthermore, if withdrawal fails and she becomes pregnant, it is obviously his fault, and her feelings about men are verified. Use of any other method implies an interest and a consent that she denies.

Ms. House describes women who enforce use of the condom as being angry at men and distrustful. They consider men to be weak, disappointing, and unable to equal the strength and qualities of women. Dating and marriage are deals—sex for sociality and security. They believe that all sex is essentially prostitution, and a male-female love relationship cannot be perceived. A subconscious self-image of whore appears in this circumstance, and the woman spends her entire life reacting to it. She punishes and controls men by insisting that they accept full contraceptive responsibility and by forcing them to use this particular pleasure-interfering, disruptive method. She figuratively rejects men through the use of a barrier to exclude their dirty semen and to exclude any direct contact with the repugnant penis. Or she may attempt purification of her self-image by the white cloak of holy motherhood. A more efficient method might deprive her of the potentiality of expiation by pregnancy and leave her simply a pleasure-bent harlot. The condom is convincing visual evidence of protection from men and sex.

Those women employing intravaginal foams and jellies are described as passive, motherhood-family directed, and highly satisfied with their femininity. Such women are joyfully dependent on men and see them as strong, supportive, protective, and responsible. Women should make men happy, and men should make their families happy. "Everybody lives happily ever after." Sex, love, pregnancy, motherhood, and family are all well integrated and pleasurable. Highly effective contraceptive methods, especially if they exclude the mutual sharing of love and semen, conflict with her needs for passivity, for giving, and for motherhood.

The diaphragm user is considered independent, self-reliant, logical, career oriented, and competitive with men. She likes to be in control of herself and her sexuality and of the males in the world about her. She may feel superior to men and contemptuous of them, but at the same time she retains a need for romance, love, male attention, and approval. Her sexual responsivity may be quite variable, depending on her degree of need to control and her competitiveness in achieving the same abandon and pleasure as the man. She tends to be hypochondriacal and threatened by illness, symptoms, or potential body changes that she cannot control. The intrauterine device and oral contraceptives are feared in this light. The diaphragm is under her reassuring observation and direct control. It allows her to dictate the sexual scene, prevents any unbecoming, uncontrolled, and unstructured spontaneity, and suits her work ethic.

The user of the intrauterine device is not as completely characterized as the others but is believed to be comfortable with her body, loving, masturbatory, and highly orgasmic. She is fully accepting of the mutuality, "messiness," and spontaneity of pleasurable sexual activity. She is accepting of pregnancy and childbirth and is neither repulsed nor fearful when considering them. She is not anxious in passivity and does not feel threatened by events and situations beyond her control.

The woman who happily chooses and uses oral contraceptives is modern, active, opportunistic, ambitious, accepting of the new role of women, acquisitive, and desirous of freedom. Men, children, and other contraceptive methods are restrictors of personal freedom and indulgence, and they also restrict the pursuit of personal opportunities. She is not as secure, however, as this picture paints her. Her desires for freedom, control, and personal mastery over fate are in conflict with desires to be cared for and tended. But passivity is threatening; although marriage may not be seen in that light, pregnancy and childbirth are. Personal control of a totally efficient contraceptive method relieves concerns of potential personal imprisonment in a stereotyped woman's role.

As engaging and as superficially reasonable as these personality vignettes may seem, it must be recognized that they are generalities and were never offered as all encompassing. Additionally, they relate to only half of the population, women. The vignettes may occasionally be used to direct certain women to the variety of contraception most appealing to their personalities and needs, but they have considerably greater virtue in helping dispensers of contraceptives to recognize that there is no contraceptive that is ideal for all. The vignettes may also convey the message that impressing one's own concepts of contraceptive use on another is inconsiderate and defeating. It certainly behooves all dispensers of contraceptives to try to achieve tolerance for the personalities and tastes of others and to recognize and accept the concept of "different strokes for different folks."

The achievement of this tolerance is exceptionally useful in the handling and understanding of a sizable and probably more important segment of our population, the frequent or regular nonuser of contraceptives. In general and in direct contrast to effective contraceptive users, contraceptive nonusers may be characterized as immature, dependent, insecure, impulsive, and indecisive. They often have low self-esteem and little desire to control their lives or the world about them. They have a limited capacity to assume responsibility, to complete self-assumed tasks, to tolerate frustration, and to appreciate long range goals.

This generality, like the others, contains certain aspects of truth but describes only the most blatant and flagrant of contraceptive nonusers. Far more subtle personality characteristics and psychological factors control contraceptive disuse, misuse, or rejection in most people. In reality, only a very small proportion of the copulating population has never used any form of contraception and totally and chronically rejects its use. Far more commonly, known and available contraceptive methods are sporadically and intermittently ignored.

It would be as difficult to draw a picture of the typical contraceptive disuser as it would be to draw a composite picture of the population of the United States. Essentially every one has indulged in intercourse without a contraceptive, some more commonly than others. The rationalizations and self-explanations of appropriateness of action that rapidly come to mind are not pertinent; the fact remains that people knowledgeably indulge in unprotected coitus when pregnancy is not desired. Assuredly, an overwhelming number of such coital engagements do not result in pregnancy. For some couples, in some situation, however, they do. In what way are these couples or these situations different? In some, quite probably, pregnancy is subconsciously sought by one or the other of the pair or both. In the remainder, however, pregnancy occurs simply as a result of bad luck, regardless of any establishment of short ended odds. The psychological forces leading to these engagements are common to everyone. A person may selectively fall prey more to one than to another, but the entire panoply of human psychological energies is operative in this area.

The degree of attention or inattention to contraceptive use varies with the number, variety, and strength of the psychological forces that are operative. It also varies with age, stage of life, partner, experience, frequency, setting, time, mood, recent events, emotional attachment, actions or opinions of others, ad infinitum. Vacillations between contraceptive use and nonuse, although unfortunate, should not be regarded as abnormal or reprehensible. Contraception is merely one aspect of a person's existence, and it moves in synergy with all other aspects of that person's personality and emotional structure. Contraception is not an entity in itself. To understand a person's use or nonuse of contraceptives requires an understanding of that person and of his or her partner at the moment in question.

The following pages categorize and at least partially explain some of the psychological forces that are involved in the disuse or rejection of contraception. There is no effort or claim to be all inclusive; the number of categories may be nearly as endless as the variety of examples in each. An overlap of certain of the categories is obvious, and some of the examples given under one category could just as readily be employed under another. Only the state of mind of the person at the moment in question could resolve any argument as to which of the forces was the most operative.

In some categories and instances, pregnancy acquisition is obviously the objective. In others, pregnancy may occur simply as a by-product of the lack of contraception and is not deliberately sought.

Contraceptive nonuse due to mental derangement, honest ignorance, forced intercourse, or other specific instances in which the volitional use of contraception was prevented has been intentionally omitted (see Table III).

Denial

An unwillingness to acknowledge reality is one of the most common bases for contraceptive nonuse. It is especially

TABLE III
Arbitrary Categorization of Psychological Bases for Contraceptive Misuse or Rejection

1. Denial
2. Opportunism (desperation)
3. Sexual identity conflicts
4. Love
5. Guilt
6. Shame (embarrassment)
7. Hostility
8. Coital gamesmanship
9. Masochism
10. Eroticism
11. Entrapment
12. Nihilism
13. Emotional poverty
14. Fear and anxiety
15. Availability of abortion
16. Iatrogenesis

operative during the early coital trials and experiences of high school and college students. It may simply be a denial that coitus will occur, a denial that resolve may disappear or appear irrational in the heat of desire. It may be a denial that impregnation is possible, an assumption of invulnerability. For example: "Pregnancy happens to other people. It can't happen to me." Or "I won't get pregnant. I'll be careful."

Or the person may deny that contraception really works. Thus, it is hardly worth the effort to acquire or use a contraceptive. Each of the methods may be explained away by a reassuring generalization, such as, "All my friends who use the diaphragm get pregnant anyway." Or the rationalizational dismissal of one of the methods is accepted as adequate to eliminate any necessity to consider the others. Such a person simply does not want contraception but needs to try to placate or quiet a social conscience. This need to accommodate conscience while also accommodating a need that requires action contrary to conscience appears repetitively in this and many other categories. Rationalization and denial are the mechanisms most often employed in this process.

Denial of personal responsibility for contraceptive use may also be present, but categorically the psychological content here is often not denial in psychiatric terms but denial as a response to hostility and interpersonal gamesmanship.

Opportunism (Desperation)

An exceptionally prevalent basis for contraceptive nonuse is simple opportunism, the availability of a coital opportunity and the unwillingness for whatever reason to put it off until a contraceptive can be obtained. The opportunity may be to initiate, cement, or protract a relationship, to gain status, to obtain infrequently available affection, to relieve peer group pressure, to be accepted, or a host of other reasons that offer a reward of some nature for immediate and undelayed coitus.

In some circumstances, the opportunity and reward may merely be to please a partner. In most cases, however, the opportunity is that of obtaining immediate personal sensual pleasure. In any event, the psychological setting in nearly all such circumstances contains an aspect of desperation documented by an inability to wait until a contraceptive is obtained. Consequently, both headings are used for this single category.

Sexual Identity Conflicts

Personal evaluation of self is closely correlated with one's attitude regarding his or her sexual identity and sexual adequacy. Self-worth and self-esteem are frequently judged on the basis of virility, as demonstrated by impregnation, and femininity, as demonstrated by fecundity. The necessity for these demonstrations is lessened in proportion to the number and importance of accomplishments in other areas of life and to the degree of ego strength in the entire area of sexuality. If ego rewards in life are minimal and self-esteem can neither be built nor sustained through other efforts, the creative, productive accomplishment of pregnancy and reproduction may be compensatory and may be used as repetitively as required. The birth of an infant is not always demanded. Simple demonstration of virility and femininity by means of a pregnancy that is subsequently and deliberately aborted may be quite sufficient. Indeed, it is highly likely that a substantial number of the pregnancies currently being legally aborted were generated on just this basis. For the majority of such persons, a single demonstration is very frequently so sufficiently reassuring that contraception can be regularly and reliably used thereafter. Manhood or womanhood has been proved.

Contraceptive nonuse emanating from fragility of sexual ego strength may also be seen in the insecure man who uses sexual activity to reinforce a marginal self-esteem. He may fear that the use of a contraceptive will diminish his partner's desire and responsiveness and thus reduce the availability of his sexual outlet. Conversely, he may anticipate that contraception will eliminate her fear of pregnancy and accentuate her lustful demands beyond his ability to fulfill them. This would injure his pride and spotlight his vulnerability to further anguish through her potential infidelity. Such castration anxieties may even lead to impotence or other male

sexual dysfunction. These persons do not accept contraception with equanimity.

Being rejected by a mate or partner may also reinforce feelings of insecurity, low self-worth, and sexual inadequacy. Restitution may require proof of one's sexual ability or desirability through sexual activity with another or with many. In some instances this may require that contraceptives not be used and that pregnancy be achieved as demonstrative proof of worth. Identical scenes may also be generated from the energies of hostility.

Also in this category are certain childless women in their thirties (or occasionally even younger) who sense their aging with despair. They develop an engulfing, irresistable urge to demonstate their femininity with motherhood before their capacity for it is withdrawn. The socially acceptable cloak of marriage is preferred, but the need for motherhood is often greater than that for social compliance.

Love

Risk taking and self-sacrifice are readily accepted in this society as both romantic and realistic demonstrations of one's love for another. And this risk taking extends to the willful risking of pregnancy. Such a demonstration of love may be bilaterally offered and fully shared. More commonly, it is offered by one to the other. Such a demonstration can be very satisfying and fulfilling to the giver, who may often like to risk as much as romantically possible without actually risking the ultimate, one's life. It may be equally gratifying and reassuring to the receiver, for it is the odd person who does not enjoy being loved and having that love demonstrated and reinforced.

In other instances, risk taking is either not considered or is not believed to be adequate. Giving and self-sacrifice are the necessary ingredients of the demonstration. The actual gift of pregnancy may be chosen as the offering with or without the knowledge or solicitation of the partner. This gift of pregnancy may be offered simply to allow the man to demonstrate his virility, or it may be chosen with the actual gift of an infant in mind.

Occasionally, the rejection of contraception may arise from naive and idealistic adoration and an ethereal concept of the requirements of romantic devotion. "To protect myself from him would be a rejection, a denial of my love." "To place a contraceptive between us would be to withhold, to deny myself the love I feel." "My love is so great I want to surrender in totality, to give over every part of my being."

Additionally, in some minds a positive declaration for contraception destroys the illusion that coitus is a spontaneous, uncontrollable, and overwhelming consequence of love. The acquisition of a contraceptive is a cold-blooded confession and an unromantic acceptance of one's yearning for sensual pleasure.

Guilt

Intuitively one might anticipate that a desire to minimize guilt by preventing pregnancy would most frequently drive persons to the regular use of a contraceptive. However, innumerable avenues are available for the development of a type and a quantity of guilt sufficient to totally dissuade persons from any consideration of contraceptive use. For example, to be sexually accessible at all times because of the use of noncoitally connected contraception can be very distressing to some women. Accessibility is tantamount to prostitution and promiscuity, an open invitation to be used (or raped) rather than to be romantically seduced and loved. Additionally, many people have been raised to believe that sex was designed by God for making babies. Sex with contraception must be accepted as sex for lustful and sensual pleasure. To this they cannot emotionally accommodate. The potential for pregnancy must exist in order to obviate any sense of guilt arising from their enjoyment. For some, simply accepting a risk may not be adequate to assuage that guilt. Actual punishment in the form of impregnation may be sought. This may also be seen in the expiation of sinfulness derived from other sexual or "immoral" activities.

Shame (Embarrassment)

The presence or potentiality of feelings of shame or embarrassment is also counter-productive to the acquisition or use of a contraceptive. Embarrassment sufficient to preclude contraceptive use may arise from a necessity to admit ignorance to a partner, to a peer group, or to a physician. This ignorance may be related to contraception alone, or it may relate to sexuality or to sexual activity in general. Embarrassment may also arise from the potentiality of discovery by parents, children, relatives, friends, or others that a contraceptive has been sought or is being used. This feeling is particularly prevalent among adolescents and those acting counter to their social or religious teachings. A considerable degree of inner security, positive self-image, firmness of purpose, independence, and a sense of rightness regarding one's sexual decisions are required for a person of any age to socially expose himself or herself in obtaining contraceptive attention. These are not, for example, the ordinary characteristics of the home-based, financially dependent, and socio-parentally controlled adolescent. Nor are they the characteristics of a substantial number of older, married, and even parous women.

This potentiality that embarrassment or shame will prevent contraceptive use is accentuated in situations in which the community is small, peer group support is minimal, or physicians or clinic personnel are reputed to be judgmental, excessively inquisitive, distant, or unapproving. The impact of an intemperate, opinionated, guilt-provoking physician on the marginally secure contraceptive seeker may be enormous. Rarely do tirades, threats, or rejections result in the elimination of sexual desires or even in significant modification of sexual activity. A consequent pregnancy in a person driven from contraception by a demeaning, authoritarian physician can very appropriately be labeled as iatrogenic, a category to be discussed later in more detail.

Hostility

Resentment and hostility are frequently seen as motivating forces for contraceptive rejection. This is easily seen in the case of a hostile woman who, by rejecting contraception, can also reject her partner, using the fear of potential pregnancy as her socially approved weapon. For the man, the hostile act may be to provoke fear, or it may be a revengeful enforcing of impregnation on a wife or mistress for any of a multitude of reasons. For others, it may be a deliberate seeking of pregnancy to injure a parent, to rebel against a social group, to escape an undesirable environment, to punish a straying mate with guilt and additional responsibility, to retaliate against rejection, and so on.

In many instances, the initial rejection of contraception may not be pregnancy oriented, as it is in most of the examples above. It may simply be used as a statement to the partner that discontent exists and that noncontraceptive sequelae, celibacy or pregnancy, will result if the current resentment is not tended and resolved. Or it may possibly result from resentment against a shift in contraceptive responsibility. "Don't give me that job. I'm not going to use those things. If you don't want pregnancy, take care of it yourself."

Coital Gamesmanship

The last several examples describe rejection of contraception on the basis of a hostile and punitive attitude, but the identical action in essentially the same situation may be undertaken as a ploy in the struggle for interpersonal control. This is, in essence, the male-female power struggle taken to bed. It may arise from a bilateral desire to control or manipulate or simply from a reactive expression of self-defense against a partner who would otherwise dominate to the point of obtaining total submissiveness and subservience. In this sense it is a struggle to maintain a desired degree of independence and self-identity.

In the area of contraception and coital gamesmanship, the question may relate to who is going to control the frequency of coitus, recognizing that the use of coitally related and less effective contraceptives usually offers the female greater control and vice versa. Or the question may relate to who is going to be forced to accept the demeaning role of contraceptor and who is going to be forced to accept being the recipient of accusations of responsibility in the event of pregnancy. Thus, the balance of power in a relationship may well be the deciding factor regarding contraceptive use, and this balance of power may shift from time to time.

Masochism

Hostility may, in many circumstances, be inwardly directed by persons having feelings of worthlessness and may manifest itself in self-deprecating and self-punishing behavior. Overt expressions of such a psychological force may include the infliction of potentially self-destructive injury. This may occur through life-threatening self-abortion, necessitated or generated by deliberate contraceptive nonuse. Far milder forces may only require a sense of self-vilification through allowing oneself to be used sexually. The concurrent nonuse of a contraceptive may add the threat of pregnancy for a double fulfillment of self-punishment. Or pregnancy may be directly sought as a demeaning, degrading, socially reprehensible, imprisoning, figure-destroying subjugation—the price to be paid for recountable or unrecountable sins or for simply existing.

Eroticism

A different approach to contraceptive nonuse is seen in persons who have a desire for self-indulgence, who have a rather insistent urge constantly to supersede previous pleasures. For some, this may amount to a total life-style. For most others, it is intermittent and largely opportunistic. Regardless, for many, such pleasures are procurable through sensual enrichment achievable by risk taking. In the sexual sphere, this may simply result in fornication in a semipublic place, where newness of locale and the sharing of an erotic secret are components of the thrill, and the imminent potential of discovery is the risk. Or it may consist of coitus in a hazardous environment, where the risk actually relates to the danger of bodily harm. In a far more subtle way, the erotic sensualization may be obtained simply by taking the risk of pregnancy through contraceptive nonuse.

The flagrant and consciously deliberate seeking of eroticism through this means is certainly existent but probably infrequent. It is very likely, however, that this is a palpable although infrequently self-assessed element in practically all instances of unprotected coitus. To risk is anxiety provoking, but to win is thrilling and ego satisfying in any endeavor, and the thrill is usually directly proportional to the degree of initial anxiety. In this game of risking pregnancy, most people win most of the time. Consequently, reattainment of this satisfaction seems likely and may be repetitively risked as long as anxieties are manageable. At a minimum, satisfaction in winning is accepted in postmenstrual smugness.

Coercion of the woman into coitus without contraception, a game of coital chicken, could be perceived as the pursuit of eroticism through contraceptive nonuse. But its unilateral demand and its one-sided, willful subjugation of the woman to the narcissistic and selfish pleasures of the man could place this activity in any of several categories, depending on the true motivation of the man and the resultant retrospective feelings of the woman.

Entrapment

Entrapment by impregnation, achievable through contraceptive nonuse or maluse, is becoming decreasingly effective. This is due to current shifts of moral tone, the availability of abortion, and the gradual male acceptance of the proclamation of independence and self-sufficiency by liberated womanhood. But such attitudes and their acceptance are not all pervasive in the culture as yet, and this psychological force for contraceptive nonuse remains both available and operative.

The acquisition of pregnancy may be used to trap a partner into marriage or into a closer commitment to self or family. It may be used to prevent separation or divorce or to force a partner into providing previously limited emotional or financial support. It may even be undertaken to force the partner to confess socially that coitus has been occurring.

Hostility and masochism may be companion dynamics. If the device fails and the partner leaves, full justification is then available for overt expressions of long residing resentment and also for assumption of the stance of martyrdom.

Nihilism

Feelings of apathy, hopelessness, and insurmountable poverty are not conducive to effortful and planned activity, including activity aimed at pregnancy prevention. Sufficiently grave emotional and intellectual nihilism may result in cessation of sexual activity, but this is uncommon except in the most severely depressed states. Sexual activity persists, and, although pregnancy itself is rarely sought, the dispatch of effort to prevent it is inconsistent with the nihilistic outlook over-all. The unremitting bleakness of yesterday and today is projected to tomorrow. A hopeless fatalism prevails. Contraception has little to offer. Nothing will change whether it is used or not. Contraception is obviously difficult to sell in this atmosphere. It has low priority on a long list of needs and is unlikely to be sought or accepted until more urgent necessities become securely available.

Affectional Poverty

Poverty need not be restricted to the financial and social forms. Destitution in any sphere, including that of affection, connotes impoverishment. Unless nihilistic and depressive feelings are overwhelming, most persons make some attempt to respond to existing affectional impoverishment. These attempts, unfortunately, are often misdirected, inadequate, or distorted. Chronic or acute deprivation of love, companionship, and the feeling of being needed is an example of such impoverishment and is frequently accompanied by conflicts regarding sexual identity. An unmet need to be needed and loved is commonly seen and socially anticipated in the unmarried. Indulgence in requested coitus after an ego-gratifying pursuit is a common method for temporary fulfillment of this need. A more emphatic and persistent need may be met by forgoing contraception, achieving pregnancy, and acquiring fulfillment through the acquisition of a needful and loving infant.

This, of course, may also occur within marriage whenever emotional and affectional gratification becomes unavailable for whatever reason. The most commonly used example is the woman whose children are leaving the nest and whose husband has become indifferent and has transferred his attentions to matters outside the home. A new infant obtained from rationalized contraceptive omission or an unconscious sabotage of the current method may eliminate her affectional poverty in a conscience-free fashion.

The recent loss of a friend, parent, relative, partner, or even a deeply loved pet is a common finding in studies of women seeking abortion. For many, the loss of emotional support, love, or companionship may be temporarily mollified through coitus. And in these therapeutic encounters, contraception is often ignored or rejected for any of a number of reasons. It may be because of nihilistic inaction or depressive indecision if the grief is sufficiently deep. Or it may stem from a need for punishment if there is a feeling of guilt concerning the circumstances of the loss. Or it may simply be an unrealistic and probably unconscious attempt to retrieve, through pregnancy, the person or the sense of companionship or love that has been lost.

Fear and Anxiety

Both physically and emotionally directed fears or anxieties may be quite adequate to cause certain persons to eschew specific types of contraception or contraception in general. These anxieties are naturally and rationally used by most persons in the process of selecting their contraceptive method. They are frequently used, however, as rationalizations by those who have greater ends to serve by contraceptive nonuse but who need to escape the social or conjugal stigma of not avoiding conception. There may be fears of manipulating, altering, or harming the body or of infection, cancer, uterine perforation, blood clots, or unknown diseases. The woman may fear a loss of personal control and the initiation of irrepressible sexual aggression or promiscuity if the threat of pregnancy is lifted. Or, conversely, there may be a fear of frigidity or loss of libido as a contraceptive side effect. The fear may relate to the potential of interference with the person's all-important, identity-supporting, future fertility. Or it may simply relate to the awesome responsibility

one then has to control and to decide on one's reproductive fate. Many people prefer to accept fate and to suffer nobly and volubly from its treatment rather than to create a life pattern for themselves and accept personal culpability for resultant failures or unhappiness. Reproductive independence requires strength of personality. Immature and insecure persons commonly choose the less efficient methods and use them irregularly.

Abortion Availability

In light of the United States Supreme Court's decision regarding the legality of induced abortion, abortion availability becomes a rationally acceptable basis for using a less efficient but more acceptable means of contraception or for regular or, at least, occasional rejection of contraception. This is especially true for persons who have infrequent coitus, couples with apparent low fertility, or others in whom the potentiality for impregnation appears to be slight. Abortion, although undesirable, is sufficiently inexpensive and safe to be accepted as a legitimate escape from an undesirable situation and, in many minds, is not an undue price to pay if sensual gambles fail.

For a good many people, abortion even represents an escape from a desirable situation, one that becomes undesirable, however, if allowed to proceed. Becoming pregnant and having a child are often totally separate thoughts, totally different desires, and may serve totally different goals. Abortion can be exceptionally salvaging and useful for the person who needs to demonstrate fecundity but for whom an infant would currently be anathema. Abortion offers the best of two worlds, satisfaction through achievement of pregnancy without a demanding requisite for protracted responsibility.

Only 5 to 10 per cent of women having an abortion have either a subsequent abortion or an illegitimate birth; 90 to 95 per cent do not repeat the circumstance. For these women, it is probable that something positive has been gained or demonstrated and that pregnancy has served a useful function. It may have satisfied a vital, acute, and nonrecurring need. It may have proved a point or provided reassurance or demonstrated inappropriateness of previous action or response. It may have substituted reality for a previous denial or helped to resolve any one of the host of psychological concerns described above. The availability and use of abortion seems to be of definite benefit to the majority of these women.

Iatrogenesis

The final category and the most bitter because of its closeness to home and its pathetic needlessness is that of iatrogenesis. The counsel and opinion of physicians are sought with as much or greater frequency than are their diagnostic and therapeutic skills. Their opinions are usually held in respect, and their attitudes, especially in the area of contraception, are very influential. Too frequently, the physician's attitude toward contraceptive use by others is colored by his own moral, religious, and social philosophy. And, unfortunately, his advice in this area often relates more to himself than to the patient's needs and desires. For example, he may refuse to insert an intrauterine device into a nulligravidous and unmarried adolescent, despite her request and her willingness to accept potential side effects. Or he may withhold oral contraceptives or a diaphragm from another because of his feeling that she is irresponsible or promiscuous. Moreover, the patient's partner is rarely consulted, despite the fact that the partner is half of the contraceptive team and can scuttle essentially any contraceptive method with which he or she disagrees. Additionally, monetarily directed physicians find that it consumes far less time to impose a specific contraceptive on a patient than it does to help that patient arrive at a personal choice. Some physicians with contraceptive prejudice simply refuse to insert any intrauterine devices or prescribe any oral contraceptives, despite the widespread acceptance of these by governmental regulatory agencies and their regular use by the physician's own intellectual peers. Such a physician may impress a diaphragm on a patient before she realizes that she has an option. A diaphragm may be a very compatible form of contraception at the doctor's house, but in the

patient's home it may turn out to be constraining, disruptive, and unused.

Conversely, because of its absolute efficiency, oral contraceptives may be stoutly encouraged by a doctor who has no contraceptive prejudice and whose only regard is the woman's best interest. But, if in his enthusiasm he fails to hear her poorly verbalized fears regarding the pill, he will truly have worked against her best interest, and she will be confused, disappointed, hurt, and uncomprehending when she subsequently becomes pregnant.

The demeaning, opinionated, intimidating, and pronatalist attitude of some physicians; the ignorance, apathy, or inconsiderate unconcern of others; and the embarrassment, ambivalence, or punitiveness of still others are destructive of contraceptive enthusiasm and are substantial factors in patient's misuse or nonuse of contraception. Perhaps less diabolical but equally reprehensible is the much more common aspect of simple oversight. Far too many physicians, for example, fail to give any consideration to alternative contraceptive methods when they advise the temporary cessation of the current method. They are remiss in their duties if they simply assume that the patient will be careful or that coitus will cease in the interim.

Conclusion

From the breadth of this categorical listing and the recognition that there are thousands of nuances and combinations of these circumstances and forces that can exist, it should be obvious that there is an incredible number of situations in which contraception is misused or rejected for psychological reasons. In fact, if one looks closely, there are probably more reasons not to use contraception than there are to use it. These all speak to the fact that contraceptive knowledge and immediate availability cannot and do not ensure regular contraceptive use. As long as conception control is volitional and despite the fact that many persons prefer to deny that contraception pertains to them, each person must come to a personal decision as to where and when contraception fits into his or her psychological structure and life.

Without doubt, the provision of information to all persons regarding all aspects of contraception and the provision of insight into the psychological makeup of themselves and their partners are requisite for optimal decision making. Contraceptive information should be and can be dispensed to persons of all ages. Enormous national progress has already been made in this regard. Honest ignorance is a very uncommon cause for contraceptive nonuse. The provision of insight into personal psychological makeup and potential reasons for contraceptive nonuse is far more complex. It would be ideal if insight could be imparted before the age of first intercourse, but this is perhaps too lofty a goal to seek at present. However, physicians can help to provide such insight for persons who are obviously in the process of flirting with pregnancy. Such persons come to the attention of all doctors. The major concern should not be that these persons are avoiding contraception in order to express themselves but that they be made aware that they are doing so and be made aware of the possible psychological reasons for their actions. It may be possible then to help them to explore and find more appropriate and quite possibly more effective avenues for such expression.

One should always recognize, however, that adequate expression for some can only be achieved by the acquisition of pregnancy. If this mode of expression is unmodifiable by insight, one ought to accept it and offer them help in determining whether the acquisition of an infant is also a necessary component or whether their goal is achievable by pregnancy itself. In the latter eventuality, many need additional supportive counseling to extricate themselves from the situation. Although the path may seem unduly arduous and frustrating, the payoff is substantial in that relatively few will choose or need this avenue again. Seen in this light, abortion can be more readily accepted as a positive and desirable therapeutic implement.

REFERENCES

*Calderone, M., editor. *Manual of Family Planning and Contraceptive Practice.* Williams & Wilkins, Baltimore, 1970.

13.7 Abortion

HRAIR MOSES BABIKIAN, M.D.

Definition

Abortion is the expulsion of a previable fetus from the uterus before gestation is complete. The abortion may be spontaneous or artificially induced.

History

Abortion has been practiced since the beginning of organized society. A glimpse at history reveals that the laws governing abortion have been varied. However, in almost all instances, the laws have been made with the primary purpose of preserving the fabric and structure of a particular society. The fetus was considered to have no rights and was disposed of whenever it threatened any of the values of a given society.

The ancient Greeks thought that the fetus had no soul. Plato, in *The Republic*, lists incest and over-age parents as indications for abortion. He states that, if incest occurred, he would prescribe "strict orders to prevent any embryo which may come into being from seeing the light." Aristotle even suggested that abortion should be practiced when the couple has had the normal quota of children.

Many primitive societies seemed to approach abortion with similar perspectives.

Acceptable conditions for induced abortion ranged from fear of childbirth to pregnancy resulting from rape or improper paternity. Evidently, abortion was sanctioned in order to maintain the equilibrium of a given society. Gradually, social reasons gave way to medical indications, which became the acceptable ones. Therapeutic abortions were condoned whenever it was felt that the fetus made the mother sick or aggravated an existing illness.

The advance of medical technology introduced new problems. Medical indications for therapeutic abortions became limited to a few severe conditions, such as hypertensive diseases, renal failure, and uncontrolled, protracted diabetes. At the same time, induced abortion became a much safer procedure. Before 1940, almost all indications for therapeutic abortions were medical. After this date, there was increasing use of psychiatry to extend the range of indications for therapeutic abortion. By 1950, psychiatric reasons accounted for more than 50 per cent of all abortions. By 1960, society was questioning social, cultural, moral, and ethical values, and ultimately, the issues of individual rights and freedom. Despite the fact that sophisticated birth control methods removed the fear of pregnancy from sexual activity, social pressures increased to such an extent that the medical model, even with the leeway provided by psychiatry, was inadequate. Frustrated psychiatrists became increasingly aware of being used to solve a social problem. Their protest resulted in the Group for the Advancement of Psychiatry report of 1968, which emphasized that psychiatrists must recognize their limitations and not accept responsibility for making decisions that belong to the community. It was felt that psychiatrists should not allow themselves to be exploited by society's need to make abortions easier.

By 1970, four states had liberalized their abortion laws. On January 23, 1973, the United States Supreme Court settled the legal battle by overruling all state laws that prohibit or restrict a woman's right to obtain an abortion during her first 3 months of pregnancy. The vote was seven to two. The major points can be summarized as follows.

1.   During the first trimester, the right to have an abortion lies with the woman and her doctor. The state's interest in her welfare is not compelling enough to warrant any interference.

2.   For the next 6 months of pregnancy, the state may "regulate the abortion procedure in ways that are reasonably related to maternal health," such as licensing and regulating the persons and facilities involved.

3.   For the last 10 weeks of pregnancy, the period during which the fetus is judged to be capable of surviving if born, any state may prohibit abortion, if it wishes, except where it may be necessary to preserve the life or health of the mother.

Spontaneous and Habitual Abortion

Spontaneous abortion may be defined as the expulsion of a previable fetus in the absence of external manipulation. Habitual abortion is characterized by three or more consecutive spontaneous abortions (see Table I).

The cause of spontaneous abortion is as yet unknown. Many factors have been suspected;

TABLE I
Types of Abortion

Spontaneous abortion—the spontaneous expulsion of a previable fetus.
Habitual abortion—three or more consecutive spontaneous abortions.
Missed abortion—a state wherein a dead fetus is not expelled within 2 months.
Threatened abortion—more than one missed period with bleeding and cramps.
Incomplete abortion—continuous bleeding with the expulsion of chorionic tissue.
Therapeutic abortion—an inducted abortion for medical indications. With the increasing sophistication of medical techniques, these indications have diminished markedly. Currently, the two main indications are psychiatric and the potential abnormality of the fetus.
Induced abortion—an abortion purposefully brought on by outside forces. The abortion may be criminal or medical. The technique used depends on the duration of the pregnancy; the principal techniques are dilation and curettage, suction curettage, saline injection into the amniotic sac at about the eighteenth week of gestation, and hysterotomy.

studies have focused on microscopic pathology, nutrition, endocrinology, and pathology. Many of the widely favored theories do not seem to stand the test of scrutiny. The conceptus of spontaneous aborters does not seem to be significantly different from that of nonaborters. Similarly, there does not seem to be any significant deficiency in vitamins C and E or in thyroid hormone. Only a small percentage of fetuses from spontaneous abortions show fetal abnormalities. Factors known to affect spontaneous abortion have been summarized by Tupper and Mann as follows.

1. Low hormone levels that seem to fluctuate with emotional stress.

2. The presence of microscopic degenerative changes in the chorionic villi of the majority of the abortions.

3. An incompetent cervix, which accounts for about 13 per cent of all spontaneous abortions.

4. Psychological factors.

Most investigators seem to weigh psychological factors heavily in the etiology of spontaneous abortions. Empirical clinical evidence, as reported by Tupper and Mann, seems to substantiate this theory. Treatment of spontaneous abortion in medical literature is varied; different authors emphasize different causes and cures, and most claim good results. Mann (1959) attributes good results to the doctor-patient relationship rather than to the medical treatment itself. He reports a success rate of 80 per cent for those women who receive supportive psychotherapy.

There are a number of consistent findings in women suffering from habitual abortion. Family dynamics seems to fall usually into the following pattern. The mothers of these patients are often dominant, overpowering women who have difficulty in separating themselves from their children. The patients remain tied to their mothers from early infancy, never actually maturing as persons. The mother sees to it that her daughter remains dependent on her for all physical and emotional needs. The process of separation and individuation does not take place. This extreme overprotectiveness suffocates and impairs the growth of the daughter. She seldom learns any degree of independent action and fails to develop an acceptance of her own body and sexuality. Her interpersonal relationships with adults are characterized by infantile dependence.

The father of the patient follows no consistent pattern. He may be absent, emotionally distant, or too involved and concerned with his daughter. He often fails to establish any kind of loving or caring relationship with her; instead, he tends to have many obsessive concerns over her possible sexual acting out. Therefore, these patients grow up in a relatively sterile environment.

As children, they are described as nice, quiet, and obedient. They are careful and constantly concerned about their physical health and well-being and often somatize their emotional problems. This type of behavior continues into adolescence, when there is little attempt at individuation, rebellion, and separation. Furthermore, they never show much curiosity or even interest in the changes taking place within their own bodies. Knowledge of their own reproductive organs is minimal, and, even when taught about reproduction in school, they seem not to assimilate the material. They go through adolescence with numerous psychosomatic illnesses and complaints but with very little sexual exploration.

The clinical picture of women having habitual abortions is usually presented in one of three ways. First, she is seen as a very dependent, immature person who has terrible fears of her own growth and acceptance of herself as a woman. She usually marries a man who is very protective and, in this way, replaces her own mother. Childish and immature, she remains throughout her married life deeply attached to her mother, often seeing her daily. The second type of woman usually seems extremely independent. She is career oriented and wants to be a successful, strong, and independent businesswoman. It is hard for her to accept womanhood, which she equates with dependence, weakness, and submission. Her behavior seems to be a counterphobic maneuver geared at handling underlying fears of dependence. The third type of woman is presented as a rather hysterical and somewhat narcissistic person. Her self-esteem is dependent primarily on her perception of her body and the preservation of her looks. Pregnancy represents an intolerable threat to her body image.

Induced Abortion

Induced abortion is a unique issue; it permeates every aspect of human relations and goes deep into the fabric of society. It touches on almost everything. It is at once political, social, religious, economic, medical, legal, moral, and ethical. Each proponent and each person affected responds with something akin to fanaticism. As a matter of fact, it is difficult to approach abortion without a bias. Since 1968, there have been innumerable articles both for and against abortion. In each article, the first paragraph reveals the bias of the author, even when the author claims to look at the issue objectively. Cries of genocide, murder, rights for life, rights of freedom, and rights of privacy have all been raised. It would be presumptuous of this author to admit no bias. The choice of having an abortion should be available to every human being. However, the responsibility of each person to make such a decision and to carry it through has to be tempered by a healthy respect for human life.

The most heated arguments concerning induced abortion seem to cluster around three main issues. First, at what point does life begin? Second, has the individual woman the right to control her own body? Third, what are the psychological consequences, if any? The last question concerns the impact of abortion on the emotional and mental health of the patient and the effects of unwanted pregnancy and rejection on the mental health of the children.

In ancient Greek civilizations, neither Plato nor Aristotle considered the fetus as alive. In the Ottoman empire, Turkish rulers used to have a woman in each harem called the "bloody midwife" whose function was to terminate unwanted pregnancies. The official doctrine of the Roman Catholic Church from 1591 until 1869 was that the fetus became alive with the first signs of quickening—that is, between the twelfth and fourteenth weeks of gestation. After 1869, after the proclamation of Pope Pius X, life was thought to begin at conception. Indeed, the laws of

Western civilization have been very ambivalent concerning the issue of life and abortion. The woman who actively seeks abortion or who attempts to abort herself is not actually punished by law; the abortionist is considered the criminal.

In January 1973, in a decision concerning abortions, Supreme Court justices rejected the idea that the fetus became a person on conception and was thus entitled to the due process and equal protection guaranteed by the Constitution. Justice Blackmun stated that the word "person" as used in the fourteenth amendment does not include the unborn.

It is this author's observation that most women experience life with the onset of quickening, when they begin to refer to the fetus as "the baby." The existence of independent movement within the body sets in motion a relationship between mother and fetus, mother and baby. At that point, the baby assumes a psychic reality.

PSYCHIATRIC IMPLICATIONS

Role of the psychiatrist. The psychiatrist's role in this complex issue steadily increased in the 1950's and 1960's. Rosen, in his book *Abortion in America,* states that abortions for psychiatric reasons have skyrocketed. It seems as if the psychiatrist was exploited in an attempt to satisfy a social need within the context of the medical model. He was the link that provided an adequate justification for abortion, but, with increased demand, the system became inadequate, expensive, and cumbersome.

In the late 1960's and early 1970's, the majority of psychiatrists voiced the complaint that psychiatry was being exploited and that abortion should be an issue between the woman and her gynecologist. It was not an accident that the psychiatrist was drawn into this conflict. First, his medical background leads him to consider the health and welfare of his primary patient (the mother). Second, his training makes him think in terms of prevention. By preventing the birth of unwanted children, he can diminish or prevent the incidence of mental and emotional illness.

Emotional factors in pregnancy. The physiological changes brought about by pregnancy activate many emotional counterparts. Pregnancy causes both emotional and physiological stress. It disrupts the existing homeostasis, necessitating changes in an attempt to achieve a new adaptive balance.

The first trimester is characterized by ambivalence, no matter how planned and desired the conception was. Dormant unconscious fears are reactivated; when reinforced by physiological processes, such as rises in hormone levels, these fears give rise to symptoms. The patient also experiences new feelings, such as the need to mother and the wish to be mothered, to be taken care of. The outcome of this conflict is determined by the mental and emotional health of the woman and by her environmental support or its lack. In the relatively healthy pregnant woman, the wish to be taken care of manifests itself in various little eccentricities, such as requests for pickles at midnight, that reassure her of the love and care of the person close to her.

With the onset of quickening, in the twelfth to fourteenth week of gestation, the fetus becomes a reality. With the acceptance of this fact, the balance usually shifts to gratification of the need to mother. Refusal to accept the fetus as a psychological reality results in prolongation of the conflict, resulting in denial of pregnancy, psychosomatic ailments, or efforts at aborting the fetus. Everyday experiences with women who go to extremes to terminate pregnancies and with women who have babies despite grave danger to their own lives are proof enough of the intensity of the conflict.

In the second and third trimesters the fetus becomes a baby, an accepted reality, assuming a definite place in the psychic life of the woman. The subsequent development of feelings aroused by pregnancy has a maturing effect on the woman. Pregnancy is viewed as a developmental milestone similar to puberty, menarche, and menopause. Its manner of resolution deeply affects the emotional maturation of the woman.

Motivations for abortion. Motivations for seeking an induced abortion are many. Initially, there may be an impulse to remove the disrupting factor and regain homeostasis. Social and moral considerations may contribute to feelings of shame and disgrace and concern over responsibility and the burden of financial support. Induced abortions are frequently sought to terminate pregnancy after rape, incest, sexual acting out, and "accidents." The married women who seek abortion because of too many children or for economic reasons seem to respond better than single women. Possibly their mothering needs are fulfilled by the presence of children, or they are able to postpone the gratification of these needs.

In considering abortion, the psychiatrist has to be keenly aware that pregnancy disrupts an existing homeostasis, reactivates unconscious fears and conflicts, and awakens the need to mother—setting in motion a whole set of psychic constellations designed to meet the stress at hand. Abortion is a second assault, one that brings to a halt a process already set in motion.

Psychiatric considerations. The 1950's and 1960's witnessed an expanding psychiatric literature concerned with establishing guidelines for the psychiatric indications for abortion. Now, after the Supreme Court decision, this question seems academic. Furthermore, certain basic operational concepts proved to be wrong, such as the notion that impending psychoses or serious threats of psychotic decompensation and serious risks of suicide were indications for abortion. Experience has shown that psychotic women are not better or worse after abortion. It is not possible to evaluate how serious is the problem of abortion-related suicide. Statistics point out that suicide in pregnant women is extremely rare. However, a pregnant woman who wanted an abortion desperately could get a criminal abortion or attempt to abort herself. Suicide statistics could change dramatically if these two avenues were totally cut off to her. In the emergency rooms of large city hospitals, huge numbers of women are admitted bleeding with incomplete abortions—proof enough for such an assumption.

The psychiatrist as a clinician has to evaluate the effect of increased stress on the mental health or illness of the patient and the ability of the already sick person to deal with the crisis at hand. He has to consider and evaluate seriously every threat to life, no matter how small the statistical risk. He has the delicate task of delineating the fine line between human misery and mental illness.

With the change in the law, he has to consider the possible contraindications to abortion. Patients who feel coerced by familial or social forces need help to sort out their feelings and to cope more effectively with the problem. Many patients need help to terminate the ongoing pregnancy and to resolve conflicts aroused by the abortion. With the removal of legal restrictions, the psychiatrist is in a better position to do what he is trained to do—help the patient resolve her conflicts and reach a healthy psychic balance.

In a society that has divergent moral values and beliefs concerning induced abortions, the experience can be harrowing. The patient has to cope with her personal feelings of guilt and deal with overt and covert attitudes of the personnel directly administering to her.

The nursing staff have to resolve some important issues within themselves. Nurses have difficulty in accepting the shift in their professional role from one of bringing life and sharing their own mothering experiences with new mothers to one of being accomplices to death. Often, they do not know how to relate to the patient, whether to congratulate her or to be sad. The strongest reaction is usually seen among the staff working with patients who were given saline injections for salting out. The delivery of fetuses with almost-formed human features is very disturbing. Nurses frequently become angry with the physician, who is blamed for committing the abortion and leaving the dirty work to them. Furthermore, intrastaff hostility and jealousy may also develop. Some hospitals respect religious restrictions and do not assign Catholic nurses and aides to duty on the abortion service. Such a policy gives rise to resentment on the part of nonCatholic members of the staff, and this resentment is displaced onto the patients, who may be regarded as immoral prostitutes, especially the repeaters. The growing experience of hospitals performing abortions points toward separating the abortion service from the delivery service and instituting group sessions with the staff, including the obstetricians, with the goal of expressing their feelings and

coming to terms with this totally new kind of patient care.

Psychiatric sequelae. It is extremely difficult to evaluate the literature dealing with psychiatric consequences of induced abortions. There has been a virtual deluge of papers that describe them as serious and others that label these findings as nonexistent myths. Such diametrically opposite views indicate the injection of prejudice and emotion into the evaluation and interpretation of data.

In evaluating consequences of induced abortion, one must consider three aspects:

1.   Immediate psychological effects of induced abortion.

2.   Long term psychological consequences of induced abortion.

3.   Long term psychological effects on unwanted children born to women denied induced abortion.

Most authors agree that the immediate reaction to abortion is relief. The patient who has developed the least attachment to the fetus—that is, the woman who refers to the pregnancy as a "blood clot" or "tissue"— usually does best clinically. She has not allowed any changes to occur in her adaptive balance. Pregnancy is experienced as a disrupting factor; its removal restores her to her previous homeostasis. Studies of most authors confirm that the best time for termination of pregnancy is up to the twelfth to fourteenth week of gestation. An exception is the medically sick woman who has to have a therapeutic abortion and experiences the loss of the fetus with reactive depression. Hers is a true loss of an already highly cathected loved object. Grief, mourning, and varying degrees of depression are necessary steps in the resolution of such a loss.

The most consistent postabortion psychiatric finding is guilt. A study conducted at Metropolitan Hospital Center in 1970 found that a majority of patients scored higher on guilt on the Hamilton Depression Scale after an abortion. The healthier patients were the least disturbed; they were better able to cope with guilt feelings. Patients who were sicker before abortion had more serious postabortion problems. This is a paradoxical situation, since one of the most accepted psychiatric indications for induced abortion has been a pre-existing psychiatric illness.

The data in the psychiatric literature highlight the issue of guilt. One of the best studies reported is by Ekblad (1955), who studied 479 Swedish women who had undergone legal abortion; 65 per cent of the women stated that they had no self-reproaches, 14 per cent had mild self-reproaches, and 11 per cent had serious self-reproaches or regretted having had the abortion. Malmords, in another Swedish study, reports that 37 per cent of those he interviewed admitted to guilt feelings. In Japan, where abortion is legal on demand, guilt seems to be prevalent and has a high incidence. The Mainichi survey in 1965 reported that, of 3,600 married women, 18 per cent did not feel anything in particular, 28 per cent felt that they had done something wrong, 35 per cent felt sorry for the fetus; 4.3 per cent had fears of sterility, 6.5 per cent had a variety of responses, and 7.9 per cent did not answer. It can be concluded that 80 per cent of these women felt some degree of guilt.

Studies done in the United States seem to focus on the absence of serious psychiatric sequelae in induced abortions. The majority of papers published after 1967 stress the point that induced abortions performed in a medical setting produced little if any sequelae and that patients who were psychiatrically ill before abortion did poorly, whereas patients who were psychiatrically healthy did well. One of the first such reports was published by Marder after his experience with the liberalized California Therapeutic Abortion Act of 1967. Of a total 550 therapeutic abortions, he reported that only a few women experienced serious emotional problems of guilt or remorse.

Peck and Marcus studied 50 women who had undergone therapeutic abortions at Mt. Sinai Hospital in New York. Only one case of acute psychotic reaction was reported; 20 per cent showed mild guilt. Nyswander and Patterson (1967), in a study of 116 patients, found that few women expressed regrets, and even these regrets tended to disappear by the time of the follow-up study, 8 months later. The literature on the subject is voluminous.

The question of induced voluntary abortion is too charged an issue at this time for objective studies to emerge. It is the impression of this author that guilt is fairly common and that the ability of the woman to cope with guilt determines both the presence and the seriousness of the symptoms. The available data support this view; the woman who is psychologically vulnerable is more apt to develop psychiatric symptoms after abortion. Her ego is weaker and, therefore, less able to handle the guilt.

What are the long term effects of such an experience in shaping and changing the life pattern of the woman concerned? It is probably too early to determine. Psychoanalytic studies testify to the difficulty in assimilating the abortion experience. Wallerstein et al. report the postabortion course of 22 women who were studied intensively at 5 to 7 months postabortion and then were reinterviewed at 12 to 14 months. At 5 to 7 months postabortion, the young women in the study were believed to have only a 50 per cent chance of mastering the pregnancy and abortion experience to the point of reconstructing their previous state of psychosocial functioning. Interviewed again at 14 months, they showed no improvement in the interim. The psychiatrist should look beyond the immediate symptoms and acute decompensation. He is interested in the nature of the assimilation of the experience with its subsequent impact on the quality of life.

The latter concern applies not only to the woman but also to the unwanted child born after an abortion has been refused. If one has to single out one factor as most responsible for psychopathology, one can safely point to rejection. The effects of rejection, albeit before birth, can be crippling. The best documented study of this subject is by Forssman and Thuwe (1966) in Sweden. They investigated the mental health, social adjustment, and educational level of 120 children, up to age 21, who were born after therapeutic abortion had been refused. They compared these children with an equally large control series. The unwanted children received more psychiatric care, exhibited more antisocial and criminal behavior, and received more public assistance. Far fewer pursued their studies above what was obligatory. The difference in the two series was statistically significant. Forssman and Thuwe concluded that the child born to a woman wanting an abortion had to surmount far greater social and mental handicaps than his peers.

CONCLUSION

The psychiatric literature has been inundated with papers dealing with the issue of induced abortion. Despite the claim for objectivity, a review of 200 papers on abortion reveals that each author had an emotional committment to either the protagonist or antagonist camp. However, there are certain points of general agreement. Psychiatric indications for therapeutic abortion did not stand the test of scrutiny. Women suffering from psychiatric illness before abortion showed no significant improvement after abortion and had more difficulty in coping with the stress of abortion than psychologically healthier women. With the advances in medical technology, medical indications for therapeutic abortion are becoming fewer. Therefore, the decision for induced abortion has to be made by the woman. She must be able to exercise control over her life-style and her sexual and reproductive functions. In a pluralistic society, with divergent moral and ethical codes, laws become unduly restrictive on one group or another. These laws are apt to be obscure, ineffective, unenforceable, and, therefore, broken. The final decision rests with the personal morality of the woman in question. The morality of both Eastern and Western civilizations for centuries has upheld life as sacred. The trend in the 20th century has continued to emphasize prolonging and improving the quality of life. It is extremely difficult and perhaps unwise to escape from the influence of such basic and deep rooted principles.

The psychiatrist finds himself with a whole new set of problems. First, he must help the woman with her decision, resolve her ambivalence, and ascertain if her expressed wishes are consistent with her inner feelings. With increasing experience, he will anticipate problems and provide help. For example, women who have fantasies of the baby before abor-

tion are more apt to develop symptoms than are women who do not have such fantasies. Second, the psychiatrist must help the hospital staff with their feelings and reactions to the patients and to abortion. Third, the psychiatrist must provide help, not only to the few women who undergo psychiatric decompensation but to all who seek help in assimilating the experience and reconstructing their lives.

REFERENCES

*Callahan, D. *Abortion: Law, Choice, and Morality*. Collier Books, London, 1970.

Char, W. F., and McDermott, J. F., Jr. Abortions and acute identity crisis in nurses. Am. J. Psychiatry, *128:* 8, 1972.

Dunbar, F. Emotional factors in spontaneous abortion. In *Psychosomatic Gynecology, Obstetrics, and Endocrinology*, Kroger, editor. ch. vi., Charles C Thomas, Springfield, Ill., 1963.

*Ekblad, M. Induced abortion on psychiatric grounds: A follow-up study of 479 women. Acta Psychiatr. Neurol. Scand., *99:* 3, 1955.

Ewing, J. A., and Rouse, B. E. Therapeutic abortion and a prior psychiatric history. Am. J. Psychiatry, *130:* 1, 1973.

Floyd, M. K. *Abortion Bibliography for 1970*. Whitston, Troy, N.Y. 1972.

Floyd, M. K. *Abortion Bibliography for 1971*. Whitston, Troy, N.Y. 1973.

Forssman, H., and Thuwe, I. One hundred and twenty children born after application for therapuetic abortion refused. Acta Psychiatr. Scand., *42:* 71, 1966.

*Group for the Advancement of Psychiatry. *The Right to Abortion: A Psychiatric View*. Charles Scribner's Sons, New York, 1970.

Lebensohn, Z. M. Abortion, psychiatry, and the quality of life. Am. J. Psychiatry, *128:* 3, 1972.

*Mann, E. C. Habitual abortion. Am. J. Obstet. Gynecol., *77:* 706, 1959.

Mann, E. C. *Spontaneous Abortions and Miscarriage in Modern Perspectives in Psycho-Obstetrics*. J. G. Howells, editor. Brunner Mazel, New York, 1972.

Marder, L. Psychiatric experience with a liberalized therapeutic abortion law. Am. J. Psychiatry, *126:* 1230, 1970.

*Minoro, M., editor. *Japan's Experience in Family Planning—Past and Present*. Family Planning Federation of Japan, Tokyo, 1967.

Nyswander, K., and Patterson, R. Psychologic reaction to therapeutic abortion. Obstet. Gynecol., *29:* 702, 1967.

Osofsky, J. D., and Osofsky, J. H. The psychological reaction of patients to legalized abortion. Am. J. Orthopsychiatry, *42:* 48, 1972.

Patt, S. L., Rappaport, R. G., and Barglow, P. Follow-up of therapeutic abortion. Arch. Gen. Psychiatry, *20:* 408, 1969.

*Rosen, H. *Abortion in America.* Beacon Press, Boston, 1954.

Senay, E. C. Therapeutic abortion. Arch. Gen. Psychiatry, *23:* 408, 1970.

Tupper, W. R. The problem of spontaneous abortion. Am. J. Obstet. Gynecol., *73:* 73, 1957.

Wallerstein, J. S., Kurtz, P., and Bar-Din, M. Psychosocial sequelae of therapeutic abortion in young unmarried women. Arch. Gen. Psychiatry, *27:* 828, 1972.

chapter 14 Sexual Behavior and Mental Illness

IVER F. SMALL, M.D.,
and JOYCE G. SMALL, M.D.

Introduction

Until the last few years, the role of sexuality was considered to be of central importance in normal and abnormal personality development. Many psychiatrists still hold such views and believe that sexual functions are likely to be disturbed in mental disorders and, further, that recovery from such illnesses may be retarded or endangered by patients' sexual activities (Pinderhughes et al., 1972). Others theorize that the struggle for mastery of the sex drive in adolescence must be won, or psychosis will result. Avoidance or postponement of the struggle may lead to characterological deficiencies, whereas neuroses may be derived from unresolved psychosexual conflicts.

However, many of these contentions must now be viewed in the light of evidence from recent human and animal research. Masserman (1966) has adopted the viewpoint that sexual dysfunctions are usually secondary considerations in human maladjustment, an opinion based on work with experimental neuroses in animals and on his own clinical experience. He concedes that behavior is mostly motivated by physiological needs but regards sexual desires as relatively unimportant because they are episodic, transient, and, viewed dispassionately, dispensable. In his framework, more important issues in the understanding of mental disturbances include the unique capacities and maturity of the patient, individual experience, and the range of adaptive behaviors. Hunt (1965) went further and questioned whether some behavior is even motivated or whether emotional attachments are necessarily related to

gratification of libidinal needs. Such opinions are supported by many studies of patients with various kinds of mental illnesses who have shown little or no evidence of sexual maladjustment. On the other hand, there is at least one clinical entity, hysteria, in which there are definite sexual concomitants. Moreover, studies of patients with particular kinds of deviant sexual behavior often do show an increased incidence of mental and emotional difficulties.

In the presence of contradictory opinions and incomplete information on the subject, it is perhaps best at the present time to take the position that sexual function and dysfunction should be viewed as one facet of behavior that may or may not be affected by mental or, for that matter, physical disease. In this section, some of the data about sexual activity and behavior as they occur in association with some of the diagnostic entities listed in the *Diagnostic and Statistical Manual of Mental Disorders,* second edition (DSM-II), are reviewed. Efforts are made to relate this information to normative data and to studies of specific kinds of sexual deviant behavior.

Mental Retardation

Much attention has been given to the sexual behavior of the mentally deficient, particularly with regard to eugenic considerations and the desirability of sterilization. However, the sexual development and physical growth of the mentally retarded person is often inversely proportional to the degree of mental subnormality (Roberts and Clayton, 1969). Therefore, it is unusual for profoundly or severely retarded persons to engage in heterosexual relationships. Generally, they exhibit primitive sexual behaviors, such as individual or mutual masturbation. On the other hand, less retarded persons are capable of mature heterosexual relationships, including marriage.

Some of the sexual problems that have been reported in association with mental deficiency include sexual behavior that is appropriate for persons of younger chronological age, thus creating adjustment problems when the mentally deficient child attempts to function within normal groups (Simmons, 1968). Other difficulties have to do with homosexual or heterosexual exploitation of dull or gullible persons. There are also parental conflicts about accepting the sexuality of their mentally retarded children.

In Turner's survey (1970), 20 per cent of the parents polled thought that their mentally defective child was having difficulty in sexual adjustment, with most of them concerned about excessive masturbation. Sterilization had been proposed at some time for 8 per cent of these brain-damaged or mongoloid children.

Low intelligence has frequently been cited as a contributing factor in disturbances of sexual behavior, such as promiscuity, prostitution, and illegitimate pregnancy. However, many of the studies of groups exhibiting these kinds of behaviors do not reveal lower intelligence than is found in comparative samples. Also, Malmquist et al. (1966) did not find that mental retardation was a significant factor in multiple illegitimate births. Kinsey reported that bestiality with domestic animals was common in mentally retarded males living on the farm. Otherwise, associations of mental deficiency with socially troublesome sexual behavior do not appear to exist. Recently, de la Cruz and LaVeck (1973) have edited a comprehensive survey of what is known about multidisciplinary aspects of sexuality and mental retardation with recommendations for guidance of parents and professionals and with proposals for experimental programs and future research.

Organic Brain Syndromes

It is known that organic lesions of the brain may produce various kinds of sexual aberrations, depending on the extent and the area of the brain involved. The classic Kluver-Bucy syndrome associated with bilateral lesions of the temporal lobes is a striking example of specific effects on sexual behavior. Characteristic of the syndrome in both animals and man is bizarre hypersexuality, which can probably be interpreted as release phenomena in the Jacksonian sense (Oppenheimer, 1971). More commonly, structural pathology of the central nervous system is associated with nonspecific changes in sexual behavior that may be understood in terms of dissolution, with a retreat toward lower or more primitive levels of behavioral organization. Commonly, such pathology is associated with a loss of social controls, with sexual behavior occurring at inappropriate times or circumstances, rather than hypersexuality or particular kinds of sexual deviations in the usual sense of these terms. Other considerations have to do with pre-existing personality characteristics. Further, it has been shown by Roth (1972) that the extent of intellectual and social deterioration in senile brain disease is directly proportional to the amount of neuropathological degeneration as measured by neurofibrillary tangles, ventricular size, senile plaques, and brain weight.

In other instances, patients with early organic disorders of the brain may present in depressed states, as in presenile dementia and in neurosyphilis (Marsden and Harrison, 1972; Dewhurst, 1969; and Hooshmand et al., 1972). It may reasonably be assumed that sexual activity and interests are reduced in the presence of clinical depression.

Sexual behavior has been examined explicitly in case studies of Huntington's disease. Dewhurst et al. (1970) evaluated 102 patients and their families in a 16-year follow-up study. It was found that 38 per cent of the married patients were divorced after onset of the illness. Abnormal sexual behavior was found in 30 of 48 adults on whom data on sexual activities were obtained. Such behavior included manifestations of sexual jealousy, exhibitionism, homosexual aggression, sodomy, voyeurism, and promiscuity. Hypersexual behavior in several instances led to hospitalization. Wives of the male patients described them as demanding an inordinate amount of sexual satisfaction at inappropriate times and places. If the patients were rebuffed, they sometimes became abusive and violent. In women, hypersexuality occurred in the form of promiscuity, illegitimate pregnancy, and sometimes sexual exposure. Reduction of sexual interest was present in 11 cases; 6 were frigid.

Relatively more attention has been focused on sexual deviations appearing in association with epilepsy, particularly with psychomotor or temporal lobe epilepsy. Much of the early literature proposed a link between temporal lobe epilepsy and various kinds of mental aberrations, including uncontrolled violence and aggressive sexual behavior. However, more recent controlled studies of patients with psychomotor epilepsy compared with patients with other types of seizure disorders and medical illnesses have not confirmed that there are any such specific associations. Recent data suggest that the severity of the seizure disorder and the side, extent, and localization of the epileptogenic focus determine how much social disability, mental disturbance, and, by inference, sexual difficulty occur in the patient with epilepsy (Stevens, 1966; Mignone et al., 1970; Flor-Henry, 1972). Impotence and hyposexuality have been described as interictal characteristics of psychomotor epilepsy (Johnson, 1965; Hierons and Saunders, 1966; Blumer and Walker, 1967) that may resolve after temporal lobectomy. However, hypersexuality can occur as part of ictal or preictal phenomena (Hoenig and Hamilton, 1960; Blumer, 1970). Considerable literature links sexual deviation, including transvestism and fetishism, to temporal lobe damage as evidenced by electroencephalographic studies (Walinder, 1965; Kolarsky et al., 1967; Epstein, 1973). However, the case reports do not furnish information on the frequency of these particular kinds of sexual disturbances in the absence of electroencephalographic evidence of temporal lobe injury or on the incidence of temporal spiking and other paroxysmal characteristics in patients without sexual problems. In any case, the association of sexual deviation with temporal lobe lesions is of interest in the light of the evolution of sexual functions within the brain as discussed by MacLean (1973).

Head trauma with resultant brain damage is well known to be followed by emotional and psychiatric disturbances. In Lishman's (1968) series of 670 patients, 144 were thought to have psychiatric disability after head injuries—psychiatric disability defined as disturbance in any area of mental life, including cognitive and intellectual functions, affective disorder, behavioral problem, or somatic complaint without demonstrable physical basis or a formal psychiatric diagnosis. Lesions of the orbital and frontal lobes were more apt to affect sexual behavior than were traumatic lesions elsewhere. Typical changes included hypersexuality, with disregard for the partner, and criminality with sexual offenses. More psychiatric disability was associated with wounds in the right frontal lobe than with those on the dominant side. However, significant sexual disturbances were found in only eight patients. Other sequelae of head injuries are perhaps best classified as psy-

chosomatic, since both physical injury and emotional reactions appear to be involved. Most commonly, symptoms such as dizziness, emotional instability, depressed mood, and impairment of concentration follow significant head trauma. These relate to the severity and extent of the head injury and also to psychological characteristics prior to the injury. Compensation factors, particularly if settlements are delayed, are also known to play an important role. Sexual dysfunctions may accompany some of the physical and psychological reactions, although their extent and severity have not been documented (Merskey and Woodforde, 1972).

A specific instance of brain trauma is that of prefrontal lobotomy. Concerns about sexual behavior after such neurosurgical procedures, particularly about unrestrained hypersexual behavior, have frequently been expressed. Variable results have been reported by different investigators, with the postoperative incidence of hypersexuality ranging from as high as 25 per cent of cases to nearly 0 per cent. Some of the differences may be related to the time of follow-up after surgery, the preoperative status of the patient, and the area and the extent of the surgical lesions. Levine and Albert (1951) examined 40 patients at intervals of 6 months to 4 years after lobotomy, explicitly inquiring about changes in sexual behavior. They found a decrease in inhibitions—such as guilt, modesty, and embarrassment—about sexual behavior in 27 patients, which, for the most part, was regarded as an improvement in interpersonal adjustment. Four of the male patients who had been impotent or had had preoperative difficulties with premature ejaculation functioned adequately after lobotomy. In only four patients did sexual behavior after the operation cause social concerns, but three of these patients had similar troubles before surgery. Homosexuality did not arise de novo after lobotomy, and three patients who were troubled with homosexual fantasies preoperatively were less disturbed afterward. Most patients maintained their usual modes of sexual expression, with a general decrease in feelings of guilt, modesty, anxiety in association with such behavior. Long term follow-up studies by Post et al. (1968) and by Shobe and Gildea (1968) reported similar findings, with an improvement in adjustment and very little socially objectionable or uninhibited sexual behavior on follow-up several years after the procedure. However, the importance of selection of appropriate cases was stressed. Freeman (1971) described his long term follow-up results with lobotomy in 415 cases of early schizophrenia. In his series, the majority experienced improvement in functioning with minor undesirable sequelae.

DSM-II lists psychosis with childbirth organic brain syndrome. By definition, this illness relates to sexual behavior insofar as pregnancy is a requirement for the diagnosis. Although endocrinological phenomena illnesses, other variables relating to sexual behavior, such as the acceptance of and desire for the pregnancy and satisfaction with sexual and marital adjustment, may play roles. Nilsson et al. (1967) found a statistically significant association between unplanned pregnancy and mental disorder, during both pregnancy and the postpartum period. The presumptive dynamics and possible factors contributing to postpartum emotional problems have been recently reviewed (Douglas, 1968; Butts, 1969). Other psychiatrists question whether postpartum mental illness is really distinct from other psychiatric conditions, since such illnesses often mimic schizophrenia, affective psychosis, and organic confusional states. Further, they generally follow a longitudinal course similar to such illnesses occurring in the absence of a postpartum onset (Wilson et al., 1972). Nevertheless, the sharp increase in such reactions in the month after delivery suggests that pregnancy is an important precipitating event (Hamilton, 1972).

Most of the studies of patients with presenting complaints of particular sexual dysfunctions do not mention organic brain disease as a significant factor. One exception is that of the elderly sex offender. Whiskin (1967) found that nine of 15 sexual offenders, age 60 years or more, had chronic brain syndromes associated with senile or arteriosclerotic central nervous system changes.

Major Affective Disorders

There is relatively little information about specific sexual functions and dysfunctions in the major affective disorders. Libido and potency may be reduced or abolished in endogenous depression, but, sexual interests and desires are likely affected as a general consequence of the depressed state rather than because of any specific physiological mechanism. Decreases in libido and impotence have been described in manic-depressive patients (Cassidy et al., 1957), but increased interest in sex is commonly associated with hypomanic episodes, with an increased incidence of promiscuity and illegitimate pregnancies (Arieti, 1967). Sexual preoccupations and delusions are often found in patients during hypomanic and manic episodes. In the authors' experience, these delusions sometimes take the form of pseudocyesis. Another sexual problem that creates difficulties in the marital adjustment of manic-depressive patients is the common wish by the hypomanic patient for another pregnancy. This wish may arise in either male or female patients. This demand, coupled with impaired social and financial judgment and other typical features of the illness, frequently precipitates separation and divorce. However, follow-up studies have shown that the long range prognosis in manic-depressive illness is relatively favorable, with a high percentage of patients achieving a good marital and social adjustment (Shobe and Brion, 1971).

It is questionable whether involutional melancholia and paranoid states should be considered as separate diagnostic entities, since the clinical phenomena accompanying such disorders do not differ appreciably from those characterizing affective disturbances at other periods in life. Nevertheless, there are unique endocrine, physiological, and psychological events that occur in the involutional age that warrant their separate consideration. A comprehensive review of the involutional syndrome was written by Rosenthal (1968).

Classically, the depressive and paranoid psychoses are superimposed on a premorbid personality described as rigid, overconscientious, and restricted, with lifelong repression of sexual and aggressive drives. Obsessive-compulsive defenses predominate, and the illness may be viewed as a decompensation of this defensive system. Sexual adjustment is generally described as poor.

Some authors have stressed the importance of the role of motherhood in female patients with involutional melancholia and state that decompensation may be related to children's leaving home as well as to the aging process. However, a recent normative study raises some questions about the relevance of some of these proposed dynamics (Lowenthal and Chiriboga, 1972). An interview study of 54 middle-age men and women that was conducted at the time the youngest child left home revealed that this time of life was not necessarily a period of crisis or of severe separation longings. In fact, the majority of parents regarded the departure of their last child in a positive light, with a sense of satisfaction and relief, and their marital and sexual adjustment improved.

Some of the declining interest in sex in association with affective disorders, particularly depression, has also been related to advancing age. This, too, must be questioned in the light of recent normative studies showing that sexual interests and activities persist at a high level in normal geriatric populations (Poinsard, 1967; Verwoerdt et al., 1969).

Studies of populations presenting with various complaints about sexual functioning show a relatively low incidence of psychotic illness in general and of affective disorders in particular. Only six of the 40 husbands and wives consulting Masters and Johnson for treatment of sexual dysfunctions meet even partial criteria for a diagnosis of depression (Maurice and Guze, 1970).

Schizophrenia

Considerable pathology in sexual development and its expression might be expected in schizophrenia, which is postulated by some to have an unresolved pregenital conflict at its core. Moreover, hormonal and metabolic alterations have been demonstrated in schizophrenic patients (Rosenbaum, 1968). Deviations in sexual functioning and responsiveness in schizophrenia would also be anticipated in the light of the lower rates of marriage and fertility among such patients and their well known tendency to avoid close relationships. However, it has been said that physical sexual intimacy may be accomplished quite easily by the schizophrenic patient but that such activity is detached from the partner and remains uncommitted, with frequent sick qualities, such as sadism and other hostile or perverted characteristics (Frank, 1969).

Winokur et al. (1959a) interviewed a group of 50 psychotic female outpatients, 64 per cent of whom were assigned a diagnosis of schizophrenia, and compared their responses with those of 50 neurotic patients and 100 nonpsychiatric patients. The patients were asked about their sexual behavior, including orgastic frequency and enjoyment, frequency of coitus, miscarriages, pregnancies, and the menopause. Very few reliable differences were found between the three groups. In other observations, the same authors (1959b) reported more

nocturnal orgasms in female psychiatric outpatients than in medical and surgical controls, but no significant differences were found between patients with psychoses and those with other emotional disturbances.

McCulloch and Stewart (1960) compared the sexual histories of psychiatric outpatients with those of normal women. No differences in sexual satisfaction were found between normal, neurotic, and schizophrenic subjects. Another report by Lukianowicz (1963) described the sexual behavior of a group of 100 hospitalized schizophrenic men, comparing them with age-matched normals and depressed patients. Unfortunately, no diagnostic criteria were specified, nor were statistical analyses of the data reported. However, increases in sexual desire and frequency of sexual gratification were reported in the initial stages of the illness, with more autoerotic activity in both married and single schizophrenic males as compared with normals, depressives, and their own premorbid levels. The author postulated that such behavior may be related to a failure of inhibition. He provided further commentary about how female schizophrenics are more apt to exhibit "unrestrained and degraded sexual behavior" during the psychosis than are men. However, the source of the data from which these conclusions were derived was not mentioned.

Varsamis and Adamson (1971) described the phenomenology of prodromal features of schizophrenia in a retrospective interview of 44 hospitalized patients, most of whom met diagnostic criteria for process schizophrenia. Decreased sexual drive was the most common sexual dysfunction reported, but 24 per cent noted an increase in sexual interest toward the end of the prodromal period, with more frequent masturbation, coitus, nocturnal emissions, and sexual arousal.

In other work, Nameche et al. (1964) reported that sexual acting out and antisocial behavior—such as running away, theft, and truancy—may characterize the childhood history of future schizophrenics. Robins' (1966) work also bears this out, in that the children who received an adult diagnosis of schizophrenia were more often described in childhood as antisocial, rather than shy or withdrawn. In a related area, Rutter et al.'s (1967) follow-up study of psychotic children indicated that very few of them developed mature heterosexual interests, although specific sexual difficulties were rare.

There have been other studies of the impact of the schizophrenic illness on marriage and the spouse. Johnston and Planansky (1968) examined the effects of chronically ill schizophrenic husbands on their wives. A gradual withdrawal from the situation and, finally, rejection were described over time, progressing through phases of acceptance, blame, avoidance, ambivalence, and divorce, separation, or annulment after several years of the illness. In another study of the husbands of paranoid women, Dupont and Grunebaum (1968) found a rather stable marital syndrome in which the husbands were passive, socially isolated, and unable to express angry and sexual feelings directly. Psychosis in the wife was associated with cessation of sexual relationships, and the husbands' inabilities to set limits on the wives' aggressiveness finally led to hospitalization. However, the marital system seemed to be quite stable in that both husband and wife behaved in ways to restore the status quo and to be resistant to therapy. The authors described the husbands as "willing victims" in a marital equilibrium that appeared to consist of the wives' expressing anger and dissatisfaction in the marriage, which the husbands could not do; instead, the husbands maintained passive, apparently reasonable attitudes. Planansky and Johnston (1967) also conducted a study of the wives of 96 schizophrenic male patients, comparing the wives' retrospective descriptions of their spouses at the time of courtship with similar descriptions from wives with husbands who did not have any major psychiatric disorder. It was found that the wives of the schizophrenics were more active in pursuit of the spouse during courtship than were the controls. The future patients were seen as passive, sensitive, shy, and introverted, whereas the wives of the normal men described their husbands as active, socially desirable men. Grunebaum et al. (1971) also examined knowledge of family planning and practices of 20 married hospitalized female psychiatric patients, the majority of whom were loosely categorized as psychotic. There was a high incidence of divorce, separation, and marital difficulties in this sample, as well as unwanted pregnancies and unreliable use of contraceptives.

Other studies have examined thought content in male and female schizophrenics as related to subjective ideas of sexual change and olfactory and gustatory hallucinations (Gittleson and Levine, 1966; Gittleson and Dawson-Butterworth, 1967; Connolly and Gittleson, 1971). Seventy hospitalized male patients were asked whether their illnesses were associated with a change in heterosexual interests, as well as questions about their ability to achieve erection, unusual or abnormal genital feelings, and worries about changes in genitalia or sex assignment. Forty-five patients with other psychiatric diagnoses, mainly depression, who were older than the schizophrenics, served as controls. Reduction of heterosexual interest was reported more often in the controls, whereas genital hallucinosis and delusions of sex change occurred in nearly one third of the schizophrenics. Such delusions were more apt to occur in unmarried patients. A similar study of hospitalized female schizophrenics revealed that the women, too, were more likely to retain heterosexual interests than were the controls. In this study, the age of the control group was not significantly different. However, schizophrenic women were less likely to retain heterosexual interests than were schizophrenic men. Genital hallucinations and delusions appeared with about the same incidence in men and women. Moreover, schizophrenic patients with delusions of sexual change were more apt to have olfactory and gustatory hallucinations than were those who did not have such delusions.

There is considerable psychological literature on how schizophrenic patients perceive their sex roles in terms of performance on various psychological tests. Likewise, there have been combined physiological and clinical studies of their reactions to sexual and nonsexual stimuli and reports of dream content with and without association with penile erection and nocturnal orgasm. There has also been interest in the genetic aspects, with reports of a higher incidence of positive sex chromatin males in psychiatric hospitals with diagnoses of schizophrenia and other mental illnesses (Negulici and Christodorescu, 1967; Wakeling, 1972). Although schizophrenic patients have not been described in significant proportions among patients who consult physicians for treatment of specific kinds of sexual difficulties, it is well known that drugs used in the treatment of schizophrenia may be associated with impaired sexual performance, such as altered libido, difficulties in sustaining erection, and ejaculatory failure.

Neuroses

Psychoanalytic theory predicts that behavioral expression of sexuality will be inhibited or deviant in illnesses thought to result from unresolved conflicts arising during psychosexual phases of development. Again, the available evidence does not support such a position. Studies by McCulloch and Stewart (1960) and Winokur et al. (1959a, 1959b) found very few differences between neurotic, psychotic, and normal control groups as far as their sexual behavior and enjoyment of sex were concerned. Nevertheless, many of the clinical descriptions of anxiety neurosis and the other kinds of neurotic disorders do mention sexual maladjustments.

Roth (1969) described some measure of impotence and lack of warmth in sexual relations as characteristic of anxiety neurosis. Templer's (1972) review of the obsessive-compulsive neurosis did not describe specific sexual problems. However, Goodwin et al. (1969) reviewed 13 follow-up studies from seven countries and found that apparent precipitating factors in obsessional illnesses may include pregnancy, childbirth, and sexual difficulties. Woodruff et al. (1972) examined the incidence of divorce among psychiatric outpatients and details about their sexual behavior, including age of first intercourse, extramarital affairs, homosexual experiences, sexual indifference, frigidity, and impotence. No positive or negative correlations with a diagnosis of neurosis were evident, nor was the likelihood of divorce higher in the neurotic patients.

Other aspects of the association between sexual problems on the one hand and neurotic disorders on the other have been provided by surveys and studies of patients who present with specific sexual difficulties. Maurice and Guze (1970) studied 20 marital couples treated by Masters and Johnson. These people were referred for a variety of sexual dysfunctions, including premature ejaculation, primary and secondary impotence, and primary and situational orgastic dysfunction—all specifically defined. Only one person received a diagnosis of psychoneurosis. Cooper (1968) studied neurosis and disorders of male sexual potency, with clinical interviews and psychological testing of 53 patients complaining of impotence. Only 15 patients, 28 per cent of the sample, were regarded as neurotic. It was concluded that neurosis and neurotic tendencies are associated relatively infrequently with primary disorders of sexual potency.

In another paper, Cooper (1972) considered psychological factors—such as anxiety, fear, and hostility—as important in psychogenic impotence, but such factors do not confer a diagnosis of psychoneurosis. Cooper (1968) also examined personality factors in frigidity, finding high anxiety in such patients but neuroticism scores within normal limits. On the other hand, Paulson and Lin (1970) thought that frigidity was associated with severe deep-lying psychological conflicts. However, they based these impressions on a review of the literature about presumed dynamics plus repeated self-ratings by six patients in group psychotherapy.

Ovesey and Meyers (1968) reviewed the literature on retarded ejaculation, citing psychoanalytic and other formulations about the meaning of this symptom. They reviewed 10 consecutive cases and categorized six of them as obsessive-paranoid and four as paranoid-depressed. They concluded that the symbolism of the symptom was important, the major dynamics having to do with rivalry with other men and symbolic displacement of hostile and destructive impulses to sexual acts

with women. Psychoanalysis was regarded as the treatment of choice. De Moor (1972) reviewed the literature on vaginismus and noted that several workers have emphasized that such problems are not accompanied by neurotic symptoms.

Other associations of sexual disorders and neurotic features have been identified in studies of particular populations, many of them college students. Halleck (1967) reported that permissive sexual behavior was much more common in college women who consulted a psychiatric outpatient clinic than it was in nonpatient students. He raised the question of whether this relationship may be explained on the basis of causality—that is, sexual behavior inducing the neurotic disturbances. However, he thought it much more likely that being mentally ill made a person more susceptible to casual sex, or perhaps there are underlying variables accounting for both permissive sexuality and neurotic disorders.

Raboch and Bartak (1968a, 1968b) examined personal and background factors in the lives of 279 married women with diminished or absent orgastic capacity and 360 married controls with good capacity for orgasm. The women, drawn from a group of medical patients, were administered a standard series of 170 questions. No differences were found between the two groups with regard to neurotic manifestations.

Eastman et al. (1969) evaluated unmarried undergraduate women who consulted the psychiatric section of the student health service. The women were divided into three groups on the basis of whether the presenting complaint was a primary concern about sexual behavior or whether sexual difficulties were mentioned but were not regarded as the main issue. A control group of women who consulted the service but who did not express concerns about sexual behavior was also evaluated. Both interview data and Minnesota Multiphasic Personality Inventory (MMPI) scores were compared. The results indicated that the women who presented with primary sexual complaints were healthier in terms of both psychiatric evaluations and MMPI profiles than either those who had sexual problems that were not regarded as paramount or the comparison group who denied concerns about sexual behavior. Thus, those who more readily admitted that sex was a problem seemed to be better adjusted. Moreover, admitted promiscuity was more common in the women who did not present with primary sexual complaints.

Fink (1970) examined the correlations between Freud's actual neurosis and the works of Masters and Johnson, which he regarded as providing some scientific corroboration of Freud's ideas. The actual neurosis, which was described in terms interchangeable with anxiety neurosis, was defined as a state of increased excitement, with free-floating or expectant anxiety and such physical symptoms as palpitations, perspiration, and tremor. These kinds of phenomena, Freud postulated, are related to some disturbance in the course of sexual arousal, such as coitus interruptus, frustrated excitement, or abstinence—all situations in which there is a lack of discharge in orgasm or adequate gratification. Masters and Johnson have shown objectively that women who do not achieve orgasm develop pelvic vasocongestion and various symptoms, such as irritability, difficulty in sleeping, and back pain. Most of these findings were discovered in studies of prostitutes who were maintained at excitement-phase levels during prolonged coital exposure without orgasm. However, automanipulation to orgasm brought almost immediate relief, with congestion reduced by an estimated 50 per cent in 5 minutes. Other possibly related observations included findings that neurotic symptoms and sexual dysfunction may sometimes improve during pregnancy, the symptoms and dysfunction being attributed to a loss of worry about contraception. Masters and Johnson also found that nonorgastic women may become orgastic for the first time during the second trimester, but the researchers offered the alternate explanation that the increased pelvic congestion of the pregnancy itself may bring women closer to the orgastic threshold. Thus, there is some peripheral physiological evidence for sexual frustration to be related to some of the symptoms of anxiety neurosis, although not to the specific diagnostic entity (Feighner et al., 1972).

A variety of psychological test instruments have been applied to studies of sexual behavior and its disturbances in relation to neurotic features. The majority of the studies show more neurotic features or, more usually, factor loadings suggesting more emotional difficulties in people who have problems with sexual adjustment than in those who do not. However, the explicit diagnostic criteria for neurosis are not usually considered. In fact, many such studies have made use of nonclinical populations, with neurosis defined in terms of cutting scores on various psychological test measures and personality inventories.

Personality Disorders

Literature relating sexual behavior to characterological deficiencies is scarce, with the exception of studies of the antisocial personality and hysterical personality. In regard to the latter, there is some semantic confusion as DSM-II has adopted the term hysterical personality to refer mostly to a syndrome defined and described in the literature as hysteria or Briquet's syndrome. Since the criteria for the latter are much more explicit and include more information about sexual behavior, the latter definition will be used herein.

HYSTERICAL PERSONALITY

The hysterical personality or hysteria is the only psychiatric diagnostic entity for which sexual dysfunctions have been specifically demonstrated.

Purtell et al. (1951) reported that 86 per cent of conversion hysterics had sexual problems, as compared with 29 per cent of a control group. The most common difficulty among hysterical women was that of sexual indifference. Winokur and Leonard (1963) subsequently found a wide variety of sexual behaviors in hysterics (sexual symptoms not required for diagnosis) and concluded that hysteria was not invariably associated with sexual disturbances. Woodruff et al. (1971) have continued studies of Briquet's syndrome, stressing that the criteria for firm diagnosis require a minimum of 25 complaints in at least nine of 10 symptom groups, only one of which describes such problems as sexual indifference, frigidity, dyspareunia, vomiting throughout pregnancy, and hyperemesis gravidarum. Woodruff (1971) estimated the incidence of hysteria to be approximately 2 per cent of the general female population. Curiously, the incidence of hysteria among women generally has mainly been investigated in postpartum samples. Not surprisingly, a high incidence of sexual indifference was found among such women, although the incidence of the complete clinical picture was rare (Farley et al., 1968) Prosen (1967) described two patients who met diagnostic criteria for hysteria but who possessed an unusual ability to enjoy sexual pleasure and coitus, again emphasizing that sexual maladjustment is neither necessary nor sufficient for the diagnosis.

Woodruff et al. (1971) were cautious about making the diagnosis of hysteria in males. There were only three men in their series; one developed a brain tumor, another was later diagnosed schizophrenic, and a third had prominent compensation factors. However, Luisada and Pittard (1973) described a series of 24 men who met the DSM-II definition of hysterical personality and found that limited sexual satisfaction, tendency to marry older mates, and some of the other clinical features were similar for men and women. However, there were differences in that higher incidence of polysurgery was present in females, whereas the men were more apt to have a history of criminal acts and excessive drinking.

There have been many discussions of the possible dynamics of hysteria. Hojer-Pedersen (1965) surveyed the psychoanalytic literature about the hysterical personality type that stresses the characteristic dramatic quality of social interactions. He mentioned that the flirtatiousness of the female hysteric serves as a method to seduce or conquer rather than to express sexual feelings and that such people are not often able to achieve orgastic fulfillment. Jones (1971) viewed the hysteric personality in an ethological context, describing hysteric behavior as attention seeking and a way of using sexual signals to convey nonsexual messages. Such behavior has also been encountered in nonhuman primates, particularly for the purpose of placation of aggression. In some species, same sex and opposite-sex mounting may also indicate nonaggression or a greeting, rather than sexual interest.

Many studies have suggested a relationship between hysteria or the hysterical personality and antisocial personality. In Robins' (1966) work, children from a child guidance clinic who received an adult diagnosis of either hysteria or antisocial personality had similar childhood characteristics. Females who became adult hysterics had a very high rate of juvenile sexual offenses, as did the sociopathic group (80 per cent as compared with 86 per cent). An episode of rape under age 18 was reported in one third of a group of girls who became hysterics, as compared with 21 per cent of the future sociopaths. Seventy-five per cent of the hysterics had voluntary premarital sexual experiences. Accompanying such behavior were reports of incorrigibility, associations with undesirable company, and a history of running away and vagrancy. However, the incidence of stealing and, correspondingly, the number of arrests were lower than in the future antisocial women. Other characteristics of the future hysterics included a lack of energy and apparent laziness, which occurred at a higher rate than in any other future adult psychiatric diagnostic category. Likewise, somatic symptoms were recorded in about one third of the cases. Forty-one per cent of the children who became either hysterics or sociopaths as adults experienced some somatic symptoms prior to the age of 8. The longitudinal history with childhood antecedents resembling those of antisocial behavior supports the inclusion of hysteria among the personality disorders rather than among the neuroses. Robins (1966) postulated that somaticization and focus on physical illness may cur-

tail the promiscuity, drinking, and other acting-out symptoms that are typical of the sociopath, perhaps simply by absorbing them in alternate activities. The prominence of hysterics among female criminals, female relatives of male criminals, and wives of convicted felons also suggests some link with antisocial personality (Guze et al., 1969, 1970; Cloninger and Guze, 1970a, 1970b).

A number of psychological studies have investigated the relationship of sexuality to personality. The work of Eysenck (1971) deserves special mention. He postulated that hysterics are characterized by high extroversion and low neuroticism scores, making for conflicts between sexual attitudes and behavior. Such a hypothesis was confirmed in extreme scoring groups selected from a large number of male and female college students. Many other psychological evaluations of students and other groups displaying hysteric-like traits generally support the theoretical position that hysteria is characterized by conflicts between sexual motivation and behavior. Physiological studies, too, have tended to support the relative importance of sexual conflicts in hysteria in terms of differential responses to sexual and nonsexual stimuli.

ANTISOCIAL PERSONALITY

Much of what has been said about the hysterical personality can be applied to the patient with an antisocial personality disorder. However, there are sex differences. More men than women present with antisocial personalities, whereas females predominate among the hysterics. As indicated before, delinquent and antisocial behavior in childhood is highly predictive of both adult sociopathy and hysteria (Robins, 1966). Increased sexual activity and interest in sex was more typical of the girls than of the boys who became sociopathic adults.

Guze et al. (1969, 1970) found the incidence of antisocial personality among male prisoners to be between 56 and 81 per cent. Sexual problems, such as repeated venereal disease, flagrant promiscuity, and sexual deviations were among their criteria for diagnosis. Only one prisoner was considered to be homosexual, although 18 per cent of the sample of more than 200 prisoners had had one or more homosexual experiences. These figures are less than

Kinsey's incidence of homosexual contacts in 22 to 24 per cent of nonpenal male populations of similar age and education. Despite the widespread belief that homosexual practices are common in incarceration, many of the men reported that their homosexual experiences had occurred only outside of prison.

Cloninger and Guze (1970a) studied 66 female felons; 65 per cent met diagnostic criteria for sociopathy. Such sociopathy was associated with other diagnostic entities in the majority: with alcoholism, 60 per cent; hysteria, 40 per cent; drug dependency, 30 per cent; and homosexuality, 28 per cent. Nine women reported some overt homosexual experience; in five, this experience was limited to the period of imprisonment. Differences between the studies of male and female prisoners included the greater prevalence of hysteria and a higher incidence of homosexuality among the women (higher than Kinsey's figures for normal females). Other characteristics of the sexual behavior of the female prisoners included early premarital sexual intercourse, rape, prostitution, and veneral disease. Seventy-nine per cent of the prisoners reported sexual inadequacy; 67 per cent, sexual indifference; 52 per cent, frigidity; and 36 per cent, dyspareunia. Divorce or separation was reported by the majority who had been married. Fifty-five had been pregnant at least once, with a total of 144 children, 40 per cent of whom were conceived out of wedlock.

Cloninger and Guze (1970a, 1970b) also studied the first degree relatives of criminals and the spouses of male felons. These studies showed that both male and female prisoners came from similar family backgrounds, with a high incidence of antisocial and hysterical personality disorders. Social and family disruption was more common among the female felons than among the men. Also, spouses of the male prisoners showed similar psychopathology, suggesting assortative mating, with marriage of persons from similar backgrounds. This fact, combined with environmental factors, makes for dismal predictions about the offspring.

Lukianowicz (1971) examined 50 female juvenile offenders who were remanded to a training school in Northern Ireland. He found an association between age and the nature of the offense, with sexual offenses being the most characteristic problem in the age group from 14 years to over 17. Girls 12 to 13 years old were more frequently charged with property offenses. The most common sexual offenses were promiscuity and unrestrained sexual behavior in general. This behavior was not correlated with mental deficiency, and the rate of illegitimacy was relatively low (6 per cent, as compared with the expected figure for the general population of about 5 per cent). Sexual activity began in 80 per cent of the delinquent girls before the age of 13, with an 8 per cent rate of incest with fathers early in life. Despite normal intelligence, educational achievement was poor. After a 2- to 5-year follow-up, more than 60 per cent of the girls were adjusting reasonably well in the community. None of the girls who were released had reverted to antisocial behavior, and most were able to adjust their sexual behavior to meet community standards.

As would be expected, there is also a high incidence of persons with antisocial personality disorders among populations of patients who are charged with sexual offenses. Cuthbert (1970) reported experience with psychiatric examinations of nearly 70 murderers, excluding cases of infanticide and suicide pacts. He was impressed with the contribution of sexual jealousy in homicidal attacks and reported that half of his cases had a sexual aspect of some kind. Stürup (1968) reported that the risk of recidivism in first time sexual offenders is about 6.9 per cent. This rate increased to 40 per cent after the third offense. He mentioned that in Denmark about 10 per cent of serious sexual offenders request permission for castration. Long term follow-up showed that relapse rates after surgery dropped to about 2 per cent, often accompanied by considerable personal satisfaction on the part of the patient.

There have been many psychological studies of personality and sexual adjustment and investigations of the relationship between aggressive and sexual drives in humans and animals. This has peripheral relevance to the antisocial and other personality disorders. Likewise, endocrine studies have shown that hormones exert effects on both sexual and aggressive behavior and may be used therapeutically to modify both.

PASSIVE-AGGRESSIVE PERSONALITY

Very little has been written about the sexual behavior of patients with a diagnosis of passive-aggressive personality disorder. This fact may be related to difficulties in defining the syndrome, as in a 7- to 15-year followup study by Small et al. (1970).

In another paper, Small and Small (1971) gave more detailed descriptions of the sexual behavior of their sample of 100 probands, comparing them with other psychiatric patients. The incidences of both marriage and divorce were higher in the cohort of passive-aggressives, with at least half having been divorced or remarried during the course of the follow-up study. One third of the subjects admitted to promiscuity—that is, multiple extramarital sexual relationships with more than one partner. The incidence of promiscuity among passive-aggressives was similar to the incidence in manic-depressive illness, particularly the bipolar type of the illness, but was higher than in schizophrenia. None of the passive-aggressive subjects was preferentially homosexual or had indulged in deviant sexual practices. Persistent frigidity and impotence were uncommon. Heightened or reduced sexual interest was often associated with exacerbation of symptoms and disturbances in interpersonal relationships. Unlike patients with antisocial personality disorders, the passive-aggressive subjects reported enduring relationships with other people, with sustained sexual attachments that had more than a physical basis. Some 15 years later, the majority had achieved stable marital relationships.

EMOTIONALLY UNSTABLE PERSONALITY

This diagnosis was included in DSM-I but was deleted from DSM-II and incorporated under the heading of hysterical personality. However, there have been some recent studies suggesting that it is possible to separate the emotionally unstable personality from both hysterical and passive-aggressive personality disorders (Rifkin et al., 1972a). This separation was done on the basis of the presenting clinical phenomena, response to drug treatment, and clinical outcome (Rifkin et al., 1972b; Klein et al., 1973). Patients with emotionally unstable character disorders, particularly women, often experience sexual problems, with frequent promiscuous behavior. Such was found to be true of the patients who either did or did not improve over time. The occurrence of improvement, particularly in relation to drug treatment with chlorpromazine or lithium, was stressed as one of the features that differentiates this illness from other kinds of personality disorders.

Psychophysiological Disorders

Mechanic (1972) described how a variety of such factors as vulnerability, social and cultural influences, responses to perceived illnesses, and emotional distress contribute to the kind of symptoms that patients develop. Moreover, learning and social conditioning and the reactive components in physical illnesses are important considerations in diagnosis and in management. Many times the symptoms of emotional distress associated with the physical illness may persist well beyond the normal course of somatic disturbance. Physicians may reinforce continued distress by their own instructions, expectations, or other behaviors.

Tyrer (1973) pointed out that the James-Lange theory of emotion is no longer tenable in the light of current neurophysiological knowledge. However, in a modified form, it can be stated that, in normal emotion, bodily feelings and sensations are relatively unimportant, but in morbid states, these feelings and sensations may become so predominant that they become almost the sole manifestations of mood change. He also emphasized the role of other such factors as social class and cultural background, which may confer a predisposition to respond in a particular way to a stimulus. Once established, such a pattern of response tends to be stable.

If such theoretical considerations are supported by further data, symptomatic treatment of either physical or emotional states may gain wider acceptance instead of the usual criticisms for encouraging so-called symptom substitution. Such general comments bear on sexual disturbances and on other psychophysiological abnormalities that characterize these diagnostic categories.

Hypersexuality

Nymphomania and satyriasis are descriptive terms signifying excessive or pathological heterosexual interests and desires for coitus in women and in men, respectively. Although there is considerable descriptive literature, particularly about nymphomania, there have been few scientific studies.

Ellis (1936) wrote a monograph on nymphomania, and Diethelm (1966) summarized the medical literature about the subject. No comparable works have appeared about satyriasis. Kinsey tended to dismiss both states on the basis that they are nothing more than extreme positions on a distribution curve. Moreover, Jensen (1973) had indicated that hypersexuality is the rule, not the exception, in subhuman primates, from which human sexual behavior has evolved. The popular literature has tended to glamorize hypersexuality in both sexes. However, the medical descriptions of the subject mostly state that hypersexuality is associated with a lack of sexual gratification or release of tension and is accompanied by psychological difficulties. Pumpian-Mindlin (1967) described such patients as intensely narcissistic, with disregard of other people and a lack of ability for heterosexual satisfaction. The incidence of such problems is difficult to ascertain since the definition of "excessive" has never been made precise. However, Burnap and Golden (1967) described the sexual problems encountered in the practices of physicians in different medical specialties. Nymphomania was number 18 on a list of sexual problems with 16 estimated cases seen per year by 60 physicians. Satyriasis was number 20, with five cases seen per year.

Male promiscuity, which is also termed the Don Juan syndrome, has been the subject of few studies. Noy et al. (1966) described Don Juan behavior in 11 of 25 patients who were suffering from impotence of nonorganic causes. Excessive sexual behavior by these patients was interpreted as efforts to prove themselves, and their personal relationships with the women involved were devoid of much emotion. Don Juanism has also been described in male hysterics (Luisada and Pittard, 1973). Guiora (1966) reviewed some of the presumed psychodynamics of the promiscuous man as relating to oedipal conflicts, with a continuing search for mother love in relationships with other women. The effects of such behavior on the daughters of such men were reported in three cases; all the daughters were diagnosed as suffering from anxiety hysteria, which was hypothesized to result from constant exposure to sexual stimuli and fantasies, combined with repeated rejections by the father with his many affairs. Jens (1970) discussed the treatment of hypersexual behavior in men, reporting on 15 cases treated with female hormones and psychotherapy. The subjects came from mental hospitals or prisons or were referred for treatment of some kind of sexual offense. It was found that sexual drive was reduced with hormone treatment but that it returned when the medication was discontinued, although the drive did not generally reach pretreatment levels, a fact that was related, in part, to the effects of insight-oriented psychotherapy. Laschet (1973) has reviewed the generally effective results of antiandrogenic treatment of sex offenders.

Promiscuity in women has received relatively more attention than it has in men. However, the definition of such behavior, particularly in a climate of rapidly changing sexual mores, is critical and makes generalizations of data from different sources and time periods very difficult. Willis (1967) defined promiscuity as indiscriminate sexual pairing with frequent partners, with an absence of consideration or love for the partner. He suggested that such behavior may represent anxiety about close relationships, and, paradoxically, physical intimacy may actually maintain emotional distance. There have been many reports of increasing sexual activity among the unmarried, particularly on college campuses. However, most writers agree that increased sexual freedom does not mean promiscuity in the sense of repeated coitus with strangers but usually involves a meaningful partnership and loving relationship with someone else. Walters (1965) believes that promiscuity in adolescent girls indicates a failure of ego development, with loss of impulse control, failure of self-esteem, and a lack of development of selectivity. Naiman (1966) interviewed 14 unmarried and 18 married mothers (controls). He did not find that overt or conscious guilt or knowledge of contraception was of causative significance in the unmarried pregnancies, but impulsivity was significant. Likewise, the unmarried women were more promiscuous in the sense of having more sexual partners and proceeding to intercourse after a shorter period of acquaintance. The unmarried women also had poorer abilities to form stable relationships.

Another significant correlation with promiscuity is that of venereal disease. Ekström (1966) studied 100 teen-agers in Denmark who were infected with gonorrhea. The sample included 63 females and 37 males. They had a high incidence of social problems, such as poor family background, early dropout from school, and lack of vocational training. Immaturity, low intelligence, and emotional and behavior problems were also common. The age of first coitus was quite young, 15½ years on the average for the girls and 15 years for the boys. Many of the teen-agers reported brief sexual liaisons and previous venereal infections. Among the girls, illegitimate pregnancies and prostitution were common; 24 of the 63 girls had been prostitutes.

Another association with female promiscuity was identified by Tennent et al. (1971) in a study of 56 arsonists who were hospitalized in special facilities for the care of psychiatric patients who commit criminal acts. They were compared with a control group of age-matched patients from the same institutions. The arsonists were significantly less physically aggressive than the controls, but they had more sexual difficulties, including severe dysmenorrhea, earlier age of first sexual experience, fewer marriages, more promiscuity, and more convictions for prostitution. Psychiatric symptoms and diagnoses were similar in the two groups. This study confirmed earlier findings and supported hypotheses concerning the underlying sexual root of fire setting, although the relative lack of physical aggressiveness in the arsonists was in contrast to some other studies, mainly of men.

There have been several formal studies of prostitutes and their clients. The clients were studied by Gibbens and Silberman (1960), who examined a sample of 230 men who consorted with prostitutes. The men were gathered from venereal disease clinics in England. The majority were between 20 and 40 years of age, and, whether married or not, their first intercourse had often been with a prostitute. Only 15 per cent of the men had contacted the same prostitute more than once or had expressed any friendly feelings toward them. Transient occupations among the men were common. Characteristically, they were described as passive and of good reputation, often coming from parental constellations of a dominant mother and a passive or absent father.

Other workers have described the background and training of prostitutes. Bryan (1970) studied the backgrounds of 33 prostitutes or call girls and detailed the role of pimps, the apprenticeship period, and the various organizational details involved in the profession. The author judged that prostitution is really an unskilled job, requiring few skills and little training. Moreover, the occupation is unstable and liable to exploitation and criminal prosecution. Bullough (1970) reviewed the literature on prostitution and described the difficulties that are involved in establishing the extent of the problem and conducting adequate research. Most studies agree that the woman who becomes a prostitute is young, poorly educated, impoverished, and likely to be from a broken home. However, most of the data come from police records and venereal disease clinics, so that the samples are biased toward those who are least proficient in the occupation. Ellis (1936) and many subsequent workers have stressed the lack of sensuality and the absence of sexual satisfaction in prostitutes' relationships with their customers. Others, including Glover (1945), have proposed that prostitutes are sexually frigid, with unconscious hostility toward men and, possibly, latent homosexuality. However, Pomeroy's (1965) data are contradictory, in that he found prostitutes to be more orgastic than normal women. A few studies of middle-and upper-class prostitutes have been done, including an anonymous English study (1955) and work by Greenwald (1958), who concluded that maternal deprivation was an important predisposing factor. However, comprehensive studies of the problem have yet to be made.

An article by Winick and Kinsie (1972) presents an analysis of the presenty-day status of prostitution in America; it objects to the legal penalties for such behavior and questions whether current trends toward the sanctioning of sexual freedom and the use of surrogates may ultimately reduce the need for commercialized sex. Grold (1970) has also raised the issue of whether casual sexual encounters (swinging) are really pathological or more an expression of changing cultural mores. The subject of the current status of extramarital sex in contemporary society has also been reviewed and considered in depth by Smith and Smith (1973).

REFERENCES

American Psychiatric Association. *Diagnostic and Statistical Manual of Mental Disorders*, ed. 2. American Psychiatric Association, Washington, 1968.

Arieti, S. Sexual conflict in psychotic disorders. In *Sexual Problems: Diagnosis and Treatment in Medical Practice*, C. W. Wahl, editor, p. 228. Free Press (Macmillan), New York, 1967.

Blumer, D. Hypersexual episodes in temporal lobe epilepsy. Am. J. Psychiatry, *126:* 1099, 1970.

Blumer, D., and Walker, A. E. Sexual behavior in temporal lobe epilepsy. Arch. Neurol., *16:* 37, 1967.

Bryan, J. H. Apprenticeships in prostitution. In *Studies in Human Sexual Behavior: The American Scene*, A. Shiloh, editor, p. 420. Charles C Thomas, Springfield, Ill., 1970.

Bullough, V. L. Problems and methods for research in prostitution and the behavioral sciences. In *Studies in Human Sexual Behavior: The American Scene*, A. Shiloh, editor, p. 14. Charles C Thomas, Springfield, Ill., 1970.

Burnap, D. W., and Golden, J. S. Sexual problems in medical practice. J. Med. Educ., *42:* 673, 1967.

Butts, H. F. Post-partum psychiatric problems. J. Natl. Med. Assoc., *61:* 136, 1969.

Cassidy, W. L., Flanagan, N. B., Spellman, M., and Cohen, M. E. Clinical observations in manic-depressive disease. J. A. M. A., *164:* 1535, 1957.

Cloninger, C. R., and Guze, S. B. Psychiatric illness and female criminality: The role of sociopathy and hysteria in the antisocial woman. Am. J. Psychiatry, *127:* 303, 1970a.

Cloninger, C. R., and Guze, S. B. Female criminals: Their personal, familial, and social backgrounds. Arch. Gen. Psychiatry, *23:* 554, 1970b.

Connolly, F. H., and Gittleson, N. L. The relationship between delusions of sexual change and olfactory and gustatory hallucinations in schizophrenia. Br. J. Psychiatry, *119:* 443, 1971.

Cooper, A. J. "Neurosis" and disorders of sexual potency in the male. J. Psychosom. Res., *12:* 141, 1968.

Cooper, A. J. Factors in male sexual inadequacy: A review. J. Nerv. Ment. Dis., *149:* 337, 1969.

Cooper, A. J. Some personality factors in frigidity. J. Psychosom. Res., *13:* 149, 1969.

Cooper, A. J. The causes and management of impotence. Postgrad. Med. J., *48:* 548, 1972.

Cuthbert, T. M. A portfolio of murders. Br. J. Psychiatry, *116:* 1, 1970.

*de la Cruz, F. F., and LaVeck, G. D. *Human Sexuality and the Mentally Retarded*. Brunner/Mazel, New York, 1973.

DeMoor, W. Vaginismus: Etiology and treatment. Am. J. Psychother., *26:* 207, 1972.

Dewhurst, K. The neurosyphilitic psychoses today. Br. J. Psychiatry, *115:* 31, 1969.

Dewhurst, K., Oliver, J. E., and McKnight, A. L. Socio-psychiatric consequences of Huntington's disease. Br. J. Psychiatry, *116:* 255, 1970.

Diethelm, O. La surexcitation sexuelle: Historique et discussion clinique. Evol. Psychiatr. (Paris), *31:* 233, 1966.

Douglas, G. Some emotional disorders of the puerperium. J. Psychosom. Res., *12:* 101, 1968.

Dupont, R. L., and Grunebaum, H. Willing victims: The husbands of paranoid women. Am. J. Psychiatry, *125:* 151, 1968.

Eastman, W. F., Fromhart, M. V., and Fulghum, M. S. Sexual problems and personality adjustment of college women. J. Am. Coll. Health Assoc., *18:* 144, 1969.

Ekström, K. One hundred teenagers in Copenhagen infected with gonorrheoa. Br. J. Vener. Dis., *42:* 162, 1966.

Ellis. H. *Studies in the Psychology of Sex,* vol. 2. Random House, New York, 1936.

Epstein, A. W. The relationship of altered brain states to sexual psychopathology. In *Contemporary Sexual Behavior,* J. Zubin and J. Money, editors, p. 297. Johns Hopkins University Press, Baltimore, 1973.

Eysenck, H. J. Hysterical personality and sexual adjustment, attitudes, and behaviour, J. Sex Res., *7:* 274, 1971.

Farley, J., Woodruff, R. A., and Guze, S. B. The prevalence of hysteria and conversion symptoms. Br. J. Psychiatry, *114:* 1121, 1968.

Feighner, J. P., Robins, E., Guze, S. B., Woodruff, R. A., Winokur, G., and Munoz, R. Diagnostic criteria for use in psychiatric research. Arch. Gen. Psychiatry, *26:* 57, 1972.

Fink, P. J. Correlations between "actual" neurosis and the work of Masters and Johnson. Psychoanal. Q., *39:* 38, 1970.

*Flor-Henry, P. Ictal and interictal psychiatric manifestations in epilepsy: Specific or nonspecific? Epilepsia, *13:* 773, 1972.

Frank, L. Humanizing and dehumanizing aspects of human sexuality. Dis. Nerv. Syst., *30:* 781, 1969.

Freeman, W. Frontal lobotomy in early schizophrenia—long follow-up in 415 cases. Br. J. Psychiatry, *119:* 621, 1971.

Gibbens, T. C. N., and Silberman, M. The clients of prostitutes. Br. J. Vener. Dis., *36:* 113, 1960.

Gittleson, N. L., and Dawson-Butterworth, K. Subjective ideas of sexual change in female schizophrenics. Br. J. Psychiatry, *113:* 491, 1967.

Gittleson, N. L., and Levine, S. Subjective ideas of sexual change in male schizophrenics. Br. J. Psychiatry, *112:* 779, 1966.

Glover, E. *The Psycho-pathology of Prostitution.* Institute for the Scientific Treatment of Delinquency, London, 1945.

Gold, L., Crain, I. J., Kaufman, S. S., Frank, L., and Berman, L. H. Panel on the humanistic approach to sexuality. Dis. Nerv. Syst., *30:* 771, 1969.

Goodwin, D. W., Guze, S. B., and Robins, E. Follow-up studies in obsessional neurosis. Arch. Gen. Psychiatry, *20:* 182, 1969.

Greenwald, H. *Call Girl: A Social and Psychoanalytic Study.* Ballentine, New York, 1958.

Grold, L. J. Swinging: Sexual freedom or neurotic escapism? Am. J. Psychiatry, *127:* 521, 1970.

Grunebaum, H. U., Abernethy, V. D., Rofman, E. S., and Weiss, J. L. The family planning attitudes, practices, and motivations of mental patients. Am. J. Psychiatry, *128:* 740, 1971.

Guiora, A. Z. Daughter of a Don Juan: A syndrome. Psychiatr. Q., *40:* 71, 1966.

Guze, S. B., Goodwin, D. W., and Crane, J. B. Criminality and psychiatric disorders. Arch. Gen. Psychiatry, *20:* 583, 1969.

Guze, S. B., Goodwin, D. W., and Crane, J. B. A psychiatric study of the wives of convicted felons: An example of assortative mating. Am. J. Psychiatry, *126:* 1773, 1970.

Halleck, S. L. Sex and mental health on the campus. J. A. M. A., *200:* 684, 1967.

Hamilton, J. A. Postpartum psychoses. In *Davis' Gynecology and Obstetrics,* vol. II, J. J. Rovinsky, editor, p. 1. Harper & Row, Hagerstown, Md., 1972.

Hierons, R., and Saunders, M. Impotence in patients with temporal-lobe lesions. Lancet, *2:* 761, 1966.

Hóenig, J., and Hamilton, C. M. Epilepsy and sexual orgasm. Acta Psychiatr. Neurol. Scand., *35:* 448, 1960.

Hojer-Pedersen, W. The hysterical personality type. Acta Psychiatr. Scand., *41:* 122, 1965.

*Hooshmand, H., Escobar, M. R., and Kopf, S. W. Neurosyphilis: A study of 241 patients. J. A. M. A., *219:* 726, 1972.

Hunt, J. McV. Traditional personality theory in the light of recent evidence. Am. Sci., *53:* 80, 1965.

Jens, R. Male hypersexual behavior: Suggested treatment. In *Studies in Human Sexual Behavior: The American Scene,* A. Shiloh, editor, p. 373. Charles C Thomas, Springfield, Ill., 1970.

Jensen, G. D. Human sexual behavior in primate perspective. In *Contemporary Sexual Behavior,* J. Zubin and J. Money, editors, p. 17. Johns Hopkins University Press, Baltimore, 1973.

Johnson, J. Sexual impotence and the limbic system. Br. J. Psychiatry, *111:* 300, 1965.

Johnston, R., and Planansky, K. Schizophrenia in men: The impact on their wives. Psychiatr. Q., *42:* 146, 1968.

Jones, I. H. Ethology and psychiatry, Aust. N. Z. J. Psychiatry, *5:* 258, 1971.

Klein, D. F., Honigfeld, G., and Feldman, S. Prediction of drug effect in personality disorders. J. Nerv. Ment. Dis., *156:* 183, 1973.

Kolarsky, A., Freund, K., Machek, J., and Polak, O. Male sexual deviation. Arch. Gen. Psychiatry, *17:* 735, 1967.

Laschet. U. Antiandrogen in the treatment of sex offenders: Mode of action and therapeutic outcome. In *Contemporary Sexual Behavior,* J. Zubin and J. Money, editors, p. 311. Johns Hopkins University Press, Baltimore, 1973.

Levine, J., and Albert, H. Sexual behavior after lobotomy, J. Nerv. Ment. Dis., *113:* 332, 1951.

Lishman, W. A. Brain damage in relation to psychiatric disability after head injury. Br. J. Psychiatry, *114:* 373, 1968.

Lowenthal, M. F., and Chiriboga, D. Transition to the empty nest. Arch. Gen. Psychiatry, *26:* 8, 1972.

Luisada, P. V., and Pittard, B. A. The hysterical personality in males. In *Scientific Proceedings in Summary Form from the 126th Annual Meeting of the*

American Psychiatric Assoc., p. 313. American Psychiatric Association, Washington, 1973.

Lukianowicz, N. Sexual drive and its gratification in schizophrenia. Int. J. Soc. Psychiatry, *9:* 250, 1963.

Lukianowicz, N. Juvenile offenders. Acta Psychiatr. Scand., *47:* 1, 1971.

MacLean, P. D. Special award lecture: New findings on brain function and sociosexual behavior. In *Contemporary Sexual Behavior,* J. Zubin and J. Money, editors, p. 53, Johns Hopkins University Press, Baltimore, 1973.

Malmquist, C. P., Kiresuk, T. J., and Spano, R. M. Personality characteristics of women with repeated illegitimacies: Descriptive aspects. Am. J. Orthopsychiatry, *36:* 476, 1966.

Marsden, C. D. and Harrison, M. J. G. Outcome of investigation of patients with presenile dementia. Br. Med. J., *2:* 249, 1972.

Masserman, J. H. Sexuality re-evaluated. Can. Psychiatr. Assoc. J., *11:* 379, 1966.

Maurice, W. L., and Guze, S. B. Sexual dysfunction and associated psychiatric disorders. Compr. Psychiatry, *11:* 539, 1970.

McCulloch, D. J., and Stewart, J. C. Sexual norms in a psychiatric population. J. Nerv. Ment. Dis., *131:* 70, 1960.

Mechanic, D. Social psychologic factors affecting the presentation of bodily complaints. N. Engl. J. Med., *286:* 1132, 1972.

Merskey, H., and Woodforde, J. M. Psychiatric sequelae of minor head injury. Brain, *95:* 521, 1972.

Mignone, R. J., Donnelly, E. F., and Sadowsky, D. Psychological and neurological comparisons of psychomotor and nonpsychomotor epileptic patients. Epilepsia, *11:* 345, 1970.

Naiman, J. A comparative study of unmarried and married mothers. Can. Psychiatr. Assoc. J., *11:* 465, 1966.

Nameche, G., Waring, M., and Ricks, D. Early indicators of outcome in schizophrenia. J. Nerv. Ment. Dis., *139:* 232, 1964.

Negulici, E., and Christodorescu, D. Paranoid schizophrenia and Klinefelter's syndrome. Psychiatr. Neurol. (Basel), *154:* 27, 1967.

Nilsson, A., Kaij, L., and Jacobson, L. Postpartum mental disorder in an unselected sample: The importance of the unplanned pregnancy. J. Psychosom. Res., *10:* 341, 1967.

Noy, P., Wollstein, S., and Kaplan-De-Nour, A. Clinical observations on the psychogenesis of impotence. Br. J. Med. Psychol., *39:* 43, 1966.

*Oppenheimer, H. *Clinical Psychiatry: Issues and Challenges.* Harper & Row, New York, 1971.

Ovesey, L., and Meyers, H. Retarded ejaculation. Am. J. Psychother., *22:* 185, 1968.

Paulson, M. J., and Lin, T. T. Frigidity: A factor analytic study of a psychosomatic theory. Psychosomatics, *11:* 112, 1970.

Pinderhughes, C. A., Grace, E. B., and Reyna, L. J. Psychiatric disorders and sexual functioning. Am. J. Psychiatry, *128:* 1276, 1972.

Planansky, K., and Johnston, R. Mate selection in schizophrenia. Acta Psychiatr. Scand., *43:* 397, 1967.

Poinsard, P. J. Psychiatric aspects of the woman over sixty-five. Clin. Obstet. Gynecol., *10:* 532, 1967.

Pomeroy, W. B. Some aspects of prostitution. J. Sex Res., *1:* 177, 1965.

Post, F., Rees, W. L., and Schurr, P. H. An evaluation of bimedial leucotomy. Br. J. Psychiatry, *114:* 1223, 1968.

Prosen, H. Sexuality in females with "hysteria." Am. J. Psychiatry, *124:* 687, 1967.

Pumpian-Mindlin, E. Nymphomania and satyriasis. In *Sexual Problems: Diagnosis and Treatment in Medical Practice,* C. W. Wahl, editor, p. 163. Free Press (Macmillan), New York, 1967.

Purtell, J. J., Robins, E., and Cohen, M. E. Observations on clinical aspects of hysteria. J. A. M. A., *146:* 902, 1951.

Raboch, J., and Bartak, V. A contribution to the study of the anesthetic-frigid syndrome in women. Cesk. Psychiatr., *64:* 230, 1968a.

Raboch, J., and Bartak, V. The sexual life of frigid women. Psychiatr. Neurol. Med. Psychol., *20:* 368, 1968b.

Rifkin, A. Levitan, S. J. Galewski, J., and Klein, D. F. Emotionally unstable character disorder—a follow-up study. I. Description of patients and Outcome Biol. Psychiatry, *4:* 65, 1972a.

Rifkin, A., Levitan, S. J., Galewski, J., and Klein, D. F. Emotionally unstable character disorder—a follow-up study. II. Prediction of outcome. Biol. Psychiatry, *4:* 81, 1972b.

Roberts, G. E., and Clayton, B. E. Some findings arising out of a survey of mentally retarded children. Part II. Physical growth and development. Dev. Med. Child Neurol., *11:* 584, 1969.

*Robins, L. N. *Deviant Children Grown Up.* Williams & Wilkins, Baltimore, 1966.

Rolph, C., editor. Women of the Streets. Seeker & Warburg, London, 1955.

Rosenbaum, C. P. Metabolic, physiological, anatomic, and genetic studies in the schizophrenias: A review and analysis. J. Nerv. Ment. Dis., *146:* 103, 1968.

Rosenthal, S. H. The involutional depressive syndrome. Am. J. Psychiatry, *124:* 21, 1968.

Roth, M. Anxiety neuroses and phobic states. I. Clinical features. Br. Med. J., *1:* 489, 1969.

Roth, M. Recent progress in the psychiatry of old age and its bearing on certain problems of psychiatry in earlier life. Biol. Psychiatry, *5:* 103, 1972.

Rutter, M., Greenfeld, D., and Lockyer, L. A five to fifteen year follow-up study of infantile psychosis. Br. J. Psychiatry, *113:* 1183, 1967.

*Shiloh, A., editor. *Studies in Human Sexual Behavior: The American Scene.* Charles C Thomas, Springfield, Ill., 1970.

Shobe, F. O., and Brion, P. Long-term prognosis in manic-depressive illness. Arch. Gen. Psychiatry, *24:* 334, 1971.

Shobe, F. O., and Gildea, M. C.-L. Long-term follow-up of selected lobotomized private patients, J. A. M. A., *206:* 327, 1968.

Simmons, J. Q. Emotional problems in mental retardation. Pediatr. Clin. North Am., *15:* 957, 1968.

Small, I. F., and Small, J. G. Sex and the passive-aggressive personality. Med. Aspects Hum. Sexuality, *5:* 78, 1971.

Small, I. F., Small, J. G., Alig, V. B., and Moore, D. F.

Passive-aggressive personality disorder: A search for a syndrome. Am. J. Psychiatry, *126:* 973, 1970.

Smith, L. G., and Smith, J. R. Co-marital sex: The incorporation of extramarital sex into the marriage relationship. In *Contemporary Sexual Behavior,* J. Zubin and J. Money, editors, p. 391. Johns Hopkins University Press, Baltimore, 1973.

Stevens, J. R. Psychiatric implications of psychomotor epilepsy. Arch. Gen. Psychiatry, *14:* 461, 1966.

Sturup, G. K. Will this man be dangerous? Int. Psychiatr. Clin., *5:* 5, 1968.

Templer, D. I. The obsessive-compulsive neurosis: Review of research findings. Compr. Psychiatry, *13:* 375, 1972.

Tennent, T. G., McQuaid, A., Loughnane, T., and Hands, A. J. Female arsonists. Br. J. Psychiatry, *119:* 497, 1971.

Turner, E. T. Attitudes of parents of deficient children toward their child's sexual behavior. J. Sch. Health., *40:* 548, 1970.

Tyrer, P. J. Relevance of bodily feelings in emotion. Lancet, *1:* 915, 1973.

Varsamis, J., and Adamson, J. D. Early schizophrenia. Can. Psychiatr. Assoc. J., *16:* 487, 1971.

Verwoerdt, A., Pfeiffer, E., and Wang, H. S. Sexual behavior in senescence. Geriatrics, *24:* 137, 1969.

*Wahl, C. W. *Sexual Problems: Diagnosis and Treatment in Medical Practice.* Free Press (Macmillan), New York, 1967.

Wakeling, A. Comparative study of psychiatric patients with Klinefelter's syndrome and hypogonadism. Psychol. Med., *2:* 139, 1972.

Walinder, J. Transvestism, definition and evidence in favor of occasional derivation from cerebral dysfunction. Int. J. Neuropsychiatry, *1:* 567, 1965.

Walters, P. A. Promiscuity in adolescence. Am. J. Orthopsychiatry, *35:* 670, 1965.

Whiskin, F. E. The geriatric sex offender. Geriatrics, *22:* 168, 1967.

Willis, S. E. Sexual promiscuity as a symptom of anxiety. In *Sexual Problems: Diagnosis and Treatment in Medical Practice,* C. W. Wahl, editor, p. 172. Free Press (Macmillan), New York, 1967.

Wilson, J. E., Barglow, P., and Shipman, W. The prognosis of postpartum mental illness. Compr. Psychiatry, *13:* 305, 1972.

Winick, C., and Kinsie, P. M. Prostitutes. Psychol. Today, *6:* 57, 1972.

Winokur, G., Guze, S. B., and Pfeiffer, E. Developmental and sexual factors in women: A comparison between control, neurotic, and psychotic groups. Am. J. Psychiatry, *115:* 1097, 1959a.

Winokur, G., Guze, S. B., and Pfeiffer, E. Nocturnal orgasm in women. Arch. Gen. Psychiatry, *1:* 180, 1959b.

Winokur, G., and Leonard, C. Sexual life in patients with hysteria. Dis. Nerv. Syst., *24:* 337, 1963.

Woodruff, R. A., Clayton, P. J., and Guze, S. B. Hysteria: Studies of diagnosis, outcome, and prevalence, J. A. M. A., *215:* 425, 1971.

Woodruff, R. A., Guze, S. B., and Clayton, P. J. Divorce among psychiatric outpatients. Br. J. Psychiatry, *121:* 289, 1972.

*Zubin J., and Money J., editors. *Contemporary sexual behavior: Critical Issues in the 1970's.* Johns Hopkins University Press, Baltimore, 1973.

chapter **15** Sexual Variants and Sexual Disorders

15.1 Homosexuality and Sexual Orientation Disturbances

JUDD MARMOR, M.D.

Introduction

Homosexual behavior as a variant form of sexuality occurs in most, if not all, human societies, advanced as well as primitive, and is probably as old as humanity. Evidence of its existence can be found in the writings and graphic arts of the most ancient of civilizations. Because it is a subject in which moral and religious issues and cultural value systems are deeply implicated, it is difficult to approach it with dispassionate scientific objectivity; nevertheless, such objectivity is essential if the psychiatrist it to deal constructively with the psychosocial problems involved in such behavior.

Definition

Homosexuality was listed as a sexual deviation under the broad rubric of "personality disorders and certain other nonpsychiatric mental disorders" in the second edition of the American Psychiatric Association's *Diagnostic and Statistical Manual of Mental Disorders*. This classification reflected a more tolerant approach to this condition than existed in the previous edition's listing, which included sexual deviation under the category of "sociopathic personality disturbance," or in earlier classifications, which placed it in the group of psychopathic personalities with pathological sexuality. The question of whether homosexuality belongs in the category of mental disorders at all has become a hotly debated issue in recent years, and in April, 1974, in a history-making decision, the American Psychiatric Association ruled that homosexuality would no longer be listed as a mental disorder. In its place they created a category of "sexual orientation disturbance" and described it as follows:

This category is for individuals whose sexual interests are directed primarily toward people of the same sex and who are either disturbed by, in conflict with, or wish to change their sexual orientation. This diagnostic category is distinguished from homosexuality, which by itself does not necessarily constitute a psychiatric disorder. Homosexuality per se is one form of sexual behavior and, like other forms of sexual behavior which are not by themselves psychiatric disorders, is not listed in this nomenclature of mental disorders.

The definition of homosexuality is far from a clear-cut matter. It can be defined in simple operational terms as any behavior involving sexual relations with a member of the same sex. Such a definition, however, fails to do justice to the wide variety of motivations that can underlie such behavior. Some persons enter into homosexual liaisons only because heterosexual objects are not available to them; others do so out of loneliness, boredom, rebelliousness, curiosity, or a neurotic need to please. Homosexual behavior also occurs among many adolescents and preadolescents as an expression of their intense sexual strivings in a society that forbids them the heterosexual explorations that they would prefer if they were free to choose.

Thompson (1964) deals with the same issues in stating:

[H]omosexuality is not a clinical entity, but a symptom with different meanings in different personality setups . . . . [O]vert homosexuality may express fear of the opposite sex, fear of adult responsibility, a need to defy authority, or an attempt to cope with hatred of or competitive attitudes to members of one's own sex; it may represent a flight from reality . . . or it may be a symptom of destructiveness of oneself or others. These do not exhaust the possibilites of its meaning . . . .

Rado (1956), in a similar vein, distinguishes five types of homosexual behavior indulged in: (1) because females are unavailable; (2) incidental homosexuality, in which homosexual behavior is transitory and sporadic, as in preadolescents and adolescents; (3) disorganized schizophrenia, where the homosexual behavior is an expression of chaotic behavior; (4) "surpiue variation" behavior, in which the homosexual behavior is the expression of sexual curiosity and wishes for diverse sexual experience; and (5) reparative homosexuality, where the homosexual pattern is an adaptive response to "hidden but incapacitating fears of the opposite sex."

The definition of homosexuality is further complicated by the fact that homosexual and heterosexual behaviors in human beings are not always or clearly differentiated patterns. Rather, they are points on a continuum that ranges from exclusive heterosexuality to exclusive homosexuality, with various grada-tions of bisexual patterns in between. Kinsey and his associates (1948) have suggested a seven-point scale for this continuum, based on both psychological reactions and overt experience: 0 on the scale denotes exclusively heterosexual; 1, predominantly heterosexual, only incidentally homosexual; 2, predominantly heterosexual but more than incidentally homosexual; 3, equally heterosexual and homosexual; 4, predominantly homosexual but more than incidentally heterosexual; 5, predominantly homosexual, only incidentally heterosexual; and 6, exclusively homosexual.

Others have suggested the terms "facultative homosexual" for people who are 1 and 2 on the scale, "bisexual" for those who rate 3 and 4, and "obligatory homosexual" for those who rate 5 and 6.

In this discussion, the definition of homosexuality is restricted to persons with a strong preferential erotic attraction to members of their own sex. It implies the same spontaneous capacity to be aroused by members of one's own sex as heterosexuality implies in regard to members of the opposite sex. It is the preferential arousal pattern that is crucial in this definition, not the manifest behavior. Indeed, some persons with such feelings may never indulge in overt homosexual behavior because of intense social fears or moral prohibitions; in this regard, they function analogously to inhibited or repressed heterosexuals.

Epidemiology

Homosexual activities of some kind probably occur in almost all societies, but the attitudes of different societies toward such practices vary widely. In a study of 76 societies other than their own, Ford and Beach (1952) observed that in 64 per cent of them homosexual activities were considered normal and socially acceptable, at least for certain members of the community. In some societies—like the Keraki of New Guinea, the Aranda of Australia, and the Siwans of North Africa—male homosexual activities were universal, although this activity did not preclude heterosexual relationships. Among the Mohave Indians, there was also a recognized class of exclusively homosexual women (Devereux, 1937). Among the 36 per cent of societies in which homosexual expression was condemned and prohibited, there was evidence in some that such practices continued to take place in secret.

These variant societal attitudes toward homosexual behavior make the scientific study of its prevalence extremely difficult. Mead (1961) has pointed out that statements on the absence of homosexual behavior in cross-cultural studies must be viewed with caution because of such factors as language barriers, unbreakable cultural taboos, need for personal privacy, distrust of Caucasian investigators, retrospective falsification, and, in some nonliterate societies, conventions of courtesy that demand telling a questioner what he presumably wants to hear. Another complication stems from the fact that different investigators often use widely varying defintions of homosexuality—from the exploratory same-sex play of adolescents to highly institutionalized, often religious, gender role changes to genuine adult homoerotic practices.

Similar difficulties attend efforts to study the prevalence of homosexuality in American culture. Here, homosexuals can be encountered in all walks of life, at all socio-economic levels, among all racial and ethnic groups, and in rural as well as urban areas. Their actual numbers are almost impossible to ascertain because many persons withhold this information from investigators because of opprobrium with which such inclinations are regarded. Thus, it is probable that actual incidence figures are higher than studies have reported.

The Kinsey study (1948), based on interviews with more than 5,000 white American men, concluded that 37 per cent of the men in this society have had at least some overt homosexual experience to the point of orgasm between adolescence and old age. The significance of this figure is diluted by Kinsey's inclusion in it of transitory adolescent practices and incidental prison experiences. A more relevant statistic is the finding that 10 per cent of white men are more or less exclusively homosexual—that is, on the Kinsey scale they rate 5 or 6—for at least 3 years between the ages of 16 and 55, and 4 per cent of them are exclusively homosexual throughout their

lives, from adolescence onward. Another meaningful finding was that about 13 per cent of the sample revealed a potentiality for homosexual behavior, in that they reacted erotically to other males, despite the fact that they had no overt homosexual contacts after the onset of adolescence.

Comparable studies of American women by the Kinsey group (1953) revealed a lower incidence of homosexuality among them, as compared with men, although the figures were substantially higher for unmarried women that for married ones. Between 2 and 6 per cent of the unmarried women in the sample but less than 1 per cent of the married ones had been more or less exclusively homosexual—that is, on the Kinsey scale they rated 5 or 6—in each of the years between 20 and 35 years of age. On the other hand, about 28 per cent of the women in the study reported some homosexual experiences or arousal in the course of their lives, 13 per cent of them to the point of orgasm. An additional significant finding was that 14 to 19 per cent of the unmarried women, 5 to 8 per cent of the previously married, and 1 to 3 per cent of the married ones had never had *any* sociosexual responses, either heterosexual or homosexual, between the ages of 20 and 35.

The Kinsey reports suffer from a number of sampling biases, particularly the failure to include racial and ethnic minority groups. Nevertheless, they represent the most thorough and extensive surveys done to date. A number of European surveys have been made, most of which are in approximate agreement with the Kinsey findings. Römer (1906), in a study of 600 male university students in Holland, arrived at a figure of about 2 per cent exclusive homosexuality plus 4 per cent bisexuality. Hirschfeld (1920), in a survey of 3,665 German men, calculated that 2.3 per cent were exclusively homosexual and 3.4 per cent bisexual. Friedeberg (1953) studied about 500 men in West Germany and found that 23 per cent of them admitted to postpubertal homosexual experiences; he did not obtain figures for exclusive homosexuality. Giese (Schoof, unpublished data, 1967) studied 2,835 male and 831 female college students in North Germany and found that 19 per cent of the men and 4 per cent of the women reported overt homosexual experiences, but most of these may have been adolescent experiences between the ages of 12 and 18. Within the previous 12 months, only 3 per cent of the men and 1 per cent of the women had had a homosexual contact. Schofield (1965) surveyed, 1,873 unmarried young people in England, almost equally divided among men and women in the 15 to 19 age group. Although he made no special effort to ascertain the incidence of homosexuality, 5 per cent of the men and 2 per cent of the women reported homosexual experiences.

It is clear from all these various surveys, despite their considerable limitations, that the propensity for homosexual reactivity is rather widespread, even in a society such as this one, which strongly discourages it. The psychiatrically intriguing question is why so substantial a number of men and women become preferentially motivated toward such behavior in spite of the powerful cultural taboos against it.

Causes

Nineteenth century scientists leaned toward a genetic explanation of homosexuality or else regarded it as a stigma of some degenerative disease of the nervous system. With the advent of embryology, the ancient Greek conception of organic bisexuality was revived, resting its case on the apparent hermaphroditic characteristics of the early human embryo. Psychoanalytic explanations, which have been the most influential contemporary ones, have combined this concept of bisexuality with a developmental theory based on psychosocial factors. Freud's view was that there is a normal psychic bisexuality, based on a biological bisexual predisposition in all human beings, and that all persons go through a homoerotic phase in childhood in the regular course of development. According to this view, if homosexuality develops in later life, it is the result of an arrest of normal development or else of regression as a result of castration anxiety mobilized by pathogenic family relationships. Moreover, even if development proceeds normally, certain vestiges of the homoerotic phase remain as permanent aspects of the personality. These latent homosexual tendencies are universal, Freud believed, and are reflected in sublimated patterns of affection for members of one's own sex or in certain passive tendencies in men and aggressive tendencies on women.

A more recent view, advocated by Bieber and others (1962), rejects the theory of psychic bisexuality and argues that heterosexuality is the biological norm in all mammals, including humans, and that the development of homosexuality is always a pathological consequence of fears of heterosexual functioning that have been produced by unfavorable life experiences. This, in contrast to the Freudian hypothesis that latent homosexual tendencies exist in all heterosexuals, the Bieber thesis is that "all homosexuals are latent heterosexuals."

With the development of modern genetics and endocrinology, many efforts have been directed toward attempting to demonstrate either a genetic predisposition or a hormonal basis for homosexual behavior. Kallman (1952) studied 85 homosexuals who were twins, and, although the concordance rates for overt homosexual behavior (5 and 6 on the Kinsey scale) were only slightly higher than normal for the 45 dizygotic pairs, it was 100 per cent for the 40 monozygotic pairs. This finding suggests the presence of a definite and decisive genetic factor in homosexuality, but Kallman's findings have not been comfirmed by other investigators. Thus, Kolb (1963) has described 7 monozygotic homosexual twins in which there was no concordance at all with their twin siblings. Moreover, it does not necessarily follow that a higher concordance rate in twins is due to a genetic factor; the powerful identification between them may result in a greater tendency to indulge in preadolescent and adolescent homosexual activities with each other with less inhibiting guilt than exists between other siblings. Given other facilitating and fixating familial and environmental circumstances, such activites may well result in a greater preponderance of concordant homosexual patterns. Nevertheless, the generally higher incidence of homosexual concordance in monozygotic as compared with dizygotic twins suggests that the possibility of a hidden genetic predisposition interacting with subsequent environmental experiences cannot be entirely ruled out at this stage of knowledge.

Chromosomal studies have thus far been unable to differentiate homosexuals from heterosexuals. Although an occasional patient with Klinefelter's syndrome (XXY or XXXY) or Turner's syndrome (XO) turns out to be homosexual, this finding is not considered significant, inasmuch as most persons with these chromosomal abnormalities are not homosexual. Some geneticists have suggested that the shift to the right in the birth orders of homosexuals as compared with heterosexuals—that is, they are born later in the sibship—may be indicative of some as yet undemonstrable chromosomal abnormality. However, such a postulate may not be necessary. The shift to the right may simply indicate that later siblings are more apt to be exposed to the kind of intrafamilial experience that tends to increase the susceptibility to the development of homosexual patterns; for example, mothers may become more deeply involved emotionally with later children, especially if they arrive at a time when their husband's conjugal ardors have begun to cool. Also, a younger sibling is more apt to be babied, to develop feelings of inadequacy in relation to older siblings, or to be the target of bullying or homosexual seduction by them.

Until recently, hormonal studies of homosexuals have failed to demonstrate any consistent difference between them and heterosexual controls. Recent technological advances in assay methods have begun to turn up some intriguing findings. Loraine et al. (1970) have reported finding abnormally low 24-hour urinary testosterone levels in two exclusive homosexual men, in contrast to normal findings in a bisexual subject. Margolese (1970) studied 24-hour urine samples from 24 Caucasian men, of whom 10 were healthy homosexuals, 10 healthy heterosexuals, and four heterosexuals "not in good health" (three were depressed and one had diabetes mellitus). Analyses of these samples for two breakdown products of testosterone—androsterone (A) and etiocholanolone (E)—revealed a clear difference between

the healthy homosexual and heterosexual groups. In seven of the homosexual group, the E values were greater than the A values; in one, A and E were equal; and in two, the A was very slightly greater than the E. On the other hand, in all 10 healthy heterosexuals, A was distinctly greater than E. However, the sick heterosexuals all had A to E ratios closer to those in the homosexual group, suggesting that an altered A to E ratio can result from physiological states other then homosexuality. Nevertheless, because women also tend to have higher E's than A's in their urine, Margolese hypothesizes that:

the metabolic condition which results in a relatively high A value is the cause of sexual preference for females by either sex, whereas a relatively low A value is associated with sexual preference for males by either sex.

These studies of Loraine and Margolese remain to be validated on larger samples and by other workers, and many other variables will have to be ruled out. For example, not only illness can affect these hormonal levels but also, as Rose et al. (1969) have shown, nonspecific physical and emotional stress may result in reversed A to E ratios. Furthermore, as Perloff (1965) has pointed out, hormonal studies involving urinary excretory products are

fraught with difficulty because many metabolic metamorphoses occur between formation of a hormone within a gland, secretion from the gland, binding to the protein and transportation within the body, degradation within the liver, and conversion into a form excretable by the kidney into the urine.

Plasma testosterone studies represent still another approach that is commanding new attention. Kolodny et al. (1971) have reported finding significantly lower plasma testosterone levels in a group of homosexuals (5 and 6 on the Kinsey scale) as compared with a matched control group of heterosexuals. These findings, too, remain to be validated, and the possible role of other variables—such as general health, diet, drug use, cigarette smoking, sexual activity, and physical and emotional stress—will have to be ruled out.

One subsequent study by Tourney and Hatfield (1973) has failed to confirm the results of either Kolodny or Margolese. Another study by Doerr et al. (in press) also failed to replicate these findings but did find significant differences in plasma estradiol levels between a group of male homosexuals and a control group of heterosexuals. For the time being, therefore, the question of whether there may be innate genetic or endocrinological differences between obligatory homosexuals and heterosexuals must be regarded as still unsettled. An additional fact that lends some persuasiveness to the possibility that there may be an innate constitutional factor in at least some forms of homosexuality is the recent research in lower animals indicating that action of fetal hormones on the hypothalamus of the developing embryo may play an important role in subsequent adult sexual functioning. A failure of the fetal hormones to function at the critical period may have important effects in these animals even though there may be no abnormalities in their external anatomy. Dörner (1967) has demonstrated that in geno- and phenotypical normal rats which have been castrated on the first day of life, female sexual behavior will be induced by androgens given after they have achieved maturity. If, however, after such castration they are given a small injection of testosterone on the third day of life, they will exhibit perfectly normal heterosexual behavior after androgen treatment in adulthood. This suggests the possibility that an absolute or relative androgen deficiency in the human male fetus during the critical period of differentiation may effect the direction of the sex drive, even in the subsequent presence of normal testosterone production. Money (1967) while warning that one must be careful not to draw parallels from such lower animals to primates, nevertheless indicates that they raise the question of whether or not some homosexuals may be born with a "hidden predisposition, perhaps lurking in the neurohumoral system of the brain, that makes [them] more vulnerable to differentiate a psychosexual identity as a homosexual—not in any automatic or mechanistic sense, but only if the social environment happens to provide the right confluence of circumstances."

The most prevalent theory concerning the cause of homosexuality is that which attributes it to a pathogenic family background. Bieber et al. (1962), in a psychoanalytic study of 106 male homosexual patients, based on the clinical findings of 77 cooperating psychoanalysts, conclude that the most significant factor in the genesis of homosexuality or "severe homosexual problems" is a parental constellation of a detached, hostile father and a close-binding, seductive mother who dominates and minimizes her husband. Although the Bieber group recognizes that there are variants to this pattern—such as disinterested or hostile mothers or overly close but demeaning fathers—they believe that a truly loving father precludes the development of homosexuality in a son, even though a homosexually inductive mother may be present.

That such parental constellations are frequently found in the background of homosexual men has long been known. As far back as 1905, in Freud's "Three Essays on the Theory of Sexuality" he indicated that men with weak or absent fathers and frustrating mothers are apt to become homosexual. The common denominator described in a host of clinical studies appears to be a background that results in a failure to form a satisfactory identification with an adequate father figure and in an originally close but ambivalent relationship with a mother figure, resulting, presumably, in a strong, unconscious fear or hatred of women. Various family patterns have been described in addition to the Bieber group pattern—for example, distant or hostile mothers and overly close fathers, ambivalent relationships with an older brother, absent mothers, absent fathers, idealized fathers, and broken homes.

However, the fact that many heterosexual men have similar backgrounds and do not go on to become homosexual suggests that these familial patterns are not adequate in themselves as sole etiological explanations. Marmor (1965) has suggested that the cause of homosexuality is not only "multiply determined by psychodynamic, socio-cultural, biological, and situational factors" but also "reflects the significance of subtle temporal as well as qualitative and quantitative variables." For example, if the strong mother/weak-or-absent father parental constellation were a crucial determinant in and of itself, one would expect to find a much higher incidence of male homosexuality among urban blacks, inasmuch as life in the ghetto has for decades produced large numbers of broken homes in which the mother is the mainstay of family life. However, although no definitive statistics on this subject exist as yet, available evidence does not suggest any significant difference in the incidence of homosexuality in black and white men. The reasons may lie in a number of other significant acculturating factors. First, as Harlow and Harlow (1965) have shown, good peer associations can often override the negative effect of a pathogenic mother relationship. It is possible that the readily available, numerous peer relationships of ghetto life present models for masculine identification that compensate for the absence of such models within the family. Second, there is substantial clincial evidence suggesting that both male and female homosexuality tend to develop more frequently in an atmosphere of sexual puritanism; the mores of ghetto life do not usually reflect the pervasive antiheterosexual bias that so often characterizes the middle-class upbringing.

Another relevant social factor is the existence of homosexual communities that present an accepting social milieu in which wavering, confused, and guilt-ridden young homosexuals can find, often for the first time in their lives, others like themselves who offer them affection and available sexual gratification. In urban centers, as Hooker (1965) notes, the gay bars that constitute a prominent aspect of the homosexual community function as "social institutions where friends can be met, the news of the homosexual world heard, gossip exchanged, invitations to parties issued, and warnings about current danger spots and attitudes of the police given. The reassurance and experience gained in these training centers may provide the turning point for some young men and women that starts their active and open participation in homosexual behavior, a phenomenon referred to in the gay world as "coming out."

Economic factors may also play a contributory role in the genesis of homosexual behavior, particularly in men. A number of writers have speculated that the increasing complexity of Western civilization makes it more difficult for contemporary men to achieve a secure masculine identity and enhances any latent existing tendencies to flee from the demands and responsibilities of the masculine role. Parallels exist in a number of primitive cultures also. For example, among the Chukchee of northeastern Siberia, the high incidence of homosexual behavior seems to be correlated with the difficulty in accumulating the high purchase price of a wife.

Clinical Features

Homosexuals may indulge in all the erotic practices that characterize heterosexual relations except for the limitations imposed by their same-sex anatomies. Kissing, tongue play, petting, mutual masturbation (either by hand or body friction), oral-genital relations, breast stimulation and kissing (by women), and anal intercourse (by men) are all common practices, although some persons may show a preference for certain patterns and a distaste for others. The use of artificial phalluses (dildoes) to simulate male-female intercourse is rare between homosexual women, although they are often used in exhibitions and stag movies intended for male viewers.

Contrary to popular assumption, most homosexuals do not fall into active or passive categories in their relations with one another. Even though they may have role preferences, in practice the majority vary their techniques, assuming the active and passive roles alternately or taking different roles with different partners. Moreover, there is no reliable correlation between physical appearance, social mannerisms, and preferred sexual practices. Masculine types frequently assume passive sexual roles, and effeminate types may prefer active roles.

Male homosexuals are often quite promiscuous in their sexual behavior. Part of the explanation may lie in certain common underlying psychodynamic patterns. If their avoidance of heterosexual involvement is related, as it often is, to the fears of interpersonal commitment, intimacy, or responsibility that such involvement may entail, the same fears operate with regard to homosexual relationships. Part of the safety of homosexual liaisons rests precisely on the fact that they do not entail expectations of marriage or the possibility of children.

On the other hand, a substantial element in homosexual promiscuity may well be sociologically rather than psychodynamically determined. If heterosexual exchanges were as easily available as homosexual ones, is there any reason to doubt that heterosexual men would be just as promiscuous? In actual fact, there has been an enormous increase in heterosexual promiscuity in recent years, since the advent of the pill has made women less fearful of pregnancy and, consequently, less inhibited about undertaking sexual relations. Another element underlying homosexual promiscuity is the fact that—in a society in which exposure as a homosexual carries legal, occupational, and social risks—there may seem to be less danger of such exposure in transitory sexual contacts than in openly living with someone in a long term relationship.

Gay bars, public baths, autos, and certain streets, parks, and public rest rooms are the locales where homosexuals meet one another, and, in some of them—the baths, parks, and rest rooms—liaisons frequently take place. Often, these liaisons are entirely anonymous; in public rest rooms, partners may not even see each other's faces. In some men, the drive for such contacts takes on an enormously compulsive quality, so that they may be involved in a dozen or more sexual transactions in the course of a single day or evening. These patterns, when they occur, have an obvious strong neurotic component, and such persons are constantly flirting with the danger of being apprehended. This danger, for some, is part of the excitement, and many of these men do, indeed, get into repeated difficulties with the law.

The popular conception that all men who pursue these practices are obligatory homosexuals bears little relationship to the actual facts. Humphreys (1970), in a study of participants in the impersonal sex of the public rest rooms (often called "tearooms" by their frequenters), found that 54 per cent of them were married and living with their wives and children in middle-class homes and, for all intents and purposes, just "average guys next door." As a group, they tended to be on the politically conservative side, and many were regular churchgoers. About 40 per cent of them were Roman Catholic, and only about 16 per cent professed no religious affiliation. About 10 per cent were black. Only 38 per cent fell into the type 5 and 6 Kinsey groups, and 24 per cent could be categorized as being type 3 or 4 on the Kinsey scale. This "heterosexual" group usually functioned as fellatees, rather than fellators, and apparently viewed their experiences not as homosexual encounters but, rather, as a "quick, inexpensive, and impersonal" way of achieving an orgasm. They were largely emotionally withdrawn men whose marriages had deteriorated and whose sex lives with their wives had become unsatisfactory.

Despite the relative ease with which homosexual contacts can be made, not all homosexuals pursue patterns of promiscuity. The more emotionally mature the person, the more likely he or she is to seek some kind of stable liaison with a genuine love object. Since such relationships have no legal bonds, it is not surprising to find that many of them do not last very long, breaking up after a year or two or even less. Quite probably, however, many heterosexual relationships would end in divorce much sooner if there were no legal restraints or children involved. On the other hand, some homosexual marriages between stable persons go on for many years. Unfortunately, not enough is known about these relationships because such persons generally lead quiet and discreet lives and are less likely to seek psychotherapy or to appear in the statistics of investigators. Such stable relationships are more frequent among female homosexuals than among male homosexuals.

Although most male homosexuals seem to be drawn to partners with attributes reflecting a high degree of masculinity—well developed physiques and, particularly, large penises—there are wide variations of preference. Some are attracted by qualities of intellect or by cultural achievement, and some reach out for partners with obvious feminine characteristics, mannerisms, or dress. The popular assumption that homosexuals constitute a threat to young children is an unwarranted myth; in fact, the seeking out of children as sexual objects is much less common among homosexuals than among heterosexuals.

Psychopatnology

Despite the fact that countless articles and books have been written about the homosexual personality, there is no reason to assume that 'here is a specific psychodynamic structure to homosexuality any more than there is to heterosexuality. There is just as wide a range of variation among homosexual personalities as there is among heterosexuals, and their psychiatric diagnoses, leaving aside their homosexuality, run the gamut of modern nosology. Nevertheless, although no adequate comparative studies have been possible thus far, it may well be that there is a higher incidence of neurotic personality distortion among homosexuals than among heterosexuals; but this distortion is not necessarily attributable to the homosexuality itself. In a culture like this, in which being homosexual is labeled as being queer and means being subjected to ridicule, humiliation, contempt, and rejection, it would be remarkable, indeed, if most persons who found themselves growing up with such yearnings did not suffer from an impaired self-image, feelings of emotional insecurity, and various defensive personality consequences. Still, there is as wide a personality variation among homosexuals as among heterosexuals, from passive ones to aggressive ones; from shy introverts to loud, raucous extroverts; from theatrical, hysterical personalities to rigid, compulsive-obsessive ones; from sexually inhibited, timid types to sexually promiscuous flamboyant ones; from radical activists to staunch conservatives; from defiant atheists to devout churchgoers; and from unconscionable sociopaths to highly responsible, law-abiding citizens.

A question remains as to whether or not there are any primary psychodynamic characteristics that are etiologically relevant or unique to homosexual object choice as distinguished from those patterns that are secondary to such a choice in this culture. A number of psychodynamic patterns have been described within the context of psychoanalytic theory as essential features in the development of a homosexual preference. The most commonly mentioned is the presence of an unconscious castration anxiety that turns all women into phobic objects because their lack of penis calls to mind the feared state of castration; The castration anxiety is assumed to be a consequence of repressed incestuous wishes toward the seductive mother and fear of retaliation from the father. The difficulty with this construction is that unconscious castration anxiety is regularly uncovered in the analyses of all heterosexual patients also, and it has been offered in explication of such a wide variety of psychopathological syndromes that it has become almost a cliche. When a theory explains everything, it becomes a ritualistic formula that ultimately explains nothing.

Another frequently mentioned psychodynamic pattern is a fear and hatred of women based on a relationship with a controlling, possessive, castrating mother whose attitude toward men is symbolically represented by the dentate vagina. Another popular view stresses the assumption that the homosexual love object is a narcissistic extension of the homosexual himself—that is, the homosexual seeks someone like himself or like his idealized self. Still another theory is that the homosexual pattern rests primarily on an identification with the mother, either because she was the more loving and important parent or because she was seen as the real source of power and danger in the family (identification with the aggressor).

Some of these patterns are mutually contradictory. Nevertheless, there is little doubt that, in the course of psychoanalytic therapy, one or another of them can be elicited from male homosexual patients, especially those who rate 5 or 6 on the Kinsey scale. The crucial question, however, is whether these patterns can be shown to exist also in male heterosexual patients; this author believes they do. If so, not one of these patterns can be considered as pathognomonic in itself or a crucial determinant of a homosexual object choice.

Another formulation about which there is considerable disagreement is Rado's dictum that "hidden and incapacitating fears of the opposite sex" are always present in type 5 and type 6 homosexuals. That this cannot be true of all homosexuals is obvious from the fact that many type 3 and type 4 homosexuals function heterosexually without anxiety and with full satisfaction. Moreover, from what is now known of how sexual object choice develops in human beings, there is no reason to assume categorically that homosexual object choice, even in type 5 and type 6 homosexuals, cannot occasionally develop as a consequence of positive conditioning toward same-sex objects rather than always on the basis of aversive conditioning toward heterosexual objects. The author has encountered a number of persons in clinical practice in whom the homosexual object preference clearly was established as a result of repeated positive reinforcement by gratifying sexual relations in childhood with an admired older brother or friend. Freud seems to have recognized such a possibility also in his conjecture that the extent of male homosexuality in ancient Greece may have been due to the fact that Greek children were brought up by male slaves. It should not be inferred from the foregoing, however, that overt homosexual relationships in childhood are frequent factors in the development of same-sex object preference. On the contrary, most obligatory homosexuals report an awareness of such object preference early in their lives without any prior exposure to actual homosexual experience.

Female Homosexuality

There are a number of significant differences between male and female homosexuals that deserve elaboration. Most importantly, American culture does not attach as much stigma to sexual intimacies between women as it does to those between men. Women can kiss each other on the lips, embrace, or walk down the street hand in hand with hardly any eyebrow being lifted; not so, men. Two women who live together are taken for granted; not so, men. The girl tomboy is often a source of pride; not so, the boy sissy. Women can wear male attire, and, as long as their behavior and mannerisms are

not too butch, no one pays much attention; men who dress or behave effeminately are immediately suspect.

What this means in practical terms is that the female homosexual is not as likely as is her male counterpart to suffer from fears of disclosure, threats of blackmail, or feelings of insecurity and inadequacy. As a result, a greater proportion of female homosexuals maintain stable patterns of social adjustment than do male homosexuals, the degree of promiscuity among female homosexuals is much less, and there is a higher proportion of long term relationships among them.

Although figures concerning the incidence of homosexual behavior are just as unreliable for women as they are for men, most studies agree that the incidence of type 5 and type 6 homosexuality in women is only about half that for men. There are a number of reasons. First, the achievement of a feminine identity is less difficult in this society than is the achievement of masculine identity; dependency patterns constitute an acceptable adaptation for women and are more easily achieved than are the patterns of self-reliance and vocational and paternal responsibility required of men. Second, in the sexual act itself, it is much easier for a woman to simulate competence than it is for a man. It is no surprise to find, therefore, that, in contrast to males, the degree of exclusive homosexuality in women is quite low. Most homosexual women have had some exposure to heterosexual relations. Third, women who have a fear of or aversion to heterosexuality have an option open to them that is evidently quite rare among men—witness the 14 to 19 per cent of unmarried women and the 5 to 8 per cent of previously married women whose sexual needs have become so repressed that they never have any sociosexual responses through all their adult years. The double sexual standard of this culture finds such asexuality acceptable in women but not in men. Thus, large numbers of women who might otherwise be driven by their heterosexual aversions into homosexual patterns are able, instead, to take refuge in lives of no sexual involvement at all.

The cause of female homosexuality is, if anything, more obscure than that of male homosexuality, partly because far fewer of them have sought psychiatric help for their problems and, thus, fewer have been studied. In recent years, more determined and systematic efforts have been made to investigate groups of lesbians (Saghir and Robins, 1973), and the evidence appears to be that their family backgrounds are as diverse as are those of male homosexuals. Some lesbians have had hostile, domineering mothers and detached, unassertive fathers, similar to those found in the families of male homosexuals. Others, however, have had intense, seductive relationships with their fathers and had narcissistic, detached mothers. In others, the parental background does not appear particularly exceptional. In still others, strong rivalry patterns with male siblings appear to have had a decisive influence, with resultant hostility to men and rejection of the female sex role. Others have grown up feeling that their parents would have preferred them to be boys. A common factor in most of their backgrounds is a strong antiheterosexual pattern in the home—stemming sometimes from the mother, sometimes from the father. As a result, relations with boys tend to be powerfully discouraged and laden with guilt and fear, but crushes on girls are either disregarded or covertly encouraged. Much more research is needed in this whole area particularly with nonpatient populations of lesbians, since most current psychiatric knowledge is based on a skew sampling of female homosexuals who are patients.

Sociological factors are probably relevant in female homosexuality. Significant numbers of women choose the homosexual route because—for reasons of unattractiveness, shyness, fears of rejection, or lack of available men—they feel closed off from the heterosexual relationships they might otherwise prefer. This factor may become increasingly important as the disproportion in the numbers of women as compared with available men in most Western populations, particularly in the middle-age and older-age groups, continues to increase. Still another significant sociological factor in the latter half of the 20th century has been the rise of the women's liberation movement. A by-product of the resentment that it has unleashed toward male "sexist" attitudes has

been a tendency among its more revolutionary members to reject men sexually and turn toward women for sexual release. At the very least, bisexual patterns among women have become more accepted and acceptable as a consequence.

Psychological Tests

There are no psychological tests that pathognomonically differentiate homosexuals from heterosexuals in the absence of a clinical history. The presence of items on Rorschach responses indicating anal interests or feminine identification or hostility to women are often, but not always, found on testing of homosexuals and can also be found in heterosexuals. The same holds true for a high M-F score on the Minnesota Multiphasic Personality Inventory (MMPI). The difficulty with most reports of psychological testing of homosexuals is that the tests deal with homosexual patients rather than with the nonpatient population, and the findings are, therefore, biased by the presence of other psychopathology. Where efforts have been made to compare matched groups of nonpatient samples of homosexuals and heterosexuals with each other, the results have been essentially negative. Thus, Dean and Richardson (1964), in a comparison of the Minnesota Multiphasic Personality Inventory profiles of 40 college-educated overt male homosexuals with a matched control group, concluded that there were no significant differences between the two groups. Hooker (1957) conducted a comparative study of 30 male homosexuals and 30 male heterosexuals who were matched for age. I.Q., and education. The homosexuals were all rated 6 and the heterosexuals 0 on the Kinsey scale. None of the subjects was in therapy. Two judges independently, without prior knowledge of which subjects were which, reviewed the Rorschach protocols, Thematic Apperception Tests, and Make-a-Picture-Story responses, and tried to distinguish the homosexuals from the heterosexuals, but they were unable to do so. The two groups did not differ significantly in the ratings received. Hooker's conclusions were that homosexuality is not a single clinical entity and that there is no necessary correlation between a homosexual orientation and other aspects of a person's intrapsychic or interpersonal functioning.

Homosexuality and Mental Illness

This is one of the most disputed issues related to the subject of homosexuality. Should a homosexual orientation properly be regarded and classified as an illness requiring psychotherapeutic intervention whenever possible? Or is it merely a different way of life that falls within a normal psychobiological range but that happens to be regarded with disfavor in today's culture? Freud did not consider it an illness. In his "Three Essays on the Theory of Sexuality," he wrote that it

is found in people who exhibit no other serious deviations from the normal . . . whose efficiency is unimpaired, and who are indeed distinguished by specially high intellectual development and ethical culture.

In his "Letter to an American Mother," Freud wrote:

Homosexuality is assuredly no advantage, but it is nothing to be ashamed of, no vice, no degradation, it cannot be classified as an illness; we consider it to be a variation of the sexual functions produced by a certain arrest of sexual development.

Ironically, however, many contemporary psychoanalysts do tend to consider homosexuality as a form of psychopathology "incompatible with a reasonably happy life" (Bieber). One probable reason for this belief is that most psychiatrists derive their views about homosexuality not from the homosexual population at large but almost exclusively from homosexual patients. If psychiatrists' impressions of the general heterosexual population were based only on their experience with patients, would they not end up with an equally skewed impression about the problems of being heterosexual?

Psychiatric views in favor of considering homosexuality as a form of psychopathology generally rest on three major arguments: (1) that homosexuals are the product of disordered sexual development, (2) that they represent a deviation from the biological norm, and (3) that they are uniformly deeply disturbed, unhappy people.

When examined closely, the statement that homosexuality is the result of disordered sexual development really says nothing other than that the outcome of that development is not considered to be normal. All personality differences are the result of variations in developmental background. Any careful reconstruction of life histories reveals plausible reasons for the idiosyncratic way in which each person lives and acts. The background development of homosexuals, although tending to fall into certain patterns, is by no means uniform, as has been noted. Moreover, many heterosexuals can and do emerge from backgrounds essentially similar to those described for homosexuals. In the final analysis, the psychiatric categorization of the homosexual outcome as psychopathological is fundamentally a reflection of society's disapproval of that outcome, and psychiatrists are unwittingly acting as agents of social control in so labeling it. A century ago, some medical forebears, on the same basis, authoritatively labeled the tendency to frequent masturbation as indicative of serious mental disturbances.

Psychiatrists must seriously consider whether it is proper to attach a label of deviancy to behavior simply because if differs from that favored by the majority. As a matter of fact, psychiatrists do not always do so, except where they are themselves reflecting the culture's prejudice toward a particular form of deviance. For example, psychiatrists do not classify adherents of astrology, numerology, spiritualism, or certain unusual religious sects as being ipso facto mentally ill. In a democratic society, they recognize the rights of persons to adhere to widely divergent ideological or religious patterns, so long as they do not attempt to force their beliefs on others. Psychiatrists react differently, however, toward "deviant" sexual preferences because moral values are involved.

Some psychiatrists argue that all such unusual life-styles are indeed neurotic and a consequence of disordered development. It was on this basis that some psychoanalysts once asserted that all political radicalism was the expression of neurotic rebellion against paternal authority or that women who sought careers for themselves were being neurotically competitive with men. Such labeling tends to define normality in terms of adjustment to social conventions and makes psychiatry an agent of cultural control.

One must not forget that other cultures have had, and do have, quite different attitudes toward homosexuality. Moreover, sexual mores are constantly in the process of change and evolution. Many patterns considered deviant only a decade ago are now widely accepted as normal, and it would be a serious error to assume that this society's current reaction to homosexuality is sacrosanct or eternal. Indeed, there is a discernible trend in the mores of the present counterculture toward the acceptance and practice of patterns of bisexuality.

The second major argument for the psychopathology of homosexuality is that it is biologically abnormal. It is, indeed, true that exclusive homosexuality is rarely seen in lower animals, except under extreme and unusual environmental conditions. By the same token, however, exclusive and obligatory heterosexuality is equally unusual. The wide occurrence of both obligatory homosexuality and obligatory heterosexuality is unique to human society. All lower animals, including the infrahuman primates, display patterns of homosexual behavior from time to time, even though heterosexual responses are the usual ones. Indeed, homosexual reactions take place even in the presence of available heterosexual partners, although homosexual reactions are more frequent when heterosexual partners are unavailable. They occur between females as well as between males but are observed more often among young males. In general, the higher an animal is on the evolutionary scale, the more varied and extensive are both its autoerotic and its homoerotic practices.

It is sometimes argued that such mounting behavior in lower animals is simply a dominance reaction and has nothing to do with sexuality. As every cattle breeder knows, however, a young bull is often used as a teaser to induce not only mounting but also ejaculation in the breeding bull, and this teasing is a method used to obtain semen for

artificial insemination. Indeed, if this teasing is done too often, the bull begins to react more readily to his own sex than to a female. On the basis of all the evidence from comparative zoology. Beach (1948) concluded:

Human homosexuality reflects the essential bisexual character of our mammalian inheritance. The extreme modifiability of man's sex life makes possible the conversion of this essential bisexuality into a form of unisexuality with the result that a member of the same sex eventually becomes the only acceptable stimulus to arousal.

The speciousness of the biological argument becomes more apparent when one realizes that all civilized human behavior, from the wearing of clothes to the cooking of food, is a departure from the strictly natural. Moreover, one does not label vegetarianism or sexual celibacy as automatic evidences of psychopathology, even though they do not follow "natural" biological patterns. Clearly, the biological argument is but another rationalization for this society's moral disapproval of homosexual behavior.

The third contention concerning the pathology of homosexuality is that any indepth, intrapsychic study of homosexuals reveals them all to be deeply disturbed and unhappy people. This thesis, put forward primarily by psychoanalysts, is obviously based on therapeutic experience with homosexual patients and is as unwarranted as any similar generalization about heterosexuals would be if it were based only on work with disturbed or deeply troubled persons. The issue here is not whether many or even most homosexuals in this society are neurotically disturbed; it would be surprising if most of them were not, considering the contempt and contumely with which their way of life is regarded. The question, rather, is whether all homosexuals should be so labeled solely on the basis of their sex object preference. It seems to the author, quite apart from studies such as those of Hooker, that any objective appraisal of nonpatient homosexuals can only lead to the conclusion that such stereotyping is quite unwarranted. Many homosexuals, both male and female, function responsibly and honorably, often in positions of the highest trust, and live emotionally stable, mature, and well adjusted lives, psychodynamically indistinguishable from well adjusted heterosexuals, except for their alternative sexual preferences. One must recognize that mental health is, at best, a relative concept. No one is so absolutely or perfectly healthy that an in-depth exploration of his unconscious fantasies and wishes would not reveal deviations from the ideal.

This issue of the psychiatric classification of homosexuals is not just a harmless theoretical one. The social and legal consequences of stereotypically labeling an entire group of human beings as mentally ill—or "suffering from psychopathology," a euphemistic alternative—are quite serious, particularly in these days of computer banks of instantaneously available information about private lives. Psychiatric labeling of homosexuality as ipso facto a form of mental disorder lends authoritative weight to the basis on which homosexuals are often subjected to discrimination in employment, discharged from military service without honor, deprived of various legal rights, and sometimes confined involuntarily in mental institutions. In this author's opinion, it is more objective for psychiatry to treat the issue of homosexual object choice as essentially irrelevant to the issue of mental illness and to base diagnostic judgments about homosexuals on the existence of specific underlying mental disorders.

Latent Homosexuality

The concept of latent homosexuality rests on Freud's theory of psychic bisexuality, a theory open to considerable doubt. It assumes that vestiges of an original homosexual phase of development remain in all persons and are manifested in sublimated form in tender feelings toward members of one's own sex and in certain psychic patterns considered to be identified with the opposite sex. Passive tendencies in men and aggressive tendencies in women fall into this category.

However, the assumption that certain psychological traits are innately masculine or feminine is questionable. Gender role patterns vary widely in different cultures and in different historical periods and are strongly influenced by the acculturation processes that the infant encounters in the first several years of life. Although, in the aggregate, males tend to be more aggressive and more physically active than females, the distributions of these traits in males and females constitute overlapping curves, with many perfectly normal female infants being constitutionally more aggressive and vigorous than many perfectly normal male infants, even without taking into consideration the highly important effect of subsequent environmental experiences which can either accentuate or negate these initial differences.

Apart from its dubious theoretical basis, the concept of latent homosexuality carries with it some questionable clinical inferences. It is widely assumed, for example, that the syndrome of homosexual panic is due to life situations that have unduly stimulated the latent homosexuality of certain men to a point at which their egos become overwhelmed by the fear that these homosexual impulses may emerge. Although it is true that, in some instances, this kind of mechanism may be operative, it would probably be more accurate to speak of such persons as repressed homosexuals, rather than latent ones. Some men do have strong erotic interests in other men that they have repressed or suppressed—witness the 13 per cent of men described by Kinsey who gave histories of reacting erotically to other men, even though they had never had any overt homosexual contacts.

In many cases of homosexual panic, however, the problem involves not homosexual anxiety but what Ovesey (1955) has described as "pseudohomosexual anxiety." In a culture such as this one, where homosexuality is associated in the popular mind with weakness and effeminacy, many men who have doubts about their masculinity express these doubts in the form of fears that they may be homosexual or will be so considered by others. This is a common clinical phenomenon in this culture, and to attempt to reassure such men that everyone has latent homosexual tendencies usually has an antitherapeutic effect. More often than not, the presence of such fears in cases of homosexual panic and in men in general is not related to any repressed homoerotic tendencies but to profound feelings of masculine inadequacy, and psychotherapeutic work directed along these lines proves to be more fruitful and effective.

The entire issue, both of homosexual anxiety and pseudohomosexual anxiety is closely related to what is coming to be known as *homophobia*—a pathological fear of homosexuality. As indicated above, such fears are often indicative of deep-seated insecurity in an individual about his or her own gender identity, but they are also, of course, reflective of widespread prejudice against homosexuality in our culture. Homophobia is usually manifested in patterns of intense antagonism to, abhorrence of, or discomfort with homosexuals—generally cloaked in religious, legal, moral, or scientific rationalizations. Although accessible to individual psychotherapy, the ultimate solution of this problem rests on the dissemination of improved understanding of homosexuality through educational, religious, and scientific channels.

Prevention and Treatment

The issue of the prevention of homosexuality arouses a good deal of irritation among gay liberation spokesmen because it conveys a pejorative implication that homosexuality is something to be avoided. This reaction is quite understandable, yet it seems to this author that, until sexual mores have reached a point at which homosexuality is as fully acceptable culturally as is heterosexuality, the issue of preventing its development is legitimate. Indeed, questionnaires of homosexuals themselves, dealing with whether they would want their children to be gay also, indicate that a large majority of them reply in the negative because of the difficulties that a homosexual way of life encounters in this culture. Obviously, almost all heterosexual parents feel this way also.

Assuming, in the absence of any definitive evidence to the contrary for the time being, that most homosexual patterns are acquired rather than innate, the optimal time for preventive measures is in early childhood, prepubertally—before, rather than after, sexual object choice has begun to take clear form. The growing understanding of family dynamics should make it possible to pinpoint the kinds of patterns that may tend to create personalities more susceptible to later homosexual object choice. Children and preadolescents who are failing to develop sex-appropriate gender role identifications or satisfactory peer relationships should be considered potentially vulnerable to homosexual development, and adequate family diagnosis and treatment should be undertaken as early as possible. The family as a whole should be regarded as the problem, not just the child. Emphasis in treatment should be placed on those aspects of the family dynamics that are interfering with the child's development of a positive identification with the same-sex parent, affectionate and unambivalent feelings toward the opposite parent, and good peer relationships. Important to explore are not only the patterns of mothering and fathering but also the antisexual bias that often exists in these families.

Once a homosexual predilection has clearly emerged, the question of whether treatment should be undertaken rests fundamentally on the person's motivation. Psychiatrists are often importuned by distraught parents to treat a teen-age boy or girl in whom a homosexual propensity has been discovered, but, unless the adolescent wishes to change, not much can be accomplished in this regard, and it is more constructive to try to help the parents approach the issue of homosexuality with greater tolerance and understanding and, above all, not to reject their children on this account. At the same time, an effort should also be made in such instances to help the homosexual youngsters to accept themselves without shame or guilt, and to cope more effectively with the social consequences of their varient sexual preference.

In this writer's opinion, there is never any justification for forcing treatment on any unwilling or uncooperative homosexual. If a homosexual's behavior violates public decency or involves the seduction of a minor, it is a matter for the application of legal sanctions, just as would be corresponding behavior in a heterosexual; but homosexual relationships between consenting adults in private should be neither the law's nor psychiatry's business. There seems to be a slowly growing acceptance of this view throughout the Western world.

Homosexuals do present themselves for treatment, however, and for a wide variety of reasons. Some come for help for problems analogous to those presented by heterosexuals—difficulties in attracting partners, break-up of important dyadic relationships, problems in self-realization, various neuroses, and depressive reactions. Most of these patients are not interested in changing their sexual orientation and should be treated as any corresponding heterosexual patient would be.

Other patients, however, are unhappy with their homosexual adaptation and would like to function heterosexually, if possible. These patients fall into the new diagnostic category of "sexual orientation disturbance." Although some gay liberationists argue that it would be preferable to help these persons accept their homosexuality, this writer is of the opinion that, if they wish to change, they deserve an opportunity to try, with all the help that psychiatry can give them. Whether one likes it or not, the fact remains that a homosexual adaptation imposes special stresses on a person in the current culture, and in the effort to assist such a person—when he or she wishes—to achieve a heterosexual adaptation, the psychiatrist, like any other physician, is endeavoring to help his patient achieve an optimally homeostatic relationship with his environment. If the psychotherapeutic process fails in the achievement of that goal, then clearly the effort should be directed toward enabling these patients to accept their homosexual identity without shame or self-derogation and to function as mature and responsible people within the context of that identity.

The myth that homosexuality is untreatable still has wide currency among the public at large and among homosexuals themselves. This view is often linked to the assumption that homosexuality is constitutionally or genetically determined. This conviction of untreatability also serves an ego-defensive purpose for many homosexuals. As the understanding of the adaptive nature of most homosexual behavior has become more widespread, however, there has evolved a greater therapeutic optimism about the possibilities for change, and progressively more hopeful results are being reported.

It is true, nevertheless, that the treatment of homosexuality, at least at this stage of knowledge, is not easy. Part of the difficulty is the same as is found in any behavioral pattern in which the chief "symptom" carries with it a high potential for gratification. Obviously, the degree to which any deviant behavior is ego syntonic or dystonic plays a major role in the degree of motivation for change on the part of the patient. The profound pleasure that most homosexuals obtain from their behavior is a major determinant in the fact that only a small proportion of them voluntarily seek psychiatric help. Counterbalancing this, however, is the pressure of the social milieu, the impairment of self-image, and the unsatisfactory interpersonal adjustment that often accompany a homosexual way of life in this culture. The reasons for seeking help have an important bearing on what can be expected from therapy. Those who undertake therapy for the specific purpose of altering their sexual patterns, all other things being equal, offer the best prognosis for achieving such change. At the opposite end of the pole, those who come unwillingly because of court orders growing out of legal violations tend to be least promising.

No specific form of therapy has as yet clearly established its superiority over any other. The difficulty in evaluating results of various approaches rests in part that patient samples differ widely and are often not adequately defined as to whether they are 3, 4, 5, or 6 on the Kinsey scale. Moreover, follow-ups are often unsatisfactory, and criteria for improvement are inconsistent. For example, a change for the better in the general life adjustment of a homosexual would certainly constitute a positive therapeutic result, yet it falls into a different category of improvement from a shift in object preference from homosexual to heterosexual.

Granting these difficulties of evaluation, there is little doubt that a genuine shift in preferential sex object choice can and does take place in somewhere between 20 and 50 per cent of patients with homosexual behavior who seek psychotherapy with this end in mind. The single most important prerequisite to reversibility is a powerful motivation to achieve such a change. Given such motivation, other favorable prognostic indices are (1) youth—patients under 35 tend to do better; (2) previous heterosexual behavior or responsiveness; (3) recency of onset of homosexual activity; and (4) in men, aggressive personality patterns, as contrasted to strongly passive patterns and effeminate mannerisms, especially if they date back to childhood.

The treatment techniques used vary widely—from psychoanalysis, 4 to 5 times weekly, to psychoanalytically oriented psychotherapies, 1 to 3 times weekly, to group therapy, some with mixed groups and others exclusively homosexual in makeup, to conditioning techniques using aversive and reinforcing stimuli. Despite differences in approach, all these methods share certain features in common. All require a high degree of motivation and cooperation from the patient. All, either implicitly or explicitly, tend to discourage homosexual behavior and encourage heterosexual behavior, but without any derogation of the homosexual patient by the therapist in the interpersonal transaction. The dynamic psychotherapies, in addition, place stress on other aspects of the patient's personality functioning, with special emphasis on increasing his self-esteem and his self-assertiveness. In those instances in which therapy proves unsuccessful in reversing the homosexual pattern, efforts are usually directed at the alternate objective of enabling the patient to achieve a mature, stable relationship with one partner and to avoid the reality dangers involved in cruising and in violations of public decency.

Although reports of treatment of women are less frequent than those of men, primarily because far fewer female homosexuals present themselves for treatment, most indications are that such treatment is at least as successful with them as with men.

At best, however, all therapeutic approaches are of limited value in relation to the problem of homosexuality in its broadest aspects. The large majority of homosexuals do not seek to change their sexual patterns. A humane society must develop greater acceptance of homosexuality as an alternative lifestyle. Legal sanctions against homosexual behavior have not proved effective; homosexuality is no more common in France, Sweden, and the Netherlands, where it is not a crime, than in the United States, where it is. Recognizing this fact, Great Britain, in 1967,

legalized homosexual behavior between consenting adults in private. There is a beginning trend in this direction in the United States also. The American Psychiatric Association is officially on record as favoring such legislation and deploring "all public and private discrimination against homosexuals in such areas as employment, housing, public accommodation, and licensing." Eight states—Colorado, Connecticut, Delaware, Hawaii, Illinois, North Dakota, Ohio, and Oregon—have already adopted such legislation, and the American Law Institute has gone on record as being in favor of it. Such laws do not condone the seduction of minors or violations of reasonable standards of public decency; such behavior, whether homosexual or heterosexual, remains illegal. It is to be hoped that ultimately such statutes legalizing homosexuality will become universal and presage a basic change in society's current discriminatory attitudes toward the millions of men and women whose life experiences, through no fault of their own, have rendered them erotically responsive to members of their own sex.

REFERENCES

*Bieber, I., Dain, H. J., Dince, O. R., Drellich, M. G., Grand, H. G., Gundlack, R. H., Kremer, M. W., Rifkin, A. H., Wilbur, C. B. and Bieber, T. B. *Homosexuality: A Psychoanalytic Study.* Basic Books, New York, 1962.

*Churchill, W. *Homosexual Behavior Among Males.* Hawthorn Books, New York, 1967.

Dean, R. B., and Richardson, H. Analysis of MMPI profiles of forty college-educated overt male homosexuals. J. Consult. Psychol., *28:* 483, 1964.

Devereux, G. Institutionalized homosexuality of the Mohave Indians. Hum. Biol., *9:* 498, 1937.

Dörner, G. Tierexperimentalle undersuchungen zur frage einer hormonellen pathogenese der homosexualitet. Acta Biol. Med. Germ., *19:* 569-584, 1967.

Ford, C. S. and Beach, F. A. *Patterns of Sexual Behavior.* Harper & Bros., New York, 1952.

Freud, S. Letter to an American mother. Am. J. Psychiatry, *102:* 786, 1951.

*Freud, S. Three essays on the theory of sexuality. *In Standard Edition of the Complete Psychological Works of Sigmund Freud,* J. Strachey. editor, vol. 7, pp. 135-243. Hogarth Press, London, 1953.

Friedeburg, L. von. Die umfrage in der intimphäre. beitr. z. Sexualforschung, *4:* 1953.

Harlow, H. F., and Harlow, M. D. The affectional systems. In Behavior of Non-human Primates. A. M.,

Schrier, H. F. Harlow, and F. Stollwitz, editors, vol. 2, p. 287, Academic Press, New York, 1965.

Hirschfeld, M. *Die Homosexualität des Mannes und des Weibes.* L. Marcus, Berlin, 1920.

Hooker, E. The adjustment of the male overt homosexual. J. Prof. Technol., *21:* 18, 1957.

Hooker, E. Male homosexuals and their worlds. In *Sexual Inversion,* J. Marmor, editor, pp. 83-103. Basic Books, New York, 1965.

Humphreys, L. *Tearoom Trade: Impersonal Sex in Public Places.* Aldine-Atherton, Chicago, 1970.

Kallman, F. J. A comparative twin study on the genetic aspects of male homosexuality. J. Nerv. Ment. Dis., *115:* 283, 1952.

*Kinsey, A. C., Pomeroy, W. B., and Martin, C. E. *Sexual Behavior in the Human Male.* W. B. Saunders, Philadelphia, 1948.

*Kinsey, A. C., Pomeroy, W. B., Martin, C. E., and Gebhard, P. H. *Sexual Behavior in the Human Female.* W. B. Saunders, Philadelphia, 1953.

Kolb, L. S. Therapy of homosexuality. In *Current Psychiatric Therapies,* J. Masserman, editor, vol. 3, p. 131. Grune & Stratton, New York, 1963.

Kolodny, R. C., et al. Plasma testosterone and semen analysis in male homosexuals, N. Engl. J. Med., *285:* 1170, 1971.

Loraine, J. A., Ismael, A. A. Adamopoulos, P. A. and Dove, G. A. Endocrine function in male and female homosexuals. Br. Med. J., *4:* 406, 1970.

Margolese, M. S. Homosexuality: A new endocrine correlate. Horm. Behav., *1:* 151, 1970.

*Marmor, J., editor. *Sexual Inversion: The Multiple Roots of Homosexuality.* Basic Books, New York, 1965.

Mead, M. Cultural determinants of sexual behavior. In *Sex and Internal Secretions,* W. C. Young, editor, ed. 3, vol. 2, pp. 1433-1479. Williams & Wilkins, Baltimore, 1961.

Money, J. Sexual dimorphism and homosexual gender identity. Working paper prepared for the NIMH Task Force on Homosexuality. Unpublished, 1967.

Ovesey, L. Pseudohomosexuality and homosexuality in men. In *Sexual Inversion,* J. Marmor, editor, pp. 221-233. Basic Books, New York, 1965.

Perloff, W. H. Hormones and homosexuality. In *Sexual Inversion,* J. Marmor, editor, pp. 211-233. Basic Books, New York, 1965.

Rado, S. *Psychoanalysis of Behavior,* vol. 1. Grune & Stratton, New York, 1956.

Römer, L. von. Die uranische familie. Beitr. z. Erkentniss des Uranismus, 1, 1906.

Rose, R. M., Bourne, P. G., Poe, R. O., Mougey, E. M., Collins, D. K. and Mason, J. W. Androgen responses to stress. Psychosom. Med., *31:* 418, 1969.

*Saghir, M. T., and Robins, E. *Male and Female Homosexuality.* Williams & Wilkins, Baltimore, 1973.

Schofield, M. *The Sexual Behavior of Young People.* Little, Brown, Boston, 1965.

Thompson, C. M. *Interpersonal Psychoanalysis: The Selected Papers of Clara M. Thompson.* Basic Books, New York, 1964.

Tourney, G., and Hatfield, L. M. Androgen metabolism in schizophrenics, homosexuals, and normal controls, Biol. Psychiatry, *6:* 23, 1973.

15.2   Sexual Deviations in Children

JOSEPH D. TEICHER, M.D.

Definition

Sexual deviation is a label that should rarely be used in childhood. All human beings are bisexual anatomically, physiologically, and psychologically. Fixed disorders in adolescence may warrant a diagnostic term. But it should be used only when the condition is regarded as the major personality disturbance, with such a degree of chronicity and pervasiveness in personality functioning as to dominate the adolescent's orientation toward social life. Confusion, disturbance, or deviation in heterosexual identifications and sexually deviant behavior may occur in a variety of pictures and should be classified under other headings. Some transiently homosexual behavior is known to be characteristic of many healthy boys and girls in the late preadolescent and early adolescent years.

The label of sexual deviation applied to a

child is associated with more immature emotional development than it would when applied to an adult. One must also realize that what is normal in one development period may sometimes be considered a "deviation" in a later period. How sexual feelings are expressed—whether sexual behavior is carried out at home or openly exhibited—is generally decided by society. Since the expression of sexuality must relate to society's demands, individual sexual expressions that violate societal prohibitions may be considered sexual deviations.

All small children obtain sexual pleasure from the use of other organs than the genitals, obtaining, in fact, greater sexual pleasure from these other organs. This stage of development passes as the child solves the Oedipus situation, which ends with the primacy of the genitals, the early pregenital pleasures being relegated to the minor role of forepleasure in the sexual act. Also, small children are oriented to both homosexual and heterosexual objects, the homosexual predominating during the latency period. With adolescence, the homosexual orientation is repressed and becomes sublimated into friendship and companionship so that the heterosexual orientation may be dominant. The ego accepts the fact that a homosexual orientation exists but demands that its expression take a sublimated pathway. If, however, the ego rejects the homosexual orientation completely, it finds expression in the form of a neurosis—perhaps with the symptom of being afraid of persons of the same sex. If the ego approves of the homosexual orientation, it appears as an overt perversion.

Epidemiology

The following section is based on material from Work (1967).

The fact that many sexual activities, such as masturbation, are practically universal in society does not mean that they are necessarily normal. How a child achieves genital sexual satisfaction usually depends on his period of sexual development. In normal development, he passes through periods of early masturbation, homosexual attachment to peers, and sexual strivings that lead toward intercourse with a mature partner of the opposite sex. However normal development does not always proceed smoothly. There may be departures from the normal sexual patterns at any point during childhood. As Work (1967) states:

If the child during his normal development subdues all his sexual impulses, the public is not particularly concerned. In this sense then, asceticism, with its complete inhibition of sexual drives, evokes only public apathy. However, when the child is overstimulated and develops an abnormal sexual appetite in any direction heterosexual or homosexual, the promiscuity that evolves arouses public concern.

What this society expects and allows with regard to sexual activity varies widely. In general, the moral tone is set by the middle class, whose sexual codes are the most organized. Although the long accepted notion of the girl as basically passive and the male as active is being challenged, most segments of society are still more willing to accept sexual activity on the part of the male. Although it is true that earlier and more open heterosexual behavior is being condoned, homosexuality is still fairly consistently frowned on by most members of American culture. There is evidence that this too is changing, especially in those parts of society that have been quick to accept overt heterosexuality. Since what is considered pathological is determined by society, pathology is only brought to medical attention when it violates societal mores.

Sexual abnormalities are not only a function of society's mores. They may be approached as part of the child's relationship to the parent as the child goes through the normal stages of development. Certain aspects of parent-child relations seem to stimulate sex activity, and such stimulating activity may be quite common in some segments of society. When there is overcrowding, with children and adults sharing sleeping quarters, children cannot help but witness and sometime become involved in adult sexual activity. Parents may even sometimes make overt attempts to stimulate sexual activity by the children. Mothers who live alone with their sons may in many unconscious aspects of living with them serve as stimulants to the child's developing sexuality. In those cases in which the mother sleeps with her son, an abnormal kind of sexual activity may be aroused without either being consciously aware of the distortion. This practice makes the boy anxious and may lead to his acting out and becoming sexually overactive as he goes into his adolescence.

Work (1967) points out that excessive inhibition of the childhood manifestations of sexuality also plays a role in the development of symptoms. The expressions of parental taboos often carry a message of intrigue and salacious delight, which serves to stir up the child. The value of activity is increased by being forbidden. The development of specific deviations in these instances may relate to the emphasis used in suppressing the particular acts of the child. Coupled with more general anxieties, a mode of symptomatic expression is clearly demonstrated.

Masturbation

Children begin masturbating when they are very young. One- and 2-year-olds play with their genitalia and obtain satisfaction from doing so. Some children continue to masturbate more actively than others, in which cases the activity is almost always stimulated, consciously or unconsciously, by the parents. Small gangs, usually of boys, sometimes use masturbation as an acting-out behavior. Oral copulation and other kinds of sexual deviation are frequently associated with it. Adolescent masturbation is characterized by an end point of satisfaction and is thus a more overt sexual activity. Childhood masturbation is normal and is only regarded as pathological when it is excessive or when it is a source of anxiety for the child. Children who masturbate excessively usually suffer from guilt, as a result of cultural values imparted to them by their parents. However, there is some evidence that this guilt seems to be decreasing. Some young children become excessively involved with masturbation and seem to have a compulsion to carry it on. These children usually masturbate because of anxiety. They freely talk about how they feel such pressure to masturbate that they cannot stop. Such children are nearly always involved with other sexual activities at the same time.

FANTASIES

Masturbation is accompanied by fantasies. There seems to be a difference between the way the child masturbates during the oral and early anal-sadistic periods and the way he masturbates later. Perhaps during these first periods the child does not have sufficient concepts or is too unaware of his concepts either to have or to be aware of any fantasies. He is aware only of the pleasure in the sensory experience. On the other hand, the content of the masturbation fantasies during the latter part of the anal-sadistic period and during the phallic and latency periods and adolescence is erotic or aggressive or both. The erotic fantasies are sensual in nature, and the love object is the parent of the opposite sex if the fantasy is heterosexual and the parent of the same sex if homosexual. Since aggression is combined with the erotic sensual drives, the fantasies also have a sadistic or masochistic and an active or passive coloring. The aggressive fantasies are hostile and destructive in nature and have as the object one or the other parent.

The severe conflicts between the fantasies themselves, between the fantasies at various levels of the unconscious, between the conscious content of the fantasies and the feelings the child consciously has toward his parents, and between the conscious content of the fantasies and the possibility that he may really act them out produce great mental torture and severe feelings of fear, guilt, and horror. The suffering becomes more than the child can tolerate. He tries to get rid of it by altering his behavior. Since he has the fantasies while masturbating, he comes to regard the masturbation as the cause of the fantasies, although actually they are coincidental. Therefore, he becomes frightened of his desire to masturbate and tries hard to stop it. At the same time he tries to deny the fantasies either by repressing them or by thinking of other things. That is why there is partial or complete cessation of masturbation during the latency period. During adolescence the sexual desires and, therefore, the desire to masturbate are increased because of the physiological changes of puberty. This increase reactivates the unconscious fantasies, which attempt to break through the repression and become conscious again. This attempt of the repressed fantasies to become conscious is the cause of the adolescent's worry about the effects of masturbation on him. He is unconsciously afraid that the old horrifying repressed fantasies will return to torment him or will come true. Under these circumstances, the child has great difficulty in stopping his masturbation and may come to feel that his sexual wishes bring only mental misery but are too strong to resist. And his turmoil is only increased by threats, warnings, or punishments by the parents.

COMPULSIVE MASTURBATION

This differs from normal masturbation clinically and in its fantasy content. It is performed as if the supply of sexual desire were inexhaustible, and, therefore, it is not associated with real pleasure and satisfaction, as is ordinary masturbation. In fact, there is often no real pleasurable feeling connected with it. No matter how often the act is performed, it can never satisfy the type of fantasy needed. Older children and adults may masturbate compulsively as an attempt to hurt and injure themselves—that is, to castrate themselves. It is as if the person said, "I must not masturbate because it is forbidden to me to get pleasure from it, so I will stop. But I cannot stop: therefore, I will masturbate to punish myself by self-injury for wanting to masturbate." In this way an instinctual desire is experienced by the person as a superego command.

Sexual Orientation Disturbance

It is sometimes difficult to decide when there is deviation in this area, since it is normal for the child to engage in nongenital relationships with peers of his own sex. As he begins adolescence the youngster develops relationships with children of both sexes. Homosexuality can then be regarded by the psychiatrist as part of the older child's confusion about his sexual identity. Whenever children are placed together in institutions, such as schools and residential homes, there is a stirring up of homosexual activity, manifested both by overt sexual relations and by the fears that children have about such relations.

There are some children who seem to have confused gender identification and demonstrate at a young age that they are uncomfortable with the opposite sex. Typical is the boy who is overly attached to his mother and dresses and behaves in a feminine manner. It is, of course, normal for the small boy to be dependent on his mother, but clinging to her beyond the normal oedipal resolution is a sign of pathology. Although such youngsters are concerned about relationships between sexes, they themselves are more feminine than masculine in their identity.

Certain preconditions in the family unit contribute to the development of homosexuality. Often stressed is the combination of a weak or absent father and a dominating, harsh mother. Boys who grow up in such households are unable to form an appropriate identification with the anatomical, psychological, and social roles of the man. Their attitudes toward women are distorted by sadomasochistic impulses, and toward men they develop passive and submissive homosexual attitudes. A primitive psychological mechanism may come into play, a splitting of the ego so that at times the boy feels he is male and at other times he feels he is female in his attitude toward his father. If the conflict thus engendered remains unresolved, homosexual fantasies and perverse activities such as fetishism develop. Under the pressure of the increased sexual drive during adolescence, the fantasies may lead to overt homosexual activity. In girls, the same fear of and aggression toward the mother may be observed. The girl harbors a secret wish to be loved exclusively by the father and interprets his indifference as rejection because of her phallic deficiency. During adolescence she may turn away from men entirely and seek the company, admiration, or love of other females.

More classically, the small boy, in order to cope with his intrapsychic problems, may identify himself with his mother for a number of reasons that are revealed in the type of object chosen by the homosexual. Freud states that a homosexual orientation is caused by an intense but short lived fixation by identifying himself with the mother and so taking himself as the sexual object; proceeding on a narcissistic basis, he looks for young men to love as he wished his mother had loved. Or the boy has experienced severe frustrations at his mother's hands and identifies himself with her in order to avoid further frustration, as if he were saying, "If my mother does not love me and always frustrates me, I will be my mother, and then I can control the frustrations I experience." This, too, results in the person's taking as a homosexual object a boy younger than himself and behaving toward him as he would have liked his mother to behave. He identifies himself with his mother and his homosexual object with himself. Sometimes the identification with the mother takes place because the small boy fears her displeasure if he openly expresses his hatred of a younger brother. He represses the hate and acts in an overloving way toward him, the way the mother acts. The homosexuality is, then, an overcompensation for hatred, and here the age of the partner does not matter. If the identification with the mother is associated with a fixation at the anal-sadistic stage, the homosexuality expresses the wish to enjoy sexual pleasure the way the mother does. Here the partner is usually older, and the homosexual person is passive in the relationship. In one type of homosexual orientation only—the active, aggressive male homosexual—the homosexuality is caused by the displacement of the excitation produced by a relationship with a female onto a male object. Once this has happened, it may become repetitive.

The sexual aim in the homosexual relations shows no uniformity. It may be the anus, mutual masturbation (this is the most common method in men), or the mouth (this is the method preferred by homosexual women).

In early adolescence the avoidance of girls is a homosexual defense that may carry over into the late teens. Usually, there are homosexual fantasies of mutual masturbation and fellatio, a seductive mother and a passive, retiring father. Already noted are the frequent transient homosexual episodes common in adolescence. The occurrence of homosexual behavior or the fear of being a homosexual is often related to anxiety over not attaining the masculine ideal. To most adolescents and adults in this society, the term "homosexual" implies slight of build,

not interested in girls, and nonmasculine interests. The adolescent who feels he possesses these attributes is in the precarious position of beginning to believe that he may be a homosexual. This chronic anxiety soon leads to an avoidance of girls and a growing apathy until the youngster comes to believe he is incapable of becoming interested in girls and interprets his apathy and avoidance as an indication that he is a homosexual. The self-label homosexual often carries with it the expectation of failure in a heterosexual relation. A perception of marked deviance from the masculine ideal is one antecedent of the feeling that one has homosexual wishes and facilitates the probability of engaging in homosexual behavior.

The troubled adolescent inspects the genitals of little girls to assure himself that he is not afraid of a person without a penis. Also, he does so with the hope that the girl does, after all, have a penis—that there is no reality in his ideas of castration.

He fears his homosexuality. If he can prove to himself that he is really most interested in girls, he will not have to become aware of his homosexual desires. His interest in girls and their genitals is, therefore, a compulsive denial of his homosexuality, indicated by the fact that he only looks—he does not attempt a genital union. Furthermore, the inspection takes place under such circumstances that he is almost sure of being discovered and punished. He seems, in other words, to use the voyeurism as a way of assuaging his sense of guilt. In the same category falls his boasting to the mother about his behavior, knowing that she will be displeased and angry.

Exhibitionism

This pregenital act refers to genital exhibitionism. The little child examines and displays his genitals with pride. In the adult, various activites like exhibiting, looking, and stroking are preludes to the sexual act. Where exhibiting becomes an end in itself, it is a perversion. Such behavior always serves as a reassurance against castration, genital injury. The purpose is not to seduce; actually, seeing a nude female body destroys sexual desire. Exhibitionists enjoy the terror and fear engendered in the spectator. They confess to impotence with girls and have scorn and hatred for them. Often shy, they fear close relationships but seek admiration and reassurance about genital development in their display of it. Usually, there is a history of self-examination before the mirror, which serves the voyeuristic purpose to see the female figure but with reassurance that their penis is really there. Unconsciously, the fantasy is that their supermasculinity is what they are displaying, but it is done with a passive feminine orientation—to be looked at, to be admired, to be sought after. In their fantasies they see women becoming sexually excited if exposed to the sight of their organ. "I will allow you to look, as I was not permitted to do. This is what can be seen—a penis only. Everybody has a penis." The exhibitionist who ejaculates is also saying he has no need of the woman and thus negates any incestuous pattern.

Transvestitism

In transvestitism the child may be said to be deprived of normal gender identity. This development phenomenon may or may not be related to homosexuality. The child who practices transvestitism is usually involved in a pathological relationship with the parent of the opposite sex. For example, a mother may dress her son in girl's clothing when he is very young and may encourage him to enjoy play and other activities normally associated with girls. Unconsciously and consciously reared as a girl, he grows up with an exaggerated and deviant understanding of his own sexual role and eventually appears to prefer the habitus and activities of a girl. These kinds of developmental phenomena appear to be increasing, but they can be prevented if they are recognized and treated early. Transvestitism is not yet clearly understood in the fullest sense. Transvestitism is transitory but undetected in most adolescents. The boy really wishes to see the female figure—garbed in bra, swim suit, corset—but with the reassurance that his penis is there.

Abnormal Relations

Adults sometimes use children for their own sexual pleasure and have also been known to encourage youngsters to indulge in sexual activity with animals and objects. It is common to find that children who are brought to a psychiatrist because of excessive sexual activity have suffered from adult sexual exploitation, including rape. Consummated incest is most common between fathers and daughters, but a *forme fruste* occurs frequently between mothers and sons. Because they are exposed to such intense sexual stimulation, these children have a compulsive need to relieve their own sexual tension.

Fetishism

As the child gradually separates from the parent he may want to cling to an object—a blanket, toy, or similar item—that for him represents the parent. This is an entirely normal development and can only be considered a deviation when the object becomes the primary choice of sexual satisfaction—a situation that can only develop much later. Fetishism can be a translation from an earlier transitory object. It is normal and not uncommon for adolescents to use an object to enhance sexual satisfaction.

Prostitution

Parents today tend to push heterosexuality and sexual experiences too early. When standards are low at home, girls often engage in sexual relations quite early. When there has been considerable sexual seduction of the girl by the father or another man, the sexual drive is often intensified in adolescence. When coldness and rejection exist in the family and there is an aura of self-depreciation, girls often seek warmth and acceptance in physical contact, even though it may be destructive. When girls become involved in excessive sexual activity early in adolescence it is almost always brought on by their having been exploited and sexually stimulated by adults. The deviant behavior leads to an increase in the neurotic tension, which can only be relieved by excessive sexual activity. Classically, these adolescents present a bland, hysterical personality pattern. The psychiatrist sees such deviant sexual behavior as part of the total psychic activity of the adolescent.

Other Deviations

DSM-II lists other sexual deviations, but they are rarely seen in children and adolescents. Pedophilia, molesting a child sexually, is occasionally seen in adolescents. Sadism and masochism do occur, but they are clinical curiosities.

Prognosis and Treatment

Psychiatrists are not in full agreement about treatment methods for sexual deviates. This lack of consensus reflects societal attitudes about sexual deviation—that is, each therapist tends to view such deviation in terms of the moral attitudes of his community. Nonetheless, treatment consists mainly of understanding what the symptom means to the patient, understanding the compulsion and its repetitive activity, and relieving the patient's tension and redirecting his growth into healthy channels by attempting to make the compulsive process less satisfying to him.

Most sexual deviations must be viewed in the context of the over-all personality, since they are really exaggerations of normal developmental processes. The prognosis in these cases depends to a great extent on how early the child receives treatment and on how well the therapist is able to understand the family pattern and to view the symptoms as part of the child's total life experience. Management should involve a combination of psychiatric and legal approaches. Unfortunately, by separating such people from the rest of society and placing them together, the law unwittingly exaggerates the problem by providing a stimulating environment for the sexual deviate.

Sexual deviation is best treated as part of the entire neurotic process. Unfortunately, older children are less responsive to treatment. When sexual deviation is present in the younger child he can be treated along with the entire family, thus exposing intrafamily tensions and abnormal relationships to therapeutic intervention. Workers have reported success with behavior modification therapy. It should also be noted that those adolescents who are not actually engaging in homosexual activity but are rather using homosexual defenses seem to respond well to dynamically oriented treatment.

REFERENCES

Bender, L., and Grugett, A. E. A follow-up report of children who had atypical sex experience. Am. J. Orthopsychiatry, 22: 825, 1952.
*Bieber, I., et al. *Homosexuality.* Basic Books, New York, 1962.
*Freud, S. Three essays on the theory of sexuality. In *Standard Edition of the Complete Psychological Works of Sigmund Freud,* vol. 7, p. 135. Hogarth Press, London, 1953.
Harrison, S. I. A girl reared as a boy. J. Am. Acad. Child Psychiatry, 4: 53, 1965.
Henry, G. W. *Sex Variants.* Harper & Row, New York, 1948.
Holemon, R. E., and Winokur, G. Effeminate homosexuality: A disease of childhood. Am. J. Orthopsychiatry, 35: 48, 1965.
*Sperling, M. A study of deviate sexual behavior in children. In *Dynamic Psychopathology in Childhood,* L. Jessner and E. Pavenstedt, editors, p. 221, Gruen & Stratton, New York, 1959.
*Taylor, G. R. *Sex in History.* Thames & Hudson, London, 1962.
*_Wolfenden Report._ Stein & Day, New York, 1963.
*Work, H. H. Sociopathic personality disorders. II. Sexual deviations. In *Comprehensive Textbook of Psychiatry,* A. M. Freedman and Harold I. Kaplan, editors, p. 1426. Williams & Wilkins, Baltimore, 1967.

15.3 Frigidity, Dyspareunia, and Vaginismus

JUDD MARMOR, M.D.

Introduction

When emotional factors are thought to be playing a major role in their genesis, frigidity, dyspareunia, and vaginismus are classified as psychophysiological genitourinary disorders in the American Psychiatric Association's *Diagnostic and Statistical Manual of Mental Disorders*. Obviously, if the reasons for these dysfunctions are primarily anatomical or physiological, they should not be classified as mental disorders. Somatic and psychogenic factors can, however, coexist.

Until the second half of the 20th century, disorders of sexual function in women were given relatively little attention and were poorly understood. The physiological basis of female orgasmic response was shrouded in obscurity, and its psychiatric evaluation was colored by varying degrees of cultural prejudice and by a double standard of sexual behavior for men and women. Respectable women were expected to tolerate sex, but the question of whether they enjoyed it, let alone were orgasmic, was regarded as a matter of minor importance. It was not until Sigmund Freud's views on the importance of sexual repression in the genesis of neurotic disorders began to influence psychiatric thought that disorders of sexual function in women began to come under greater clinical scrutiny.

Frigidity

DEFINITION

Frigidity or sexual anesthesia is a term applied to a wide range of inhibited sexual responses in women, from a complete lack of response to sexual stimulation to various inadequacies in orgasmic response, despite the fact that the woman finds sex otherwise pleasurable. The traditional psychoanalytically oriented definition of frigidity as "the incapacity of a woman to have a *vaginal orgasm*" (Hitschman and Bergler, 1936) can no longer be considered adequate in the light of recent research findings concerning feminine sexual physiology (Masters and Johnson, 1966). Freud's assumption (1933) that, in the mature female, "the clitoris must give up to the vagina its sensitivity, and with it, its importance either wholly or in part," is now known to have been misleading. Clitoral sensitivity remains a factor of paramount importance in the sexual response of the normal woman, and, although the female orgasm may vary in intensity and duration under different circumstances, its fundamental physiology is identical, regardless of the location or mode of the erotic stimulation.

There are those who assert, nevertheless, that the designation of frigidity should be applied whenever a woman is unable to achieve an orgasm by means of vaginal intercourse specifically, regardless of whether she is able to achieve it in other ways. Others, however, argue that "a more enlightened attitude toward sex should avoid assigning priorities to particular methods of achieving sexual satisfaction" (Salzman, 1968), and that, therefore, so long as a woman is able to achieve an orgasm in the process of mutual lovemaking, she should not be labeled as frigid.

Masters and Johnson (1970) dispense with the value-laden term of frigidity entirely and, instead, refer descriptively to orgasmic dysfunction. They consider primary orgasmic dysfunction as a condition in which a woman has never experienced an orgasm, either in masturbation, love play, or coitus. The term secondary or situational orgasmic dysfunction is used to refer to a condition in which the woman has experienced at least one previous orgasm, regardless of how or under what circumstances it was induced. Masters and Johnson subdivide secondary orgasmic dysfunction into three subcategories: (1) masturbatory orgasmic inadequacy, in which a woman is unable to achieve orgasmic release by manipulation, either by her partner or herself, but is able to achieve orgasm in coitus; (2) coital orgasmic inadequacy, in which a woman has never been able to achieve orgasm in coitus but can respond orgasmically to digital manipulation, oral-genital stimulation, or other stimulative techniques; this subgroup represents the largest number of orgasmic inadequacies and encompasses the traditional definition of frigidity; and (3) random orgasmic inadequacy, referring to a state in which the woman tends to be rarely orgasmic but can be both coitally and manipulatively responsive on occasion. Women in this subgroup seem to feel little or no physical need for sexual release.

INCIDENCE

Dickinson and Beam (1931) in a study of 1,000 married women found that only two of every five women in their sample experienced orgasms during intercourse, a figure roughly corroborated by other investigators. A Kinsey study (1953)—based on approximately 6,000 representative white, non-prison, American women ranging in age mainly from 16 to 50 years—revealed that about 36 per cent of the married women had never experienced orgasm from any source before marriage. In the total sample, 47 per cent of the women in their late teens had yet to experience their first orgasm, and 28 to 39 per cent of the unmarried older women had never had an orgasm. Among married women, the percentage who had never experienced orgasm dropped to as low as 5 per cent, but a large proportion of these responded only occasionally.

These figures indicate that orgasmic inadequacy in women is a frequent finding in this culture. Whether this is true in most other societies is not certain, since adequate comparable studies have not been done. The fact, however, that in some societies, as in that of the Crow Indian, most women expect and achieve orgasm more or less regularly suggests that the frequency of this problem in Western society is not a function of any physiological differences between the sexes—indeed, physiologically women are capable of more frequent and more intense orgasms than are men—but is a consequence of the greater degree of sexual repression to which women in this culture are subjected, as compared with men. The Kinsey statistics indicate that there has been a gradual diminution in the incidence of orgasmic difficulties in women born in successive decades after 1900. It is possible that the continuing liberalization of sexual mores in the decades to come may result in a further decrease in the incidence of these disorders in women.

CAUSES

In the absence of detectable organic factors, it is fair to assume that the vast majority of orgasmic inadequacies in women are basically psychogenic. The underlying causes, however, are complex and multiple.

To begin with, girls growing up in societies dominated by a double sexual standard are generally subjected to considerably more sexual repression in the process of growing up than are boys. Little girls are expected to be cleaner, daintier, and gentler than boys and to use more refined language. From a very early age they are taught to beware of sexual advances from men as something not only dirty and sinful but also dangerous. Apart from such indoctrination, sex is often never discussed at home, so that both explicitly and implicitly the subject of sex becomes negatively conditioned as a taboo area, surrounded by ignorance, fear, and guilt. These patterns are observable with particular frequency in families dominated by orthodox religious convictions.

Because of this differential in early acculturation, a woman's ability to be sexually responsive is usually more dependent than is a man's on feelings of trust, security, tenderness, intimacy, and affection in the relation with her partner. Any life experiences that have rendered her less open to such feelings impair her capacity for orgasmic responsiveness. Such experiences may be the witnessing of intense and open conflict between the parents or feelings of being unloved by either parent, particularly the father. Traumatic sexual events—such as a particularly unpleasant first coital experience, rape, early molestation, witnessing and misunderstanding a primal scene in childhood—may lead to the conviction that sex is an act of violent aggression, carrying with it the threat of physical injury from the penis. Orgasm may be unconsciously associated with loss of control or a state of dangerous vulnerability. Occasionally, too intense an involvement with a seductive father may be the basis for subsequent frigidity based on incest-guilt. An underlying homosexual fixation, with conscious or unconscious hostility to men, may exist in some instances. In still others, conflict over being a woman, with strong underlying penis envy, may be involved; or there may be an intense fear of pregnancy and childbirth. These background factors are not mutually exclusive, and often a number of them are present in the same person.

Women with such backgrounds frequently present themselves with a history of never having had an orgasmic experience, either through manipulation or coitus. This kind of primary orgasmic dysfunction in women has no parallel in men, almost all of whom experience frequent orgasms, if only by means of masturbation, by the time they reach their late teens.

When, however, women have experienced orgasms, one way or another, but are unable to achieve them with a particular partner, the root of the difficulty almost invariably can be found in the nature of the relation with that partner. A frequent presenting factor is the partner's premature ejaculation, which does not allow the woman sufficient time to build up the erotic tension necessary for orgasmic release. Women in such instances often end up with feelings of being used, and their consequent resentment then becomes a pressure on the partner to perform that contributes still further to his own anxiety and sexual inadequacy. The mutuality of this interaction makes it important for such partners to be treated together as a unit for optimal therapeutic results.

Perhaps even more frequent as a cause of secondary orgasmic problems in women is a disturbance in the nonsexual interpersonal relationship with the partner. Feelings of being neglected, competitive attitudes, quarrels over money or the children, reactions to distasteful habits, lack of personal hygiene, lack of tenderness or demonstrativeness in the partner, and a host of other sources of interpersonal friction can become the basis for a failure of orgasmic responsiveness in a woman. Occasionally, specific traumatic experiences, such as the discovery of infidelity on the part of the mate or a rape experience, can become the basis for secondary orgasmic inhibition.

Marmor (1954) has suggested that these psychodynamic factors operate through inhibitory impulses from the cerebral cortex acting on the spinal center that controls the final common pathways to orgastic discharge.

Orgasmic dysfunction can be a secondary consequence of any severe debilitating disease, general ill health, extreme fatigue, and excessive indulgence in alcohol or other depressant drugs. It also occurs as a consequence of the falling off of libido in depressive states.

Hormonal factors are not usually involved in orgasmic inadequacy, nor is the administration of estrogen therapeutically effective. As Benedek (1950) points out, only in rare cases of severe hypogonadism does frigidity seem to be a consequence of ovarian disorder.

In all other instances, women may have any form and degree of frigidity, and at the same time, normal gonadal function.

By the same token, removal of the gonads in a mature, normally orgasmic woman has no inhibiting effect on her subsequent capacity to respond orgasmically.

TREATMENT

Until recently, the most common therapeutic approach to orgasmic dysfunction was that of psychoanalysis or psychoanalytically oriented psychotherapy. Although this approach eventuated in the significant elucidation of the psychodynamic sources of the dysfunction, the therapeutic results, even after years of therapy, were, in general, rather unsatisfactory. In recent years, the therapeutic program initiated by Masters and Johnson (1970) has enabled these disorders to be treated with a considerably higher rate of success.

The reasons for this difference in therapeutic outcome are several. First, when dealing with patterns of behavior that are deeply engrained and enmeshed in a lifetime of fears, taboos, and guilt feelings, as are these disorders, the therapist must do more than improve the woman's insight to alter her behavior. As in the treatment of phobias, he often needs to use specific measures designed to desensitize the patient's fears and guilt feelings and to enable the patient to confront the anxiety-provoking situation directly and in a new way. The Masters and Johnson technique provides such desensitization and behavior modification.

Second, in almost every instance of orgasmic dysfunction, the relation with the sexual partner must be taken into account. Frequently, the husband is equally inhibited about sexual matters; the partners never discuss their sexual needs, feelings, or concerns with each other; the husband may have potency or ejaculatory problems that accentuate the woman's orgasmic difficulties; or there may be significant interpersonal problems between them, engendering anxieties or hostilities that are contributing to the sexual disturbance in the woman. To deal only with the intrapsychic reverberations of these problems in the dysorgasmic woman is, at best, a highly inefficient way of dealing with her disorder; at worst, it can be totally ineffective. The Masters and Johnson (1970) approach, operating on the concept that "there is no such thing as an uninvolved partner in any marriage in which there is some form of sexual inadequacy," insists on treating the two sexual partners as a unit and on involving the cooperation of both in all aspects of the treatment program. The marital couple is considered the patient, never the wife alone. By dealing with the systemic disturbance in this way, the therapist is more apt to achieve better therapeutic results than with traditional one-to-one therapy.

Masters and Johnson (1970) are also of the firm conviction that the treatment process should be conducted by a dual-sex team, on the grounds that "no man will ever fully understand woman's sexual function or dysfunction," and that the converse applies to a woman in relation to a man's sexual reactions. They also feel that a dual-sex team offers each partner a friend in court and prevents the development of transference reactions to a single therapist that may act as a resistance in the therapeutic transactions.

Although these are persuasive arguments, it has been this writer's observation that it is possible for a single therapist to work effectively with a marital unit in such therapy, provided the therapist is free from sexist prejudices and can remain objective and empathic with both partners. A single-therapist approach has the advantage of reducing the cost to the patient and of using precious person-power more efficiently.

The basic concepts of the Masters and Johnson approach can be modified in other ways also. Recently, successes have been reported, for example, in using this approach in once a week group therapy of several marital units simultaneously (Kaplan, 1974). The use of such an approach obviates neither the value of a psychodynamic understanding of the background factors in the patient's sexual dysfunction nor the need for dynamic psychotherapy when neurotic complications are present.

Dyspareunia and Vaginismus

DEFINITION

These two disorders are discussed together because in actual practice they often coexist and have similar causative origins. Dyspareunia refers to painful intercourse. When present, it is usually but not always accompanied by vaginismus, which is an involuntary spasm of the pelvic musculature and lower third of the vagina. This spasm makes penile entry difficult, if not impossible, and there are instances in which it has prevented a marriage from being consummated for years. Under such circumstances, it often eventuates in the husband's impotence.

INCIDENCE

Adequate figures on the incidence of dyspareunia and vaginismus are not available, but these disorders probably constitute only a small proportion of the total number of functional orgasmic disorders. The Kinsey study (1953) made no inquiries concerning these problems. Masters and Johnson, however, indicate that, of 342 women with orgasmic dysfunction whom they treated, 29—8½ per cent—also suffered from vaginismus.

CAUSES

When dyspareunia and vaginismus are psychogenic, the background factors are identical to those already described for frigidity. The pain in coition and the subsequent spasm are often the result of a failure in vaginal lubrication. Such failure is to be expected when there is a total inhibition of erotic reactivity as a consequence of intense guilt or fear underlying the sexual act. If these disorders have been manifest from the first attempt at coitus, one is dealing with psychodynamic factors identical to those in primary orgasmic dysfunction, although they are often more intense in these disorders. On the other hand, if these symptoms appear in a woman who was previously orgasmic in coitus, one must consider—once organic factors are excluded—the situational factors already described for secondary orgasmic dysfunction. However, in the absence of any obvious traumatizing experience, such as a rape or a beating from a mate, there is a strong presumption that a somatic problem has intervened and is accounting for the painful coitus; a careful gynecological examination is indicated.

The kinds of somatic pathology that may be involved in cases of dyspareunia and vaginismus are manifold. They include (1) disorders of the vaginal outlet—intact hymen or irritated hymenal remnants; painful scars, either traumatic or postepisiotomy; Bartholin gland infection; (2) clitoral disorders—irritations or traumata; (3) disorders of the vagina—infectious vaginitis; allergic sensitivity reactions to douches, creams, jellies, or to the latex in condoms or diaphragms; senile vaginitis, with shrinking and loss of sensitivity of the vaginal barrel; radiation vaginitis; painful scarring of the roof of the vagina after a hysterectomy; (4) pelvic pathology—laceration of the broad ligaments, pelvic infection, endometriosis, tumors, or cysts.

Occasionally, after a hysterectomy or other genital tract surgery, a transitory vaginismus may occur that is due not to any somatic factor but to the woman's anxiety that she may be hurt in coitus. Medical reassurance and a patient, gentle approach on the part of the sexual partner usually overcome this problem.

TREATMENT

In addition to the general principles involved in the therapy of the orgasmic disorders, the treatment of dyspareunia and vaginismus may require certain specific technical interventions, particularly the use of graduated vaginal dilators within the framework of the Masters and Johnson approach. Obviously, if somatic factors are involved, they must be taken care of appropriately.

ORGASMIC DYSFUNCTION AND AGING

There is no basis in fact for the myth that postmenopausal women are doomed to lose both the desire and the capacity for sexual pleasure. When this loss does occur, it is usually a consequence of the absence of sexual outlets—loss of the partner or withdrawal of sexual interest on his part—or else it represents a rationalized retreat from sexual participation on the part of a woman who has always been totally or relatively frigid.

Although the physiological reactions involved in the various phases of the sexual response cycle of the postmenopausal woman tend to be slowed or diminished in intensity in some respects, the capacity for orgasmic pleasure remains intact. Indeed, it is not unusual for some postmenopausal women to go through a phase of intensified libidinal desire and sexual responsiveness. The reasons for this intensification are psychological, rather than physiological. In such instances, the removal of fears of becoming pregnant and the need for reassurance that—despite the narcissistic injury of menopause and aging—they are still desirable sexual and love objects serve to potentiate their erotic interests.

The aging process also initiates a number of changes in the female genital apparatus as a result of the diminution in the production of the sex steroids. From the standpoint of sexual function, the most pertinent of these changes are the thinning of the vaginal mucosal lining and the gradual contracture of the vaginal barrel. In addition, the loss of fatty tissue in the area of the mons and the labia renders the clitoral glans and shaft more susceptible to irritation by manipulation and coitus. The consequence of these involutional changes is that, in the absence of sex-steroid replacement, sexual intercourse may become painful to the aging woman. Adequate sex-steroid replacement therapy retards these changes and prevents such secondary dyspareunia and vaginismus. However, if sexual intercourse continues regularly throughout the menopausal and postmenopausal years, this in itself, even without sex-steroid therapy, tends to retard the development of involutional changes in the vaginal mucosa and barrel. The loss of libido and orgasmic response that is often reported by elderly women is neither physiologically nor psychologically an inevitable accompaniment of the aging

process but, rather, is a consequence of disuse. With regular intercourse, women can retain the capacity for orgasmic gratification well into the seventh decade of life and beyond.

REFERENCES

*Benedek, T. The functions of the sexual apparatus and their disturbances. In *Psychosomatic Medicine,* F. Alexander, editor, p. 247. W. W. Norton, New York, 1950.

Dickinson, R. L., and Beam, L. *A Thousand Marriages.* Williams & Wilkins, Baltimore, 1931.

*Freud, S. The psychology of women. In *New Introductory Lectures in Psychoanalysis,* p. 161. W. W. Norton, New York, 1933.

Hitschman, E., and Bergler, E. *Frigidity in Women.* Nervous and Mental Disease. Publishing, New York, 1936.

Kaplan, H. S. *The New Sex Therapy.* Brunner/Mazel, New York, 1974.

Kinsey, A. C., Pomeroy, W. B., Martin, C. E., and Gebhard, P. H. *Sexual Behavior in the Human Female.* W. B. Saunders, Philadelphia, 1953.

*Marmor, J. Some considerations concerning orgasm in the female. *Psychosom. Med., 16:* 240, 1954.

*Masters, W. H., and Johnson, V. E. *Human Sexual Response.* Little, Brown, Boston, 1966.

*Masters, W. H., and Johnson, V. E. *Human Sexual Inadequacy.* Little, Brown, Boston, 1970.

*Salzman, L. Sexuality in psychoanalytic theory. In *Modern Psychoanalysis,* J. Marmor, editor, p. 135. Basic Books, New York, 1968.

15.4   Impotence and Ejaculatory Disturbances

JUDD MARMOR, M.D.

Introduction

Although human sexual behavior, like that of other mammals, is rooted in instinctual processes that are essential to the survival of the species, its patterning is subject to enormous individual variation because instinctual patterns become more and more capable of modification by environmental influences as one moves up the evolutionary scale of the animal kingdom. This process reaches its apogee in man and is a major factor in the extraordinary scope of human adaptability.

Such susceptibility to environmental influence, however, carries with it a considerable potential for dysfunction in the expression of these instinctual processes. This is particularly true with regard to sexuality; the natural biological processes become profoundly affected by a wide variety of conscious and unconscious intrapsychic, interpersonal, moral, esthetic, religious, and cultural influences. Thus, it is not surprising to find that human sexual disturbances can usually be traced to factors such as these and are classified as psychophysiological disorders in the American Psychiatric Association's *Diagnostic and Statistical Manual of Mental Disorders* (DSM II).

Impotence

DEFINITION

The term sexual impotence refers to the inability of a man to achieve a quality of erection sufficient to enable him to achieve coitus successfully. Impotence may be either primary or secondary and may occur in homosexuals as well as heterosexuals. In primary impotence, the man has never been able to achieve a satisfactory coital erection. In secondary impotence, the man has been potent and has developed his impotence subsequently. The diagnosis of impotence should not be used to refer to an occasional erective failure caused by extreme fatigue, excessive alcohol, or some other transient unfavorable circumstance; such reactions are quite common in otherwise normal men. If, however, the erective failure becomes a frequently repetitive pattern—Masters and Johnson suggest the arbitrary figure of failure in 25 per cent of coital attempts—a diagnosis of secondary impotence is warranted. To avoid confusion, the therapist should limit the term "impotence" to failure in erection and should not use the term to refer to premature or retarded ejaculation. The term ejaculatory disturbance is reserved for such conditions.

INCIDENCE

Accurate figures concerning the incidence of primary and secondary impotence are difficult to come by, largely because to have such a problem is generally a source of shame and embarrassment in a society that places a high premium on masculine coital effectiveness. The existence of these dysfunctions is apt to be denied in sexual questionnaires,

especially among less educated and lower class men, in whom the cult of masculinity is particularly strong. The Kinsey study (1948) declared impotence to be a relatively rare occurrence in men up to the age of 35, but the validity of this finding is open to question for the reasons stated above; problems of impotence in younger men are not unusual in clinical psychiatric practice. The Kinsey statistics do reveal a gradual rise in the incidence of impotence with age, particularly after 45, with a more rapid increase after 55. By age 70, 27 per cent of the white men in the Kinsey study reported impotence; by age 75, 55 per cent; and by 80, 75 per cent. No reliable statistics are available concerning impotence among minority groups or in other cultures. Further research is indicated in this area.

CAUSES

Impotence can be caused by a broad spectrum of physical disorders and drugs, but in clinical practice such cases constitute only a small percentage of the total number of presenting potency problems. This may be the result, in part at least, of the fact that when sexual difficulties are incidental to a serious physiological disorder libido is also usually impaired; the sexual problem then becomes a matter of secondary importance to the patient and may not be his presenting complaint. Masters and Johnson (1970) report that in their series of 213 men referred for treatment of secondary impotence, only seven of the cases were found to be based on physiological dysfunction. Nevertheless, although there is general agreement among clinicians that most potency and ejaculatory disorders are psychogenic, good clinical practice requires that organic factors be ruled out before instituting psychotherapy.

Psychological causes. Primary impotence that has existed unremittingly from the onset of a man's sexual liaisons is usually indicative of more serious intrapsychic disturbance than is impotence of secondary or situational origin. Men suffering from primary impotence often come from sexually repressed or religiously orthodox family backgrounds, where sex was either never discussed or else treated as sinful, immoral, or ugly. They have often had abnormally close relations with seductive mothers and thus develop strong unconscious feelings of incest-guilt and castration anxiety in their later attempts at heterosexual functioning. In some such men, homosexual patterns develop that may become a bar to subsequent heterosexual performance.

Apart from specific mother-son relation factors, any life experiences that shape the personality of a man in such a way as to make him unusually fearful of intimacy and unable to love or feel loved, inordinately immature or inadequate, or deeply distrustful of, fearful of, or hostile to women may render him impotent whenever he attempts to function sexually with a woman. Contributing factors to such reactions may include a rejecting or derogating mother or father, dominant older siblings, intense parental quarrelling, feelings of being physically unattractive or uncoordinated, and rejection by peers.

Added to such critical early life experiences is the cultural ambience, particularly in middle-class groups, that make sexual intercourse a difficult process to achieve in reality because it is surrounded by many taboos and societal restrictions. A young man, already full of fears and feelings of inadequacy, who makes his first sexual attempts in the back seat of a car or in a corner of the park or in some similar setting, where there is a high danger of discovery or surprise, may be so beset by anxiety and tension that he fails to achieve an erection. Once having failed, the fear of failing again haunts his subsequent efforts, and his initial impotence may become reinforced by successive failures. In other instances, the initial erective failure is triggered by the resistance or vaginismus of a frightened virginal woman; this reaction intensifies the pre-existing guilt and anxiety of the man and may become the basis for a pattern of subsequent repeated and persistent erectile failure in intercourse.

Similar background factors can be found in patients with secondary impotence, although the effect of these factors has not been so severe as to preclude some capacity for subsequent potency. In actuality, there is a gradient of potency disturbances, depending on the configuration of causative variables,

ranging from intractable cases of primary impotence to cases that are relatively easy to treat, and from severe cases of secondary impotence in patients who rarely function successfully, to milder cases in patients who tend to become easily dysfunctional yet function successfully much of the time.

As might be expected, situational factors play a major role in the causation of secondary impotence. One such factor is excessive indulgence in alcohol, which may trigger an episode of impotence that becomes the basis for intense subsequent performance anxiety and a pattern of repeated failures. Another major factor, probably the most frequent of all, is a pre-existing pattern of premature ejaculation that leads to tension and unhappiness in the female partner and thus to increasing fears of failure and eventual secondary impotence on the part of the man. Other factors are economic or work tensions, depressive reactions, marital discord, loss of attractiveness of the partner, and specific traumatic experiences that either arouse feelings of hostility or rejection toward the partner or make the man feel particularly inadequate or guilty. Examples of these factors may be the discovery of infidelity in the wife, her having been raped, the man's contracting a venereal disease, or the couple's being surprised in sexual intercourse by their children.

Somatic causes. Any severe or debilitating illness can be a cause of impotence and is usually associated with loss of libido. In certain illnesses, such as cardiorespiratory disease, libido may be relatively intact, but the serious impairment of cardiac or pulmonary reserve may make sexual excitement and functioning difficult. In some cases of angina pectoris, the inhibiting factor may not be an actual physiological incapacity but, rather, the fear of triggering an attack of angina.

Diabetes mellitus appears to be particularly capable of causing impotence, although the mechanism is obscure. The impotence seems to occur regardless of the duration or mode of treatment for the diabetes, whether with insulin or with oral agents. There is, however, some correlation with age and duration of the disease; the older the patient and the longer he has been diabetic, the greater is the likelihood of impotence. The cumulative index of impotence in diabetic men is reported to be 2 to 5 times higher than in the male population at large. Keen (1959) has suggested that diabetic impotence may be a consequence of a visceral neuropathy. Other metabolic conditions that may be associated with impotence are myxedema, thyrotoxicosis, pituitary disease, and Addison's disease.

Contrary to what might be expected, the role of sex hormone deficiencies in disturbances of potency is not of major importance. As Perloff (1965) has shown, there is no correlation between sexual ability and the level of urinary 17-ketosteroids. Impotent men may demonstrate above-average levels of urinary 17-ketosteroids, and the reverse can also be true. Testicular castration before puberty usually leads to primary impotence, but postpubertal castration need not, indicating that, after puberty, cortical centers are capable of compensating for the loss of testicular activity. In general, the older a man is when castrated, the less effect it has on his libido and his capacity to function sexually.

The ingestion or administration of large amounts of estrogen results in loss of libido and impotence in men, but the administration of testosterone to normal men has no significant effect on either libido or potency. Men with Klinefelter's syndrome, although hypogonadic, usually have intact libido and sexual potency, but impairment of both can occur in this syndrome.

Any neurological disorder that destroys the function of the sacral cord or of the lower thoracolumbar sympathetic fibers can cause impotence. Hypothalmic lesions and temporal lobe lesions may also cause impotence, although temporal lobe lesions are sometimes associated with hypersexuality.

Local anatomical defects or diseases of the genital tract can create sexual dysfunction. Prostatectomy, particularly perineal prosatectomy, may result in impotence.

A wide variety of drugs, when ingested, can interfere with sexual potency. The most frequently implicated drug is alcohol, but all addictive drugs can produce secondary impotence and loss of libido. Most psychotropic drugs, the phenothiazines, antidepressant drugs (both the monoamine oxidase and the nonmonoamine oxidase inhibitors), the amphetamines, the barbiturates, and reserpine, among others, are capable, in large doses, of interfering with erectile and ejaculatory potency. The phenothiazines sometimes produce an inability to ejaculate, with the sensation of orgasm remaining intact.

EFFECTS OF AGING

Although the Kinsey statistics show a rapidly increasing incidence of impotence after the age of 55, the correlation between the aging process and impotence is not an inevitable one. With age, almost all normal men experience a gradual lessening of libidinal urgency, and the frequency of the need for sexual discharge diminishes. However, the capacity for erection continues to an advanced age, even though the attainment of erection under sexual stimulation may take place more slowly than it did in the man's youth. On the positive side, once erection is achieved, the aging man is generally able to maintain it for longer periods of time before experiencing ejaculatory urgency, thus often making him a more satisfying partner than in his youth. The strength of the ejaculatory reaction also diminishes with age, but this diminution in no way detracts from the intensity of pleasure experienced. The refractory period after orgasm is also considerably increased in older men, so that, in contrast to younger men, repetitive coital connections on the same occasion become more difficult.

Thus, the available evidence indicates that, with available opportunities for coitus, men can retain the capacity for satisfactory sexual intercourse well into their eighties. The diminished frequency of such opportunities and the consequent nonexercise of coital function are far more relevant to the increased incidence of impotence in older men than is the aging process itself.

However, one variety of secondary impotence develops in older men who do have available partners. This impotence occurs when either the man or his partner or both are unaware of the natural diminution in libidinal urgency that occurs in aging, and pressure develops—usually from the woman—for more frequent coital contacts than the man is motivated for. Or the man himself may develop an increasing concern over the fact that it is taking him longer to achieve erection than it used to. The result in such instances can be the development of performance anxiety in the man, with consequent secondary impotence. With motivated and cooperative partners, a clarification of the underlying physiological and psychological factors, together with simple reassurance, is often all that is necessary to resolve this problem.

TREATMENT

Efforts at treating impotence date back to antiquity, and the earliest treatments consisted of various magic potions and aphrodisiacs that worked, if at all, essentially by virtue of their placebo effects. Later efforts were often based on fallacious theories concerning the supposed physiological or anatomical causes of impotence. These treatments included such procedures as prostatic massage, irrigation of the bladder, passage of cold sounds, testicular diathermy, ligation of the dorsal vein of the penis, and cauterizing or painting of the posterior urethra with a silver nitrate solution. Surgical procedures have included tightening the supposedly weak perineal musculature and various forms of internal splinting of the penis by the introduction of rigid materials (plastic or cartilage) into the corpora cavernosa. Mechanical external splints have also been advocated and are still marketed. More recently, male sex hormones have occasionally been given by physicians who assume that the impotence is the result of a deficiency of such hormones. Inasmuch as such a causative basis is extremely rare in the absence of a well defined endocrinopathy, such therapeutic efforts are almost always futile, but in the occasional instance in which some benefit is derived, it is almost certainly a placebo effect.

Contemporary treatment of impotence leans heavily on the contributions of Masters and Johnson (1970), who have demonstrated that—by treating the impotent man and his female partner together, enlisting the empathic help and cooperation of the woman, and desensitizing the performance anxiety—they can achieve better therapeutic results than those obtained by traditional psychoanalytically oriented psychotherapy of the man alone. Nevertheless, dynamic psychotherapy may continue to be indicated as a prelude to or a concomitant of the Masters and Johnson approach, particularly in cases of primary impotence, in which underlying feelings of sexual guilt, anxiety, and emotional immaturity may be great. In cases of secondary impotence, attention must be given to the factors involved in the onset of the symptom, and these factors must be dealt with by appropriate psychotherapeutic techniques, including conjoint marital therapy where indicated. Masters and Johnson report a success rate, after a 5-year follow-up, of 60 per cent in cases of primary impotence and about 75 per cent in cases of secondary impotence. Others who use their approach report similar figures. As experience grows in combining this approach with dynamic psychotherapy, even better results may ultimately be attained.

Ejaculatory Disturbances

Disorders of ejaculation fall into two main groups, premature ejaculation *(ejaculatio praecox)* and retarded or inhibited ejaculation *(ejaculatio retardata, impotentia ejaculandi)*.

PREMATURE EJACULATION

Definition. There is considerable disagreement among authorities about what constitutes premature ejaculation. One definition limits use of the term to the condition in which orgasm or ejaculation persistently occurs before or immediately after penetration of the female introitus during coitus. No one would disagree that such a condition constitutes premature ejaculation, but some consider such a definition too narrow. Others broaden the definition to include ejaculations that occur within the first 30 or 60 seconds after intromission, implying that the ability to postpone ejaculation beyond such a time period is within normal limits. Hastings (1966) defines premature ejaculation even more flexibly as a condition in which a man arrives at orgasm and ejaculation "before he desires to do so." Masters and Johnson (1970) suggest a relativistic concept that considers a man to be a premature ejaculator

if he cannot control his ejaculatory process for a sufficient length of time during intravaginal containment to satisfy his partner in at least 50 per cent of their coital connections.

However, they concede that their definition has no validity if the female partner is persistently nonorgasmic for reasons that have nothing to do with the man's rapidity of ejaculation. Kinsey (1948), on the other hand, did not think that premature ejaculation is a valid clinical syndrome at all. He pointed to the rapidity with which most male mammals, including the higher primates, achieve ejaculatory discharge and argued that such rapidity of discharge, far from being pathological, is quite normal and possibly even biologically superior. Kinsey's view is not generally accepted by most clinicians, however, because it ignores the intrapsychic and interpersonal elements that almost always are associated with premature ejaculation in human beings.

One of the chief reasons for the difficulty in defining premature ejaculation is that the term is relative to the ability to satisfy a female partner, whose own time of response depends not only on her own psychodynamic patterns but also on the degree to which the man has or has not made an effort to bring her to a high pitch of excitement during coital foreplay. Under some circumstances, 60 seconds of intravaginal penile movement is quite sufficient to bring both partners to a mutually gratifying climax; under other circumstances, 5 or 10 minutes or more of vigorous intravaginal penile activity leave the woman unsatisfied, and the man, as a result, feels inadequate. In an attempt to take some of these factors into consideration, therefore, the author defines premature ejaculation as that condition in which a man, with any woman, achieves orgasm before or within seconds after vaginal intromission or in which a man, despite having a partner capable of achieving an orgasm without difficulty, is unable to delay his orgasm or ejaculation

during intravaginal coitus for a sufficient length of time to satisfy her in at least half of their coital connections.

Incidence. Although no adequate studies exist concerning the incidence of premature ejaculation, clinical experience indicates that it is probably the commonest of all disturbances in male sexual function. The frequency with which it is reported or complained of, however, is in large part a reflection of the social climate and sexual mores of the time. It is more than likely that in the Victorian era, when respectable women were not expected to enjoy sex, men with a tendency toward premature ejaculation hardly gave it a second thought. More than that, it is probable that the wives of that period were equally unconcerned about the brevity of such sexual contacts and even grateful for it. With the gradual lessening of the double sexual standard in contemporary society and with the growing awareness of women about their capacity for, and their right to, sexual pleasure, the existence of premature ejaculation has become a matter of increasing concern to both sexes, particularly among better educated people, and therapeutic help for it is, consequently, being sought more frequently.

Causes. Clinical evidence strongly suggests that difficulty in ejaculatory control tends to be closely associated with the existence of anxiety during the sexual act. It is not surprising, therefore, that in this culture premature ejaculation is a widespread phenomenon. Because of the wide prevalence of sexual guilt and anxiety, as well as the prevailing sexual taboos against premarital sex, the initial coital attempts of young men are apt to take place under circumstances of tension, haste, and fear of discovery that militate strongly against adequate sexual performance; or the initial attempt may be with a prostitute who for obvious reasons does everything she can to hasten the youth's ejaculation and get the act over with. Men are thus often conditioned from the onset to have coitus rapidly, with a predominant focus on the orgasm as the essence of the sexual act and a downgrading of the other sensual and interpersonal aspects of lovemaking. In addition, if the young man belongs to that group who has developed an awareness about the importance of female satisfaction in coitus, such rapidity of ejaculation becomes the nexus for the development of anxiety about his sexual performance. This anxiety compounds his difficulties, and a vicious cycle of premature ejaculation—performance anxiety—premature ejaculation ensues and is repetitively reinforced.

In ongoing relations, the reaction of the female partner becomes an additional contributing factor. Obviously, if the woman is disinterested in sex, she gives the man no motivational basis for changing his premature ejaculatory pattern, and she may even be covertly encouraging it. On the other hand, if she does want and seeks a more gratifying experience for herself, a different kind of interaction ensues. Initially, the woman is apt to be understanding and encouraging with the premature ejaculator. This attitude can sometimes be therapeutic, and it is not uncommon for a man's control to improve substantially as he gains confidence with a familiar and reassuring partner. If his problem persists, however, and the woman is repeatedly left in a state of frustrated tension, her empathy often changes to irritation and reproach. Unfortunately, this change usually has the effect of compounding the problem, leading to increased performance anxiety, heightened feelings of masculine inadequacy, and, not infrequently, to impotence in the male partner.

Although these situational factors probably account for the widespread existence of premature ejaculation in general in this society, the psychiatrist should not ignore the idiosyncratic variations that make certain persons more prone to its development than others and that make for differences in its severity. Here, the background factors described in the section on impotence become relevant and should be looked for. In general, they are of the same nature but apt to be somewhat less severe qualitatively and quantitatively in premature ejaculation than in impotence.

Treatment. Most early attempts at treating premature ejaculation were based on one of two major assumptions. The first of these assumptions rested on the belief that the symptom was due to excessive excitement, either at the psychic level or at the phallic

sensory level. To inhibit the psychic excitement, patients were advised to concentrate on nonsexual fantasies during coitus, use cerebral depressants or sedatives, or distract themselves by tightening the anal sphincter, pinching the skin, or biting the cheek or tongue. Not only have these methods been of no avail in the vast majority of cases, but they tend to impair further the quality of the sexual process for both partners. At the sensory level, efforts have been made to diminish penile sensitivity by the application of anesthetic ointments to the glans penis, the wearing of a condom, inhibiting penile movements within the vagina, or masturbating before intercourse. These approaches, too, have proved to be of dubious value in most instances.

The other major assumption was the psychoanalytic hypothesis that the premature ejaculation was the consequence of unconscious incest-guilt or castration anxiety or was motivated by unconscious fear of the vagina or by hostility to the woman (frustrating her, soiling her). On the basis of this assumption, patients with premature ejaculation have been subjected to years of psychoanalytic treatment, with meticulous exploration and clarification of such unconscious intrapsychic factors, but with only indifferent results as far as the amelioration of the presenting symptom is concerned.

A major advance in the treatment of premature ejaculation was achieved by Masters and Johnson (1970) when they approached premature ejaculation not as the man's problem alone but, rather, as a problem of an interacting sexual couple. Using their method—which involves desensitization of sexual guilt, removal of performance anxiety, and a practiced lowering of the threshold of penile excitability, all in a dyadic context—Masters and Johnson have been able to report almost 98 per cent success in the amelioration of premature ejaculation within a matter of weeks. Comparable rates of success have subsequently been reported by others who use this method or modifications of it. The lowering of the threshold of penile excitability is achieved by a squeeze technique that the female partner uses when the man begins to experience a sense of ejaculatory urgency.

This technique is a modification of a method first described by Semans (1956).

RETARDED OR INHIBITED EJACULATION

Definition. This disorder, the reverse of premature ejaculation, is sometimes called ejaculatory incompetence. It is a condition in which the man manifests difficulty or inability in achieving ejaculation during coitus. It can be designated as primary when it has always been present and as secondary when it develops after previous normal functioning.

Incidence. Retarded ejaculation is considerably less common than premature ejaculation, but accurate incidence figures in the adult male population are not available. Johnson (1968) found this problem in only 3 per cent of men referred to a psychiatric clinic for treatment of potency disorders. Masters and Johnson had 3.8 per cent in their series, a total of 17 such cases of 448 men referred with sexual potency problems.

Causes. When retarded or inhibited ejaculation during coitus has always been present, the precursory factors are often similar to those described for primary impotence. These factors include puritanical or orthodox religious backgrounds in which guilt and anxiety concerning sex have been strongly fostered. Fears of impregnating the partner, unconscious anxieties concerning the vagina as a contaminated organ, or anxious-hostile fantasies of the ejaculate as a contaminating substance that will defile the woman may be involved. Often, these men are rigidly compulsive personalities to whom orgasm means a terrifying loss of control, which they dare not chance, or their security systems are built around tightly holding on to everything they have, and they are incapable of the giving of themselves that ejaculation may symbolize for them.

Secondary ejaculatory incompetence of psychogenic origin is invariably the result of disturbances in the interpersonal relation between the man and his partner. The causative factors may include reactions to such situations as pressure from a wife who wants to become pregnant, which the man, consciously or unconsciously, is rejecting; a demand from an unmarried partner for marriage or some other form of commitment that the man fears; a loss of sexual attraction to the partner; interpersonal friction, resulting in hostility to the partner; and some specific traumatic experience, such as the rape of the partner or the discovery of an infidelity.

Ejaculatory difficulty may, however, be the result of organic factors, and these factors must always be ruled out. Neurological disorders interfering with the sympathetic innervation to the genitalia, such as lumbar sympathectomy and syringomyelia, may cause a ejaculatory incompetence. The condition has also been described in cases of parkinsonism and is probably of central thalamic origin in such cases. Drugs with antiadrenergic action, such as guanethidine and methyldopa (both used in the treatment of hypertension), have been reported as causing ejaculatory inhibition, as have various phenothiazine drugs, particularly thioridazine.

Treatment. When the symptom of ejaculatory retardation or inhibition is a reflection of a deep seated personality disorder, as it often is in the primary form, analytically oriented psychotherapy may be necessary to work through the symbolic distortions being expressed in the ejaculatory symptom. When the symptom is secondary to some situational problem, that problem must be dealt with by appropriate measures, including conjoint marital therapy where indicated. In addition to these traditional approaches, however, Masters and Johnson have found that a direct approach to the symptom itself, working with both partners, can often be effective. Their technique, over and above the standard measures they use in the treatment of impotence, involves enabling the woman to bring about an orgasm in the man by means of manual manipulation and then on subsequent occasions rapidly inserting the penis into her vagina as the man approaches the stage of ejaculatory inevitability, so that he is enabled to have the orgasm intravaginally. After this experience is repeated successfully on a number of occasions, the man is usually able to achieve ejaculation normally. Masters and Johnson report 14 successes with this technique out of 17 cases of ejaculatory incompetence referred to them.

REFERENCES

*Hastings, D. W. *Impotence and Frigidity*. Little, Brown, Boston, 1963.
*Johnson, J. *Disorders of Sexual Potency in the Male*. Pergamon Press, Oxford, 1968.
Kaplan, H. S. *The New Sex Therapy*. Brunner/Mazel, New York, 1974.
*Keen, H. Autonomic neuropathy in diabetes mellitus. Postgrad. Med. Jour., *35:* 272, 1959.

Kinsey, A. C., Pomeroy, W. B., and Martin, C. E. *Sexual Behavior in the Human Male*. W. B. Saunders, Philadelphia, 1948.
*Masters, W. H., and Johnson, V. E. *Human Sexual Inadequacy*. Little, Brown, Boston, 1970.
*Perloff, W. H. Hormones and homosexuality. In *Sexual Inversion: The Multiple Roots of Homosexuality,* J. Marmor, editor, p. 44. Basic Books, New York, 1965.
*Semans, J. H. Premature ejaculation: A new approach. South. Med. J., *49:* 353, 1956.

15.5 The Unconsummated Marriage

VIRGINIA A. SADOCK, M.D.

Introduction

Studies by gynecologists, family physicians, and sexual therapy clinics reveal that the unconsummated marriage is not a rare complaint. Couples present with this problem after having been married several months or several years. Masters and Johnson have reported an unconsummated marriage of 17 years' duration.

The couple involved in an unconsummated marriage is typically uninformed and inhibited about sexuality. Their feelings of guilt, shame, or inadequacy are only increased by their problem, and they are conflicted by a need to seek help and a need to conceal their difficulty.

Frequently, the couple does not seek help directly, but the woman may reveal the problem to her gynecologist on a visit ostensibly concerned with vague vaginal or somatic complaints. On examining her, the gynecologist may find an intact hymen. In some cases the wife may have undergone a hymenectomy. This surgical procedure is another stress, however, and often serves to increase the feelings of inadequacy in the couple. The wife may feel put upon, abused, or mutilated, and the husband's concern about his manliness is increased. It usually aggravates the situation without solving the basic problem. The physician's questioning, if he is comfortable dealing with sexual problems, may be the first opening to frank discussion of the couple's distress. Often, the pretext of the medical visit is a discussion of contraceptive methods or, even more ironically, a request for an infertility work-up.

Once presented, however, this complaint can often be successfully treated. The duration of the problem does not significantly affect the prognosis or outcome of the case.

Causes

Lack of sexual education, sexual prohibitions overly stressed by parents or society, neurotic problems of an oedipal nature, immaturity in both partners, overdependence on primary families, and problems in sexual identification all contribute to nonconsummation of a marriage. Religious orthodoxy, with severe control of sexual and social development or the equation of sexuality with sin or uncleanliness, has also been cited as a dominant etiological agent.

Clinical Features

In the unconsummated marriage, the husband frequently has a problem with impotence, and many wives present with vaginismus. It is often difficult to determine which problem arose first, as there has frequently been no premarital sexual experience for either partner. The woman may develop vaginismus after repeated sexual encounters with a dysfunctional man have caused her to feel rejected and frustrated; or the man may develop impotence due to the same feelings after unsuccessful attempts at intercourse with a woman suffering from vaginismus. Occasionally, one partner is able to function outside of the marital situation, and, frequently, either partner would function better sexually with a less dysfunctional mate.

The man in these cases usually bears the burden of guilt for dysfunction, but the woman suffers equally, feeling that she is not sufficiently desirable or attractive to arouse her mate.

A frequent dynamic in the unconsummated marriage involves a husband who has been taught that there are 2 types of women—one for love and one for sex—and a wife who has been brought up to expect the man to make all the advances. Their sexual life is paralyzed, as he is unable to move sexually toward his good woman, and she fears losing his love and her own self-respect if she is sexually aggressive with him. With little or no sexual play between them, they remain more attached to their primary families than to each other, which reinforces their sexual problem.

Another common pattern involves the couple for whom marriage is a power struggle and sex the major battlefield. The wife appears aggressive and controlling, and the husband appears passive and submissive. In bed, however, the husband withholds sex through impotence or premature ejaculation, and the wife is left feeling rejected and unfulfilled. She usually has her own sexual problems and is hesitant about self-stimulation or has difficulty in achieving climax. Both partners end up feeling inadequate and frustrated.

Mr. and Mrs. H. were a young, white, middle-class couple; both were 23 and had been married for 2 years when they came for treatment. They had never had intercourse together. Mr. H. was unable to achieve a strong erection during sex play with his wife. He had no problem when he masturbated himself two or three times a week,

however, Mr. H. had no previous sexual experience. Mrs. H. had had one sexual relationship prior to her marriage. She stated that she had enjoyed her previous experience with intercourse but had not been able to achieve orgasm. She had no masturbatory history.

Mrs. H. supported herself and her husband by working as a buyer for a department store, while Mr. H. completed his graduate studies. She planned to return to school when he finished his education. Neither contemplated his taking a part time or summer job. Mr. H. shouldered a good share of the household chores. However, both Mr. and Mrs. H. represented Mrs. H. as nagging—"Pick up your socks; put your laundry in the hamper." Mrs. H. was pictured as ventilating her feelings regularly, actually scolding a great deal. Mr. H. expressed upset or anger by withdrawal and silence. He stated that he would often sulk at home when provoked by events at school. In short, she came across as the dominant mother and he as the child.

Both felt deprived of nurturing as children. Mrs. H. was the oldest of 4 childen and described her mother as a harried, rejecting woman. Mrs. H. had had to assume much of the care of her younger siblings. The couple currently shared a 2-family house with her parents, and she stated that when she heard her mother yelling at her remaining unmarried sister, it tied her up in knots. The husband was the second youngest of 6 children. His mother had died when he was 7 years old. Both Mr. and Mrs. H. had fathers who worked long hours to provide for their families but had little time to romp with the children or replace the missing maternal care. Fearful of being overwhelmed by their unmet dependency needs, each partner had chosen a defense that led to problems in the marriage.

Mrs. H. had identified with her mother's aggressive characteristics and found if difficult to be vulnerable and sexually receptive to her husband. Mr. H. chose retreat, both emotionally and sexually, and physically withdrew from his wife.

Increasing the verbal as well as the physical communication and providing the support that enabled each partner to become vulnerable to his mate made up a major part of the therapy in this case.

Treatment

The problem of the unconsummated marriage is best treated by seeing both members of the couple. Dual-sex therapy involving a male-female co-therapy team has been markedly effective. However, other forms of conjoint therapy, marital counseling, traditional psychotherapy on a one-to-one basis, and counseling from a sensitive family physician, gynecologist, or urologist are all helpful.

The couple needs to receive factual sexual information from a sympathetic, accepting, but authoritative source. They need permission and encouragement to function sexually and to build confidence and pride in their own sexuality. Couples who come for treatment with this problem have usually proved to be highly motivated and have responded quickly and positively to therapy.

The therapists represent for them authority or parental figures who for the first time recognize, accept, and encourage their sexuality. The therapists act as sex educators and provide positive models for sexual identification. In dual-sex therapy they take over the sexual lives of the couple by directing, through various prescribed sexual exercises, the patients' sexual play. In this way, the therapists suspend the couple's prohibitive and inhibiting superegos and introduce new and more permissive standards of appropriate sexual behavior.

In the following case history the couple was seen in dual-sex therapy. They were treated by a male-female co-therapy team and given specific instructions regarding their sexual behavior. Initially, intercourse was prohibited and sexual contact was limited to, first, general body caressing and, later, genital caressing. This initial limitation removed the pressure to perform from both partners and allowed a respite from what had become an increasingly tense situation. Before attempting intercourse, the couple learned to become physically comfortable with each other. At the same time, they were receiving factual information regarding anatomy and sexual physiology and were being helped to restructure their attitudes toward sexuality.

Mr. and Mrs. A. were a young, attractive, middle-class couple raised in the Midwest. They had been married for 1 year at the time they were first seen in treatment. Mrs. A. was 22, recently graduated from college, and erratically involved in job hunting. The husband was 24 and halfway toward achieving a doctoral degree. Both sets of parents contributed to the couple's support. Both the man and the woman came from strongly re-

ligious families, with parents who held markedly puritanical attitudes toward sex. Factual sex education was nonexistent, and both were virgins at the time of their marriage. The husband had a history of masturbation, and he masturbated about once a week; he would not use his hands, however, but rubbed himself against the bed. The wife denied any masturbation but was able to enjoy, to the point of orgasm, erotic fantasies with strong exhibitionistic components.

Their mutual premarital sex play had involved genital stimulation of the woman by the man. She refused to remove all her underclothing, however, and refused to stimulate him by touching his genitals. At this time, Mr. A. was rebelling against his religious upbringing, but the woman insisted that he return to the fold as a condition of their marriage. On their wedding night, the wife consciously anticipated a very painful ordeal. The man was able to achieve a strong erection, but at the time of intromission the woman screamed loudly in pain, and he became impotent. Subsequent attempts at intercourse met with failure, and the husband developed an increasing problem with impotence, becoming unable to gain an erection at all.

A great deal of work was done with the wife in the initial sessions to get her to assume equal responsibility for the lack of consummation of the marriage; to face her own sexual difficulties; to face her conflicting desires to have her husband passive in areas regarding household matters, feelings toward religion, and reaction to his in-laws but assertive sexually; and to alleviate the rejection she felt because of her husband's impotence.

Much of this work was accomplished simply by explaining that it was normal and desirable for women to stimulate men, that men did not automatically achieve erections at the sight of a nude woman, and that intercourse was not usually a painful experience; by dealing with her negative and unrealistic self-image; and by encouraging her strong, if suppressed, sexual drive.

Relieved of some of his feelings of inadequacy and guilt for not consummating the marriage, the husband was able to overcome somewhat his tendency toward passivity and to express differences of opinion with his wife. Many extrasexual areas were discussed—interference by both sets of in-laws, money problems, the wife's desire to continue her education, and the lack of desire in both partners for children in spite of parental pressure to have them.

The husband regained his erections early in treatment, and the wife's avoidance of sexual contact was unmasked and dealt with by direct confrontation. She was encouraged to masturbate, explore her vagina with her fingers, and indulge in her erotic fantasies. After seven sessions the couple was able to consummate the marriage. At the time of discharge from treatment, the couple was working on remaining problems of passivity in the husband. The wife had not yet experienced an orgasm while containing her husband's penis, but she was able to masturbate to orgasm, and the couple was having intercourse once a week.

In spite of their sexually repressive backgrounds and moderate personality problems, this couple had enough motivation and ego strength to respond positively to therapy and move toward a good sexual adjustment.

But when one or both partners present a more serious maturational failure, when fear of the opposite sex is deeply ingrained or sexual identification is markedly distorted, or when there is less contact with reality or only a superficial commitment to the marriage, the couple presents a much poorer prognosis.

Mr. and Mrs. B. came for treatment of their unconsummated marriage 2 years after their wedding. They were a white, middle-class couple; the man was 29, with a promising career as an accountant; the woman was 27, a music teacher in a private elementary school. They had grown up in the same town and were children of professional families in the same social circle. They had both left home and gone to separate schools for university and graduate education, but it had been expected that they would marry. Both partners expressed fondness for each other, but they gave the impression that they simply fell into the marriage. Neither had experienced a serious relationship or significant sexual activity with anyone else.

At the time they came for treatment, their sexual play consisted of mutual attempts at manual stimulation once or twice a month. This stimulation was partially satisfactory for the husband, who would sometimes achieve an erection and ejaculate. But, when the couple attempted sex play with intercourse as a goal, he was impotent.

The wife was able to achieve orgasm by the manipulation of her vaginal lips by her husband. She would not allow her husband to insert his fingers into her vagina, however, complaining of severe pain at any attempt of his to do so. (One can imagine her reaction to his penis.) She refused to touch herself at all.

Individual interviews revealed that the husband had strong fears of being homosexual, although he had not indulged in homosexual acts. The wife suffered from the feeling that her vagina was closed and that she, in fact, had no vaginal space.

Early sessions showed extreme resistance in both partners to communicate openly about their fears, to use sexual exercises, or to change their life pattern in any way to enable them to spend more time together. Mr. B. would stay late in the office several times a week, and Mrs. B. would reciprocate by working on her lesson plans on those evenings when he was home.

The couple shared severe personality problems, which were reflected in their sexual confusion. They did not seem either sufficiently motivated or capable of focusing on their sexual problems directly. Mr. B. did not feel attracted to his wife. Mrs. B.'s feelings about her vagina amounted to a somatic delusion. Short term treatment was considered unsuitable for this couple, and individual analysis was recommended.

Many women involved in unconsummated marriages have distorted concepts about their vaginas. As with Mrs. B., there can be a fear of having no opening, fear of being too small or too soft, or a confusion of the vagina with the rectum, leading to feelings of being unclean. The man may share in these distortions of the vagina and, in addition, perceive it as dangerous to himself. Similarly, both partners may share distortions about the man's penis, perceiving it as a weapon, as too large, or as too small. In contrast to Mrs. B., however, many of these patients can be helped by simple education about genital anatomy and physiology, by suggestions for self-exploration, and by corrective information from a physician.

Both partners in an unconsummated marriage contribute to the problem. Thus, it is desirable to see the couple in treatment. Improvement or change in attitude in one partner, however, may be sufficient to enable him or her to help the mate.

Within the appropriate therapeutic milieu the partners and couples are often able to achieve a degree of growth and emotional maturity that enable them to start functioning sexually together.

REFERENCES

*Ellis, H. *Studies in the Psychology of Sex.* Random House, New York, 1942.
*Friedman, L. J. *Virgin Wives: A Study of Unconsummated Marriages.* J. B. Lippincott, Philadelphia, 1962.
*Hastings, D. W. *Impotence and Frigidity.* Little, Brown, Boston, 1963.
*Masters, W., and Johnson, V. *Human Sexual Inadequacy.* Little, Brown, Boston, 1970.

15.6   Incest

D. JAMES HENDERSON, M.D.

Introduction

Incest is a group of clinical syndromes the importance of which in psychiatry vastly outweighs their somewhat infrequent occurrence. The incest theme, on thoughtful inquiry, is found to be universal—it probably preoccupies or has preoccupied every individual, group, and culture in human history. Although clinical incest is not particularly common, in virtually every culture or civilization the social threat of incestuous behavior, as defined by that culture, exists or is tacitly acknowledged in an interlocking complex of institutions whose function is in part to minimize this threat. The incest taboo is perhaps the most binding and ubiquitous moral constraint known to man.

The incest theme is pervasive in the literature and folklore of most civilizations, further reflecting the curious paradox of this forbidden matter. Although there is convincing evidence that incest is a universal preoccupation of man, frank and open discussion of it—at least outside modern professional circles—practically does not occur. Even among psychiatrists and in psychiatric and psychoanalytic literature, the attention devoted to the subject of incest falls far short of its importance as the kingpin of psychodynamic formulation and, indeed, of its very importance as a group of clinical syndromes.

Incest has been described in virtually all periods of history and in all types of civilizations. Although the issue is debatable, some forms of incest may have been condoned or at least tacitly accepted within the royal families of classical Egypt, Greece, Peru, and Japan, and perhaps among some ruling families in medieval Europe. Incest seems to be recognized almost everywhere, and, in some form, is regarded as taboo by most primitive societies. Within Western societies, it is condemned as sinful by the Church and as an indictable offense before the law.

Incest is an ever recurring theme of the literature and mythologies of many civilizations.

Among the Greeks, Zeus is alleged to have murdered his father, Uranos, married his mother, Hera, and begotten by her a family of lesser gods.

Within the Bible's Old Testament, the two most outstanding examples of father-daughter incest are those of the daughters of Lot, where liaison occurs after the loss of the girls' mother, and Salome. In the latter, the incestuous stepfather is, moreover, the girl's uncle. In the Book of Leviticus, an entire chapter surveys the rulings for God's people regarding sexual relations and the integrity of family life.

Sophocles' *Oedipus Rex* recounts in literary form the tragic marriage of Oedipus to his mother, Jocasta. Interestingly, in view of Freud's subsequent theory of the primal father, Sophocles invokes the concept of original curse, which closely parallels in Greek legend the more familiar doctrine of original sin, wherein succeeding generations pay a never ending penalty for ancestral crime. In the legend of Oedipus, the House of Labdacus is cursed by the Delphic Oracle's prophecy to the royal family, Laius and Jocasta, that their son will slay his father and marry his mother. Hoping to evade the Oracle's decree, they give their first born son to a shepherd, instructing him to let the infant die of exposure on a mountain. But the infant Oedipus is adopted by King Polybus of Corinth. Learning of the Oracle's prophecy, Oedipus later flees Corinth believing that the prophesy refers to his Corinthian foster parents. On the way to Delphi, he becomes involved in an altercation with a stranger, whom he slays, not realizing that the stranger is his true father, Laius.

Oedipus then continues to Thebes and saves the city by guessing the Sphinx's riddle, to be received by the Thebans as a savior and offered Laius's throne and the queen, Jocasta. Through a complex series of disclosures, Oedipus learns that Jocasta is his mother. Jocasta commits suicide and Oedipus gouges out his eyes, symbolically punishing his eyes for failing to perceive his dreadful act. Oedipus' guilt lay not in marrying Jocasta, for he was ignorant at first of her true identity, but rather in the deliberate quest for power which secured his doubtfully enviable immortality.

In the legend of Electra, Electra incites her brother, Orestes, to avenge the murder of their father, Agamemnon, by their mother, Clytemnestra. In the tragedies by Euripides and Sophocles, Electra is almost delusional in her hatred of Clytemnestra and, according to Euripides, she becomes deranged with guilt after her brother, Orestes, has slain her mother and the latter's lover.

Describing the Phaedra complex, Messer (1969) related the account of the Phaedra legend in Euripedes' play *Hippolytus*. Theseus, King of Athens, returns with his bride, Phaedra, to the town where his son by Antiope has grown to be a strong and handsome young man. Phaedra falls in love with her stepson, Hippolytus and, spurned by him, kills herself, leaving a note for Theseus falsely accusing the young boy of violating her. Hippolytus dies violently when a sea monster frightens his horse and wrecks his chariot. Theseus learns too late of his son's innocence and the king's violent death closes the tragedy. Drawing on Euripedes' play, the term Phaedra complex may be used to refer to any physical attraction between stepparent and stepchild.

Definition and History

Most definitions of incest describe it as the occurrence of sexual relations between blood relatives. However, this definition does not include certain clinically incestuous situations so described throughout the relevant literature. For example, sexual relations between stepfather and stepdaughter or among stepsiblings are usually considered incestuous, although no blood relationship exists. In the *kevutza,* the socialization unit of the Israeli kibbutz, sexual relations between agemates within the kibbutz are proscribed, presumably because they are somehow akin to sibling incest.

To define incest as the occurrence of sexual relations within the socialization unit of a particular culture other than between husband and wife (or that culture's equivalent of this relationship) seems at first glance to circumvent the problem. However, if close blood relatives are separated at birth and later indulge in sexual relations, that is usually considered incestuous. Such was, of course, the case with Oedipus and his mother, and to accept a definition of incest that excludes the behavior of Oedipus would call for the rewriting of much psychiatric and psychoanalytic theory.

In discussing homosexual incest, the very term "sexual relations" raises interesting problems of definition. Physical contact, even intimate physical contact between father and son, is surely healthy! This is obviously a gray area. At exactly what point does healthy physical contact between father and son or between mother and daughter or between same-sexed siblings become "sexual relations"?

In psychiatry, to define is often to choose between a simple and often scientifically unsatisfactory definition, which nevertheless approximates the usual clinical usage of a term, on the one hand, and a more elaborate and often unwieldy but more scientific definition on the other. But a compromise is possible. Incest denotes intimate physical contact accompanied by conscious sexual excitement between individuals within the same socialization unit other than husband and wife or the cultural equivalent, or between individuals who are close blood relatives.

Epidemiology

Incest, as defined by a specific culture, is universally prohibited but everywhere recognized. It is definable in most or all cultures, modern and primitive, and has been reported in almost all civilized societies. However, reliable estimates of its incidence and prevalence are not available. The vigor of the incest taboo and the shame and guilt associated with overt incest make full reporting impossible. Differential reporting according to social class further distorts data; incestuous behavior in families of lower socio-economic status and among persons with a history of social deviance is more likely to be detected and reported than incest in prosperous, respectable families.

However, it is useful to consider some representative statistics. In Sweden, where every incest offender receives a mandatory pretrial psychiatric study, Weinberg (1955) estimated the yearly incidence at 0.73 case per million population. Comparable figures from United States sources are: 1.2 cases per million (1910); 1.9 cases per million (1920); and 1.1 cases per million (1930). Estimates of incest offenses as a percentage of total sex offenses vary from 2.4 per cent to 6.3 per cent.

Father-daughter incest receives the most attention. Weinberg (1955) studied 203 Illinois cases and reported 159 cases of father-daughter incest (78 per cent), 37 cases of brother-sister incest (18 per cent), two cases of mother-son incest (1 per cent), and five cases of multiple incestuous relationships (3 per cent). Lukianowicz (1972), studying unselected female cases from a child guidance clinic and hospital catchment areas in County Antrim in Northern Ireland (including girls referred by courts in other counties), found 26 cases of father-daughter incest among 650 unselected patients or about 4 per cent of the patient sample. Using similar material (but including male patients and excluding court referrals), the comparable figures for other forms of incest from 700 unselected cases were 29 cases, or again about 4 per cent. Among the 29 latter cases were 15 cases of sibling incest, five cases of grandfather-granddaughter incest, four cases of uncle-niece incest, three cases of mother-son incest, and two cases of aunt-nephew incest.

The older participant in an incestuous relationship is much likelier to be male than female, reflecting, perhaps, the relatively stronger taboo against mother-son incest and its symbolic equivalents than against father-daughter or sibling incest. Cross-culturally, only mother-son incest appears to be universally prohibited.

The importance of socio-economic variables is disputed and debatable. Sonden (1936) noted a rural preponderance of Swedish incest cases and stressed poor housing and geographic isolation as factors that promoted the seeking of emotional and social satisfactions within the family. There

appears to be an inverse relationship between the occurrence of incest and socioeconomic status; incest is commoner in poorer working-class and isolated rural groups, where poverty, inadequate housing, crowding, and poor sanitary facilities lead to an enforced physical proximity in the absence of good opportunities for emotional investment outside the family. Lutier (1961) emphasized social isolation as the major demographic variable associated with incest and suggested that the simpler and regressive rural milieu recapitulates the conditions found in primitive societies, where certain forms of incest were sometimes accepted. Rhinehart (1961) associated incest with socioeconomic disadvantages accompanied by social disorganization in a milieu where moral restrictions are lax. Fathers who are barred from sexual relations with their usual partner in a setting of personal, social, and economic decline may institute an incestuous relationship with a daughter. In the United States, Weinberg (1955) noted the disproportionate incidence of Polish peasant background in foreign-born incest offenders and feels that this reflects an increased tolerance for incest in the Polish peasant community.

But these data about socio-economic and demographic variables related to incest are seriously biased by the unfortunate sampling procedures in the study designs. For example, samples drawn from criminal and court records surely reflect the generally higher conviction rates for all personal crimes among the lower social classes. The majority of persons appearing in criminal courts are of lower social position, borderline economic means, and crowded living quarters, so that a sample of incest cases drawn from such a population naturally reflects this bias.

There is little firm evidence that poverty, overcrowding, and social isolation are of more than secondary etiological importance. Rates of incest in the United States and England do not clearly parallel population density, population growth, or fluctuations of the business cycle. The socio-economic variables apparently associated with incest in a given study may be merely those characterizing the population from which the study sample is drawn.

CROSS-CULTURAL DATA

Since definitions of incest are culturally determined and since the occurrence of different forms of incest varies so widely from culture to culture, any consideration of the epidemiology of this condition must include an examination of cross-cultural data.

Kardiner (1939) analyzed data from several cultural groups to delineate the interaction of personality and culture. He observed that the Oedipus conflict took different forms according to the nature of fundamental social institutions specific to a particular culture. The nature and rigidity of the incest taboo varied from culture to culture, and only mother-son incest was found to be universally prohibited.

The incest taboo varies from culture to culture. In ancient Egyptian civilization, marriage between sister and brother was not uncommon. Incest was not strictly defined as such between brother and sister by the same father, but sexual activity between offspring of the same mother was not permitted. Some groups permit marriage between first cousins; others, second cousins; and still others, only very distant nonblood relatives. Wolf (1968) described Chinese families that adopt and raise young girls, who are thus socialized into the same family unit into which they later marry. Aging parents are thus assured of their daughter-in-law's unending loyalty.

Devereux (1939) regarded myths as a culture's collective day-dreaming and traced the incest theme in many aspects of Mohave Indian culture. Wherever he found sexual relations between close relatives, one or both participants were shamans possessing evil powers. Although Mohave are sometimes lenient toward social deviance, persons who commit witchcraft and incest are regarded as a threat to the tribe and their conduct is vigorously resented. Perhaps the Mohave's own repressed incestuous wishes motivate this condemnatory attitude. Incestuous behavior characterizes the unsocialized Mohave, who fails to achieve the wide distribution of libido characteristic of his culture and invests it instead on his next of kin (the unresolved Oedipus complex). The shaman fulfills these criteria. This observation is likely related to the association of incest and schizophrenia in our own culture.

Fox (1962), surveying cross-cultural evidence and discussing mainly sibling incest, named several characteristics of the institutions surrounding a culture's family which affect the intensity of the incest taboo: matrilineal versus patrilineal or bilateral descent, degree of temptation (availability of the siblings and other sex objects), the premium on the girl's virginity, customs relating to illegitimate children, age of marriage, and sibling relationship in adult life. His hypothesis is that "the intensity of heterosexual attraction between co-socialized children after puberty is inversely proportionate to the intensity of heterosexual activities between them before puberty." Fox supports his hypothesis with a behaviorist viewpoint: frustration, anger, and aggression that result from heightened sexual excitement but failure to climax after mutual stimulation between brother and sister negatively reinforce such behavior, and when sexual maturity is reached sexual approaches to sibling objects are avoided. However, the Fox hypothesis seems equally compatible with the simpler explanation that exploratory sexual activity among siblings is associated with a healthier and less inhibited, nonincestuous heterosexual orientation in adult life with less need to resort to "forbidden" incestuous activity, the forbidden-ness of the incestuous activity being determined by a separate and complex set of factors.

Fox's review of cross-cultural data is noteworthy. The matrilineal Trobrianders are obsessed with the problem of sibling incest and public disclosure, and denunciation leads to suicide. The Tallensi and Pondo, where descent is based on patrilineages and clans, permit affectionate and even sexual play and intimacy among young siblings, and simply regard sibling incest as matter-of-factly unthinkable; little in the way of formal sanctions or punishments are provided.

Among the Chiricahua Apache, descent is bilateral, avoidance of sex play is strongly inculcated among siblings, and the youngsters are denied alternative sex objects. Among the Chiricahua, there is vigorous resentment of incestuous activity and offenders will commit suicide rather than face punishment inflicted by an irate society. The Mountain Arapesh are patrilineal, and children have complete freedom of interaction. The Arapesh are indifferent about incest and treat the matter with academic detachment.

The Tikopia are patrilineal, and the children are allowed freedom of interaction. But the situation is more complicated, with occurrences of incest apparently regarded as ego-dystonic and viewed either as a momentary passion or as a trick played by the spirits. There is an extremely high premium on virginity. The supposed sanction on occurrence of incest is suicide.

Etiology

The occurrence of clinical incest is multidetermined.

FACTORS DETERMINING THE INCEST TABOO

The incest taboo is an appealing area for theorists and has apparently lent itself to simplistic and unitary formulations. More accurately, the incest taboo is determined by a variety of instigating and sustaining factors.

In 1913, Freud (1955) posed the question as follows: "What is the ultimate source of the horror of incest which must be recognized as the root of exogamy?" Freud invoked the concept of the primal horde and supported a hypothesis that in such a primal horde the younger men banded together and murdered a paternal tyrant who had jealously kept the women of the tribe to himself. There ensued rivalry and quarreling among the young "brothers," leading to ruinous disruption of the social organization. To prevent such rivalry and social disintegration, the incest prohibition was erected. Furthermore, Freud added, "We may safely assume that no generation is able to conceal its more important mental processes from its successor." Recognizing the shortcomings of this hypothesis, Freud described "the inheritance of psychic dispositions which, however, need certain incentives in the individual's life to become effective."

Accordingly, in the oedipal situation, the child feels excluded from the passionate love between his parents, wishes to possess his mother (the incestuous wish), and regards his father as, in part, a hated rival. He perceives (or perhaps projects) a jealousy and prohibitive demeanor in his father and responds to the perceived threat and to his own projected aggression with guilt and castration anxiety. The dreaded retaliation of his father revives anxieties from an earlier age when his more basic fear was not that of being castrated but of being abandoned. Thus, pregenital experience shapes castration anxiety arising in the phallic phase.

Dubreuil (1962) postulated instrumentalism applied to man in a socio-cultural setting. Man functions at three levels; as an individual who uses others for security and power, as an individual who sees others in a reciprocal relationship with himself, and as one at the service of his culture. The incestuous man fails to progress beyond the first level and sees a demand for a reciprocal relationship as an attack on his autonomy. He reconstructs his family on the model of a kingdom where his authority is total.

Speaking from anthropological viewpoint, Dubreuil postulated that incest was infrequent and sporadic in primitive cultures by the very nature of social existence; incest was uncommon and, like other special arts, was at the same time an offense among the lower classes and a privilege and freedom among the upper. Just as unrestricted homicide would endanger the very structure of society, so also incest would be socially isolating and destructive. However, both incest and homicide are institutionalized and legitimate where appearing to benefit the social interest. Anthropologists have shown that the nature of the incest taboo is culturally determined. Sociologists have pointed out the role of the incest taboo in facilitating socialization and role learning, forcing members of a nuclear family to choose love objects outside their group.

Biological factors may have some role in determining the incest taboo. A human group practicing incest is selectively disadvantaged by the lesser fitness resulting from inbreeding vis-à-vis outbreeding human groups. Modern studies have demonstrated a higher incidence of death, mental retardation, and congenital defect in infants of incestuous unions than in control groups. From random variation in patterns of mating from society to society, human groups that insist on outbreeding are favored and preserved by the process of survival of the fittest. This formulation does not imply that the groups involved understood the consequences of inbreeding—natural selection is not mediated by conscious awareness on the part of the individual organism—but it is possible that primitive man may indeed have noted a connection between incest and physical abnormality. There are convincing data to support the lesser fitness of human and subhuman groups practicing inbreeding.

The incest taboo, like clinical incest, is multidetermined.

FACTORS PROMOTING BREAKDOWN OF THE INCEST TABOO

First, incestuous acts are, at least to some degree, collusive. In father-daughter incest, for example, the father is aided and abetted in his liaison by conscious or unconscious seduction by his daughter, and by his wife's collusion related to her hostility toward her daughter. The mother forces a heavy burden of responsibility onto her daughter by causing her to assume the role of wife and lover with her own father, thus absolving the mother of this unwanted role.

Viewing incest in a transactional framework, Lustig et al. (1966) proposed that incest is a transaction that serves defensively to protect and maintain a dysfunctional family structure. Incest, as a noninstitutionalized role relationship, reduces family tension by preventing confrontation with underlying conflicts. Such a defensive maneuver succeeds to a degree while each member can maintain a façade of role competence. For example, father-daughter incest serves as a partial alleviation of the parents' pregenital dependency needs, as an avoidance of feelings of sexual insufficiency, as a mechanism for the daughter's revenge against the non-nurturing mother, as a mechanism for reducing separation anxiety, and as an aid in the maintenance of a façade of role competence for all members. The role reversal between mother and daughter is an idiosyncratic solution to the tensions of a dysfunctional family that is too sick to use culturally approved patterns of interaction. Both parents define the daughter as a maternal object, with displacement onto her of their respective maternal and sexual fantasies. Certain latently homosexual fathers are vicariously able to

gratify their female introjects by identifying with a daughter-partner. If the father is simultaneously serving as the vehicle for the mother's unconscious homosexual impulses toward her daughter, she can vicariously enjoy the father's role in the incestuous relationship. Clearly a vulnerability to regressive ego states is a condition of this phenomenon.

Lustig defined five conditions of the dysfunctional family that foster breakdown of the incest barrier: (1) emergence of the daughter as the central female figure of the household in place of the mother; (2) some degree of sexual incompatibility between the parents with unrelieved sexual tension in the father; (3) unwillingness of the father to seek a partner outside the nuclear family because he needs to maintain the public façade of stable and competent patriarch; (4) shared fears of family disintegration and abandonment making the family desperate for an alternative to disintegration; (5) covert sanction by the nonparticipant mother, who condones and colludes with the assumption by the daughter of a sexual role with her father.

Sociological factors associated with a breakdown of incest barriers are overcrowding with physical proximity; alcoholism; geographic isolation such that extrafamilial social and emotional contacts are effectively impossible (facultative incest); in the case of father-daughter incest, prolonged absence of father from the home with his subsequent return to find an aging wife and a young, attractive, and tempting daughter; and loss of the wife by divorce, separation, or death, leaving the father alone with an adolescent daughter. The contemporary pattern of small, mobile, vertical family units and the loss of the extended family may foster incestuous relationships. Within such compact families, each individual's need for affection and physical intimacy must be satisfied largely from within the nuclear unit, although, in the light of cross-cultural data, this proximity might be expected to strengthen rather than weaken the taboo. Age of family members is an important variable. Generally in cases of father-daughter incest the father is in his late thirties or early forties, a period during which marital stress often develops.

"Neurotic endogamy" is a term that describes individuals who cannot establish object relationships outside the kinship group and therefore tend to marry cousins or other relatives. Incest in the nuclear family may be related to an extension of such a neurotic developmental process. Desertion anxiety is often strikingly prominent in incestuous partners and their families.

Major mental illness is a factor in incestuous behavior, according to some studies. Magal (1968) described five incestuous families, with major mental illness occurring in four of the five. Magal described a paranoid mother, a "borderline" father, a paranoid psychotic father, and, in one family, both father and mother psychotically depressed and suicidal.

Intellectual deficiency and constitutional inferiority may play a part in some cases of clinical incest.

Psychodynamics of Incest

The Oedipus complex and Electra complex in some form are universal, and the psychodynamics of incest are therefore universal in their applicability. The incestuous fantasy inherent in the oedipal situation is now considered to have extensive roots in the pre-oedipal period.

The phenomenon of sexual latency in children of Western civilizations may derive, in part, from environmental and social forces rather than from an inherent tendency. In India, for example, infantile marriage has been customary for centuries, and the 1921 census of India lists 2 million wives and 100,000 widows under the age of 10 years. The *Memoirs of Casanova* and the *Confessions of La Marquise de Brincilliers* attest to the sexual precocity of certain children. Such factors as constitutional intolerance of denial of satisfaction, very charming and attractive personalities, mental deficiency, emotional deprivation, and abnormal stimulation of children's urges by adults are factors that may facilitate the retention of overt sex interest into the latency period.

The psychodynamics of father-daughter incest have been described in detail by Kaufman (1954). In his series, desertion anxiety is a pervasive theme. The fathers (or stepfathers) deserted the children at some time, through divorce, living away from home, alcoholism, or frank desertion. Similarly, maternal grandfathers had deserted their families and the daughters' mothers deserted their husbands, leaving the daughter to assume the maternal role. The maternal grandmothers were consistently stern, demanding, cold, and hostile, and reacted to desertion by their husbands by singling out one daughter, whom they compared to the maternal grandfather and upon whom they lavished displaced feelings of hostility and resentment. These daughters, who became the mothers of the incestuous daughters, were hard, infantile, and dependent, and they married men who were similarly dependent and infantile. The mothers regarded themselves as worthless, yet were tied to the maternal grandmother in the futile hope of receiving the love and encouragement they never felt.

These mothers single out one daughter, whom they overindulge and develop into a replica of the maternal grandmother, then displace onto these chosen daughters hostility arising in their own unresolved oedipal conflict. They desert their husbands sexually and force their daughters to assume the role of sexual partner for their husbands. The mothers feel guilty and deny the incestuous liaison, even in the face of obvious or very suggestive evidence of it.

Incest usually has its onset when the father and daughter feel abandoned because of the mother's giving birth to a new sibling, turning to the maternal grandmother, or developing some outside interest. The girls, lonely and fearful, then accept their fathers' sexual advances as expressions of affection, acquiescing in the tacit encouragement they receive from their mothers. Although the father-daughter liaison is genital, the meaning is pregenital, and, indeed, the reactions to sexuality in these girls take such pregenital forms as promiscuity, asceticism, and homosexuality. The role of the nonparticipating member (mothers in cases of father-daughter incest) is crucial. Her denial freezes role relations and preserves them from change. Paranoid traits and unconscious homosexual strivings are common in incestuous fathers.

The paranoid component is related to strong unconscious hostility toward the paternal grandmother subsequently transferred to the wife and daughter. The behavior of incestuous fathers reflects not only a displaced positive oedipal striving toward their mothers, but also severe pregenital and genital conflicts, notably the fusion of oral aggression and positive sexual strivings. Incest among fathers is an expression of unconscious hostility fused with primitive genital impulses discharged toward the daughter. Some fathers appear to have had a disturbed relationship with their own harsh and authoritarian father, who was ambivalently hated, but admired; ensuing passive homosexual longings promote a process whereby the father obtains a fantasied affection from his own father through an incestuous liaison with a daughter.

Incestuous fathers are commonly preoccupied with having supposedly hurt their daughters and with the fear of subsequent retaliation. The discharge of the incestuous impulse in the face of the incest taboo is facilitated by perception of the daughter as incapable of retaliation, a tendency of the father to act on aggression that he suffered passively as an infant, and seductiveness on the part of the daughter.

Rascovsky and Rascovsky (1950) provided a detailed analysis of a young girl who had been a party to father-daughter incest. An extreme frustration in relation to the girl's mother and attempts at restoration from the basic depressive position led to a precocious transition to the oral search for a father. In a situation dominated by extreme anxiety, there occurred an overevaluation of the father's penis. The aggressive component against the partial object sought satisfaction in the form of an urge to castrate. The incorporation of the penis as a substitute for the primary relation with the mother's breast led the daughter to a masculine identification with the penis and there followed the choice of a feminine object disguised as a womanly man. Nymphomania resulted from anxiety over failure to obtain an orgasm and the ego developed a greater capacity for sublimation favored by the real satisfaction afforded by incest.

As a general principle, unconscious impulses may often be used for the purpose of warding off other contents. Conscious or unconscious incestuous wishes may conceal deeper pregenital wishes of an oral character. The incestuous fantasy may accordingly reflect not only the symbolic wish of a sexual nature for the parent, but also a deeper pregenital wish to be loved and protected by the mother to the exclusion of the world. Sexuality may be not only genital, but also pregenital and oral-receptive. (The hysteric is approached as a woman, but wishes to be taken as a child.) Oral fixations may give the Oedipus complex of hysterical women a strong pregenital component. A woman who is apparently heterosexual may use a man as a weapon in a preoedipal struggle with her mother. Freud asserted that the hostile attitude of the daughter to the mother may originate in the preceeding oral-dependent phase and simply finds in the Oedipus situation reinforcement and later reawakening. Activity with father or a father-substitute also satisfies revenge wishes against the mother for preoedipal frustrations.

Weich (1968) proposed that one of the functions of the terms "mother" and "father" relates to a verbal taboo such that these terms function to minimize incestuous conflicts. Children refer to parents through the use of labels rather than by proper names to describe a part of the individual, a function, and avoid consideration of the total being—his feelings, sexuality, desires, and so on. This verbal institution helps maintain the incest taboo. Weich notes a transient phase (about age 2½) when children do refer to their parents by first names, however this phase usually does not persist beyond the age of 6, being repressed under the influence of oedipal anxiety. The use of parental first names may again appear in early adolescence, this time by a taunting, mischievous adolescent. The parents' anger at such "disrespect" may reflect their discomfort as an unconscious incestuous conflict is brought nearer to consciousness.

Clinical Features

Families in which father-daughter incest occurs merit special attention, but many patterns of incest other than paternal will be described.

FATHERS IN FATHER-DAUGHTER INCEST

There is little consensus as to the severity of emotional disturbance among incestuous fathers; reports vary from the finding of little psychological abnormality to a heavy preponderance of psychotic disorder. Lukianowicz (1972) reported that of the fathers in 26 cases of father-daughter incest drawn from an unselected outpatient population 14 were inadequate psychopaths, five were aggressive psychopaths, and four were alcoholics. The men were allegedly of average intelligence but five were described as having unusually strong sex drives and weak inhibitions. There were no cases of psychosis, frank neuroses, or special disability, although one father twice developed a reactive depression that nevertheless did not prevent further incestuous activity from occurring.

Weinberg (1955) listed three categories of incestuous fathers: the first, an introversive personality with an extreme endogamic orientation and disproportionate investment in the nuclear family; the second, a psychopathic personality characterized by indiscriminate promiscuity; the third, a psychosexually immature father with pedophilic craving extending to sexual involvement with his own daughter.

Once initiated, the incestuous activity often continues for a substantial period of time. Incestuous fathers typically begin the liaison about the age of 40; they begin with the oldest daughter and subsequently may initiate incest with her younger sisters. Incestuous fathers have made poor sexual adjustments. Wives of such men often describe their sexual relations as devoid of affection and state that their husbands appeared to derive an exclusively physical satisfaction from intercourse. Pseudoheterosexuality often appears to mask latent homosexual urges. The inability of these men to achieve a stable heterosexual orientation is reflected in a variety of coping mechanisms: sexual withdrawal, hypersexuality, flagrant promiscuity, and virtual abstinence.

Incestuous fathers may suffer from some degree of guilt and depression during their incestuous activity, but most often they become remorseful and repentant after the incest has been disclosed. The incest taboo is strict and incestuous fathers show a variety of defensive maneuvers to cope with their pervasive sense of guilt. Such rationalization as parental duty, a necessity to teach facts of life, and pacification of an angry daughter are used to try to cope with the massive guilt resulting from violation of the incest taboo. However, the guilt may arise not only from the incestuous behavior, but also from the disgrace and embarrassment rendered to families.

Incestuous fathers seem to come from backgrounds of social deprivation in the form of parental conflict or broken home, marginal economic circumstances or parental unemployment, poor education and occupational instability. Population sample biases may account for some of these preponderances. Recidivism after disclosure of incest is not common; however, public disclosure often precipitates disruption of the family. Apparently, the disposition toward incestuous behavior is not correlated with more general criminal tendencies.

WIVES OF INCESTUOUS FATHERS

The wives of incestuous fathers are often dependent and infantile, pathologically attached to their own mothers, and prone to panic in the face of responsibility. They promote the occurrence of incestuous liaison by frustrating their husbands sexually or symbolically deserting them, and by promoting a dysfunctional role allocation wherein the daughter is more or less subtly encouraged to assume the role of sexual partner for the father. These mothers push their daughters prematurely into a mothering role, and that eventually includes sexual partnership with father. For whatever reason, the wives do not usually report the incestuous activity. As a rule, they tolerate it with little protest, or exercise such massive denial that the liaison continues apparently unbeknown to them. Conceivably, such wives identify with their daughters and gratify in fantasy their childhood incestuous wishes toward their own fathers.

If the wife does report the incestuous liaison, her doing so is often precipitated by anger over some other matter and appears as much linked to that as an expression of real objection to what is taking place between father and daughter. The wives are perhaps too guilty about their own collusion or too fond of their husbands to report the offense. Moreover, they are often extremely dependent on their husbands and seem prepared to pay a great price emotionally in order to remain with them.

Promiscuity among the wives of incestuous fathers is not uncommon and has been largely overlooked as a possible factor contributing to the denial exercised by them vis-à-vis the husband-daughter liaison, and to their tendency not to report it to authorities. Occasionally, promiscuity and elopement by the mother precedes and perhaps precipitates incestuous activity between father and daughter.

Lukianowicz (1972), describing the girls' mothers in the 26 cases of father-daughter incest mentioned above, reported 12 who showed no gross personality deviations, eight psychopathic and promiscuous, two frigid with symptoms of hysterical personality, and three "excessively" anxious. (One mother was unavailable.) None of the mothers was psychotic and most preserved at least a façade of normalcy.

DAUGHTERS IN FATHER-DAUGHTER INCEST

The daughters collude in the incestuous liaison and play an active and even initiating role in establishing the pattern. The girls may be frightened and lonely and welcome their fathers' advances as expression of parental love. The incestuous activity often continues until it is discovered, and the girls do not act as though they were injured. Generally, it is the eldest daughter whom the father selects for his incestuous involvement, proceeding later toward activity with her younger sisters.

Lukianowicz (1972), describing the daughters in the 26 cases already mentioned, found 11 with character disorders (promiscuity, prostitution, and antisocial behavior), five with frigidity (and of these three with hysterical personality disorders), four with frank neurosis (one case of acute anxiety reaction and three cases of depressive reactions with suicidal attempts), and six who

showed no apparent ill effects from their incestuous relationship.

Incestuous daughters often have a façade of pseudomaturity—they may be precocious in learning, reality-mastery, and motility, but object relations, feminine identification, and adolescent ego development are disturbed or impaired. The girls tend to develop character disorders rather than neuroses or psychoses, and regression after the interruption of incest leads to promiscuity, antisocial behavior, frigidity, homosexuality, learning disabilities, and depression.

Like her mother, the incestuous daughter is unlikely to report the liaison at first or to protest about it. If she eventually does, it is as much precipitated by anger at her father for something else or jealousy of his relationship with another woman, as a real objection to his incestuous behavior. Oedipal guilt may play a role in this reluctance to accuse the father. If an accusation is made, it is often a desire for revenge evoked by a perceived withdrawal of the father's attention. Some girls avoid guilt feelings through a denial of pleasure and by assuming a consistently passive role in the relationship.

Daughters who regret the incestuous behavior may seek forgiveness from their mothers even though the latter have not objected to their behavior or condemned them. The daughters' guilt may accordingly stem not only from violation of the incest taboo, but also from hostile impulses toward the mother.

Psychological tests. Kaufman (1954) reported psychological testing data for the daughters in 7 of 11 studied cases of father-daughter incest. The tests administered included a Stanford-Binet or Wechsler-Bellevue Intelligence Test, a Rorschach Test, a Thematic Apperception Test (TAT), and the Goodenough Draw-a-Man Test.

Performance scores for these girls were generally higher than verbal scores. The Rorschachs revealed depression, anxiety, confusion over sexual identification, fear of sexuality, oral deprivation, and oral sadism and aggression. Denial, repression, and sometimes projection were the chief defense mechanisms revealed by Rorschach data and the TAT. In the TAT, mother figures were seen as cruel and depriving and father figures as nurturant, weak and ineffectual, or frightening.

OTHER FORMS OF INCEST

Sibling incest. The prohibition against sibling incest varies cross-culturally and is somewhat variable within our own culture. Studies usually report sibling incest to be less common than father-daughter incest, but the near normalcy of sibling incest per se leads one to speculate that it may well be rather common and that cases coming to clinical attention are the minority where other emotional difficulties happen to be present. The older participant tends to be male. The commonest pattern is of normal sexual play and exploration leading eventually to heterosexual intercourse but subsequent substitution of sibling partners with exogamous partners, with no particular psychological harm to either participant. Parents usually deny the incestuous behavior—the absence of strong sanctions or punishments minimizes feelings of guilt among the participants. Prepubertal sibling incest may be viewed as a normal variant of heterosexual development which tends to occur in crowded, isolated, and/or lower socio-economic class families. Occasionally, sibling incest is associated with more serious psychopathology; this is more likely the case when the pattern is prolonged rather than a transitional developmental phase.

Mother-son incest. The prohibition against mother-son incest is the most consistent cross-culturally and much the strongest within most cultures. It occurs much less commonly than father-daughter or sibling incest. Raphling et al. (1967) described a family in which all three forms of incest occurred and observed that the central perpetrator of multiple incestuous liaisons within the family was nevertheless revulsed by his mother's attempt to seduce him and bore a continuing hostility for her thereafter.

Generally, the occurrence of mother-son incest bespeaks more severe psychopathology among the participants than does father-daughter incest (where personality disorder is common) or sibling incest (which is sometimes almost normal). Lukianowicz (1972) described three cases: of the three mothers, one was schizophrenic, one was "neurotic," and the third developed an involutional depression after the occurrence; of the three sons, one was schizophrenic, one mentally subnormal, and the third apparently normal. The psychodynamics of mother-son incest include the mother's profound dependency on her son to whom she turns for emotional support and protection and eventually sexual gratification. The son is idealized and the mother's youthful fantasy of a romantic lover is invested in her own son. The mother is angry with her husband and may even blame him for her incestuous behavior.

Grandfather-granddaughter incest. This syndrome is clinically and dynamically similar to father-daughter incest, with a tendency for the granddaughters to turn to promiscuity or show features of personality disorders after termination of the incestuous liaison. Lukianowicz (1972) described a case where the male participant had sexual relations for variable periods of time with each of five granddaughters; he had previously had incestuous relations with two of his own three daughters and one of the granddaughters was probably also his daughter. Social isolation characterized this case.

Uncle-niece incest. Uncle-niece incest is similar to father-daughter incest—in fact, the incestuous object choices made by the uncle and niece symbolically represent the daughter and father, respectively. Lukianowicz (1972) described three of four incestuous uncles as normal (though perhaps "oversexed"); the fourth was alcoholic with psychopathic traits.

Aunt-nephew incest. Like mother-son incest, aunt-nephew incestuous relationships are very uncommon and bespeak more severe emotional disorder among the participants than do other forms of incestuous activity. Of two cases described by Lukianowicz (1972), one aunt was clearly hypomanic, the other promiscuous and perhaps slightly elated; one of the two nephews was described as shy, withdrawn, and passive and the other was described as normal.

Homosexual incest. In Western cultures, the sanctions against homosexuality and incest are both strong, and the clinical occurrence of homosexual incest is very uncommon. Important dynamic determinants appear to be avoidance of feared but desired heterosexual incest, profound distortions of intrafamilial roles and boundaries (the dysfunctional family), collusion by the opposite-sexed nonparticipant family members, and the maintenance of "family secrets."

In a case described by Raybin (1969), the central figure was a highly intelligent professor in his mid-40's who became depressed and guilty when his 20-year-old son became acutely psychotic during an intrafamilial homosexual affair. The father's psychiatric diagnosis was felt to be borderline state or pseudoneurotic schizophrenia—he believed his homosexual advances may have precipitated his son's psychosis. The son was bright and articulate but had been experimenting with psychodysleptic drugs before his acute psychosis, and developed the somatic delusion that his limbs were gangrenous. The father's incestuous activity had apparently included his own father (described as patriarchal and ambivalently loved and hated), his brother, his cousin, and his son. In therapy, the patient talked readily about incestuous, homosexual, sadomasochistic, and murderous themes, perhaps as a defensive maneuver against an incestuous wish for his mother. He displayed both compulsive and hysterical traits. The patient appeared to be perpetuating a family fantasy between grandfather, father, and son that the family inheritance was exclusively in the male line. Women were viewed in very hostile terms. They silently colluded with the incestuous activity.

Course and Prognosis

It has already been noted that in cases of father-daughter incest the father usually begins the relationship with his oldest daughter then proceeds to include one or more of her younger sisters. The activity may proceed for some time before discovery or disclosure, but after that recidivism is uncommon and breakup of the family unit often occurs.

As a rule, if the adults involved in an incestuous relationship between father and daughter harbor little anxiety or guilt about it, the daughter will do the same. This is especially true if the nonparticipating adult is permissive and allows or encourages the incestuous behavior to be expressed in an open and forthright way. The incestuous daughter may be relatively free of guilt feelings until she is exposed to censure from parents or authorities. Sometimes, however, the daughter's sense of guilt causes her to give up the relationship of her own accord, and sometimes she may give up incestuous activity with the father only to turn to compulsive and reckless promiscuity with other men, perhaps as an equivalent of neurotic symptom formation.

There is little agreement about the role of father-daughter incest as a cause of serious subsequent psychopathology. Among those girls who become involved in therapy, a façade of maturity, competence, and responsibility is often found to mask a hostile-dependent way of relating to older women and a proneness to making impossible demands and acting out seriously when their demands are frustrated. One view is that a parent who uses a child sexually produces conflict between the stimulated adult genital sexuality and the more appropriate social tendency for sublimation of sexuality in school and play, fostering lasting confusion and ambivalence in attitudes toward family relationships.

However, incestuous relationships do not always seem to have a traumatic effect. The father-daughter liaison satisfies instinctual drives in a setting where mutual alliance with an omnipotent adult condones the transgression. Moreover, the act offers an opportunity to test in reality an infantile fantasy whose consequences are found to be gratifying and pleasurable. It has even been suggested that the ego's capacity for sublimation is favored by the pleasure afforded by incest and that such incestuous activity diminishes the subject's chance of psychosis and allows a better adjustment to the external world. There is often found to be little deleterious influence on the subsequent personality of the incestuous daughter. One study found the vast majority of them to be none the worse for the experience—many were married with children and several were respected members of their communities.

Bender and Blau (1937) reported that

daughters show immediate harmful effects in the form of prolongation of the infantile stage with sacrifice of the stage of latency, and in some instances mental retardation, anxiety states, and, in prepubertal girls, a premature development of adolescent interests and independence. A preoccupation with fantasies and a withdrawal from childhood activities in some cases led to the appearance of stupidity or a schizoid personality.

Kaufman et al. (1954) reported that daughters manifested depression and guilt after disclosure of incest. However, the guilt apparently derived as much from disruption of the home as from the act of incest. Some girls were suicidal, others showed mood swings, and most had the somatic complaints of depression—fatigue, loss of appetite, generalized aches and pains, inability to concentrate, and sleep disturbances. Several girls exhibited learning difficulties, several were sexually promiscuous, and many experienced somatic symptoms referable to the abdomen and accompanied by fantasies of pregnancy. They displayed a variety of behavioral methods of coping with their feelings, including the seeking of forgiveness from mother, resort to delinquency, sexual promiscuity, and the seeking of punishment. They appeared well integrated while permitted to act out, but became depressed when confined. The sexuality of the girls of course led to the arrest and incarceration of their fathers and to the disruption of their homes. The experience of having destructive omnipotent fantasies realized has a particularly damaging effect upon ego development and structure.

Anthropological literature quotes abundant instances of a disruptive and harmful effect of incest on its participants and of the dread or anger with which it is viewed by primitive cultures. Among the Trobrianders, Chiricahua Apache, and Tikopia, public disclosure of sibling incest called for suicide as the actual or supposed sanction. Devereux (1939) reported a Mohave shaman who committed incest with a married daughter. The daughter came to believe she had been bewitched and became ill with a fatal mental illness. Her mother and sister subsequently became psychotic and died.

Divergent findings about the harmfulness of incest are age- and culture-related. Occurrence and especially disclosure of incest in a culture where that form of incest is strongly proscribed or carries institutionalized punishment is, of course, more damaging to the participants than if the cultural attitude is mild or indifferent. For father-daughter incest, the preadolescent daughter appears less harmed by the occurrence than the older girl. This difference may be a consequence of the greater strength of inhibiting mechanisms after puberty, with adolescents considering incest socially reprehensible while children react to it no differently than to other forms of sexual activity. (The childhood incestuous liaison is usually repressed and forgotten, perhaps to reappear in later life in the form of neurotic conflicts). However, a sampling error may underly this generalization: bearing in mind the active or even initiating role of the daughter, greater age of the participant daughter may be a reflection of her already more serious psychopathology than would be the case if she were younger.

Treatment

The prevention and treatment of clinical incest are complicated by the multidetermined nature of its occurrence, by difficulty in ascertaining what weight to assign to each of the many contributing factors, and by the limited accessibility of many of these factors to post facto therapy. Furthermore, is the occurrence of incest necessarily pathological at all? A culturally determined moral imperative has been violated—the need for and choice of treatment must be decided on the basis of the response of the participants to their alleged transgression, and to personal factors that may or may not be particularly related to the occurrence of incest.

PREVENTION

Messer (1969) suggested some specific preventive measures. Legal adoption of stepchildren and (in reconstituted families) relinquishing of financial support provided by the absent parent may serve to strengthen the family structure and thereby strengthen the incest taboo and diminish the likelihood of clinical incest. A couple may usefully reinvigorate and reconfirm their mutuality through second honeymoons whereby exclusive possession in the children's absence is asserted. The marital bond is strengthened and the temptation to seek romantic gratification from a child is diminished. In reconstituted families, open discussion of the fact that remarriage involved no deliberate disloyalty to the deceased or departed spouse may help foster healthier relationships. Openly affectionate parents give their children firm models upon which to develop a healthy heterosexual role identification.

The use of names is important. Weich (1968) observed that the terms "mother" and "father" serve to buttress the incest taboo, and he suggested that children should be discouraged from referring to their parents by first names. However, parents should probably be encouraged to recognize the normalcy of the family romance, even to institutionalize it as a greater part of the family's conscious awareness. It is surely normal to wish for or fantasize a child or parent in a sexual role—this fact is frequently recognized in smiles or gestures, or as a reaction formation by avoidance.

THERAPY

When appropriate and warranted, intensive psychotherapy or psychoanalysis can be recommended. Other approaches to treatment include open and frank discussion of sex emphasizing the normalcy of incestuous feelings and wishes but the inadvisability of acting upon such wishes, substitution of alternative modes of (symbolic) expression in play or social interaction, and healthy affection from other adults in the environment. Where major emotional or psychiatric difficulties exist, institutionalization may be required.

Clinical incest may usefully be viewed as a symptom of family maladjustment, and family therapy aimed at a healthier role allocation may be indicated. Interpretive work should focus on the pervasive use of denial as a defense, stressing not only the denial of the incestuous act but also of the extensive dysfunctional role relationships within the family and of the collusion of nonparticipating members.

Evaluation of therapy. Incest is an act, or series of acts, more than a condition or illness—indeed, whether or not it is necessarily pathological per se can be vigorously debated. Since it is difficult to define the very act of incest, the necessity for and nature of treatment is accordingly variable, and its outcome is difficult to discuss in a general way.

To avoid a lengthy discourse of dubious relevance, one may reasonably state that where the incestuous act occurs in association with acute psychiatric illness effective treatment of the latter is very likely to lead to a remission of symptoms. Once incestuous behavior is disclosed and discussed, it is not likely to recur.

REFERENCES

Barry, M. J., and Johnson, A. M. The incest barrier. Psychoanal. Q., 27: 485, 1958.

Bender, L., and Blau, A. The reaction of children to sexual relations with adults. Am. J. Orthopsychiatry, 7: 500, 1937.

Cavallin, H. Incestuous fathers: A clinical report. Am. J. Psychiatry, 122:14 1132, 1966.

Cormier, B. M., Kennedy, M., and Sangowicz, J. Psychodynamics of father-daughter incest. Can. Psychiatr. Assoc. J., 7: 203, 1962.

Devereux, G. The social and cultural implications of incest among the Mohave Indians. Psychoanal. Q., 8: 510, 1939.

Dubreuil, G. Les bases psycho-culturelles du tabou de l'inceste, Can. Psychiatr. Assoc. J., 7: 218, 1962.

Fox, J. R. Sibling incest. Br. J. Sociol., 13: 128, 1962.

*Freud, S. Totem and Taboo (1912-13). In Standard Edition of the Complete Psychological Works of Sigmund Freud, J. Strachey, editor, vol. 13. Hogarth Press, London, 1955.

Gordon, L. Incest as revenge against the pre-oedipal mother. Psychoanal. Rev., 42: 284, 1955.

Heims, L. W., and Kaufman, I. Variations on a theme of incest. Am. J. Orthopsychiatry, 33: 311, 1963.

*Henderson, D. J. Incest: A synthesis of data. Can. Psychiatr. Assoc. J., 17: 299, 1972.

Kardiner, A. The Individual and His Society: The Psychodynamics of Primitive Social Organizations. Columbia University Press, New York, 1939.

*Kaufman, I., Peck, A. L., and Tagiuri, C. K. The family constellation and overt incestuous relations between father and daughter. Am. J. Orthopsychiatry, 24: 266, 1954.

Lindzey, G. Some remarks concerning incest, the incest taboo, and psychoanalytic theory. Am. J. Psychol., 22: 1051, 1967.

*Lukianowicz, N. Incest. Br. J. Psychiatry, 120: 301, 1972.

*Lustig, N., Dresser, J. W., Spellman, S. W., and Murray, T. B. Incest: A family group survival pattern. Arch. Gen. Psychiatry, *14:* 31, 1966.

Lutier, J. Role des facteurs culturels et psycho-sociaux dans les delits incestueux en milieu rural. Ann. Med. Leg., *41:* 80, 1961.

Machotka, P., Pittman, F. S., and Flomenhaft, K. Incest as a family affair. Fam. Proc., *6:* 98, 1967.

Magal, V., and Winnik, H. Z. Role of incest in family structure. Isr. Ann. Psychiatry. *5:* 173, 1968.

*Messer, A. A. The "Phaedra complex." Arch. Gen. Psychiatry, *21:* 213, 1969.

Raphling, D. L., Carpenter, B. L., and Davis, A. Incest: A genealogical study. Arch. Gen. Psychiatry, *16:* 505, 1967.

Rascovsky, P., and Rascovsky, M., The prohibition of incest, filicide and the sociocultural process. Int. J. Psychoanal., *53:* 271, 1972.

Rascovsky, M., and Rascovsky, A. On consummated incest, Int. J. Psychoanal., *31:* 42, 1950.

Raybin, J. B. Homosexual incest. J. Nerv. Ment. Dis., *148:* 105, 1969.

Rhinehart, J. W. Genesis of overt incest. Compr. Psychiatry, *2:* 338, 1961.

Riemer, S. Research notes on incest. Am. J. Sociol., *7:* 566, 1940.

Slater, M. Ecological factors in the origin of incest. Am. Anthropol., *61:* 1042, 1959.

Sloane, P., and Karpinski, E. Effect of incest on the participants. Am. J. Orthopsychiatry, *12:* 666, 1942.

Sonden, T. Die Inzestverbrechen in Schweden und Ihre Ursachen. Acta Psychiatr. Neurol., *11:* 379, 1936.

Szabo, D. Problemes de socialisation et d'integration socio-culturelles: Contribution a l'etiologie de l'inceste. Can. Psychiatr. Assoc. J., *7:* 235, 1962.

Talcott-Parsons, T. The incest taboo in relation to social structure and the socialization of the child. Br. J. Sociol., *5:* 101, 1954.

Weich, M. J. The terms "Mother" and "Father" as a defense against incest. J. Am. Psychoanal. Assoc., *16:* 783, 1968.

Weinberg, S. K. *Incest Behavior.* Citadel Press, New York, 1955.

Weiner, I. B. Father-daughter incest: A clinical report. Psychiatr. Q., *36:* 607, 1962.

*Weiner, I. B. On incest: A survey. Excerpta Criminol., *4:* 137, 1964.

Wolf, A. P. Adopt a daughter-in-law, marry a sister: A Chinese solution to the problem of the incest taboo. Am. Anthropol., *70:* 864, 1968.

15.7   Other Sexual Deviations

ROBERT L. SADOFF, M.D.

Introduction and Definition

The American Psychiatric Association's *Diagnostic and Statistical Manual of Mental Disorders* defines sexual deviations as follows.

This category is for individuals whose sexual interests are directed primarily toward objects other than people of the opposite sex, toward sexual acts not usually associated with coitus or toward coitus performed under bizarre circumstances as in necrophilia, pedophilia, sexual sadism and fetishism. Even though many find their practices distasteful they remain unable to substitute normal sexual behavior for them. This diagnosis is not appropriate for individuals who perform deviant sexual acts because normal sexual objects are not available to them.

In April 1974, the Association's official list of mental disorders was changed to include the term *sexual orientation disturbance* describing individuals whose sexual interests are directed toward persons of the same sex and who are disturbed by or in conflict with that orientation, or persons who wish to change. This diagnostic category is distinguished from homosexuality which by itself does not constitute a psychiatric disorder.

The list of deviations includes fetishism, pedophilia, transvestism, exhibitionism, voyeurism, sadism, masochism, and other sexual deviations. Others that may be added are rape, lust murder, necrophilia, bestiality, and sodomy. This section will not consider homosexuality, since it has been considered elsewhere. The sexual deviations may be subcategorized by the object of the sexual activity:

1. Sexual behavior involving other human beings includes rape, lust murder, necrophilia, pedophilia, sadomasochism, exhibitionism, voyeurism, sodomy, and incest.
2. Sexual behavior involving other than human beings includes bestiality, fetishism, and transvestism.

Friedman (1959) states:

Broadly speaking we designate as sexual deviations or perversions any patterns of sexual behavior which differ from normal coitus and serve as major sources of sexual gratification rather than as foreplay to coital activity.

Thus the deviation is considered only if that behavior is substituted for normal penovaginal coital relationship. Deviant acts must be distinguished from deviancy—that is, much foreplay may be in the form of deviant acts, but if these acts serve only to stimulate for normal coitus they are not considered part of a deviational pattern or performed by a sexual deviate.

Psychoanalytic theory indicates that sexual deviation is either a regression to or a fixation at an earlier level of psychosexual development resulting in a repetitive pattern of sexual behavior that is not mature or genital in its application and expression. One of the classic works on this phenomenon was Freud's "Three Essays on the Theory of Sexuality" (1905), which describes regression and fixation. Lorand and Schneer present the psychoanalytic interpretation of sexual deviation in the first edition of this textbook. They indicate that "infantile forms of libidinal aggressive drive expression are the raw materials of sexual deviation."

Psychoanalytic theory also states that castration anxiety is common to all sexual deviations. The genital individual psychosexually is able to express sex and love simultaneously or to express love with sexual contact at a fairly mature level. The sexual deviate, however, utilizes sex as a vehicle for the expression of other feelings such as hostility or anxiety and is either regressed or fixated at an earlier psychosexual level of development. Basically,

the sexual deviate is attempting to handle his anxieties regarding his sexual urges and his relationship with others especially of the opposite sex.

Early descriptions of sexual deviations may be found in Krafft-Ebing's book, *Psychopathia Sexualis* (1922). Krafft-Ebing felt that the deviations were hereditary or constitutional. Kraepelin referred to the sexual deviation as a form of degeneracy. This appellation has been carried through by psychiatrists and has influenced the law in negative and harsh punishment for sexual deviants.

Aggressive Deviations

A classification that is useful in understanding sexual deviations is that distinguishing the "anonymous sexual deviants" from the "aggressive sexual deviants." The aggressive deviants include those who commit rape, lust murder, sadomasochism, pedophilia, necrophilia, and sodomy. The aggression is directed toward another human being, alive or dead, using the vehicle of sexuality for the expression of the aggression and hostility. Thus, the rapist may, with sufficient aggressive force, become a lust murderer, and those who commit lust murder may also practice necrophilia. The sadist and/or masochist may be directly or passively aggressive with his partner.

Sodomy is a general legal term usually referring to unnatural sex acts and including almost anything that is not penovaginal intercourse. However, its common usage is for pederasty or penile-anal relationships or oral-genital contact. In heterosexual relationships, if anal intercourse is found to be exclusively satisfying without considering penovaginal contact, then it is considered an aggressive deviation. Incest is also a directly aggressive deviation from the normal since there are taboos against sexual contact within families. Pedophilia (the love of children or sexual contact with children) is also considered a directly aggressive deviation.

Anonymous Deviations

Anonymous sexual deviations refer to a group of sexual deviations that appear to be on a continuum and yet involve gradually decreasing contact with the object of the sexual desire. The first of these is frottage, in which the deviant is one who touches in public places. The usual object of his touching is the breast or buttocks of a female in a crowded train or elevator. He wishes no further contact with the individual and appears to obtain gratification from this fleeting physical touch. He is called a frotteur, or one who touches. Usually, the frotteur does not go beyond this form of touching and is not considered to be dangerous or likely to be involved in more serious or dangerous aggressive sexual deviations.

EXHIBITIONISM

The next in line on the continuum is the exhibitionist, who exposes his genitals either directly to an unwitting female or females, or passively in a group, or at the window of his home. There are a number of ways in which the exhibitionist expresses this deviation, and often he is not apprehended until he has exposed himself a number of times. The mode of operation is usually quite consistent and, in many cases, involves his own automobile. A number of exhibitionists have indicated that they would not break their usual pattern for fear of apprehension. Some have exposed themselves on buses and subways and others by walking down the street. There is often a hint of pedophilia with the exhibitionist who will expose himself primarily to young girls. The exhibitionist also is attempting to resolve particular problems within himself and is not considered to be a dangerous individual, nor will he "graduate" to more serious sexual deviations.

VOYEURISM

The next in the continuum is the voyeur or peeping tom. He is also not particularly interested in making specific contact with his victim or the object of his sexual desires. His primary interest is to achieve orgasmic expression through viewing others involved either in sexual relations or through viewing a woman in the nude in her home. He is usually apprehended for loitering and prowling and rarely does he go on to become a more serious sexual deviant.

OBSCENE TELEPHONE CALLING

The obscene telephone caller is the next on the continuum. He achieves sexual gratification from calling young women on the phone and making obscene remarks that suggest that the woman on the other end will meet him and perform sexual relations. The obscene telephone caller may be apprehended by having the woman he calls plan to meet him at a certain place, where the police can be available. For some reason, the phone caller is näive enough to accept the invitation and is usually apprehended.

OBSCENE LETTER WRITING

Next is the obscene letter writer, who is at a further distance from the object of his sexual desires since he merely writes a letter and does not make physical contact by voice on the telephone.

A clear example of the dynamics involved in this deviation is a 26-year-old man who wrote about 200 letters over a 10-year period to other men, indicating that he was going to spread-eagle them with the help of several of his friends and penetrate their anus with his very large phallus. When he was apprehended, after 10 years of such letter writing, he indicated that he had no idea why he was writing these letters but that he seemed to be compelled to do so. Careful examination of his earlier history revealed that at the age of 16 he was so spread-eagled himself by four other boys in the locker room after school. He used this method of working out the anxiety of this traumatic experience, which he had revealed to no one, much like the youngster who comes home and plays dentist after having a dental trauma in early childhood.

FETISHISM

Further away from the object of sexual desire is the fetishist, who is interested in his sexual object only through a displacement to a part of her clothing, either a shoe or a stocking or underwear or a brassiere. Often, the fetishist is one who is able to achieve orgasm only through masturbation with the object of the fetish nearby. There are two types of fetishists, the hard and soft. The hard fetishist is involved with rubber and leather objects; the soft fetishist uses fur, feathers, and other such materials. These individuals may be arrested for burglary or for stealing the objects of their fetishistic desires.

General Considerations of Deviations

The purpose of this section is to indicate the relationship between and among the sexual deviations on other than castration-anxiety grounds. The continuum described is based on anxiety of direct confrontation or contact with the desired sexual object. Thus, the series of deviant behaviors representing continually decreasing closeness to the sexual object has been labeled anonymous sexual deviation, since the deviate wants little or no direct confrontation. Sexual intercourse may be fantasied but is rare in these types of deviations; although, on occasion, the deviate may be able to have normal penovaginal intercourse. These deviations are primarily, but not exclusively, male behaviors. There have been instances in which a woman has been arrested for lewdness for exposing herself in public, but this exposure is usually connected with an entertainment or other commercial enterprise.

Frequently, the exhibitionist will masturbate as he is exposing himself, as will the voyeur as he is peeping. Occasionally, they will return to their homes and fantasy the experience of either exposing or watching and masturbate to the fantasy. At other times, there will be no masturbatory activity.

GROUP VERSUS INDIVIDUAL ACTIVITY

These kinds of deviations are usually conducted alone. One does not usually see groups of exhibitionists or voyeurs. Sometimes two or three adolescent girls will make obscene telephone calls; rarely will more than one be involved in letter writing, which becomes a specific resolution to internal conflicts. Sometimes, young adolescent boys will get together in crowds to practice frottage, but in adult life these deviations are usually committed by one person rather than in group functions. The groups are more likely seen in adolescent behavior.

With respect to groups of people in sexual deviations, group sex has recently become more openly discussed and practiced. Group deviations may also be observed in terms of sodomy, oral and anal sex, and lack of privacy with voyeuristic and exhibitionistic tendencies occurring in group activity. Wife swapping, or "swinging," especially if conducted in public, or if the sexual relations are viewed by the other spouses, may be seen as having sexual qualities. Menage a trois, in which two individuals of the same sex and one of the opposite sex perform sexual acts on each other, reveals homosexual tendencies as well as other voyeuristic and exhibitionistic tendencies.

Group rape, or "gang bang," as it is often called by adolescents, has homosexual qualities in the sense that a number of men are inserting their genitals into the same receptacle and sharing a fairly intimate activity.

The individual sexual deviations are considered below.

Rape

Rape is the penetration of the female by the male genital by means of force, fraud, or fear. Rape may be regarded as a fusion of aggressive and sexual impulses expressed in a single act. Others may see rape as utilizing sexual behavior as a vehicle for the expression of hostility, especially toward women. Often, rape is not considered a sexual deviation unless it is aggravated or there is force attached. Fraud, deception, statutory rape, or other forms of manipulation may be considered expressions of the masculine urge to coital activity, although some of the partners may not be fully cooperative or willing. Some men are repeated rapists and have a specific compulsive urge to harm the object of their sexual relations. This may be an expression of a need to expiate guilt and hostility toward the seductive mother. Incarceration tends to keep the rapist from performing his deviant behavior, but, after freedom from incarceration, he has been known to return to this activity without having learned or been able to control himself by virtue of his earlier periods of confinement. For some, the rape activity is a temporary expression that is not repeated.

Lust Murder

The more serious expression of this fusion of hostility and sexual urge may be seen in the lust murder or the rape murder cases, which, fortunately, are rare and often occur in clusters or groups. This type of behavior is extreme and usually is highly publicized—an example is the Boston Strangler, the community rapist and murderer. Often, the victims are prostitutes or women whom the rapist finds to be immoral or guilt ridden, or for whom he feels a calling to destroy. In these cases, the rape comes first and the murder may be conducted at the time of the rape or shortly after it. On the other hand, necrophilia—sexual intercourse with a corpse—is seen rarely but most frequently after a murder, where the rapist has sexual relations with the victim he has killed.

Sadomasochism

Lust murder may be related to the much more common phenomenon of sadomasochism. The sadist is an individual who wishes to express harm or gain sexual satisfaction from harming another person. The masochist, on the other hand, gains sexual gratification by experiencing pain before, during, or after a sexual act. Sometimes, the sexual pain may be in lieu of sexual relationships. The sadist takes his name from the Marquis de Sade, who was known for his cruel and brutal attacks on people, especially women. The term masochist comes from the 19th-century Austrian novelist, Leopold von Sacher-Masoch. There are by far many fewer sadists than there are masochists, and it is often difficult to find a "good sadist" who will gratify the masochist in the most optimal manner. Often, sadists are prostitutes who get paid for acting sadistic and perform a role that is expected of them and for which they are instructed by the masochist. Masochists are most often men who enjoy being flagellated, bound, whipped, or insulted preliminary to sexual relationships. Many women make a good living using such accessories as black stockings, high black heels, leather gloves, a leather whip, and other black or leather paraphernalia.

Part of the masochistic ritual includes a fetishistic experience and often a transvestite approach. Many men prefer to undergo their masochistic experiences while dressed in women's clothes. The fetishist may prefer a private experience in which he achieves orgasm by use of an inanimate object which reminds him of the primary love object that is not available to him. The transvestite and the masochist and the fetishist may also have homosexual tendencies and prefer to have the whippings performed by a male while they are in "drag" costume.

Sodomy

The laws of many states refer to any abnormal sexual act other than penovaginal coitus between lawfully married male and female as sodomy. Sodomy specifically refers to pederasty or anal intercourse between homosexuals and takes its name from the ancient city of Sodom, in which much sinful activity was observed. Sodomy also is used to describe abnormal acts with animals, which is now called bestiality or zoophilia. An individual may achieve orgasm or sexual gratification by having sexual contact with animals rather than human beings. This may be due in part to the lack of availability of human beings, especially in the case of shepherds who are known to have intercourse with animals in their flock. Some people have sexual relations or activities with pets such as dogs or cats or other animals such as chickens. If the activity with animals is primary and excludes human contact, it is considered to be a deviation or perversion. However, if the activity is sporadic and occurs only when human beings are not available for sexual expression, the diagnosis of deviation does not really apply.

Transvestism

The transvestite—usually a male—obtains sexual pleasure by wearing the clothing of the opposite sex and often masturbating while so dressed. This deviation is also related to castration anxiety in that the male reassures himself that even the female has a penis because he is the embodiment of that conclusion. He cannot tolerate the notion that some people are without a penis, or "castrated." He thus identifies with the woman who has a penis and also sees her as his love object. The transvestite is often homosexual, preferring males; he may also reveal fetishistic and masochistic aspects.

The transvestite in adolescence may pose a danger to his own life. Occasionally, death results from strangulation in a rare deviation in which the adolescent boy dresses up in his mother's clothes and attempts to achieve orgasm through near-asphyxiation by strangulation with one of her stockings. The boy will be found dead in a closet with evidence of seminal discharge indicating sexual involvement. Histories from other adolescents who have not died in this manner indicate that they are able to achieve sexual orgasm at the height of the asphyxiation and then are able to cut themselves down without succumbing. However, in many cases, the deviate goes too far and dies from strangulation shortly after orgasm.

Incest

Incest is seen most frequently in families that are isolated from the mainstream of society or are found in highly clustered urban ghettos. Mostly, the incestuous behavior is between father and daughter or between siblings. Cases of mother-son incest have been reported but none without the finding of either mother or son, or both, to be psychotic. The taboo against mother-son incest is the strongest of all sexual taboos. The rationalization by the father is that he is teaching his daughter how to love a man or he is taking what is rightly his, and often alludes to passages in the Bible which he may claim, justify his behavior. Occasionally, this type of Bible-rattling is found in psychotic men.

PEDOPHILIA

Pedophilia literally means love of children, but it is generally used to signify a sexual deviation in which an individual has an abnormal erotic sexual desire for children. Pedophilia may be homosexual or heterosexual. The pedophile is usually visualized as the "monster on the corner" who is ready to pick up innocent children. Thus, schools and parents warn children never to take rides with strangers. There are a number of individuals who are pedophilic in their

orientation and who do commit predatory acts and go after young children. However, by far the greatest amount of pedophilic behavior is in families or among friends and neighbors. Often it is a one-time activity in which a male who has been denied or deprived of adult female sexual gratification becomes intoxicated and turns to the children.

The pedophile may feel impotent or unable to perform adequately with adult females. Often, his pedophilic behavior will be expressed after a fight with his wife or a put-down by a friend or neighbor. The wife not only denies her husband sexually but also may berate him and make him feel less than a man. Unconscious feelings of hostility, resentment, and vindictiveness toward women may be expressed in the pedophilic behavior. It should be pointed out here that this type of psychodynamic relationship between husband and wife in which this berating activity occurs may lead to sexual deviations other than pedophilia, including exhibitionism, sexual assault, sodomy, or rape. The following illustrates the dynamics involved in an incestuous pedophilic relationship.

Jack is a 45-year-old, separated black male with three children. When his oldest daughter was about 9, his wife attended church meetings on a regular nightly basis. She refused her daughter's request to leave the house and Jack had to stay with the children. During his wife's religious preoccupation, Jack was denied sexual relations, and he began to suspect that his wife was seeing another man. He drank beer when his wife was away and began to observe his daughter maturing. His daughter became rebellious against the mother and lay in her bed in seductive positions while her father waited for his wife to come home. On several occasions, she would approach him, kiss him good night, and then go to her room. Later, the contact between father and daughter began to increase and expand to lap-sitting and mouth-kissing, which became deeper and longer. Jack knew he was becoming increasingly involved with his daughter and, after several experiences at penovaginal relations with her, he attempted to stop the relationship. He was unable to stop, however, because his daughter became more seductive and encouraged continuation with the threat that she would tell her mother if he stopped.

Cases of pedophilia typically involve alcohol and a berating wife. The pedophile needs to leave home to find companionship and sexual satisfaction. He chooses an immature sexual object because of his fear of the castrating, aggressive, mother-wife adult female.

In the United States, the pedophile is defined as one whose sexual contact is with a child under the age of 12 or up to the age of 14. The molester is 10 years or more older than the victim. In Canada, Mohr et al. (1964) indicate that the maximum age for their study on pedophilia was 15. Other studies have gone as high as 16 for the maximum age of the victim.

Exhibitionism

Exhibitionism is related to pedophilia in that the exhibitionist has a specific need to expose himself to others, often young women, in order to note their shocked response at the sight of his penis. The dynamics behind exhibitionism and pedophilia often are similar. There is a fear of castration and the need to reassure oneself that one is able to perform. Again, these are male-dominated deviations in which the individual either exposes himself or has relations with a young child in order to prove to himself that he still has masculine ability and has not lost his manhood because of his wife's tirades or mistreatment by other women in his early life.

The exhibitionist always indicates that he is exposing himself, supposedly to make contact with the woman and thereby get her to have sexual relations with him. However, rarely does an exhibitionist succeed in enticing a woman to have relations with him by exposing his penis to her, and yet all continue this compulsive, repetitive behavior. In fact, if a woman were to show interest in the exhibitionist, the great majority would run the other way, preferring not to have to prove what they already fear, that they are sexually inadequate. It is thus important that they choose a victim who is unlikely to offer this type of confrontation.

An example of the compulsive nature of exhibitionism is to be found in a 47-year-old, married, white, skilled laborer, who began exposing himself in public at the age of 18. He was apprehended frequently and given probation early in his adult life. After his third arrest, however, he was given a 2-year jail sentence. Shortly after he emerged from prison, he exposed himself again and spent another 2 years in prison. His repetitive exhibitionism led to a total of 18 years in prison by the time he was 43 years old. He had been married at age 25 and had continued difficulties with his wife, who berated him and toward whom he felt no love, but mostly anxiety and anger. He could clearly point to the times when he felt inadequate with his wife and immediately went out and exposed himself.

After his divorce from his wife, it was presumed that his exhibitionistic tendencies would improve. However, he was arrested shortly after his divorce and spent another year in prison. Upon his release, he met a woman with whom he began to have frequent sexual relations. He had no sexual difficulties with her; in fact, he felt quite adequate and potent. Often, he would brag about his sexual abilities with this woman, whom he later married. Shortly after his marriage began, he found that he was impotent with his wife. He then began exposing himself again and was soon apprehended and placed on probation. Shortly before the birth of his first and only child, he exposed himself again and was placed on further probation.

His wife was brought into the treatment in order to help maintain external controls, since his internal controls were not functioning effectively. He described substitute behavior for exposing himself, namely, calling lewd names to young girls from his open car window. He also began making obscene telephone calls, which he readily admitted to his wife and shortly discontinued. He had a specific means of exposing himself in his car and never exposed himself while walking on the street or in any other vehicle.

It was decided that the only way of helping him would be to prohibit him from driving in his car alone to and from work, or at any other time. His wife was determined to keep him out of his car alone to prevent further arrest. On one occasion, she slipped in her vigilance and he yielded to his compulsive need and was rearrested. For the past 2 years, he has not driven in his automobile alone and has not exposed himself again. He indicates that he continues to have the urge to do so and finds young girls appealing, seductive, and inviting. When his urges to expose himself are heightened, his ability to perform sexually with his wife diminishes.

This case clearly indicates the compulsive character of the exhibitionistic urge and the need for external controls after the specific mode of exhibitionism has been defined. Years of individual and group psychotherapy were ineffective in controlling the behavior, but were helpful for this patient understanding his underlying conflict and in relating more effectively to his wife and family.

Bestiality

The human being who engages in bestiality (zoophilia) achieves sexual gratification by having intercourse with a living animal. In Kinsey's sampling, intercourse with animals was the least frequent form of human sexual behavior; it was most common in the preadolescent years and in rural areas. One-third of the males who lived in rural areas and were in the upper educational level had had sexual intercourse with an animal to the point of orgasm.

The animal symbolizes the phallus. Identification with a small animal gratifies the wish for tender, loving care that the helpless animal (child) requires; a large animal enables identification with the parental role in the child-parent relationship.

A pet may rub its genitalia against the leg of a child or an adult in the family. The acquiescent human's role in this as a possible masturbatory equivalent is denied, thus sparing self-implication. An active role may be played when the human masturbates the animal by rubbing its genitalia. Rubbing the human genitals against the fur of the animal is a more direct form of masturbation. Fellatio and cunnilingus are frequent techniques.

For adolescents, the use of an animal as a transitional object in avoidance of incestuous and masturbation conflicts is usually relinquished when success in socialization with peers of the opposite sex occurs. When the bestiality persists into adulthood, the underlying disorder should be treated by psychoanalytic psychotherapy or psychoanalysis.

Hypersexuality

This condition in men (satyriasis) or women (nymphomania) is characterized by an excessive and constant preoccupation with the desire for coitus. It is usually associated with compulsive masturbation. It may result from organic dysfunction such as temporal lobe disorders, cerebral syphilis, or excessive use of drugs, particularly marijuana, cocaine, or testosterone. Psychological causes include the need to prove one's masculinity or femininity, the search for intimacy and love, or manifestations of unresolved oedipal conflicts in which the individual is constantly searching unconsciously for the opposite-sex parent.

Excretory Perversions

Coprophilia. Sexual pleasure associated with the desire to defecate on a partner or to be defecated upon or to eat feces (coprophagia) are perversions associated with fixations at the anal stage of psychosexual development. Symbolically the individual attempts to deny castration fears via the equation *feces=penis*. A variant of the perversion is the compulsive utterance of obscene words (coprolalia) in which the person attempts to master sexual fears by "magical" incantations. Coprolalia is also associated with Gilles de la Tourette's disease with accompanying spasmodic tics and echolalia.

Urolagnia. Sexual pleasure associated with the desire to urinate on a partner or to be urinated upon is a form of urethral eroticism. It has been observed in persons who tended to be overprotected by mothers who had extreme ambitions for their children. Urethral eroticism may be associated with masturbatory techniques involving the insertion of foreign objects into the urethra for sexual stimulation in both men and women.

Multiple Deviations

Most textbooks tend to separate these deviations into specific categories, but it is quite clear that in any one individual a number of the deviations may occur at any one time.

An example of this overlap occurred, in a 33-year-old male art teacher who was arrested for indecent assault on a minor male child. The charge was that he touched the penis of a 15-year-old boy who was working in his art studio. He had the boy dress up in leather boots, pants, and jacket and was taking a picture of him. Allegedly, he wanted the boy to have an erection while in the leather material. What did not emerge in the official transcript, but was revealed in several evaluation sessions was that the sexual offender was a deviate, having primary fetishistic problems, preferring leather while achieving orgasm; having homosexual tendencies; possessing pedophilic inclinations in that he preferred sexual contact with young boys; and had the experience as well as the fantasies of being bound and whipped during orgasm and during masturbatory activities. He has also dressed in leather himself and in female clothes.

In this one individual, we see a number of deviations, including fetishism, masochism, homosexuality, pedophilia, and transvestism. If one wishes to include sodomy for oral-genital relations, as most laws do, then the list becomes even longer.

Socio-legal Considerations

Each individual deviate has a specific set of dynamics that he is attempting to handle in a specific manner. Disgnoses of sex deviations may include psychosis, organic brain damage, personality disorders, or psychoneurosis. The sexual deviate may fall into any category of diagnostic label as well as his behavioristic one based on his deviation. All sexual deviates are not dangerous and must not be treated as such. However, the aggressive sexual deviates may be quite dangerous and must be treated accordingly. It is not enough to say that castration anxiety is the common element in all sexual deviations. This may be true and may be helpful in psychoanalytic treatment of certain deviations. However, the protection of society and the prediction of violent sex offenders requires a more practical orientation. Most sexual deviants do not present themselves for voluntary treatment and cannot afford psychoanalytic therapy. They may be sent for treatment by courts or lawyers.

The laws are becoming more liberal and people are beginning to tolerate more deviational behavior as long as it is not threatening or dangerous. A number of people privately seek gratification of their sexual urges in the way they know best. Psychiatrists can help those who suffer or cause others to suffer from such deviations because of the regressive elements involved. However, many people prefer to experience their deviations and do so within controlled nonthreatening private situations. These people ought to be allowed the freedom to continue their private experiences as long as they do not offend or harm others. Just as homosexuality has been increasingly considered an alternate means of sexual expression rather than a deviation, so too other deviational acts, may eventually gain such acceptance.

A 25-year-old man with a leather fetish was arrested for pedophilic behavior. He felt more strongly about the leather problems than he did about his pedophilic assault. Once the legal charges were cleared and he was placed on probation, however, he was not as concerned about his interest in leather as he was previously. He preferred to maintain it because it brought him pleasure and he was not about to give it up as long as it would not lead to difficulty. For him, the treatment was focused on the control of his behavior with young boys so that he did not put himself in jeopardy of arrest for assaulting or attacking youngsters. He has learned how to enjoy the use of leather on individuals he wishes to be with in a most socially acceptable manner, without harming them.

Treatment

Thus, there are a number of alternate forms of sexual expression to penovaginal coital relations between male and female. A number of these practices occur in foreplay to penovaginal contact and are not considered deviations unless they are expressed exclusively and never lead to penovaginal coital relations. Some people prefer the "deviations" to "normal" sexual intercourse, often because of anxieties or feelings of inadequacy. As long as these experiences are practiced among consenting adults in private, without force and without involving children, there is no problem. It is only when these practices are disturbing to the participants that they may become available for psychiatric treatment.

The law may mandate psychiatric treatment for sexual offenders who practice these deviations when they place a person in a hospital or on probation. Men are sometimes placed in group psychotherapy and are able to learn from each other about controlling or regulating their behavior. More often than not, the sexual deviation is not "cured" by the treatment but behavior is regulated so that the individual does not continue to recidivate and get into further difficulty with the law. Treatment for many of the deviations is quite difficult, especially if there is a fixation at an earlier level of psychosexual development. The individual who has expressed his deviation under stress or under the influence of alcohol, leading to a temporary regression, is a much more successful candidate for treatment. More often than not, he learns what stresses bother him and how he has traditionally handled the stress by drinking, producing regressive sexual behavior.

Many in treatment, after initial arrest, are able to decrease alcohol intake and to recognize signs in their lives that could lead to deviational behavior. Primarily, treatment allows for use of greater judgment in the expression of the deviation to prevent rearrest, but often does not rid the patient of his deviational urges unless long term psychoanalytic treatment or aversive techniques are utilized.

REFERENCES

American Psychiatric Association. *Diagnostic and Statistical Manual of Mental Disorders,* ed. 2. Washington, D.C., 1968.

Ellis, H., *Psychology of Sex.* Hawthorn Books, New York, 1961.

*Freud, S. Three essays on the theory of sexuality. In *Standard Edition of the Complete Psychological Works of Sigmund Freud,* vol. 7, p. 123. Hogarth Press, London, 1953.

Friedman, P. Sexual deviations. American Handbook of Psychiatry, S. Arieti, editor, p. 589. Basic Books, New York, 1959.

Gagnon, J., and Simon, W., editors. *Sexual Deviance.* Harper & Row, New York, 1967.

Krafft-Ebing, R. V. *Psychopathia Sexualis.* Physicians and Surgeons, Brooklyn, N. Y., 1922.

*Mohr, J. W., Turner, R. E., and Jerry, M. D. *Pedophilic and Exhibitionism.* University of Toronto Press, Toronto, 1964.

*Peters, J. J., and Sadoff, R. L. Clinical observations of child molesters. Med. Asp. Hum. Sex., *4:* 20, 1970.

*Sadoff, R. L. Sexually deviated offenders. Temple Law Q., *40:* 205, 1967.

*Slovenko, R. *Sexual Behavior and the Law.* Charles C. Thomas, Springfield, Ill., 1965.

Wolfenden Report. Lancer, New York, 1964.

chapter 16 Treatment of Sexual Disorders

16.1 Individual Psychotherapy of Sexual Disorders

JON K. MEYER, M.D.

Introduction

By individual psychotherapy is meant treatment in the dyadic setting, involving a focus on patient associations, a nondidactic approach, an open-ended time frame, a skill in the use of transference, and a familiarity with psychodynamic and psychogenetic constructs. Frequency of sessions is not an issue here. Included are dynamically oriented, open-ended psychotherapy ranging from once a week to four or five times a week. There are obvious differences within this spectrum in depth of fantasy material, strength and accessibility of transference, and degree of therapist activity, but these techniques are separable in concept from behavioral, counseling, and group approaches. Excluded, from the point of view of this definition, are such treament modalities as systematic desensitization, classical aversive conditioning, and positive training (Yates, 1970); masturbation therapy (LoPiccolo and Lobitz, 1972); and group therapy (Parloff, 1968). Because of the excellence of reported results and the increasing utilization of the Masters and Johnson (1970) mode in treating sexual dis-

abilities, special mention is made of its relationship to dynamic therapy.

Symptom-Disease Controversy

There is a debate in contemporary psychiatry surrounding the view of a presenting psychological, behavioral, or psychosomatic difficulty as the disease itself or as a symptom, representing an underlying conflict operating out of awareness. In no area of interest is this controversy more heated than in sexual dysfunction. The proposed dichotomy between sexual disabilities with neurosis and those without neurosis has provided a point of controversy or, less benignly, an area of warfare between practitioners of directly interventive techniques and practitioners of dynamic psychotherapy. Both may react to the symptom-disease controversy in a reflex manner.

That it may be possible for sexual disabilities to derive from two sources, internal conflict and inappropriate learning, was suggested in 1905 by Freud in "Three Essays on the Theory of Sexuality":

. . . anyone who is in any way . . . abnormal mentally is invariably abnormal also in his sexual life. But many people are abnormal in their sexual life who in every other respect approximate to the average. . . .[They] passed through the process of human cultural development, in which sexuality remains the weak spot.

Clearly stated is the association between the neuroses and sexual dysfunction. Stated with equal clarity is the observation that sexual disabilities may occur as an outgrowth of inadequate or inappropriate acculturation. There are two issues: the degree to which sexual disability appears in pure culture, unassociated with neurotic or character disorders; and the degree to which the neurosis or character disorder, if present, may be separated from the dysfunction for purposes of treatment.

Masters and Johnson (1970), in speaking of selection procedures for their treatment program, indicated that "the psychoneurotic is acceptable . . . ." They take the position that sexual dysfunction may be productively separated from other neurotic problems— with the assumption that, if all goes well, psychotherapy could deal with the remainder in a facilitated manner. They go on to state that

Sociocultural deprivation and ignorance of sexual physiology, rather than psychiatric or medical illness, constitute the etiologic background for most sexual dysfunction.

The majority of marital units were not felt to evidence psychiatric problems, ignorance and deprivation constituting the etiological factors. In fact, psychosocial complications were felt to be derivative of the long standing sexual disability.

Support for the observations of Masters and Johnson has come from Maurice and Guze (1970). In a study of 20 couples in treatment at the Reproductive Biology Research Foundation, they reported that "the majority of patients were without any definable psychiatric disorder other than the sexual dysfunction." Psychiatric diagnoses, excluding sexual dysfunctions, were appended to one quarter of the men and one third of the women. Coexisting psychiatric dysfunction was considered to exist if treatment had been required or if there had been interferences with the patient's normal functioning.

Cooper (1968) has challenged the idea that neurosis has a high association with male potency disorders. He evaluated 53 patients with impotence, premature ejaculation, and ejaculatory incompetence. Neurosis was diagnosed clinically if the patient had defined symptoms of anxiety obsessional behavior, hysterical conversion, dissociation, or depressed mood sufficiently severe to impair work or social capacity. Only 10 per cent were felt to be suffering from a clinical neurosis, the anxiety and neuroticism being concentrated among the premature ejaculators. Cooper specifically excluded abnormalities of personality from consideration.

Other clinical findings have differed from those of Maurice and Guze and Cooper. O'Connor and Stern (1972a), in reviewing 96 patients with sexual dysfunction treated in individual psychotherapy and analysis, indicated that 65 per cent were classified as having character disorders, 33 per cent as neurotic, and 2 per cent as schizophrenic. As they state: "It was our impression that the sexual symptom was just one manifestation of a total personality problem . . . ." There is a possible difference in their sample from those of the previous authors, however, in that the sexual disability was not necessarily the motivating factor leading to consultation.

On the other hand, the author (unpublished data, 1973) reviewed data from clinical interviews of 26 sexual partnerships (52 individuals) and six singles (3 men and 3 women) who presented complaining of a primary sexual disability and requesting "Masters and Johnson treatment." A sexual dysfunction, without discernible other psychopathology, was found in 17 per cent of both men and women. Both sexual and associated neurotic or character pathology were diagnosed in 38 per cent of the men and 55 per cent of the women. Other psychiatric diagnoses, with no apparent sexual dysfunction, was found in 24 per cent of the men and 14 per cent of the women. Another 21 per cent of the men and 14 per cent of the women were felt to be free of any psychopathology, representing symptom-free partners. In this clinic population, it appears that sexual diagnoses are more common in association with other psychiatric disorders than in uncontaminated form.

The 26 partnerships were then compared for coexisting pathology. The singles, lacking a partner, were excluded. In no case was psychopathology absent from the partnership; one or the other partner exhibited sexual or other psychiatric disability. In 27 per cent of the partnerships, all psychopathology was resident in one partner. Both partners were felt to deserve primary sexual and other psychiatric diagnoses in 23 per cent of the cases. In 50 per cent of the couples, both partners were felt to have conditions justifying either a sexual or another diagnosis.

Others have observed that neurosis of a degree to interfere with gross functioning, as defined by Maurice and Guze and by Cooper, is an infrequent accompaniment of sexual disorders. O'Connor and Stern (1972a) have observed that gross life functioning appeared adequate in their 96 patients, although mature relationships were virtually absent. Lidberg (1972) observed that most patients with potency disorders displayed outer conformity in social situations, were industrious and devoted, and often held extra jobs. They were also found to exhibit severe personality and characterologic problems in areas of interpersonal relations.

In the author's experience, the sexual disability, a major area of malfunction, and some apparently minor symptoms—a phobia for heights, an obsessive thought of minor inconvenience, or derealization in certain circumstances—stand as the twin peaks of a massive underlying neurotic or character disorder constellation. The ramifications and interrelations of these symptoms are manifest only after treatment of the major symptom is instituted. This is the obverse of the situation, also frequent, in which the primary complaints are of anxiety, disturbing obsessions, compulsions, phobias, or character problems; sexual difficulty is only mentioned in passing or may be denied altogether. Six months later nothing may be reviewed but an extensive list of sexual grievances.

That the appearance of neurosis in their population continues to be an issue was testified to recently by Masters and Johnson (1973):

> Yet another problem area to emerge in the last few years has been the obvious failure of the referring authority . . . to associate superficial complaints of physical sexual dysfunction with a depth of underlying psychosocial trauma.

They indicate that it is "equally delimiting" conceptually to categorically assign underlying pathology to all complaints of sexual dysfunction. They feel that "probably" equal or greater numbers of persons develop sexual inadequacy "without evidencing symptoms of accompanying severe psychopathology." There is apparently, increased caution between 1970 and 1973 regarding the existence and contributing role of underlying psychopathology in sexual problems.

If much clinical experience has indicated that neurosis is a frequent concomitant of sexual disability, to what extent may the sexual pathology be productively separated from the neurosis or character pathology for treatment purposes? In 1910 Freud pointed

out that lack of sexual satisfaction can occur where there is no lack of normal intercourse and that sexual trends often find only poor outlets in coitus. He captured what has become the basis of the dynamic approach to this issue:

> [N]ervous symptoms arise from a conflict between two forces— . . . libido (which has as a rule become excessive) and . . . repression . . . . [I]f they were [neurotics] without their inner resistances, the strength of the instinct itself would point the way to satisfaction for them.

Within this framework, reservations may be expressed regarding didactic, directional approaches to sexual difficulties in the face of neurotic illness. "Symptoms arise from a conflict between two forces," the drive toward sexual satisfaction, which may be of high intensity, and correspondingly strong or stronger repressive forces. The psychodynamic model predicts difficulty with directive techniques in that the conflict, with its fantasied and historical substructure, is actively extruded from awareness and, therefore, is inaccessible to rational thought, conscious memory, immediate experience, and the mediating influence of suggestion.

Psychodynamic Concept of Sexual Development

Inherent to the dynamic treatment of sexual disabilities is a certain conceptualization of sexual development. This conceptualization includes the biological, the maturational, and the developmental, as follows: innate predisposition, intrauterine maturation, infantile mothering experiences, gender development, infantile sexuality and the component drives, the family triangle (oedipal phase), latency, drive resurgence and physical maturity at adolescence, and maturity (capacity for emotional and physical intimacy and parenthood).

BIOLOGICAL FACTORS

By innate predisposition is meant those constitutional outer limits of capacity within which experience is operative. Included are temperamental predilections that put a cast on mental and emotional life. In terms of sexual functioning, there are issues of physical vigor, drive level, and the extent of innate emotional bisexuality.

In a variety of his writings (as outlined by Stoller, 1973b), Freud developed the concept of bisexuality on which later psychosexual development was anchored. On the biological side, bisexuality has subsequently been well established (Jost, 1972). Physical anlagen for internal male and female development are present in the fetus. The primordial external genitalia are bipotential. The pivotal factor in determining the direction of differentiation is the presence or absence of androgens. The basic principle of early hormonal influence is that androgen masculinizes. In its absence, female developmental pathways are followed. An extension of this pattern and its implications for female and male sexuality are found in Sherfey (1966).

Of significance also is the influence of testosterone on central nervous system structures. An acyclic (male) versus cyclic (female) release of pituitary gonadotrophins is influenced by the action of testosterone on the hypothalamus (Gadpaille, 1972). There are also behavioral effects of early prenatal androgen exposure. In a variety of infrahuman mammals, adult sexual behavior of a dimorphic (masculine versus feminine) type is influenced by androgen exposure—or the lack of it—during species-specific critical periods in fetal life (Gadpaille, 1972; Money and Ehrhardt, 1971). Observations of natural and iatrogenic conditions in the human being have indicated that certain behaviors along a broad masculinity-femininity spectrum, particularly those related to degree of overt aggression, are affected by intrauterine androgen excess or insufficiency (Ehrhardt et. al., 1968a, 1968b; I. Yalom and N. Fisk, unpublished data, 1973; Gadpaille, 1972). Relative increases in active play, tomboyishness, and aggressivity have been observed in androgen-exposed girls; a relative passivity, less active play, and effeminacy have been observed in estrogen-exposed boys.

Inheritance, fetal maturation, and hormonal conditioning may provide the physical wherewithal and the general range of the emotional thermostat as substrata for sexual development. There is no convincing evidence in human beings to date indicating that such factors are related to sexual object choice, sexual preference, or the capacity for intimacy.

EARLY MOTHERING

The development of a sexual person psychologically and socially begins with extra-uterine life. Development proceeds against the template of the parents, primarily the mother in the earliest years. As Stoller (1972b) has stated:

Freud told us . . . that parents have the greatest possible influence on their children's development, that children create psychic structure in response, that adult sexual life can be traced back to effects in infancy, and that sexual desire and gratification find origins in infancy.

The earliest intimacy is with the mothering person. That intimacy establishes the foundation for subsequent experiences, including sexual experiences. Under optimal circumstances, mothering experiences with need gratification and mutuality of purpose establish the foundation for future comfortable intimacy. Ambivalent or ambiguous mothering, early and late, sets the stage for fear of hurt and loss and for reactive, retaliatory rage with subsequent potentially intimate experiences.

GENDER IDENTITY

A body of observation with intersex persons has indicated the importance of external genitalia for setting into motion a variety of cultural and idiosyncratic rearing practices that begin the process of gender differentiation (Hampson and Hampson, 1961). Gender identity—the basic sense of maleness or femaleness—is usually well differentiated by 2½ to 4 years of age. As Kleeman (1971) stated:

Cognitive functions play a more significant role in core gender identity formation than previously believed and probably are more universally contributory at this early age (before 3) than identification mechanisms, envy of male penis, or castration anxiety.

Some cognitive factors are the observation of differences in dress and hair style and other appurtenances between boys and girls, the testimony of one's own genitals and those of others, and the constantly reiterated dichotomies of "girls do this" and "boys do that." However, certain aspects of identification and introjection in gender formation do not operate by way of conscious cognition.

INFANTILE SEXUALITY AND COMPONENT DRIVES

During development, certain bodily zones temporarily become the focus of interchange with the environment, tension discharge, and socialization. These zones, as originally observed by Freud 1905, are the oral, the anal, and the phallic. Component drives of orality and incorporation and then anality and elimination become manifest in a relatively phase-specific way. Later, awareness of intense sensations from the penis and the clitoris and concerns about the presence or absence of phalli mark the beginning of the phallic phase.

In the expression of such drives there is potential for psychological trauma. Frustration or overindulgence in the physical stimulation or fantasies associated with these stages tend to induce conflict. When there is excessive conflict, development is skewed, with a weakness in the personality structure referred to as a fixation point. These fixation points leave a mark on the character and intrapsychic processes serving as levels to which regression may occur in the face of future conflict or frustration.

Two factors other than the obvious procreative potential of the genitals are of importance in the subsequent use of these zones in sexual relations; their capacity to discharge tension and the childhood fantasies that invest them. In fantasy, preoccupation, or behavior, these early stages of development may be reflected in adult sexual performance. Representatives of oral and anal sexuality are commonly seen during foreplay. In an overdeveloped, obligatory, and compensatory form, they are seen in the perversions and the neuroses.

OEDIPAL SITUATION: THE FAMILY TRIANGLE

With increasing maturity, usually ages 4 to 6, the child's genitals become invested with urgency of feeling, and motility, physical vigor, and language development allow some possibility of direct expression.

Regardless of the degree of conflict-free or conflicted development to that point, the oedipal situation presents a formidable challenge. The primary objects of the child's concern are his parents, who receive the brunt of his genitally occasioned fantasy and activity. For both sexes, the previously perceived anatomical distinction between the sexes takes on new meaning in terms of phallic inadequacy or deprivation. For the girl, there are fantasies of having been denied a phallus; for the boy, there are concerns about its loss.

The child's sexual immaturity leads to frustration. The possessiveness with which the adult partners regard one another leads to fear. Fantasies of conquest of one or the other parent and of retribution become part of the mix. The child is powerfully attracted, affectively and sexually, to both parents to some degree and is, at the same time, fearful of the implications and consequences of that attraction. At one and the same time or with rapid oscillation, desirous and rivalrous feelings are expressed toward both parents. Only at the simplest level can the triangular situation be viewed as attraction toward the parent of the opposite sex and rivalry with the same-sex parent. There is also attraction toward same-sex parent and rivalry with the other.

The parents, of course, bring their own conflicts and distortions to the situation. Johnson (1953) and Benedek (1959) have observed that the child's ego is less stable in those areas corresponding to unresolved conflicts of the mother, father, or significant surrogates.

The constellation of sexually and aggressively colored, fantasy-interwoven oedipal relationships that children have with their parents is reported in repressed memory and fantasy and is represented by behavior in the treatment of adults and children. A number of authors—for example, Money (1973)—have criticized the generalizability of oedipal theory. However, as Stoller (1972b) has said:

What varies from family to family and culture to culture is how much conflict there is in the complex, but not whether families are made up of mothers, fathers, and children each with attributes of power and sex more or less as Freud noted in Vienna.

The oedipal situation, then, is an amalgam of affections, rivalries, physical strivings, issues of dependence and independence, and identifications based on pre-oedipal constructs. The eventual abandonment of oedipal strivings leaves behind certain more or less realistic repressions, inhibitions, unconscious proscriptions, unconscious fantasies of success and the consequences of success, and crystallized identifications.

At this pivotal point, the psychic structures are differentiated and set into place. Childhood sexual fantasies become submerged with conscience formation, not disappearing, but remaining more or less operative at an unconscious level, depending on the energy investing them. The strength of the drive, the power of fantasy, the innate coping capacity of the ego, the behavior of the parents, and the unconscious parental motivation and fantasy—all contribute to the person's particular resolution of the Oedipus conflict. The issue is always the success of repression and the cost of that success.

LATENCY

In the normal situation, the turmoil of the oedipal phase is followed by the relative quiet of latency. During this time, peer relationships and social and intellectual skills are pursued. In the normal situation, manifestations of sexuality are largely repressed. Overt sexual behavior and concern during this period are largely reflective of family pathology coming to expression in the child. (Peller, 1958, Bornstein, 1951, 1953).

ADOLESCENCE

There is a resurgence of sexual activity and pressure at adolescence, with accompanying physical maturity. Earlier conflicts become aroused once more, but the wider latitude of peer contacts and free-ranging motion in the environment does much to defuse serious recrudescence of oedipal strivings and possible physical consummation. Nevertheless, when oedipal and pre-oedipal concerns remain at issue and when there is undue parental receptivity or competition with the re-emergent sexuality, emotional and behavioral symptoms may be evoked.

The adolescent physical capacity for coitus and reproduction does not indicate a similar capacity for intimacy. There is an adolescent protointimacy, which consists of superficial protestations of love (exemplified in popular music) and some real tenderness but without the constancy of self-representation and the capacity to assume responsibility for self and others that allows for the development of true intimacy. In this light, certain articles about

the new morality seem curiously adolescent—see, for example, Smith and Smith (1973).

MATURITY

Mature sexuality requires a capacity for intimate assertiveness and receptiveness and acceptance of the partner as a real person rather than a stand-in for childhood figures. This assumes that early experiences with intimacy have been satisfactory, that partial drives have been incorporated under genital dominance or otherwise sublimated, that gender is secure, that identifications are stable rather than oscillating, that conscience and oedipal conflicts have mellowed, that peer relationships have provided adequate opportunity for sexual experimentation, and that biological capacities are not unduly limiting.

There is a mature constancy of sense of self that, as a derivative, allows a type of relatedness to others, with gradually increasing familiarity, comfort, and reliability. The driven necessity for risk taking in sexual liaison and the narcissistic requirement for flattering attention yields to an awareness that sexual attributes and capacities are roughly equivalent among persons, whereas satisfaction, as distinct from simple discharge, depends on the individual. Procreation and the rearing of children hopefully stem from such a mature base.

As the parent influences the child, the child has a reciprocal role. Parents meet in children, to paraphrase Benedek (1959), not only the promise of their hopes and ambitions but also the incorporated projections of their own conflicts. Conflicts institutionalized when the adult was a child are reworked through the experiences of parenthood. Through a successful relationship with children, the parental superego loses some of its harshness, recognizing in a retrospective mirror of the child its own infantile origins (Benedek, 1959). This gradual relaxation of harshness may have, as a consequence, an increased freedom to indulge and to achieve satisfaction in sexual relations. In women, the physical capacity to obtain high levels of sexual tension and orgasmic release may be increased by vascular and other tissue distention occasioned by pregnancy (Sherfey, 1966).

Maturity and the capacity for intimacy in the sexual sphere are not primarily limited, in this day and age, by physical disease, war, pestilence, social restrictions, ignorance, poverty, or any of a series of other ills. They are limited by the vicissitudes of personal development in the context provided by those important persons on whom the person has been dependent and with whom he has been intimate.

Sexual Disorders

Clinical experience indicates that the selection of a specific symptom is idiosyncratic, based on the most serviceable compromise and taking into account a variety of conflicting experiences, fantasies, and fears. However, the sexual symptom as a compromise represents an adaptive effort to retain sexual fulfillment and personal interrelatedness as well as pathology.

O'Connor and Stern (1972a) reviewed the past life experiences of both male and female patients with sexual dysfunctions. They found a high degree of disturbance, with a striking frequency of such gross familial pathology as psychosis, alcoholism, abnormal sexual behavior, and brutality; 57 per cent of their patients had at least one parent who manifested one such psychopathological pattern; 32 per cent of both male and female patients were partners to some form of bizarre sexual activity in the family setting. There was also a high incidence of death in the family and prolonged separation from one or the other parent.

FEMALE

Various dysfunctional syndromes are included among female patients who seek consultation regarding a sexual disability. The common clinically reported syndromes—frigidity (anorgasmia), dyspareunia, and vaginismus—may be considered as failures of performance, or orgasm, or of satisfaction. Failures of performance include a variety of conditions preventing sexual contact or adequate stimulation, such as spasm of the perivaginal musculature, pain on intercourse, and repugnance to genital contact. Failures of orgasm include lack of orgastic achievement under any and all circumstances, orgasm with masturbation but not with coitus, and absence of coital orgasm with certain partners deemed important by the patient. Failures of satisfaction may occur under situations in which there is no lack of contact and apparent release and may be related to unrealistic expectations, dissatisfaction with the partner, and moral scrupulosity. It is common to find a mixture of these conditions or all three in any given patient.

Most dissatisfactions in female sexual life have been covered in the literature under the term "frigidity." Frigidity, as Faulk (1973) notes, has been used to refer to "nonconsummation, severe vaginismus, orgasmic inadequacy, or other disturbances of sexual experience. In the literature and popularly, a distinction has been made between clitoral and vaginal orgasms. A person who experienced only clitoral orgasms was considered frigid by some authors (Bergler, 1944; Fenichel, 1946). The transfer of erogenicity from the clitoris to the vagina was postulated as necessary for true orgasm. The presumed physiological distinction between vaginal and clitoral orgasm, however, has not survived Masters and Johnson's direct observations (1966). In a subjective sense, nonetheless, the difference cannot be described as specious (LoPiccolo and Lobitz, 1972). Clinically (Stoller, 1972b), female patients do distinguish between orgasms stimulated by a vibrator, hand manipulation, manipulation by a partner, or even usual intercourse and those experienced with receptivity to a partner. Among dysfunctional women there is no dearth of orgasm with masturbation, with or without appliances; there is, however, a shortage of those dysfunctional women who can be accepting of the partner's penis and personal involvement.

Among women, O'Connor and Stern (1972b) observed the following fantasy factors in association with sexual inadequacy: fear of direct injury from the male organ (frequently displaced to fear of pregnancy), with dreams of blood and vaginal injury; inability to trust a sexual partner, related to previous experiences of loss and separation; and fear of loss of control if sexual feelings were let loose.

Certain dynamic factors have achieved prominence in clinical experience (Moore, 1964). Among these factors are the assumption of phallic deficiency and genital damage. Sexual difficulties have also been ascribed to flight from related masochistic fantasies associated with genital contact and coitus. Such assumptions of genital damage or insufficiency may give rise to wishes for vengeance that find expression in a variety of ways—for example, vaginismus with denial of entry, fantasies of vaginal mutilation of the penis, the wish to disappoint or humiliate the man, and an envy of male prerogatives.

Identification with parental attitudes may be related to adult sexual difficulty. The female child ordinarily identifies with the mother and her affectional and erotic attachments. If the mother has conflicts in sexual interest and expression, these conflicts are reflected in the daughter. The father's attitudes toward eroticism and acceptance of love from a woman are also reflected in the daughter.

Identification with the mother in the normal case is accompanied by the desire to be loved by the father and to have a child by him. This wish can be gratified, provided the attachment to the father is transferred to another man. If it is not, a spiteful rivalry with the mother may develop, with an accompanying sense of guilt that requires abandonment of the maternal role (Deutsch, 1933). A strong and persistent attachment to the father may determine the choice of a husband. In this situation the husband is a stand-in, with the liability of stand-ins to be unsatisfying, regardless of their innate potential.

MALE

The usual clinical syndromes are premature ejaculation and impotence; ejaculatory incompetence is less frequent. The paraphilias in clinically overt form are much more common among men than among women. See Masters and Johnson, 1970, and Hastings, 1963, for definitions.

The disorders of performance, orgasm, and satisfaction seen in woman have their male counterparts. Less frequent among men than among women are disorders of orgasm (ejaculatory incompetence and ejaculation without sensation) and disorders of painful intercourse (male dyspareunia). Conversely, disorders of performance are of major concern, involving failure to attain or maintain a sufficient erection. Disorders of satisfaction, however, are more common than generally supposed and are related to such items as sense of inadequacy as a man, disappointments with the partner, a frustrated wish to satisfy the partner, and the withholding of emotional involvement.

Cooper (1969) has listed the following general psychic factors or effects, among others, held to be associated with potency disorders; anxiety or fear, hostility and resentment, disgust, inhibition, and ignorance and misinformation. From a dynamic perspective he has listed other factors held in the literature to be causative: fear of punishment, fear of disease, fear of inducing pregnancy, castration anxiety, and fear of the unknown. In a more social context, anxiety and guilt associated with unsuccessful adolescent sexual adventures, fear of detection, fear of social condemnation for acts felt to be immoral, fear of female rejection, and anxiety related to the use of contraceptive devices have been suggested. Among the global personality factors noted by Cooper (1969) in his review were the following: immature personality, hysterical personality, inadequacy, difficulties in forming stable relationships, inability to engage in affectionate relationships, failure to reach genital primacy, psychopathia, and excessive shyness.

Fantasy factors found by O'Connor and Stern (1972b) in the treatment of male patients with sexual problems included the following: fear of castration and injury viewed as a result of a vulnerability incurred by opening up to others, fear of harming or destroying the woman through intercourse, and fear of retaliation from other men at successful sexual relations. Ginsberg et al. (1972) have reported observations of impotence among young men related to a demand for sexual performance on the part of the female partner. Ovesey and Meyers (1968) have found in cases of retarded ejaculation that the central conflict lay in rivalry with and fantasied retaliation from other men.

Poor identifications, fear of genital damage, rivalry, and incorporation of skewed parental attitudes contribute to male and female sexual difficulty.

A general principle useful in understanding the roots of common sexual dysfunctions in men and women is that the dynamics most directly related to the sexual difficulty are oedipal in origin, whereas the experiences that made the patient vulnerable to oedipal complications occurred earlier. Both must be dealt with in comprehensive treatment.

PERVERSIONS

The perversions are sexual disorders in which there is the inclusion of some striking form of behavior as a relatively necessary component of the performance and enjoyment of the sexual act. Aspects of the general syndrome are greater or lesser degrees of failure of reality testing, incomplete integration of masculine and feminine personality components, risk taking to heighten arousal, employment of sexuality as a tension releaser, and the presence of component drives in blatant form. The more common clinical forms, in the author's experience, are homosexuality, fetishism (particularly transvestism), sadomasochism, and the gender dysphoria syndrome (transsexualism). The perversions in their overt form are considerably more common among men than among women, appearing as a special liability of male psychosexual development. There is a multiplicity of levels of compulsiveness, associated personality damage, and clinical manifestations in all sexual disorders. The variation in intensity among the perversions, however, is particularly wide (Greenacre, 1968).

The concepts of deviance and perversion are often used interchangeably. By deviation is understood a statistical abnormality. A deviation describes an act not usually performed in certain circumstances within a given cultural milieu. Perversion implies an obligatory inclusion in the sexual act of defensive, alternate, or partial gratifications that allow genital release but usually not emotional intimacy.

Greenacre (1968) has outlined a failure of satisfactory maternal care in the perversions, with the mother either depriving or overwhelming the infant. This failure does not determine the specific perverse content, but it does establish a situation conducive to oscillations in relationship, an impairment in capacity to relate, and an increase in aggression through frustration. Difficulty in early relationships with the maternal figure and the secondary increase of rage set the stage for intensification of oedipal fantasy. Bak (1956, 1968) also calls attention to the overstimulus of aggression and the defenses surrounding aggression, with the adoption of perverse sexuality in a regressive way to protect interpersonal relatedness from the aggressive threat.

The raw materials of perversion are supplied by the constituent drives (oral, anal, and phallic) of infantile sexuality, but a clinical perversion is elaborated beyond that point. A piece of infantile sexuality is used as a compromise, allowing some sexual discharge but suppressing the rest. The compromise is instituted as a defense against the fantasied oedipal dangers in heterosexual genitality, an anxiety prepared for by earlier disordered relationships with parental figures. In the families of perverse persons, heterosexuality was distorted, and pregenital activities were encouraged, usually by way of supplying vicarious satisfaction to the parents. The adult conscience is tolerant of pregenital behavior, since it is representative of what was originally condoned by the parents (Gillespie, 1956; Greenacre, 1968).

A special problem for the male that has relevance for the perversions was pointed out by Greenson (1968). Not only does the mother provide the male child with an initial heterosexual object relationship (a service not provided for the girl) but, for both boy and girl, provides the first person with whom to identify. Disidentification from the mother's femaleness is a special task for the boy. In the perversions, disidentification from the mother is poor. Bak (1968) has pointed out the function of perversions in denying sexual differences.

Fetishism. Greenacre (1968) has made a special contribution to the study of fetishism, which she defines as follows:

> a distortion of sexual behavior in which there is the obligatory use of some nongenital object . . . without which gratification cannot be obtained. The fetish usually must possess qualities representing, in only slightly concealed form, body parts, and body attributes.

The fetish is used to bolster an uncertain masculinity, an effect that becomes apparent during sexual performance.

Greenacre (1969) has compared the fetish and the transitional object (Winnicott, 1953). The transitional object selected by the infant is usually an old blanket, a special pacifier, or a piece of some material used to provide comfort and relatedness under situations of uncertainty or separation. The fetish also serves as a bridge to relatedness and as a contact point to femininity and the mother. Both are security props serving to bring an anxiety-laden situation under control. The clothes fetish of the transvestite operates in a similar way.

Homosexuality. Anyone who has reviewed the dynamic concepts of homosexuality can only be appalled at the diversity of formulations (Saul and Beck, 1961; Socarides, 1960, 1963; Bieber et al., 1962). With regard to the multiplicity of interpersonal, historical, and intrapsychic contributions to male homosexuality, Bieber et al. (1962) make the following points:

> Neither Freud nor his followers assumed that only one mechanism underlies homosexuality in any given case. In most cases, various kinds of feelings toward the mother and the father are acted-out through many homosexual symbolizations.

Socarides (1963) has similar reservations regarding specific etiological factors in female homosexuality.

Freud postulated several basic contributions to a homosexual outcome: bisexuality of the sexual impulse, constitutional predisposition, and subsequent events in life. The persistence of strong narcissistic components in the personality, overvaluation of phallic attributes, anxiety associated with incestuous wishes toward the mother, and fear regarding rivalry with the father were further elaborations (Bieber et al., 1962).

Thompson (1947) felt that homosexuality derived from over-all character deformations and that, when the character problems were solved, homoerotic activity disappeared. Rado (1949) attributed homosexuality to incapacitating fear of the opposite sex.

Ovesey (1954, 1955) classified homosexuality into true homosexuality and pseudohomosexuality. True homosexuality was attributed to early and excessive discipline in sexual matters, with homosexuality being resorted to in order to achieve orgastic satisfaction. Pseudohomosexuality, found often in neurotic disorders, was related to wishes for dependency gratification or as a consequence of inhibited assertiveness, both regarded as earmarks of subjugation and thus related to femininity and homosexuality.

Kolb and Johnson (1955) felt that the impetus to overt, as distinct from latent, homosexual behavior resulted from parental support, wishes, or encouragement in that direction, in either clandestine or open form.

Bieber et al. (1962), in reviewing work with 106 homosexual subjects and a comparison group of 100, felt that the homosexual adaptation was the result of a covert but incapacitating fear of the opposite sex. There was evidence of an excessively close, seductive mother-son relationship and suppression of any heterosexual response. Unusual hostility was displayed by the father. There were essential contributions by both parents in the molding of the homosexual, the triangular relationship within the family being characterized by extremely disturbed interactions. The homosexual son occupied a special point within the family structure, emerging as the focus of the most profound parental psychopathology.

Socarides (1963) reviewed theoretical and clinical material regarding overt female homosexuality. He indicated that there is a strong unconscious ambivalent attachment to both parents on the part of homosexual women. Bergler (Socarides, 1963) felt that the following constellation characterizes female homosexuality: an aggressive, dominating mother who, in the face of a weak father, is the dominant educator of the child; a markedly ambivalent attachment to the mother based on their early relationship; a consequent failure of intense oedipal rivalry or

heterosexual interest; and a masochistic attachment to the mother and other women, sometimes covered by a pseudoaggressive façade.

Wilbur (1965) related the roots of female homosexuality not only to certain types of experience within the nuclear family, shared but others who do not become homosexual, by also to the kinds of persons the parents are. The typical mother was described as overbearing, dominant in the family, and excessively controlling of the daughter. Attempts by the mother to dominate, conquer, and control were induced by the techniques of threatened rejection, depreciation, and guilt induction. The child developed a great hostility toward the mother and at the same time a longing for affection and approval. The typical father was detached or concerned and overanxious about the girl. He did not present a strong masculine ideal in respect to which a complementary feminine sexual orientation could be achieved.

Sadomasochism. Sadism and masochism are paired phenomena, aspects of both being found within the same person. In the interpersonal sphere, a masochist cannot function without at least the fantasied presence of a sadist and vice versa. As used here, sadism and masochism refer specifically to those conditions in which sexual excitement and release depend, at least to some extent, on inflicting or suffering pain. Moral masochism is not included in this discussion.

Traumata or frustrations during development lead to diffuse states of tension that are exciting as well as unpleasant. The subsequent release of suspense or tension is pleasurable. Children practice inducing a threat, followed by pleasure in its removal. Such seduction of the aggressor, found in all children, contains building blocks that may serve in the construction of later masochistic behavior. Stein (1956) notes that there is a

seeking for situations that entail danger, fear, and unpleasure, and their attenuation through the loving, erotic complicity of the threatening parent. The pleasure in this behavior is derived, not from pain but from its removal, from cessation of the threat through a loving reunion with the parent.

Eventually, induction of discomfort and its removal may become condensed. Frequent pairing of these phenomena, especially when eroticized by the parent, links them to sexual functioning. In certain forms of masochistic suffering, particularly bondage practices, the end point of the suffering may be death (Stein, 1956; Litman and Swearingen, 1972; Resnik, 1972).

Gender dysphoria syndrome (transsexualism). The term "gender dysphoria syndrome", originally suggested by Fisk (unpublished data, 1973) is preferred to "transsexualism" to describe the condition manifested by applicants for sex reassignment surgery. Stoller has outlined the dynamics of the "true" transsexual condition for men (1968, 1971) and for women (1972). Clinical interviews and psychological testing of parents have indicated that covert gender confusion, sexual conflicts, unfortunate rearing experiences with fixation, and confusion of generational boundaries are part of their psychological history and dynamics when there is overt gender dysphoria in the offspring.

In the adult, the gender dysphoric picture is closely related to the perversions. Admixed conditions include sadomasochism, transvestism, homosexuality, and polymorphous sexual activity. Oscillating and frustrating relations with the parents, difficulties with aggression (frequently self-directed), and gaps in the reality sense (but not overt psychosis) are shared with the perversions. The gender development and sexual identification are dysphoric in the sense of being conflictual. The author has not seen a patient of this type with core gender reversal (Ovesey and Person, 1973) in an unconflicted sense. What is observed in children with cross-gender behavior is a simulant femininity (in boys) and masculinity (in girls).

Treatment

The psychotherapies based on dynamic principles take cognizance of the motive force of fantasy and conflict, particularly those that are unconscious. Sexual difficulties are considered, in this framework, to develop out of the same matrix as other personality and neurotic problems. An important treatment assumption is that there is a sufficiently strong propensity for the expression and enjoyment of sexuality that, without the impediment of conflict, satisfaction is obtainable.

Fromm-Reichmann (1950) has outlined the purpose and technique of dynamic psychotherapy somewhat as follows. Through the intervention of psychotherapy, there is to be a clarification of difficulties with others and oneself, including sexual difficulties. This clarification is accomplished through the recall of forgotten memories and affects in the special context of the relationship with the psychiatrist. This relationship is itself the subject of intensive scrutiny. There is resistance to this process. In the light of the memories and the therapeutic relationship, communication and operations are interpreted to provide essential clarification. Certain basic assumptions in this process require further expansion.

First, there is the assumption that the sexual problem is most often simply one manifestation, although an extremely important one, of a neurotic or personality disorder. Sexual gratification is held to be a single aspect of a more manifold capacity to feel positively toward persons and to secure bodily satisfaction from them (Fisher and Osofsky, 1967). Despite a monosymptomatic presentation, increasing respect develops for the pervasiveness, strength, and attachments of the neurosis and its character ramifications. For the patient, this respect comes at the point where healthy components of the personality assert themselves and he sees that things, indeed, could have been and can be different.

Second, there needs to be the assumption on the part of both patient and psychiatrist that treatment is open ended. Treatment will take as long as necessary, until the patient is satisfied. Artificial time parameters focus the work but allow resistance to cover embarrassing or conflictual material.

Third, the patient's responsibility is to report history, thoughts, fantasies, bodily feelings, and affects as they come to mind. He may be assured that agreement with this principle is easy but that implementation is hard. Much important material seems embarrassing, trivial, offensive, or in violation of some external confidence. The stance of the therapist is that the patient is to be as nonjudgmental in reporting the material as the psychiatrist is in hearing it.

Fourth, it is the therapist's responsibility to aid the patient as much as possible in self-exploration, by which is not meant pats on the back, approval, disapproval, or attempts at manipulating external reality. Open-ended questions about the material at hand are helpful in furthering the work of exploration. The psychiatrist's responsibility is not to exhort toward success but to remove the road blocks to it—the resistances. This removal is done most effectively by noting and commenting on apparent roadblocks to free association and communication when they occur. If sufficient material is available to relate the presenting resistance to other patterns of behavior, this relation may also be useful. Metaphorically, when growing lettuce, the ground is prepared and maintained with essentials, and the weeds are pulled. One does not stand over the seeds, encouraging them to grow. Unless the seeds are inherently and irremediably faulty, they have an innate capacity to germinate, sprout, and grow within the limits of constitutional endowment.

Fifth, one can make no promise of cure. But as history is reviewed, thoughts noted, affects expressed, and fantasies examined, certain capabilities come to the fore. As resistances are overcome and conflict comes into the forum of conscious consideration, the patient begins to report improvement in troublesome areas almost as an aside. The as-a-matter-of-course quality of the improvement often surprises the patient and the inexperienced therapist.

Sixth, the treating physician has a special responsibility for maintaining the structure of the situation in which treatment occurs. A time is selected when he can reliably be present and punctual. Freedom from other concerns—telephones and administrative matters—during this time is essential. The fee, of whatever magnitude, is worked out in advance and is acceptable to both.

Fromm-Reichmann (1950) speaks of the respect due the patient. Such respect extends from the fact that the patient's problems in living are not very different in kind, although perhaps in degree, from those the psychiatrist may have faced. In addition, the patient's sexual difficulties are often a source of embarrassment, they are of moment to him, the onset of treatment is a frightening experience, and a high degree of hope is riding on the outcome. Humility on the part of the therapist is in order. Special mention is needed about the therapist with sexual problems. Although such problems may make him empathic, unless he is treated himself, the outcome may well be that his anxiety becomes so alarming that extrication from the scene is effected or treatment is defensively used for self-aggrandizement or self-treatment. The physician should be nothing less than interested, compassionate, dependable, and concerned with his patient. As Freud noted, genuine concern for the patient does not extend to acting on the temptation to share one's own experiences, intimacies, fallacies, and problems with the patient on an assumption of quid pro quo.

TRANSFERENCE

The factor that brings conflicts and fantasies into awareness with the necessary immediacy to be convincing and to allow modification is the transference. Most of the truly effective therapeutic work is in the context of the transference. A useful definition is from Mack and Semrad (1967):

> [T]o an increasing extent the patient's feelings toward the analyst replicate his feelings toward the specific people he is talking about . . . . The special type of object displacement . . . is called transference.

The expression of reaction patterns, affects, and fantasies in a current time frame, with immediacy, and in a personalized context is the living experience of the transference. The transference brings vividly alive, in a controlled and observed setting, both the unsatisfied claims for love and sexual release and the prohibited aggressive feelings. This phenomenon offers opportunity for real work. One cannot dismantle a neurotic construction purely in retrospect or, as Freud (1912) put it, "in absentia." Free association, interpretation of resistance, and relative abstinence of immediate gratification in the treatment setting are the precursors of transference development.

Novey (1968) has commented on the importance of transference in treatment, as follows:

> In the transference situation it is necessary . . . to . . . reexperience the old emotional states . . . repeated in attenuated form and re-examined by means of a current replica of a historically significant person . . . . [T]he old emotionally laden experiences are lived out . . . in a diluted form . . . in which they can be detoxified.

Transference operates in a dual way, both as the most powerful determinant of treatment and as the most powerful resistance to successful outcome. Prototypic patterns are given up only slowly and grudgingly, after considerable effort to justify rather than relinquish them. Care must be taken to emphasize that transference is essential in human interchange, being neither good nor bad in and of itself. The end point is not a patient free of transference but one in whom the unrealistic, insatiable, and detrimental aspects have been examined and incorporated in a more mature frame of reference.

Over the course of treatment, the transference coalesces into a transference neurosis. As Freud (1914) stated:

> [W]e regularly succeed in giving all the symptoms of the illness a new transference meaning and in replacing his ordinary neurosis with a transference neurosis . . . . The transference thus creates an intermediate region between illness and real life through which the transition from one to the other is made.

This transference neurosis represents an artificial illness, being occasioned by special circumstances. It is, nonetheless, real in its effects and has the advantage of accessibility.

The tool used in resolving the transference neurosis is the interpretation. As Strachey (1934) pointed out in an old but extremely useful paper, the interpretation to be "mutative" must be given in repeated small doses, timed to coincide with the emergence in the patient of emotionally laden material, tinged with archaic fantasy, and directed toward the therapist as a transference object. Strachey observes that the therapist must exercise caution and restraint in offering interpretations to avoid siding with warring factions within the patient. The therapist's ally is reality in life—often a weak commodity at the height of the transference.

In his early works, Freud (1912) outlined characteristics of the transference particularly important for those patients with a sexual problem:

> Each individual . . . has acquired a specific method of his own in his conduct of his erotic life . . . . This produces what might be described as a stereotype plate . . . which is constantly repeated . . . in the course of the person's life.

Portions of this template have passed through the process of maturation and development. Others have been detoured or deferred. These detoured or deferred libidinal strivings are unlikely to be satisfied by events and persons within the sphere of reality. They are held ready in anticipation, responding to existing prototypes and actively structuring elements in persons encountered to fit that prototype. The physician is reacted to in a similar vein, regardless of sex. Erotic transference to the doctor, despite its semblance of reality, exceeds, both in amount and

in nature, anything justifiable on rational grounds.

Transference manifestations are not to be expected simply in terms of verbal communications of affection or hate. They are also manifest in repetitive behavior both within the treatment hour and outside. When this behavior is explored, its relation to history, fantasy, and affect is revealed. Freud observed that the greater the resistance to remembering and reporting, the more are these modalities replaced by repetitive behavior. This is particularly true of persons whose pathology is reflected primarily in character malformations, as in some perversions.

A difficulty for the male psychiatrist is presented by the female patient who falls in love. (This is not to say that female psychiatrists and those of whatever sexual persuasion do not have similar difficulties.) As Freud (1915) pointed out, the patient's falling in love is induced by the treatment situation and "is not to be attributed to the charms . . . of the psychiatrist." The effects of this love are to distort the purposes of treatment, cause them to be regarded as inconsequential, and prevent further intellectual or affective products. Love seems to come precisely when the most difficult and painful material seemed likely to emerge.

It is equally unfortunate if the patient's desire for love is satisfied and if it is suppressed. It is as necessary not to impede the transference love as it is to withhold resolutely any response to it. It is particularly difficult simply to let the transference emerge without indulging in defensive maneuvers when a homosexual liaison is the aimed-for outcome. Dahlberg (1970) has indicated the untoward consequences of sexual intimacy, heterosexual or homosexual, with patients. Treatment terminated unhappily, the patient at first feeling elated at the attention and triumphant at removing the psychiatrist from his pedestal but, in the final analysis, feeling betrayed. The more plain it is that the treating physician is neither tempted nor offended, the more readily the patient is able to extract benefit from the situation. Once the patient feels safe enough to express the preconditions for loving, the fantasies springing from erotic desires, and the detailed characteristics of being in love, the infantile and conflicted roots come to light.

SPECIAL PROBLEMS

A multiplicity of difficulties may be reflected in the sexual dysfunction, since sexuality is plastic and multifaceted, involves other people or their representations in fantasy, and is nonobligatory for an individual's life. In some instances, the most effective progress is made by direct pursuit of history and fantasies related to the sexual disability; in others, consideration of more peripheral material is highly therapeutic.

Issues of physical disability related to sexual malfunctions are more frequently seen by other medical specialists. Nonetheless, one should not overlook the psychic consequences of, for example, anomalous internal or external genitalia, the untoward masculinization of the adrenogenital syndrome, or the loss of self-esteem in microphallus or penile agenesis. Inherent variations in drive level seem to account for some disharmony among partners that requires help in adjustment or alternative modes of release.

The capacity to trust sufficiently for mature intimacy is frequently limited by unresolved grief related to early separations, loss, or psychological distancing. Until this grief is dealt with, there is constant fear of repeated loss, human relationships being approached with detachment, isolation, and a façade of independence. In treatment, the sense of deprivation and ultimately the anger must be lived through. In this situation, the reliability and the punctuality of the therapist are essential.

Gender identity problems are seen more frequently by surgeons than by psychiatrists as part of a request for sex reassignment procedures. General pessimism exists in the literature regarding psychiatric interventions in the gender dysphoria syndromes, particularly in adolescents and adults. In part this pessimism derives from an assumption of nonconflictual core gender reversal, whereas it is axiomatic in psychiatry that conflict presages therapeutic opportunity. In most cases, however, it seems that the apparent gender reversal is a compromise formation that, like the perversions, is superficially ego syntonic. Some patients electively respond to the suggestion for exploratory work. Since such work is in the patient's own best interest, it may reasonably be requested as part of any evaluation for sex reassignment procedures.

In the perversions the sexual aspect of the condition is frequently exciting, gratifying, and, to some extent, ego syntonic.

Frequently, external parameters are part of the initial treatment contact—for example, court referral, pressure from the spouse, and insistence by employers. Once the anxiety or depressive precursors of the perverse action are dissected out, the activity may lose some of its seductiveness. There are always issues of heterosexual fear. The patient's capacity to maintain any relationship, including the therapeutic one, may be a limiting factor in some cases.

For most patients, the overtly sexual material in the treatment takes on oedipal shadings. Desires for physical and emotional possession of the therapist are pursued not simply for personal satisfaction alone but also in the context of a presumed competition with other patients or other figures in the therapist's life.

For the psychiatrist who, by virtue of serendipity or hard work, has achieved a reputation as a sex doctor, the erotic transference may take on a special coloration. There is a tendency on the part of some patients to attribute personal lovemaking techniques and physical capacities that are, unfortunately, not often possessed. The assumption is that, if things are not progressing well, this situation could be corrected by accepting them as pupils or partners rather than as patients. If this opportunity is declined, such unwillingness may be interpreted as willful withholding or as demonstrating that the therapist is a paper tiger. An interest in sexual problems is interpreted as an elaborate overcompensation for a basic deficiency.

Masturbation serves to some extent as a stand-in for adequate interpersonal relationships and, in many respects, serves to insulate the person from feared wounds to his self-esteem. Time, place, occasion, frequency, and fantasies of masturbation carry the kernel of drives to sexual gratification and aggressive outlet, the prohibitions of conscience, and the attempts to mediate conflicting demands intrapsychically, culturally, and interpersonally. Hammerman (1961) has referred to masturbatory practices as the embodiment of character traits and fantasied constructs that are helpful in understanding the precipitates of the patient's history. Uncovering the full depth of masturbatory practices

will yield a more rapid and fruitful understanding of the character structure, along with the emotional abreaction necessary to insure conviction in the patient.

A number of patients present with problems of multiple pseudointimacies that seem adolescent in many respects but that are based on earlier conflicts.

A special comment might be made on the treatment of swinging couples or persons. The swinging provides the element of risk taking so addicting in neurotic and perverse sexual lives, it offers far easier gratification and discharge than is possible through a therapeutic process, it operates in the service of denial, and it provides narcissistic rewards. Similar secondary gain is apparent in the less well rationalized and institutionalized affairs that one encounters more frequently. Nonetheless, in some situations swinging operates as a seemingly perverse refinement of the more usual neurotic triangular situation and is maintained in a more exhibitionistic fashion.

After a couple has been treated with the Masters and Johnson techniques, one partner or both may realize for the first time the presence of internal resistances to working through a problem initially seen as educational and mechanical. These issues will become more frequent as the Masters and Johnson techniques and other behavioral measures are more widely employed. A request for further individual work may then be forthcoming. This request invariably has three components: genuine recognition of a personal difficulty, the operations of transference, and the difficulty with separation. In most cases, this circumstance is far better dealt with by referral. If one is inclined to take the patient into further work, it is best done after reasonable elapsed time. Pure erotic transference and separation anxiety do not survive well until the 6-month follow-up visit. At this point, however, continued recognition of personal difficulty and clear motivation for further work deserve consideration. Even under these circumstances, individual treatment should be undertaken only if one realizes and is prepared to cope with certain factors—namely, that the patient will have an unresolved transference and expectation based on a previous and different therapeutic encounter with the therapist; second, that the above considerations about his abilities as a lover and teacher will pertain; and, third, that the patient's spouse will have more than the usual questions about events in the treatment situation.

In the treatment of sexual problems there is a particular problem with a type of auditory voyeurism among certain therapists; they become so enthralled with hearing about the patient's sexual peccadilloes that other aspects of the patient's life are ignored, even though, over the long haul, these aspects may be more significant in the resolution of his difficulties.

Above all else, the patient should not be put in the position of having to reassure the physician regarding his (the physician's) attractiveness, sexual prowess, or liberated outlook. The psychiatrist may be superior to the patient sexually only in terms of his anatomical knowledge and clinical experience. It may be the easiest thing in the world for a sexually dysfunctional patient to talk about the dysfunction in an exhibitionistic way. There may be great difficulty in talking about friendly, tender, and asexual loving interpersonal relationships (Fromm-Reichmann, 1950).

RESULTS

Reports on the results from individual therapy of any substantial series of general sexual disabilities have been in short supply in the literature. Recently, however, O'Connor and Stern (1972b) published a retrospective survey of the effects of psychotherapy and psychoanalysis on sexual symptoms in 96 cases, 61 women and 35 men, treated in the psychoanalytic clinic of Columbia University.

Without considering the specific sexual disability, they found that 25 per cent of the women and 57 per cent of the men were cured. Improvement rates were 36 per cent and 17 per cent for the women and the men, respectively. Improvement for the women included more pleasure in the sexual act, positive attitudinal changes, and orgasm during foreplay but no orgasm during intercourse itself. As the authors point out, it is easier for the woman to improve without cure than for the man, since male difficulty is primarily a failure of performance rather than a failure of satisfaction. The more serious the psychopathology and the longer standing the symptom, the less likelihood there was for successful outcome. Patients treated analytically showed an improvement rate of

77 per cent versus 46 per cent for those in standard psychotherapy.

Clearly, further effort, largely prospective, is required to document the therapeutic effectiveness, mechanisms of effect, limitations, parameters of patient selection, and other aspects of the dynamic therapies in relation to other treatment modalities. Cooper (1969) has made relevant suggestions as to the necessary components of such research:

Specific needs include: (1) greater empiricism; (2) more stringent criteria for inclusion in any study which should be explicit, prospective, controlled, modest . . . and replicable by others; (3) the use of objectively validated measuring instruments . . .to supplement clinical data; and (4) the application of appropriate statistical methods.

Conclusion

One of the striking findings from any comprehensive review of the literature surrounding sexual practice and treatment is the manifold disagreement. At this time, however, the formulations of dynamic psychiatry provide a comprehensive and clinically substantiated approach to the understanding and treatment of emotional disorders, including sexual ones.

Learning theory and behavioral modification paradigms come closest to a similar comprehensivity. That behavioral approaches have value in a variety of disorders goes almost without saying. Since few other centers have had as much experience as Masters and Johnson, critiques of their techniques have to be taken with reservations. In the author's experience, however, techniques such as those of Masters and Johnson are useful within certain limits. They are useful within the restraints of consciously accessible motivation and unconflicted behavior. In other respects their success is like that of a transference cure, dependent on the continued presence of therapists. Changes are induced by the overwhelming rather than by the modification of conflict and resistances. There seems to be insufficient time for assimilation of character or intrapsychic change. With Masters and Johnson techniques, dramatic effects may be expected over the short term. To the extent that there are neurotic or character problems, there seems to be reason for concern about backsliding when the co-

therapists are no longer present. The greater the degree of neurotic conflict underlying the sexual disability, the less likely, it seems, are the gains to persist.

The precise point and significance of the dynamic observations is that much of what is operative in human life is inaccessible to conscious recollection without special effort. This material is accessible only under circumstances that have, as their base, long contact with the patient, the use of free association, and observation of the uses to which the therapist is put.

In initial evaluation the sexual difficulty may seem to be an isolated phenomenon. Whether such conclusions would be maintained through a course of treatment is problematical. It is more common at initial evaluation to find sexual and other psychiatric difficulties in association. The accumulated clinical experience in dynamic therapy indicates that sexual disabilities rarely occur free of character and neurotic problems and that the sexual disability cannot be dissected entirely free from contributory, intrapsychic conflict. These conflicts, without being dealt with, impose limitations on the degree of emotional and physical rehabilitation over the short term, on the capacity for intimacy, and on the maintenance of improvement.

This is not quite the whole story, however. Many of the ramifications of neurosis or character disorder may yield while the sexual dysfunction tenaciously repeats itself. Perhaps the closest approximation to clinical validity at this point would be that the sexual disability in most cases has both components—a dynamic mode founded on unconscious fantasy and archaic experience and a learned, preconscious or conscious mode based on ignorance, social skewing, and the conditioned response of repeated partial gratifications.

Since it is less time consuming, the Masters and Johnson approach is the treatment of choice for those persons who have ignorance, social deprivation, or lack of practice to thank for their sexual disability. The Masters and Johnson techniques have real but limited usefulness among the neurotic and character disorders. The limits are determined by the extent to which the nuclear elements of the problem are interpersonal (between husband and wife), are conscious or preconscious (intrapsychically), and are relatively free of serious unconscious determinants. In addition, one cannot gainsay the role of the Masters and Johnson treatment as an initial, supportive step toward therapy, a step some persons are able to take only with the security of their spouse's company.

In terms of the breadth and depth of what may be accomplished, the author finds individual, dynamically based psychotherapy the ultimate treatment of choice for sexual problems with neurotic and characterologic bases. As related to other treatment modalities, it is thought of in several special contexts. Increasingly, therapists using individual psychotherapy need to treat adverse reactions occasioned by short term treatment techniques for sexual dysfunction. In a more positive sense, there are also patients who have increased awareness of personal conflict and a motivation for change by virtue of their experience with more limited forms of treatment.

Individual psychotherapy is the primary modality of treatment for the sexual problems in the neuroses, character disorders, and perversions. In and of itself such treatment usually leads to restoration of adequate sexual functioning, along with relief from other symptoms or life problems. The special role of individual psychotherapy, however, is as a releaser from intrapsychic conflict. This release allows the patient to be teachable by life and by peers, which is most common, or, if necessary, by didactic, hierarchial forms of therapy.

Although the conflicts investing genital functioning may be resolved through psychotherapy and psychoanalysis, adult self-constancy and interrelatedness with others may be achieved only through experience with real persons. This is a process of learning based on a freedom to learn that, if hindered, may be unshackled by therapy. In such treatment, the patient becomes educable but perhaps only partially educated. Kestenberg (1968) stated the point of educability very well:

In psychoanalytic treatment the patient becomes teachable, but the treatment situation does not allow for training, which only performance of function can give. That must be relegated to the physical sphere of learning . . . if need be, taught by those practitioners who devise pedagogical methods to inculcate skills.

To develop adequate sexual function requires a capacity to learn, which may be disabled by the conflicts investing sexual life. These conflicts are best removed through dynamically oriented, individual psychotherapy. It is at that point that short term, didactic treatment, which also involves the partner of the now-educable patient, is perhaps most efficacious.

Most of the social, educational, and interpersonal factors given weight in many discussions of sexual disability are logically subject to the corrective factors of experience, education, and social manipulation. If they are not in a given person, it is only within the context of that person's history, interactions, conflicts, and fantasies (often unconscious in their operative force) that they become comprehensible. It is within a comprehensive theory of intrapsychic development that they become explicable. And it is within the context of the ongoing dynamically oriented treatment situation that they become reversible.

REFERENCES

Bak, R. Aggression and perversion. In *Perversions: Psychodynamics and Therapy*, S. Lorand, editor, p. 231. Random House, New York, 1956.

Bak, R. The phallic woman: The ubiquitous fantasy in perversion. Psychoanal. Study Child, *23:* 15, 1968.

Benedek, T. Parenthood as a developmental phase: A contribution to the libido theory. J. Am. Psychoanal. Assoc. *7:* 389, 1959.

Bergler, E. The problem of frigidity. Psychoanal. Q. *18:* 374, 1944.

Bieber, I., Dain, H., Dince, P., Drellich, M., Grand, H., Gundlach, R., Kremer, M., Rifkin, A., Wilbur, C., and Bieber, T. *Homosexuality: A Psychoanaltyic Study*. Basic Books, New York, 1962.

Bornstein, B. On latency. Psychoanal. Study Child, *6:* 279, 1951.

Bornstein, B. Masturbation in the latency period. Psychoanal. Study Child, *8:* 65, 1953.

Cooper, A. "Neurosis" and disorders of sexual potency in the male. J. Psychosom. Res., *12:* 141, 1968.

Cooper, A. Factors in male sexual inadequacy: A review. J. Nerv. Ment. Dis. *149:* 337, 1969.

Dahlberg, C. Sexual contact between patient and therapist. Contem. Psychoanal., *6:* 107, 1970.

Deutsch, H. Homosexuality in women. Int. J. Psychoanal., *14:* 34, 1933.

Ehrhardt, A., Epstein, R., and Money, J. Fetal androgens and female gender identity in the early-treated adrenogenital syndrome. Johns Hopkins Med. J., *122:* 160, 1968a.

Ehrhardt, A., Evers, K., and Money, J. Influence of androgen on some aspects of sexually dimorphic behavior in women with the late-treated adrenogenital syndrome. Johns Hopkins Med. J., *123:* 115, 1968b.

Faulk, M. "Frigidity": A critical review. Arch. Sex. Behav., *2:* 257, 1973.

Fenichel, O. *Psychoanalytic Theory of the Neuroses.* Routledge and Kegan Paul, London, 1946.

Fisher, S., and Osofsky, H. Sexual responsiveness in women: Psychological correlates. Arch. Gen. Psychiatry, *17:* 214, 1967.

*Freud, S. Three essays on the theory of sexuality, In *Standard Edition of the Complete Psychological Works of Sigmund Freud, J. Strachey, editor.* J. Strachey, editor, vol. 7, p. 30., Hogarth Press, London, 1953.

*Freud, S. "Wild" psychoanalysis. In *Standard Edition of the Psychological Works of Sigmund Freud, J. Strachey, editor, vol. 11, p. 221.* Hogarth Press, London, 1953.

Freud, S. The dynamics of the transference. In *Standard Edition of the Psychological Works of Sigmund Freud, J. Strachey, editor, vol. 12, p. 99.* Hogarth Press, London, 1958.

Freud, S. Recommendation to physicians practising psychoanalysis. In *Standard Edition of the Psychological Works of Sigmund Freud, J. Strachey, editor, vol. 12, p. 111.* Hogarth Press, London, 1958.

Freud, S. Remembering, repeating, and working-through. In *Standard Edition of the Psychological Works of Sigmund Freud, J. Strachey, editor, vol. 12, p. 147,* Hogarth Press, London, 1958.

Freud, S. Observations on transference-love. In *Standard Edition of the Psychological Works of Sigmund Freud, J. Strachey, editor, vol. 12, p. 159.* Hogarth Press, London, 1958.

Freud, S. The ego and the id. In *Standard Edition of the Psychological Works of Sigmund Freud, J. Strachey, editor, vol. 19, p. 12.* Hogarth Press, London, 1958.

*Fromm-Reichmann, F. *Principles of Intensive Psychotherapy.* University of Chicago Press, Chicago, 1950.

Gadpaille, W. Research into the physiology of maleness and femaleness. Arch. Gen. Psychiatry, *26:* 193, 1972.

Gillespie, W. The general theory of sexual perversion. Int. J. Psychoanal., *37:* 396, 1956.

Ginsberg, G., Frosch, W., and Shapiro, T. The new impotence. Arch. Gen. Psychiatry, *26:* 218, 1972.

Greenacre, P. Perversions: General considerations regarding their genetic and dynamic background. Psychoanal. Study Child, *23:* 47, 1968.

Greenacre, P. The fetish and the transitional object. Psychoanal. Study Child, *24:* 144, 1969.

Greenson, R. Dis-identifying from the mother: Its special importance for the boy. Int. J. Psychoanal., *49:* 370, 1968.

Hammerman, S. Masturbation and character. J. Am. Psychoanal. Assoc., *9:* 287, 1961.

Hampson, J.L., and Hampson, J.G. The ontogenesis of sexual behavior in man. In *Sex and Internal Secretions,* E. Young, editor, vol. II, p. 1401. Williams & Wilkins, Baltimore, 1961.

Hastings, D. *Impotence and Frigidity.* Little, Brown, Boston, 1963.

Johnson, A. Factors in the etiology of fixations and symptom choice. Psychoanal. Q., *22:* 475, 1953.

Jost, A. A new look at mechanisms controlling sex differentiation in mammals. Johns Hopkins Med. J., *130:* 38, 1972.

*Kestenberg, J. Outside and inside: Male and female. J. Am. Psychoanal. Assoc., *16:* 457, 1968.

Kleeman, J. The establishment of core gender identity in normal girls. Arch. Sex. Behav., *1:* 1, 1971.

Kolb, L., and Johnson, A. Etiology and therapy of overt homosexuality. Psychoanal. Q., *24:* 506, 1955.

Lidberg, L. Social and psychiatric aspects of impotence and premature ejaculation. Arch. Sex. Behav., *2:* 135, 1972.

Litman, R., and Swearingen, C. Bondage and suicide. Arch. Gen. Psychiatry, *27:* 80, 1972.

LoPiccolo, J., and Lobitz, W. The role of masturbation in the treatment of orgasmic dysfunction. Arch. Sex. Behav., *2:* 163, 1972.

Mack, J., and Semrad, E. Classical psychoanalysis. In *Comprehensive Textbook of Psychiatry,* A. Freedman and H. Kaplan, editors, edition 1, p. 269. Williams & Wilkins, Baltimore, 1967.

Masters, W., and Johnson, V. *Human Sexual Response.* Little, Brown, Boston, 1966.

Masters, W., and Johnson, V. *Human Sexual Inadequacy.* Churchill, London, 1970.

Masters, W., and Johnson, V. Current status of the research programs. In *Contemporary Sexual Behavior,* J. Zubin and J. Money, editors, p. 279. Johns Hopkins University Press, Baltimore, 1973.

Maurice, W., and Guze, S. Sexual dysfunction and associated psychiatric disorders. Compr. Psychiatry, *11:* 539, 1970.

Money, J. Pornography in the home: A topic in medical education. In *Contemporary Sexual Behavior,* J. Zubin and J. Money, editors, p. 409. Johns Hopkins University Press, Baltimore, 1973.

Money, J., and Ehrhardt, A. Fetal hormones and the brain: Effect on sexual dimorphism of behavior—a review. Arch. Sex. Behav., *1:* 241, 1971.

Moore, B. Frigidity: A review of the psychoanalytic literature. Psychoanal. Q., *22:* 323, 1964.

*Novey, S. *The Second Look: The Reconstruction of Personal History in Psychiatry and Psychoanalysis.* Johns Hopkins University Press, Baltimore, 1968.

O'Connor, J., and Stern, L. Developmental factors in functional sexual disorders. N.Y. State J. Med., *72:* 1838, 1972a.

O'Connor, J., and Stern, L. Results of treatment in functional sexual disorders. N.Y. State J. Med., *72:* 1927, 1972b.

Ovesey, L. The homosexual conflict. Psychiatry, *17:* 234, 1954.

Ovesey, L. The pseudohomosexual anxiety. Psychiatry, *18:* 17, 1955.

Ovesey, L., and Meyers, H. Retarded ejaculation: Psychodynamics and pschotherapy. Am. J. Psychoth., *22:* 185, 1968.

Ovesey, L., and Person, E. Gender identity and sexual psychopathology in men: A psychodynamic analysis of homosexuality, transsexualism, and transvestism. J. Am. Acad. Psychoanal., *1:* 53, 1973.

Parloff, M. Analytic group psychotherapy. In *Modern Psychoanalysis,* J. Marmor, editor, p. 492. Basic Books, New York, 1968.

Peller, L. Reading and daydreams in latency, boy-girl differences. J. Am. Psychoanal. Assoc., *6:* 57, 1958.

Rado, S. An adaptational view of sexual behavior. In *Psychosexual Development in Health and Disease,* P. Hoch and J. Zubin, editors. Grune & Stratton, New York, 1949.

Resnik, H. Eroticized repetitive hangings: A form of self-destructive behavior. Am. J. Psychoth., *26:* 4, 1972.

Saul, L., and Beck, A. Psychodynamics of male homosexuality. Int. J. Psychoanal., *42:* 43, 1961.

Sherfey, M. The evolution and nature of female sexuality in relation to psychoanalytic theory. J. Am. Psychoanal. Assoc., *14:* 28, 1966.

Smith, L., and Smith, J. Co-marital sex: The incorporation of extramarital sex into the marriage relationship. In *Contemporary Sexual Behavior.* J. Zubin and J. Money, editors, p. 391. Johns Hopkins University Press, 1973.

Socarides, C. Theoretical and clinical aspects of overt male homosexuality. J. Am. Psychoanal. Assoc., *8:* 552, 1960.

Socarides, C. The historical development of theoretical and clinical concepts of overt female homosexuality. J. Am. Psychoanal. Assoc., *11:* 386, 1963.

Stein, M. The problem of masochism in the theory and technique of psychoanalysis. J. Am. Psychoanal. Assoc., *4:* 526, 1956.

Stoller, R. *Sex and Gender.* Science House, New York, 1968.

Stoller, R. The term "transvestism." Arch. Gen. Psychiatry, *24:* 230, 1971.

Stroller, R. Etiological factors in female transsexualism: A first approximation. Arch. Sex. Behav., *2:* 47, 1972a.

*Stoller, R. Impact of new advances in sex research on psychoanalytic theory. Am. J. Psychiatry, *130:* 241, 1973.

Strachey, J. The nature of the therapeutic action of psycho-analysis. Int. J. Psychoanal., *15:* 127, 1934.

Thompson, C. Changing concepts of homosexuality in psychoanalysis. Psychiatry, *10:* 2, 1947.

Wilbur, C. Clinical aspects of female homosexuality. In *Sexual Inversion.* J. Marmor, editor, p. 268. Basic Books, New York, 1965.

Winnicott, D. Transitional objects and transitional phenomena. Int. J. Psychoanal., *34:* 89, 1953.

Yates, A. *Behavior Therapy.* John Wiley, New York, 1970.

16.2 Behavior Therapy of Sexual Disorders

JOHN PAUL BRADY, M.D.

Introduction

As in other problem areas, the first step in a behavioral approach to sexual disorders is to conduct a behavioral analysis or assessment. This analysis consists of specifying in as explicit and quantitative terms as possible the various disordered behaviors that constitute the clinical problem. The description includes those behavioral and environmental variables that are functionally related to the patient's symptomatic behaviors—for example, situational factors that occasion episodes of sexual dysfunction and the reinforcing (rewarding) reactions of a spouse that may help maintain the dysfunction. The second step is to design and execute a behavioral treatment program that evolves from the behavioral analysis. The interacting processes of behavioral analysis and treatment are illustrated below in the context of a common disorder—sexual frigidity in women.

Sexual Frigidity

Frigidity is an unfortunate term because of its misleading and pejorative connotation, but it is well established in the language. It may be defined broadly as persistent or repeated inadequate sexual responsiveness in appropriate sexual situations. Many circumstances may lead to this complaint, and a thorough evaluation is necessary in every case to identify the nature of the problem and the appropriate mode of treatment. The evaluation must include a general medical, psychiatric, and behavioral assessment. The assessment must also include the patient's sexual partner, both to corroborate the sexual history given by the patient and to ascertain his role in the total clinical picture.

Cases of frigidity tend to fall into one or more of the following four categories.

GENERAL MEDICAL OR GYNECOLOGICAL CONDITIONS

Many metabolic and other chronic diseases may be associated with loss of sexual interest and arousability—for example, hypothyroidism. Local pelvic disease, such as chronic infection and endometriosis, may cause painful coitus, with the subsequent development of anticipatory anxiety and avoidance. The primary treatment of these patients is medical and gynecological. However, the long association of pain with sexual activity may require behavioral treatment after the physical condition is corrected.

PERVASIVE PSYCHIATRIC CONDITIONS

Disruption of sexual function is a common accompaniment of many psychiatric disorders, especially depression and schizophrenia. Here treatment should be directed primarily at these disorders.

MARITAL CONFLICT

Difficulties in a marriage or with a particular sexual partner are probably the most common causes of frigidity. Some women are simply unable to behave sexually or become sexually aroused with a man toward whom they feel angry or resentful or with whom they are in conflict. In other cases, the apparent frigidity may have a manipulative component. In any case, the treatment here must be directed primarily at the marital relationship; behavioral procedures such as contingency contracting may be helpful. The sexual adjustment usually improves as progress is made in the relationship in general.

PRIMARY SEXUAL INHIBITION

This is a common problem that occurs in varying degrees of severity. At one end of the continuum is the recently married and sexually inexperienced woman who eagerly enters sexual activity but has difficulty reaching an orgasm. Reassurance, en-

couragement, and instruction in basic sexual techniques may be sufficient treatment. Toward the other end of the continuum is the woman who has tried for years without success to become relaxed and comfortable in sexual situations. However, sexual approaches by her husband may still elicit anxiety, guilt, or other inappropriate emotional responses that inhibit sexual arousal and abort sexual activity. When sexual maladjustment is severe and prolonged, it almost always has deleterious effects on the marital relationship. Here, however, the marital problems are a consequence rather than a cause of the sexual problems. Sometimes this distinction is not easily made, and some cases represent an admixture of both.

Although the behavioral treatment of primary sexual inhibition must be tailored to each patient's needs, common procedures are outlined below. They are listed in order from the simplest and least time-consuming procedures to the most complex and specialized procedures. In general, the latter are used only if the simpler techniques prove to be insufficient.

Detailed sexual history. Although part of the assessment procedure with every couple, this is also the first step in treatment. Often, inhibited couples have been unable to confide in each other in this area, and a good deal of desensitization occurs as a result of candid and thorough discussions of sexual matters. In addition to interviewing the patient and her husband alone, the therapist should see them conjointly and discuss such topics as the specific types of sexual foreplay and coital activity that each likes and dislikes.

Counseling in sexual techniques. Misinformation and lack of experience play a surprisingly large role in many cases of sexual maladjustment. Knowledge of such simple measures as the use of an artificial lubricant when vaginal secretions are inadequate for coitus—as is often the case with anxious and inhibited brides—can make a great difference. Well written marriage manuals can also be helpful. Here an effective strategy is to have the couple take turns reading the book out loud to each other and then discuss the information after reading each chapter. In addition to the factual information acquired by this process, a good deal of emotional learning takes place. The reading and discussion facilitate further dialogue about sexual concerns between the couple, and some of the anxiety attached to sexual issues is extinguished.

Controlled masturbation. This technique is especially useful with the patient whose chief complaint is her inability to become sexually aroused or to reach an orgasm in coitus with her partner. If she can become sexually aroused to orgasm by herself by manual stimulation or with a mechanical vibrator, it is reassuring evidence to the patient and her therapist that orgasm during coitus is physiologically possible. In a sense, the problem then is one of changing the stimulus conditions under which sexual arousal and orgasm occur from autosexual to heterosexual circumstances. As in many other behavioral procedures, this change can often be accomplished by a shaping process—that is, progressing by small steps from the present conditions that elicit the response to new desirable conditions. Thus, the patient may progress from being aroused to orgasm only with the aid of a mechanical vibrator while alone to orgasm with manual stimulation of her own genitalia to orgasm by manual stimulation by her partner, and eventually to orgasm with coitus. A priming process may be helpful here. For example, the patient may first become sexually aroused but short of orgasm by self-stimulation and then have her partner enter the room and continue the stimulation.

Systematic desensitization. This procedure has wide application in behavior therapy. It is especially useful with the sexually inhibited patient who reports that sexual approaches by her partner elicit anxiety, anger, or other disruptive affects. This writer has found a variant of this procedure, Brevital-aided desensitization, especially useful with such patients (Brady, 1966, 1971). This procedure consists of 3 steps.

First, with the aid of the therapist, the patient constructs a graded list of hierarchy of scenes that provoke increasing degrees of emotional discomfort. In a severe case, a fantasized scene of being kissed on the cheek by the husband may elicit a small but detectable amount of anxiety. This may be the first or least anxiety-provoking scene. The

second may be being kissed on the lips by the husband and so forth. Typically, the last or most anxiety-provoking scene entails some variety of intercourse. The intervening 15 to 20 scenes involve other sexual activities.

The second step is the induction of a psychophysiological state that is inhibitory of anxiety. This is accomplished by having the patient relax in a comfortable couch or reclining chair with the aid of subanesthetic doses of methohexital sodium (Brevital). The use of this ultrashort acting intravenous barbiturate obviates the need for preliminary training in deep muscular relaxation, as is usually done in desensitization therapy. To be maximally effective, it is essential that the procedure involve little discomfort and that the general setting be conducive to relaxation. A sharp, disposable number 22 needle is used in a single venipuncture, and the patient is advised that the drug will facilitate relaxation and freedom from tension but that she must work along with it. As can be seen in Figure 1, the general setting of the room is intentionally casual and nonclinical. A female nurse is also present, in part for medical-legal reasons. Typically, about 2.5 ml. of the 1 per cent solution (25 mg.) are sufficient to induce a state of deep muscular relaxation without marked drowsiness or sleep. Verbal suggestions of relaxation and calm are given at the same time. Usually the patient is in a deeply relaxed and tension-free state within 4 to 5 minutes.

The third step consists of instructing the patient to imagine vividly the first or least anxiety-provoking scene of the hierarchy. The theory is that the psychophysiological state brought about by the drug and the verbal suggestions will inhibit or countercondition the disphoric affects attached to sexual scenes. Small additional amounts of Brevital may be given to the patient by means of the same venipuncture during a 20-minute treatment session. As elsewhere in desensitization therapy, the patient proceeds systematically along her hierarchy of scenes from session to session until the last scene can be vividly imagined with equanimity.

The Brevital-aided desensitization procedure is both safe and effective. The incidence of side effects and complications is low, especially when some procedural details are

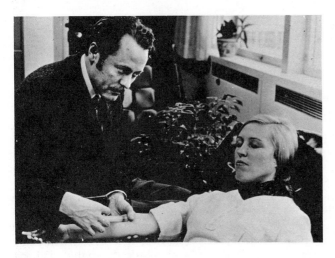

FIGURE 1. Deep relaxation induced with the aid of intravenous methohexital sodium. The patient is being modeled by a research nurse.

followed (Brady, 1967; Munjack and Razani, 1974).

It is important to include the patient's husband in the treatment plan. The nature of the treatment is explained to the couple in a joint interview before treatment begins. They are advised that sexual contacts during the treatment are desirable since this insures good carry over from the imaginal to the real-life situation. However, it is stressed that sexual activity must always stop short of emotional or physical discomfort to the patient. Usually, this means stopping short of the point that has been deconditioned in treatment. This is essential, since a traumatic sexual encounter may resensitize the patient, and therapeutic progress may be lost. Some clinicians have included the husband in the treatment in a more active manner, such as having him present during treatment sessions to verbally present the hierarchy scenes. This technique has obvious advantages.

Impotence and Premature Ejaculation

The causes of impotence are as varied as those of frigidity, and analogous diagnostic categories can be identified. (1) Although general medical and urogenital conditions account for only a small percentage of instances of impotence, their role is sometimes underestimated. In addition to lesions of the spinal cord and local organs, temporal lobe lesions (Hierons and Saunders, 1966), long standing diabetes mellitus (Ellenberg, 1971),

and the chronic abuse of ethanol (Lemere and Smith, 1973) and other drugs may lead to persistent impotence. (2) Depression and other pervasive psychiatric disorders may be associated with impotence. (3) Marital conflict may also play a role. (4) Impotence may be a manifestation of psychogenic sexual inadequacy that is usually mediated by anxiety. Sometimes the anxiety is in response to heterosexual activity itself. Fear of sexual failure is often an important component. The same procedures described above for the treatment of primary sexual inhibition in women are applicable here, including Brevital-aided systematic desensitization (Friedman, 1968). However, an in vivo variant of desensitization therapy is especially powerful for the treatment of impotence, especially when there is a large component of fear of failure.

A commonly occurring story in cases of impotence is that the problem began or was exacerbated by a failure to maintain erection during coitus for more or less adequate reasons—intoxication, being interrupted, extreme fatigue, for example. However, the failure experience resulted in the patient's anticipating failure on the next occasion, when conditions were good. However, the anticipatory anxiety interfered with persistent erection, which led to a further sense of failure, inadequacy, and anticipatory anxiety, and a vicious circle was set up.

The in vivo desensitization procedure consists in reversing these negative expectations (Wolpe, 1969). The treatment requires the skillful and understanding cooperation of a sexual partner who, along with the patient, is apprised of both the rationale and the mechanics of the procedure. In brief, the patient and his partner are told that they are to approach coitus through a series of small steps over a number of sexual occasions. Typically, they are instructed that the first such session is to consist simply in mild forms of foreplay without coitus and with minimal genital contacts. This strategy takes the pressure off the patient to perform up to some standard. The second session may go a little further, perhaps to the point of genital petting but with no expectation of persistent erection, orgasm, or coitus. In this process the patient's self-confidence is restored, and the growing sexual arousal associated with these activities may be expected to inhibit remaining anxiety responses. The rate at which sexual activity progresses is set by the rate at which the patient's self-confidence and performance is restored. Often, an adequate erection and coitus are accomplished after five to 10 such sessions.

Patients who are subject to impotence by this mechanism of intense anticipatory anxiety about sexual performance often lack self-confidence in other areas. They may benefit from additional modes of treatment. However, this in vivo desensitization procedure is surprisingly effective in restoring sexual function and, indirectly, a greater sense of mastery and adequacy in other areas.

Premature ejaculation may be treated by an analogous procedure of gradually increasing the intensity and duration of sexual stimulation across sexual situations with the aid of a cooperative partner. Masters and Johnson (1970) have written extensively on these techniques.

Homosexuality

Patients with this complaint require detailed assessment of their social and sexual behavior and current adjustment to ascertain the locus of the problem and to design an effective treatment program. Favorable prognostic signs include a strong motivation to become exclusively heterosexual and a past history of some heterosexual behavior. Some of the commonly indicated treatment procedures are given below. In most cases a combination of procedures is required.

DECONDITIONING HETEROSEXUAL ANXIETY

Clinicians of various theoretical persuasions have stressed that homosexual behavior in many male patients is related to fear of women—in particular, fear of sexual contact with them (Bieber, 1969; Kraft, 1967). For whatever historical or developmental reasons, sexual closeness to women elicits anxiety. The homosexual adjustment may be viewed as a defensive reaction to this situation or as a substitute gratification of sexual needs. A number of clinicians have used systematic desensitization successfully in the treatment of homosexuals (Kraft, 1967; LoPiccolo, 1971). Typical hierarchies in these cases involve scenes of increasing sexual intimacy with women. This is especially useful for ameliorating anxiety elicited by specific sexual stimuli.

A related procedure, called assertive training, is useful for ameliorating the excessive shyness, submissiveness, or fearfulness shown by some homosexuals in even nonsexual encounters with women. This procedure consists of helping the patient become appropriately assertive or aggressive with women across a wide range of everyday situations. Several related techniques are involved. One is behavioral rehearsal, in which the patient imagines he is in real-life situations with women that give him difficulty—dealing with a hostile waitress in a restaurant, a coquettish secretary where he works, or a domineering female relative. With the aid of the therapist, he rehearses specific behavioral responses to these situations. Both the content of what he says and the manner of delivery (tone, loudness, eye contact) are important (Serber, 1972). In addition, the therapist may role play particular situations with him. A female therapist is useful in this technique. Finally, the patient may be given particular assignments to be completed between treatment sessions. He may be instructed to intentionally enter troublesome situations in order to practice recently rehearsed assertive behavior in vivo. Usually, he begins with the easier situations first, as in systematic desensitization therapy. The therapist makes use of his therapeutic relationship with the patient by delivering strong social reinforcement in the form of approval and praise as the patient successfully completes each assignment. Thus, the patient learns to be comfortable in a new role. The anxiety previously associated with overly submissive and timid behavior is counterconditioned by more masculine, assertive responses. Usually, the response of women to these newly acquired behaviors of the patient is inherently rewarding; hence, the new behavior is reinforced in the natural environment.

ORGASMIC RECONDITIONING

This procedure is based on the theory that stimuli can come to elicit sexual arousal and sexual behavior by being paired with the release of sexual tension (Marquis, 1970). In the treatment of male homosexuals, it consists of having the patient masturbate with whatever homosexual fantasies are necessary until he senses that orgasm is inevitable. There is usually a 2 to 4-second interval between this awareness and actual orgasm (Masters and Johnson, 1966). During this critical interval the patient switches his homosexual fantasy to an appropriate heterosexual one. The idea is that an association will be formed between intense sexual arousal and the reinforcing release of sexual tension and heterosexual cues. Usually, the patient carries out this exercise on a daily basis at home.

Once he is successful in timing the sequence properly, he can begin to introduce the heterosexual fantasies earlier in time—that is, before orgasm is inevitable. A marked decrease in sexual arousal after switching fantasies is generally evidence that he has introduced the heterosexual fantasies too soon on that occasion. He can remedy this situation by switching back to the original fantasy until sexual arousal is again present and then, when closer to orgasm, again switching to heterosexual cues.

In time, many patients are able to successfully introduce heterosexual stimuli early in masturbation and remain aroused. This is evidence that previously neutral or weak heterosexual cues are now functioning as conditioned stimuli and can elicit or facilitate sexual arousal. This arousability usually carries over to actual heterosexual encounters.

In addition, an analogous reconditioning technique may be used in actual sexual situations with female partners. Here the patient may fantasize a homosexual situation until orgasm is imminent. He then focuses on the actual, ongoing, heterosexual situation. This procedure is especially useful in the treatment of homosexual men who report difficulty in being aroused in heterosexual situations.

AVERSIVE CONDITIONING PROCEDURES

To this writer these techniques have at most an adjunctive use in the treatment of homosexuality. The mere suppression of maladaptive homosexual behavior, without the development of alternative behaviors that are socially and sexually gratifying, may result in anxiety or depression in the patient. They are best used in conjunction with or after procedures directed at developing new, heterosexual behaviors. Various aversive conditioning procedures have been described for the treatment of homosexuality. The relative efficacy and modus operandi of these procedures is by no means clear (McConaghy and Barr, 1973). Some follow a Pavlovian, conditioned-aversion paradigm, in which homosexual cues are paired with drug-induced nausea and vomiting. Others follow a punishment paradigm—the viewing of sexually arousing stimuli, in the form of male photographs projected on a screen, is followed by harmless but painful electric shock. Still others have an avoidance component in that the patient can avoid electric shocks on some conditioning trials by operating a button that terminates the projected image. For reviews of these procedures, the reader is referred to Barlow (1972), Feldman (1966) and Rachman and Teasdale (1969).

SOCIOSEXUAL COUNSELING

Many homosexual patients have little or no experience of a sexual or general social nature with women. Even when the patient is eager to form heterosexual relationships, his current behavioral repertoire is not equal to the task. Social and sexual counseling is needed. Behavioral rehearsal and role playing are useful here, as are graded in vivo exercises that are repeated and discussed with the therapist.

Female homosexuals seek treatment less often than male homosexuals. However, the procedures described above are generally applicable to them, too.

Sexual Deviation

The treatment of fetishism, pedophilia, exhibitionism, voyeurism, and other deviations depends critically on a behavioral analysis of the individual patient. Often these patients prove to be overly passive and submissive, and assertive training is beneficial. The deconditioning of heterosexual anxiety and sociosexual training is essential in many patients.

Conditioned aversion has been used extensively with these disorders, but this treatment should be adjunctive. Orgasmic reconditioning, described above, is especially useful in the treatment of sexual deviates who fail to become adequately aroused by socially acceptable, heterosexual stimuli (Marquis, 1970). For example, a patient with a pedophilic problem may report that he can become intensely aroused during masturbation by having fantasies of sexual play with little girls. In daily treatment exercises at home he may be instructed to do this but to switch his fantasies to adult women when orgasm is imminent. As in the use of this treatment with homosexual persons, he should then progressively move the adult female fantasy to an earlier point in the masturbation-to-orgasm sequence so that, in time, both fantasied and overt sexual activity with adult women are arousing and satisfying. Other forms of behavioral intervention are also indicated.

Conclusions

This brief review by no means includes all the behavioral procedures that have been described for the treatment of sexual disorders, and additional procedures will be developed as more is known about the acquisition and elimination of sexual habits as learned behavior.

REFERENCES

Barlow, D. H. Aversive procedures. In *Behavior Modification: Principles and Clinical Applications.* W. S. Agras, editor, pp. 87-125. Little, Brown, Boston, 1972.

Bieber, I. *Homosexuality: A Psychoanalytic Study.* Holt, Rinehart & Winston, 1969.

*Brady, J. P. Brevital-relaxation treatment of frigidity. Behav. Res. Ther., *4:* 71, 1966.

Brady, J. P. Comments on methohexitone-aided systematic desensitization. Behav. Res. Ther., *5:* 257, 1967.

Brady, J. P. Brevital-aided systematic desensitization. In *Advances in Behavior Therapy, 1969.* R. D. Rubin, H. Fensterheim, A. A. Lazarus, and C. M. Franks, editors, pp. 77-83. Academic Press, New York, 1971.

*Brady, J. P. Systematic desensitization. In *Behavior Modification: Principles and Clinical Applications,* W. S. Agras, editor, pp. 127-150. Little, Brown, Boston, 1972.

Ellenberg, M. Impotence in diabetes: The neurological fact. Ann. Intern. Med., *75:* 213, 1971.

Feldman, M. P. Aversion therapy for sexual deviations: A critical review. Psychol. Bull., *65:* 65, 1966.

Friedman, D. The treatment of impotence by Brevital relaxation therapy. Behav. Res. Ther., *6:* 257, 1968.

Hierons, R., and Saunders, M. Impotence in patients with temporal-lobe lesions. Lancet, *2:* 761, 1966.

Kraft, T. A case of homosexuality treated by systematic desensitization. Am. J. Psychother., *21:* 815, 1967.

Lemere, F., and Smith, J. W. Alcohol-induced sexual impotence. Am. J. Psychiatry, *130:* 212, 1973.

LoPiccolo, J. Case study: Systematic desensitization of homosexuality. Behav. Ther., *2:* 394, 1971.

*Marquis, J. N. Orgasmic reconditioning: Changing sexual object choice through controlling masturbation fantasies. J. Behav. Ther. Exp. Psychiatry, *1:* 263, 1970.

Masters, W. H., and Johnson, V. E. *Human Sexual Response.* Little, Brown, Boston, 1966.

Masters, W. H., and Johnson, V. E. *Human Sexual Inadequacy.* Little, Brown, Boston, 1970.

*McConaghy, N., and Barr, R. F. Classical, avoidance and backward conditioning treatments of homosexuality. Br. J. Psychiatry, *122:* 151, 1973.

Munjack, D., and Razani, J. Side effects of Brevital-aided desensitization. Behav. Ther., 1974.

Rachman, S., and Teasdale, J. *Aversion Therapy and Behavior Disorders.* University of Miami Press, Coral Gables, Fla., 1969.

Serber, M. Teaching the nonverbal components of assertive training. J. Behav. Ther. Exp. Psychiatry, *3:* 179, 1972.

*Wolpe, J. *The Practice of Behavior Therapy.* Pergamon, New York, 1969.

16.3   Dual-Sex Therapy

VIRGINIA A. SADOCK, M.D.,
and BENJAMIN J. SADOCK, M.D.

Introduction

Historians, authors, and anthropologists have recorded human sexual practices, specifically or by inference, throughout man's history. Pioneers in psychiatry like Havelock Ellis, Krafft-Ebing, and Freud focused broadly on man's sexuality. Recently there has been more specific research by Kinsey and by Masters and Johnson. The sexual mores of each civilization have influenced or stood in contrast to individual sexual practices. Certainly, they have influenced public behavior. Sexual codes have varied from culture to culture and era to era.

American society is currently experiencing radical changes in its prevalent sexual attitudes. With the advent of effective birth control methods and legalized abortion, sexual activity as a pleasurable function has been clearly differentiated from procreation. Women are sharing sexual responsibility with men as both seek to gratify their needs. The Kinsey reports of 1948 and 1953 published the degree, type, and frequency of sexual activity occurring in this country, bringing sexual practices from the realm of inference and secrecy into accepted, if still private, reality. The recent Presidential Commission on Pornography advised against sexual repression, encouraging the candid discussion of sexuality in society and the acceptability of frankly sexually stimulating material. One of the results of this sexual revolution has been the demand for sexual counseling by individuals and couples.

Sexual counseling programs—patterned on the therapy at the Reproductive Biology Research Foundation in St. Louis, Missouri, offered by William Masters and Virginia Johnson—are springing up throughout the country. Masters and Johnson did pioneer research on physiological responses to sexual stimulation and originated a treatment method to deal with specific sexual complaints.

Most of these programs accept only married couples for treatment. Basic to the therapy is the concept of the marital-unit problem. There is no acceptance of a sick half of a patient couple. Both are involved in a relationship in which there is sexual distress, and both, therefore, must participate in the therapy program.

Presenting complaints may include premature ejaculation, primary or secondary impotence, or ejaculatory incompetence in the man; lack of orgasmic response, dyspareunia, and vaginismus in the woman, and general sexual incompatibility resulting from lack of interest or desire in either the man or the woman.

The presenting sexual problem often reflects other areas of disharmony or misunderstanding in the marriage. The marital relationship as a whole is treated, with emphasis on sexual functioning as a part of that relationship. Psychological and physiological aspects of sexual functioning are discussed, and an educative attitude is employed. Suggestions are made for specific sexual activity, and these suggestions are followed in the privacy of the couple's home.

The crux of the program is the round-table session in which a male and female therapy team clarifies, discusses, and works through the problems with the couple. These four-way sessions require active participation on the part of the patients. The aim of the therapy is to establish or re-establish communication within the marital unit. Sex is emphasized as a natural function that flourishes in the appropriate domestic climate, and improved communication is encouraged toward that end.

The therapy team approach is an essential part of the treatment plan. The woman of the patient couple is represented by the female therapist and the man by the male therapist. In this type of treatment, support, challenge, criticism, and encouragement are best accepted when offered by the therapist of the same sex. By the same token, a patient may really listen to his or her mate's words for the first time when they are restated or represented by the opposite-sex therapist.

Treatment is short term and is behaviorally oriented. The co-therapists attempt to reflect the situation as they see it rather than interpret underlying dynamics. An undistorted picture of the relationship presented by a dual-sex team often corrects the myopic, narrow view held individually by each marriage partner. This new perspective can disrupt the vicious cycle of relating in which the couple has been caught, and improved, more effective communication can be encouraged.

In the Masters and Johnson treatment, couples undergo thorough physical exams, laboratory work-ups, hormonal studies, for example, and psychological examinations before therapy proceeds. Initial histories are taken to determine suitability for this type of treatment. When there is evidence of major underlying psychopathology, further psychiatric evaluation is suggested, and participation in the program may be deferred until the patient seems more able to benefit from it. Concurrent psychotherapy with a psychiatrist while participating in these programs is frequently recommended by such workers as Schumacher.

Each patient is interviewed individually by both the male and the female therapist prior to the round-table sessions. A complete sexual history is obtained, and this history is later reflected back to the couple with the aim of helping them understand their present problem. The individual sessions also enable the therapists to understand the life-style of the patients and enable them to make suggestions that fit into that life-style.

Specific exercises are prescribed for the couple to help them with their particular problem. Most forms of sexual inadequacy involve lack of information, misinformation, and fear of performance. The couples are, therefore, specifically prohibited from any sexual play other than that prescribed by the therapists. Beginning exercises usually focus on heightening sensory awareness to touch, sight, sound, and smell. Initially, intercourse is interdicted, and couples learn to give and receive bodily pleasure without the pressure of performance. They are simultaneously learning how to communicate nonverbally in a mutually satisfactory way and learning that sexual foreplay is as important as intercourse and orgasm. Genital stimulation is eventually added to general body stimulation. The couple are instructed sequentially to try various positions for intercourse, without necessarily completing the union, and to use varieties of stimulating techniques before they are instructed to proceed with intercourse. The approaches vary with different presenting complaints, but the over-all goal is always to initiate an educational process, to diminish fears of performance felt by both sexes, and to facilitate communication with the marital unit in sexual and nonsexual areas.

Round-table sessions follow each new exercise period, and problems and satisfactions, both sexual and in other areas of the couple's lives, are discussed. Specific instructions and the introduction of new exercises geared to the individual couple's progress are reviewed in each session. Gradually, the couple gains confidence and learns or relearns to communicate, verbally and sexually. Masters and Johnson report an over-all success rate of 80 per cent in the varieties of sexual disorders that they have treated, and these results have been replicated in other centers.

Improved Communication

Specific instructions are given in the areas of verbal and nonverbal communication. Couples are urged to set aside prescribed periods each day just to talk to each other in order to overcome frequent patterns of withdrawal into silence or busy work. As far as possible, phone conversations, involvement with children, and television watching are banned during these periods of time. The couples are also taught techniques of communication that can help them keep in touch with their own feelings and express them to their partners. Each is encouraged to start as many sentences as possible with the word "I"—"I feel . . ." "I think . . ." "I believe . . ."— and to question his mate directly rather than to guess what the partner is thinking or feeling. The couples are also urged to use their angry feelings as a signal that they are severely threatened or hurt and to explore their anger within that framework. The need to be vulnerable to one's mate if there is to be effective communication is stressed throughout the sessions. These techniques force the patients to be conscious of their own reactions to situations, to limit projection, to equalize responsibility for communication, and often to break the cycle of interaction when there is one attacking and one victimized or a mutually withdrawn couple.

At the end of a round-table session early in treatment, a couple were given specific instructions regarding foreplay. The wife, a talkative woman, became anxious and kept asking her husband, "Do you understand?" The husband, a passive-aggressive man, became enraged and followed his usual pattern of withdrawal, which only increased the woman's anxiety. When she was able to express her anxiety directly and say, "I'm getting nervous and confused. I know I won't remember the directions; will you?" the husband was put in a protective position, in which to withdraw would be openly rejecting.

Treatment
IMPOTENCE

Sexual functioning in the human male is influenced by complex conscious and unconscious psychic factors, by such physiological factors as neurological and endocrine status and age, and by such socio-cultural factors as income and education and the prevailing sexual mores and attitudes about women. These are all taken into account prior to dual-sex therapy. The patient is physically examined and questioned as to type and quantity of drug intake, and he undergoes laboratory tests, psychological tests, and a psychiatric interview.

Impotence is that condition wherein the man cannot obtain or maintain an erection satisfactory for purposes of heterosexual coitus. In primary impotence the man is never able to obtain an erection sufficient for vaginal insertion. In secondary impotence the man has successfully achieved vaginal penetration at some time in his sexual life but is later unable to do so. In selective impotence the man is able to have coitus in come circumstances but not in others. Impotence is a relatively common condition; it is a particularly distressing one in the younger years of adult life. Masters and Johnson report the fear of impotence in all men over 40, which reflects the fear of loss of virility with growing old.

Kinsey et al. found that impotence increases with age, with few men in their sample being impotent at age 35, and 77 per cent impotent at age 80. But impotence is not a regularly occurring phenomenon in the aged. Studies by Finkle and Moyers and by Newman and Nichols indicate that having an available sexual partner is more closely related to continuing potency in the aging man than is age per se, and Masters found that the more active the sex life was earlier in life, the more active it is in old age.

After the initial history taking and examination, the couple and the dual-sex team proceed with the round-table sessions. A good portion of these sessions deal with the extrasexual interaction of the couple to enable them to work through daily or long standing hostilities, misunderstandings, and fears and to increase their communication. At the same time, they are given specific instructions in how to communicate physically. When impotence is the main complaint, intercourse is forbidden, and the couple begin with a series of nongenital caressing exercises. The couple's approach to and interaction during these exercises are often a microcosm of their usual way of relating. The man and the woman are alternately assigned the role of initiating a session of caressing, so the responsibility for their sexual interaction is shared and does not rest with one partner. The man is encouraged to enjoy the passive role of being caressed as well as the active role of caresser, and the couple is relieved of having to praise each other, since the session is silent. With emphasis removed not only from intercourse but even from the genitalia, the couple relearns the more general pleasures of touching each other. The man, in particular, is relieved of the pressure to perform—with intercourse forbidden, an erection is no longer a necessity—and this relief in itself is often enough to allow him to gain an erection quite easily. The couple next includes genital stimulation in their sessions of physical caressing, with each alternately guiding the partner's hand in the patterns of touch found most pleasing. This technique reinforces the idea of responsibility for one's own sexuality, while being a practical way of instructing one's partner. At this stage, the patients may manipulate each other to orgasm when they so desire.

When the couple has had enough good sexual experiences without intercourse and can, therefore, tolerate the idea of an unsuccessful coital experience, they are advised to try intercourse. The burden of the union is lightened for the man in that the woman is instructed to assume the superior position and encouraged to take charge of inserting the man's penis into her vagina. This helps the man through what is frequently his most vulnerable moment, that of insertion, and is also more practical, since the woman has a much better sense of the angle of her vagina than her partner does.

At this time, when the man has been achieving erections for several weeks and is able to sustain it through insertion and entry, the pathology of the woman may often emerge more clearly. Previously, her mate's impotence may have protected her from facing her own fears or negative feelings about intercourse. She may balk at accepting equal responsibility for their sexual interactions or responsibility for her own sexuality. Usually, her attitudes have been apparent to the therapists from the time of the initial history taking and have been discussed from the early sessions, making them easier to work on at this point.

When the couple is quite at ease with insertion and entry, they are instructed to carry intercourse as far as they care to, including orgasm.

Set-backs are examined and learned from, and the couple is encouraged to take an optimistic attitude and to rely on sexual techniques not involving intercourse during difficult periods. The experience that sexual satisfaction can be achieved in other ways and the equal valuation of alternative methods by the therapists continue to relieve the man of performance pressure and the woman of her frustrations.

Mr. and Mrs. A.—he was 48, and she was 43—had been married for 20 years when they came for therapy. They were a white, middle-class couple, living in the suburb of a large city. Both evaluated their relationship as quite good. They had two children, one away at college and one in high school. The husband owned his own business, and the wife was involved in community affairs and worked as a legal secretary 1 day a week.

The husband had had two brief sexual experiences prior to his marriage. The wife was a virgin when they married. Neither had had extramarital affairs. They described their sexual relationship as good until 2 years before they were seen. They had had intercourse twice a week, and, although the husband had increasing difficulty in maintaining an erection in the vagina, his wife was able to achieve orgasm both vaginally and by clitoral manipulation. They used the male superior position consistently during coitus. During the past 2 years the husband had had an increasing problem with impotence, and the couple had had no physical contact, although they shared a bed, for 8 months before they were seen in therapy.

The wife could think of no precipitating event but felt that she contributed to the continuing condition because she was "tight as a drum" when her husband approached her, thinking, "If we try and fail, it's even worse than not trying at all." The husband felt that he was being punished for masturbating as an adolescent and revealed with great shame that he still masturbated on occasion.

A good part of the initial sessions were devoted to exploring masturbatory myths and representing the husband's current masturbatory practices as evidence of a still strong sexual drive. The prohibition of intercourse relieved the enormous pressure on the husband to get an erection and enabled the wife to approach him and receive his attentions in a relaxed manner. Her responsiveness was an important stimulant for her husband, and he quickly began responding with erections. The couple moved quickly to the stage of intercourse. At this point the wife began complaining bitterly about the female superior position, stating that she had never had an orgasm that way and that she did not like manual manipulation after her husband's orgasm.

With confrontation, as well as encouragement and support from the therapists, she was then able to examine her own contributions to their difficulties. She had a reservoir of anger over what she perceived as taking second place to her in-laws, particularly her mother-in-law, and to her husband's business and was expressing this anger through their sexual play. She learned to confront her husband more directly, and he responded with greater attentiveness out of bed. At the time of discharge from therapy, the couple was having intercourse once a week, alternating male and female superior positions and occasionally lateral positions. They were also having at least two sessions of caressing or manual stimulation a week.

UNCONSUMMATED MARRIAGE

Couples come with this complaint after suffering lack of consummation for periods varying from several months to several years. In spite of the extremity of lack of sexual contact in such a couple, this is an unusually easy disorder to treat. The couple determined to remain together in spite of extreme sexual difficulties is highly motivated and makes good material for this type of treatment. Typically, with this complaint, both husband and wife are misinformed or uninformed regarding all areas of sexuality and are very inexperienced. It is not unusual for both partners to be virgins at the time of their marriage. Sexual prohibitions absorbed from parents and society in general and lack of sexual education play large parts in the unconsummated marriage.

The couple is educated jointly about their sexual anatomy and physiology. They are then instructed in techniques of foreplay and genital stimulation. Initial prohibitions of intercourse allay the usually present fear of penetration in the woman until she becomes more comfortable with her own sexuality. It also relieves performance pressure from the man. It is vital, early in therapy, to make clear that successful intercourse depends on both partners, as it is usually the husband in these cases who has assumed total responsibility for the couple's failure to function sexually. In addition to relieving pressure from the husband, this mutual responsibility enables the wife to examine her own sexual attitudes and actions. The wife is instructed early in treatment on the techniques of masturbation and is encouraged to enjoy her own sexuality. If she suffers from vaginismus, she is instructed in the use of size-graded dilators. Fears of or desires for pregnancy in both partners are also discussed, as these can be contributing factors to lack of sexual union.

Usually, the immediate relief of pressure to have intercourse, a sound sexual education, contraceptive advice (where necessary), dilators patiently used to alleviate vaginal constriction, and the presence of authority figures (in the form of the therapists) who encourage sexual interaction enable the couple to make rapid progress in treatment and to consummate their union. With this complaint, the couple is advised to have intercourse first in the male superior position, as this position is generally most acceptable to both partners. The wife is, nonetheless, expected to help her husband during the process of intromission. Once successful intercourse has been experienced, the couple is able to repeat the experience with less and less anxiety. When the wife is suffering from vaginismus—involuntary spasm of the muscles surrounding the vagina, making the vaginal space virtually impenetrable—the wife directs and aids the husband in inserting dilators graduated in size into her vagina prior to penile penetration. Follow-up sessions are held to help the couple through inevitable set-backs until they are secure enough to sustain an occasional unsuccessful attempt at coitus. At that point they are discharged.

Mr. and Mrs. B. were a young, attractive, middle-class couple raised in the Middle West. They had been married for 1 year at the time they were first seen in treatment. Mrs. B. was 22, recently graduated from college, and erratically involved in job hunting. Mr. B. was 24 and half way toward achieving a doctoral degree. Both sets of parents contributed to the couple's support. Both the man and the woman came from strongly religious families, with parents who held markedly puritanical attitudes toward sex. Factual sex education was nonexistent, and both were virgins at the time of their marriage. The husband had a history of masturbation, and he masturbated about once a week; he would not use his hands, however, but rubbed himself against the bed. The wife denied any masturbation but was able to enjoy erotic fantasies, with strong exhibitionistic components, to the point of orgasm.

Their mutual premarital sex play had involved genital stimulation of the wife by the husband. She had refused to remove all her underclothing, however, and had refused to stimulate him by touching his genitals. At this point, the husband had been rebelling against his religious upbringing, but Mrs. B. had insisted he return to the fold as a condition of their marriage. On their wedding night the wife consciously anticipated a very painful ordeal. The man was able to achieve a strong erection, but at the time of intromission the woman screamed loudly in pain, and he became impotent. Subsequent attempts at intercourse met with failure, and the husband developed an increasing problem with impotence, becoming unable to gain an erection at all.

A great deal of work was done with the wife in the initial sessions; to get her to assume equal responsibility for the lack of consummation of the marriage, to face her own sexual difficulties, to face her conflicting desires to have her husband passive in certain areas (regarding household matters, feelings toward religion, reaction to his in-laws) though assertive sexually, and to alleviate the rejection she felt because of her husband's impotence.

Much of this work was accomplished simply by explaining that it was normal and desirable for women to stimulate men, that men did not automatically achieve erections at the sight of a nude woman, and that intercourse was not usually a painful experience; by dealing with her negative and unrealistic self-image; and by encouraging her strong, if suppressed, sexual drive.

Relieved of some of his feelings of inadequacy and guilt for not consummating the marriage, the husband was able to overcome somewhat his tendency toward passivity and to express differences of opinion with his wife. Many extrasexual areas were discussed: interference by both sets of in-laws, money problems, the wife's desire to continue her education, and the lack of desire by both partners for children in spite of parental pressure to have them.

The husband regained his erections early in treatment, and the wife's avoidance of sexual contact was unmasked and dealt with by direct confrontation. She was encouraged to masturbate, to explore her vagina with her fingers, and to indulge in her erotic fantasies. After seven sessions the couple was able to consummate the marriage. At the time of discharge from therapy, the couple was working on the remaining problems of passivity in the husband. The wife had not yet experienced an orgasm while containing the husband's penis, but she was able to masturbate to orgasm, and the couple was having intercourse once a week.

PREMATURE EJACULATION

In premature ejaculation the man arrives at orgasm and ejaculation before he wishes to do so. Often used to describe the extreme condition, wherein the man ejaculates immediately after entering the vagina or even before and the sexual attempt ends in a fiasco, the term also applies to all degrees of prematurity wherein the man is dissatisfied with his performance. The dissatisfaction invariably relates to his having ejaculated and lost his erection before his sexual partner has reached orgasm.

Masters and Johnson define the condition in terms of the marital unit. Thus, premature ejaculation is present when the penis is not in the vagina long enough to produce orgasm in the woman 50 per cent of the time. Premature ejaculation is more common in college-educated men, and it relates to their concern for partner satisfaction. Men who did not attend college have less concern about their partner's achieving orgasm and do not consider ejaculatory control as a desirable technique.

Establishing the climate. The first step in treating this complaint is to re-establish a climate of comfort and acceptance for the couple's sexual interaction. By the time the couple comes for treatment, the husband's sense of inadequacy and the wife's sense of frustration have usually led to a pattern of very infrequent intercourse. This infrequency of intercourse only increases the problem, as a longer time between ejaculatory experiences in itself leads to increased rapidity of ejaculation. The couple is made aware of this fact, the man is encouraged to masturbate, and a moratorium is placed on intercourse. The couple is re-educated to enjoy touch and body stimulation in general. When the anxiety of physical closeness has been diminished, they are instructed to proceed to genital stimulation and then intercourse and are simultaneously given specific techniques to deal with the premature ejaculation.

Altering the threshold of excitability. The man or the wife stimulates the erect penis until the premonitory sensations of impending orgasm and ejaculation are felt. The penile stimulation is stopped abruptly. A variant of this technique is the squeezing of the coronal ridge of the penis by the female. Sexual excitement and possibly the erection subside over the course of the ensuing minutes. The stimulation is then started again, and, as before, it is stopped at the first sensations of impending orgasm. This technique appears to train the threshold of excitability to be more tolerant of the stimuli. This exercise is done two or three times a day for 20 to 30 minutes, and after several days coitus is usually prolonged. Masters and Johnson report that this therapy for premature ejaculation is successful in 98 per cent of the cases treated.

Reducing the tactile component. This technique involves reducing the amount or the intensity of vaginal friction or reducing the excitability of the receptor organs in the glans penis. Some find condoms to be a solution to their problem of premature ejaculation. The amount of vaginal friction may also be reduced by limiting the frequency of thrusts or the extent of penis travel within the vagina.

The female co-therapist must enlist the wife's cooperation in treating this complaint. With the knowledge that her own sexual needs will eventually be better met, with emphasis on the fact that the problem has been beyond the husband's conscious control, and with encouragement of manual stimulation and satisfaction of the wife by the husband, the wife is usually able to be a constructive and supportive part of the treatment program.

Mr. and Mrs. C. were newly married when they were seen in treatment, although they had been having sexual relations for more than a year. It was the second marriage for both. Mrs. C. was an exceptionally attractive housewife with two school-age children. She had sporadically done secretarial work. Between marriages she had lived near her parents, and her mother was actively involved in raising her two children. Her father was an alternately seductive and rejecting man. Her previous husband had been a brutal, irresponsible man, but he was, according to the wife, very adequate sexually and "capable of going on all night." She had been orgasmic with him and was orgasmic on occasion with her present husband. However, she was frequently unsatisfied after sexual relations with Mr. C. and would fake an orgasm to "boost his ego." She had experienced satisfactory intercourse with several men before her second marriage, and she "couldn't believe it" when she learned of Mr. C.'s difficulties.

Mr. C. was a handsome, professional man in his mid-thirties. He had three children by his first marriage, and the couple saw them on alternate weekends. He had been the only child of elderly parents. He had few memories of his father, who died when he was 5, and he portrayed his mother as a cold, demanding, and ambitious woman. He married his first wife when he was 20, after she "mistakenly informed him she was pregnant." He

had had only one sexual experience with a prostitute before his marriage, and his sexual relations with his first wife were erratic, with premature ejaculation and at times impotence a problem from the beginning.

Early in treatment the couple was informed that their problem was not unique, a fact that in itself reassured both the husband and the wife. The fact of entering treatment alleviated the wife's sense of responsibility for Mr. C.'s reaction to his sexual problems, and she was able to be honest with him about her own sexual reactions.

During the round-table sessions she verbalized her fears about his commitment to her—fears accentuated by his sexual problems, his general lack of communicativeness, and his tolerance of interference in their lives by his first wife. This new outlet for her pressures and resentment, optimism as to the outcome of treatment, and her own good previous sexual experiences enabled her to function as a supportive part of the therapeutic program.

As Mr. C. began to function more effectively sexually, he was able to deal more assertively with both his ex-wife and his present wife; he became increasingly talkative as the sessions progressed.

At the time of discharge from therapy, he was able to sustain an erection in the vagina for a period of 4 to 5 minutes. The couple was having intercourse two or three times a week, and Mrs. C. was being brought to orgasm manually by her husband after or preceding coitus. Both Mr. and Mrs. C. were optimistic about continuing improvement in their sexual relations.

VAGINISMUS AND DYSPAREUNIA

Dyspareunia, painful or difficult sexual intercourse, and vaginismus, an involuntary spasm of the muscles surrounding the vagina that results in constriction of the vagina, are differentiated from frigidity, but the same underlying fear, hostility, and guilt lead to these consequences. Dyspareunia and vaginismus are less prevalent than frigidity and generally indicate the presence of more severe pathology.

In vaginismus, the involuntary muscle spasm that prevents penile penetration and renders coitus impossible may express the force with which the woman desires to prevent penile entrance into her body. Her perception of the male sexual organ as a dangerous weapon leads her to lose her capacity for sensation. Her concern with her inability to participate in sexual intercourse reinforces her distress and her fears that she is unfeminine or homosexual. Similarly, in dyspareunia the psychogenic fear of anticipated pain makes intercourse unbearable or unpleasant.

Ideally, the therapeutic plan includes education of both partners to bring increased awareness of sexual technique and relationship pitfalls and increased understanding of the part that each partner plays in the problem of the other. Social and internal pressures that characterize female development in society; ignorance of sexual techniques; moral, religious, and parental prohibitions; fear of dependency and of the expression of aggressive impulses; and excessive guilt and fear of coitus—all impinge on the freedom of the woman to develop her capacity for sexual pleasure.

Treatment of vaginismus. A vital part of the treatment of vaginismus is the physical examination, with the husband present so that he is able to see the spasm of muscles resulting in constriction of the vagina. The involuntary nature of this spasm is explained to him by the therapist to lessen his feeling of rejection and to enable him to be supportive and encouraging of his wife throughout treatment. Intercourse is initially prohibited, relieving the wife of fears of penetration, pain, and her own sense of inadequacy and relieving the husband of his frustration in literally coming up against a wall. The couple are then able to enjoy each other physically in a nongenital manner.

The wife is encouraged to take responsibility for her own problems and is, taught to introduce dilators into her vagina in graduated sizes, beginning with a narrow size that could easily be accommodated by a virgin. Since she is performing these exercises herself, she is controlling the anxiety that may be caused by conscious or unconscious rape fantasies, by fear of hurting herself, and by her own vaginal manipulation, and she can stop the exercise at any time. The husband is thus relieved of the role of intruder or aggressor, and she is literally placed in touch with her own sexuality and encouraged to be conscious of it. Treatment usually proceeds rapidly, and intercourse is allowed only when the wife is comfortable with insertion of the largest size in the series of dilators. By that time she has also become more comfortable with her husband's penis through exercises in which she has manually stimulated him to orgasm.

Treatment of dyspareunia. A thorough obstetrical examination is necessary to assure both the patient and the therapist that there is no physical cause for the woman's pain. The couple can then be informed that the dyspareunia is a result of lack of sufficient lubrication and excitement in the woman, involuntary muscle spasm—as in vaginismus—or sensation that is perceived as pain for psychological reasons.

With the initial prohibition of intercourse, the wife is relieved of her fears of penetration and anticipation of pain and is able to learn to relax and enjoy herself in sexual situations with her husband.

The prohibition of intercourse, which is often seen as a threat, may in itself be sufficient to allow her to respond to other genital stimulation. This response enables the husband to learn what is most stimulating to her sexually and to restore the confidence he may have lost during their previous distressing sexual encounters.

Before the couple has intercourse, the husband is satisfied by the wife with either manual or oral manipulation of his genitals. In addition to fulfilling his needs, this manipulation enables the wife to be giving and active sexually and to become comfortable with her husband's genitalia.

She is encouraged to explore herself and to masturbate, and her husband also stimulates her manually before intercourse is attempted. At the first attempt at intercourse during treatment, a sterile lubricant may be prescribed to facilitate entry.

The female superior position is used during coitus because it accentuates the active role being cultivated in the woman and seems less threatening to women who approach intercourse with fear. The wife is responsible for inserting the husband's penis into her vagina, and she feels more in control of what has previously been a threatening situation. In addition, the husband is free to play with the rest of her body in the ways that he has learned please her. For most women, this position also allows for more clitoral stimulation. Intercourse is experienced gradually. First there is simple intromission. Only after the couple can achieve intromission easily and with pleasure do they proceed to movement and eventually to completion.

Mr. and Mrs. Y., a middle-aged couple, had been married for 15 years. For 2 years before being seen in treatment, the wife had been suffering from vaginismus, and the husband, not surprisingly, had recently developed a problem of impotence. He had been a successful salesman but was unemployed at the time the couple was first seen, although he was able to contribute some dividends from a small amount of accumulated stock to the family income. The wife was an administrative assistant to a highly placed executive in an advertising firm. Her job introduced her to many people daily, and she was then the main financial support of the family. They had no children.

Mrs. Y. had been raised very strictly in a non-practicing Catholic family. Her parents held a puritanical attitude toward sex. Her father had been doting but had restricted her social behavior severely, and she had little dating and no sexual experience or sexual education before her marriage. Her mother was an exceptionally pretty but infantile woman who was competitive with Mrs. Y. A paternal aunt who lived with the family had been the primary nurturing figure; she had shown a good deal of warmth and acceptance of Mrs. Y., but she, too, had difficulty accepting sexuality and upheld the father in his social restrictions of the patient. The patient's family was not accepting of Mr. Y. but did not actively oppose the marriage. Neither partner desired children. During the early years of her marriage, Mrs. Y. was able to enter into physical relations with her husband without any complaints but without any pleasure. About 5 years after their marriage, she began to experience pain during intercourse, and their frequency of intercourse was markedly reduced.

At that time, Mrs. Y. became sexually involved with a client of her firm. He was married but had a great deal of freedom of movement and was very experienced sexually. The affair lasted 4 years, and Mrs. Y. was able to respond to him fully; she frequently experienced orgasm. They stopped seeing each other when he moved to a different area.

During and for a time after this affair, Mrs. Y. was able to respond more comfortably to her husband. But 5 years before entering treatment, she began to experience dyspareunia again and, shortly after her husband lost his job, vaginismus.

Mr. Y. was 36 when he married. He was very attacted to his wife and admired her capabilities but was aware of her sexually innocent background and was afraid to express his own sexual needs. As a salesman, he had done considerable traveling and

had had a great deal of sexual experience, primarily with prostitutes. However, he never shared his experiences with his wife verbally or nonverbally, as he was afraid they would be repellent to her.

He was an intelligent man who had worked himself up from a financially impoverished background. He was the second of four children. His father had been communicative and accepting but was an invalid, and his mother had been the main support of the family. Mr. Y. felt she had loved her children but was always too overworked to be able to express it. She was portrayed as a non-demonstrative—even cold—woman.

The standard treatment with dilators, prohibition of intercourse, and reintroduction of nongenital bodily stimulation worked well with this couple. A major factor in the success of treatment here, though, was verbal communication. The couple was encouraged to express their sexual needs and preferences to each other. With help from the therapists, they were able to see each other realistically as sexual people, and they quickly responded to each other on a sexual level. Mr. Y. was surprised but reassured by his wife's interest in his sexual knowledge. It was extremely important for Mrs. Y. to see her husband as a sexually experienced and adept man, which he was, and to feel that he could accept her as a sexual woman. At the time of discharge from therapy, the couple was having intercourse at least three times a week, and Mrs. Y. was frequently orgasmic. In addition, Mr. Y. was much more actively looking for work and had a probable and appealing job prospect.

NONORGASM

Frigidity or sexual anesthesia designates a variety of sexual disorders related to the inhibition of female sexual response, ranging from unsatisfactory orgasm but otherwise vigorous sexual response to complete lack of response to sexual stimulation.

Nonorgasm refers specifically to the inability to achieve orgasm by means of masturbation or coitus. Many women can achieve orgasm through masturbation but not coitus and should not be categorized as nonorgasmic, although some degree of sexual inhibition can be postulated in these instances. Kinsey reported that, by age 35, more than 90 per cent of women have experienced orgasm by means of coitus or masturbation. The psychological factors associated with nonorgasm are variously ascribed to fear of impregnation, fear of rejection by the sexual partner, envy or hostility toward the man, guilt regarding the impropriety of the sex act, and fear of mutilation.

Unresponsiveness may be used as a weapon against the man. To the woman who feels inferior and, therefore, hostile toward the man because of anatomical differences and social roles or because of her dependency on him, sexual nonparticipation may be a bid for independence. Frigidity may also be a defense against earlier unacceptable impulses, such as competitiveness with the mother or forbidden sexual fantasies. Orgasm may also be equated with loss of control and with aggressive, destructive, or violent behavior. Fear of these impulses contributes to sexual inhibition, which is expressed as nonorgastic response.

In addition to psychoanalysis and psychotherapy, the dual-sex therapy approach has been remarkably successful in the treatment of these disorders. The nonorgasmic woman is educated about her sexual anatomy and physiology in conjunction with her partner. The man is instructed in the techniques of foreplay, particularly genital stimulation. In addition, the woman receives specific instructions in masturbatory techniques and may experience her first orgasm by this method applied by her husband or autoerotically.

She then shares with her husband what she has learned through self-stimulation. The couple proceeds slowly from general body and genital stimulation to penile penetration, with the woman in the female superior position. This position allows her freedom of movement and facilitates a teasing technique, in which intercourse is interrupted by periods of rest and non-genital body contact. These enforced interruptions allow for progressive stimulation without the demand for a climax. The man is usually brought to orgasm manually or orally during these sessions. Only toward the end of treatment, when the woman has been able to achieve climax with manual stimulation, is the couple instructed to complete intercourse.

Mr. and Mrs. Z. were a childless couple, both in their late twenties. She was a college instructor, and he was a free-lance writer. The couple had been married for 4 years and came to therapy with a mutual complaint of steadily lessening sexual desire. During the year before they were seen, they had had intercourse six times. In the initial interview Mrs. Z. stated that she had never been able to have an orgasm with her husband and had never experienced an orgasm during intercourse. Her continuing frustration made her increasingly rejecting of her husband sexually, and the tenseness surrounding their sexual interaction began to pervade the rest of their relationship. Mrs. Z. was able to masturbate to orgasm while indulging in masochistic fantasies, but she did so very infrequently.

She was the oldest of four children, raised in an intellectual but undemonstrative and highly controlled family. She attended religious schools until the age of 12. She stated that she had been a very docile child and adolescent but openly rebelled in marrying her husband. Her parents disapproved of him, since he came from a different religious background and a different area of the country. Mrs. Z.'s father particularly objected, and relations between Mr. Z. and his father-in-law were still extremely strained. Mrs. Z. stated that she often felt caught between them.

Mr. Z. was the middle child and the only boy in a family of three children. There was a 20-year age difference between his parents, and the father was not actively involved with the children. His mother had complete charge of their upbringing and allowed them little privacy. He felt that he had always been her pet.

Mr. and Mrs. Z. met while in college, and, although neither was sexually experienced, they were strongly attracted to one another and indulged in enjoyable sexual play, short of intercourse. Mrs. Z. perceived her husband as a very assertive man and was impressed by the way he stood up to her family. When he completed school, a year ahead of Mrs. Z., he broke off the relationship with her and returned home, where he got a job with the local newspaper. During that year Mrs. Z. became involved with another man and enjoyed sexual play with him. She did not have intercourse with him but frequently came to orgasm through manual or oral manipulation. At the time of her graduation, she terminated this relationship and managed to get a job in Mr. Z.'s home town, a large city 1,000 miles from her own home. Two weeks after her arrival, the couple married.

Intercourse had been a disappointment to Mrs. Z. from the beginning. She felt teased instead of fulfilled, but she did not know how to change things.

Her husband felt increasingly rejected and inadequate. The couple was well motivated, intelligent, and quite devoted to each other. They were reassured simply by the fact of coming into therapy and responded well to instructions regarding physical contact. Their premarital expectations were discussed. In effect, each had expected more assertiveness from the other, and, in reality, each had some problem with passivity. Several sessions were also spent dealing with relations with in-laws. Mrs. Z. was encouraged to give priority to her relationship with her husband, and Mr. Z. was encouraged to face and restrain his competitiveness with her father. This changed relationship became easier for both as their sexual contact increased in both quantity and quality.

At the time of their discharge from therapy, the couple was having intercourse several times a week. Mrs. Z. was occasionally able to reach orgasm during intercourse and was frequently able to achieve climax after coitus through manual stimulation. Their extrasexual interaction had been greatly eased, and their appreciation of each other became more realistic.

RETARDED EJACULATION

This disorder is characterized by the inability to achieve orgasm, even though the erection is satisfactory. It must be differentiated from orgasm with ejaculation, which is common in those men receiving thioridazine (Mellaril). At times, retarded ejaculation is selective. The man is able to achieve orgasm as a result of masturbation but not during coitus. There are usually severe conflicts present in these men, including deep seated fears of women. In some, histories of incest with the mother are found. Hostility toward or fear of women and unconscious confusion of the wife with the mother are the dynamics most often encountered.

The couples are treated in an authoritarian, behavioral manner. Increased communication helps clear up projections and distorted perceptions of the opposite sex.

The support of the woman must be enlisted if therapy is to succeed. The way the woman plays into her husband's problem may emerge and be dealt with as treatment progresses. Physically, the couple moves first to general caressing and then to genital caressing. The wife is guided by her husband to stimulate him satisfactorily. The couple stays with manual stimulation until the husband is thoroughly comfortable in coming to orgasm in front of his wife this way. The couple continues manual stimulation until the husband feels that he is approaching orgasm. Only then does he attempt penetration. Once he has been able to ejaculate in his partner's vagina, the spell is broken, and successive attempts become easier, with the man being able to enter the woman earlier in sexual play.

Mr. and Mrs. D. had been married for 3 years. They were 25 and 23, respectively. Although they had frequent intercourse and Mrs. D. was fully responsive, Mr. D. had never been able to ejaculate in her vagina. This fact had been denied and ignored by both partners since the beginning of their marriage.

Mrs. D., who had been a virgin at the time of her marriage, sensed that something was wrong but was reluctant to question her husband directly. Mr. D. was ashamed to bring up the matter himself. He had never been able to ejaculate in any woman's vagina, although he had had numerous premarital sexual encounters, and he had strong feelings of inadequacy. He was able to ejaculate when he masturbated himself. Facing their problem became unavoidable when the couple decided to have a baby. Even then, several joint conversations with Mrs. D.'s gynecologist had been necessary before the couple would come for therapy.

The partners came from similar white, middle-class backgrounds and met when Mrs. D. was in high school and Mr. D. in the service. They liked each other right away and had a pleasant, uneventful courtship.

Mr. D. had been the only son in a family that prized males. He had two sisters, a doting mother, and an overinvolved father. Through the time the couple were seen, Mr. D.'s father called several times daily and insisted on knowing the couple's plans and activities. Mr. D. accepted this involvement as inevitable, and although Mrs. D. resented it, she inadvertently tightened the bonds with her in-laws by enlisting her willing mother-in-law as an ally against Mr. D.'s father.

Mr. D.'s family had always had a raging battle of the sexes going, and both his parents accepted a sexual double standard. In addition, his mother made him fully aware of the pain she experienced during childbirth and of her fear of ever undergoing another such ordeal.

Mr. D. perceived women as simultaneously dangerous and victimized. Ejaculation was, therefore, seen as both hostile and degrading toward his wife. These interpretations were never directly made, but the couple was encouraged to maintain a certain distance from Mr. D.'s family throughout therapy and their mutual interaction was changed through treatment.

Mrs. D. had played directly into her husband's problems with her own fears and inhibitions. Although responsive, she believed that her unattractiveness had caused her husband's problem. She was, in fact, a pleasant-looking young woman. Unable to confront him directly with her fears, she would nag him and increase his well entrenched wariness of women. She also fitted too well into a maternal image. She felt her husband had married her only for her domestic capabilities, and she was afraid to be seductive. She had specific inhibitions about sexual language.

During therapy she was encouraged to express her strong sexual impulses and to confront her husband with her sexuality. She was specifically told to use the words "penis," "vagina," "intercourse," and, other phrases instead of "it" and "down there." This change in her expression of sexual matters helped Mr. D. blur the lines he had made between pure and impure women and allowed him to see that his wife valued and did not fear his sexuality.

With the relief of finally facing their problem and with the encouragement that the prognosis was very good, they were able to disengage themselves somewhat from the influence of Mr. D.'s family. Each partner actually valued the other highly, and they were able to communicate more openly than at any time since before their marriage. Physical interaction progressed rapidly.

Mr. D. was first forbidden to ejaculate in his wife's vagina, which relieved him of 3 years' pressure to do so. In their sexual play Mrs. D. could be brought to orgasm through intercourse (short of his ejaculation) and by manual and oral manipulation, and Mr. D. was instructed to bring himself to climax in front of his wife. Once he was able to do this, Mrs. D. was instructed to place her hand over her husband's hand. Eventually, she performed all the manual manipulation. At this point, after 4 weeks of treatment, Mrs. D. was told to manipulate her husband manually until he felt the urge to ejaculate, at which time he would enter her. The couple moved into this phase easily and smoothly. At the time of discharge from therapy, they were having intercourse with mutual orgasmic response four or five times a week.

Taking a Sexual History

A general psychiatric interview is given to couples who come for dual-sex therapy. The chief complaint, however, is sexual distress, and special attention is paid to the sexual history of the couple, as individuals and as a unit (Figures 1 and 2).

During the initial history-taking period, the male patient is interviewed by the male co-therapist, and the female patient is interviewed by the female co-therapist. This procedure allows the therapists to enlarge on the initial interviews, to develop sensitive areas, to pool their impressions to form a more thorough picture, and to note significant omissions or additions of information.

As with all psychiatric interviews, the sexual history taking not only is an information-gathering time but permits the development of a positive doctor-patient relationship. Essential to the development of confidence and rapport is an accepting atmosphere and a nonjudgmental attitude on the part of the therapists toward the patients' sexual values, ideas, and practices.

The taking of the sexual history is more structured than the rest of the interview, although the patient is encouraged to take his own lead in areas having great personal significance. In general, the therapist structures the interview so that he can cover both recent and early sexual history. The therapist must ascertain the specific current sexual complaint, the couple's sexual practices and pattern of interaction, the individual's sexual goal and fantasies, the masturbatory history, the presence or extent of extramarital relationships, and the degree of commitment to the marriage and the partner. The patient describes his view of the problem and when it began. The courtship, honeymoon, and reproductive history are examined in detail. Premarital expectations, mutual physical attraction, periods of separation, the type of contraception used, and the effect of children on the couple's sexual life are covered. The satisfying aspects of the marriage must also be discussed. The patient is particularly asked to evaluate his own and his partner's contribution to their present distress.

Early sexual development and education are also thoroughly discussed. The interviewer asks for the patient's view of his parents' marriage as seen in retrospect and as perceived in childhood. Relationships to peers, siblings, and important familial figures other than parents are also explored. Particular attention is paid to ways in which affection was expressed in the family and the degree of physical contact between family members. The sexual climate in which the patient grew up is seen through parental attitudes, memories of sexual games played as a child, the way in which the patient learned sexual facts, the specifics of religious training, relations to masturbation and nocturnal

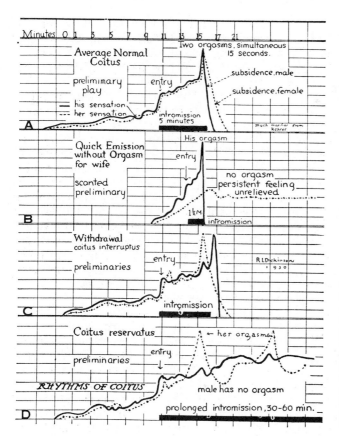

FIGURE 1. The varieties of sexual potency disorders are depicted graphically as they affect both the male and the female partner. *A.* Average coitus. *B.* Premature ejaculation 1½ minutes after intromission with non-orgasmic return in the female. *C.* Coitus interruptus in which both partners achieve orgasm, the male extravaginally. *D.* Retarded ejaculation in which the female has multiple orgasms but the male does not ejaculate even after 60 minutes of penile thrusting. (From Dickinson, R. L. *Atlas of Human Sex Anatomy,* ed. 2. Williams & Wilkins, Baltimore, 1949, Fig. 127.)

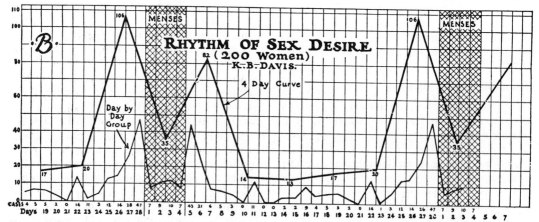

FIGURE 2. Note the peak of sexual desire during the premenstrual state in this series of 200 women. Individual variations exist, however. (From Dickinson, R. L. *Atlas of Human Sex Anatomy,* ed. 2. Williams & Wilkins, Baltimore, 1949, Fig. 42.)

emissions or the menarche, dating patterns, an adolescent rebellious phase, and any significant premarital involvements. Ethnic background and the socio-economic level of the patient's primary family are also taken into account. As the interview progresses, the patient's self-image emerges. The interviewer must be sensitive to any event that was exceptional in the patient's sexual life in either a destructive or a highly pleasant manner and should take particular note of those people who contributed to the patient's sexual education, identity, and mores.

The interviewer must also ask specific questions to elicit information that may be outside the patient's view of the socially acceptable, such as premarital and extramarital affairs, group sex, homosexual involvements, and abortions.

Results

Masters and Johnson report that approximately 80 per cent of persons treated for all types of sexual dysfunction have a successful outcome with the dual-sex therapy method. This figure has been replicated at other centers including the Department of Human Sexuality at Long Island Jewish Hospital under Schumacher and the Sexual Therapy Center of New York Medical College under Sadock and Sloan. There is variability in the success rate according to the particular disorder as indicated in Table I.

Ethics and Standards

The rapid growth of treatment centers for couples experiencing sexual dysfunction is an indication of the extent of patient demand for this particular service. Unfortunately, the extent of this need also gives rise to centers or persons not professionally qualified to deliver treatment. Care available to the patient ranges from pseudotherapy to competent, responsible psychotherapy.

Imperative for the growth and development of this field of treatment and, above all, for the welfare of the patient is the establishment of a system of self-regulation supported by psychiatry and the medical profession in general. Such a system would involve the development of standards for therapeutic competence, adequate training programs, and review of treatment techniques and results.

As Masters has stated:

Organized medicine must take a definitive position publicly as a first step in patient protection. Subsequently, the behavioral and theological disciplines should be invited to join in establishing and supporting ethical standards for diagnosis and treatment of the distresses of sexual inadequacy.

Without such safeguards there is no protection for patient or therapist.

REFERENCES

*Finkle, A. L., and Moyers, T. G. Sexual potency in aging males. J. Urol., *84:* 152, 1960.

*Hastings, D. W. *Impotence and Frigidity,* Little, Brown, Boston, 1963.

*Kinsey, A. C., Pomeroy, W. B., and Martin, C. E. *Sexual Behavior in the Human Male.* W. B. Saunders, Philadelphia, 1948.

*Kinsey, A. C., Pomeroy, W. B., and Martin, C. E. *Sexual Behavior in the Human Female.* W. B. Saunders, Philadelphia, 1953.

TABLE I
*Success Rate Summary**

Male Complaint	Success Rate	Female Complaint	Success Rate
	%		%
Premature ejaculation	97	Mastubatory orgasmic	
Retarded ejaculation	72	dysfunction	91
Secondary impotence	69	Primary orgasmic	
Primary impotence	49	dysfunction	82
		Coital orgasmic	
		dysfunction	80

*After Masters and Johnson data.

*Masters, W. H., and Johnson, V. E. *Human Sexual Response*. Little, Brown, Boston, 1966.

*Masters, W. H., and Johnson, V. E. *Human Sexual Inadequacy*. Little, Brown, Boston, 1970.

Newman, G., and Nichols, C. R. Sexual activities and attitudes in older persons. J. A. M. A., *173:* 33, 1960.

Paulson, M. J., and Lin, T. T. Frigidity: A factor analytic study of a psychosomatic therapy. Psychosomatics, *11:* 112, 1970.

Schumacher, S. S. The reproductive biology research foundation treatment approach to sexual inadequacy. Prof. Psychol., *2:* 263, 1971.

Sherfey, M. J. The evolution and nature of female sexuality in relation to psychoanalytic theory. J. Am. Psychoanal. Assoc., *14:* 28, 1966.

16.4   Group Psychotherapy of Sexual Disorders

BENJAMIN J. SADOCK, M.D., and HENRY I. SPITZ, M.D.

Introduction

The field of group psychotherapy has undergone a tremendous expansion in recent years. New treatment techniques have emerged, and group methods are now being applied to an ever widening variety of behavioral problems. One of the most prominent of these problems is sexual dysfunction.

Since sexual problems often lend themselves to a range of therapeutic modalities, the role of the group leader becomes particularly significant. His theoretical and technical orientation strongly affect the choice of treatment technique employed. A survey of the group methods used for treating sexual problems indicates that nearly all major schools of psychotherapeutic thought are included.

Group therapy offers distinct advantages and adds some new options for the clinician in his quest for an efficient and reliable method in treating a patient who seeks help for a sexual problem. In addition, the application of group methods to sexual dysfunction has added new meaning to certain core issues in group therapy. For example, the decision to compose a group with a heterogeneous or a homogeneous membership is a classic issue in group circles. When the factor that the prospective group members share is a sexual problem, some special management problems arise. If the therapist is alert to these phenomena, they do not emerge as roadblocks in therapy but, in fact, serve a catalytic function in the therapeutic process.

History

The history of the group psychotherapy movement in the early 1920's reveals some theoretical issues that eventually formed the groundwork for present-day group treatment of sexual disorders. McDougall's observations about the group's potential for increased emotional intensity and Le Bon's concept of emotional contagion among members were key developments. These came at a time when Freud was dealing with group phenomena, as evidenced by his publication of "Group Psychology and the Analysis of the Ego" in 1921. Freud devoted part of this work to a consideration of the role of repressed sexual feelings and the way in which they operate as motivational factors in determining group behavior. He also underscored the part played by identification and empathy as potent forces in the service of constructive group function.

Paul Schilder's emphasis on body image in his group work in the 1930's was another important avenue of pursuit. This idea has been integrated into contemporary group approaches which explore sexual attitudes in relation to the perception of body configuration and physiologic states. These methods can be readily seen in the sensitivity and encounter group movements.

The post-World War II era saw a dramatic period of growth in the field of group process. Therapists began to experiment with new techniques and became aware of technical problems ensuing from those techniques. For example, the analytically oriented groups had to deal with the problem of sexual acting out among group members. Wolf and other analysts (1954) felt that these issues were of critical import in therapy. This concern reflected itself in the group literature, which abounded with books and journal articles devoted to the management of sexual feelings in group therapy.

It was not until the 1950's that group therapy designed specifically to treat sexual problems was seen as a discrete entity. One such effort in this area was Levine's work with sexual problems in marriage (1956). She reported experiences with groups that included members with such problems as azoospermia, potency difficulty, infertility, and miscarriage. Marital problems of a sexual and nonsexual nature and premarital sexual counseling were also part of this program.

At this point, it seemed a logical step to extend work in the field to encompass homosexuality, sexual offenders, and other sexually related problems. Litman (1961), Mintz (1966), and others worked along these lines during the 1960's. Their studies reflect some of the trends in modern-day group work with sexual problems and typify the kinds of issues that have led to further study in the 1970's.

Rationale and Treatment Goals

Most sexual problems occur in an interpersonal sphere and are often more complex than just the symptom of dysfunction that surfaces. The group setting, with its built-in properties for the examination and resolution of relationship difficulties, offers the person with a sexual problem a safe atmosphere for change. The group provides an in vivo laboratory setting in which the patient can experiment with alternatives to his present maladaptive behavior.

With proper composition of the group and mature judgment on the part of the leader, factors that facilitate positive change emerge freely. The effect of group cohesion in coming to the support of a member who feels ashamed, guilty, and anxious about his sexual problem is often dramatic. When group pressure is mobilized in the service of positive reinforcement for adaptive behavior, a dimension not present in dyadic approaches can be observed.

The function of the group as a reality-testing device is particularly beneficial to the person suffering from myths or misconceptions in the area of sex. The varied life experiences of other group members and the challenging of his irrational beliefs help to accomplish an educational function regarding sexual information. In the same way, groups are effective in countering the denial and projective mechanisms that form a key part of the defensive structure seen in patients with anxiety related to sexual issues. This effectiveness is most obvious in a group of married couples in which both members of a marriage share in an inaccurate explanation for their sexual difficulties, rather than deal with their underlying anxieties. The group confrontation and the alternatives that are present in other members with different coping styles tend to lessen the defensive bond between the partners and allow for more open, realistic viewing of the problem.

An outgrowth of the aspect of group therapy that concerns itself with relationship problems is the potential that therapeutic groups have for dealing with the problems of intimacy, closeness, and dependency. This potential is particularly advantageous, since these problems tap, many of the psychodynamic issues that translate themselves behaviorally into sexual dysfunction. An effective group experience can be emotionally corrective when the patient concretely sees his own positive behavior and emerges with a sense of mastery over his problems and fears. The social reinforcement that the group offers tends to increase the likelihood of this new behavior generalizing and showing itself in improvement on other areas of impaired function in the patient's life.

Group methods share with other forms of therapy the goal of symptom removal when sexual function is impaired. The personality factors involved in each case guide the group therapist in choosing the most appropriate group methods likely to result in symptom removal. For instance, the impotent man who has a history of overwhelming anxiety in the presence of women and who almost phobically avoids them learns through the group that his fears are unjustified as he gains insight into his own psychological processes. At the same time, he can experience himself in relation to women in the group. The therapist can select a number of procedures that may further develop this theme. Here is where techniques like role playing, psychodrama, and behavior rehearsal have been used with great success.

The issue of identification takes on added meaning in groups that have members with sexual problems. Groups increase the number of persons with whom the patient can identify. Group studies have shown that shifting levels of identification take place in the life of a group. These identifications give a sexually dysfunctional member a chance to imitate and adopt successful behavior he sees in others and to identify with healthy role models who have been successful in dealing with the same problem he experiences. The result shows itself in increased self-esteem and in countering feelings of hopelessness about his inability to resolve his problem.

Communication problems frequently accompany sexual problems. Lack of communication is apparent in many married couples who request therapy for such problems as impotence and orgasmic dysfunction. A clear-cut goal of group therapy in such situations is to improve communcation about sexual subjects. This improvement can be facilitated by group techniques of different kinds. In married couples group therapy, the presence of other couples in the therapy setting lends support and tends to diminish the apprehension about discussing sexual habits, fantasies, and problems. The other couples also serve to lessen feelings of isolation and uniqueness, both of which inhibit people sexually.

At times, a male-female co-therapy team may lead the group in order to set the example of a relationship that can communicate effectively about sexual themes. In a couples group, a theme that often emerges and serves as a barrier to normal communication centers on confused role definitions in the marriage. This confusion plays itself out in the area of sex and results in sexual problems.

Since a group stimulates feelings related to those experienced in one's family of origin, a therapy group that is oriented along psychoanalytic lines allows for an examination of childhood sexual attitudes and experiences. The examination of transference phenomena, resistance, and dream material in the group opens the door to an understanding of the psychodynamic factors that influence sexual behavior. Oedipal problems, sibling problems, and authority problems are common repetitive themes in groups that attempt to deal with sexual problems. Working on both peer member to member and authority member to therapist levels allows for a rapid emergence of sexual conflicts related to siblings and to parents.

A college student was engaged to be married soon, and he was deeply concerned about his sexual relationship with his fiancée. He was having anxiety attacks and was becoming almost phobic in his avoidance of sexual contact. His previous sexual experiences with women were limited, and he had experienced premature ejaculation on almost all those occasions. His family background included an overprotective mother who discouraged his dating and other social activities during his adolescence. His father was described as passive and somewhat detached emotionally. The young man had one older sister, with whom he fought constantly throughout childhood.

The psychodynamic factors related to this man's problem of premature ejaculation became clear in one group session. The group leader, who had an electric orientation, used one session to ask the group members to discuss their dreams. The young man in question presented a dream he had had the evening after attempting unsuccessful intercourse with his fiancée.

The dream content and subsequent analysis made it clear to the group that he had a poor image of himself as a man; based in part on his identification with his weak father. His attitudes toward women were shaped mostly by his experiences with his mother and his sister; consequently, his expectations in regard to heterosexual relationships were fearful and unrealistic.

Other factors present in groups that are useful in dealing with sexual problems include the socialization function that groups provide. Socialization comes as a result of being a member of an ongoing group and of having established relationships on an emotional level with other people. The emphasis on interaction in group therapy promotes involvement with others and fosters an orientation toward open and honest communication. In this kind of atmosphere, it is possible to reduce anxiety and to provide the ego support necessary to encourage serious work on solutions to personal problem.

Treatment Techniques

WITH HOMOSEXUALITY

Group therapists have learned that much of what determines the success or failure of a group experience takes place before the first group meeting, underscoring the significance of such issues as group composition, preparation of patients, and screening. When the therapist considers in which group to place a male homosexual, group composition takes on added meaning. The most prominent decision the therapist has to make is whether to place the homosexual in a homogeneous (all homosexual) group or in a heterogeneous (homosexual-heterosexual) group.

Workers, like Hadden (1966), who favor homogenity in groups treating homosexuals do so for the following reasons: (1) The homogeneous group members share a baseline of similar experience as adults, which serves both to facilitate communication and to counter rationalizations about homosexual issues. (2) They have had similar developmental experiences, which permits quicker entrance into an understanding of the psychodynamic features of childhood and family life. (3) Homogeneous groups offer a corrective experience in a peer vector. This experience is in sharp contrast to the defective peer experiences of many homosexuals in preadolescent and adolescent periods. (4) The anxiety level about openly discussing homosexual behavior is less in a homogeneous group than in a mixed group. This advantage offsets the homosexuals' feelings of uniqueness and isolation and allows for the emergence of these themes for exploration by the group. (5) The chance of being scapegoated or rejected by heterosexual group members is significantly reduced. (6) The

ability to identify with a member who is in the process of becoming heterosexual is increased.

The exponents of the heterogeneous approach feel that the mixed group offers close contact with members of the opposite sex. The corrective peer experience holds true for these groups as well. In addition, the development of group cohesion is a potent force against the homosexual's desire to drop out during anxiety-laden periods in therapy. Heterogeneous groups afford an opportunity to experience heterosexual feelings and fantasies toward other group members. The homosexual man, for example, can gain firsthand information from women regarding their sexual attitudes.

Despite these differing theoretical considerations about group composition, actual clinical practice shows that there is considerable overlap in group process and group dynamics. Early stages of the groups are characterized by anxiety about homosexual problems and by denial and rationalization as defensive means of dealing with this anxiety. With the emergence of group cohesion and trust, there is movement in the direction of acceptance of homosexuality as a problem and a desire for change or, conversely, as a desirable way of life with the goal being self-acceptance and enhancement of self-esteem as a homosexual.

The leader's role is critical. The leader working alone can provide an experience of acceptance in a parental vector at the stage when patients most fear rejection and humiliation. The attitude of the therapist is extremely important, and factors like his activity or passivity, rather than his or her own biological sex, often determine the members' perception of him. For this reason, some group leaders elect to work in mixed-sex co-therapy teams to afford the group members a chance to work simultaneously on masculine and feminine problems.

The most popular format for groups oriented to treat homosexuals is a once-a-week meeting for 1½ hours, with a group size of from 4 to 10 members. The groups are close in composition for factors such as age and level of intelligence but vary widely with regard to specific sexual behavior and homosexual life-styles. Most groups also emphasize the fact that neurotic traits other than homosexuality are in evidence, and they hold over-all improvement in major areas of function as a common goal. Outcome studies show general improvement in behavior in most members and change to heterosexual orientation in about one third.

It should be emphasized that an increasing number of homosexual persons are oriented solely toward a more successful adaptation to the homosexual life-style. These members do not enter the group with the conscious or unconscious desire to change their sexual orientation. In such instances the therapist must be aware of any bias he may have against helping the individual attain his or her goal and also remain alert to any subtle pressures from other group members toward changing the persons sexual orientation.

WITH GENDER IDENTITY PROBLEMS

Groups composed of children with gender identity problems were recently reported by Green and Fuller (1973). They describe a method used to treat young boys who show evidence of feminine traits—that is, boys who dress in female clothing, prefer to play with girls rather than boys, and show mannerisms and speech patterns that appear clearly feminine. The structure of the therapy setting resembles an operant condition model. The group is led by a male therapist who uses verbal reinforcement for masculine activities as one of the cornerstones of the technique. His presence also serves as a healthy male role model. The group meets in a recreational setting, where the leader can foster male-male peer play and strengthen efforts at masculine athletic activities.

Another part of the process is the separate group meetings for the mothers and fathers of the boys. The preliminary results of this method are promising and show significant decreases in all the above-noted feminine traits.

WITH ADOLESCENT SEXUALITY

The use of the group as an instrument of preventive psychiatry is illustrated in groups designed for purposes of sex education. Such groups enable the members to share information about sex.

A sex education course for second-year high school students was started. The program included a lecture series about sexual physiology, with group discussions after the lectures. The groups were composed of 10 to 12 boys and girls from the sophomore class, with a man and a woman as co-leaders. One of the leaders was a physician, either a psychiatrist or a pediatrician, and the other leader was a teacher or a nurse, The students were encouraged to ask questions and to discuss any area of interest related to the lecture material.

In one group a boy said that a friend of his was told that masturbation in adolescence could lead to sexual problems and sterility as an adult. It became apparent that he had struck a responsive chord in the other group members, as evidenced by their nonverbal behavior, their giggling, the serious discussion that followed. It emerged that many of the students shared a variety of concerns about masturbation but were afraid to mention the subject for fear of humiliation or embarrassment in the eyes of both peers and adults.

WITH SEXUAL PROBLEMS IN MARRIAGE

A number of group techniques have been created to meet the needs of the sexually dysfunctional couple. Work by Masters and Johnson (1970), who emphasized rapid and effective treatment of sexual problems—such as impotence, premature ejaculation, and orgasmic dysfunction—gave rise to increased professional awareness of the possible use of groups. Group therapists interested in the field of sexual dysfunction have found aspects of group dynamics in the Masters and Johnson approach, which consists of a group of four—two therapists and two patients, the dysfunctional couple.

Married couples group therapy has mixed origins. When used to treat sexually dysfunctional couples, it blends elements from analytically oriented group therapy, family therapy, round-table sexual counseling, and behavior therapy. The work of therapy takes place on several levels—intrapsychic, interpersonal, and educational. The focus of many groups begins with the here and now transactions of group members and moves into historical material when appropriate. Couples have the chance to see similar sexual problems in the relationships of other couples, which tends to establish early rapport and trust. The emphasis on treating the couple together for the sexual problem has the effect of interrupting neurotic blame patterns that may exist in the relationship. It also lessens feelings of shame and guilt about sex and encourages realistically based appraisal of the sexual difficulty.

Midway during the course of long term psychotherapy with a group composed of married couples whose primary complaint was marital or sexual difficulties, a recently married woman was confronted by several other members of the group about her constant avoidance of sexual topics in group discussions. In an emotional moment, she broke into tears and expressed her fears of having to talk about her sexual relationship with her husband because she could not reach orgasm with him.

The response she evoked from the group was very different from the one she had anticipated. Instead of being humiliated or rejected, she received supportive feedback. Other group members related similar difficulties in their marriages, thereby helping to counter her feelings of uniqueness and isolation. Furthermore, they made a serious attempt to understand her and the evolution of her present difficulty, much of which had to do with her insecure feelings about her role as a woman. She was afraid that she was inadequate sexually, but she was fearful of what she called "successful sexual relations" because she was also afraid of becoming pregnant. Pregnancy carried with it fears of dirtiness and disfigurement—attitudes that were clearly transmitted to her by her mother.

When couples become involved with the group, it is possible to select tasks or homework assignments specifically designed to desensitize them to their sexual anxiety. Additional techniques, like videotape recording and playback, are employed at other stages. Videotape helps couples to deal with body image problems that may be contributing to their sexual difficulties. Feelings related to sexual attractiveness, distortions of body perception, and physical inadequacy are common themes that emerge in taped sessions. Usually, a segment of a group session is recorded and played back within the same meeting. Each member is asked to describe his response to the playback and to comment on it as it relates to himself and his spouse. Other group members are encouraged to give feedback in the hope of further objectifying whatever misperceptions may be present.

The videotape also has other functions,

including the dramatization of nonverbal behavior and illustration of faulty communication patterns in couples. In the sexual therapy group, videotape is used to study both content and metacommunication levels of the couple's interchange on sexual topics. The effect of hearing and seeing oneself repeatedly on tape serves to lessen self-consciousness and to reduce social inhibition. This effect has obvious carry-over into general aspects of the marriage and to sexual behavior in particular.

Therapists who lead couples groups must be aware of two potential problems that stem from composing a group of marital pairs. The first is subgroup formation, and the second is pseudocohesion. Subgroup formation may occur because these members had ongoing established relationships before entry in the group. Husbands and wives tend to sit next to one another, and, during anxious moments, they communicate with one another (side-to-side pattern) rather than with the group. This is a force counter to interaction and cohesion, and it presents a roadblock to therapeutic progress. Simple maneuvers, like changing the seating arrangements so that the couple sit across from one another, have the effect of interrupting their nonverbal cue systems and allowing their conversation to be available to the group.

Subgroup formation can also present itself in the form of extragroup sexual relationships. This is a relatively infrequent occurrence, but it is noteworthy because of its inhibitory effect on the therapist. Some leaders shy away from dealing with sexual problems in couples groups, for fear that open discussions of sexual feelings among the members will foster sexual acting out. Data from this type of group work show that the reverse is true. Reality-based, frank group discussions about sex tend to discourage unrealistic fantasies and neurotic desires for extramarital sexual contact.

False cohesion is seen when couples are anxious and huddle together because they are frightened. This huddling may be misperceived as closeness or cohesiveness, but it is not. Anxiety-evoking group techniques —confrontation, Gestalt exercises, and videotape—should not be introduced unless true cohesion, with member-to-member support, is present to offset the anxiety.

WITH MIXED SEXUAL DISORDERS

An appreciable number of therapists are in favor of groups composed of patients with different sexual problems. This format has been used with success in Europe, particularly in England and Germany.

The mixed group has been used in varied clinical settings, ranging from prisons to inpatient and outpatient departments of psychiatric and general hospitals. An increasingly popular application of the mixed group is in the field of student health. A good deal of work has come from using this approach with the sexual problems presented by students seen in mental health clinics and in the counseling services affiliated with colleges and universities. Short term, closed-ended (fixed-membership), small group meetings with a psychoanalytically oriented focus have traditionally been the main group type. Recent trends tend toward expansion of this model, incorporating encounter and sensitivity group experiences and behavior therapy techniques.

The groups conducted by Rosen (1964) afford a model for further study in this area of mixed sexual disorders.

A sensitivity group for nurses contained one member who was a nun. After a group session that concerned itself largely with feelings about pregnancy and sex, she approached the leader, appearing quite upset, and asked for an individual interview. Her request was granted, and in the session she related her apprehensiveness about a recurrent dream she had. In the dream she was running in the country and came to a dense forest. Suddenly, she looked at the trees and to her amazement found that they had turned into penises. Needless to say, the dream troubled her greatly. In fact, she questioned her own motives so intensely that she considered leaving the convent.

The group leader encouraged her to discuss some of these feelings in the group, and she did so. The result was dramatic. Most members felt positively toward her and were able to identify with her struggle to adjust to her sexual ideas. She experienced a great sense of relief in learning that she was human, just like everyone else, and that her guilt feelings and self-deprecation were unncessary.

Members of these groups include exhibitionists, voyeurs, transvestites, and fetishists. Many members are referred directly by the courts as sexual offenders. The groups are mostly male; an attempt is made to keep the ages and intellectual abilities of the members somewhat similar; and adolescents are seen not in adult groups but in their own peer groups. Otherwise, the groups are heterogeneous.

It is desirable in outpatient settings to keep groups of this nature larger in size because of the potentially high dropout rate. The repetitive nature of the condition for which the patients are being treated means that one or more may be apprehended and arrested at some point during therapy. Impulsivity is another feature common to this patient population, and it also contributes to the danger of group dropouts. The group size is about six to 10 in institutional settings and 10 to 15 on an outpatient basis.

A woman was troubled by a compulsive wish to stare at men's genitals. She became distressed after she was nearly caught peeping into a neighbor's window. She consulted a psychiatrist because she was afraid that the voyeuristic impulse was out of control. It became apparent that the nature of her problem significantly interfered with any attempts to establish normal heterosexual relationships.

The psychiatrist placed her in a setting where she was most apt to gain insight into her own psychological processes, while she simultaneously had a here-and-now opportunity to work through her difficulties with men. The group chosen for her was one in which many of the methods of traditional psychoanalysis were used in a group environment. The interpretation of dreams, fantasy material, and free association were among the methods used. Frequently, her interactions with other group members were used as a focal point for stimulating associative connections to the past. In this way she was able to recapture many repressed memories and experiences directly related to the origins of her neurosis.

A group with different sexual problems has, as its therapeutic rationale, the concept that the members often have similar underlying psychological problems. The early group meetings highlight this fact. Group discussions consistently center on themes of impulse control—control of sexual impulses but control of aggressive impulses as well. Members soon learn that they share a common bond. Group goals crystallize more readily when this bond is defined. The therapist is then in a position to use this feeling of relatedness to further behavioral change. Members are encouraged to delve deeper into their feelings about their particular sexual disturbances. What emerges is emotionally charged material related to the implications of members' acts for their family lives and job functions. Other social consequences, such as fear of public awareness of one's sexual problem, are also sources of great concern.

When members can openly share their feelings in group sessions, they experience an increasing sense of stability and positive regard for the group. Some report using the attitudes of the group or of a group member as a deterrant to acting on impulses outside the group. Sharing also takes place on the level of sexual beliefs. The group members can confide in one another their fears about homosexuality, women, masturbation, and the effects of their early childhood sexual experiences.

Since all group members easily relate to these feelings, the affect level of the group is intensified. This affect level provides an emotional substrate within the individual member on which attempts at effective control can be made. This internal control is in favorable contrast to such concepts as imprisonment and punishment, which try to impose external controls on deviant sexual behavior.

A short term group therapy experience was provided for enlisted men stationed at a remote Army base in the Midwest. Opportunities for normal heterosexual contacts were almost nonexistent. As a result, many of the men engaged in relations with farm animals. In a group of eight members, three had practiced bestiality. This information emerged in a group session centering on the stresses of being isolated and on the ways various members of the group dealt with their sexual feelings during this period.

Generally speaking, the inhibited, shy adolescent or adult is a better candidate for a mixed group than is the person with a compulsive, impulse-driven character structure. Most participants in this kind of group experience can learn to moderate the extremes of their behavior by substituting normal control mechanisms, like intellectualization.

A man in his early twenties was refused induction into military service because it was discovered that he had a shoe fetish. His particular pattern was to steal women's tennis shoes and then masturbate with the shoelaces wrapped around his penis. He experienced an overwhelming sense of shame when asked to discuss his fetish, and he very much wanted to rid himself of this long term problem.

He had never experienced genital contact with a woman, nor had he engaged in homosexual activities. Social situations evoked tremendous anxiety and fears that his problem would become known to others. His daily life was further complicated by his tendency to fantasize about the fetish. His ability to concentrate and study was impaired, and his school career was in jeopardy.

A form of behavior therapy—aversion therapy—was used to help extinguish the fetishistic activity and to diminish the time spent daydreaming about the fetish-related themes. Although this technique was successful, it had limitations. His interpersonal anxiety and poorly developed social skills persisted as a by-product of living with this long term problem and still had to be dealt with. Therefore, the patient was put in a therapy group composed of members with a range of sexual problems.

The group reaction to this new member was important and helped bring about a positive outcome. As an extension of his individual therapy, the group reinforced new ways of acting by offering approval. They also aided in the negative reinforcement aspect of behavior therapy by putting group pressure on the patient to give up his fetish. Firm group support and group pressure were used to advantage in treating this patient's fetishism.

Groups designed to deal with diverse sexual problems are also seen in psychosomatic clinics for problems related to infertility. In the course of pretherapy screening interviews, significant difficulties in sexual functioning are observed. These difficulties include vaginismus, incapacitating menstrual disorders, orgasmic dysfunction, and dyspareunia. Groups formed to deal directly with these sexual dysfunctions see a mixture of themes emerge. Disturbed parent-child relationships in the members' families of origin are almost universally present, as are difficulties in viewing their husbands as procreators. Feelings of shame and guilt regarding intercourse are also prevalent. Some studies revealed that, after group therapy for these problems, as many as eight out of 10 group members were able to conceive and carry to term. The menstrual disorders and problems with intercourse were also overcome.

In structured interactional group psychotherapy, Kaplan and Sadock (1971) introduce subject sessions which deal with specific sexual themes such as masturbation, infidelity, techniques of coitus, oralism, and exhibitionism. Group members share thoughts and feelings about these highly charged subjects with salutary effects. On occasion, movies with specific erotic themes and imagery may be shown to the group with the members free associating to the material.

A single man in his thirties had a history of one arrest; he had been caught exhibiting himself to school children in a playground. After this episode he was pressured by his parents and the court to seek psychotherapy. He was willing to enter therapy on an individual basis but had reservations about bringing up his problem in front of a group of strangers.

To deal with this reluctance, the group therapist decided to use the structured interactional approach. This method allows the group to focus on a single member throughout a session, which usually lasts 1½ hours. Over a period of some weeks or months, each member is up for discussion on a rotational basis until all members have been included in a cycle. Then the leader has the option of continuing the same format and repeating the rotation or of changing to another method, such as spontaneous interaction.

In a group milieu such as this, it becomes increasingly more difficult for a group member to hide or to edit his thoughts and feelings. This technique can be used to advantage with an exhibitionist, a voyeur, and a sexual offender, such as a rapist. It also has wide applicability for nonsexual problems. The group can concentrate in depth on an individual and often deal with material that might ordinarily take much longer to emerge.

SPECIAL THERAPEUTIC CONSIDERATIONS

The group therapist must be aware of the common pitfalls encountered in working with patients and their sexual problems in a group setting. Of paramount importance is the therapist's self-awareness regarding his own sexual feelings. If not properly understood, his own feelings intrude themselves into the therapeutic process. For example, the therapist may elicit inadequate data during pregroup sexual history taking. Therapists must be sufficiently free of their own inhibitions and unrealistic beliefs to allow for clear and direct communication with their patients.

It is often very difficult to elicit information about incestuous feelings or behavior in a group setting, especially if group mores inhibit the introduction of such topics. In one group, however, a schizophrenic woman came to a session in an obviously intoxicated state. At one point she broke into tears and recounted a scene from her childhood in which she had relations several times with her father. Her mother was promiscuous and often encouraged double dates, introducing her daughter as her sister. The mother and father were divorced, and shortly thereafter the mother remarried. In the same group meeting, the patient told of her sexual relations with her stepfather. The mother seemed to be aware of this activity but said nothing. The pattern repeated itself once more when the mother divorced the stepfather and married another man. The patient claimed he also raped her.

In individual interviews after the group meeting, the story was confirmed by one of the men involved. The reaction of most of the group members was one of shock and disbelief. The whole topic was so anxiety provoking that two members got up and left the session, and others withdrew in less dramatic ways. In later sessions, the group was able to handle this highly charged material successfully.

In the therapy process, sexual feelings are often stimulated in the leader, which can be anxiety evoking. These feelings are sometimes directly related to sexual stimuli arising from the events in the lives of the group members. More often, the discomfort reflects an unresolved problem of the therapist's that is operating out of his awareness. Treatment of couples is notorious for precipitating these countertransference problems. The oedipal problems and sibling problems that affect the couple can easily affect the therapist, too. In addition, the therapist must have a realistic view of his own interpersonal relationships, specifically the ones with his spouse, his family of origin, and his co-therapist. Attention to these matters guards against taking sides and covert alliances with group members and allows the therapist to maintain a posture of objectivity. It also helps ensure that the multiple transferences essential to the group process are fully explored and not blocked by the leader's blind spots.

The susceptible therapist may be caught in the process of identification that takes place in all therapy groups. Neurotic needs of the leader, such as a desire to help his own marriage or sexual relationship through the group process, can make him vulnerable to this danger. Or the therapist who opposes divorce may encourage couples who are incompatible, sexually and emotionally, to remain together. Once caught in this web, the therapist is no longer the impartial leader he set out to be. On the other hand, therapists who anticipate these problems and deal with them in advance of the group and as they emerge in therapy do fulfill the roles of catalyst, reality tester, and interpreter that are vital to their function.

NUDE GROUP THERAPY

This highly controversial field has been characterized by its exponents as not only a bona fide treatment method but the technique of choice for some sexual problems. It has been called "offensive" by the American Psychiatric Association Task force on Encounter Groups and Psychiatry and cited as a prime example of acting out and regression to instinctual gratification on the part of the group therapist by other critics.

Nude group therapy, also called nude intimacy training and nude marathon encounter therapy, has as its theoretical basis the impact of repression as an inhibitory force in people's lives. One of the primary aims of nude groups is to counter repression and so allow for the fullest expression of many emotions including those of sexuality. The groups can be large in size, often numbering 16 to 18 members. Sometimes the activities in a nude group include meditation and massage. Many groups are organized to discourage and exclude those persons who might seek this experience for anti-therapeutic reasons. This is accomplished by pre-group screening to assess motivation and by clearly defining the group standards, goals and limitations. Sexual intercourse is usually prohibited, although some groups may allow hugging, kissing, and body exploration to occur.

When used to work on sexual problems, the nude group focuses on body image themes. Attitudes about aging, physical deformities, obesity, genital size in men, and breast size in women are examples of sexually related themes that develop in nude groups.

The natural connection between nudity and sexual feelings accounts for the opinion by leaders of nude groups that this experience works well as a form of therapy. Nude group therapy is not the sole form of therapy employed in every case. Sometimes a time-limited experience in a nude group is recommended as an adjunct to another primary form of treatment, in the hope that the nude group will mobilize or unfreeze areas that have become obstacles to progress in the main therapy relationship.

The place of the nude group in the future of psychiatry is open to serious question; however, the reality of its presence today makes it important to consider here. The authors do not intend to deny categorically the potential therapeutic value of nudity. But its use as a treatment device has yet to be demonstrated.

Conclusion

There is a distinct movement today in the direction of comprehensive, short term, economical programs for treating sexual problems and the group therapy field clearly reflects this movement. Programs that emphasize an over-all approach incorporating more than one psychotherapeutic technique are in the vanguard of emerging developments. Here, group methods are being effectively joined with other therapeutic modalities.

The psychological and physiological factors that contribute to ejaculatory and potency disturbances in men and orgastic difficulties in women are efficiently attended to in settings that include group experiences. In addition, couples group therapy is concurrently used to deal more intensively with the marital relationship and the individual psychopathology of the spouses. The group deals with the motivational factors that prevent the couple from successfully resolving their sexual problems. Aversion to intercourse, fears of injury or of pregnancy, problems with depression, alcohol, and drugs, and impulse control problems are some of the more common issues handled in the group. The group experience often continues after successful problem solving and serves as an ongoing source of contact with therapy.

The combination of behavior therapy and group psychotherapy also lends itself well to this scheme. Assertive training, behavior rehearsal, systematic desensitization, and some of the aversive procedures have all been included with ease in combined individual and group therapy.

Finally, it is especially essential that the hallmarks of sound psychotherapy—such as warmth, empathy, ethics, responsibility, care, concern, and integrity—be adhered to by therapists as these newer applications of the group method of treatment expand even further.

REFERENCES

*American Psychiatric Association. *Task Force Report on Encounter Groups and Psychiatry.* American Psychiatric Association, Washington, 1970.
*Bieber, T. Group therapy with homosexuals. In *Comprehensive Group Psychotherapy,* H. I. Kaplan and B. J. Sadock, editors, p. 518. Williams & Wilkins, Baltimore, 1971.
Birk, L., and Miller, E. Group psychotherapy for homosexual men by male-female co-therapists. Acta Psychiatr. Scand., *218* (Suppl.): 7, 1970.
Foulkes, S. H., and Anthony, E. J. *Group Psychotherapy: The Psychoanalytic Approach,* ed. 2. Penguin Books, Baltimore, 1965.
Framo, J. L. Marriage therapy in a couples group. Seminars in Psychiatry, *5:* 207, 1973.
Freud, S. Group psychology and the analysis of the ego. In *Standard Edition of the Complete Psychological Works of Sigmund Freud,* vol. 18, p. 69. Hogarth Press, London, 1955.
Green, R., and Fuller, M. Group therapy with feminine boys and their parents. Int. J. Group Psychother., *23:* 54, 1973.
Hadden, S. B. Treatment of male homosexuals in groups. Int. J. Group Psychother. *16:* 13, 1966.
*Kaplan, H. I., and Sadock, B. J. *Comprehensive Group Psychotherapy.* Williams & Wilkins, Baltimore, 1971.
*Kaplan, H. I., and Sadock, B. J. Structured Interactional Group Psychotherapy. N.Y. St. J. Med., *71:* 13, 1971.
Levine, L. Sex and marriage problems. In *The Fields of Group Psychotherapy,* S. Slavson, editor, International Universities Press, New York, 1956.
Litman, R. E. Psychotherapy of a homosexual man in a heterosexual group. Int. J. Group Psychother., *11:* 440, 1961.
Masters, W., and Johnson, V. *Human Sexual Response.* Little, Brown, Boston, 1966.
Masters, W., and Johnson, V. *Human Sexual Inadequacy.* Little, Brown, Boston, 1970.
Mintz, E. E. Group and individual treatment. J. Consult. Psychol., *30:* 193, 1966.
Rosen, I. *The Pathology and Treatment of Sexual Deviation.* Oxford University Press, London, 1964.
Schilder, P. *The Image and Appearance of the Human Body.* International Universities Press, New York, 1950.
Singer, M., and Fisher, R. Group psychotherapy of male homosexuals by a male and female co-therapy team. Int. J. Group Psychother., *17:* 44, 1967.
*Spitz, H. I., and Sadock, B. J. Psychiatric training of graduate nursing students: The use of small interactional groups. N. Y. St. J. Med., *73:* 1334, 1973.
*Wolf, A. Sexual acting out in the psychoanalysis of groups. Int. J. Group Psychother., *4:* 22, 1954.

16.5   Family Therapy

JAY HALEY, M.A.

Introduction

DEFINITION

Family therapy is not a treatment method but a clinical orientation that includes many different therapeutic approaches. Having developed independently in different parts of the United States, each school of family therapy has different operations. Some family therapists continued with an individual orientation and theory of change and merely added more people in the interview room. Others made a radical shift and instituted entirely new procedures and new theories of change. What distinguishes the family approach from that of other therapy is the basic premise that the unit with the problem is not the single individual but two or more people. It is not that there is a patient with something wrong who is put under stress by other people, but that symptomatic behavior is a contract between two or more people. How to change such contracts is the focus of the many different family therapy approaches.

APPROACHES

Some forms of family therapy are spontaneous and unplanned with the therapist using interpretations and uncovering techniques (Ackerman, 1966; Ferber and Beels, 1970). Other forms are carefully planned and the outcome is documented (Patterson et al., 1967; Stuart, 1970). Some therapists require that the whole family always come to each interview (Sonne et al., 1962), while others are quite willing to interview individuals or sections of families (Pittman et al., 1971). This reflects the fact that some family therapists are method oriented (Boszormenyi-Nagy and Framo, 1965) and others are problem oriented in the sense that they change their approach depending on the problem (Haley, 1970). In some approaches, the therapist is central and works hard in negotiating among family members (Zuk, 1969), whereas in others the therapist focuses the family members on each other (Kempler, 1968) and may even spend most of the time out of the room behind a one-way mirror watching the family work by itself (Fulweiler, 1967). Family therapy can range from being a happening (Whitaker, 1966) to an occasion of planned directives (Haley, 1973). The focus can be on expressing emotions (Paul, 1967; Rubenstein, 1968) or on changing family structure (Minuchin and Montalvo, 1967).

Some family therapists work largely with the marriage as the fundamental dyad in the family or at least the nuclear family (Satir, 1964); others emphasize the importance of bringing in the network of extended kin and even friends and neighbors on the supposition that everyone in the system is involved (Speck and Attneave, 1973). In multiple family therapy, a number of families are seen together in a large group (Laqueur, 1970; Curry, 1965). Of course, many family therapists change their approach over time as they find new ways of working. For example,

Bowen shifted from hospitalizing the whole family (Bowen, 1961) to largely seeing individual family members to seeing couples or families in groups (Bowen, 1966).

Family therapy sessions may range from the 45-minute hour to marathon sessions of many hours a day, as in Multiple Impact Family Therapy (MacGregor et al., 1964), which is geared to families who cannot attend regular sessions because of long distance travel problems. As family therapy has developed in Canada (Epstein, 1962), in Latin America (Sluzki, 1968), and Europe (Vassilou, 1970) the number of different approaches tends to multiply (Glick and Haley, 1971).

Indications and Contraindications

When all therapy is considered from a family orientation, one cannot say that family therapy is indicated in one case and individual therapy in another. From the family point of view, individual therapy is, in fact, one way of intervening in a family. To interview a child alone and not see the parents is a way of doing therapy with a family, even if the therapist thinks he is engaged in individual therapy. To hospitalize an adolescent, whether the parents are interviewed or not, is a clinical intervention into a family. Therefore, the question is not when is family therapy indicated but when is it appropriate to interview one person and when to interview several people. For example, if a married couple is in crisis and violent, the first interview might better be individual until the groundwork is laid for seeing the family members together.

Family Theory

There is no comprehensive, coherent theory of family therapy; as with psychodynamic theory, more emphasis is placed on a theory of pathology than a theory of therapy. What characterizes a family orientation is the fact that the choice of who is to be the focus of diagnosis and therapy is made arbitrarily. An individual, a dyad, or a triad can be chosen. For example, the same problem can be regarded in the following ways:

1. Individual. A 10-year-old boy will not go outside the house alone, claiming to be afraid of dogs. From the individual point of view, he has a dog phobia. Inside him is a fear of dogs.

2. **Dyad.** If one notices the boy's mother is constantly with him because of this problem and that she has no interest in life except him and his fears, one can say that the unit with the problem is the dyad of mother-child. The fear of dogs helps to maintain an overinvolved relationship between mother and child.

3. **Triad.** If one observes the sequence between mother, father, and child, it becomes apparent that mother and father avoid each other except in relation to the son's problem. When mother and father have too much conflict, they make peace by consoling each other about the boy's fears. In the triadic view, the boy helps to hold the marriage together by having this problem.

Although these are ostensibly descriptions of the same problem, obviously the therapeutic intervention will be quite different in each case—helping a boy to get over his introjected fear of dogs, changing a mother-child relationship, or changing a triangulated child-parent relationship involve different interventions.

TERMINOLOGY

The dyad is the smallest unit in family theory, and so most problem descriptions are of that unit or larger ones. To formulate a scientific description of these units is difficult, since there is no language for relationships and all terminology is based on individual characteristics. One can use the word "symptom" to mean the way one person responds to another, but the word carries a connotation of individual psychopathology. To speak of a depression, a phobia, a compulsion, or a psychotic episode as adaptive behavior involving several people leads to confusion; as originally developed, those terms were not meant to describe more than one person. Thus, traditional psychiatric diagnostic categories are not appropriate to family therapy. Equally inappropriate is the traditional intake procedure in which an individual is interviewed, given psychological tests, and classified. The appropriate intake procedure is to bring together all the people involved in the situation.

NATURAL GROUPS

By the term "family," many family therapists mean a unit of several people but not necessarily blood relatives. Family therapy actually concerns itself with natural groups—any relationship with a history and a future. A man can manifest symptoms in relation to his work if the people there are highly significant to him and he has long term patterns of behavior established with them. A child's disturbance may relate to the family or to school or to a conflict between home and school. The more disturbed the child, the more there is a replication of conflictual relationships in different settings. For example, a patient's psychotic episode on a hospital ward can be a response to a covert conflict between his therapist and ward administrator, as was pointed out as long ago as 1954 (Stanton and Schwartz, 1954). However, if the situation is examined more fully, it usually becomes clear that he is in a similar situation in a variety of contexts. At the same time he is responding to a covert conflict between his parents, he is also caught in a conflict between parents and hospital staff. When it was discovered that symptoms have a function in relation to other people, the total interpersonal context became part of the diagnosis of a psychiatric problem.

Theoretical Models

Because most family therapists were originally concerned with individuals, it was natural that theories about changing individuals would be adapted and expanded by the family therapy theoreticians. Just as therapists made interpretations to individuals to bring their unconscious ideas into awareness, they did so with whole families gathered together. In the early days, therapists would interpret the transference and help the family members to understand their unconscious dynamics. This approach changed when therapists shifted to making interpretations to family members about how they were dealing with each other. Wives might be helped to understand, for example, that they were provoking their husbands, and if a wife objected to this interpretation she could be offered an interpretation about her resistance and transference involvement. Therapists also carried from individual therapy into family therapy the idea that if an individual expressed his feelings he would change. Therefore, early family therapists tried to encourage the expression of affect.

As family therapists gained more experience, they began to do therapy on the basis of new premises, ones that had not existed previously in individual therapy. One theoretical approach was based on the communication theory ideas that were developing as whole families were observed. In this approach, the therapist emphasized specificity and clarity of communication as a cause of therapeutic change because of the increased harmony and togetherness brought about (Satir, 1964). Another set of theories about change developed around the idea of differentiating people from one another. As it was recognized how intimately involved family members could be, therapy focused on shifting the family members toward more independence and autonomy. The goal was not to bring about family togetherness but disengagement (Bowen, 1966).

SYSTEMS THEORY AND STRUCTURAL THEORY

As family therapy moved further from individual theory, the theoretical model that emerged as most characteristic of family therapy was one based on cybernetics. The concept of a system of repeating sequences limited by governors was proposed in the 1940's (Wiener, 1948) and began to influence the social sciences. It appeared in psychiatry with the recognition that change in one person could affect, sometimes adversely, another person in the family (Jackson, 1957). From that point on, families began to be described as made up of people responding to one another in repeating ways so that the system was stable, as in any governed system. For example, if the father exceeds the limits of behavior within the system, the mother reacts, and if the mother introduces new behavior, the father reacts. Should the mother and father behave in ways that exceed the limits of the system, the child will react. Stability is maintained because the participants respond in "error activated" ways to any deviation from the habitual behavior within the system. When that habitual behavior includes psychiatric symptoms

expressed by one or more family members, then the symptoms cannot change unless the behaviors of the various family members change. Family therapy became a way of changing sequences of behavior among intimates in ongoing, ruled governed systems.

Although the cybernetic, or systems, model became the most popular one with family therapists, other theoretical dimensions are also important. One is the concept of family structure. All learning animals organize in hierarchies based on power and status. Family structure can be described in terms of hierarchy, and most family theorists argue that pathology expressed by an individual occurs when there is a confusion in a hierarchy or a violation of rules innate in hierarchical organizations. For example, if a mother sides consistently with child against father, she is breaching generation lines and so violating the rules of hierarchical structures. Similarly, if a grandmother consistently forms a coalition with a child against the child's mother, the levels of hierarchy in the organization are in confusion and the individuals will experience distress (Haley, 1967). These structural principles apply to other natural groups besides families. If a ward doctor consistently sides with a mental hospital patient against a psychiatric resident, a hierarchical confusion occurs and odd behavior will result.

This point of view does not assume that it is pathological for a mother occasionally to save a child from father's wrath. Coalitions form and change in any flexible system. It is the consistent, repeating, cross-generational coalitions that lead to distress, particularly when they are secret. The ward doctor who is constantly siding covertly with a patient against a resident is expressing a pathological situation, but this does not mean that it is pathological occasionally to protect a patient from a resident.

It is in relation to repetitive sequences that systems theory and structural theory come together. In a dynamic system, structure appears with the repetition of sequences. When one observes a person repeatedly telling another what to do and the other doing it, one concludes that there is a hierarchical structure with two people of different status. A hierarchical structure is shaped by the behavior of the people involved, and, insofar as the behavior is repetitive and redundant, it is an error-activated, governed system. If one person deviates from the repeating behavior, the other reacts against that deviation.

Pathological behavior appears when the repeating sequences simultaneously define two opposite hierarchies, or when the hierarchy is unstable because the behavior indicates one shape at one time and another at other times, as when parents sometimes take charge and at other times accept their child as an authority over them.

The following is an example of the repeating behavior in an abnormal system:

A mother and her 11-year-old boy are in an overinvolved relationship of mutual exasperation. The mother insists that the boy be more independent while simultaneously condemning him if he becomes so. The father is peripheral to the family, holding down two jobs and seldom at home. In the typical family sequence, the mother becomes overtaxed in dealing with her son, and in exasperation asks her husband for assistance and support. Her behavior defines the hierarchy as two parents dealing jointly together as authorities in relation to the child. The husband steps in to deal with the son, usually demanding from the son more independent behavior and less fear and dependence on his mother. When this occurs, the mother reacts and condemns that father for not understanding the son, shifting to a coalition with the son against the father. The father withdraws to the periphery. The mother has redefined the hierarchy as one in which she and her son have special status and the father is not to interfere. Later, in exasperation with the son, the mother will ask for support from the father. She defines them as two parents in charge of the child. The father begins to deal with the son or advise his wife how to deal with him, and the mother reacts against the father, indicating that he is not to interfere. Once again, the husband withdraws to the periphery. This sequence repeats itself endlessly and the hierarchy is undefined and confused. The homeostatic process prevents a clarification of the hierarchy or a resolution of symptomatic behavior.

FAMILY DEVELOPMENT

Besides a theory of systems and of hierarchical structure, there is a third dimension of family theory. A recent concern has been with the stages of family development over time (Haley, 1973). It is obvious that families change over the years as part of a natural process. As children mature and parents and grandparents age, coalition structures shift and the hierarchy changes. In the family life cycle, there is a major reversal of the hierarchical structure. Children shift from being taken care of by their parents to being peers of parents to taking care of parents in their old age. Some spontaneous change in families may be related to this developmental process over time; sometimes, therapy is given credit for a change that is a product of a natural process.

In summary, a comprehensive family theory, if developed, would have to include the homeostatic behavior of intimates, the nature of hierarchical structure, and developmental changes in the life cycle of natural groups. Family research has found a complication that makes the task of creating theory more difficult. Just as it was discovered that an individual behaves differently in different contexts, it has become apparent that families change in different contexts of observation. Family members can respond to each other in one way in a research setting and in another way in a therapy setting. To accumulate evidence in support of a hypothesis can be a problem when the data fluctuate with the circumstances under which they are gathered.

Theory of Therapeutic Change

Family theory, particularly homeostatic theory, has provided a model for explaining how a system remains unchanged. The clinical problem lies in providing a theory of how to bring change about. Granting that one needs a theory of how to stabilize a change when it is obtained in therapy, it is also necessary to theorize about how to start a change happening.

TWO MAJOR APPROACHES

In recent years, family therapy ideas have led to a concern with how to produce systematic changes in governed systems. Two major approaches characterize many diverse family therapies (Hoffman, 1971). In one approach, the therapist introduces a small change in the system and begins to amplify it. As this deviation from usual behavior is amplified, the entire system must go through a reorganization to adapt to the deviation. Thus, the system is changed. The other approach is just the opposite. A therapist forces a change in the family by introducing a crisis. To adapt to this new extreme situation, the family must reorganize.

For example, in a structure in which a grandmother joins in a coalition against the mother, the grandmother takes care of the grandchild while the mother withdraws. At a certain point, the grandmother insists that the mother take responsibility for the child. As the mother does so, the grandmother intrudes and insists that the mother does not know how to take care of the child or is irresponsible, and she takes over. The mother withdraws while the grandmother takes care of the grandchild. At another point, the grandmother insists that the mother take care of the child, and the sequence begins again. The hierarchy is confused because the grandmother is crossing generation lines and joining with a child against its mother. The goal of the therapy is to put the mother in charge of her child and the grandmother in an advisory capacity, dealing with the grandchild through the mother.

In this kind of situation, the goal can be achieved by a step-by-step process. The therapist can encourage the mother to take care of the child in one small area and restrain the grandmother from interfering in that area. As this change is accepted, it can be enlarged by having the mother deal with the child effectively in another small area while the grandmother is restrained. The therapist introduces a small deviation and then amplifies it, forcing the system to reorganize to adapt to the deviation.

In the crisis approach, the therapist might insist that for a period of 2 weeks the grandmother have full care of the grandchild while the mother does as she pleases. If the child misbehaves, the grandmother must deal with it. After 2 weeks of this burden, the therapist shifts to the opposite extreme. He insists that for the next 2 weeks the mother is to have full responsibility for the child. If the child misbehaves, the mother must deal with it. At the end of the second 2 weeks, the therapist has the family adopt an organization whereby the mother is primarily in charge and the grandmother is her adviser. (Often, the grandmother accepts this arrangement, since she is threatened with having full charge of the child if she does not.) To adapt to the crisis of an extreme change, the organization has had to shift.

Certain premises follow from conceiving of the problem of therapy as one of changing a governed, stable system. One premise is that change can most easily be accomplished if the family situation is unstable, which is often the case when a person with a problem first enters treatment. If the therapist intervenes actively at the beginning with a crisis approach, he takes advantage of the instability that led to the call for help. This approach is not feasible if the psychiatrist is functioning as an agent of social control and is stabilizing problem people for the community. If he uses drugs and custody to quiet a problem person or situation, or if he does extensive diagnosis, the problem sequence becomes stabilized and after that it is difficult to change.

The family systems view leads logically to the idea that therapy should be active and directive, but it also leads to a change in past ideas about therapeutic change. Since the problem is defined as changing the behavior of more than one person, focusing on insight and self-understanding, expressing affect, or exploring fantasies or the past is not relevant to therapy. Therapeutic change is defined as a shift in the interaction of intimates, including the interaction with the therapist. The therapist should not interview a person alone to help him understand his fantasies, but he can interview him alone to change the way he is dealing with an intimate.

STAGES OF THERAPY

In the systems approach, whereby individual change is brought about by changing the system, therapy must proceed through stages. One cannot go directly from the problem situation to the structure that is the goal. For example, stages of therapy can be applied to the problem of an overinvolved mother and child, and peripheral father, with the boy expressing a symptom of a fear of dogs. In the first stage of the therapy, the therapist insists that the father deal with the child in relation to a dog while the mother withdraws from the scene. As father and child become more involved, the mother will become upset at being left out and will attempt to re-engage herself. If she is blocked off from dealing with the child, she will deal with the father, complaining about his neglect of her and lack of appreciation of her problems. The therapy then enters the next stage, in which the emphasis is on the married couple. The child is moved out to dealing with peers rather than parents. The hierarchy has been stabilized in a structure in which parents are together in relation to child. If the marriage issues are resolved and the marriage is stabilized, the therapist can leave the system with the problem solved.

Therapist Coalitions

In the systems approach, a crucial problem for a therapist is the way he becomes part of the coalition patterns in families. A fundamental rule in family therapy is that one should not *consistently* side with any one member or part of a family against any other. If this happens, therapy has a poor outcome. To be helplessly caught in coalitions is a therapeutic misfortune. For example, when a therapist involuntarily and without plan attempts to rescue a child from his parents, he has formed a coalition with the child against the parents. Often, he is duplicating a family situation whereby someone of higher status, such as a grandmother, attempts to rescue the child from the parents. Thus, he is not introducing change but stabilizing an abnormal structural pattern. Similarly, to side consistently with a wife against a husband or with parents against in-laws can lead to poor outcome.

As one observes therapists at work, it becomes evident how difficult it is for a therapist not to join one faction of a family against another as he becomes personally involved. For example, if the therapist is young he tends to side with adolescents against parents. There is a generational pull that he can hardly resist. If the therapist is older and having problems with his own children, he may side with parents against their problem child. These coalitions are formed even if the therapist is not interviewing the whole family. The therapist who hospitalizes and medicates an adolescent is aligning himself with the family faction that presents the child as the problem even if he has never met the family.

A further premise of the systems view is that the therapeutic milieu can replicate the problem situations of patients. For example, a child can become disturbed if the mother and grandmother are in a struggle in which they use the child in their conflict. Yet, a "child" can also be disturbed if a psychiatric resident and his supervisor are in a struggle in which they use the patient in their conflict. Should the supervisor attempt to rescue the patient from a resident he considers incompetent or too emotionally involved, and the resident attempt to save the patient from the supervisor, who is too inhuman, a typical family pattern is being reproduced that consistently leads to symptoms.

From a systems view, the interaction of a psychiatric staff becomes as important as the interaction of family members. If a resident is assigned a patient for intensive individual therapy while a social worker sees the parents, each professional can respond with conflictual territorial struggles that replicate the behavior in a problem family. Unlike other therapeutic modalities, the family view requires a contextual view of the problem in that everyone involved must be considered as part of the problem situation.

Training in Family Therapy

While developing a new idea of therapeutic change, many family therapists continued to be trained in traditional ways. At first, teachers of family therapy modeled their training on individual therapy. Since psychodynamic therapy assumed that the patient must totally reveal himself, it was expected that the student therapist should totally reveal himself. Supervisors explored countertransference problems and encouraged students to enter therapy to discover and reveal personal problems—with the idea this would improve the student's skill as a therapist. In the beginning, student family therapists were also asked to reveal themselves totally, and a student's ideas about his mother were a legitimate subject for exploration by a teacher of family therapy. Since training was often in groups, student family therapists could be expected to publicly expose their personal family relationships in group exercises, such as family sculpting. This was supposed to improve a therapist's skill. Later, a revulsion developed against requiring this confessional kind of behavior from therapy students. Unless a teacher could show that the student's feelings about his mother interfered with his therapy and that talking about those feelings would change how the student dealt with a family, the student's personal life was not intruded upon.

Just as a patient's statements about his family seemed quite different from what a therapist observed when he saw the family, so what a therapist says about an interview appears quite different from what a supervisor observes. One-way mirrors and videotapes have made it possible for a supervisor actually to watch the student. He can observe the therapist's technical difficulties and teach him basic skills. The one-way observation mirror also allows live supervision; the supervisor can call the student on the telephone, or the student can come out of the interview room and discuss the problem. This kind of on-the-spot guidance has proven to be an effective way for a student to learn and is a way to protect a family from a therapist's inexperience.

In summary, the introduction of training in family therapy in a clinical department requires many innovations. Whole families must be brought in, not only individuals. The focus in the treatment is on what to do to bring about change, rather than on diagnosis. Teachers and students must conceptualize therapy in terms of how the therapist's involvement will bring about change, not how to encourage family understanding or affect expression. A one-way mirror and videotape arrangement is expected, and with it teachers can demonstrate therapy and guide students while the student does therapy. The focus is on the skill of the student doing the therapy, not on his personal problems. Finally, the training of a psychiatrist as a consultant also shifts when the emphasis is on family therapy. Rather than meet with a group and talk about a patient's diagnosis, the consultant is expected to have ideas about what to do.

As this form of therapy intrudes more into the field, the issue of the difference between the professionals also arises. When the problem unit was the individual, the psychologist, social worker, and psychiatrist each had a separate function defined by their training. When the unit is the family, all clinicians tend to do the same work and the difference between the professionals becomes obscured. This situation has provided a problem for many psychiatry departments. If residents are trained with an individual orientation and in the use of medication, they can maintain their professional identity and status in the field as the most extensively trained professionals. Yet, if the orientation of therapy becomes more social so that the emphasis is on changing families and other natural groups, the psychiatrist trained to use medication and psychodynamic therapy will be regarded as old fashioned and not relevant to therapy. To avoid falling behind when techniques of therapy change, psychiatry departments can train their residents to do family therapy and focus on social interventions, but, if they do so, they are not training psychiatrists to work any differently from psychologists or social workers who are learning the same skills. The separate identity of a psychiatrist can be in jeopardy as well as his higher status in the clinical community. The solution of many departments is to train residents in a broad way so that they are familiar with family therapy theory while they continue to practice as psychiatrists have in the past. This seems to be only a temporary solution to the dilemma.

REFERENCES

Ackerman, N. *Treating the Troubled Family.* Basic Books, New York, 1966.

Boszormenyi-Nagy, I., and Framo, J. L., editors. *Intensive Family Therapy.* Harper & Row, New York, 1965.

Bowen, M. Family psychotherapy. Am. J. Orthopsychiatry, *31:* 40, 1961.

Bowen, M. The use of family theory in clinical practice. Compr. Psychiatry, *7:* 345, 1966.

Curry, A. Therapeutic management of multiple family group. *Int. J. Group Psychother., 15:* 90, 1965.

Epstein, N. B. Family therapy. Can. Ment. Health, *10:* 5, 1962.

Ferber, A. S., and Beels, C. C. Changing family behavior programs. In *Family Therapy in Transition,* N. W. Ackerman, editor. Little, Brown, Boston, 1970.

Fulweiler, C. No man's land. In *Techniques of Family Therapy,* J. Haley and L. Hoffman, editors. Basic Books, New York, 1967.

*Glick, I., and Haley, J. *Family Therapy Research: An Annotated Bibliography.* Grune & Stratton, New York, 1971.

Haley, J. The perverse triangle. In *Family Therapy and Disturbed Families,* G. Zuk and I. Boszormenyi-Nagy, editors. Science and Behavior Books, Palo Alto, Calif., 1967.

Haley, J. Approaches to family therapy. Int. J. Psychiatry, *9:* 233, 1970.

*Haley, J. *Uncommon Therapy.* W. W. Norton, New York, 1973.

Hoffman, L. Deviation-amplifying process in natural groups. In *Changing Families,* J. Haley, editor. Grune & Stratton, New York, 1971.

*Jackson, D. D. The question of family homeostasis. Psychiatr. *31:* (Suppl.) 79, 1957.

Kempler, W. Experiential psychotherapy with families. Fam. Proc., *7:* 88, 1968.

Laqueur, H. P. Multiple family therapy and general systems theory. Int. Psychiatry Clin., *7:* 99, 1970.

MacGregor, R., Ritchie, A. M., Serrano, A. C., Schuster, F. P., MacDonald, E. C., and Goolishian, H. A. *Multiple Impact Therapy with Families.* MacGraw-Hill, New York, 1964.

*Minuchin, S., and Montalvo, B. Techniques for working with disorganized low socioeconomic families. Am. J. Orthopsychiatry, *37:* 880, 1967.

Patterson, G. R., MacNeal, S., Hawkins, N., and Phelps, R. Reprogramming the social environment. J. Child Psychol. Psychiatry, *8:* 181, 1967.

Paul, N. The use of empathy in the resolution of grief. Perspect. Biol. Med., *11:* 153, 1967.

*Pittman, F. S., Langsley, D. G., Flomenhaft, K., De-Young., C. D., and Machotka, I. Therapy techniques of the family treatment unit. In *Changing Families,* J. Haley, editor. Grune & Stratton, New York, 1971.

Rubenstein, D. Family therapy. In *Progress in Neurology and Psychiatry,* E. A. Speigel, editor, vol. 23. Grune & Stratton, New York, 1968.

Satir, V. *Conjoint Family Therapy.* Science and Behavior Books, Palo Alto, Calif., 1964.

Sluzki, C. E. Family interaction and symptoms. Interam. Psycol., *2:* 283, 1968.

Sonne, J. C., Speck., R. V., and Jungerie, J. E. The absent member maneuver as a resistance in family therapy of schizophrenia. Fam. Proc., *1:* 44, 1962.

*Speck, R. V., and Attneave, C. *Retribalization and Healing.* Pantheon Books, New York, 1973.

Stanton, A. H., and Schwartz, M. S. *The Mental Hospital.* Basic Books, New York, 1954.

Stuart, R. B. *Trick or Treatment; How and When Psychotherapy Fails.* Research Press, Champaign, Ill., 1970.

Vassilou, G. Milieu specificity in family therapy. In *Family Therapy in Transition,* N. W. Ackerman, editor. Little, Brown, Boston, 1970.

Whitaker, C. Family treatment of a psychopathic personality. Compr. Psychiatry, *7:* 397, 1966.

Wiener, N. *Cybernetics.* John Wiley, New York, 1948.

Zuk, G. Triadic based family therapy. Int. J. Psychiatry, *8:* 539, 1969.

16.6   Marital Therapy

VIRGINIA A. SADOCK, M.D.

Introduction

Although marriage tends to be regarded everywhere as a permanent tie, unsuccessful unions may be terminated, as indeed they are, in most societies. In spite of this, many marriages that do not end in separation or divorce are seriously disturbed. People marry for a variety of reasons—emotional, social, economic, and political, among others. In considering marital problems, the clinician is concerned not only with the persons involved but also with the marital unit itself. How any marriage works out relates to the partners selected, the personality organization or disorganization of each, the interaction between them, and the reasons behind the union in the first place.

Ideal Marriage

Is there an ideal marriage? If so, at what point along a continuum of deviation from that ideal is intervention required? The goal of constructing a model for a sound marriage, taking into account the changing values of the society and of the persons involved, is most important, and several workers in the field have attempted to define marital adjustment. Lidz (1968) describes the following qualities in a good marriage:

It forms a stabilizing influence for both spouses and a new opportunity for self-realization. Life becomes a new adventure filled with opportunity to live out what has long been imagined. Each partner relishes having another person so interested in his or her well-being and feels secure in being the center of the spouse's interest and love. Activity, thought, and fantasy have a new tangible and legitimate focus, which gives a new coherence to one's life. The companionship banishes loneliness, and sexual satisfaction brings a sense of release and fulfillment that mobilizes energies for the pursuit of incentives derived from the marriage . . . . Each partner makes mistakes and is apt to misunderstand, but evidence of love negates any intent to hurt.

Other models have been described elsewhere in this textbook, models ranging from the traditional marriage presented by Reed to the open marriage described by O'Neill and O'Neill. Ackerman (1958) has defined an ideal that is characterized by the following qualities:

Strivings and values would be shared to a reasonable degree by both partners and would be relatively realistic, stable, and flexible. There would be a reasonable degree of compatability in the main areas of shared experiences—the emotional, social, sexual, economic, and parental areas. Conflicts would not be excessive, would be under control, and would have mainly a realistic rather than an irrational content. There would be empathic tolerance of differences based on mutual understanding and equality and tolerance as well as residual immaturities of need that might be present in either partner. There would be a sharing of pleasure, responsibility, and authority. There would be reasonable fulfilment of goals both for the relationship and for the further development of each partner as an individual.

These descriptions, if taken as the ideal, would lead persons to have great expectations of marriage. At the very least, people expect love, affection, and companionship when they marry; but, as the oft-quoted statistic that one of every four marriages in this country ends in divorce seems to attest, all too often they find hostility, isolation, and loneliness in the marriage from which they expected the opposite.

History

Marital therapy has existed in one form or another since antiquity. Egyptian deities existed solely for the purpose of assuring a happy union in addition to a fertile one. The early Hebrews were known to prescribe a variety of ritualistic behaviors that, if followed, would provide for a joyous marriage. And the various Hindu and Arabian love manuals were as much marriage manuals as they were instructions in sexual techniques.

In more recent times, when families consisted of relatives, grandparents, parents, and children living under the same roof, assistance could be obtained from one or more members of the extended family with whom one or both partners had rapport. But, with the contraction of the extended family, this source of informal help is no longer accessible. Similarly, religion played a more important role than it does now in the maintenance of family stability. The wise religious leader was available to provide sought-after counseling; but, even though these leaders still exist and in many ways are more knowledgeable than their forbears, they are not sought out to the extent that they once were, a reflection of the decline of religious influence for large segments of the population.

Both the extended family and religion not only provided guidance for the couple in distress but also prevented dissolution of the marriage by virtue of the social pressure that each exerted on the couple to stay together. This pressure was a mixed blessing. For some persons who may have preferred to flee rather than fight, being forced to confront their differences served as a stimulus for growth when the capacity for change existed. For others, unhappily, the same social pressure acted as a prison from which there was no escape, and aired differences only furthered conflict and, at best, resigned alienation. As family, religious, and societal pressures relaxed, legal procedures for relatively easy separation and divorce expanded. Concurrently, the need for formalized marriage counseling services developed.

Definition

Marital therapy is designed to modify psychologically the interaction of two married people who are in conflict with one another along one or a variety of parameters—social, emotional, sexual, economic. Marital therapy is a form of psychotherapy in that a trained person establishes a professional contract with the patient-couple and, through definite types of communication, attempts to alleviate the disturbance, reverse or change maladaptive patterns of behavior, and encourage personality growth and development.

Attempts to distinguish marital therapy from marital counseling lead to difficulties, since there are more similarities than differences. Marriage counseling may be considered more limited in scope in that only a particular conflict related to the immediate concerns of the family is discussed. Or it may be primarily task oriented, geared to solving a specific problem, such as child rearing. In marriage therapy, there is a greater emphasis on restructuring the interaction between the couple, including, at times, an exploration of the psychodynamics of each of the partners. Most workers, including the author, regard this dichotomy as largely artificial. Both therapy and counseling place emphasis on helping the marital partners to cope more effectively with their problems. Most important is the definition of appropriate and realistic goals, which may involve extensive reconstruction of the union, problem-solving approaches, or a combination of both.

Types of Therapy

The therapy of emotional disorders began with psychoanalytic theory and practice, which established the rule that each spouse has to be treated in separate sessions and by a different therapist. This dyadic model was questioned by several early analysts who saw the patient as functioning within a social system from which he could not be isolated. Psychiatrists began to work with couples individually and jointly with favorable results, and Ackerman (1958) described the importance of the joint interview, in which the husband and wife are seen together so as to enable the therapist to appreciate fully the neurotic interaction of a particular marriage. As interest in group psychotherapy developed, successful reports of married couples group therapy emerged (Papanek, 1971). At the present time, treatment techniques for the dysfunctional couple are myriad, and a

sometimes confusing array of approaches is in use.

INDIVIDUAL THERAPY

Marital partners may be seen by different therapists, who may not necessarily communicate with one another. Indeed, they may not even know one another. Treatment in these situations is individually oriented, with the goal being to strengthen the adaptive capacities of each partner, so that they may relate to one another as more uniquely individualized people. At times, only one of the partners is in treatment; in such cases a visit by the spouse who is not in treatment with the therapist may be of value for several reasons: The visiting partner may provide the therapist with data about the patient that may otherwise be overlooked; overt or covert anxiety in the visiting partner as a result of change in the patient can be identified and dealt with; irrational beliefs about treatment events can be corrected; and attempts by the partner to consciously or unconsciously sabotage the treatment of the patient can be examined.

INDIVIDUAL MARITAL THERAPY

This form of treatment involves each of the marriage partners in therapy. When the same therapist conducts the treatment, it is called *concurrent* therapy; when one therapist sees one of the partners and a different therapist the other, it is called *collaborative* therapy. In collaborative therapy it is extremely important that the collaborating therapists do not work at cross-purposes with one another. They need not hold to the same theoretical view of emotional or marital disorders, but they must respect one another's abilities and therapeutic skill. Any dissonance between the therapists that remains unresolved will be communicated to the patients and only aggravate the discord that brought the couple into treatment in the first place. Collaborative therapists must also avoid taking an advocacy position with their respective patients and, in a well meaning attempt to provide support for one, end up by attacking the other.

CONJOINT THERAPY

Conjoint therapy is the treatment of partners in joint sessions conducted by either one or two therapists; it is the most common treatment method used in marital therapy. There is some advantage in co-therapy with therapists of both sexes working with a couple. This format prevents a particular patient from feeling ganged up on when confronted by two members of the opposite sex. For example, the female partner in a marriage may feel intimidated by having only a male therapist in conjoint therapy; she may imagine that he will side with her husband against her. Having a female therapist in the treatment setting reduces that anxiety. Additionally, in these times of rapidly changing gender and sexual roles—themes that almost always emerge in marital therapy—the presence of a male therapist and a female therapist can be most salutary. The therapist, male or female, working alone must be especially careful that he or she is aware of any biases, prejudices, or problems that may interfere countertransferentially with effective therapy in this type of setting.

FOUR-WAY SESSION

In this approach each partner is seen by a different therapist, with regular joint sessions in which all four participate. Papanek (1971) refers to these meetings as the square interview and reports the following case history:

At the age of 20, before her marriage to Charles, Greta started therapy. Charles, 24 years old, was referred to another therapist by his friend, a former patient. He would never have accepted a referral by Greta's therapist, whom he did not trust.

The marriage had been a stormy one from the beginning, since neither one of the young people had had adequate mothering, and both were immature and dependent. They had hardly anything in common. Their national and religious backgrounds were different; Charles' tendencies were toward hippie culture and the radical left; Greta espoused middle-class values. They were unprepared for their two small children, whose conceptions were accidental. They fought about everything and made each other continually miserable. They remained together because of the children and because each was afraid of isolation and loneliness. Charles had seen Greta's therapist a few times and was convinced that Greta's doctor was against him, since the doctor reinforced her middle-class values and expected Charles to conform.

The young people fought especially about basic decisions, such as the appearance and location of their apartment, the handling of money, and who should take care of the children. Charles' therapist suggested to Greta's that they meet the couple on their home ground. Greta and Charles had subjective and very different images of their apartment. It was a dirty, depressing hovel for her and an expensive, cheerful place for him. The therapists decided to make their own inspection in order to get a more objective image.

The apartment was partly a hovel and partly bright and pleasant, depending on whether you looked at its rear or front, whether you paid attention to its location in a dismal house and street or focused on the apartment itself and the view over the roofs of New York.

Subjectivity of viewpoints, values, and the hierarchy of what seems to be immediately important became crystal clear. The therapists saw that the differences of opinion between Greta and Charles could be solved easily. Each hid behind the shield of superficial difficulties a deep fear of being swallowed up by the other one and of losing his own identity.

The meeting of both therapists with both patients in their life space and seeing their children and stage of their quarrels not only enabled the two therapists to communicate with each other and to rectify their errors but also helped to demonstrate to the couple the strengths and weaknesses of the marriage. The greatest impact of the visit was an awareness on the part of all four people involved that each person is different from the other but that mutual respect and consideration for each other can prevail. Acceptance of this attitude became the realistic goal for this family, leading to mutual appreciation for each other, therapists included.

Charles' progress in therapy and his development of a more secure and more giving relation with Greta was to a great extent based on the square interview. Both therapists recognized the lack of communication between the spouses, the intensity of their fear to give in and thereby be obliterated by the other. This fear had grown steadily during their therapy; each felt that the "enemy" therapist had strengthened his own patient's attitudes and viewpoints against the spouse. This fear disappeared when the four faced each other and communicated freely.

The therapists understood the mutuality of their patients' neurotic transactions. Each therapist liked and was nice to his own patient but felt a responsibility for the family unit. Therefore, the therapists were firmly committed to help their patients to be less afraid, less stubborn, more helpful, and more accepting of the spouse. It took approximately 20 months for this one interview to bear fruit in the therapeutic process, but all through this time the memory of the common experience influenced all four people.

A variation of the four-way session is the round-table interview, developed by Masters and Johnson for the rapid treatment of sexually dysfunctional couples. Two patients and two opposite-sex therapists meet regularly in sessions that may also be considered a particular form of marital therapy.

GROUP PSYCHOTHERAPY

Therapy for married couples placed in a group, usually three to four couples and one or two therapists, allows for a variety of group dynamics to exert their effects on the married units involved. The couples identify with one another and recognize that others have similar problems; each gains support and empathy from fellow group members of the same or opposite sex; they explore sexual attitudes and have the opportunity to gain new information from their peer group; each receives specific feedback about his or her behavior, either negative or positive, that may have more meaning and be better assimilated coming from a more neutral nonspouse member.

When only one partner is in a therapy group, the other spouse may visit the group on occasion, so as to allow the members to test reality more effectively, especially if the visitor does not turn out to be the ogre that he or she had been presented as being. At times, a group may be so organized that only one married couple is part of the larger group. Depending on a variety of factors, especially careful selection, such a situation can be of benefit to the couple involved and to the rest of the group. At times, however, such placement may present specific problems of its own, as in the following case history:

A husband was admitted to his wife's group after she had been a member for a period of time because the therapist felt that this couple could benefit from such interaction. In addition, he felt confident of his ability to maintain his objectivity toward both patients. And, finally, he knew, from the data obtained in the course of their individual treatment, that these partners knew everything there was to know about each other. On the sur-

face, then, his decision was a valid one. However, 1 week after her husband entered the group, the wife took steps to establish herself as the center of the group's interest and concern (and divert attention from her husband). Apparently, she felt sufficiently threatened by his presence to initiate her first extramarital affair, thus obviating the less complicated marital relationship which had existed previously.

COMBINED THERAPY

In this instance combined therapy refers to any or all of the above described techniques used concurrently or in combination. Thus, a particular patient-couple may begin treatment with one or both partners in individual psychotherapy, continue to conjoint therapy with his or her partner, and terminate therapy after a course of treatment in a married couples group. The rationale for combined therapy is that no single approach to marital problems has been demonstrated as superior to another. Familiarity with a variety of approaches allows the therapist a degree of flexibility that will provide maximum benefit for the couple in distress.

In deciding on a particular appoach, the therapist must make a careful diagnostic evaluation. This evaluation includes individual interviews with each spouse to obtain a complete psychiatric history and mental status, to establish areas of psychopathology, and to allow each of the partners to reveal material he or she may otherwise conceal in a joint interview. After these interviews, the couple should be seen together and their interaction observed. Several individual or joint interviews may be needed before the therapist has enough data to recommend a particular course of treatment. At times, the process of evaluation may, in and of itself, provide certain couples with sufficient input to resolve their difficulties.

Indications for Treatment

Regardless of the specific therapeutic technique used, certain guidelines for starting marital therapy are agreed on: when methods of individual therapy have failed to resolve the marital difficulties or would be likely to fail because of insufficient motivation, when the onset of distress in one or both partners clearly relates to marital events, and when marital therapy is requested by a couple who is in conflict and unable to resolve it.

Problems in communication between partners are a prime indication for marital therapy. In such instances, one spouse may be intimidated by the other, may react with anxiety when attempting to tell the other about thoughts or feelings, or may project onto the other unconscious expectations. The therapy is geared to enable each of the partners to see the other more realistically, as unique persons with problems that often existed before the marriage.

Marital therapy is also indicated when a problem is related to the series of complex interactions that, when improperly carried out, cause the marriage to deviate from the ideal described earlier. Thus, conflicts in one or several areas, such as the partners' sexual life, are indications for treatment. Similarly, difficulty in establishing satisfactory roles in the social, economic, parental, or emotional area is an indication for help. Toward this end, the clinician should evaluate all aspects of the marital relationship before attempting to treat only one problem, which may be a symptom of a more pervasive marital disorder.

Contraindications for Treatment

In general, contraindications for marital therapy are few. They include the following: patients with severe forms of psychosis, particularly those with paranoid elements and patients in whom the homeostatic mechanism of the marriage is a protection against psychosis; one or both of the partners really wants to get a divorce; one spouse refuses to participate because of anxiety or fear. Some workers have suggested that conjoint therapy is contraindicated when secrets of which the other partner is unaware are present, particularly infidelity or homosexuality. Others, including the author, believe that family secrets more often create disharmony and feelings of guilt. Accordingly, whenever possible, the sharing of such secrets is encouraged. It is important, however, that such revelations be well timed and occur within the framework of an ongoing therapeutic relationship in which both patients and the therapist have developed feelings of trust and warmth.

A 32-year-old man had a history of bestiality, in which he had copulated with sheep. Before his marriage, he decided to withhold this information from his fiancee, for fear that she would not marry him if she knew this aspect of his past. After the marriage, however, he became troubled and guilt ridden about his secret and sought professional help. In the individual diagnostic interview, the bestiality was found to be associated with puberty, at which time he had lived on a farm and participated in this activity with other adolescents. Accordingly, the therapist was first able to reassure the man that his behavior was not abnormal under the circumstances. The patient's relief at having expressed his secret to the therapist without punitive rejection enabled him, after a few individual sessions, to accept the suggestion that he share this information with his wife. In a joint session he revealed his history. The wife was surprised but not repulsed and, although she had some questions about its normality, was reassured by the therapist.

Models of Therapy

As in all types of psychotherapeutic approaches, a variety of schools are represented in the ways marital therapists work. Techniques vary from allowing the patients to interact spontaneously, with little or no direction from the therapist, to structuring the sessions so that most communication is directed toward the therapist, who actively participates. Certain combinations of theory and techniques are most commonly practiced.

PSYCHOANALYTIC MODEL

Marital therapy based on psychoanalytic principles assumes that conscious and unconscious feelings exist between the spouses and that these feelings are based on the past familial experiences of each. The therapist sees marital conflict emerging from unfulfilled infantile expectations that one or both partners hope the other will gratify. In therapy, these strivings are interpreted, as are the various transferences made by the partners toward the therapist.

BEHAVIORAL MODEL

In therapy based on learning theory, particularly operant conditioning, the therapist shapes the behavior of each of the spouses in such a way that destructive patterns are replaced by constructive patterns.

As behavior changes, a reciprocal reward system is established between the partners and between the partners and the therapist, who, by his approval or disapproval, reinforces healthy interaction.

CLIENT-CENTERED MODEL

This approach, based on the work of Carl Rogers, helps the couple to clarify their own thinking and feelings about issues. The therapist follows the lead of the patients and does not introduce material based on a preconceived scheme, other than the basic assumption that the client possesses the ability to improve.

TRANSACTIONAL MODEL

In therapy based on the theories of Eric Berne, the therapist examines the transactions between the spouses as they occur in the here-and-now. A determination is made about whether the patient is acting as parent, child, or adult—different ego states assumed at various times. The therapist provides the couple with active feedback about their interactions as they occur.

SYSTEMS THEORY MODEL

Derived from general systems theory, this model sees the marital unit as a system in equilibrium. Disequilibrium is equivalent to discomfort and produces stress, which is felt by the partners. The role of the therapist is to monitor the emotional forces from moment to moment as they unfold through the interactions of the couple. Therapy is geared to modify whatever tension states exist (Bowen, 1971).

ECLECTIC MODEL

This model, to which the author subscribes, requires that the therapist be able to take the best of a variety of schools and apply them where applicable. Accordingly, the therapist may be a participant-observer at one moment—active, forthright, open—and a passive observer of the couple's interaction the next. If a psychoanalytic interpretation is called for, it is made. If, on the other hand, a didactic presentation of sexual technique or child-rearing practices is required, that is given. In practice, most experienced therapists do the same things with most patients, regardless of their particular theoretical orientations.

Goals

Ackerman (1966) has defined the aims of marital therapy as follows:

The goals of therapy for marital disorders are to alleviate emotional distress and disability and to promote the levels of well-being of both together and of each partner as an individual. In a general way, the therapist moves toward these goals by strengthening the shared resources for problem-solving; encouraging the substitution of more adequate controls and defenses for pathogenic ones; enhancing immunity against the disintegrative effects of emotional upset; enhancing the complementarity of the relationship; and promoting the growth of the relationship and of each partner as an individual.

Included in the therapeutic task is the notion that each partner in the marriage must take responsibility in attempting to understand the psychodynamic makeup of his or her personality. Accountability for the effects of behavior on one's own life, the life of the spouse, and the lives of others in the environment is emphasized. This emphasis often results in a deeper understanding of the problems that created marital discord and in a working through of individual psychopathology.

Marital therapy does not ensure the maintenance of any marriage. Rather, in certain instances it may serve to clarify for the partners that they are, for a variety of reasons, in a nonviable union that should be dissolved. As difficult as such a decision is to make, there is some gratification in the knowledge that every attempt to save the marriage was made. The partners not only separate with less feeling of guilt but provide themselves with some assurance that they have gained sufficient self-awareness to prevent a similar situation from occurring again.

Conclusion

The field of marital therapy draws upon the resources of the traditional mental health professionals—psychiatrists, psychologists, psychiatric social workers, nurses, and the

FIGURE 1. A rare print (circa 1790) depicting the marriage ceremony of the Laplanders of the Arctic region. (Courtesy of Virginia A. Sadock, M.D.)

clergy. The field is growing rapidly, and there is real concern about the professional training and qualifications of those who present themselves as marital therapists and marriage counselors. It is up to the various state licensing agencies, working in cooperation with local mental health associations, to determine adequate measures to protect the public against unscrupulous practitioners.

As long as the family remains the basic unit of society, the need for increased knowledge about the dynamics of family life will be necessary to provide a framework in which each member can realize his or her potential. Marriage has been and will continue to be the great bulwark against anxiety and the most effective source of love, sexual expression, affection, and companionship for the overwhelming majority of people throughout the world (see Figure 1). Marital therapy directs itself to maintaining this longest and most enduring of all adult human relationships.

REFERENCES

*Ackerman, N. W. *The Psychodynamics of Family Life.* Basic Books, New York, 1958.
*Ackerman, N. W. *Treating the Troubled Family,* p. 114. Basic Books, New York, 1966.
*Bowen, M. Family therapy and family group therapy. In *Comprehensive Group Psychotherapy,* H. I. Kaplan and B. J. Sadock, editors, p. 384. Williams & Wilkins, Baltimore, 1971.
*Lidz, T. *The Person.* Basic Books, p. 411. New York, 1968.
*Papanek, H. Group psychotherapy with married couples. In *Comprehensive Group Psychotherapy,* H. I. Kaplan and B. J. Sadock, editors, p. 691. Williams & Wilkins, Baltimore, 1971.
*Mudd, E. H. *The Practice of Marriage Counseling.* Association Press, New York, 1951.

16.7 The Physician's Role in Sex Therapy

BENJAMIN J. SADOCK, M.D.,
and HAROLD I. KAPLAN, M.D.

Introduction

With increased sexual awareness on the part of the public and with increased emphasis on sexual matters in daily life, more and more physicians are being asked to deal with and manage sex-related problems in their daily practices. Yet, despite the obvious need for informed sexual counseling, doctors are often uncomfortable about sexual matters and about the fact that patients tend to look to them as authorities on sexual problems, even though many physicians have no special expertise in this area. There are a number of reasons for patients' endowing physicians with such special qualifications regarding sexual matters. Doctors study and treat the human body, and they are privy to the intimate secrets of various patients. The incorrect assumption by patients that doctors have received specific sexual training and the equally unrealistic concept of the wise and omniscient family doctor combine to create an aura of authority, knowledge, and omnipotence.

Rather, physicians frequently offer poor sexual advice, based on their own prejudices, inhibitions, motivations, and feelings. Sometimes they even abandon traditional methods of diagnosis and therapy to offer medical advice that is often no more than a statement of individual opinion or personal bias.

Physician's Qualifications Regarding Sex

Most doctors treat a fairly varied patient population in regard to age, background, and education. Ironically, however, although they are asked to comment and advise on a variety of sexual life-styles and disabilities, they themselves are frequently overcontrolled and conservative regarding sex. Their usual lack of training in this area does not help. According to sex researchers Masters and Johnson, physicians know no more and no less about the subject than do other college graduates. A 1959 survey of the medical graduates and the faculty of a Philadelphia medical school revealed that half of the students correlated masturbation with mental illness. A University of Virginia study of law students and medical students revealed that, as freshmen, these students were equal in their knowledge of sexual matters and that, although senior medical students knew more than senior law students about sex, they still missed 10 of 80 questions in a questionnaire designed for educated laymen.

Although sexual dysfunction and its consequences have been sadly neglected in most medical educational programs—even gynecologists and psychiatrists report inadequate training in areas that help them to deal with marital and sexual problems—the picture is improving steadily today as physicians recognize their responsibility to provide expert advice in all areas related to human sexual behavior. Most medical schools now include some training on sexual problems.

Physician's Responsibilities Regarding Sex

The general practitioner, the gynecologist, the obstetrician, the urologist, the pediatrician—all have ample opportunities to introduce sex information into their regular medical examination and to respond to patients' implicit or explicit queries about sexual matters. Sex should be discussed with adolescents, with the hemiplegic, with cardiac patients, and with those who have had spinal cord injuries, colostomies, ileostomies, hysterectomies, or mastectomies. The husbands of nonorgasmic wives and the wives of impotent men are urgently in need of sex therapy, even if they are reluctant to state this need openly. In fact, few areas or disabilities are totally unrelated to sexual factors.

In offering advice or setting up a program of sex therapy, the physician must rely on more than his fundamental knowledge of anatomy, which is about the "sexual"

training the average physician has received. Anatomy may help the teen-ager understand his or her body, but it does not ease the suffering of the guilt-ridden 16-year-old who has defied her parents and had sexual intercourse. Nor is it sufficient to reassure the 18-year-old boy who is worried about the size of his penis. Counseling patients, uncovering sexual difficulties, and helping patients to overcome embarrassment require both knowledge and a sensitive, well defined, well thought out approach. Implied as well is the physician's willingness to involve himself in what many doctors still regard as strictly private matters.

The physician who deals successfully with the sexual problems of his patients must, above all, recognize that his own biases must be cast aside before he can offer objective advice without value judgments and moralistic preaching. The physician who considers certain practices repugnant or perverse will find it difficult to communicate the accepting, nonjudgmental attitude that is necessary in effective sex therapy. The doctor must be willing to tolerate the varying sexual habits of different segments of the population. The young doctor in the youth culture may find that he is unsympathetic or uninformed about the sexual behavior of older people. The puritanical, middle-class physician may be shocked at the sexual behavior of some of his patients. The physician must also know the patient he is dealing with; he must have a sense of the patient's mores and attitudes so that he can communicate with him appropriately. And at all times in dealing with sexual matters, the physician must remember that even the most sophisticated patient is likely to see him as an authority figure and that the knowledge he imparts and the advice he gives are endowed with this special authority.

Approaches

How a particular medical doctor approaches sex therapy depends on his specialty, on his style of practice, and on his perception of the particular problem and the particular type of patient. Some, like sex therapists Masters and Johnson, consider sexual technique and attitudes all important, and in their work with patients they impart accurate sex information, accept without sanctions their patients' feelings, and provide a program of sexual reawakening and readjustment. Basic to this type of therapy, which is being practiced successfully in sex counseling programs throughout the country, is the notion that sexual dysfunction is a shared problem and that for most couples it is fruitless to consider one partner as sick and the other as well. Although most programs based on the Masters and Johnson approach prefer to treat couples, some of the techniques employed can be applied to single people as well. The physician can adapt many aspects of the Masters and Johnson educative and supportive program for use with a variety of patients with sexual problems.

Some doctors feel that this kind of behavioral approach is not sufficient to relieve sexual problems in any meaningful way and that deeper probing is needed to uncover the deeper causes of sexual dysfunction. In such cases, psychiatric referral is indicated. However, an impressive number of cases of sexual unhappiness and dysfunction are the result of ignorance, inhibition, and embarrassment, which the understanding, informed, and supportive physician can do much to alleviate.

Family Planning

One of the responsibilities of the physician, particularly the general practitioner and the obstetrician-gynecologist, is to advise couples and individual patients about contraception and family planning. Many authorities feel that this responsibility can be effectively integrated into a total program not only of contraception but of sexual and marital adjustment, infertility treatment, family counseling, and detection and treatment of venereal disease. In this type of approach, doctors help to deal with social problems of marital discord, sexual incompatibility or dysfunction, divorce, abortion, and child abuse while cooperating with schools and community and religious organizations.

Sexual History

Regardless of whether the patient's presenting complaint is sexual or whether the physician suspects that sexual problems underlie the patient's disorder, a sexual history is an excellent means of eliciting information. It is also a good way for the doctor to communicate his interest and involvement in the sexual aspects of the patient's life. When no sexual history is taken and there is no mention of sex in the doctor-patient interview, the patient may conclude that the doctor thinks sex is taboo or unimportant and, therefore, may be reluctant to discuss it.

The physician should communicate to the patient, both directly and by means of a reassuring attitude, that all information elicited is strictly confidential. To avoid embarrassment and to facilitate ease of communication, the physician may sometimes use a written questionnaire, although a verbal history is preferable. In either case, written or oral, questions should be detailed and presented in language familiar to the patient. Although technical language should be avoided if there is reason to think the patient will be intimidated by it or ignorant of its meaning, scientific language is often desirable in dealing with the informed, educated person, who may be offended by slang or what he considers condescending terminology. The interviewer must not only concern himself about his language but evaluate the content of the language of the patient and be certain that definitions are clear. A woman who has orgasms at night but not in the morning is not frigid, and a man who can perform with his mistress but not his wife is not impotent, although both these patients may be seriously concerned about their sexual impairment.

Questions should be as specific as possible. Questions such as, "How often do you have intercourse? At what age did you begin to masturbate?" are designed to elicit truthful responses with a minimum of embarrassment and shame. In an oral interview, pausing between questions encourages the patient to elaborate and assures him of the interviewer's interest and approval. In the case of married couples, it is important to interview both partners, usually both separately and together, if possible.

How the physician communicates with his patient has much to do with how easily he can uncover the sexual difficulty and how effective he is in treating the patient. It is important that his manner be completely professional and that he inspire confidence by allowing ample time—20 minutes is usually sufficient—for interviewing. He should be alert to nonverbal cues; clenched fists, averted eyes, and a tense posture may suggest anger and anxiety not revealed by the patient's spoken message. Comments like, "You seem unhappy; is there something bothering you that you haven't told me about?" can help open up the embarrassed or inhibited patient.

An outline prepared by the Group for Advancement of Psychiatry based on the sexual performance evaluation questionnaire of the Marriage Council of Philadelphia—which is affiliated with the division of family study, department of psychiatry, University of Pennsylvania School of Medicine—indicates the lines of inquiry to be considered in obtaining a sexual history. It is not intended as a questionnaire to which patients should be subjected. Depending on the individual clinical situation, one or more lines of inquiry in this comprehensive review of possible topics could be sufficient and appropriate.

I. Identifying data
  A. Patient
    1. Age
    2. Sex
    3. Marital status (single, number of times previously married, currently married, separated, divorced, remarried)
  B. Parents
    1. Ages
    2. Dates of death and ages at death
    3. Birthplace
    4. Marital status (married, separated, divorced, remarried)
    5. Religion
    6. Education
    7. Occupation
    8. Congeniality
    9. Demonstration of affection
    10. Feelings toward parents
  C. Siblings (as indicated)
  D. Marital partner
    1. Age
    2. Marital status (number of times previously married; remarried, if divorced)
    3. Place of birth
    4. Religion
    5. Education
    6. Occupation
    7. Cultural background
  E. Children
    1. Ages
    2. Sex
    3. Assets
    4. Problems

II. Childhood sexuality
  A. Family attitudes about sex
    1. Degree of parents' openness or reserve about sex
    2. Parents' attitude about nudity and modesty
    3. Behavior about nudity and modesty: (a) parents; (b) patient
  B. Learning about sex
    1. Asking parents about sex: (a) which parent; (b) answers given; (c) at what age; (d) nature of questions; (e) feelings about it
    2. Information volunteered by parents: (a) which parent; (b) what information; (c) at what age; (d) feelings about it
    3. Explanations by either parent (indicate which parent or parent substitute): (a) sex play; (b) pregnancy; (c) birth; (d) intercourse; (e) masturbation; (f) nocturnal emissions; (g) menstruation; (h) homosexuality; (i) venereal disease; (j) age at the time of each explanation; feelings about such learning
  C. Childhood sex activity
    1. First sight of nude body of same sex: (a) age ("how young"); (b) feelings; (c) circumstances
    2. Of opposite sex: (a) age ("how young"); (b) feelings; (c) circumstances
    3. Genital self-stimulation: (a) age ("how young") *before adolescence* at first occurrence; (b) manner; (c) orgasm? (how often?); (d) feelings (pleasure, guilt); (e) consequences, if apprehended.
    4. Other solitary sexual activities (bathroom sensual activity regarding urine, feces, odors)
    5. First sexual exploration or play (playing doctor) with another child (possible reply may be *never*): (a) age; (b) sex and age of other child; (c) nature of activity (looking, manual touching, genital touching, vaginal penetration, oral-genital contact, anal contact, other; (d) feelings (pleasure, guilt); (e) consequences, if apprehended (what and by whom)

6. Other episodes of sexual exploration or play with other children *before adolescence* (subcategories as in 5 above)
7. Sex activity with older persons: (a) at what ages; (b) ages of other persons; (c) nature of activity; (d) willing or unwilling; (e) force or actual attack involved? (f) (feelings)
D. Primal scene
   1. Parents' intercourse: (a) hearing; (b) seeing; (c) feelings
   2. Other than parents: (a) hearing; (b) seeing; (c) feelings
E. Childhood sexual theories or myths
   1. Thoughts about conception and birth
   2. Functions of male and female genitals in sexuality
   3. Roles of other body orifices or parts (such as umbilicus) in sexuality and reproduction (such as oral impregnation, anal intercourse, anal birth, pregnancy by kissing)
F. Other childhood sexuality
III. Onset of adolescence
A. In girls
   1. Preparation for menstruation: (a) informant; (b) nature of information; (c) age given; (d) feelings about way in which the information was given; (e) about the information itself
   2. Age: (a) at first period; (b) when breasts began developing; (c) of appearance of pubic and axillary hair
   3. Menstruation: (a) regularity (initial, subsequent, present); (b) frequency; (c) discomfort? (d) medication? (e) duration; (f) hygienic method (Kotex, tampons); (g) feelings about first period (surprise, distaste, interest, anticipation, guilt, shyness); (h) about subsequent periods
B. In boys
   1. Preparation for adolescence: (a) informant; (b) nature of information; (c) age given
   2. Age: (a) of appearance of pubic and axillary hair; (b) change of voice; (c) of first orgasm; (d) with or without ejaculation; (e) frequency of orgasm; (f) for how many years?
   3. Emotional reaction: (a) to early or delayed onset of adolescence; (b) to first orgasm
IV. Orgastic experiences

A. Nocturnal emissions (male) or orgasm during sleep (female)
   1. Frequency: (a) premarital; (b) postmarital
   2. Accompanying dreams
B. Masturbation
   1. Age when begun
   2. Ever punished?
   3. Frequency per week: (a) during teens; (b) during twenties; (c) during thirties, etc.
   4. Method: (a) usual; (b) others tried; (c) others used
   5. Marital partner's knowledge of past or present masturbation
   6. Practiced with others: (a) before marriage; (b) with spouse
   7. Emotional reactions
   8. Accompanying fantasies
C. Necking and petting ("making out")
   1. Age when begun
   2. Frequency
   3. Number of partners
   4. Types of activity
D. Intercourse (see also section IX below)
   1. Frequency of occurrence
   2. Number of partners
   3. Kinds of partners (fiancée, lover, friend, prostitute, unselective)
   4. Contraceptives used
   5. Feelings about premarital intercourse: (a) for girls; (b) for boys; (c) for different ages
E. Orgastic frequency (over-all)
   1. During teens
   2. During twenties
   3. During thirties
   4. During forties, etc.
V. Feelings about self as masculine/feminine
A. The male patient
   1. Does he feel masculine?
   2. Popular?
   3. Sexually adequate?
   4. Any feelings about being a "sissy"?
   5. Does he feel accepted by his peers? (belongs to a group?)
   6. Feelings about: (a) body size (height, weight, etc.); (b) appearance (handsomeness, virility); (c) voice; (d) hair distribution; (e) genitalia (size, circumcision, undescended testicle, virility, potency, ability to respond sexually); (f) cross-dressing (any experience in doing so)
B. The female patient
   1. Does she seem feminine?
   2. Popular?

3. Sexually adequate?
4. Was she ever a "tomboy"?
5. Does she feel accepted by her peers? (belongs to a group?)
6. Feelings about: (a) body size (height, weight, etc.); (b) appearance (beauty); (c) breast size, hips; (d) distribution of hair; (e) cross-dressing (any experience in doing so)

VI. Sexual fantasies and dreams
  A. Nature of sex dreams
  B. Nature of fantasies
    1. During masturbation
    2. During intercourse

VII. Dating
  A. Age ("how young")
    1. First date
    2. First kissing: (a) lips; (b) deep
    3. First petting or "making out": feelings
    4. First going steady: feelings
  B. Frequency: feelings about frequency of dating

VIII. Engagement
  A. Age (formal or informal?)
  B. Sex activity during engagement period
    1. With fiancée: (a) kissing; (b) petting; (c) intercourse
    2. With others: (a) number of persons; (b) frequency; (c) nature of activity

IX. Marriage
  A. Vital statistics
    1. Date of marriage
    2. Age: (a) interviewee; (b) spouse
    3. Spouse's occupation
    4. Is spouse present at interview?
    5. Previous marriage(s): (a) interviewee; (b) spouse
    6. Reason for termination of previous marriage (death, divorce): (a) interviewee; (b) spouse
    7. Number, sex, and ages of children from previous marriage: (a) interviewee; (b) spouse
  B. Premarital sex with spouse (if not previously covered)
    1. Petting: (a) frequency; (b) feelings about it
    2. Intercourse: (a) frequency; (b) feelings about it
    3. Contraceptives (identify kind used, if any)
  C. Wedding trip (honeymoon)
    1. Social and geographic particulars: (a) where; (b) duration; (c) generally pleasant or unpleasant?
    2. Sexual considerations: (a) frequency of intercourse; (b) was sex pleasant or unpleasant? (c) was the wife aroused? (d) was orgasm achieved (occasionally, always, never)? (e) was spouse considerate? (f) any complications (impotence, frigidity, pain, difficulty in penetration, honeymoon cystitis)
  D. Sex in marriage
    1. General satisfaction or dissatisfaction
    2. Thoughts about general satisfaction or dissatisfaction of spouse
  E. Pregnancies
    1. Number
    2. At what ages
    3. Results (normal births, cesarean delivery, miscarriages, abortions)
    4. Effects on sexual adjustment (fear of pregnancy)
    5. Number wanted and number unwanted
    6. Sex of child wanted or unwanted

X. Extramarital sex
  A. Emotional attachments
    1. Number of different attachments
    2. Frequency of contacts
    3. Feelings about extramarital emotional attachment
  B. Sexual intercourse
    1. Number of different partners
    2. Frequency of incidents
    3. Feelings about extramarital intercourse
  C. Postmarital masturbation
    1. Frequency
    2. How recent?
  D. Postmarital homosexuality
    1. Frequency
    2. How recent?
  E. Multiple sex ("swinging")

XI. Sex after widowhood, separation, or divorce
  A. Outlet
    1. Orgasms in sleep
    2. Masturbation
    3. Petting
    4. Intercourse
    5. Homosexuality
    6. Other
  B. Frequency of past or current resort to outlet
  C. Feelings about such experiences

XII. Sexual variants and sexual disorders
  A. Homosexuality
    1. First experience: (a) age ("how young"); (b) age and number of persons involved; (c) how often repeated; (d) nature of activity

(looking, manual, oral, anal); (e) active or passive (in seeking the activity, in performance)? (f) circumstances (childhood sex play, seduction by elders)

2. During and since adolescence: (a) patient's age; (b) age and number of persons involved; (c) frequency; (d) recency; (e) nature of activity (looking, manual, oral, anal); (f) usual circumstances (at movies or gay bars, in public toilets or turkish baths, with minors); (g) penalties (blackmail, being "rolled," being arrested); (h) interest or desire and whether fulfilled or unfulfilled

B. Sexual contact with animals
 1. When: (a) childhood; (b) in adolescence; (c) since adolescence
 2. Nature of contact: (a) vaginal penetration; (b) anal penetration; (c) licking by animal; (d) masturbation on or of an animal
 3. Frequency
 4. Recency
 5. Feelings about sexual contact with animals

C. Voyeurism
 1. Interest or pleasure in looking at objects connoting sex (genitals, nudes, etc.): (a) in childhood; (b) in adolescence; (c) since adolescence; (d) frequency; (e) recency; (f) circumstances; (g) consequences; (h) arousal or masturbation while looking
 2. Sexual interest or pleasure from looking into mirror: (a) in childhood; (b) in adolescence; (c) since adolescence; (d) frequency; (e) recency
 3. Interest in pornographic pictures: (a) in childhood; (b) during adolescence; (c) since adolescence; (d) frequency; (e) recency; (f) feelings about them (pleasure, disgust); (g) response (arousal, masturbation)
 4. Peeping: (a) in childhood; (b) in adolescence; (c) since adolescence; (d) frequency; (e) recency; (f) circumstances (in bathhouses, public toilets, lighted windows at night, by use of field glasses, etc.); (g) consequences, if apprehended; (h) feelings about peeping

D. Exhibitionism (deriving pleasure from displaying genitals)

1. To whom: (a) children; (b) adults
2. When: (a) in childhood; (b) in adolescence; (c) since adolescence; (d) frequency; (e) recency; (f) circumstances (in bathhouses, public toilets, lighted windows at night, etc.); (g) consequences, if apprehended; (h) feelings about exhibitionism

E. Fetishes, tranvestism
 1. Nature of fetish (underwear, other clothing, objects of sexual attraction): (a) when adopted; (b) sexual behavior associated with it (such as masturbation); (c) frequency; (d) recency; (e) consequences
 2. Nature of transvestite activity: (a) when adopted; (b) sexual behavior associated with it; (c) frequency; (d) recency; (e) consequences

F. Sadomasochism
 1. Nature of activity: (a) pain inflicted; (b) pain undergone; (c) means employed
 2. Sexual response: (a) to activity itself; (b) to fantasies of such activity
 3. Frequency
 4. Recency
 5. Consequences

G. Seduction and rape
 1. Has the patient seduced or raped another person? (a) frequency; (b) recency; (c) circumstances; (d) consequences
 2. Has the patient been seduced or raped? (a) frequency; (b) recency; (c) circumstances; (d) consequences

H. Incest
 1. Nature of sex play or sexual activity with: (a) brother; (b) sister; (c) mother; (d) father; (e) son; (f) daughter; (g) other
 2. Period of activity: (a) in childhood; (b) in adolescence; (c) since adolescence
 3. Frequency
 4. Recency
 5. Consequences

I. Prostitution
 1. Has patient accepted or paid money for sex: (a) when in life? (b) frequency; (c) recency
 2. Has patient "rolled" someone or ever been "rolled"?
 3. Feelings about prostitution
 4. Types of sexual practices: (a) actual; (b) tolerated; (c) preferred

5. Types of clients accepted or paid for

XIII. Certain effects of sex activities
  A. Venereal disease
    1. Age ("how young") of learning about venereal disease
    2. Venereal disease contracted: (a) gonorrhea (when, treatment, effects); (b) syphilis (when, treatment, effects)
  B. Illegitimate pregnancy
    1. Having an illegitimate pregnancy (female patient): (a) how often; (b) at what age; (c) disposition of pregnancy (miscarriage, abortion, adoption, marriage; kept baby; kept baby without marriage); (d) feelings about it
    2. Causing an illegitimate pregnancy (male patient): (a) how often; (b) at what age; (c) disposition of pregnancy; (d) feelings about it
  C. Abortion
    1. Why performed?
    2. At what age(s)?
    3. How often?
    4. Before or after marriage?
    5. Circumstances: (a) who; (b) where; (c) how
    6. Feelings about abortion: (a) at the time; (b) in retrospect; (c) anniversary reaction

XIV. Use of erotic material
  A. Response to erotic or pornographic literature, pictures, movies
    1. Sexual pleasure arousal
    2. Mild pleasure
    3. Disinterest
    4. Disgust
  B. Use in connection with sexual activity
    1. Type of material
    2. Frequency of use
    3. Use accompanying or preceding: (a) intercourse; (b) masturbation; (c) other sexual activity

Sexual Problems in Family Medicine

In a number of ways the family practitioner is well suited to counsel patients who have sexual problems or difficulties. In many cases there is no one else available who can offer advice on sexual matters. The family practitioner generally knows his patients and has a built-in rapport based on confidence and trust. He can conveniently work counseling into general treatment, since sexual problems are often symptomatic of other difficulties.

The average generalist sees a great variety of problems related to sex—the mother concerned about her son's masturbation, the adolescent worried that he has a venereal disease, the young couple seeking advice about contraception, the husband who is afraid that he is becoming impotent, the nonorgasmic wife, the homosexual, the wife who suspects her husband of infidelity, and those people who have undergone surgery or suffered illnesses or accidents that affect sexual functioning.

Most sexual problems are related to guilt, misinformation, or concepts of inadequacy or some combination of these factors. Physicians report that few patients come in with a frank sexual problem; the presenting complaint is usually one of vague illness or discomfort, and only through careful probing is the sexual difficulty brought out.

More women than men seek out sexual advice, which is consistent with the fact that more women than men seek medical advice in general. A woman may complain of lower back pain, vague abdominal discomfort, vaginal discharge, dyspareunia, fatigue, or menstrual difficulties. The sensitive physician is alert to possible underlying sexual difficulties while treating the presenting complaint. The woman who complains about postpartum fatigue may also be talking about her fears that her husband is being unfaithful to her. The women who declares she cannot enjoy sex may really be revealing her husband's impotence. It is common for a man's impotence to be presented to the physician by his wife; the husband is usually too embarrassed and frustrated to discuss it with a physician.

The man who complains to his physician about his wife's frigidity, coldness, and unresponsiveness is frequently really complaining about himself, just as his wife may be revealing his impotence by complaining about her lack of pleasure in sex. Impotence or fear of impotence, premature ejaculation, pain associated with coitus, and contraception are some of the sexual issues that men bring to the general practitioner. In most cases, as with women, the presenting complaint is not sexual, and the sexual problem is often brought up as a seemingly casual after-thought.

SEX AND MEDICATION

Here the power of suggestion is vitally important. The man who is forewarned that the drug he is taking will affect his libido may oblige by fulfilling this prophecy; since in most cases the sex-impairing side effects cannot be predicted accurately, the physician is well advised to avoid any mention of these effects but to be prepared to discuss them if the patient brings them up later. Sometimes a change in medication solves the problem. There is no harm in changing oral contraceptives, for example, if the patient thinks that the one she is taking is affecting her sexual drive.

Once the patient has spoken of his sexual problems, the physician can decide how to treat him. With married couples it is best to see both partners. Both married and single people can benefit immediately from frankly presented information. Direct physical causes of the problem can be ruled out by a careful examination; if there are physical components, they will be discovered by the examination and careful interviewing. Simply reassuring the patient that his complaint is understandable, that he is not alone in the problem, and that the difficulty is curable are most helpful to him. Some physicians recommend sex manuals or set up specific programs of instruction based on the techniques of sex therapists like Masters and Johnson.

Every general practitioner sees men and women seeking advice about contraception. In the case of married people, he need only present the various means of birth control and discuss the comparative virtues of each. The single woman seeking advice about birth control may fear that the physician will make a judgment about her sexual activity or in some way impose his views about sexual behavior in the unmarried. Unless he is requested to do so, the physician should refrain from offering such opinions and should limit himself to providing his single patients with up-to-date contraceptive information. Venereal disease, encountered in both married and single patients, should be treated in a similar nonjudgmental fashion, although it is vitally important that those with whom the affected patient has had sexual contact be notified; this requires tactful management on the part of the physician.

MARRIAGE COUNSELING

With today's increased sexual freedom and elevated expectations regarding the rewards of sexual experience, many couples have become aware that their sex lives, although not necessarily fraught with anxiety or even particularly troublesome in the marriage, are lacking in quality and depth. Others, made aware of sexual practices and norms as a result of increased emphasis in the media and in society in general, realize that their sexual experiences are decidedly inferior and a source of anxiety and displeasure. Many of these dissatisfied people discuss their problems with the general practitioner. It has been estimated that the average busy practitioner sees about three sex-related cases each week.

In treating marital problems, the physician must keep himself abreast of the latest developments in sex therapy and marital counseling. He must be able to devote a good deal of time to these patients, to establish a comfortable and authoritative relationship with both partners, and to help them to communicate freely with each other and with him. Certain difficult cases, in which marital dissatisfaction and sexual discord have reached complicated proportions, are best referred to a psychotherapist or other specialist in marital and sexual counseling. But a great many of the sexual problems of marriage can be handled effectively and relatively simply by a dedicated and sensitive physician. The physician must remember, however, that his patients represent different backgrounds, cultural norms, and ideational notions. He must be careful not to impose on them his own often conservative and sometimes incorrect concepts of normal and acceptable. For example, he might keep in mind that normal frequency of coitus varies from once in 3 months to 30 times in 7 days.

After making a careful physical examination of both partners and reassuring them that they are physically normal, the doctor should stress the emotional aspects of sexual difficulty, pointing out that discord and lack of satisfaction usually result from a combination of complicated factors. He must remind the couple that sex problems are interpersonal problems and that both partners must be involved and committed to alleviating the difficulty. Speaking in terms of the healthy partner and the sick partner should be avoided. The emphasis should be placed on giving pleasure, rather than on demanding pleasure; for example, the wife of an impotent husband may try to help her husband by manipulation, instead of demanding that he provide her with satisfaction.

The physician who is familiar with the work of such sex counselors as Masters and Johnson can advise his patients about ways to increase their sexual responsiveness and their sexual adequacy. A sequential program of exercises—building up from heightening sensory awareness, learning to give and receive general bodily pleasure, and on to genital stimulation—should be instituted before the couple even attempts intercourse. Although the Masters and Johnson methods involve an elaborate program of co-therapy, round-table discussion, psychological examinations, and individual and marital therapy, some of their techniques can be successfully used by the general practitioner. Presenting complaints of premature ejaculation, primary or secondary impotence, dyspareunia, vaginismus, and general sexual incompatibility may respond well to this type of therapy.

Sex Therapy and Adolescent

All physicians who see adolescents in clinics and private practice—pediatricians, internists, gynecologists, family practitioners—should be alert to sexual difficulties and should be prepared to identify such problems, counsel youngsters, and make referrals as part of routine health care. Such problems as venereal disease, unwanted pregnancies, and emotional concerns about body image, sex roles, and self-control of physiological urges loom large during the junior high school and high school years.

Girls are typically concerned about the size of their breasts; very large breasts are frequently more of a source of unhappiness and embarrassment than are too small ones. Problems of menstruation can also contribute to some adolescents' anxieties. Boys worry about penis size, masturbation, nocturnal emissions, and early-morning erections. Both sexes are often disturbed by homosexual fantasies and by the powerful sexual feelings that they are beginning to experience and that they frequently find difficult to channel. Conflicts with parents about sexual and social matters are also common in this age period.

TECHNIQUES

The physician can be of great help to the adolescent by treating him or her in a noncondescending and nonjudgmental manner. He should impart information calmly and gently and as honestly as possible. Since teen-agers may be reluctant to present their problems directly, he should be able to probe in a casual way, asking questions that at all times suggest that the youngster's problems and experiences are natural and normal.

Sexual counseling should begin in the preadolescent years. Casual questions, begun when the child is 9 or 10, are conducted during routine physical examinations; questions about dating, sexual feelings, and masturbation can do much to alleviate and to pave the way for open communication about sexual matters. Many physicians find that pamphlets and charts are useful in augmenting the face-to-face contacts.

CONTRACEPTION

One of the most critical sexual issues in the adolescent years is the matter of birth control. Nearly 50 per cent of all out-of-wedlock births occur among teen-agers. Although authorities are not in agreement about whether or not contraceptive information should be given to teen-agers—some feel that it leads to promiscuity—most agree that unwanted births are undesirable. Abortion, when legal, is advisable, but contraception is certainly preferable.

Adolescents have difficulty in obtaining straightforward advice about birth control; despite the increased availability of information, an astonishing number of teen-agers still rely on such primitive devices as Saran Wrap and Coca-Cola douches. Older teen-agers do not give information to younger ones, thus continuing the cycle of ignorance and misinformation begun by many parents. The wise physician can fill this gap. For the sexually active youngster who is not using any contraception, the physician should present the choices available and perhaps prescribe an interim method, such as spermicidal foam for a girl or the condom for a boy.

Along with asking about contraception, the adolescent may be really asking for a sanction for his or her sexual feelings or behavior. The virgin under peer pressure to engage in sexual relations may be asking the physician to help her to make this decision. In such cases the doctor can only reassure the patient that many girls her age are virgins, despite what her friends say, and try to confirm her own attitude that sexual activity should be accompanied by some feeling for the partner. For the nonvirgin, it is medically advisable to prescribe contraception. Moral lectures about the pros and cons of sexual intercourse in the unmarried tend to be of little use in such cases. What is useful, however, is to talk with the patient about her sexual feelings, since many youngsters engage in sex that is devoid of pleasurable feeling and may be associated with anxiety, fear, and pain. A sensitive and sympathetic physician can help to clear up confusion and perhaps help the adolescent to gain a greater understanding of her own sexuality.

Of the available contraceptive methods, the oral contraceptive and intrauterine device (IUD) are well suited to teen-agers; there is no evidence that these contraceptives are responsible for promiscuity. Both the condom and the diaphragm-jelly method tend to be inconvenient and can sometimes lead to embarrassment and error. The use of the condom, in particular, requires a degree of sexual control that most teen-age boys do not possess. Coitus interruptus, practiced by many young people, is to be discouraged, since it is an extremely unreliable way of preventing conception and, more important from a sexual point of view, it can seriously hamper healthy sexual adjustment for both the boy and the girl.

The decision whether or not to discuss contraception with the patient's parents is a sensitive one. In some states the physician is legally required to consult with the parents. In states where consultation is not required, confidentiality is usually advisable to preserve the youngster's privacy and to protect the confidence he has in the doctor. Some teen-

agers tell their parents about their sexual activity, even though they know their parents disapprove of such activity. There are many reasons youngsters do this, including a desire for punishment because of the guilt they feel, a desire to provoke indifferent or uncaring parents, and a desire to obtain approval for what they feel is acceptable behavior.

Sex Therapy in Obstetrics and Gynecology

This speciality, by its very nature, is intimately involved in sexual matters, yet many gynecologists are reluctant to involve themselves in their patients' sexual problems. Patients with sexual problems may complain of anxiety, nervous tension, sleeplessness, pruritus, leukorrhea, and dysmenorrhea. The patient may display fear, anxiety, and depression triggered by sexual problems; during the examination her hands and face and general tension may reveal her concerns. The nonorgasmic woman may be suffering as a result of her own psychogenic difficulties or because her partner is somehow failing to arouse her. Gentle, matter-of-fact questioning usually provides enough information about the problem for the physician to offer a program of therapy. As with so much sexual dysfunctioning, ignorance is often the main culprit. Clearly presented advice about coital positions, male-female anatomy, the function of foreplay and sexual stimulation—augmented by reassurance of the normality of all sexual behavior between partners—is often sufficient to alleviate the problem. Sexual dysfunctioning is usually due to a subtle interplay of many factors, rather than the result of one specific inadequacy. The physician should try to help the patient and her partner to communicate with one another openly and honestly regarding their sexual feelings and attitudes.

Since fear of pregnancy is the cause of sexual inhibition and displeasure for many women, sound advice about contraception should be offered. Pain or irritation connected with sexual intercourse is sometimes caused by local infection in the urinary tract or in the vaginal canal; curing the infection usually removes the pain. However, pain and discomfort connected with sexual activity are more often caused by psychological factors.

Menopausal and older women present particular problems regarding sex. Menstrual cessation and estrogen deficiency can lead to irritation, tearfulness, and anxiety. Intercourse may be painful because of a reduction in vaginal secretions. Moreover, if married, the older woman may be faced with the problem of an impotent or uninterested husband. Both married and single older women usually have sexual needs, although they may be unwilling or unable to acknowledge this fact. The sensitive gynecologist should be able to evaluate his older patient's sexual needs and help her to find ways to fulfill them. He must be able to listen to what she does not say as well as what she does say. Such deeper, unconscious concerns as fear of loss of femininity and loss of sexual function may lie behind routine complaints of fatigue and boredom.

Infertility is another sex-related problem of concern to the gynecologist. A couple undergoing prolonged testing and treatment for infertility is subjected to great strain, sexual and nonsexual. Their sexual activity—monitored, timed, and sometimes relentlessly investigated—becomes a tension-filled, systematic means to an end, rather than a source of pleasure and tension relief. Such circumstances challenge the best of relationships, a fact that every gynecologist should keep in mind. Admonitions to "relax and forget about it" or to "take a vacation together" are of little help; what is helpful is to present to the couple an organized plan, describing the procedures as clearly as possible and reminding both the husband and the wife that their sexual relations may in some ways be affected by the experience. Open communication about the matter helps to prevent sexual discord and difficulty. It is of some note that, when a previously infertile couple does succeed in having a baby, the longed-for child sometimes takes the place of sexual satisfaction, particularly for the wife.

Impotence

Although there are some organic causes of impotence—multiple sclerosis, temporal epilepsy, certain drugs and hormones, among them—the overwhelming majority of cases of impotence result from psychological factors. The over-40 man is often plagued by financial worries and by the uneasy realization that life's goals have not been attained, that there are things he has failed to accomplish. He is bothered by a lack of privacy—at this age he is likely to have teen-age children—and by concerns that his wife may become pregnant. The general complexity and stress of modern life and the reassignment of sexually determined roles today contribute to the problem of sexual inadequacy in men.

Impotence may begin with premature ejaculation and proceed to no ejaculation or to no pleasure gained from sex, even with orgasm, and, finally, to the inability to attain or maintain an erection. As stated earlier, most men are reluctant to discuss impotence with a physician and do so only in the most indirect fashion. An understanding attitude of acceptance and casualness is the physician's best ally in dealing with the impotent patient. Some doctors have successfully treated this problem with antidepressant or tranquilizing drugs; others have found that alcohol in moderation is helpful. In either case, it is likely that the power of suggestion and the sympathetic, supportive attitude of the physician are more effective than the medication. Impotence must be treated as a symptom in a whole constellation of symptoms. The total person must be evaluated and the psychodynamics of his disorder understood.

Medical and Surgical Problems

MASTECTOMY

Depression, emotional trauma, despair, and feelings of sexual inadequacy are to be expected as a consequence of this mutilating surgery. Although the patient's fears and anxieties may center on the life-threatening aspect of cancer and the concomitant uncertainties, she is inevitably concerned as well about her image as a woman and about her ability to maintain a normal sex life. Ervin (1973) describes a program of counseling, support, and active medical involvement aimed at easing the patient's adjustment to a mastectomy. He often encourages the patient's husband to involve himself in the case. He suggests that the surgeon talk privately to the husband and impress on him the importance of reassuring his wife that he still loves her and that she is still an attractive and feminine person. Having the husband change her dressing and massage his wife's affected arm helps to involve him in her recovery and softens for both partners the shock of seeing the results of the surgery. Ervin finds that fitting the patient with a temporary prosthesis even before she leaves the hospital is a great aid in emotional recovery. He also makes a point of mentioning casually to the patient that she can resume sexual activity as soon as she wants to, thus reassuring her that he takes it for granted that her sex experience will not be affected by the operation.

COLOSTOMY AND ILEOSTOMY

Although this type of surgery relieves the disabling and, to many, life-threatening symptoms, it also introduces new problems of social and personal acceptance, threatened self-esteem, and disturbed body image. Sexual activity may be directly affected. To help the patient to readjust requires the cooperation of the surgeon and the family physician.

Sexual consequences are usually not discussed before surgery; the surgeon cannot predict the patient's sexual response, and, since this type of surgery is often life saving, sexual matters are of secondary importance initially. When there is no preparation for sexual readjustment, the patient may fall victim to myths and misinformation. Every man fears that he will be impotent; every woman wonders whether she will still be desirable. Dlin et al. (1969) found that maintenance of sexual interest and activity was an important index of total social adjustment. The typical ostomate continues to enjoy sex and engages in sexual activity, although there is usually some reduction in performance. The physician can help the patient to work out his feelings of worthlessness and repulsiveness by providing him with active support, guidance, and information. Problems about odor, increased intestinal activity, and appearance must be uncovered and are readily resolved.

SPINAL CORD INJURIES

One of the primary concerns of cord-injured people is whether or not they will be able to regain sexual functioning. In most cases the answer cannot be known immediately; therefore, physicians must handle the patient's anxieties and questions with a great deal of tact and delicacy. Most physicians refuse to make early commitments or predictions and, instead, suggest that the patient attempt intercourse after readjusting to his home situation. This advice enables the doctor to make specific suggestions after he learns what the patient can and cannot do. Patients who can have coitus but are unable to ejaculate are sometimes helped by mechanical massagers or by such alternate experiences as fellatio or masturbation. Prosthetic devices are sometimes indicated for patients who cannot maintain an erection.

The doctor who advises the cord-injured person about sexual activity must exercise extreme sensitivity. Although the doctor should not withhold information from the patient and his partner, he must be careful in deciding how and when to disclose material. To inform a recently injured man that he will never again have an erection will obviously do little to further rehabilitation and recovery. Moreover, prognosis in many cases is not that clear. Some physicians are too eager to embark on a program of sexual rehabilitation without delving deeply into the attitudes and psychosocial makeup of the patient and his partner. For example, motion pictures or printed material designed to illustrate alternate sexual activity for spine-injured patients may be enormously helpful for one couple but turn another couple off sex forever. As with all sex therapy, the doctor must take into account the timing of communication, the appropriateness, and the nature of his own relationship with the patient and the partner.

CARDIAC PATIENTS

The keynote in sexual counseling of the patient who has suffered a heart attack is individually tailored therapy and advice. The great majority of heart attack victims can resume normal sexual activity; how soon and how often varies from case to case. The physician must impress on his patient that—although sexual intercourse does place a strain on the heart, being associated with increased pulse and respiratory rate—many other experiences, such as family anxieties and arguments and business worries, are even more stressful. Abstaining from sex can lead to impotence and to an unhealthy self-image, which, in turn, can lead to anxiety and anger, both of which place a strain on coronary function.

The physician should reassure both the patient and the spouse that the patient is not likely to die as a result of sexual activity. Fewer than 1 per cent of heart patients die while having intercourse; of those, the majority were not having intercourse with their spouses. The doctor should back up his reassurance with appropriate therapy and counseling. Although he may advise nitroglycerine for anginal pain, to suggest that the patient take nitroglycerine before intercourse implies that the doctor fears that sex will be detrimental, if not fatal, to the patient's health.

REFERENCES

Bors, E.. and Comarr, A. E. Neurological disturbance of sexual functioning with special reference to 529 patients with spinal cord injury. Urol. Surv., *10:* 141, 1960.

Brecher, R., and Brecher, E., editors. *An Analysis of Human Sexual Response.* Little, Brown, Boston, 1966.

*Burnap, D. W., and Golden, J. S. Sexual problems in medical practice. J. Med. Educ., *42:* 673, 1967.

Dlin, B. M., Perlman, A., and Ringold, E. Psychosexual response to ileostomy and colostomy. Am. J. Psychiatry, *126:* 3, 1969.

Ervin, E. V. Psychological adjustment to mastectomy. Med. Aspects Human Sex., *7:* 42, 1973.

*Gadpaille, W. J. Research into the physiology of maleness and femaleness: Its contribution to the etiology and psychodynamics of homosexuality. Arch. Gen. Psychiatry, *26:* 193, 1972.

Heersema, P. H. Homosexuality and the physician. J. A. M. A., *193:* 159, 1965.

Hofman, A. D., and Shenker, I. R. Medical care of adolescents and the law. N. Y. State J. Med., *70:* 2603, 1970.

*Lief, H. I. Preparing the physician to become a sex counselor and educator. Pediatr. Clin. North Am., *14:* 447, 1969.

*Masters, W. H., and Johnson, V. E. *Human Sexual Response.* Little, Brown, Boston, 1966.

*Masters, W. H., and Johnson, V. E. *Human Sexual Inadequacy.* Little, Brown, Boston, 1970.

Nash, E. M., Jessner, L., and Abse, D. W., editors. *Marriage Counseling in Medical Practice.* University of North Carolina Press, Chapel Hill, 1964.

*Pauly, I. B., and Goldstein, S. Physicians' perception of their education of human sexuality. J. Med. Educ., *54:* 745, 1970.

Vincent, C. E. *Human Sexuality in Medical Education and Practice.* Charles C Thomas, Springfield, Ill., 1968.

chapter 17 Education for Sexuality

MARY S. CALDERONE, M.D.

Introduction

The previous edition of this book discussed normal and abnormal sexuality primarily in terms of genital activity. This section considers education for sexuality in broad terms, considering sexuality as one aspect of personality structure, including genital or erotic activity as one part of sexuality but focusing principally on questions related to formalized or planned educational approaches to the achievement of healthy sexuality in the developing child, within those social institutions that are the most logical and likely loci for such formalized approaches: the school, the college, and the church or synagogue.

Healthy Sexuality and Education

What is healthy sexuality? A simple working definition of a sexually healthy person is: one who is correct and certain about his or her gender identity; who enjoys the gender role that has been programed by his or her surrounding culture; who is free to enjoy his or her genitality but, as maturity advances, has an increasing sense of responsibility not only in its use but toward assuring the fulfilling or positive effects of such enjoyment for the self, the partner, and the society.

In the foregoing, it is presupposed that the psychosexual evolution or differentiation (Money and Ehrhardt, 1972) of the human being is the result of numerous environmental factors, conscious and unconscious, direct and indirect, biological and social, interacting with the person's genetic inheritance. Phyletically, some of this interaction may take place in utero between the moments of conception and of birth, but most of it is postnatal.

ROLE OF THE PARENTS

Perhaps the forces that are the most powerful in their immediate and long term psychosexual postnatal effects are those direct yet unconscious ones exerted by the parents or parent surrogates on the child in his first 5 years of life. The differentiation of core gender identity and of gender role behavior appropriate to both the identity and the chromosomal-anatomical sex should, under normal circumstances, be congruent. The programing or imprinting of parental sexual attitudes and self-images affects the child's early eroticism and, therefore, the feelings the child holds about his own body as a legitimate source of pleasure and his self-image as one who is attractive and lovable to others—or the opposite.

These early effects constitute the anlagen out of which can eventually come a sexually healthy adult—or not. Cognitive input or sex education, appropriately provided in appropriate ways at appropriate times by such institutions as the school, presumably serve to solidify or support such anlagen as are positive in nature and so facilitate the growth of a sexually mature personality. But, in the face of birth-to-5 years of negative sexual anlagen, information alone, no matter when provided, cannot be expected to fill the gaps or accomplish the ideal.

ROLE OF THE SCHOOL

The first years of school inevitably gather together children who are in all stages of early or late, successful or unsuccessful, psychosexual differentiation, including children who have already been psychosexually traumatized and a statistically definite if small percentage whose future lies in various forms or degrees of homosexual, bisexual, transsexual, transvestic, fetishist, sadomasochistic, or other variant sexual minority behaviors or identities. Therefore, planning consciously for much needed positive sex education of a direct, pedagogic nature is today, given our ignorance, still a kind of monumental Russian roulette. The best one can do, in the face of the flood of children entering school from families that are totally unaware of their own crucial roles in the psychosexual differentiation of their children, is to construct and provide a network of sexual and reproductive information that is considered basic and desirable for everyone to master in the course of moving from childhood to adulthood and to devise a pedagogic framework by which these facts can be made freely available, with the most positive attitudes possible on the part of the conveyors. How much corrective or preventive influence such programing may achieve remains to be researched. In point of fact, in the present state of knowledge, the very possibility of successfully providing positive programing to correct negative sexual imprinting or positive sexual imprinting that has been absent at the appropriate moments must remain conjectural.

ROLE OF THE CHURCH

Religious institutions, particularly Christian faiths and denominations, have followed in almost parallel fashion the interest in sex education occurring in nonreligious schools. At the national level, the Roman Catholic church and the major Protestant denominations have recognized the same needs, prepared special curricular materials, and trained their own teachers. A bibliography of religious curricular materials and general materials on human sexuality (Sex Information and Education Council of the United States (SIECUS), 1972) shows how intensive such religiously oriented efforts have been and how deeply the Christian sector is presently committed to the concept of sexuality as an integral part of the human condition.

The church is one of the institutions of society to which any discussion related to school activities in the realm of sexuality clearly applies, even though every denomination has its own opposition groups whose organization, rationales, and tactics are the same as those of the public sector.

OPPOSITION TO SCHOOL PROGRAMS

A number of hypothetical informational programs have been constructed for various age groups in schools, and some have been implemented. What must constantly be borne in mind is that, regardless of what the school as a prototype social institution may do for the children under its care, many parents today are so uninstructed or so traumatized themselves in the area of sex that they may attempt to obstruct or may succeed in destroying whatever the institution, with the best of intentions, hopes or tries to accomplish. Marmor et al. (1960) have speculated on the psychopathology of those who systematically oppose such public health programs as fluoridation and mental health, and their discussion is easily extrapolated into the area of sex education. Specifically, Baker (1969) has detailed the nature and lack of rationality behind the massive 1969-1971 attacks on sex education in schools, and the United Methodist Church (1969) has documented the sources, purposes, and methods of these attacks. A few physicians (Parsons, 1969; Douglas, 1969) have played prominent roles in the attacks, which continue as the same opposition forces regroup for fresh attacks (Anchell, 1971). Rarely do such physicians, some of whom are described as psychiatrists, appear to be well versed in the growing literature on human sexuality.

For such reasons, emphasis needs to be placed on the role of total community involvement, at least in understanding the importance and, indeed, the inevitable necessity of what the school may be attempting to plan. Programing in any institutional setting falls naturally into broad categories: informational and experiential treatment of human sexuality for age groups 5 to 9, 10 to 12, and 13 to 16 and in the college setting for the young adult group of 17 to 21.

Sex Education Programs

Sex education programs are not a recent phenomenon in American schools, some of which have had elements of such programs for 35 years or more, others of which had them and then dropped them because of lack of qualified staff or objections from parents or the public. Most early efforts dealt primarily with physical changes at puberty, menstruation (specifically for girls), reproduction, and venereal diseases. In the early 1960's came a nationwide concern for school-sponsored sex education programs, sparked in many cases by rising teen-age pregnancy rates and the disturbing rise in venereal disease statistics. Then, the late 1960's witnessed the organized reaction against school sex education programs by right-wing organizations and fundamentalist religious groups, which claimed that such programs were undermining parental authority, promoting permissive attitudes, and generally corrupting the moral fiber of youth.

Valid rationales for sex education programs have emerged out of new knowledge about psychosexual development of children and youth (group for the Advancement of Psychiatry, 1968); out of better information on the range and variety of sexual behavior (Kinsey, 1948, 1953); from systematic investigations of concerns and questions of children and youth (Group for the Advancement of Byler et al., 1969); out of evolving changes in society related to alternative life styles, the role of women, and premarital sexual standards (Reiss, 1973); and out of studies demonstrating the depths of sexual ignorance of college-age youth (Zelnik and Kantner, 1972). Perhaps the most pervasive factor has been the increasingly frank treatment of sex in the professional and mass media. Sex has become not only permissible but respectable and relevant as a topic of discussion at many levels in American society.

In response both to new knowledge, particularly from social scientists and child development specialists, and to changes in cultural attitudes, the present comprehensive view of education for human sexuality has emerged. From an almost exclusive concern with the anatomy and physiology of reproduction, today's views of sex education recognize sexuality as an integral part of total personality development. Educational programing in human sexuality must, therefore, be developmental in nature, with appropriate content and learning experiences from early childhood through adulthood, including parent education.

COMMUNITY INVOLVEMENT

Programs in human sexuality education are most likely to be accepted through broad-based community understanding and support. The interdisciplinary academic aspects of sexuality, plus their sensitive and sometimes controversial place in the school curriculum, call for input from many sectors of the community. Such support assures comprehensive attention to the subject and lends professional and parental authority to any program that the school administration and staff have recognized as requiring implementation. Many communities have begun planning their programs through a community advisory council or planning committee made up of representatives from medical, public health, social welfare, religious, youth services, and parent-teacher sectors. An advisory body that is broadly representative of the community can formulate goals and suggest guidelines for the program and help to interpret the program to the community at large.

TRAINING OF TEACHERS AND OTHER PROFESSIONALS

The major shortcoming to more widespread acceptance of sex education programs has been the lack of trained staff (Malfetti and Rubin, 1967). Yet, much progress has been made from the time the local doctor was invited into the school auditorium to lecture on reproduction or venereal disease. Many state colleges and universities are now offering courses on both content and methods in sex education, usually in departments of health education or home and family life. Between 50 and 100 university summer workshops are listed each year for the sex education training of elementary and secondary teachers; large school systems have organized their own in-service programs; several major religious denominations and social agencies have begun to institute training programs tailored to their specific needs. There now exists a sizable cadre of trained professionals working in the educational and health fields.

The unknown factors are the competency

of those who are already teaching in the field and the adequacy of their training, which may have varied from a 3-day workshop to a full academic year of study at the master's degree level. Efforts to upgrade and set standards for the training of sex educators were begun by the American Association of Sex Educators and Counselors with the publication of *The Professional Training and Preparation of Sex Educators* in 1972. Three areas were identified as essential for teaching in sex education: content in human sexuality, personal and professional attitudes, and professional skills. Content includes such areas as reproductive biology, psychosexual development, variations in sexual orientation and behavior, sex and gender, dynamics of interpersonal relationships in marriage, the family, and alternative life-styles. Personal and professional attitudes include a healthy and positive understanding and appreciation of one's own sexuality and a nonjudgmental and tolerant attitude toward the range of opinions and attitudes about sexual matters commonly found in today's pluralistic society. Professional skills include effectiveness in group leadership, knowledge of the dynamics of group discussion, familiarity with a variety of teaching and experiential methods appropriate to various age levels and to the content being presented, knowledge of printed and audiovisual resources, and ability to work with the community and parent groups.

Although training programs should provide many opportunities for obtaining basic content and skills and for developing sound attitudes, a continuing need is for on-the-job training under skilled supervision.

Objectives of Human Sexuality Education

Many statements of goals and objectives are found in the literature of sex education, but the SIECUS Guide No. 1, *Sex Education* (Kirkendall, 1965), provides a summary that has been used by many school systems as a basis for their own curriculum development in human sexuality education. The outlined goals are:

1. To provide for the individual an adequate knowledge of his own physical, mental, and emotional maturation processes as related to sex.

2. To eliminate fears and anxieties relative to individual sexual development and adjustments.

3. To develop objective and understanding attitudes toward sex in all of its various manifestations—in the individual and in others.

4. To give the individual insight concerning his relationships to members of both sexes and to help him understand his obligations and responsibilities to others.

5. To provide an appreciation of the positive satisfaction that wholesome human relations can bring in both individual and family living.

6. To build an understanding of the need for the moral values that are essential to provide rational bases for making decisions.

7. To provide enough knowledge about the misuses and aberrations of sex to enable the individual to protect himself against exploitation and against injury to his physical and mental health.

8. To provide an incentive to work for a society in which such evils as prostitution and illegitimacy, archaic sex laws, irrational fears of sex, and sexual exploitation are nonexistent.

9. To provide the understanding and conditioning that will enable each individual to use his sexuality effectively and creatively in his several roles as spouse, parent, community member, and citizen.

Curriculum Content

Moving from a broad statement of objectives to specific content and learning activities is the direct responsibility of the teachers and curriculum development staff and of the publishers of educational materials. At this time, no standard curriculum exists for human sexuality education, although several resources can assist curriculum planners (American School Health Association, 1967; Schulz and Williams, 1969; Kilander, 1970; Burt and Brower, 1970; Somerville, 1972).

AGES 5 TO 9

In the primary and intermediate grades, content in human sexuality is usually integrated into ongoing units in health, science, social studies, and language arts. Reproductive information may come up in a unit on pets, providing good opportunities to learn proper terminology for all parts of the body. Information about babies can be presented naturally through stories or in children's own writing on the arrival of a new baby in the family of one of the students. Considerable attention is given to sex roles in the comparative study of families throughout the world in social studies, including changing roles in today's American family. Attitudes about healthy interpersonal relationships are probably best dealt with in the day-to-day experience of living together in the classroom, but many teachers devote special attention to dealing with feelings and emotions in the family setting and among peers.

AGES 10 TO 12

Anticipating the physical and emotional changes that occur at puberty, content at this level deals with the normal range of growth changes and rates; the role of hormones in the onset of puberty; systematic information about the reproductive process; sound information and attitudes about menstruation, nocturnal emissions, and masturbation; the roles of heredity and environment as determinants of physical traits and personality; continuing attention to the understanding and control of one's emotions; and clarification of today's wide range of differential behavior related to masculine and feminine roles.

AGES 13 TO 15

At this stage, many programs focus on self-identity, with units of study under such titles as "Who Am I?" and "What Kind of Person Am I?" Content deals with the nature of personality, understanding one's emotions, getting along with others, boy-girl relationships, differences in male and female attitudes, dating, family conflicts, establishing values to live by, and a review of male and female reproductive processes, with attention to contraception. Venereal disease education may be included in the sex education program, but it is frequently offered in a health education unit on communicable diseases.

AGES 16 TO 18

At this level, when many young people are dating and some are involved in sexual experiences, content must reflect the reality of the youth scene and prepare youth for possible future goals of marriage and parenthood. Common topics are boy-girl relationships, the double standard, courtship, choosing a marriage partner, family planning and conception control, alternative life styles, homosexuality, premarital sex, abortion, pornography, parenthood, and moral and ethical issues related to sexual behavior.

COLLEGE LEVEL

College courses on human sexuality are increasingly widespread and usually very popular. Content tends to reflect the department under which the course is given—health education, psychology, sociology, or anthropology. In many cases, it is simply a more sophisticated treatment of content covered in high school, but for many students it is their first systematic exposure in an academic setting to the field of human sexuality. Other informal educational experiences are found on many campuses in the form of symposiums, extensive discussion groups, and student information services.

SPECIAL GROUPS

Concurrently with awareness of the general need for sex education programs, awareness has emerged of the equal needs of children and young people who fall into such special categories as those with physical or mental handicaps. It had not been generally recognized that the assumption existed that a person was automatically desexualized by his handicap. The first efforts to correct this impression were made on behalf of the mentally retarded (SIECUS and American Association for Health, Physical Education, and Recreation Joint Committee, 1971; Kempton et al., 1971; Klappholz, 1971; Bass, 1972; de la Cruz and LaVeck, 1973).

Current efforts are being made on behalf of the visually handicapped under the auspices of the American Foundation for the Blind and SIECUS; by the United Cerebral Palsy Association; by the United Ostomy Association (Dlin and Perlman, 1972; Binder, 1973;

Gambrell, 1973; Gambrell and Norris, 1972); and at the University of Minnesota Medical School on behalf of paraplegics. Others are beginning efforts on behalf of the deaf, the emotionally disturbed, and the aging. Generally, the working premise is that all such groups have the same sexual drives as do the nonhandicapped but that the particular handicap poses special problems, not only in fulfilling these normal drives but in the area of education toward the achievement of satisfactory sexual self-image and other-images and of satisfying and productive gender roles.

The general philosophy emerging is that society has an obligation to aid the handicapped to achieve these goals as far as possible and to offer not only the means toward attaining them but the real possibility for handicapped persons to live out their sexual lives in as satisfactory and normal a fashion as possible.

Evaluation of Sex Education

It is difficult to evaluate sex education programs in terms of models traditionally found for other areas of the curriculum (Burleson, 1973). Acquisition of information is relatively easy to measure, but the more nebulous attitudinal goals of human sexuality programs require long range research (Bidgood, 1973). At this writing, it is not possible to pinpoint school-sponsored programs in a cause-and-effect relationship when it comes to sexual attitudes and behavior, for the school is only one agent in attitude formation and is unlikely to be as influential as the home, peers, mass media, and society in general. Nevertheless, behavioral change as a result of involvement in institutional sex education programs, as reported in research, tends to be in the direction of increased ease and openness in discussing sexual topics and better parent-child communication about sex (Crosby, 1971; Carton and Carton, 1971).

In 1969, Ellis and Mooney (unpublished data) carried out a study of eleventh and twelfth grades, in which the study group of 115 students had a course in sex education 35 minutes a day for 6 school weeks and the control group of 88 students did not. Attitude scales and a vocabulary test were administered to both groups simultaneously before and after the course. The findings indicated that the opportunity to hear and understand the ideas and concerns of one's peers as related to human sexual behavior and social interaction has a sobering influence on the attitudes of adolescents and leads to the development of an individualized and personal social ethic that has been thought through in the course of discussion.

Professional and public concern about venereal disease and out-of-wedlock pregnancies is real, but current research provides little to show that school sex education programs have any direct effect on reducing these troubling statistics. On the other hand, surveys of both adolescents and adults who contract venereal disease or conceive out of wedlock show gross ignorance of basic anatomy and reproductive information as well as preventive measures in these two problem areas. The solution to this dilemma appears to point to better programs and better research. Rather than continue to look for attitude and behavioral change as a direct consequence of current education programs, one must scrutinize the educational processes through which attitudes and values are confronted and clarified (Kohlberg, 1972).

The present state of the art of formalized education for healthy sexuality is in an early embryonic stage. There is a crucial need for research on many questions, research that will cross and perhaps erase existing rigid boundary lines between anthropology, developmental embryology, endocrinology, education, fetology, neurology, prenatal and postnatal gender differentiation, physiology, psychiatry, psychology, and sociology, to name the major areas and disciplines involved. The human being is, beyond imagination, sexually complex. If, in one family, doing nothing to teach about sex has apparently benign results in three children but malign results in a fourth; if one child apparently suffers little from sexual molestation, even by a parent or close relative, but a neighbor's child suffers permanent damage, perhaps not from the incident itself so much as from what the surrounding adults make of it; if a girl grows up and never experiences orgasm until her early forties, when she becomes phenomenally multiorgasmic, whereas a second girl who has masturbated to orgasm from infancy remains mono-orgasmic or even nonorgasmic in coitus throughout her life; if one man requires only one or two sex outlets per month, but another requires one or two sex outlets per day—these are a few of the presently unexplainably variant ways that human beings differ from each other sexually, with sidetracking of some away from any orderly process toward healthy sexual maturity.

As regards formalized sex education in schools and other institutions, however, one thing over and over again becomes clear. Louis Maslinoff, in his unpublished doctoral dissertation, *Toward a Definition of Sex Education,* stated it well:

Unless an enlightened citizen population can come to grips with social problems related to sexuality, the best that sex education programs can hope to do is help children to accommodate themselves to a hostile environment.

Such accommodation—as has been remarked by Duane (1962), Byler and her colleagues (1969), and Barbey (1972)—is, at present, most fruitfully engendered by a simple resort to truth. Offer children and young people all the opportunities they themselves want in an open environment to ask their sex questions and get them answered honestly and comfortably by people trained to have or to find out the facts. The experience of having their long standing puzzlements cleared up in open discussion is new and healing, especially of the anxieties brought on by fear, guilt, and ignorance. Psychiatrists can attest to how often release of anxietal tensions results in observable abatement of acting out or counterproductive behavior, whether sexual or otherwise.

Conclusions

The past decade has seen an extraordinarily rapid evolution and acceptance, among professionals of many disciplines, of sexuality not merely as an erotic drive to be turned on or off or controlled by social or religious rules but as a profoundly vital element of the self and of the life of every human being at every age level. So essential to most persons is the sense of sexual selfhood that, directly and indirectly, it becomes a part of their daily actions and interactions with each other,

whether consummated in erotic contact or not.

But the same decade has also witnessed an almost cataclysmic outburst of social pathology over the world as a concomitant of urbanization. Like the nerve that is traumatized by being enmeshed in callus formation after a fracture, human psychosexual evolution, at best fragile in its susceptibility to a hostile social environment, has massively suffered distortions as perhaps never before in history. Therefore, as Calderone (1971) has stated:

"To achieve . . . a desirable state of preventive medicine will require the combined understanding and efforts of child psychiatrists, pediatricians, psychologists, social scientists, educators, and clergymen in teaching parents what their own roles are, not only in active education of their own children, but in not obstructing the serious efforts now being engaged in by these professionals to provide a better, more rational climate in which children can learn about this great universal component of life.

In other words, education for sexuality is not a curriculum, a course, or a series of lectures, nor will it be found in books or films alone. At present, education for sexuality within such institutional settings as the school, church, and university should form a coherent part of a lifelong experiential continuum, in which many people who meet the child have roles to play. Truthful information about human sexual behavior must be conveyed to all growing children and young people when they themselves desire it, but the manner and attitudes with which it is conveyed remain the most important factors of all. A massive re-educational program of the society regarding human sexuality, particularly of parents in relation to their own vital roles as primary sex educators of their children, may eventually eliminate the need for institutional programs. Until this re-education is accomplished, the school, church, and university have no other option than to develop and apply programs based on the broad principles outlined here.

REFERENCES

American Association of Sex Educators and Counselors. *The Professional Training and Preparation of Sex Educators.* American Association of Sex Educators and Counselors, Washington, 1972.

American School Health Association. *Growth Patterns and Sex Education.* American School Health Association, Kent, Ohio, 1967.

Anchell, M. *Sex and Sanity.* Macmillan, New York, 1971.

Baker, L. G. The rising furor over sex education. Fam. Coordinator, *3:* 210, 1969.

Barbey, M. A. Education sexuelle de la jeunesse, Canton de Vaud, Suisse. Bull. Centre Medico-Social Fam. Nos. 5, 6, and 7, Lausanne, 1972.

Bass, M. S. *Developing Community Acceptance of Sex Education for the Mentally Retarded.* Sex Information and Education Council of the United States, New York, 1972.

Bidgood, F. E. The effects of sex education: A summary of the literature. SIECUS Report, *1:* 11, 1973.

Binder, D. *Sex, Courtship and the Single Ostomate.* United Ostomy Association, Los Angeles, 1973.

*Broderick, C. D., and Bernard, J., editors. *The Individual, Sex, and Society: A SIECUS Handbook for Teachers and Counselors.* Johns Hopkins Press, Baltimore, 1969.

Burleson, D. L. Evaluation in sex education: A wasteland. SIECUS Report, *1:* 1, 1973.

Burt, J. J., and Brower, L. A. *Education for Sexuality: Concepts and Programs for Teaching.* W. B. Saunders, Philadelphia, 1970.

*Byler, R., Lewis, G., and Totman, R. *Teach Us What We Want to Know.* Connecticut State Board of Education, Mental Health Materials Center, New York, 1969.

Calderone, M. S., editor. *The Manual of Family Planning and Contraceptive Practice,* ed. 2 Williams & Wilkins, Baltimore, 1970.

Calderone, M. S. Sexual education of the child. Child Psychiatry Hum. Dev., *1:* 211, 1971.

Calderwood, D. Adolescents' views on sex education. J. Marriage Fam. May, 1965.

Carton, J., and Carton, J. Evaluation of a sex education program for children and their parents: Attitude and interactional changes. Fam. Coordinator, *20:* 377, 1971.

Comfort, A., editor. *The Joy of Sex: A Gourmet Guide to Lovemaking.* Crown, New York, 1972.

Crosby, J. F. The effects of family life education on the values and attitudes of adolescents. Fam. Coordinator, *20:* 137, 1971.

de la Cruz, F. F., and La Veck, G. D., editors. *Human Sexuality and the Mentally Retarded.* Brunner/Mazel, New York, 1973.

*Demarest, R. J., and Sciarra, J. J. *Conception, Birth and Contraception: A Visual Presentation.* McGraw-Hill, New York, 1969.

*Dickinson, R. L. *Atlas of Human Sex Anatomy.* Williams & Wilkins, Baltimore, 1969.

Dlin, B. M., and Perlman, A. Sex after ileostomy or colostomy. Med. Asp. Hum. Sex., *6:* 32, 1972.

Douglass, W. The jet sex. J. Sarasota County Med. Soc., *16:* 2, 1969.

Duane, M. Sex education: A small experiment. J. Fam. Planning Assoc. (London), *2:* 27, 1962.

Ellis, A., and Abarbanel, A., editors. *Encyclopedia of Sexual Behavior.* Hawthorn, New York, 1967.

Gambrell, E. *Sex and the Male Ostomate.* United Ostomy Association, Los Angeles, 1973.

Gambrell, E., and Norris, C. *Sex, Pregnancy and the Female Ostomate.* United Ostomy Association, Los Angeles, 1972.

Group for the Advancement of Psychiatry. *Normal Adolescence.* Report No. 68, Mental Health Materials Center, New York, 1968.

Katchadourian, H. A., and Lunde, D.T. *Fundamentals of Human Sexuality.* Holt, Rinehart and Winston, New York, 1972.

Kempton, W., Bass, M. S., and Gordon, S. *Love, Sex, and Birth Control for the Mentally Retarded.* Planned Parenthood Association of Southeastern Pennsylvania, Philadelphia, and Family Planning and Population Information Center, Syracuse, 1971.

Kilander, H. F. *Sex Education in the Schools.* Macmillan, New York, 1970.

Kinsey, A. C., Pomeroy, W. B., and Martin, C. E. *Sexual Behavior in the Human Male.* W. B. Saunders, Philadelphia, 1948.

Kinsey, A. C., Pomeroy, W. B., Martin, C. E., and Gebhard, P. E. *Sexual Behavior in the Human Female.* W. B. Saunders, Philadelphia, 1953.

Kirkendall, L. A. *Sex Education.* SIECUS Study Guide No. 1. Sex Information and Education Council of the United States, New York, 1965.

Klappholz, L., editor. *A Resource Guide in Sex Education for the Mentally Retarded.* Sex Information and Education Council of the United States, New York, and American Association for Health, Physical Education, and Recreation, Washington, 1971.

Kohlberg, L. A cognitive developmental approach to moral education. The Humanist. *32:* 13, 1972.

Malfetti, J. L., and Eidlitz, E. M., editors. *Perspectives on Sexuality.* Holt, Rinehart and Winston, New York, 1972.

Malfetti, J., and Rubin, A. Sex education: Who is teaching the teachers? Teachers College Rec., *69:* 214, 1967.

Marmor, J., Bernard, V. W., and Ottingberg, P. Psychodynamics of group opposition to health programs. Am. J. Orthopsychiatry, *30:* 330, 1960.

Masters, W. H., and Johnson, V. E. *Human Sexual Response.* Little, Brown, Boston, 1965.

Masters, W. H., and Johnson, V. E. *Human Sexual Inadequacy.* Little, Brown, Boston, 1970.

McCary, J. L. *Sexual Myths and Fallacies.* Van Nostrand Reinhold, New York, 1971.

*Money, J., and Ehrhardt, A. A. *Man and Woman, Boy and Girl.* Johns Hopkins Press, Baltimore, 1972.

Parsons, J. M. Sex education vs. the "no-no" moralists. J. Sarasota County Med. Soc., *16:* 15, 1969.

*Reiss, I. L. Changing trends, attitudes, and values on premarital sexual behavior in the United States. In *Human Sexuality and the Mentally Retarded,* F. F. de la Cruz and G. D. La Veck, editors. Brunner/Mazel, New York, 1973.

Schulz, E. D., and Williams, S. R. *Family Life and Sex Education: Curriculum and Instruction.* Harcourt Brace Jovanovich, New York, 1969.

Sex Information and Education Council of the United States. Bibliography of religious publications on sexuality and sex education. SIECUS Newsletter, *7:* 10, 1972.

Sex Information and Education Council of the United States American Association for Health, Physical Education, and Recreation Joint Committee. *A

Resource Guide for the Mentally Retarded. Sex Information and Education Council of the United States, New York, 1971.

Silverman, H. L., editor. *Marital Therapy: Moral, Sociological, and Psychological Factors.* Charles C Thomas, Springfield, Ill., 1972.

Somerville, R. *Introduction to Family Life and Sex Education.* Prentice-Hall, New York, 1972.

Task Group on Sex Education of General Committee on Family Life. *Memorandum to Pastors and Coordinators of Family Ministries.* United Methodist Church, Nashville, 1969.

Zelnik, M., and Kanter, J. F. Sexual experience of young unmarried women in the United States. Fam. Plann. Perspect., *4:* 9, 1972.

*The author is greatly indebted to Derek L. Burleson, Ed.D., SIECUS Director of Educational and Research Services, for his contribution of the sections on school and college programs, evaluation of programs, and teacher training.

chapter 18 Sex and the Arts

KLAUS LAEMMEL, M.D.

Introduction

Sexuality is the elemental creative force in nature. Life is a continual cycle of death and rebirth, and in its primitive stage these two processes are one and the same event. Division by cellular fission is a merging of decay and regeneration. A human being's birth and death, however, are separated in time. Unlike the lower forms of life, he is aware of his own finiteness. From this consciousness springs the fear of death and the yearning for immortality. All human endeavors in the final analysis are motivated by the desire to be reborn, to deny death its power.

Since death is a physical reality, it can be transcended only through spiritual striving. Hence man's eternal search for meaning. Traditionally, his need for significance has been answered by religion. But a person who is not gifted with faith in an everlasting life necessarily experiences existence as ultimately absurd. He attempts to fill this vacuum by creating his own personal meaning. To secure himself from the threat of nothingness, he aims at achieving a sense of completeness apart from any divine plan. Traditional values are replaced by individual ones, and total self-realization is seen as a person's highest possible accomplishment.

The artist, by virtue of his genius, is in a unique position to achieve this goal. In Arthur Miller's essay, "On Social Plays," (1955) he affirms that

like every act man commits, the drama is a struggle against his mortality, and meaning is the ultimate reward for having lived.

By the very act of fulfilling his own potential, the artist communicates a message of universal significance. He crystallizes and intensifies the human experience—the awareness of death, the suffering and joy of life.

A work of art appeals to the senses as well as to spiritual needs. It is a perfect amalgamation of the sensual and transcendent aspects of beauty. The human esthetic experience is a glimpse of the eternal. Likewise, the sensual pleasure of the sexual union, in its highest intensity, takes on a divine dimension. As Mozart has Papageno sing in his opera *The Magic Flute:*

Its [Love's] noble aim shows clear in life:
No greater good than man and wife.
Wife and man and man and wife
Reach the height of godly life.

There is a close affinity between religious, esthetic, and sexual ecstasy. The joy felt at these moments compensates for the suffering inherent in consciousness. At the same time it holds the promise of regeneration, although on a far higher plane than that of insentient nature's death and rebirth. It is, therefore, not surprising that the key to the understanding of any given culture is the study of its art and of human sexual behavior. The evolution of world consciousness, of which the religious attitude is an intrinsic part, is directly reflected in these two areas of human activity. Thus, the story of how man coped with his sexual drives is also the story of how he handled and harnessed the creative impulse.

Beginnings in Religion

As indicated above, religion and sexuality, still closely linked today, sprang from one and the same source. Primitive people, powerfully impressed by the seasonal changes, realized that their own survival depended on the annual revival of nature. They saw the renewal of life on earth as an earthly counterpart and outcome of the sexual union of the gods. Seeking to aid their deities in their struggle against the principle of death, they dramatized this myth in their fertility cults. Sexual intercourse with the sacred prostitutes, the representatives of the goddess of fertility, expressed the worshipers' belief that they shared in the divine life force and were furthering the reproduction of fruits, animals, and people.

The re-enactment of a natural process rests on the familiar magic principle that any desired effect can be achieved by merely imitating the action that leads to it. The early beginnings of the religious rituals constituted an imitation of nature, which is Aristotle's definition of art. And, indeed, most art forms appear to have their roots in these rites. Ritualistic intercourse was eventually replaced by symbolic representation through dance. The ceremonies became more elaborate in time and gradually included primitive forms of music, storytelling, sculpture, painting, and architecture. The most famous extant example is the Venus of Wilendorf, a fertility goddess.

Originally, all members of the tribe participated in the ritual, but the increasing complexity of the ceremony later called for a select group of initiates, who evolved into the priesthood. The priest became the mediator between the human and the divine. The artist's role as imitator of nature evolved into that of interpreter of life. Sexuality remained an integral part of both art and religion. Religion either execrated sexuality and by this very fact acknowledged its potency or consecrated sexuality as a means for an ultimate mystical realization. The Christian church regarded sexuality as a symptom of man's fallenness and as a force to be expunged. In some early forms of Eastern religions, on the other hand, literal sexual union was practiced as symbolic identification with a deity consti-

tuting supreme spiritual bliss. Celibacy and ascetic morals were rejected, and a general indulgence of the senses was approved.

Early Civilization

The earliest traces of our civilization revolve around the central theme of fertility. Clay fragments of bas reliefs excavated from the Sumerian city of Ur and dating back more than 5,000 years depict a variety of sexual scenes attended by nude female musicians. In Babylonian-Assyrian culture, Ishtar, the fertility goddess, was the most important deity of all. She is frequently represented holding her breasts with one hand and covering her genitals with the other, a position that is symbolic of the mystery of regeneration (Klaf and Hurwood, 1964).

GREEK

Mesopotamia and Egypt contributed to the culture and religious thought of Greece. Dionysus—the Greek god of the vine and, more importantly, of fertility—hailed from Thrace. Greek drama originated with the worship of Dionysus, the chief rites being a festal procession of revelers, with dancing and singing, and dramatic performances. Tragedy is generally acknowledged to have developed from the dithyramb, a choral hymn sung to Dionysus on these occasions. Comedy owes its name to the Greek *komoidia,* the song of the *komos* or revel. According to Aristotle, its origin was with the leaders of these processions. The phallic *komos* developed in primitive times when it was discovered that the phallus and the female genitalia were directly related to the production of children. The ceremony took place at the festivals of Demeter, a grain goddess, and Dionysus to ensure the fertility of the crops. Occasionally, the rite included intercourse in the fields so that the fertility of the participants might affect the fertility of the land. Aristophanic comedy raised and modified these primitive performances into art, but it retained vestiges of the old ritual. The phallus took a prominent part in the costuming and staging of the play, with male actors carrying six-foot-long thongs attached to the waist. The comedy generally ended in a *gamos* or festive union of the sexes, either at a party or in marriages.

The golden age in Greece was a turning point in the human world view. Logical thinking and scientific observation developed a new consciousness. Greek art was intellectual, the art of men who were clear and lucid thinkers. One of the changes brought about was the discovery of beauty, especially the beauty of the human body. The concept of beauty itself had its beginning in the Mesopotamian and Egyptian cultures, but Greece raised it to a revered ideal. In representative art the sex organs became de-emphasized. Instead, the beauty of the human godlike body was the focus of artistic creation. Male statues were shaped with feminine delicacy, and females were represented with definite masculine traits. The Greek ideal of beauty found its expression in the mythological union of Hermes and Aphrodite, from which sprang Hermaphroditus, an embodiment of divine perfection. Narcissus was the spiritual descendant of Hermaphroditus. Leaning over the waters of a fountain one day, Narcissus conceived such a lively passion for his own reflection that he could not tear himself away from it. He died there of languor but was changed into the flower that bears his name. This myth was to be a preferred subject of the visual arts for centuries to come. The vision of the human being as possessing divine beauty finally culminated in the resurgence of the Greek ideal during the Renaissance.

In the field of literature and philosophy, Plato's writing offers a superb insight into the idea of beauty as experienced in the Greek world. The *Symposium,* a one-act play, dramatizes a philosophical discussion on Eros by a group of eminent speakers at a party given in honor of the tragic poet, Agathon (416–415). The center of interest lies in the discourse of Socrates, which he professes to have learned in his youth from the priestess Diotima of Mantinea. She described love as the soul's ascent to an ultimately divine vision, for the object that awakens love in all its forms is beauty, and beauty is eternal. Love is a way, also, of yearning for immortality. Its lowest form is sexual attraction, which in reality seeks to perpetuate itself in physical offspring. A more spiritual

form of the craving for eternity is the desire to win immortal fame by political action. On a still higher level is the endeavor to combine with chosen minds to give birth to ideas and thus enrich philosophy and science. The true achievement of immortality, however, is effected only by a vision of the supreme beauty that is the cause and source of all beauties discerned by the soul on its journey upward. Eros is seen neither as a god nor as a mortal but as a mediating spirit between the human being and god. Raised to the highest level, it becomes the symbol of divine communion. Love for absolute beauty can render a human immortal.

Heterosexual love, on the other hand, is mentioned as valuable for procreation only. In fact, the first speaker begins the dialogue with a eulogy on homosexual relationships, and throughout the work it is implied that women are excluded from higher forms of love. The reason for this low esteem of heterosexual relationships lies in the fact that Athenian women received no education whatsoever and, therefore, could not be expected to participate in intellectual discussions and spiritual communion. Indeed, even as sexual partners, men were often preferred for the same reason.

Although Plato ultimately valued the transcendent above the sensuous aspect of beauty, he recognized the sensuous as the indispensable first step in the soul's ascent. By the same token, his contemporary world did not deny the pleasure of the senses. On the contrary, the classical Greek's appreciation of beauty enhanced a general affirmative attitude toward life. It encouraged behavior totally accepting of sex as an integral part of a joyful human existence. Beauty was seen as both sensuous and supersensuous perfection. It was that which pleased the beholder. Greek artists, never denying the importance of the body, saw in it a spiritual significance.

As far as the common man was concerned, however, the joy of life and sexual freedom expressed itself in more earthy terms. These qualities are best reflected in the plays of Aristophanes, the most outstanding comic author of the time. He wrote for the masses, rather than the educated populace, and his primary purpose was to instruct the people.

Lysistrata, a play famous for its ribaldry, had a very serious purpose—to convince the Athenian people of the necessity of political compromise. The Peloponnesian war was raging outside the city gates at the time, and there was no end in sight. The Athenian expedition to Sicily (415–413 B.C.) was a dismal failure, severely crippling the city state. While Athen's colonies were revolting, the Spartans were uniting with the Persians to control the Aegean. Yet the constant warfare eventually strained the Spartans' strength, so that both sides, except for a few headstrong factions, were ready for a peace settlement. In Aristophanes' comedy, Athenian and Spartan women ally themselves in the common cause; they start a sex strike to force their men to negotiate a peace. It is their intent to

stir so amorous a feeling among the men that they stand as firm as sticks

and no longer desire to fight. The dialogue is filled with double meanings. Even the names are phallic, suggesting perpetual erection. The male protagonist's name, Cinesias, derives from the Greek word kinein, to move, which also means to make love; and he, as well as his fellow warriors in the course of the action, experience an increasing discomfort due to their unrelieved sexual drives. Their erections are so immense that they can scarcely walk. In one episode the men blame their own blindness for their dire plight. They have invited the women's rebelliousness and paved the way to cuckoldry by their own actions:

For female depravity, gentlemen, we stand guilty—we, their teachers, preceptors of prurience, accomplices before the fact of fornication. We sowed them in sexual license, now we reap rebellion.

The proof?

Consider. Off we trip to the goldsmith's to leave an order:

"That bangle you fashioned last spring for my wife is sprung. She was thrashing around last night, and the prong popped out of the bracket. I'll be tied up all day—I'm boarding the ferry right now—but my wife'll be home. If you get the time, please stop by the house in a bit and see if you can't do something—anything—to fit a new prong into the bracket of her bangle."

And bang.

Another one ups to a cobbler—young, but no apprentice, full kit of tools, ready to give his awl—and delivers this gem:

"My wife's new sandals are tight. The cinch pinches her pinkie right where she's sensitive. Drop in at noon with something to stretch her cinch and give it a little play."

In contrast to Aristophanic comedy, Greek tragedy embodied the Hellenic ideal of nothing in excess, an attitude distinguished by love of harmony and peace and deep sympathy for human weakness. Its dominant theme was the conflict between man and the universe. The tragic fate that befell the main characters in these plays was brought on by the fact that someone had committed a crime against society, thereby offending the moral scheme of the universe. Punishment must follow to balance the scale of justice. Greek tragedy did not merely depict suffering and interpret human actions but portrayed the exemplary conduct of the ideal Greek in a painful situation. According to Aristotle, another purpose was to purify the emotions of the audience by arousing their pity and fear.

The two most famous exponents of this type of drama were Aeschylus and Sophocles. In Sophocles' *Oedipus Rex,* probably the most emotionally gripping of all Greek tragedies, the inevitability of Oedipus' doom is a paradigm of Aristotelian catharsis as the character, following the prediction of the Delphic oracle, unknowingly kills his own father and marries his mother. Freud later picked up the theme of a child's sexual attraction for the parent of the opposite sex and the death wish for the other parent to define what he saw as the central conflict in human existence—the Oedipus complex.

The supreme achievements in tragic drama were paralleled in Greek sculpture and architecture. Probably even more than literature, these arts reflected the true character of Hellenic civilization. Sculpture, embodying Greek ideals, represented men as androgynous, godlike creatures and gods as beautiful men.

The same attitude expressed itself in sexual behavior, which was inspired less by the attraction of the opposite sex than by the beauty of the human being per se. As a result, homosexuality was an accepted practice. Decorations on vases of that period display a variety of homosexual as well as heterosexual scenes. Sappho, the greatest poetess of antiquity (6th century B.C.), who had made herself the leader of a group of women on the island of Lesbos, wrote lyrics expressive of homosexual feelings unsurpassed for depth, passion, and grace. But she appears to have been equally susceptible to male charm. Legend has it that, in despair over her unrequited love of Phaon, a sailor, she plunged into the sea from the Leucadian rock.

The social, political, and economic changes that took place after the death of Alexander the Great in 323 B.C. and the disintegration of his vast empire had a deteriorating effect on art. No giants of art appeared on the Hellenistic horizon with the notable exception of Theocritus of Syracuse (315–264 B.C.). His poetry marked the beginning of a long pastoral tradition. The growth of urban civilization had given rise to a new appreciation of the charms of the countryside. Theocritus gave vivid expression to this nostalgia. He developed the idyll (*eidyllion,* little picture), which conveyed with great feeling the Greek love for soil and stream, sky and pasture, the world of shepherds and goatherds. One of his best known idyllic poems, later imitated by Virgil and Ovid, tells of Polyphemus, the Cyclops, who falls passionately in love with the sea nymph Galatea and uses bucolic similes to describe her beauty:

> white Galatea, why dost thou repulse thy lover— whiter than curd to look upon, softer than the lamb, more skittish than the calf, sleeker than the unripe grape.

The idealized country life, as opposed to the corrupt city, subsequently has become a recurrent theme in world literature.

After Alexander's death, the center of power shifted to Alexandria, Egypt; Greek thought and art were on the decline. The balance of esthetic enjoyment tipped in favor of the pleasure of the senses; thus Eros, the Platonian god of love, changed his character to that of lust. The spirit of moderation, the golden mean, as expounded by Aristotle, was abandoned. Greek ideas of excellence gave way to concerns for carnal pleasure, and a profound distrust of intellectuality, authority, and religion set in. Corinth, the first Greek city state to fall to the Romans (146 B.C.), was notorious for its debauchery, its vast number of prostitutes, and its commercially run brothels. Few great names in the field of art appear during that period. Only two Greek writers are worthy of note: Plutarch (46–120) and the satirist Lucian of Samosata (125–200). Lucian poked fun at philosophers, gods, and historians, but Plutarch, in his *Parallel Lives,* idealized figures from the past for the edification of the lesser men of his own day. His rambling style and the uncritical piety displayed in a number of shorter works under the title of *Moralia* show that the intellectual tide of Greece was well on the ebb.

ROMAN

The Roman Empire took over where Greek culture left off. In literature and philosophy the Romans were essentially preservers and disseminators of Hellenistic culture. At the beginning, Roman writers did little more than translate Greek works into Latin, and sculptors copied Greek models. Nevertheless, Rome experienced a golden age of its own, with works expressive of a changing ethos. During the Hellenic period Greek culture had moved from the severe style of Phidias (5th century B.C.), whose unsmiling statues embodied the Greek concept of *sophrosyne* (moderation and restraint) to the new soft style of Praxiteles (4th century B.C.). This period—which produced fleshlike, realistic portraits, works of increasing emotional expression and sensuality—appealed to the Romans and inspired their art. Thanks to their enthusiasm, present-day art lovers can still enjoy works like the underhandedly erotic Venus of Cnidos and the sensuously tactile Aphrodite of Syracuse.

In art, as well as in life, the Romans continued in the Greek vein of exuberance, but eventually their insatiable lust for power and wealth led them to the excesses that accompanied the decline of their empire. The two greatest playwrights of the early period were Plautus and Terence, comic authors who borrowed heavily from Greek comedy and who, in turn, supplied the sources for many Shakespearean plays. Their works contained elements of farce, with boisterous sexual scenes abounding with bawdy jokes. The Augustan period, also known as the golden age, produced some of the greatest Roman love poets, such as Catullus, Ovid, Horace, Tibullus, and Propertius. Many of their works were explicitly sexual, a fact that may amaze the modern student of Latin, since most editions have been expurgated for use in the classroom. Putnam (1936) calls Horace

one of the outstanding rakes of history, a Casanova of his day.

With the cruel ironical wit of the rogue, Horace describes his casual relationships with courtesans and is very frank about his excitement over boys and young girls. His exploits earned him the nickname of *penis putissimus* (the constantly put-in penis) by the emperor Augustus. The theme of impotence, which later became prevalent in Roman literature, is already present in his writings.

Catullus, in *Carmina,* mingled obscenities with poignant poetic beauty. Early Christian censors destroyed a large part of his work, but tidbits such as the following offer a glimpse of his facile sense of humor:

Here's a good one for you, Cato:
I caught a kid humping his lass,
and the chance was too good to pass;
a true son of Venus,
I whipped out my penis,
and pronged a piece off his ass.

What secured him a place in history, however, are passionate lyrics to Lesbia, expressing both love's rapture and its agony. They belong to the most magnificent verses ever written in the Latin tongue. Even translations convey a glimmer of the poetic power of the original (Atkins, 1972):

My Lesbia, let us live and strain
our love through all Time's pores, I pray—
till we don't care a tinker's curse
for moral men that slander love.
Suns drop to earth yet lift again—
for us when the quick circle of light
gutters away, the sky above
shuts with a thick unbroken night.
And so, my Lesbia, let's rehearse
our game of kisses while we may . . .

a thousand first, a hundred then;
a second thousand from our store;
a hundred—or a thousand, say;
and then another hundred more.

The subject of the poet's passion was a married woman, Clodia, known for her beauty and promiscuity. Eventually, she wearied of his kisses and turned to other lovers, a fact that radically changed the mood of his poems:

Caelius, that Lesbia, my woman,
that—that Lesbia, whom once I, Catullus,
loved above himself and closest cronies,
now rubs up the grandsons of lordly Remus
on the corners and in the narrow alleys.

Catullus named her Lesbia in memory of Sappho, whose poems he translated and frequently imitated. Both he and Horace died in their midthirties reportedly as a result of their sexual indulgence and physical exhaustion. Poetically, Catullus carried on the theme of passion spent in amorous exploits. Indeed, a chronicle of impotence can be traced all the way from Horace to Martial and down to Petronius.

The great poet laureate of erotic love, however, was Ovid. His fame began with the publication of *Amores,* racy couplets about an unnamed courtesan, audacious and sensual, a veritable litany of promiscuity. Apparently, his personal life was also devoted to the pursuit of women. His famous *Ars Amatoria* is a comprehensive manual of seduction, an emotionally detached description of how to find and win a mistress, how to keep her interested, and the many means and ways by which a woman can hold her lover. He emphasizes the mutuality of giving and receiving sexual pleasure and thereby reveals a remarkable insight into the psychology of Roman men and women. Although he reduced sexual love to a mere skill in technique and psychological manipulation, an attitude quite different from the Greek delight in its beauty, his poetic genius produced a literary masterpiece. In the introduction to *Ars Amatoria,* he speaks of the art of love as something to be mastered, like the steering of a sailboat or the holding of a horse's reins. His scintillating wit and elegant verse attest to an equal skill in handling words. The following lines—although in modern translation—reflect this unusual gift:

Let the man be the first to make the approach and entreaty,
    Let the girl be the one willing to wait and be kind.
Ask her outright: that's all any girl has been waiting for really,
    Give her a cause, an excuse, just so you give her a start.
Jove himself would go and beg the girls for their favors:
    He was seducer, in love; no girl solicited Jove.
Yet, if you find that your pleas inspire an arrogant coldness,
    Stop what you may have begun, take a few steps in retreat.
Many a girl desires the coy and hates the aggressive:
    Take it a little bit slow, don't let her weary of you.
Don't always show in your talk that you know you are going to get her—
    What you are eager to be, tell her, is *Only a friend.*
I have seen this work, on the most unwilling of women—
    Only a friend, who was found more than proficient in bed!

The death of Augustus in 14 A.D. began a long period of decadence that reached its nadir under the despotic emperors Caligula and Nero. A few courageous writers during that time invented a new literary genre, the satire, to use against the bad taste of Roman society.

Petronius savagely indicted the life-style of his contemporaries in *Satyricon,* a rambling, picaresque novel teeming with obscenities. Only parts of the work are extant. They contain a long description of a banquet given by a vulgar, immensely rich Roman citizen, who is a caricature of the nouveau riche not only of Petronius' time but of every age. Petronius, whom Tacitus called the arbiter of elegance, was for a while the semiofficial master of the revels at Nero's court, but, after having given a detailed recording of the emperor's vices, he fell out of favor and was ordered to commit suicide.

Two other satirists, incensed by the corruption everywhere and the deterioration of the Roman character, were Martial and Juvenal. Martial's love lyrics were to boys only, and he composed bitter verses about women's frailties and treacheries. Juvenal also aimed his most virulent attacks against women, claiming that there was scarcely a Roman woman worth marrying.

Rome's last great writer was Apuleius. His most famous work, *The Golden Ass,* is a picaresque romance satirizing the vices of the age. Its plot is taken from a Greek tale, of which the episode of Cupid and Psyche is a rare literary gem:

A merchant's daughter of radiant beauty incurs the jealousy of Venus. The goddess sends her son Cupid to make the girl fall in love with a monster. But Cupid disobeys. Enamored with the lovely virgin, he hides her in a castle. He makes her his wife and visits her nightly but forbids her to look at his face. For a while she is content not to see him, but at last, giving in to her envious sister's suspicious needling, she begins to fear that he may be a hideous creature. At night, when he is sleeping, she lights a lamp, takes a look at him, and is enthralled with his beauty. He awakes, however, and, reproaching her for her lack of faith, he vanishes. The castle disappears at the same moment, and the maiden is thrown into solitude. She starts wandering over the earth in search of Eros. Venus keeps pursuing her and submitting her to a series of terrible ordeals, which even include a descent into the underworld. Yet, thanks to mysterious assistance, the girl succeeds in overcoming them all. Finally, touched by the suffering and repentance of his unhappy spouse, Eros implores Jupiter to take pity on her. Since Venus refuses to recognize her son's marriage with a mortal, Jupiter confers immortality upon her and names her Psyche, which in Greek means soul.

This story has been understood as an allegory of the salvation of the soul through love and suffering. It signifies, at any rate, an important step forward in the evolution of the Eros-Cupid concept. The early Greek idea of Eros or love was an inseparable part of cosmogony. In the beginning was Chaos, out of which the universe was created. According to the Greek Orphic myth, Eros had an important hand in the process, for he was the offspring of a fertilized egg that had been laid in Chaos by Chronos, the time spirit. The role of Eros was to coordinate the elements that constitute the universe. He brought harmony to chaos and permitted life to develop. At this time he was still a primitive deity, a semiabstract personification of cosmic force.

Most myths of origin shared the imagery of cosmic sexuality and the idea of an initial fertilization as the source of all being. Thereby, they endowed elemental cosmic forces with human properties and functions. Eventual deification of these powers paved the way to the fundamental notion that sexuality is intrinsically divine and that the sexual impulse in humans and animals is the sensible presence of creative or, to account for its opposite, destructive divinity. As Putnam (1936) points out, Eros the unifier was also a destroyer. Even later, as he developed into the winged, rosy-cheeked, and gracious child, he displayed malicious traits, using his bow and arrow for pranks that caused much suffering among humans and gods.

The dichotomy of Eros' nature can be traced back in history to the Vedic mythology, in which Siva, who was to be worshiped as the Generator and Begetter, was originally adored as the destructive member of the divine triad—Brahma created, Vishnu preserved, and Siva was to destroy the universe.

In the course of time, Eros took on many shapes, but for centuries he was looked on as a benign power. During the Greek golden age he stood for something sublime, man's road to beauty and the good. Later on, as the quality of Greek and Roman life began to deteriorate, he became almost synonymous with lust. In the story of Cupid and Psyche are both aspects of Eros, the destroyer and the redeemer, but with an important difference—the erstwhile universal forces have been translated into human terms. Now they wreak havoc in the human soul. Eros, a god, gets involved with Psyche, a mortal. They are in harmony as long as Psyche is blindly content. However, her mind, her doubts, and her curiosity cause conflict. She is impelled to disobedience, for which she pays a heavy price. But then her initial lack of faith is redeemed through suffering and repentance. This spiritual quality, as well as her instinctual drive to be united with Cupid, finally saves her.

The story signaled the discovery of suffering that lies in love. It contains the seed of the conflict between the heart and the mind, which from then on was to be a dominant theme in literature down the ages, reaching its peak during the Romantic period.

Although Eros in representational art has remained the pudgy, playful, little child armed with bow and arrow, the concept of Eros in literature has taken on all the shades and complexities of the divided human soul. In his commentary on *The Secret of the Golden Flower,* Jung (1932) outlines the strife of these conflicting impulses. In effect, he identifies Eros with instinct, intuition, as set over against the reason, the intellect. Starting from the premise that spirit and intellect vie for control over human sexual drives, Jung concludes that only the spirit—something higher than the intellect, since it also includes feelings—can effect a harmonious balance by modifying and elevating instinct into a positive, creative force. Consequently, love can be an integrated part of the human psyche only if it allies itself with intuition, rather than with reason. Jung writes:

I can only take the reaction which begins in the West, against the intellect in favor of eros, and in favor of intuition, as a work of cultural advance, a widening of consciousness beyond the too narrow limits set by tyrannical intellect.

Christianity and the Middle Ages

RELIGIOUS EXPRESSION

Christianity deepened the gulf between instinct and spirit. It used reason as a weapon to combat instinctive-intuitive manifestations of Eros in favor of all spiritual, otherworldly concerns. Erotic love or instinct, having come to be equated with lust, was condemned as a degenerative symptom. The spiritual vacuum left by the collapse of the Roman culture had created a powerful impetus for the belief in a future world that was free of corruption and salaciousness. When St. Paul arrived on the scene, therefore, his teaching of a new kingdom of God, a new era of hope and joy, fell on fertile ground.

Paul was a scholarly Pharisee, born a Roman citizen, who became a Christian through a dramatic conversion, which turned him into an indefatigable worker for the

Christian cause. His injunctions against fornication and his advice against marriage to those who had the necessary willpower for abstinence—

I say it is well for them to remain single as I do. But if they cannot exercise self-control, they should marry. For it is better to marry than to be aflame with passion.

—laid the cornerstone for later Christian doctrine. Eros eventually became identified with evil, something to be ashamed of and repressed.

It has to be remembered, however, that it was not Paul's intent to legislate sexuality out of existence. He fully realized its power as an integral part of human nature, just as he recognized all human worldly drives and concerns. His teaching was motivated by the firm conviction that judgment day was near. The second coming of Christ was to happen in his lifetime. He was concerned with people's spiritual preparation for this event—hence, his advice to keep the same occupation, to remain in the same state without change. The slave should not seek freedom, the uncircumcised should not ask for circumcision:

I think in view of the impending distress, it is well for a person to remain as he is.

It is in this light that Paul's famous passage in praise of love in his letter to the Corinthians must be understood.

So faith, hope, love abide, these three; but the greatest of these is love.

A future resurrection of all Christians was a certain hope to all those who had faith in Jesus Christ as the Son of God. Love was to be valued as the highest because it was the Christians' response to God's love and mercy. By loving their neighbors, they glorified their Creator. Thus, the joyous love feasts of the early Christians were held in celebration of God's power. Although the reports of rampant immorality at these agape feasts must be dismissed, since they emanated from the wagging tongues of enemies, it is quite possible that the intimate communion among these people still had a strongly sensual character. Even Paul, though not accusing the Corinthians of licentiousness, objects to the lack of dignity and to the greediness and drunkenness of some.

If any one is hungry, let him eat at home.

However, the new transcendent dimension of love, as introduced by Paul, did not have the effect of welding instinct and spirit. On the contrary, it drove a wedge between the two by means of reason. This condition eventually hardened and was to dominate Christian culture and art throughout the Middle Ages.

The Bible provides the best illustration of the change the concept of love underwent with the new age. Several passages in the New Testament speak of the relationship of Christ with his disciples and the people of the church as that of a bridegroom to his bride; but the intimacy of the relationship is merely hinted at:

Can the wedding guests mourn as long as the bridegroom is with them?

In contrast to these chaste intimations, the Old Testament contains a wealth of sensuous poetry devoted to the same theme of love between God and his people, or so at least goes the allegorical interpretation:

I am my beloved's,
    and his desire is for me.
Come, my beloved,
    let us go forth into the fields,
    and lodge in the villages;
let us go out early to the vineyards,
    and see whether the vines have
    budded,
whether the grape blossoms have
    opened
    and the pomegranates are in bloom.
There I will give you my love.

The above quotation is from the Song of Solomon or Song of Songs. The Song of Solomon consists of a series of melodious love poems, rich with sensuous imagery, spoken in dialogue form between a man and a woman. Of its various interpretations, the cultic one seems to be the most plausible. It implies that the Song of Solomon is a remnant element of an ancient Sumerian fertility cult, also practiced in ancient

Canaan, in which ritual marriages took place between the king and a goddess, in which the goddess was perhaps represented by a temple prostitute or a priestess. Since popular ceremonies in springtime happened to coincide with the celebration of Passover, a fusing of the two events in the course of time could easily have happened. This explanation also solves the puzzle of pagan cult songs having found their way into the Hebrew canon of holy scriptures.

Although the New Testament is free from the explicitly erotic material present in Hebrew scriptures, Eros soon found its way back into Christian literature. Since art came to be identified with paganism, sensuality, and decadence, the Church sought to ban all secular artistic expression. Throughout the Middle Ages, therefore, art was centered on religion, and sensuality appeared clothed in otherworldly garb.

St. Augustine, the 4th century philosopher, reintroduced platonic mysticism, reconciling it with Christian teaching. With its stress on faith and the spirit as opposed to reason, it opened the road to sensual artistic expressions of religious ecstasy. St. Augustine is one of a number of Christian fathers—among them St. Jerome (347–420)—who, before their spiritual conversions, had fully indulged in the life of the senses. St. Augustine's ardent *Confessions* reveal a man with unabated passion, although it served the glory of God in a perfect fusion of artistic inspiration and religious ecstasy.

He who knows truth knows that light,
and he who knows that light knows eternity.
Love knows it.
O eternal truth and true love and beloved eternity!
You are my God;
to you I sigh by day and night.
And when I first knew you, you raised me up
so that I could see that there was something to see.

St. Augustine was followed by a long line of Christian mystics who delighted in singing of divine love. Eros, to them, was the soul's desire to be united with God. Christian mysticism saw man as separated from God by an abyss that cannot be bridged without the merciful initiative of God Himself. Only He may, by the infusion of grace, illuminate and

elevate the human soul. In this descending movement of divine love (agape), He may meet the ascending loving aspiration of the soul (eros). The mystic's life was spent in preparation for the soul's ultimate union with God. The processes involved, the individual steps leading to this goal, were of a spiritual nature, transcending sense, and could be described only symbolically. Mystics, therefore, continuing the biblical tradition of the Song of Solomon, often related the exaltation of a spiritual union with God in highly sensual terms, comparing God to the spouse and the soul to His bride.

One of the greatest representatives of this art is St. John of the Cross, a 16th century Spanish theologian, poet, and scholar. The poetry and musicality of his verses are of unequaled beauty, giving expression to the highest intensity of emotion. To describe the soul's deepening relationship with God, he uses the image of the mutual attraction of lovers, their courtship, betrothal, and marriage. The ascending soul is likened to the preparation of young maidens for the marriage bed

with certain ointments of myrrh and other spices. These unctions are so subtle and so delicate in their anointing that they penetrate the inmost sweetness of the depth of the soul, preparing it and filling it with sweetness in such a way that its suffering and fainting with desire in the boundless emptiness of these caverns is likewise boundless.

The double-edged sweetness of suffering and bliss is inherent in any intense experience. It is, therefore, a recurrent theme in religious as well as secular act. It is also expressed in St. Theresa's autobiography, which relates her spiritual progress and beatific vision. St. Theresa and St. John of the Cross were friends and cofounders of the order of the Discalced Carmelites. Her place in Spanish literature was well secured by her own works; however, what made her truly immortal in the eyes of posterity is the magnificent statue by Giovanni Lorenzo Bernini (1598–1680) in the Cornaro Chapel of Rome, showing the saint at the supreme moment of transverberation—the piercing of her heart by the arrow of divine love. That moment was described by her as a moment of infinite pain and infinite pleasure that she wished could last forever.

Her facial expression reflects the passion of a woman in orgasm. The statue is a graphic illustration of the close kinship of religious, sexual, and esthetic ecstasy. All three partake of the ineffable, of a truth that eludes description. A successful attempt to communicate this experience is by nature artistic, for art expresses the inexpressible. By the same token, the spectator, receiving and responding to this communication, participates in a mystical event that is beyond the power of words.

Divine love, which was the subject of Christian literature throughout the Middle Ages, would seem to be exclusively a manifestation of Eros the creator. However, the suffering inherent in the soul's struggle for enlightenment and Christ's passion as a demonstration of God's love and mercy point to the other side of Eros, that of the destroyer.

Although the development took many centuries, Christianity completely changed the appearance of the two-faced god. Eros the destroyer eventually became the dominant theme in representative art. The mysticism of the Orient, which expressed itself in elaborately ornamental art, exercised a considerable influence on Western culture. The originally transcendent deity of the Jews took on human features in Jesus Christ, the son of God, though in the beginning the stress still lay on His almighty power. In early Christian art the Savior was generally portrayed as the risen Christ, sitting in awe-inspiring dignity on the heavenly throne. But gradually a new conception began to predominate. Both theologians and the common people began to emphasize Jesus' human experience, recognizing in his suffering and humiliation their own earthly miseries. Artists increasingly represented the tortured and dying Christ on the cross, a portrayal of human agony that would have been anathema to the sensibilities of the classical Greeks. Eros was transformed into a sadomasochistic tendency toward necrophilia that seemed to be taking hold of medieval people, not loosening its grip until the time of the Renaissance, when hope for a better life after death gave way to a more optimistic view of life here on earth.

However, even during the Middle Ages the human desire for beauty, love, and warmth could not be totally repressed. Eros, the creator, met this need through the cult of the Virgin. The more human view of Jesus and the love of Mary as the mother of God were reflected most clearly in Christian sculpture and painting. The infant Jesus in early portraits appeared as a regal figure, but later He came to look like any baby held in the arms of his fond mother. The representation of Mary, who personified the Christian ideals of love and charity, underwent a similar change. She developed from a rigid female figure with a serious facial expression to a tender virgin of otherworldly beauty.

SECULAR EXPRESSION

In secular art, the open expression of eroticism had practically disappeared with the cultural darkness that enveloped Europe for the first centuries after the sack of Rome. Around the beginning of the 12th century, with the emergence of what came to be known as the High Middle Ages, medieval literature underwent two principal developments: Ancient myths and legends sung by bards appeared in written form, and vernacular languages began to compete with Latin, which hitherto had been the common tongue of the monks, who were just about the only people able to read and write.

The new literature extolled heroism, honor, and loyalty and provided entertainment for the knightly class. Eventually, chivalry, with its glorification of women and its emphasis on gentility, displaced the ideals of the battlefield. The first literary works to reflect and in part to inspire this change were the songs of the troubadours, the migratory poets who originated in Provence, in southern France. They initiated a movement of profound importance in late medieval literature. For the first time since the days of pagan authors, a poetry of passion appeared in Europe. Woman, who had once been condemned by monks and Church fathers as the very incarnation of evil, was put on a pedestal by some and was actively pursued as a sexual object by others.

Those knights who idealized the woman of their passion often expressed their yearning in such devout and prayerful terms as to render the subject of their adoration almost indistinguishable from the holy Virgin. Conversely, it was a common practice for Christian mystics to use strongly erotic symbolism in their religious poetry. One of the outstanding representatives of this genre during the 12th century was the Spaniard Alfonso el Sabio, who used the most palpable sensual imagery to describe the Virgin Mary. Another great Spanish poet of original and varied genius, who was equally at home in the areas of worldly and divine love, was Juan Ruiz, whose *Book of Virtuous Love* is a fantastic mixture of tales, fables, and devotional poems unified by a history of his own love affairs.

The author of romantic songs, as a rule, addressed himself to the wife of another. It was held that true love was possible only between knight and mistress, never between husband and wife. The adulterous basis of such romantic passion can easily be explained in the light of medieval marriage conventions and the attitude of the Church to marital love, which could have done little to encourage deeply felt devotion between the spouses. Marriage was usually a business contract, involving property and military power but little sentiment, and the Church frowned on any kind of sexual activity that did not serve the purpose of procreation exclusively.

In France the literary tradition of the troubadours was continued by the northern trouvères and gave rise to a new genre, the romance. The new convention spread from there into Italy, England, and Germany. The romantic ballads most famous for their colorful narrative and poetic beauty are those of Chrétien de Troyes' Arthurian cycle, Wolfram von Eschenbach's *Parzival,* and Gottfried von Strassburg's *Tristan und Isolde,* which was completed by Ulrich von Turheim and Heinrich von Freiberg.

Tristan und Isolde was one of the first romances to take up and elaborate on the theme of suffering as a part of love, the germ of which is found is the ancient myth of Cupid and Psyche. The story focuses on Tristan's journey to Ireland on behalf of his uncle, King Mark of Cornwall, to bring back Isolde as the king's bride. On the way, the couple accidentally drink a magic love potion that causes them to fall passionately and eternally in love. Isolde has to stand trial for adultery, but the lovers are able to outwit the king. Eventually, however, they are discovered *in flagrante delicto,* and Tristan flees to Brittany, where he marries another woman named Isolde. In the course of further adventures, Tristan receives a wound from a poisoned spear, which can be healed only by the first Isolde, now Mark's wife. She is summoned from Cornwall. Tristan is advised that a white sail will be the sign that Isolde is on board the returning ship. As the boat carrying Isolde is sighted, however, Tristan's jealous wife tells him that the sail is black. When Isolde arrives, she finds Tristan dead, and, overcome with grief, she joins her lover in death.

As Gottfried von Strassburg stated in the prologue to his poem, his purpose was to show that love, by virtue of its inherent suffering, ennobles the soul. Thus, the love potion, the equivalent to Cupid's dart, becomes the mere outward symbol of a situation brought about by the inner nature of the relationship between the lovers. Now Eros the creator and Eros the destroyer are inseparably linked. In this case it is an adulterous relationship, which causes an irreconcilable conflict between the lovers' emotions and society's conventions. The adulterous union is condemned by law; but seen from the medieval perspective, only this kind of love can achieve spontaneity and completeness.

Another type of poem was the allegorical, moralistic, or didactic, in which the characters are abstract virtues and vices, such as Love, Hate, and Envy. A great example is *Le Roman de la Rose,* a work consecutively written by two poets. Its general theme is the art of love and gallantry, reminiscent of Ovid's *Ars Amatoria,* yet with a refreshing breeze of satire on the mores of the time.

While the chivalric romances appealed to the nobility, the rising bourgeoisie came to prefer another type of secular literature—the *fabliaux* (fables). Unlike the heroic and idyllic tales of courtly love, the *fabliaux* dealt with everyday life. Often richly spiced with obscenities, they reveal a contempt for the trappings of chivalry, with its romanticized love and pursuit of adventure.

One of the most popular of the *fabliaux* was *Aucassin et Nicolette.* Its main theme is the tyrannical demands of impetuous love. Aucassin, the son of a Provençal count and indifferent to the fact that his soul's salvation may be in jeopardy, falls hopelessly in love with Nicolette, a slave captured from the Saracens. The lovers are separated by imprisonment, but they escape, and after many perilous adventures they are reunited forever. The naturalism of this story and others of its kind clearly foreshadow the secular spirit of the Renaissance.

In Italy courtly love was sung by the *stilnovisti* (new style) poets, whose tender ballads dealing with beautiful and saintly women were thematic forerunners of a great masterpiece that was to dwarf almost all other poetry past and future—Dante's *Divine Comedy.*

The Florentine poet was born in the 13th century, a few years in advance of the official beginning of the Renaissance, but his work is a timeless monument rising above ordinary classification. Dante's idealization of Beatrice reaches far beyond simple romantic sentiment. *The Divine Comedy* is a Christian epic of universal scope. It is a presentation and interpretation of the nature of human existence, focusing on the human need for spiritual enlightenment, at the same time presenting a grand synthesis of medieval theology and philosophy.

La Vita Nuova (new life) is the story of the poet's young love for Beatrice and is an inseparable introduction to *The Divine Comedy.* Dante saw Beatrice for the first time when they were both only 10 years old. Several years later they met again, exchanging bashful smiles. That was the beginning and the end of their romance. Beatrice married the son of a rich banker and died shortly after, but she remained "the glorious lady of [his] mind."

The Divine Comedy is constructed as an allegorical tale, describing the experience of human souls after death. It is divided into three equal parts: Inferno, Purgatory, and Paradise. It begins when Dante loses his way in a gloomy forest, where he encounters the spirit of the Roman poet Virgil, who leads him through hell and purgatory; then Beatrice guides him into paradise.

The underlying theme of the poem is reminiscent of Socrates' conception of Eros in Plato's *Symposium.* Whereas the Greek soul aspires to absolute beauty, the Christian soul moves toward a union with God. In both cases, however, love is the motivating force behind the spiritual journey. Neither Plato nor Dante saw love initially as an abstract principle to be defined philosophically; it was an intense emotional experience in which a man's desire is focused on a specific human being. Dante's passion for Beatrice starts him on the road to salvation. She, the ideal of Christian womanhood, forces him to raise his vision ever higher, until he is brought face to face with his Creator. This theme of a spiritual love that is rooted in romantic-sexual attraction gives the poem its universal meaning. The theme was to be reiterated by all the masters of literature down to the present time.

Goethe, one of the future giants, immortalized man's yearning for the sublime in *Faust.* In this play Faust's soul is ultimately saved and reunited with that of Gretchen because, as the chorus of angels in heaven explains,

He whose strivings never cease
Is ours for his redeeming.

But the driving force behind these aspirations is always woman:

Here the ineffable
Wins life through love;
Eternal Womanhood
Leads us above.

Renaissance

Only a generation after Dante, Francesco Petrarca (Petrarch), the Florentine poet, was born. He marks the shift from medieval to modern times. Although Dante knew the classics, he philosophically remained a medieval man, but Petrarch had a passion for classic literature and was deeply influenced by it. Without repudiating his Christian allegiance, he warmly embraced pagan values. His enthusiasm for ancient learning earned him the admiration and respect of his contemporaries, and today he is regarded as the founder of Renaissance humanism. His love sonnets, for which he is most famous, are addressed to Laura, a beautiful matron. The unattainable lady inspired him with a passion that has become proverbial for its constancy and purity. His odes partook of the same spirit as the chivalrous love poetry of the 13th century troubadours.

A more robust humanism than Petrarch's was displayed by Giovanni Boccaccio (1313–1375), a compatriot and close friend of Petrarch's. Like Petrarch, Boccaccio was a scholar and a great lover of ancient learning. His writings were markedly pagan in spirit. *La Fiammetta,* sometimes called a forerunner of the psychological novel, makes no reference to Christian faith and doctrine. His best known work, the *Decameron,* is, in fact, decidedly anticlerical. It directs its shaft at the Church and its dignitaries under the guise of sexual ribaldry. It consists of a hundred stories told by seven young women and three men who are waiting for 10 days (whence the name *Decameron*) outside of Florence for the plague in the city to subside. Some of the stories are poetically beautiful; others are seasoned with bawdy humor. All of them have a larger purpose than to amuse; they basically treat the human struggle in coping with an existence that seems to be controlled by fate, rather than by a benign, divine power.

Boccaccio selected the plots of his stories from popular fiction of his day, especially the *fabliaux,* thus presenting medieval material in classical form. Chaucer, his famous contemporary from across the English Channel, borrowed largely from these tales.

Geoffrey Chaucer's (1345–1400) *Canterbury Tales* relates the stories exchanged by a group of people on a pilgrimage to the shrine of Canterbury. It exhibits a rare combination of scholarship, sophistication, insight, and earthy humor and has been most lauded for its fine characterizations of the persons telling the stories. The best known character is probably the wife of Bath, whose reminiscences of marital bliss are a comic masterpiece.

In France, the beginning of the 15th century saw an outburst of lyric poetry. At that time, this art form no longer constituted the exclusive entertainment for genteel audiences. It was made available to the common people by students at the new universities who were equally at home in cloister, marketplace, and tavern. These bards could sing hymns to the Virgin with as much enthusiasm and talent as they belted out a bawdy song.

The undisputed king of French lyric poetry was François Villon (1431–1463). He was educated at the Sorbonne, but his private life was divided between tavern and brothel. After he had killed a priest in a quarrel, he left Paris and fell in with a band of rogues who ravaged the countryside after the Hundred Years' War. His main work consists of two compositions, the *Testament* and the *Lais,* or *Little Testament,* lyrics of extraordinary beauty, vigor, and pathos. These ballads relate intimate details of lusty exploits alongside anguished prayers for the salvation of his soul.

In the fields of literature and philosophy, the French Renaissance produced, among others, an outstanding writer in François Rabelais (1490–1553). He was educated as a monk, but, soon after taking Holy Orders, he left the monastery to study medicine. His work expresses in a most exuberant manner the newly found joy of life after centuries of medieval restraint. He wrote primarily to amuse. However, the thick layer of obscenities and broad humor concealed a deadly weapon with which he satirized the practices of the Church and ridiculed all forms of bigotry and repression. He mingled serious ideas with overwhelming nonsense to attack everything he detested. His account of the adventures of Gargantua and Pantagruel, two lengendary giants with marvelous strength and gross appetites, served as a vehicle to express his philosophy of individual freedom and to glorify natural and healthy instincts. Rabelaisian humor today has become identified with coarsely bawdy jokes; but Rabelais' exuberance, in typical humanistic fashion, reached into all areas of life. The thirst and hunger of his two principal characters exemplified not only epicurean appetites but also the passion for unlimited experience and knowledge. In that, they epitomized the coming of modern times.

After the end of the Middle Ages, Europe experienced an upheaval of political and social changes, accompanied by fresh ideas about the nature of man and his place in the universe. No longer was the universe conceived of as a finite system of concentric spheres revolving around the earth and existing for the glory and ultimate salvation of human beings. New scientific theories suggested a cosmos of infinitely greater extent that could not so easily be explained in terms of Christian dogma, which placed man at the center of things, but for a higher, otherworldly purpose. Human beings were merely cogs in the wheel of a grand design. The Renaissance view replaced the divine puppet at the center with man's own creative, rational, and esthetic powers. It glorified the divine in the human—hence the term "humanism," which was the heart and soul of the Renaissance. The concomitant ideals of optimism, worldliness, naturalism, individualism, hedonism—all celebrated human powers. If the humanists seldom renounced religion, it was often treated as a formality or as an extension of man's knowledge.

In its more restricted meaning humanism also referred to the new enthusiasm for the classical writings, which conveyed the same confidence in all things human. The good life during those years (1400–1650) was one that pleased man's senses, intellect, and esthetic faculties.

PAINTING

Literature enjoyed a far greater freedom of sexual expression than did other arts. The spirit of humanism burst forth brilliantly in the visual arts, but the portrayal of beauty took precedence over explicit sexuality.

Greek myths now rivaled the Christian epic in popularity. Greek and Roman goddesses often replaced the Virgin Mary as subject matter. A revival of interest in the human body can be traced from the first careful, tentative demonstrations—such as Domenico Veneziano's *St. John of the Desert*, which shows the saint taking off his clothes to change into a hair coat, thereby exposing a handsome, athletic physique—to Giorgione (1478–1510), who rediscovered the female body as an artistic motif. Giorgione's *Sleeping Beauty* started a trend in Western art that is sensuous but not sexual, erotic but never lewd. The female nude painted in many guises—goddess, nymph, courtesan, lady of fashion—became a veritable cult. Botticelli's *Birth of Venus* shows the goddess of love as a woman of unearthly beauty floating ashore on a seashell. The work is considered to be the zenith of Renaissance painting.

Titian's *Venus of Urbino* is a beautiful example of palpable sensuality breaking through the veil of intellectual respectability. The seductively reclining nude, looking directly into the eyes of the viewer, has a very self-pleasing air about her. Her modest gesture of covering the pudendum has more the effect of drawing the spectator's attention to than away from it.

This painting seems to support Freud's contention that an artist's work provides important clues to his personality. For, in his private life, Titian often threw off his cloak of respectability. He fully enjoyed the free spirit of his time, holding company with Pietro Aretino, an Italian author notorious for his sexually extreme, explicit sonnets and dialogues.

Active eroticism breaks through in Titian's painting of *Danae*, which depicts Zeus visiting a young maiden in the form of a shower of gold. The classical theme only thinly veils the work's unabashedly erotic content: Danae is pictured in the position of a woman ready to receive her lover. It is but one of many works showing Titian's interest in erotic myths.

The same painter's *Sacred and Profane Love* is the very embodiment of the Renaissance spirit. Profane love is represented as a richly draped woman, adorned with jewelry, whereas sacred love is a nude holding the burning lamp of divine love. To the Renaissance man the beauty of a naked body was not profane but to be revered as an example of God's creation.

The renewed interest in the classical Greeks' ideal of beauty is starkly evident in many masters of the time, especially in Leonardo da Vinci's ephebic youths, such as *St. John the Baptist,* in Caravaggio's *Narcissus,* and in the numerous representations of Bacchus done in this period.

The Renaissance was much more than the revival of pagan values. The legacy of the Middle Ages was very strong, and, especially in German and Flemish art, religious themes were greatly favored. The most famous works of the Italian Renaissance, in a radiant blend of Christianity and classicism, depicted an ideal world with beautiful people, but the artists north of the Alps were still more concerned with human fallenness. The zeitgeist of the northern regions was dominated by the puritanical leaders of the Reformation. The symbolic paintings of Bosch (1460–1516) and Bruegel (1566–1637) abound with nightmarish demons and show scenes of hellish wastelands. Bosch's canvases are pervaded with an almost perverted eroticism, an illustration of what Freud, some 400 years later, saw in the polymorphous perversions of the id.

Albrecht Dürer (1471–1528), Hans Baldung (1476–1545), and Hans Holbein the younger (1497–1543) reflected the prevalent preoccupation with death, sin, and punishment. The medieval concept of the dance of death, which probably originated in a mimed dance or a morality play, was a favorite motif. A famous example are Hans Holbein's woodcuts dealing with this stern reminder of the inevitability of death, which constitutes a summons to repentance and amendment of life.

Sin being all but synonymous with sex and vanity, the theme of beautiful female nudes clutched in the hands of death or the devil recurrently appeared in Northern art. In Baldung's symbolic painting *The Three Ages of Women,* Vanity is depicted as a lovely nude admiring herself in the looking glass. Behind her stands Age, a figure of undetermined sex, trying to ward off Death, who is holding the hourglass over Vanity's head, while Childhood, sitting on the ground, is hopefully looking up. In the face of inevitable doom, the center figure of the nude, despite her self-absorption, presents a moving picture of innocence in her complete unawareness.

Another work by Baldung shows Eve flirting with Death as well as the Devil. Half-hiding the apple of temptation, she touches the serpent, which bites the figure of Death, who in turn grasps Eve by the arm. The symbol of womanhood remains unmoved by the evil presence of Death, which, displaying a cloven hoof, teaches an obvious lesson: Sin leads to Death and from there inescapably to hell. This painting dimly foreshadows the Romantic period, which is characterized by a fascination with and, in its extreme forms, almost a love of death.

France, largely because of its geographical position, was specially predisposed to serve as a ground of understanding and conciliation between Northern and Southern influences. Freed from Gothic inhibitions by the liberating force of the Italian Renaissance, artists in the 16th century began to exalt the female body. Sometimes it was done under the pretext of mythology, but just as often nudity was celebrated in works dealing with subjects from everyday, albeit royal, life, as exemplified by the school of Fontainebleau. These artists portrayed unclad, courtly ladies, giving them a frail and porcelain-like appearance. The effect is one of sensuality injected with elements of mystery.

One enigmatic painting of this school that has received many different interpretations is that of two naked women in a bath, one holding the other's nipple between two dainty fingers (1594). It is generally agreed that the painting shows the mistress of Henri IV, Gabrielle d'Estrées, and her sister, the Duchesse de Villars. In the 16th century it was common practice for people to bathe together, but why the Duchesse is pinching her sister's nipple still remains a mystery. Some experts believe that the gesture indicates that the royal mistress was soon to give birth. Other details of the canvas, such as the sewing nurse in the background, seem to support this theory. A ring held by Gabrielle has been said to symbolize her hope of marrying the king. The painting, without doubt, has symbolic meaning. The deliberate detachment with which the artist has treated the subject, the symmetrical composition, and the solemn stiffness of the two women all point to a message, the content of which is open to speculation.

SHAKESPEARE

The Renaissance also witnessed the rebirth of the theater, with William Shakespeare as its foremost representative. The advent of Christianity had forced the drama into an eclipse for hundreds of years. However, the natural urge to play, to imitate, and to embellish the ordinary is too strong to be forever repressed. Like other arts, the drama was absorbed into the service of the Church. It started with semidramatic dialogues that formed part of the Easter service. These tropes, as they were called, eventually developed into more elaborate passion plays.

Around the year 1000 medieval theater emerged, retaining the religious character of its forerunners. There were three main genres: The mystery plays, very popular in England, dealt with the fall and salvation. Miracle plays enacted the miraculous intervention of the Virgin Mary or various saints in the exigencies of life. The morality plays presented characters as abstract personifications, such as Truth, Mercy, and Envy. In France and Italy these plays eventually became indistinguishable from farce. William Shakespeare (1564–1616) absorbed into his work elements from all these types of drama.

Many works in this period of English literature were characterized by explicitly sexual content. Renaissance writers struggled to delineate the often thin line between physical desire that is love and physical desire that is lust. Shakespeare defined the two principles in his poem *Venus and Adonis:*

Love comforteth like sunshine after rain,
But Lust's effect is tempest after sun.
Love's gentle spring doth always fresh remain;
Lust's winter comes ere summer half be done.
Love surfeits not, Lust like a glutton dies;
Love is all truth, Lust full of forged lies.

The theme of Eros the creator, as opposed to Eros the destroyer, is reiterated in Shakespeare's plays in a myriad of variations. Yet his attitude toward sex defies categorizing. Being an astute observer of human behavior, he illuminated all forms and shades in which love manifests itself. His treatment of sex is as multifaceted as is the number of his dramatic personages. Having an unrivaled gift for making his actors speak in character, his language perforce is staggering in richness and diversity. A true appreciation of his works requires the study of a comprehensive glossary. For sexual imagery alone, he borrows metaphors from all fields of human life, as well as from the animal world. His moods range from the loftiest lyricism and idealism to the most brutal prose and materialism, and his unique gift of expression is adequate to underline them all. The sexual wit of the highborn courtier is as authentic as the bawdry of lower characters, the poetry of romantic love as captivating as the manifestations of lust are repugnant.

Little is known about Shakespeare's private life. He was an actor before he started writing plays. It has been speculated that he was estranged from his wife, since he lived alone in London for nearly 20 years and since his will left all his land to his first-born daughter; to his wife he bequeathed the "second-best bed."

It has been suggested that Shakespeare was a homosexual. However, his plays show evidence to the contrary. References to homosexuality are very few, and they reveal the kind of tolerance that any intelligent person would hold. There is, on the other hand, ample proof that in matters of heterosexual love he spoke from personal experience. Many scholars agree with Partridge (1969) that Shakespeare was apparently an

exceedingly knowledgeable amorist . . . a highly artistic, an ingeniously skillful practitioner of love-making, who could have taught Ovid rather more than that facile doctrinaire could have taught him.

The fact that the majority of his sonnets are addressed to a man has been explained on the basis of Renaissance custom. Artists used to dedicate their works to the patrons who supported them financially. It has also been maintained that the tone of the sonnets glorifying the idea of friendship between men is common to this period. The Renaissance used the violent, sensuous terms for friendship between men that later generations reserved for sexual love (Chute, 1949).

Although speculations about Shakespeare's own sexual preferences seem to be futile, his dramas yield a wealth of information on his view of Renaissance life and love. In his intense love of things human and earthly he is akin to Boccaccio and Rabelais. His conviction that beauty and goodness are synonymous recalls the ancient Greeks' ideal. But he adds a spiritual dimension, which gives his work its universality.

Long before Freud defined the term "libido," Shakespeare recognized the erotic impulse as an inheritance from an animal and human past, with all its capacity for both good and evil. Using an appropriate metaphor for this powerful driving force in humans, he termed it "blood." Blood is intensity, passion, life's untutored energy. If not ruled by reason or tempered by spirit, it easily turns into destructive lust and violence.

Even in the plays of his early period, which is marked by a somewhat restrained optimism, love, as an irresistible and potentially dangerous attraction, is always lurking behind its apparently playful manifestations. From these works it is apparent that Shakespeare held the human ideal to be a proper balance of blood and judgment—that is, emotions balanced with reason. It is this ideal that Hamlet admires in his stoic friend, Horatio, and that he himself vainly struggles for:

> . . . and blest are those
> Whose blood and judgment are so well
>   commeddled
> That they are not a pipe for Fortune's finger
> To sound what stop she please. Give me that man
> That is not passion's slave, and I will wear him
> In my heart's core, ay, in my heart of heart,
> As I do thee.

Eventually, however, Shakespeare—like Jung 3 centuries later—opted for spirit over reason, for reason can, at best, achieve order; only spirit can elicit harmony.

For complete spiritual triumph one has to look in Shakespeare's later plays, although its groundwork has been laid in the very beginning. It is found in *Romeo and Juliet,* where youthful passion is sanctified by its very purity and innocence. In contrast to this tender love story, *Antony and Cleopatra* presents the violent stormy passion of two people at the very apex of their lives. Antony's is clearly a conflict of passion over reason. He is torn between his love for the enchantress of the Nile, the woman to whose charms Julius Caesar had succumbed, and the compelling demands of Rome. Although love wins out over his sense of duty, it does not diminish his greatness, for in this play Shakespeare has abandoned the idea of mingling blood and judgment in favor of a purified passion. Somehow in the course of the action, sexual passion is being transformed from a social weakness into a spiritual value. Cleopatra, the object of Antony's devotion, has changed from an alluring slut, who wallows in sensual pleasure, to a goddess of love. Here is how Enobarbus evaluates her—and women in general—at the beginning of the play:

> Under a compelling occasion, let women die. It were pity to cast them away for nothing, though between them and a great cause they should be esteemed nothing. Cleopatra, catching but the least noise of this, dies instantly; I have seen her die twenty times upon far poorer moment. I do think there is mettle in death, which commits some loving act upon her, she hath such a celerity in dying.

"To die" in Elizabethan English also means to have a sexual orgasm. This is another indication that the idea of death and rebirth is in some mysterious way related to the sexual experience and is deeply rooted in human consciousness. In Shakespeare's plays, at any rate, it offers the occasion for numerous sexual puns.

Cleopatra, then, is initially portrayed as a woman wholly concerned with sensual pleasure. However, at the close of the play, when the dying queen exclaims,

> Husband, I come!
> Now to that name my courage prove my title!
> I am fire and air; my other elements
> I give to baser life.

it strikes the reader as a genuine perception of the divine element in her love. The couple's death is a spiritual triumph, an ultimate fulfillment of their immortal love, as expressed in Cleopatra's words:

> The stroke of death is as a lover's pinch,
> Which hurts, and is desir'd.

In contrast to Antony, who sacrifices all to love, his adversary, Octavius Caesar, sacrifices all to his ambition, which embodies cold rationality. One is almost tempted to read the play as an allegory on the virtues of blood, which in its purity and untainted vitality is closer to divinity than when it is fettered by reason.

Shakespeare's ultimate reconciliation of blood and spirit is realized in *King Lear.* Eros the destroyer is contrasted with Eros the redeemer, love that transcends sexual passion. Nowhere is Shakespeare's conviction of the radical link between violence and lust more manifest than in Lear's daughters Goneril and Regan. In these women lust is coupled with cold reason. They belong to a gallery of the most inhuman characters ever created. Shakespeare reserved some of his most poignant sexual imagery to paint these monsters of the deep, for Lear has these two daughters in mind when he vents his rage and nausea over woman:

Behold yond simp'ring dame,
Whose face between her forks presageth snow,
That minces virtue, and does shake the head
To hear of pleasure's name—
The fitchew nor the soiled horse goes to 't
With a more riotous appetite.
Down from the waist they are Centaurs,
Though women all above.
But to the girdle do the gods inherit,
Beneath is all the fiend's;
There's hell, there's darkness, there's the sulphurous pit,
Burning, scalding, stench, consumption.

This is Eros the destroyer personified. Goneril and Regan are its embodiment. Their characters combine lust for power with carnal desire. They stoop to any means to achieve their end, from extravagant hypocritical protestations of love for their father in order to gain his kingdom to fratricide for the purpose of winning Edmund, the archvillain of the play, for their beds.

Cordelia, the antithesis of her sisters, is Eros in its most sublime form. She is present on stage only at the beginning and at the end of the play, but her spirit guides Lear through his growth from infantile egotism to spiritual maturity, from a man possessing worldly power to one endowed with human greatness. Her power of love helps transform King Lear from a bad king into a good man.

The seed of this theme was evident in the earlier plays. In *King Lear* Shakespeare achieves a final synthesis. Its ringing message is the eternal truth that the redemption of man from lust and violence lies in his power to rise to the spiritual without ever abandoning the sensual—that is, his humanity. It is the commingling of blood with spirit. Yet spirit manifests itself not only through love, humility, and patient acceptance but also through imagination, esthetic experience. The spiritual beauty of Cordelia is an esthete's delight. She joins all the seemingly fragile representatives of beauty pitted against the ugly powers of destruction in Shakespeare's play. Dreams, the quality of innocence, ideal love, art in every form—all partaking in the spirit of imagination—ultimately prevail over brute force. Thus, Eros the creator is linked with art, and both are raised into the realm of religion. This theme may have been subconscious in Shakespeare's writing. But the affinity of art and religion was to find explicit expression in many great works of the future.

Baroque and Rococo

The Renaissance was followed by the baroque and rococo periods, which sought to preserve the classical ideals recaptured and celebrated during the previous 200 years. These ideals were especially adhered to in French literature. Neoclassical reformers established new dramatic rules in accordance with Aristotle's guidelines. The two principal exponents of this genre were Pierre Corneille (1606–1684) and Jean Racine (1639–1699). Racine developed tragedy somewhat further than Corneille, who treated grandeur and heroism, rather than love. Racine concentrated on the passion of love, especially in his heroines, who have little choice and are caught up in situations that are beyond the power of free will.

The novel during that period was just in its beginning stages. One example has been hailed as an outstanding masterpiece: Madame de La Fayette's *La Princesse de Clèves*

(1678). Concentrating on a central moral problem, it is in its psychology and restrained pathos a perfect example of modern classical art. The story centers on the familiar theme of conflict between passion and principle, the heart and the mind. The heroine chooses principle. She never succumbs to her love for another man, but confesses her secret desires to her husband. Ironically, her scrupulous integrity ruins her own as well as her husband's happiness. Instead of presenting the story from the point of view of an outside observer, the author introduced an early form of the interior monologue, which made her work a precursor of the psychological novel.

The baroque spirit found a somewhat different expression in the visual arts. The period saw a hitherto unequaled growth of powerful dynastic states and tremendous wealth acquired through the discovery of new continents and the ensuing commercial revolution. Although the neoclassicists followed in the footsteps of the humanists, their art, reflecting these changes, was more grandiose and extravagant. The word "baroque" means excessive or eccentric. Yet the worldliness engendered by this opulence was counteracted by opposing forces, which made for extreme contrasts within the era. While Kepler, Galileo, Harvey, and other scientists reshaped the knowledge of the world and Descartes extolled the virtue of reason, superstition was rampant, and the Inquisition wreaked havoc among the masses. The power and wealth of the leading classes often led to corruption and licentiousness. On the other hand, a great number of people, artists and writers among them, sought to escape from these excesses. The response to these diverging tendencies was an outpouring of magnificent art, ranging from the mystical to the sensual.

The exemplar of baroque art was the Flemish painter Peter Paul Rubens (1577–1640). He covered a wide range of themes, from romantic and mythological subjects to those of the Christian faith. His paintings are charged with movement and vigor, his voluptuous nudes representing a celebration of the human body as a work of God. *The Fall of the Damned,* considered his greatest masterpiece, shows panoramic masses of well fed naked figures strung like garlands across the picture surface. A closer study reveals details of diabolical creatures pushing, pulling, and tearing the flesh off the damned. The naked bodies—shown from all angles in twisted positions, with distorted faces, crying out in agony—give the picture a powerful erotic quality of orgiastic emotionality. Eros has made an about-face—from that of the creator to that of the destroyer. Sensuous colors, usually expressing the joy of life, serve here to warn of its overindulgence and the dangers lurking just beneath the surface. Rubens' treatment of the theme vividly contrasts with the almost detached and pretty depiction of the Last Judgment rendered by Bosch, the early Renaissance artist.

Speaking for Rubens' great versatility are his 21 canvases of the life of queen Marie de Medici, done by commission for the new Luxembourg Palace and treating a subject of quite a different sort. Ennobling a queen whose looks were not striking and whose life lacked the glamour expected of her was no small feat. Rubens solved the problem by clothing truth in allegory, surrounding the lady with nude Greek gods and goddesses in striking, sensuous poses. *The Garden of Love* shows noble couples at leisure, frolicking with numerous cupids hovering about, pushing, pulling, and shooting their arrows from all directions. Above the scene a fountain made of a fleshy nude riding on a fish pours water from her breasts. The whole canvas seems to be overflowing with abundance—flowers, dogs, birds, musical instruments—all join the richly dressed company in an exuberant celebration of love.

The later baroque style of the 18th century, known as rococo, became more and more playful. It took its name from the fantastic scrolls and shell-like designs used for ornamentation in French architecture. Rules in art became less rigid but not as lax as those of social conduct. It was a period of great permissiveness, especially in France, where secret lesbian clubs sprang up, transvestism became stylish, and the court inspired ridiculously elaborate fashions. It was the age that made a Marquis de Sade (1740–1814) possible. Although probably psychotic, he had a brilliant mind. As one of the first to deal with the mechanics of sensual man—exposing the naked force of Eros the destroyer within the human soul—he deserves the credit not only for having influenced future literary works down to the present time but for offering a major contribution to the study of psychopathology: In the form of fairytales, he rendered the first system of perversions. By doing so, he gave the human drive of sadism its name, a drive that is as mysterious as the forces of life and death, with which it is inextricably linked.

The painters of France, sustained largely by royal and aristocratic patronage, produced works marked by charm, repose, and grace, reflecting the indolent ease and elegance of the court of Louis XV, which had replaced the earlier struggle for power. The painters were serving a doomed social order, but their work reveals no sign of the impending holocaust. They participated in the mass delusion characterized by the slogan, *Après nous le déluge!* (After us, the deluge.)

With the outbreak of the French Revolution a strong reaction set in against the elegant rococo style of the Old Regime. The result was manifold. No one style was predominant anymore; several coexisted. In France, instead of launching a new tradition, the artists of the Revolution simply went back to what was supposed to be a pure classicism, on the assumption that this style would be in harmony with the rationalist ideals of the new order. The style's foremost representatives were Jean Auguste Ingres (1780–1867) and Jacques David (1748–1825). Their work was characterized by order, restraint, and a liberal choice of themes from Greek and Roman mythology. Ingres was concerned not with naturalism but with the spiritual world of form. He created abstract designs into which the forms of the natural world were shaped into an eloquent pattern. Thus, the composition of his paintings has an unreal, near geometrical smoothness. The sensuality of his nudes is thereby checked by a certain sterility. The *Baigneueses* (Bathers) and *Le Bain Turc* (Turkish Bath) reveal Ingres' conception of the erotic as an intangible sensuality. The attraction lies in its unattainability. The *Turkish Bath* is not merely a tasteful display of erotic morsels. It shows an unlikely assemblage of 25 nude women amusing themselves by the petty diversions of a harem. They dance, eat and drink, and tickle each other. The viewer senses erotic delight, but he is barred from participating either emotionally or intellectually.

Romanticism

While Ingres' and David's classicism remained the official style in France for a century, romantic painters everywhere revolted against official styles of any sort and against academic rules of painting. One of the earliest rebels, not merely against accepted artistic standards but against political and social restraints as well, was the Spanish painter Francisco Goya (1746–1828). He detested the aristocracy, despised the Church, and ridiculed the hypocrisy of respectable society. He was visionary in his time, and his social conscience was sensitive to the tyranny, civil strife, and poverty that he saw everywhere in his native country. He dramatized the horror of war and man's capacity for cruelty, aspects that his French contemporaries, the glorifiers of heroism, chose to ignore. Another theme that engrossed him was the similarity between the wild joys of a crowd and the real insanity of truly deranged people, the madness common to the revelers at a fiesta and the inmates of the asylum. His works are variations on the theme of the two-faced Eros.

This extremely versatile painter also recreated Eros in one of the few nude portraits ever painted in Spain, the other famous portrait being Velazquez' Venus. Goya's *Naked Maja*—sultry, desirable, and seductively immodest—is one of the most provocative and magnetic figures ever put on canvas. She is no goddess but a living woman, yet alluringly romanticized.

In Goya's etchings, several series of prints, among them the "Caprichos" (Caprices, published in 1799), and the "Disparates" (Follies) or "Proverbios" (Proverbs), he explores the dark underside of a pretentious world, that of the corrupted Spanish royal court. His captions to the illustrations reveal a gift for pungent writing. The following from the "Caprichos" provides the theme for the entire work:

When man allows his reason to sleep, the creatures of the irrational world control his life; only with the awakening of reason will these hobgoblins finally disappear.

Indeed, throughout the series animal imagery symbolizes human folly. Men and women are half-human and half-animal, or they are tied down, acted on, and sexually assaulted by inhuman creatures. In Goya's view, Eros the creator, if unrestrained by reason, becomes the destroyer. By the same token, Eros, by embracing reason, becomes the creator, the symbol of rebirth and Truth itself.

In his "Disaster" series, Truth is shown as a beautiful bare-breasted maiden. One etching depicts her funeral, presided over by a cleric, while Justice stands by, hiding her eyes in the shadows. Rays of light emanate from the dead Truth. The figures in the background still have human faces, but those in the next etching have taken on animal features; the light radiating from the still lifeless Truth now pierces their dark world, indicating that a new spirit of reason may rise from the ashes of irrational war. The illustration that concludes this series shows a beaming, robust, full-breasted Truth, well and alive. She is addressing a bearded old farmer, suggesting not only that Spain's ravaged lands may flourish again but that Truth prevails. She is the midwife assisting the inevitable rebirth of man's better nature. She is an integral part of the creative capacity.

Goya is the father of 19th century art and of all modern art. His best and truest heirs were to be found in France until Spain produced another universal genius in Picasso.

In France the spirit of Romanticism was checked for the first two decades of the 19th century by the vigor of the classical revival. After the defeat of Napoleon at Waterloo, however, the age of enlightenment was seen as a closed chapter, and the force of the romantic influence, already well established in literature and philosophy, could no longer be denied in painting. It was an age to compare with the Italian Renaissance, a great

cultural transformation based on a revolution of human consciousness. It was the rebellion of passion against reason, imagination against logic, idealism against cynicism. The romantics had rediscovered not only poetry but also the uses of history and myth, the supernatural, the beauties of nature in the Alps and the exotic Mediterranean. The belief that the individual is the center of life triggered an intense interest in the psychic and sexual mysteries of the self.

The most brilliant exponent of romanticism was Eugène Delacroix (1798–1863), whose dazzling colors were to change the course of modern painting. Indulging in the romantic predilection for the exotic, he traveled to Algiers, where he was inspired to create some of his most popular works, paintings of the Moorish court and its concubines. Believing in the imagination above reason and knowledge, he injected excitement and movement into his work. His lurid emotionalism reveals the heavy legacy of the Marquis de Sade. Delacroix delights in scenes where blood is as freely poured as wine. His riotous splashes of color give his spectacles of slaughter an orgiastic quality. His paintings abound with naked, tortured, raped, imprisoned, and murdered women. *Death of Sardanapalus,* an illustration of one of Marquis de Sade's tales related on the occasion of an orgy, shows the Assyrian king on his deathbed, overlooking with an air of contentment the hecatomb of his concubines, naked beauties in the throes of death sprawled all over the canvas. To this king the experience of his final hour seems no different from his usual erotic diversions.

The latent awareness of the close link between terror and pleasure, expressed in works of art throughout the ages, finally surfaced into consciousness in the 18th century. Poems such as the *Ode to Fear* by William Collins and the exciting 18th century gothic tales—characterized by horror and violence, usually set against the background of ghost-ridden gloomy castles, in which tragic-romantic heroes and heroines met their destiny—marked the beginning of a new trend in literature. Goethe's dictum, *Das Schaudern ist der Menschheit bestes Teil* (Shuddering is the spice of life), sanctioned the thoughts expressed in the essays by the English critics John and Anna Aikins (1773) "On the Pleasure Derived from Objects of Terror" and "Enquiry into These Kinds of Distress Which Excite Agreeable Sensations."

Entirely new and peculiar to this period, however, was the recognition of pain as an integral part of sensual pleasure—hence, the fascination with a wild, barbaric Orient, epitomized by the orgy of colors in paintings and the depiction of lust and murder. The joy of love was no longer accompanied by suffering due to external circumstances. Lust and cruelty, on a purely sensual level, were now experienced as one and the same. Pain used to be inherent in pleasure; now pleasure was inherent in pain. Friedrich von Hardenberg Novalis (1772–1801), a German poet, sometimes called the prophet of romanticism expressed this new awareness in his "Psychological Fragments":

It seems strange that people have not long ago realized that the concurrence of sensual gratification, religion, and cruelty point to their interrelatedness and a common root. Amazing that sexuality should be the source of cruelty.

The new sensibility brought about a profound change in esthetic ideals. Romantic artists were intrigued by the tale of Medusa, one of the Greek Gorgons, who, as described by Aeschylus, were

monsters abhorred by mortals, with locks of serpents, whom none look upon without perishing.

Perseus, so the saga goes, finally decapitated Medusa by fixing his eyes on her reflection in the polished surface of his shield. A painting of her ghastly head, first ascribed to Leonardo da Vinci but now believed to be the work of an unknown Flemish artist, inspired Shelley to dedicate a lengthy ode to this embodiment of the romantic ideal of beauty:

It lieth, gazing on the midnight sky,
   Upon the cloudy mountain-peak supine;
Below, far lands are seen tremblingly;
Its horror and its beauty are divine.
Upon its lips and eyelids seems to lie
   Loveliness like a shadow, from which shine,

Fiery and lurid, struggling underneath,
The agonies of anguish and of death.
Yet it is less the horror than the grace
   Which turns the gazer's spirit into stone.

The same sentiment is expressed in Goethe's *Faust*. The following scene, taken from the Walpurgisnacht (Witches Sabbath), has been vividly illustrated by Eugène Delacroix, replete with monsters, snakes, and hellish fire. Faust and Mephistopheles are witnessing the gathering of witches and evil spirits. Faust discovers a solitary figure standing apart from the action, a pale young beauty resembling Margarethe. He approaches her, but Mephistopheles warns him:

	Let that alone! Such thoughts can do no good.
	This is a witchery, a phantom, dead;
	To meet with it is luckless, full of dread,
	Its frigid stare congeals the gazer's blood,
	Till stony death through all the limbs is spread—
	Of Medusa, Sir, you must have read.
Faust:	Indeed, indeed, the eyes are of the dead,
	Eyes that no hand has closed or comforted.
	That bosom Gretchen yielded, lovely, warm,
	I took my joy of that dear, gentle form.
Mephistopheles:	That is the witchcraft, poor deluded fool:
	Each sees in her the sweetheart of his soul.
Faust:	What longing love, what ecstasy and woe!
	This haunting gaze will never let me go,
	And strangely clear, around her lovely throat,
	She has a single cord of red,
	Thin as a knife-blade is the thread.

"What ecstasy and woe!" This is romanticism in a nutshell.

Although in later life Goethe (1749–1832) rejected these emotional excesses and declared that classicism represented sanity but that romanticism was madness, he had helped initiate the movement in his youth with the influential novel *The Sorrows of Young Werther*. In his own words, it is the story of a young man

gifted with sentiment and penetrating intelligence, who loses himself in fantastic dreams, undermines himself in speculative thought until finally, torn by hopeless passions, especially by infinite love, he shoots himself in the head.

Unrequited love was a persistent leitmotif in romantic literature, and suicide the ultimate romantic gesture. After the publication of Goethe's book, many young readers, no longer able to distinguish between life and fiction, took their own lives for unhappy love or a general feeling of *Weltschmerz*. The young man endowed with special gifts, particularly the poet or the artist, doomed by his genius to loneliness and misunderstanding, was another theme that appeared during that time. It has come down to the present day in many variations, especially in the *Kuenstlerroman*, novels that trace the development of the artist.

Another salient figure of the period was Charles Baudelaire (1821–1867), the embodiment of alienation in his life, as well as in his work. He was a poet standing apart from any school, but he paved the way for the symbolists, poets of the decadent 1890's. Their doctrine was based on the Hegelian belief that the world perceived by the senses is a reflection of the spiritual universe. They strove to express the truth behind appearances by means of symbols. Baudelaire, some 40 years before their time, asserted that natural phenomena—colors, scents, and sounds—were the multiple symbols of a single reality and that it was the poet's task to rediscover the mysterious unity beneath their diversity. At the same time, however, he was attached to the ethos of romanticism, especially in his fascination with death and the macabre. He read the Marquis de Sade, admired Delacroix's paintings immensely, and was deeply drawn to Edgar Allan Poe, whose international fame he secured by his admirable translations. In his notebook Baudelaire defines beauty as something glowing yet infinitely sad, as epitomized by a seductive

woman who at once arouses dreams of sensual pleasure, melancholia, satiety, fiery passion, lust for life, bitterness, deprivation, and despair. His idea of perfect male beauty was Milton's Satan. In his best known book, *Les Fleurs du Mal* (Flowers of Evil), he extols the beauty of evil and conjures up the bittersweet quality of pain. In his poems he compares the clinging embraces of love to a surgical operation, for love is torture, and the lovers are its voluntary victims. He envisions scenes worthy of the Marquis de Sade, such as black masses with his black mistress, Jeanne, and Apollonia, a woman he knew only casually at the time of writing his poems.

His book was not well received. In fact, he was prosecuted and asked to obliterate some of the more offensive verses, since they were judged to be injurious to public morals. The following poem is one of these that met the court's disapproval:

What a Pair of Eyes Can Promise

I love, pale one, your lifted eyebrows bridging
   Twin darknesses of flowing depth.
But however deep they are, they carry me
   Another way than that of death.

Your eyes, doubly echoing your hair's darkness
   —That leaping, running mane—
Your eyes, though languidly, instruct me: "Poet
   And connoisseur of love made plain,

If you desire fulfilment of the promise,
   The ecstasy that is your trade,
You can confirm the truth, from thigh to navel,
   Of all that we have said.

You will find my white breasts heavy
   With the weight of their rough, bronze coins,
And, under a soft as velvet, rounded belly,
   Poised between ambered loins,

A fleece, not golden, but for richness sister
   To that hair with darkness bright,
Supple and springing—and as boundless
   As a deep, starless night!"

Realism

Before the middle of the turbulent 19th century, the romantic movement as a literary force was dying. Many writers, especially novelists, rejected the emotional excesses of its exponents and sought to depict life without idealization, true to experience.

Gustave Flaubert (1821–1880), by temperament a romantic, pitilessly curbed his tendency to emotional extravagance when he wrote his masterpiece, *Madame Bovary*. He wanted to purge romanticism of its defects: sentimentality, perceptual vagueness, and intellectual confusion. He hated these trends, prevalent in fashionable society, as well as the stupidity and vulgarity of bourgeois and provincial life. His novel is a devastating exposure of these ills.

Flaubert had a mystical view of art. He saw the true artist's work as an act of love inspired by a religious devotion, his only goal must be the search for beauty. This ideal led him to the unremitting struggle for perfect form, the striving for the artistically correct word. In *Madame Bovary* the beauty of style compensates for the ugliness of the subject matter. The novel, therefore, represents an early form of the *Kuenstlerroman,* with the very process of writing as the central meaning of the work. *"Madame Bovary, c'est moi,"* Flaubert has been reported saying: "I am Madame Bovary."

Emma Bovary is as much a symbol as an actual woman of flesh and blood. She embodies everything Flaubert detested. She is emotional but not warm-hearted, sentimental without poetic sensibility, and sensual rather than spiritual. Her early education, instead of giving her a true appreciation of learning and higher values, inspired her with a longing for glamour and romance. Her marriage to a country doctor quickly disappointed her expectations. Sexual intimacy disgusted her. In place of a perfumed, handsome lover in velvet and lace, her husband was a dullwitted man who reeked of medicines and drugs. Languishing in boredom, she tried to free herself from her straitjacket by escaping into a series of adulterous affairs. Finally, ruined and heavily in debt, abandoned by her insensitive lovers, she saw no way out but suicide. She died the victim of a grossly materialistic society as much as of her own deluded, romantic notions.

Flaubert's contemporaries did not see beyond Emma's immoral conduct. They perceived the book as a glorification of adultery and persecuted the author for indecency. He was acquitted, albeit with a severe censure.

The novel, in fact, contains not a single explicit description of lovemaking. Flaubert's great art lies precisely in his style, which, through the use of the most vivid imagery, conveys Emma's sexuality without ever showing her indulge in it. All her responses, down to her last breath, are sensuous. Emma died the way she had lived:

The priest stood up and took the crucifix; she stretched out her head like someone thirsting; and pressing her lips to the body of the God-Man, she imprinted on it, with every ounce of her failing strength, the most passionate love-kiss she had ever given. Then he recited the *Misereatur* and the *Indulgentiam,* dipped his right thumb in the oil, and began the unctions. First he anointed her eyes, once so covetous of caressing breezes and amorous scents; then her mouth, so prompt to lie, so defiant in pride, so loud in lust; then her hands, that had thrilled to voluptuous contacts; and finally the soles of her feet, once so swift when she had hastened to slake her desires, and now never to walk again.

Thus, false romanticism dies from an inherent disease: Eros the destroyer in the form of lust, coupled with a misdirected search for meaning. Flaubert obviously saw the creator only in a purged, spiritualized eros as it manifests itself in the love of art.

Flaubert was one of the first to embrace the doctrine of *L'art pour l'art* (Art for art's sake). During the French Revolution art had been regarded primarily as an instrument of propaganda. As a reaction to this notion, a French school of poets, the Parnassians, emerged and turned their backs on the social concerns of the romantics. They devoted themselves to objective poetry, from which the personality of the writer was entirely removed.

The principle of objectivity, being opposed to the natural impulses of poetry, was soon abandoned. The idea of art for art's sake, however, was there to stay. Painters and artists from other fields picked up the battle cry. This new attitude was also related to and influenced by the artists' relationship with the general public. Their status had undergone a fundamental change since the Renaissance. Formerly the most respected member of society and generously supported by kings and nobles, the artist had become a superior artisan, compelled to satisfy public taste, obedient to commands, treating the well defined subject that was expected of him. Now the artist gave priority to his own inclination, and the public could take it or leave it. This attitude contributed to his alienation. His style of life became more and more eccentric, and he was increasingly looked on as a character, a bohemian.

Impressionism

In the visual arts the new mood expressed by the slogan "To hell with the public!" held true especially for the impressionists, a school of painting whose chief aim it was to capture a momentary glimpse of a subject, sometimes rendering several impressions of the same object or scene to demonstrate that objective reality is different to the viewer at different times of the day. The basic premise was that truth lies in the artist's personal vision, not in external reality.

Traditional concepts of painting gave way to highly individualistic uses of perspective, color, and form. The artists tried to preserve in the finished painting the spontaneous quality of a sketch. The desire to reproduce life in the open air induced them for the first time to take the easel out of doors. They had recourse to quick outlines and to short brush strokes that transcribed light and atmosphere quickly and accurately. The beauty of woman was celebrated as part of nature's bounty, but almost any scene was worthy of their attention as long as it lent itself to catching the living light and the instant changes it produces. There is little intentional erotic art, at least in the works of the first representatives of this genre.

Nevertheless, some paintings caused quite a stir, not only because of the revolutionary techniques employed but also because of their so-called immorality. Édouard Manet's *Dejeuner sur l'Herbe* was pronounced immodest by the Emperor and rejected as vulgar by many critics. It shows a picnic scene with two dressed gentlemen lounging on a ground shaded with trees. They are joined by a sitting nude casually posing as if for a snapshot. Her matter-of-fact facial expression betrays no self-consciousness, despite the somewhat unorthodox gathering. In the background another young woman, barely covered, is just emerging from a little stream. Ironically, the theme for which Manet was attacked was derived from classical masters, for he was often inspired by works of the past. In this case, he had adapted an engraving by Raphael, whose figures, however, are all in the nude. It has been suggested that he was also influenced by Giorgione's *Fète Champètre,* an equally puzzling composition, showing an open-air scene with two male musicians, fully clad, and two female nudes.

Manet's *Olympia,* which met a similar storm of protest, was a humorous and, so it was deemed, disrespectful take-off on Titian's *Venus of Urbino.* Manet's figure is an individualized portrait of a well known Parisian model who dispensed her favors liberally. In contrast to the innocently sensuous Venus by Titian, Manet's Olympia, with her brazen stare, is provocatively self-assertive. Her household connotes her profession—an exotic-looking servant presenting her with a bouquet from a lover and a sinister black cat standing at her feet and arching its back, as if to symbolize Eros the destroyer, lurking in the lovely shape of the seductive nude. Not only the theme but also the execution of the painting offers a fascinating contrast to its classical model. Instead of faithfully rendering the details, Manet suggested the texture of each part for the general appearance of the whole. Such a clear, fresh, and direct rendition outraged the critics, partly because it was so close to a sketch.

Another member of the impressionist group, Edgar Degas (1834–1917), never completely severed his link with classical tradition, but he was more revolutionary in the subjects he chose. Preoccupied with contemporary life in all its manifestations, he seldom did landscapes. Instead, he focused his attention on the human figure. His central theme was woman. He sought her out in the theater, the opera, the boudoir, and the laundry. Primarily interested in movement, he painted numerous studies of ballerinas, bodies submitted to rigorous discipline, others in the process of getting dressed, laundresses moving the iron over rumpled clothes, nudes bathing. Critics who accused him of toppling the woman goddess by painting banal scenes of everyday life may, in reality, have been offended by his intellectual detachment. The spirit that animates his work is that of an almost dispassionate observer. He sees the driving force behind life's movement as mind, rather than Eros.

Quite the opposite is true for Pierre Auguste Renoir's (1841–1919) art. His primary concern was the well rounded feminine forms of Parisian women, expressed in the portrait during the first part of his life and in the nude during the second part of his life. He took sensuous delight in his work. His view of woman—the fertility goddess, the giver of life, comfort, and sexuality—is reflected in numerous studies of enchanting, graceful nudes, innocent nymphs seemingly unaware of their great sensual beauty. He loved bright colors, which he applied in short, whipping strokes, using their different tones to create form. Renoir is so famous for this technique that his name immediately calls to mind the warm and luscious hues of his canvases. His exuberance of expression and fullness of forms are reminiscent of Rubens. He makes the viewer feel the blood pulsating under the skin of each model. His *Nude in the Sun* (1876) captures the 18th century rococo spirit with his unique individual stamp: The painting offers the spectacle of capricious lights and shadows falling through the foliage of a tree and dancing on the model's nude body.

A somewhat less optimistic view of life and sex is presented by a contemporary, Henri de Toulouse-Lautrec (1864–1901). He was the descendant of one of the oldest French aristocratic families. Because of an accident in his childhood, he remained a cripple for the rest of his life. Unable to participate in most activities of the young, he grew up to be a shrewd and detached observer of human behavior. In later years he joined the bohemian world of Montmartre, where he found the themes most congenial to his cool, analytical mind. He became a familiar figure in the bars, nightclubs, and brothels, the places that inspired most of his art. He was the first Western painter to illustrate life and sexual practices in brothels. He preferred to create his works on location, where he felt himself in immediate emotional contact with his subjects. The result was a firsthand image of the decadent milieu in which he moved. His portraits of prostitutes, actresses, singers, circus performers, and patrons of both fashionable and sleazy bars sometimes have a cruel truthfulness, their psychology illuminated by the background. However, there is no real pessimism or bitterness in Toulouse-Lautrec's work. He was both in and above his sordid environment. His painting is not mere reporting, nor is it social criticism. Treating with sympathy the human scramble to escape inner loneliness, his paintings testify to a mind seeking to understand humans, rather than to bemoan them.

Postimpressionism

The impressionist period lasted a little less than 20 years. A reaction to the movement was already fermenting with Gauguin and van Gogh. Earlier impressionists followed the principles of art for art's sake. Gauguin and van Gogh, although in very different ways, more consciously than any painters before them sought to express their search for meaning through art. They richly charged their work with complex ideas, a tendency vigorously resisted by pure impressionists. Tortured spirits both, they gave themselves over to painting with a passion approaching mysticism. This common basic attitude explains the two men's friendship and belief that they could accomplish their life's work together, an error that was bound to end in tragedy.

Gauguin went through a development from synthesism—a movement corresponding to the idea of symbolism current in literature—to a style uniquely his own. His Tahitian landscapes exhibit a range of perfect forms, at once barbaric and refined, inspired and reasoned, a mixture of symbolic content and decorative quality. Despite their exotic sumptuousness, his nudes transcend eroticism. They are part of the mystery of the existential landscape, which his art is attempting to explore. The theme of search for meaning is exemplified by the work subtitled *D'où venons-nous? Qui sommes-nous? Où allons-nous?* (Where do we come from? Who are we? Where are we going?) A mixture of mythical and biblical allegory juxtaposing man, nature, and deity—it represents a synthesis of the artist's major work.

Van Gogh bared his soul as much in his paintings as in his letters. He created fiery, passionate portraits, expressive of the subject filtered through the screen of his own personality. Sensuality is less expressed in his view of the subject than an inherent part of his creative impulse. The primary importance of woman is her role as a life-giving force, as mother of the race. In *La Berceuse* (The Wet Nurse), for instance, the subject is rendered with a deliberate enlargement of the breasts and hips, as if to epitomize the earth mother he sees in every woman.

Both artists felt they had a mission to accomplish. In spirit they foreshadowed Joyce's priest of the imagination. Ironically, both died in poverty and unrecognized by the public. Nevertheless, their immortality was ensured not only by the legacy of their works but also by the influence they exerted on the future development of art. In particular, van Gogh's distortions imposed on nature with his flaming trees, blazing suns, and twisted branches prepared the way for expressionism.

Naturalism

The profound social, intellectual, and scientific changes taking place during the impressionist period had their impact on literature as well. Realism gave way to the more radical naturalism, popularized by Émile Zola (1840–1902). In his essay "Le Roman Expérimental" (The Experimental Novel), dated 1880, Zola maintained that the novelist, like the scientist, should be performing an experiment, independent of moral conventions, and basing his work on careful documentation. Influenced by social Darwinism, Zola believed that human behavior is determined by heredity and environment. However, his purpose was not merely to prove his ideas by depicting life down to the last sordid detail. The impulse behind his brutal exposure of what he saw as the conditioning factors of a person's deprived existence was a moral one: The end

was to instigate reform, a concern the realists did not share with him.

Zola carried out his theories in such works as *Thérèse Raquin* (1868) and *L'Assommoir* (1877) and later in an ambitious series of novels called *Les Rougon-Macquart,* stories loosely connected by the individual fates of members of one family. The three branches of the clan stretch into different social spheres, thus presenting a total picture and with it a powerful indictment of the social decay of Second Empire society. *Nana,* although not the best written, is the best known for its purported obscenity. It follows the rise and fall of a thoroughly atypical prostitute. The whole book is a ruthless denial of the romantic and sentimental view of harlots presented by earlier writers. Nana is vulgar, greedy, and heartless. She has irresistible erotic appeal. Her *belles cuisses, hanches roulantes,* and *gorge superbe* attract men from all social classes. Once under her spell, they are prepared not only to gamble away their fortunes for her sake but to lose their human dignity as well. She is discovered while appearing near nude in a play called "The Blonde Venus" and from then on sleeps her way up the social ladder, mercilessly discarding suitors for better opportunities. Neither a lover's suicide nor a lover's financial ruin can sway her delirious rush toward her own inevitable downfall. She thrives on those she destroys on the way. One of her ardent pursuers goes so far as to submit to her every whim, even to the point of crawling on the floor like an animal, while Nana happily mocks his ridiculous nudity. Fate, however, catches up with her at last. Dying of smallpox, the once-beautiful body rots away in a lonely room, deserted by all.

For Zola, sex is the Achilles' heel of humanity, the root of all evil in society. If the energies of the rich were spent and wasted in fruitless, tiring sexual exploits, the poor turned to sex as the only pleasure they could afford. But they paid for it in further degradation and misery. Even in novels like *L'Assommoir,* which is ostensibly a sermon against drink, the main characters' sexual incontinence is ultimately responsible for their ruin. The naked, middle-aged count Muffat, beaten by Nana as he crawls on all fours like a dog, is a symbol of Eros the destroyer.

Zola realized the link between sexual passion and violence. Brute force is a constant feature of his novels. Together with sexuality—portrayed by promiscuous, invariably corrupt, slothful, and weak people—brute force signifies the self-destructive, corrupt elements in life. Adultery, for instance, is treated from many angles but always as a source of murder, suicide, madness, or general decay. Only sexuality leading to responsible parenthood was recognized by Zola as a positive force. This social pessimism and sexual despair had its root in the writer's personal life. His first wife, Alexandrine, was unable to bear him children. As can be gleaned from his autobiographical novel, *La Joie de Vivre,* the thought of death without leaving offspring was a horrifying spectre to a man who believed in the progressive evolution of mankind. It meant that he would have no part in an ultimately perfect society of the future. Zola's gloomy outlook seemed to change after his fruitful union with another woman, Jeanne Rozerat. Although this union saved him from morbidity, his creativity seemed to be faltering. His literary position, however, was secured, and he strongly influenced the trend that future literature was to take.

Contemporary Art

Zola's naturalism anticipated a new era of psychological awareness, but the advent of Sigmund Freud had the decisive impact on subsequent writers and all of 20th century culture. In *Introductory Lectures on Psychoanalysis* (1920), *Collected Works* (1925), and a series of monographs, Freud expounded his theory of art, which was based on psychoanalytic doctrine. He saw art as a means of assuaging unfulfilled, infantile wishes, both in the creator and in the spectator. These desires, mainly erotic and egotistical, are in conflict with opposing forces from within and without. Art, like a dream or fantasy, fulfills these desires. The creative process resolves the artist's conflict, which would otherwise lead to neurosis. Unlike a dream or fantasy, a work of art has great reality value, and it meets the artist's and society's approval. Art, therefore, constitutes a unique reconciliation of pleasure

and reality principles. The creative experience and the esthetic experience gratify the artist's and the spectator's repressed desires.

Freud, in other words, saw art essentially as a product of infantile impulses. Such reductionism does not do justice to one of the most complex aspects of human experience. Freud's scientific bent obscured his view of the mystical dimension of art, which defies causalistic explanation.

The psychoanalytic movement coincided with a number of other developments, all contributing to a general disillusionment in man as a rational being. Darwin's theory had already shattered the world by proving that a human, far from being godlike, is simply a particularly crafty cousin of the ape. Freud's discovery of unconscious, irrational forces and their enormous influence on human behavior compounded the impact of the blow dealt by Darwin. The voices of doom and nihilism were strengthened by World War I and by the advanced technology used for the purpose of destruction. Depression, the rise of dictatorships, the horror of extermination camps, and the explosion of the atomic bomb had a devastating effect, especially on those who had believed in the power of reason and the perfectibility of humans.

No wonder existentialism became the leading philosophy of the time. Its tenet proclaimed that existence precedes essence, which means that a person, through his actions, creates his essence, his own personal meaning. There is no divine plan laid out for him. A person's decisions must be his own, and he is wholly responsible.

These developments spurred fundamental changes in accepted mores. A revolt against reason appeared in every aspect of culture. Eros, out of hiding, became more and more the subject of explicit artistic depiction. Yet, once seen as the sure destroyer of inner loneliness, sex became a particularly poignant expression of it.

Henry Miller's *Tropic of Cancer,* originally banned for its obscenity, uses frequent, sordid, and detailed description of sexual encounters as a tool—not for pornographic purposes but to shock the reader into awareness of a reality, which is unrelieved despair and alienation. There is a similar intent in the rough and obscene language used by the characters in Norman Mailer's *The Naked and The Dead*. The language serves to highlight the central theme of the novel, the dehumanizing and brutalizing effects of war.

The leading existentialist philosopher and novelist, Jean-Paul Sartre (1905–   ), insists on the loneliness of the human soul and on the need to preserve this loneliness from the encroaching invasions of other people. Yet in *Road to Freedom* he uses the sexual theme to illustrate a conception, expounded in *Being and Nothingness,* that allows human relationships without denying each person's essential separateness.

The dominant themes in contemporary literature and drama—eroticism, life as a meaningless absurdity, the individual preoccupied with himself—were predated by the visual arts. The artistic evolution of the late 19th century became a revolution as the 20th century proceeded. Pablo Picasso (1881–1973), the greatest and most protean artist of this century, went through the whole development of art history in his own work. Starting out in the traditional style, his paintings increasingly expressed his personal vision, reflecting his well known gargantuan lust for life.

Out of the multitude of his productions, *Suite 347* (1968) is of particular interest. Schiff (1972) called these engravings

the most comprehensive statement made by an artist about his philosophy of painting and of life.

Picasso in this sequence identifies Eros as one of the main sources of inspiration, manifested by the central motif of a nude woman. He also sees himself as a torchbearer of the great humanistic tradition of painting. He perceives the artist as a godlike creator. In an engraving reminiscent of Michelangelo's *Creation of Adam,* Picasso portrays himself with paintbrush in hand, less a tool of his trade than a symbol of his creative power, and, like God's finger, it brings the figure on the canvas to life.

Picasso's total identification of the creative and procreative act is revealed in another series of engravings, the 24 variations of Ingres' *Raphael Painting Fornarina.* Ingres'

original shows the painter Raphael, a beautiful nude girl on his knees, contemplating her nearly completed portrait. Picasso's series, taking off where Ingres stopped, depicts Raphael going through progressively passionate steps of lovemaking, finally completing the act by inserting his penis into her vagina. Throughout this development the artist never relinquishes his brush and painting equipment. In one parallel thrust of phallus and brush, he symbolically links the creative and sexual act more explicitly than any other artist has ever done.

Whatever the variations in styles and techniques, the contemporary trend in all art remains basically expressionistic, for it conveys, above all, the artist's personal experience of existence, as potently demonstrated by Picasso's work. The work of George Grosz (1893–1959), one of the leading exponents of expressionism, could serve as an illustration for Henry Miller's writing. His series of erotic watercolors, dating back to the late 1920's, are a poignant social commentary in the line of Goya, Daumier, and Toulouse-Lautrec, albeit with a graphic frankness unheard of by his forerunners. In these pictures Grosz dwells on repulsively unattractive people engaged in a loveless game of mutual titilation. The intentionally brutal treatment of human sexual activity conveys a sense of intense existential nausea.

Surrealism, another expression of the prevailing sentiment of absurdity, is greatly indebted to psychoanalytic theory. Dealing in terms of the irrational, surrealism sought to exalt the unconscious into an active, creative role. Its best known exponent in painting is the Spaniard Salvador Dali (1904–   ). He has produced a multitude of etchings and lithographs that show every aspect of sexual behavior. His style is asensual and intentionally repulsive.

Erotic Art (Kronhausen and Kronhausen, 1968 and 1970), a two-volume collection of explicit sexual material, testifies to the tremendous outpouring of eroticism in contemporary Western art. In contrast to the East, where sexuality was not repressed, Western culture required a major revolution to liberate these forces. Perusal of these two volumes not only affords a glimpse into

Everyman's bedroom but leads the spectator on a fantastic voyage to the interior of his mind. Every imaginable version of sexual behavior—heterosexuality, homosexuality, autoeroticism, bestiality, group sex, voyeurism—has been represented in a multitude of styles and media. Pure flights of the imagination attest to the validity of psychoanalytic theories. Tomi Ungerer's female nudes devour penises taken from a sardine can or gather them like flowers in a field, inserting them orally and vaginally in an illustration of penis envy and castration anxiety.

During the past two decades a new trend has become apparent, cutting across all media. Art seems to have come to a dead end. As the unspeakable has been expressed, the unseeable shown, and Eros robbed of its mystical quality, only boredom and experimentation are left. This is the realm of the avant-garde. Now art, to command attention, has to be stark and mind-boggling. As nothing makes sense any longer, one indulges in non-sense. Art changes to antiart. Rudolf Schwarzkogel, in a ghoulish demonstration of the prevailing *Zeitgeist,* amputated his penis inch by inch while a photographer recorded the event. The pictures were exhibited at a show of Western art in Kassel, Germany, in 1972. Successive acts of self-mutilation finally cost the enthusiast his life. He died in 1969 at the age of 29, a martyr to his art.

The painter Muehl, in another variation of body art, exhibits his feces neatly packed in tin cans as *Merde de l' Artiste.* Hermann Nittsch's *Orgies Mysteries Theater,* performed in New York City in 1972, consisted of the artist's covering himself, the room, and everyone in view with animal blood and guts. As a *dernier cri,* Vito Acconi built a ramp and crawled around on it while masturbating. Hughes (1972) terms these extravaganzas "the last rictus of expressionism."

MOTION PICTURES

The 20th century witnessed the birth of an entirely new art form: motion pictures. Because of its possibilities for verisimilitude, this medium is uniquely suited for the expression of sexuality as an aspect of human behavior. The treatment of sex in films has been explored by Knight and Alpert (1956–1974) in a comprehensive series of articles, "The History of Sex in Cinema." Movies as an unconscious sexual expression of those creatively involved in moviemaking has also been pointed out by Geduld (1972):

> The essence of cinema, like the sex act itself, is movement . . . a caressing with the camera, acting as the visual equivalent of the hand.

And Sergei Eisenstein, the great Russian moviemaker, compared the act of editing with copulating: linking image to image, sound to sound in one creative act.

With the advent of this new medium, however, militant moralists, bent on protecting society from erotic stimulation, found a new target, and censorship severely curtailed the movies' vast artistic possibilities.

The movies did, indeed, begin as peep shows, and the element of voyeurism is still retained in the roving eye of the camera. The camera can be said to allow the spectator to be privy to intimacy without guilt feelings. This factor, as well as the identification with the hero, may well explain some of the mass appeal of the movies, which makes then an unusual sociocultural document. As with no other art form, the filmmaker's economic survival depends on box office success, which, as a function of popular appeal, reflects both conscious and unconscious concerns of the audience.

Before World War I the movies were dominated by the theme of the other woman, the vamp who broke up a happy family by luring away the only weakly resisting husband. This was the theme of the classic William Fox movie, *A Fool There Was* (1914), with the famous Theda Bara, the high priestess of the vamp cult, in the lead. The vamp, the embodiment of Eros the destroyer, is a whimsical and darkly alluring goddess who charms men into submission and ultimate ruin. She is typified by Marlene Dietrich opposite Emile Jannings in the movie classic *The Blue Angel* (1930). Professor Unrath, an authoritarian teacher, meets Lola, a nightclub singer, and is immediately under her spell. He marries her and travels with her troupe; he winds up playing the clown as part of their act while his faithless wife gratifies her insatiable desires elsewhere. The erstwhile imposing figure of the professor crumbles to a shadow of his former self. In a belated awareness of his downfall, he tries to strangle the pernicious woman.

The jazz age brought about decisive changes in the mores and ideals of sexual behavior. The new slogan was, "If you can't be good, be careful." Hollywood became notorious for its scandals; sex orgies, dope addiction, and suicide made the headlines. These scandals led to the introduction of the Code of the Motion Picture Industry in 1927, the first handbook of movie censorship. It influenced and hampered the development of American movies until late in the 1950's. But great stars continued to project a sensual image, and directors worked their way around the strict rules with a number of gimmicks, such as dramatizing reprehensible subject matter and then sternly condemning it.

In the early 1930's a series of movies taking place in the prohibition era were produced. Sadistic sexuality and cruelty were the specialty of great movie idols. James Cagney projected the image of the slap-happy tough guy, while his private life was advertised as that of an exemplary husband and father. American morality, with characteristic ambivalence, accepted and welcomed Cagney as a hero with whom people could identify.

A no-nonsense approach to sexuality was introduced by Mae West's appearance in the 1930's. Her approach is epitomized by her classic line, "When I'm good, I'm good, but when I'm bad, I'm better," announced in *I'm No Angel* (1934). The pressure of censorship, however, soon drove normal sexuality from the American screen. Mae West was replaced by a number of stars who played roles of hysterical women with obviously ambivalent feelings about sex. The actress, in her eternal role as the good girl gone astray and saved, seemed to meet the infantile needs of those caught in a prostitute-Virgin Mary complex.

Another version of perverted sexuality was the bitch heroine, as exemplified by Bette Davis, playing a sadomasochistic, insatiable woman in *Of Human Bondage* (1934), and by Vivien Leigh as the intractable Scarlett O'Hara in *Gone with the Wind* (1939).

Increasing sexual freedom had its profound influence on all the arts but especially on the movies. Legal censorship has been eroded in most Western countries, where the voices holding traditional values have been shouted down by the outspoken defenders of the new morality.

After World War II the movies experienced a burst of artistic growth, increasingly incorporating explicit sexuality. The Swedish director Ingmar Bergman came out with his first film in 1945. Over the next several years he made a number of solemn dramas, probing the relationship between man and woman in love. Later movies were concerned with broader existential topics. Throughout his work he uses ostensibly erotic themes to examine and illuminate the nature of good and evil, fear of death, and struggle for faith in a disintegrating, meaningless universe. *Through a Glass Darkly* (1961) depicts on the surface the progressive deterioration of a psychotic young woman. Fanatically religious but unable to love her husband, she experiences sexual ecstasy whenever she hears the voice of God. Her insanity is a metaphor for man's alienation from God and from his own true being. The spiritual relationship with God cannot be divorced from the act of living and participation in the human world. On the contrary, it manifests itself through love for fellow human beings. The heroine of Bergman's movie, by eroticizing her love for God while rejecting her husband, cuts herself off from both God and man.

In *The Silence* (1962) promiscuity, lesbianism, masturbation, and voyeurism are the graphic vehicles used to convey a powerful message to the same effect: God is dead, and the rest is silence. The moral wasteland depicted is that of a universe that has ceased to be informed by the life-giving power of a benign divine being. Thrown back on their own resources, humans are condemned to a sterile existence, devoid of love and warmth.

History was made by Michelangelo Antonioni and Federico Fellini, the leading Italian film-makers of the recent past, with artistically outstanding movies unmasking the aimless amorality of the overprivileged classes in contemporary Italy. *La Dolce Vita,* in Fellini's own words, was a

trip into anguish and despair, a report on Sodom and Gomorrah.

It follows the protagonist, played by Marcello Mastroianni, on a 3-hour odyssey through a man-made hell. Perverted sexuality graphically serves to underline the focal theme of alienation and despair, concluding the shattering revelation with an orgy replete with homosexuals, transvestites, and a grotesque striptease by an overendowed matron.

Fellini's *8½* is a psychoanalytic exploration of the dynamics that formed his personality. Sexuality is used as a means to trace his maturation. In a collage of facts and fantasy, sexual encounters lead him from inauthentic role-playing through crisis to an ultimate synthesis.

Like Fellini, Antonioni deals with the decadence of upper-middle-class society. Unlike Fellini, however, Antonioni is not a participant but a detached observer. His cerebral approach to the portrayal of desensualized sexuality gives his movies a surrealist quality. This quality is especially evident in *Blow-Up,* the account of one day in the life of a young fashion photographer, a day that turns out to be full of unsettling experiences. The movie, set in London, examines the restless, empty lives of its swinging pacesetters. The only discernible evidence of love in this movie is that of the male protagonist, played by David Hemmings, for his work. Sex is only a mechanical activity, a scanty diversion from life's boredom. His art, however, compensates for the inner void that cannot be filled by human interaction. During a photographic session with a half-nude model, the intensity of his concentration, expressed in his movements and short commands, seems to arouse the writhing girl to a sexual climax. Thereupon, he abruptly leaves, handing the camera over to an assistant. His act, in which the camera literally did the caressing, is completed.

In a number of American-English coproductions, the newly won freedom has allowed for a wider expansion of erotic themes. The bawdiness of *Tom Jones* (1963) was followed by artistically valuable movies that openly treat the subjects of homosexuality and promiscuity. Bernardo Bertolucci's *Last Tango in Paris* (1973) confirmed the general acceptance of sexuality as a means for expressing deeper underlying topics. As in all true works of art, nudity and sex are not incidental but integral to the theme of this film, which explores the role that sex plays in people's lives. Here modern Eros seems neither the creator nor the destroyer. It simply serves as a tool, sometimes to destroy and sometimes to comfort. In either case, a potentially beneficial force is being misused and sapped of its strength, leaving the human being locked in inner loneliness and despair.

A Clockwork Orange (1972) casts an even dimmer view into the future, when the destroyer will take over completely. As epitomized by the rape scene, it is a horrifying vision of unbridled violence combined with sex.

Recently, a distinctive turning away from the central theme of sexuality can be discerned. Such movies as *Midnight Cowboy* (1969), which focused on a relationship between two men, were followed by a series of films shifting the focus from sexual relationships to camaraderie, as in *Papillon* and *The Sting.*

The excessive use of sexuality in the sexploitation movies has blunted the senses of viewers and led to boredom, the product of all overexposure. *The Exorcist* answered the craving for ever-more-battering experiences. Capitalizing on the new obsession with parapsychology and the occult, it blended sexuality with demonology. Recently, a new genre of movies, revolving around the central theme of catastrophe *(Airport 75, Earthquake, The Towering Inferno),* have drawn large crowds. This phenomenon may be explained by the public's need for catharsis in a prevailing mood of doom and by its demand for stronger stimulation.

DANCE AND MUSIC

The 20th century spirit of disintegration and rebellion against restricting rules also made itself felt in dance and music, two closely related art forms.

Dance, which uses the movement of the human body as a means of expression is, by definition, the most sensual of all arts. The early courtly dances of the Renaissance and the baroque periods, however, tightly harnessed the sexual impulse. Their highly stylized and manneristic forms left little room for spontaneity. But when Isadora Duncan introduced the modern dance movement at the beginning of the 20th century, a major change occurred. Her primary concern was to allow the body to express itself freely, without being hampered by confining clothes or restricting rules. She encouraged a total abandonment to emotions through movement. The result was a virtual revival of pagan dances, with all their unrestrained sensuality.

Modern dance found many adherents and underwent certain modifications throughout the decades. As an art form, it never enjoyed the wide popularity of the other arts. The reason may lie in the fact that it is uniquely enjoyed by participation, rather than observation; since few people are artists, yet all respond to its sensuous appeal, it had to yield to social dancing, its popular branch.

As a spectator art, however, modern dance had a great impact on the trend of future entertainment. It played an important part in the movie spectaculars of the 1930's and 1940's, in which the influence of jazz and South American music inspired lavish and sexually suggestive dance scenes, only slightly toned down—sometimes even heightened—by the prudish measures taken to satisfy the censors.

The musical, an art form peculiar to America, was another area that was particularly suited to dance and that made extensive use of it. With increasing sexual liberation, not only has nudity become a common phenomenon on stage but choreographies have provided for more sensuous entertainment, including simulated sex acts.

The ballet, having thrown off some of its conventional shackles, has itself undergone considerable modifications. A performance of the Stuttgart Ballet Company described by Malkin (1974) would have been inconceivable a few years ago:

For 26 minutes the dancers flit and fit around each other, like a set of oiled and animated corkscrews inspired by the Kama Sutra. The two couples slide through a visual glissando of sexual exercises, yet so subtle in execution that the intimacies never shock.

In contrast to this highly eroticized ballet, social dancing has changed in the opposite direction. It has developed from the controlled intimacies of the Viennese waltz (1800) to the sensual movements inspired by Spanish and Mexican tunes and the intimate body-to-body dancing of the jazz age, only to reverse the trend completely in the 1960's and 1970's. Rock and roll dancers today do not touch but groove to the music in detached self-abandon.

Music, like dance, was one of the earliest forms of art. It has brightened human life since time immemorial—at work, at play, and in the pursuit of sex. Cave paintings, dating back at least 17,000 years, indicate the presence of musical instruments, as do the first reliefs found in Mesopotamia, the cradle of civilization. The design of musical instruments used in the fertility rites of primitive tribes is meant to symbolize the source of fertility as much as to produce a sound. The split drum, found in many areas of the world, is suggestive of the vulva, and it is played with a phallic drumstick. To dispel any doubts of intention, coital movements, gestures, and songs clearly explained the sexual symbolism.

Primitive music was purposely sexual, but music during the Middle Ages, like all other arts, became spiritualized as part of the religious ritual. The music was predominantly vocal. Around the beginning of the second millenium, secular music started to flourish again with the arrival of the troubadours (the word comes from *trobar,* to compose), who often accompanied their songs with the fiddle or the lute. Their tunes were simple, but the lyrics were appropriately sensuous.

A major breakthrough came with the discovery of the triad, a chord of three tones, and the subsequent development of modal harmony, which opened the door to more elaborate tunes around 1500. Composers began to write instrumental music for listening, not just for dancing. The madrigal was the love song par excellence of the Renaissance. Claudio Monteverdi (1567–1643), the last madrigalist, was also the first Italian operatic composer, starting a tradition that brought forth some of the greatest feasts of erotic music in Western culture.

It was the baroque period, however, that became the golden age of instrumental music. During this period music was probably at the pinnacle of its prestige and influence. Every cultivated person was thoroughly familiar with and enthralled by the works of a Johann Sebastian Bach (1685–1750), Antonio Vivaldi (1675–1741), and George Frederic Handel

(1685–1759). The diarist Samuel Pepys' comment on a concert he attended serves not only as a cultural document of his time but also as a reminder that even music at its highest and most abstract can kindle sensual feelings and associations. His entry reads:

That which pleased me beyond anything was the wind music . . . which is so sweet that it ravished me . . . just as I have formerly been when in love with my wife.

The great baroque composers celebrated mainly celestial bliss, but love as an earthly joy was praised by the classicists. They concentrated more on secular works than their predecessors. Wolfgang Amadeus Mozart (1756–1791) composed the music for several operas dealing with sexual love. The best known is probably *Don Giovanni,* which immortalizes the Don Juan theme. The overture to this work initiated the romantic movement in music by dramatizing the eternal battle between the sexes.

Ludwig von Beethoven (1770–1827) bridged the classical and the romantic styles. His early works were similar to those of Mozart and Haydn, but then, true to his tempestuous character, he responded with gusto to the romantic spirit. His music is marked by heightened drama, suspense, and brilliant climaxes reflecting his passionate nature. He remained unmarried, but he is reported to have been eternally infatuated with some woman or other.

Many of the romantics were inspired by tumultuous love affairs fraught with frustrations. The whole movement seemed to thrive in a climate of sexual tension. The German composer Richard Wagner (1813–1883), a great innovator of style, is considered a foremost representative of musical eroticism. His opera *Tristan and Isolde* (1857–1859) was called by MacDougald (1961):

a deliberately conceived, soul-moving apotheosis of carnal love.

The opera was inspired by Wagner's hopeless love for Mathilde Wesendonk, the wife of a rich friend and patron.

Wagner influenced the early work of Claude Debussy (1862–1918), but Debussy soon branched off into a more experimental and individual style. He introduced new techniques and effects with the aim of evoking clear images in the listener's mind. His *tonmalerei* produced pictures in sound, which led his compositions to be described as musical impressionism. His first work to bring him fame, the *Prélude à l'Après-midi d'un Faun* (Prelude to an Afternoon of a Faun) paints images of lovers and all kinds of real and imaginary creatures.

The new psychology, which made naturalism in painting and literature impossible, and the disillusionment that reached a climax after World War I first made themselves felt in the work of Gustav Mahler (1860–1911). He represents a link between the late romantic style and the revolutionary compositions of Arnold Schoenberg (1874–1951) and his followers. Mahler, as a contemporary of Freud, was greatly influenced by psychoanalysis. He was the first composer to be concerned with the dynamics of the unconscious and to incorporate their new awareness into his art.

What followed was Schoenberg's atonality and Igor Stravinsky's (1882–1971) polytonality, schools of musical expressionism characterized by highly dissonant sounds. Their aim was less to please the listener's ears than to convey the composer's subjective ideas. The result often had a deeply emotional effect.

Stravinsky participated in the contemporary outburst of musical primitivism, which shared with other forms of art a renewed interest in their ritualistic origins. His stylized fertility rite, *Le Sacré du Printemps* (The Rite of Spring), performed in Paris in 1913, was one of the most influential works in the history of music. It had all the ingredients of vehement barbaric ritualism: nature worship, tribal drums, a brute outbreak of elementary eroticism.

The age of electronics, which allows a profusion of styles to be exposed to an audience of unprecedented number, has also had an enormous impact on the development of musical tastes. Classical, jazz, rock, folk, country—all concurrent genres—are mutually influencing each other.

Jazz, the first major American contribution to art, was created by black musicians and had its origin in African rhythms. Its erotic roots are strong. The very name is derived from the Creole patois word *jass,* which is a sexual term for the Congo dances.

Rock music grew out of jazz. It reached an artistic pinnacle during the 1960's with the arrival of the Beatles. Combining great musical talent with lyrics that were tuned in with the prevailing antiwar sentiment and drug escapism, their influence reached beyond their own field. By wearing their hair a few inches longer than usual, they initiated the trend toward a unisex culture and influenced fashions for years to come. Many a staid and whiskered gentleman today may have forgotten that he owes his looks to four unconventional young men whose singing voices and outlandish appearance used to sweep multitudes of teenage girls off their feet.

Presently, hard rock, with its androgynous performers and undisguised lyrics, is most popular with young people. Alice Cooper, like many other successful rock idols, projects a strange transvestite image that draws big crowds. Cooper, in a sadomasochistic performance, brings the enthusiastic response of his audience to a peak with his frantic orgiastic song, *Dead Babies.* In his act, he suggestively rips off a doll's clothes, then tears it apart and flings the limbs to a hysterical audience. He accompanies this performance with a demented semiwhine that passes for singing.

The appeal of these hermaphroditic performers may lie in the fact that they pose little threat to a generation whose gender identity has been increasingly effaced by the vanishing differentiation of clear-cut male and female roles. Or they may be just a manifestation of the present craze for the bizarre and the macabre.

Art and Society

Today's art, diverse as it may be, has a common denominator: the glorification of unreason. The quality of the absurd is the symptom of a world that has lost its direction. As the existentialist psychiatrist R. D. Laing contends, to be well adjusted in this bedlam is a sign rather of insanity than of a healthy mind and soul. In this culture the fine line between sickness and mental health has been blurred.

The fact that it is often difficult to distinguish between the work of the insane and that of some acknowledged artists, even if one discounts the excesses of body art, gives support to Laing's claim. It follows that the relationship between certain personality patterns and creative genius is also difficult to establish. Even in periods of history when societies were relatively stable, outstanding artistic work has been done by persons ranging from the healthy to the severely pathological.

The new psychology, however, has made use of art in diagnosing and treating the emotionally disturbed, and some interesting insights have been gained in the process. It has been commonly observed that some acutely psychotic patients exhibit a burst of creative activity, often concretely or symbolically revealing their problem areas. Frequently, their art is blatantly erotic. As a rule, the patients' creativity subsides along with the psychotic episode. This observation seems to confirm the idea that the creative impulse is innately human but that the adjustment to everyday life seems to exact the price of suppression and, consequently, of mediocrity.

In this context it may be worthwhile to mention that many outstanding artists were reputedly suffering from central nervous system syphilis. However, it cannot be determined to which degree this illness contributed to or influenced their artistic creation. Equally uncertain is the matter of the relationship between homosexuality and creative talent. Many artists were or are believed to have been homosexuals—Leonardo da Vinci, Michelangelo, Raphael, Blake, Wilde, Tschaikowski, Gide, Genet, Cocteau, not to mention the Greeks of the golden age and many Roman artists. There is no evidence that homosexuality predisposes to artistic creativity, as maintained by some, nor that homosexuality is an obstacle to artistic creativity.

Another question that has been the subject of debate for many years is the striking dearth of great women artists. There is no prominent female composer, painter, sculptor, or architect known in history. It stands to reason that the age-old suppression of women is to blame for this condition. This view is supported by the fact that art forms considered to be more feminine have produced some outstanding female representatives—Sappho, Marie de France, George Sand, Jane Austen, the Brontë sisters, Virginia Woolf, and Simone de Beauvoir, to name a few in the field of literature. Women have also made extraordinary contributions to the interpretive arts, such as dance, drama, and music.

Obviously, society so far has not allowed women to unfold their creative potentials to the same degree as men. The relationship between the artist and society is a complex one and cannot easily be pinpointed, although the event of certain changes throughout the centuries can be deduced. At any rate, there is little doubt that the creative genius is almost irreconcilable with conformity. The artist is isolated by virtue of his unique gifts, and, being exceptionally sensitive, he is also more keenly aware of his intrinsic separateness than is the average person.

Although the explicit treatment of the theme of alienation is a fairly recent phenomenon, there is evidence that ever since history was first recorded, alienation has been an aspect of the artist's life. Sophocles in his play *Philoctetes* (409 B.C.) deals with what has been interpreted by scholars and artists as a parable of human character. Specifically, Philoctetes has been seen as the archetype of the artist and the peculiar position he holds in society.

Philoctetes, a member of the Greek campaign to Troy, receives from the demigod Heracles a bow that never misses its target. On the way to Troy, the Greeks stop off at the island of Chrysè to sacrifice to the local deity. Philoctetes, approaching the shrine first, is bitten in the foot by a snake. As a result, he develops a festering wound that is so malodorous and so painful that his companions cannot bear to have him around and to listen to his cries and curses. They leave him on the island of Lemnos and sail to Troy without him. Philoctetes languishes in exile for 10 years, seething with rage, his infection never healing. The Greeks are finally told by a soothsayer that they can conquer the city only with the help of Philoctetes and his bow. Odysseus thereupon devises a scheme to trick him into handing over the magic tool. The plan miscarries, however, because Neoptolemus, Achilles' son, who was to be used as bait, refuses to participate in treach-

ery. Instead, the boy persuades Philoctetes to set his grievances aside and to come to his people's aid. As a result, Philoctetes' wound is healed and the Greek campaign is saved.

The bow and the wound have come to be regarded as symbols of the artist's divine gift and of his unique knowledge gained through suffering. The power of insight is the result of a tortured spirit, a festering disease. The artist is the victim not only of this inner wound but, all too often, of society's misunderstanding and rejection. Yet his fellow human beings need him. It is through art and religion that human beings have the opportunity to break the fetters of a purely earthly existence—hence, the sacrificial roots of Philoctetes' infliction.

What finally bridges the abyss between the artist and society, as illustrated in this play, is the common bond of essential humanity established by the divine qualities of love and truth. Neoptolemus' compassion for the sick outcast and his refusal to betray him effected a miracle that could not have been accomplished by an army of sly and cunning Odysseuses. Eros the creator is ubiquitous, but it appears in protean disguises. Recognizing and embracing it is a creative act in itself.

Conclusion

Sex and art are human ways of reaching for immortality. Siring and giving birth to children ensure continuation, and so does a work of art in the mind of posterity. Shakespeare assured the friend to whom he dedicated his sonnets that the tyrant Time and even inexorable Death would have no power over him because he would live on in the poet's work:

But were some child of yours alive that time,
You should live twice—in it and in my rhyme.

Both art and sex also offer humans a glimpse of eternity here on earth. Many artists have acknowledged this mystical dimension. To them, art is an act of devotion, be it religious or sensual. Henri Matisse (1869–1954), the French postimpressionist, declared that his paintings were inspired by a religious feeling. *(C'est toujours un sentiment religieux qui m'a poussé vers l'art.)* Artur

Rubinstein (1886–   ) confessed to the kinship of artistic and sexual experience. To him, playing the piano is making love. Renoir is reported to have said, *Je peins avec ma queue.* (I paint with my penis.)

Art is communication, for it relates the artist's innermost feelings and personal vision of the world. It strives for communion. So does sex. Having intercourse with another human being is an attempt to break through one's intrinsic loneliness.

Besides being a means of communication in itself, art has assisted humans in the pursuit of sex since the dawn of history. The urge to ornament oneself springs from the desire to charm a sexual partner.

This trend can be traced all the way to primitive people and the animal world. The work of fashion designers serves the same purpose as the brilliant plumage of some birds and the multicolored furs of many animals. Often, these designers borrow their materials from feathered friends and furry beasts. And the nightingale's mating call is comparable to the love songs of the troubadours. The mosaics of stones and other bright objects arranged by bowerbirds to attract females also attest to an instinctive drive in animals that is akin to that in humans. Witness the caveman's pathetic venuses, who are bedecked with an array of necklaces. These are early signs of the human need to embellish. They are the ancestors of representative art.

Human esthetics, the very concept of beauty, is based on the element of attraction, a subjective quality that may explain its changeability throughout the ages. Another dimension to the human creative impulse is the pervasive need for beauty, pure and simple—the desire to escape one's humdrum existence by flights of the imagination. Art is the highest form of play, of make-believe. The fleeting moments of the esthetic experience paradoxically reveal a higher truth than reality. They purge life of the ugly and the ordinary. Art is a form of recreation, a pleasurable activity that fortifies and prepares a person for the daily toil. Sex obviously fulfills the same need.

Within this general framework, art serves many psychological functions, the dynamics of which are intimately related to the artist's personality and environment.

It lies in the nature of all civilization to curtail or control the free expression of sexuality. This repression may, paradoxically, have beneficial effects on artistic creativity. Freud held the view that the basis of culture lies in the ability of people to forgo immediate gratification, sexual and otherwise, in favor of time and circumstances more conducive to lasting benefit.

This theory points to a correlation between the relative permissiveness of a culture and its creative output. Kavolis (1971) made a study comparing certain periods that were characterized by great creativity with the prevailing sexual customs of the time. He came to the conclusion that severe sexual repression, as at the beginning of Christianity in Rome, has never produced outstanding works of art. Conversely, the golden age of Greece and the Renaissance, eras of life-affirming attitudes and sexual freedom, reached artistic heights. But the most licentious cultures are not noted for their creativity.

Art apparently springs from a tension, a favorable climate not present in a totally unrestrained culture. But the polarity generated in a repressive society seems to have the same leveling effect.

Freud developed a psychological theory based on the assumption that artistic motivation is a function of repressed sexual impulses. According to this principle, art is the product of psychological defense mechanisms, such as sublimation, substitution, repression, and reaction formation. This is undoubtedly true in many cases. But, unless an artist can be analyzed in person, his psychodynamics are, at best, a matter of speculation based on the fragmentary information of unreliable sources.

There is also ample evidence that not all art is a product of repressed sexual impulses. Picasso's life of many loves is the most prominent exception to the rule. Artistic creativity has in many instances directly gratified erotic desires, allowing the artist, as well as the spectator or reader, to indulge in sensory delights. Creativity has served as a catharsis for poets, writers, and painters who have dealt extensively with sexual topics in a number of ways. Humorous, poetic, and realistic accounts of personal experiences and fantasies have all helped release intensive inner conflicts and emotions.

Erotic imagery has been used by artists in all fields to express their view of external reality as well. Throughout the ages deadly shafts have been directed at social institutions and certain segments of society in the guise of blatantly erotic material. Sexuality in this case fulfills the double purpose of attracting the audience's attention and hiding the real target of the attack.

In the course of time, an incredible amount of erotic art by reputable artists of acknowledged genius has been suppressed and hidden away. Many painters have depicted the genitalia or the act of copulation in their sketches and in privately held paintings. The vaults of most museums in the world, notably the Vatican, contain erotica that prudery has banished from the eyes of the world.

It is not surprising that cultural repression of sexuality has called for censorship, which made a definition of pornography necessary. Nobody has yet succeeded in drawing that filament between erotic art and the lascivious. The reason lies not only in the constant changes of sexual mores and attitudes but also in the subjectivity of the individual esthetic experience. Pornography is as elusive a concept as art itself, but the term would become meaningless at the moment of total disclosure. If all the expurgated texts were published, all the dark cellars opened, and all the supposedly pornographic material out in the open, it would be up to each person to decide and choose. Some would respond as they do to art. Others would soon return to their favorite magazine stand on 42nd Street.

Freud started a trend to examine works of art with the tool of psychoanalytic theory. The best papers of this kind have been assembled by Phillips (1957). Fascinating as these studies may be, they are based on conjecture and are written from a rather limited perspective. It should also be kept in mind that so-called psychoanalysis of a work of art is a far cry from understanding it in its totality and hardly contributes to the enjoyment of it. Diagnosing Hamlet's oedipal fixation only obscures the deeper existential meaning of this most enigmatic of all Shakespearean plays.

An examination of the artist's life can throw revealing light on his work, but a work of art always speaks for itself and has a life of its own. The odyssey through a long line of monuments testifies to man's genius and although one cannot come face to face with the creators, one stands in solemn wonder of their creations.

REFERENCES

Aratow, P. *100 Years of Erotica: A Photographic Portfolio of Mainstream American Subculture, 1845–1945.* Straight Arrow Books, San Francisco, 1973.

Aristophanes. *Lysistrata.* New American Library, New York, 1970.

*Atkins, J. *Sex in Literature.* Grove Press, New York, 1972.

Besidine, M. Michelangelo: The homosexual element in the life and work. Med. Aspects Hum. Sex., *4:* 127, 1970.

Bleuel, H. P. *Sex and Society in Nazi Germany.* Bantam Books, New York, 1973.

Brusendorff, O., and Henningson, P. *A History of Eroticism.* Lyle Stuart, New York, 1961–1970.

Burdick, J. *Theater.* Newsweek Books, New York, 1974.

Chute, N. *Shakespeare of London.* Dutton, New York, 1949.

Cole, W. C. *Sex and Love in the Bible.* Association Press, New York, 1959.

DeBecker, R. *The Other Face of Love.* Bell, New York, 1969.

Edwardes, A. *Erotica Judica: A Sexual History of the Jews.* Julian Press, New York, 1967.

Elisoforn, E., and Watts, A. *Erotic Spirituality.* Macmillan, New York, 1971.

Ellis, A. Art and sex. In *Encyclopedia of Sex,* A. Ellis and A. Abarbanel, editors, p. 161. Jason Aronson, New York, 1973.

Fitch, R. E. *The Decline and Fall of Sex.* Greenwood, New York, 1973.

Foster, J. H. *Sex Variant Women in Literature.* Bantam Press, New York, 1956.

Franz, D. O. Lewd priapans and Renaissance pornography. Studies Eng. Lit., 1500–1800, *12:* 157, 1972.

Freud, S. *Introductory Lectures on Psychoanalysis.* G. Allen & Unwin, London, 1922.

Freud, S. *Collected Papers.* Basic Books, New York, 1959.

Garde, N. I. *Jonathan to Gide; The Homosexual in Literature.* Vantage Press, New York, 1964.

Geduld, H. M. A note on eroticism in the movies. Film J., *2:* 28, 1972.

Goddard, H. C. *The Meaning of Shakespeare,* 2 vols. Phoenix Books, Chicago, 1968.

Grunfeld, F. V. *Music.* Newsweek Books, New York, 1974.

Hess, T. B., and Baker, E. C. *Art and Sexual Politics.* Collier Books, New York, 1971.

Hughes, R. The Decline and Fall of the Avant-Garde. Time, *100:* 111, Dec. 18, 1972.

Hunninghuer, B. *The Origin of the Theater.* Hill & Wang, New York, 1966.

Kahmen, V. *Erotic Art Today.* New York Graphic Society, Greenwich, Conn., 1972.

Katchadourian, H. A., and Lunde, D. T. *Fundamentals of Human Sexuality.* Holt, Rinehart & Winston, New York, 1972.

Kavolis, V. Sex norms, emotionality and artistic creativity. Psychoanal. Rev., *58:* 22, 1971.

Kiell, N. *Psychosexuality in Literature.* International Universities Press, New York, 1973.

*Klaf, F. S., and Hurwood, B. J. *A Psychiatrist Looks at Erotica.* Ace Books, New York, 1964.

Kris, E. *Psychoanalytic Explorations in Art.* International Universities Press, New York, 1952.

*Kronhausen, P., and Kronhausen, E. *Erotic Art,* 2 vols. Grove Press, New York, 1968 and 1970.

Kronhausen, P., and Kronhausen, E. *Pornography and the Law.* Ballantine Books, New York, 1959.

Lacey, P. *The History of the Nude in Photography.* Bantam Books, New York, 1964.

Laemmel, R. *Der Moderne Tanz (Modern Dance).* Ostergaard, Berlin, 1928.

Legman, G. A. *The Horn Book: Studies in Erotic Folklore and Bibliography.* New York University Books, New Hyde Park, N.Y., 1966.

Leish, K. W. *Cinema.* Newsweek Books, New York, 1974.

*Lewinsohn, R. *A History of Sexual Customs.* Bell, New York, 1958.

Loftus, J. Sex in the art of Toulouse-Lautrec. Med. Aspects Hum. Sex., *6:* 64, 1972.

MacDougald, D. *Music and Sex.* In *Encyclopedia Of Sexual Behavior,* A. Ellis and A. Abarbanel, editors, p. 746. Jason Aronson, New York, 1973.

Malfetti, J. L., and Fidlitz, E. *Perspectives on Sexuality.* Holt Rinehart & Winston, New York, 1972.

Malkin, L. *New Start in Stuttgart.* Time, *103:* 92, June 17, 1974.

Marcus, S. *The Other Victorians: A Study of Sexuality and Pornography in Mid-19th Century England.* Basic Books, New York, 1966.

Martin, G. Van Gogh: A study in torment. Med. Aspects Hum. Sex., *7:* 34, 1973.

Melville, R. *Erotic Art of the West.* Putnam, New York, 1973.

Miller, A. On Social Plays: Introduction to *"A View from the Bridge".* Viking Press, New York, 1955.

Pacion, S. J. Leonardo da Vinci: A psychosexual enigma. Med. Aspects Hum. Sex., *5:* 35, 1971.

Partridge, E. *Shakespeare's Bawdy.* Dutton, New York, 1969.

Phillips, W. editor. *Art and Psychoanalysis.* Criterion Books, New York, 1957.

*Putnam, S. Literature and love. In *Encyclopedia Sexualis,* V. Robinson. editor, p. 451. Dingwall Rock, New York, 1936.

Rawson, P. *Primitive Erotic Art.* Putnam, New York, 1973.

Rawson, P. *Erotic Art of the East.* Putnam, New York, 1968.

Riess, K. *Erotica! Erotica! Das Buch der Verbotenen Buecher.* Hoffman & Campe, Hamburg, 1967.

Rotsler, W. *Contemporary Erotic Cinema.* Ballantine Books, New York, 1973.

*Schiff, G. Picasso's Suite 347: Or painting as an act of love. In *Woman as Sex Object,* T. B. Hess and L. Nochlin, editors, p. 239. Newsweek Books, New York, 1972.

Sterba, R. The problem of art in Freud's writings. Psychoanal. Q., *9:* 256, 1940.

Trilling, L. Art and neurosis. In *Art and Psychoanalysis,* W. Phillips, editor, p. 502 Criterion Books, New York, 1957.

Van Dowski, L. *Genie und Eros (Genius and Eros).* Delphi, Bern, 1947.

Vatsyayna. *Kama Sutra: The Classic Hindu Treatise on Love and Social Conduct.* Dutton, New York, 1962.

Wilson, A. *Emile Zola.* Morrow, New York, 1952.

Winick, C. Sex and dancing. Med. Aspects Hum. Sex., *4:* 122, 1970.

Winick, C. Popular music and sex. Med. Aspects Hum. Sex., *4:* 148, 1970.

Winick, C. The beige epoche: Depolarization of sex roles in America. Med. Aspects Hum. Sex., *3:* 69, 1969.

Young, W. H. *Eros Denied: Sex in Western Society.* Grove Press, New York, 1964.

chapter 19 Sex and the Law

ROBERT L. SADOFF, M.D.

Introduction

A number of areas dealing with human sexuality are covered by legal regulations. This section will discuss the legal and psychological aspects of sex offenses, homosexuality, prostitution, rape, castration, sterilization, bigamy, illegitimacy, artificial insemination, and abortion.

The Sex Offender

As defined by the law, the sex offender is that individual who commits a crime involving expression of sexual urges. These traditionally include rape, indecent assault, incest, assault with intent to commit sodomy, sodomy, assault with intent to ravish or rape, indecent exposure, child molestation, and homosexuality. A number of sexual deviations are not considered sex offenses, including transvestitism, fetishism, and coprophilia. These are not included as offenses unless other offenses such as burglary or larceny are involved in obtaining the object of the fetish or for cross-dressing. Other crimes that may have sexual connotation are: burglary, car theft, carrying a concealed deadly weapon such as a knife or a gun, shoplifting, and excessive fire setting.

CLASSIFICATION OF SEX OFFENDERS

The law has tended to group all individuals committing crimes with sexual connotation into a class of criminals called "sex offenders" or "sexual psychopaths." Since 1938, a number of states have passed the so-called sexual psychopath statutes, aimed at the protection of society and the treatment of the offender. Most of these laws impose indeterminate sentences on the individual and provide for treatment or rehabilitation within a hospital or prison. Placing all these individuals into a single classification in order to provide treatment is fallacious and fraught with difficulty. All sex offenders are not alike and may have various emotional disturbances ranging from a personality problem to gross psychotic illness or organic brain disease. A helpful classification system has been suggested by Ellis and Brancale (1956):

1. Normal sex offenders, who are not sexual deviates but who commit illegal sex acts.

2. Sex deviates who commit illegal sex acts but who are sufficiently stable and well integrated to maintain their deviational patterns without usually getting into official difficulty.

3. Sexually and psychiatrically deviated offenders who commit illegal sex acts and who are so emotionally disturbed and mentally impaired that they frequently come to official attention.

4. Psychiatrically deviated but sexually nondeviated offenders who commit illicit sex acts because of their general rather than their sexual disturbances, and who are often officially apprehended.

MYTHS ABOUT SEX OFFENSES

Many of the difficulties of handling sex offenders arise from the myths that people have about sexual behavior and sex offenses. Tappan (1955) lists 11 popular myths concerning sex offenders, including the feeling that sex offenders are usually recidivists, that the minor sex offender, if unchecked, will progress to more serious types of crime, that it is possible to predict the danger of serious crimes by sexual deviates, that sexual psychopathy or sexual deviation is a clinical entity, and that reasonably effective treatment methods to cure sexual offenders are known and employed.

Psychiatry has aided in preserving the myths that have led to harsh and unusual treatment of the sex offender. Krafft-Ebing (1922), Kraepelin, and other leading psychiatrists of the late 19th and early 20th centuries considered sexual perversion essentially a form of degeneracy caused by hereditary taint and often associated with physical stigmata of degeneracy. As recently as 1951, a California judge denied the emotional component to sexual deviation and said that there is no treatment for these harmful tendencies. Psychiatrists must educate the law on the variable diagnoses and difficulties of sex offenders and must recommend individual treatment for each kind of offense, rather than allow all "sex offenders" to be lumped together. For example, pedophiles may be psychotic or sociopathic, and each offender needs to be treated differently, even though all have engaged in pedophilic behavior.

The most recidivistic of all sex offenses is exhibitionism and that offense usually does not progress to more serious sexual crimes. The offender has a particular psychodynamic conflict that needs to be resolved; when it is acted on, it may lead to arrest. Despite the relatively high recidivism rate for exhibitionism as compared to other sexual offenses, the general recidivism rate of all sex offenses is low compared to other crimes.

Homosexuality

Homosexual behavior is illegal in all states except one—Illinois—where homosexual behavior between consenting adults is decriminalized. The Wolfenden Report (1964) also recommends decriminalizing homosexual acts by consenting adults. Historically, homosexuality has been practiced in almost every culture and has been prohibited in most. Earlier, the prohibition was related to the inability to procreate by this method and the fear of extinction of the species if homosexual

behavior became excessive without heterosexual contact. Today, this is no longer the fear; rather, the concern is with how such behavior will influence the adolescent's developing sexual identity. Recently, noted sex researcher William Masters stated very clearly that homosexual behavior is not necessarily an abnormal expression of the human sexual urge.

Laws remain, however, to inhibit or prohibit homosexual behavior, and vice squads in the police departments are active in rooting out homosexuals in the community. It is not true that there is greater violence in homosexual relationships or homosexual triangles than there is in heterosexual triangles. The etiology of homosexuality remains unknown and many hypotheses and theories have been propounded to explain its occurrence. Recently, the gay activist movement has emerged from underground to express its feelings and to demand acceptance. Psychiatrists have been criticized for continuing to call homosexuality a deviation rather than an alternation of sexual functioning. Homosexuals function in every phase of life, including psychiatry and other professions. In the military, homosexual behavior is prohibited ostensibly because of the fear of exposure and blackmail. There is a good deal of pressure to liberalize the law and to decriminalize homosexual behavior among consenting adults. However, legal change is slow in coming. One of the problems is that because of the stigma traditionally attached to homosexuality lawmakers are reluctant to sponsor bills for fear of being labeled homosexual.

The danger of homosexual behavior exists in the forced situations between adults and also in adults' enticing children or adolescents to perform homosexual acts. The forced relationships and the relationships with youngsters continue to be prohibited in all jurisdictions. The penalties for homosexual behavior appear to be excessively harsh, and the methods of arresting often seem underhanded, including entrapment in washrooms of bus stations and train depots by members of vice squads.

Some homosexuals prefer to dress "in drag," or in women's clothes, and may thus be accused of "disturbing the peace" or being "nuisances." They may be harrassed for their transvestite behavior. In some municipalities on certain occasions, transvestite homosexuals are encouraged to appear in public as a means of entertainment without harrassment.

Prostitution

Prostitution is defined as sexual activity for pay. A commercial venture, it includes not only sexual intercourse but all forms of sexual encounter, homosexual or heterosexual. This discussion will be limited to the heterosexual prostitute. The prostitute has been studied primarily from a sociological and legal point of view. Some researchers have described the prostitute as having sexual problems that can be masked or hidden within her profession. Gagnon and Simon (1967) present a number of instances in which the prostitute feels that she is different from others and has problems not encountered by the "straight" woman. Many prostitutes prefer sexual relations with women and confine their sexual life with men to the commercial enterprise.

Although many prostitutes have serious sexual and social difficulties, including frigidity and hostility toward men, some appear to engage in prostitution primarily for economic reasons. Groups of middle-class, suburban housewives have been known to maintain flourishing prostitution rings, presumably to add to their families' income, although other motivations may also have been present.

KINDS OF PROSTITUTES

There are two principal types of prostitutes.

1. The street prostitute abounds in large cities, where men are accosted on the street. Many of these women have difficulties with the law and are frequently arrested. Others contract venereal diseases which they pass on to subsequent customers. There is no regulation of these prostitutes.

2. The private prostitute is contracted by a middleman or a pimp who sets up private arrangements with women in their own apartments. Other prostitutes working privately are on their own and make their own arrange-

ments with repeat customers. Some have very elaborate routines designed for the tired businessman or executive.

REGULATION OF PROSTITUTION

Prostitution has always existed in almost every culture and locale, and it is quite likely that there will always be a market for this service. It has been encouraged in some societies on religious grounds and has also been encouraged in wartime to help the morale of the soldiers.

Some psychiatrists find prostitution a therapeutic tool for a number of their patients who have sexual inhibitions and occasionally refer patients to prostitutes who have high sensitivity for men with sexual difficulties.

In many municipalities in this country, prostitution was allowed until recently. One municipality in Nevada openly supports prostitution and is proud of the medical attention it gives its tourist attractions.

However, in most communities in the United States, prostitution is outlawed and police departments have vice squads whose job is to round up the prostitutes and get them off the streets. New York City has recently run into a difficult problem with aggressive street prostitutes who work in groups and sometimes attack potential customers and rob them. England has attempted to regulate prostitution after the Wolfenden Report indicated that discreet prostitution was tolerable but open lewdness on the street was not to be accepted or tolerated. Regulating prostitution with medical control appears to have social merit since the criminal laws against prostitution are relatively ineffective in discouraging this behavior.

Prostitution continues to thrive in the large cities of most countries of the world. The recommendations of the Wolfenden Report appear to be most appropriate and significant. Prostitution should be regulated and controlled by the government. Unregulated prostitution, which is quite common, may lead to difficult social problems, including venereal disease and increased indication for therapeutic abortion. It may add to the welfare problem as well as to the number of criminals in the society. Violence is not unknown among prostitutes, their pimps, and their customers. Regulation of prostitution will have social benefits, including therapeutic advantages for patients with sexual inhibitions. Many will not go to an illegal or street prostitute but would under a regulated system.

Rape

Rape may be defined as sexual intercourse by use of force, fear or fraud between individuals of the same sex or the opposite sex.

HOMOSEXUAL RAPE

This occurs primarily in closed institutions such as prisons or maximum security hospitals. Homosexual rape is more frequent among men and usually denotes a hostile, aggressive attitude rather than a sexual one. The rapist in these cases often does not see himself as a homosexual but sees the victim as a punk, or passive homosexual. The one who is raped often feels that he has been ruined and fears that he may become homosexual because of being attacked. Mostly, however, these attacks have little to do with homosexuality; the sexual behavior is used as a vehicle for the expression of violence.

HETEROSEXUAL RAPE

Rape has been called the easiest crime to accuse or charge and the most difficult to prove. Rape is defined in the law as penetration of the penis beyond the introitus. Whether ejaculation occurs is irrelevant. By definition, a man who cannot have an erection is unable to commit rape. Oral sex is not rape; neither are other indecent touchings or assaults. In the law, rape is seen as a very serious offense and when rapes are reported with great frequency legislatures are usually stimulated to provide more severe penalties. In some states, rape may be punishable by death, especially in cases of miscegenous rape. In others, rape is punishable by much less severe penalties, such as probation or a short term in prison. Some jurisdictions have a classification called aggravated rape, which includes rape by force with a deadly weapon or harm or assault in addition to rape.

STATUTORY RAPE

Statutory rape refers to the unlawful sexual intercourse between a male over the age of 16 and a female under the age of consent, which varies from 14 to 21, depending on the jurisdiction. This means that if a male of 18 has intercourse with a girl of 15 and the intercourse is consensual, the man may still be held for statutory rape if the girl or her parents wish to press charges. This type of rape is not seen as a deviation, except when the age discrepancy is excessive, in which case the deviation is called pedophilia. (This definition requires that the age discrepancy be in excess of 10 years or that the female be 12 or under.) Ploscowe (1962) states that 82 per cent of all rape convictions in a 10-year period in New York City were for statutory rape.

PROSECUTING RAPE CASES

One of the great difficulties in prosecuting rape is the cooperation of the victim, who has to be examined by a physician to prove that there has been penetration, or evidence of semen at the time of her complaint, or evidence of bruises or other physical damage as a result of the assault. Often, the victim encounters negative attitudes by police and other examiners, who question whether she "enjoyed it" and test to see whether or not she succumbed to temptation or was actually forced into a sexual act. J. J. Peters has been studying the effect of rape on the victim at Philadelphia General Hospital and is developing a set of objective criteria for evidence of rape and credibility of the victim.

NATURE OF THE RAPIST

Usually, the rapist is a one-timer, using poor judgment or forcing the issue under the influence of alcohol or drugs. At other times, he is a repetitive, aggressive individual who has a pattern of reaction that is uncontrollable for him. The psychodynamics of the rapist may involve a fusion of the aggressive and sexual drives that results in an act that is both hostile and sexual. In rare circumstances, prolonged patterns of aggressive rapes in one community attributable to one disturbed individual are noted. Equally rare are the lust murderers, those who rape and then kill their victims. A typical lust murder is the case of the deviant who seeks out a prostitute in order to kill her to prove that she is evil and he is the servant of goodness and morality.

Women are rarely arrested for rape, but a woman may be an accessory to rape by bringing unsuspecting victims for her mate to attack. Other women have actually held the victim down while a boyfriend rapes her.

Castration

In some places in the world, sex offenders of serious aggressive tendencies are castrated in order to allow them to remain free from incarceration for long periods of time. At the Herstedvester Clinic in Denmark, rapists and other sex offenders have been castrated by X-ray or by surgery in order to allow them to return to the community without danger to others. Occasionally, antitestosterone is used to effect a similar change.

Recently, an experiment was considered in Michigan to remove the amygdaloid nucleus of violent sex offenders in order to render them less dangerous. Because of legal rights considerations, that research has been challenged in the courts. From the standpoint of the sex offender himself, many would prefer to be castrated than to be locked up for the rest of their lives as some of the sex offender laws have mandated. However, the American Civil Liberties Union and other civil rights groups have questioned whether it is appropriate for these men to have to make such a choice and whether their freedom to give informed consent to the procedure is abrogated by undue coercion by virtue of their indefinite or indeterminate sentence.

Sterilization

Sterilization procedures are means of rendering an individual incapable of reproduction. In the male, the sterilization procedure is usually accomplished by vasectomy, a ligation of the vas deferens, a relatively easily performed operation that can be done in the physician's office and is frequently done in countries with high birth rates, such as India. For the female, the sterilization procedure is a tubal ligation, a ligation of her fallopian tubes. This is often done at the time of a therapeutic abortion or after the birth of an unexpected child.

VOLUNTARY STERILIZATION

About 100,000 women are said to submit annually to voluntary sterilization, primarily as a means of permanent contraception. Some states use legal formulae to determine whether such a procedure should be allowed. In one state, the formula is a multiplication of the woman's age by the number of her children; if that number is 100 or greater, she may have the procedure. Sterilizing an unwed woman occasionally presents problems in the event that she marries and her husband wishes to have children. The husband-to-be must be informed that the woman is sterile before he marries her, and he must do so with the understanding that there will be no children. If he is not informed, he may file for annulment on the basis of fraud or concealment of essential information.

In the event of a failure of the sterilization procedure and a resultant pregnancy, there may be a law suit against the physician who performed the procedure unless he has carefully advised the couple that there is not a 100 per cent guarantee that there is a very minimal risk or chance of becoming pregnant again even with the procedure intact. Voluntary sterilization produces relatively few legal ramifications. Among men, about 750,000 vasectomies are performed each year.

EUGENIC STERILIZATION

Eugenic sterilization—the sterilization of people in order to prevent certain characteristics from being passed on to offspring—presents a number of legal difficulties. Ordinarily, this procedure is designed for mentally retarded females in order to allow them to live outside of institutions without procreating mentally retarded children. Schizophrenic women are also encouraged to have sterilization to keep from producing schizophrenic children. As of 1970, the estimated total number of sterilizations for eugenic purposes has been more than 65,000. More than half were performed on the mentally deficient and about 40 per cent on the mentally ill. More than 2,000 others were performed for a number of other reasons, including epilepsy.

The classic case in eugenic sterilization is *Buck v. Bell* (1927), which upholds the statute for compulsory sterilization. Larrie Buck was a feebleminded daughter of a feebleminded mother and the mother of an illegitimate feebleminded child. She was connected to the State Colony for Epileptics and Feebleminded in Virginia. At age 18 in 1924, she was ordered by the court to have a salpingectomy for sterilization. The Supreme Court of the United States upheld the judgment of the lower court with the following reasoning:

"It is better for all the world, instead of waiting to execute degenerate offspring for crime, or to let them starve for their imbecility, society can prevent those who are manifestly unfit from continuing their kind. The principle that sustains compulsory vaccination is broad enough to cover cutting the fallopian tubes."

Many new statutes have been written since that decision, some of which have been found unconstitutional. Included in these statutes are provisions for sterilization of hereditary criminals, sex offenders, and syphilitics, as well as the mentally retarded and epileptic. The American Civil Liberties Union and other human rights groups have been challenging the legality and ethical considerations of such sterilization procedures.

Bigamy

Bigamy is the condition of having two spouses; having more than two spouses is called polygamy. A woman who has more than one husband is engaged in polyandry. A man who has more than one wife is polygynous. The Mormons were, until recently, polygamists, and the rulers of some Middle Eastern cultures historically had harems of wives. Bigamy has been outlawed in the United States; marriage is not only a personal commitment but also a legal commitment in this society. The complexity of society and the intimate relationship between husband and wife prohibit the taking of more than one spouse at a time. Inheritance problems, legal structural contracts, and other complexities of the contract of marriage are significant in maintaining a monogamous society.

In some cultures and some jurisdictions, common law marriage is recognized without benefit of license or clergy. If two people of opposite sex present themselves as married, and particularly if they raise a family, they may be assumed to have the same rights and

liabilities as legally married people, especially when questions of inheritance or distribution of money arise. In some areas, the cost of obtaining a divorce is prohibitive and people may separate without obtaining a valid divorce certificate. The understanding is that they are divorced or separated and free to find other mates. Occasionally, a man will marry another woman before he has achieved a valid divorce from his first wife and does not mention his previous marriage to anyone. Under the law, the second marriage is invalid, null and void, if it is contested.

Another type of "unintentional" bigamy is the case of a man who falls into a fugue state from a neurotic dissociative reaction and leaves his home and family to seek a new life. He may be unaware that he has been previously married and may take a second wife and raise a family with her. If it is discovered subsequently that he has a first wife and children living, the second marriage is null and void. However, he may not be charged with deliberate bigamy, which is a misdemeanor, because it may be shown that his mental illness—that is, his fugue state or dissociative reaction—led to a loss of memory for which he cannot be held consciously responsible.

Illegitimacy

The term "illegitimacy" refers to both parents and children. A mother is not usually referred to as an illegitimate mother because she bears the child and is the natural parent. However, the natural father who is not legally married to the mother of the child is called the illegitimate father. The child is referred to as an illegitimate child, born out of wedlock. Until recently, the plight of the illegitimate child has been a serious one in which he had no legal rights and was an unfortunate individual within the law. He could not inherit from his father nor could he take his father's name.

The law, in its attempt to legitimize as many children as possible, has liberalized its formerly stringent views on illegitimate relationships. Any child born to a married woman was considered legitimate and considered to be the offspring of the woman's husband, whether it was medically possible or not for the husband to have fathered the child.

Thus, it is the unwed mother that is of concern here. Ordinarily, the mother of the child had the right and the option to keep the child or give it out for foster care. The illegitimate father was never consulted, nor did he have any rights in this regard. In a recent case, the Supreme Court of Illinois declared that the illegitimate father had special rights to his natural child, as did the child have rights to his natural father. The rights of children, in many respects, are beginning to be observed and considered and legal representation is given to the child in child custody battles, child battering cases, and tort actions involving the child as plaintiff.

New York State has recently amended its statute involving inheritance by the illegitimate child by the following rules:

1. An illegitimate child is the legitimate child of his mother so that he and his issue inherit from his mother and from his maternal kindred.

2. An illegitimate child is the legitimate child of his father so that he and his issue inherit from his father if a court of competent jurisdiction shall have found the decedent to be the father of such child it shall have made an order of filiation declaring paternity in a proceeding instituted during the pregnancy of the mother or within 2 years from the birth of the child.

Artificial Insemination

Artificial insemination is the injection of viable sperm into the vagina of the female in order to induce a pregnancy. This is done by artificial means and not through the natural manner of penovaginal coitus. The sperm may be from a neutral donor or may be the woman's husband's sperm, condensed to make it more viable. In some cases, the donor's and the husband's sperm are mixed, so as to have open the question of biological paternity.

Many couples in which the male is infertile and the wife normally fertile find artificial insemination a better solution than adoption; they reason that biologically the child will be half theirs and that the wife will not be denied the experience of child bearing. Furthermore, the child born of such a conception need never know about the artificial insemination and thus will never have to make the adjustment the adopted child must make. Some couples find the notion repugnant; some husbands feel threatened by the idea of their wives being impregnated by an anonymous donor.

The child born of artificial insemination has all the rights of a natural child and is legitimized. All records of the procedure—in most states a legal release is required of both husband and wife—are kept confidential. Artificial insemination is used almost exclusively with married women with consent of their husbands. If a woman is impregnated by artificial means without the consent of her husband, a legal battle may ensue in which the husband may disown any claim to the pregnancy or the child by virtue of not having been consulted and not having given his consent.

Artificial insemination may have its dangers for the woman, especially in cases of divorce. An example is the case of Orford v. Orford (1921), a Canadian case in which Mrs. Orford sued her husband for alimony upon divorce. Her husband defended by claiming adultery, indicating that she had given birth to a child in England after they had been separated for more than 3 years. Mrs. Orford stated that her marriage had never been consummated because of her inability to have sexual intercourse and that her husband had agreed to have her see a doctor, which she did. The doctor then artificially inseminated her, resulting in the pregnancy. The court did not believe her story and found her guilty of adultery "in the ordinary natural way."

This court also found that the essence of the offense of adultery

"consists not in the moral turpitude of the act of sexual intercourse, but in the voluntary surrender to another person of the reproductive powers or faculties of the guilty person; and any submission of those powers to the service or enjoyment of any person other than the husband or the wife comes within the definition of 'adultery.' "

About 7,000 children are born each year in the United States as a result of artificial insemination. It appears that greater legal regulations will be required for proper interpretation of the results of this procedure, which is being used with greater frequency.

Abortion

The term "abortion" describes the termination of pregnancy, which can be spontaneous (often called a miscarriage) or induced. Induced abortions can be the therapeutic or criminal.

Until recently, all induced abortions that were not performed to save the life of the mother were considered illegal. A number of medical conditions in the mother could warrant a therapeutic termination of pregnancy. All other reasons for terminating the pregnancy were considered to be inappropriate, unethical, and illegal. Many women who wanted an abortion found that they could get no help from the medical profession because of the stringent rules and laws and had to resort to an abortionist, often an untrained or unqualified person whose equipment and methods were primitive and dangerous. In the late 1950's, the number of illegal abortions in the United States was estimated to range from 200,000 to one million per year.

The high mortality rate of such illegal abortions, plus the increasing awareness of women's rights has resulted in gradual change in the laws of various states regarding therapeutic abortion.

Women began to influence legislators and others to consider the point of view that they should have some control over what happened to their bodies and that the law should not impose upon the privacy of a decision that they felt ought to be left up to the patient and her physician. Several states began to apply a liberal approach to the standards for therapeutic abortion to include not only sparing the life of the mother but also her mental health.

PSYCHIATRY AND ABORTION

Until recently, psychiatrists had not been involved in the consultation for therapeutic abortion unless the mother was considered suicidal and likely to kill herself during the course of her pregnancy. This occurrence has been found to be extremely rare and the prediction of such suicidal behavior has not always been accurate. Serious mental illnesses, such as schizophrenia or profound depression, were also considered appropriate reasons for therapeutic abortions. Most hospitals had established abortion committees consisting of representatives of the department of obstetrics and gynecology, the

department of psychiatry, and other staff members to evaluate each request for therapeutic abortion. When the states began to include incestuous relationships, miscegenous relationships, and rape situations as appropriate reason for therapeutic abortion, the psychiatrist and his consultation became more significant.

The role of the psychiatrist in consulting in therapeutic abortions was changing because of the need to aid the obstetrician and the patient. Many psychiatrists had considered it their duty to find justifiable reasons for therapeutic termination of pregnancy such as suicide potential and serious mental illness, including schizophrenia and depression. In fact, many of these criteria were social, economic, or personality conveniences, rather than life or health risks. In the case of abortion, the psychiatrist's role is to advise his medical colleague about psychological risks that may attend performing the procedure. Advice regarding treatment is appropriate, should the anticipated psychological difficulties arise.

Some states found that their laws on therapeutic abortion were so vague that, in essence, they had very little criteria for prohibiting therapeutic abortion except by individual interpretation. Many were concerned that if they broadened and liberalized their abortion statutes, their states would become "abortion mills" and people would travel great distances in order to take advantage of their liberal approach. New York was one of the first states to offer liberal therapeutic abortions without residency requirements. Maternal mortality rates dropped as therapeutic abortion incidence increased and criminal abortion frequency decreased. In this and other states that introduced abortion reform, the important goal was to provide adequate medical care for women who would seek termination of their pregnancies at any cost—often the cost of their own lives—from untrained and unskilled abortionists.

As many states debated the issues and contemplated making changes in their abortion statutes, the United States Supreme Court, in 1973, held the following:

1. The decision to have an abortion during the first three months of pregnancy and the manner in which it is performed is de-

pendent solely upon the medical judgment of the physician and may not be prohibited by the state.

2. Until viability, i.e., between the twenty-fourth and twenty-eighth week of pregnancy, the state may regulate abortion procedures.

3. After the twenty-eighth week the state may regulate or forbid abortion unless medical judgment indicates to the contrary for the life or health of the mother.

In essence, the Supreme Court decision confirms the professional judgment of the physician in deciding when a therapeutic abortion is necessary; the state may regulate only later in the pregnancy. This holding affects all jurisdictions of the United States.

REFERENCES

*Ellis, A., and Brancale, R. *The Psychology of Sex Offenders*. Charles C. Thomas, Springfield, Ill., 1956.

*Gagnon, J., and Simon, W., editors. *Sexual Deviance.* Harper & Row, New York, 1967.

Krafft-Ebing, R. V. *Psychopathia Sexualis.* Physicians and Surgeons, Brooklyn, N.Y., 1922.

*Ploscowe, M. *Sex and the Law,* Ace Books, New York, 1962.

*Sadoff, R.L. Sexually deviated offenders. Temple Law Q., *40:* 1967.

*Tappan, P. Some myths about the sex offender. Fed. Prob., *19:* 7, 1955.

**Wolfenden Report*. Lancer Books, New York, 1964.

chapter 20 Laws Relevant to Marriage and Divorce

SIMON M. KOENIG, LL.B.

Introduction

Divorce is the interment of a dead marriage, the resolution of the socio-economic and legal obligations between the spouses, and the fixing of the obligation of each of the spouses to the other and to their children.

Only in recent times has the concept of divorce been socially accepted. Originally and for the longest time thereafter, the marriage relationship was for better or worse, as usually provided for in the marriage oath. Only in exceptional cases and for good cause was a marriage dissolved, and then both parties to the divorce suffered some social rejection.

When a legal marriage does not exist, a divorce is not necessary, and a court cannot grant a divorce. In fact, as part of the petition to the court for a divorce, there must be set forth the allegation that the parties are married to each other.

Marriage

From a legal viewpoint, marriage

is a mutual, voluntary compact, springing from sentiment, emotion, affection, and parties' desire for sacrifice and surrender to each other, and is properly based on mutual regard and love, suitably ratified, for the purposes of living together as husband and wife until death and constituting a family for preservation of moral and social purity, propagation of children, and their nurture, training, and preparation for family welfare, and general good of society. (Amsterdam v. Amsterdam, 1945, 56 N.Y.S. 2d 19)

Although marriage is often considered a religious sacrament, it is, legally speaking, a civil contract.

'Marriage' is a civil contract between a man and a woman, but it is also especially a status of personal relation in which the state is deeply concerned and over which the state has exercise of exclusive dominion; it is a foundation upon which society depends for its very survival. (Morris v. Morris, 1961, 31 Misc. 2d 548, 220 N.Y.S. 2d 590)

But the marriage contract is an exception to the rules governing civil contracts.

Marriage is more than a personal relation between man and woman and is status founded on contract and established by law, and constitutes an institution involving the highest interests of society and is regulated and controlled by law based on principles of public policy affecting welfare of people of state, the state as well as the parties being party to every marriage (Reese v. Reese, 1943, 179 Misc. 665, 40 N.Y.S. 2d 468, affirmed 268 App. Div. 993, 51 N.Y.S. 2d 685)

It [marriage] is declared a civil contract for certain purposes, but it is not thereby made synonymous with the word contract employed in the common law or statutes . . . . It cannot be dissolved by the parties when consummated, nor released with or without consideration. The relation is always regulated by government. It is more than a contract. It requires certain acts of the parties to constitute marriage, independent of and beyond the contract. It partakes more of the character of an institution regulated and controlled by public authority, upon principles of public policy, for the benefit of the community. (Wade v. Kalbfleisch, 1874, 58 N.Y. 282, 17 AM Rep. 250)

The parties to a marriage cannot alter or waive their rights under the contract. But the marriage contract can be modified by society, even though society was not privy to the contract, without violating the protection given to ordinary civil contracts by state and federal constitutions and by laws existing at the time the contract was entered into.

ESTABLISHING THE MARRIAGE RELATIONSHIP

Each jurisdiction has reserved to itself the right to establish the marriage relationship and has promulgated rules, regulations, and laws concerning the establishment of the marriage relationship. The actual marriage relationship in most jurisdictions can be established only by the prescribed formality of obtaining a license or permit to marry from the duly designated authority and by the execution of a written contract of marriage. The marriage license itself does not create the married relationship.

In a relatively few jurisdictions the marriage relationship can be created by the couple themselves, without a license or a written marriage contract, provided, however, that they comply with all the laws governing the legal age, incest, polygamy, and serological tests. A marriage contracted without a formal license is often referred to as a common-law marriage.

Where the couple are required by local statutes to obtain a marriage license to enter into the marriage relationship, they are usually required to go through certain procedures and submit proof of certain conditions:

1. Submit to serological tests to determine their freedom from certain venereal diseases in most jurisdictions, from sickle cell anemia in a relatively few jurisdictions, and from infectious tuberculosis in a few jurisdictions; in some jurisdictions a general good health certificate is required. In the United States, only Nevada and South Carolina do not require a blood test.

2. Produce proof that they are of legal age, permitting them to contract the marriage relationship without parental consent; when parental consent is necessary, the consenting parent must be present and give written approval at the time the license is issued. In some jurisdictions, parental consent is waived when the couple are under the legal age of consent if a child has been born to them or if the female partner is pregnant. In most jurisdictions, the laws permit a young woman to enter into the marriage relationship at an earlier age than a young man. Since the age factor differs in each jurisdiction, local laws must be consulted to determine the legal age of consent and the age below which a parent's consent is required. In addition, laws in each jurisdiction establish an age below which marriage cannot be entered into.

3. Produce proof of freedom from any prior marriage relationship and, where applicable, proof that all prior marriages have been legally terminated.

4. Produce proof of mental capacity to enter into the relationship in some jurisdictions.

5. Produce proof that the blood relationship of the couple does not violate the local incest statutes. These incest statutes vary from jurisdiction to jurisdiction. Incest is usually defined as a sexual relationship between a legitimate or illegitimate ancestor and a descendant, between a brother and a sister, between a half-brother and a half-sister, between an uncle and a niece, and between an aunt and a nephew, although uncle-niece and aunt-nephew marriages are permitted in some jurisdictions. As a general rule, a marriage legally permitted to be contracted in the jurisdiction where it is entered into is given recognition in all other jurisdictions, unless the marriage is polygamous or incestuous in a degree regarded generally as within the prohibition of natural law.

6. Physically obtain the marriage license from the proper issuing authority within the prescribed time after the serological and physical examinations required by statute.

There is usually a waiting period between the time of the serological and physical examinations and the time the license is issued. This waiting period can usually be waived by the proper authority for appropriate reasons. In most jurisdictions, the maximum elapsed time permitted between the examinations and the issuance of the marriage license is 30 days.

After the couple obtain the marriage license, a written contract of marriage must be entered into according to local law. In some jurisdictions, there is a waiting period between the date the marriage license is issued and the time the marriage is solemnized or the written marriage contract is signed. This waiting time can be waived by a designated authority for various reasons.

MARRIAGE CEREMONY

The marriage ceremony, often religious in nature, is actually the execution of the marital contract in the presence of witnesses and under the guidance or supervision of a duly authorized clergyman or government official. The marriage ceremony must be performed with the couple present, except where proxy marriages are permitted. The judicial officer or clergyman who presides over the ceremony must make sure the marriage contract is properly filed with the designated legal authority charged with recording the contract. In general terms, the marriage contract sets forth the obligations that the couple assume for themselves with respect to the other and to the community.

COMMON-LAW MARRIAGE

A common-law marriage is an agreement between a man and a woman, who are legally competent to contract a marriage, that they take each other as husband and wife. It differs from a ceremonial marriage only in that the agreement does not have to be in the presence of witnesses or pronounced by an official with the legal authority to perform marriage ceremonies. Cohabitation is regarded as evidence that such an agreement was made. Sometimes it is the only available evidence of such agreement, but cohabitation does not constitute a marriage and is not a substitute for or the equivalent of the actual agreement.

The marriage relationship is established by words spoken by the couple to each other in the present tense and by acts and deeds of the couple with reference to each other in the presence of the local society. The couple must agree to take each other as husband and wife. Mere cohabitation, sexual relations, use of the same name, and belief by others that the couple are husband and wife are not sufficient proof of a common-law marriage. However, in some jurisdictions the courts will assume that an agreement exists between the couple.

According to the opinion of the Court of Civil Appeals of Texas . . . "the essential elements of a common-law marriage are: (1) an express or implied agreement to enter into marriage; (2) cohabitation as husband and wife; (3) holding themselves out to the public as being married." The Supreme Court of the United States has held that parties' conduct towards each other "was equivalent, in law, to a declaration by each that they did, and during their joint lives were to, occupy the relation of husband and wife." Such a declaration was as effective to establish the status of marriage in New Jersey as if it had been made in words of the present tense. (Travers v. Reinhardt, 205 U.S. 423, 440, 27 S. Ct. 563, 569, 51 L.Ed. 865)

Proof that the couple created a marriage relationship by words spoken to each other may be difficult to establish after one of them dies, since the couple usually do not obtain a license, undergo physical or serological tests, or partake in the usual formal ceremony.

Common-law marriages properly established in a United States jurisdiction that permits such marriages are usually recognized in all other United States jurisdictions and are, in fact, protected by the United States Constitution, except when they violate the laws of incest or polygamy.

The common-law marriage, once having been properly established by a couple competent to enter into the relationship, entitles them to all the rights and obligations of the ceremonial marriage. A common-law marriage can be dissolved only in the same manner as a ceremonial marriage is dissolved.

At this time, a common-law marriage can be established in the District of Columbia and 13 states: Alabama, Colorado, Delaware, Georgia, Idaho, Iowa, Kansas, New Hampshire, Ohio, Oklahoma, Pennsylvania, South Carolina, and Texas.

Another 13 states recognize common-law marriages if the relationship originated within their jurisdiction prior to the date noted: California (1895), Florida (January 1, 1968), Illinois (June 30, 1905), Indiana (January 1, 1958), Michigan (January 1, 1959), Minnesota (April 26, 1941), Mississippi (April 5, 1956), Missouri (March 31, 1921), Nebraska (January 1, 1923), Nevada (March 29, 1943), New Jersey (December 1, 1939), New York (April 29, 1933), and South Dakota (1959).

VOID MARRIAGE

A void marriage is defined as one in which either one of the couple was legally unable to enter into the marriage relationship because of a prior existing marriage or a prohibited incestuous relationship or for a specific legal reason. When the couple are underage, most jurisdictions treat the marriage as voidable.

A void marriage, being invalid from its inception, technically does not exist and, therefore, does not require judicial intervention to bring it to an end; but it does form the basis for seeking from a court a decree declaring it a nullity. The practical purpose of such a legal declaration is to avoid future problems and claims.

As a rule, once a marriage has been established, it is given recognition by other jurisdictions. But there is an exception to this rule when the marriage violates the incest and polygamy laws of the place where the couple seek to establish their home.

Many jurisdictions permit the spouse of a person sentenced to death or to life imprisonment the option of unilaterally declaring the existing marriage as terminated and void. No court decree is required, and remarriage is permitted. Anyone sentenced to death is considered civilly dead, and his marriage is thereby dissolved, at least at the election or choice of his spouse. And in many jurisdictions, the penal law declares a person convicted and sentenced to life imprisonment to be civilly dead, freeing the spouse to remarry.

Once the spouse makes the election to dissolve the marriage, a later pardon or release of the convicted spouse from prison does not restore the marriage relationship or affect the legal status of a remarriage.

VOIDABLE MARRIAGE AND ANNULMENT

A voidable marriage is one that appears to be proper in every aspect, but an underlying premarital impediment, fault, or fraud disturbs the marriage contract. A voidable marriage is in full force and effect until a competent court, on application by either spouse or by a person properly having an interest in the marriage relationship, requests the court to dissolve the relationship. The dissolution is referred to as an annulment. It is necessary to examine the laws of each jurisdiction to determine the exact basis for an annulment.

Premarital fraudulent intent or misrepresentation is often necessary. The misrepresentation must be such that the deceived spouse would not have entered into the marriage had it not been for the misrepresentation. However, the deceived spouse must cease cohabitation immediately after discovering the fraud. Except under extraordinary circumstances, a spouse who claims fraud must discover it within a reasonable time after the marriage and, on discovery, must disavow the marriage.

When the annulment is based on fraud or misrepresentation, that fraud or misrepresentation must concern something vital. For example, a promise, express or implied, to have normal sex relations with a view toward procreation is vital to the marriage.

A marriage in violation of the statutes pertaining to the marriage of a common drunkard, an imbecile, a feebleminded person, an idiot, an insane person, or a person afflicted with a contagious disease may be annulled.

In addition, an annulment may be granted when (1) the consent of one spouse was obtained by the duress, force, or fraud of the other spouse; (2) one spouse was underage, lacked mental capacity, or was incapable of entering into a sexual relationship; (3) the rules and regulations concerning the obtaining of a license or the performance of the marriage ceremony were not complied with; (4) the spouses entered into the marriage with the intent not to cohabit or not to discharge to each other their various marital obligations and rights; (5) it is a mock or trial marriage; (6) an unresolved prior marriage exists; (7) the relationship is incestuous. Also, proxy marriages may be annulled where they are prohibited.

Since an annulment is based on facts and representations existing or made before the marriage, it may not be granted on the basis of any events that occurred after the establishment of the marriage relationship. An annulment differs from a divorce in that an annulment is not a dissolution of a marriage but a judicial declaration that no marriage had ever existed.

When children are born or conceived as a result of a union that is later annulled, they are in most jurisdictions declared by law to be the legitimate children of both parents. And, since such children are legitimate, they are entitled to all the rights established for them by law. Each of the parents is subject to all the obligations chargeable to parents.

Separation

A separation is often referred to as a limited divorce—a divorce from bed and board. In all instances, the couple remain legally and factually married to each other.

A legal separation, either by court decree or by a voluntary written agreement, permits the couple to live separate and apart and to lead separate private lives, free from interference or obligation to the other, except that neither is free to enter into a new marital relationship and neither may engage in sexual relations with anyone other than each other. A decree of judgment of separation remains in full force until a court, on proper application based on the reconciliation of the couple, revokes the decree. And the courts look favorably on reconciliation.

GROUNDS FOR SEPARATION

The grounds for separation in most jurisdictions cover physical and mental cruelty, nonsupport, adultery, desertion, abandonment, alcoholism, insanity, bigamy, drug addiction, refusal to have sexual relations, false accusations of infidelity or insanity, incompatibility, the procuring of an invalid divorce decree, refusal to establish a proper marital home, indiscreet conduct, and compelling an abortion.

When a separation is granted on the basis of the insanity of one of the spouses, the courts are apt to decree a separation limited to the length of time the spouse is deemed insane. An insane spouse is permitted to bring an action for a separation or a divorce.

A decree or judgment of separation usually indicates that one of the spouses was guilty of one or more acts sufficient in law to grant the other spouse the right to live separate and apart; to relieve the guiltless spouse of some of the marriage vows, including the right or obligation to engage in sexual relations with the other spouse; to provide for the financial needs of the spouse or provide that the spouse, as a result of the conduct complained of, is not entitled to financial assistance; to provide for the support, custody, and visitation of any children; and to provide for the sole use and occupancy of jointly owned property. A decree of separation or a separation agreement establishes the financial obligation of each spouse to the other and prevents future lawsuits by creditors or shopkeepers seeking to hold a husband liable for the extension of credit to the wife.

All issues presented to the court for determination and adjudicated by the court are deemed resolved for all time, and these issues cannot be relitigated in any other action between the spouses. The judgment of separation bars an action for annulment. In some jurisdictions the legal separation, either by court decree or by written agreement, forms the basis for a no-fault divorce.

When the spouses are of legal age and mentally competent to understand the nature of their acts, they are permitted to enter into a separation agreement, in which they may agree to live separate and apart from each other, each waiving conjugal rights, establishing financial obligations to each other within the limits as provided by law, disposing of jointly owned property, relinquishing property rights, waiving the right to participate in each other's estate, and providing for custody and support of any children born of the marriage, bearing in mind that the rights of the children are subject to review by the courts. As a general rule, the spouses are free to enter into a meaningful agreement as to their own future, provided the terms of the agreement are fair, adequate, and equitable.

A separation agreement—properly and fairly entered into by the parties and complied with by the husband, insofar as his financial obligations are concerned—prevents his further liability and exposure to liability for any obligation or expenditures on the part of the wife or children until the agreement is modified.

When the spouses enter into a fair, equitable, and adequate written separation agreement, the courts as a rule will not modify or change the agreement's terms except in cases of fraud or overreaching by one of the spouses.

The legislature in each state has the power to enact specific statutes regulating the drawing, execution, and enforceability of separation agreements. The agreement usually provides that it is subject to interpretation, as provided by the laws of the jurisdiction where it was drawn and executed, even though one or both spouses move from the jurisdiction.

Subject to statutes and court intervention, the spouses in a separation agreement may set up for themselves their obligations to their children. The court reserves for itself the right to review any agreement, so as to make sure that the welfare and best interests of the children are protected. Regardless of the provisions of a separation agreement, the agreement cannot affect the parents' obligation to support their children.

When an agreement is drawn, a duty is placed on the husband to be fair and to disclose the true picture of his financial assets. Laws in some jurisdictions permit a wife who waived her support in a separation agreement to bring a later action to establish her right to alimony.

In most jurisdictions a husband and wife cannot enter into an agreement in which the wife waives her alimony. If a wife becomes a public charge, the courts in some instances are permitted to open the agreement and to assess the husband or ex-husband an additional amount, rather than permit the wife or ex-wife to become a public charge.

The separation agreement remains in effect until a court sets it aside or until the spouses, by willful acts and intent, set it aside or abandon it. However, cohabitation and sexual intercourse between the spouses after the execution of the separation agreement do not vitiate the agreement. The spouses must intend to reconcile and abrogate the agreement.

Divorce

Divorce is defined as the severance of the marital obligations each spouse has to the other. In some jurisdictions the word "divorce" has been replaced by the word "dissolution."

JURISDICTION

The United States does not have a national divorce law, although an effort is being made to create such a law. Each state has reserved for itself the full power to create and establish its own matrimonial laws, including laws of divorce. When a state has jurisdiction and makes a judicial determination, the United States Constitution provides that all the other states accord the determination full faith and credit, except when the rights of children, the custody of children, and the support of children are concerned.

A gray area exists if the spouses have voluntarily subjected themselves to the jurisdiction of a court other than one in the place where they reside. Under certain circumstances, a state may refuse to recognize the sister-state judgment.

Decrees of divorce issued by a foreign government having proper jurisdiction over the spouses may be entitled to recognition by virtue of a treaty between that government and the United States. But when a state as a matter of public policy or express statute prohibits the recognition of a foreign decree, the divorce is sometimes not recognized.

Until recently, spouses in some jurisdictions, because of the archaic nature of the existing statutes, were compelled to commit perjury to obtain a divorce; other spouses were compelled to leave their home jurisdiction and travel to another jurisdiction in order to avoid committing perjury to obtain a divorce; and in some jurisdictions the spouses were compelled to stay married, albeit in name only. However, in most jurisdictions the grounds for divorce have been broadened, and in some jurisdictions a divorce can be obtained on a no-fault basis.

Although in the past the divorced person was looked down on, society does not discriminate against the divorced person, now that about a third of all marriages end in divorce. However, the laws in some jurisdictions still create a penalty for the divorced person, especially in those states in which adultery is the grounds for divorce: In Pennsylvania, the guilty spouse cannot marry the paramour while the former spouse is alive; in South Dakota, the guilty spouse cannot remarry except to the ex-spouse or until the death of the ex-spouse; in Mississippi, the court may prohibit the remarriage of the guilty spouse, but the prohibition can be lifted after 1 year on the basis of good conduct; in

Virginia, the guilty spouse is prohibited from remarrying, but after 6 months the court for good reason may lift the prohibition.

Remarriage after divorce, except to each other, is prohibited in Alabama for 60 days, in Delaware for 3 months at the court's discretion, in Georgia at the court's discretion, in Kentucky for 60 days, in Michigan for not more than 2 years at the court's discretion, in Minnesota for 6 months, in North Dakota at the court's discretion, in Oklahoma for 6 months, in Oregon for 60 days, in Texas for 60 days, in Utah for 3 months, and in Wisconsin for 6 months.

In Hawaii, the final decree is not entered for 6 months if the spouses are under 21 years of age. And in Nebraska, the divorce decree does not become effective until 6 months after its rendition.

NO-FAULT DIVORCE

Many jurisdictions have created a no-fault divorce. Under this concept neither of the spouses is deemed to be the culprit at the expense of the other; in fact, this procedure is not an adversary proceeding. Often, it is called a dissolution of marriage, not a divorce. In a no-fault divorce one or both spouses charge that irreconcilable differences have caused an irremediable or irretrievable breakdown of the marriage relationship.

At the time this section was written, the Virgin Islands and 15 states had adopted a no-fault form of divorce: Alabama, Arizona, California, Colorado, Delaware, Florida, Hawaii, Idaho, Iowa, Kentucky, Michigan, Nebraska, New Hampshire, North Dakota, and Oregon. Many states have a no-fault type of law under consideration.

FAULT DIVORCE

Some jurisdictions grant only divorces in which one spouse must accuse and prove to the court's satisfaction that sufficient grounds exist for the court to award a divorce to the aggrieved party. The decree in a fault divorce spells out the grounds for divorce. And in some jurisdictions the spouse at fault is made to suffer a penalty or must seek the court's permission to remarry.

In some fault jurisdictions a divorce can be obtained on a no-fault basis. The statutes usually provide that, if the spouse had entered into a valid written separation agreement or

had been living under a decree of separation for a prescribed period of time and had complied with the terms of the agreement or the separation decree, the court will grant a divorce based on the dead-marriage concept.

The usual grounds for divorce are adultery, mental or physical cruelty, abandonment for a specific period of time, continuing to live separate and apart for 1 year or more after a decree of separation by a court or after the couple entered into a separation agreement and lived apart and complied with the terms of the agreement, conviction of a crime that resulted in a declaration of civil death or in incarceration for a specified number of consecutive years, drug addiction, conviction of an infamous crime, alcoholism for a specified period of time, impotency, nonsupport, and incompatibility.

Desertion or abandonment for a specified period of time forms the basis for a divorce in the District of Columbia and 37 states: Alabama, Alaska, Arizona, Arkansas, Connecticut, Delaware, Georgia, Idaho, Illinois, Indiana, Kansas, Maine, Maryland, Massachusetts, Minnesota, Mississippi, Missouri, Montana, Nevada, New Hampshire, New Jersey, New York, North Dakota, Ohio, Oklahoma, Pennsylvania, Rhode Island, South Carolina, South Dakota, Tennessee, Texas, Utah, Virginia, Washington, West Virginia, Wisconsin, and Wyoming.

Living separate and apart for a period of years forms the basis for a divorce in the District of Columbia and 24 states: Alabama, Arizona, Arkansas, Connecticut, Delaware, Hawaii, Idaho, Louisiana, Minnesota, Maryland, Nevada, New Hampshire, New Jersey, New York, North Carolina, Rhode Island, South Carolina, Texas, Vermont, Virginia, Washington, West Virginia, Wisconsin, and Wyoming.

Incompatibility is one of the grounds for a divorce in the Virgin Islands and eight states: Alaska, Alabama, Delaware (if for a period of 2 years), Kansas, Nevada, New Mexico, Oklahoma, and Texas.

DUAL DIVORCE

In some instances each of the spouses is entitled to obtain a divorce from the other. In these cases the grounds for divorce used by one spouse must not contradict the grounds alleged by the other.

Dual divorce is possible in the Virgin Islands and 15 states: Alaska, California, Florida,

Georgia, Idaho, Illinois, Kansas, Kentucky, Montana, New Jersey, New York, North Dakota, Oklahoma, Utah, and Washington.

DIVISIBLE DIVORCE

A court sometimes grants a divorce but does not alter the financial obligations of the spouses toward each other. Under this divisible divorce concept, the divorce decree dissolves the marriage but does not extinguish all the husband's obligations, including the duty to support his former wife.

REFERENCES

*Foster and Freed. *Law and the Family.* Lawyers' Cooperative Publishing Co., 1972.
*Grossman, M. L. *New York Law of Domestic Relations.* Dennis & Co., Buffalo, 1942, 1962 Supplement.
**New York Supplement,* series 2. West Publishing Co.
**Clark's Digest Annotation.* Kimball-Clark Publishing Co., Boonton, N.J., 1932–1937.

chapter 21 Pornography

MORRIS A. LIPTON, M.D., Ph.D.

Introduction

Obscenity and pornography are poorly defined terms with equally poorly defined consequences in the genesis or perpetuation of antisocial behavior. Despite this, or perhaps because the effects are much less clearly demonstrable than are the questions and fantasies that surround the consequences of exposure to explicitly erotic sexual material, the problem of obscenity and pornography became a matter of sufficient national concern, in the eyes of the 1967 Congress, to warrant the establishment of a national advisory commission. The function of this commission, established in 1968, was,

after a thorough study which shall include a study of the causal relationship of such material to antisocial behavior, to recommend advisable, appropriate and constitutional means to deal effectively with such traffic in obscenity and pornography.

Although some of the possible consequences of exposure to explicitly erotic materials fall within the domain of psychiatry and may include rape, pederasty, exhibitionism, and other sexual crimes or deviations, there are clearly other issues that must be considered. These are legal, moral and aesthetic—matters that are invariably intertwined and that may often be in conflict with each other. Thus, the First Amendment to the Constitution guarantees free speech and a free press. To what extent do legal restrictions on the manufacture, distribution, and sale of pornographic material constitute a violation or at least a threat to the guarantees of the First Amendment? At the very least, an answer to this question requires an acceptable definition of pornography. Such a definition does not come easily.

All religions attempt to influence man's social behavior through the establishment of rules of conduct. Some of these rules are in the sexual area. The growth of premarital and extramarital sex and of divorce is, therefore, a matter of great concern to religion and its leaders. There is also the concern that if religious proscription crumbles in one area it will be threatened in others. Sexual permissiveness is seen by some as a cause for diminished church attendance and the rapid decline in students who aspire to the ministry. Some church leaders are concerned that if the availability of explicit sexual material fosters the decline of accepted sexual practices and moral values might it not lead to other feared consequences, like crime, drug abuse, and loss of commitment to the family, community, and country? Some political leaders ascribe diminution in patriotism to sexual permissiveness engendered by the availability of pornography. And the description of man—his actions, creations, and fantasies has always properly been a subject of art. The human body was graphically recorded in ancient history. All recorded literature and drama attempt to describe man and his complexity as he copes with the joys and sorrows of the human existence. Sexual activity is part of this existence, and the artist has always fought control over his freedom to describe man as he sees fit. The artist, as both a member and a contributor to society, has often tested religious precepts and the law in fighting for his right to express himself. Does this right include the description of all of man's sexual acts and fantasies?

The establishment of the Commission on Obscenity and Pornography was an attempt to examine the problem from many perspectives before making recommendations to the Congress and the President. It may be considered a hallmark in congressional and presidential responsibility in its concern for the origins and consequences of an area of significant human behavior. The Congress asked specific questions of the commission. President Johnson selected the commissioners for professional interest and competence. Two years and about $2 million were available for the studies. The President recognized that the problem was one of concern to lawyers, social scientists, theologians, representatives of the arts, and behavioral scientists. This multidisciplinary nature of the commission was reflected in the fact that, of its 18 members, five were attorneys or judges, four were concerned with the publication and dissemination of books, television, and movies; three were ministers of the Catholic, Protestant, and Judaic faiths, three were sociologists; two were psychiatrists; and one was an educator. A supporting staff of professionals examined the existing literature and did its own research. More than 50 contracts for needed research were let throughout this country and abroad. Public hearings were held.

In general, the strategy of the commission followed the specific tasks assigned to it by the Congress in Public Law 90-100. A legal panel was established "to analyze the laws pertaining to the control of obscenity and pornography: and to recommend definitions of obscenity and pornography." A traffic and distribution panel had the task "to ascertain the methods employed in the distribution of obscene and pornographic material and to explore the nature and volume of traffic in such material. An effects panel was established to "study the effect of obscenity and pornography upon the public and particularly minors, and its relationship to crime and other antisocial behavior." A positive approaches panel undertook the task "to recommend such legislative, administrative or other advisable and appropriate action as the Commission deems necessary to regulate effec-

tively the flow of such traffic, without in any way interfering with constitutional rights."

The work of the commission generated much more information about the nature of the industry, the characteristics of users, and the consequences of exposure than had hitherto been available. The results of the commission's work and its recommendations are available from the United States Government Printing Office as a substantial volume entitled *The Report of the Commission on Obscenity and Pornography*. Ten volumes of the technical documents on which the commission report is based are also available. Nothing that refutes the findings of the commission has been published in the scientific literature since 1970, although many criticisms of its methods and, especially, its conclusions and recommendations have appeared in the lay press.

The data obtained by the commission formed the basis for its recommendations. The information obtained to answer the major and subsidiary questions posed by the Congress is incomplete and imperfect, yet not only is that information a vast improvement over what was available before the commission began its work, but everything pointed in the same direction. The information was insufficiently conclusive to permit a unanimous report. Instead, 12 of the 18 commissioners voted for the basic recommendation that "federal, state and local legislation prohibiting the sale, exhibition and distribution of sexual materials to consenting adults should be repealed." Three of the dissenters were clergymen. A fourth dissenter, a woman educator, subscribed to the bulk of the report but felt that the evidence was too weak to warrant repeal of all restrictions. The fifth dissenter was the Attorney General of California. One abstainer actually dissented and wrote a minority report castigating the majority. He was the only commissioner appointed by President Nixon, and he was a lawyer whose position was established long before his appointment to the commission because he was the head of a national antismut organization called the Citizens for Decent Literature.

The full commission depended greatly on the data generated by the effects panel in determining its recommendations. It is the law of the land, expressed in the opinion of the Supreme Court written by Judge Oliver Wendell Holmes, Jr., in 1919, that the right of free speech does not apply if there is evidence that such speech may result in "clear and present danger." One has no constitutional right to commit libel or to yell "fire" in a crowded theater when there is no fire. Had detrimental results of pornography been found, the position of the moralists would have been strengthened, and the entire panel would have recommended restrictive legislation. The failure of the effects panel to find persuasive evidence of such danger was a major determinant of the recommendations of those commissioners who attempted to base their conclusions on evidence. However, it had no effect on those commissioners who based their judgments on religious morality or other values unsusceptible to influence by collected data. The effects panel limited itself to the question of the influence of exposure to erotic material on sexual attitudes, conduct, and mental health. Neither the effects panel nor any of the other panels attempted to gather and assess evidence relating the influence of pornography on political attitudes, religious activity, or attitudes toward patriotism, war, violence, drug taking, ecology, or the myriad of social problems that beset the country.

The conclusions of the commission were perhaps unique insofar as it found no evidence to sustain the view that the availability of sexually stimulating material has consequences of grave national import. The commission, by a vote of 12 to 6, recommended liberalization of existing laws. The President rejected the report and its recommendations. The Supreme Court, by a 5 to 4 vote in June 1973, voted to make laws even more restrictive. The facts that the commission was unable to reach a unanimous opinion and that the Supreme Court, by the narrowest of margins, went against the recommendations of the commission are testimony to the conflicting values that go into legislative and judicial judgments. In the report, the effects panel wrote, ... "if a case is to be made against 'pornography' in 1970, it will have to be made on grounds other than effects of a damaging personal or social nature." The case has been made by the President and the Supreme Court on moral, aesthetic, and perhaps political grounds.

Legal Considerations

The term "obscene" is often equated with "pornographic." Strictly speaking, this is incorrect because material may be deemed obscene—abhorrent—in a variety of contents: religious, political, sexual, scatological, violent, and so on. Pornography, on the other hand, refers specifically to sexually exciting material. The application of obscenity laws has been devoted almost exclusively to sexual obscenity, so that the two words have tended to become legally identical.

Yet, neither word is precisely defined in the courts. Historically, censorship for political and religious reasons dates back to Greek and Roman times and permeates medieval law, but sexual permissiveness in art, literature, and drama was not censored until the 17th century, when, during the Puritan influence in England, profanity was prohibited, and playhouses were closed. They were opened shortly after, during the Restoration. The first legislation in England authorizing the prosecution of obscene materials was enacted in 1824. In Massachusetts, a statute enacted in 1711 was entitled "an act against intemperance, immorality and profaneness and in Reformation of Manners." These and similar statutes were not directed against explicit sexual materials as such. Rather, they were designed to criminalize sexual matter incorporated into materials that directly attacked religious institutions and beliefs. The earliest prosecutions pertained to sexual works that were explicitly antireligious. The first English conviction dealt with the publisher of a book entitled, *Venus in the Cloister, or the Nun in Her Smock.*

In 1868, the English courts offered a test of obscenity. It was

whether the tendency of the matter is to deprave and corrupt those whose minds are open to such immoral influences and into whose hands a publication of this sort may fall.

In the United States, blasphemy and other offenses against religion were heavily punished during the 17th and 18th centuries, but there are no recorded convictions for purely sexual material until the *Fanny Hill* case of 1821. Shortly thereafter, Vermont, Connecticut, and Pennsylvania passed antiobscenity statutes, and Massachusetts broadened its statute to define obscene works as "manifestly tending to the corruption of the morals of youth." The first federal statute was a customs law of 1842 that prohibited the import of indecent and obscene prints, paintings, and books. In 1865, Congress passed the first mail obscenity law. In 1868, Anthony Comstock persuaded New York to legislate against obscene literature, and in 1873 Congress broadened its 1865 law to what is essentially its present form. Comstock was made a special federal agent in charge of enforcing these laws. States that had previously not had obscenity legislation quickly followed, and by the beginning of the 20th century more than 30 states had such legislation.

The basic definition of obscenity used in such legislation between 1850 and 1957 was similar to that offered by the English courts in 1868—that is, whether such material "will deprave and corrupt those whose minds are open to such immoral influences." During these years, the dissemination of printed and photographed material increased enormously. As it did, material with sexual content slowly but persistently increased in advertisements, literature, and art. An exposed ankle or bare back, which might have been considered obscene at one point, became conventional, even in advertisements for clothing. In the interest of increased sales, purveyors of girlie magazines have always tested the limits of the law. Photographs of the bare back were extended down to include the buttocks, and the body was rotated to give a partial view of the abdomen and breasts. Coverings of these parts became increasingly transparent, full breasts were exposed and, after some years, acquired nipples, and the crotch recently developed pubic hair. These changes are subtle and almost imperceptible as public acceptance and legal permissiveness increases.

In 1957, in the case of Roth versus the United States, the question was finally asked as to whether there was a constitutional basis for obscenity prohibitions. Before the Roth decision, many lower court judges argued that the dissemination of speech was protected by the First and Fourteenth Amendments unless the subject matter created a "clear and present danger" of significant social harm. In the 1957 Roth decision, the court did not apply the test of clear and present danger but,

rather, simply determined that "obscenity is not within the area of constitutionally protected speech or press." The Court decision was based on two findings: (1) When the Constitution was written and adopted, states already had statutes prohibiting libel, blasphemy, and profanity. Hence, in their view, "the unconditional phrasing of the First Amendment was not intended to protect every utterance." (2) The Court also noted a universal judgment that obscenity should be restrained, a judgment reflected in the existence of antiobscenity laws in more than 50 nations, in the obscenity laws of all 48 states, and in the 20 obscenity laws enacted by the Congress from 1842 to 1956.

In the Roth decision and in the litigation that has followed it, a working definition of obscenity evolved. This definition had three criteria: (1) For the average person, the dominant theme of the material, taken as a whole, must appeal to a "prurient" interest in sex. (2) The material must be "patently" offensive because it affronts "contemporary community standards" regarding the depiction of sexual matters. (3) The material must be "utterly lacking in redeeming social value." All three criteria must coalesce before material may be deemed obscene for adults.

This definition of obscenity is superbly ambiguous and has resulted in much litigation. Who is the average person? What is a community? Is it the nation as a whole, or is it the state, city, county, or even neighborhood where the distribution occurs? How does one determine community standards? Is it by a majority vote? A plurality of the Court (not a majority) held that unless the material is "utterly" without redeeming social value it may not be considered obscene. A minority felt that a small degree of social value may be outweighed by prurience and offensiveness. Furthermore, the Court has not defined what values are redeeming social values. Does entertainment have social value?

The Court further heightened the ambiguity in 1969 in the Georgia versus Stanley decision, when it decided that the First and Fourteenth Amendments prohibit making mere private possession of obscene material a crime. It therefore permits a person to privately possess and use material that he may not legally be permitted to purchase.

In June 1973, in Kaplan versus California,

the Supreme Court clarified some of the issues and complicated still others. In a 5 to 4 decision, the minority advocated accepting the recommendations of the Commission on Obscenity and Pornography and eliminating all federal statutes regarding the control of the availability of obscene material to consenting adults. The majority of 5, however, upheld the Roth decision that obscenity was not protected by the Constitution and altered the definition of obscenity in a restrictive direction. (1) It removed the word "utterly" from its redeeming value judgment and substituted "serious literary, artistic, political, or scientific value." It does not include entertainment, educational, or philosophical value. (2) The Court specifically included states as a defined community, since it permits prosecution under state, rather than federal, statutes. It does not, however, define whether a city, town, county or neighborhood is a legitimate community for this purpose. (3) The Court demanded that offensiveness or the nature of the material appealing to prurient interests be specifically described. Only "works which depict or describe sexual conduct" can be outlawed, and that conduct "must be specified by state law." Since few states have such specificity in their existing statutes, it is likely that many previous convictions based on general statutes will now be appealed. (4) In principle, the Court made it unnecessary for prosecutors to prove that material is obscene. Instead, defendants must prove that the material is "serious" by using experts who will testify as to the literary, artistic, political, or scientific value. This Supreme Court decision will very likely result in a flurry of legislative and prosecutory activity at state and lower levels and in repeated tests in the Supreme Court. The initial outcome of the Supreme Court ruling will undoubtedly lead to a retreat by purveyors of pornography and even by publishers, editors, writers, and film makers who have introduced explicit sexual material into serious presentations. The long range outcome is difficult to predict, except that confusion will reign while new statutes are drafted, new prosecutions are made, and these cases are tested in the courts. Already, the Association of American Publishers has filed a brief with the Supreme Court asking it to reconsider the antiobscenity ruling, which they say has "reduced the rule of law to a matter of taste."

As stated previously, the word "obscene" is not limited to the sexual area, although it has, through usage, become identified in this way. The many types of illegal political activity that have recently been revealed may properly be called obscene. One can only be wryly concerned about the public political immorality of some of those who press hard for the legislation of private sexual morality.

Effects of Exposure to Pornographic Materials

METHODS

The strongest justification for the legal control of the distribution of explicit sexually arousing material would be the demonstration that it constitutes a "clear and present danger," insofar as it causes delinquent or criminally sexual behavior among youth or adults. If such a case cannot be made, then controls must be justified on other grounds. The 1973 Supreme Court decision justifies such controls on the grounds that states have a right to protect "the quality of life and the tone of commerce in great city centers."

To examine the proposition that exposure to such material results in aberrant sexual behavior, The Commission on Obscenity and Pornography used several strategies: (1) The existing research literature on the effects of sexually arousing material on behavior was examined. (2) The recorded opinions of behavioral scientists, law enforcement officials, and persons concerned with youth and morality were collected and examined. (3) A national public opinion survey was conducted by the commission to determine the nature and extent of exposure to erotic materials by a random sample of adults and youth and to describe the opinions of this sample with respect to community standards. This same survey attempted to determine public opinions regarding the effects of this exposure. (4) A survey was undertaken to determine the opinions of behavioral scientists, clinicians, and law enforcement officials on the effects of exposure to erotica. (5) Quasiexperiments were conducted in which groups of persons who manifested a supposed consequence of exposure to erotica (delinquents and sex offenders) were compared retrospectively with groups similar in most characteristics except the misbehavior in terms of past experiences with erotic materials. (6) An international comparison was made between Denmark, where erotic material is readily available, and countries where it is not, with respect to the incidence of delinquency and sexual crime. Similarly, in countries where there had been a change in laws in recent times, the consequences of the change were examined in terms of delinquency and sex crime statistics. (7) Controlled psychophysiological experiments were performed in which two or more groups of persons were given a controlled differential exposure to sexual materials and the consequences were observed later. Fourteen such studies were conducted. The subjects included married adults, young unmarried men and women, and incarcerated sex offenders and nonoffenders. The erotic materials were textual or visual. Follow-up studies extended to 2 months.

The emphasis in the studies sponsored by the commission was on the relationships between the availability of erotica and juvenile and adult sex offenses, with particular emphasis on forcible crime. Similarities and differences in experience with erotica between delinquents and nondelinquents, between sex offender adults and nonoffender adults, and between controls and sex deviants (such as homosexuals and transvestites) were examined. Other behavior that might be regarded as antisocial was not examined. No data were obtained with regard to the influence of such material on venereal disease or divorce.

RESULTS

Formulations from scientific literature. The research literature before 1970 was limited to immediate sexual arousal responses and failed to consider how this arousal might effect overt behavior, attitudes governing be-havior, and mental health. This literature showed that a large proportion of adults could become sexually aroused by pictures and words. Persons differed considerably in their preference for and response to sexual stimuli; for example, sexual stimuli for women differed from that for men. The social context of the viewing significantly determined the extent of arousal.

Formulations from popular literature. Such formulations covered a wide range: (1) Erotica is an offense against community standards of good taste; (2) Exposure is harmful to people; (3) Erotica has harmful consequences to society; and (4) Erotica is harmless or beneficial to people.

The commission report offers many samples of such opinions. They range from the opinion that pornography is a stench in the public nostril "quite analogous to keeping a goat in a residential area or urinating in public" to

The open distribution of pornography would encourage heterosexuality and discourage impotence and frigidity. As such it is life giving, a stimulus to joy and a source of socially harmless pleasure.

Thirty-six categories of opinions were recorded. These opinions included 26 presumed harmful effects, ranging from causing sexually aggressive acts of a criminal nature to suicide, ennui, and submission to authoritarianism. Ten neutral or beneficial effects were noted. These ranged from offering sexual information to entertainment and discharge of antisocial sexual appetites. None of these opinions were supported by data. In general, law enforcement officials tended to see pornography as more dangerous than did behavioral scientists, but several psychiatrists—including Lawrence Kubie, Ernest Van den Haag, Max Levin, and Natalie Shainess—rendered strong opinions about the damaging effects of erotica.

Survey of professionals. Psychiatrists who see damage resulting from exposure to erotica are in a small minority. A total of 3,423 psychiatrists and clinical psychologists responded to a commission sponsored questionnaire on the subject; 80 per cent reported that they had never encountered a case in which pornography appeared to be a factor in producing antisocial sexual behavior, 9 per cent suspected such cases, and 7 per cent were convinced of such a case. Similarly, professional workers in child guidance, psychiatry, psychology, and social work responded to the question, "Do you think reading obscene books plays a significant role in causing juvenile delinquency?" with 77 per cent "No," 12 per cent "Yes," and 10 per cent "Don't know." In marked contrast, police chiefs responded to the same question with 31 per cent "No," 58 per cent "Yes," and 11 per cent "Don't know."

Survey of current public opinion

Restrictions on availability. In a survey involving face-to-face interviews of 2,500 adults and 769 persons in the 15-to-20 age range, the question was asked: "Would you please tell me what you think are the two or three most serious problems facing the country today [1970]?" Only 2 per cent answered concern about erotic materials, whereas 33 per cent were more concerned with the economy, racial conflict, or Vietnam. This question was phrased badly in limiting itself to the two or three most important issues, since conceivably a large number would have rated concern over erotic materials among the 10 most important social issues. A large majority of the adults and youth surveyed admitted experience with specifically erotic materials.

The results of this survey differ from Gallup and Harris polls in 1969 that revealed that 75-to-85 per cent of adults wanted stricter laws on pornography and felt that smut was taking the beauty out of sex. The discrepancy may be accounted for by the subtleties of survey questionnaires. For example, in the commission survey, more than 50 per cent felt that their opinions as to the availability of sexually arousing material would depend on whether or not the material was shown to be harmful. About one third of the public would oppose availability even if no harm could be demonstrated.

Effects. Diversity characterizes public opinion about the effects of erotica. There is no presumed effect on which more than two thirds of the surveyed population agreed.

More than 45 per cent of the adult population felt that erotica excited people sexually, provided sexual information, provided entertainment, led to a breakdown of morals, led people to commit rape, improved sexual relations in marriage, made people bored, led to loss of respect for women, and made people do things with their spouses. Clearly, some of these responses refer to desirable and some to undesirable or even dangerous effects.

These same respondents, when asked what the effects were on them in contrast to others known personally, always responded that the desirable effects occurred with them but that the undesirable effects occurred with others. Of the 49 per cent who felt that it led to rape, none reported that it did it to them, but 9 per cent reported knowing someone who had been incited to rape by sexual material. Such a figure could not possibly be true, since it would result in several million rapes annually, a figure much higher than the actual incidence.

Survey results have distinct limitations, but the survey revealed that, in general, positive or neutral effects of explicit sexual material were associated with higher levels of education, greater exposure, and relative youth. Older, less educated, and sexually conservative people tended to see more undesirable effects.

Direct experiments

Nature of arousing materials. A number of experimental studies show that 60 to 85 per cent of both men and women experience sexual arousal when reading or viewing certain erotic stimuli. Women tend to be more aroused than men by written material and less aroused by visual material. Most sexual themes of petting and heterosexual coitus are equally arousing to both sexes, but group oral sex is more arousing to men. Arousal during exposure to erotica diminishes with age. Incarcerated sexual offenders tend to be aroused by the same types of materials as controls, but sexual deviants respond to literary or depicted stimuli similar to those that they encounter in real life. Thus, transsexual men are likely to find clothing more erotic than nudity or coitus.

Consequences of arousal. Several retrospective studies and at least one direct experiment show that repeated exposure to erotica rapidly leads to satiation. In the direct experiment, subjects were required to spend 90 minutes daily, 5 days a week, for several weeks, in a room in which a large supply of erotic books, pictures, and movies were freely available. Also freely available were conventional books, magazines, and newspapers. It was found that viewing time with erotica dropped rapidly from 90 per cent to about 40 per cent in less than 5 days. Physiological indices of arousal dropped equally rapidly. At no time in this experiment did the daily 90-minute exposure significantly affect sleep, mood, study, or work habits. Satiation was specific to erotic material and did not affect the subjects' personal sexual activities. A large number of studies show that between ages 18 and 50 established patterns of premarital, extramarital, and marital coitus, petting, homosexual activity, and sexual fantasy are very stable and are not altered by exposure to explicit sexual stimuli. In some circumstances, exposure to erotica temporarily activates sexual behavior, but, when this occurs, it is short lived and follows previously established patterns of sexual activity. Thus, for unmarried men and women, there may be a 24-hour increase in masturbation. In those with regular sexual partners, there may be increased coitus. Unusual sexual activity, such as fellatio and cunnilingus, did not increase significantly after viewing such activity, but sexual dreams and sexual conversation increased for a brief time.

Erotica and antisocial and criminal behavior. Studies in this area depend on correlations, on retrospective examinations of sex offenders, and on comparative data from other countries. The data are not fully conclusive; collectively, they suggest a lack of correlation between the availability of erotica and sex crime. For example, in the period 1960 to 1969, the availability of erotica increased by several hundred per cent. The number of arrests for nonsexual crimes increased by 108 per cent, for forcible rape by 85 per cent, and for prostitution by 119 per cent, but for all sex offenses lumped together arrests decreased by 4.5 per cent. This decline is partly the result of liberalization of law enforcement in the areas of homosexuality and exhibitionism. But even

in arrests for prostitution and rape, where laws have not been liberalized, the contribution of juveniles is very low—1.5 per cent for prostitution in 1960 and 2.1 per cent in 1969; 17.3 per cent for rape in 1960 and 20.6 per cent in 1969. Small increases in these crimes versus very large increases in the availability of pornography do not support the thesis that increased availability leads to sex crime in juveniles, but neither do they disprove it.

The data relating availability of erotica to illegitimacy are confusing. In the period 1940 to 1965, illegitimacy rose in all age groups from 15 to 35. From 1965 to 1968, it rose substantially among teen-agers but dropped in all other age groups. Probably, this trend results from the increased availability of contraception and abortion to older women, but one cannot be certain. Again, the data do not support the argument that experience with erotica causes increased risk of illegitimate pregnancy.

Examination of the data concerning the time, nature, and extent of exposure to erotica between delinquent and nondelinquent youth shows no significant differences. Both groups showed considerable experience with such materials.

Adult criminal behavior of all sorts has increased from 1960 to 1969. Robbery, auto theft, and grand larceny represent the greatest increases. Rape increased less than these crimes. Furthermore, arrests for all sex offenses constituted less than 2 per cent of all arrests. During the same time period, the availability of pornography increased enormously. If there was a causal correlation, one would expect a much larger increase in sex crimes. The failure to find it suggests, but does not prove, the absence of causal correlation.

Studies of adult sex offenders reveal that this population responds to erotic materials to about the same degree as does a control population. However, a comparison of incarcerated sex offenders with nonsex offenders revealed that rapists had their first exposure to erotica at age 18, but the nonsex offenders were first exposed to erotica at age 15. Control populations of college students and members of men's clubs also had earlier and more extensive experience with erotica than did rapists. In terms of recent exposure, sex deviants, such as transsexuals and homosexuals, had about as much recent exposure as the controls, but rapists and pedophiles had less. In general, sex offenders report sexually repressive backgrounds and immature and inadequate sexual histories.

Finally, the Danish experience, in which erotic materials have been fully available to the public since 1965, shows a significant reduction in all types of sex crimes since that time.

When all these results are put together, it appears clear that there is no data base for the belief that exposure to erotic materials is a significant determining factor in causing sex crimes or delinquency. This is a statistical statement, for it is also evident that it will never be possible to state that on no occasion and under no conditions will erotic materials ever contribute in any way to the likelihood of any person's committing a sex crime. The decision to pass prohibitory laws is not based on rare individual cases, but rather on statistical likelihoods. On the basis of the available data, it is not possible to conclude that erotic material is a statistically significant cause of sex crime.

Recommendations of the Commission

Although no single bit of evidence was totally conclusive, the many lines of evidence obtained from diverse research strategies all pointed in the same direction: Exposure of adults to erotic materials offers no clear and present danger. There was no support for the thesis that there is a meaningful causal relationship, or even a significant correlation, between exposure to erotica and immediate or delayed antisocial behavior among adults. The best evidence points to satiation and boredom as a consequence of repeated exposure. Pornography may be vulgar, distasteful, wasteful of money, and dull. It may be a nuisance, but it does not appear to be a significant evil.

On the basis of these findings and others about the nature of the industry, its purveyors, and its consumers, the commission recommended the elimination of all restric-

tions on the availability of such materials for adults.

The commission lacked adequate evidence for making a judgment on the effect of pornography on juveniles. Although there is substantial evidence that children always have obtained and always will obtain pornographic material, often by creating their own age-appropriate graffiti, it was not ethically possible to conduct direct exposure experiments on juveniles. However, there is clear evidence from public opinion polls that parents do not wish their children to be exposed to erotica. Consequently, the commission felt that the rights of parents to raise their children as they saw fit and to limit their exposure to questionable materials must be respected. The commission therefore prepared and recommended a model statute controlling the availability of such material to juveniles.

By the same reasoning, it was felt that the right of persons to be protected from exposure to materials they considered immoral or offensive must also be protected. Hence, model statutes controlling advertising and public displays were also prepared and recommended.

The majority of the commission recognized that society is in a period of rapidly changing values regarding premarital sex, marriage, divorce, contraception, abortion, and the right to have as many children as one chooses. Such changes may be offensive to moral absolutists but seem inevitable nonetheless. There is also a gradual change in what may be defined as healthy sexual attitudes. Whatever these may be, the majority of the commission members thought that age-appropriate sex education, presented accurately and truthfully in an appropriate aesthetic and moral context, would go further in reducing interest in hard core pornography than would restrictive legislation. Furthermore, sex education could do so without raising the controversies that exist regarding definitions of obscenity and pornography and the kinds of materials that may or may not be protected by the First Amendment. The commission, therefore, recommended large increases in sex education programs for both children and adults and further recommended citizen participation in the organization and presentation of such programs. Finally, the commission recognized the imperfections of much of its time-limited research and strongly recommended support of more and better longitudinal research.

Critics of these recommendations have called them a "Magna Carta for pornographers." They are not. In fact, they are much more stringent than are existing laws regarding the advertisement, exhibition, and sale of the tools of violence.

REFERENCE

*The Commission on Obscenity and Pornography *The Report of the Commission on Obscenity and Pornography.* United States Government Printing Office, Washington, D.C., 1970.

chapter 22 Prostitution

BARBARA E. BESS, M.D.,
and SAMUEL S. JANUS, Ph.D.

History

Prostitution is called the oldest profession. The earliest reference to prostitution is in the Bible, Genesis 38. It reads, "Tamar thy daughter-in-law hath played the harlot; and also, behold, she is with child by whoredom."

Sacred or temple prostitution unites religion with prostitution. It is thought to have originated in the Orient about 300 B.C. Temple prostitution was also highly developed in Cyprus, Babylonia, and Egypt. Sacred men attached to the temples acted as homosexual prostitutes.

GREECE

The Greeks almost eliminated love from the marriage relationship. Love and sexual stimulation were derived from prostitutes, who were necessary in preventing adultery. The Grecian brothels were sanctuaries within which one was immune from debts and creditors and from irate wives. Three classes of ancient Grecian prostitution are clearly documented: Hetairae were the aristocrats of Greek prostitution and were likened to the European courtesans or the American call girls. The word "hetairae" means companions. These women were often the intellectual companions of influential Greek men, and they were known for their beauty and wit. Auletrides were the dancers and flute players who, in addition to entertaining, performed sexual services. Dicteriades were the streetwalkers and the brothel prostitutes.

ROME

Roman prostitution vacillates from one extreme to the other. Early Rome severely regulated and restricted prostitution. Later, prostitution became rampant. Prostitutes worked in taverns, in parks, and on beaches; they walked the streets and worked in both lavish and wretched brothels. The Roman period is most notorious for its baths, the forerunners of the modern massage parlors. Male and female prostitutes worked in the baths and gave a variety of sexual services. Prostitutes also frequented the Roman amphitheaters. The arches or fornices of the theaters formed secluded places and served as brothels. The word fornication is derived from "fornix." In Rome, homosexual prostitution was as prevalent as heterosexual prostitution. Sexual exploitation of children was commonplace. Nursing babies were used to perform fellatio. Girls as young as 5 or 6 died of venereal diseases.

EUROPE

In the early Christian era the Church both tolerated and sanctioned prostitution, but soon it adopted the antisexual view of the older Hebraic code. The end of the Middle Ages saw the establishment of red-light districts. Bawdy houses were so designated by hanging red lanterns at the doors. Prostitution flourished throughout Europe in every major city.

The Renaissance brought the emergence of the great courtesans. The wearing of lipstick was originated by prostitutes in the Middle East during this period. Lipstick was supposed to make the lips resemble the vulva and was worn by women who specialized in fellatio. Wealthy and powerful nobles married courtesans. Pope Alexander VI (1431–1503) was known to entertain these women at the Vatican.

In the 16th century, venereal disease was first associated with sexual promiscuity. This association initiated the regulation and the suppression of prostitution. However, French and British prostitution continued to flourish throughout the 18th century. This period in France became known as the golden age of prostitution.

UNITED STATES

American prostitution began with the settlers and the Indians. Indian women were treated badly by their spouses and were willing to give themselves sexually to white men in exchange for a few trinkets. Indian poverty and sexual freedom paved the way for massive Indian prostitution.

Indian prostitution was largely replaced by the sexual exploitation of female slaves. Men of great distinction purchased slave women for sexual use. Female offspring of white and slave unions were sold to the brothels as prostitutes. They were in high demand and were called fancy girls. This was the fate of daughters of President Thomas Jefferson and President John Tyler.

The industrial revolution and the gold rush of 1849 impelled a change in prostitution. Along the Eastern seaboard, many young women gravitated to work in factories in the large cities. The long hours and low wages were inadequate and disheartening. These girls were not acquainted with young men for desirable marriages. To fight poverty and to meet men, some turned to prostitution. The industrial revolution also brought an influx of European immigrants. European prostitutes were encouraged to migrate or were deported to America. The European immigrants and prostitutes, destitute and unable to make their way, established the first American brothels. The gold rush to the West Coast brought large numbers of adventuresome women, who traveled after the young men. Brothels sprang up near the mining camps and towns.

The last part of the 19th century and the first part of the 20th century are known as the golden age of brothels in America. The sexual double standard gave rise to the establishment of American red-light districts; they were legal in Louisiana, Arkansas, and New Mexico and were tolerated in every major city. Registration, licensing, and medical regulation were at times imposed. A house of prostitution was called a bordello, cathouse, cat wagon, joy house, parlor house, house of ill repute, whorehouse, or sport house. Some of the bordellos gained national and international fame. Red-light districts in New York, San Francisco, Chicago, and New Orleans were especially notorious.

The most successful and lavish house was run by the Everleigh sisters in Chicago from 1900 to 1911. They invested $55,000 in their house and retired in 1911 with more than a million dollars. Basin Street in New Orleans was infamous for houses from the most wretched to the most lavish. *The Little Blue Book,* a guide to pleasure in New Orleans, became the most famous guidebook to expensive bordellos. Nell Kimball and Kate Townsend were the prosperous madams in New Orleans. The brothels of New York were concentrated between West 28th Street and West 30th Street and on the lower East Side in tenement areas. Polly Adler was the most famous New York madam.

Seven distinct types of prostitution establishments are described by Burnett and Seegar: (1) Clip joints or panel houses—while a customer was sexually occupied, his money was stolen by an accomplice through a panel in a closet. (2) Whore houses—assembly-line businesses where a customer was time-limited. (3) Houses of assignation—traffic control centers for call girls. (4) Cribs—single rooms large enough for only a bed; the prostitutes solicited through open windows and doorways. (5) Brothels—two-story buildings with bedrooms upstairs and a living room on the first floor, where there was socializing before sex. (6) Sporting houses—expensive houses that featured fine liquor and music and imposed no time limits. (7) Mansions—the elite of houses, where evening gowns were worn and champagne was served; there was socializing first with beautifully dressed and coiffed prostitutes, and elegant gourmet dining was available.

In the 1920's and 1930's brothels

flourished. After World War I, soldiers who had been exposed to French organized prostitution returned to the United States and became the clientele for these brothels. Even during the depression, prostitution continued on the rise. Egos, deflated because of the decline in earning power, drove some men to the brothels, where they could assert their masculinity. Unemployment made time available. The emotional struggles at home often made wives withdraw from sex, and men sought gratification from prostitutes. Fees were lowered during the depression. Some women became part-time prostitutes to supplement their family income. Prostitution became associated with venereal disease and criminality during this period. The Mann Act of 1911 penalized the transportation across state lines of women for immoral purposes.

Brothels did not decline in numbers until after World War II. With the decline of brothels, prostitution became less organized. The major shift in prostitution in the past three decades has been from organized business to individual entrepreneurship. Call houses arose. A client could call a number to make an appointment to meet a girl at an agreed-on place. With the close of the brothels, prostitutes were forced into the streets, bars, and taverns. Prostitution was not eliminated; streetwalking replaced the brothels.

With the decline of organized prostitution, it is more difficult to estimate the extent of prostitution in the United States. Prostitution is often a symbol of conspicuous consumption and power. Call girls are frequently entertained in certain elite political and business circles. In the United States, the prostitute of today is the chief means by which a man can gratify unusual sexual desires. At present, Nevada is the only state that recognizes legal prostitution.

Prostitutes

Prostitution may be defined as the granting of nonmarital access established by mutual agreement of the woman, her client, and her employer for remuneration that provides part or all of her livelihood. Often called the oldest profession, prostitution is a trade. It differs from other trades in that the woman rents her body; it is similar in that she has a service to sell. Few prostitutes claim that they like their work; in fact, they find it repetitious and boring. Most find prostitution degrading. Modern prostitutes work shorter hours than did the brothel prostitutes of the 1920's, but many work 10 hours a day, 7 days a week.

TYPES

Call girl

Greenwald states, "The call girls are the aristocrats of prostitution." Call girls live in the most expensive residential sections of large cities. They dress in rich, good taste. They charge a minimum of $25 for each sexual contact. Many women receive fees of $50 to $100 for a sexual contact and as much as $250 for all-night arrangements. Call girls earn between $30,000 and $100,000 a year, all tax-free. However, the call girls have heavy expenses and live so extravagantly that very few manage to accumulate any sizable savings. Expenses include telephone and answering services, expensive apartments and clothing, and high laundry bills. Call girls must take particular care of their personal hygiene and their appearance. Therefore, a great deal of money is spent on cosmetics, perfumes, beauty shops, physicians' examinations, abortions, and prophylactic doses of antibiotics. A large expense is the payoff and protection money to landlords, superintendents, doormen, and the police. Call girls are also generous tippers.

Call girls usually acquire their clients from satisfied customers or from other call girls. Often, call girls work for a madam who provides clients. Wealthy businessmen may provide call girl services for their business associates. Contact is made through a phone call, and arrangements are made for a visit to either the caller's apartment or the call girl's apartment. If business is particularly slow, a call girl may initiate a call from her black book, which contains names of clients in code, the fees paid, and sexual preferences. Black books are bought and sold for thousands of dollars. Cocktail lounges and restaurants are sometimes the haunts of call girls, and bartenders and managers sometimes act as intermediaries and introduce potential clients. Call girls generally work between the hours of 3 P.M. and 3 A.M. In-town customers prefer late afternoons; out-of-towners prefer evening hours.

Call girls are better educated than other prostitutes. Some are college graduates. They often come from middle-class backgrounds, and all have greater self-discipline than other prostitutes. The call girl is more skillful than her colleagues in the erotic arts. She knows her customer, his sexual preferences and fantasies. She creates the illusion that time is unimportant, and she simulates pleasure and orgastic responses. The most accurate and representative portrayal of a call girl was given by Jane Fonda in the film "Klute."

The call girl has fewer sexual contacts than her colleagues. Status is very important to the call girl, and all call girls disassociate themselves from other types of prostitutes. Call girls are usually in their twenties and thirties.

Brothel worker

Few cities have large brothels now. However, some houses are in operation today and are quite lavish. The brothel prostitutes closely resemble the call girls in life-style.

Streetwalker

Most prostitutes are streetwalkers. They are most visible as they ply their trade on the streets in large cities. With the suppression of brothels, streetwalking immediately increased. Streetwalkers are the most difficult prostitutes to suppress, since they are highly mobile, moving from street to street, area to area, city to city, and state to state.

Streetwalkers receive lower fees than call girls do. It is not unusual for a streetwalker to get $5 for a quickie. Streetwalkers are generally less attractive than call girls; they contract and spread venereal disease more readily, are less fastidious in their personal hygiene, and dress more uniformly, often in hot pants or miniskirts and high boots. Streetwalkers congregate in business areas, where there is much street traffic. They are frequently arrested, since they have a high degree of exposure to the police. The street-walker who makes continuous contacts with unknown customers is apt to be robbed,

beaten, or victimized by dangerous sexual deviates. Streetwalkers are younger than call girls; many are in their teens and early twenties. Most black women in prostitution are streetwalkers. Most streetwalkers keep pimps.

Bar girl

Bar girls work out of bars and taverns that cater to a blue-collar, drinking clientele. Bar girls tend to be whites from lower-class backgrounds; they have less than a high school education, and most quickly become alcoholics. Much of their time is spent in bars, consuming drinks while waiting for a client. Fees are relatively low, and often they are not collected because the prostitute passes out or is too drunk to remember. Bar prostitutes live in cheap rooming houses and hotels, and they change their addresses frequently. Some are quite attractive when they enter the life. They rapidly age and lose their appearance. Poor diets, excess alcohol, and poor hygiene contribute to a rapid deterioration. Bar prostitutes operate alone and do not have pimps.

A fleabag is an old-time bar prostitute, often 60 or 70 years of age. Her clientele are skid-row alcoholics and derelicts. Her fee is as low as 50 cents or whatever she can get.

Baby pro

The baby pro is usually less than 16 years old. She works conventions, resorts, and hotels. In recent years there has been an increasing demand for pubertal prostitutes. Many baby pros turn to the streets or, if attractive and ambitious enough, are soon working under the tutelage of an experienced call girl or pimp. But mobility in prostitution is generally downward.

BACKGROUND

Family

Prostitutes generally come from intact families with poor family relationships or from broken homes. With the exception of call girls, prostitutes are usually from a low economic class status; many are from rural and farming communities. Many come from an existence of relative material deprivation. Often, prostitution was covertly encouraged by their mothers, who were living with men in nonmarital arrangements. The mothers were overprotective, rigid, competitive, and neglectful. The fathers were absent either physically or emotionally. Hostility toward the fathers was universal. Many prostitutes report that their fathers had shown overt interest in their sexuality. Sexual relations with family members is fairly common. The attitude of both parents toward their children was one of complete rejection. The parental rejection gave the daughters a feeling of complete worthlessness.

Religion

Studies show that 41 per cent of prostitutes are Catholic, 39 per cent are Protestant, 12 per cent are Jewish, and 7 per cent are of other faiths. These big city statistics are considered representative.

Education

Few prostitutes are well educated. Call girls generally have a high school or college education. Many prostitutes are school dropouts. They completed elementary school, but few finished high school. School was seen by prostitutes as too regimented and as an obstacle toward immediate gratification. Truancy was frequent. Prostitutes are not feeble-minded; most are of average intelligence.

Work experience

Before taking to prostitution, they were unskilled workers, such as clerks and waitresses. Jobs are seen as boring and financially unrewarding. No escape other than prostitution is seen possible. Some prostitutes are aspiring actresses and models who used sexuality for entry into a glamorous and exciting world. While working at conventional jobs, many became sexually involved with their bosses to ease their work conditions and to obtain favors.

Peer relationships

Prostitutes usually associate with others of similar backgrounds. Often, as adolescents they were members of juvenile gangs and were considered semidelinquent. A history of poor interpersonal relationships is common.

Sexuality

Sexual promiscuity is frequently reported in the sexual history of prostitutes. Coming from backgrounds that promote sexual behavior, these women were introduced to sex at early ages. They frequently observed parents and peers engaging in sex. Sexual relations with family members was much more the rule than the exception. Many first engaged in sex at age 10. Most had their initial sexual experiences between ages 14 and 16. These women usually entered prostitution about 2 years after their initial sex experiences.

ENTERING PROSTITUTION

Understanding the background is important in considering why women turn to prostitution. During the course of history, women turned to prostitution because of severe economic deprivation. This is no longer the case, but economic considerations remain an important underlying factor. Today, a woman who becomes a prostitute does so voluntarily.

Dislike of regimen and discipline in conventional jobs is often a motivating factor. Boredom is associated with the square world, and a woman looking for glamour and excitement sees prostitution as the way to this glamorous world.

Many women consider themselves ugly and unwanted. Through prostitution they can have men who would not otherwise be available to them. Some see prostitution as the only field in which they may meet important and exciting men. Some women hold the fantasy that a Prince Charming will rescue them. This fantasy is not necessarily unfounded, since a number of prostitutes have married respected and wealthy clients. The success rate of these marriages, however, is poor.

For some unskilled women who wish to achieve status and wear good clothing, prostitution is the only means for achieving upward economic mobility. Recently, many women addicts have been driven to prostitution to support their habit. Lack of success in the mainstream of society's vocational opportunities may encourage women to enter prostitution. In ghetto areas, where prostitution is taken for granted and where conventional opportunities are limited, minority women can make large sums of money in prostitution. Women from small towns and rural communities come to big cities looking for fantasied opportunities. Demoralized by loneliness, poverty, and the lack of success, some turn to prostitution.

Many women, because of intrapsychic and social disorganization, feel worthless. In their families, they discovered at an early age, that they could receive affection and interest by giving sexual gratification. They carry this method into their adult life, where they acquire the skill of seduction and, in return, obtain favors and money.

Peer associates may introduce women into prostitution. Sociologist Edwin Sutherland refers to differential association. Women who become prostitutes have often been associated with other prostitutes or pimps, who have enticed and introduced the women to prostitution. Traditional tales relate that madams have forced virginal young women into the life. Today, a madam has more applicants for work than she can accommodate. Prostitutes frequently give tearful stories to clients to elicit sympathy, tips, and higher fees. Few prostitutes report having been traumatized by their initiation into prostitution.

Karl Abraham saw prostitution as an act of hostility directed against the father. He stated:

> Just as Don Juan avenges himself on all women for the disappointment he once received from the first woman who entered his life, so the prostitute avenges herself on every man for the gift that she had expected from her father and had not received.

Edward Glover sees prostitution as a fixation at the oedipal phase. A prostitute is still tied to her father, but prostitution is a way of denying the attachment. Helene Deutsch also sees the oedipal situation's importance in that a girl views her mother's sex life with her father with rage and jealousy. Seeing the father's unfaithfulness to them, girls retaliate with their own unfaithfulness to all men, instead of to one. Caprio sees prostitution as a defense against homosexuality.

Prostitutes felt biparental rejection. Replacing sexual interest in one with sexual interest in many serves as a defense by denying that originally there was a parental love object. Revenge against men—they must pay for the sexual contact—is symbolic of revenge against the father—that is, revenge for not caring or revenge for parental seduction. The moral humiliation of prostitution may reflect an extreme masochism and guilt about early sexuality.

The prostitute may also be seen in light of biparental deprivation. Deprivation from the nurturing mother, as well as the father, gives rise to desperate needs to receive from anyone. Because of this need, the prostitute may never develop to later stages of psychosexual development; she maintains her polymorphous perverse status. Money is the symbol of nurturance, love, warmth, and acceptance; but money is only symbolic, not satisfying. Money buys the pimp and tries to buy the love and warmth. Unsure of their femininity, prostitutes have many men in attempts to reassure themselves.

Hostility is omnipresent in prostitutes. However, the hostility is usually expressed against themselves, whereas their pimps direct their hostility outward. Suicide and risk-taking behavior are occupational hazards. An estimated nine out of 10 prostitutes make suicide attempts—some, unfortunately, successful.

Psychoanalytic studies stress the frigidity of prostitutes. However, prostitutes often experience sex on an intense level with a pimp or a boyfriend. With clients, a prostitute experiences lack of involvement in the sexual act. Perhaps, if the act is not pleasurable, a prostitute experiences less guilt.

LEAVING PROSTITUTION

Squaring up or leaving the life is the renunciation of prostitution. Giving up prostitution is extremely difficult. Difficulties lie in the financial area. Working as a prostitute, a woman can earn up to $2,000 a week. To take a $90 or $150 a week clerical job is emotionally and financially unrewarding. Also, many prostitutes establish interdependent relationships with pimps, and they find these relationships difficult to relinquish. The maturing-out theory of prostitution suggests that women advance in age, lose their attractiveness and clientele, and drift out of prostitution.

Janus and Bess found that many prostitutes renounce prostitution because of any combination of the following: (1) arrest and threat of long term incarceration; (2) legal agencies insisting on foster care, adoption, and loss of their children; (3) the fear of loss of an eligible man's love; and (4) knowledge that a girlfriend was the victim of violence during the course of work. Women who leave and successfully stay out of prostitution usually marry or get their status needs met with higher level vocational retraining and entry into more exciting and gratifying jobs than before. Nursing, social work, sales, stewardessing, and hostessing are common fields of employment chosen by ex-prostitutes. The number of autobiographies and novels indicates that many become authors.

Madams

From the golden days of the brothel, the madam is primarily a historical figure and is the best known of commercialized prostitution's third persons. The madam was the manager-hostess of the brothel. Many madams enjoyed both national and international fame. They possessed remarkable personalities and financial finesse. Madams often referred to each other as landladies. The madam of a brothel had her women reside in the brothel and was ultimately in charge of all aspects of their lives. The madam of a call house did not have residential quarters but had women available during specified hours. With the prohibition of prostitution, the number of madams diminished. Present-day madams operate only call houses. The famous madam of the 1970's is Xaviera Hollander, author of *The Happy Hooker*, who is reputed to have managed the most expensive call house in New York City. The house was closed through the efforts of the Knapp Commission.

Most madams are ex-prostitutes who consider themselves detached from their earlier role. The personalities of the madams, allowing for individual differences, have basic common traits. Madams are usually of superior intelligence, they are very ambitious, and they have self-discipline. The self-discipline

enables the madam to achieve her goals and to function as a supportive figure for her women. Madams have leadership qualities; they are aggressive, firm, and consistent but warm. They must be astute judges of character to survive. Madams boast of their ability to spot police officers in mufti and to recognize a potential troublesome client or an unmanageable girl. They relate well with people from all walks of life, from underworld figures to politicians. The madam has to be constantly alert to unhappy customers and must work to appease them.

The madam recruits the women for her house. She becomes the educator of these women, teaching them the tricks of the trade. Often, one-way mirrors are installed in houses so that a madam may observe a girl and her client. The madam uses this mirror as a teaching device; she watches the on-the-job performance and later intructs or praises the girl. In addition, the madam gives instruction on how to dress, speak, use cosmetics, manage money, and maintain personal hygiene. A madam is the Professor Higgins for her Eliza Doolittles.

In the 1920's and 1930's, the madam assumed a tremendous responsibility in managing a house. She was the person responsible for the total maintenance of the brothel. The madam had to both attract and retain customers and prostitutes. She had to ameliorate arguments and jealousies among her women and had to be sensitive to a client's needs. She established contacts with the police for security and protection.

The madam is characterized by her maternalism. A house becomes a home and family for many prostitutes; in fact, the madam is often called "Mother." At times, the madam had strong emotional attachments to her women. Only rarely did she encourage lesbian relationships, since such relationships would undermine her authority.

A madam usually has an important man in her life—half-lover, half-pimp. The madam regularly gives him money and lavish gifts but never regards him as a pimp. The paramour has little or nothing to do with the management of the house. In general, madams detest pimps, some of whom represent competition. They refuse to employ women controlled by pimps. A few madams cooperate with pimps, since they see this relationship as a way to keep the prostitutes in line.

Usually, madams do not have sexual relationships with clients. They do not want to risk a competitive relationship between them and the women working for them. They clearly demarcate the status difference between prostitute and madam. Beverly Davis, a famous madam and the author of *Call House Madam*, states,

> The ethics of a parlor house require that the madam does not compete with her girls.

Madams are subject to arrest more readily than are prostitutes, and they must pay higher fines and stricter penalties. Madams who are imprisoned usually return to their vocation after release. Some famous madams speak of being incarcerated dozens of times. Madams leave their vocation after having been driven out by the law. Some have gone on to other vocations. Many wrote autobiographies. Polly Adler, a famous New York madam and the author of *A House Is Not a Home,* began a college education on the West Coast. Some madams leave the vocation destitute; others retire with great wealth. The Everleigh sisters of Chicago retired to New York, and, through wise investments with the million dollars made in their brothel, they lived in wealth until their deaths.

Pimps

The pimp is the paid companion-master of the prostitute, and he derives all or most of his earnings from the prostitute. The pimp is not usually a procurer or panderer.

A procurer, also known as a panderer, is the go-between for the prostitute and the client. He may also serve as an intermediary between a pimp and a prospective prostitute. Panderers are rarely pimps; however, pimps are occasionally panderers. Procurers often introduce women into prostitution and arrange their appointments. Bartenders and businessmen are often procurers. All states have laws that prosecute procurers, but some have laws more stringent than others.

The pimp's functions include obtaining money from their women, providing bail if the prostitute is arrested, being alert to arrest, securing a lawyer if needed, and providing shelter, food, clothing, and pocket money for the prostitute. Very important is the provision of companionship. For the prostitute, the relationship between herself and her pimp is an emotional one. For the pimp it is a business relationship, with the emotionality as a necessary evil.

The pimp is associated with the underworld or gray world. He may be engaged in part-time criminal activity. He associates only with these connections and with prostitutes. Pimps have their own code of ethics apart from society's moral code. Pimps are proud of their manner of living. In fact, they live in such a way as to bring attention to their status as pimp. They live luxuriously in expensive apartments, dress flamboyantly and in characteristic flashy, bright, lacy, and frilly apparel. Leather and furs are preferences. No successful pimp is deprived of a mink coat. Conspicuous automobiles, the pimpmobile, are *sine qua nons*. Customized Cadillacs, Continentals, and expensive prestige foreign cars, upholstered with furs and glitter, are standard for pimps.

A pimp's typical day may include rising late, dining at a good restaurant, gambling, checking out his women, in the early hours having a cup of coffee with several of his women, and retiring with or without one of the women to his home. Copping new women or narcotics is another major activity. The life span of the pimp-prostitute relationship is relatively short. The prostitute may be arrested and jailed, may leave the pimp, or may become financially unproductive. Since the pimp depends on the earnings of the prostitute, he must always be recruiting new women. Recruitment may come from loitering in the courts and posting bail for prostitutes without money or through social activities, such as parties and after-hours clubs. The pimp is an expert in luring women into the life. By faking emotional involvement, offering false promises, and making drugs, especially cocaine, available, he can manipulate a woman to prostitute for him.

Pimps assume fancy and unusual names like Black Devil, Red Devil, Silky, Pretty

Boy, Big Colossal, Bomber, and Snake. The prostitute-pimp relationship has a characteristic vocabulary. Prostitutes are referred to as whores, girls, working girls, harlots, strumpets, tarts, and hookers. Prostitutes working for one pimp are in his stable and are called wives. The women of the same pimp refer to themselves as wives-in-law. An outlaw is a prostitute unattached to a pimp. The bottom woman is the favorite in a stable.

During the 1920's and 1930's pimps were predominantly Jewish and Italian. Sociologist Sara Harris estimates that 90 per cent of present-day pimps in the United States are black or Puerto Rican. Black pimps prefer white women, who make more money, have an easier time soliciting tricks, and have less difficulty with police and society. It is said that white prostitutes more readily accept the situation of being one among others in a stable. By exploiting white women, the black pimp may feel that he is getting revenge in a society that has suppressed the black male ego.

There is a high incidence of drug addiction and alcoholism among pimps. Many pimps use drugs to relax and combat sexual anxiety. Pimps claim that drugs enhance their sexual activity by prolonging erections and thereby giving them a sense of manhood. Many pimps are narcotic pushers who introduce their women to drugs. A pimp is better able to bind a drug-dependent woman to him. Hooked on heroin or cocaine, a prostitute depends on her pimp as the source of her drugs.

There are many sexual myths about the prostitute-pimp relationship. Stories about the great sexual prowess of pimps have never been validated. In fact, the sexual aspect of the relationship is least important. Neither the pimp nor the prostitute is able to enter into a genuine affectionate and intimate sex-love relationship. Each finds the other's sexual and intimate incapacity less threatening than a more mature reciprocal relationship. Although prostitutes report that they are more orgastic and fulfilled physically with their pimps than with clients, their sexual relationships are frequently limited to oral sex. Pimps prefer fellatio, and, by engaging in cunnilingus, they can gratify several of their women in a shorter period of time.

Preference for oral sex may reflect the pimp's passivity and his nurturing needs. It does not challenge his potency.

The pimp gives the prostitute an illusion that she is needed and that someone really cares. Prostitution, despite the frequency of contacts, gives rise to profound loneliness. The pimp is usually the only object of affection in a prostitute's life. He provides her with the companionship she desperately needs and the semblance of a family life. This companionship is the most motivating factor in sustaining the relationship. With her pimp, the prostitute can relax, converse, discuss her work, and, in general, be herself. The pimp is someone to meet after work hours for a drink and someone to go home to, even though he is shared. After entering the life, the prostitute cuts herself off from her family and former associates. the pimp becomes a surrogate husband, father, mother, relative, and friend. The pimp provides the stability, discipline, and encouragement to continue in prostitution.

Because of his connection with the underworld, the pimp can provide his women with protection against theft, which they are frequently subject to, since prostitutes do not complain to the police.

The prostitute's need for masochistic dominance is an important factor in their relationship. Often, the prostitute will do anything to placate her pimp. She resolves disagreements by, typically, assuming the entire blame and punishment. Often, she is the victim of brutal beatings, which leave her injured and bleeding. The prostitute excuses her pimp with the rationalization that she deserved punishment. She shares with the pimp the belief that these beatings are demonstrations of love. Masochism is an important dynamic in the relationship. Violence is used as an emotional communication.

Prostitutes need pimps to upgrade their own position, and they symbolically say of their pimps, "They are the only things lower than me." Prostitutes do not testify against their pimps, making the apprehension of pimps very difficult. Pimps tend to remain in their vocation until driven out by law enforcement. They subsequently drift into some other illegal activities.

The commonly held psychodynamic formulation concerning the character of the pimp is as follows: The pimp is an extremely passive-dependent person who needs total and continuous nurturance. Being kept by a prostitute is the regression to being cared for by the all-giving and forgiving mother. The pimp's preference for oral sex is seen as a mother fixation. Castration fears and impotence are motivating factors. A pimp's sense of self and male identity is impaired. A reaction formation ensues, with the stress on the supermasculine, superaggressive, totally controlling, virile, and tough image. Many pimps have strong latent homosexual drives. The supermasculine image serves as a cover; the vicarious relationship with other men through the prostitute's contacts with clients defends the homosexual theory. In addition, by being the man singled out by a woman who has hundreds of contacts with other men and by having this woman readily succumb to his control and dominance, the pimp reassures himself of his manhood. A pimp both gratifies his passive cravings and simultaneously denies them. The relationship with the prostitute both bolsters the pimp's self-esteem and undermines it. The pimp may feel supremacy with his control and dominance and his flashy cars and clothes, but he is constantly reminded that his livelihood from the prostitute makes him the lowest of the low. Only his externalization of his aggression prevents a feeling of complete worthlessness, self-destruction, and suicidal tendencies.

Lesbian pimps are usually former prostitutes who have made an association, usually while in jail. The lesbian pimp typically assumes the butch or bull dyke role and adopts male clothing. The lesbian pimp and her prostitute live together. Most lesbian pimps are black and have only one woman at a time.

Customers

The customer or client of a prostitute is most frequently referred to as a john or a trick. Other names are sucker, meatball, patron, and beefbuyer.

The Kinsey study in 1948 reported that two-thirds of American men had had at least one contact with a prostitute and that 15 to 20 per cent had had multiple contacts; 74 per cent of nonhigh school graduate men had had sexual experiences with prostitutes. Today, it is estimated that the same number of men visit prostitutes but that the number of contacts has decreased since the closing of the brothels. Many more adolescent and single men were clients in the 1940's. At present, 75 per cent of clients are in their 40's or 50's and are overwhelmingly married men. The decline in the younger clientele is attributed to the loosening of sexual restrictions. In the 1940's, 25 per cent of American men's first sexual experience was with a prostitute. In the late 1960's, only 5 per cent had their initial sexual experience with a prostitute.

OCCASIONAL JOHNS

These clients make up about 60 per cent of all clientele. These are often salesmen out of town who want the services of a woman. Sailors in port for a short time also frequent prostitutes. Many occasional johns are respectable family men and businessmen who seek a change and find sex with a prostitute less threatening to the marriage relationship than a romantic affair would be. Extramarital relationships demand emotional involvement.

HABITUAL JOHNS

These clients frequent prostitutes more than the occasional johns do, but they are not driven to them. Often, they try to establish relationships that are beyond the sexual. Married men who are habitual johns seek sexual variety that is not practiced at home, especially oral sex. Often, they desire sex more frequently than their wives do, and so they turn to prostitutes for sexual gratification. Frequently, sexual deprivation in the marriage sends men to prostitutes. Also, men who are without women for long periods of time and who do not wish to or cannot make other relationships become habitual johns. Wealthy and prominent men—sometimes celebrities on stage, in sports, and in politics who want to avoid entangling alliances—patronize expensive call girls. Frequently, this type of client also provides prostitute companions for business associates.

COMPULSIVE JOHNS

These clients are the men who are driven to prostitutes for their major sexual gratification. Despite guilt and frequently made resolutions, they cannot keep away. In this category are men who seek out prostitutes for sexual activity because of preference.

One type of compulsive john is the man who can be potent only with a prostitute. He has so identified sex with sin and has so separated love and sex that sex is possible only with a degraded woman, and love is possible only in a sexless relationship. Freud states,

Where they love, they can feel no passion, and where they feel passion, they cannot love.

This dichotomy is known in the vernacular as the Madonna-harlot complex.

The physically handicapped may have gratification only with prostitutes. Toulouse-Lautrec, who was grotesquely deformed, had sex only with prostitutes.

Some compulsive johns are unable to establish intimate relationships. They avoid female contacts with the excuse that such contacts demand emotional entanglements and moral obligations and involve the risk of pregnancy.

Many compulsive johns are men who have deviant sexual needs that can rarely be satisfied except through paid sexual relations. Perversions are specialties of prostitutes. Exhibitionism, voyeurism, and sadomasochism are common. Watching two women perform simulated sex or taking part in a *ménage à trois* are some preferences. Transvestite clients can cross-dress with a prostitute. Coprolalia—the use of obscene language—is the only sexual turn-on for some men. Rather than degrade their mates, these men prefer prostitutes to be the initiator or recipient. Fetishists are also found among the compulsive johns. Enthusiastic compulsive johns are those requiring discipline—that is, sadomasochistic sexual practices: whippings, beatings, being tied up, or tying up the prostitute. These johns frequent prostitutes often enough that prostitutes wear dresses with cloth belts, so that, when they are beaten, their own belts are used. For the most part, the beatings are symbolic, but occasionally an enthusiastic client gets so carried away that the prostitute is severely injured. Even more bizarre sexual practices are sometimes demanded. Some brothels had rooms decorated as funeral chapels for those men who wanted to simulate intercourse with a corpse. Prostitutes defecate on and urinate, as either donor or recipient. The more bizarre the john's perversion, the higher the fee.

It is estimated that increasing numbers of johns of all types are seeking oral relations and that nine out of 10 customers today want some form of oral gratification, most commonly fellatio, also called frenching. In contrast, the service most frequently sought before World War II was genital-genital intercourse. The increase in oral sexual needs reflects the changing sexual mores and the fact that sexual intercourse is readily available today outside of prostitution. Oral sex, although a common sexual practice, is still seen by some as a sexual perversion and is often denied in the marriage arrangement.

Clients' reactions to the circumstances under which they visit prostitutes differ. Some resent the speed and the businesslike manner. Others are so needy that they are oblivious of all but the sexual gratification, no matter how brief. An experience with a prostitute can evoke extreme anxiety, depression, or tremendous elation. During his initial visit, the customer often experiences sexual difficulty in performance, often impotence. Clients use fictitious names to avoid exposure. Frequently, a client has the fantasy of reforming the prostitute and taking her out of the life. This fantasy is frequently shared and encouraged by the prostitute.

Venereal Disease

Throughout the centuries, venereal disease has been the major medical hazard for prostitutes and their clients. Prostitution was the single greatest source of venereal infections until the advent of penicillin. This is not the case today, but too often prostitution is blamed for the spread of venereal disease.

At the time of World War I, 23 per cent of prostitutes showed overt signs of syphilis, and 74 per cent showed a positive Wassermann test. Before 1939, three-fourths of all venereal disease was contracted through prostitution.

In 1946, an estimated 21 per cent of prostitutes had syphilis and in 1956 only 8.5 per cent. Present estimates show that female prostitutes account for only 5 per cent of American venereal disease cases. Male homosexuals and homosexual prostitution probably account for many present cases. There has been a great increase in venereal disease among uneducated minors. However, the decline in brothels may also be a major factor in the upsurge in venereal disease in the United States in the past two decades. In 1921 Wolbarst demonstrated that the suppression of prostitution increases venereal infection. Suppression results in clandestine and amateur prostitution, followed by an increase in venereal disease.

In 1958 Italian brothels were closed. Before they were closed, the reported venereal disease cases numbered 1,679. By 1963 the cases numbered 16,395. Prohibition of prostitution drives women into the streets, and these women are less likely to seek medical attention. For years it has been routine for women in call houses to examine clients for chancres and signs of gonorrhea and to get periodic medical and prophylactic treatment.

Professional prostitutes now regularly take prophylactic oral or injectable penicillin. In the United States penicillin has sharply reduced the likelihood that the professional prostitute is the major source of venereal disease.

The Military

The problem of prostitution in times of war has always been of concern to the military. The practice of prostitution changes with the wars and law enforcement. Whenever healthy young men in their sexual prime are isolated and segregated, sexual outlets become necessary. Their health and welfare become chief concerns. Prostitution has been seen as a moral and physical hazard by authorities who feel the need for suppression and elimination.

There is an increase in prostitution during wartime, explained by the changes in social life. Young men no longer live under parental control and are freer to do as they please. The camaraderie with peers often leads them to experiment with prostitutes. The stress of being together only with men and the stress of being together only with men and the stress of the military life make them seek some outlet. A sense of masculine identity and competition is associated with visiting prostitutes. The uncertainty of being alive tomorrow causes one to live it up tonight. Wherever armies travel or are stationed, they are usually accompanied by prostitutes, who look after the personal and sexual needs of the men.

Before World War I, organized prostitution and segregated areas with brothels flourished. An increase in amateur prostitutes was seen in 1917 and 1918. These women, filled with patriotism, traveled to the training camps and were eager to be of help. Not being able to support themselves, they drifted into prostitution. They became known as victory girls and were well known to the populace during World War I. Some women who were left behind at home—manless, bored, and unable to support themselves— also drifted into part-time prostitution.

Venereal disease increased dramatically. The primitive treatment available was ineffective. This disease problem brought attention to the problem of prostitution. Venereal disease incapacitated soldiers for active duty. In 1917 the venereal disease rate in the army was 108 per 1,000. The military then took steps to regulate and suppress prostitution.

The Training Camp Activities Commission adopted a four-point program: (1) Occupy the soldiers' time with wholesome activities. (2) Educate them about prostitution and venereal disease. (3) Enforce the law against prostitution. (4) Give medical treatment for venereal disease. As a result, recreational and social centers were created. Houses of detention and reformation were established to treat women engaged in prostitution with military personnel. Section 17 of the draft act prohibited prostitution near training camps. As a result of the military's concern and law enforcement, every red-light district in every major city was eliminated by the end of World War I. European brothels were placed off limits.

The abolition of segregated prostitution only created a dispersion of prostitution, and prostitutes were still readily available. The military did not take into consideration the sexual needs of the young men. At the end of the war and military rule, prostitution continued to flourish.

In World War II there was again a resurgence of prostitution in military areas. Young women flocked to areas frequented by servicemen and defense workers. Victory girls re-emerged. The eight-point agreement formulated by the U.S. Public Health Service, the American Social Health Association, and the armed forces aimed at the eradication of prostitution. Other committees were formed to control venereal disease, but they shifted their emphasis to the eradication of prostitution. The Mann Act was passed by Congress in July 1941; it prohibited prostitution near naval and military establishments. The enforcement of this act was carried out by the Federal Bureau of Investigation. Since 1926, penalties and disciplinary action had been taken against those contracting venereal disease. In September 1944 the penalties were eliminated, and the provision of medical care was established.

The eight-point agreement was not effective overseas, where the military could not place foreign private establishments off limits. It became impractical to suppress prostitution abroad. For the first time, the military acknowledged the need for sexual release and sought regulation. Soldiers were allowed free access to certain areas in Casablanca in December 1942. Brothels were set aside for the American troops and were closely supervised. In Naples and Sicily, military officers were stationed to make sure the men received prophylactic treatment after leaving the houses. This procedure was practiced in all the European and Oriental theaters of war. A different type of regulated prostitution prevailed in Manila. Benny boys, transvestite male homosexual prostitutes, serviced the military personnel who were too drunk to realize the sex of the prostitute.

Commercialized prostitution hit an all-time low in 1945. However, after World War II, there was an upsurge in prostitution. Commercialized prostitution flourished in American cities between 1945 and 1948. In 1950 the trend was reversed because of rigid law enforcement.

The Korean war of the early 1950's once again brought attention to prostitution, since Korea had legalized segregated brothels. In Okinawa, the prostitutes relied on the American troops for most of their business. Brothels were far enough away from the military establishments to escape regulation but close enough for ready access.

The Vietnam war gave rise to controlled prostitution for the benefit of American servicemen. Brothels were built exclusively for Americans in Ankhe. Boum-boum parlors were extremely popular and, though managed by Vietnamese, were patrolled by the American military police, who checked the pass of every entering soldier. Prostitutes had to have special entertainers' cards and receive weekly medical examinations. Servicemen had to pick up prophylactics before entering the houses, were instructed by the police in proper hygiene to avoid venereal disease, and were given prophylactic treatment before leaving. American servicemen were provided ready access to prostitution. Thousands visited Taipei and Taiwan each month on rest and relaxation leaves. Pamphlets showed the servicemen how to get access to a girl. In the Vietnam war, the military officers came to recognize the effect that sexual continence had on the morale of their men.

Espionage

Espionage and prostitution have a long joint history. Among the most famous historical figures was Mata Hari, whose name has become synonymous with sex and spying. Her activities during World War I in the service of the Germans are reputed to have cost the lives of 50,000 Frenchmen. Political leaks are suspected to occur when politicians patronize call girls.

Drug Addiction

Narcotic addiction and abuse have dramatically increased among prostitutes. In the times of the great brothels, drug use was minimal. Madams did not tolerate drug use, and they kept a tight control on the drug traffic in the brothels. Prostitutes who were addicted or resorting to drugs were immediately expelled from the houses. The brothel provided the family and social relationships and a sense of security and companionship that made drugs unnecessary. The suppression of the brothels is an important factor in the rise of narcotic addiction among prostitutes.

It is important to distinguish between the prostitute who is also an addict and the addict who becomes a prostitute solely to support her drug habit. The former, the prostitute-addict, has freely chosen prostitution as a vocation. She may enter prostitution first and then turn to drugs or do both simultaneously. Prostitute-addicts prefer heroin, cocaine, or some mixture of the two. Prostitutes claim that drugs make it easier for them to ply their trade and that with drugs they are better able to cope with the stresses of their work. They often use drugs to combat the boredom they experience while waiting for clients. Prostitutes are frequently introduced to drugs by their pimps. The pimps encourage their women to use drugs, since the drugs foster dependency and loyalty and reassure them that their women will continue in prostitution.

The addict-prostitute often turns to prostitution only after she is addicted. Prostitution becomes her primary means of earning money to support her narcotic habit. Teenage prostitutes are almost always narcotic addicts who turn to the streets to get money for drugs. Some addicts become streetwalkers when they are as young as 12 years of age. Most teenage addict-prostitutes come from impoverished and minority groups. Some large cities are becoming centers for addict-prostitutes because both drugs and clients are readily available. New York City is the largest center for addict-prostitutes. One-half of all prostitutes in New York are addicts.

Alcohol is generally not abused by streetwalkers and call girls. Alcohol reduces sexual performance and control, and a drunk prostitute is rarely a desirable partner. Skid-row and bar prostitutes are almost always alcoholics. They consume large quantities of alcohol during the hours they sit in bars waiting for a client. Call girls cautiously sip drinks, usually watered-down ones.

Male Homosexuals

Male homosexual prostitution is universal in the Western world. Homosexual prostitutes are frequently visible in England, Germany, France, Italy, Spain, Holland, Scandinavia, and the United States.

The male homosexual prostitute is called a hustler. The client is called a score. The hustler is between 15 and 25 years old. Young men and boys are the most popular.

Most hustlers deny their homosexuality. They insist that they are primarily motivated by making money, and, since they scorn conventional work, they turn to prostitution. However, most hustlers are relatively poor and have little money at any given time.

The hustler is more aware of his client's physical appearance, age, and dress than is his female counterpart. The hustler may adjust his price accordingly. The emphasis on age and the willingness to lower a fee for an attractive client, even taking an attractive free client, suggest the homosexuality of the hustler. The hustler often denies an attraction to his score or a sexual desire, but the fact that he gets an erection and ejaculation indicates a homosexual response. Follow-up studies show that ex-hustlers become exclusively homosexual.

In large cities, parks, street corners, public bathrooms, movie theaters, docks, and steam baths are the locations where hustlers work. These same areas are used for cruising by nonprostitute homosexuals. Hustlers loiter while trying to make contact with a score. They move from seat to seat in all-night movie houses until a contact is made and terms agreed on. They may engage in fellatio or masturbation.

The homosexual client and the prostitute may begin contact on a meat block, a section where male prostitutes are likely to be visible. West 42nd Street in New York City and the Tenderloin section of San Francisco are popular locations. A series of nonverbal acknowledgments ensues and leads to conversation and sparring for 3 to 4 minutes until the matter of payment is settled. Bargaining over price is used to reassure the hustler that he is essentially straight and that he is primarily interested in money.

Some hustlers obviously dress and behave effeminately. Most hustlers, however, are recognizable only by those who are in the life. The majority try to cultivate a supermasculine image by favoring leather jackets and jeans as the usual dress. The clothes are worn tightly to emphasize and delineate their genitals.

Male hustlers are highly mobile and change residences frequently. Often, they live in fly-by-night hotels. Frequently, they have no homes, and they score for a place to shower, shave, stay the night or longer, or have a meal. Hustlers' fees are low. They usually average between $5 and $15 a contact, but often the hustler accepts $1, especially if the client is appealing.

During the age of the brothels, certain houses specialized in male homosexual prostitution and were known as peg houses. With the decline of these houses, turkish baths are used to make homosexual contacts. A hustler retires to a cubicle with a bed, and he lies nude with the door ajar. Scores pace before the doors until they choose one; then they come to monetary terms and engage in sex. Massage parlors employ young hustlers who, in addition to giving a massage, perform other sexual acts if the price is right.

Some male homosexual prostitutes dress in drag and offer fellatio to a client who does not know that the prostitute is a man. Other clients prefer this type of contact and are attracted to the man in female attire. Female impersonators, working in nightclubs, attest to this preference, and they often freelance as prostitutes.

Male homosexual prostitution is probably a major cause of the spread of venereal disease and accounts for some of the recent increase.

Transsexuals

Within the past decade transsexual prostitution has emerged. A transsexual, as used in this context, is a man who actually believes that he is a woman, trapped in the wrong body. He wishes to have his physical state in agreement with his emotional state. He seeks hormonal castration, surgical removal of his genitals, and reconstructive vaginal and vulval surgery. Often, after surgery, there is a need to prove one's femaleness and to reassure oneself. This need often leads to sexual promiscuity and prostitution. The period of prostitution is time-limited, since marriage is a better proof of femininity.

A transsexual may also turn to prostitution for economic reasons. The difficulty in finding a job because of lack of proper identification and credentials may lead to prostitution. Once legal matters are clarified and adjusted, the prostitution ceases. Transsexuals who have not yet been operated on and thus are not legally female may turn to prostitution in order to earn enough money for the costly operation. They do not indulge in coitus or genital fondling, which would expose them. They limit their sexual activity to fellatio.

The Law

Prostitution, like drug addiction, is considered a legal problem, but, unlike drug addiction, prostitution has never been considered a social-medical problem. The long association of prostitution with vice and crime is established. Vice may be only a matter of personal conduct, but both vice and crime are treated in the same manner.

In the United States the laws to suppress and abate prostitution are under state jurisdiction. Laws and penalties differ from state to state. At present, every state, except Nevada, prohibits prostitution. These laws have been in effect since the 1920's but have not always been enforced. Recently, laws have become more stringent, but still the enforcement varies according to the community and the political administration. At election time, campaigns to clean up the streets and abate prostitution take the forefront; shortly after elections, the laxity in enforcement resumes. Streetwalkers, who are highly visible, are the most frequently apprehended. Brothel prostitutes and call girls are rarely arrested, for they are not seen in public places, and they offer large payoffs for police protection. The recent publicity concerning the arrest of Xaviera Hollander of *Happy Hooker* fame indicates the longevity of call houses and the tremendous network of payoffs for protection.

In most large cities where prostitution is prevalent, moral and vice squads are formed to deal with it. Prostitutes quickly learn to identify members of the squads who are posing as clients. Vice squad officers try many approaches to apprehend prostitutes. In the entrapment method they pick up a woman, follow her to a room, and try to entice her to disrobe, so that they may note any identifying marks that can be used in court. Once the woman negotiates the price and offers sexual activity, the policeman identifies himself and makes the arrest. Often, the police stake out suspected places of prostitution, and, when contact between client and prostitute is made, the police move in and raid the place. Informers are frequent aides of the vice squad. Another widely used method is the decoy method. Prostitutes, aware of this method, try to kiss the suspected customer on the lips. Police decoys avoid kissing, since they may be implicated in initiating sexual play. The decoy method is used chiefly in New York City. Wiretapping is often used for obtaining evidence against call girls.

In most jurisdictions, prostitution is considered a misdemeanor, but pimping and pandering are felonies. Third persons involved are treated more severely than prostitutes. Often, streetwalkers are arrested to harass them. These arrests do not result in prosecution but merely detain the women overnight on the charge of disorderly conduct. They are fined and released the next morning.

Prostitutes are more concerned about fines and sentences than actual arrests. Low fines enable them to return to the streets quickly. High fines may drive prostitutes from the area. In some communities, judges seem to be lenient, and some even favor rehabilitation, rather than punishment. In New York City, one-half of all women arrested for prostitution are discharged. In areas where there are mild penalties, the incidence of prostitution rises. In 1967 in New York City, prostitution was considered a violation, and a 15-day maximum sentence was the penalty. Women from all over the country flocked to New York. In 1969 the maximum sentence was increased to 90 days, and there was a decline in prostitution. High fines in New Haven and Hartford have served as deterrents to prostitution. In Philadelphia, prostitution has dramatically declined as a result of vigorous law enforcement.

Nevada is the only state that permits prostitution. Houses of prostitution may be maintained as long as they are not on principal business streets or within 400 yards of a schoolhouse or church and do not disturb the peace of the neighborhood. Prostitutes carry identification cards and are required to have weekly medical examinations. However, Reno in Washoe County and Las Vegas in Clark County have enacted ordinances that make prostitution illegal.

The enactment and enforcement of laws against prostitution creates graft, and police are accused of taking payoff money. The temptation to accept a bribe may be increased because most policemen feel that the prostitute is not committing a genuine crime and that they, the police, are degrading themselves in making the arrests. A few attorneys and usurious bondsmen monopolize the prostitutes' legal business, and there is often an alliance between them.

Four major approaches to prostitution are prohibitionist, abolitionist, regulationist, and neoregulationist. The United States is committed to the prohibitionist approach, the least workable approach. All prostitution is prohibited, and prostitution is a criminal act. There are many problems with this approach. Rights of individuals, prostitutes and clients, are denied. Prohibition has never worked at any time or in any place. When prostitution is prohibited, the prostitutes continue to ply their trade but in association with the underworld. Exploitation by panderers, pimps, bondsmen, attorneys, and the police is encouraged. Law enforcement agencies and their members are corrupted.

Most countries tend toward the abolitionist approach. Abolitionists admit that, although prohibition is desirable, it is unobtainable. England is an example of an abolitionist country. Exploiters and clients are punished. Prostitutes are not punished; instead, they are given access to medical, educational, and rehabilitative assistance. This system eliminates the vice squad.

The regulationist approach is perhaps the oldest method, but it is not commonly adhered to today. It permits prostitution in brothels and restricted areas. Often, prostitutes are not permitted to leave these areas. Düsseldorf uses this method, and it has built a million-dollar wall confining 250 prostitutes. This extreme may not be necessary. The regulationist method essentially limits prostitutes to given areas, and it controls prostitution so that the venereal disease rate is kept down and the prostitutes are not exploited or abused. Hamburg has used this approach in a sensible and flexible manner.

The neoregulationist approach is similar to the abolitionist approach, but prostitutes carry cards and must submit to periodic medical examinations and treatment if they are infected.

Legislation is aimed not just at penalizing the prostitute. Usually, those who are considered exploiters are subject to more severe penalties than are the prostitutes. However, they are usually less visible, more difficult to apprehend, and, therefore, less frequently penalized. The law prohibits and punishes operators of brothels and call houses, procurers and panderers, abductors, pimps, husbands of prostitutes, customers, employees of houses of prostitution, and informants. However, in many states, despite the law, customers are not harassed, arrested, or prosecuted. Customers detained in connection with the arrest of a prostitute are usually asked to post so small a bond that its forfeiture is not difficult if they do not appear in court. A prostitute may be jailed without loss to society, but a customer is often the support of his family, someone important in the community, business, church, state, and areas that would disrupt life and society. Some clients are prominent law men and lawmakers.

Prostitution, at present, is primarily an individual entrepreneurship controlled by pimps, especially black pimps. Prostitution was once closely associated with organized crime. The Capone gang controlled prostitution in Chicago in the 1930's. In New York, Lucky Luciano and his mob dominated the prostitution business. Gambling and prostitution have a long association. Sexual activity and gambling have similar enticements. Criminal syndicates not only controlled prostitution but even sought refuge in the brothels. Thus, brothels became hideouts for organized crime figures.

REFERENCES

Abraham, K. *Selected Papers on Psychoanalysis.* Basic Books, New York, 1953.

Adler, P. *A House Is Not a Home.* Rinehart, New York, 1953.

Ball, J. D., and Thomas, G. H. A sociological, neurological, serological, and psychiatric study of a group of prostitutes. Am. J. Insanity, *74:* 647, 1918.

*Benjamin, H., and Masters, R. E. L. *Prostitution and Morality.* Souvenir Press, London, 1965.

Bloch, I. *Marquis de Sade: His Life and Works.* Britany, New York, 1961.

British Social Biology Council. *Women of the Streets.* Secker & Warburg, London, 1955.

*Bullough, V. L. History of prostitution in the United States. Hum. Sex., *4:* 64, 1970.

Bullough, V. L. The American brothel. Hum. Sex., *7:* 198, 1973.

Burnett, S., and Seegar, A. *Prostitution around the World.* Derby, Conn., 1963.

Caprio, F. S. *Female Homosexuality.* Citadel Press, New York, 1954.

*Choisy, M. *Psychoanalysis of the Prostitute.* Pyramid Books, New York, 1962.

Deutsch, H. *The Psychology of Women.* Grune & Stratton, New York, 1945.

Ellis, A. Why married men visit prostitutes. Sexology, *25:* 344, 1959.

Gibbens, T. C. N., and Silberman, M. The clients of prostitutes. Br. J. Vener. Dis., *36:* 113, 1960.

Glover, E. G., and Hollender, M. H. Prostitution, the body and human relatedness. Int. J. Psychoanal., *42:* 404, 1964.

Gover, R. *One Hundred Dollar Misunderstanding.* Grove Press, New York, 1962.

*Greenwald, H. *The Elegant Prostitute: A Social and Psychoanalytic Study.* Ballantine, New York, 1970.

Hall, S., and Adelman, B. *Gentleman of Leisure.* Signet, New York, 1973.

*Henriques, F. *Stews and Strumpets: A Survey of Prostitution,* Vol. 1. MacGibon & Kee, London, 1961.

Hirschi, T. The professional prostitute. Berkeley J. Sociol., *7:* 33, 1962.

Hollander, X. *The Happy Hooker.* Warner, New York, 1972.

*Kinsey, A. C., Pomeroy, W. B., and Martin, C. E. *Sexual Behavior in the Human Male.* Saunders, Philadelphia, 1948.

Kinsey, A. C., Pomeroy, W. B., Martin, C. E., and Gebhard, P. H. *Sexual Behavior in the Human Female.* Saunders, Philadelphia, 1953.

Murtagh, M., and Harris, S. *Cast the First Stone.* McGraw-Hill, New York, 1957.

*Reitman, B. *Prostitution: Contemporary Social Problems.* Harcourt Brace, New York, 1961.

Robbins, J. *The Anatomy of a Prostitute.* Signet, New York, 1974.

Sanger, W. L. *The History of Prostitution.* Harper & Bros., New York, 1858.

Seymour-Smith, M. *Fallen Women.* Nelson and Sons, London, 1969.

*Winick, C., and Kinsie, P. *The Lively Commerce.* Quadrangle Books, Chicago, 1971.

Wolbarst, A. The suppression of public prostitution—a factor in the spread of venereal diseases. N.Y. Med. J. Med. Rec., *113:* 648, May 4, 1921.

Woolston, H. B. *Prostitution in the United States.* Century, New York, 1921.

chapter 23 Religion and Sexuality

ABRAHAM N. FRANZBLAU, M.D., Ph.D., L.H.D.

Introduction

The caduceus is universally recognized as the symbol of medicine and its practitioners. It is the herald's wand, the wand of Hermes (Mercury), the messenger of the gods. It takes the form of two intertwined serpents surmounted by a pair of wings. In primitive religious mythology, the two snakes are recognized as the monster serpent and the naked goddess, symbols of the generative force of Nature, pairing to create the world. The wings are the symbol of the winged Ker (Eros).

In later mythology, the god of healing is Aesculapius (Asklepious), son of Apollo, whose worship was introduced at Athens in 421 B.C., probably in relation to the great plague. The staff on which Aesculapius leans has entwined about it a single snake, not two snakes, and, unlike the caduceus, it is not winged. Aesculapius was himself originally a snake god, like Enki, whom ancient Sumerian tablets (6000-4000 B.C.) describe as the Lord of Wisdom, the god "who brings life." The serpent of the Garden of Eden, too, guarded the tree of knowledge and the tree of life.

The caduceus thus telescopes millennia of human religious development, all the way from the crude worship of the gravid uterus and the fecundating phallus to the present day. In it are symbols of the god of wisdom and life and the god of love, religion, and sexuality, bound in an inseparable union, under the aegis of the wings of Cupid.

Definitions

In the second edition of *Webster's New International Dictionary, religion* is defined as

an apprehension, awareness, or conviction of the existence of a supreme being; or more widely, of supernatural powers or influences controlling one's own or humanity's or nature's destiny . . . . the service and adoration of God or a god, expressed in forms of worship, obedience to divine commands as found in accepted sacred writings or as declared by recognized teachers, and in the pursuit of a way of life regarded as incumbent on true believers.

Religion includes a system of faith, worship, and prescribed rituals and observances.

The definition of sexuality, according to Webster's, is, "The constitution and life of the individual as related to sex."

This definition includes all of sexuality's physical, emotional, and interpersonal manifestations and its developmental progression from infancy throughout life.

Pastoral counseling is the service rendered by a minister to a parishioner who seeks help in dealing with a problem or dysfunction in the realm of his family relations, his work, his social relations, his ethical values and behavior, or his ideational processes. This dysfunction does not constitute a breakdown but remains within the context of normality.

PREHISTORIC AND PRECIVILIZED MAN

"Very deep is the well of the past," said Thomas Mann. During the past century and a half of discovery, science has opened up parts of this long covered well and has afforded a sample of what it contains. The evidence covers more than 100,000 years of human development and extends over the entire face of the globe. Millennia separated Neanderthal man from Cro-Magnon man and these from *Pithecanthropus erectus*. The ascent to *Homo sapiens* has undoubtedly been even longer and harder. As to how early man lived and died, what he imagined the universe to be like, and what he believed came after life, one can scarcely even conjecture on the basis of the fragmentary evidence available. One catches illuminating glimpses here and there from the evidence brought back by anthropologists who have lived among present-day primitive tribes whose level of culture approximates that of the early aborigines.

Primitive man was probably sure of only one thing—that life was a fierce struggle for survival against the cruel and capricious forces of nature, the predatory beasts of the jungle, and the rapacious foes of his own species who sought to make food out of him and his offspring. When he learned to follow the herds of the herbivores as they roamed the grassy steppes and ultimately to domesticate small flocks for his use, fertility became the key to survival. He curried the favor of whatever forces he believed to foster it and pacified those hostile to it, thus creating the benevolent and malevolent local deities whom he worshiped. Their rites were largely sexual, and their names and shapes were legion. By and large, their gender was female.

This emphasis on the female was quite logical, for the female was, to primitive man, not only the eternal presence but the eternal mystery. In pregnancy, her ballooning abdomen afforded visible proof of her fertility. No male could actually duplicate this mystery in his own body in reality, although many examples exist in legend. Kumarbi bit the loins of the god Anu and became pregnant with three monsters; Zeus gave birth to Athena from his head and Dionysus from his thigh; Adam gave birth to Eve from his rib.

The female functions were the source not only of envy and worship but of fear. The blood of menstruation, defloration, and childbirth was to primitive man a source of mortal danger because he imagined it to be the natural due of the demons, a draft that was theirs by right. One still finds a craving for human blood in current myths about vampires. Hence, primitive man devised rites of separation and purification to protect himself from the bleeding female genital.

Some of these myths and rites appear to have come down to the present time, although in greatly modified strength and form. Examples are the avoidance of intercourse during menstruation; the Mikvah or Jewish ritual purification bath; cabalistic talismans and incantations in the confinement room against Lilith, the baby-snatching demon; the veiling of the bride and the great secrecy as to the site of the honeymoon; the breaking of the glass at Jewish weddings; and the pealing of the bells at church weddings. (Demons are rapacious but stupid and easily frightened off by noises.) All these examples are warding-off phenomena, which seem to fall under Wundt's famous warning, which applies in all generations, "Beware of the wrath of the demons!"

An example of how far into historic times this fear of the blood thirst of the demons persisted and of how it could find its way even into Holy Writ is found in chapters VI to VIII of the Book of Tobit in the Apocrypha, written in Aramaic between 190 and 170 B.C. It narrates the story of Sara, the lovely and virtuous daughter of Raguel, who married seven husbands. They died, one after another, on their wedding night, "before they had lain with her." The evil spirit Asmodeus, who loved her, was entitled to the blood of her defloration and would allow no man to rob him of his due. Death was the penalty of all seven men for trying. However, the Angel Azarias supplied special magic, with the aid of which Asmodeus was frightened off, and Sara and Tobit could marry and "live happily ever after." The right of the feudal lord to the first night with every bride of his domain (the *jus primae noctis* or the *droit du seigneur*) probably springs from this same source. The demons did not dare to attack the person of the lord (God), the bridegroom was saved, and his bride, deflowered, was free of the demon's power.

There can be no doubt that, for prehistoric and precivilized man, religion and sexuality were as intertwined as the snakes in the caduceus.

EARLY HISTORY AND THE DAWN OF CIVILIZATION

With the rise of the arts of agriculture, the nomadic period of man's existence gradually came to a close. As man settled on the soil, the gravid womb became less important than the fertile field. To fertilize a womb required little aggressive effort on the part of the male beyond the onetime act of impregnation, but it took toil and sweat, skill and patience to wrest a living from the land. The rise of the city-states required rulers who were strong and skilled in the arts of war, as well as in those of peace. The female goddesses were now gradually replaced by male gods, with males as their priests.

The transition is well exemplified in the classical story of old Grandmother Tiamat, chief of all the goddesses, from the Ugaritic Gilgamesh cycle. Tiamat created hosts of young gods but found them, after a while, to be a noisy, bothersome, and unruly lot, and she devised a plan to destroy them all. But her grandson, Marduk the Mighty, thwarted her wicked plan and vanquished her instead. Splitting her carcass like an oyster, he made half of it into the firmament of heaven and the other half into the fountains of the earth. Thus was the world created (Gaster, 1952).

The female fertility goddesses—Ishtar (Aphrodite), Venus, Isis, Athena, Cybele, Vesta, and a host of others—ultimately yielded to the male gods. The fecundating phallus assumed ascendancy over the gravid uterus. However, the fertility cults remained a powerful influence, and their often awesome and savage rites continued side by side with the growth of religion as it is now known.

As long as man remained ignorant of science, with its laws of cause and effect, he relied on magic, and the sway of the gods and demons to whom he prayed to work this magic remained undiminished. He saw his early rulers as divine, and their potency, even their life, was the price that they had to pay to assure their fields' fertility. Frazer, in *The Golden Bough* (1965), gives many examples of the ritual sacrifice of the king, in his role as the god, at special festivals designed to transfer his potency and fertility to the soil. The first born son was also declared sacred or taboo, and his sacrifice, too, was required by the gods. Then it became the first born of the flocks and the first ripe fruits of the harvest that were declared sacred. It was a great step forward when an article of some monetary value or money itself could be substituted. Finally, a prayer, instead of a sacrifice, became acceptable. Thus, a sacrifice *to* the god replaced the sacrifice *of* the god.

The original concept was summed up by Freud, in "Totem and Taboo" in 1913 (1957): It is " . . . as though the whole dangerous ('taboo') charge had been transmitted over to . . . all special individuals, such as kings, priests, or new-born babies, to all exceptional states, such as the physical state of menstruation, puberty, or birth, and to all uncanny things, such as sickness and death . . . ." The motivation of these religious practices was seen by Freud to stem from the killing of the primeval father by his sons, which boomeranged into "the stuff for . . . his supreme triumph," for the sons had an ambivalent attitude toward the father, and their affectionate emotions ultimately triumphed over their hostile emotions. The sacrifice offered satisfaction to the father for the outrage inflicted on him and allayed the guilt of the sons for their dastardly act.

The nature of worship subsequently underwent great changes. Socrates (469-399 B.C.) protested the formula "Do ut des" (I give that you may give to me) as making the practice of holiness "an art in which gods and men do business with each other." In a later day, Plutarch (46-120 A.D.) labeled the demon-worship formula of earlier times, "Do ut abeas" (I give that you may go away), as rank superstition, beneath the notice of any intelligent person. This sacrifice was always rife with sexual overtones, as was the ritual that attended it—for example, sacred prostitution and the self-castration of the novitiates in the rites of Cybele.

These sexual aspects of the sacrifice, involving the transfer of the potency of the person directly to the soil, died out. So did the rituals of the year religions, related to the birth and death of the gods, who, dying with the autumn solstice and being buried in deep caves in the nether regions, were resurrected joyously with the coming of the spring solstice. The characteristic formula is seen in the Attis ritual, " . . . suddenly a light shone in the darkness, the tomb was opened; the god had risen from the dead." It also occurs in the Osiris legend, in the Babylonian Tammuz story, the Syrian Adonis rites, the Greek Orpheus and Persephone tales, and even in a little known Hebrew David mystery uncovered by Morgenstern in 1966. The relation of the Christ story bears examination.

However, the onward and upward dynamism of religious development was strong and irresistible. Man left his primitive superstitions, his dependency on the undependable magic of his highly anthropomorphic deities, and began to see larger forces in control of his universe. He began to interpret these forces as laws, ultimately as God's law, and crude sexuality departed from worship.

Man's cultural and intellectual range had increased so greatly that these developments were able to proceed at a rapid pace. Having learned to use fire and having invented the wheel and other machines and instruments to multiply his power and lighten his work, writing to broaden his communications, history to link his past with his present and future, numbers and mathematics and astronomy to tie heaven and earth together, and functionaries like kings, priests, tax collectors, architects, builders, skilled artisans, and creative artists to serve his new collective needs, he was ready for the millennia of civilization.

Man came to see that his personal and sexual life, as well, had to come under some kind of discipline or law, and he began to seek rules and regulations for guidance in the conduct of his relations within his small family and with his fellow man in the larger community of which he was a part.

The impish Cupid who shot his arrows whithersoever his caprice impelled him was ready to become the God of Love, the foundation stone of the structure of the human family, supplying strength, solidity, and permanence to its dimensions.

RELIGION AND SEXUALITY IN THE JUDEO-CHRISTIAN TRADITION

It took man 2,000 years or more to address himself seriously and with some effectiveness to the larger questions with which religion and philosophy concern themselves. Such questions are the whys and wherefores of existence; the relatedness of man to his fellows; the inequities of the forces in the universe that bring calamity, disease, and death to the innocent and guilty alike; and the question of what happens after this life. Immediate questions that had to be dealt with concerned the administration of justice, criminality and delinquency, property rights, marriage, divorce and child rights, and a great many others, which the exigencies of daily living forced on man's attention.

The Code of Hammurabi (c. 2000-1700 B.C.) is one of the earlier formulations of laws governing daily living. Although known for its humanitarian principles, in comparison with the rules by which man lived in primitive societies, it also contains some penalties that, according to the modern point of view, are harsh and savage. The growth of the Judeo-Christian tradition represents the high point in the moral and spiritual development of man. In the Ten Commandments and the Holiness Code (Exodus XX and Leviticus XIX), which came 1,000 to 1,500 years after the Code of Hammurabi, and in the Sermon on the Mount, which came 2,000 years after it, one sees an enormous advance.

The answers to man's questions were no longer couched in the ancient magical formulas that served him in early days. He created complex religious systems, dealing with all aspects of his life, here and hereafter, with special personnel, priests, prophets, and lawmakers to cope with the problems, offer plausible and workable answers, and administer them in the temples, courts, and market places. As the city-states gave way to larger aggregations of men, nations began to form. These were shaped often by the rude swords of conquerors. The peculiar gods of the conquered nations were conquered and taken over, like their warring armies, and syncretism diminished the hordes of heaven. They could not long survive the ineffable logic of the prophets, who, gradually forsaking their roles as soothsayers and masters of witchcraft and magic, became cosmic thinkers and moral guides to mankind.

Higher and higher soared their spiritual sensitivity, their ethical insights, the visions that they inspired in their fellow men, and more and more unified became their concept of the universe and its laws. Inevitably came the incontestable conclusion that one law in the universe presupposed one God to rule over it.

Monotheism had been hinted at broadly in the Prayer of Ikhnaton (1375-1358 B.C.), although it was the sun that was seen by him as the supreme ruler of the universe. But his monotheistic religious ideas came to a disastrous end with the collapse of his reign and almost his entire empire.

In the Judeo-Christian tradition, monotheism came into its own, and Islam followed that tradition. Today, 2,000 years later, the world's monotheistic religions number more than 2½ billion adherents.

Within the Judeo-Christian tradition, there has developed what religion regards, with some justification, as the highest step on the ladder of physical, psychological, and social evolution—the monogamous human family. Here man can attain, religion says, what is finest and best in human sexual experience, and here he can rear his offspring in loving security and moral integrity. The perservation of the sanctity of marriage and the family has become a major objective of all modern religions, however much they may differ in dogma or ritual. This, they maintain, is the real gateway to freedom and the cornerstone of civilization. Only through the intact, loving, and happy human family, as the architectural unit of man's life here on earth, can a moral universe ever be created. As love has endured and grown as the cement that holds human hearts together, the winged Ker has become truly god-like.

THE CRITICS

Religious systems and institutions and the sexual code of conduct that they have advocated over the years have not been without their critics. The most widely known and most severely criticized critic of both is undoubtedly Freud. It is interesting to examine his original arguments, set forth in *The Future of an Illusion* in 1921 (1961) and then to note a surprising addendum in the latter part of the same work.

Religion evolves, Freud said, first, because nature is cruel and capricious, showing man no favor; he must battle for his existence or perish. Therefore, he personifies the benevolent or malevolent forces in his environment as gods, propitiating the benevolent and flattering the malevolent.

Second, as far as man knows, death is the inescapable end of life, there being no shred of evidence to the contrary. But man cannot bring himself to accept this end, so he invents immortality and the hereafter as a means of outwitting death. God is needed as the accountant who tallies man's good and bad deeds and who stands guard over the turnstiles of heaven and hell.

Third, to survive, man needs the help of his fellow men, for he cannot face the hazards of living in a ruthless world alone. Therefore, he invents God to sanction the commandment "Love thy neighbor as thyself," knowing all the time that he will have to yield a measure of his personal libidinous gratifications as the price of the benefits he derives from communal living.

To Freud, religion was a neurotic, rather than a mature, resolution of the conflicts of daily living, and he called it "the universal obsessional neurosis of humanity."

It is true that among primitive religions Freud's formulations find ample confirmation. But Freud himself, in the treatise that is his major work setting forth his atheistic position, apparently punctures his own balloon and makes this statement:

"You must not be surprised if I plead on behalf of retaining the religious doctrinal system as the basis of education . . . . Since we are obliged to impose on the growing child some doctrinal system . . . it seems to me that the religious system is by far the most suitable."

Einstein, too, who affiliated himself with no organized religious group, felt the need of some larger orientation to life and to the universe than that which science alone afforded, and he said, "Science without religion is lame, and religion without science is blind." Religion adds, as its basic position: Sex without love and discipline is a mirage.

Although dogma may substitute conviction for evidence, it cannot do so for long. The new scientific and intellectual advances of each age exert their indomitable influence on the religious thinking of some leaders in every religious group, and they gradually prevail. The orthodoxies cling tenaciously to their ancient conceptions of revealed and immutable truth, but religious reform has been a rejuvenating fountain of life in all faiths, guaranteeing to religion unending continuity through the relentless process of change. That religion and the family, which it safeguards, survive all the vicissitudes of time proves this point. Most critics attack orthodoxy; none attack reform. The final grudging accolade that the doubting Freud accorded to the religious doctrinal system was that it allows a refinement and sublimation of ideas, which makes it possible for it to be divested of primitive and infantile thinking.

According to the criteria of modern dynamic theories, when may a religion be regarded as having divested itself of primitive and infantile thinking and thus be worthy of being designated mature?

A religion may, perhaps, be designated as mature when it fulfills the following criteria:

When the family and sexual morality to which it subscribes is robust and realistic, rather than guilt laden and ascetic.

When it is man fostering, according man goodness and worth as well as human dignity, rather than man flagellating, using fear of punishment in the here or the hereafter as its motivation.

When it is centrifugal, moving outward in its tropism to concern with others and societal melioration, rather than centripetal, moving inward to concern with personal salvation and the hereafter.

When its ethical system is deed centered, with guilt feelings and repentance stemming from violations of principles of human interrelationships, rather than creed-centered, with guilt feelings and repentance stemming from violations of ecclesiastical rules and regulations.

When its approach to evil is thisworldly and healthily aggressive to root it out, rather than otherworldly and passive, relying on supernatural agencies to cure it.

When it relies on the power of the human mind to perceive right and wrong and on science and reason to discover the laws by which nature and the universe are governed and by which the human psyche operates, rather than relying for these discoveries on supernatural revelation.

Religions manifesting this type of maturity, divesting themselves of primitive and infantile thinking, would attract the best minds of the day, many of whom find little inspiration within the more traditional faiths.

RELIGION AND THE SEXUAL REVOLUTION

Reading some of the current literature on marriage and the family is apt to be a disheartening experience for those who believe in the value systems of the past that were calculated to bring happiness and fulfillment to man.

It is a well known fact that one out of every four marriages ends in divorce, that the family is falling apart, that the adolescents of today are a lost generation, that the women of today no longer accept the role their elders did as wives and mothers, that to place any restrictions on sexual behavior is iniquitous, and so forth.

As the Red Queen said to Alice, "That is a well-known fact, so well-known that it may not be true at all."

For example, the statement that one out of every four marriages ends in divorce is an oft-quoted bit of statistical misinformation. It stems from the ratio of divorces newly granted to marriages newly performed in any single year, and that ratio is about 1 to 4. However, quoting this statistic as an indication of how many marriages end in divorce leaves out of consideration all those people who are already married and those who divorce only to remarry. There were over 75 million married people in the United States in 1971, and only about 4½ million divorced people, although the divorce rate is definitely climbing—from 0.8 per 1,000 in 1901 to 2.4 per 1,000 in 1951 to 3.7 per 1,000 in 1971.

People turn to a minister when they want to get married. The typical bride's dream is to walk down the aisle dressed in white (for purity), on the arm of her father who "gives her away," thereby publicly attesting that all oedipal feelings have been resolved. By and large, ministers are the ones who ask, "Do you?" rather than judges, justices of the peace, and other civil functionaries. This function affords the clergy a unique opportunity for premarital counseling and establishes the possibility for bringing needed help to the young couple during their period of adjustment.

As for the well known fact that the family is falling apart, if one compares the statistics for 1950, 1960, and 1970, the opposite is apparent. From 1950 to 1960, the population of the United States increased from 152 million to 180 million, about 18 per cent. The number of households over the same period increased from 42 million to 53 million, an increase of almost 24 per cent. From 1960 to 1970, the population increased from 180 million to 205 million, about 13 per cent, but the households increased from 53 million to 62 million, almost 19 per cent. These figures do not seem to support the statement that the family is falling apart.

The argument may be advanced that, although the number of households is not decreasing, the fact that the mothers are leaving their homes to enter the labor force may be destroying the family's integrity. It is true that from 1950, with 8 million married women working, although they had husbands present in the family, the number of married working women grew to 12 million in 1960 and to 18 million in 1970. Unquestionably, the impetus came from the labor shortages of World War II, when it was a patriotic duty for every woman who could be spared to join the war effort by taking some kind of job.

This movement of women out of the home has snowballed under economic and other pressures since the war. However, although some mothers go to work at the cost of their youngsters' welfare, a large percentage of them wait to seek employment until their children are of school age or older, and then they make responsible provision for the care of their children until they get home from work. The rise of day care centers is a bulwark safeguarding the families of many working mothers. Many are quick to blame the working wife, but the troublesome delinquencies of the younger generation are not limited to broken homes, poverty areas, or the homes of working mothers. Very often, the problem lies in the kind of rearing the home affords the children. Not all mothers are happiest when they have to be homemakers. They may be better wives and mothers when they pursue careers for which they are qualified by training and experience, provided that they delegate their home obligations responsibly.

With respect to the lost generation of today's adolescents, the problem is not entirely unique to the present time, as can be seen in the following quotation: "The children now love luxury, they have bad manners, contempt for authority . . . they no longer rise when elders enter the room. They contradict their parents, chatter before company, and tyrannize their elders." The author was

Socrates and the date 430 B.C. Society's progress seems to be characterized by zigs and zags. The country is now in a serious zag period because of disillusionment with the Vietnam war and politics and for other reasons. The drug scene cannot be ignored; nor can the sexplosion and the antagonism toward education, religion, and the Establishment be ignored.

However, the return movement in the younger generation is unmistakable. The drug scene has clearly abated from enormous involvement in certain age and social groups to a great diminution in the ranks of regular users, and there has been a great drop in the number of new recruits. The sex mores are changing from a pattern of almost compulsive, casual sex relations with any youngster who chances to be contiguous. There is a noticeable lengthening and deepening of relations, along with an increasing degree of commitment, even though marriage may not, as yet, be the in thing. Youngsters are going back to college to learn, rather than to burn. Their impact on the faculty, curriculum, and regulations has been tremendous and, in the main, healthy. The most interesting zig phenomenon is, perhaps, the Jesus freaks, the youngsters desperately seeking an ideal personal image from whom to draw some values. This is a reaction to the desert created for them by the one whom they now recognize as a false prophet, the one who counseled, "Tune in, turn on, drop out!"

Parents have a great role to play in this turnabout if they have the ability to say "No!" to their children's inordinate demands that the dictates of their conscience or their religious principles tell them are wrong. It takes stamina to say, as Justice Cardoza did, "Just so that you may know my decision is final, I will give you no reason." This parental firmness alone can raise the level of integrity in their offspring. Goethe, too, had relevant advice for youngsters: "It is not doing the thing we like to do but liking the thing we have to do that makes life blessed."

Mae West, the greatest sex symbol of her time, said, "Marriage is a great institution; no family should be without it." In days gone by, there was no possibility of a family without it, but today some women claim that not only is marriage unnecessary for a family but husbands are unnecessary, too. Any man suitable for insemination serves their purpose, and they are intent on proving that they can bear and rear their children without either a resident husband or any of the other appurtenances of normal family life. What this innovation will breed remains to be seen, but it is certainly a misuse of children, who have no choice in the matter, to make them serve the needs of their unconventional mothers.

On the other side of the coin, there is a remarkable breakdown in the social, occupational, and legal restrictions against homosexuals. There is a movement by some homosexual couples to gain permission of the courts to marry. The religious establishment has been unanimous against this movement until recently, when some cracks developed in their ranks. Here and there, homosexual religious congregations have cropped up, seeking admission to the national religious organizations. The repercussions in the ranks of the more traditionally minded groups have been tremendous. However, if the sexual freedom that is the credo of gay liberation, women's liberation, and the like is to prevail, much more of the same will no doubt occur.

To claim that it is iniquitous to place any restrictions on sexual behavior leaves out of consideration the fact that such things as exhibitionism, voyeurism, pedophilia, pornography for youngsters, and rape are included in the catalogue of sexual behavior. Whatever may be condoned among consenting adults in their private sex life and whatever may be regarded as outside the jurisdiction of the law, there is no doubt that some of these practices, as well as the public exposure of immature youngsters to premature sexual stimulation, cannot be tolerated in a healthy society.

One may expect that religion will always remain in the child protectionist ranks and be stalwart in its defense of the home and family.

The Religions and Sexuality

When Freud first expounded his sexual theories, he was attacked as a licentious and prurient instrument of Satan, even though personally he was, as Hunt (1957) notes, a

rather puritanical, romantic and inhibited young man . . . chaste before his marriage, devotedly monogamous after it.

At this date, almost a century later, there is scarcely a place in the Western world that has not been profoundly influenced by his ideas and scarcely a home in which his constructive contributions to the theory and practice of sex, marriage, homemaking, and child rearing are not being applied.

As for religion, the points of agreement with psychoanalysis far exceed the points of disagreement. Both are in total agreement about the importance of a good and lasting marriage, a mother's loving arms, a father's protective potency and strength. Both regard as indispensable the development of a sound value system in the child, with a strong, but nonpunitive and realistic, conscience as its safeguard. Both want a stable home to enable the child to grow to maturity, relinquishing dependency on the parents when the right time comes, so that he can move forth into independent and responsible adulthood.

However, the points of difference among the various religions and their denominational dissents on specific sexual principles and practices are so numerous that one cannot categorize any one position as the point of view of religion on sex and marriage. Most observers agree that, by and large, the Jewish point of view on sex and marriage, as exemplefied in Ecclesiastes, "Enjoy life with the wife that thou lovest," is a robust and open one, that the Catholic position is more ascetic, and that the Protestant groups fall, in the main, between the two.

The attitude of St. Paul expressed in Corinthians 1 has long been forsaken insofar as the Christian layman is concerned:

It is good for a man not to touch a woman . . . . . But if they cannot contain, let them marry: for it is better to marry than to burn.

Marriage is universally regarded as the optimal condition for the good life, and sexuality is not seen as a lustful degradation of the married partners but as an act of sanctification, expressing all that is finest and holiest in life.

This attitude persists, despite the strong defense of celibacy for the Catholic religious orders against the challenges within the hierarchy. The example of the celibacy of the highest devotees of the Catholic Church and of such theological doctrines as the virgin birth must influence laymen, if unconsciously, and create guilt feelings that may hamper full and free sexual expression. Nietszche expressed it in his quip, "Christianity poured a drop of poison into the cup of Eros."

The Bible enjoins husbands not to withhold the conjugal rights of their wives, and the Talmud enjoins wives to use cosmetics and ornaments in order to be attractive to their husbands, not only in their youth but also in old age. The Talmud also encourages all forms of sex play between husband and wife.

Rabbi Meir, in the 2nd century A.D. urged as the ideal that the sex experience be always as fresh and exciting as the first union on the wedding night.

Regardless of the religious persuasion of the partners, *penis normalis dosim repetatur* is an essential ingredient in any happy marriage, as Chrobak is reputed to have quipped to Freud. This is totally in line with the view of the modern advocates of women's right to sexual gratification and orgasm.

On divorce, Catholicism is unyielding, since it regards the preservation of the integrity of the home and family as flowing from its rigid prohibition of divorce. Among Protestants, there is far greater leniency, as there is among Jews, except that divorce is less common among Jews. "The altar sheds tears over him who divorces his wife," says the Talmud. However, childlessness after 10 years of marriage is regarded as making divorce obligatory, except by special dispensation. This is because the first positive command in the Bible is, "Be fruitful and multiply," and a man is expected to beget at least two children. However, this command does not enjoin the use of contraceptives. The command, applying only to Jewish men, does not proscribe the use of contraceptives by Jewish women, who are free to take on themselves full responsibility for family planning.

The Protestant denominations generally favor the use of contraceptives for ethical purposes, such as family planning and protecting the health of mother and child. Among Catholics, the use of all contraceptive procedures, except abstinence and the rhythm method, is prohibited and is regarded as sinful.

Abortion is also unequivocally forbidden by the Catholic Church, even if it is necessary to save the life of the mother, since the church holds the view that the soul is born at the moment of conception. Hence, a living being is "murdered" in the process of abortion, and no one can decree to let one human being die in the place of another. The only case in which abortion is sanctioned is when the fetus has no right to be there, as in ectopic pregnancy. Officially, the Jewish religion is just as strongly opposed to abortion as an elective device for limiting the size of families as is Catholicism, except in the case of the saving of the life of the mother or when the child is certain to be born deformed, diseased, or defective. Among Protestants, the rules about abortion are much more relaxed, and the right of the persons involved to decide the matter for themselves, in consultation with medical authorities, is fairly well established. However, statistics of actual attendance at birth control and abortion clinics show little relation to denomination population percentages.

Masturbation, regarded as sinful in Catholicism, is equally frowned on in official Protestant and Jewish doctrine. However, there has been a marked relaxation of parental attitudes in recent years under the influence of modern psychosexual theory and practice. The main difference among the religious groups appears to be not in how much masturbation actually takes place, for all sex studies to date agree that it is almost universal at one stage or another among boys and quite widespread among girls, but in how much guilt it arouses in the person.

Intermarriage is another subject on which wide differences exist among the religious groups. Interracial marriages, especially with blacks, were, until recently, almost universally refused in this country by ministers of all faiths, and the barriers are still quite strong. Interfaith marriages are forbidden by Catholicism, except under strict promises intended to safeguard the faith of the home and the offspring. Among Protestants, there are fewer restrictions. The official position of the Jews closely approximates that of the Catholics. Among Orthodox Jews, the prohibitions are even more severe, a parent mourning as dead a child who marries outside of the faith. Conversion, of course, removes all the obstacles.

The general theory of religious dogma regarding sexuality and the restrictions that it imposes claims not only to preserve the sanctity of the home and family but to guarantee in this fashion the highest level of sexual gratification over the longest period of time. According to religion, twenty-fifth and fiftieth wedding anniversaries are called silver and golden for sound reasons. These marriages—not the sordid, revolving door romances that the tabloids chronicle daily and the divorce reports that follow soon after—are the real triumphs of Cupid.

Religion, Sexuality, and the Home

The home is the locus of the most important function in human life, that of child rearing, and it is an area where religion and sexuality have a great commonality of interest. The parents' sex life creates the family, and they create the character and integrity of their offspring by the manner in which they conduct themselves as parents. The peak point in the process is the early years of childhood. Here, conscience, the mold in which the sexuality of the child is cast in his future life, and his religious orientation to the universe—or his lack of religious orientation—are shaped and formed.

In all these areas, often the greatest influence is not what the parents say but what they do, not the overt curriculum but the occult curriculum, which is imprinted and absorbed and which insinuates itself subtly from the actual behavior and attitudes of the elders who surround the child. Religion maintains that it is the most potent ally of the occult curriculum.

The young child has crude and almost savage impulses that demand almost instantaneous gratification, lest he give vent to screaming fury, which, if he were not so weak and impotent, would have murderous force. As the child grows, he is inconsiderate, egoistic, selfish, dirty, odoriferous, shameless, greedy, cruel, and destructive, and, greatest sin of all, he plays with his sexual organs. This behavior confronts parents with a constant dilemma: How shall they handle their child's crude impulses?

There are three ways: first, the way of free and untrammeled expression, which Rousseau advocated; second, the way exemplified in Anna Freud's story of the mother who told the maid to go see what the children are doing and tell them to stop it—that is, to thwart and suppress the child's natural impulses; third, the way of sublimation, which molds, disciplines, and elevates the child's natural impulses into forms of expression that bring him gratification yet are acceptable in civilized society. Few religions follow the first way, that of free and untrammeled ex-

pression. Many tend to favor the thwarting and suppression of much of the original nature of man. A few favor the way of sublimation.

Because, from the moment he is born, the mother stands by, 24 hours a day, to serve him and satisfy all his desires, the infant develops ideas of omnipotence. However, in time he learns that there are others in the family who share her—brothers and sisters and, particularly, the father. The child has to do what she wants if she is to do what he wants, and he has to love her so that she may love him.

The conflict out of which conscience is born comes when he wants a certain thing and the mother forbids it. How is it resolved in a loving home? The child ultimately learns to use the old politician's dictum, "If you can't lick 'em, join 'em." By introjecting his mother, her authority becomes his authority, and her power becomes his power.

The child must believe, "I am so strong in my mother's love that I can yield to her without feeling defeated." This mechanism is also involved when the religious person introjects the image of a loving God or a concept of the good, the true, and the beautiful. There being no damage to self-respect, there is no inordinate need to rebel. The time comes when the person becomes the sole owner of his own soul. Free will is thus not identical, either psychologically or religiously, with infantile omnipotence, the fantasy that one can do whatever one wills. One must, instead, freely accept and incorporate within oneself the yoke of heaven—namely, discipline, with conscience as its guardian, self-accepted because of love. This is the cornerstone of civilization, according to both religion and psychoanalysis. This is also the high road out of the world of infantile fantasy into the world of adult reality.

The mother is gradually joined by other authority figures—the father, teachers, peers, employers, and government officials. In many homes, among the most important authority figures who influence the character and conscience of the child are the religious leaders and the church. Religion claims that it operates to add the dimension of past experience and divine revelation, over the generations, to enlarge the child's moral heritage. With its help, he can stand on the shoulders of many who came before him as he grows toward moral and ethical maturity.

In that little trio of phrases—the surrender of infantile omnipotency; the achievement of mature, ethical, self-reliant competency; and the avoidance of traumatic, love-starved impotency—the whole story of human development can be told.

OEDIPAL PROBLEMS

The future sexuality of every child is determined by the manner in which his oedipal strivings are resolved in the home. Starting out with a desire for exclusive possession of the mother and a wish to have the interfering father out of the way, how does this resolution come about?

One might think that no good can possibly emerge from such incestuous and murderous wishes. But, in a loving home, only good emerges, or, to put it another way, only in a loving home does good emerge. In a disturbed or broken home, oedipal problems that are unresolved or only partially resolved haunt the children and cause them untold misery all their lives. When the contribution that religion makes enhances the love of the parents for each other and their loving responsibility toward their children, it must be labeled a beneficial force.

The story of the oedipal resolution is different in the case of boys and girls, since they both start out loving a woman, their mother. This is the way the male child must wind up, but the female child must accomplish a turnabout and wind up loving a man instead. The delicacy of the job indicates why any force that operates to stabilize the home and enrich the relation between the parents, fostering their love and lending security and durability to their marital relationship, as religion claims it does, leads to healthier psychosexual development in the children. Any force that operates in the opposite direction—as does moral laxity, infidelity, child neglect, or shirking of responsibility as a parent—leads to many problems in the offspring, including sexual delinquency.

Every child comes into the world knowing how to express anger but not knowing how to love. Under the tutelage of his mother, he learns this fast. She naturally becomes the target and the magnet of his affections. But this is only a temporary condition. Under the influence of his divided feelings toward his father—fear of what may happen if the father learns the truth about the child's passion for his mother on the one hand, and love for this wonderful man who loves him, on the otherhand—he gives up his passion for his mother and replaces it with a tender feeling for her, which he also develops for his father, his former rival.

However, in his relations with both of them, he learns important lessons that stand him in good stead for the rest of his life. First, he learns to shoot love arrows and hit the bull's eye, deflecting them from his mother to the love of his life, who comes on the scene later. He always has tender but not passionate feelings toward his mother and toward all other women but his wife. Out of the hostility that was built up toward his father in the toddling years comes a reservoir of healthy aggression, ambition, zeal, drive, perseverance, courage, patience, and ingenuity. Since he winds up with tender feelings for his father, he also gains the capacity to compete with others without having to make a killing to win and without feeling emasculated if he loses. This is indeed, a rich legacy from the resolution of the boy's oedipal situation in a loving home.

The girl has a more difficult task in attaining psychosexual maturity. It is, therefore, much more important for her to have a loving home, with a loving father and mother, for the girl has five special hurdles to get over that the boy does not: First, she shifts the sex of her love object from a woman to a man. Second, she shifts the organ of sexual pleasure from the clitoris, which she knows about from infancy, to the vagina, the existence of which she is ignorant about until much later. Third, she has a biological barrier, related to her function as a potential mother—she is the Prometheus of procreation, bound to her rock of child rearing until her family is grown. Fourth, although she, of all females in creation, has the capacity to enjoy sex at will—in and out of heat, morning, noon, and night—she has tied her destiny to love, and she needs a loving mate and a stable home in which to fulfill herself. Fifth, she is dependent for her sexual pleasure on her man's potency, without which she is a sad creature.

The girl resolves her oedipal wishes by means of a double shift—from her mother as her love object to her father as her love object and ultimately from him to the love of her life. This may be why girls are so often found to be more religious than boys—they find a heavenly father to be a useful supplement when their earthly father falls short. It is a difficult task for any father to fulfill for a daughter, even under optimal conditions. This may also be why girls tend to mature sexually and marry earlier than boys. Object finding and object fixation settles them comfortably and securely in their life niche. The man has a more difficult time winning his way in the world and carving out a niche for himself. In a man's adoration (or denial) of God may lie, in part, some displacement or derivative of the love of his father. In the atheist's or nihilist's violent denial may be concealed the need to deny that very important homosexual love that can be the precursor of superego.

OTHER PARENTAL INFLUENCES

Much of the child's religious orientation to the universe is influenced by the kind of family and sexual relationship that exists in the home. In a home in which the mother cherishes her femininity, both as a wife and as a mother, where the father is the prototype of strength and masculine procreativity, and where the child is regarded as having worth and dignity in his own right, the child conceives of a friendly universe, ruled over by a good, kind, loving, and supporting God.

However, in a home in which the parental figures are unloving, quarrelsome, cruel, rejecting, punitive, and demeaning in their attitude toward their children, there the concept of the father in heaven is apt to be identical with that of the father on earth, and the relationship between God and man is a projection of the child's experience in the home.

If one traces the personal history of some of the great religious and literary figures, like Kierkegaard and Kafka, this theory appears to be confirmed. Their austere theological concepts and their inability to enter into a close and intimate relationship with any woman seem to stem from a family in which a harsh and punitive father crushed all possibility of tenderness and love out of their lives. This father is just like the harsh and punitive God they project in their writings. One's orientation to the universe and the immutable laws by which it is governed need not be one of surly rebellion or of abject, fear-laden submission if this is not one's orientation to sex and family life.

Why is Cupid always depicted as an infant? There may be a deep unconscious reason. In the development of sexuality in the human, from the cradle onward there are some remarkable parallels between the strange state of being in love and the state of being an infant in the cradle. The infant wants the exclusive love of his mother; the lover wants the exclusive love of his beloved. The infant tremendously overvalues his love object; so do lovers. The infant has fantasies of omnipotence; so has the man who has won a girl and sets out to lay the world at her feet. The infant sees the commonplace as exciting; so do lovers—in each sunset, opening bud, and bird's song. The infant in his sexuality is what Freud called polymorphous perverse; so are lovers as they sample the joys of every erogenous zone of each other's bodies. Perhaps most touching of all, no matter how much the mother whispers her sweet nothings into her infant's ear, one frown can change ecstasy into misery; it is even more so with lovers.

This is another way of saying that the roots of romantic love stem from the cradle and have a long and complex developmental history. The future psychosexual development of offspring is affected by everything that happens in the home—the relationship of the parents to each other, their children, their parents, siblings, relatives, friends, and perhaps all their fellow men.

Pastoral Counseling of Sexual Problems

In a recent survey in the United States, it was found that 12.5 per cent of all members of the American Psychiatric Association provide some kind of psychiatric service to religious institutions. Part of this service is devoted to training ministers in pastoral counseling. Today, thousands of ministers have had clinical training in pastoral counseling. The medical profession, and psychiatrists in particular, has been cooperative in this program and has been made aware of the contribution that the ministry can make. For the maximum of cooperation and the minimum of conflict, it is important that the distinctive functions of the two professions be clearly defined.

MINISTERS' AND PSYCHIATRISTS' ROLES

Generally speaking, the minister deals with his parishioner's problems within a context of normality. When the problem involves a serious breakdown in the person's capacity to function normally in his sex and family relations, his work, his social relations, his ideational processes, and even in his ethical behavior and values in some instances, the pastor is wise to look to the psychiatrist for professional help. Conversely, when a psychiatric patient brings in a problem that appears to have at its root a breakdown in some religious area, such as his belief in God or the exaggerated performance of some ritual (scrupulosity), the psychiatrist is wise to look to the patient's pastor for an understanding of the manifestations of the problem or for guidance in handling it.

The minister, both by training and by inclination, is uniquely situated to perform the pastoral counseling function, whether it be in the sexual or any other area. In fact, he has certain advantages that the psychiatrist does not have. In addition to his constant contact with his parishioner from the pulpit, in the classroom, and in the vestry, the minister has the privilege of making unannounced calls in the home, which no other professional has, not even the family doctor.

When a couple ask a minister to marry them, they must meet his conditions and criteria. He may require them to come for premarital counseling as frequently as the procedures that he has established dictate. If there are problems involving the parents of the couple, he may request consultations with them before consenting to perform the marriage. After the couple are married, they often turn to him for help with their problems of adjustment, and, when children arrive, they look to him for help with certain child rearing problems and crises. If in-law problems or other difficulties—vocational, financial, social, and the like—arise, they may again ask for their minister's help. It has been shown in various studies that, when confronted by some disturbing problem, a far larger percentage of people turn to their minister first than to their doctor, lawyer, or other professional.

The minister, in offering pastoral counseling, also has a far wider range of permissible activities than the psychiatrist has. The minister may permissibly allow a personal relationship to develop, a relationship that can include the parishioner's entire family and that usually includes the minister's family, especially his wife, continuing on over the generations. Inevitably, this relationship places the minister in a more difficult position than a psychiatrist in handling certain intimate sexual problems, and he must be sure that his training is so expert that countertransference problems do not get in his way. The minister may offer specific advice in situations brought to him, and he may even offer material goods and services that his various church organizations provide, all of which the psychiatrist cannot do.

The minister, being committed to the maintenance of the moral and ethical code of his religion, may speak out against any improper behavior in his parishioner and may correct and castigate when he feels that such correcting is necessary or justified. The same holds for misbehavior or misfeasance in the public life of his community, which he may denounce in his preaching and in the press.

In some confessions, he is empowered to grant or withhold absolution for sins, for he is the ordained representative of God. In tragedy, the minister is often there to offer solace and comfort. If he is trained for such situations, he can begin to handle the depression that usually accompanies bereavement. The minister can teach and inspire, encourage and strengthen; he can clear clouded vision and restore judgment; and, believing in the efficacy of prayer, he can pray with or for his parishioner.

The minister's charisma has transference and countertransference implications that are altogether different from those of the psychiatrist. It is hard for him to be nonjudgmental in the face of violations of the sexual and moral code to which he is committed or totally objective in dealing with nonbelievers or scoffers. In certain confessions, he may be committed to definitions of sexual or other guilt that may influence his handling of problems brought to him in a manner completely different from the psychiatrist's way of handling them. This difference may also apply to his position on aspects of problems bordering on life in the here and in the hereafter. If his dogmatic orientation stresses dependency on divine help, he may counsel his parishioners with sexual problems in a different manner from a psychiatrist in the same situation.

The multiplicity of roles that the minister

must fulfill—preacher, priest (performing whatever sacraments his religion includes), teacher, administrator, community leader, and pastor—places him under the obligation to diversify his time, efforts, and talents. The psychiatrist can function in a more unified role.

SEXUAL PROBLEMS

Pastoral counseling of sexual problems is a complex matter that starts with the pastor's decision as to whether or not to perform a certain marriage. If his decision is favorable, he goes on to premarital counseling. After the wedding, he may be called on to counsel in crises of a sexual origin and, in extreme conditions, to guide a couple through a separation and divorce.

Decision to marry. The decision as to whether or not to perform the marriage ceremony is easier when the pastor already knows one or both of the partners. In any event, he must make certain legal determinations—for instance, whether church and state regulations permit such marriages because of the religion or race of the two parties, consanguinity considerations, and a previous marriage.

Premarital counseling. The minister feels an obligation to see to it that the couple get off to as good a start as possible in their marriage. To do so, he may require a number of premarital counseling sessions. These sessions may help the couple to clear up misunderstandings and acquire useful information that enable them to set up successful and rewarding sex and living patterns and a proper home environment in which to rear their children. If the minister sees shoals ahead, he can warn the couple, prepare them as best he can before the wedding, and offer to continue counseling them after the wedding.

Even if he fears that the couple are not suited to each other and that the marriage is destined to be short lived and even if he informs the couple fully of the grounds for his misgivings, he must recognize that he is not likely to influence them. The decision to refuse to perform the marriage ceremony is difficult, for no man can be sure of his prophecy. The couple are sure that love conquers all and are certain that they will live happily ever after. Sometimes a minister makes, and a couple accepts, a psychiatric referral before marrying if his misgivings are extreme.

In premarital counseling sessions, the minister looks carefully into the present and the past of the couple and the circumstances that brought them together. Among the factors that he considers and explores are these:

The age factor. Warning signals: marrying too young; too old; too great a disparity in age between the couple.

The romance. Warning signals: Pickup or other unconventional first meeting; rapid sexual involvement; pregnancy or abortion; forced marriage; too brief a time lapse before engagement and marriage; overt pressure to marry, with greater love and affection displayed on the part of one than the other.

Past marital history. Warning signals: brief or repeated past marriages and divorces; predivorce sexual involvement of the couple; repeated sexual liasons on the part of one or both; illegitimate children; evidence or suspicion of bisexuality.

Background differences. Warning signals: racial or marked religious difference, suggesting a rebellion phenomenon at its root; wide disparity between the couple in educational, socio-cultural, or economic status; unhappy parents' marital situation or broken home; an aged parent to support or live with; siblings with disturbed psychosocial or marital situations.

Personal habits and patterns. Warning signals: addictions to drinking, gambling, drugs, food, going out, or television; money attitudes—spendthrift or miserly; carelessness with personal hygiene or overneatness and orderliness; dislike of children; suspected sociopathology or psychopathology; resistance to authority.

Any of these warning signals merit exploration and counseling. Some instances merit deeper attention, perhaps a referral for psychotherapy.

When the minister has satisfied himself that he can, in good conscience, marry the couple, he can proceed to set the date and make the necessary arrangements. Sometimes this step signals the outbreak of the wedding blues that precede the wedding bells. It often triggers the recrudescence of family grievances and hostilities that have long lain dormant. The wedding arrangements can be the subject of great debates and the beginnings of in-law trouble that will long fester. The wise counsel of the minister should be available at such times for clarification and conciliation. His counsel can also prevent last minute breakups, or he can stop couples from being pushed into marriage for the wrong reasons.

Prospective marital partners must be as well informed as possible about the anatomy and physiology of sex and about what constitutes good sex techniques for each partner to bring the other to gratification and orgasm. However, the pastoral counselor, as a religious guide, should not undertake this instruction. He should, rather, recommend one of the many excellent manuals available today and refer the couple to their family physicians for more specific guidance if need be. If the couple need guidance in other medical matters, such as contraception, if this is not contrary to the pastor's religious position, he may refer them to a gynecologist or a family planning clinic. Transference and countertransference complications can be troublesome when the pastor undertakes to do this counseling himself.

Sexual crises. The third important area of pastoral counseling of sexual problems is the handling of couples who have been married for long periods of time. They often come for other than sexual reasons—problems related to money, differences about the rearing of the children, in-law problems, disagreements about their friends and their social life, conflicting cultural interests. But when their sex life is vigorous and gratifying or when it is helped to become so, the other problems grow insignificant. There may also be a complication when the problem brought to him involves infidelity. His religious and ethical position may make it difficult to speak with openness, robbing the counselor of complete revelation and the patient of his impartiality.

When a couple come for counseling and their chief complaint is that they are not happy together, the number of years that they have been married makes a great difference. In some instances, a separation or divorce may be appropriate and necessary, even after a long number of years of married life together, but this condition is rare. In the 12 states in the United States that keep such statistics, the median length of time during which couples stay together before a divorce or annulment occurs is about 6 years. If a marriage is not going to work, the parties

usually know it in a relatively short time, and the marriage ends early rather than late.

In other situations the couple want the privilege of complaining to each other, to their children, to various and sundry relatives, and to friends, but basically they want to do so while they stay together. Investigation usually reveals that, in a large proportion of such cases, their sex life goes on with a frequency and intensity that belie their complaints, even when their sex life is one of the things they complain about most. Any attempts to advise, persuade, or help them to divorce are met with complete resistance and end in failure, the couple electing to remain together.

In such cases, one must conclude that the conscious and unhappy part of their relationship is only one eighth of the iceberg, what appears above the surface. This part is all that they can see and deal with. The remainder, the submerged seven-eighths of the iceberg, consists of their unconscious needs, the satisfaction of which holds them together. It is obvious that to counsel separation or divorce in such cases would be fruitless.

The pastoral counselor can give such cases symptomatic treatment. The specific complaints can be aired, preferably in joint sessions. Mechanisms for eliminating the roadblocks and the hurdles can be suggested and compromises worked out. The positives in their long relationship can be stressed (the glass is half full, rather than half empty), and the road can be left open for further consultations in the future, should things again get difficult.

It helps to get the couple to work out a budget if they complain of mismanagement of their money or unfairness in the allocation of it. If the problem relates to the children, the practices that cause the conflict can often be spotted in the counseling session and remedied. Problems with in-laws, social relations, and cultural interest differences can often be handled effectively by ventilation, analysis of the points of irritation and conflict, and suggestions by the parties themselves as to what changes in the spouse's behavior would please them. In general, the application of common sense, rather than any profound principles of dynamics or counseling techniques, is most helpful. The sex aspects need rarely be the subject of sole concentration. They improve with the rest of the relationship.

Some of the common types of such iceberg marriages are:

The marriage of convenience. It is based on the exchange of marriage vows by one partner for some urgently desired good—such as money, a position or share in a business, a title of nobility, or high social position—supplied by the other partner. As long as the contract is fulfilled, the partners may complain, but the marriage lasts.

The escapist marriage. One or both parties see in the marriage an opportunity to escape from intolerable home, economic, geographic, or other conditions to which return is unthinkable. They have made their bed and will lie in it.

The oedipal marriage. One or, more usually, both parties have failed to work out their separation from the opposite-sex parent, hence they seek a parent-substitute partner, with whom they can gain the unconscious sexual gratifications that they have never renounced. Examples: an alcoholic or other addict; a member of another race (the exotic is erotic); an obviously blemished person, physically, mentally, or morally; a liason obviously intended to punish a parent.

The combat marriage. Sexual activity having been interpreted from childhood as a form of fighting between the parents, the stimulation of a combat is needed in their sex life to arouse and satisfy the partners.

The reversed-role marriage. An aggressive, domineering woman married to a passive, yielding man. In the extreme form, the woman goes out and earns the living, and the man, under some pretext or other (he is writing the great American novel or is working on a world-revolutionizing invention), stays home and does the housework, cooking, cleaning, and shopping.

The question of what constitutes a good marriage from a sexual or other point of view can not easily be answered. Basically, the pastoral counselor does not go far wrong if he concludes that a good marriage is a lasting marriage. If it meets and matches unconscious needs of a couple, then, regardless of what their words may be, the melody lingers on.

REFERENCES

Bevan, E. R., and Singer, C., editors. *The Legacy of Israel.* Clarendon Press, Oxford, 1927.

Bier, W. C., editor. *Pastoral Psychology.* Fordham University Press, New York, 1964.

Campbell, J. *The Masks of God: Primitive Mythology.* Viking Press, New York, 1959.

Cherry, H. *Understanding Pregnancy and Childbirth.* Bobbs-Merrill, Indianapolis, 1973.

Clinical and theoretic aspects of religious belief. J. Am. Psychoanal. Assoc., *12:* 1964.

Cohen, I. M., editor. *Family Structure, Dynamics and Therapy.* American Psychiatric Association, Washington, 1966.

Cole, G. *Sex in Christianity and Psychoanalysis.* Oxford University Press, New York, 1955.

*Draper, E. *Psychiatry and Pastoral Care.* Fortress Press, Philadelphia, 1965.

Eisenstein, V. W. *Neurotic Interaction in Marriage.* Basic Books, New York, 1956.

Elman, P., editor. *Jewish Marriage.* Soncino Press, New York, 1967.

Flanagan, G. L. *The First Nine Months of Life.* Simon & Schuster, New York, 1962.

*Franzblau, A. N. *The Road to Sexual Maturity.* Simon & Schuster, New York, 1954.

*Franzblau, A. N., and Franzblau, R. N. *A Sane and Happy Life.* Harcourt, Brace & World, New York, 1963.

*Frazer, J. G. *The Golden Bough,* 1-vol. abridged ed., Macmillan, New York, 1965.

Freud, A. *Psychoanalysis for Teachers and Parents.* Emerson, Books, New York, 1947.

*Freud, S. Three Essays on the theory of sexuality. In *The Complete Psychosological Works of Sigmund Freud,* vol. 7, pp. 125-248. Hogarth Press, London, 1953.

Freud, S. Totem and taboo. In *The Complete Psychological Works of Sigmund Freud,* vol. 13, pp. 1-162. Hogarth Press, London, 1957.

Freud, S. The future of an illusion. In *The Complete Psychological of Works of Sigmund Freud,* vol. 21, pp. 5-56. Hogarth Press, London, 1961.

Gaster, T. H. *The Oldest Stories in the World.* Beacon Press, Boston, 1952.

Ginott, G. *Between Parent and Child.* Macmillan, New York, 1965.

Group for the Advancement of Psychiatry. *The Psychic Function of Religion in Mental Illness and Health.* Group for the Advancement of Psychiatry, New York, 1968.

Harnack, A. *History of Dogma.* Dover, New York, 1961.

Harrison, J. *Prolegomena to the Study of Greek Religion.* ed. 3. Cambridge University Press, London, 1922.

Hawkes, J. *Dawn of the Gods.* Random House, New York, 1968. Kelly, A. *A Catholic Parent's Guide to Sex Education.* Hawthorn Books, New York, 1962.

Klausner, S. Z. *Psychiatry and Religion.* Free Press of Glencoe (Macmillan), New York, 1964.

Lipton, L. *The Erotic Revolution.* Sherbourne Press, Los Angeles, 1965.

Mace, D., and Mace, V. *Marriage East and West.* Macgibbon & Kee, London, 1960.

Montague, A., editor. *Marriage Past and Present.* Porter Sargent, Boston, 1956.

Morgenstern, J. *Some Significant Antecedents of Christianity.* E. S. Brill, Leiden, 1966.

Morris, J. *Premarital Counseling.* Prentice-Hall, Englewood Cliffs, N.J., 1960.

*Murray, A. *Myth and Mythmaking*. George Braziller, New York, 1960.

Pattison, E. M. *Clinical Psychiatry and Religion*. Little, Brown, Boston, 1969.

Peterson, J. A., editor. *Marriage and Family Counseling*. Association Press, New York, 1968.

Silver, A. H. *Where Judaism Differed*. Macmillan, New York, 1956.

Stone, A., and Levine, L. *The Premarital Consultation*. Grune & Stratton, New York, 1956.

Stone, H. M., and Stone, A. *A Marriage Manual*. Simon & Schuster, New York, 1952.

van de Velde, T. H. *Ideal Marriage*. Random House, New York, 1930.

van den Haag, E. *The Jewish Mystique*. Stein & Day, New York, 1969.

Weatherhead, L. D. *The Christian Agnostic*. Abingdon Press, New York, 1965.

*Westberg, G. E. *Minister and Doctor Meet*. Harper & Bro., New York, 1961.

chapter 24 The Women's Movement

ELIZABETH JANEWAY

Introduction

A study of the women's movement must begin with three descriptive statements. First, in its present phase, it is historically quite new. Second, it is diverse. Third, it has arisen in response to qualitative changes in the social and economic circumstances of women's lives. Since the movement is controversial, an awareness of these facts is helpful as a means of avoiding false assessments and attributions. As with any social movement, a core area of agreement is surrounded by ongoing discussions and, indeed, disputes. These can best be understood as processes testing hypotheses explaining woman's role, position, and potentiality against the reality of lived experience and as actual efforts to adjust life-styles and behavior to new roles that women either feel themselves compelled to enter into or are desirous of undertaking. But, although the movement at present is still in a stage of experimentation and of rapid evolutionary development, it has already established itself as a substantial and influential entity. Moreover, since it stems from a reaction to long term and continuing trends in society, its interests and purposes reflect and illuminate the concerns of many women who are not conscious adherents of its tenets. Students of the women's movement should bear in mind that the experiences to which it is a response affect many times the number of women who think of themselves as being, or even as wanting to be, "women's libbers."

History of the Movement

Although the present phase of the movement began only in the 1960's, its roots run far back in time. A convention of women held in Seneca Falls, New York, in 1848 under the leadership of Lucretia Mott and Elizabeth Cady Stanton is often cited as the inception of feminist activity in this country. Early efforts concentrated on removing legal disabilities from women and obtaining for them such rights as that of married women to hold property in their own names, to sue for divorce, to gain educations on a par with those of men, and, as a major and central goal, to vote. This last right of suffrage was achieved by the Nineteenth Amendment to the Constitution, ratified in 1920. After the vote was won, the first wave of feminist activity died down, although women moved into professional careers during the next decades more freely than ever before. During World War II, their labor contributed greatly to the war effort, and the work they did included many categories of heavy labor that were usually reserved for men. No organized movement protected their interests, however, or spoke for their rights. Unions were, and for the most part still are, uninterested in sponsoring demands for equal opportunity for women, and management has generally consigned them to areas of "women's work," where wages are low and jobs tend to be routine and dead-end.

When men returned to the civilian work force at the end of the war, many women left their jobs to return home and to concentrate on traditional family interests. The atmosphere of the late 1940's and the 1950's was one of "togetherness," in which the large family was highly approved. The birth rate rose significantly, although some of this rise was due to a catch-up in births delayed by the economic depression of the 1930's and the absence of men during the war years. A classic expression of proper female behavior of the time can be found in *Modern Woman: The Lost Sex* by Lundberg and Farnham, who urged women to find fulfillment in the traditional nurturing role and assured them that neurotic unhappiness was the fate preparing itself for those who did not.

A convenient sign of the changing times that witnessed the rise of the present women's movement was the publication in 1963 of *The Feminine Mystique* by Friedan. There had, of course, been other statements of feminist and liberationist feelings, even during the years when the women's movement was hardly existent. De Beauvoir's thoughtful, wide ranging, and, in the end, highly influential work *The Second Sex* first appeared in 1949 in France and was published in the United States in 1953. But Friedan's book came at a time when an eager audience was ready to hear its message, and it spoke in a tone of passionate commitment that evoked a fervent response.

Originally, the typical response was private discussion, of the sort that later came to be called consciousness raising. But in 1966 the oldest, largest, and most structured organization of the movement was founded, the National Organization for Women (NOW). Three hundred educators, advertising copywriters, businesswomen, editors, and government officials joined Ms. Friedan in setting up this organization which declared itself to be

dedicated to the proposition that women, first and foremost, are human beings, who, like all other people in our society, must have the chance to develop their fullest human potential.

The board of NOW, which includes men, entered on a course of intervention in public and political affairs in the cause of equal rights for women. NOW has become a nation-wide organization, whose activities include backing legal actions to bring about equal employment opportunities for women, the passage of the Equal Rights Amendment, and such social issues as the institution and spread of child care centers. Although NOW has increasingly concerned itself with the problems of poor women, including those on welfare, it has been attacked by more radical groups as not only middle-class but overly pragmatic and basically reformist in policy.

Diversity of the Movement

Historically speaking, divisions within the movement were soon apparent. The disputes are numerous, and many have been ephemeral. However, this diversity of interest, giving rise to contests over priorities as well as over opinions, should not be taken as a sign of weakness but rather as a sign of the range of appeal of the movement and, equally, of its youth. The women's movement is challenging a formidable number of assumptions basic to American society and is challenging them not only at the public, institutional level but at the private, psychological level. Some of these challenges will, in the course of time, prove to be more valid and of greater significance than others. Some issues will be discarded or left to one side. Some will be seen later as distractions. Some will be outmoded by continuing social change. A similar process can be noted in the previous history of the women's movement, during the 19th and early 20th centuries, when, for example, an alliance was formed first with the abolitionists and then with temperance groups, while such private matters as free love, which might now be titled "open marriage," were shunted aside.

Nonetheless, certain questions have already proved themselves to be matters for continuing discussion among women. Issues involving women's occupational roles are those on which most overt action has been centered. These issues are the ones most open to agreement and action. Demands for equal wages for women receive the widest adherence. These are closely followed by demands for equal opportunity, which involves opening professional schools and job-training programs at all levels to women, on a par with men. Government support for these demands is evidenced by legislative action and executive orders that instruct all educational institutions and government contractors holding contracts above a minimum level to meet equal opportunity standards or to file affirmative action plans that will enable the organization to meet such standards promptly.

Questions involving other segments of woman's role are felt as equally pressing, but they are a great deal less amenable to direct public action or even to agreement on proper action. Much of woman's role has to do with her activities, obligations, and behavior in what is thought of as the private sphere—within the family, as a wife and mother. In fact, the role of the family as a subsystem of society is not widely understood today, and part of the difficulty in grappling with women's new demands is that they seem to have to do only with private matters, although, in fact, they stem from social changes outside the family. A growing awareness of these public-private connections can be found throughout the women's movement, but it has not as yet been thoroughly ventilated or coherently articulated. As so many general questions do, this awareness is surfacing by way of particular issues. This diversity of issues and interests gives an air of confusion to the movement, but many of them are inter-related.

The proper role of the woman at home, in her relationship to her husband and children, is a major subject of consideration and reconsideration among women today. In terms of her function as wife, some of the questions now being debated are: Is the woman to think of herself mainly as support to her husband? Is his vocation to come first in every case? Is the relation of the family to the community to be maintained by the husband, while the wife's activities are confined to the home or to approved volunteer or leisure-time associations? If not, how are duties and obligations to be divided? Some couples have worked out detailed marriage contracts, touching on the division of money earned by both partners and on home duties, including housework and responsibility for child care, and providing for a reconsideration of arrangements, including the marriage itself, at timed intervals.

Other obligations considered within marriage deal with sexual relationships. How valid are the traditional mores? Will sexual experience outside marriage enrich or disrupt the union, and can extramarital sex be undertaken by the woman as freely as by the man? How useful and advisable are less formal relationships for living together? Can patterns of life that differ from the normal

coupling be sustained, such as long term three-way relationships or group marriages among several adults, with children being raised by all members of the older generation? Should homosexual couples be deemed acceptable? Can children born to one member of such a couple be raised successfully be lesbian mothers? How is female sexuality conditioned by women's physiology, and does her physiology have a bearing on activities and behavior other than sexual?

Debate over a woman's proper role as wife slips easily into the question of the mother role. Should children be raised primarily by the mother, or should the father also be engaged? If so, at what age? Are child care facilities outside the home helpful, baneful, or neutral? Should the use of mother substitutes be encouraged, and, if so, is a plurality wise? What about single-parent families? If women or couples decide to have no children, will their lives be as fulfilled as those of parents, or can psychological difficulties be expected? Should the family function as a democratic group, or are rules to be laid down by the parents and, if so, in what areas? How rigid should such rules be, and how are they to be enforced?

The position of women members of minority groups is another factor making for diversity in the women's movement. Black women, in particular, are concerned to define their priorities. Should they support the efforts of black men to step forward to full equality before they insist on their own rights? Have oppression and deprivation produced a family structure differing significantly from the white home, and, if so, what effect does this difference have on the larger social structure? The range of behavior among black women is perhaps even wider than that among whites. At one end, women are more numerous among black professionals than among white professionals; at the other end, veiled black women can be seen publicly in America, and some black women actually argue for polygyny as a deliberate re-creation of the African background and in order that they may "share the good men," as expressed by a spokeswoman at a seminar held by the William Alanson White Institute.

These very different responses clearly indicate that black women face choices and decisions even more complex than their white counterparts. In addition, the disproportionate ratio of disadvantaged blacks in regard to educational opportunities, earnings, job openings, and over-all employment puts a continuing strain on blacks and on none more than the women who are charged with the task of raising the next generation. What are their goals to be? It is not surprising that racial discrimination and economic inequities seem to many black women to be more pressing than the demands raised by the women's movement. Yet, at the same time, black women are aware of their position as workers receiving the lowest wages, the fewest training opportunities, and the least legal protection. The women's movement is committed to work for the eradication of these old injustices, but this very commitment means that debates over tactics and strategy occur.

Another factor making for confusion over priorities is age differences. Older women formed their life-styles at a time when traditional roles were less questioned, and it was assumed that marriage and motherhood would set the pattern for their years of maturity. Many are now employed, but they usually see their work as secondary and peripheral to their husbands' careers and, often, to their roles as housewife and homemaker. But young women appear more and more to be looking to a future that will include work and are, therefore, planning their lives differently. Their educational programs are changing, since the prospect of continuing employment makes the early acquisition of professional skills attractive. This change means that women's education increasingly parallels that of men. In addition, the expectation of carrying on a vocation progressively invalidates the old concept that the choice of marriage partner is women's most significant life decision. No longer is a woman's status automatically dependent on that of her husband, for the work that she will very likely undertake serves as another determinant of her position.

Abstract and theoretical questions also occupy the attention of the women's movement, adding to its diversity of interest. Is polarization of the sexes healthy, or should the common humanity of both sexes be emphasized?

Can sex-role stereotypes be avoided or changed, and how? To what extent are psychological differences between the sexes innate, and to what extent are they the product of social training? Beyond these philosophical matters, are questions of methodology. If change is necessary, how is it to be brought about? Are the changes needed of a revolutionary scale?

The Movement as Response and Reaction

The diversity suggested by this sampling of issues is, in itself, evidence of the newness of the movement, but, perhaps more important, it indicates that widespread questioning of tradition is occurring in many fields. This questioning has arisen spontaneously wherever traditional patterns of behavior have proved themselves inadequate to new demands. Criticism of or disappointment in the movement because it is not cohesive is thus a misjudgment of its origins. The movement is fundamentally a reaction to drastic social, economic, and cultural changes that have taken place and are still taking place. The very validity of the movement derives from its responsiveness to these fundamental shifts in contemporary lives, both social and individual. Its adherents and spokeswomen are still in a stage of what might be called "primitive accumulation" of data, and efforts to arrive at a central ideology will be premature until the process of historic change is better apprehended.

Role conflicts, however, can already be traced to social shifts. Thus, the changes in women's occupational roles can be understood only in the context of long term economic trends. Women have worked throughout history, but they have usually done so within a family group, which functioned as an economic unit. Cottage industry and the family farm are familiar examples. Such work did not remove them in space from their children. Indeed, the children quite often participated in it, as part of the training that formed their education for adult life.

The introduction of the factory system, some 200 years ago, put an end to the ancient family work group. Few families have ever sustained themselves by the labor of the man alone, so the working wife and mother is nothing new. But the removal of the locus of work from the home has produced increasing strain and faces many women with a dilemma. Their earnings are needed to support the family, but, in order to win these earnings, they must leave the children whose support is sustained by the earnings. Over the last generation women have left home in a steady stream until, currently, 50 per cent of women with children between the ages of 6 and 18 hold jobs. Most of them do so because of objective economic need. Six million women are listed in the 1970 census as heads of families. Sixteen million women are cited in Labor Department statistics as contributing the wages that keep their families above the poverty line. Subjectively, the problem of these working mothers was summed up in a letter to *Time* magazine in June 1973:

As long as we live in an inflated economy, the imperative for a working-class woman to be employed . . . will increase with each child . . . . Leaving the work-force was a luxury I could afford only before I became a mother.

Carolyn Foust
Memphis

This influx of women over 35 into the labor force shows no signs of abating. In fact, younger married women with preschool children have joined this trend increasingly since 1950. In 1970, one third of married women, aged 20 to 24 with preschool children, in marriages with husbands present, were at work. This situation is supported not only by the need for married women to earn but by objective demand for their labor. Oppenheimer reports that "the level of demand for women workers has risen to such an extent that no demographic changes that are at all likely to occur can return us to the situation that existed in 1940," the last year when the census reported that young women typically left their jobs either at marriage or at the birth of their first child.

It is clear that an economic situation that can offer women remunerative work only away from the home will strain family relationships predicated on the presence of the wife and mother in the home. Efforts of the women's movement both to redefine the mother's and housewife's obligations within the home and to support her by advocating an increase in child care centers outside the home thus offer an example of response to a pressing existent situation. Since it is a situation involving many millions of women who are not in any way declared supporters of the movement, the emphasis laid on it by the movement indicates how useful a study of movement concerns and programs can be for understanding over-all social circumstances. To borrow a phrase from economics, the women's movement often operates as a system of leading indicators for growing social problems, which have psychological effects.

Questions Raised by the Women's Movement

Knowledge of present actuality is clearly of fundamental importance to physicians and therapists dealing with mental health and disability. The first question posed by the women's movement for practitioners of psychiatry is one of definition: What is normal? As Offer and Sabshin wrote in the first edition of this book:

A definitive answer to the question, "What is mental health or normality?" . . . must evolve out of new research and new experience.

Certainly the position of women, both in the exterior world and as reflected in their own self-images, has been changing with extreme rapidity. The women's movement is by no means the only source of data, but its insistence on the need to broaden the "normal" limits of femininity and of the acceptable female role makes it a central resource.

The second question raised by the movement is at least as philosophical: How are norms to be established? Are they to be drawn from innate biological factors, or is normality the product of social training and experiential learning? Is it man-made and thus subject to change, or is it immutable and to be discovered within natural law? Most philosophers would doubtless declare that both elements play a part. The thrust of the women's movement here is to lay increased emphasis on the role of social training or acculturation. This emphasis appears to be a judgment much in line with the development of analytical theory itself, which has steadily moved from the Freudian position, where innate drives and instincts are seen as primary with the infant's environment, functioning causally only as a source of frustration or distortion, to such theories as that of Erikson, by whom the self is understood to grow throughout life in continuing interaction with its ambience. In this sense, the women's movement and analytical theory may be said to be moving on similar lines toward a shared goal: that of securing to the person a greater degree of responsible and active control of her or his life, this control to be gained through reasoned interaction with the environment.

Anterior to these questions is the basic postulate of the women's movement, for it explains the need to raise them at all. Whereas, in the past, women have been held to have special capabilities and disabilities, special characteristics and special limitations, the movement believes in a fundamental equality of talent, mental capacity, and character strength within men and women alike. This equality does not imply sameness. Rather, in its opposition to sex stereotyping, it posits individual diversity as great for women as for men. Most profoundly, it declares that women's lives, emotions, and aims are as important and significant as those of men.

This point is worth dwelling on, for it is here that any dispute between the women's movement and traditional psychiatric theory is grounded. Both consciously and unconsciously, orthodox theory and orthodox therapy have approached women as members of the second sex. The male role is seen as primary and that of women as an adjunct. Perhaps by analogy with the supporting role assigned to the nurturing woman, female psychology is seen as ancillary to male psychology.

This tendency can be found in much analytical literature. Discussions of character formation, of psychological processes, of sexuality, and of psychopathology begin with studies of what one would suppose to be human experience. But then follows an addendum on female character formation or sexuality or development of the superego by

way of the female castration complex. This not to deny the historical reality of separate and different female experience. But an analysis of that experience is almost always undertaken as a study of a deviation from the norm because the norm is arrived at by a study of male experience.

The corollary of this view of normal human psychology as based on male experience and behavior in a male context is perhaps even more disturbing to the women's movement. Not only are women's psychological difficulties diagnosed in relation to male norms, which may or may not apply, but treatment is prescribed according to a definition of normality not primary to women but derived by men from male experience. Female norms are thus ascribed to and projected onto women from an external point of view—a point of view, moreover, arrived at on the basis of experience different from that of women. The movement is speaking for many women outside its membership and supporters when it declares that the ascribed norms are no longer realistic. Take one example documented above: Have theory and therapy fully accepted and adjusted to the fact that most women now spend some years at work outside the home? Ninety per cent of women alive today will hold, are holding, or have held a job at some time in their lives. The return of married women to the work force after 1940, and after 1950, at an earlier and earlier age, assures that women's occupational role now increasingly resembles that of men and that holding a job is normal. Do therapists fully agree to this? And if they do, are they aware of the strain sustained by working mothers who also feel themselves primarily responsible for the task of child raising? And how do they counsel women on dealing with these strains, inevitable in the present situation? This is, admittedly, a rather *ad hominem* approach to the problem, but it is used here to illustrate the way in which outdated norms are believed by the movement to diminish or even to undermine the value of therapy. The conflict felt by a working mother between her obligation to help support or, when she is the only parent present, to support her children entirely and her obligation to be present and primarily active in their upbringing arises from social and economic pressures inherent in today's way of life. It cannot be resolved on a personal level.

Another sort of conflict between the directions to women of the traditional role and the realities of current lived experience affects women who are strongly motivated to work full time in fields in which they are competent, or, to be brief, career women. They, too, almost always regard themselves as the marriage partner chiefly responsible for the maintenance of the home and the welfare of the family. Committing themselves to a career in a world in which the extended family is a thing of the past and domestic help is approaching the vanishing point (two relatively new factors) raises a choice that is not an option but a dilemma: What comes first, family or career? Either solution sets up its own strains, as has been well documented by Ginzberg. Psychologically, the personal problem is compounded by the lack of community support in the way of adequate child care centers or crèches or of programs for training professional mothers' helpers. Consequently, an increasing number of professional women plan either not to marry or to marry but not to bear children. Another reaction is that of women, able to support a child by their own earnings, who have children without marrying. Here, apparently, it is the role of wife rather than of mother that these women find difficult to combine with a full time work load. No doubt the incidence of working divorceés who support their children makes the out-of-wedlock baby seem a possible option for the working woman.

Another fact of change deeply affects the present situation of women: the option to choose when or whether to bear children—an option that has been signally increased by new contraceptive methods. The decline in the birth rate, combined with the growing lifespan of women, has now reduced the proportionate amount of time spent in actual mothering to an historical low. This reduction dramatically changed the pattern of women's lives in the last generation, as has been outlined above, drawing them back to work in their thirties and, increasingly, in their twenties. What effect this drastic shift in occupation, from work to home to work again,

has on the ego identity of women is a question that deserves exploration. This shift clearly invalidates the old proposition that the chief and central role of any woman is motherhood. Certainly, most women enjoy their years of motherhood, but they can no longer accept them as being the normative experience defining the value of their lives.

The diversity of reaction within the women's movement to these circumstances can be confusing and, in fact, makes it difficult to sum up any structured opposition on which positive solutions can be based. But, once more, this diversity should be seen as evidence of the large number of women who are affected by social change and who find the traditional definition of woman's proper role at best insufficient and often crippling and distorting. In this sense, the women's movement began, not so long ago, as protest, and many of its strongest statements are negative because they arise from dissatisfaction with past standards that have become unrealistic today. To those who are still satisfied with the status quo, these statements seem to be attacks on the way things are, and the women's movement is consequently said to be turning women away from marriage and motherhood and even from normal heterosexual relationships. Certainly, many statements are sharp, even bitter. Some examples from seminal works may be cited:

Germaine Greer on marriage:

Every wife must live with the knowledge that she has nothing else but home and family, while her house is ideally a base which her tired warrior-hunter can withdraw to and express his worst manners, his least amusing conversation, while he licks his wounds and is prepared by laundry and toilet and lunch-box for another sortie. Obviously any woman who thinks in the simplest terms of liberating herself to enjoy life and create expression for her own potential cannot accept such a role.

Kate Millett on sex roles (reprinted from *Sexual Politics*, 1969, 1970, by permission of Doubleday & Co., Inc.):

As the whole subject of sex is covered with shame, ridicule and silence, any failure to conform to stereotype reduces the individual . . . to an abysmal feeling of guilt, unworthiness and confusion . . . . Unalterably born into one group or another, every subject is forced, moment to moment, to *prove* he or she is, in fact, male or female by deference to the ascribed characteristics of masculine and feminine. There is no way out of such a dilemma but to rebel and be broken, stigmatized, and cured. Until the radical spirit revives to free us, we remain imprisoned in the vast gray stockades of the sexual reaction.

Shulamith Firestone on the female sex stereotype:

Sex privatization stereotypes women: it encourages men to see women as "dolls" differentiated only by superficial attributes—not as the same species as themselves—and it blinds women to their sexploitation as a class, keeping them from uniting against it, thus effectively segregating the two classes. A side-effect is the converse: if women are differentiated only by superficial physical attributes, men appear more individual and irreplaceable than they really are.

Juliett Mitchell on child raising:

The need for intensive care in the early years of a child's life does not mean that the present single sanctioned form of socialization—marriage and family—is inevitable. Nor that the mother is the only possible nurse. Far from it. The fundamental characteristic of the present system of marriage and family is in our society its *monolithism;* there is only one institutionalized form of inter-sexual or intergenerational relationship possible. It is that or nothing. This is why it is essentially a denial of life.

Many more statements by writers accepted as spokeswomen for the movement on various aspects of dissatisfaction with traditional patterns of life can be found, but those cited are both typical and taken from widely read publications. It is worth noting that, although they are negative in approach, this negativism is directed to special areas of irritation. Many of these writers go on to suggest alternative ways of dealing with these problems. In short, these may be revolutionary statements—and Firestone imagines a deliberately extreme Utopia as an antidote to negativism—but they are not intended to be destructive of emotional life, happiness, and order—only of what seem to the writers to be restrictions, arising from outdated rules, on the free expression of emotional life necessary to happiness and order. The picture of the movement as led and womanned by furious females out to attack and destroy men is not supported by any of the serious literature. The anger voiced therein is clearly related to specific past causes, and attempts are often made to suggest cures and alternatives. Many writers, such as Millett, believe that too rigid sex roles are inhibiting for men as well as women and the greater flexibility would promote the happiness of both sexes. The desire to reach equality but no supremacy is everywhere present in the literature, and fear that the women's movement is working toward a reversal of roles, replacing male by female dominance, simply cannot be supported. Any statements to this effect should be regarded with suspicion as attributions by outsiders that arise from ignorance, misunderstanding, or outright hostility to the aims of the movement. Movement statements may express anger and resentment against men or the system, but the desire for a dominant role over men is absent from them.

The women's movement is grounded in the realities of everyday life in America today, especially as they affect the interplay between women's place in the family and the labor force. In many ways, current experience has undermined the value and the usefulness of the orthodox feminine pattern of occupation, ideals, and behavior. The part played by the movement is largely to record, analyze, and publicize this major social phenomenon, with its concomitant shifts in psychological norms. These norms should now be understood to include many years of work outside the home, quite often coinciding with the period of active mothering. The decision of married women to work is induced in a substantial majority of cases by economic pressures and is felt to be both a reality-oriented response to need and a proper supportive procedure for the family. In many cases, of course, a desire to work in order to use individual talents, to maintain a connection with the world outside the home, or to hold on to one's independence is also present, but it is a mistake to assume that most working women see themselves as having a free option to work or to stay home.

Sociologists report that marriages that include a working wife may experience somewhat greater strains than those that do not, but these marriages also produce greater happiness for both partners (Orden and Bradburn). Such strains as are felt, it is suggested, should be seen by psychiatrists and analysts as arising from or exacerbated by social causes and not simply as resulting from the personal decision to work of a woman with a free option to do so or not to do so. In any case, the working wife and mother is now so common a figure that she must be counted as a normal variant, not a deviate from the accepted feminine role, even if this change of view means enlarging the parameters of that role.

Effects of Shifts in Sexual Norms

The realities of everyday life have greatly changed not only the approved and practiced occupational roles of women but also the sexual activities now considered acceptable for them. The women's movement should be seen less as a spearhead of change than as an attempt to respond with some coherence to changes already set in motion by impersonal forces. Some of these continuing historical forces are economic, connected with the increased ability of women to get and hold jobs that pay a living wage for individual work and also with the disappearance of family groups working together, as on the subsistence farm or the peasant holding. By achieving the ability to support themselves, single women have gained immeasureably in independence and, therefore, in their freedom to choose a marriage partner, to abstain from marriage, or to end a marriage that has become painful. Other forces for change in sex behavior are the products of medical technology, like the improved and more widely available methods of contraception, backed up most recently by access to abortion on demand. The effects of the cultural phenomenon denoted by "permissiveness" can be seen in the more frequent involvement in sexual activities at an earlier age by both men and women. These activities are also less confined to a traditional "normal" pattern. Various practices once considered perversions are now quite widely accepted.

The psychiatric profession has almost unanimously approved this spread of unashamed and open sexual activity. From Freud to Masters and Johnson, the crippling results of sexual repression have been noted and deplored. Comfort goes so far as to say:

Sex is the one place where we today can learn to treat people as people.

Moreover, while a century ago the pleasures of sex were almost exclusively a male prerogative, with eminent Victorian physicians like Dr. William Acton taking female frigidity for granted, but women are now understood to be fully orgasmic. Indeed, the decline in female frigidity can be traced, decade by decade, through the figures given in the Kinsey report on women, and the data supplied by Masters and Johnson appear to indicate that women are capable of longer, more sustained, and more quickly repeated orgasm than are men.

But, like the profound changes in the occupational role of women, these changes in sexual attitudes and behavior have effects that are less clearly understood. The idea that liberation for women walks hand in hand with the sexual revolution, although widely held, is a mistaken oversimplification. Once more, an example may illuminate the divergence. Neither liberation nor the sexual revolution has yet made it acceptable for women to appear as initiators in sexual encounters. When they do initiate sexual encounters, either they are declassed as a group (prostitutes), or, like the groupies who offer themselves to popular singing stars, they are acting out an existential inferiority to the men they seek. The position of initiator is thus still reserved to men unless the woman takes on the traditional role of inferior.

Even less obvious but still strongly influential in the approach to sexual encounter is a corollary to the male right of initiative. In the past, this right was balanced by a female right to refuse the man's request on general grounds of morality or propriety. Acceptance was seen as a personal sign of affection and favor, but refusal carried no stigma of personal rejection. This view has now changed. The assumptions that women enjoy sex as much as men and that it is proper for them to do so have been extended to the expectation that they will respond to a request for sexual relations by agreeing. Consequently, a woman's refusal becomes as personally pejorative as her acceptance was personally rewarding in the older situation. The result is that, although a man retains full choice in a sexual encounter, since he can approach the woman or not as he chooses, the woman has not gained full choice, and her decision to make the disapproved choice—that is, to say "No"—involves her in an apparent personal disparagement of the man. This is not only unpleasant at the time, but it shadows the future of the relationship in a way that refusal never used to do.

Thus, the assumption that sex is enjoyable per se sometimes functions as a positive pressure on a woman to accept the advance of any man who approaches her, since a refusal is seen as a personal rejection. She is not understood to be making some general statement ("I don't much like having sex with a stranger,") or to be heeding her own physical desires or lack of them. Rather, a refusal is interpreted as meaning, "I don't like *you*." Thus, although it is perfectly possible for a woman to refuse an invitation, for example, to a concert on the grounds that the program is not to her taste or to a movie on the grounds that she would rather do something active, refusal to take part in sexual activity can be invidious. The woman's awareness of this situation, plus her continuing sense of herself as a secondary person who cannot, for instance, initiate a sexual encounter, means that the man's invitation now seems to contain an element of compulsion. As a result, men assume that sexual freedom is as complete for women as it is for themselves, but women do not find this to be the case.

Interpreters of the psychology of women must be aware of complications of this sort. The idea is widespread that current acceptance of female pleasure in sex frees women fully from the disabilities that haunted them in the past, but this is not so. The content of the female sexual role has changed, but the format has not. A study of recent books and current periodicals addressed to the mass market indicates beyond a doubt that, at this level of class and culture, initiative in sexual matters is still a male prerogative, and the role of the woman is traditionally submissive and pleasing. She is instructed to be seduc-tive, sexually provocative, alert to her partner's desires rather than to her own, and always ready to accept his advances. This is as true in publications directed to women, such as *The Cosmopolitan Love Guide,* as it is in those directed to men like *Playboy* and *Penthouse.* Clearly, here is a basic divergence between the ideals of increased independence for women upheld by the women's movement and the practices advocated by the sexual revolution, as it is generally defined. This is not to judge between these positions but simply to point out the conflict. Until sexual freedom allows women the right to initiate sexual encounters and to refuse them if they so choose, with equal rights of refusal allowed to men, it cannot be equated with liberation. Consequently, it is a mistake to imagine that the forces working for these two different ends are operating in tandem. They are not, and they must, therefore, be expected to set up cross-riffs.

Lesbianism

A view occasionally advanced in the press attributes a large incidence of lesbianism to adherents of the women's movement. The movement does, indeed, include lesbians, fully approves their right to take part in the sexual activity they prefer and to advocate it for others, and supports their insistence on the social acceptability of such a preference. This stand should be understood as part of the diversity of the movement, which refuses either to advocate or to condemn any particular form of sexual activity undertaken by consenting adults. A statement of the point of view that combines radical feminism with lesbianism can be found in *Lesbian Nation, the Feminist Solution* by Johnston. Other women have reported on lesbian experience and related it to dissatisfaction and personal unhappiness resulting from heterosexual relations, which appear to them to be based on male dominance. Outstanding among these personal testaments is *Combat in the Erogenous Zone* by Bengis.

However, these statements represent individual responses to pressures that are seen as resulting from sex stereotyping. In desiring the end of one set of stereotypes, the movement should not be taken to wish the institution of another set. Enlarging "normal behavior" to include homosexual relationships as a way of life for those who choose them freely is simply a part of the general rewriting of norms to match present circumstances, which the movement approves—and approves, equally, for men.

Effects of Social Change on the Mother Role

In the discussion of the changes in occupational roles of women, the effect on the mother role has already been touched on, evidence in itself of the complicated interplay of forces that the women's movement finds itself attempting to deal with. The need for mothers to leave the home in order to work if their earnings are necessary for family support is a difficulty in itself. It also points to a wider problem—namely, the current isolation of the family from the wider world of activity. The elimination of the breadwinning father from an effective role in child raising, both as present model and as active teacher and disciplinarian, is often overlooked, but his absence is as great an historical anomaly as the partially absent mother. In addition, other sorts of isolation now cut the family off from the community. A study undertaken for the Massachusetts Advisory Council on Education by the Massachusetts Early Education Project (Rowe) lists some as follows:

1. The isolation of wage earners from spouses and children, caused by the wage earners' absorption into the world of work.

2. The complementary isolation of young children from the occupational world of parents and other adults.

3. The general isolation of young children from persons of different ages, both adults and older children.

4. The residential isolation of families from persons of different social, ethnic, religious, and racial backgrounds.

5. The isolation of family members from kin and neighbors.

As a result, this study points out, parents are discouraged from becoming involved in major aspects of their children's lives. Both young children and youth are growing up without the benefit of a variety of adult role models. Children are becoming increasingly ignorant about the world of paid work. Parents are increasingly replaced by three other socializing agents: the schools, the peer group, and the mass media.

The economic and social factors responsible for the contemporary isolation of families cannot be dealt with by the women's movement alone. But these factors are fundamental reasons for the desire felt by many responsible mothers to engage fathers more deeply in interaction with children, thus preventing dependence on the mother alone, a dependence easily productive of intense and binding intimacy. Efforts to overcome family isolation and to provide easy connections with other adults also play a part in the support for adequate child care centers, with the women's movement joining in this support. The most pressing need for responsible child care outside the home arises from the requirements of working mothers, but the social isolation of the family is also a factor acknowledged by many families. In fact, when family income is sufficient to pay for good out-of-home care in nursery schools, kindergartens, and play groups, attendance rises sharply from an average of a third or less for low income families to a full half for those making more than $15,000.

The endeavor to engage adults other than the mother in active and continuing child care should be seen not as an attempt to replace the mother but rather as an effort to support her socializing function. Much anthropological evidence and data from earlier periods of American history can be cited to indicate that the present American pattern of consigning small children to the sole care of the mother is unusual (Minturn and Lambert).

Much has been written recently, both for the general public and for more psychiatric-oriented readers, on the psychological difficulties that can be induced in the family relationship by isolation from the community and overintimacy within the family group (Keniston; Laing; Janeway). Briefly, a consensus points to the danger of confining women to vicarious living through others by binding them to a narrow and isolated home situation. The inability of a woman to gain public reward and acknowledgment of success for individual activity and the injunction to find her reward in the success of husband and children tend to produce a manipulative and devious personality that seeks covert power, since independent open endeavor is denied her. The influence of such a woman on children in her care has sometimes been found to be alienating or even schizophrenegenic. Far from downgrading or belittling the mother role, the women's movement emphasizes the importance of child raising and socialization to the community at large by seeking the participation of others in this process. Such participation provides the positive result of variety in role models and avoids the negative effect of binding the child too tightly within the maternal relationship.

Theoretical Considerations

Students of psychiatry may find it useful to become aware of instances in which the women's movement is in fundamental disagreement with orthodox psychoanalytic theory. Much of this disagreement can be surmised from the statements made above, but specific examples can be helpful.

The work of Freud and his disciples has borne the brunt of attacks by feminists, no doubt because it is the most influential but also because the analytical psychology of Jung, especially Jung's conception of animus and anima—that is, the presence in each sex of an undeveloped and significant aspect of the other—has seemed to run counter to the masculine dominance found in Freudian theory. This is not to suggest that Freud's theories are totally and blindly denied. Mitchell, Firestone, and Janeway, for example, have all publicly noted the influence of Freud's powerful concepts and brilliant analysis on their own thinking. But aspects of Freud's theory are challenged, first, by the primary postulate of the women's movement—namely, the equal significance of women's lives and experience with men's—and, second, by the evidence of experiential divergence from theory arising from the changes in social circumstances since Freud wrote.

Freud grounded the inferiority of women in their physiological difference from men and saw their recognition of this inferiority as a necessary and necessarily limiting part of their progress toward maturity (the female castration complex and penis envy), but the women's movement sees female inferiority as attributed to women by dominant men in the social circumstances of a particular time and place. Freudian theory declares the primacy of the man as innate, based on biology. Possession of a penis is the cause of this primacy. The women's movement holds that male primacy is a social construct, fabricated, whether consciously or not, as a means of upholding male dominance in power relationships. Penis envy is not denied, but it is understood as envy of the male position of dominance in society and in the family, and possession of a penis is not the cause but the symbol of this dominance.

Freud himself, by consistently using the concept of female castration (which is symbolic, since no female has ever been castrated), appears to accept a symbolic interpretation of the physiological difference between man and woman. The whole question of male superiority is taken as axiomatic by Freud and is never explored. The child is assumed to recognize that possession of a penis signifies the right to dominance, but no attempt is made to explain why this recognition should occur. The problem is seen only in reverse: If the girl child rebels against the meaning of right to dominance assigned to possession of a penis, this rebellion is a sign of immaturity, which must be overcome. But to assume that male superiority is validated by possession of a penis implies awareness of this superiority in the child at the time he or she learns of the physiological difference between the sexes; else why should the connection be made at all? "Penis means dominance" is a syllogism that could be formed only in a context of already understood male dominance, which is to say that the concept is a justification of a pre-existing belief and not a logical cause of the belief.

It is possible that Freud was aware of the symbolism of penis envy in a submerged way, just as references can be found throughout his work to the character structure of women as the product not simply of biological forces but of social forces as well. Nonetheless, he was largely content to derive theories of female development from the biological base of penis envy, with the maternal urge seen as a transfer of desire for a penis to desire for a child. However, some of his followers, notably the well known female analysts Marie Bonaparte and Helene Deutsch, took up a brief suggestion of Freud to the effect that femininity may have "some secret relationship with masochism." The idea that women are by nature masochistic clearly grounds their inferiority even more securely in physiology. This explanation appeared to account both for the high incidence of frigidity noted among women two generations ago and for the concurrent assumption of a self-sacrificial or even martyr role of many mothers. In addition, the idea that it is natural for women to wish to suffer justified the existing inferiority of the sex. And the insistence on a passive role for women in sexual activity, tied up with the theory of vaginal orgasm as the only norm, follows from the premise of female masochism.

Challenges to these ideas have arisen over the years. Alfred Adler did not deny to women the common drive toward superiority that he perceived as basic to humanity, although he assumed that the social situation of his time would usually prevent this masculine protest from achieving any real success. A generation ago, Karen Horney declared that, when considering the cause of feminine masochism, "one has to look not for biological reasons but for cultural ones." Horney analyzes the effect of social pressures on women, especially "the cultural situation which has led women to regard love as the only value that counts in life." Horney notes that neurotic fear of aging, which decreases a woman's attractiveness, follows from this, as does a general sense of insecurity and self-devaluation, and, indeed, that "all-embracing expectations that are joined to love account to some extent for that discontentment with the female roles that Freud ascribes to penis-envy," since these expectations are, in the nature of things, rarely achieved in full.

These theoretical difficulties have been reinforced both by the actual experience of many women, whose lives no longer conform to the traditional pattern, and also by scientific advances. Direct research into sexual practice and sexual response, undertaken by Masters and Johnson, has overthrown forever the assumption of female passivity, of less frequent and lower female response, and of a necessary evolution during maturation in women from clitoral to vaginal orgasm. Some women appeared capable of multiorgasmic response to stimulation far beyond the capacity of men, but, over-all, Masters and Johnson found "parallels in reaction to effective stimulation [to] emphasize the physiological similarities in male and female responses rather than the differences." These physical findings call into dispute the theories based on lowered sexual drive in women being the result of their biological makeup and the theories that a passive nonorgasmic reaction is normal, as put forward by Deutsch and Bonaparte.

Another scientific discovery challenging old theories was announced in 1953 by the French endocrinologist Jost and developed by the work of Barr, Burns, Van Wyk, and Witschi. This discovery is reported and commented on most accessibly by Sherfey:

Genetic sex is established at fertilization; but the influence of the sex genes is not brought to bear until the fifth to the sixth week of fetal life [in human beings]. During these first weeks, all embryos are morphologically females. If the fetal gonads are removed before differentiation occurs, the embryo will develop into a normal female, lacking only ovaries, regardless of the genetic sex.

Burns, Sherfey reports, suggests that the femaleness of the mammalian embryo is directly related to viviparity, since in reptiles and birds all embryos are innately male, with the female hormone acting as the inductor of sex difference. In mammals, however, intrauterine life would expose a basically male embryo to feminization, even without the intervention of female hormone. The hypothesis is that, in the evolution of mammals, the inducing hormones became the androgens, and the innate embryo became female through an early adaptation. However that may be, it is now apparent that analytical theories that see women as immature or partially developed men have lost any genetic grounding. Obviously, no more should be assumed from the original femaleness of the embryo in mammals than from the maleness of the embryo in oviparous vertibrates. Both appear to be adaptations to changing evolutionary circumstances. But the discovery does emphasize the danger of arguing from physiology to psychology in too simplified a way.

Conclusions

The appearance of a new women's movement in the 1960's was, in itself, a challenge to many psychological assumptions about women. The very suddenness of its advent contributed to this effect of challenge; but, in another way, it raised the question of the seriousness and extent of the movement. In addition, the time frame of its appearance made it, originally at least, seem to be a mere addendum to other rebellions of the 1960's: that of blacks, demanding civil rights, and that of the young of both sexes, which culminated in the unrest on campus so widespread during that decade.

However, the women's movement is deep rooted and promises to be long lasting. No doubt the climate of the 1960's promoted—or provoked—movements for social change, which merely suggests that the old orthodoxies were proving themselves inadequate in many fields at once. Just so, over a century before, in the 1840's, movements of economic and political protest surfaced together throughout Western society. Already attitudes toward women and women-oriented demands for social justice and a wider role in active life can be seen to have changed, in areas ranging from employment standards to the literature addressed to women (as in popular magazines), to an extent that cannot be appreciated without examining the period of the early 1960's, before these reactions began. Much re-examination of basic thinking about women and their proper behavior is taking place, among both women and men.

Specifically, the traditional roles of women have changed and are now seen to have changed in all aspects. The occupational role of women has changed, and the employment of married women and mothers, even mothers of young children, has risen steadily. This shift has increased the similarity of experience for men and women. What this similarity may mean for future relations between the sexes cannot be predicted, but it is certainly simplistic to imagine that simi-

larity of experience will reduce sexual attraction. Erich Fromm has expressed concern that a lessened polarization of sex roles will produce such an effect, and this may be so; but, equally, extreme polarization has been accompanied by a high degree of homosexuality in the past, notably in Periclean Greece and Victorian England. One cannot predict the direct effect of women's new occupational role on their sexual activities, beyond the unmistakable evidence that an increase in independence will make for a greater degree of freedom of choice in love object for both sexes and, thus, will make for greater diversity.

The effect of changes in women's occupational role on the mother-child relationship is also apparent. Predictions of how these changes will affect child raising in the future can be no more than guesses. The most that can be said is that it seems probable that the narrowing down of the family to one parent present in the home, with almost no other adults regularly available for child care, has reached its peak. It seems likely that involvement of the father, interaction with other parents or adults (as in communal living), and out-of-the-home child care will become increasingly common. These changes can be expected to reduce the intensity of the mother-child bond that has recently characterized American life, a bond that has been exalted as the central and most significant relationship for the mother and, at the same time, vilified by critics as disparate as Philip Wylie and Philip Roth as a crippling silver cord for the child. Perhaps a loosening of this ambiguous tie will produce a healthy reduction of tension within the family.

Turning to women's estimates of themselves, it appears that society is experiencing a revolution of rising expectations. Todays college generation of women is planning to undertake demanding careers to a greater extent than ever before; and it is a generation much more numerous than the earlier ambitious feminists of the 1910's and 1920's. The trend toward later motherhood and a lower birth rate, combined with a lengthened life expectancy, means that women will necesarily have more time and energy to spend outside the home. This generation, however, is not content merely to see itself as replicating male experience and acting out male roles. Women are increasingly seeking a new self-image for themselves. The women's studies programs found on many campuses today are a response to these desires. Older women are also reconsidering the form and content of their lives. This does not mean that they will or should downgrade their special experience as wives and mothers but, rather, that they may find new substance in evaluating it and new bases for extending their experience into activity in other fields as this extension becomes possible for them.

The women's movement is best understood as a response to deep environmental change in society. One must expect these changes to continue and the movement to change in its practical emphasis and immediate interests. Already, these interests are very diverse, representing the areas of response of women of all kinds and classes, all races and regions, diverse backgrounds and individual characters. Fundamentally, however, the premise that women's lives are of equal importance with men's, to women themselves and to society, will endure and grow stronger. In a time of rapid change like the present, the application to women of standards extrapolated from the past will often be felt as distorting to the psyche. At the same time, however, the talents and energies of women are becoming newly available as resources for coping with demands of change. The teaching and practice of psychiatry can only profit from using the rich experience of women in seeking to understand the effects of such change.

REFERENCES

Bengis, I. *Combat in the Erogenous Zone.* Alfred A. Knopf, New York, 1972.
Bird, C. *Born Female.* McKay, New York, 1968.
Comfort, A. *The Joy of Sex.* Crown, New York, 1972.

de Beauvoir, S. *The Second Sex.* Alfred A. Knopf, New York, 1953.
Firestone, S. *The Dialectic of Sex.* Morrow, New York, 1970.
Foust, C. Letter. *Time,* No. 26, vol. 101, p. 4. June 15, 1973.
*Freeman, J. The origins of the women's liberation movement. In *Changing Women in a Changing Society,* J. Huber, editor, p. 30. Chicago Press, Chicago, 1973.
Freud, S. Female sexuality. In *Standard Edition of the Complete Psychological Works of Sigmund Freud,* vol. 21, p. 225. Hogarth Press, London, 1961.
Friedan, B. *The Feminine Mystique.* W. W. Norton, New York, 1963.
Ginzberg, E. *Life Styles of Educated Women.* Columbia University Press, New York, 1966.
Greer, G. *The Female Eunuch.* McGraw-Hill, New York, 1971.
*Horney, K. *New Ways in Psychoanalysis.* W. W. Norton, New York, 1939.
Huber, J., editor. *Changing Women in a Changing Society.* University of Chicago Press, Chicago, 1973.
*Janeway, E. *Man's World, Woman's Place.* Morrow, New York, 1971.
Johnston, J. *Lesbian Nation, the Feminist Solution.* Simon & Schuster, New York, 1973.
Keniston, K. *The Uncommitted.* Harcourt, Brace & World, New York, 1965.
Kinsey, A. C., et al. *Sexual Behavior in the Human Female.* W. B. Saunders, Philadelphia, 1948.
Laing, R. D. *The Divided Self.* Penguin, London, 1965.
Laing, R. D. *The Politics of Experience.* Ballantine, New York, 1967.
Laing, R. D. *Self and Others.* Pantheon, New York, 1969.
Lerner, G., editor. *Black Women in White America.* Pantheon, New York, 1972.
Lundberg, F., and Farnham, M. *Modern Woman: The Lost Sex.* Harper, New York, 1947.
*Masters, W. H., and Johnson, V. E. *Human Sexual Response.* Little Brown, Boston, 1966.
*Millett, K. *Sexual Politics.* Doubleday, New York, 1970.
Minturn, L., and Lambert, W. W., editors. *Mothers of Six Cultures.* John Wiley, New York, 1964.
Mitchell, J. *Woman's Estate.* Patheon, New York, 1971.
Oppenheimer, V. K. Demographic influence on female employment and the status of women. In *Changing Women in a Changing Society,* J. Huber, editor. University of Chicago Press, Chicago, 1943.
*Orden, S. R., and Bradburn, N. M. *Working Wives and Marriage Happiness.* Am. J. Sociol., January, 1969.
Sherfey, M. J. *The Nature and Evolution of Female Sexuality.* Random House, New York, 1972.

Glossary

Abdominal pregnancy. A pregnancy in which the embryo is implanted and develops within the abdomen.

Aberration, sexual. A deviation from usual sexual practices. *See also* Algolagnia, Autoerotism, Bestiality, Exhibitionism, Flagellantism, Frottage, Homosexuality, Masochism, Necrophilia, Ozolagnia, Pedophilia, Pygmalionism, Sadism, Scopophilia, Sexual deviation, Transsexualism, Transvestitism, Urolagnia, Voyeurism.

Abnormal. Deviating from the average or normal.

Abortifacient. An agent, usually a drug, that causes abortion.

Abortion. The expulsion of an embryo or fetus before it has reached the stage of viability—that is, before about 20 weeks of gestation. The abortion may be either spontaneous or induced. *See also* Criminal abortion, Premature birth, Therapeutic abortion.

Abstinence. Refraining from the use of certain substances, such as food or drugs. In psychoanalysis, abstinence refers to refraining from sexual intercourse.

Acid. Slang for lysergic acid diethylamide (LSD).

Adolescence. Period of growth from puberty to maturity. The beginning of adolescence is marked by the appearance of secondary sexual characteristics, usually at about age 12, and the termination is marked by the achievement of sexual maturity at about age 20. *See also* Psychosexual development.

Adultery. Voluntary sexual intercourse between a married person and someone other than his or her spouse. *See also* Fornication.

Afterbirth. The placenta and membranes that are extruded after the birth of the infant. *See also* Placenta.

Agape. The Greek concept of spiritual love, in contrast to eros, physical love. *See also* Eros.

Aggression. Forceful, goal-directed behavior that may be verbal or physical. It is the motor counterpart of the affects of rage, anger, and hostility.

Aggressive drive. Destructive impulse directed at oneself or another. It is also known as the death instinct. According to contemporary psychoanalytic psychology, it is one of the two basic drives; sexual drive is the other one. Sexual drive operates on the pleasure-pain principle, whereas aggressive drive operates on the repetition-compulsion principle. *See also* Aggression, Libido theory, Sexual drive.

Algolagnia. A sexual deviation in which sexual pleasure is associated with pain; it includes both the giving and the receiving of pain. *See also* Masochism, Sadism.

Amastia. Absence of breasts.

Ambisexuality. *See* Bisexuality.

Amenorrhea. The absence or abnormal cessation of the menses. Primary amenorrhea is the failure of menstruation to occur during puberty. Secondary amenorrhea is the cessation of menstruation, although it had appeared during adolescence. *See also* Dysmenorrhea, Menopause.

Amor purus. An element in the ideal of courtly love in which the completed sex act was considered less desirable than unconsummated intercourse.

Anal erotism. *See* Anal phase.

Analingus. Stimulation of the anus of one person with the mouth, tongue, or lips of another.

Anal phase. The second stage in Freud's theory of psychosexual development. It occurs when the child is between the ages of 1 and 3. During this period, the child's activities, interests, and concerns are centered on his anal zone and bowel function. The pleasurable experience felt in this area is called anal erotism. *See also* Coprophilia, Genital phase, Infantile sexuality, Latency phase, Oral phase, Phallic phase.

Anaphrodisiac. A drug or other agent that represses or abolishes sexual desire. The opiates have this effect. *See also* Aphrodisiac.

Androgen. A hormone that has masculinizing properties. It is produced in the testes and the adrenal glands. *See also* Estrogen, Testosterone.

Androgyny. A combination of female and male characteristics in one person. *See also* Bisexuality.

Anhedonia. Absence of the capacity to experience pleasure. *See also* Hedonism.

Animism. A system of thought in which nature and all objects, animate and inanimate, are conceived of as having spirits and conscious lives of their own. The development of the concept of animism is felt to have resulted, in prehistoric times, in the emergence of sex as a social activity with both emotional and instinctual significance.

Anomaly. Excessive deviation from some standard.

Anxiety. An unpleasurable affect consisting of psychophysiological changes in response to an intrapsychic conflict. In contrast to fear, in which the danger is real, anxiety is marked by an unreal danger or threat. Physiological changes during a state of anxiety consist of increased heart rate, disturbed breathing, trembling, sweating, and vasomotor changes. Psychological changes during anxiety consist of an uncomfortable feeling of impending danger, accompanied by an overwhelming awareness of being powerless, the inability to perceive the unreality of the threat, a prolonged feeling of tension, and exhaustive readiness for the expected danger. *See also* Fear.

Aphrodisiac. A substance, usually a drug, that excites sexual desire. *See also* Anaphrodisiac.

Areola. The dark area surrounding the nipple. It is found in both men and women.

Artificial insemination. The introduction of sperm into the uterus without coitus.

Asexual. Not sexual.

Assertive therapy. A behavioral therapy technique in which healthy interpersonal communication is encouraged by open and frank discussion of feelings.

Autocunnilingus. Use of one's mouth or tongue to stimulate one's own vulva. *See also* Cunnilingus.

Autoerotism. Sexual arousal of oneself without the participation of another person. The term, introduced by Havelock Ellis, is at present used interchangeably with masturbation. In psychoanalysis, autoerotism is a primitive phase in object relationship development, preceding the narcissistic state. In narcissism there is a love object, but there is no love object in autoerotism. *See also* Dildo, Narcissism.

Autofellatio. The putting of one's penis in one's own mouth. *See also* Fellatio.

Aversive control. The utilization of unpleasant stimuli to change behavior. *See also* aversive therapy.

Aversive therapy. A form of conditioning therapy in which the patient is made to associate an unpleasant or painful experience with undesirable behavior in an effort to eliminate undesirable behavior patterns. It has been used to treat certain sexual deviations. *See also* Behavioral psychotherapy.

Axillism. Sexual gratification through the use of the axilla.

Bartholin's gland. One of two small glands located on either side of the vagina. The gland empties mucus into the labia. *See also* Cowper's gland.

Behavioral psychotherapy. Therapy that focuses on overt and objectively observable behavior, rather than on thoughts and feelings. It aims at symptomatic improvement and the elimination of suffering and maladaptive habits. Various conditioning and anxiety-eliminating techniques derived from learning theory are combined with didactic discussions and techniques adapted from other systems of treatment. It has been used in the treatment of sexual deviations. *See also* Aversive therapy.

Bestiality. A sexual deviation in which a person engages in sexual relations with an animal. *See also* Zoophilia.

Bigamy. Marriage in which a spouse has two mates at one time. *See also* Polyandry, Polygamy, Polygyny.

Birth control. An effort to avoid the birth of a child through contraception or sterilization.

Birth trauma. Otto Rank's term to describe what he considered the basic source of anxiety in human beings, the birth process.

Bisexuality. The existence of the qualities of both sexes in the same person. Freud postulated that both biologically and psychologically the sexes differentiated from a common core; that differentiation between the two sexes was relative, rather than absolute; and that regression to the common core occurs to varying degrees in both normal and abnormal conditions. An adult person who engages in bisexual behavior is sexually attracted to and has contact with members of both sexes. He is also known in lay terms as an AC-DC person. *See also* Androgyny, Hermaphrodite, Heterosexuality, Homosexuality, Latent homosexuality, Overt homosexuality.

Body image. One's image, conscious and unconscious, of one's own body at any particular time.

Body language. The system by which a person expresses his thoughts and feelings through his bodily activity.

Bowdlerize. To expurgate according to prudish standards. This term is derived from the name of Thomas Bowdler, who published an expurgated edition of Shakespeare in 1818.

Breast. One of two milk-producing and erogenous organs in a woman. *See also* Amastia, Galactorrhea, Gynecomastia.

Buggery. Anal intercourse. *See also* Pederasty, Sodomy.

Bundling. A custom in which young men and women spend time together in bed without removing their clothing.

Carpopedal spasm. Flexor contraction of the feet commonly seen during orgasm.

Castration. Excision of the gonads, causing a person to be incapable of reproduction. *See also* Eunuch, Sterilization.

Castration anxiety. Fear concerning the loss or injury of the genitalia. *See also* Castration complex.

Castration complex. Imagined danger to the penis. In the Oedipus complex, the child wants to eliminate his archrival, his father, and anticipates retaliation in the form of deprivation of his penis. *See also* Oedipus complex.

Celibacy. Abstention from sexual intercourse or marriage. *See also* Chastity, Continence, Virgin.

Chancre. An indurated ulcer that is characteristic of primary syphilis.

Change of life. *See* Menopause.

Chastity. Abstention from sexual intercourse. *See also* Celibacy, Continence, Virgin.

Circumcision. Surgical removal of all or part of the foreskin.

Climacteric. Menopause. The term is sometimes used to refer to the same age period in men.

Climax. *See* Orgasm.

Clitoridectomy. Removal of the clitoris. *See also* Clitorism.

Clitoris. The organ of sexual stimulation at the anterior part of the vulva. *See also* Clitoridectomy, Clitorism, Glans clitoridis, Smegma.

Clitorism. Overdevelopment or continuous erection of the clitoris. *See also* Clitoridectomy, Priapism.

Codpiece. Pouch or flap covering the male genitalia.

Coitus. Sexual union between a man and a woman involving insertion of the penis into the vagina. It is also termed coition, copulation, and sexual intercourse.

Coitus a tergo. Coitus from the rear.

Coitus in ano. Anal intercourse.

Coitus inter femora. Coitus in which the penis is inserted between the pressed thighs of the partner.

Coitus interruptus. Sexual intercourse that is interrupted before the man ejaculates.

Coitus reservatus. Sexual intercourse in which there is deliberate suppression of ejaculation. It is also known as coitus retardata. *See also* Ejaculatio retardata.

Conception. The fertilization of an ovum; the act of becoming pregnant. *See also* Impregnation.

Condom. A covering for the penis that is worn during coitus to prevent infection or conception. *See also* Diaphragm, Intrauterine device, Pill.

Congenital. Present at birth. A congenital condition may be hereditary or the result of prenatal development or the process of birth itself.

Conscious. One of the three divisions of the psyche, according to Freud's topographical psychology. The conscious includes all the material within the realm of awareness at all times. *See also* Preconscious, Unconscious.

Continence. Self-restraint from yielding to desire. *See also* Celibacy, Chastity, Virgin.

Contraception. The prevention of conception. *See also* Condom, Diaphragm, Pill, Sterilization.

Coprolalia. The involuntary use of vulgar or obscene words. It is observed in some cases of schizophrenia. *See also* Gilles de la Tourette's disease.

Coprophagy. The eating of feces. *See also* Coprophilia.

Coprophilia. Sexual pleasure associated with feces. Coprophilic perversions are associated with fixations at the anal stage of psychosexual development. *See also* Coprophagy.

Copulation. *See* Coitus.

Corona glandis. The rim of the glans penis; the most sensitive area of the penis.

Courtesan. A high-class prostitute or mistress.

Courtly love. An ideal or code about male-female relationships that appeared in France during the 11th and 12th centuries. *See also* Amor purus.

Cowper's gland. One of a pair of glands located on either side of the urethra in the male. The gland secretes material that forms part of the seminal fluid. *See also* Bartholin's gland.

Crab. *See* Pediculus pubis.

Criminal abortion. The illegal interruption of pregnancy by any means. *See also* Therapeutic abortion.

Cryptorchidism. Failure of a testis to descend into the scrotum. It is also called undescended testis.

Cunnilingus. Use of the mouth or tongue to stimulate the female genitalia. *See also* Autocunnilingus, Oragenitalism.

Cunnus. *See* Vulva.

Death instinct. *See* Aggressive drive.

Defloration. Rupture of the hymen. This term is usually used to describe the first coitus, a ritual breaking of the hymen, or rupture during a vaginal examination.

Detumescence. The subsiding of a penile erection. The term is also used to describe the subsiding of genital engorgement in both sexes.

Deviation. *See* Aberration, sexual.

Diagnostic and Statistical Manual of Mental Disorders. A handbook for the classification of mental illnesses. Formulated by the American Psychiatric Association, it was first issued in 1952 (DSM-I). The second edition (DSM-II), issued in 1968, correlates closely with the World Health Organization's *International Classification of Diseases*.

Diana complex. A female wish to become a male. *See also* Penis envy.

Diaphragm. A dome-shaped contraceptive device, usually made of rubber, that obstructs the cervical os. *See also* Condom, Intrauterine device, Pill.

Dildo. An artificial penis. Usually made of rubber, it is used for self-stimulation. *See also* Autoerotism, Olisbos.

Disinhibition. The removal of inhibition. Chemical substances, such as alcohol, can remove inhibitions by interfering with cerebral cortex functions.

Douche. The cleansing of the vagina with water or a special solution.

Dry orgasm. Male climax without ejaculation.

Dual-sex therapy. A form of therapy, developed by William Masters and Virginia Johnson, in which treatment is focused on a particular sexual disorder. The crux of the program is the round-table session, in which a male and female therapy team suggest special exercises for the couple to diminish the fears of sexual performance felt by both sexes and to facilitate communication in sexual and nonsexual areas. *See also* Excitement phase, Orgasmic phase, Plateau phase, Refractory period, Resolution phase, Sex flush, Sweating phenomenon.

Dysmenorrhea. Painful menstruation. *See also* Amenorrhea.

Dyspareunia. Physical pain in sexual intercourse experienced by women. Usually emotionally caused, it may result from cystitis, urethritis, or other organic condition. *See also* Frigidity.

Ectopic pregnancy. A pregnancy in which the embryo is implanted and develops outside of the uterus. *See also* Abdominal pregnancy, Ovarian pregnancy, Pregnancy, Tubal pregnancy.

Egg. *See* Ovum.

Ego. One of the three components of the psychic apparatus in Freud's structural framework. Although the ego has some conscious components, many of its operations are automatic. It serves to mediate between the person and external reality. It evaluates, coordinates, and integrates perceptions so that internal demands can be adjusted to external requirements. It is also responsible for certain defensive functions to protect the person against the demands of the id and the superego. Adaptation to reality is perhaps its most important function. *See also* Id, Superego.

Ejaculatio deficiens. *See* Dry orgasm.

Ejaculation. The emission of seminal fluid. *See also* Orgasm.

Ejaculatio praecox. *See* Premature ejaculation.

Ejaculatio retardata. The excessive delay of ejaculation during intercourse. *See also* Coitus reservatus.

Electra complex. According to Freudian theory, an inordinate amount of emotional involvement by a daughter with her father. *See also* Oedipus complex.

Emasculation. *See* Castration.

Embryo. The earliest stage of an organism's development. In humans, it is the period from conception until the beginning of the third month of intrauterine development. *See also* Fetus.

Emission. The discharge of a substance; the flow of semen out of the penis. *See also* Nocturnal emission.

Endogamy. Marriage within a specific group. *See also* Exogamy.

End-pleasure. Satisfaction associated with the genital stage of development. *See also* Foreplay, Psychosexual development.

Eonism. Male tranvestitism.

Erection. Stiffening of the penis as a result of engorgement with blood. Erection usually occurs 10 to 20 seconds after sexual excitement begins. *See also* Detumescence, Orgasm.

Erogenous zone. A region of the body that is exceptionally sensitive to sexual stimulation, such as the mouth, breast, vagina, penis, urethra, and anus. Sometimes called erotogenic zone.

Eros. The Greek god of love; physical love. In Freudian psychoanalysis, it is the life instinct. *See also* Agape, Sexual drive.

Erotic. Sexually stimulating.

Eroticize. To invest with erotic or sexual feeling.

Erotolalia. Obscene speech that is usually sexually arousing and used in sexual intercourse.

Escutcheon. Pattern of pubic hair. The female escutcheon is typically an inverted triangle.

Estrogen. A hormone that is produced mainly by the ovaries. The estrogens produce the development of the female reproductive organs and secondary sex characteristics. Important estrogens include estradiol, estriol, and estrone. *See also* Androgen.

Estrus. A period of intense sexual urge in female animals.

Eunuch. A man castrated before puberty who then develops the secondary sexual characteristics of a woman.

Eunuchoid. Possessing the characteristics of a eunuch without actually being castrated.

Excitement phase. The first stage in the human sexual response after sexual stimulation. The phase was first described by Masters and Johnson. *See also* Orgasmic phase, Plateau phase, Refractory period, Resolution phase, Sex flush, Sweating phenomenon.

Exhibitionism. A sexual deviation characterized by a compulsive need to expose one's body, particularly the genitals.

Exogamy. Marriage outside of a specific group. In a biological sense, it is the union of gametes of unrelated parents. *See also* Endogamy.

Extramarital relations. Sexual intercourse outside of marriage.

Fantasy. Daydream; fabricated mental picture or chain of events. A form of thinking dominated by unconscious material and primary processes, it seeks wish fulfillment and immediate solutions to conflicts. Fantasy may serve as the matrix for creativity or for neurotic distortions of reality.

Fear. An unpleasurable affect consisting of psychophysiological changes in response to a realistic threat or danger to one's existence. *See also* Anxiety.

Fellatio. Use of the mouth or tongue to stimulate the penis. *See also* Autofellatio, Irrumation, Oragenitalism.

Femaleness. Anatomic characteristics relating to the female procreative role.

Feminine identity. Well-developed sense of gender affiliation with females. *See also* Gender identity.

Fertility. Ability to produce offspring.

Fertilization. The union of egg and sperm. *See also* Gamete, Zygote.

Fetish. An object, usually inanimate, that a person endows with sexual symbolism.

Fetishism. A sexual deviation in which a person achieves sexual excitement and gratification by substituting an inanimate object—such as a shoe, a piece of underwear, or other article of clothing—for a human love object.

Fetus. An unborn child from the third month after conception until birth. *See also* Embryo.

Fixation. The arrest of psychosexual development at any stage before complete maturation; a close and paralyzing attachment to another person, such as one's mother or father. *See also* Anal phase, Latency phase, Genital phase, Oral phase, Phallic phase.

Flagellantism. A sexual deviation in which the sexual partners are aroused and gratified by whipping or being whipped.

Fliess, Wilhelm (1858–1928). Berlin nose and throat specialist. He shared an early interest with Freud in the physiology of sex and entered into a prolonged correspondence that figures importantly in the records of Freud's self-analysis. Freud was influenced by Fliess's concept of bisexuality and his theory of the periodicity of the sex functions.

Foreplay. The sexual play that precedes sexual intercourse. It is also called fore-pleasure. *See also* End-pleasure.

Foreskin. The covering over the penis or clitoris; prepuce. *See also* Circumcision, Smegma.

Fornication. Sexual intercourse between persons not married to one another. *See also* Adultery.

Freud, Sigmund (1856–1939). Austrian psychiatrist and the founder of psychoanalysis. With Josef Breuer, he explored the potentialities of cathartic therapy, then went on to develop the analytic technique and such fundamental concepts of mental phenomena as the unconscious, infantile sexuality, repression, sublimation, superego, ego, and id formation and their applications throughout all spheres of human behavior.

Frigidity. Lack of sexual response or feeling in a woman, ranging from complete anesthesia to incomplete climax. *See also* Dyspareunia, Impotence, Vaginismus.

Frottage. A sexual deviation in which the deviant touches the object of his or her sexual desire in public places. The male deviant usually touches the breast or buttocks of a woman in a crowded train or elevator. *See also* Frotteur.

Frotteur. A person who becomes sexually aroused by rubbing up against someone, usually without specific genital contact, as in a crowd. *See also* Frottage.

Frustration. The thwarting of an impulse or drive. The ability to tolerate frustration and delay gratification is considered a sign of maturity and good ego strength.

Fulfillment. Satisfaction of needs that may be either real or illusory.

Galactorrhea. Excessive or spontaneous flow of milk from the breast. It may be a result of the endocrine influence of phenothiazine drugs.

Gamete. A sex cell that unites with another germ cell to form a zygote. *See also* Fertilization.

Gamophobia. Fear of marriage.

Gender. The attributes that characterize masculinity or femininity. *See also* Sex.

Gender dysphoria syndrome. *See* Transsexualism.

Gender identity. The culturally determined sets of attitudes, behavior patterns, and physical attributes usually associated with masculinity and femininity. *See also* Masculine identity.

Gender role. Public declaration of gender identity.

Genetic counseling. The presenting and discussing of the scientific factors involved in inherited pathological conditions. The counselor investigates a couple's genetic background, indicates to the prospective parents how likely or unlikely they are to transmit certain characteristics, and in many cases helps them make appropriate plans based on all available scientific evidence.

Genital organ. Sex or reproductive organ.

Genital phase. The final stage of psychosexual development. It usually occurs during puberty. In this stage the person's psychosexual development is so organized that he can achieve sexual gratification from genital-to-genital contact and has the capacity for a mature, affectionate relationship with someone of the opposite sex. *See also* Anal phase, End-pleasure, Infantile sexuality, Latency phase, Oral phase, Phallic phase.

Genotype. The genetic inheritance of a person, the set of genes that he receives from both parents at the time of conception.

Germ cell. A cell that transmits hereditary characteristics. *See also* Gamete, Zygote.

Gerontophilia. Sexual attraction for the old and the aged by a young person.

Gestation. Pregnancy; the period from conception to birth.

Gilles de la Tourette's disease. A rare illness that has its onset in childhood. First described by a Paris physician, Gilles de la Tourette, the illness is characterized by involuntary muscular movements and motor incoordination, accompanied by echolalia and coprolalia.

Glans clitoris. The head of the clitoris.

Glans penis. The head of the penis. *See also* Corona glandis.

Gonad. A sex gland; a testis (male) or ovary (female). *See also* Castration, Germ cell.

Gonadotropin. A hormone having a stimulating effect on the gonads.

Gonorrhea. A venereal disease, caused by *Neisseria gonorrhoeae* and transmitted chiefly through sexual intercourse, that produces a contagious catarrhal inflammation of the genital mucous membranes.

Granuloma inguinale. A veneral disease, caused by *Donovanio granulomatis* and most often affecting the genitals, that is characterized by widespread ulceration and scarring of the skin and underlying tissues.

Gynecomastia. Female-like development of the male breasts.

Gynophobia. Fear of women.

Hedonism. Seeking after pleasure. *See also* Anhedonia.

Heredity. The transmission of bodily traits and characteristics or of diseases from parents to offspring. *See also* Germ cell.

Herma. A four-sided column with the head of the god Hermes at the top and a protruding phallus in the middle.

Hermaphrodite. A person who has both female and male sexual organs, usually with one sex dominating. *See also* Bisexuality.

Heterosexuality. Sexual attraction or contact between opposite-sex persons. The capacity for heterosexual arousal is probably innate, biologically programmed, and triggered in very early life, perhaps by olfactory modalities, as seen in lower animals. *See also* Bisexuality, Homosexuality.

Hirsutism. Excessive hairiness, especially in women. *See also* Virilization.

Homosexuality. Sexual attraction or contact between same-sex persons. Some authors distinguish two types: overt and latent. *See also* Bisexuality, Heterosexuality, Inversion, Isophilic, Lesbianism.

Homosexual panic. Sudden, acute onset of severe anxiety, precipitated by the unconscious fear or conflict that one may be a homosexual or act out homosexual impulses. *See also* Homosexuality.

Hormone. A substance produced by a gland that has a specific effect on the functioning of other organs in the body. *See also* Androgen, Estrogen.

Hymen. The tissue that partly covers the entrance to the vagina. It is stretched or broken during coitus. If a hymen is imperforate, it completely closes the vaginal opening. The hymen is also called the maidenhead. *See also* Defloration.

Id. Part of Freud's concept of the psychic apparatus. According to his structural theory of mental functioning, the id harbors the energy that stems from the instinctual drives and desires of a person. The id is completely in the unconscious realm, unorganized and under the influence of the primary processes. *See also* Conscious, Ego, Preconscious, Primary process, Superego, Unconscious.

Impotence. Inability to achieve an erection of the penis. Also known as ejaculatory incompetence. *See also* Frigidity, Sterility.

Impregnation. The act of fertilization. *See also* Conception.

Incest. Sexual activity between members of a family. Common patterns are father-daughter, mother-son, and between siblings. Incest may also be homosexually oriented.

Infantile sexuality. Freudian concept regarding the erotic life of infants and children. Freud observed that, from birth, infants are capable of erotic activities. Infantile sexuality encompasses the overlapping phases of psychosexual development during the first 6 years of life and includes the oral phase (birth to 18 months), when erotic activity centers on the mouth; the anal phase (ages 1 to 3), when erotic activity centers on the rectum; and the phallic phase (ages 2 to 6), when erotic activity centers on the genital region. *See also* Psychosexual development.

Infibulation. A primitive African practice that involved sewing up the vaginal opening. A small hole was left open for urination. Just before marriage, the vagina was opened with a model of the penis made to the specific dimensions of the husband-to-be.

Insemination. The deposit of semen within the vagina. *See also* Artificial insemination.

Intercourse. *See* Sexual intercourse.

Intrauterine device (IUD). A device placed in the uterus to prevent pregnancy. *See also* Condom, Diaphragm, Pill.

Introitus. The entrance into the vagina.

Intromission. Insertion of the penis into the vagina.

Inversion. Synonym for homosexuality. Inversion was the term used by Freud and his predecessors. *See also* Homosexuality, Latent homosexuality, Overt homosexuality.

Invert. A homosexual.

Irrumation. Fellatio.

Isophilic. Term used by Harry Stack Sullivan to mean liking or feeling affectionate toward people of the same sex, without the genital aspects of homosexuality.

IUD. *See* Intrauterine device.

Jus primae noctis. The medieval custom, with parallels in other periods of history, of the right of the lord of the manor to have the first intercourse with a maiden under his jurisdiction on the first night of her marriage.

Koro. An acute anxiety reaction characterized by the patient's fear that his penis is shrinking and may disappear into his abdomen, in which case he will die. This psychogenic disorder is found only among the people of the Malay archipelago and among the South Chinese.

Labia majora. *See* Labium majus pudendi.

Labia minora. *See* Labium minus pudendi.

Labium majus pudendi. One of two outer folds or lips of the vagina covering the vaginal opening. The plural is labia majora. *See also* Labium minus pudendi.

Labium minus pudendi. One of two small inner folds or lips of the vagina. The plural is labia minora. *See also* Labium majus pudendi.

Latency phase. Stage of psychosexual development extending from age 5 to the beginning of adolescence at age 12. Freud's work on ego psychology showed that the apparent cessation of sexual preoccupation during this period stems from a strong, aggressive blockade of libidinal and sexual impulses in an effort to avoid the dangers of the oedipal relationship. During the latency period, boys and girls are inclined to choose friends and join groups of their own sex. *See also* Anal phase, Genital phase, Infantile sexuality, Oral phase, Phallic phase.

Latent homosexuality. Unexpressed conscious or unconscious homoerotic wishes that are held in check. Freud's theory of bisexuality postulated the existence of a constitutionally determined, although experientially influenced, instinctual masculine-feminine duality. Normally, the opposite-sex component is dormant, but a breakdown in the defenses of repression and sublimation may activate latent instincts and result in overt homoerotism. Many writers have questioned the validity of the theory of a universal latent homoerotism. *See also* Bisexuality, Homosexuality, Overt homosexuality.

Lesbian. A female homosexual. *See also* Tribade.

Lesbianism. Femal homosexuality. About 600 B.C. on the island of Lesbos in the Aegean Sea, the poetess Sappho encouraged young women to engage in mutual sex practices. Lesbianism is also known as Sapphism. *See also* Bisexuality, Homosexuality, Latent homosexuality, Overt homosexuality.

Libido. The energy of the sexual impulse; the sexual drive of a person.

Libido theory. Freudian theory of sexual instinct, its complex process of development, and its accompanying physical and mental manifestations. Before Freud's introduction and completion of the dual-instinct theory (sexual and aggressive) in 1920, all instinctual manifestations were related to the sexual instinct, making for some confusion at that time. Current psychoanalytic practice assumes the existence of two instincts: sexual (libido) and aggressive (death). *See also* Aggressive drive, Sexual drive.

Life instinct. *See* Sexual drive.

Lust dynamism. A term used by Harry Stack Sullivan to describe clearly stated sexual desires and abilities.

Maidenhead. *See* Hymen.

Marital counseling. Process whereby a trained counselor helps married couples resolve problems that arise and trouble them in their relationship.

Masculine identity. Well-developed sense of gender affiliation with males. *See also* Gender identity.

Masculine protest. The Adlerian doctrine that depicts a universal human tendency to move from a passive and feminine role to a masculine and active role. This doctrine is an extension of his ideas about organic inferiority. It became the prime motivational force in normal and neurotic behavior in the Adlerian system.

Masculinity-femininity scale. Any scale on a psychological test that assesses the relative masculinity or femininity of the testee. Scales vary and may focus, for example, on basic identification with either sex or preference for a particular sex role.

Masochism. A sexual deviation in which sexual gratification is derived from being maltreated by the partner or oneself. It was first described by an Austrian novelist, Leopold von Sacher-Masoch (1836–1895). *See also* Algolagnia, Sadism, Sadomasochistic relationship.

Masters and Johnson. Sex researchers William Masters and Virginia Johnson, who developed a system of sex therapy at the Reproductive Biology Research Foundation in St. Louis, Missouri. *See also* Dual-sex therapy, Excitement phase, Orgasmic phase, Plateau phase, Refractory period, Resolution phase, Sex flush, Sweating phenomenon.

Masturbation. *See* Autoerotism.

Ménage à trois. *See* Troilism.

Menarche. The onset of menstruation.

Menopause. Permanent cessation of menstruation, usually between the ages of 45 and 50. *See also* Amenorrhea, Climacteric.

Menstruation. Periodic discharge of blood from the uterus, usually occurring every 28 days.

Monogamy. Marriage between one man and one woman.

Mons pubis. Fatty tissue in women just over the pubic bone. It becomes covered with hair at puberty. It is also called the mons veneris.

Mons veneris. *See* Mons pubis.

Multipara. Woman who has given birth to more than one child. *See also* Nullipara, Primipara.

Myotonia. Increased muscular tension.

Narcissism. Self-love. It is linked to autoerotism but is devoid of genitality. The word is derived from Narcissus, a Greek mythology figure who fell in love with his own reflected image. In psychoanalytic theory, it is divided into primary and secondary types. Primary narcissism refers to the early infantile phase of object relationship development, when the child has not differentiated himself from the outside world. All sources of pleasure are unrealistically recognized as coming from within himself, giving him a false sense of omnipotence. Secondary narcissism results when the libido once attached to external love objects is redirected back to the self. *See also* Autoerotism.

Natelism. Predominant use of the buttocks (nates) during intercourse.

Necrophilia. A sexual deviation in which a person is sexually aroused at the sight or thought of a corpse. *See also* Necrosadism.

Necrosadism. Sadism inflicted on a corpse. *See also* Necrophilia.

Neurosyphilis. Syphilitic infection of the nervous system. *See also* Syphilis.

Nocturnal emission. Seminal ejaculation during sleep. It is also called spermatorrhea and wet dream.

Nullipara. A woman who has never given birth to a child. *See also* Multipara, Primipara.

Nymphomania. Morbid, insatiable need in women for sexual intercourse. *See also* Satyriasis.

Oedipus complex. A distinct group of associated ideas, aims, instinctual drives, and fears that are generally observed in children when they are from 3 to 6 years of age. During this period, which coincides with the peak of the phallic phase of psychosexual development, the child's sexual interest is attached chiefly to the parent of the opposite sex and is accompanied by aggressive feelings and wishes about the parent of the same sex. One of Freud's most important concepts, the Oedipus complex was discovered in 1897 as a result of his self-analysis. *See also* Castration complex. Electra complex, Totem and Taboo.

Olisbos. A type of dildo used in ancient Greece.

Onanism. Coitus interruptus or masturbation.

Oragenitalism. Sexual activity in which the mouth of one partner stimulates the genitalia of the other partner, as in fellatio and cunnilingus.

Oral phase. The earliest stage in Freud's theory of psychosexual development. It lasts through the first 18 months of life. During this period the oral zone is the center of the infant's needs, expression, and pleasurable erotic experiences. This stage has a strong influence on the organization and development of the child's psyche. *See also* Anal phase, Genital phase, Infantile sexuality, Latency phase, Phallic phase.

Orgasm. The peak of excitation in the genitals. *See also* Dry orgasm, Ejaculation, Erection, Orgasmic phase.

Orgasmic dysfunction. A woman's inability to achieve orgasm through physical stimulation. In primary orgasmic dysfunction, the woman has never had an orgasm. In secondary dysfunction there has been at least one instance of orgasm.

Orgasmic phase. The third stage in the human sexual response cycle as described by Masters and Johnson. In this phase, orgasm occurs. *See also* Excitement phase, Plateau phase, Refractory period, Resolution phase, Sex flush, Sweating phenomenon.

Orgasmic platform. The outer third of the vagina, which displays marked vasocogestion and contraction in the plateau phase of the female sexual response, as described by Masters and Johnson.

Ovarian pregnancy. A pregnancy in which the embryo is implanted and develops within an ovarian follicle.

Ovary. One of two femal reproductive glands. *See also* Gonad, Testes.

Overt homosexuality. Behaviorally expressed homoerotism, as distinct from unconsciously held homosexual wishes or conscious wishes that are held in check. *See also* Homosexuality, Latent homosexuality.

Ovum. Female germ cell. It is also called an egg. *See also* Fertilization, Gamete, Sperm, Zygote.

Ozolagnia. A sexual deviation in which sexual pleasure is derived from body odors.

Pain-pleasure principle. A psychoanalytic concept stating that, in psychic functioning, a person tends to seek pleasure and avoid pain. *See also* Pleasure principle.

Paraphilia. Sexual deviation.

Parthenogenesis. Virgin birth, reproduction without fertilization.

Pederasty. Anal intercourse between a man and a boy. *See also* Buggery, Sodomy.

Pediculus pubis. Pubic louse. *See also* Crab.

Pedophilia. A sexual deviation in which a person has an erotic desire for children. Pedophilia may be homosexual or heterosexual.

Penile containment. Location of the penis in the vagina, usually without thrusting.

Penis. The male organ of copulation and urination. *See also* Glans penis, Koro, Smegma.

Penis envy. A concept developed by Freud that maintains that the woman envies the man for his possession of a penis. It is sometimes used to refer to the woman's generalized envy of the man. *See also* Diana complex, Phallic overbearance.

Perversion. A deviation from the expected norm. In psychiatry, it commonly signifies sexual perversion. *See also* Sexual deviation.

Phallic overbearance. Domination of another person by aggressive means. It is generally associated with masculinity in its negative aspects. *See also* Penis envy.

Phallic phase. The third stage in Freud's theory of psychosexual development. It occurs when the child is from 2 to 6 years of age. During this period, the child's interest, curiosity, and pleasurable experiences are centered on the penis in boys and the clitoris in girls. *See also* Anal phase, Genital phase, Infantile sexuality, Latency phase, Oral phase.

Phallus. Penis. *See also* Herma.

Phantasy. *See* Fantasy.

Pill. Oral contraceptive. *See also* Condom, Diaphragm.

Placenta. The organ that connects the fetus to the maternal uterus and that makes metabolic exchanges possible. *See also* Afterbirth.

Plateau phase. The second stage in the human sexual response cycle, as described by Masters and Johnson. This phase precedes orgasm. *See also* Excitement phase, Orgasmic phase, Orgasmic platform, Refractory period, Resolution phase, Sex flush, Sweating phenomenon.

Platonic love. A strong emotional attachment between two persons without any accompanying sexual relations.

Pleasure principle. In psychoanalytic theory, the notion that a person tries to gain pleasure and gratification and to avoid pain and discomfort. *See also* Pain-pleasure principle.

Polyandry. Marriage in which a wife has more than one husband at a time. *See also* Bigamy, Polygamy, Polygyny.

Polygamy. Marriage in which a spouse has more than one mate at a time. *See also* Bigamy, Polyandry, Polygyny.

Polygyny. Marriage in which a husband has more than one wife at a time. *See also* Bigamy, Polyandry, Polygamy.

Pornography. Written or graphic matter portraying sexual activity that is intended to sexually stimulate the person seeing it.

Postpartum psychosis. Symptoms of psychosis such as hallucinations or delusions which follow childbirth.

Potency. A male's ability to perform the sexual act.

Preconscious. In psychoanalysis, one of the three divisions of the psyche, according to Freud's topographical psychology. The preconscious includes all ideas, thoughts, past experiences, and other memory impressions that can be consciously recalled with effort. *See also* Conscious, Unconscious.

Pregenital. In psychoanalytic theory, the oral and anal periods, before the genitals become a dominating force in sexual development.

Pregnancy. The period from conception to birth. *See also* Abdominal pregnancy, Ectopic pregnancy, Gestation, Ovarian pregnancy, Pseudocyesis, Tubal pregnancy.

Premature birth. Birth of a fetus after it has reached the stage of viability—that is, after about 20 weeks of gestation—but before it has reached full term. *See also* Abortion.

Premature ejaculation. Ejaculation before, during, or immediately after intromission.

Prenatal. Existing or occurring before birth.

Prepuce. *See* Foreskin.

Priapism. Persistent penile erection. *See also* Clitorism.

Primary process. In psychoanalysis, the mental process directly related to the functions of the id and characteristic of unconscious mental activity. The primary process is marked by unorganized, illogical thinking and by the tendency to seek immediate discharge and gratification of instinctual demands. *See also* Secondary process.

Primipara. A woman who has given birth to only one child. *See also* Multipara, Nullipara.

Promiscuity. Casual and indiscriminate sexual activity with a number of partners.

Prophylactic. Guarding against disease; condom.

Prostitute. A person who engages in sexual relationships for money.

Prudery. Excessive, exaggerated concern with and displays of morality, modesty, and decorum. It is felt that prudery in most instances represents a reaction-formation. *See also* Bowdlerize.

Pseudocyesis. False pregnancy.

Psychoanalysis. Freud's method of psychic investigation and form of psychotherapy. As a technique for exploring the mental processes, psychoanalysis includes the use of free association and the analysis and interpretation of dreams, resistances, and transferences. As a form of psychotherapy, it uses the investigative technique, guided by Freud's libido and instinct theories and by ego psychology, to gain insight into a person's unconscious motivations, conflicts, and symbols and thus to effect a change in his maladaptive behavior. Several schools of thought are loosely referred to as psychoanalytic at present. Psychoanalysis is also known as analysis in depth, and its practitioners are known as psychoanalysts.

Psychosexual development. Maturation and development of the psychic phase of sexuality from birth to adult life. Its phases are oral, anal, phallic, latency, and genital. *See also* End-pleasure, Fixation, Infantile sexuality.

Pudendum. *See* Vulva.

Pygmalionism. A sexual deviation in which a

person falls in love with an object of his own creation.

Rape. Forcible sexual intercourse.

Refractory period. A temporary state of psychophysiological resistance to sexual stimulation immediately after orgasm, as described by Masters and Johnson. *See also* Excitement phase, Orgasmic phase, Plateau phase, Resolution phase, Sex flush, Sweating phenomenon.

Resolution phase. The final stage in the human sexual response cycle, during which the sexual system returns to its normal, nonexcited state. The term was introduced by Masters and Johnson. *See also* Excitement phase, Orgasmic phase, Plateau phase, Refractory period, Sex flush, Sweating phenomenon.

Sadism. A sexual deviation in which sexual gratification is achieved by inflicting pain and humiliation on the partner. *See also* Algolagnia, Masochism, Necrosadism, Sadomasochistic relationship.

Sadomasochistic relationship. A relationship in which the enjoyment of suffering by one person and the enjoyment of inflicting pain by the other person are important and complementary attractions in their ongoing relationship. *See also* Masochism, Sadism.

Sapphism. *See* Lesbianism.

Satyriasis. Morbid, insatiable sexual needs or desires in men. It may be caused by organic or psychiatric factors. *See also* Nymphomania.

Scopophilia. A sexual deviation in which a person achieves sexual gratification by viewing sexual acts or the genitals of others. *See also* Voyeurism.

Scoptophilia. *See* Scopophilia.

Scrotum. Sac containing the testes. *See also* Cryptorchidism.

Secondary process. In psychoanalysis, the mental process directly related to the functions of the ego and characteristic of conscious and preconscious mental activities. The secondary process is marked by logical thinking and by the tendency to delay gratification by regulation of discharge of instinctual demands. *See also* Primary process.

Secondary sexual characteristics. The physical characteristics, other than the external sexual organs, that distinguish male from female. *See also* Adolescence.

Semen. The secretion of the male reproductive organs. It is ejaculated from the penis and contains sperm.

Sex. The biological attributes that characterize a male or a female. *See also* Gender.

Sex flush. The superficial vasocongestive skin response to increasing sexual arousal that begins in the plateau phase. *See also* Excitement phase, Masters and Johnson, Orgasmic phase, Refractory period, Resolution phase, Sweating phenomenon.

Sexual deviation. A mental disorder characterized by sexual interests and behaviors other than those culturally accepted. *See also* Algolagnia, Autoerotism, Bestiality, Exhibitionism, Fetishism, Flagellantism, Frottage, Masochism, Necrophilia, Ozolagnia, Pedophilia, Pygmalionism, Sadism, Scopophilia, Transsexualism, Transvestitism, Urolagnia, Voyeurism.

Sexual drive. One of the two primal instincts (the other is the aggressive drive), according to Freud's dual-instinct theory of 1920. It is also known as eros and life instinct. Its main goal is to preserve and maintain life. It operates under the influence of the pleasure principle. *See also* Aggressive drive, Libido theory.

Sexual intercourse. Sexual union of two persons. *See also* Coitus.

Sexual orientation disturbance. A diagnostic category for individuals whose sexual interests are directed toward persons of the same sex and who are disturbed about their orientation.

Sixty-nine. The act of simultaneous fellatio and cunnilingus in which the two persons are in a head-to-foot position.

Smegma. The whitish secretion that accumulates under the prepuce of the clitoris or the penis.

Sodomy. Anal copulation. It is also a general legal term that includes all sexual acts other than penis-vagina coitus. *See also* Buggery, Pederasty.

Sperm. Male germ cell. It is also called a spermatozoön (plural, spermatozoa). *See also* Fertilization, Gamete, Ovum, Semen, Zygote.

Spermatogenesis. Sperm formation and development.

Spermatorrhea. *See* Nocturnal emission.

Sperm duct. *See* Vas deferens.

Spermicide. An agent that destroys sperm.

Sterility. Inability to produce offspring. *See also* Fertility, Impotence.

Sterilization. The process of making a person permanently infertile. It may be accomplished by cutting and tying a man's seminal ducts or by tying a woman's fallopian tubes. *See also* Castration, Contraception, Vasectomy.

Sublimation. An unconscious defense mechanism in which unacceptable instinctual drives are diverted into personally and socially acceptable channels. Unlike other defense mechanisms, sublimation offers some minimal gratification of the instinctual drive or impulse.

Superego. One of the three component parts of the psychic apparatus. The other two are the ego and the id. Freud created the theoretical concept of the superego to describe the psychic functions that are expressed in moral attitudes, conscience, and a sense of guilt. The superego results from the internalization of the ethical standards of the society in which the person lives, and it develops by identification with the attitudes of his parents. It is mainly unconscious and is believed to develop as a reaction to the Oedipus complex. It has a protective and rewarding function, referred to as the ego ideal, and a critical and punishing function, which evokes the sense of guilt. *See also* Ego, Id.

Sweating phenomenon. The appearance of droplets of fluid on the walls of the vagina early in the excitement phase of the female sexual response cycle, as described by Masters and Johnson. *See also* Orgasmic phase, Plateau phase, Refractory period, Resolution phase, Sex flush, Vaginal lubrication.

Syphilis. A venereal disease caused by *Treponema pallidum*. It can lead to an organic psychosis if it is left untreated. *See also* Chancre, Neurosyphilis, VDRL test, Wassermann test.

Testicle. *See* Testis.

Testis. One of two male reproductive glands. *See also* Cryptorchidism, Gonad, Ovary.

Testosterone. An androgen produced in the testes. This hormone produces the secondary sex characteristics of the male, such as pubic hair and deepening of the voice.

Therapeutic abortion. The induced interruption of a pregnancy for medical reasons. *See also* Criminal abortion.

Three Essays on the Theory of Sexuality. The title of a book by Freud published in 1905. It applied the libido theory to the successive phases of sex instinct maturation in the infant, child, and adolescent. It made possible the integration of a vast diversity of clinical observations and promoted the direct observation of child development.

Tinea cruris. A fungus infection causing irritation to the skin in the genital region.

Totem and Taboo. The title of a book by Freud published in 1913. Applying his concepts to the data of anthropology, he showed the meaning of tribal organizations and customs.

Transsexualism. A sexual deviation in which a person shows a desire to change his sex. Some male transsexuals, many of whom have adopted the role of a female since childhood, have undergone sex-changing surgical procedures, accompanied by intensive hormonal therapy and psychotherapy, in order to live as women.

Transvestitism. A sexual deviation in which a person dresses in the clothing of the opposite sex. *See also* Eonism.

Tribade. A lesbian who rubs her external genitalia against those of another woman. The tribade may have an unusually large clitoris.

Troilism. Sexual activity involving three people, one of them of the opposite sex. It usually includes both homosexual and heterosexual acts. It is called ménage à trois when all three live together.

Tubal pregnancy. A pregnancy in which the embryo is implanted and develops in the oviduct.

Tumescence. Engorgement; erection of the penis or the clitoris.

Unconscious. 1. (Noun) Structural division of the mind in which the psychic material—primitive drives, repressed desires, and memories—is not directly accessible to awareness. 2. (Adjective) In a state of insensibility, with absence of orientation and perception. *See also* Conscious, Preconscious.

Undescended testis. *See* Cryptorchidism.

Urethra. The canal that conducts urine from the bladder to the outside of the body.

Urolagnia. A sexual deviation in which sexual pleasure is derived from urinating on someone else, being urinated on, or drinking urine.

Uterus. The female organ in which the zygote develops. It is also called the womb.

Vagina. The female genital canal, extending from the vulva to the uterus, that receives the penis during coitus. It is also known as the vaginal barrel.

Vagina dentata. A theory proposed by Freud which states that an unconscious fantasy exists in certain persons who are afraid of women and who believe that there are "biting teeth" in the vagina.

Vaginal agenesis. Absence of the vagina at birth.

Vaginal barrel. *See* Vagina.

Vaginal lubrication. The transudate that appears on the walls of the vagina 10 to 20 seconds after the onset of sexual stimulation. *See also* Excitement phase, Sweating phenomenon.

Vaginismus. Vaginal spasm that causes pain during sexual intercourse. *See also* Frigidity.

Vaginitis. Inflammation of the vagina.

Vas deferens. One of two ducts in the male that conduct sperm from the epididymis to the urethra. It is also known as the seminal duct, the ductus deferens, and the sperm duct.

Vasectomy. Sterilization procedure in men in which the seminal ducts are tied off, eliminating the production of sperm. Potency and sexuality are unaffected.

Vasocongestion. Engorgement of the blood vessels; congestion of the veins in the genital area during sexual excitement.

VDRL test. A blood test for syphilis developed by the Venereal Disease Research Laboratory. *See also* Wassermann test.

Venereal disease. A contagious disease that is usually transmitted by sexual intercourse.

Vestibule vaginae. The entrance to the vagina.

Vibrator. A device, either electrical or battery-powered, that is used to stimulate and massage a body part. A vibrator may be used to stimulate the penis, clitoris, labia, or nipples, or it may be inserted in the vagina itself.

Victorianism. A moral ethic that had as its central ideal the denial or repression of sexual drives. Victorianism was characterized by prudishness with respect to sexual matters, stress on the sanctity of the home, and belief in the innate purity of women and children.

Virgin. A person who has never had sexual intercourse. *See also* Celibacy, Chastity, Continence.

Virilization. The development in a female of male secondary sex characters, including enlargement of the clitoris, hirsutism, deepening of the voice, decreased breast size, and baldness. *See also* Tribade.

Voyeurism. A sexual deviation in which a person has a desire to look at sexual organs or observe sexual acts by others.

Vulva. The female external genital organs, including the vestibule vaginae, clitoris, mons pubis, labia majora, and labia minora. It is also called the cunnus.

Wassermann test. A blood test for syphilis that uses the complement-fixation method. *See also* VDRL test.

Wet dream. *See* Nocturnal emission.

Withdrawal. *See* Coitus interruptus.

Womb. Uterus.

Zoophilia. An abnormally intense fondness for animals which usually consists of the attainment of sexual pleasure from the handling or petting of animals. *See also* Bestiality.

Zygote. The single-celled product of the fusion of a sperm and an egg. It is also known as a fertilized egg.

Index